W9-APH-331

THE FINAL FOUR *of* EVERYTHING

Contents

The Brackets

Introduction *by Mark Reiter*

AMERICANA

1 **Magical Numbers** *by Richard Sandomir*
2 **American Guns** *by Stephen Hunter*
3 **Jim Henson Creations** *by Michael Davis*
4 **American Products** *by Lee Eisenberg*
5 **Cars That Made a Difference** *by Phil Patton*
6 **Protestant Hymns** *by Nancy Gibbs*
7 **License Plates** *by Tom Vanderbilt*
8 **State Birds** *by Scott Mowbray*
9 **Pseudonyms** *by Stanley Bing*
10 **Iconic Photographs** *by James Danziger*
11 **Ridiculous Celebrity Auctions** *by Leila Dunbar*
12 **Board Games** *by Stefan Fatsis*
13 **Magic Tricks** *by Joshua Jay*
14 **Roller Coasters** *by Scott Rutherford*
15 **SAT Success Strategies** *by Laura Wilson*
16 **Screen Cowboys** *by Neil Amdur*
17 **A New National Anthem** *by Richard Sandomir*

HISTORY AND POLITICS

18 **Vestiges of the 20th Century** *by Kurt Andersen*
19 **Conservative Texts** *by Mary Matalin*
20 **First Ladies** *by Gail Collins*
21 **Panic Attacks** *by Jack Hitt*
22 **Memorable Speech Lines** *by Jeff Shesol*
23 **Innovators** *by Harold Evans*
24 **Supreme Court Decisions** *by Adam Liptak*
25 **Presidential Pardons** *by P.S. Ruckman, Jr.*
26 **Military Heroes** *by Richard Goldstein*
27 **Enduring One-Liners** *by Jan Van Meter*
28 **Financial Villains** *by Joe Nocera*
29 **Political Rivalries** *by Adam Clymer*
30 **Presidential Speeches** *by Curt Smith*
31 **Influential Radicals and Extremists** *by David Oshinsky*
32 **Biographies** *by James McGrath Morris*

PEOPLE

33 **Astronauts** *by Jeffrey Kluger*
34 **Supermodels** *by Crystal Renn and Marjorie Ingall*
35 **Celebrity Mugshots** *by Willie Geist*
36 **Mary** *by Mary C. Curtis*
37 **Bald Guys** *by Richard Sandomir*
38 **Geniuses** *by Peter Richmond*
39 **Celebrity Baby Names** *by Linda Rosenkrantz and Pamela Redmond Satran*
40 **Untimely Deaths** *by Mark Reiter*
41 **David** *by David Fisher*
42 **Celebrity Memoirs** *by Charles Leerhsen*
43 **Lousy Husbands** *by Kari Boyer*
44 **William et. al.** *by William/Bill Geist*
45 **Disappearing Acts** *by Franz Lidz*
46 **Richard vs. Dick** *by Richard Sandomir*
47 **American Pinups** *by Gregory Curtis*
48 **Pundits** *by Franklin Foer*
49 **Great Brother Acts** *by Mark Reiter*
50 **Tom vs. Thomas** *by Tom Chiarella*
51 **Immigrants** *by Tony Quinn*

SPORTS

52 **Olympic Athletes** *by David Maraniss*
53 **NFL Team Logos** *by D.W. Pine*
54 **Dallas Cowboys** *by Jeff Pearlman*
55 **Jewish Baseball Players** *by Daniel Okrent*
56 **All-Time Fantasy Sports Performances** *by Matt Pitzer*
57 **21st-Century Sports Books** *by Will Leitch*
58 **Ringless Athletes** *by Dick Friedman*
59 **Donald Ross Courses** *by Bob Carney*
60 **American Hockey Players** *by Nick Paumgarten*
61 **Steroid-Era Moments** *by Shaun Assael*
62 **Sports Clichés** *by Steve Rushin*
63 **Instant Replays** *by Alan Schwarz*
64 **Sexually Inadequate Nicknames** *by Hart Seely*
65 **Baseball Moments** *by John Thorn*
66 **Absurd College Nicknames** *by Richard Sandomir and Pete Thamel*
67 **Toughest Golf Holes** *by Chris Millard*
68 **Dubious Sports Achievements** *by Richard Hoffer*
69 **From Athlete to Actor** *by Mark Reiter*
70 **Sportscasters** *by Richard Deitsch*
71 **SEC Athletes** *by Steve Eubanks*
72 **Pound-for-Pound Fighters** *by Steve Farhood*
73 **Field Goals and PATs** *by Stefan Fatsis*
74 **Golf Books** *by John Garrity*

THE FINAL FOUR *of* EVERYTHING

A celebration of all that's great, surprising, or silly in America using the foolproof method of bracketology* to determine what we love or hate – and why. The arguments begin here.

*A knockout tournament format made famous by the NCAA's March Madness basketball tournament, now applied to everything but basketball.

Edited by
Mark Reiter and Richard Sandomir

Designed by **D.W. Pine**

Simon & Schuster Paperbacks
New York London Toronto Sydney

Simon & Schuster Paperbacks
A Division of Simon & Schuster, Inc.
1230 Avenue of the Americas
New York, NY 10020

First Simon & Schuster Paperbacks edition May 2009

Designed by D.W. Pine

Manufactured in the United States of America

10 9 8 7 6 5 4 3 2 1

Library of Congress Cataloging-in-Publication Data has been applied for.

ISBN-13: 978-1-4391-2608-0
ISBN-10: 1-4391-2608-9

75 **New York Athletes** *by George Vecsey*
76 **Boston Athletes** *by Dan Shaughnessy*
77 **Sportswriters** *by Glenn Stout*
78 **Advertising Icons** *by Bryan Curtis*
79 **Greatest Sports Year** *by Mike Vaccaro*

POP CULTURE

80 **Movie Gunfights** *by Stephen Hunter*
81 **YouTube Videos** *by Virginia Heffernan*
82 **Soul Songs** *by John Leland*
83 **Paul Newman Roles** *by Mark Reiter*
84 **Sitcom Dads** *by Steven Reddicliffe*
85 **Sitcom Moms** *by Richard Sandomir*
86 **Talk-Show Graveyard** *by Bill Carter*
87 **Children's Books** *by Jon Scieszka*
88 **Cinematic Interrogatories** *by John Steinbreder*
89 **Comic Strips** *by R.C. Harvey*
90 **High School Movies** *by Rick Staehling*
91 **Stunt Scenes** *by Kevin Conley*
92 **Impressionists** *by Richard Sandomir*
93 **Literary Heroes** *by B.R. Myers*
94 **Comedy Routines** *by Bill Scheft*
95 **Worst Movies by Great Directors** *by A.O. Scott*
96 **George Carlin Hunks** *by Kelly Carlin-McCall*
97 **Cop Movies** *by Lorenzo Carcaterra*
98 **Reality TV Stars** *by Bob Boden*
99 **Fictional Lawyers** *by Thane Rosenbaum*
100 **Good Imus vs. Evil Imus** *by Richard Sandomir*
101 **Steve Earle Songs** *by Mark Reiter*
102 **Most American Superhero** *by Peter Coogan*
103 **Gangster Films** *by Lorenzo Carcaterra*
104 **Disney Animated Films** *by Richard Corliss*
105 ***Honeymooners*** *by Peter Crescenti*
106 **You Call This Acting?** *by Will Reiter*
107 **Talk Radio Hosts** *by David Hinckley*
108 **Child Actors** *by Griffin Miller*
109 **Detroit Celluloid** *by Kevin Conley*
110 **Girl Singers** *by Tom Moon*
111 **Cathartic Movie Deaths** *by David Edelstein*
112 **Game-Show Hosts** *by Steve Leblang*
113 **Grateful Dead Songs** *by John Steinbreder*
114 **Romance Novels** *by Isabel Swift*
115 **TV Catchphrases** *by Robert J. Thompson*
116 **Jazz Solos** *by Nick Trautwein*
117 **Romantic Comedies** *by David Denby*
118 **Cats and Dogs** *by Lon Tweeten*
119 **Clint Eastwood Films** *by Manohla Dargis*
120 **Comedy Teams** *by Robert Wuhl*
121 **Comic Book Superpowers** *by Peter Coogan*

NATURE

122 **Fears and Phobias** *by Roz Chast*
123 **National Parks** *by Scott Kirkwood*
124 **Dangerous Animals** *by Chris Jenkins*
125 **Best Ski Runs** *by Steve Cohen*
126 **Nothing but the Tooth** *by James Hudson, D.M.D.*
127 **Fish Tales** *by Peter Kaminsky*
128 **Energy Alternatives** *by Gwyneth Cravens*
129 **My Prized Feathers** *by Luke Dempsey*
130 **Looking Younger** *by David Leffell, M.D.*

WORDS

131 **Fatherly Advice** *by Jancee Dunn*
132 **Motherly Advice** *by Mark Reiter*
133 **Acronyms** *by Stefan Fatsis*
134 **Lazy Wit** *by Adi Ignatius*
135 **Texas Sayings** *by Anne Dingus*
136 **Seductive Foreign Accents** *by Asif Eydohno*
137 **Yogi Berra Wisdom** *by Dave Kaplan*
138 **Fortune Cookies** *by Jennifer 8. Lee*
139 **All-Purpose Banalities** *by Joe Queenan*
140 **Deadly Sins of Emailing** *by David Shipley and Will Schwalbe*
141 **Politically Correct Terms** *by Henry Beard and Christopher Cerf*
142 **Woody Allen Wisdom** *by Eric Lax*

FOOD AND DRINK

143 **It's Better with Bacon** *by Peter Kaminsky*
144 **Cocktails** *by Jonathan Miles*
145 **Breakfast Cereals** *by Drew Magary*
146 **Domestic Beers** *by Maureen Ogle*
147 **Artisan Cheeses** *by Max McCalman and David Gibbons*
148 **Regional Soda Pop** *by Bob Roe*
149 **American Wines** *by Joseph S. Ward*
150 **Classic Cookbooks** *by Katie Workman*

Blank bracket
Acknowledgments

Introduction

By Mark Reiter

Here's how to enjoy this book.

Stop reading this introduction and start flipping through the pages. Pause at the first page that catches your eye. It might be a picture that grabs you (e.g., **Nick Nolte's mugshot**). Or a name (Otis Redding). Or a song title ("God Bless America"). Or a fortune cookie ("Do or do not. There is no try"). Or a pairing of proper nouns you never expected to be linked together (**Michael Jordan** vs. John Glenn).

If you're engaged by the page, you'll start nodding your head in agreement. Or shaking it in violent disagreement. You might not agree that Paul Newman's best role was in *Absence of Malice,* or that **Mary Tyler Moore** is the greatest American named Mary – ever! Or that Crunch Berries is the best breakfast cereal and **Mark Twain** had the best pseudonym and that a brew from Louisiana named **Turbodog** is America's best beer. Or that **Maine** has the most stylish license plate and "This Land Is Your Land" is the best choice to replace our current national anthem. Or that 1941 was the greatest sports year (I prefer 2008) and **Scrabble** is a better board game than Monopoly.

Mark Twain

If you regard any of the above opinions as fighting words, then you're already enjoying this book in the way we intended. In these pages we are celebrating everything good, surprising, and silly about America – which means that (a) it's a happy, optimistic book that (b) is designed to generate arguments. If you want to have livelier conversations over family dinner, place this book at the head of the table.

MAINE
MAY
9239 NQ
Vacationland
07

On the other hand, you might have questions, such as: What does "bracketology" mean? Did you make it up? Why don't you just make a list? Who are all these people with their firm opinions? Who died and made them boss? And of course, how can I do this stuff at home?

My job here is to answer those questions.

The bracket concept is not new. It's a unique way of organizing information that dates back to the rise of the knockout (or single elimination) tournament. Its origins are not precisely known. It's possible that the first bracket was drawn by a master of jousts at a medieval jousting tournament or by an enterprising member of a Scottish golf club in the 16th century as a way of determining the club champion. We do not know, because the crude chart informing jousters and golfers whom they would face in the next round does not survive. But there was genius in the bracket design and it hasn't changed much over the years. By 1849 in London, Henry Buckle was winning the first modern chess tournament and adhering to the bracket format. Tennis, bridge, soccer, rowing, and other sports followed soon enough.

N
I
W
Abita Beer
TURBODO

You, of course, may be familiar with the bracket format via the NCAA basketball tournament pairings each March. If you've ever watched ESPN or participated in a March Madness office pool, you know the guiding concept behind this book. All we've done here is take the knockout format and apply it to every category except basketball. In areas where taste, judgment, and hard-earned wisdom really matter, we've set out to determine (as the book's cover modestly announces) the Final Four of Everything.

A bracket is not a list, nor does it aspire to be one. The world already has enough lists. To us, a list is a crude, invidious, one-dimensional device. It ranks things from best to worst, but that's all it does. It doesn't explain. It doesn't pit one item against another, allowing the two to rub together and create friction to determine the superior player.

A bracket is a more dynamic way of understanding personal preferences. The practice of parsing people, places, and things into discrete one-on-one matchups works because it's simple and the face-off happens right in front of you – in real time. In that sense, a bracket invests your opinions with a narrative of how you decided something. Thus, when **Annie Hall** and *The Front Page* go at each other in David Denby's Romantic Comedies bracket (#117), you are forced to compare the two films' merits and debits. Isn't a champion more interesting when you know who or what it had to beat to get to the top?

WOODY ALLEN
DIANE KEATON
TONY ROBERTS
CAROL KANE
PAUL SIMON
JANET MARGOLIN
SHELLEY DUVALL
CHRISTOPHER WALKEN
COLLEEN DEWHURST
"ANNIE HALL"
A new comedy.

As for the term "bracketology," it is one of those cute neologisms deployed by obsessive fans to inject greater significance into a familiar sports phenomenon – for example, threepeat or SABRmetrics or bouncebackability. I first heard bracketology used by the co-editor of this book, Richard Sandomir, in a March 2006 *New York Times* sports column, in reference to ESPN's saturation coverage of March Madness. The term was new to me (clearly, I do not watch enough ESPN), but its meaning (technically, the study of the brackets) did not sail over my head. I knew it referred to Americans' annual debate over whether the NCAA created a gross miscarriage of justice in, say, seeding Gonzaga (with their 26-3 record and a defeat early in the season of top-ranked Duke) third in the Midwest regional. So crisp and clean was the phrase, creating such a vivid picture of American men devoting their analytical powers to guessing the outcome of a series of basketball games over three long weekends in March, that I wondered, "What if that cranial energy, that heat and obsession, were placed at the service of a better, higher purpose?"

That's when I knew that bracketology could be used to establish our preferences in . . . well, everything.

We do not claim authorship of the concept. One of the earliest non-sporting uses of brackets can be found in the December 1989 issue of *Spy* magazine. But we like to think that in this book, we have taken the concept to its logical extreme.

In celebrating America, we've tried to capture the nation's greatness and glory and occasional foolishness in 150 self-contained two-page spreads of brackets. Our subject matter includes sports, of course, but ventures deeply into history, nature, people, food and drink, popular culture, and miscellaneous issues such as the most seductive foreign accent for speaking English.

We didn't do this all by ourselves. We approached experts and celebrated authorities to render the verdict of what is good, better, and best in America. Thus, you will find bestselling thriller writer (and firearm aficionado) Stephen Hunter bracketizing on **American guns.** And *New York Times* columnist Gail Collins on First Ladies. And Kelly Carlin-McCall on her father **George Carlin's** best comedy routines. And Pulitzer Prize–winning historian David Oshinsky on **extremists and radicals.** And Bill Geist on notable **Williams** and Bills.

One of the underappreciated miracles here is how a bracket can provide an essential nitroglycerine tablet of information on the most complicated topics. In Harry Evans's **Innovators** bracket (#23), you'll find an instant summary of America's most durable business breakthroughs. In Pulitzer Prize–winner David Maraniss's **Olympic Athletes** bracket (#52), you get a memory-jog about our gold-medal heroes – all adding up to what could have been a two-hour documentary. Adam Liptak's **Supreme Court** Decisions (#24) is a cheat sheet for what we will still be arguing about in decades to come. In Stefan Fatsis's **Acronyms** (#133), you get the story of the last 100 years via our shorthand. In Richard Sandomir's Magical Numbers (#1), you'll find a stealth history of the United States through the numbers that we embrace. Each in two pages.

A bracket also displays great versatility as a communications tool. In her **Fatherly Advice** bracket (#131), writer Jancee Dunn accumulates all the pearls of wisdom – solicited or not – that she has heard from her father in her lifetime. Take away the bracket format and I doubt that Dunn would ever have gathered these nuggets in one place at the same time, let alone have them compete to determine that "when you meet someone, shake their hand firmly and look them right in the eye" is the best advice her father has ever given her. Absent the bracket, she might never have known how much she values that advice – and neither would her father.

In that sense, Dunn's bracket could literally serve as her Father's Day card this year – which suggests another use for brackets: *you can do them at home.* (That's why we've provided a blank template at the end of this book.) Facing a dilemma of personal choice, don't fall back on the usual list of dos and don'ts. Draw up a bracket of one-on-one items that gives structure and depth to your many options. The process is simple: fill in the first round with any idea that pops into your mind. Then let this jumble of competing notions play out in a tournament of the mind until a clear winner emerges.

A
B
C

D
E
F

More than anything, though, a bracket can function as a decision-making engine. It lets us confirm what we're really thinking and, as a result, provides us with an incremental gain in self-knowledge. Not long ago I was at a wedding reception in upstate New York. It was a beautiful sunny day as I sipped champagne with a professor of Irish literature and a local attorney. Surveying the lovely scene and stunning weather, the professor said, "James Joyce believed that the two loveliest words in the English language are 'summer afternoon.'"

"That's nice," said the attorney, clasping his flute of champagne. "But I'm partial to 'open bar' myself."

It depends on who you are, I thought. To a schoolkid, the two happiest words might be "snow day"; to a job hunter, "You're hired"; to a childless couple, "We're pregnant"; to a cancer patient, "in remission"; to a defendant, "not guilty." And so on. Curious to know what my happiest two words were, I made a bracket that looked like this:

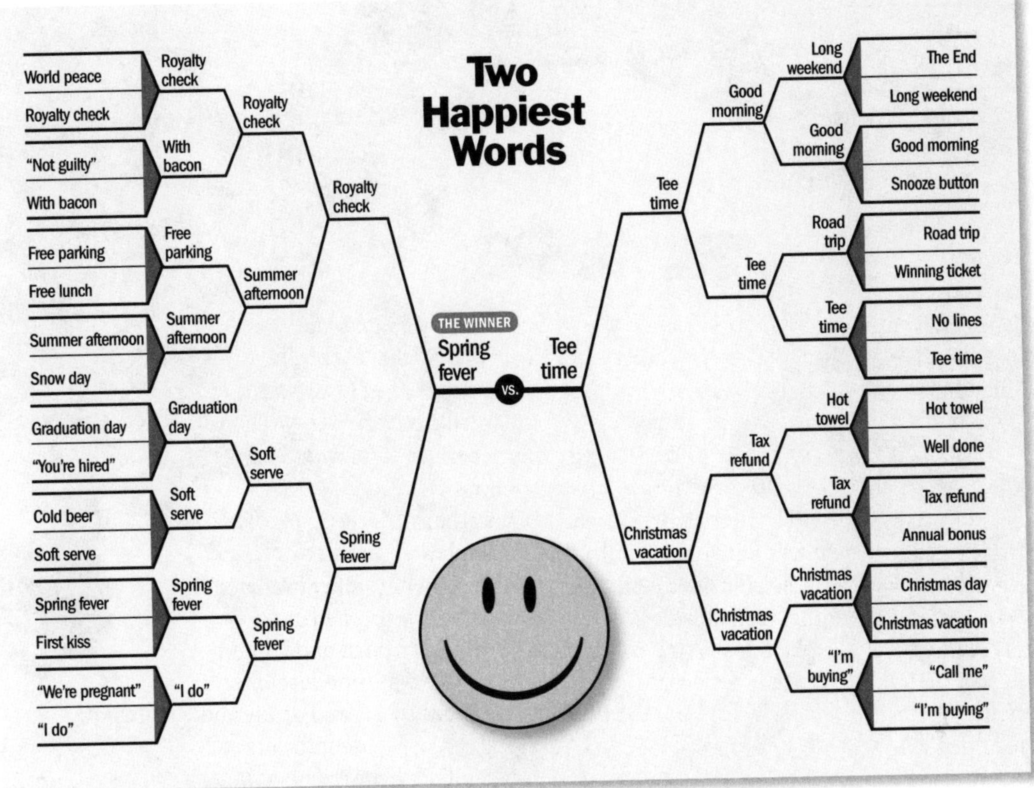

Two Happiest Words
World peace
Royalty check
"Not guilty"
With bacon
Free parking
Free lunch
Summer afternoon
Snow day
Graduation day
"You're hired"
Cold beer
Soft serve
Spring fever
First kiss
"We're pregnant"
"I do"
Royalty check
With bacon
Free parking
Summer afternoon
Graduation day
Soft serve
Spring fever
"I do"
Royalty check
Summer afternoon
Soft serve
Spring fever
Royalty check
Spring fever
THE WINNER
Spring fever
vs.
Tee time
The End
Long weekend
Good morning
Snooze button
Road trip
Winning ticket
No lines
Tee time
Hot towel
Well done
Tax refund
Annual bonus
Christmas day
Christmas vacation
"Call me"
"I'm buying"
Long weekend
Good morning
Road trip
Tee time
Hot towel
Tax refund
Christmas vacation
"I'm buying"
Good morning
Tee time
Tax refund
Christmas vacation
Tee time
Christmas vacation

If you study this bracket closely, you could come to a few reliable conclusions about my demons and desires. (Which is why I encourage you to have everyone in your immediate family fill out a similar bracket, if only for mental-health reasons.)

Frankly, I was surprised that "Tee time" reached the finals. I didn't know that playing golf made me happier than earning a living ("Royalty check"). This is particularly shocking if you've seen my golf game. As for the penumbra of happy thoughts surrounding the words "Spring fever," that's much more understandable. It takes me back to my schoolboy years, sitting in a classroom on a gorgeous day in May, scorched by a fizzy restless yearning to be anywhere outdoors. Spring fever reminds me of baseball, of graduation, of putting warm woolens away for another year. It reminds me that summer is not far away – and that golf season is beginning again. So much of what I enjoy is wrapped up in the promise contained within the words "spring fever" that I know its position as champion in my bracket is true. That's something worth discovering.

In this book, we have gathered 150 brackets about something worth discovering in the great land that we live in. You may be glad or disappointed or furious about some of the conclusions drawn here (and we appreciate that; when it comes to brackets, disagreement is music to our ears). But what we're really doing here is turning opinion into a sport.

Now so can you.

AMERICANA

Magical Numbers *by Richard Sandomir* 1
American Guns *by Stephen Hunter* 2
Jim Henson Creations *by Michael Davis* 3
American Products *by Lee Eisenberg* 4
Cars That Made a Difference *by Phil Patton* 5
Protestant Hymns *by Nancy Gibbs* 6
License Plates *by Tom Vanderbilt* 7
State Birds *by Scott Mowbray* 8
Pseudonyms *by Stanley Bing* 9
Iconic Photographs *by James Danziger* 10
Ridiculous Celebrity Auctions *by Leila Dunbar* 11
Board Games *by Stefan Fatsis* 12
Magic Tricks *by Joshua Jay* 13
Roller Coasters *by Scott Rutherford* 14
SAT Success Strategies *by Laura Wilson* 15
Screen Cowboys *by Neil Amdur* 16
A New National Anthem *by Richard Sandomir* 17

Magical Numbers

By Richard Sandomir

Richard Sandomir was born on 9/4, nearly 2 score and 12 years ago, files an annual 1040, has a 401(k) account, has read *Catch-22* (but not *Mila 18*), and has never watched *Beverly Hills: 90210*.

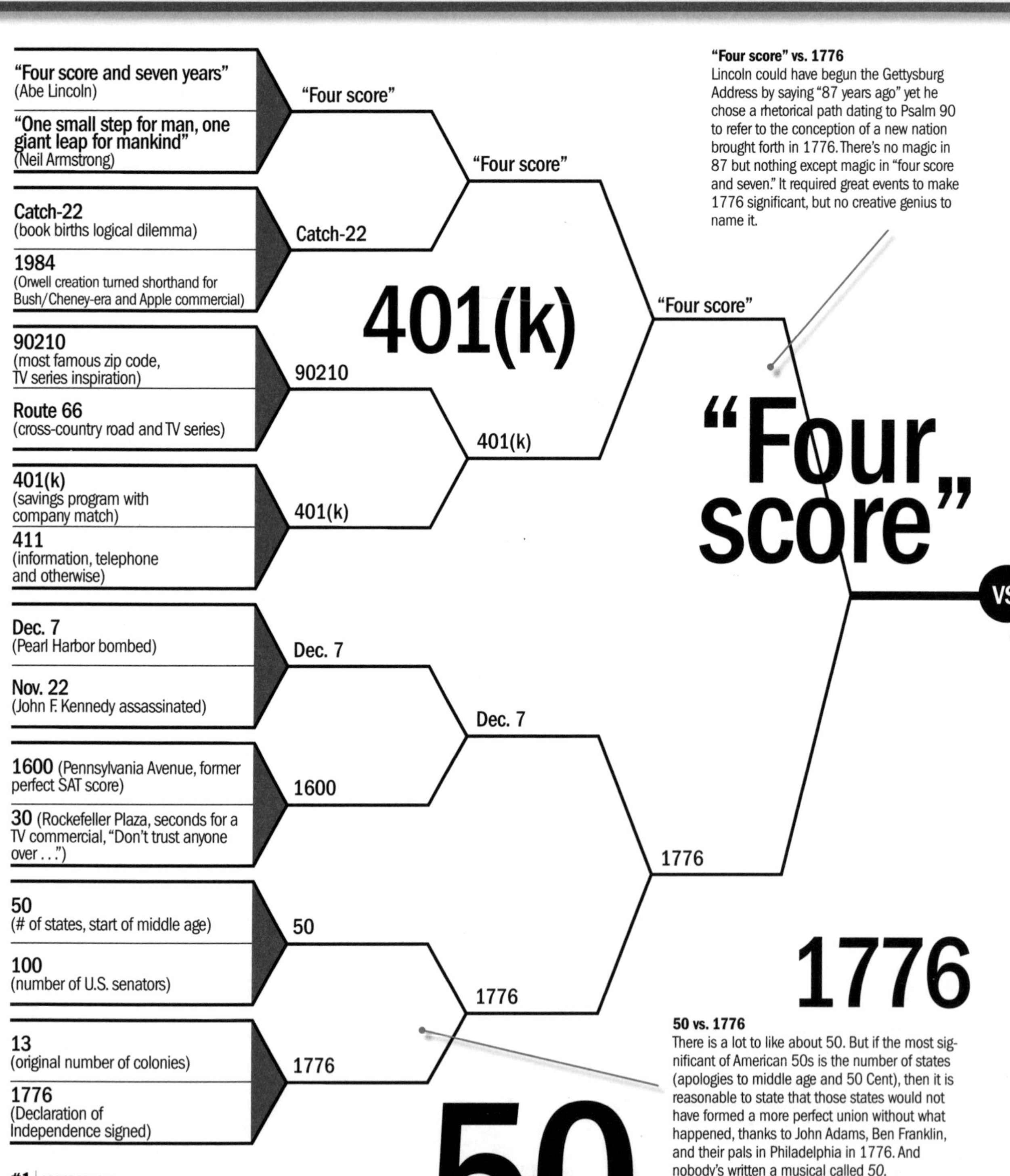

"Four score and seven years"
(Abe Lincoln)
"One small step for man, one giant leap for mankind"
(Neil Armstrong)
Catch-22
(book births logical dilemma)
1984
(Orwell creation turned shorthand for Bush/Cheney-era and Apple commercial)
90210
(most famous zip code, TV series inspiration)
Route 66
(cross-country road and TV series)
401(k)
(savings program with company match)
411
(information, telephone and otherwise)
Dec. 7
(Pearl Harbor bombed)
Nov. 22
(John F. Kennedy assassinated)
1600 (Pennsylvania Avenue, former perfect SAT score)
30 (Rockefeller Plaza, seconds for a TV commercial, "Don't trust anyone over . . .")
50
(# of states, start of middle age)
100
(number of U.S. senators)
13
(original number of colonies)
1776
(Declaration of Independence signed)
"Four score"
Catch-22
90210
401(k)
Dec. 7
1600
50
1776
"Four score"
401(k)
Dec. 7
1776
401(k)
"Four score"
1776
"Four score"
1776
50
VS.

"Four score" vs. 1776

Lincoln could have begun the Gettysburg Address by saying "87 years ago" yet he chose a rhetorical path dating to Psalm 90 to refer to the conception of a new nation brought forth in 1776. There's no magic in 87 but nothing except magic in "four score and seven." It required great events to make 1776 significant, but no creative genius to name it.

50 vs. 1776

There is a lot to like about 50. But if the most significant of American 50s is the number of states (apologies to middle age and 50 Cent), then it is reasonable to state that those states would not have formed a more perfect union without what happened, thanks to John Adams, Ben Franklin, and their pals in Philadelphia in 1776. And nobody's written a musical called *50*.

IN DAILY LIFE AND HISTORY, certain numbers slice into our subconscious, cling to our chromosomes, and alter our national language. Their magic and linguistic rightness can be sensed in an instant (the way 9/11 evokes the 2001 terror attacks) or only after repetition (the way the 401(k) section of the tax code now represents a deferred savings retirement account). If they are magical, these numbers endure, whether they spring from eloquence, snappiness, bureaucratic necessity, or just a day of the week.

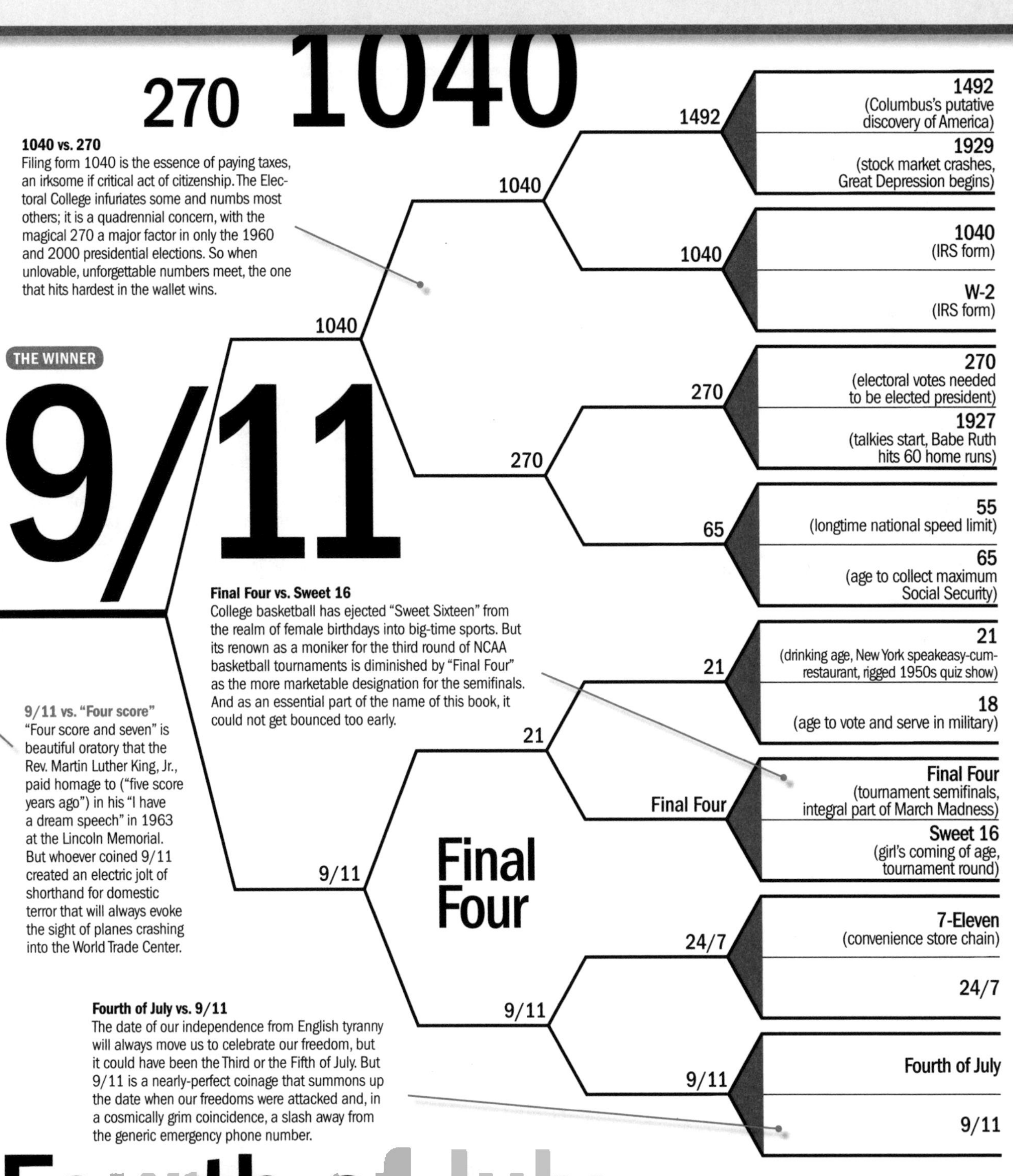

270
1040
1040 vs. 270
Filing form 1040 is the essence of paying taxes, an irksome if critical act of citizenship. The Electoral College infuriates some and numbs most others; it is a quadrennial concern, with the magical 270 a major factor in only the 1960 and 2000 presidential elections. So when unlovable, unforgettable numbers meet, the one that hits hardest in the wallet wins.
THE WINNER
9/11
9/11 vs. "Four score"
"Four score and seven" is beautiful oratory that the Rev. Martin Luther King, Jr., paid homage to ("five score years ago") in his "I have a dream speech" in 1963 at the Lincoln Memorial. But whoever coined 9/11 created an electric jolt of shorthand for domestic terror that will always evoke the sight of planes crashing into the World Trade Center.
Final Four vs. Sweet 16
College basketball has ejected "Sweet Sixteen" from the realm of female birthdays into big-time sports. But its renown as a moniker for the third round of NCAA basketball tournaments is diminished by "Final Four" as the more marketable designation for the semifinals. And as an essential part of the name of this book, it could not get bounced too early.
Final Four
Fourth of July vs. 9/11
The date of our independence from English tyranny will always move us to celebrate our freedom, but it could have been the Third or the Fifth of July. But 9/11 is a nearly-perfect coinage that summons up the date when our freedoms were attacked and, in a cosmically grim coincidence, a slash away from the generic emergency phone number.
Fourth of July
1040
1040
1492
1040
270
270
65
9/11
21
21
Final Four
9/11
24/7
9/11
1492
(Columbus's putative discovery of America)
1929
(stock market crashes, Great Depression begins)
1040
(IRS form)
W-2
(IRS form)
270
(electoral votes needed to be elected president)
1927
(talkies start, Babe Ruth hits 60 home runs)
55
(longtime national speed limit)
65
(age to collect maximum Social Security)
21
(drinking age, New York speakeasy-cum-restaurant, rigged 1950s quiz show)
18
(age to vote and serve in military)
Final Four
(tournament semifinals, integral part of March Madness)
Sweet 16
(girl's coming of age, tournament round)
7-Eleven
(convenience store chain)
24/7
Fourth of July
9/11

American Guns

By Stephen Hunter

Raconteur, war hero, gourmet chef, champion ballroom dancer. Hunter is none of those things. But he knows a lot about guns.

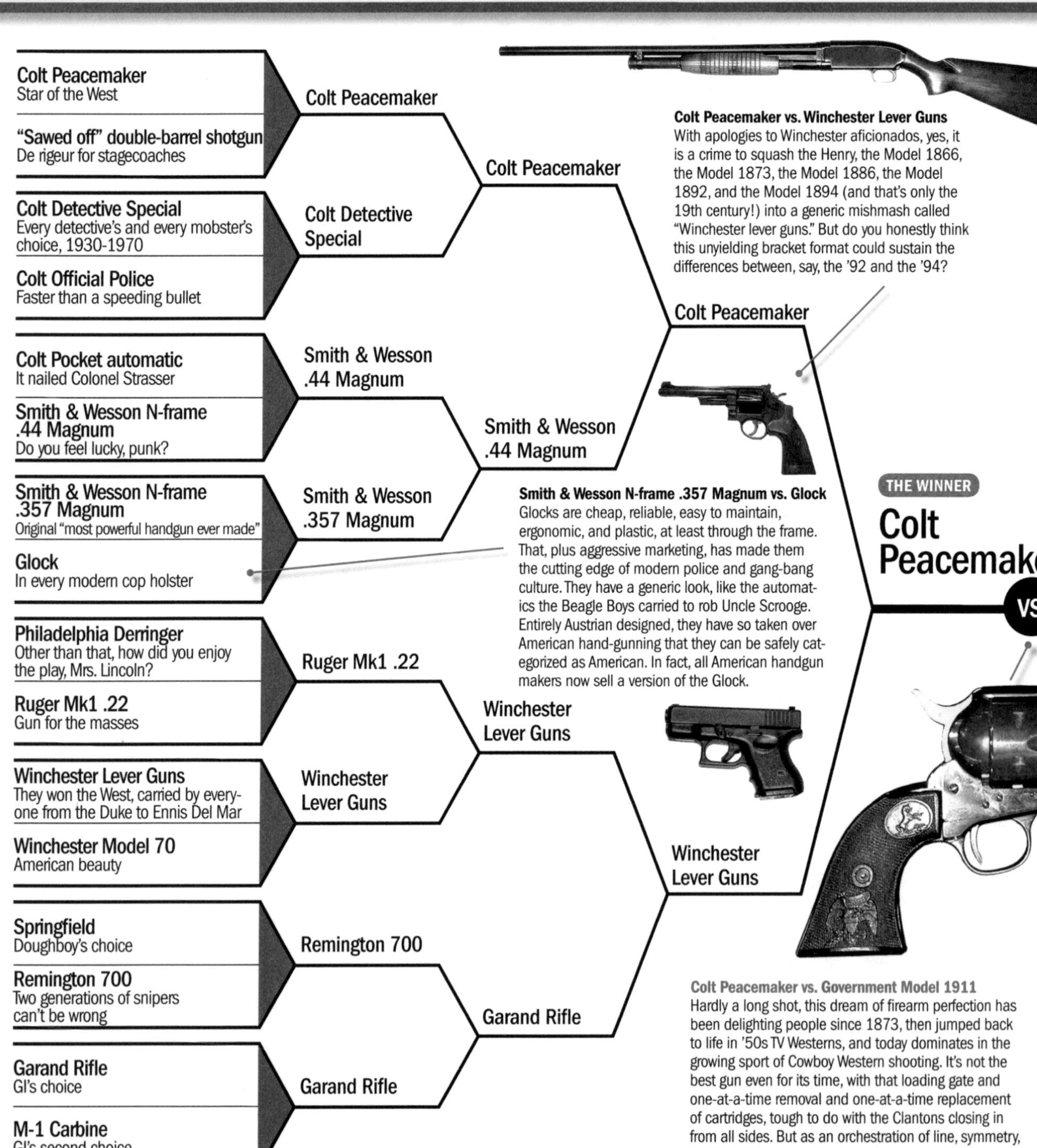

Colt Peacemaker
Star of the West
"Sawed off" double-barrel shotgun
De rigeur for stagecoaches
Colt Detective Special
Every detective's and every mobster's choice, 1930-1970
Colt Official Police
Faster than a speeding bullet
Colt Pocket automatic
It nailed Colonel Strasser
Smith & Wesson N-frame .44 Magnum
Do you feel lucky, punk?
Smith & Wesson N-frame .357 Magnum
Original "most powerful handgun ever made"
Glock
In every modern cop holster
Philadelphia Derringer
Other than that, how did you enjoy the play, Mrs. Lincoln?
Ruger Mk1 .22
Gun for the masses
Winchester Lever Guns
They won the West, carried by everyone from the Duke to Ennis Del Mar
Winchester Model 70
American beauty
Springfield
Doughboy's choice
Remington 700
Two generations of snipers can't be wrong
Garand Rifle
GI's choice
M-1 Carbine
GI's second choice
Colt Peacemaker
Colt Detective Special
Smith & Wesson .44 Magnum
Smith & Wesson .357 Magnum
Ruger Mk1 .22
Winchester Lever Guns
Remington 700
Garand Rifle
Colt Peacemaker
Smith & Wesson .44 Magnum
Winchester Lever Guns
Garand Rifle
Colt Peacemaker
Winchester Lever Guns
THE WINNER
Colt Peacemaker
VS.
Colt Peacemaker vs. Winchester Lever Guns
With apologies to Winchester aficionados, yes, it is a crime to squash the Henry, the Model 1866, the Model 1873, the Model 1886, the Model 1892, and the Model 1894 (and that's only the 19th century!) into a generic mishmash called "Winchester lever guns." But do you honestly think this unyielding bracket format could sustain the differences between, say, the '92 and the '94?
Smith & Wesson N-frame .357 Magnum vs. Glock
Glocks are cheap, reliable, easy to maintain, ergonomic, and plastic, at least through the frame. That, plus aggressive marketing, has made them the cutting edge of modern police and gang-bang culture. They have a generic look, like the automatics the Beagle Boys carried to rob Uncle Scrooge. Entirely Austrian designed, they have so taken over American hand-gunning that they can be safely categorized as American. In fact, all American handgun makers now sell a version of the Glock.
Colt Peacemaker vs. Government Model 1911
Hardly a long shot, this dream of firearm perfection has been delighting people since 1873, then jumped back to life in '50s TV Westerns, and today dominates in the growing sport of Cowboy Western shooting. It's not the best gun even for its time, with that loading gate and one-at-a-time removal and one-at-a-time replacement of cartridges, tough to do with the Clantons closing in from all sides. But as an orchestration of line, symmetry, and ergonomics, as an icon of the century, as a font of popular art, as a reliable tool for tough scrapes, you can't top Colonel Colt's equalizer.

TOOL, DEMON, ERGONOMIC MASTERPIECE, CRUSHER OF DREAMS. That's the American firearm. The criterion here is something indefinable, a memorable orchestration of lines and symmetry that compels the object to memory. History also counts for half. The entries are mostly all-American, though we include two European gizmos that have left their mark within our shores. Guns made famous by movies are favored over guns useful to history, probably because I prefer movies to history. Calibers aren't given because so many were manufactured in multiple calibers.

Thompson vs. Greasegun
America's two pre-eminent wartime subguns go head to head. The Greaser is strictly a wartime improvisation, designed for cheapness and ease of manufacture as opposed to the Thompson's more demanding manufacturing requirements. But for a piece of junk, it served well in many conflicts the globe over. Still, the Thompson's classicism rules in its many guises, first as the Zeitgeist of the '30s mob and FBI era, then as the war raiders' reliable buddy in Marine and Airborne hands, then in every cop movie made in the '50s. An American masterpiece.

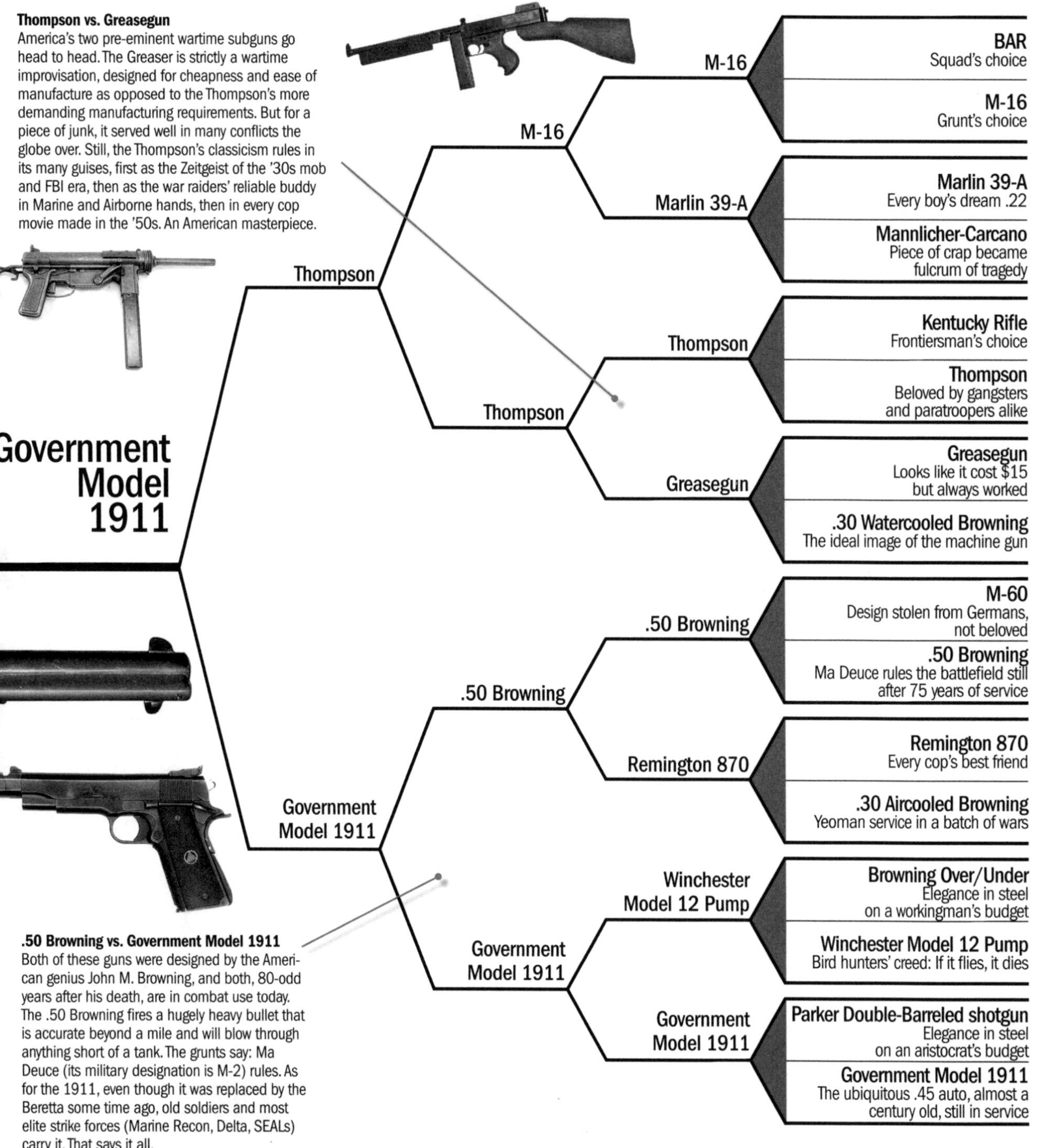
BAR
Squad's choice
M-16
Grunt's choice
Marlin 39-A
Every boy's dream .22
Mannlicher-Carcano
Piece of crap became fulcrum of tragedy
Kentucky Rifle
Frontiersman's choice
Thompson
Beloved by gangsters and paratroopers alike
Greasegun
Looks like it cost $15 but always worked
.30 Watercooled Browning
The ideal image of the machine gun
M-60
Design stolen from Germans, not beloved
.50 Browning
Ma Deuce rules the battlefield still after 75 years of service
Remington 870
Every cop's best friend
.30 Aircooled Browning
Yeoman service in a batch of wars
Browning Over/Under
Elegance in steel on a workingman's budget
Winchester Model 12 Pump
Bird hunters' creed: If it flies, it dies
Parker Double-Barreled shotgun
Elegance in steel on an aristocrat's budget
Government Model 1911
The ubiquitous .45 auto, almost a century old, still in service
M-16
Marlin 39-A
Thompson
Greasegun
.50 Browning
Remington 870
Winchester Model 12 Pump
Government Model 1911
M-16
Thompson
.50 Browning
Government Model 1911
Thompson
Government Model 1911
Government Model 1911

.50 Browning vs. Government Model 1911
Both of these guns were designed by the American genius John M. Browning, and both, 80-odd years after his death, are in combat use today. The .50 Browning fires a hugely heavy bullet that is accurate beyond a mile and will blow through anything short of a tank. The grunts say: Ma Deuce (its military designation is M-2) rules. As for the 1911, even though it was replaced by the Beretta some time ago, old soldiers and most elite strike forces (Marine Recon, Delta, SEALs) carry it. That says it all.

Jim Henson Creations

By Michael Davis

Michael Davis is the author of *Street Gang: The Complete History of Sesame Street.* Not surprisingly, hectoring balcony critics Statler and Waldorf mocked it, Oscar the Grouch trashed it, but Elmo, who can't read, loved it.

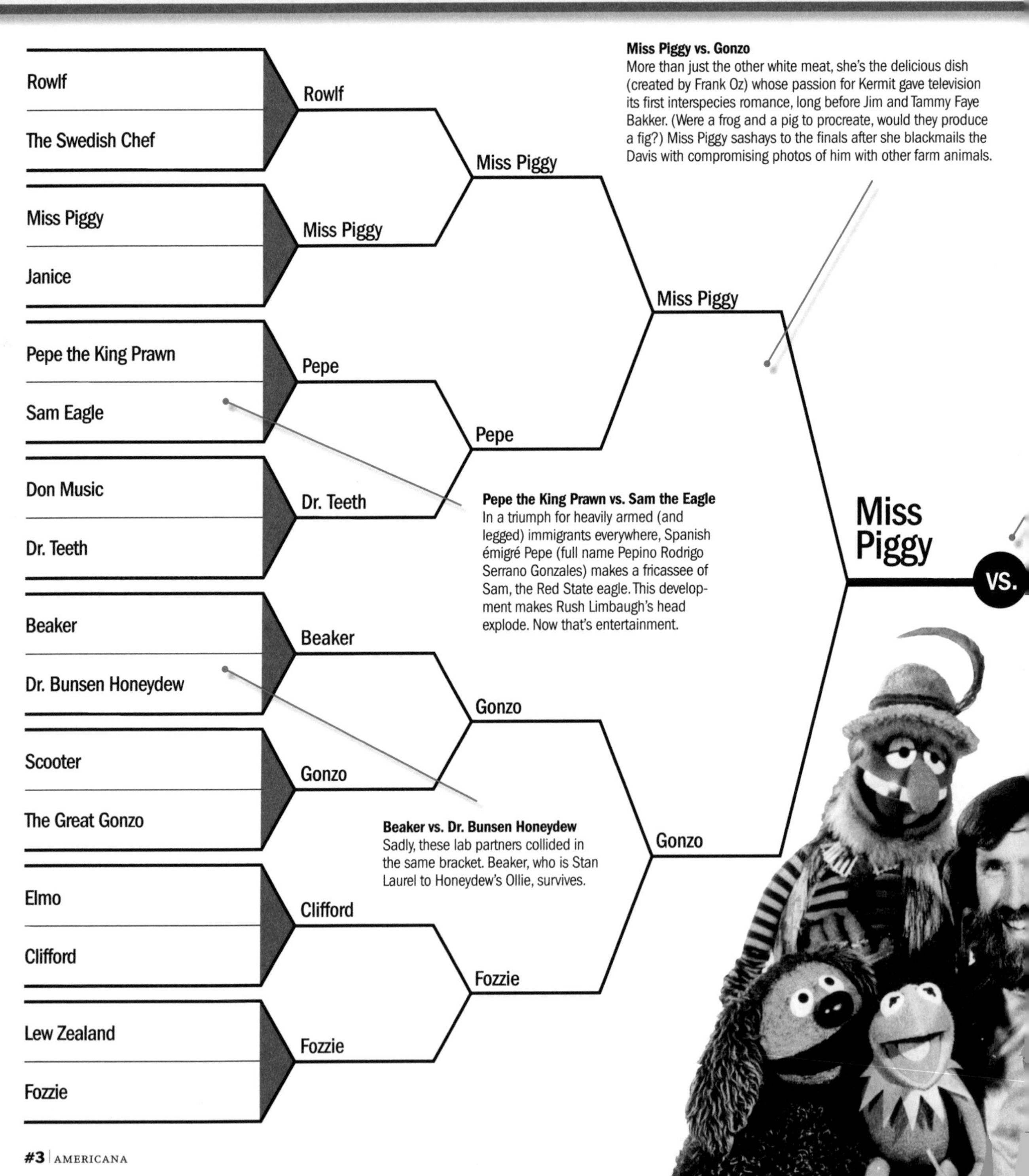
Rowlf
The Swedish Chef
Miss Piggy
Janice
Pepe the King Prawn
Sam Eagle
Don Music
Dr. Teeth
Beaker
Dr. Bunsen Honeydew
Scooter
The Great Gonzo
Elmo
Clifford
Lew Zealand
Fozzie
Rowlf
Miss Piggy
Pepe
Dr. Teeth
Beaker
Gonzo
Clifford
Fozzie
Miss Piggy
Pepe
Gonzo
Fozzie
Miss Piggy
Gonzo
Miss Piggy
VS.

Miss Piggy vs. Gonzo
More than just the other white meat, she's the delicious dish (created by Frank Oz) whose passion for Kermit gave television its first interspecies romance, long before Jim and Tammy Faye Bakker. (Were a frog and a pig to procreate, would they produce a fig?) Miss Piggy sashays to the finals after she blackmails the Davis with compromising photos of him with other farm animals.

Pepe the King Prawn vs. Sam the Eagle
In a triumph for heavily armed (and legged) immigrants everywhere, Spanish émigré Pepe (full name Pepino Rodrigo Serrano Gonzales) makes a fricassee of Sam, the Red State eagle. This development makes Rush Limbaugh's head explode. Now that's entertainment.

Beaker vs. Dr. Bunsen Honeydew
Sadly, these lab partners collided in the same bracket. Beaker, who is Stan Laurel to Honeydew's Ollie, survives.

HEREWITH, A MUPPET MATRIX pitting the late Jim Henson's sneakily subversive commentators on the human condition against one another for the first time, a puppet popularity contest to pick the top dog, frog, pig, bird, rodent, or bear. Let the fur fly!

Miss Piggy vs. Kermit
Long before Howard Stern, Kermit was king of all media. He conquered television (hosting the *Tonight* show), the movies (opposite Orson Welles in one of the great denouements in cinema history), and theme park attractions. There's even a Kermit balloon in the Macy's Thanksgiving Day Parade, this culture's highest accolade! Only a brute would hog this amiable amphibian's spotlight.

Animal vs. Cookie Monster
It's Id versus Id in this battle between the Electric Mayhem's libidinous stadium-rock drummer and *Sesame Street*'s serial nosher. Both are working through their problems with obsession, but how can you look into Cookie's hypnotically googly eyes and not move him on to Round III?

Round I	Round II	Round III	Round IV	Winner
Sweetums	Animal	Cookie	Cookie	Kermit
Animal				
Two-Headed Monster	Cookie Monster			
Cookie Monster				
Big Bird	Big Bird	Big Bird		
La Choy Dragon				
Roosevelt Franklin	Hoots			
Hoots				
The Trash Heap	The Trash Heap	Oscar	Kermit	
The Mighty Favog				
Oscar the Grouch	Oscar the Grouch			
Grover				
Bert	Ernie	Kermit		
Ernie				
Kermit	Kermit			
Rizzo				

THE WINNER

Kermit

Big Bird vs. La Choy Dragon
This battle of walk-around puppets pits an 8-foot canary from public television against a fire-breathing agent of clever commercialism from the mid-1960s. Big Bird moves on to the next round when the dragon suddenly realizes he's extinct.

Kermit vs. Ernie
His split-personality bracket features the two projections of Henson's ego, Kermit, the wry observer who is wary of the fray, and Ernie, the mischievous buddy boy. One could argue that Kermit was proto-observational comic. It wasn't easy bein' green, but he never worked blue.

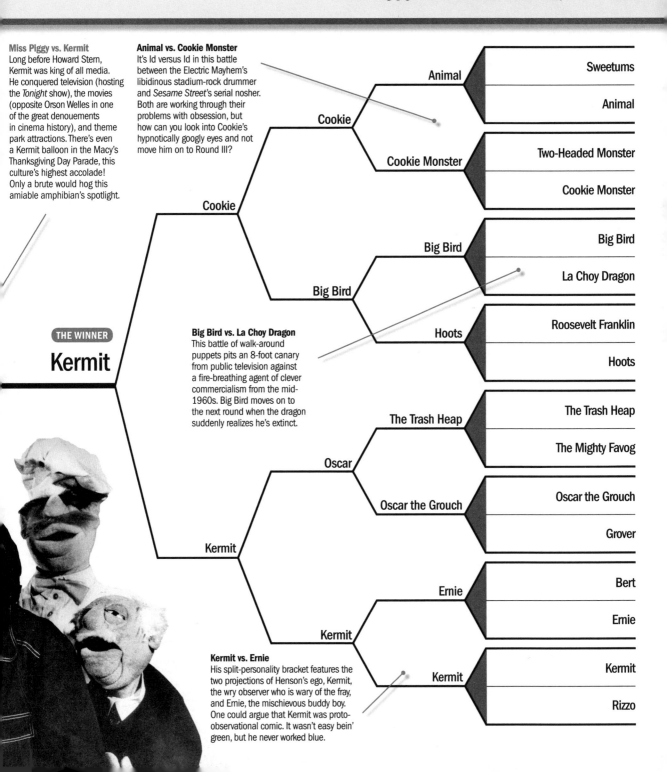

American Products

By Lee Eisenberg

Lee Eisenberg is the bestselling author of *The Number: A Different Way to Think About the Rest of Your Life* and (next) *Shoptimism: A Journey Through the Heart and Mind of the American Consumer.*

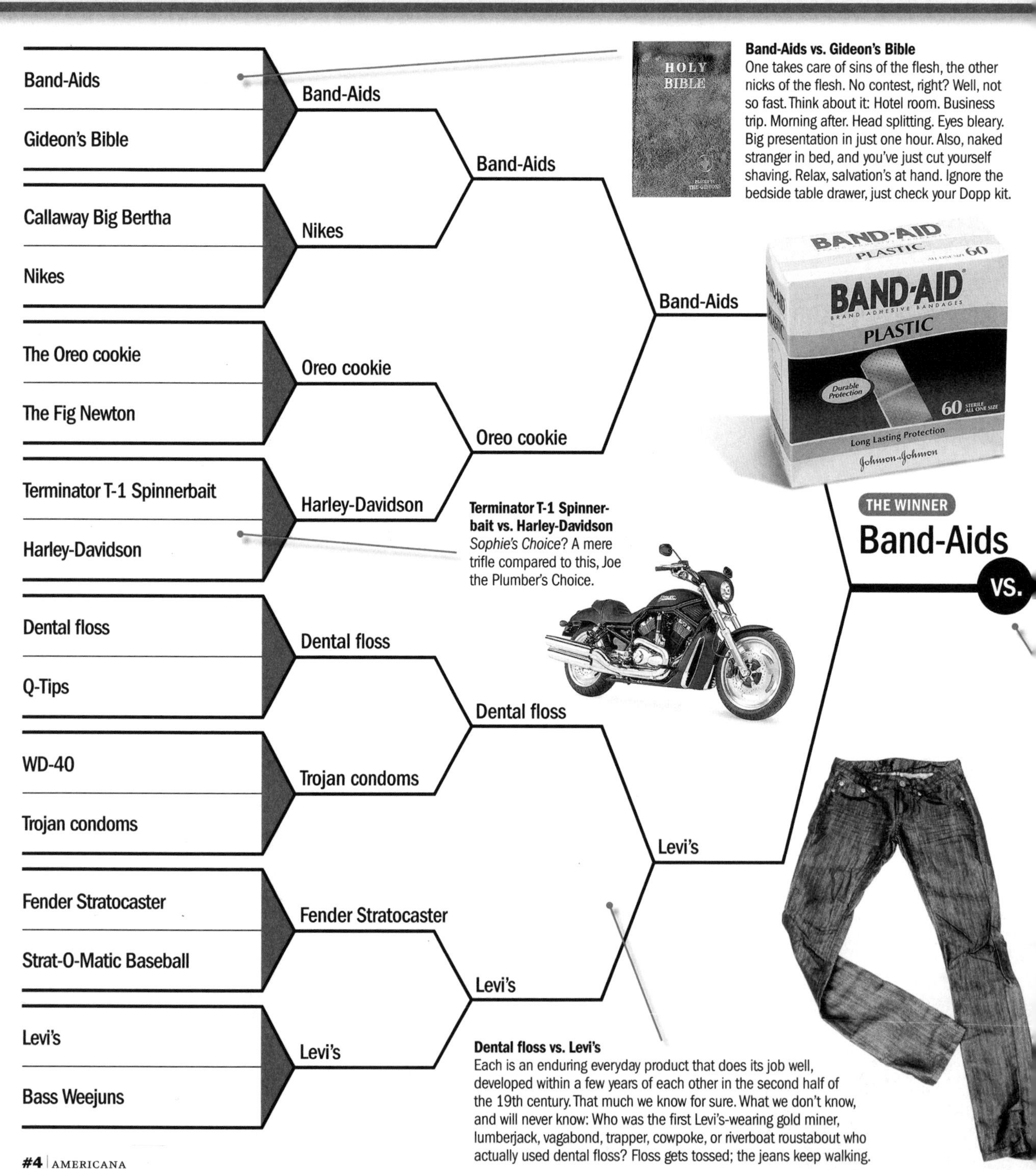

Band-Aids
Gideon's Bible
Callaway Big Bertha
Nikes
The Oreo cookie
The Fig Newton
Terminator T-1 Spinnerbait
Harley-Davidson
Dental floss
Q-Tips
WD-40
Trojan condoms
Fender Stratocaster
Strat-O-Matic Baseball
Levi's
Bass Weejuns
Band-Aids
Nikes
Oreo cookie
Harley-Davidson
Dental floss
Trojan condoms
Fender Stratocaster
Levi's
Band-Aids
Oreo cookie
Dental floss
Levi's
Band-Aids
Levi's
THE WINNER
Band-Aids
VS.
HOLY BIBLE
BAND-AID
PLASTIC
60
BAND-AID
BRAND ADHESIVE BANDAGES
PLASTIC
Durable Protection
60 STERILE ALL ONE SIZE
Long Lasting Protection
Johnson & Johnson

Band-Aids vs. Gideon's Bible
One takes care of sins of the flesh, the other nicks of the flesh. No contest, right? Well, not so fast. Think about it: Hotel room. Business trip. Morning after. Head splitting. Eyes bleary. Big presentation in just one hour. Also, naked stranger in bed, and you've just cut yourself shaving. Relax, salvation's at hand. Ignore the bedside table drawer, just check your Dopp kit.

Terminator T-1 Spinnerbait vs. Harley-Davidson
Sophie's Choice? A mere trifle compared to this, Joe the Plumber's Choice.

Dental floss vs. Levi's
Each is an enduring everyday product that does its job well, developed within a few years of each other in the second half of the 19th century. That much we know for sure. What we don't know, and will never know: Who was the first Levi's-wearing gold miner, lumberjack, vagabond, trapper, cowpoke, or riverboat roustabout who actually used dental floss? Floss gets tossed; the jeans keep walking.

IN 1890, the psychologist William James said that "a man's self is the sum total of all that he can call his . . . his clothes and his house . . . his reputation and works, his lands, and yacht and bank-account." He wasn't creating an excuse for materialism. He meant that our true temperament and values are not reflected in the mirror, but in all that's stashed in our garages, kitchens, and bathrooms. In other words, the quintessential All-American product that wins here most reflects who we are.

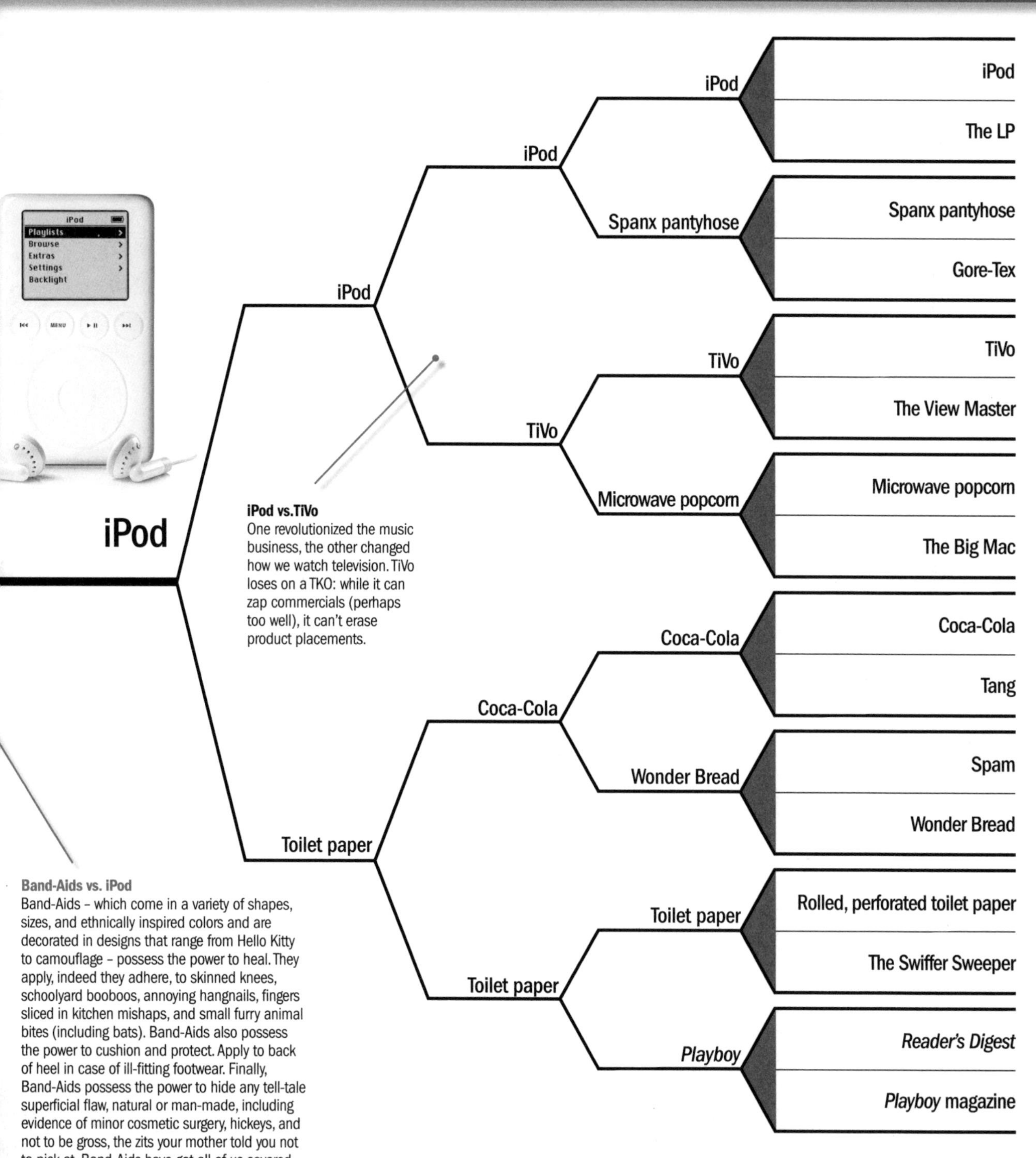

iPod
iPod
iPod
iPod
The LP
Spanx pantyhose
Spanx pantyhose
Gore-Tex
TiVo
TiVo
TiVo
The View Master
Microwave popcorn
Microwave popcorn
The Big Mac
Toilet paper
Coca-Cola
Coca-Cola
Coca-Cola
Tang
Wonder Bread
Spam
Wonder Bread
Toilet paper
Toilet paper
Rolled, perforated toilet paper
The Swiffer Sweeper
Playboy
Reader's Digest
Playboy magazine

iPod vs. TiVo
One revolutionized the music business, the other changed how we watch television. TiVo loses on a TKO: while it can zap commercials (perhaps too well), it can't erase product placements.

Band-Aids vs. iPod
Band-Aids – which come in a variety of shapes, sizes, and ethnically inspired colors and are decorated in designs that range from Hello Kitty to camouflage – possess the power to heal. They apply, indeed they adhere, to skinned knees, schoolyard booboos, annoying hangnails, fingers sliced in kitchen mishaps, and small furry animal bites (including bats). Band-Aids also possess the power to cushion and protect. Apply to back of heel in case of ill-fitting footwear. Finally, Band-Aids possess the power to hide any tell-tale superficial flaw, natural or man-made, including evidence of minor cosmetic surgery, hickeys, and not to be gross, the zits your mother told you not to pick at. Band-Aids have got all of us covered.

Cars That Made a Difference

By Phil Patton

Phil Patton is the author of a dozen books on design and culture and writes about automobiles for the *New York Times, ID, Met Home,* and other publications.

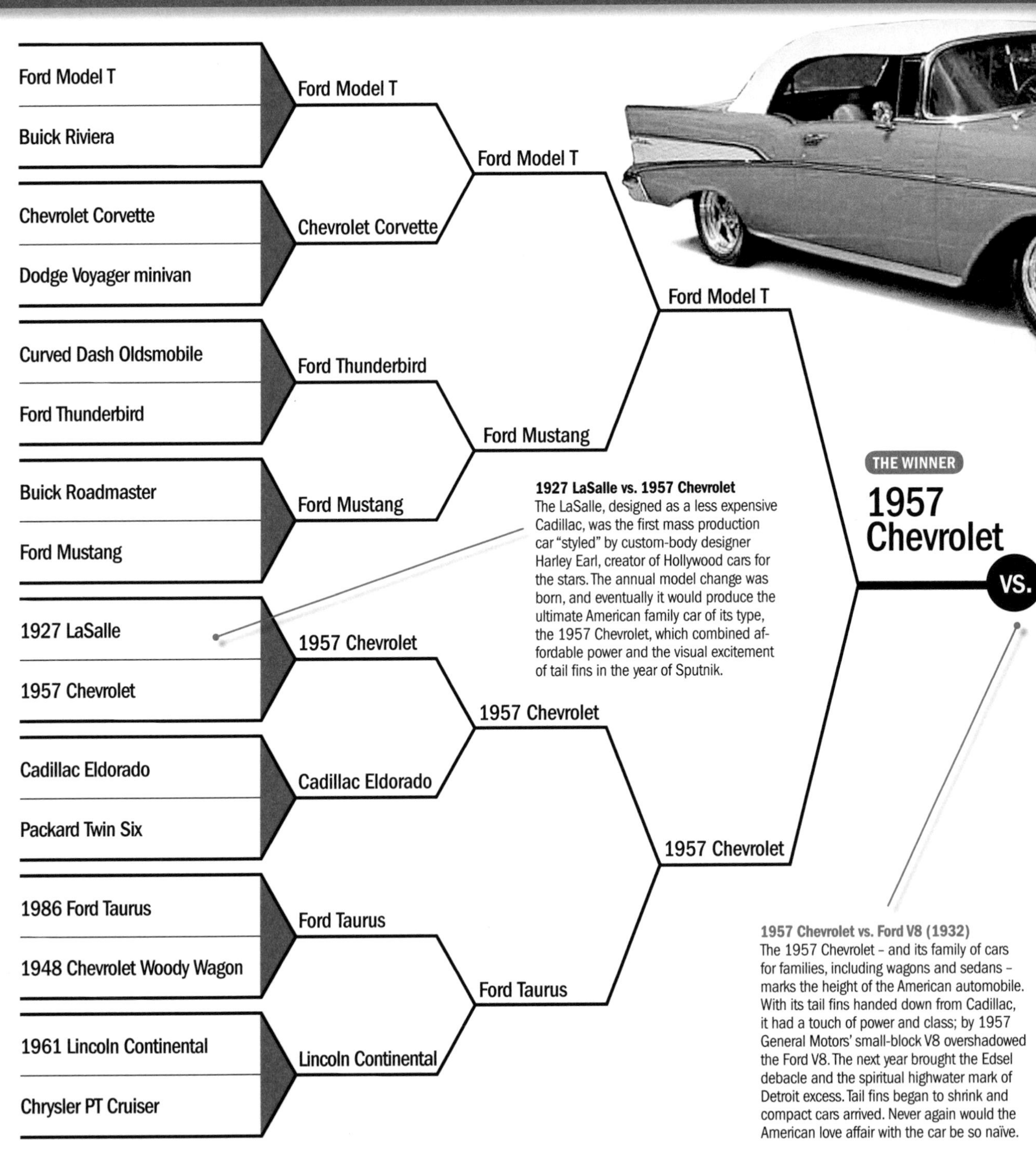
Ford Model T
Buick Riviera
Chevrolet Corvette
Dodge Voyager minivan
Curved Dash Oldsmobile
Ford Thunderbird
Buick Roadmaster
Ford Mustang
1927 LaSalle
1957 Chevrolet
Cadillac Eldorado
Packard Twin Six
1986 Ford Taurus
1948 Chevrolet Woody Wagon
1961 Lincoln Continental
Chrysler PT Cruiser
Ford Model T
Chevrolet Corvette
Ford Thunderbird
Ford Mustang
1957 Chevrolet
Cadillac Eldorado
Ford Taurus
Lincoln Continental
Ford Model T
Ford Mustang
1957 Chevrolet
Ford Taurus
Ford Model T
1957 Chevrolet
THE WINNER
1957 Chevrolet
VS.

1927 LaSalle vs. 1957 Chevrolet
The LaSalle, designed as a less expensive Cadillac, was the first mass production car "styled" by custom-body designer Harley Earl, creator of Hollywood cars for the stars. The annual model change was born, and eventually it would produce the ultimate American family car of its type, the 1957 Chevrolet, which combined affordable power and the visual excitement of tail fins in the year of Sputnik.

1957 Chevrolet vs. Ford V8 (1932)
The 1957 Chevrolet – and its family of cars for families, including wagons and sedans – marks the height of the American automobile. With its tail fins handed down from Cadillac, it had a touch of power and class; by 1957 General Motors' small-block V8 overshadowed the Ford V8. The next year brought the Edsel debacle and the spiritual highwater mark of Detroit excess. Tail fins began to shrink and compact cars arrived. Never again would the American love affair with the car be so naïve.

IN A COUNTRY CONQUERED BY THE MACHINE, the car became a perfect avatar for four-wheeled fantasies of speed, size, empowerment, and mobility. Some figured as versions of the cowboy's horse and some as versions of Cinderella's coach. Some carried ideas, like the Model T Ford, which popularized the wild and crazy notion that every family should own at least one car, while others, from Packards to Corvettes, suggested the car as a work of art, an esthetic object compounded by metal, glass, and speed.

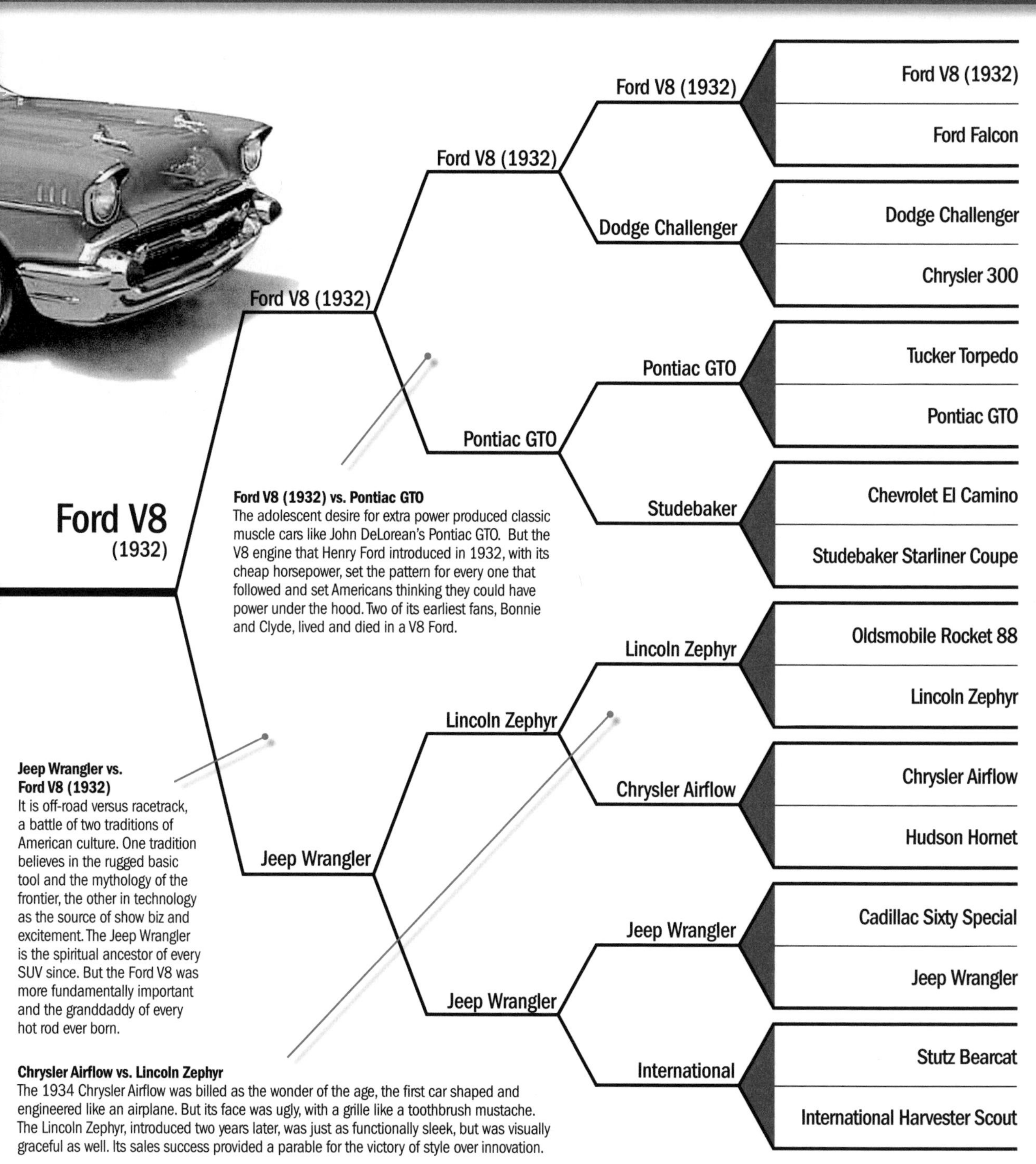

Ford V8 (1932)
Ford Falcon
Dodge Challenger
Chrysler 300
Tucker Torpedo
Pontiac GTO
Chevrolet El Camino
Studebaker Starliner Coupe
Oldsmobile Rocket 88
Lincoln Zephyr
Chrysler Airflow
Hudson Hornet
Cadillac Sixty Special
Jeep Wrangler
Stutz Bearcat
International Harvester Scout
Ford V8 (1932)
Dodge Challenger
Pontiac GTO
Studebaker
Lincoln Zephyr
Chrysler Airflow
Jeep Wrangler
International
Ford V8 (1932)
Pontiac GTO
Lincoln Zephyr
Jeep Wrangler
Ford V8 (1932)
Jeep Wrangler
Ford V8
(1932)

Ford V8 (1932) vs. Pontiac GTO
The adolescent desire for extra power produced classic muscle cars like John DeLorean's Pontiac GTO. But the V8 engine that Henry Ford introduced in 1932, with its cheap horsepower, set the pattern for every one that followed and set Americans thinking they could have power under the hood. Two of its earliest fans, Bonnie and Clyde, lived and died in a V8 Ford.

Jeep Wrangler vs. Ford V8 (1932)
It is off-road versus racetrack, a battle of two traditions of American culture. One tradition believes in the rugged basic tool and the mythology of the frontier, the other in technology as the source of show biz and excitement. The Jeep Wrangler is the spiritual ancestor of every SUV since. But the Ford V8 was more fundamentally important and the granddaddy of every hot rod ever born.

Chrysler Airflow vs. Lincoln Zephyr
The 1934 Chrysler Airflow was billed as the wonder of the age, the first car shaped and engineered like an airplane. But its face was ugly, with a grille like a toothbrush mustache. The Lincoln Zephyr, introduced two years later, was just as functionally sleek, but was visually graceful as well. Its sales success provided a parable for the victory of style over innovation.

Protestant Hymns

By Nancy Gibbs

Nancy Gibbs is an essayist and editor at large at *Time* magazine, and co-author, with Michael Duffy, of *The Preacher and the Presidents: Billy Graham in the White House.*

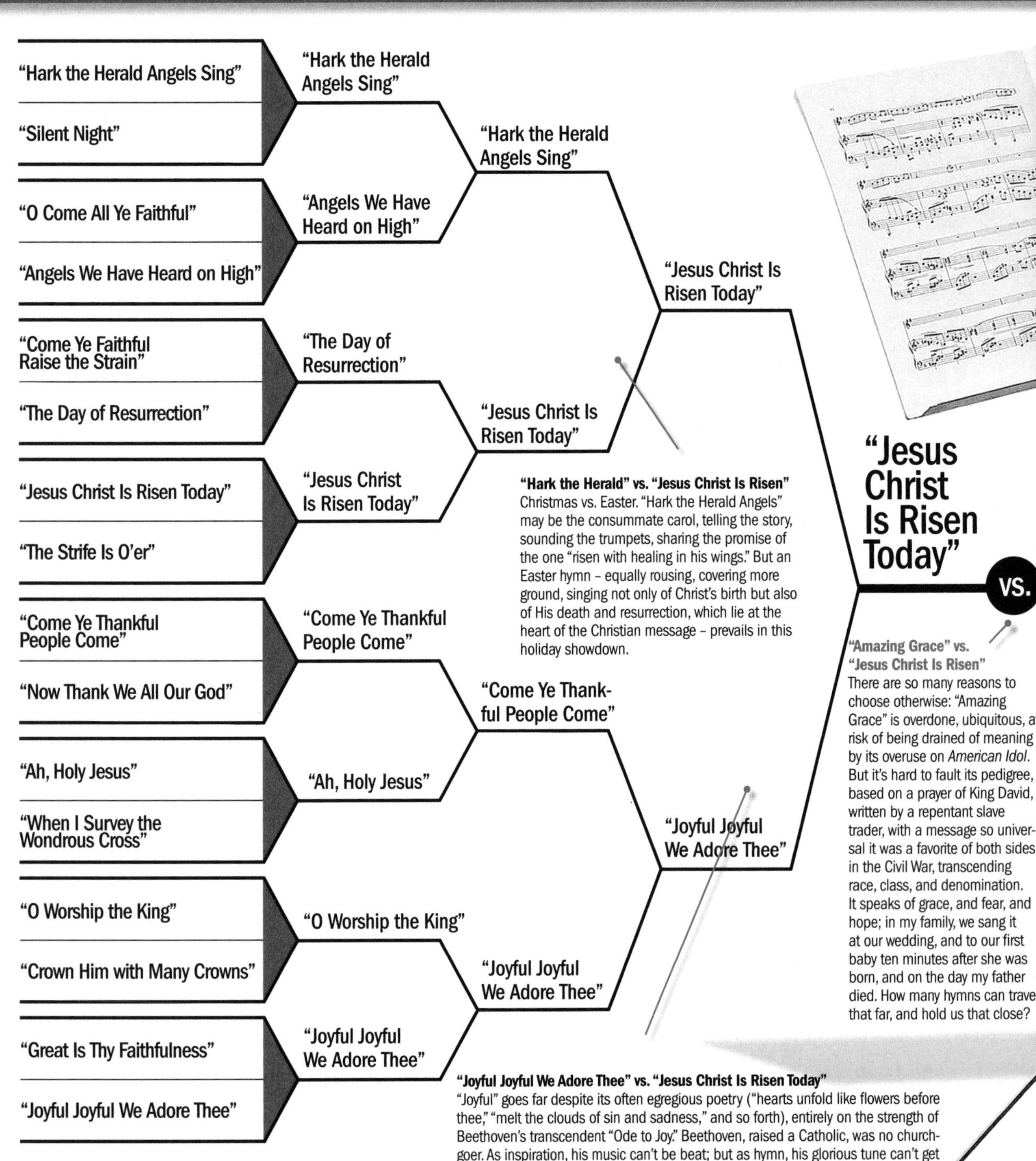
"Hark the Herald Angels Sing"
"Silent Night"
"O Come All Ye Faithful"
"Angels We Have Heard on High"
"Come Ye Faithful Raise the Strain"
"The Day of Resurrection"
"Jesus Christ Is Risen Today"
"The Strife Is O'er"
"Come Ye Thankful People Come"
"Now Thank We All Our God"
"Ah, Holy Jesus"
"When I Survey the Wondrous Cross"
"O Worship the King"
"Crown Him with Many Crowns"
"Great Is Thy Faithfulness"
"Joyful Joyful We Adore Thee"
"Hark the Herald Angels Sing"
"Angels We Have Heard on High"
"The Day of Resurrection"
"Jesus Christ Is Risen Today"
"Come Ye Thankful People Come"
"Ah, Holy Jesus"
"O Worship the King"
"Joyful Joyful We Adore Thee"
"Hark the Herald Angels Sing"
"Jesus Christ Is Risen Today"
"Come Ye Thank-ful People Come"
"Joyful Joyful We Adore Thee"
"Jesus Christ Is Risen Today"
"Joyful Joyful We Adore Thee"
"Jesus Christ Is Risen Today"
VS.

"Hark the Herald" vs. "Jesus Christ Is Risen"
Christmas vs. Easter. "Hark the Herald Angels" may be the consummate carol, telling the story, sounding the trumpets, sharing the promise of the one "risen with healing in his wings." But an Easter hymn – equally rousing, covering more ground, singing not only of Christ's birth but also of His death and resurrection, which lie at the heart of the Christian message – prevails in this holiday showdown.

"Joyful Joyful We Adore Thee" vs. "Jesus Christ Is Risen Today"
"Joyful" goes far despite its often egregious poetry ("hearts unfold like flowers before thee," "melt the clouds of sin and sadness," and so forth), entirely on the strength of Beethoven's transcendent "Ode to Joy." Beethoven, raised a Catholic, was no church-goer. As inspiration, his music can't be beat; but as hymn, his glorious tune can't get past the bright hymn of resurrection that captures the joy of Easter morning.

"Amazing Grace" vs. "Jesus Christ Is Risen"
There are so many reasons to choose otherwise: "Amazing Grace" is overdone, ubiquitous, at risk of being drained of meaning by its overuse on *American Idol*. But it's hard to fault its pedigree, based on a prayer of King David, written by a repentant slave trader, with a message so universal it was a favorite of both sides in the Civil War, transcending race, class, and denomination. It speaks of grace, and fear, and hope; in my family, we sang it at our wedding, and to our first baby ten minutes after she was born, and on the day my father died. How many hymns can travel that far, and hold us that close?

THE PROTESTANT HYMNAL HAS SURVIVED as a thing of musical and spiritual beauty, despite mighty efforts to politically correct it. I'll leave it to others to rank Christian pop, Gospel rap, the megachurch's evangelical praise music, and the black church's roof-raising spirituals (none of which you'll find here). We start with 32 "greatest hits" from the mainline hymnal in its present incarnation – Christmas carols, Easter hymns, Good Friday dirges, joyful hymns of praise, and ceremonial music that carried the country through its 9/11 mourning and recovery. Victory goes to that one that manages to lift the soul toward praise and peace.

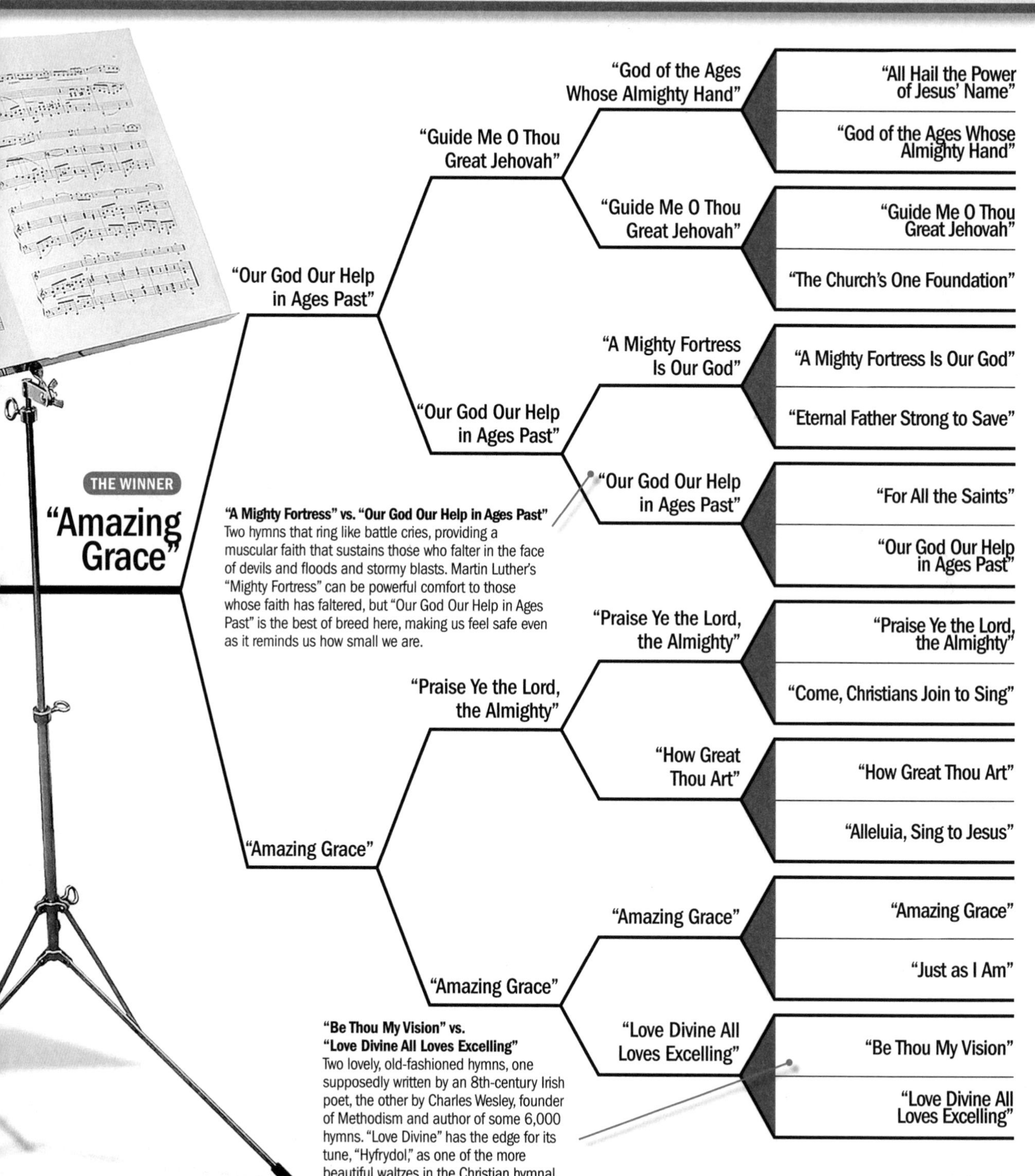

"All Hail the Power of Jesus' Name"
"God of the Ages Whose Almighty Hand"
"Guide Me O Thou Great Jehovah"
"The Church's One Foundation"
"A Mighty Fortress Is Our God"
"Eternal Father Strong to Save"
"For All the Saints"
"Our God Our Help in Ages Past"
"Praise Ye the Lord, the Almighty"
"Come, Christians Join to Sing"
"How Great Thou Art"
"Alleluia, Sing to Jesus"
"Amazing Grace"
"Just as I Am"
"Be Thou My Vision"
"Love Divine All Loves Excelling"
"God of the Ages Whose Almighty Hand"
"Guide Me O Thou Great Jehovah"
"A Mighty Fortress Is Our God"
"Our God Our Help in Ages Past"
"Praise Ye the Lord, the Almighty"
"How Great Thou Art"
"Amazing Grace"
"Love Divine All Loves Excelling"
"Guide Me O Thou Great Jehovah"
"Our God Our Help in Ages Past"
"Praise Ye the Lord, the Almighty"
"Amazing Grace"
"Our God Our Help in Ages Past"
"Amazing Grace"
THE WINNER
"Amazing Grace"

"A Mighty Fortress" vs. "Our God Our Help in Ages Past"
Two hymns that ring like battle cries, providing a muscular faith that sustains those who falter in the face of devils and floods and stormy blasts. Martin Luther's "Mighty Fortress" can be powerful comfort to those whose faith has faltered, but "Our God Our Help in Ages Past" is the best of breed here, making us feel safe even as it reminds us how small we are.

"Be Thou My Vision" vs. "Love Divine All Loves Excelling"
Two lovely, old-fashioned hymns, one supposedly written by an 8th-century Irish poet, the other by Charles Wesley, founder of Methodism and author of some 6,000 hymns. "Love Divine" has the edge for its tune, "Hyfrydol," as one of the more beautiful waltzes in the Christian hymnal.

License Plates

By Tom Vanderbilt

Tom Vanderbilt, author of the bestselling *Traffic: Why We Drive the Way We Do (and What It Says About Us),* lives in Brooklyn with his wife, Jancee Dunn (where he receives a lot of second-hand father-in-law advice; see bracket #31).

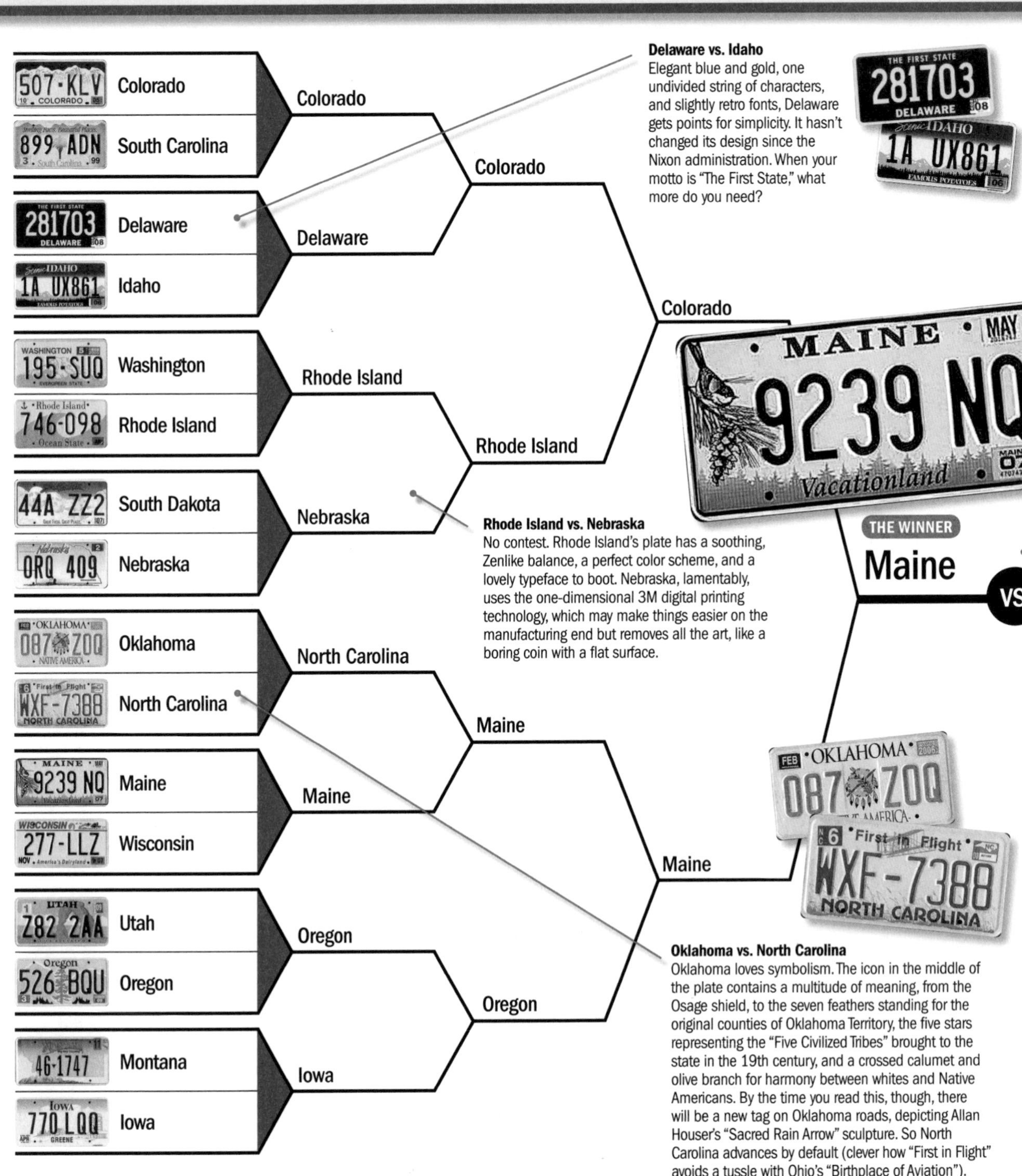

Colorado
South Carolina
Delaware
Idaho
Washington
Rhode Island
South Dakota
Nebraska
Oklahoma
North Carolina
Maine
Wisconsin
Utah
Oregon
Montana
Iowa
Colorado
Delaware
Rhode Island
Nebraska
North Carolina
Maine
Oregon
Iowa
Colorado
Rhode Island
Maine
Oregon
Colorado
Maine
THE WINNER
Maine
VS.

Delaware vs. Idaho
Elegant blue and gold, one undivided string of characters, and slightly retro fonts, Delaware gets points for simplicity. It hasn't changed its design since the Nixon administration. When your motto is "The First State," what more do you need?

Rhode Island vs. Nebraska
No contest. Rhode Island's plate has a soothing, Zenlike balance, a perfect color scheme, and a lovely typeface to boot. Nebraska, lamentably, uses the one-dimensional 3M digital printing technology, which may make things easier on the manufacturing end but removes all the art, like a boring coin with a flat surface.

Oklahoma vs. North Carolina
Oklahoma loves symbolism. The icon in the middle of the plate contains a multitude of meaning, from the Osage shield, to the seven feathers standing for the original counties of Oklahoma Territory, the five stars representing the "Five Civilized Tribes" brought to the state in the 19th century, and a crossed calumet and olive branch for harmony between whites and Native Americans. By the time you read this, though, there will be a new tag on Oklahoma roads, depicting Allan Houser's "Sacred Rain Arrow" sculpture. So North Carolina advances by default (clever how "First in Flight" avoids a tussle with Ohio's "Birthplace of Aviation").

LICENSE PLATES ARE MARKERS of identity in the otherwise anonymous world of traffic. There's a curious power in seeing a fellow resident's plate far from home, or some rare species sighting like Hawaii tags on the mainland. Once bearing nothing more than the state's name and a few letters and numbers on a slab of porcelain, the tags increasingly function as touristic come-ons or mobile billboards for civic virtue. In Ohio they can identify you as a repeat drunk driver. But one thing is constant: U.S. plates are still largely manufactured in prisons.

Maine vs. New Mexico
Whenever I see a Maine plate in front of me, I feel as if I'm no longer breathing car exhaust but the fragrance of the pines stretching across the plate's bottom, hearing not the motor but the complex call of the black-capped chickadee. I want to follow it home, this stirring postcard in stamped metal, to that magical *Vacationland*, italicized for dreamy emphasis.

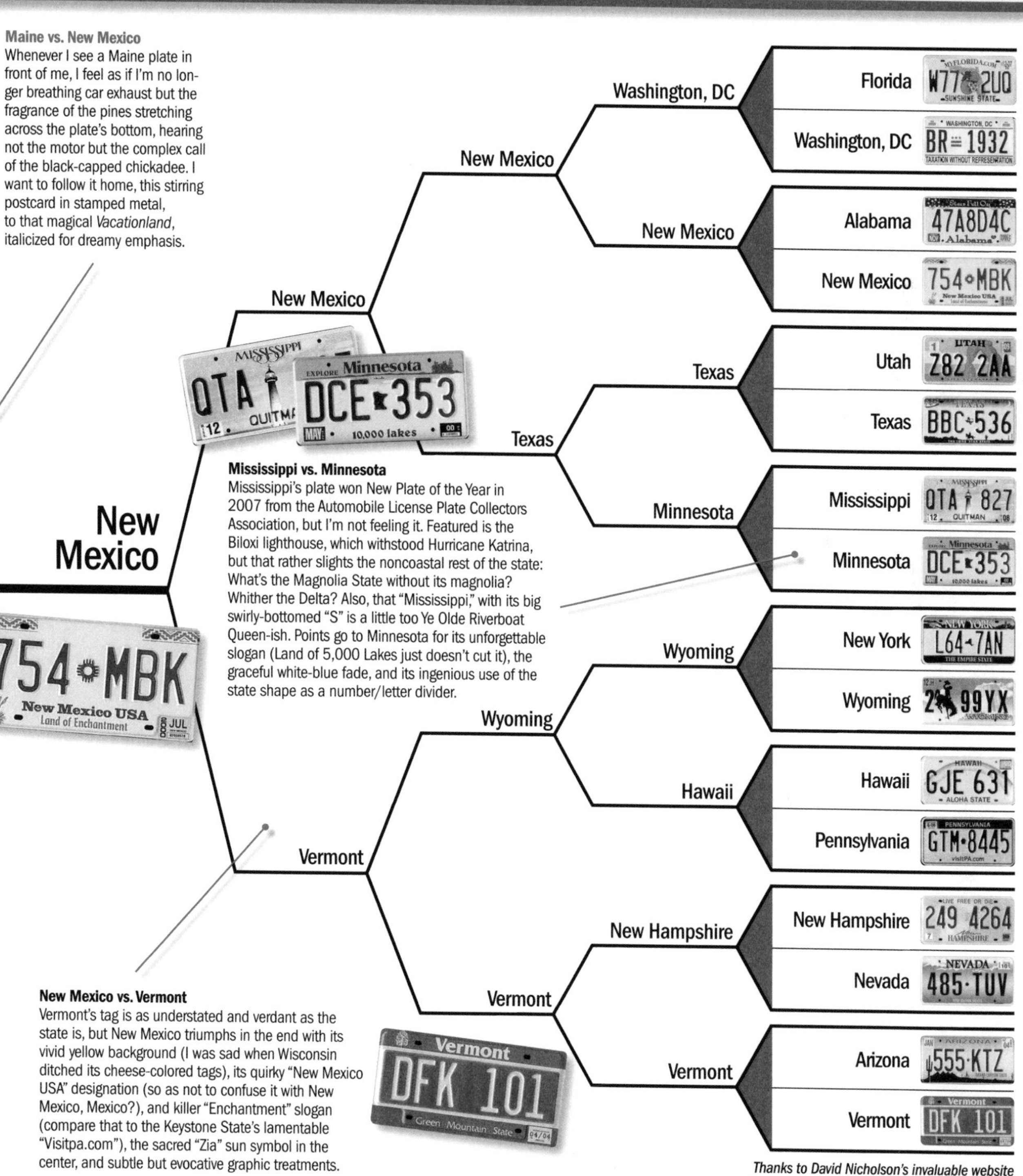

Florida
Washington, DC
Alabama
New Mexico
Utah
Texas
Mississippi
Minnesota
New York
Wyoming
Hawaii
Pennsylvania
New Hampshire
Nevada
Arizona
Vermont
Washington, DC
New Mexico
Texas
Minnesota
Wyoming
Hawaii
New Hampshire
Vermont
New Mexico
Texas
Wyoming
Vermont
New Mexico
Vermont
New Mexico

Mississippi vs. Minnesota
Mississippi's plate won New Plate of the Year in 2007 from the Automobile License Plate Collectors Association, but I'm not feeling it. Featured is the Biloxi lighthouse, which withstood Hurricane Katrina, but that rather slights the noncoastal rest of the state: What's the Magnolia State without its magnolia? Whither the Delta? Also, that "Mississippi," with its big swirly-bottomed "S" is a little too Ye Olde Riverboat Queen-ish. Points go to Minnesota for its unforgettable slogan (Land of 5,000 Lakes just doesn't cut it), the graceful white-blue fade, and its ingenious use of the state shape as a number/letter divider.

New Mexico vs. Vermont
Vermont's tag is as understated and verdant as the state is, but New Mexico triumphs in the end with its vivid yellow background (I was sad when Wisconsin ditched its cheese-colored tags), its quirky "New Mexico USA" designation (so as not to confuse it with New Mexico, Mexico?), and killer "Enchantment" slogan (compare that to the Keystone State's lamentable "Visitpa.com"), the sacred "Zia" sun symbol in the center, and subtle but evocative graphic treatments.

Thanks to David Nicholson's invaluable website (www.15q.net) for license plate information.

State Birds

By Scott Mowbray

Scott Mowbray is a Brooklyn-based magazine editor. He has been editor of *Popular Science*, Health.com, *Joe*, and *Eating Well* magazine.

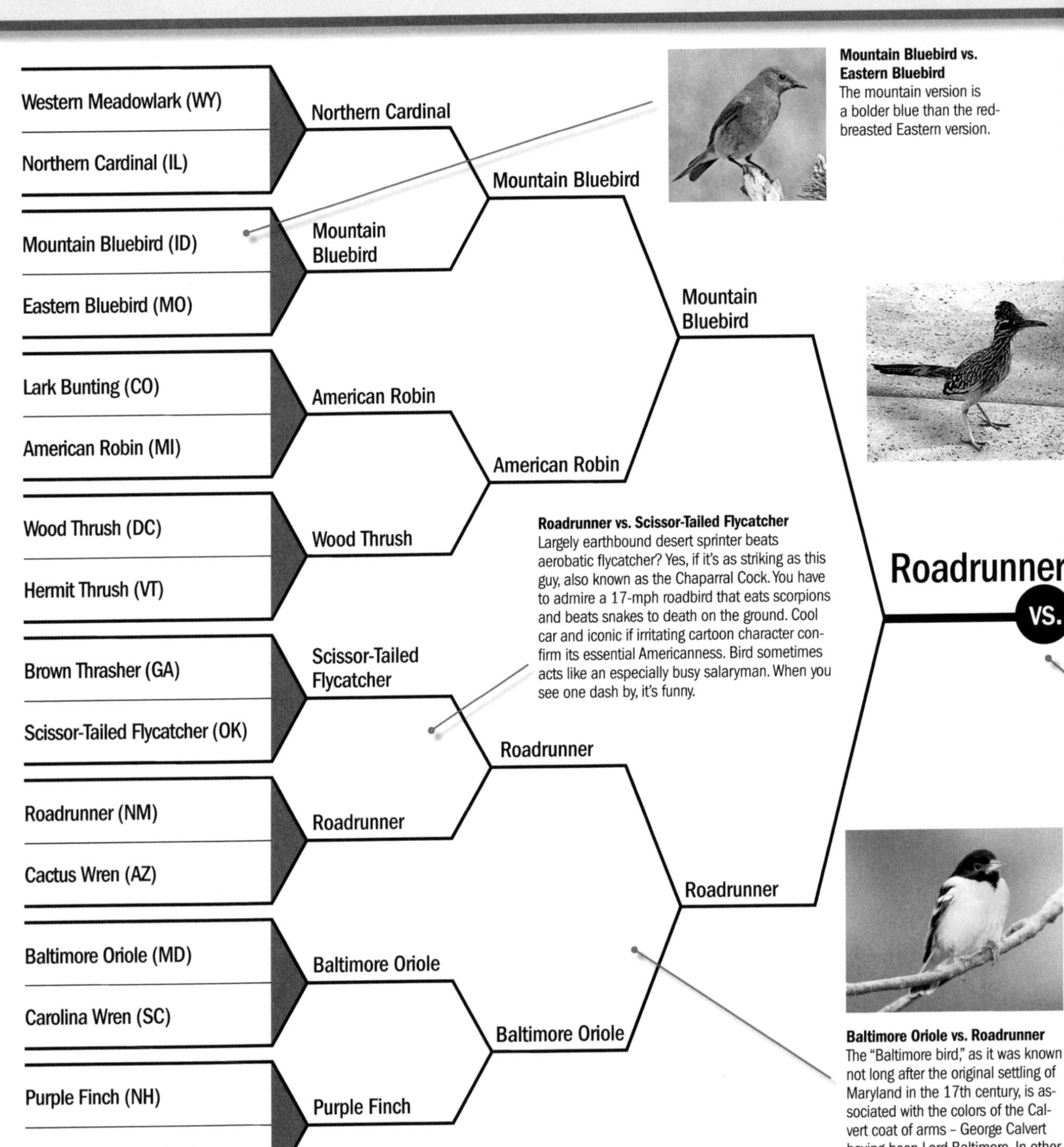

Western Meadowlark (WY)
Northern Cardinal (IL)
Mountain Bluebird (ID)
Eastern Bluebird (MO)
Lark Bunting (CO)
American Robin (MI)
Wood Thrush (DC)
Hermit Thrush (VT)
Brown Thrasher (GA)
Scissor-Tailed Flycatcher (OK)
Roadrunner (NM)
Cactus Wren (AZ)
Baltimore Oriole (MD)
Carolina Wren (SC)
Purple Finch (NH)
American Goldfinch (IA)
Northern Cardinal
Mountain Bluebird
American Robin
Wood Thrush
Scissor-Tailed Flycatcher
Roadrunner
Baltimore Oriole
Purple Finch
Mountain Bluebird
American Robin
Roadrunner
Baltimore Oriole
Mountain Bluebird
Roadrunner
Roadrunner
VS.

Mountain Bluebird vs. Eastern Bluebird
The mountain version is a bolder blue than the red-breasted Eastern version.

Roadrunner vs. Scissor-Tailed Flycatcher
Largely earthbound desert sprinter beats aerobatic flycatcher? Yes, if it's as striking as this guy, also known as the Chaparral Cock. You have to admire a 17-mph roadbird that eats scorpions and beats snakes to death on the ground. Cool car and iconic if irritating cartoon character confirm its essential Americanness. Bird sometimes acts like an especially busy salaryman. When you see one dash by, it's funny.

Baltimore Oriole vs. Roadrunner
The "Baltimore bird," as it was known not long after the original settling of Maryland in the 17th century, is associated with the colors of the Calvert coat of arms – George Calvert having been Lord Baltimore. In other words, the Baltimore bird, like the Maryland state flag, reeks of British heraldry. That doesn't win here.

THE 1920S SAW THE FIRST WAVE OF STATE-BIRD NAMINGS, but laggards included New York, which waited more than 40 years to pick the Bluebird. Seven states claimed the Cardinal between 1928 and 1950. Five picked the Mockingbird. All this me-too bird-boosting means we don't have 32 different state birds to fill this bracket, even though more than 800 species hang here, according to John James Audubon. (No one wanted the Lesser Prairie Chicken?) The first state to pick the bird – e.g., Texas grabbing the Mockingbird three months before Florida in 1927 – gets the honors here.

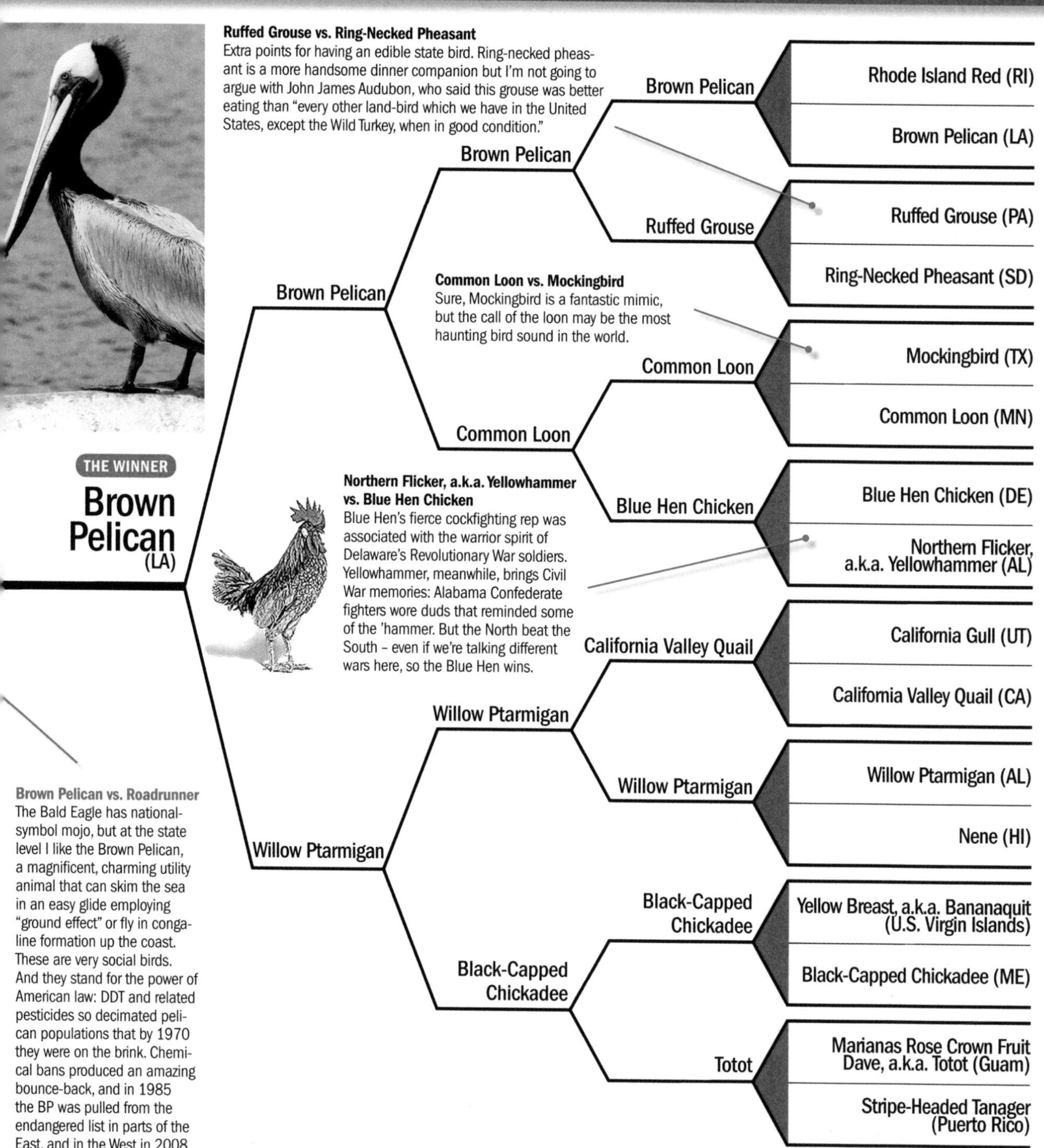

Rhode Island Red (RI)
Brown Pelican (LA)
Ruffed Grouse (PA)
Ring-Necked Pheasant (SD)
Mockingbird (TX)
Common Loon (MN)
Blue Hen Chicken (DE)
Northern Flicker, a.k.a. Yellowhammer (AL)
California Gull (UT)
California Valley Quail (CA)
Willow Ptarmigan (AL)
Nene (HI)
Yellow Breast, a.k.a. Bananaquit (U.S. Virgin Islands)
Black-Capped Chickadee (ME)
Marianas Rose Crown Fruit Dave, a.k.a. Totot (Guam)
Stripe-Headed Tanager (Puerto Rico)
Brown Pelican
Ruffed Grouse
Common Loon
Blue Hen Chicken
California Valley Quail
Willow Ptarmigan
Black-Capped Chickadee
Totot
Brown Pelican
Common Loon
Willow Ptarmigan
Black-Capped Chickadee
Brown Pelican
Willow Ptarmigan
THE WINNER
Brown Pelican (LA)

Ruffed Grouse vs. Ring-Necked Pheasant
Extra points for having an edible state bird. Ring-necked pheasant is a more handsome dinner companion but I'm not going to argue with John James Audubon, who said this grouse was better eating than "every other land-bird which we have in the United States, except the Wild Turkey, when in good condition."

Common Loon vs. Mockingbird
Sure, Mockingbird is a fantastic mimic, but the call of the loon may be the most haunting bird sound in the world.

Northern Flicker, a.k.a. Yellowhammer vs. Blue Hen Chicken
Blue Hen's fierce cockfighting rep was associated with the warrior spirit of Delaware's Revolutionary War soldiers. Yellowhammer, meanwhile, brings Civil War memories: Alabama Confederate fighters wore duds that reminded some of the 'hammer. But the North beat the South – even if we're talking different wars here, so the Blue Hen wins.

Brown Pelican vs. Roadrunner
The Bald Eagle has national-symbol mojo, but at the state level I like the Brown Pelican, a magnificent, charming utility animal that can skim the sea in an easy glide employing "ground effect" or fly in conga-line formation up the coast. These are very social birds. And they stand for the power of American law: DDT and related pesticides so decimated pelican populations that by 1970 they were on the brink. Chemical bans produced an amazing bounce-back, and in 1985 the BP was pulled from the endangered list in parts of the East, and in the West in 2008. Welcome back, champ.

Pseudonyms

By Stanley Bing

Stanley Bing is the pen name of a writer whose true identity is none of your business. You could find it anyway with Internet search engines that have taken the mystery out of everything. Bing adopted the name long ago to keep his corporate masters off his back, but it has failed miserably.

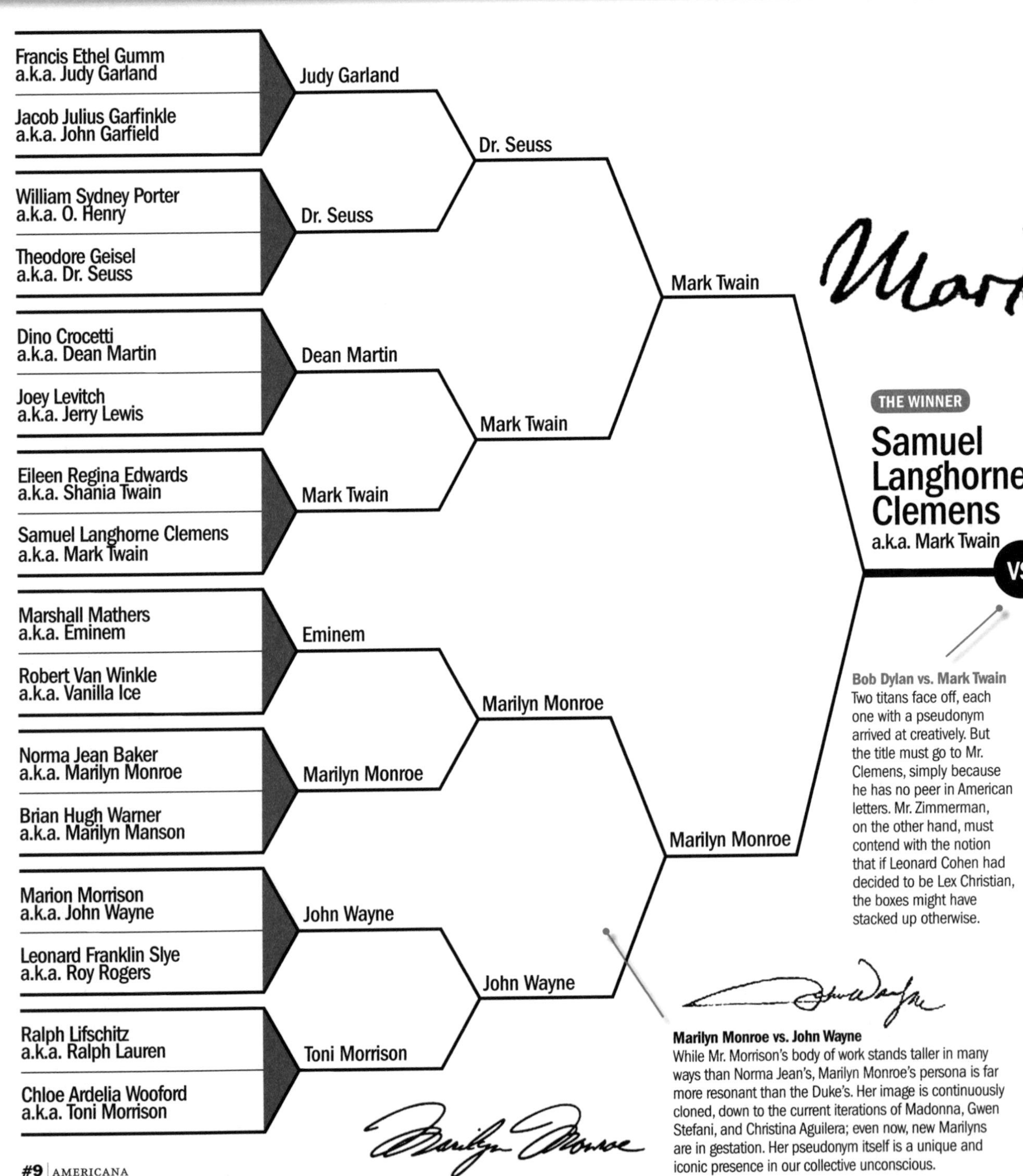

Francis Ethel Gumm a.k.a. Judy Garland
Jacob Julius Garfinkle a.k.a. John Garfield
William Sydney Porter a.k.a. O. Henry
Theodore Geisel a.k.a. Dr. Seuss
Dino Crocetti a.k.a. Dean Martin
Joey Levitch a.k.a. Jerry Lewis
Eileen Regina Edwards a.k.a. Shania Twain
Samuel Langhorne Clemens a.k.a. Mark Twain
Marshall Mathers a.k.a. Eminem
Robert Van Winkle a.k.a. Vanilla Ice
Norma Jean Baker a.k.a. Marilyn Monroe
Brian Hugh Warner a.k.a. Marilyn Manson
Marion Morrison a.k.a. John Wayne
Leonard Franklin Slye a.k.a. Roy Rogers
Ralph Lifschitz a.k.a. Ralph Lauren
Chloe Ardelia Wooford a.k.a. Toni Morrison
Judy Garland
Dr. Seuss
Dean Martin
Mark Twain
Eminem
Marilyn Monroe
John Wayne
Toni Morrison
Dr. Seuss
Mark Twain
Marilyn Monroe
John Wayne
Mark Twain
Marilyn Monroe
THE WINNER
Samuel Langhorne Clemens
a.k.a. Mark Twain
VS.

Bob Dylan vs. Mark Twain
Two titans face off, each one with a pseudonym arrived at creatively. But the title must go to Mr. Clemens, simply because he has no peer in American letters. Mr. Zimmerman, on the other hand, must contend with the notion that if Leonard Cohen had decided to be Lex Christian, the boxes might have stacked up otherwise.

Marilyn Monroe vs. John Wayne
While Mr. Morrison's body of work stands taller in many ways than Norma Jean's, Marilyn Monroe's persona is far more resonant than the Duke's. Her image is continuously cloned, down to the current iterations of Madonna, Gwen Stefani, and Christina Aguilera; even now, new Marilyns are in gestation. Her pseudonym itself is a unique and iconic presence in our collective unconscious.

THE USE OF PEN NAMES AND STAGE NAMES by writers, actors, and other obfuscators is as ancient as the human desire to morph into whatever is necessary. Some wish to appear less of whatever momentarily outré race, religion, or ethnic persuasion they might be. Some have simply been saddled with monikers that are useless in their chosen profession. Whatever the rationale, the pseudonym forever changes the fate of the individual who takes it on. The most influential men in history began as Emmanuel and Gautama, and Calcutta's poor were soothed by a sweet lady named Agnes Gonxha Bojaxhiu.

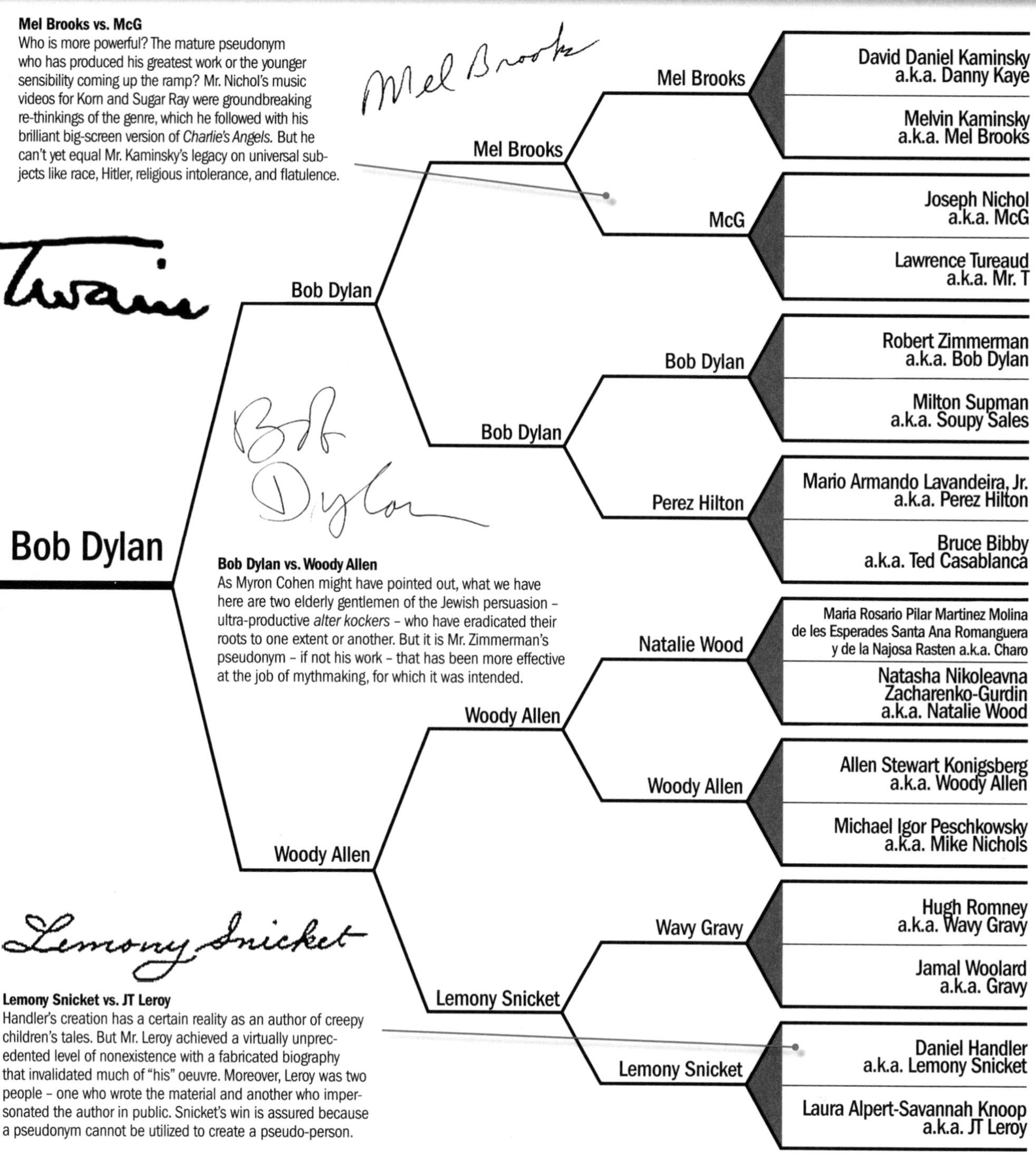
David Daniel Kaminsky a.k.a. Danny Kaye
Melvin Kaminsky a.k.a. Mel Brooks
Joseph Nichol a.k.a. McG
Lawrence Tureaud a.k.a. Mr. T
Robert Zimmerman a.k.a. Bob Dylan
Milton Supman a.k.a. Soupy Sales
Mario Armando Lavandeira, Jr. a.k.a. Perez Hilton
Bruce Bibby a.k.a. Ted Casablanca
Maria Rosario Pilar Martinez Molina de les Esperades Santa Ana Romanguera y de la Najosa Rasten a.k.a. Charo
Natasha Nikoleavna Zacharenko-Gurdin a.k.a. Natalie Wood
Allen Stewart Konigsberg a.k.a. Woody Allen
Michael Igor Peschkowsky a.k.a. Mike Nichols
Hugh Romney a.k.a. Wavy Gravy
Jamal Woolard a.k.a. Gravy
Daniel Handler a.k.a. Lemony Snicket
Laura Alpert-Savannah Knoop a.k.a. JT Leroy
Mel Brooks
McG
Bob Dylan
Perez Hilton
Natalie Wood
Woody Allen
Wavy Gravy
Lemony Snicket
Mel Brooks
Bob Dylan
Woody Allen
Lemony Snicket
Bob Dylan
Woody Allen
Bob Dylan
Mel Brooks
Twain
Bob Dylan
Lemony Snicket

Mel Brooks vs. McG
Who is more powerful? The mature pseudonym who has produced his greatest work or the younger sensibility coming up the ramp? Mr. Nichol's music videos for Korn and Sugar Ray were groundbreaking re-thinkings of the genre, which he followed with his brilliant big-screen version of *Charlie's Angels*. But he can't yet equal Mr. Kaminsky's legacy on universal subjects like race, Hitler, religious intolerance, and flatulence.

Bob Dylan vs. Woody Allen
As Myron Cohen might have pointed out, what we have here are two elderly gentlemen of the Jewish persuasion – ultra-productive *alter kockers* – who have eradicated their roots to one extent or another. But it is Mr. Zimmerman's pseudonym – if not his work – that has been more effective at the job of mythmaking, for which it was intended.

Lemony Snicket vs. JT Leroy
Handler's creation has a certain reality as an author of creepy children's tales. But Mr. Leroy achieved a virtually unprecedented level of nonexistence with a fabricated biography that invalidated much of "his" oeuvre. Moreover, Leroy was two people – one who wrote the material and another who impersonated the author in public. Snicket's win is assured because a pseudonym cannot be utilized to create a pseudo-person.

Iconic Photographs

By James Danziger

James Danziger operates Danziger Projects in New York City. He was picture editor of the *London Sunday Times Magazine* and director of Magnum Photos.

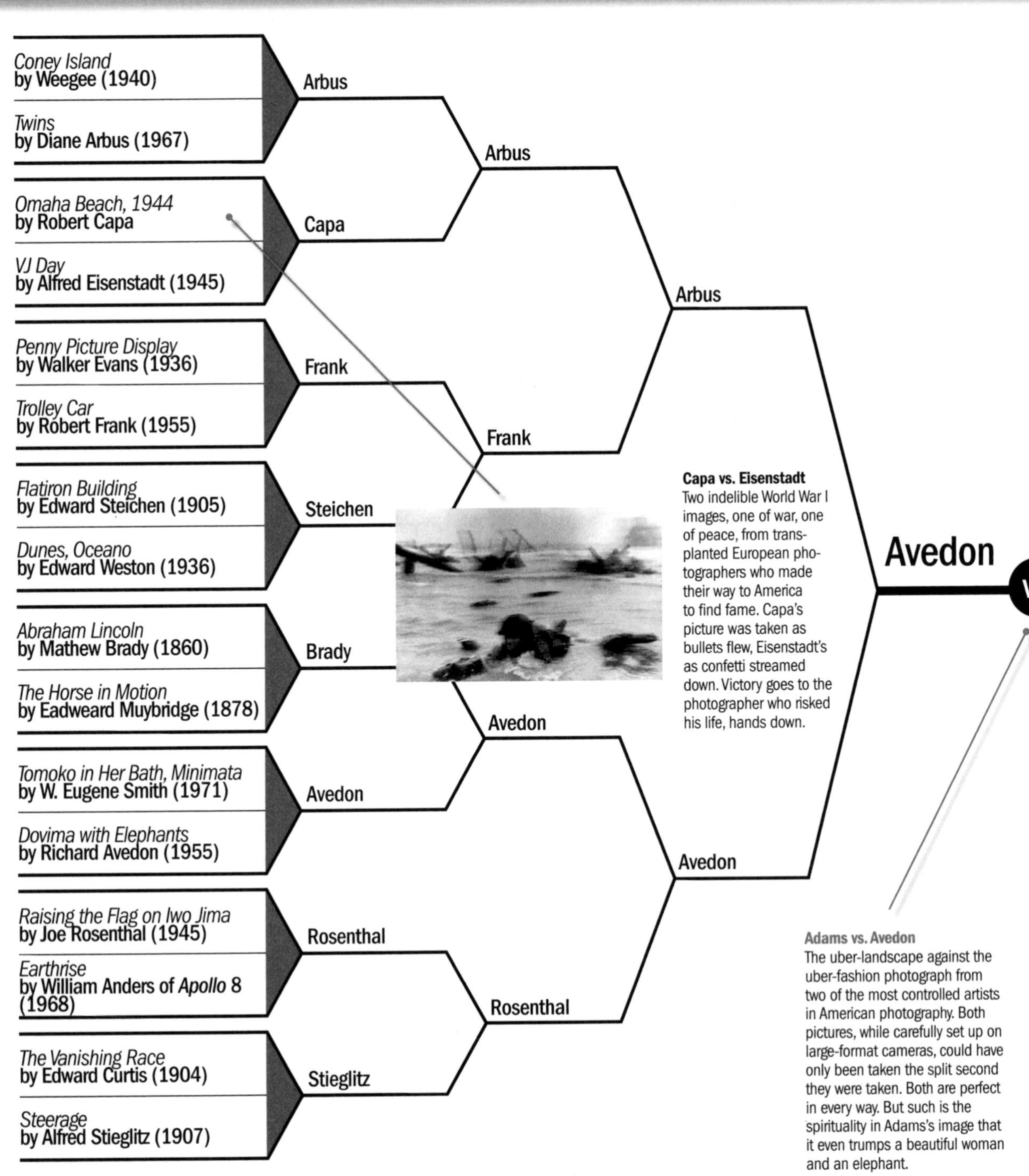

Coney Island by Weegee (1940)
Twins by Diane Arbus (1967)
Omaha Beach, 1944 by Robert Capa
VJ Day by Alfred Eisenstadt (1945)
Penny Picture Display by Walker Evans (1936)
Trolley Car by Robert Frank (1955)
Flatiron Building by Edward Steichen (1905)
Dunes, Oceano by Edward Weston (1936)
Abraham Lincoln by Mathew Brady (1860)
The Horse in Motion by Eadweard Muybridge (1878)
Tomoko in Her Bath, Minimata by W. Eugene Smith (1971)
Dovima with Elephants by Richard Avedon (1955)
Raising the Flag on Iwo Jima by Joe Rosenthal (1945)
Earthrise by William Anders of *Apollo* 8 (1968)
The Vanishing Race by Edward Curtis (1904)
Steerage by Alfred Stieglitz (1907)
Arbus
Capa
Frank
Steichen
Brady
Avedon
Rosenthal
Stieglitz
Arbus
Frank
Avedon
Rosenthal
Arbus
Avedon
Avedon
VS.

Capa vs. Eisenstadt
Two indelible World War I images, one of war, one of peace, from transplanted European photographers who made their way to America to find fame. Capa's picture was taken as bullets flew, Eisenstadt's as confetti streamed down. Victory goes to the photographer who risked his life, hands down.

Adams vs. Avedon
The uber-landscape against the uber-fashion photograph from two of the most controlled artists in American photography. Both pictures, while carefully set up on large-format cameras, could have only been taken the split second they were taken. Both are perfect in every way. But such is the spirituality in Adams's image that it even trumps a beautiful woman and an elephant.

LET'S START BY SAYING AMERICAN PHOTOGRAPHY SO DOMINATES THE MEDIUM as to make other countries' contributions a footnote. So we're really choosing the most iconic photograph of all time. And what are we looking for? A visceral image, one that is embedded in our cultural subconscious, one taken with the greatest skill by an artist whose entire body of work is capped by one transcendent image that is totally unreplicable. One that you can close your eyes to and it will come floating into the space between your mind and your eyelids, with something between a shiver and a sigh of pleasure.

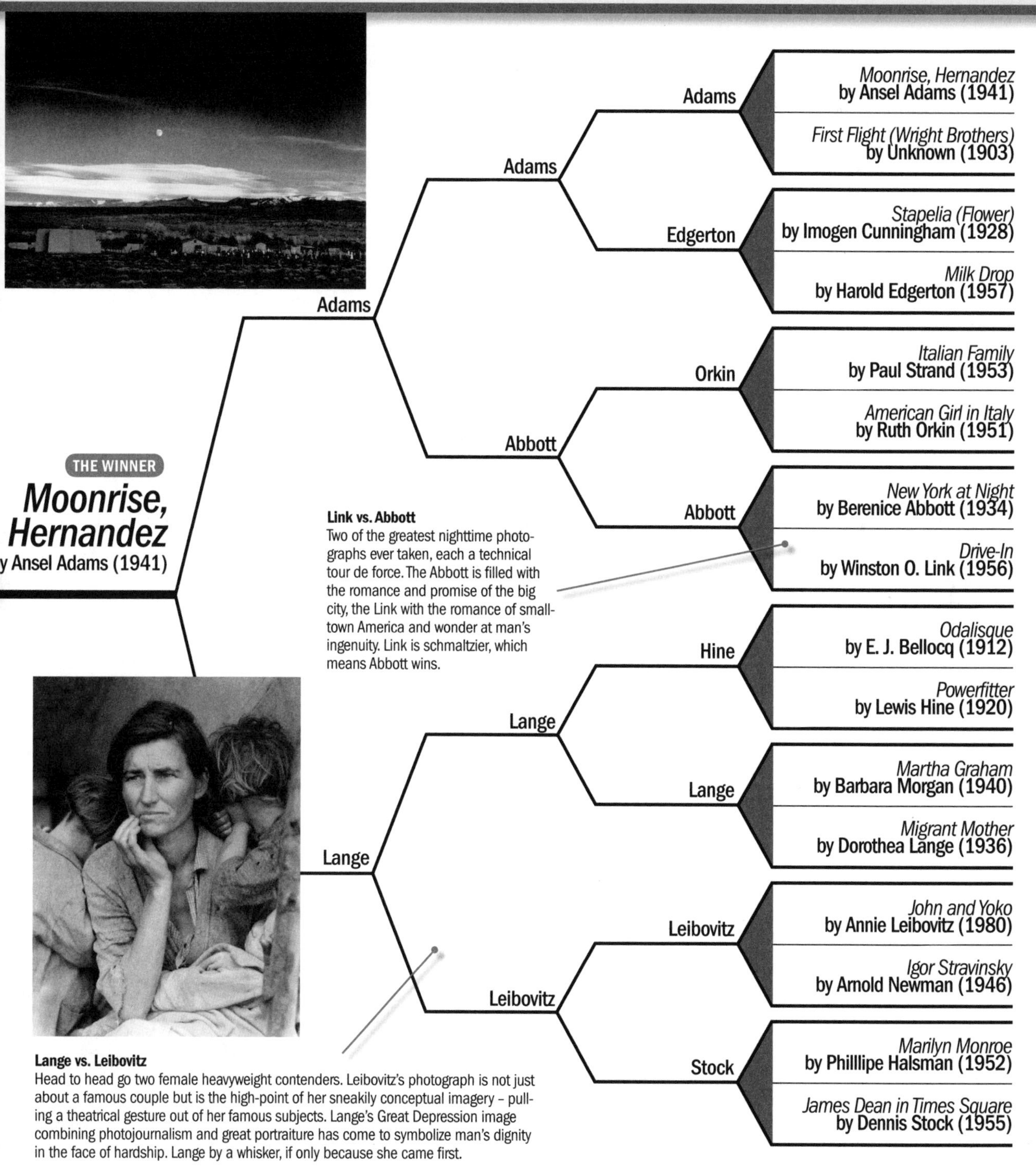
THE WINNER
Moonrise, Hernandez
by Ansel Adams (1941)
Moonrise, Hernandez by Ansel Adams (1941)
First Flight (Wright Brothers) by Unknown (1903)
Stapelia (Flower) by Imogen Cunningham (1928)
Milk Drop by Harold Edgerton (1957)
Italian Family by Paul Strand (1953)
American Girl in Italy by Ruth Orkin (1951)
New York at Night by Berenice Abbott (1934)
Drive-In by Winston O. Link (1956)
Odalisque by E. J. Bellocq (1912)
Powerfitter by Lewis Hine (1920)
Martha Graham by Barbara Morgan (1940)
Migrant Mother by Dorothea Lange (1936)
John and Yoko by Annie Leibovitz (1980)
Igor Stravinsky by Arnold Newman (1946)
Marilyn Monroe by Phillipe Halsman (1952)
James Dean in Times Square by Dennis Stock (1955)
Adams
Edgerton
Orkin
Abbott
Hine
Lange
Leibovitz
Stock
Adams
Abbott
Lange
Leibovitz
Adams
Lange

Link vs. Abbott
Two of the greatest nighttime photographs ever taken, each a technical tour de force. The Abbott is filled with the romance and promise of the big city, the Link with the romance of small-town America and wonder at man's ingenuity. Link is schmaltzier, which means Abbott wins.

Lange vs. Leibovitz
Head to head go two female heavyweight contenders. Leibovitz's photograph is not just about a famous couple but is the high-point of her sneakily conceptual imagery – pulling a theatrical gesture out of her famous subjects. Lange's Great Depression image combining photojournalism and great portraiture has come to symbolize man's dignity in the face of hardship. Lange by a whisker, if only because she came first.

Ridiculous Celebrity Auctions

By Leila Dunbar

Leila (Lee) Dunbar, who headed Sotheby's collectibles department for nine years and has been an appraiser for PBS's *Antiques Road Show* since its inception, runs her own consulting and appraisal business.

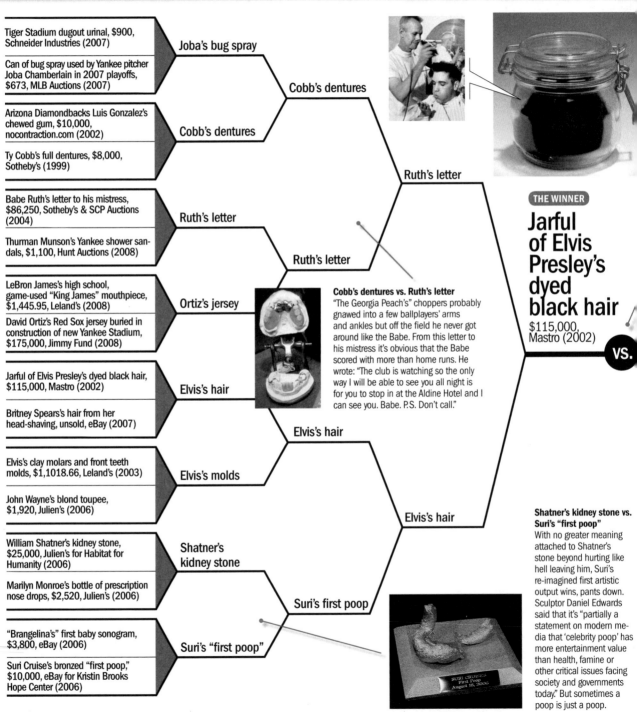

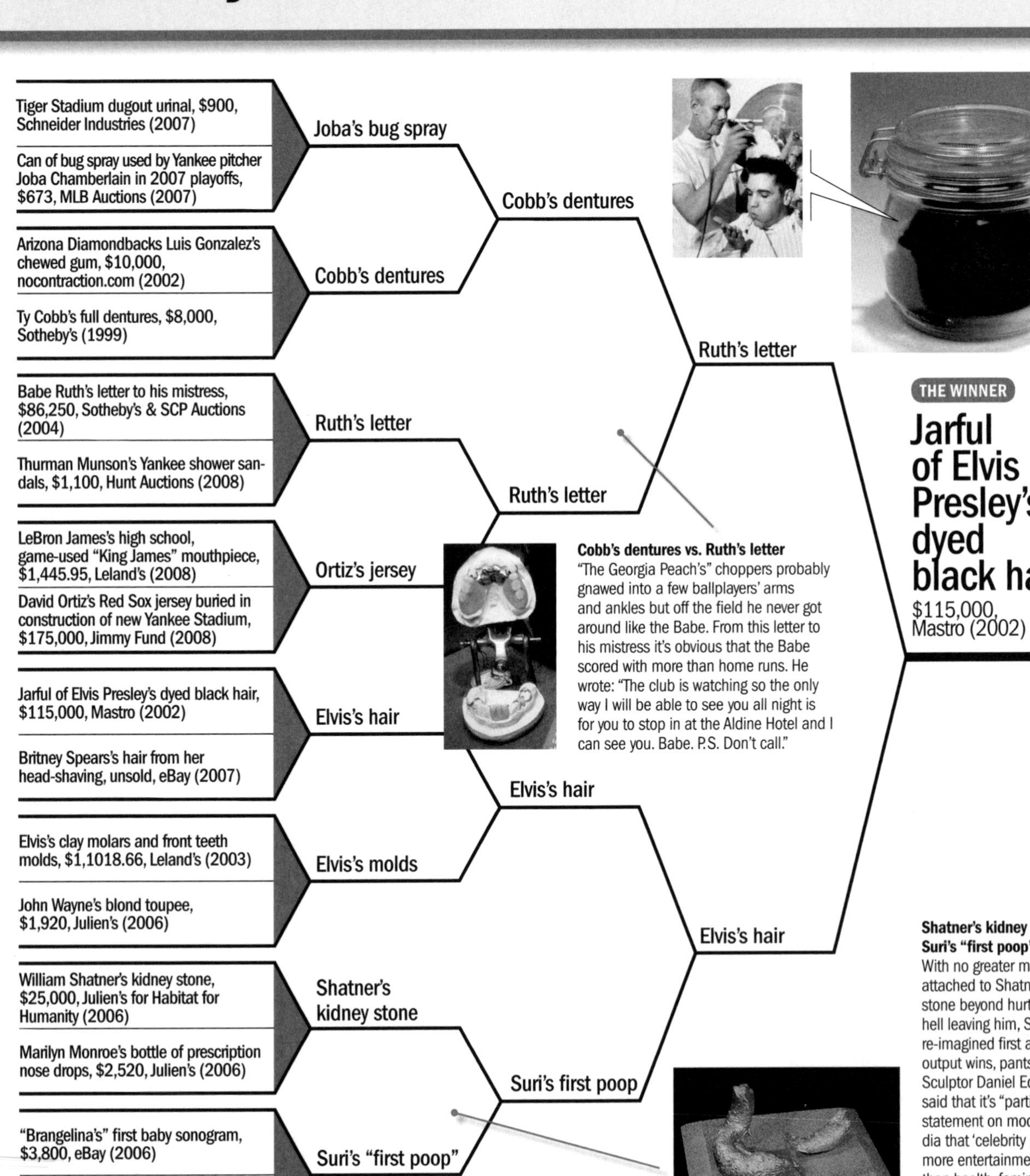
Tiger Stadium dugout urinal, $900, Schneider Industries (2007)
Can of bug spray used by Yankee pitcher Joba Chamberlain in 2007 playoffs, $673, MLB Auctions (2007)
Joba's bug spray
Arizona Diamondbacks Luis Gonzalez's chewed gum, $10,000, nocontraction.com (2002)
Ty Cobb's full dentures, $8,000, Sotheby's (1999)
Cobb's dentures
Cobb's dentures
Babe Ruth's letter to his mistress, $86,250, Sotheby's & SCP Auctions (2004)
Thurman Munson's Yankee shower sandals, $1,100, Hunt Auctions (2008)
Ruth's letter
LeBron James's high school, game-used "King James" mouthpiece, $1,445.95, Leland's (2008)
David Ortiz's Red Sox jersey buried in construction of new Yankee Stadium, $175,000, Jimmy Fund (2008)
Ortiz's jersey
Ruth's letter
Ruth's letter
Jarful of Elvis Presley's dyed black hair, $115,000, Mastro (2002)
Britney Spears's hair from her head-shaving, unsold, eBay (2007)
Elvis's hair
Elvis's clay molars and front teeth molds, $1,1018.66, Leland's (2003)
John Wayne's blond toupee, $1,920, Julien's (2006)
Elvis's molds
Elvis's hair
William Shatner's kidney stone, $25,000, Julien's for Habitat for Humanity (2006)
Marilyn Monroe's bottle of prescription nose drops, $2,520, Julien's (2006)
Shatner's kidney stone
"Brangelina's" first baby sonogram, $3,800, eBay (2006)
Suri Cruise's bronzed "first poop," $10,000, eBay for Kristin Brooks Hope Center (2006)
Suri's "first poop"
Suri's first poop
Elvis's hair
THE WINNER
Jarful of Elvis Presley's dyed black hair
$115,000, Mastro (2002)
VS.
SURI CRUISE
First Poop
August 18, 2006

Cobb's dentures vs. Ruth's letter
"The Georgia Peach's" choppers probably gnawed into a few ballplayers' arms and ankles but off the field he never got around like the Babe. From this letter to his mistress it's obvious that the Babe scored with more than home runs. He wrote: "The club is watching so the only way I will be able to see you all night is for you to stop in at the Aldine Hotel and I can see you. Babe. P.S. Don't call."

Shatner's kidney stone vs. Suri's "first poop"
With no greater meaning attached to Shatner's stone beyond hurting like hell leaving him, Suri's re-imagined first artistic output wins, pants down. Sculptor Daniel Edwards said that it's "partially a statement on modern media that 'celebrity poop' has more entertainment value than health, famine or other critical issues facing society and governments today." But sometimes a poop is just a poop.

IT SEEMS NORMAL FOR DEVOTED FANS to pay enormous sums for a game-used Babe Ruth bat, a sweat-stained Elvis jumpsuit, or Marilyn Monroe's halter dress from *The Seven Year Itch*. Far more mysterious is the impulse to acquire the underwear, toenails, or prescription medicine vials of the stars, as if a relationship with Britney Spears can be forged by bidding on her laundry lint. Celebrities beware: Unless you have a charity in mind, lock your medicine cabinets, burn your correspondence, and sweep up your own hair clippings – or everything's for sale.

Elvis's hair vs. Holly's glasses
In this battle of survival tales, the King's weird one wins. When Elvis's barber, Homer Gilleland, dyed the star's blond hair black, he cut the locks into towels and stored them in plastic bread bags. Before dying, Gilleland gave this hunka hunka hair (one of many bagged hunkas) to a friend, who put it up for auction. Confidence is high that these are authentic Elvis snippings even without a DNA test.

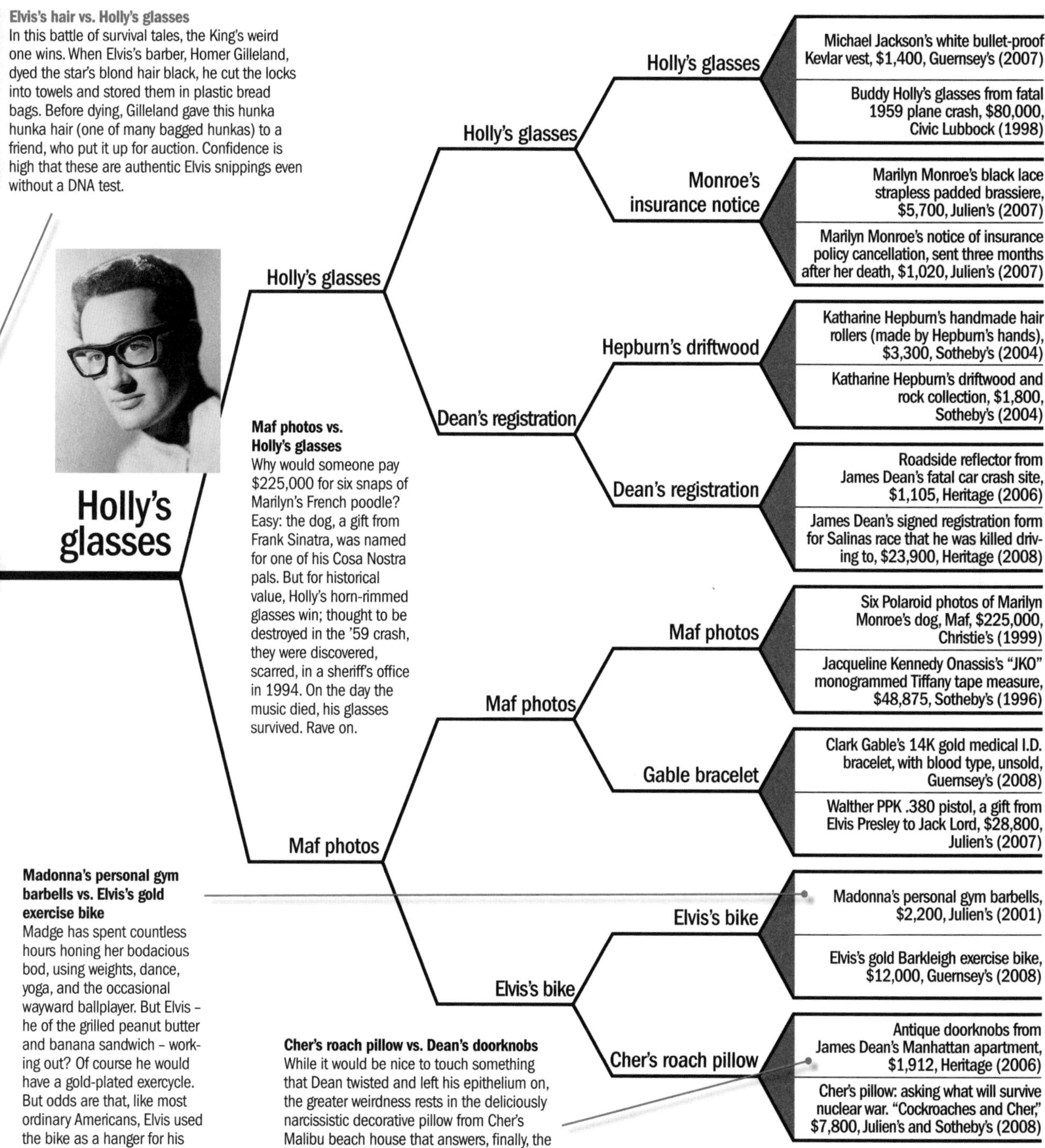

Holly's glasses
Holly's glasses
Holly's glasses
Holly's glasses
Michael Jackson's white bullet-proof Kevlar vest, $1,400, Guernsey's (2007)
Buddy Holly's glasses from fatal 1959 plane crash, $80,000, Civic Lubbock (1998)
Monroe's insurance notice
Marilyn Monroe's black lace strapless padded brassiere, $5,700, Julien's (2007)
Marilyn Monroe's notice of insurance policy cancellation, sent three months after her death, $1,020, Julien's (2007)
Dean's registration
Hepburn's driftwood
Katharine Hepburn's handmade hair rollers (made by Hepburn's hands), $3,300, Sotheby's (2004)
Katharine Hepburn's driftwood and rock collection, $1,800, Sotheby's (2004)
Dean's registration
Roadside reflector from James Dean's fatal car crash site, $1,105, Heritage (2006)
James Dean's signed registration form for Salinas race that he was killed driving to, $23,900, Heritage (2008)
Maf photos
Maf photos
Maf photos
Six Polaroid photos of Marilyn Monroe's dog, Maf, $225,000, Christie's (1999)
Jacqueline Kennedy Onassis's "JKO" monogrammed Tiffany tape measure, $48,875, Sotheby's (1996)
Gable bracelet
Clark Gable's 14K gold medical I.D. bracelet, with blood type, unsold, Guernsey's (2008)
Walther PPK .380 pistol, a gift from Elvis Presley to Jack Lord, $28,800, Julien's (2007)
Elvis's bike
Elvis's bike
Madonna's personal gym barbells, $2,200, Julien's (2001)
Elvis's gold Barkleigh exercise bike, $12,000, Guernsey's (2008)
Cher's roach pillow
Antique doorknobs from James Dean's Manhattan apartment, $1,912, Heritage (2006)
Cher's pillow: asking what will survive nuclear war. "Cockroaches and Cher," $7,800, Julien's and Sotheby's (2008)

Maf photos vs. Holly's glasses
Why would someone pay $225,000 for six snaps of Marilyn's French poodle? Easy: the dog, a gift from Frank Sinatra, was named for one of his Cosa Nostra pals. But for historical value, Holly's horn-rimmed glasses win; thought to be destroyed in the '59 crash, they were discovered, scarred, in a sheriff's office in 1994. On the day the music died, his glasses survived. Rave on.

Madonna's personal gym barbells vs. Elvis's gold exercise bike
Madge has spent countless hours honing her bodacious bod, using weights, dance, yoga, and the occasional wayward ballplayer. But Elvis – he of the grilled peanut butter and banana sandwich – working out? Of course he would have a gold-plated exercycle. But odds are that, like most ordinary Americans, Elvis used the bike as a hanger for his gold lamé jumpsuits.

Cher's roach pillow vs. Dean's doorknobs
While it would be nice to touch something that Dean twisted and left his epithelium on, the greater weirdness rests in the deliciously narcissistic decorative pillow from Cher's Malibu beach house that answers, finally, the burning question of her mortality.

Board Games

By Stefan Fatsis

Stefan Fatsis is the author of *Word Freak: Heartbreak, Triumph, Genius, and Obsession in the World of Competitive Scrabble Players,* so you know where this bracket is heading. He writes about a game contested on a board of a different kind in his latest book, *A Few Seconds of Panic: A 5-foot-8, 170-pound, 43-year-old Sportswriter Plays in the NFL*

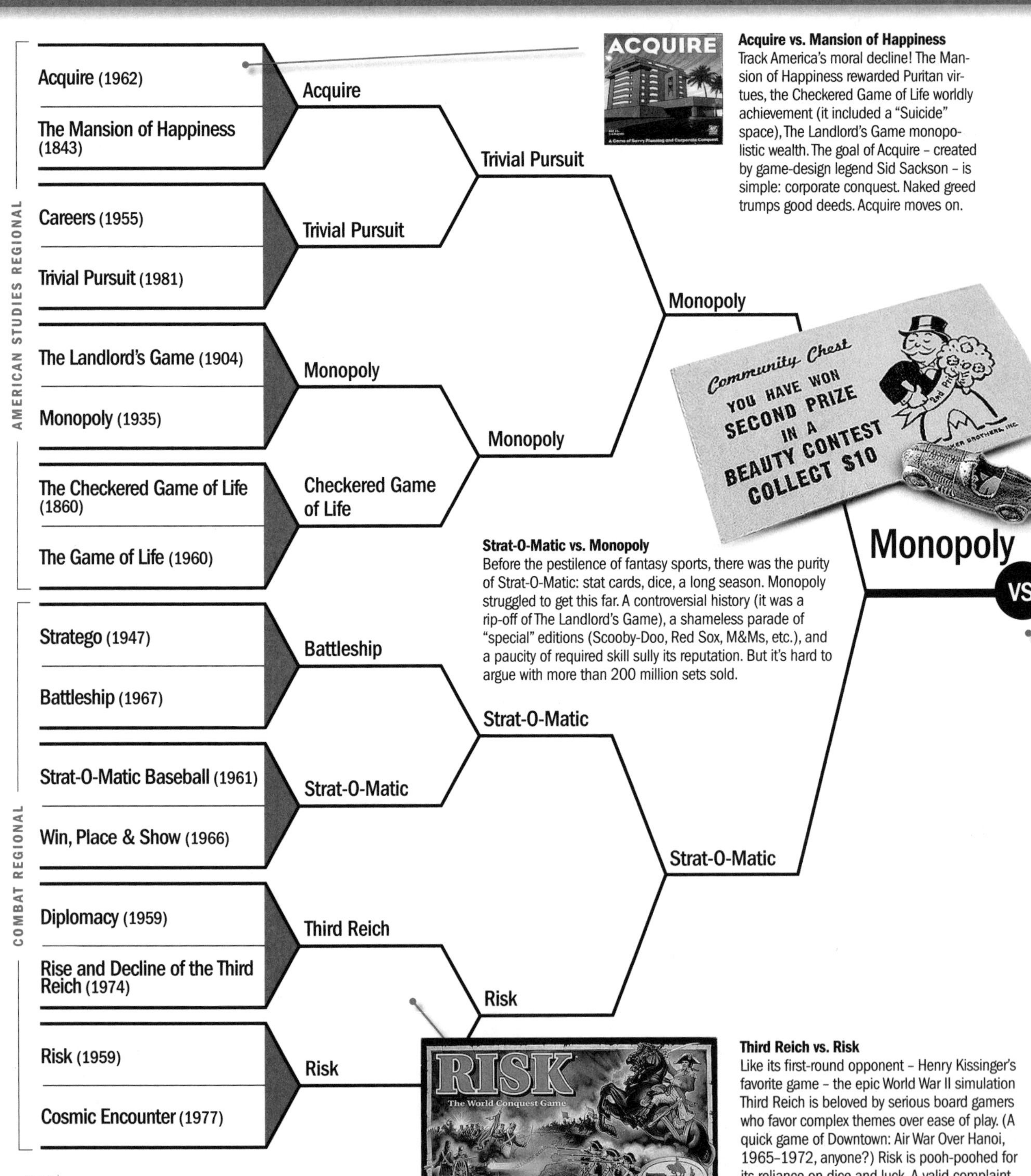

AMERICAN STUDIES REGIONAL
Acquire (1962)
The Mansion of Happiness (1843)
Careers (1955)
Trivial Pursuit (1981)
The Landlord's Game (1904)
Monopoly (1935)
The Checkered Game of Life (1860)
The Game of Life (1960)
Acquire
Trivial Pursuit
Monopoly
Checkered Game of Life
Trivial Pursuit
Monopoly
Monopoly
COMBAT REGIONAL
Stratego (1947)
Battleship (1967)
Strat-O-Matic Baseball (1961)
Win, Place & Show (1966)
Diplomacy (1959)
Rise and Decline of the Third Reich (1974)
Risk (1959)
Cosmic Encounter (1977)
Battleship
Strat-O-Matic
Third Reich
Risk
Strat-O-Matic
Risk
Strat-O-Matic
Monopoly
VS.
ACQUIRE
A Game of Savvy Planning and Corporate Conquest
Community Chest
YOU HAVE WON
SECOND PRIZE
IN A
BEAUTY CONTEST
COLLECT $10
RISK
The World Conquest Game

Acquire vs. Mansion of Happiness
Track America's moral decline! The Mansion of Happiness rewarded Puritan virtues, the Checkered Game of Life worldly achievement (it included a "Suicide" space), The Landlord's Game monopolistic wealth. The goal of Acquire – created by game-design legend Sid Sackson – is simple: corporate conquest. Naked greed trumps good deeds. Acquire moves on.

Strat-O-Matic vs. Monopoly
Before the pestilence of fantasy sports, there was the purity of Strat-O-Matic: stat cards, dice, a long season. Monopoly struggled to get this far. A controversial history (it was a rip-off of The Landlord's Game), a shameless parade of "special" editions (Scooby-Doo, Red Sox, M&Ms, etc.), and a paucity of required skill sully its reputation. But it's hard to argue with more than 200 million sets sold.

Third Reich vs. Risk
Like its first-round opponent – Henry Kissinger's favorite game – the epic World War II simulation Third Reich is beloved by serious board gamers who favor complex themes over ease of play. (A quick game of Downtown: Air War Over Hanoi, 1965–1972, anyone?) Risk is pooh-poohed for its reliance on dice and luck. A valid complaint, but the power of Irkutsk cannot be denied.

IN MY MID-30S, I BECAME OBSESSED with a board game. I believe that game belongs on Mount Rushmore with the ancient classics chess, backgammon, and Go. Others think it's something to play only when hopelessly bored. But play we all do. The first American board game – Traveller's Tour Through the United States – was published in 1822. Ever since, games have helped us endure our childhoods, stretch (and atrophy) our brains, and define our culture. Oh, and behave like idiots. I'm looking at you, Twister.

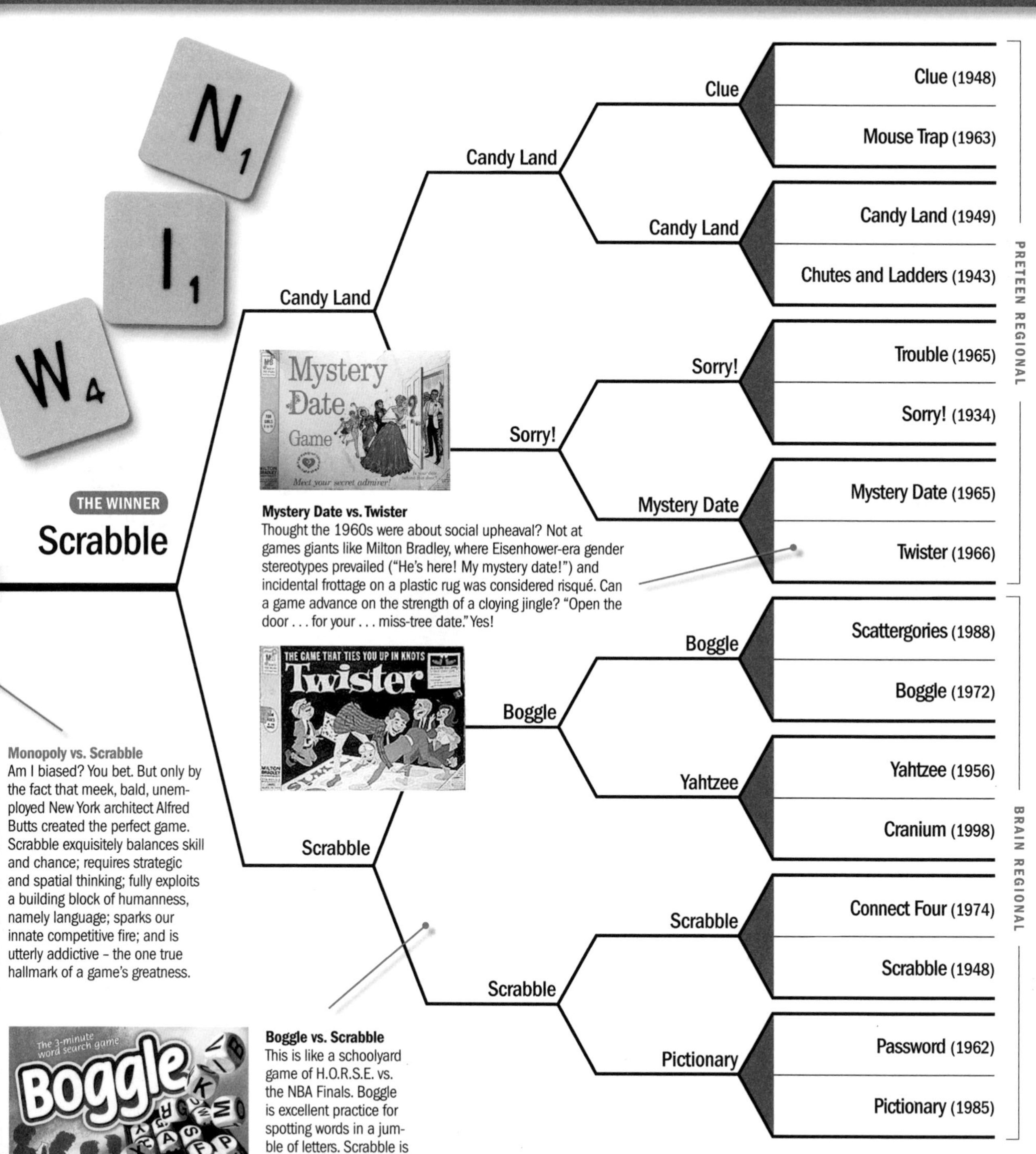

N 1
I 1
W 4
THE WINNER
Scrabble
Clue (1948)
Mouse Trap (1963)
Candy Land (1949)
Chutes and Ladders (1943)
Trouble (1965)
Sorry! (1934)
Mystery Date (1965)
Twister (1966)
PRETEEN REGIONAL
Scattergories (1988)
Boggle (1972)
Yahtzee (1956)
Cranium (1998)
Connect Four (1974)
Scrabble (1948)
Password (1962)
Pictionary (1985)
BRAIN REGIONAL
Clue
Candy Land
Sorry!
Mystery Date
Boggle
Yahtzee
Scrabble
Pictionary
Candy Land
Sorry!
Boggle
Scrabble
Candy Land
Scrabble
Mystery Date Game
Meet your secret admirer!
THE GAME THAT TIES YOU UP IN KNOTS
Twister
The 3-minute word search game
Boggle

Mystery Date vs. Twister
Thought the 1960s were about social upheaval? Not at games giants like Milton Bradley, where Eisenhower-era gender stereotypes prevailed ("He's here! My mystery date!") and incidental frottage on a plastic rug was considered risqué. Can a game advance on the strength of a cloying jingle? "Open the door . . . for your . . . miss-tree date." Yes!

Monopoly vs. Scrabble
Am I biased? You bet. But only by the fact that meek, bald, unemployed New York architect Alfred Butts created the perfect game. Scrabble exquisitely balances skill and chance; requires strategic and spatial thinking; fully exploits a building block of humanness, namely language; sparks our innate competitive fire; and is utterly addictive – the one true hallmark of a game's greatness.

Boggle vs. Scrabble
This is like a schoolyard game of H.O.R.S.E. vs. the NBA Finals. Boggle is excellent practice for spotting words in a jumble of letters. Scrabble is the artful deployment of that talent.

Magic Tricks

By Joshua Jay

Joshua Jay has performed and lectured all over the world, and won the coveted World Magic Seminar in 1998. He is the author of *MAGIC: The Complete Course* and has no desire to catch a bullet in his teeth, onstage or otherwise.

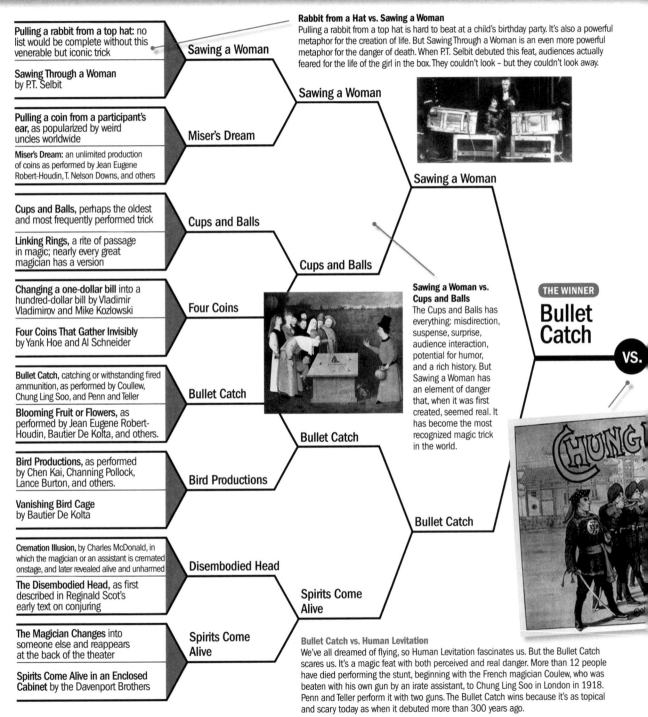

Pulling a rabbit from a top hat: no list would be complete without this venerable but iconic trick

Sawing Through a Woman by P.T. Selbit

Sawing a Woman

Pulling a coin from a participant's ear, as popularized by weird uncles worldwide

Miser's Dream: an unlimited production of coins as performed by Jean Eugene Robert-Houdin, T. Nelson Downs, and others

Miser's Dream

Sawing a Woman

Cups and Balls, perhaps the oldest and most frequently performed trick

Linking Rings, a rite of passage in magic; nearly every great magician has a version

Cups and Balls

Changing a one-dollar bill into a hundred-dollar bill by Vladimir Vladimirov and Mike Kozlowski

Four Coins That Gather Invisibly by Yank Hoe and Al Schneider

Four Coins

Cups and Balls

Sawing a Woman

Bullet Catch, catching or withstanding fired ammunition, as performed by Coullew, Chung Ling Soo, and Penn and Teller

Blooming Fruit or Flowers, as performed by Jean Eugene Robert-Houdin, Bautier De Kolta, and others.

Bullet Catch

Bird Productions, as performed by Chen Kai, Channing Pollock, Lance Burton, and others.

Vanishing Bird Cage by Bautier De Kolta

Bird Productions

Bullet Catch

Cremation Illusion, by Charles McDonald, in which the magician or an assistant is cremated onstage, and later revealed alive and unharmed

The Disembodied Head, as first described in Reginald Scot's early text on conjuring

Disembodied Head

The Magician Changes into someone else and reappears at the back of the theater

Spirits Come Alive in an Enclosed Cabinet by the Davenport Brothers

Spirits Come Alive

Spirits Come Alive

Bullet Catch

THE WINNER

Bullet Catch

VS.

Rabbit from a Hat vs. Sawing a Woman

Pulling a rabbit from a top hat is hard to beat at a child's birthday party. It's also a powerful metaphor for the creation of life. But Sawing Through a Woman is an even more powerful metaphor for the danger of death. When P.T. Selbit debuted this feat, audiences actually feared for the life of the girl in the box. They couldn't look – but they couldn't look away.

Sawing a Woman vs. Cups and Balls

The Cups and Balls has everything: misdirection, suspense, surprise, audience interaction, potential for humor, and a rich history. But Sawing a Woman has an element of danger that, when it was first created, seemed real. It has become the most recognized magic trick in the world.

Bullet Catch vs. Human Levitation

We've all dreamed of flying, so Human Levitation fascinates us. But the Bullet Catch scares us. It's a magic feat with both perceived and real danger. More than 12 people have died performing the stunt, beginning with the French magician Coulew, who was beaten with his own gun by an irate assistant, to Chung Ling Soo in London in 1918. Penn and Teller perform it with two guns. The Bullet Catch wins because it's as topical and scary today as when it debuted more than 300 years ago.

TOM ROBBINS SAID IT BEST: "Using words to describe magic is like using a screwdriver to cut roast beef." Ranking magic isn't any easier. But we can all agree about what makes magic great: the illusion of impossibility. Anything impossible is considered: telepathy, telekinesis, and unexplainable escapes are all fair game. Tricks that are topical rank high, but timeless tricks rank higher. Believable tricks are preferred, and above all else, we are in search of memorable, meaningful magic.

Spoon Bending vs. Second Sight
Magic tricks require a willing suspension of disbelief. But these two tricks look so plausible that they are accepted as genuine by audiences worldwide. When a blindfolded mentalist is able to discern the owner of a watch only by feeling it, or when he is able to call out details on someone's driver's license without looking, people attribute real psychic abilities to the performer (it's not the case, sorry). Spoon Bending wins here, precisely because it is so believable. Although the metal bends less than an inch, it appears to do so by the mind.

Mysterious Escapes in which no explanation seems possible: as performed by Houdini, Doug Henning, David Copperfield, and others.

Substitution Trunk, popularized by Houdini, in which he and his wife would transpose through a locked chest

Mysterious Escapes

Human Levitation, an ancient trick that still astounds, by practitioners like Servais Le Roy, David Copperfield, and David Blaine

The Water Torture Cell by Houdini, in which the magician, inverted and shackled in a clear tank of water, magically escapes

Human Levitation

Human Levitation

Spoon Bending, as performed by Uri Geller and others

Second Sight Acts, in which a blindfolded mentalist "sees" objects and thoughts

Spoon Bending

Pepper's Ghost, an uncanny illusion of a see-through apparition (think holographic) by Henry Dircks and John Pepper

Black Art Magic, in which people and objects levitate, vanish, and change with no cover

Pepper's Ghost

Spoon Bending

Human Levitation

Human Levitation

Indian Rope Trick vs. Light and Heavy Chest
The Indian Rope Trick is the only trick here that cannot be performed. It is mythic, fabricated, and romantically discussed as if it were real. A fakir throws a rope into the air and it is suspended, erect. A boy then climbs the rope and disappears at the top. But Robert-Houdin's Light and Heavy Chest wins this round, if only because his trick can be and has been performed.

Indian Rope Trick, wherein a rope becomes rigid in midair and a boy is able to climb it and ultimately vanish

Light and Heavy Chest by Jean Eugene Robert-Houdin

Light and Heavy Chest

Turning a Card Inside Out by Roy Walton

Magically separating red cards from black cards by Paul Curry and John Scarne

Red cards from black cards

Light and Heavy Chest

Rising Card by Abram Colorni, wherein a playing card mysteriously rises from the deck

Turning an Invisible Card Visible by Judson Brown, Joe Berg, Dai Vernon, and Eddie Fields

Ultra-Mental Deck

Vanishing the Statue of Liberty by David Copperfield and Andre Kole

The Turk: a thinking, chess-playing machine by Baron Wolfgang von Kempelen

Vanishing the Statue of Liberty

Vanishing the Statue of Liberty

Vanishing the Statue of Liberty

GSOO

DEFYING THEIR BULLETS

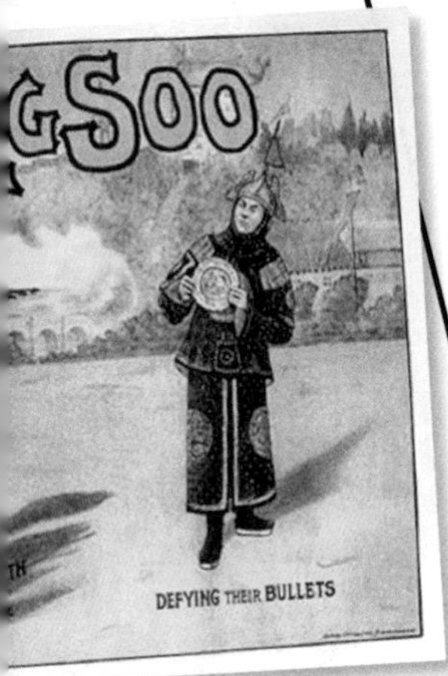

Light and Heavy Chest vs. Vanishing the Statue of Liberty
Napoleon III called Robert-Houdin to Algeria in 1856 to use his magic to quash a rebellion by a superstitious tribe called the Marabout. In a theater in Algiers, Houdin showed the Marabout how he could easily lift a small chest off the ground, then "take away" an opponent's strength; when the strongest Marabout tried to lift the small chest, it was impossible. Rebellion over. A century later, David Copperfield vanished one of the most famous landmarks in the world. Performed but once, in 1983, it is still among the most talked-about tricks ever.

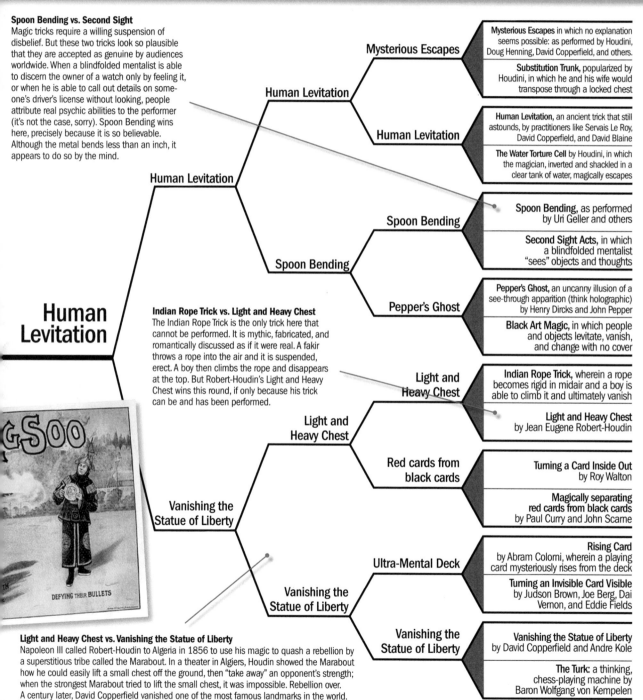

Roller Coasters

By Scott Rutherford

Scott Rutherford is senior editor/writer for the trade publication *Amusement Today* and author of *The American Roller Coaster.*

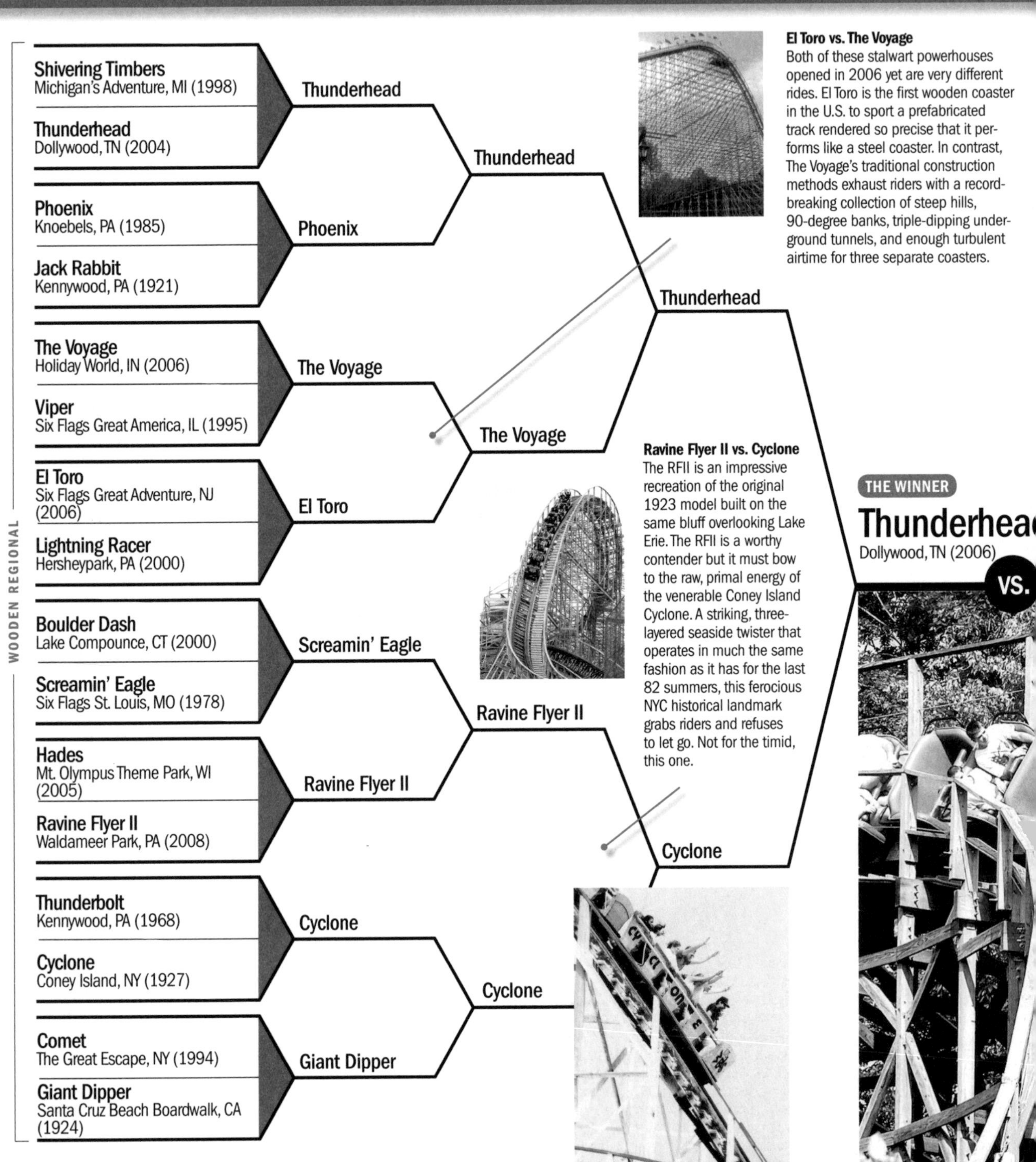
WOODEN REGIONAL
Shivering Timbers
Michigan's Adventure, MI (1998)
Thunderhead
Dollywood, TN (2004)
Phoenix
Knoebels, PA (1985)
Jack Rabbit
Kennywood, PA (1921)
The Voyage
Holiday World, IN (2006)
Viper
Six Flags Great America, IL (1995)
El Toro
Six Flags Great Adventure, NJ (2006)
Lightning Racer
Hersheypark, PA (2000)
Boulder Dash
Lake Compounce, CT (2000)
Screamin' Eagle
Six Flags St. Louis, MO (1978)
Hades
Mt. Olympus Theme Park, WI (2005)
Ravine Flyer II
Waldameer Park, PA (2008)
Thunderbolt
Kennywood, PA (1968)
Cyclone
Coney Island, NY (1927)
Comet
The Great Escape, NY (1994)
Giant Dipper
Santa Cruz Beach Boardwalk, CA (1924)
Thunderhead
Phoenix
The Voyage
El Toro
Screamin' Eagle
Ravine Flyer II
Cyclone
Giant Dipper
Thunderhead
The Voyage
Ravine Flyer II
Cyclone
Thunderhead
Cyclone
El Toro vs. The Voyage
Both of these stalwart powerhouses opened in 2006 yet are very different rides. El Toro is the first wooden coaster in the U.S. to sport a prefabricated track rendered so precise that it performs like a steel coaster. In contrast, The Voyage's traditional construction methods exhaust riders with a record-breaking collection of steep hills, 90-degree banks, triple-dipping underground tunnels, and enough turbulent airtime for three separate coasters.
Ravine Flyer II vs. Cyclone
The RFII is an impressive recreation of the original 1923 model built on the same bluff overlooking Lake Erie. The RFII is a worthy contender but it must bow to the raw, primal energy of the venerable Coney Island Cyclone. A striking, three-layered seaside twister that operates in much the same fashion as it has for the last 82 summers, this ferocious NYC historical landmark grabs riders and refuses to let go. Not for the timid, this one.
THE WINNER
Thunderhea
Dollywood, TN (2006)
VS.

(THE CAROUSEL MAY BE THE SOUL OF AN AMUSEMENT PARK, but the roller coaster is its iconic, adrenaline-filled heart. Inspired by 17th-century Russian ice slides, it took American ingenuity in 1884 at New York's Coney Island to refine the concept. More than 2,000 were built in the Roaring '20s, but only a handful from that first Golden Age survived the wave of destruction that began during the Great Depression. Today's coaster renaissance commenced in 1972 and shows no signs of faltering. The sky is quite literally the limit.)

Batman vs. Mind Bender
While these two loopers share the same German designer (Werner Stengel), they offer vastly dissimilar experiences. Swooping in as the world's first inverted coaster, Batman locks riders into floorless ski lift-style vehicles and rockets them through five rapid-fire inversions. But its senior Southern cousin excels due to its inspired concealment in a forested ravine, unexpected moments of ejector airtime, and a mere lap bar to restrain passengers. Even at 30 years old, Mind Bender still riddles the Dark Knight.

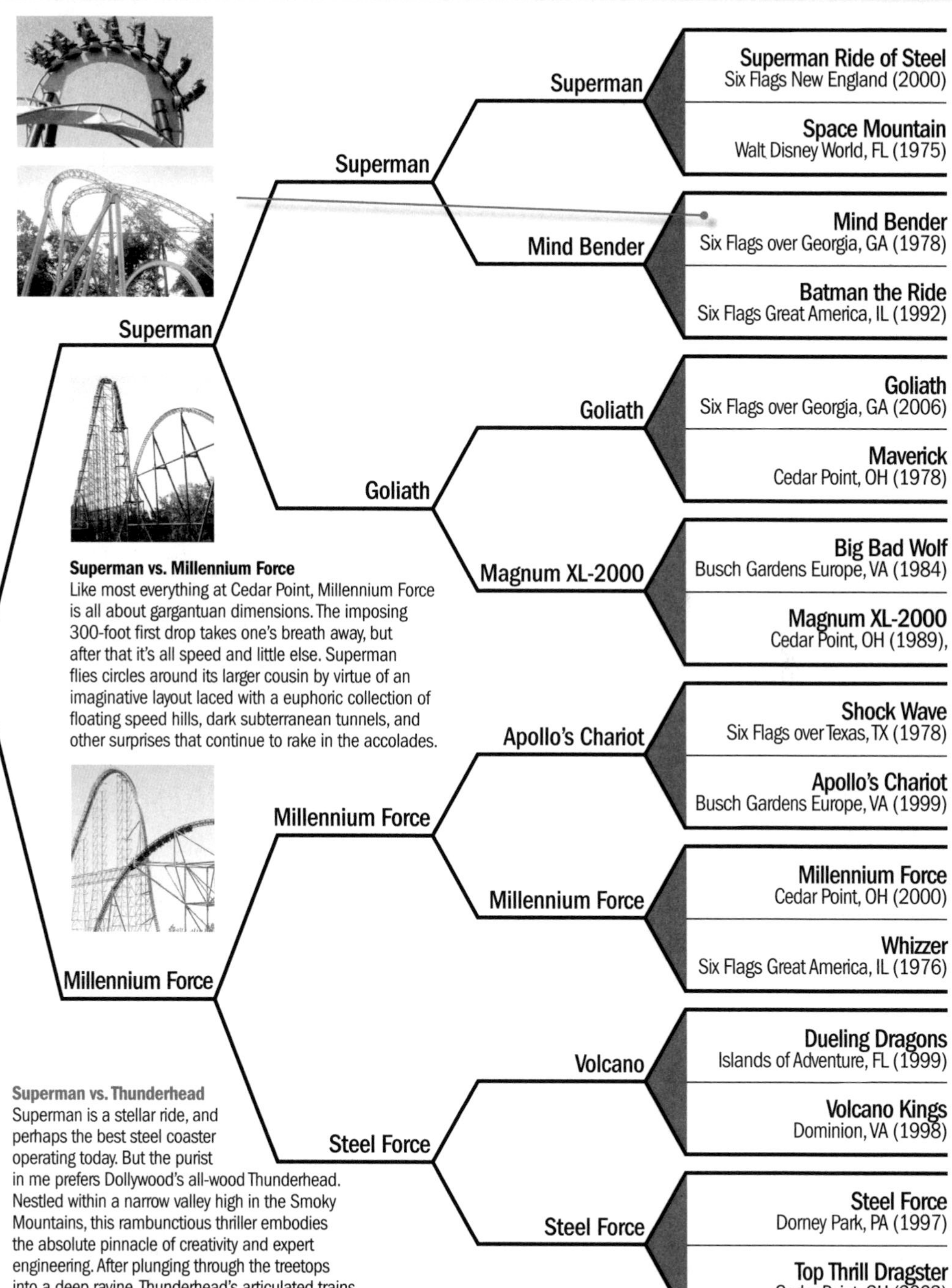

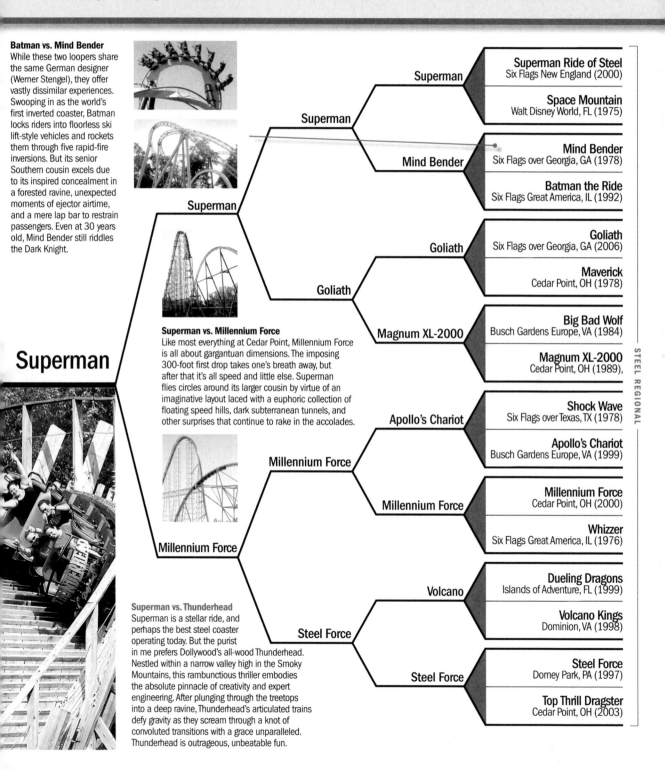

Superman Ride of Steel
Six Flags New England (2000)
Space Mountain
Walt Disney World, FL (1975)
Mind Bender
Six Flags over Georgia, GA (1978)
Batman the Ride
Six Flags Great America, IL (1992)
Goliath
Six Flags over Georgia, GA (2006)
Maverick
Cedar Point, OH (1978)
Big Bad Wolf
Busch Gardens Europe, VA (1984)
Magnum XL-2000
Cedar Point, OH (1989),
Shock Wave
Six Flags over Texas, TX (1978)
Apollo's Chariot
Busch Gardens Europe, VA (1999)
Millennium Force
Cedar Point, OH (2000)
Whizzer
Six Flags Great America, IL (1976)
Dueling Dragons
Islands of Adventure, FL (1999)
Volcano Kings
Dominion, VA (1998)
Steel Force
Dorney Park, PA (1997)
Top Thrill Dragster
Cedar Point, OH (2003)
Superman
Mind Bender
Goliath
Magnum XL-2000
Apollo's Chariot
Millennium Force
Volcano
Steel Force
Superman
Goliath
Millennium Force
Steel Force
Superman
Millennium Force
Superman
STEEL REGIONAL

Superman vs. Millennium Force
Like most everything at Cedar Point, Millennium Force is all about gargantuan dimensions. The imposing 300-foot first drop takes one's breath away, but after that it's all speed and little else. Superman flies circles around its larger cousin by virtue of an imaginative layout laced with a euphoric collection of floating speed hills, dark subterranean tunnels, and other surprises that continue to rake in the accolades.

Superman vs. Thunderhead
Superman is a stellar ride, and perhaps the best steel coaster operating today. But the purist in me prefers Dollywood's all-wood Thunderhead. Nestled within a narrow valley high in the Smoky Mountains, this rambunctious thriller embodies the absolute pinnacle of creativity and expert engineering. After plunging through the treetops into a deep ravine, Thunderhead's articulated trains defy gravity as they scream through a knot of convoluted transitions with a grace unparalleled. Thunderhead is outrageous, unbeatable fun.

SAT Success Strategies

By Laura Wilson

Laura Wilson is CEO and founder of the WilsonDailyPrep, an online SAT/ACT program, and WilsonPrep, a test prep company. She is the author of two books, *English in English* and *Write the 25-Minute SAT Essay Right.*

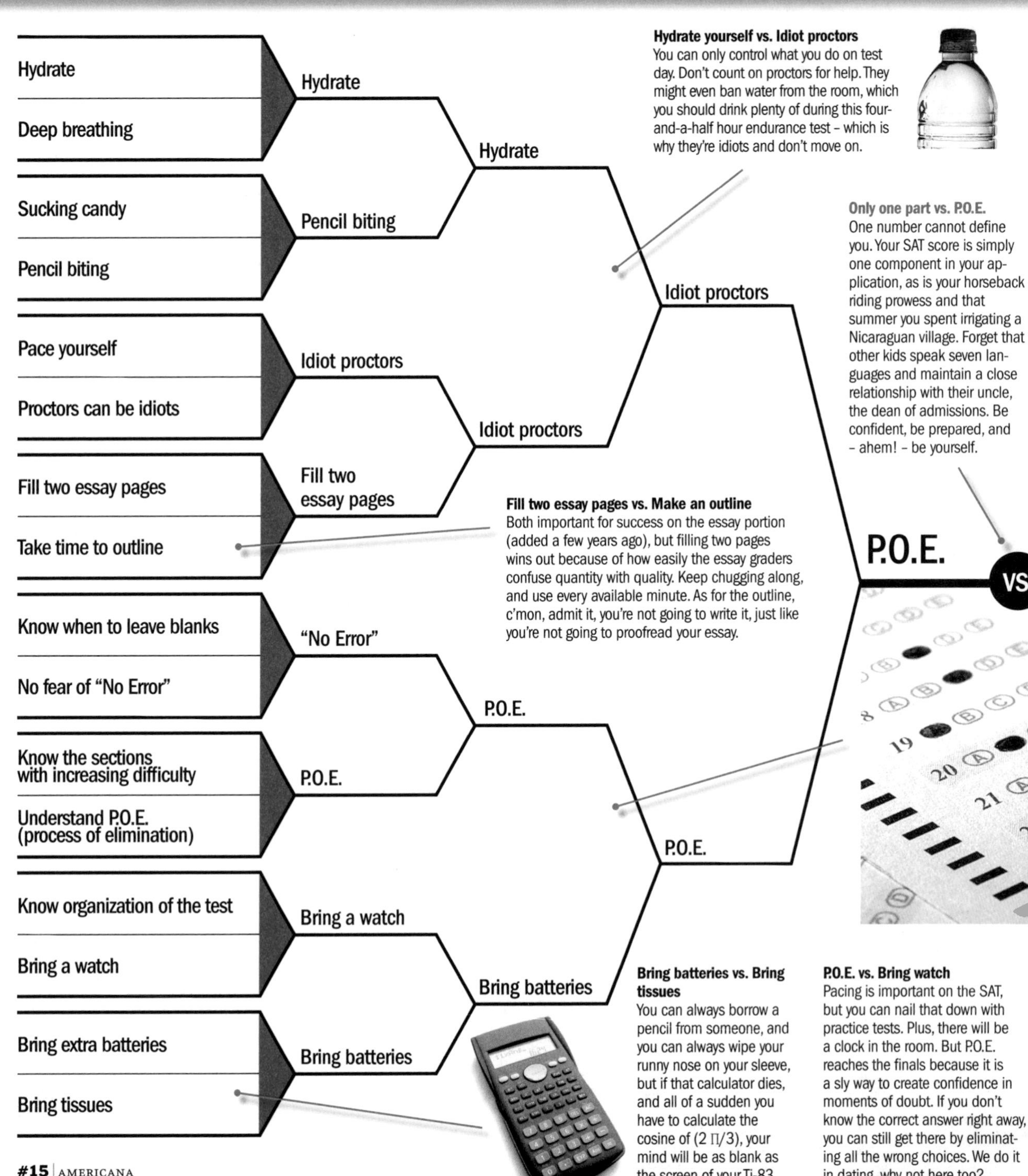
Hydrate
Deep breathing
Sucking candy
Pencil biting
Pace yourself
Proctors can be idiots
Fill two essay pages
Take time to outline
Know when to leave blanks
No fear of "No Error"
Know the sections with increasing difficulty
Understand P.O.E. (process of elimination)
Know organization of the test
Bring a watch
Bring extra batteries
Bring tissues
Hydrate
Pencil biting
Idiot proctors
Fill two essay pages
"No Error"
P.O.E.
Bring a watch
Bring batteries
Hydrate
Idiot proctors
P.O.E.
Bring batteries
Idiot proctors
P.O.E.
P.O.E.
VS.

Hydrate yourself vs. Idiot proctors
You can only control what you do on test day. Don't count on proctors for help. They might even ban water from the room, which you should drink plenty of during this four-and-a-half hour endurance test – which is why they're idiots and don't move on.

Only one part vs. P.O.E.
One number cannot define you. Your SAT score is simply one component in your application, as is your horseback riding prowess and that summer you spent irrigating a Nicaraguan village. Forget that other kids speak seven languages and maintain a close relationship with their uncle, the dean of admissions. Be confident, be prepared, and – ahem! – be yourself.

Fill two essay pages vs. Make an outline
Both important for success on the essay portion (added a few years ago), but filling two pages wins out because of how easily the essay graders confuse quantity with quality. Keep chugging along, and use every available minute. As for the outline, c'mon, admit it, you're not going to write it, just like you're not going to proofread your essay.

Bring batteries vs. Bring tissues
You can always borrow a pencil from someone, and you can always wipe your runny nose on your sleeve, but if that calculator dies, and all of a sudden you have to calculate the cosine of ($2\Pi/3$), your mind will be as blank as the screen of your Ti-83.

P.O.E. vs. Bring watch
Pacing is important on the SAT, but you can nail that down with practice tests. Plus, there will be a clock in the room. But P.O.E. reaches the finals because it is a sly way to create confidence in moments of doubt. If you don't know the correct answer right away, you can still get there by eliminating all the wrong choices. We do it in dating, why not here too?

REMEMBER THOSE HALCYON (repugnant, purgative, quotidian?) days of studying for your SAT? Our aim here is not to espouse practice (that's a given) but to rank 32 test-taking strategies that you might not have considered. They are a mixture of logistical tips, ways to feel confident, and below-the-surface eccentricities on the test itself. All of them have the same goal: to put the next generation of prodigious (precocious, perspicacious) neophytes into schools where they will feel challenged and proud of their accomplishments.

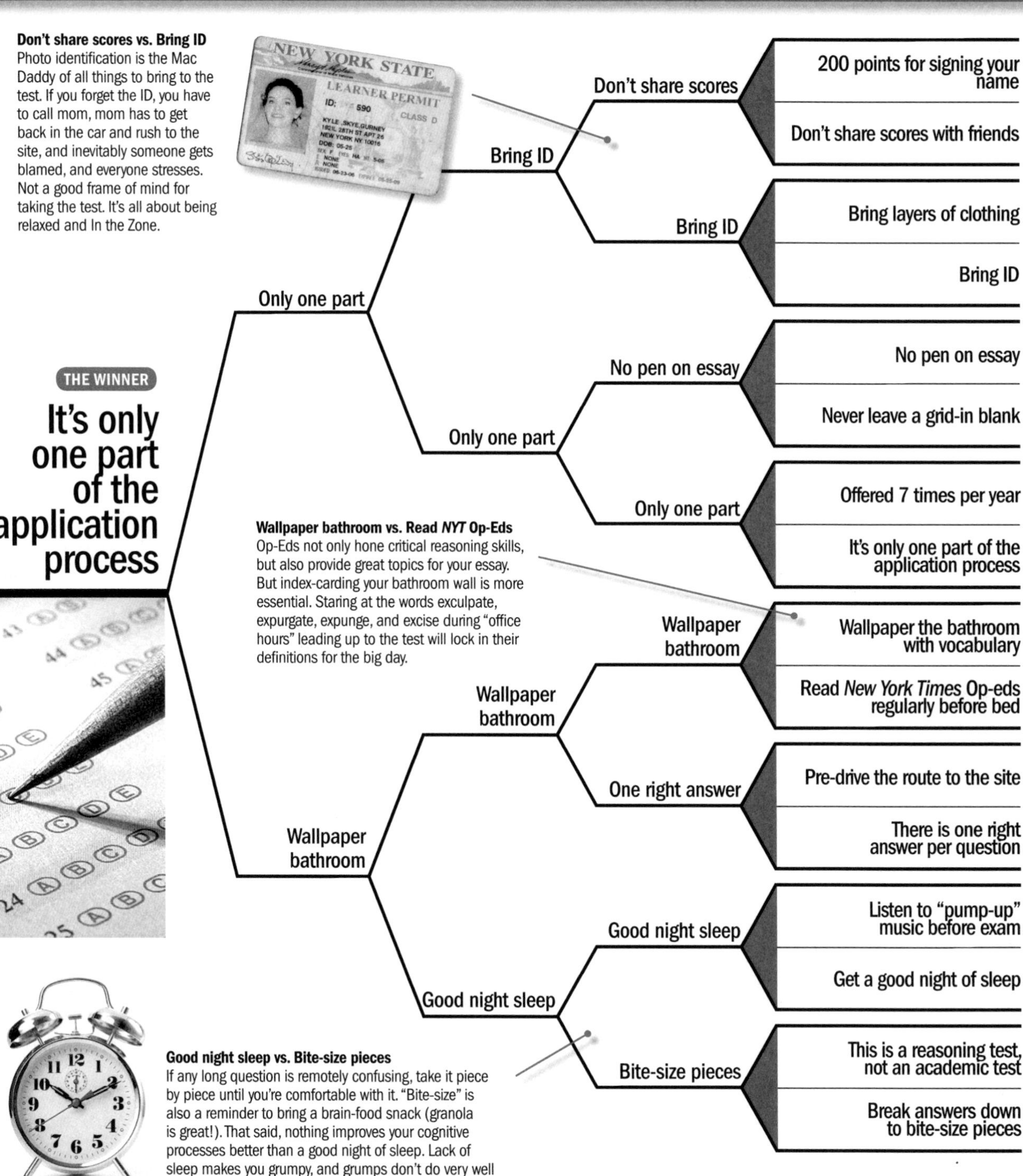

200 points for signing your name
Don't share scores with friends
Bring layers of clothing
Bring ID
No pen on essay
Never leave a grid-in blank
Offered 7 times per year
It's only one part of the application process
Wallpaper the bathroom with vocabulary
Read *New York Times* Op-eds regularly before bed
Pre-drive the route to the site
There is one right answer per question
Listen to "pump-up" music before exam
Get a good night of sleep
This is a reasoning test, not an academic test
Break answers down to bite-size pieces
Don't share scores
Bring ID
No pen on essay
Only one part
Wallpaper bathroom
One right answer
Good night sleep
Bite-size pieces
Bring ID
Only one part
Wallpaper bathroom
Good night sleep
Only one part
Wallpaper bathroom
NEW YORK STATE
LEARNER PERMIT

Don't share scores vs. Bring ID
Photo identification is the Mac Daddy of all things to bring to the test. If you forget the ID, you have to call mom, mom has to get back in the car and rush to the site, and inevitably someone gets blamed, and everyone stresses. Not a good frame of mind for taking the test. It's all about being relaxed and In the Zone.

THE WINNER

It's only one part of the application process

Wallpaper bathroom vs. Read *NYT* Op-Eds
Op-Eds not only hone critical reasoning skills, but also provide great topics for your essay. But index-carding your bathroom wall is more essential. Staring at the words exculpate, expurgate, expunge, and excise during "office hours" leading up to the test will lock in their definitions for the big day.

Good night sleep vs. Bite-size pieces
If any long question is remotely confusing, take it piece by piece until you're comfortable with it. "Bite-size" is also a reminder to bring a brain-food snack (granola is great!). That said, nothing improves your cognitive processes better than a good night of sleep. Lack of sleep makes you grumpy, and grumps don't do very well on tasks that require full concentration.

Screen Cowboys

By Neil Amdur

Neil Amdur has spent a lifetime covering tournaments of all kinds – from tennis to the Olympics – as a reporter and then as sports editor of the *New York Times* for 12 years. His knowledge of cowboys extends from childhood to manhood.

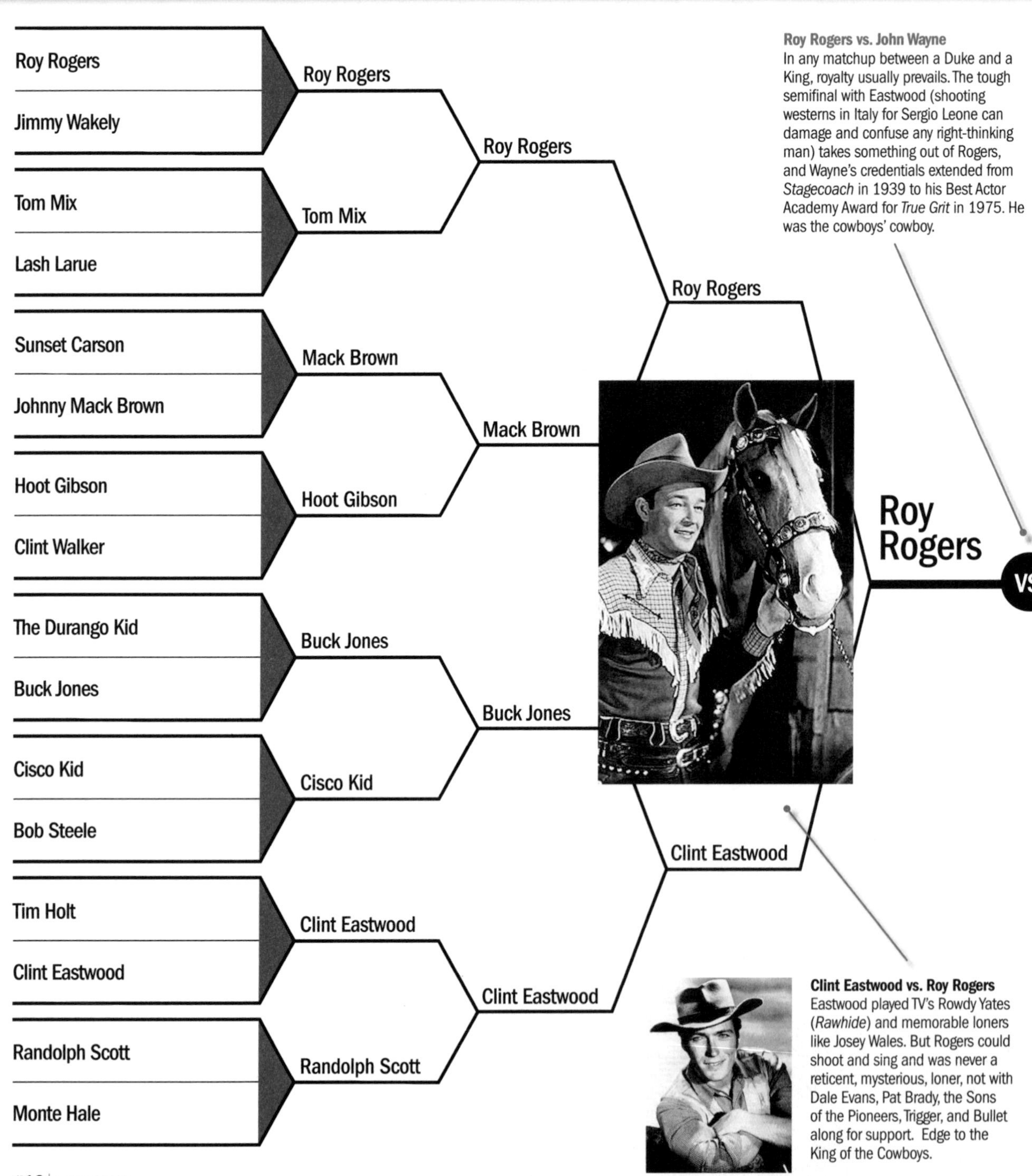

Roy Rogers
Jimmy Wakely
Tom Mix
Lash Larue
Sunset Carson
Johnny Mack Brown
Hoot Gibson
Clint Walker
The Durango Kid
Buck Jones
Cisco Kid
Bob Steele
Tim Holt
Clint Eastwood
Randolph Scott
Monte Hale
Roy Rogers
Tom Mix
Mack Brown
Hoot Gibson
Buck Jones
Cisco Kid
Clint Eastwood
Randolph Scott
Roy Rogers
Mack Brown
Buck Jones
Clint Eastwood
Roy Rogers
Clint Eastwood
Roy Rogers
VS.

Roy Rogers vs. John Wayne
In any matchup between a Duke and a King, royalty usually prevails. The tough semifinal with Eastwood (shooting westerns in Italy for Sergio Leone can damage and confuse any right-thinking man) takes something out of Rogers, and Wayne's credentials extended from *Stagecoach* in 1939 to his Best Actor Academy Award for *True Grit* in 1975. He was the cowboys' cowboy.

Clint Eastwood vs. Roy Rogers
Eastwood played TV's Rowdy Yates (*Rawhide*) and memorable loners like Josey Wales. But Rogers could shoot and sing and was never a reticent, mysterious, loner, not with Dale Evans, Pat Brady, the Sons of the Pioneers, Trigger, and Bullet along for support. Edge to the King of the Cowboys.

IN THE AMERICAN PSYCHE, cowboys were our heroes, transported from the range to movie theaters and TV screens with personalities we could only envision in our dreams. They each brought their own identity, with slick costumes, exotic horses, elaborate disguises, finely crafted hardware, diverse sidekicks, and even the ability to deliver a song amid the madness. And all in the name of law and order.

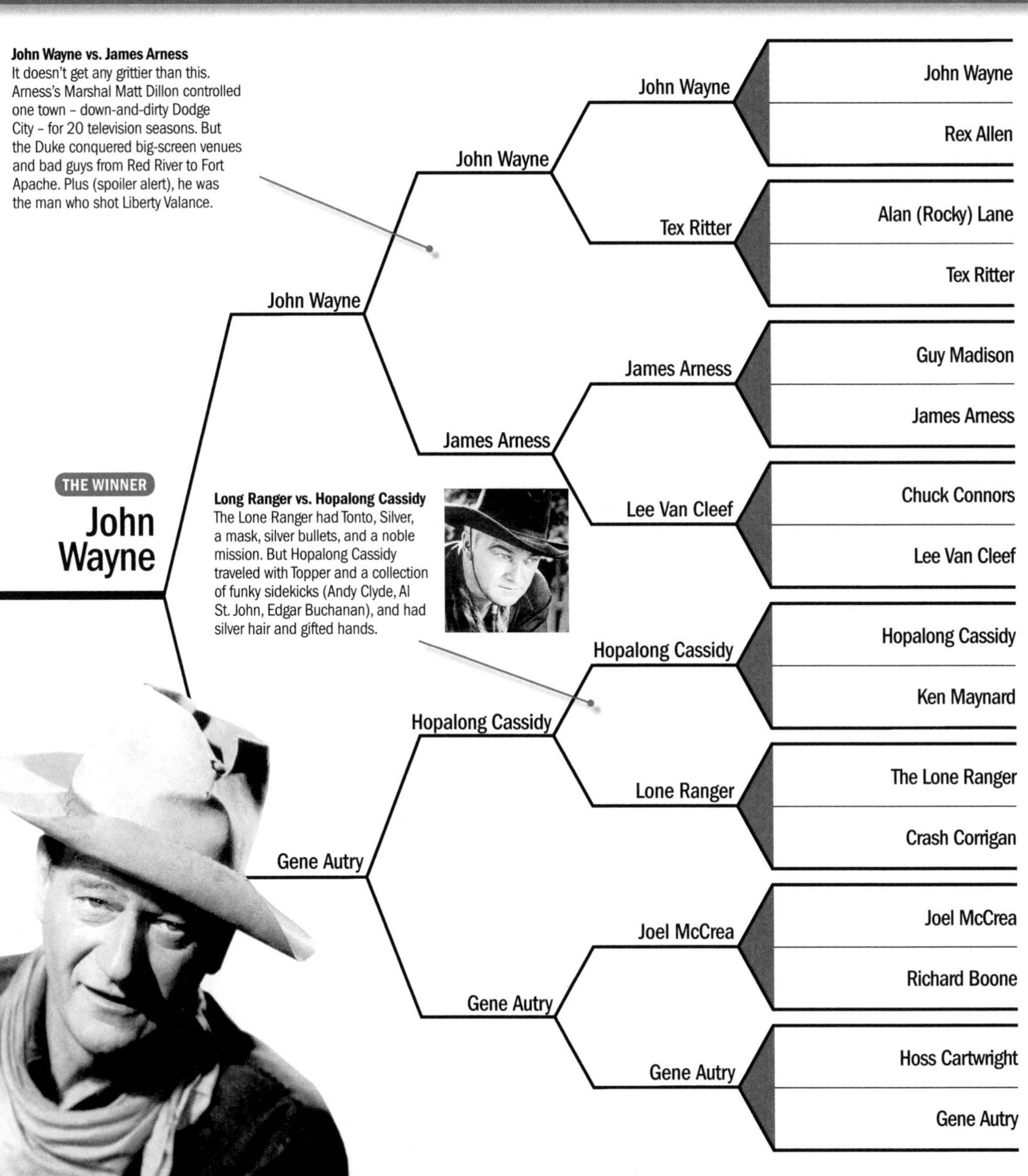

John Wayne
Rex Allen
Alan (Rocky) Lane
Tex Ritter
Guy Madison
James Arness
Chuck Connors
Lee Van Cleef
Hopalong Cassidy
Ken Maynard
The Lone Ranger
Crash Corrigan
Joel McCrea
Richard Boone
Hoss Cartwright
Gene Autry
John Wayne
Tex Ritter
James Arness
Lee Van Cleef
Hopalong Cassidy
Lone Ranger
Joel McCrea
Gene Autry
John Wayne
James Arness
Hopalong Cassidy
Gene Autry
John Wayne
Gene Autry
THE WINNER
John Wayne

John Wayne vs. James Arness
It doesn't get any grittier than this. Arness's Marshal Matt Dillon controlled one town – down-and-dirty Dodge City – for 20 television seasons. But the Duke conquered big-screen venues and bad guys from Red River to Fort Apache. Plus (spoiler alert), he was the man who shot Liberty Valance.

Long Ranger vs. Hopalong Cassidy
The Lone Ranger had Tonto, Silver, a mask, silver bullets, and a noble mission. But Hopalong Cassidy traveled with Topper and a collection of funky sidekicks (Andy Clyde, Al St. John, Edgar Buchanan), and had silver hair and gifted hands.

A New National Anthem

By Richard Sandomir

Richard Sandomir, the co-editor of this book, was instructed in eighth-grade music class to always mouth the words so that no one would hear his voice.

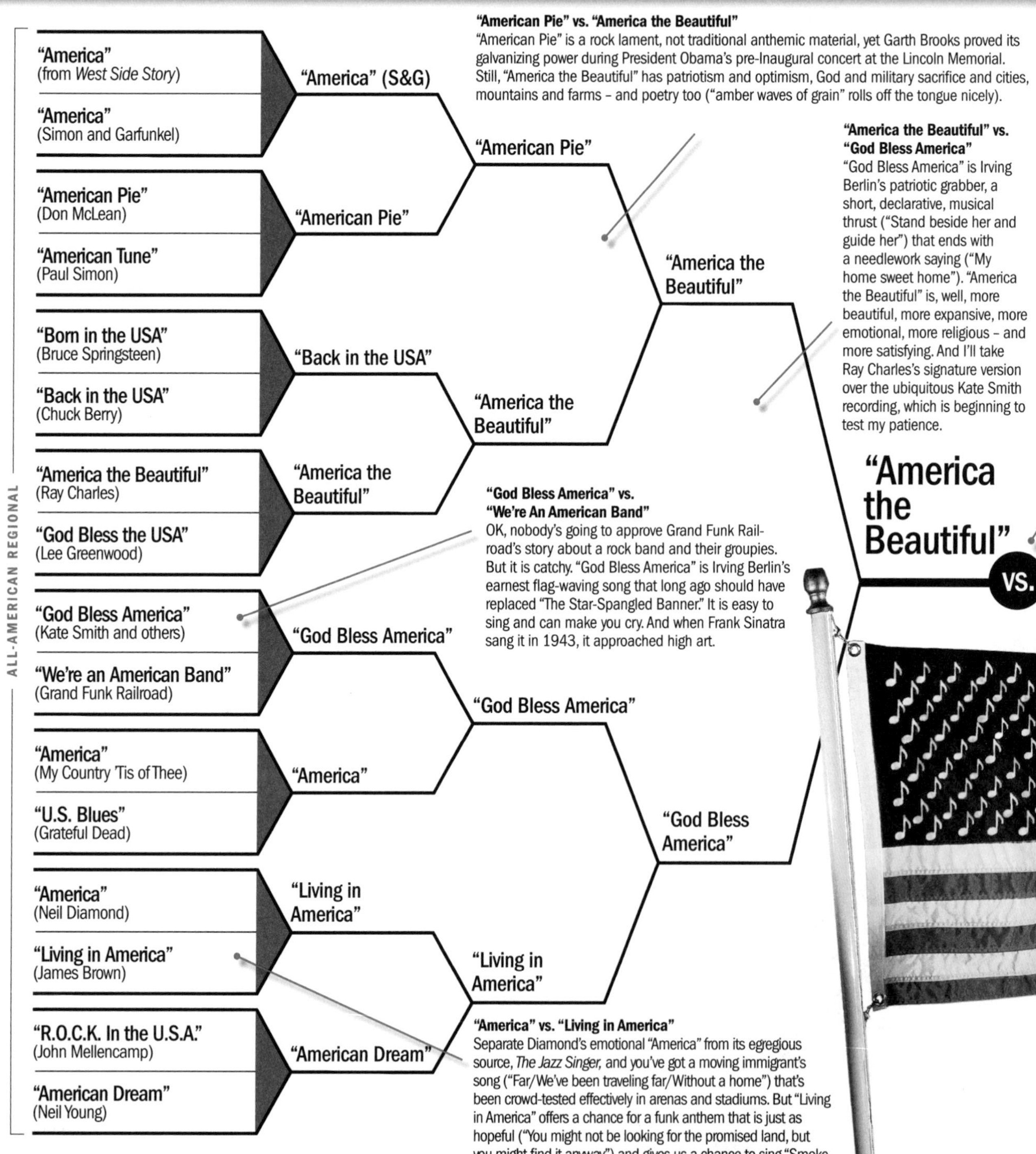

ALL-AMERICAN REGIONAL
"America" (from *West Side Story*)
"America" (Simon and Garfunkel)
"American Pie" (Don McLean)
"American Tune" (Paul Simon)
"Born in the USA" (Bruce Springsteen)
"Back in the USA" (Chuck Berry)
"America the Beautiful" (Ray Charles)
"God Bless the USA" (Lee Greenwood)
"God Bless America" (Kate Smith and others)
"We're an American Band" (Grand Funk Railroad)
"America" (My Country 'Tis of Thee)
"U.S. Blues" (Grateful Dead)
"America" (Neil Diamond)
"Living in America" (James Brown)
"R.O.C.K. In the U.S.A." (John Mellencamp)
"American Dream" (Neil Young)
"America" (S&G)
"American Pie"
"Back in the USA"
"America the Beautiful"
"God Bless America"
"America"
"Living in America"
"American Dream"
"American Pie"
"America the Beautiful"
"God Bless America"
"Living in America"
"America the Beautiful"
"God Bless America"
"America the Beautiful"
VS.

"American Pie" vs. "America the Beautiful"
"American Pie" is a rock lament, not traditional anthemic material, yet Garth Brooks proved its galvanizing power during President Obama's pre-Inaugural concert at the Lincoln Memorial. Still, "America the Beautiful" has patriotism and optimism, God and military sacrifice and cities, mountains and farms – and poetry too ("amber waves of grain" rolls off the tongue nicely).

"America the Beautiful" vs. "God Bless America"
"God Bless America" is Irving Berlin's patriotic grabber, a short, declarative, musical thrust ("Stand beside her and guide her") that ends with a needlework saying ("My home sweet home"). "America the Beautiful" is, well, more beautiful, more expansive, more emotional, more religious – and more satisfying. And I'll take Ray Charles's signature version over the ubiquitous Kate Smith recording, which is beginning to test my patience.

"God Bless America" vs. "We're An American Band"
OK, nobody's going to approve Grand Funk Railroad's story about a rock band and their groupies. But it is catchy. "God Bless America" is Irving Berlin's earnest flag-waving song that long ago should have replaced "The Star-Spangled Banner." It is easy to sing and can make you cry. And when Frank Sinatra sang it in 1943, it approached high art.

"America" vs. "Living in America"
Separate Diamond's emotional "America" from its egregious source, *The Jazz Singer,* and you've got a moving immigrant's song ("Far/We've been traveling far/Without a home") that's been crowd-tested effectively in arenas and stadiums. But "Living in America" offers a chance for a funk anthem that is just as hopeful ("You might not be looking for the promised land, but you might find it anyway") and gives us a chance to sing "Smoke-stack, fatback/Many miles of railroad track." We feel good!

SHOW OF HANDS: how many of you think "The Star Spangled Banner" must go? Polls show that most American adults don't know the words, why it was written, or why it is sung to the melody of a British drinking song. It's a tough tune to carry, with a one-and-a-half octave range and two "o'er's" just in the one verse (of four) that we sing. Here we begin the search for a song: one not mired in bellicose imagery observed from a 19th-century fort, one that prompts a mass singalong, and one that even Roseanne can sing.

"Blowin' in the Wind" vs. "Yankee Doodle"
"Yankee Doodle" is a short, jolly earwig that fails the sense test: if Yankee Doodle is Uncle Sam's nephew (an august station in life), how can he justify going to London just to ride the ponies? Would you want Whitney Houston singing that to 75,000 fans? Dylan's song, a serious part of the American folk/protest songbook, has three advantages: it is philosophical, angry, and easy to sing.

"America the Beautiful" vs. "This Land"
Guthrie's astonishing song – a folk classic and a political response to "God Bless America" – is an ode to the nation he "roamed and rambled" on foot and by train. Yes, Brother Ray gives you chills, but Woody's song crisply evokes America's coast-to-coast natural beauties and also finds him "wonderin'" about whether "this land's still made for you and me" when you and me are on relief.

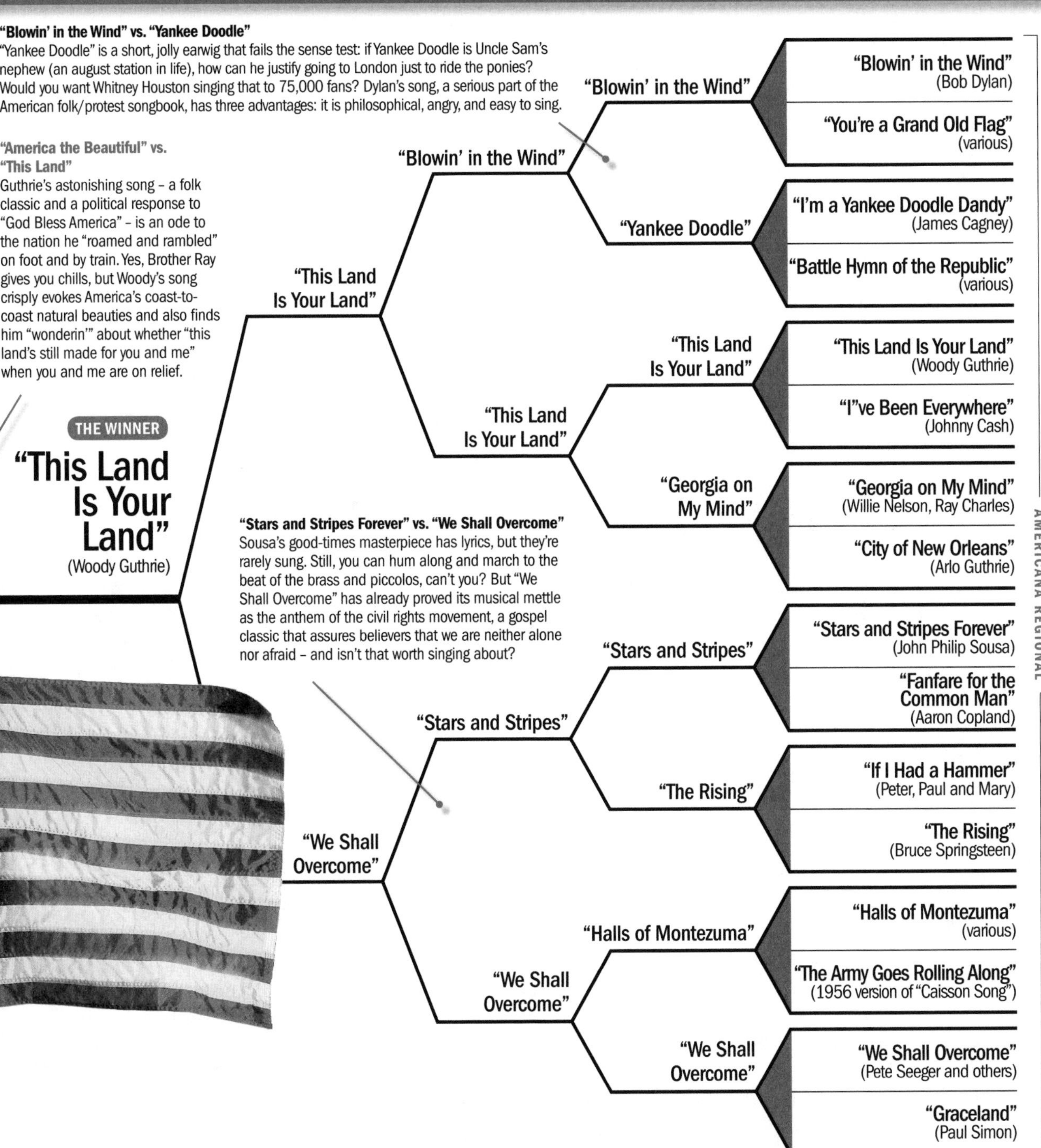

THE WINNER
"This Land Is Your Land"
(Woody Guthrie)
"This Land Is Your Land"
"We Shall Overcome"
"Blowin' in the Wind"
"This Land Is Your Land"
"Stars and Stripes"
"We Shall Overcome"
"Blowin' in the Wind"
"Yankee Doodle"
"This Land Is Your Land"
"Georgia on My Mind"
"Stars and Stripes"
"The Rising"
"Halls of Montezuma"
"We Shall Overcome"
"Blowin' in the Wind" (Bob Dylan)
"You're a Grand Old Flag" (various)
"I'm a Yankee Doodle Dandy" (James Cagney)
"Battle Hymn of the Republic" (various)
"This Land Is Your Land" (Woody Guthrie)
"I've Been Everywhere" (Johnny Cash)
"Georgia on My Mind" (Willie Nelson, Ray Charles)
"City of New Orleans" (Arlo Guthrie)
"Stars and Stripes Forever" (John Philip Sousa)
"Fanfare for the Common Man" (Aaron Copland)
"If I Had a Hammer" (Peter, Paul and Mary)
"The Rising" (Bruce Springsteen)
"Halls of Montezuma" (various)
"The Army Goes Rolling Along" (1956 version of "Caisson Song")
"We Shall Overcome" (Pete Seeger and others)
"Graceland" (Paul Simon)
AMERICANA REGIONAL

"Stars and Stripes Forever" vs. "We Shall Overcome"
Sousa's good-times masterpiece has lyrics, but they're rarely sung. Still, you can hum along and march to the beat of the brass and piccolos, can't you? But "We Shall Overcome" has already proved its musical mettle as the anthem of the civil rights movement, a gospel classic that assures believers that we are neither alone nor afraid – and isn't that worth singing about?

HISTORY & POLITICS

Vestiges of the 20th Century *by Kurt Andersen* 18
Conservative Texts *by Mary Matalin* 19
First Ladies *by Gail Collins* 20
Panic Attacks *by Jack Hitt* 21
Memorable Speech Lines *by Jeff Shesol* 22
Innovators *by Harold Evans* 23
Supreme Court Decisions *by Adam Liptak* 24
Presidential Pardons *by P.S. Ruckman, Jr.* 25
Military Heroes *by Richard Goldstein* 26
Enduring One-Liners *by Jan Van Meter* 27
Financial Villains *by Joe Nocera* 28
Political Rivalries *by Adam Clymer* 29
Presidential Speeches *by Curt Smith* 30
Influential Radicals and Extremists *by David Oshinsky* 31
Biographies *by James McGrath Morris* 32

Vestiges of the 20th Century

By Kurt Andersen

Kurt Andersen does a lot, but his obituary written near the end of the 21st century might mention that he co-founded *Spy*, edited *New York*, hosted "Studio 360," and, beginning with *Turn of the Century* and *Heyday*, wrote many critically acclaimed bestselling novels.

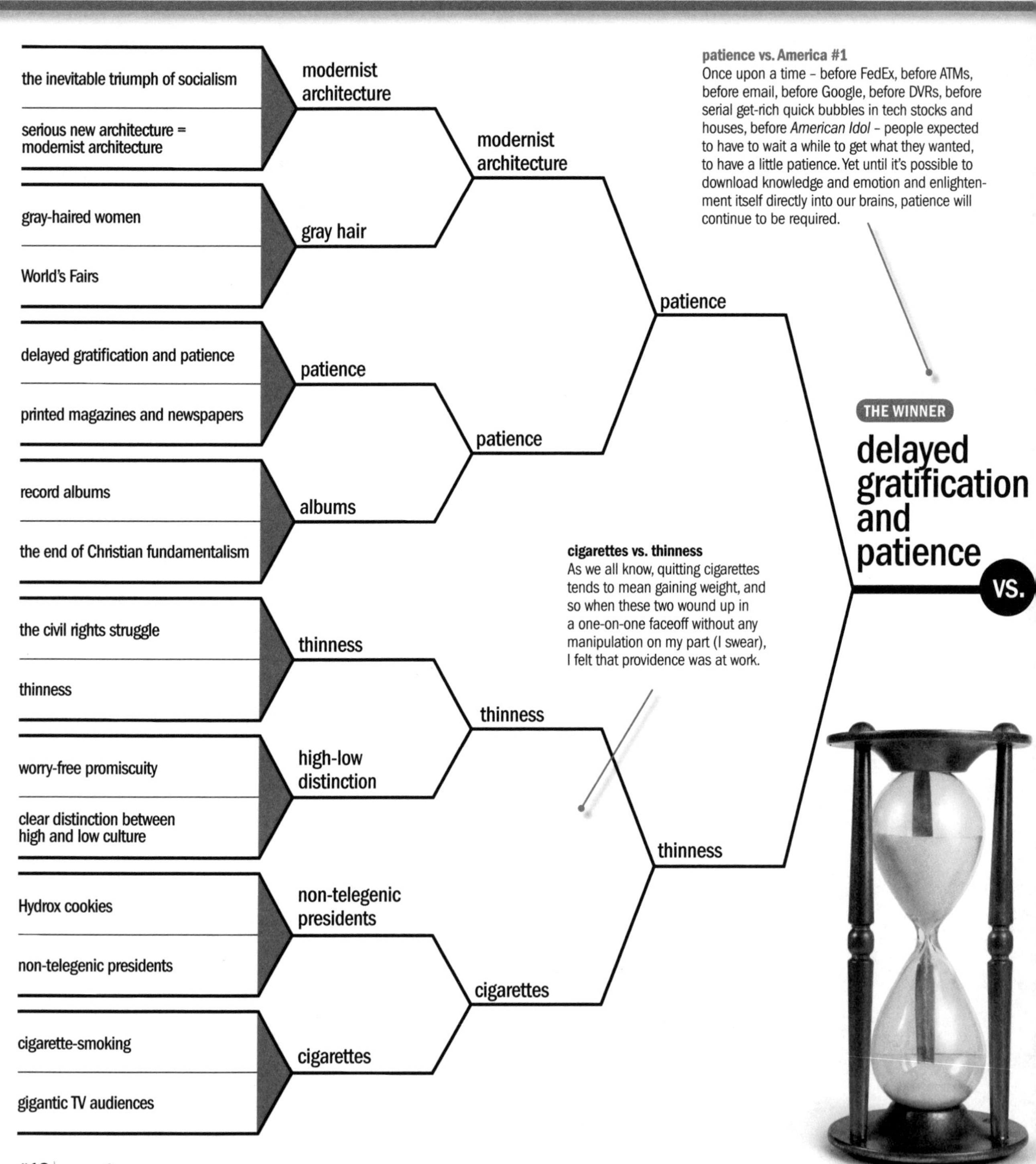

the inevitable triumph of socialism
serious new architecture = modernist architecture
gray-haired women
World's Fairs
delayed gratification and patience
printed magazines and newspapers
record albums
the end of Christian fundamentalism
the civil rights struggle
thinness
worry-free promiscuity
clear distinction between high and low culture
Hydrox cookies
non-telegenic presidents
cigarette-smoking
gigantic TV audiences
modernist architecture
gray hair
patience
albums
thinness
high-low distinction
non-telegenic presidents
cigarettes
modernist architecture
patience
thinness
cigarettes
patience
thinness
THE WINNER
delayed gratification and patience
VS.

patience vs. America #1
Once upon a time – before FedEx, before ATMs, before email, before Google, before DVRs, before serial get-rich quick bubbles in tech stocks and houses, before *American Idol* – people expected to have to wait a while to get what they wanted, to have a little patience. Yet until it's possible to download knowledge and emotion and enlightenment itself directly into our brains, patience will continue to be required.

cigarettes vs. thinness
As we all know, quitting cigarettes tends to mean gaining weight, and so when these two wound up in a one-on-one faceoff without any manipulation on my part (I swear), I felt that providence was at work.

DURING MOST OF THE 20TH CENTURY, these 32 beliefs, artifacts, habits, paradigms, and phenomena were all givens, defining features of modern life, and seemingly permanent. Yet as the century ended and this new one proceeds, we've discovered that they are, um, not. In each round the winner is the one that will take longer to peter out entirely. In the long run, and with uncanny metaphysical aptness, it turned out to be patience that triumphs.

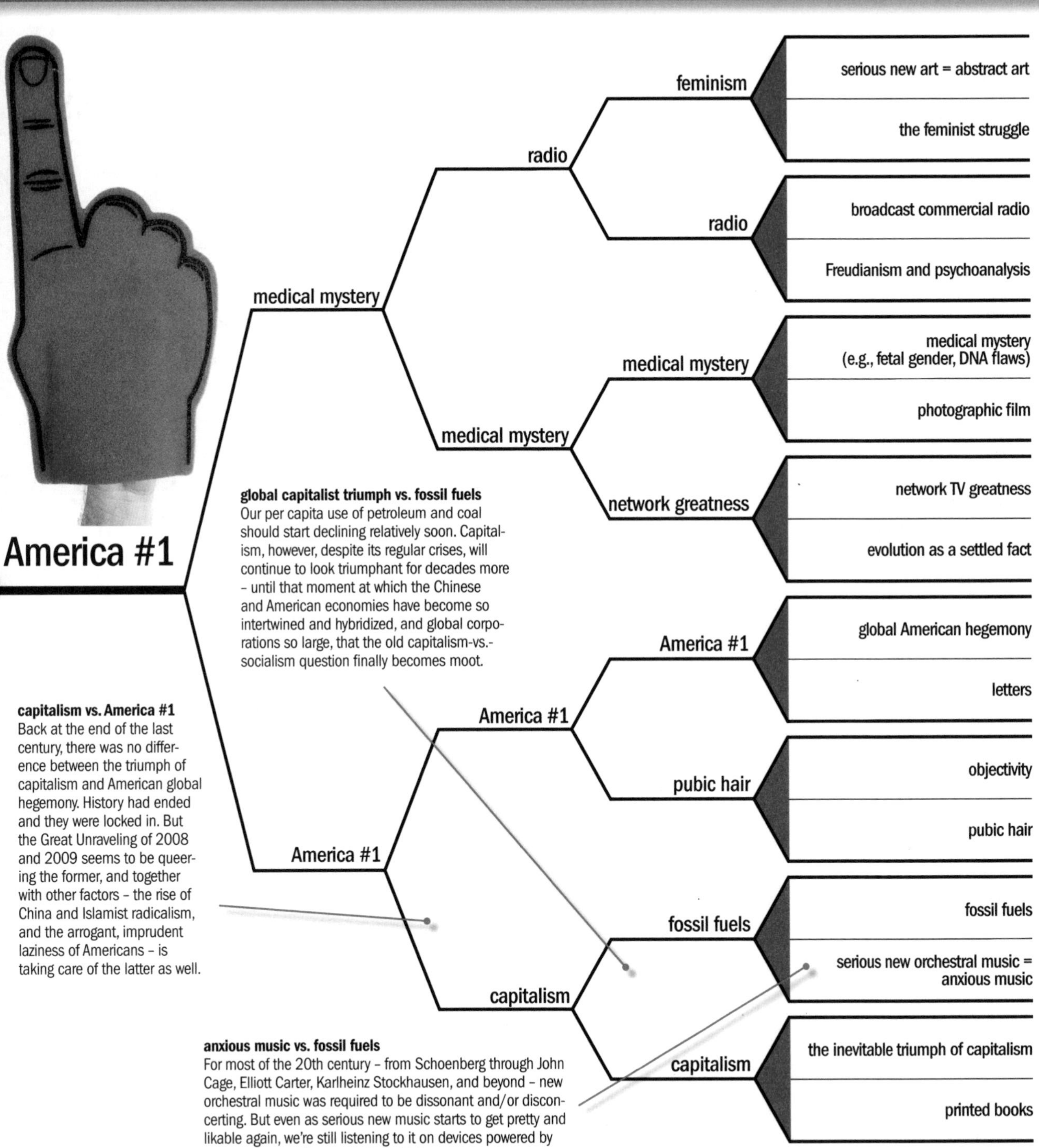
America #1
medical mystery
America #1
radio
medical mystery
America #1
capitalism
feminism
radio
medical mystery
network greatness
America #1
pubic hair
fossil fuels
capitalism
serious new art = abstract art
the feminist struggle
broadcast commercial radio
Freudianism and psychoanalysis
medical mystery (e.g., fetal gender, DNA flaws)
photographic film
network TV greatness
evolution as a settled fact
global American hegemony
letters
objectivity
pubic hair
fossil fuels
serious new orchestral music = anxious music
the inevitable triumph of capitalism
printed books

global capitalist triumph vs. fossil fuels
Our per capita use of petroleum and coal should start declining relatively soon. Capitalism, however, despite its regular crises, will continue to look triumphant for decades more – until that moment at which the Chinese and American economies have become so intertwined and hybridized, and global corporations so large, that the old capitalism-vs.-socialism question finally becomes moot.

capitalism vs. America #1
Back at the end of the last century, there was no difference between the triumph of capitalism and American global hegemony. History had ended and they were locked in. But the Great Unraveling of 2008 and 2009 seems to be queering the former, and together with other factors – the rise of China and Islamist radicalism, and the arrogant, imprudent laziness of Americans – is taking care of the latter as well.

anxious music vs. fossil fuels
For most of the 20th century – from Schoenberg through John Cage, Elliott Carter, Karlheinz Stockhausen, and beyond – new orchestral music was required to be dissonant and/or disconcerting. But even as serious new music starts to get pretty and likable again, we're still listening to it on devices powered by not-so-clean, coal-generated electricity.

Conservative Texts

By Mary Matalin

Mary Matalin, former assistant to President George W. Bush and counselor to Vice President Dick Cheney, is a conservative TV and radio commentator and publisher of Threshold, a conservative book imprint.

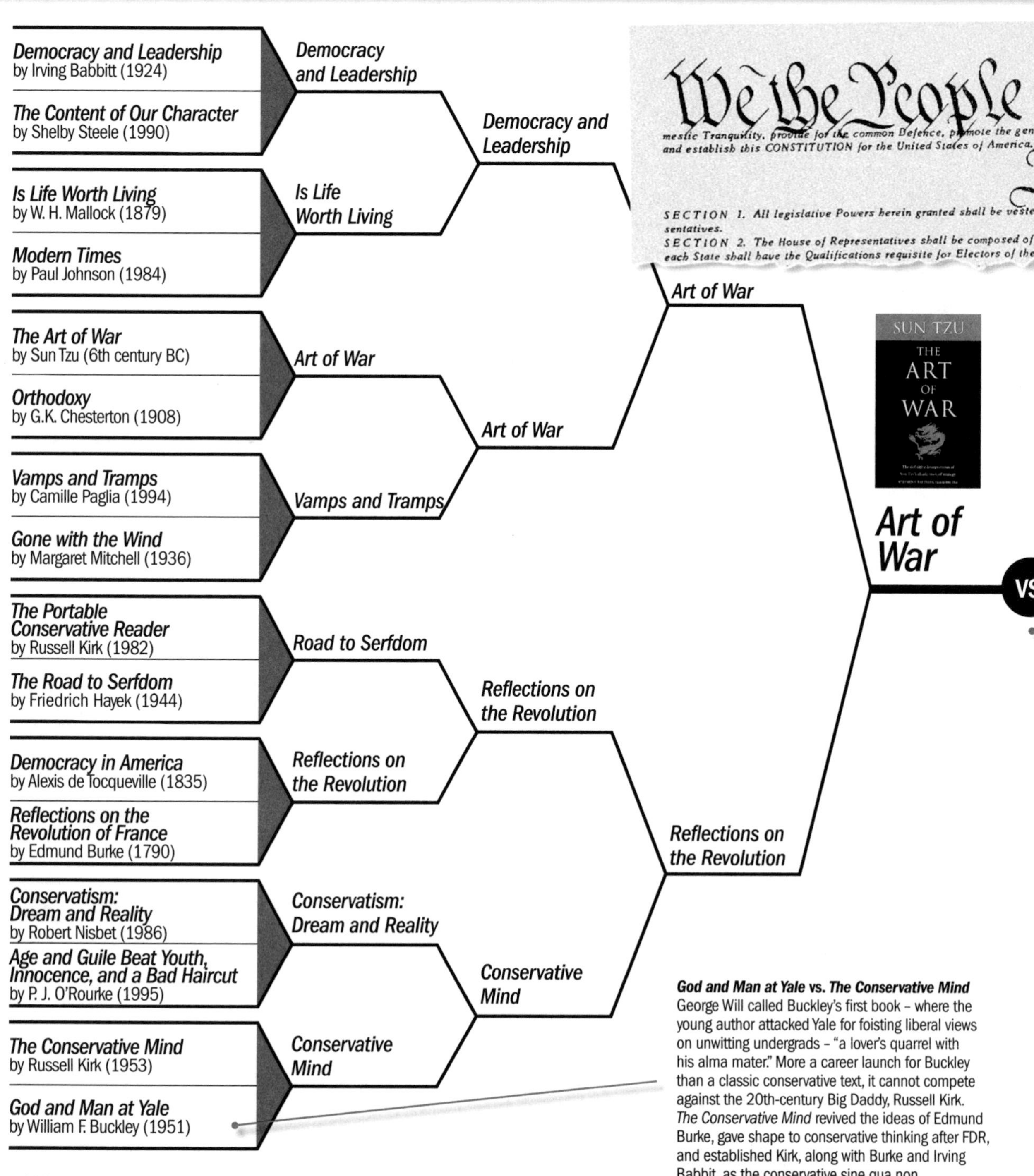
Democracy and Leadership
by Irving Babbitt (1924)
The Content of Our Character
by Shelby Steele (1990)
Is Life Worth Living
by W. H. Mallock (1879)
Modern Times
by Paul Johnson (1984)
The Art of War
by Sun Tzu (6th century BC)
Orthodoxy
by G.K. Chesterton (1908)
Vamps and Tramps
by Camille Paglia (1994)
Gone with the Wind
by Margaret Mitchell (1936)
The Portable Conservative Reader
by Russell Kirk (1982)
The Road to Serfdom
by Friedrich Hayek (1944)
Democracy in America
by Alexis de Tocqueville (1835)
Reflections on the Revolution of France
by Edmund Burke (1790)
Conservatism: Dream and Reality
by Robert Nisbet (1986)
Age and Guile Beat Youth, Innocence, and a Bad Haircut
by P. J. O'Rourke (1995)
The Conservative Mind
by Russell Kirk (1953)
God and Man at Yale
by William F. Buckley (1951)
Democracy and Leadership
Is Life Worth Living
Art of War
Vamps and Tramps
Road to Serfdom
Reflections on the Revolution
Conservatism: Dream and Reality
Conservative Mind
Democracy and Leadership
Art of War
Reflections on the Revolution
Conservative Mind
Art of War
Reflections on the Revolution
Art of War
VS.
We the People
SUN TZU
THE ART OF WAR

God and Man at Yale vs. The Conservative Mind
George Will called Buckley's first book – where the young author attacked Yale for foisting liberal views on unwitting undergrads – "a lover's quarrel with his alma mater." More a career launch for Buckley than a classic conservative text, it cannot compete against the 20th-century Big Daddy, Russell Kirk. *The Conservative Mind* revived the ideas of Edmund Burke, gave shape to conservative thinking after FDR, and established Kirk, along with Burke and Irving Babbit, as the conservative sine qua non.

CONSERVATISM IS COMMONLY, AND OFTEN MALICIOUSLY, MISCHARACTERIZED as an ideology and its adherents as ideologues. Unlike modern liberalism (not to be confused with classical liberalism), conservatism is not a product of some abstract philosophical tract or Utopian theory. From Edmund Burke (the father of political conservatism) to contemporary champions, conservative conviction comes from the accumulated experience of individuals and nations over time. Choosing the best conservative text (which is as difficult as choosing a favorite Beatles song) demands that you savor the variety of offerings, appreciating their shared common origin: individual freedom.

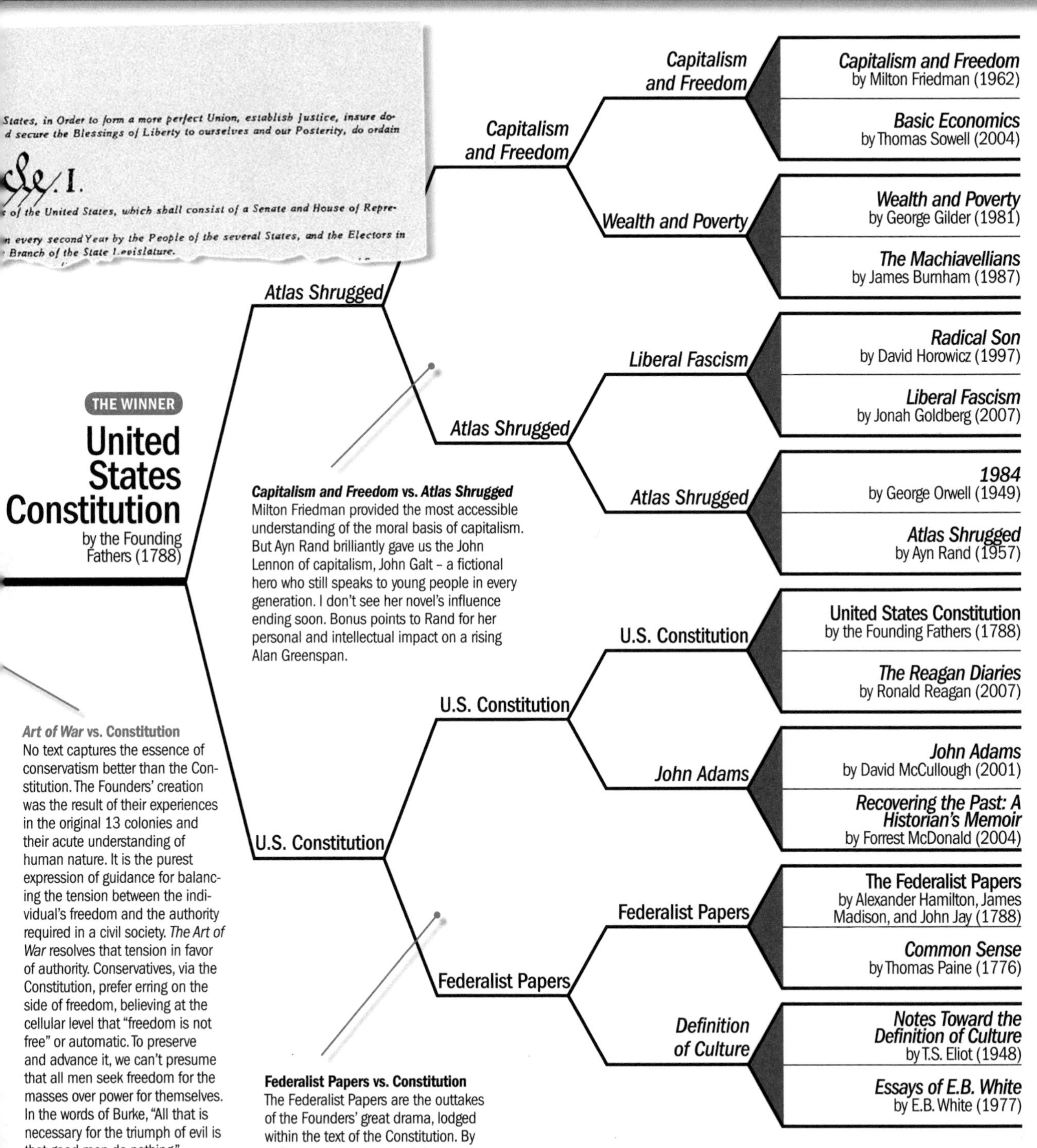
States, in Order to form a more perfect Union, establish Justice, insure do-
d secure the Blessings of Liberty to ourselves and our Posterity, do ordain
Sect. I.
of the United States, which shall consist of a Senate and House of Repre-
n every second Year by the People of the several States, and the Electors in
Branch of the State Legislature.
Capitalism and Freedom
by Milton Friedman (1962)
Basic Economics
by Thomas Sowell (2004)
Wealth and Poverty
by George Gilder (1981)
The Machiavellians
by James Burnham (1987)
Radical Son
by David Horowicz (1997)
Liberal Fascism
by Jonah Goldberg (2007)
1984
by George Orwell (1949)
Atlas Shrugged
by Ayn Rand (1957)
United States Constitution
by the Founding Fathers (1788)
The Reagan Diaries
by Ronald Reagan (2007)
John Adams
by David McCullough (2001)
Recovering the Past: A Historian's Memoir
by Forrest McDonald (2004)
The Federalist Papers
by Alexander Hamilton, James Madison, and John Jay (1788)
Common Sense
by Thomas Paine (1776)
Notes Toward the Definition of Culture
by T.S. Eliot (1948)
Essays of E.B. White
by E.B. White (1977)
Capitalism and Freedom
Wealth and Poverty
Liberal Fascism
Atlas Shrugged
U.S. Constitution
John Adams
Federalist Papers
Definition of Culture
Capitalism and Freedom
Atlas Shrugged
U.S. Constitution
Federalist Papers
Atlas Shrugged
U.S. Constitution
THE WINNER
United States Constitution
by the Founding Fathers (1788)

Capitalism and Freedom* vs. *Atlas Shrugged
Milton Friedman provided the most accessible understanding of the moral basis of capitalism. But Ayn Rand brilliantly gave us the John Lennon of capitalism, John Galt – a fictional hero who still speaks to young people in every generation. I don't see her novel's influence ending soon. Bonus points to Rand for her personal and intellectual impact on a rising Alan Greenspan.

***Art of War* vs. Constitution**
No text captures the essence of conservatism better than the Constitution. The Founders' creation was the result of their experiences in the original 13 colonies and their acute understanding of human nature. It is the purest expression of guidance for balancing the tension between the individual's freedom and the authority required in a civil society. *The Art of War* resolves that tension in favor of authority. Conservatives, via the Constitution, prefer erring on the side of freedom, believing at the cellular level that "freedom is not free" or automatic. To preserve and advance it, we can't presume that all men seek freedom for the masses over power for themselves. In the words of Burke, "All that is necessary for the triumph of evil is that good men do nothing."

Federalist Papers vs. Constitution
The Federalist Papers are the outtakes of the Founders' great drama, lodged within the text of the Constitution. By definition they must stand down.

First Ladies

By Gail Collins

Gail Collins is an op-ed columnist for the *New York Times* and the author of *America's Women: 400 Years of Dolls, Drudges, Helpmates and Heroines.*

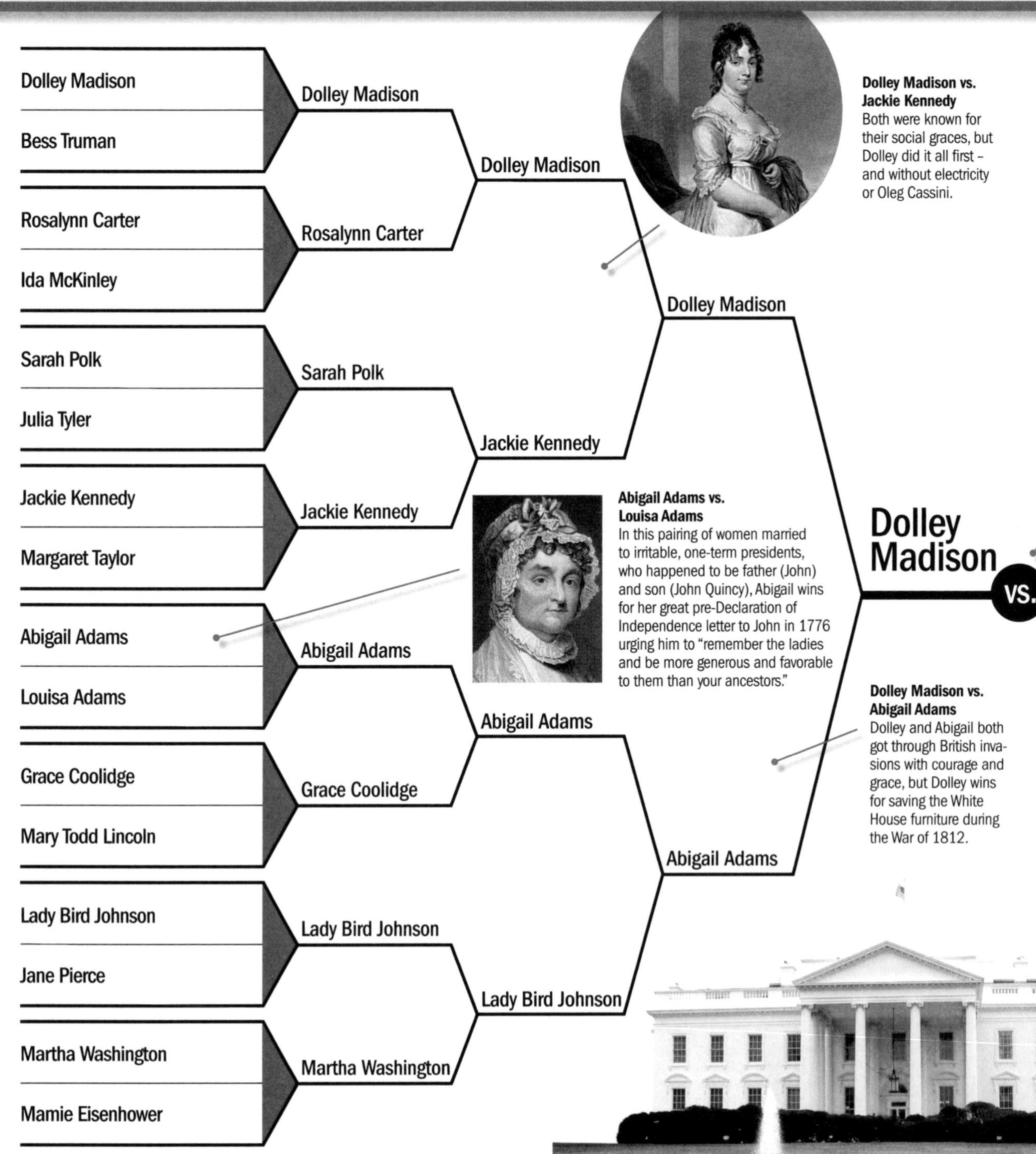
Dolley Madison
Bess Truman
Rosalynn Carter
Ida McKinley
Sarah Polk
Julia Tyler
Jackie Kennedy
Margaret Taylor
Abigail Adams
Louisa Adams
Grace Coolidge
Mary Todd Lincoln
Lady Bird Johnson
Jane Pierce
Martha Washington
Mamie Eisenhower
Dolley Madison
Rosalynn Carter
Sarah Polk
Jackie Kennedy
Abigail Adams
Grace Coolidge
Lady Bird Johnson
Martha Washington
Dolley Madison
Jackie Kennedy
Abigail Adams
Lady Bird Johnson
Dolley Madison
Abigail Adams
Dolley Madison
VS.

Dolley Madison vs. Jackie Kennedy
Both were known for their social graces, but Dolley did it all first – and without electricity or Oleg Cassini.

Abigail Adams vs. Louisa Adams
In this pairing of women married to irritable, one-term presidents, who happened to be father (John) and son (John Quincy), Abigail wins for her great pre-Declaration of Independence letter to John in 1776 urging him to "remember the ladies and be more generous and favorable to them than your ancestors."

Dolley Madison vs. Abigail Adams
Dolley and Abigail both got through British invasions with courage and grace, but Dolley wins for saving the White House furniture during the War of 1812.

THIS COMPETITION IS BIG ENOUGH to include virtually every First Lady who survived her White House tenure, from Martha Washington to Laura Bush. Preference goes to actually using the position to do something useful for the country – like Lady Bird Johnson's beautification campaign – and to setting a good example, enduring hardship, engaging the interest of the public in a positive way, and putting up with difficult, even philandering men. We'll give Michelle Obama a little more time before we push her into the playoffs.

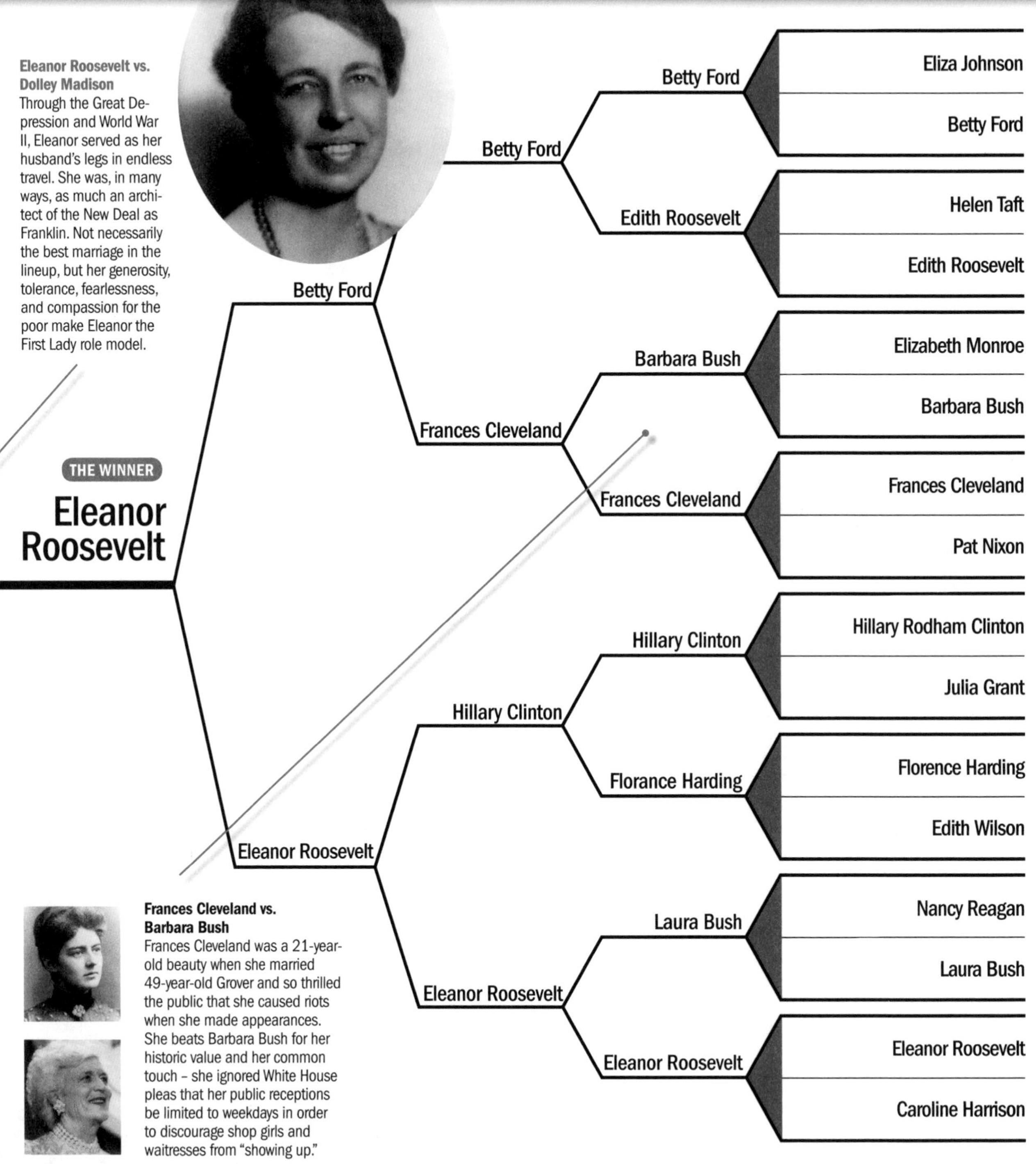

THE WINNER
Eleanor Roosevelt
Betty Ford
Eleanor Roosevelt
Betty Ford
Frances Cleveland
Hillary Clinton
Eleanor Roosevelt
Betty Ford
Edith Roosevelt
Barbara Bush
Frances Cleveland
Hillary Clinton
Florance Harding
Laura Bush
Eleanor Roosevelt
Eliza Johnson
Betty Ford
Helen Taft
Edith Roosevelt
Elizabeth Monroe
Barbara Bush
Frances Cleveland
Pat Nixon
Hillary Rodham Clinton
Julia Grant
Florence Harding
Edith Wilson
Nancy Reagan
Laura Bush
Eleanor Roosevelt
Caroline Harrison

Eleanor Roosevelt vs. Dolley Madison
Through the Great Depression and World War II, Eleanor served as her husband's legs in endless travel. She was, in many ways, as much an architect of the New Deal as Franklin. Not necessarily the best marriage in the lineup, but her generosity, tolerance, fearlessness, and compassion for the poor make Eleanor the First Lady role model.

Frances Cleveland vs. Barbara Bush
Frances Cleveland was a 21-year-old beauty when she married 49-year-old Grover and so thrilled the public that she caused riots when she made appearances. She beats Barbara Bush for her historic value and her common touch – she ignored White House pleas that her public receptions be limited to weekdays in order to discourage shop girls and waitresses from "showing up."

Panic Attacks

By Jack Hitt

Jack Hitt is a contributing writer for the *New York Times Magazine* and *Harper's*.

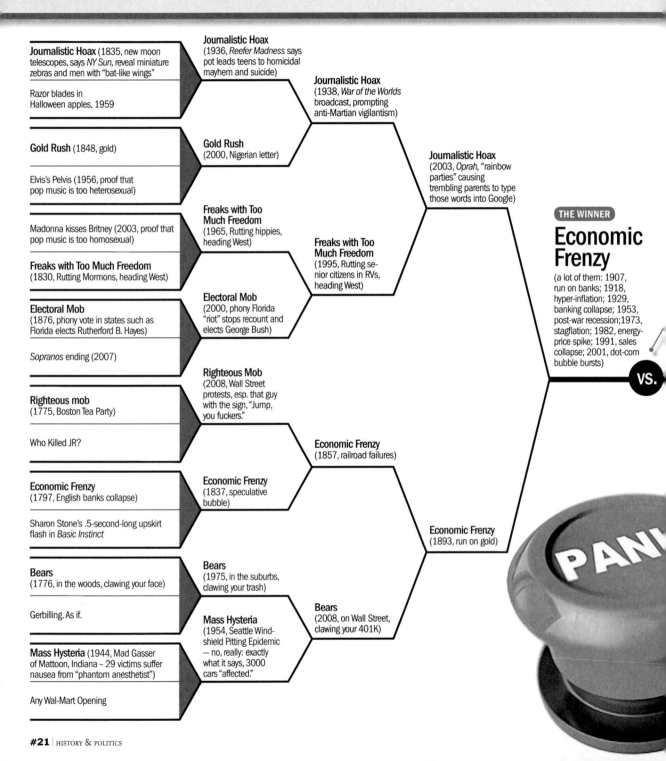

Journalistic Hoax (1835, new moon telescopes, says *NY Sun,* reveal miniature zebras and men with "bat-like wings")

Razor blades in Halloween apples, 1959

Gold Rush (1848, gold)

Elvis's Pelvis (1956, proof that pop music is too heterosexual)

Madonna kisses Britney (2003, proof that pop music is too homosexual)

Freaks with Too Much Freedom (1830, Rutting Mormons, heading West)

Electoral Mob (1876, phony vote in states such as Florida elects Rutherford B. Hayes)

Sopranos ending (2007)

Righteous mob (1775, Boston Tea Party)

Who Killed JR?

Economic Frenzy (1797, English banks collapse)

Sharon Stone's .5-second-long upskirt flash in *Basic Instinct*

Bears (1776, in the woods, clawing your face)

Gerbilling. As if.

Mass Hysteria (1944, Mad Gasser of Mattoon, Indiana – 29 victims suffer nausea from "phantom anesthetist")

Any Wal-Mart Opening

Journalistic Hoax (1936, *Reefer Madness* says pot leads teens to homicidal mayhem and suicide)

Gold Rush (2000, Nigerian letter)

Freaks with Too Much Freedom (1965, Rutting hippies, heading West)

Electoral Mob (2000, phony Florida "riot" stops recount and elects George Bush)

Righteous Mob (2008, Wall Street protests, esp. that guy with the sign, "Jump, you fuckers.")

Economic Frenzy (1837, speculative bubble)

Bears (1975, in the suburbs, clawing your trash)

Mass Hysteria (1954, Seattle Windshield Pitting Epidemic – no, really: exactly what it says, 3000 cars "affected.")

Journalistic Hoax (1938, *War of the Worlds* broadcast, prompting anti-Martian vigilantism)

Freaks with Too Much Freedom (1995, Rutting senior citizens in RVs, heading West)

Economic Frenzy (1857, railroad failures)

Bears (2008, on Wall Street, clawing your 401K)

Journalistic Hoax (2003, *Oprah,* "rainbow parties" causing trembling parents to type those words into Google)

Economic Frenzy (1893, run on gold)

THE WINNER

Economic Frenzy

(a lot of them: 1907, run on banks; 1918, hyper-inflation; 1929, banking collapse; 1953, post-war recession;1973, stagflation; 1982, energy-price spike; 1991, sales collapse; 2001, dot-com bubble bursts)

VS.

PAN

FROM THE VERY FOUNDING OF THE COUNTRY, when pioneers swore they saw vaporous demons cavorting in New World swamps, to last week's food scare, Americans love a good panic. We can freak out about anything – fingernail clippers at the airport, the latest fatigue syndrome, a Dixie Chicks song. If something barely real can't be found, we're preternaturally gifted at spotting a flying saucer or conjuring some Satanic ritual abuse to explain it.

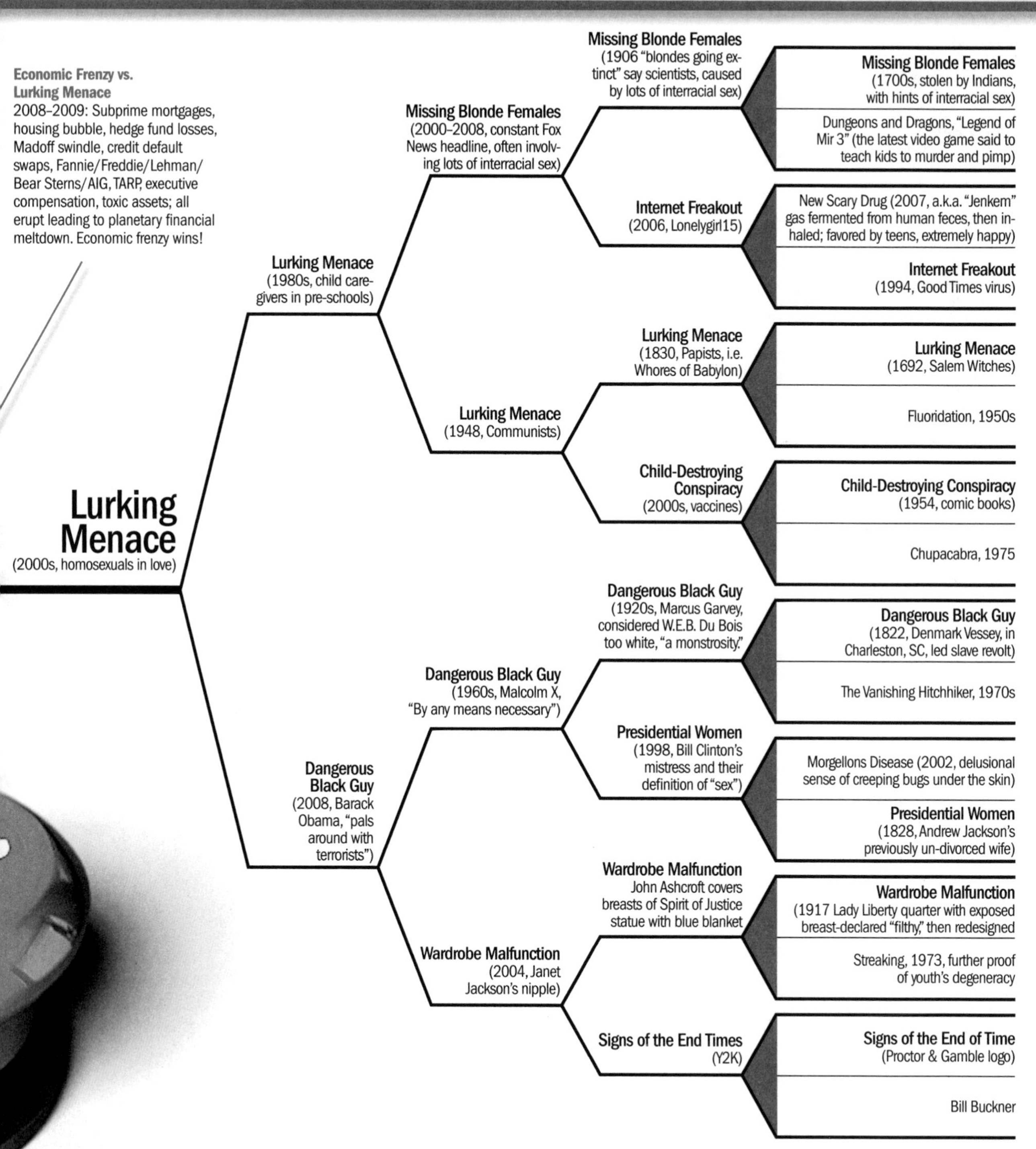

Economic Frenzy vs. Lurking Menace
2008–2009: Subprime mortgages, housing bubble, hedge fund losses, Madoff swindle, credit default swaps, Fannie/Freddie/Lehman/Bear Sterns/AIG, TARP, executive compensation, toxic assets; all erupt leading to planetary financial meltdown. Economic frenzy wins!
Lurking Menace
(2000s, homosexuals in love)
Lurking Menace
(1980s, child caregivers in pre-schools)
Dangerous Black Guy
(2008, Barack Obama, "pals around with terrorists")
Missing Blonde Females
(2000–2008, constant Fox News headline, often involving lots of interracial sex)
Lurking Menace
(1948, Communists)
Dangerous Black Guy
(1960s, Malcolm X, "By any means necessary")
Wardrobe Malfunction
(2004, Janet Jackson's nipple)
Missing Blonde Females
(1906 "blondes going extinct" say scientists, caused by lots of interracial sex)
Internet Freakout
(2006, Lonelygirl15)
Lurking Menace
(1830, Papists, i.e. Whores of Babylon)
Child-Destroying Conspiracy
(2000s, vaccines)
Dangerous Black Guy
(1920s, Marcus Garvey, considered W.E.B. Du Bois too white, "a monstrosity.")
Presidential Women
(1998, Bill Clinton's mistress and their definition of "sex")
Wardrobe Malfunction
John Ashcroft covers breasts of Spirit of Justice statue with blue blanket
Signs of the End Times
(Y2K)
Missing Blonde Females
(1700s, stolen by Indians, with hints of interracial sex)
Dungeons and Dragons, "Legend of Mir 3" (the latest video game said to teach kids to murder and pimp)
New Scary Drug (2007, a.k.a. "Jenkem" gas fermented from human feces, then inhaled; favored by teens, extremely happy)
Internet Freakout
(1994, Good Times virus)
Lurking Menace
(1692, Salem Witches)
Fluoridation, 1950s
Child-Destroying Conspiracy
(1954, comic books)
Chupacabra, 1975
Dangerous Black Guy
(1822, Denmark Vessey, in Charleston, SC, led slave revolt)
The Vanishing Hitchhiker, 1970s
Morgellons Disease (2002, delusional sense of creeping bugs under the skin)
Presidential Women
(1828, Andrew Jackson's previously un-divorced wife)
Wardrobe Malfunction
(1917 Lady Liberty quarter with exposed breast-declared "filthy," then redesigned
Streaking, 1973, further proof of youth's degeneracy
Signs of the End of Time
(Proctor & Gamble logo)
Bill Buckner

Memorable Speech Lines

By Jeff Shesol

Jeff Shesol, a former speechwriter for President Bill Clinton, is disappointed that none of his own best lines made the opening round. Shesol is the author of *Mutual Contempt: Lyndon Johnson, Robert Kennedy and the Feud That Defined a Decade.*

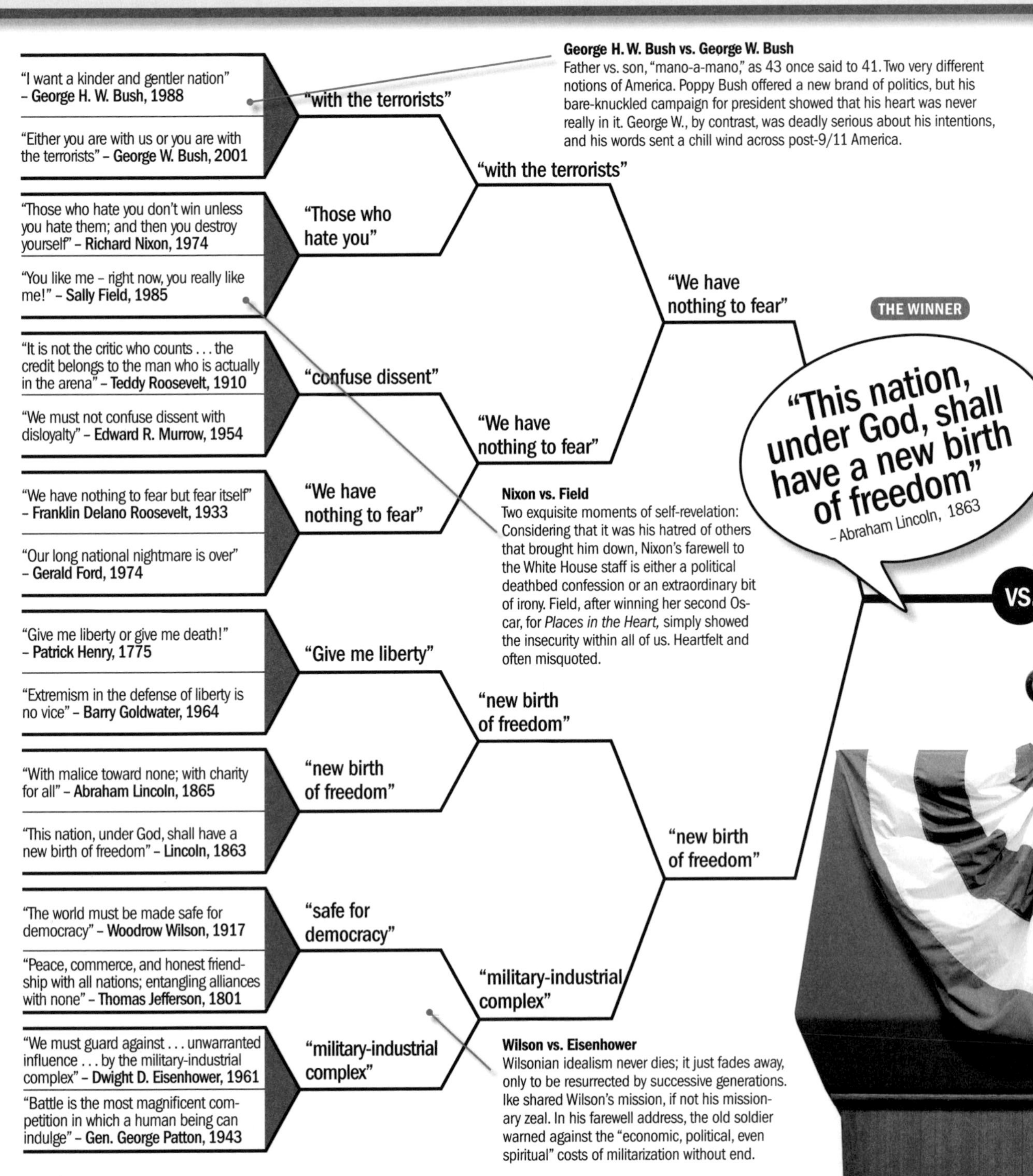

"I want a kinder and gentler nation" – George H. W. Bush, 1988
"Either you are with us or you are with the terrorists" – George W. Bush, 2001
"Those who hate you don't win unless you hate them; and then you destroy yourself" – Richard Nixon, 1974
"You like me – right now, you really like me!" – Sally Field, 1985
"It is not the critic who counts . . . the credit belongs to the man who is actually in the arena" – Teddy Roosevelt, 1910
"We must not confuse dissent with disloyalty" – Edward R. Murrow, 1954
"We have nothing to fear but fear itself" – Franklin Delano Roosevelt, 1933
"Our long national nightmare is over" – Gerald Ford, 1974
"Give me liberty or give me death!" – Patrick Henry, 1775
"Extremism in the defense of liberty is no vice" – Barry Goldwater, 1964
"With malice toward none; with charity for all" – Abraham Lincoln, 1865
"This nation, under God, shall have a new birth of freedom" – Lincoln, 1863
"The world must be made safe for democracy" – Woodrow Wilson, 1917
"Peace, commerce, and honest friendship with all nations; entangling alliances with none" – Thomas Jefferson, 1801
"We must guard against . . . unwarranted influence . . . by the military-industrial complex" – Dwight D. Eisenhower, 1961
"Battle is the most magnificent competition in which a human being can indulge" – Gen. George Patton, 1943
"with the terrorists"
"Those who hate you"
"confuse dissent"
"We have nothing to fear"
"Give me liberty"
"new birth of freedom"
"safe for democracy"
"military-industrial complex"
"with the terrorists"
"We have nothing to fear"
"new birth of freedom"
"military-industrial complex"
"We have nothing to fear"
"new birth of freedom"
THE WINNER
"This nation, under God, shall have a new birth of freedom"
– Abraham Lincoln, 1863
VS.

George H. W. Bush vs. George W. Bush
Father vs. son, "mano-a-mano," as 43 once said to 41. Two very different notions of America. Poppy Bush offered a new brand of politics, but his bare-knuckled campaign for president showed that his heart was never really in it. George W., by contrast, was deadly serious about his intentions, and his words sent a chill wind across post-9/11 America.

Nixon vs. Field
Two exquisite moments of self-revelation: Considering that it was his hatred of others that brought him down, Nixon's farewell to the White House staff is either a political deathbed confession or an extraordinary bit of irony. Field, after winning her second Oscar, for *Places in the Heart,* simply showed the insecurity within all of us. Heartfelt and often misquoted.

Wilson vs. Eisenhower
Wilsonian idealism never dies; it just fades away, only to be resurrected by successive generations. Ike shared Wilson's mission, if not his missionary zeal. In his farewell address, the old soldier warned against the "economic, political, even spiritual" costs of militarization without end.

A SOUND BITE IS LIKE A SMOKE RING – a neat trick, but gone in an instant. A truly great line transcends its time and place, and does more than simply endure. The very best lines change the way people think or act. Most of the first-round entries here are from political speeches, the majority from presidents (because they weigh in on vital issues and people pay close attention). But a few civilian speeches make the cut because they have the same effect: they redefine your reality, burrow into your brain, and get you talking.

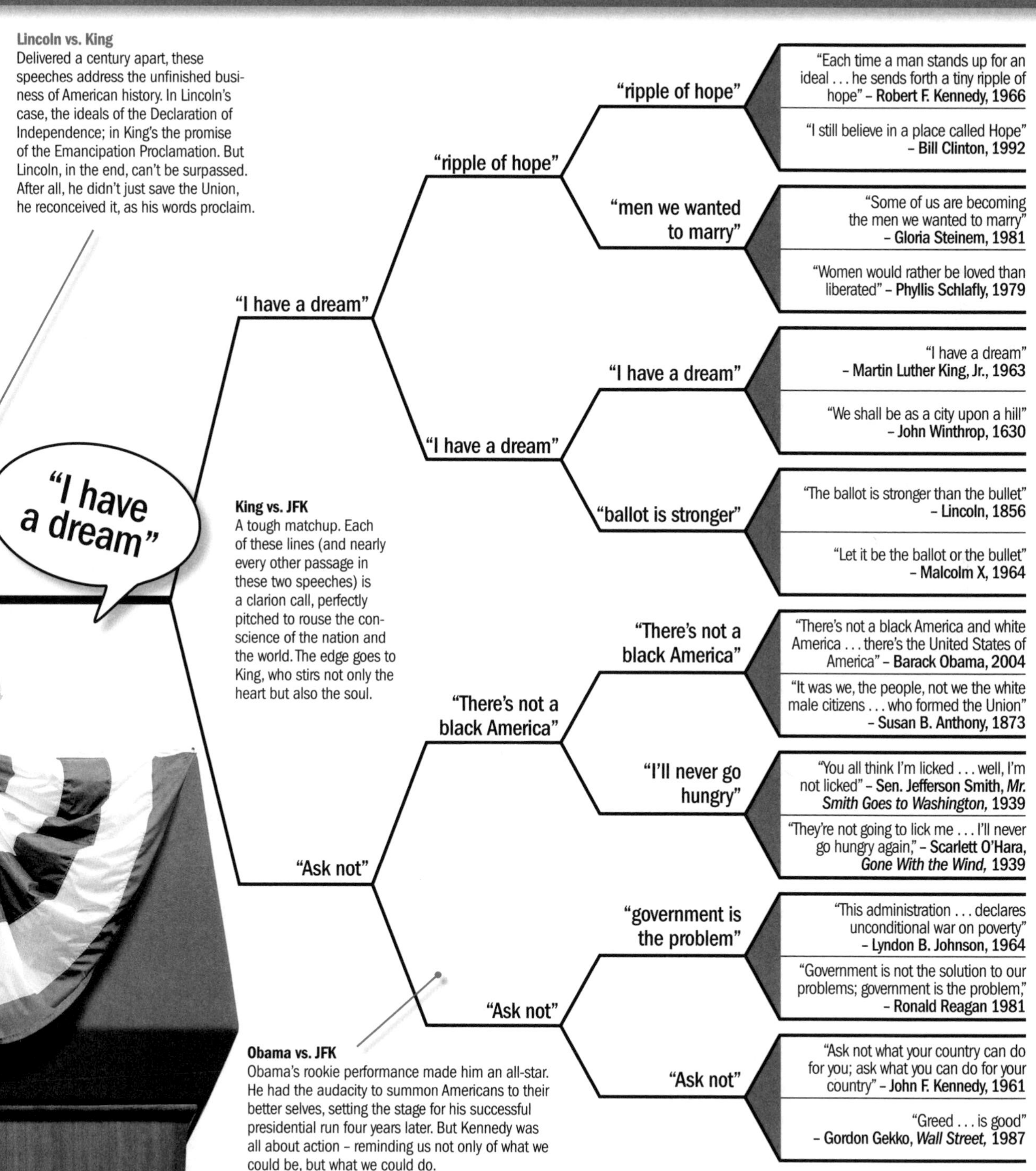

"I have a dream"
"I have a dream"
"ripple of hope"
"ripple of hope"
"Each time a man stands up for an ideal . . . he sends forth a tiny ripple of hope" – Robert F. Kennedy, 1966
"I still believe in a place called Hope" – Bill Clinton, 1992
"men we wanted to marry"
"Some of us are becoming the men we wanted to marry" – Gloria Steinem, 1981
"Women would rather be loved than liberated" – Phyllis Schlafly, 1979
"I have a dream"
"I have a dream"
"I have a dream" – Martin Luther King, Jr., 1963
"We shall be as a city upon a hill" – John Winthrop, 1630
"ballot is stronger"
"The ballot is stronger than the bullet" – Lincoln, 1856
"Let it be the ballot or the bullet" – Malcolm X, 1964
"Ask not"
"There's not a black America"
"There's not a black America"
"There's not a black America and white America . . . there's the United States of America" – Barack Obama, 2004
"It was we, the people, not we the white male citizens . . . who formed the Union" – Susan B. Anthony, 1873
"I'll never go hungry"
"You all think I'm licked . . . well, I'm not licked" – Sen. Jefferson Smith, *Mr. Smith Goes to Washington,* 1939
"They're not going to lick me . . . I'll never go hungry again," – Scarlett O'Hara, *Gone With the Wind,* 1939
"Ask not"
"government is the problem"
"This administration . . . declares unconditional war on poverty" – Lyndon B. Johnson, 1964
"Government is not the solution to our problems; government is the problem," – Ronald Reagan 1981
"Ask not"
"Ask not what your country can do for you; ask what you can do for your country" – John F. Kennedy, 1961
"Greed . . . is good" – Gordon Gekko, *Wall Street,* 1987

Lincoln vs. King
Delivered a century apart, these speeches address the unfinished business of American history. In Lincoln's case, the ideals of the Declaration of Independence; in King's the promise of the Emancipation Proclamation. But Lincoln, in the end, can't be surpassed. After all, he didn't just save the Union, he reconceived it, as his words proclaim.

King vs. JFK
A tough matchup. Each of these lines (and nearly every other passage in these two speeches) is a clarion call, perfectly pitched to rouse the conscience of the nation and the world. The edge goes to King, who stirs not only the heart but also the soul.

Obama vs. JFK
Obama's rookie performance made him an all-star. He had the audacity to summon Americans to their better selves, setting the stage for his successful presidential run four years later. But Kennedy was all about action – reminding us not only of what we could be, but what we could do.

Innovators

By Harold Evans

Harold Evans is author of *They Made America: From the Steam Engine to the Search Engine: Two Centuries of Innovators.* Now an American citizen, he was knighted for his services to journalism as editor of *The Sunday Times* and *Times of London.*

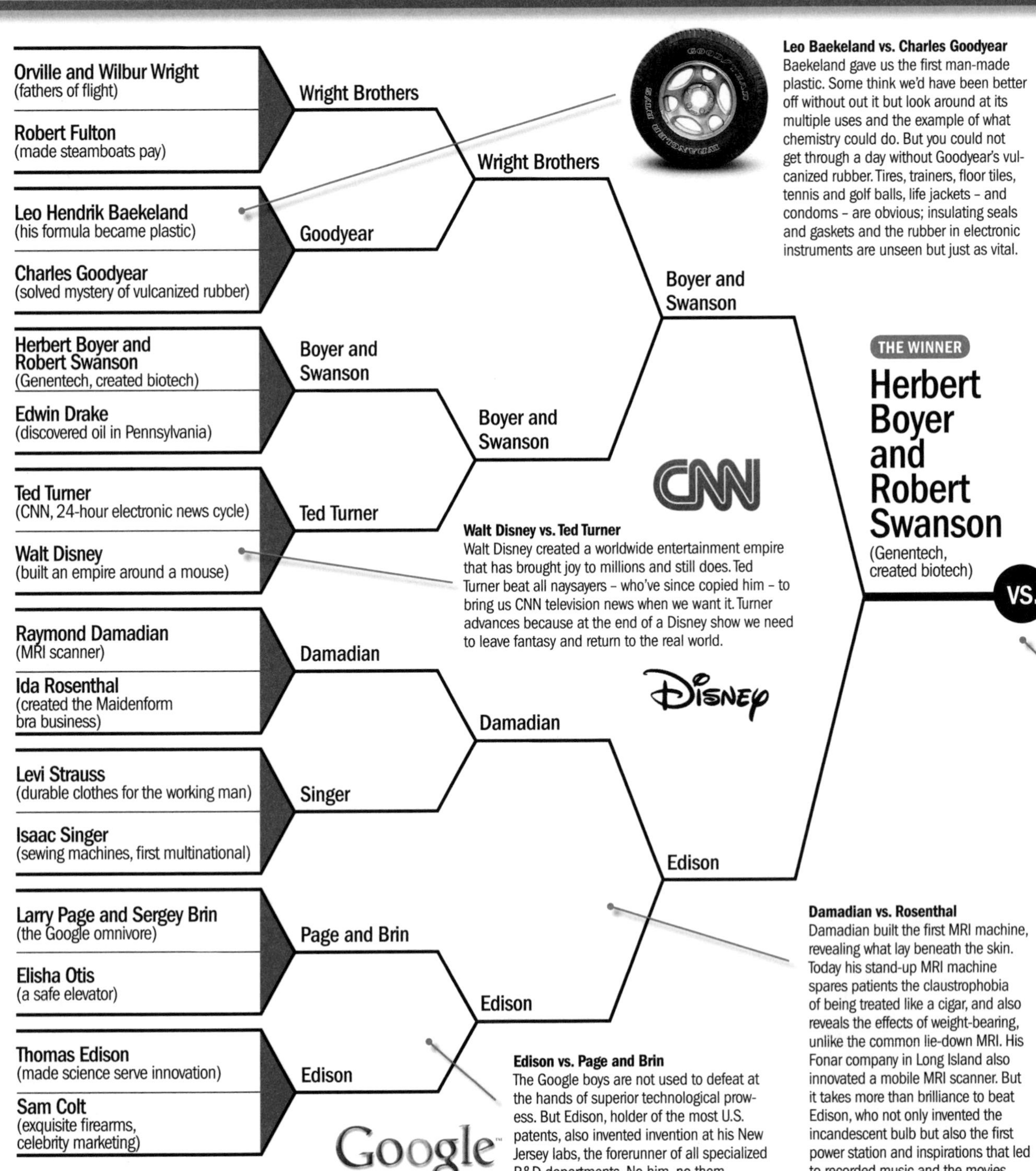

Orville and Wilbur Wright
(fathers of flight)
Robert Fulton
(made steamboats pay)
Leo Hendrik Baekeland
(his formula became plastic)
Charles Goodyear
(solved mystery of vulcanized rubber)
Herbert Boyer and Robert Swanson
(Genentech, created biotech)
Edwin Drake
(discovered oil in Pennsylvania)
Ted Turner
(CNN, 24-hour electronic news cycle)
Walt Disney
(built an empire around a mouse)
Raymond Damadian
(MRI scanner)
Ida Rosenthal
(created the Maidenform bra business)
Levi Strauss
(durable clothes for the working man)
Isaac Singer
(sewing machines, first multinational)
Larry Page and Sergey Brin
(the Google omnivore)
Elisha Otis
(a safe elevator)
Thomas Edison
(made science serve innovation)
Sam Colt
(exquisite firearms, celebrity marketing)
Wright Brothers
Goodyear
Boyer and Swanson
Ted Turner
Damadian
Singer
Page and Brin
Edison
Wright Brothers
Boyer and Swanson
Damadian
Edison
Boyer and Swanson
Edison
THE WINNER
Herbert Boyer and Robert Swanson
(Genentech, created biotech)
VS.
CNN
Disney
Google

Leo Baekeland vs. Charles Goodyear
Baekeland gave us the first man-made plastic. Some think we'd have been better off without out it but look around at its multiple uses and the example of what chemistry could do. But you could not get through a day without Goodyear's vulcanized rubber. Tires, trainers, floor tiles, tennis and golf balls, life jackets – and condoms – are obvious; insulating seals and gaskets and the rubber in electronic instruments are unseen but just as vital.

Walt Disney vs. Ted Turner
Walt Disney created a worldwide entertainment empire that has brought joy to millions and still does. Ted Turner beat all naysayers – who've since copied him – to bring us CNN television news when we want it. Turner advances because at the end of a Disney show we need to leave fantasy and return to the real world.

Damadian vs. Rosenthal
Damadian built the first MRI machine, revealing what lay beneath the skin. Today his stand-up MRI machine spares patients the claustrophobia of being treated like a cigar, and also reveals the effects of weight-bearing, unlike the common lie-down MRI. His Fonar company in Long Island also innovated a mobile MRI scanner. But it takes more than brilliance to beat Edison, who not only invented the incandescent bulb but also the first power station and inspirations that led to recorded music and the movies.

Edison vs. Page and Brin
The Google boys are not used to defeat at the hands of superior technological prowess. But Edison, holder of the most U.S. patents, also invented invention at his New Jersey labs, the forerunner of all specialized R&D departments. No him, no them.

WE LIVE IN A WORLD CREATED BY INNOVATORS. Invention and scientific discovery may be the start, but innovators do more. They take a brain wave and bring it to the bustle of the marketplace – the hard part, Thomas Edison said – so all may benefit. American innovators gave us the steamboat and air travel, personal computers and the uplift brassiere, MRI scanners and stereo FM, and container shipping, which initiated globalization. To win among these 32 great innovators of the last 200 years, your innovation must go on and on and on.

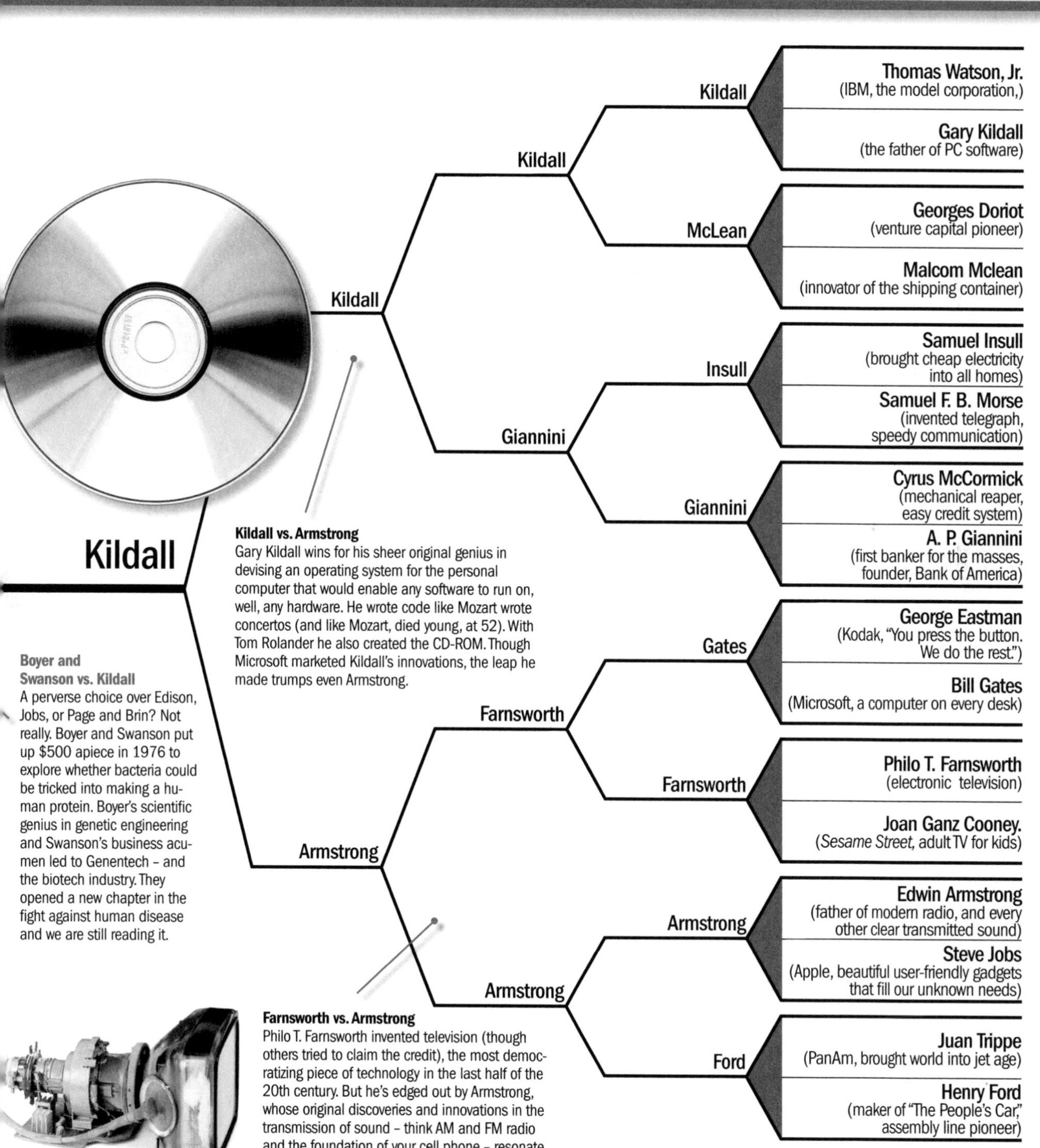

Thomas Watson, Jr.
(IBM, the model corporation,)
Gary Kildall
(the father of PC software)
Georges Doriot
(venture capital pioneer)
Malcom Mclean
(innovator of the shipping container)
Samuel Insull
(brought cheap electricity into all homes)
Samuel F. B. Morse
(invented telegraph, speedy communication)
Cyrus McCormick
(mechanical reaper, easy credit system)
A. P. Giannini
(first banker for the masses, founder, Bank of America)
George Eastman
(Kodak, "You press the button. We do the rest.")
Bill Gates
(Microsoft, a computer on every desk)
Philo T. Farnsworth
(electronic television)
Joan Ganz Cooney.
(Sesame Street, adult TV for kids)
Edwin Armstrong
(father of modern radio, and every other clear transmitted sound)
Steve Jobs
(Apple, beautiful user-friendly gadgets that fill our unknown needs)
Juan Trippe
(PanAm, brought world into jet age)
Henry Ford
(maker of "The People's Car," assembly line pioneer)
Kildall
McLean
Insull
Giannini
Gates
Farnsworth
Armstrong
Ford
Kildall
Giannini
Farnsworth
Armstrong
Kildall
Armstrong
Kildall

Kildall vs. Armstrong
Gary Kildall wins for his sheer original genius in devising an operating system for the personal computer that would enable any software to run on, well, any hardware. He wrote code like Mozart wrote concertos (and like Mozart, died young, at 52). With Tom Rolander he also created the CD-ROM. Though Microsoft marketed Kildall's innovations, the leap he made trumps even Armstrong.

Boyer and Swanson vs. Kildall
A perverse choice over Edison, Jobs, or Page and Brin? Not really. Boyer and Swanson put up $500 apiece in 1976 to explore whether bacteria could be tricked into making a human protein. Boyer's scientific genius in genetic engineering and Swanson's business acumen led to Genentech – and the biotech industry. They opened a new chapter in the fight against human disease and we are still reading it.

Farnsworth vs. Armstrong
Philo T. Farnsworth invented television (though others tried to claim the credit), the most democratizing piece of technology in the last half of the 20th century. But he's edged out by Armstrong, whose original discoveries and innovations in the transmission of sound – think AM and FM radio and the foundation of your cell phone – resonate every time we hear a clear sound over the air.

Supreme Court Decisions

By Adam Liptak
Adam Liptak covers the Supreme Court for the *New York Times.*

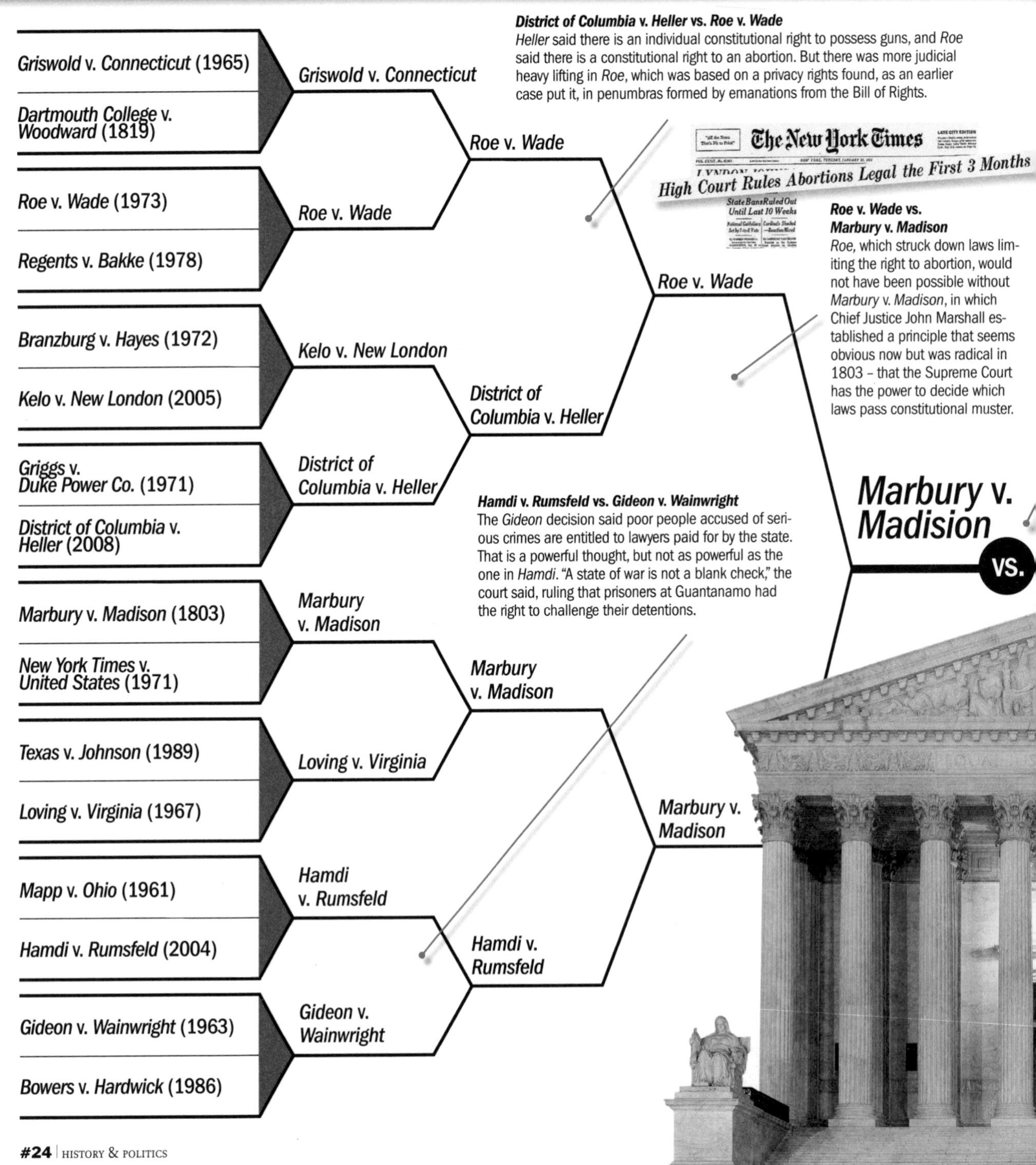
Griswold v. *Connecticut* (1965)
Dartmouth College v. *Woodward* (1819)
Roe v. *Wade* (1973)
Regents v. *Bakke* (1978)
Branzburg v. *Hayes* (1972)
Kelo v. *New London* (2005)
Griggs v. *Duke Power Co.* (1971)
District of Columbia v. *Heller* (2008)
Marbury v. *Madison* (1803)
New York Times v. *United States* (1971)
Texas v. *Johnson* (1989)
Loving v. *Virginia* (1967)
Mapp v. *Ohio* (1961)
Hamdi v. *Rumsfeld* (2004)
Gideon v. *Wainwright* (1963)
Bowers v. *Hardwick* (1986)
Griswold v. *Connecticut*
Roe v. *Wade*
Kelo v. *New London*
District of Columbia v. *Heller*
Marbury v. *Madison*
Loving v. *Virginia*
Hamdi v. *Rumsfeld*
Gideon v. *Wainwright*
Roe v. *Wade*
District of Columbia v. *Heller*
Marbury v. *Madison*
Hamdi v. *Rumsfeld*
Roe v. *Wade*
Marbury v. *Madison*
Marbury v. *Madision*
VS.
The New York Times
High Court Rules Abortions Legal the First 3 Months
State Bans Ruled Out Until Last 10 Weeks

District of Columbia* v. *Heller* vs. *Roe* v. *Wade
Heller said there is an individual constitutional right to possess guns, and *Roe* said there is a constitutional right to an abortion. But there was more judicial heavy lifting in *Roe*, which was based on a privacy rights found, as an earlier case put it, in penumbras formed by emanations from the Bill of Rights.

Roe* v. *Wade* vs. *Marbury* v. *Madison
Roe, which struck down laws limiting the right to abortion, would not have been possible without *Marbury* v. *Madison*, in which Chief Justice John Marshall established a principle that seems obvious now but was radical in 1803 – that the Supreme Court has the power to decide which laws pass constitutional muster.

Hamdi* v. *Rumsfeld* vs. *Gideon* v. *Wainwright
The *Gideon* decision said poor people accused of serious crimes are entitled to lawyers paid for by the state. That is a powerful thought, but not as powerful as the one in *Hamdi*. "A state of war is not a blank check," the court said, ruling that prisoners at Guantanamo had the right to challenge their detentions.

SOME OF THE MOST FAMOUS Supreme Court cases are ones in which the Court got it preposterously wrong, like *Dred Scott*, which said black people could be property but not citizens, or *Korematsu*, which upheld the internment of 120,000 Americans of Japanese descent in detention camps during World War II. Those cases don't get into this bracket. But unpopularity does not disqualify cases if their reasoning has lasting force or if the rulings themselves altered the social structure. It's all about impact.

Brown* v. *Board* vs. *Marbury* v. *Madison

The Supreme Court's unanimous decision in *Brown*, which said that segregating students by race in public schools was constitutionally intolerable, remains the Court's undisputed triumph. Some quarrel with its reasoning and with the studies on which it relied. No one doubts its moral power.

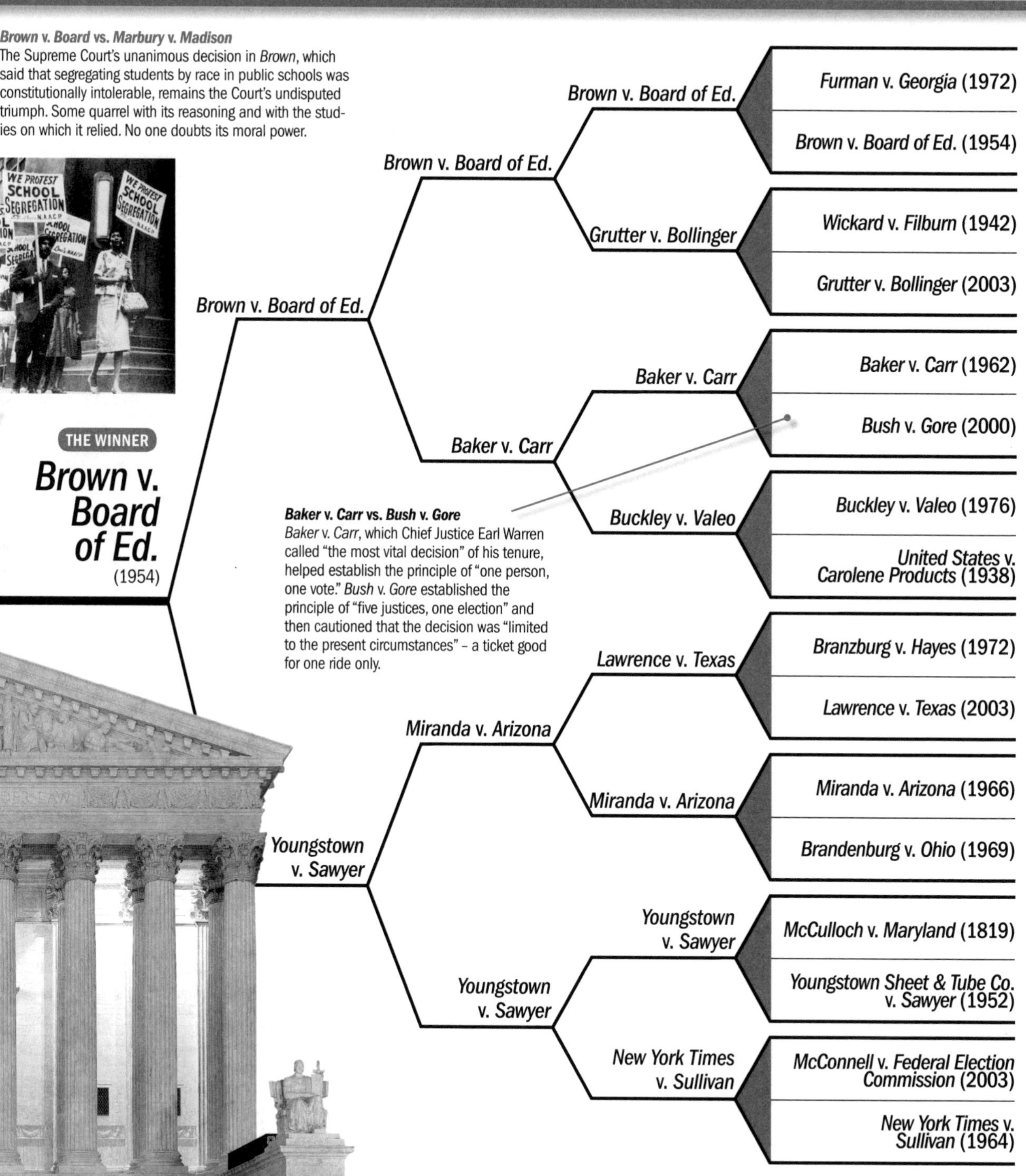

WE PROTEST SCHOOL SEGREGATION
WE PROTEST SCHOOL SEGREGATION
THE WINNER
Brown v. Board of Ed. (1954)
Furman v. Georgia (1972)
Brown v. Board of Ed. (1954)
Wickard v. Filburn (1942)
Grutter v. Bollinger (2003)
Baker v. Carr (1962)
Bush v. Gore (2000)
Buckley v. Valeo (1976)
United States v. Carolene Products (1938)
Branzburg v. Hayes (1972)
Lawrence v. Texas (2003)
Miranda v. Arizona (1966)
Brandenburg v. Ohio (1969)
McCulloch v. Maryland (1819)
Youngstown Sheet & Tube Co. v. Sawyer (1952)
McConnell v. Federal Election Commission (2003)
New York Times v. Sullivan (1964)
Brown v. Board of Ed.
Grutter v. Bollinger
Baker v. Carr
Buckley v. Valeo
Lawrence v. Texas
Miranda v. Arizona
Youngstown v. Sawyer
New York Times v. Sullivan
Brown v. Board of Ed.
Baker v. Carr
Miranda v. Arizona
Youngstown v. Sawyer
Brown v. Board of Ed.
Youngstown v. Sawyer

Baker* v. *Carr* vs. *Bush* v. *Gore

Baker v. *Carr*, which Chief Justice Earl Warren called "the most vital decision" of his tenure, helped establish the principle of "one person, one vote." *Bush* v. *Gore* established the principle of "five justices, one election" and then cautioned that the decision was "limited to the present circumstances" – a ticket good for one ride only.

Presidential Pardons

By P.S. Ruckman, Jr.

P.S. Ruckman, Jr. is the editor of the Pardon Power blog. His research on pardons appears in several social science journals and he is the author of the forthcoming book *Pardon Me, Mr. President: Adventures in Crime, Politics and Mercy.*

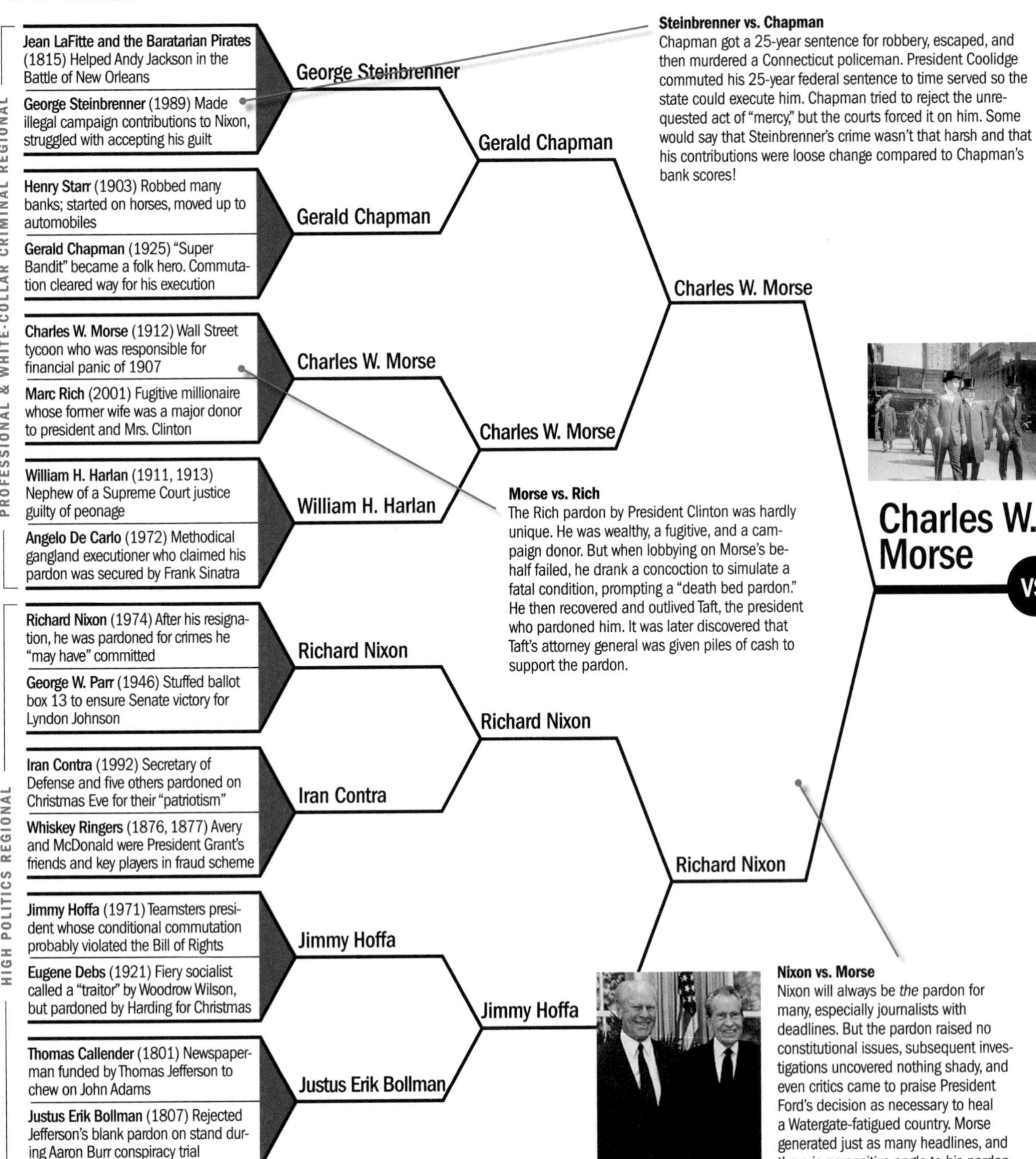
PROFESSIONAL & WHITE-COLLAR CRIMINAL REGIONAL
Jean LaFitte and the Baratarian Pirates (1815) Helped Andy Jackson in the Battle of New Orleans
George Steinbrenner (1989) Made illegal campaign contributions to Nixon, struggled with accepting his guilt
George Steinbrenner
Henry Starr (1903) Robbed many banks; started on horses, moved up to automobiles
Gerald Chapman (1925) "Super Bandit" became a folk hero. Commutation cleared way for his execution
Gerald Chapman
Gerald Chapman
Charles W. Morse (1912) Wall Street tycoon who was responsible for financial panic of 1907
Marc Rich (2001) Fugitive millionaire whose former wife was a major donor to president and Mrs. Clinton
Charles W. Morse
William H. Harlan (1911, 1913) Nephew of a Supreme Court justice guilty of peonage
Angelo De Carlo (1972) Methodical gangland executioner who claimed his pardon was secured by Frank Sinatra
William H. Harlan
Charles W. Morse
Charles W. Morse
Steinbrenner vs. Chapman
Chapman got a 25-year sentence for robbery, escaped, and then murdered a Connecticut policeman. President Coolidge commuted his 25-year federal sentence to time served so the state could execute him. Chapman tried to reject the unrequested act of "mercy," but the courts forced it on him. Some would say that Steinbrenner's crime wasn't that harsh and that his contributions were loose change compared to Chapman's bank scores!
Morse vs. Rich
The Rich pardon by President Clinton was hardly unique. He was wealthy, a fugitive, and a campaign donor. But when lobbying on Morse's behalf failed, he drank a concoction to simulate a fatal condition, prompting a "death bed pardon." He then recovered and outlived Taft, the president who pardoned him. It was later discovered that Taft's attorney general was given piles of cash to support the pardon.
Charles W. Morse
VS.
HIGH POLITICS REGIONAL
Richard Nixon (1974) After his resignation, he was pardoned for crimes he "may have" committed
George W. Parr (1946) Stuffed ballot box 13 to ensure Senate victory for Lyndon Johnson
Richard Nixon
Iran Contra (1992) Secretary of Defense and five others pardoned on Christmas Eve for their "patriotism"
Whiskey Ringers (1876, 1877) Avery and McDonald were President Grant's friends and key players in fraud scheme
Iran Contra
Richard Nixon
Jimmy Hoffa (1971) Teamsters president whose conditional commutation probably violated the Bill of Rights
Eugene Debs (1921) Fiery socialist called a "traitor" by Woodrow Wilson, but pardoned by Harding for Christmas
Jimmy Hoffa
Thomas Callender (1801) Newspaperman funded by Thomas Jefferson to chew on John Adams
Justus Erik Bollman (1807) Rejected Jefferson's blank pardon on stand during Aaron Burr conspiracy trial
Justus Erik Bollman
Jimmy Hoffa
Richard Nixon
Nixon vs. Morse
Nixon will always be *the* pardon for many, especially journalists with deadlines. But the pardon raised no constitutional issues, subsequent investigations uncovered nothing shady, and even critics came to praise President Ford's decision as necessary to heal a Watergate-fatigued country. Morse generated just as many headlines, and there is no positive angle to his pardon.

THE POWER TO GRANT PARDONS is probably the most imperial power that a president wields. It is shrouded in secrecy, virtually without limit, and suspiciously arbitrary in an age when so much of the justice system is meticulously regulated by statutes and the requirements of the due process clause. Every generation of Americans has experienced its seemingly "unforgettable" pardon(s), but the most notable have involved notorious crimes and criminals., celebrities, constitutional questions, and political hijinks.

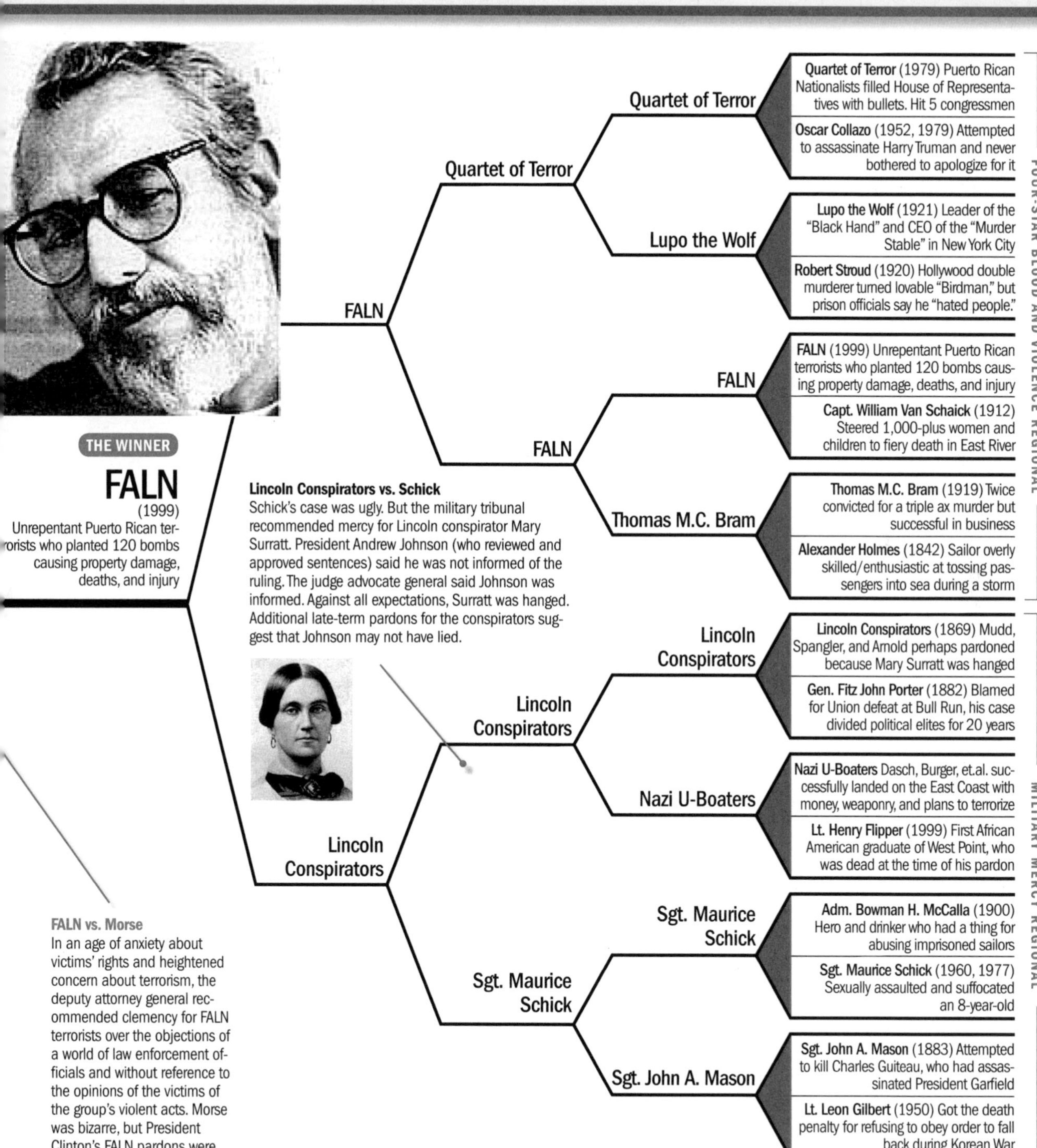

FOUR-STAR BLOOD AND VIOLENCE REGIONAL
Quartet of Terror (1979) Puerto Rican Nationalists filled House of Representatives with bullets. Hit 5 congressmen
Oscar Collazo (1952, 1979) Attempted to assassinate Harry Truman and never bothered to apologize for it
Lupo the Wolf (1921) Leader of the "Black Hand" and CEO of the "Murder Stable" in New York City
Robert Stroud (1920) Hollywood double murderer turned lovable "Birdman," but prison officials say he "hated people."
FALN (1999) Unrepentant Puerto Rican terrorists who planted 120 bombs causing property damage, deaths, and injury
Capt. William Van Schaick (1912) Steered 1,000-plus women and children to fiery death in East River
Thomas M.C. Bram (1919) Twice convicted for a triple ax murder but successful in business
Alexander Holmes (1842) Sailor overly skilled/enthusiastic at tossing passengers into sea during a storm
Quartet of Terror
Lupo the Wolf
FALN
Thomas M.C. Bram
Quartet of Terror
FALN
FALN
MILITARY MERCY REGIONAL
Lincoln Conspirators (1869) Mudd, Spangler, and Arnold perhaps pardoned because Mary Surratt was hanged
Gen. Fitz John Porter (1882) Blamed for Union defeat at Bull Run, his case divided political elites for 20 years
Nazi U-Boaters Dasch, Burger, et.al. successfully landed on the East Coast with money, weaponry, and plans to terrorize
Lt. Henry Flipper (1999) First African American graduate of West Point, who was dead at the time of his pardon
Adm. Bowman H. McCalla (1900) Hero and drinker who had a thing for abusing imprisoned sailors
Sgt. Maurice Schick (1960, 1977) Sexually assaulted and suffocated an 8-year-old
Sgt. John A. Mason (1883) Attempted to kill Charles Guiteau, who had assassinated President Garfield
Lt. Leon Gilbert (1950) Got the death penalty for refusing to obey order to fall back during Korean War
Lincoln Conspirators
Nazi U-Boaters
Sgt. Maurice Schick
Sgt. John A. Mason
Lincoln Conspirators
Sgt. Maurice Schick
Lincoln Conspirators
THE WINNER

FALN
(1999)
Unrepentant Puerto Rican terrorists who planted 120 bombs causing property damage, deaths, and injury

Lincoln Conspirators vs. Schick
Schick's case was ugly. But the military tribunal recommended mercy for Lincoln conspirator Mary Surratt. President Andrew Johnson (who reviewed and approved sentences) said he was not informed of the ruling. The judge advocate general said Johnson was informed. Against all expectations, Surratt was hanged. Additional late-term pardons for the conspirators suggest that Johnson may not have lied.

FALN vs. Morse
In an age of anxiety about victims' rights and heightened concern about terrorism, the deputy attorney general recommended clemency for FALN terrorists over the objections of a world of law enforcement officials and without reference to the opinions of the victims of the group's violent acts. Morse was bizarre, but President Clinton's FALN pardons were flabbergasting.

Military Heroes

By Richard Goldstein

Richard Goldstein is the author of *America at D-Day* and *Desperate Hours: The Epic Rescue of the Andrea Doria.*

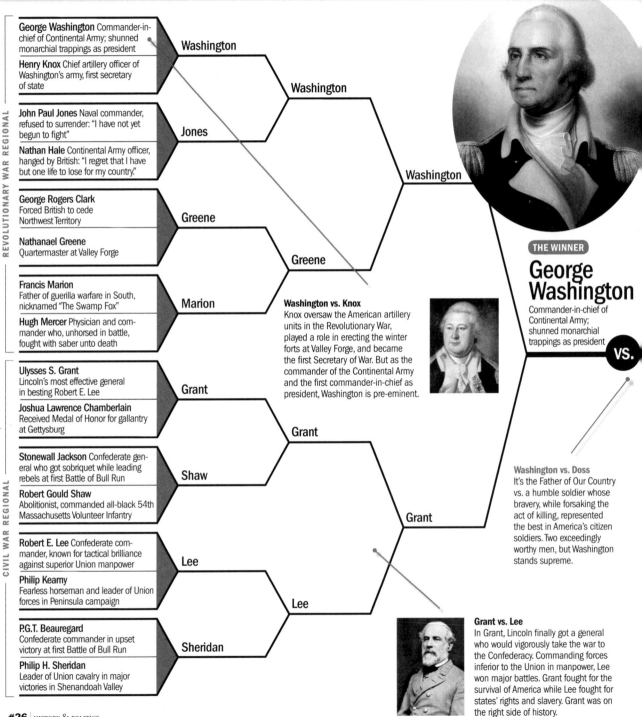

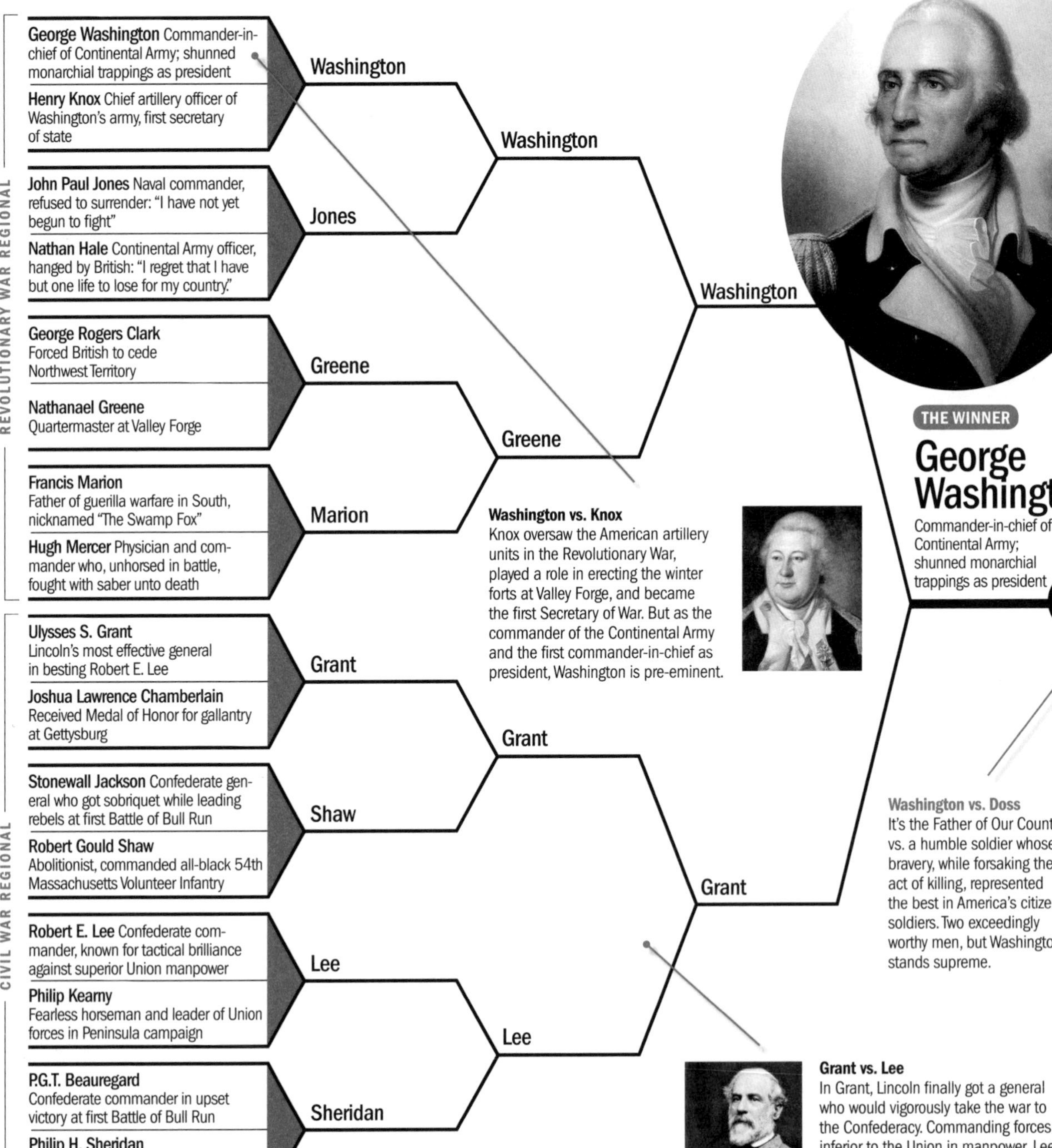
REVOLUTIONARY WAR REGIONAL
George Washington Commander-in-chief of Continental Army; shunned monarchial trappings as president
Henry Knox Chief artillery officer of Washington's army, first secretary of state
John Paul Jones Naval commander, refused to surrender: "I have not yet begun to fight"
Nathan Hale Continental Army officer, hanged by British: "I regret that I have but one life to lose for my country."
George Rogers Clark Forced British to cede Northwest Territory
Nathanael Greene Quartermaster at Valley Forge
Francis Marion Father of guerilla warfare in South, nicknamed "The Swamp Fox"
Hugh Mercer Physician and commander who, unhorsed in battle, fought with saber unto death
CIVIL WAR REGIONAL
Ulysses S. Grant Lincoln's most effective general in besting Robert E. Lee
Joshua Lawrence Chamberlain Received Medal of Honor for gallantry at Gettysburg
Stonewall Jackson Confederate general who got sobriquet while leading rebels at first Battle of Bull Run
Robert Gould Shaw Abolitionist, commanded all-black 54th Massachusetts Volunteer Infantry
Robert E. Lee Confederate commander, known for tactical brilliance against superior Union manpower
Philip Kearny Fearless horseman and leader of Union forces in Peninsula campaign
P.G.T. Beauregard Confederate commander in upset victory at first Battle of Bull Run
Philip H. Sheridan Leader of Union cavalry in major victories in Shenandoah Valley
Washington
Jones
Greene
Marion
Grant
Shaw
Lee
Sheridan
Washington
Greene
Grant
Lee
Washington
Grant
VS.

Washington vs. Knox
Knox oversaw the American artillery units in the Revolutionary War, played a role in erecting the winter forts at Valley Forge, and became the first Secretary of War. But as the commander of the Continental Army and the first commander-in-chief as president, Washington is pre-eminent.

THE WINNER

George Washington

Commander-in-chief of Continental Army; shunned monarchial trappings as president

Washington vs. Doss
It's the Father of Our Country vs. a humble soldier whose bravery, while forsaking the act of killing, represented the best in America's citizen soldiers. Two exceedingly worthy men, but Washington stands supreme.

Grant vs. Lee
In Grant, Lincoln finally got a general who would vigorously take the war to the Confederacy. Commanding forces inferior to the Union in manpower, Lee won major battles. Grant fought for the survival of America while Lee fought for states' rights and slavery. Grant was on the right side of history.

MEDAL OF HONOR RECIPIENTS invariably reject the tag of "heroes," saying that the real American heroes never come home from the wars they fought. Still, battlefield heroes acted "above and beyond the call of duty," giving their lives without regard to their own safety to protect their comrades. Men who refuted the common wisdom that they would not fight because of their race or forefathers are also heroes. So are those who have led in battle but never forgot the welfare of their soldiers and sailors.

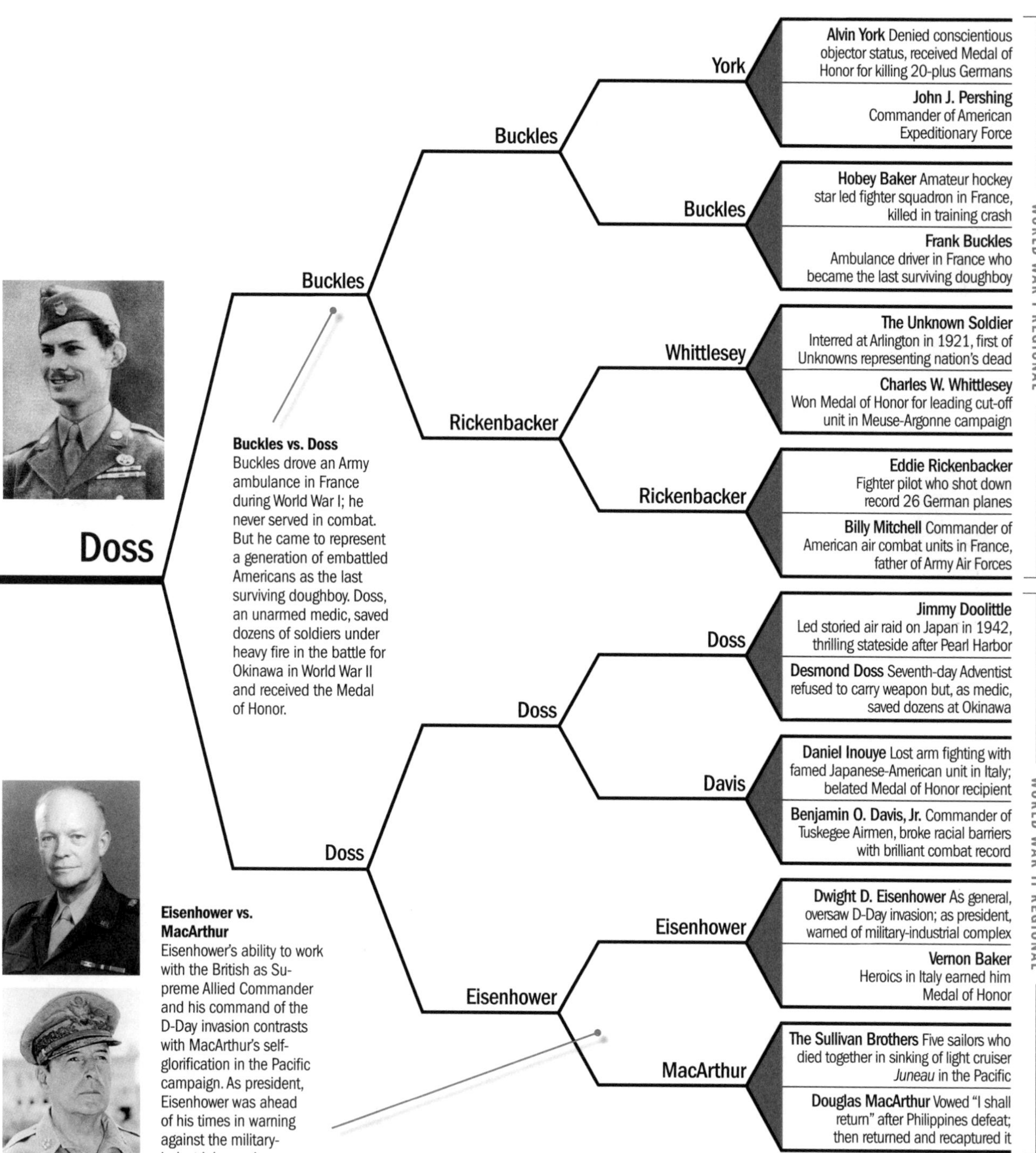

Alvin York Denied conscientious objector status, received Medal of Honor for killing 20-plus Germans
John J. Pershing Commander of American Expeditionary Force
Hobey Baker Amateur hockey star led fighter squadron in France, killed in training crash
Frank Buckles Ambulance driver in France who became the last surviving doughboy
The Unknown Soldier Interred at Arlington in 1921, first of Unknowns representing nation's dead
Charles W. Whittlesey Won Medal of Honor for leading cut-off unit in Meuse-Argonne campaign
Eddie Rickenbacker Fighter pilot who shot down record 26 German planes
Billy Mitchell Commander of American air combat units in France, father of Army Air Forces
Jimmy Doolittle Led storied air raid on Japan in 1942, thrilling stateside after Pearl Harbor
Desmond Doss Seventh-day Adventist refused to carry weapon but, as medic, saved dozens at Okinawa
Daniel Inouye Lost arm fighting with famed Japanese-American unit in Italy; belated Medal of Honor recipient
Benjamin O. Davis, Jr. Commander of Tuskegee Airmen, broke racial barriers with brilliant combat record
Dwight D. Eisenhower As general, oversaw D-Day invasion; as president, warned of military-industrial complex
Vernon Baker Heroics in Italy earned him Medal of Honor
The Sullivan Brothers Five sailors who died together in sinking of light cruiser *Juneau* in the Pacific
Douglas MacArthur Vowed "I shall return" after Philippines defeat; then returned and recaptured it
WORLD WAR I REGIONAL
WORLD WAR II REGIONAL
York
Buckles
Whittlesey
Rickenbacker
Doss
Davis
Eisenhower
MacArthur
Buckles
Rickenbacker
Doss
Eisenhower
Buckles
Doss
Doss

Buckles vs. Doss
Buckles drove an Army ambulance in France during World War I; he never served in combat. But he came to represent a generation of embattled Americans as the last surviving doughboy. Doss, an unarmed medic, saved dozens of soldiers under heavy fire in the battle for Okinawa in World War II and received the Medal of Honor.

Eisenhower vs. MacArthur
Eisenhower's ability to work with the British as Supreme Allied Commander and his command of the D-Day invasion contrasts with MacArthur's self-glorification in the Pacific campaign. As president, Eisenhower was ahead of his times in warning against the military-industrial complex. Ike gets the nod.

Enduring One-Liners

By Jan Van Meter

Jan Van Meter has had many jobs, four careers, but only one retirement, which gave him the time to research and write *Tippecanoe and Tyler Too: Famous Slogans and Catchphrases in American History.*

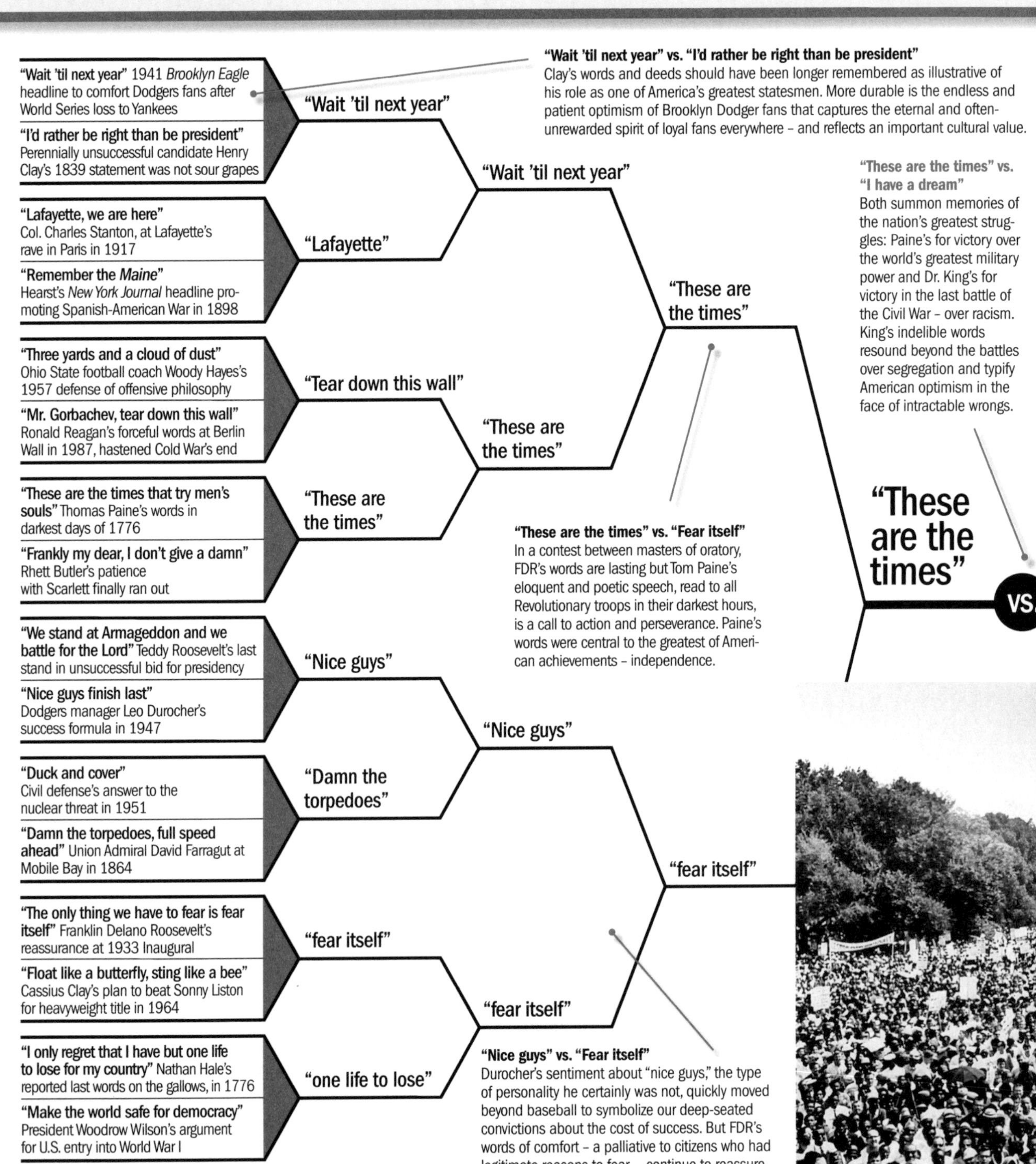

"Wait 'til next year" 1941 *Brooklyn Eagle* headline to comfort Dodgers fans after World Series loss to Yankees
"I'd rather be right than be president" Perennially unsuccessful candidate Henry Clay's 1839 statement was not sour grapes
"Lafayette, we are here" Col. Charles Stanton, at Lafayette's rave in Paris in 1917
"Remember the *Maine*" Hearst's *New York Journal* headline promoting Spanish-American War in 1898
"Three yards and a cloud of dust" Ohio State football coach Woody Hayes's 1957 defense of offensive philosophy
"Mr. Gorbachev, tear down this wall" Ronald Reagan's forceful words at Berlin Wall in 1987, hastened Cold War's end
"These are the times that try men's souls" Thomas Paine's words in darkest days of 1776
"Frankly my dear, I don't give a damn" Rhett Butler's patience with Scarlett finally ran out
"We stand at Armageddon and we battle for the Lord" Teddy Roosevelt's last stand in unsuccessful bid for presidency
"Nice guys finish last" Dodgers manager Leo Durocher's success formula in 1947
"Duck and cover" Civil defense's answer to the nuclear threat in 1951
"Damn the torpedoes, full speed ahead" Union Admiral David Farragut at Mobile Bay in 1864
"The only thing we have to fear is fear itself" Franklin Delano Roosevelt's reassurance at 1933 Inaugural
"Float like a butterfly, sting like a bee" Cassius Clay's plan to beat Sonny Liston for heavyweight title in 1964
"I only regret that I have but one life to lose for my country" Nathan Hale's reported last words on the gallows, in 1776
"Make the world safe for democracy" President Woodrow Wilson's argument for U.S. entry into World War I
"Wait 'til next year"
"Lafayette"
"Tear down this wall"
"These are the times"
"Nice guys"
"Damn the torpedoes"
"fear itself"
"one life to lose"
"Wait 'til next year"
"These are the times"
"Nice guys"
"fear itself"
"These are the times"
"fear itself"
"These are the times"
VS.
"Wait 'til next year" vs. "I'd rather be right than be president"
Clay's words and deeds should have been longer remembered as illustrative of his role as one of America's greatest statesmen. More durable is the endless and patient optimism of Brooklyn Dodger fans that captures the eternal and often-unrewarded spirit of loyal fans everywhere – and reflects an important cultural value.
"These are the times" vs. "I have a dream"
Both summon memories of the nation's greatest struggles: Paine's for victory over the world's greatest military power and Dr. King's for victory in the last battle of the Civil War – over racism. King's indelible words resound beyond the battles over segregation and typify American optimism in the face of intractable wrongs.
"These are the times" vs. "Fear itself"
In a contest between masters of oratory, FDR's words are lasting but Tom Paine's eloquent and poetic speech, read to all Revolutionary troops in their darkest hours, is a call to action and perseverance. Paine's words were central to the greatest of American achievements – independence.
"Nice guys" vs. "Fear itself"
Durocher's sentiment about "nice guys," the type of personality he certainly was not, quickly moved beyond baseball to symbolize our deep-seated convictions about the cost of success. But FDR's words of comfort – a palliative to citizens who had legitimate reasons to fear -- continue to reassure us as the country faces yet another crisis.

THAT SLOGANS AND CATCHPHRASES are part of the American character was recognized nearly a century ago, long after they had begun to accumulate. Whether they have sprung to life in battles, speeches, boxing rings, campaigns, or films, they capture historical moments, national ideals, and pervasive attitudes. Still others endure for trivial reasons. But the best survive because what they were meant to convey continues to be important to the nation.

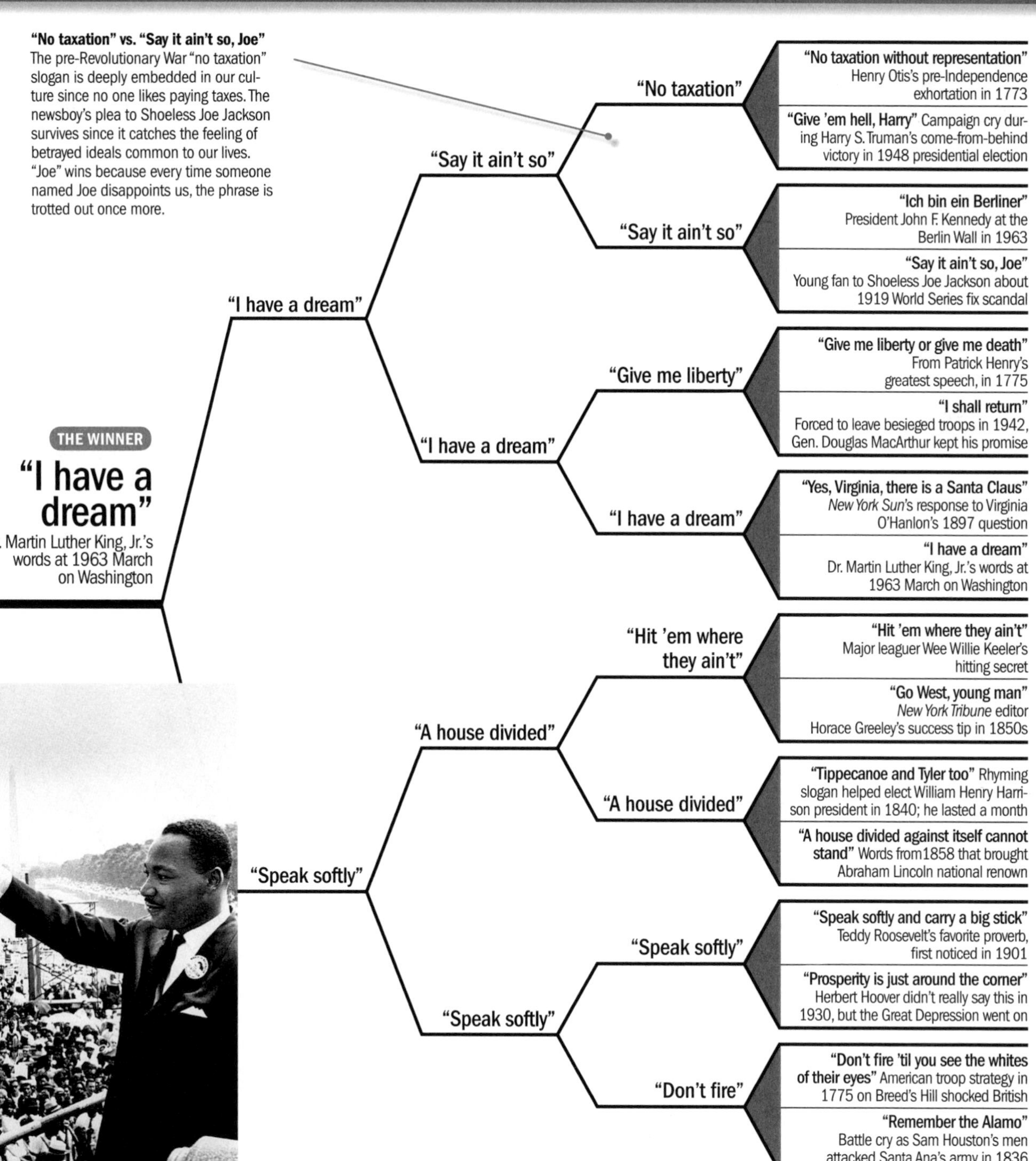

"No taxation" vs. "Say it ain't so, Joe"
The pre-Revolutionary War "no taxation" slogan is deeply embedded in our culture since no one likes paying taxes. The newsboy's plea to Shoeless Joe Jackson survives since it catches the feeling of betrayed ideals common to our lives. "Joe" wins because every time someone named Joe disappoints us, the phrase is trotted out once more.
"No taxation without representation" Henry Otis's pre-Independence exhortation in 1773
"Give 'em hell, Harry" Campaign cry during Harry S. Truman's come-from-behind victory in 1948 presidential election
"Ich bin ein Berliner" President John F. Kennedy at the Berlin Wall in 1963
"Say it ain't so, Joe" Young fan to Shoeless Joe Jackson about 1919 World Series fix scandal
"Give me liberty or give me death" From Patrick Henry's greatest speech, in 1775
"I shall return" Forced to leave besieged troops in 1942, Gen. Douglas MacArthur kept his promise
"Yes, Virginia, there is a Santa Claus" *New York Sun*'s response to Virginia O'Hanlon's 1897 question
"I have a dream" Dr. Martin Luther King, Jr.'s words at 1963 March on Washington
"Hit 'em where they ain't" Major leaguer Wee Willie Keeler's hitting secret
"Go West, young man" *New York Tribune* editor Horace Greeley's success tip in 1850s
"Tippecanoe and Tyler too" Rhyming slogan helped elect William Henry Harrison president in 1840; he lasted a month
"A house divided against itself cannot stand" Words from1858 that brought Abraham Lincoln national renown
"Speak softly and carry a big stick" Teddy Roosevelt's favorite proverb, first noticed in 1901
"Prosperity is just around the corner" Herbert Hoover didn't really say this in 1930, but the Great Depression went on
"Don't fire 'til you see the whites of their eyes" American troop strategy in 1775 on Breed's Hill shocked British
"Remember the Alamo" Battle cry as Sam Houston's men attacked Santa Ana's army in 1836
"No taxation"
"Say it ain't so"
"Give me liberty"
"I have a dream"
"Hit 'em where they ain't"
"A house divided"
"Speak softly"
"Don't fire"
"Say it ain't so"
"I have a dream"
"A house divided"
"Speak softly"
"I have a dream"
"Speak softly"
THE WINNER
"I have a dream"
Dr. Martin Luther King, Jr.'s words at 1963 March on Washington

Financial Villains

By Joe Nocera

Joe Nocera, the "Talking Business" columnist for the *New York Times*, is the author of *Good Guys and Bad Guys: Behind the Scenes with the Saints and Scoundrels of American Business (and Everything in Between)* and *A Piece of the Action: How the Middle Class Joined the Money Class.*

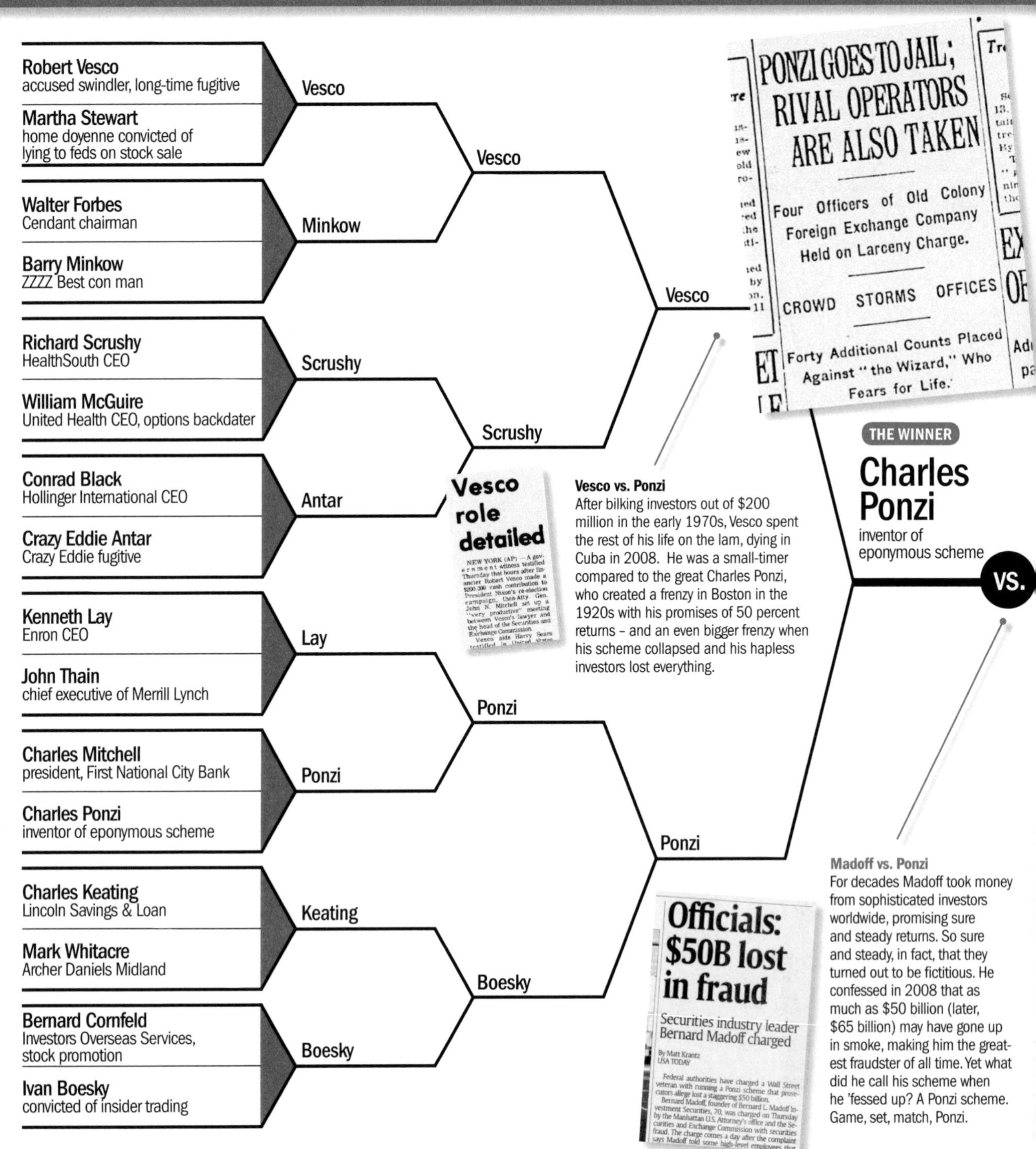

Robert Vesco
accused swindler, long-time fugitive
Martha Stewart
home doyenne convicted of lying to feds on stock sale
Walter Forbes
Cendant chairman
Barry Minkow
ZZZZ Best con man
Richard Scrushy
HealthSouth CEO
William McGuire
United Health CEO, options backdater
Conrad Black
Hollinger International CEO
Crazy Eddie Antar
Crazy Eddie fugitive
Kenneth Lay
Enron CEO
John Thain
chief executive of Merrill Lynch
Charles Mitchell
president, First National City Bank
Charles Ponzi
inventor of eponymous scheme
Charles Keating
Lincoln Savings & Loan
Mark Whitacre
Archer Daniels Midland
Bernard Cornfeld
Investors Overseas Services, stock promotion
Ivan Boesky
convicted of insider trading
Vesco
Minkow
Scrushy
Antar
Lay
Ponzi
Keating
Boesky
Vesco
Scrushy
Ponzi
Boesky
Vesco
Ponzi
VS.
THE WINNER
Charles Ponzi
inventor of eponymous scheme
PONZI GOES TO JAIL; RIVAL OPERATORS ARE ALSO TAKEN
Four Officers of Old Colony Foreign Exchange Company Held on Larceny Charge.
CROWD STORMS OFFICES
Forty Additional Counts Placed Against "the Wizard," Who Fears for Life.
Vesco role detailed
Vesco vs. Ponzi
After bilking investors out of $200 million in the early 1970s, Vesco spent the rest of his life on the lam, dying in Cuba in 2008. He was a small-timer compared to the great Charles Ponzi, who created a frenzy in Boston in the 1920s with his promises of 50 percent returns – and an even bigger frenzy when his scheme collapsed and his hapless investors lost everything.
Officials: $50B lost in fraud
Securities industry leader Bernard Madoff charged
By Matt Krantz
USA TODAY
Madoff vs. Ponzi
For decades Madoff took money from sophisticated investors worldwide, promising sure and steady returns. So sure and steady, in fact, that they turned out to be fictitious. He confessed in 2008 that as much as $50 billion (later, $65 billion) may have gone up in smoke, making him the greatest fraudster of all time. Yet what did he call his scheme when he 'fessed up? A Ponzi scheme. Game, set, match, Ponzi.

YOU CAN'T HAVE CAPITALISM WITHOUT CROOKS, or at least without the occasional harmless villainy. Okay, maybe it's not so harmless, not when investors are led astray, when people are snookered out of their savings, and when traders try to hide multi-billion dollar losses from their unsuspecting bosses, the eventual discovery of which can bring down even the mightiest of giant institutions. But the world would be a far less colorful place without financial schemers trying to put one over on us.

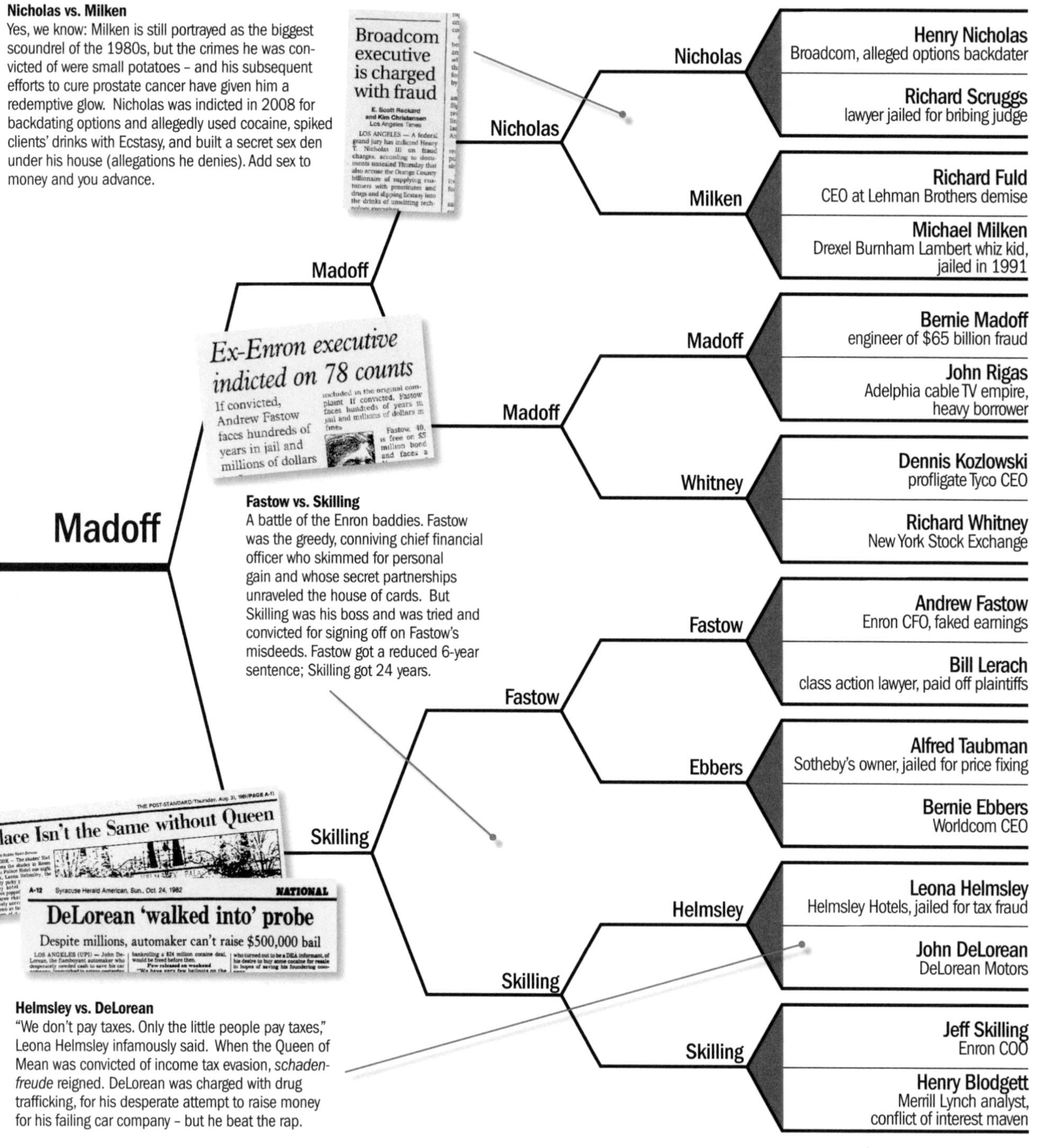

Henry Nicholas
Broadcom, alleged options backdater
Richard Scruggs
lawyer jailed for bribing judge
Richard Fuld
CEO at Lehman Brothers demise
Michael Milken
Drexel Burnham Lambert whiz kid, jailed in 1991
Bernie Madoff
engineer of $65 billion fraud
John Rigas
Adelphia cable TV empire, heavy borrower
Dennis Kozlowski
profligate Tyco CEO
Richard Whitney
New York Stock Exchange
Andrew Fastow
Enron CFO, faked earnings
Bill Lerach
class action lawyer, paid off plaintiffs
Alfred Taubman
Sotheby's owner, jailed for price fixing
Bernie Ebbers
Worldcom CEO
Leona Helmsley
Helmsley Hotels, jailed for tax fraud
John DeLorean
DeLorean Motors
Jeff Skilling
Enron COO
Henry Blodgett
Merrill Lynch analyst, conflict of interest maven
Nicholas
Milken
Madoff
Whitney
Fastow
Ebbers
Helmsley
Skilling
Nicholas
Madoff
Fastow
Skilling
Madoff
Skilling
Madoff
Broadcom executive is charged with fraud
Ex-Enron executive indicted on 78 counts
If convicted, Andrew Fastow faces hundreds of years in jail and millions of dollars
Palace Isn't the Same without Queen
DeLorean 'walked into' probe
Despite millions, automaker can't raise $500,000 bail

Nicholas vs. Milken
Yes, we know: Milken is still portrayed as the biggest scoundrel of the 1980s, but the crimes he was convicted of were small potatoes – and his subsequent efforts to cure prostate cancer have given him a redemptive glow. Nicholas was indicted in 2008 for backdating options and allegedly used cocaine, spiked clients' drinks with Ecstasy, and built a secret sex den under his house (allegations he denies). Add sex to money and you advance.

Fastow vs. Skilling
A battle of the Enron baddies. Fastow was the greedy, conniving chief financial officer who skimmed for personal gain and whose secret partnerships unraveled the house of cards. But Skilling was his boss and was tried and convicted for signing off on Fastow's misdeeds. Fastow got a reduced 6-year sentence; Skilling got 24 years.

Helmsley vs. DeLorean
"We don't pay taxes. Only the little people pay taxes," Leona Helmsley infamously said. When the Queen of Mean was convicted of income tax evasion, *schadenfreude* reigned. DeLorean was charged with drug trafficking, for his desperate attempt to raise money for his failing car company – but he beat the rap.

Political Rivalries

By Adam Clymer

Adam Clymer is the former chief Washington correspondent of the *New York Times,* author of *Edward M. Kennedy: A Biography* (1999) and *Drawing the Line at the Big Ditch: The Panama Canal Treaties and the Rise of the Right* (2008; and in the opinion of George W. Bush and Dick Cheney, "major league."

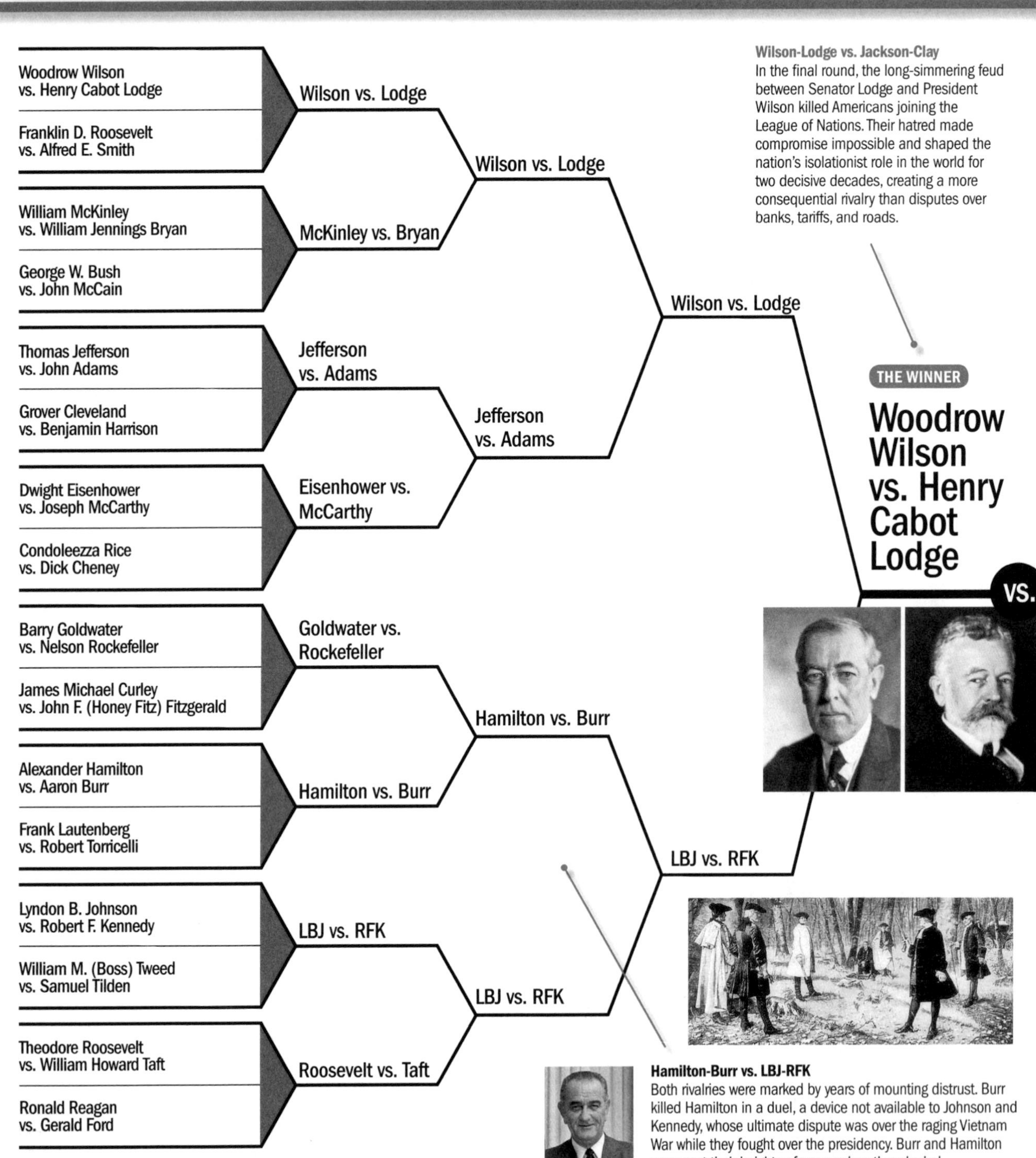
Woodrow Wilson vs. Henry Cabot Lodge
Franklin D. Roosevelt vs. Alfred E. Smith
William McKinley vs. William Jennings Bryan
George W. Bush vs. John McCain
Thomas Jefferson vs. John Adams
Grover Cleveland vs. Benjamin Harrison
Dwight Eisenhower vs. Joseph McCarthy
Condoleezza Rice vs. Dick Cheney
Barry Goldwater vs. Nelson Rockefeller
James Michael Curley vs. John F. (Honey Fitz) Fitzgerald
Alexander Hamilton vs. Aaron Burr
Frank Lautenberg vs. Robert Torricelli
Lyndon B. Johnson vs. Robert F. Kennedy
William M. (Boss) Tweed vs. Samuel Tilden
Theodore Roosevelt vs. William Howard Taft
Ronald Reagan vs. Gerald Ford
Wilson vs. Lodge
McKinley vs. Bryan
Jefferson vs. Adams
Eisenhower vs. McCarthy
Goldwater vs. Rockefeller
Hamilton vs. Burr
LBJ vs. RFK
Roosevelt vs. Taft
Wilson vs. Lodge
Jefferson vs. Adams
Hamilton vs. Burr
LBJ vs. RFK
Wilson vs. Lodge
LBJ vs. RFK
THE WINNER
Woodrow Wilson vs. Henry Cabot Lodge
VS.

Wilson-Lodge vs. Jackson-Clay
In the final round, the long-simmering feud between Senator Lodge and President Wilson killed Americans joining the League of Nations. Their hatred made compromise impossible and shaped the nation's isolationist role in the world for two decisive decades, creating a more consequential rivalry than disputes over banks, tariffs, and roads.

Hamilton-Burr vs. LBJ-RFK
Both rivalries were marked by years of mounting distrust. Burr killed Hamilton in a duel, a device not available to Johnson and Kennedy, whose ultimate dispute was over the raging Vietnam War while they fought over the presidency. Burr and Hamilton were past their heights of power when they dueled.

THE BEST POLITICAL RIVALRIES involve more than personal competition for office. They have far-reaching consequences. They are contests for power: in government, like President Truman vs. General MacArthur; in a political movement, like William F. Buckley's crusade against Robert Welch and his John Birch Society, or best of all, over the future of the nation, like Henry Clay vs. Andrew Jackson. Antipathy approaching hatred, adds luster; see Alexander Hamilton and Aaron Burr. Great rivalries last for years.

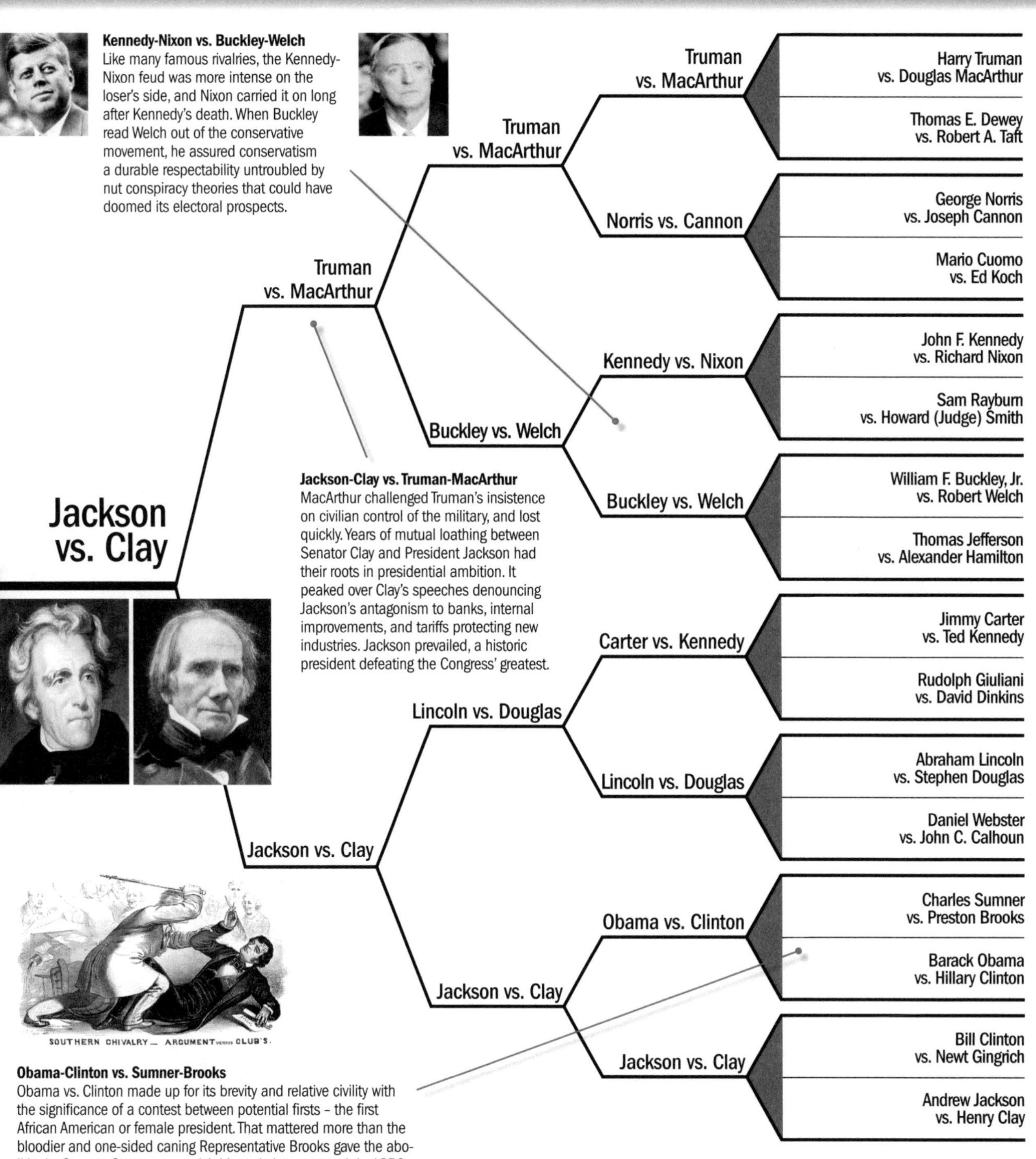
Harry Truman vs. Douglas MacArthur
Thomas E. Dewey vs. Robert A. Taft
George Norris vs. Joseph Cannon
Mario Cuomo vs. Ed Koch
John F. Kennedy vs. Richard Nixon
Sam Rayburn vs. Howard (Judge) Smith
William F. Buckley, Jr. vs. Robert Welch
Thomas Jefferson vs. Alexander Hamilton
Jimmy Carter vs. Ted Kennedy
Rudolph Giuliani vs. David Dinkins
Abraham Lincoln vs. Stephen Douglas
Daniel Webster vs. John C. Calhoun
Charles Sumner vs. Preston Brooks
Barack Obama vs. Hillary Clinton
Bill Clinton vs. Newt Gingrich
Andrew Jackson vs. Henry Clay
Truman vs. MacArthur
Norris vs. Cannon
Kennedy vs. Nixon
Buckley vs. Welch
Carter vs. Kennedy
Lincoln vs. Douglas
Obama vs. Clinton
Jackson vs. Clay
Truman vs. MacArthur
Buckley vs. Welch
Lincoln vs. Douglas
Jackson vs. Clay
Truman vs. MacArthur
Jackson vs. Clay
Jackson vs. Clay
SOUTHERN CHIVALRY — ARGUMENT versus CLUB'S.

Kennedy-Nixon vs. Buckley-Welch
Like many famous rivalries, the Kennedy-Nixon feud was more intense on the loser's side, and Nixon carried it on long after Kennedy's death. When Buckley read Welch out of the conservative movement, he assured conservatism a durable respectability untroubled by nut conspiracy theories that could have doomed its electoral prospects.

Jackson-Clay vs. Truman-MacArthur
MacArthur challenged Truman's insistence on civilian control of the military, and lost quickly. Years of mutual loathing between Senator Clay and President Jackson had their roots in presidential ambition. It peaked over Clay's speeches denouncing Jackson's antagonism to banks, internal improvements, and tariffs protecting new industries. Jackson prevailed, a historic president defeating the Congress' greatest.

Obama-Clinton vs. Sumner-Brooks
Obama vs. Clinton made up for its brevity and relative civility with the significance of a contest between potential firsts – the first African American or female president. That mattered more than the bloodier and one-sided caning Representative Brooks gave the abolitionist Senator Sumner to punish his anti-slavery speech in 1856.

Presidential Speeches

By Curt Smith

Curt Smith wrote more speeches than anyone for President George H. W. Bush. A member of the prestigious Judson Welliver Society of former presidential speechwriters, he teaches presidential rhetoric and public speaking at the University of Rochester.

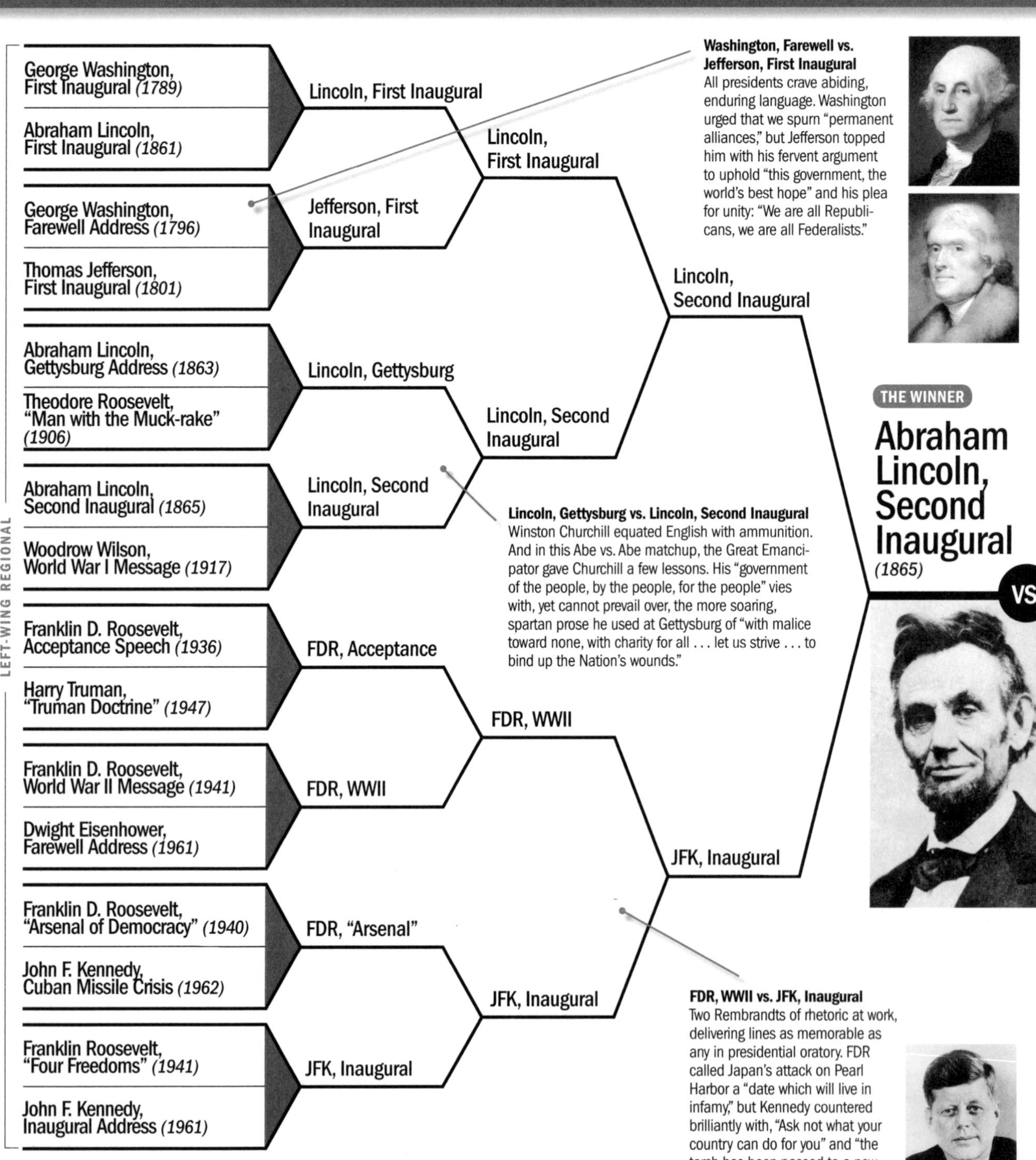

LEFT-WING REGIONAL
George Washington, First Inaugural (1789)
Abraham Lincoln, First Inaugural (1861)
George Washington, Farewell Address (1796)
Thomas Jefferson, First Inaugural (1801)
Abraham Lincoln, Gettysburg Address (1863)
Theodore Roosevelt, "Man with the Muck-rake" (1906)
Abraham Lincoln, Second Inaugural (1865)
Woodrow Wilson, World War I Message (1917)
Franklin D. Roosevelt, Acceptance Speech (1936)
Harry Truman, "Truman Doctrine" (1947)
Franklin D. Roosevelt, World War II Message (1941)
Dwight Eisenhower, Farewell Address (1961)
Franklin D. Roosevelt, "Arsenal of Democracy" (1940)
John F. Kennedy, Cuban Missile Crisis (1962)
Franklin Roosevelt, "Four Freedoms" (1941)
John F. Kennedy, Inaugural Address (1961)
Lincoln, First Inaugural
Jefferson, First Inaugural
Lincoln, Gettysburg
Lincoln, Second Inaugural
FDR, Acceptance
FDR, WWII
FDR, "Arsenal"
JFK, Inaugural
Lincoln, First Inaugural
Lincoln, Second Inaugural
FDR, WWII
JFK, Inaugural
Lincoln, Second Inaugural
JFK, Inaugural
Washington, Farewell vs. Jefferson, First Inaugural
All presidents crave abiding, enduring language. Washington urged that we spurn "permanent alliances," but Jefferson topped him with his fervent argument to uphold "this government, the world's best hope" and his plea for unity: "We are all Republicans, we are all Federalists."
Lincoln, Gettysburg vs. Lincoln, Second Inaugural
Winston Churchill equated English with ammunition. And in this Abe vs. Abe matchup, the Great Emancipator gave Churchill a few lessons. His "government of the people, by the people, for the people" vies with, yet cannot prevail over, the more soaring, spartan prose he used at Gettysburg of "with malice toward none, with charity for all . . . let us strive . . . to bind up the Nation's wounds."
FDR, WWII vs. JFK, Inaugural
Two Rembrandts of rhetoric at work, delivering lines as memorable as any in presidential oratory. FDR called Japan's attack on Pearl Harbor a "date which will live in infamy," but Kennedy countered brilliantly with, "Ask not what your country can do for you" and "the torch has been passed to a new generation of Americans."
THE WINNER
Abraham Lincoln, Second Inaugural
(1865)
VS.

THE MOST SUCCESSFUL PRESIDENTS have employed what Teddy Roosevelt labeled the "bully pulpit": the office's power to persuade. Their best speeches are remembered for social impact, political consequence, and/or rhetorical artistry, which create a form of oral history. Some of the speeches contain only two of the criteria, while others, like Abraham Lincoln's Second Inaugural and Franklin Delano Roosevelt's First Inaugural, contain all three. Memorable pre-presidential speeches such as Lincoln's 1858 "house divided speech" and Barack Obama's 2008 tour de force on race, did not qualify.

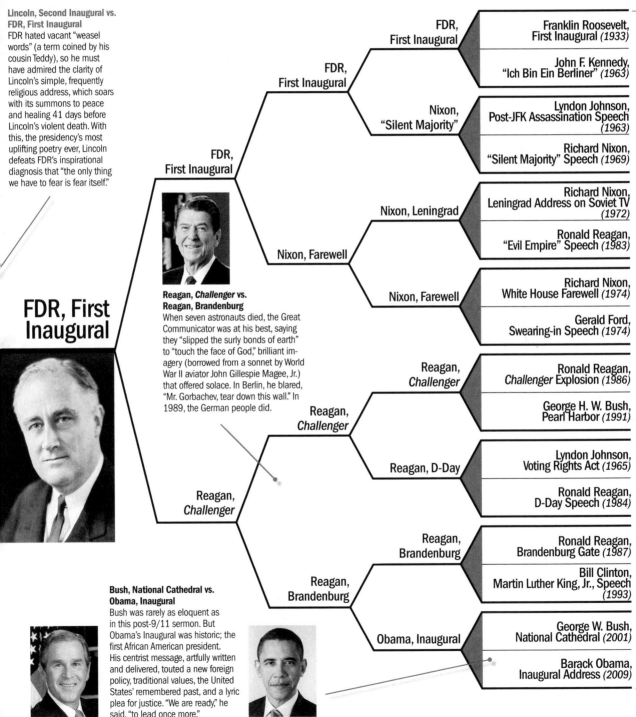

Lincoln, Second Inaugural vs. FDR, First Inaugural
FDR hated vacant "weasel words" (a term coined by his cousin Teddy), so he must have admired the clarity of Lincoln's simple, frequently religious address, which soars with its summons to peace and healing 41 days before Lincoln's violent death. With this, the presidency's most uplifting poetry ever, Lincoln defeats FDR's inspirational diagnosis that "the only thing we have to fear is fear itself."

RIGHT-WING REGIONAL

First round:
- Franklin Roosevelt, First Inaugural *(1933)*
- John F. Kennedy, "Ich Bin Ein Berliner" *(1963)*
- Lyndon Johnson, Post-JFK Assassination Speech *(1963)*
- Richard Nixon, "Silent Majority" Speech *(1969)*
- Richard Nixon, Leningrad Address on Soviet TV *(1972)*
- Ronald Reagan, "Evil Empire" Speech *(1983)*
- Richard Nixon, White House Farewell *(1974)*
- Gerald Ford, Swearing-in Speech *(1974)*
- Ronald Reagan, *Challenger* Explosion *(1986)*
- George H. W. Bush, Pearl Harbor *(1991)*
- Lyndon Johnson, Voting Rights Act *(1965)*
- Ronald Reagan, D-Day Speech *(1984)*
- Ronald Reagan, Brandenburg Gate *(1987)*
- Bill Clinton, Martin Luther King, Jr., Speech *(1993)*
- George W. Bush, National Cathedral *(2001)*
- Barack Obama, Inaugural Address *(2009)*

Second round:
- FDR, First Inaugural
- Nixon, "Silent Majority"
- Nixon, Leningrad
- Nixon, Farewell
- Reagan, *Challenger*
- Reagan, D-Day
- Reagan, Brandenburg
- Obama, Inaugural

Third round:
- FDR, First Inaugural
- Nixon, Farewell
- Reagan, *Challenger*
- Reagan, Brandenburg

Fourth round:
- FDR, First Inaugural
- Reagan, *Challenger*

Reagan, *Challenger* vs. Reagan, Brandenburg
When seven astronauts died, the Great Communicator was at his best, saying they "slipped the surly bonds of earth" to "touch the face of God," brilliant imagery (borrowed from a sonnet by World War II aviator John Gillespie Magee, Jr.) that offered solace. In Berlin, he blared, "Mr. Gorbachev, tear down this wall." In 1989, the German people did.

FDR, First Inaugural

Bush, National Cathedral vs. Obama, Inaugural
Bush was rarely as eloquent as in this post-9/11 sermon. But Obama's Inaugural was historic; the first African American president. His centrist message, artfully written and delivered, touted a new foreign policy, traditional values, the United States' remembered past, and a lyric plea for justice. "We are ready," he said, "to lead once more."

Influential Radicals and Extremists

By David Oshinsky

David Oshinsky holds the Jack S. Blanton Chair in History at the Universit of Texas and is a distinguished scholar-in-residence at New York University His latest book, *Polio: An American Story,* won the Pulitzer Prize for History.

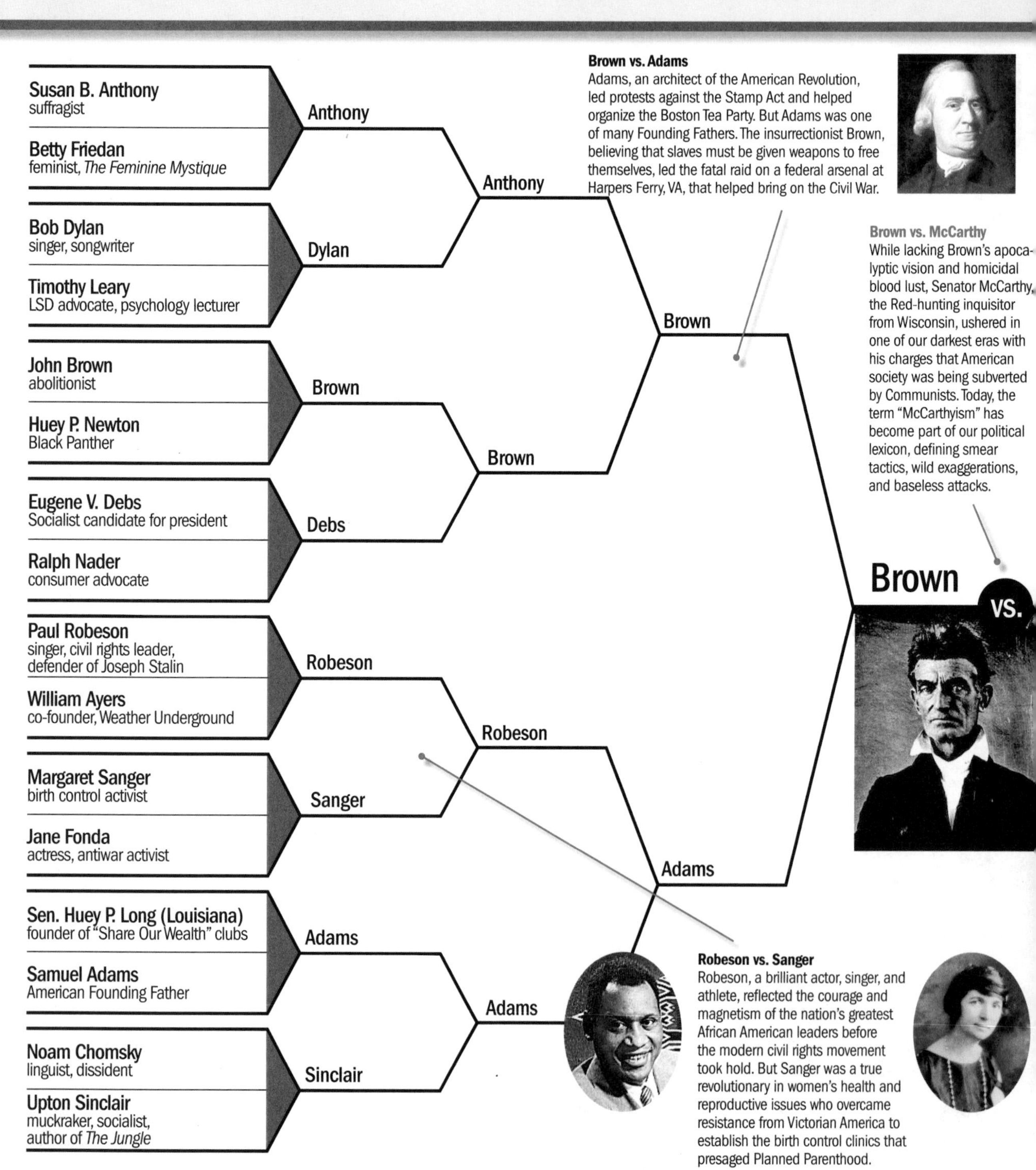
Susan B. Anthony
suffragist
Betty Friedan
feminist, *The Feminine Mystique*
Bob Dylan
singer, songwriter
Timothy Leary
LSD advocate, psychology lecturer
John Brown
abolitionist
Huey P. Newton
Black Panther
Eugene V. Debs
Socialist candidate for president
Ralph Nader
consumer advocate
Paul Robeson
singer, civil rights leader, defender of Joseph Stalin
William Ayers
co-founder, Weather Underground
Margaret Sanger
birth control activist
Jane Fonda
actress, antiwar activist
Sen. Huey P. Long (Louisiana)
founder of "Share Our Wealth" clubs
Samuel Adams
American Founding Father
Noam Chomsky
linguist, dissident
Upton Sinclair
muckraker, socialist, author of *The Jungle*
Anthony
Dylan
Brown
Debs
Robeson
Sanger
Adams
Sinclair
Anthony
Brown
Robeson
Adams
Brown
Adams
Brown
VS.

Brown vs. Adams
Adams, an architect of the American Revolution, led protests against the Stamp Act and helped organize the Boston Tea Party. But Adams was one of many Founding Fathers. The insurrectionist Brown, believing that slaves must be given weapons to free themselves, led the fatal raid on a federal arsenal at Harpers Ferry, VA, that helped bring on the Civil War.

Brown vs. McCarthy
While lacking Brown's apocalyptic vision and homicidal blood lust, Senator McCarthy, the Red-hunting inquisitor from Wisconsin, ushered in one of our darkest eras with his charges that American society was being subverted by Communists. Today, the term "McCarthyism" has become part of our political lexicon, defining smear tactics, wild exaggerations, and baseless attacks.

Robeson vs. Sanger
Robeson, a brilliant actor, singer, and athlete, reflected the courage and magnetism of the nation's greatest African American leaders before the modern civil rights movement took hold. But Sanger was a true revolutionary in women's health and reproductive issues who overcame resistance from Victorian America to establish the birth control clinics that presaged Planned Parenthood.

HISTORIANS HAVE TRIED WITH LIMITED SUCCESS to measure the influence of individuals who wrote books, pushed theories, or led movements that society considered radical or extremist. What is clear, though, is that radicals and extremists of the Right and Left have altered our history by raising fundamental questions about the tyranny of government, the expansion of human rights, the limits of national security, and the role of violent and nonviolent protest in a free society. All should be judged on their continuing impact on society.

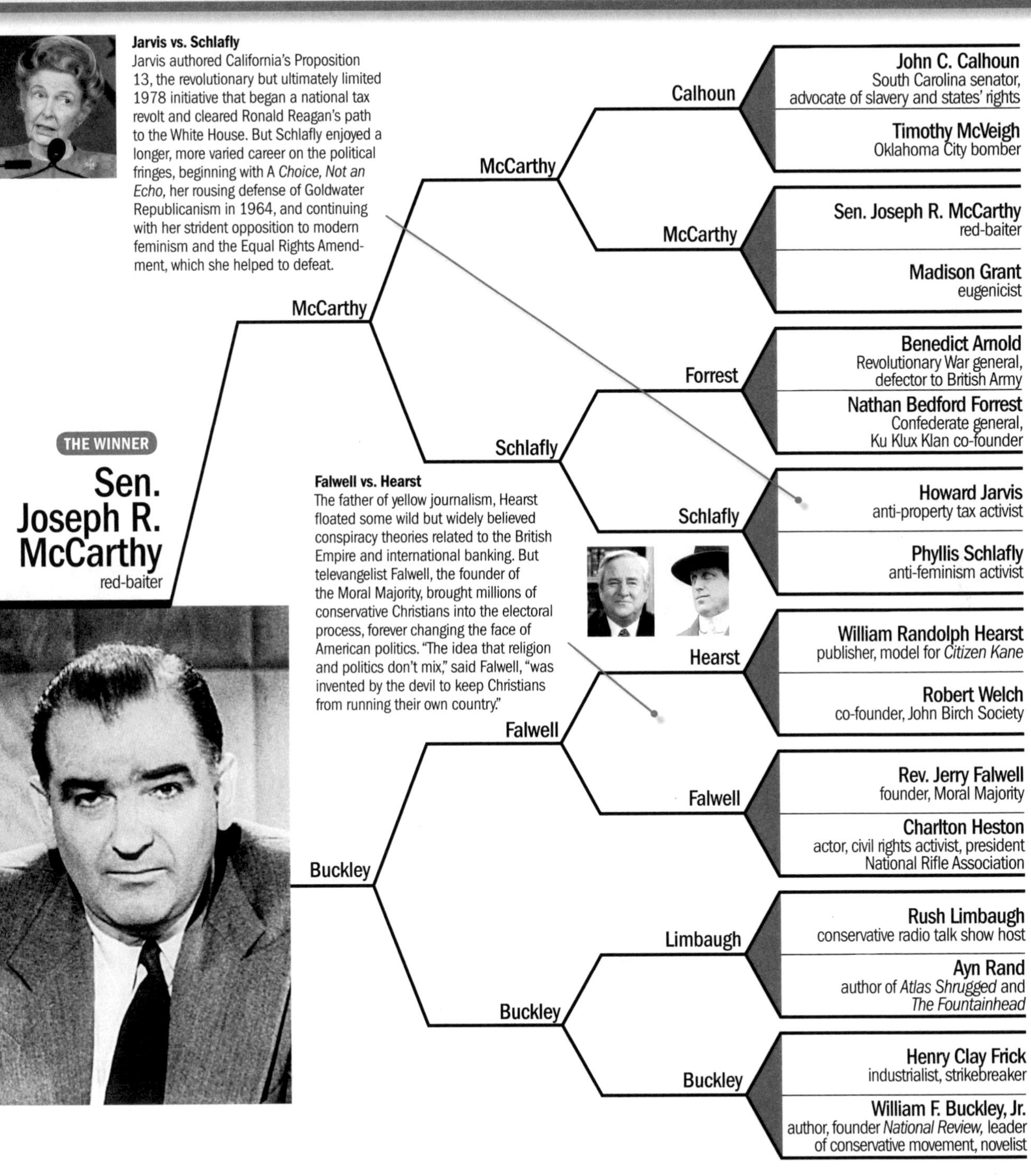
John C. Calhoun
South Carolina senator, advocate of slavery and states' rights
Timothy McVeigh
Oklahoma City bomber
Sen. Joseph R. McCarthy
red-baiter
Madison Grant
eugenicist
Benedict Arnold
Revolutionary War general, defector to British Army
Nathan Bedford Forrest
Confederate general, Ku Klux Klan co-founder
Howard Jarvis
anti-property tax activist
Phyllis Schlafly
anti-feminism activist
William Randolph Hearst
publisher, model for *Citizen Kane*
Robert Welch
co-founder, John Birch Society
Rev. Jerry Falwell
founder, Moral Majority
Charlton Heston
actor, civil rights activist, president National Rifle Association
Rush Limbaugh
conservative radio talk show host
Ayn Rand
author of *Atlas Shrugged* and *The Fountainhead*
Henry Clay Frick
industrialist, strikebreaker
William F. Buckley, Jr.
author, founder *National Review*, leader of conservative movement, novelist
Calhoun
McCarthy
Forrest
Schlafly
Hearst
Falwell
Limbaugh
Buckley
McCarthy
Schlafly
Falwell
Buckley
McCarthy
Buckley
THE WINNER
Sen. Joseph R. McCarthy
red-baiter

Jarvis vs. Schlafly

Jarvis authored California's Proposition 13, the revolutionary but ultimately limited 1978 initiative that began a national tax revolt and cleared Ronald Reagan's path to the White House. But Schlafly enjoyed a longer, more varied career on the political fringes, beginning with *A Choice, Not an Echo,* her rousing defense of Goldwater Republicanism in 1964, and continuing with her strident opposition to modern feminism and the Equal Rights Amendment, which she helped to defeat.

Falwell vs. Hearst

The father of yellow journalism, Hearst floated some wild but widely believed conspiracy theories related to the British Empire and international banking. But televangelist Falwell, the founder of the Moral Majority, brought millions of conservative Christians into the electoral process, forever changing the face of American politics. "The idea that religion and politics don't mix," said Falwell, "was invented by the devil to keep Christians from running their own country."

Biographies

By James McGrath Morris

James McGrath Morris, author of *Joseph Pulitzer: A Life in Politics, Print, and Power* and *The Rose Man of Sing Sing,* is also the editor of the monthly newsletter *The Biographer's Craft.*

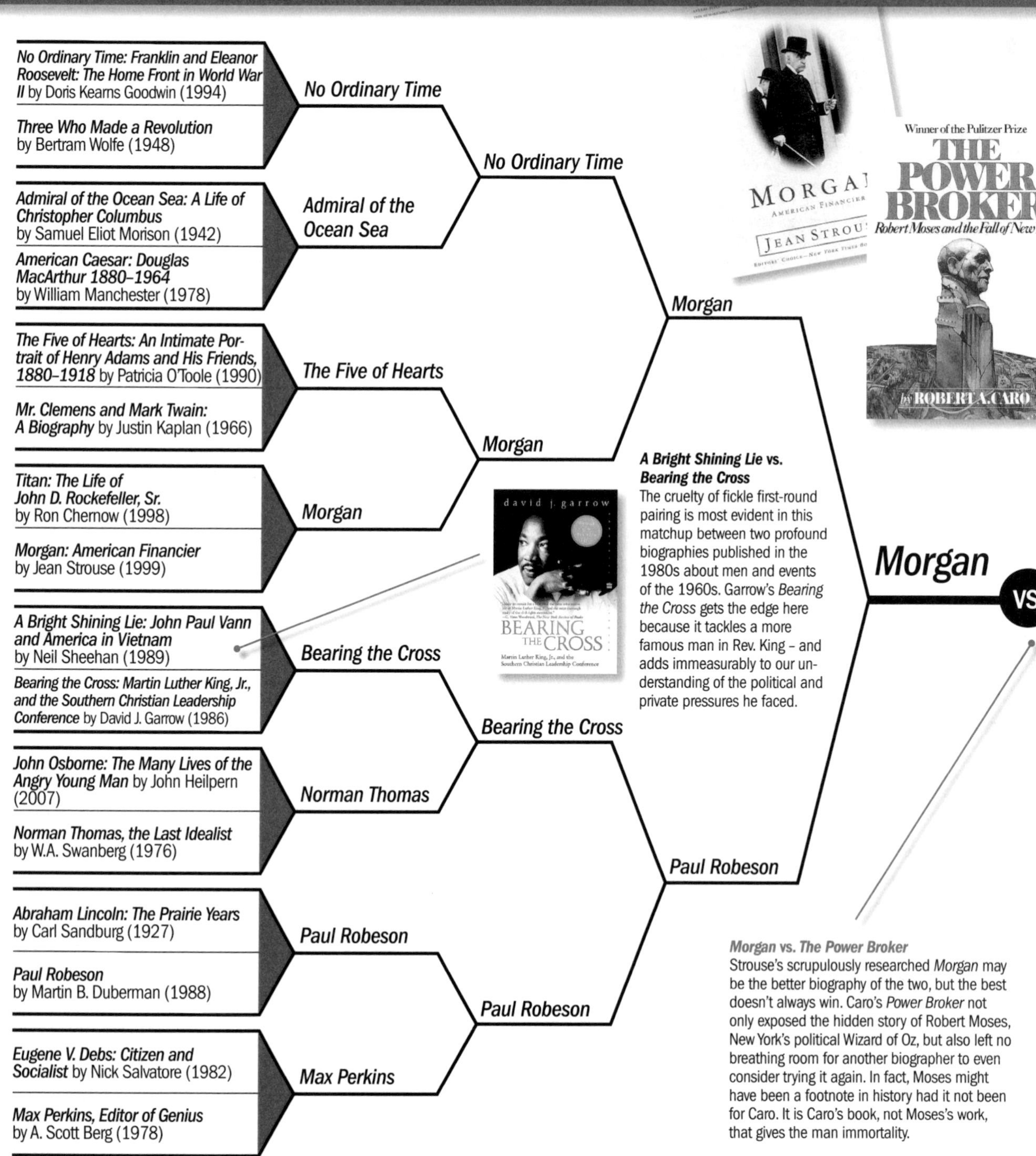
No Ordinary Time: Franklin and Eleanor Roosevelt: The Home Front in World War II by Doris Kearns Goodwin (1994)
Three Who Made a Revolution by Bertram Wolfe (1948)
Admiral of the Ocean Sea: A Life of Christopher Columbus by Samuel Eliot Morison (1942)
American Caesar: Douglas MacArthur 1880–1964 by William Manchester (1978)
The Five of Hearts: An Intimate Portrait of Henry Adams and His Friends, 1880–1918 by Patricia O'Toole (1990)
Mr. Clemens and Mark Twain: A Biography by Justin Kaplan (1966)
Titan: The Life of John D. Rockefeller, Sr. by Ron Chernow (1998)
Morgan: American Financier by Jean Strouse (1999)
A Bright Shining Lie: John Paul Vann and America in Vietnam by Neil Sheehan (1989)
Bearing the Cross: Martin Luther King, Jr., and the Southern Christian Leadership Conference by David J. Garrow (1986)
John Osborne: The Many Lives of the Angry Young Man by John Heilpern (2007)
Norman Thomas, the Last Idealist by W.A. Swanberg (1976)
Abraham Lincoln: The Prairie Years by Carl Sandburg (1927)
Paul Robeson by Martin B. Duberman (1988)
Eugene V. Debs: Citizen and Socialist by Nick Salvatore (1982)
Max Perkins, Editor of Genius by A. Scott Berg (1978)
No Ordinary Time
Admiral of the Ocean Sea
The Five of Hearts
Morgan
Bearing the Cross
Norman Thomas
Paul Robeson
Max Perkins
No Ordinary Time
Morgan
Bearing the Cross
Paul Robeson
Morgan
Paul Robeson
Morgan
VS.
david j. garrow
BEARING THE CROSS
Martin Luther King, Jr., and the Southern Christian Leadership Conference
Winner of the Pulitzer Prize
THE POWER BROKER
Robert Moses and the Fall of New York
by ROBERT A. CARO

A Bright Shining Lie* vs. *Bearing the Cross

The cruelty of fickle first-round pairing is most evident in this matchup between two profound biographies published in the 1980s about men and events of the 1960s. Garrow's *Bearing the Cross* gets the edge here because it tackles a more famous man in Rev. King – and adds immeasurably to our understanding of the political and private pressures he faced.

Morgan* vs. *The Power Broker

Strouse's scrupulously researched *Morgan* may be the better biography of the two, but the best doesn't always win. Caro's *Power Broker* not only exposed the hidden story of Robert Moses, New York's political Wizard of Oz, but also left no breathing room for another biographer to even consider trying it again. In fact, Moses might have been a footnote in history had it not been for Caro. It is Caro's book, not Moses's work, that gives the man immortality.

THE FAMOUS HAVE AN EDGE HERE. Few readers will invest $34.95 for *The Life of Lenart Elckerlijc,* who sent his kids to college, mowed his lawn on Saturdays, and bowled 300 five years before dying. Still, in biography it's the telling that counts. A great biographer scores points by weaving a great narrative. "Just the facts, ma'am" works only for the LAPD. Virginia Woolf, while writing a life of Roger Fry, asked, "How can one make a life out of six cardboard boxes full of tailors' bills, love letters and old picture postcards?" The biographers here know the answer.

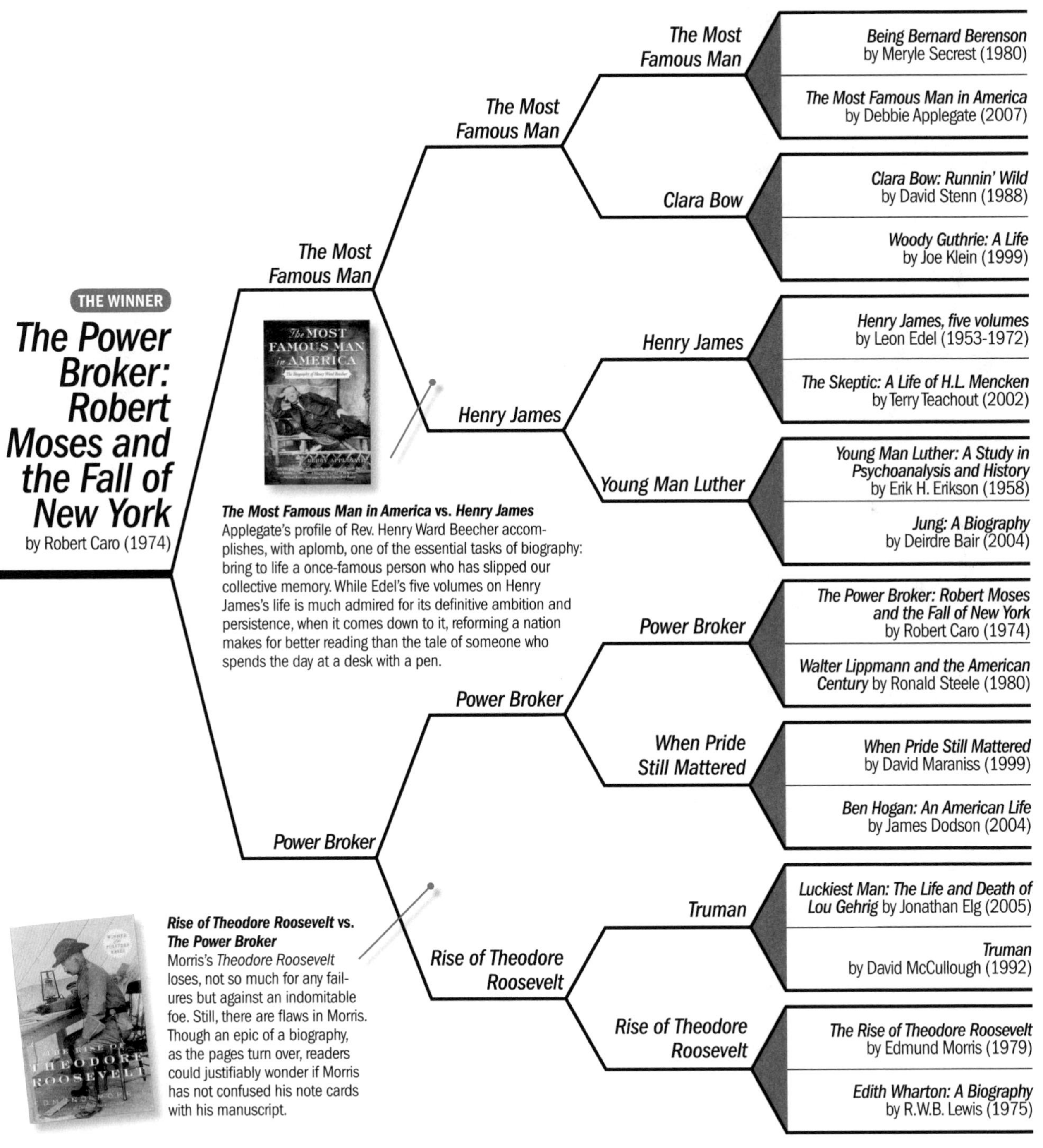

Being Bernard Berenson by Meryle Secrest (1980)
The Most Famous Man in America by Debbie Applegate (2007)
Clara Bow: Runnin' Wild by David Stenn (1988)
Woody Guthrie: A Life by Joe Klein (1999)
Henry James, five volumes by Leon Edel (1953-1972)
The Skeptic: A Life of H.L. Mencken by Terry Teachout (2002)
Young Man Luther: A Study in Psychoanalysis and History by Erik H. Erikson (1958)
Jung: A Biography by Deirdre Bair (2004)
The Power Broker: Robert Moses and the Fall of New York by Robert Caro (1974)
Walter Lippmann and the American Century by Ronald Steele (1980)
When Pride Still Mattered by David Maraniss (1999)
Ben Hogan: An American Life by James Dodson (2004)
Luckiest Man: The Life and Death of Lou Gehrig by Jonathan Elg (2005)
Truman by David McCullough (1992)
The Rise of Theodore Roosevelt by Edmund Morris (1979)
Edith Wharton: A Biography by R.W.B. Lewis (1975)
The Most Famous Man
Clara Bow
Henry James
Young Man Luther
Power Broker
When Pride Still Mattered
Truman
Rise of Theodore Roosevelt
The Most Famous Man
Henry James
Power Broker
Rise of Theodore Roosevelt
The Most Famous Man
Power Broker
THE WINNER
The Power Broker: Robert Moses and the Fall of New York
by Robert Caro (1974)
The Most Famous Man in America

The Most Famous Man in America* vs. *Henry James
Applegate's profile of Rev. Henry Ward Beecher accomplishes, with aplomb, one of the essential tasks of biography: bring to life a once-famous person who has slipped our collective memory. While Edel's five volumes on Henry James's life is much admired for its definitive ambition and persistence, when it comes down to it, reforming a nation makes for better reading than the tale of someone who spends the day at a desk with a pen.

Rise of Theodore Roosevelt* vs. *The Power Broker
Morris's *Theodore Roosevelt* loses, not so much for any failures but against an indomitable foe. Still, there are flaws in Morris. Though an epic of a biography, as the pages turn over, readers could justifiably wonder if Morris has not confused his note cards with his manuscript.

PEOPLE

Astronauts *by Jeffrey Kluger* 33
Supermodels *by Crystal Renn and Marjorie Ingall* 34
Celebrity Mugshots *by Willie Geist* 35
Mary *by Mary C. Curtis* 36
Bald Guys *by Richard Sandomir* 37
Geniuses *by Peter Richmond* 38
Celebrity Baby Names *by Linda Rosenkrantz and Pamela Redmond Satran* 39
Untimely Deaths *by Mark Reiter* 40
David *by David Fisher* 41
Celebrity Memoirs *by Charles Leerhsen* 42
Lousy Husbands *by Kari Boyer* 43
William et. al. *by William/Bill Geist* 44
Disappearing Acts *by Franz Lidz* 45
Richard vs. Dick *by Richard Sandomir* 46
American Pinups *by Gregory Curtis* 47
Pundits *by Franklin Foer* 48
Great Brother Acts *by Mark Reiter* 49
Tom vs. Thomas *by Tom Chiarella* 50
Immigrants *by Tony Quinn* 51

Astronauts

By Jeffrey Kluger

Jeffrey Kluger is the science editor of *Time* magazine and the author of numerous books, including *Apollo 13*, which served as the basis of the 1995 movie.

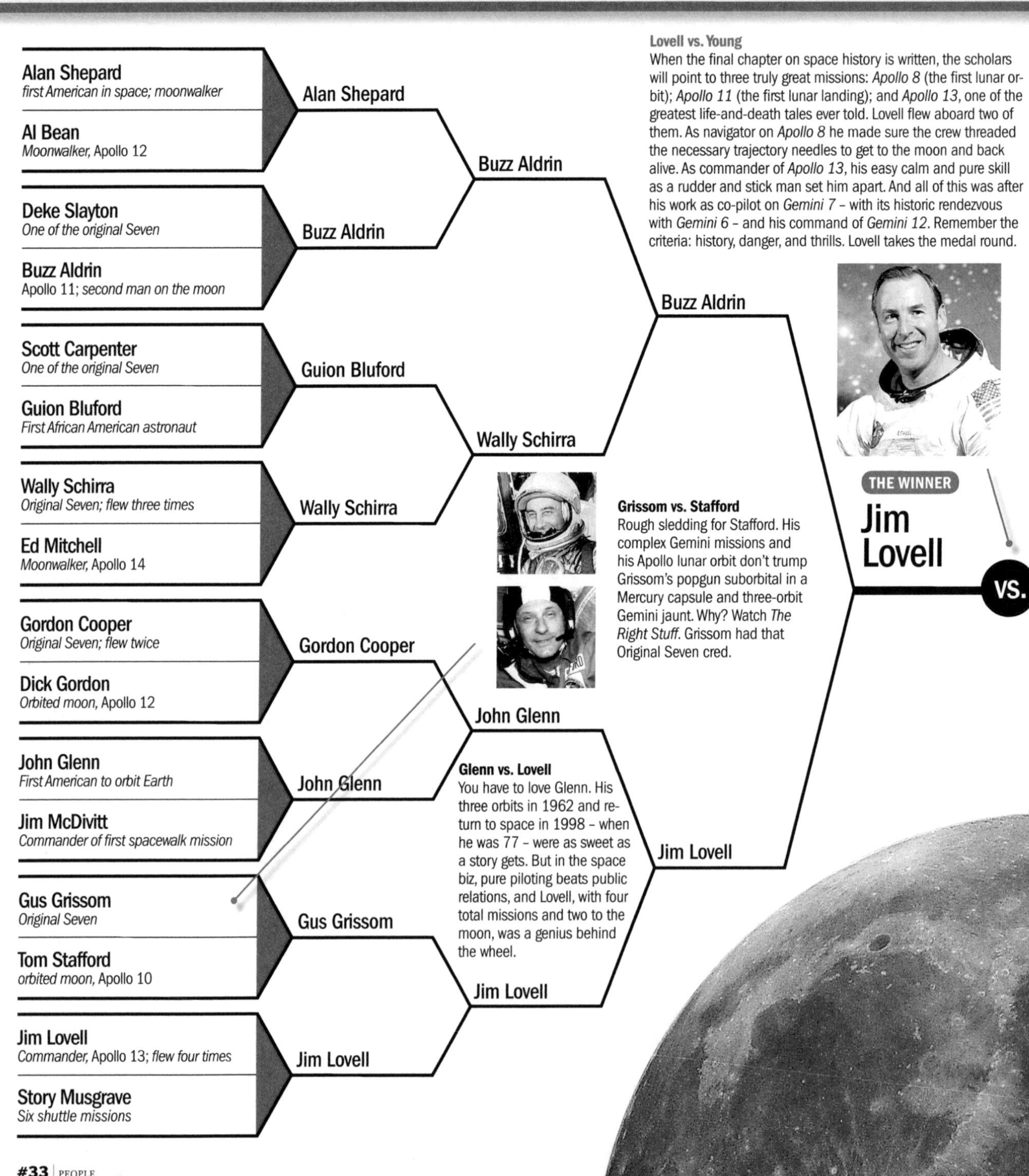

Alan Shepard
first American in space; moonwalker
Al Bean
Moonwalker, Apollo 12
Deke Slayton
One of the original Seven
Buzz Aldrin
Apollo 11; second man on the moon
Scott Carpenter
One of the original Seven
Guion Bluford
First African American astronaut
Wally Schirra
Original Seven; flew three times
Ed Mitchell
Moonwalker, Apollo 14
Gordon Cooper
Original Seven; flew twice
Dick Gordon
Orbited moon, Apollo 12
John Glenn
First American to orbit Earth
Jim McDivitt
Commander of first spacewalk mission
Gus Grissom
Original Seven
Tom Stafford
orbited moon, Apollo 10
Jim Lovell
Commander, Apollo 13; flew four times
Story Musgrave
Six shuttle missions
Alan Shepard
Buzz Aldrin
Guion Bluford
Wally Schirra
Gordon Cooper
John Glenn
Gus Grissom
Jim Lovell
Buzz Aldrin
Wally Schirra
John Glenn
Jim Lovell
Buzz Aldrin
Jim Lovell
THE WINNER
Jim Lovell
VS.

Lovell vs. Young

When the final chapter on space history is written, the scholars will point to three truly great missions: *Apollo 8* (the first lunar orbit); *Apollo 11* (the first lunar landing); and *Apollo 13*, one of the greatest life-and-death tales ever told. Lovell flew aboard two of them. As navigator on *Apollo 8* he made sure the crew threaded the necessary trajectory needles to get to the moon and back alive. As commander of *Apollo 13*, his easy calm and pure skill as a rudder and stick man set him apart. And all of this was after his work as co-pilot on *Gemini 7* – with its historic rendezvous with *Gemini 6* – and his command of *Gemini 12*. Remember the criteria: history, danger, and thrills. Lovell takes the medal round.

Grissom vs. Stafford

Rough sledding for Stafford. His complex Gemini missions and his Apollo lunar orbit don't trump Grissom's popgun suborbital in a Mercury capsule and three-orbit Gemini jaunt. Why? Watch *The Right Stuff*. Grissom had that Original Seven cred.

Glenn vs. Lovell

You have to love Glenn. His three orbits in 1962 and return to space in 1998 – when he was 77 – were as sweet as a story gets. But in the space biz, pure piloting beats public relations, and Lovell, with four total missions and two to the moon, was a genius behind the wheel.

AN UNFAIR BRACKET, SINCE THERE SHOULD BE JUST TWO SEEDS: people with the moxie to go into space and all of the rest of us. But we're starting with 32 slots and once you send out the invitations to the tournament, how do you compare guys who flew to the moon twice with a man who flew aboard a temperamental ship like the space shuttle half a dozen times and survived all six trips? What about the first man to walk in space versus the first woman to break into the hard-drinking, fast-driving, crotch-grabbing boys' club? The winner should be the astronaut who makes history, survives danger – and thrills us down to our last nerve ending.

Armstrong vs. Collins
A lot of talent in Round 1 means tough pairings. Collins could have made it deep into the competition, but for the bad luck of winding up against crewmate Armstrong. A moonwalker trumps the guy they left behind to mind the store in lunar orbit.

Armstrong vs. Young
The first man on the moon doesn't make it out of the second round? No, sir. Six missions beats two, and two lunar trips beat one. Armstrong's a hero. Young was an institution.

Young vs. Scott
Mano a mano between two giants. Scott flew three times, nearly buying the farm on *Gemini 8* and flying his LEM through lunar mountains on *Apollo 15*. But Young's longevity (including two shuttle trips) gives him the edge.

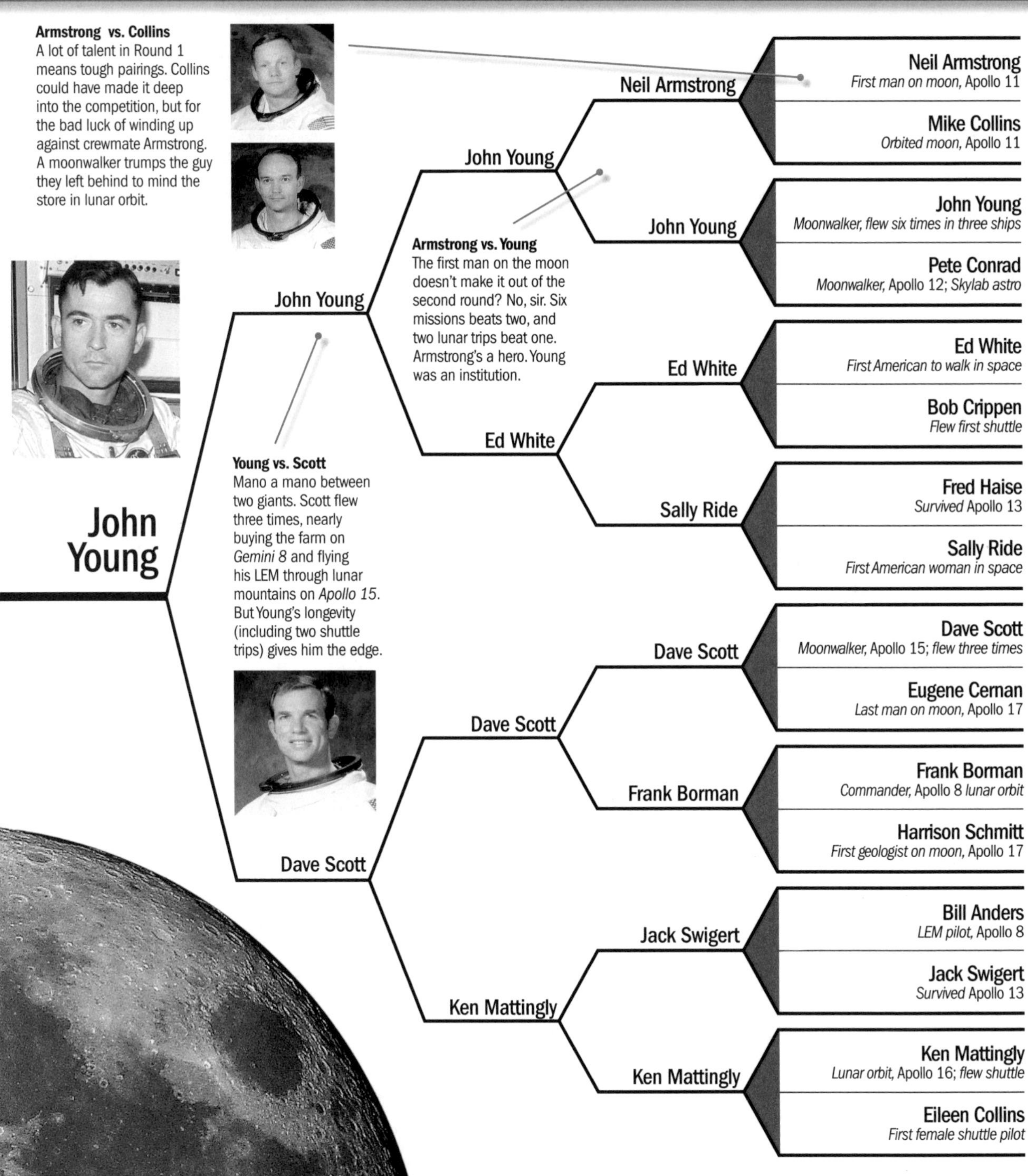

John Young
John Young
Dave Scott
John Young
Ed White
Dave Scott
Ken Mattingly
Neil Armstrong
John Young
Ed White
Sally Ride
Dave Scott
Frank Borman
Jack Swigert
Ken Mattingly
Neil Armstrong
First man on moon, Apollo 11
Mike Collins
Orbited moon, Apollo 11
John Young
Moonwalker, flew six times in three ships
Pete Conrad
Moonwalker, Apollo 12; Skylab astro
Ed White
First American to walk in space
Bob Crippen
Flew first shuttle
Fred Haise
Survived Apollo 13
Sally Ride
First American woman in space
Dave Scott
Moonwalker, Apollo 15; flew three times
Eugene Cernan
Last man on moon, Apollo 17
Frank Borman
Commander, Apollo 8 lunar orbit
Harrison Schmitt
First geologist on moon, Apollo 17
Bill Anders
LEM pilot, Apollo 8
Jack Swigert
Survived Apollo 13
Ken Mattingly
Lunar orbit, Apollo 16; flew shuttle
Eileen Collins
First female shuttle pilot

Supermodels

By Crystal Renn and Marjorie Ingall

Crystal Renn, the leading plus-size model in America, has written with Marjorie Ingall the memoir, *Hungry: A Woman's Story of Appetite, Ambition, and the Embrace of Curves.*

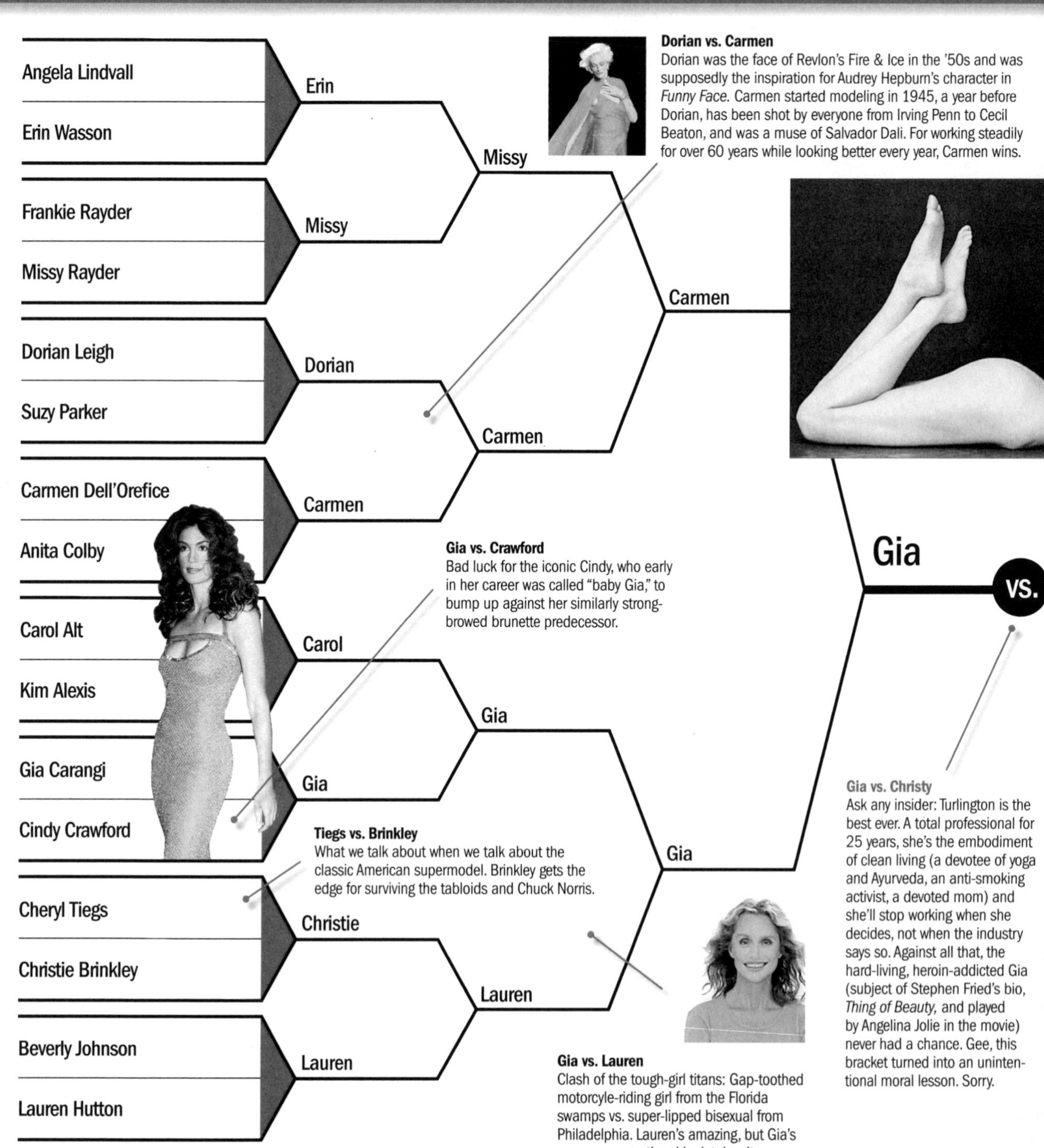

Angela Lindvall
Erin Wasson
Frankie Rayder
Missy Rayder
Dorian Leigh
Suzy Parker
Carmen Dell'Orefice
Anita Colby
Carol Alt
Kim Alexis
Gia Carangi
Cindy Crawford
Cheryl Tiegs
Christie Brinkley
Beverly Johnson
Lauren Hutton
Erin
Missy
Dorian
Carmen
Carol
Gia
Christie
Lauren
Missy
Carmen
Gia
Lauren
Carmen
Gia
Gia
vs.

Dorian vs. Carmen
Dorian was the face of Revlon's Fire & Ice in the '50s and was supposedly the inspiration for Audrey Hepburn's character in *Funny Face*. Carmen started modeling in 1945, a year before Dorian, has been shot by everyone from Irving Penn to Cecil Beaton, and was a muse of Salvador Dali. For working steadily for over 60 years while looking better every year, Carmen wins.

Gia vs. Crawford
Bad luck for the iconic Cindy, who early in her career was called "baby Gia," to bump up against her similarly strong-browed brunette predecessor.

Tiegs vs. Brinkley
What we talk about when we talk about the classic American supermodel. Brinkley gets the edge for surviving the tabloids and Chuck Norris.

Gia vs. Lauren
Clash of the tough-girl titans: Gap-toothed motorcyle-riding girl from the Florida swamps vs. super-lipped bisexual from Philadelphia. Lauren's amazing, but Gia's more unconventional look takes it.

Gia vs. Christy
Ask any insider: Turlington is the best ever. A total professional for 25 years, she's the embodiment of clean living (a devotee of yoga and Ayurveda, an anti-smoking activist, a devoted mom) and she'll stop working when she decides, not when the industry says so. Against all that, the hard-living, heroin-addicted Gia (subject of Stephen Fried's bio, *Thing of Beauty,* and played by Angelina Jolie in the movie) never had a chance. Gee, this bracket turned into an unintentional moral lesson. Sorry.

THE STEREOTYPICAL AMERICAN MODEL is a toothy sun-baked hair-tossing blonde. But we're actually a diverse lot: different races, ethnicities, body types, vibes. In the first round of this battle for foxy supremacy, we paired like with like: sisters Missy & Frankie and Dorian & Suzy; tragic contemporaries Margaux & Tina; obsessive-fan-faves Phoebe & Dovima; Victoria's Secret va-va-voomsters Jill & Tyra. We also pitted stars of the same era against each other (we're catty that way). Actresses who put their mugs on fashion mags were not invited.

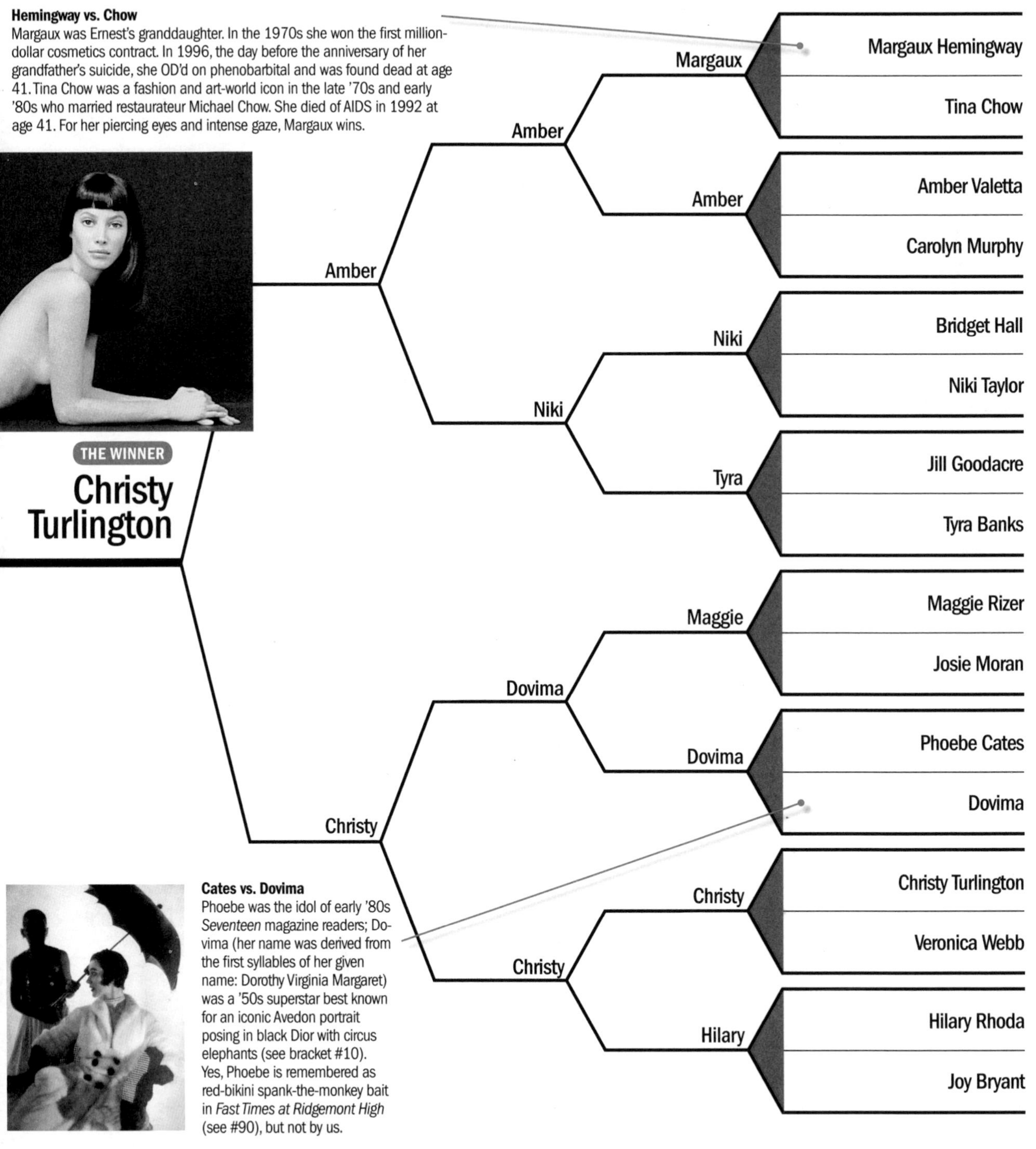

Margaux Hemingway
Tina Chow
Amber Valetta
Carolyn Murphy
Bridget Hall
Niki Taylor
Jill Goodacre
Tyra Banks
Maggie Rizer
Josie Moran
Phoebe Cates
Dovima
Christy Turlington
Veronica Webb
Hilary Rhoda
Joy Bryant
Margaux
Amber
Niki
Tyra
Maggie
Dovima
Christy
Hilary
Amber
Niki
Dovima
Christy
Amber
Christy
THE WINNER
Christy Turlington

Hemingway vs. Chow
Margaux was Ernest's granddaughter. In the 1970s she won the first million-dollar cosmetics contract. In 1996, the day before the anniversary of her grandfather's suicide, she OD'd on phenobarbital and was found dead at age 41. Tina Chow was a fashion and art-world icon in the late '70s and early '80s who married restaurateur Michael Chow. She died of AIDS in 1992 at age 41. For her piercing eyes and intense gaze, Margaux wins.

Cates vs. Dovima
Phoebe was the idol of early '80s *Seventeen* magazine readers; Dovima (her name was derived from the first syllables of her given name: Dorothy Virginia Margaret) was a '50s superstar best known for an iconic Avedon portrait posing in black Dior with circus elephants (see bracket #10). Yes, Phoebe is remembered as red-bikini spank-the-monkey bait in *Fast Times at Ridgemont High* (see #90), but not by us.

Celebrity Mugshots

By Willie Geist

Willie Geist is the co-host of MSNBC's *Morning Joe* and the host of *Zeitgeist*, a satirical video blog on MSNBC.com. There are no known mugshots of him, but he is wanted in several states across the Southwest. He has vowed never to be taken alive.

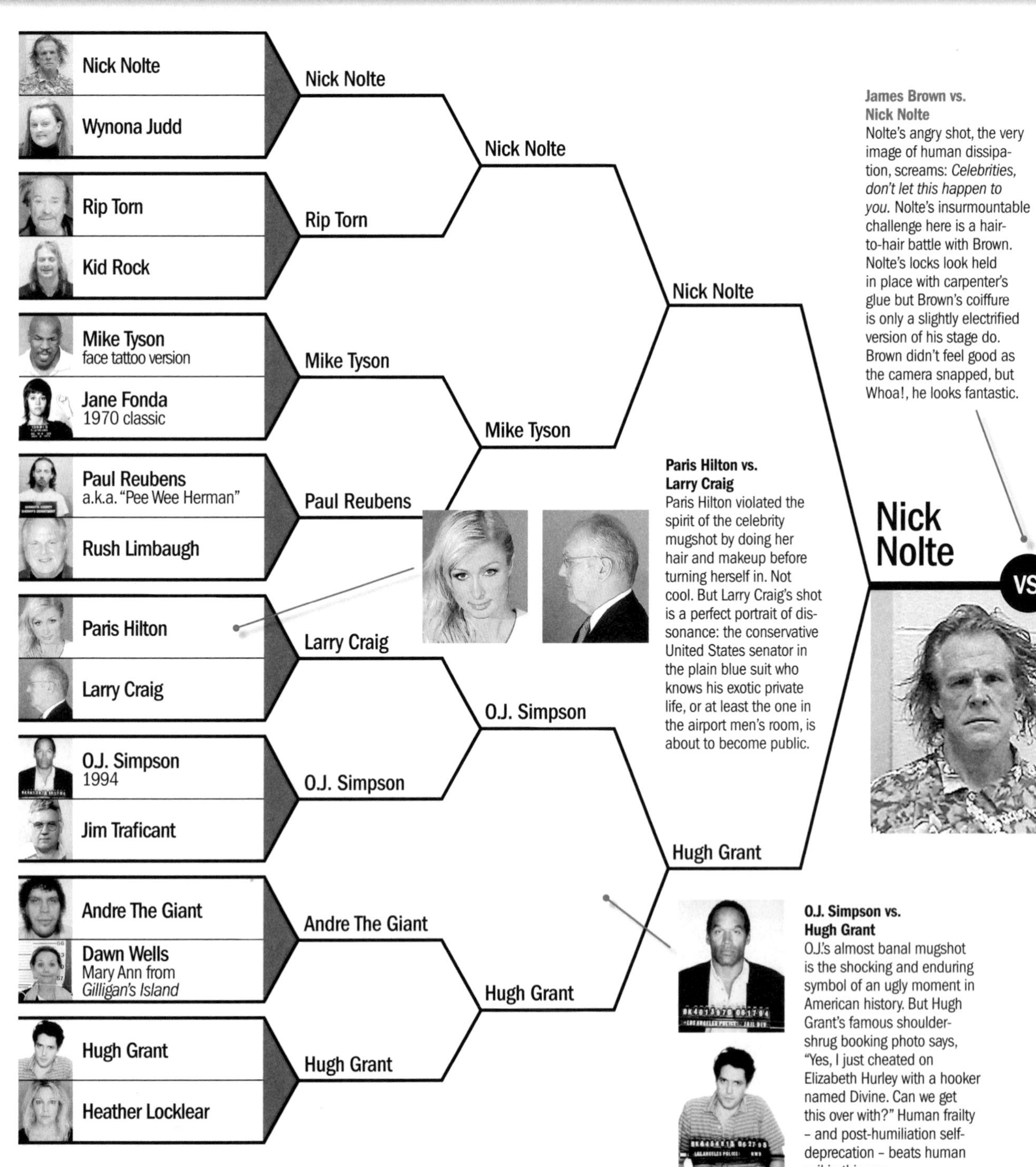

Nick Nolte
Wynona Judd
Rip Torn
Kid Rock
Mike Tyson
face tattoo version
Jane Fonda
1970 classic
Paul Reubens
a.k.a. "Pee Wee Herman"
Rush Limbaugh
Paris Hilton
Larry Craig
O.J. Simpson
1994
Jim Traficant
Andre The Giant
Dawn Wells
Mary Ann from *Gilligan's Island*
Hugh Grant
Heather Locklear
Nick Nolte
Rip Torn
Mike Tyson
Paul Reubens
Larry Craig
O.J. Simpson
Andre The Giant
Hugh Grant
Nick Nolte
Mike Tyson
O.J. Simpson
Hugh Grant
Nick Nolte
Hugh Grant
Nick Nolte
VS.

James Brown vs. Nick Nolte
Nolte's angry shot, the very image of human dissipation, screams: *Celebrities, don't let this happen to you.* Nolte's insurmountable challenge here is a hair-to-hair battle with Brown. Nolte's locks look held in place with carpenter's glue but Brown's coiffure is only a slightly electrified version of his stage do. Brown didn't feel good as the camera snapped, but Whoa!, he looks fantastic.

Paris Hilton vs. Larry Craig
Paris Hilton violated the spirit of the celebrity mugshot by doing her hair and makeup before turning herself in. Not cool. But Larry Craig's shot is a perfect portrait of dissonance: the conservative United States senator in the plain blue suit who knows his exotic private life, or at least the one in the airport men's room, is about to become public.

O.J. Simpson vs. Hugh Grant
O.J.'s almost banal mugshot is the shocking and enduring symbol of an ugly moment in American history. But Hugh Grant's famous shoulder-shrug booking photo says, "Yes, I just cheated on Elizabeth Hurley with a hooker named Divine. Can we get this over with?" Human frailty – and post-humiliation self-deprecation – beats human evil in this one.

CELEBRITIES EXIST IN A SCRIPTED, AIR-BRUSHED PARALLEL UNIVERSE where every image of them is controlled. The beauty of their mugshots is the absolute loss of control. They can't summon Annie Leibovitz for their shoots or demand a second take. Instead, they're at the mercy of fluorescent lights, cinderblock backdrops, and the officer working the night shift at the Santa Monica Police Department. A classic mugshot is the inartful result of bad photography, the absence of hairstylists, and a great backstory.

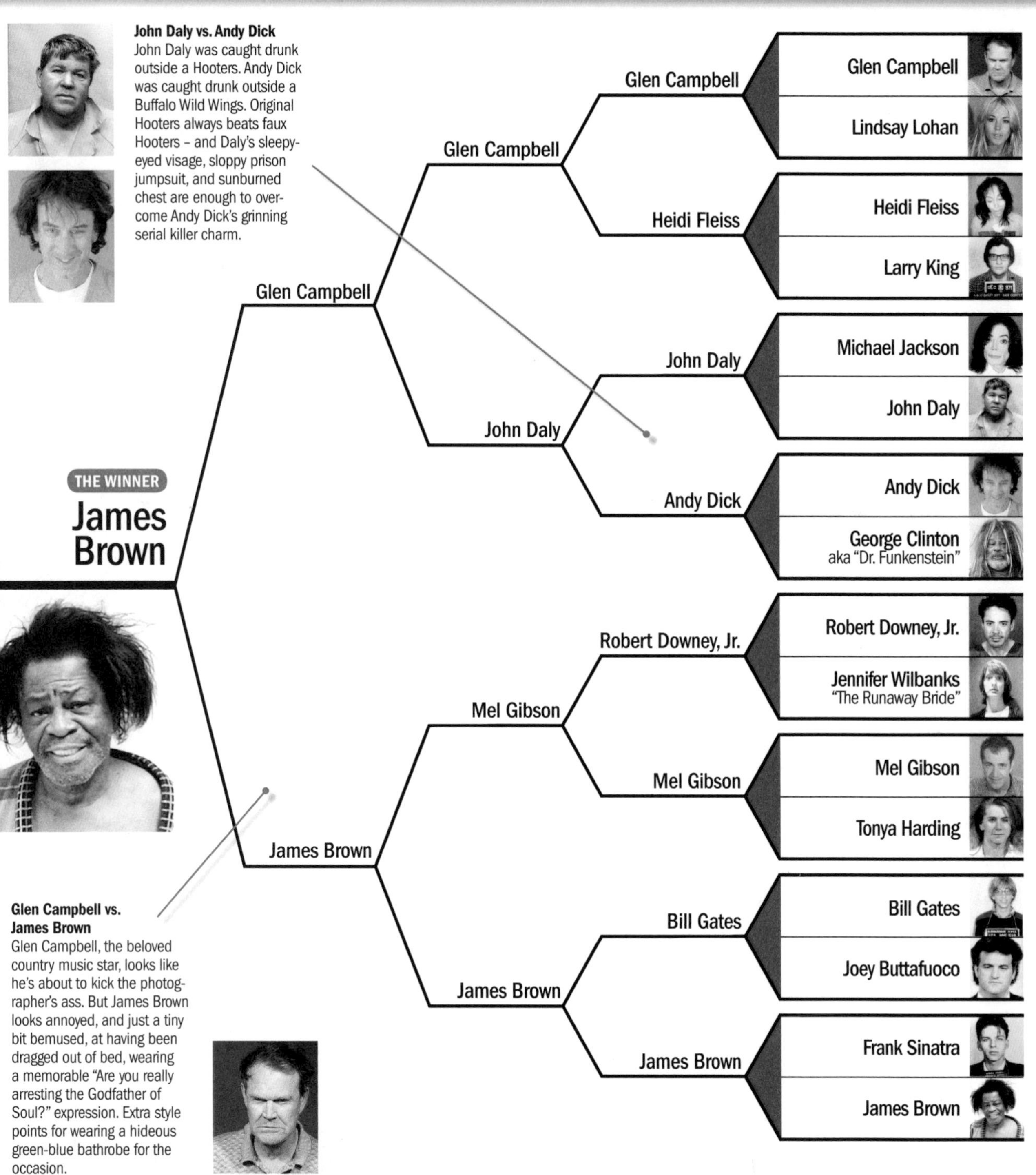

Glen Campbell
Lindsay Lohan
Heidi Fleiss
Larry King
Michael Jackson
John Daly
Andy Dick
George Clinton
aka "Dr. Funkenstein"
Robert Downey, Jr.
Jennifer Wilbanks
"The Runaway Bride"
Mel Gibson
Tonya Harding
Bill Gates
Joey Buttafuoco
Frank Sinatra
James Brown
Glen Campbell
Heidi Fleiss
John Daly
Andy Dick
Robert Downey, Jr.
Mel Gibson
Bill Gates
James Brown
Glen Campbell
John Daly
Mel Gibson
James Brown
Glen Campbell
James Brown
THE WINNER
James Brown

John Daly vs. Andy Dick
John Daly was caught drunk outside a Hooters. Andy Dick was caught drunk outside a Buffalo Wild Wings. Original Hooters always beats faux Hooters – and Daly's sleepy-eyed visage, sloppy prison jumpsuit, and sunburned chest are enough to overcome Andy Dick's grinning serial killer charm.

Glen Campbell vs. James Brown
Glen Campbell, the beloved country music star, looks like he's about to kick the photographer's ass. But James Brown looks annoyed, and just a tiny bit bemused, at having been dragged out of bed, wearing a memorable "Are you really arresting the Godfather of Soul?" expression. Extra style points for wearing a hideous green-blue bathrobe for the occasion.

Mary

By Mary C. Curtis

Mary C. Curtis, a writer and editor based in Charlotte, N.C., was named after her grandmother Mary Cecelia. As a Catholic schoolgirl in Baltimore, she was convinced that every fourth girl at St. Pius V Elementary School was named Mary.

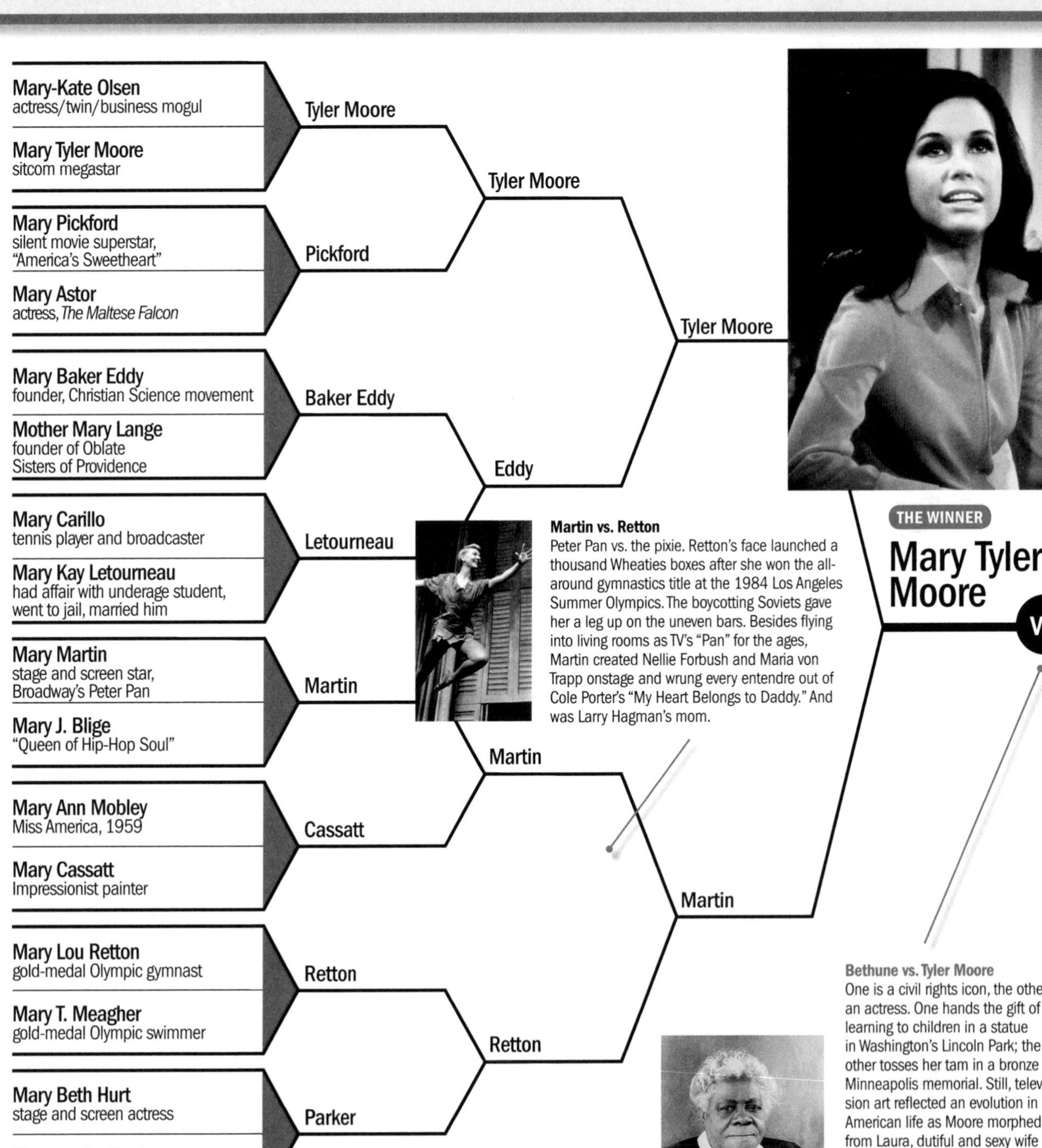

Mary-Kate Olsen
actress/twin/business mogul
Mary Tyler Moore
sitcom megastar
Mary Pickford
silent movie superstar, "America's Sweetheart"
Mary Astor
actress, *The Maltese Falcon*
Mary Baker Eddy
founder, Christian Science movement
Mother Mary Lange
founder of Oblate Sisters of Providence
Mary Carillo
tennis player and broadcaster
Mary Kay Letourneau
had affair with underage student, went to jail, married him
Mary Martin
stage and screen star, Broadway's Peter Pan
Mary J. Blige
"Queen of Hip-Hop Soul"
Mary Ann Mobley
Miss America, 1959
Mary Cassatt
Impressionist painter
Mary Lou Retton
gold-medal Olympic gymnast
Mary T. Meagher
gold-medal Olympic swimmer
Mary Beth Hurt
stage and screen actress
Mary-Louise Parker
Tony and Emmy-winning actress
Tyler Moore
Pickford
Baker Eddy
Letourneau
Martin
Cassatt
Retton
Parker
Tyler Moore
Eddy
Martin
Retton
Tyler Moore
Martin
THE WINNER
Mary Tyler Moore
VS.

Martin vs. Retton
Peter Pan vs. the pixie. Retton's face launched a thousand Wheaties boxes after she won the all-around gymnastics title at the 1984 Los Angeles Summer Olympics. The boycotting Soviets gave her a leg up on the uneven bars. Besides flying into living rooms as TV's "Pan" for the ages, Martin created Nellie Forbush and Maria von Trapp onstage and wrung every entendre out of Cole Porter's "My Heart Belongs to Daddy." And was Larry Hagman's mom.

Bethune vs. Tyler Moore
One is a civil rights icon, the other an actress. One hands the gift of learning to children in a statue in Washington's Lincoln Park; the other tosses her tam in a bronze Minneapolis memorial. Still, television art reflected an evolution in American life as Moore morphed from Laura, dutiful and sexy wife of Rob Petrie, sitcom stand-ins for Jack and Jackie Kennedy, to Mary Richards, the single career woman. And she really did turn the world on with her smile.

"PLAIN AS ANY NAME CAN BE," George M. Cohan called Mary, even as the all-American entertainer was moved to immortalize the ordinary name in song. "When her name is Mary, there is no falseness there," Cohan wrote. The name is deceptively simple, so simple many people think it needs accompaniment, which explains Mary Lou, Mary Jane, and Mary Ann. Mary is an ocean of classic calm in a sea of churning Britneys and Lindsays. Deeds noble and notorious have hidden behind its mask of sweetness. A "grand old name," indeed.

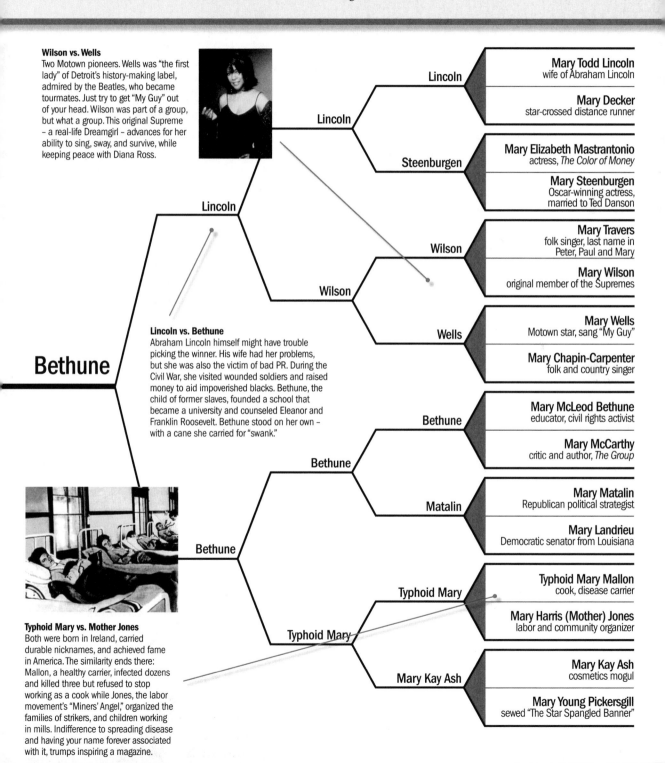

Wilson vs. Wells
Two Motown pioneers. Wells was "the first lady" of Detroit's history-making label, admired by the Beatles, who became tourmates. Just try to get "My Guy" out of your head. Wilson was part of a group, but what a group. This original Supreme – a real-life Dreamgirl – advances for her ability to sing, sway, and survive, while keeping peace with Diana Ross.

Lincoln vs. Bethune
Abraham Lincoln himself might have trouble picking the winner. His wife had her problems, but she was also the victim of bad PR. During the Civil War, she visited wounded soldiers and raised money to aid impoverished blacks. Bethune, the child of former slaves, founded a school that became a university and counseled Eleanor and Franklin Roosevelt. Bethune stood on her own – with a cane she carried for "swank."

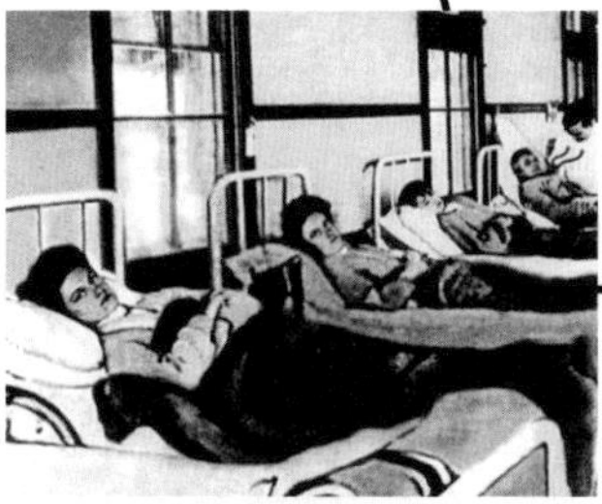

Typhoid Mary vs. Mother Jones
Both were born in Ireland, carried durable nicknames, and achieved fame in America. The similarity ends there: Mallon, a healthy carrier, infected dozens and killed three but refused to stop working as a cook while Jones, the labor movement's "Miners' Angel," organized the families of strikers, and children working in mills. Indifference to spreading disease and having your name forever associated with it, trumps inspiring a magazine.

Bethune

Lincoln / Bethune

Lincoln / Wilson / Bethune / Typhoid Mary

Lincoln / Steenburgen / Wilson / Wells / Bethune / Matalin / Typhoid Mary / Mary Kay Ash

Mary Todd Lincoln
wife of Abraham Lincoln

Mary Decker
star-crossed distance runner

Mary Elizabeth Mastrantonio
actress, *The Color of Money*

Mary Steenburgen
Oscar-winning actress, married to Ted Danson

Mary Travers
folk singer, last name in Peter, Paul and Mary

Mary Wilson
original member of the Supremes

Mary Wells
Motown star, sang "My Guy"

Mary Chapin-Carpenter
folk and country singer

Mary McLeod Bethune
educator, civil rights activist

Mary McCarthy
critic and author, *The Group*

Mary Matalin
Republican political strategist

Mary Landrieu
Democratic senator from Louisiana

Typhoid Mary Mallon
cook, disease carrier

Mary Harris (Mother) Jones
labor and community organizer

Mary Kay Ash
cosmetics mogul

Mary Young Pickersgill
sewed "The Star Spangled Banner"

Bald Guys

By Richard Sandomir

Richard Sandomir wrote a memoir of his long-faded hairline, *Bald Like Me: The Hair-Raising Adventures of Baldman*. He was stimulated to shave his Larry Fine-like fringe of unkempt hair by Charles Barkley, who told him, "Brother, what you got ain't working for you." Barkley's intervention exempts him from this competition.

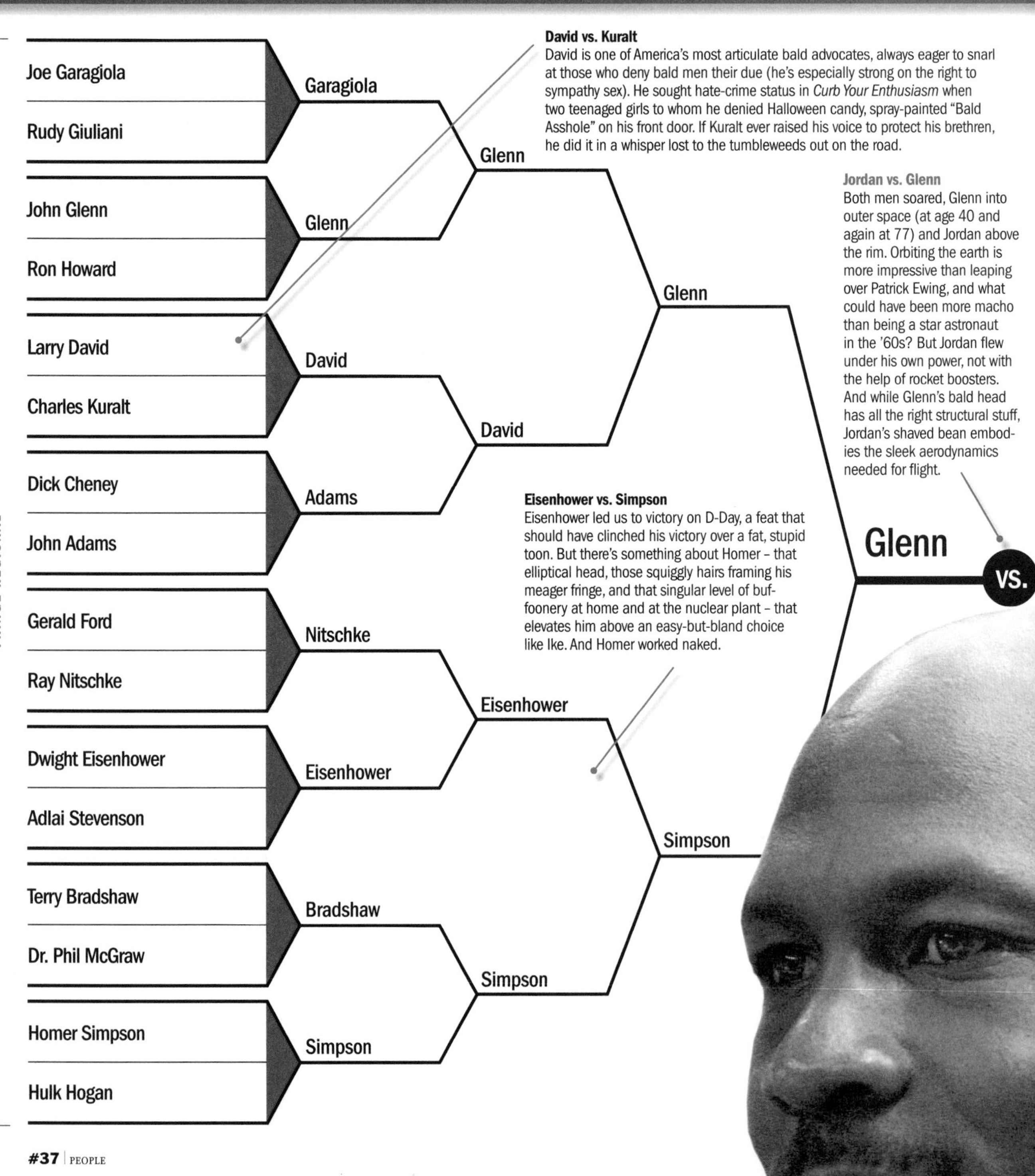

FRINGE REGIONAL
Joe Garagiola
Rudy Giuliani
John Glenn
Ron Howard
Larry David
Charles Kuralt
Dick Cheney
John Adams
Gerald Ford
Ray Nitschke
Dwight Eisenhower
Adlai Stevenson
Terry Bradshaw
Dr. Phil McGraw
Homer Simpson
Hulk Hogan
Garagiola
Glenn
David
Adams
Nitschke
Eisenhower
Bradshaw
Simpson
Glenn
David
Eisenhower
Simpson
Glenn
Simpson
Glenn
VS.

David vs. Kuralt
David is one of America's most articulate bald advocates, always eager to snarl at those who deny bald men their due (he's especially strong on the right to sympathy sex). He sought hate-crime status in *Curb Your Enthusiasm* when two teenaged girls to whom he denied Halloween candy, spray-painted "Bald Asshole" on his front door. If Kuralt ever raised his voice to protect his brethren, he did it in a whisper lost to the tumbleweeds out on the road.

Jordan vs. Glenn
Both men soared, Glenn into outer space (at age 40 and again at 77) and Jordan above the rim. Orbiting the earth is more impressive than leaping over Patrick Ewing, and what could have been more macho than being a star astronaut in the '60s? But Jordan flew under his own power, not with the help of rocket boosters. And while Glenn's bald head has all the right structural stuff, Jordan's shaved bean embodies the sleek aerodynamics needed for flight.

Eisenhower vs. Simpson
Eisenhower led us to victory on D-Day, a feat that should have clinched his victory over a fat, stupid toon. But there's something about Homer – that elliptical head, those squiggly hairs framing his meager fringe, and that singular level of buffoonery at home and at the nuclear plant – that elevates him above an easy-but-bland choice like Ike. And Homer worked naked.

WHO IS THE TRUE BALDIE: the one whose hair loss is genetically programmed or the one who shears all the hair from his head? The debate will continue unabated as long as men lose their hair or see a benefit in shaving it all off. In this celebration of both species of homo baldus, we derived spiritual guidance from the words of the fringe-haired dyspeptic, Larry David, who said: "Anyone can be confident with a full head of hair. But a confident bald man – there's your diamond in the rough."

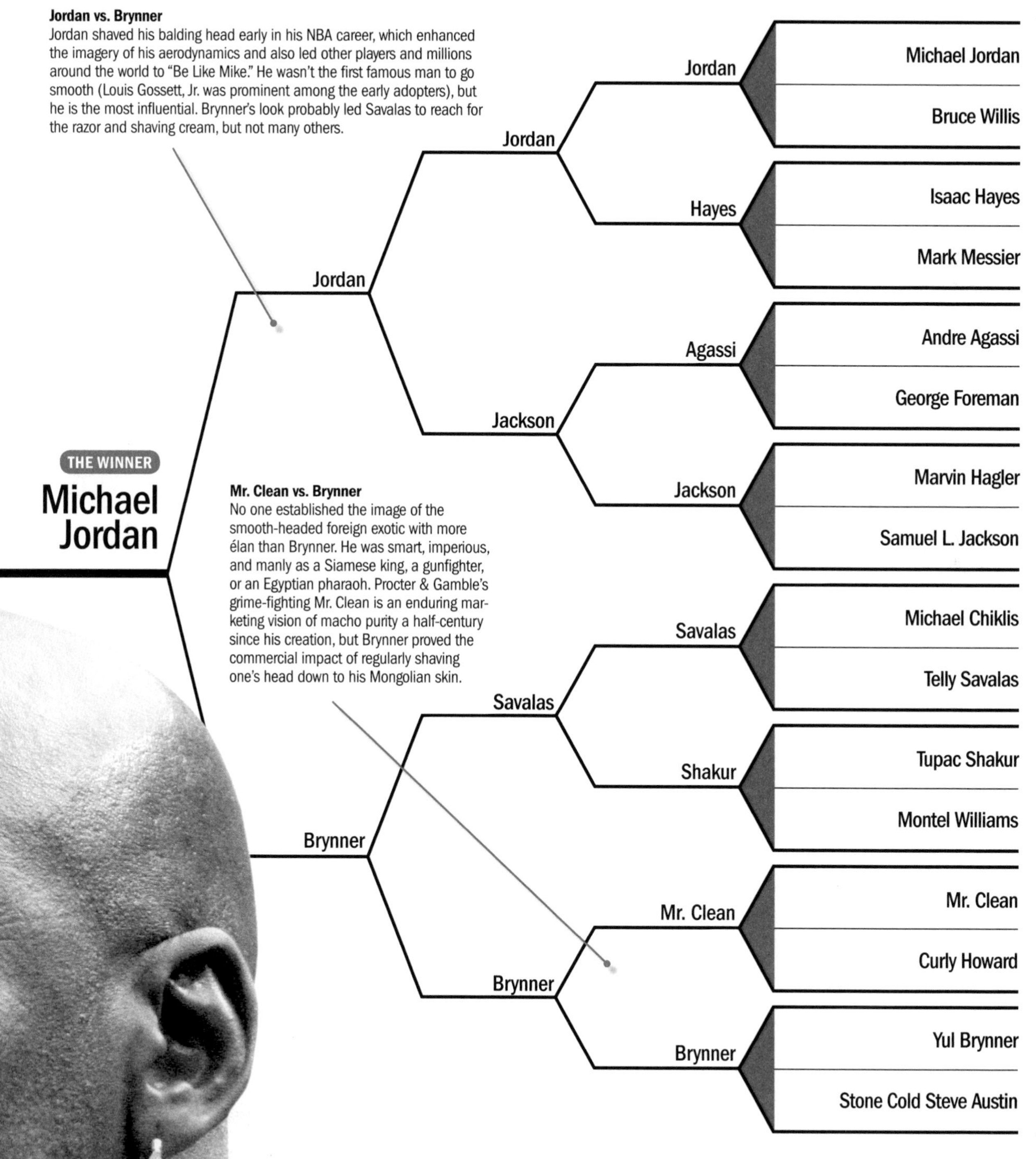

Jordan vs. Brynner
Jordan shaved his balding head early in his NBA career, which enhanced the imagery of his aerodynamics and also led other players and millions around the world to "Be Like Mike." He wasn't the first famous man to go smooth (Louis Gossett, Jr. was prominent among the early adopters), but he is the most influential. Brynner's look probably led Savalas to reach for the razor and shaving cream, but not many others.
Mr. Clean vs. Brynner
No one established the image of the smooth-headed foreign exotic with more élan than Brynner. He was smart, imperious, and manly as a Siamese king, a gunfighter, or an Egyptian pharaoh. Procter & Gamble's grime-fighting Mr. Clean is an enduring marketing vision of macho purity a half-century since his creation, but Brynner proved the commercial impact of regularly shaving one's head down to his Mongolian skin.
THE WINNER
Michael Jordan
Jordan
Brynner
Jordan
Jackson
Savalas
Brynner
Jordan
Hayes
Agassi
Jackson
Savalas
Shakur
Mr. Clean
Brynner
Michael Jordan
Bruce Willis
Isaac Hayes
Mark Messier
Andre Agassi
George Foreman
Marvin Hagler
Samuel L. Jackson
Michael Chiklis
Telly Savalas
Tupac Shakur
Montel Williams
Mr. Clean
Curly Howard
Yul Brynner
Stone Cold Steve Austin
SHAVED-HEAD REGIONAL

Geniuses

By Peter Richmond

Author and journalist Peter Richmond has interviewed hundreds of famous people, including a few geniuse But he's always found that the guy sitting next to at him at the bar in a Ruby Tuesday's just off the interstate next to the Marriott Courtyard is more interesting. Then, he's no genius. For which he is eternally grateful.

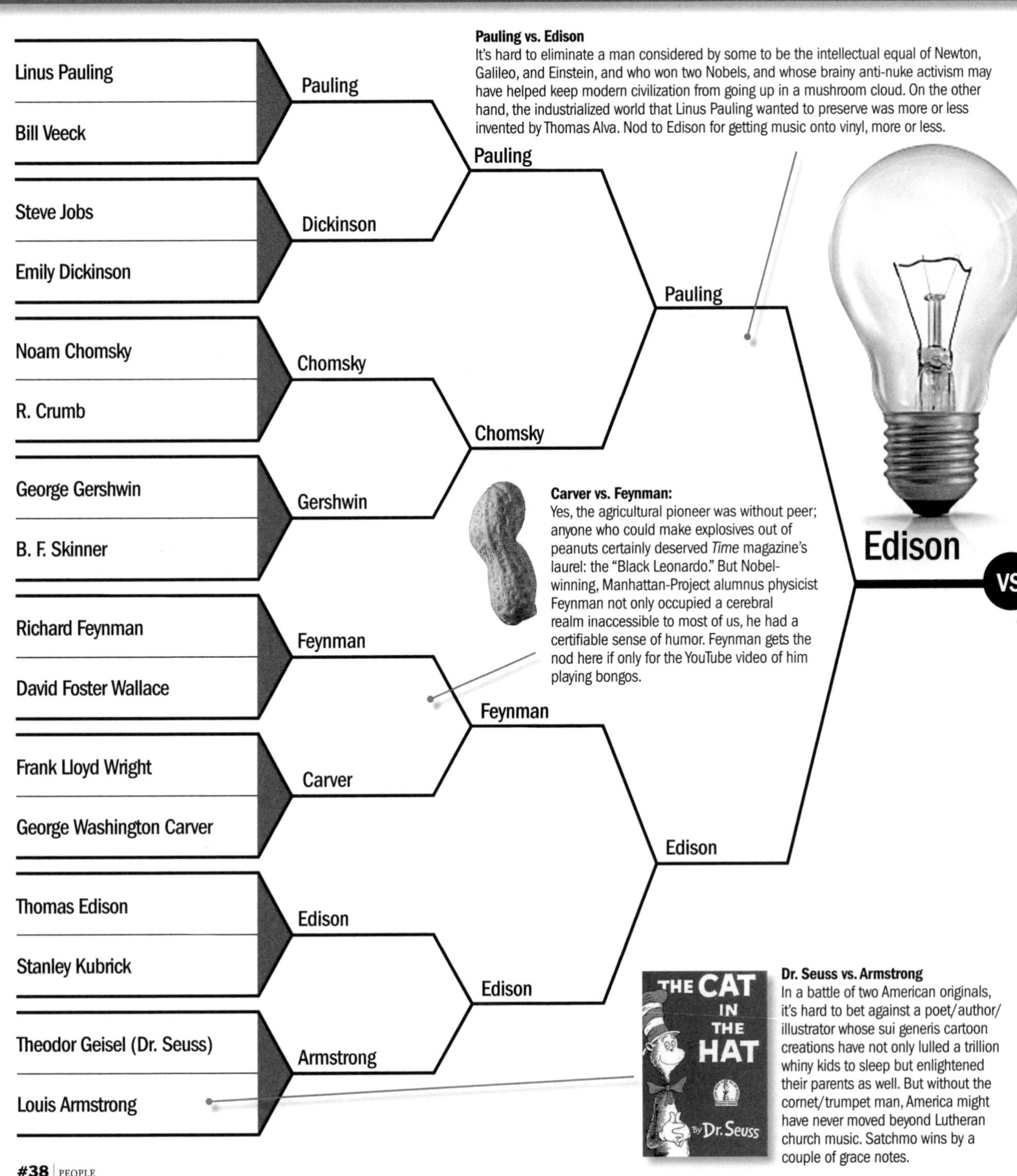

Linus Pauling
Bill Veeck
Steve Jobs
Emily Dickinson
Noam Chomsky
R. Crumb
George Gershwin
B. F. Skinner
Richard Feynman
David Foster Wallace
Frank Lloyd Wright
George Washington Carver
Thomas Edison
Stanley Kubrick
Theodor Geisel (Dr. Seuss)
Louis Armstrong
Pauling
Dickinson
Chomsky
Gershwin
Feynman
Carver
Edison
Armstrong
Pauling
Chomsky
Feynman
Edison
Pauling
Edison
Edison
VS.
THE CAT IN THE HAT
By Dr. Seuss

Pauling vs. Edison
It's hard to eliminate a man considered by some to be the intellectual equal of Newton, Galileo, and Einstein, and who won two Nobels, and whose brainy anti-nuke activism may have helped keep modern civilization from going up in a mushroom cloud. On the other hand, the industrialized world that Linus Pauling wanted to preserve was more or less invented by Thomas Alva. Nod to Edison for getting music onto vinyl, more or less.

Carver vs. Feynman:
Yes, the agricultural pioneer was without peer; anyone who could make explosives out of peanuts certainly deserved *Time* magazine's laurel: the "Black Leonardo." But Nobel-winning, Manhattan-Project alumnus physicist Feynman not only occupied a cerebral realm inaccessible to most of us, he had a certifiable sense of humor. Feynman gets the nod here if only for the YouTube video of him playing bongos.

Dr. Seuss vs. Armstrong
In a battle of two American originals, it's hard to bet against a poet/author/illustrator whose sui generis cartoon creations have not only lulled a trillion whiny kids to sleep but enlightened their parents as well. But without the cornet/trumpet man, America might have never moved beyond Lutheran church music. Satchmo wins by a couple of grace notes.

IN PICTURES, THEIR HAIR IS NEVER QUITE RIGHT and they have a weird look in their eyes. But they fascinate us in a way that the rich, beautiful, and otherwise famous cannot. After all: any of us might get rich or famous; none of us will ever be geniuses. But what, exactly, makes them geniuses? I.Q.? Historical impact? Wisdom? Talent? Self-promotional ability? I defer to Supreme Court Justice Potter Stewart's definition of obscenity in trying to define genius: "I know it when I see it." Or hear it. Or read it. Or witness it. Or, in the end, feel it in my gut.

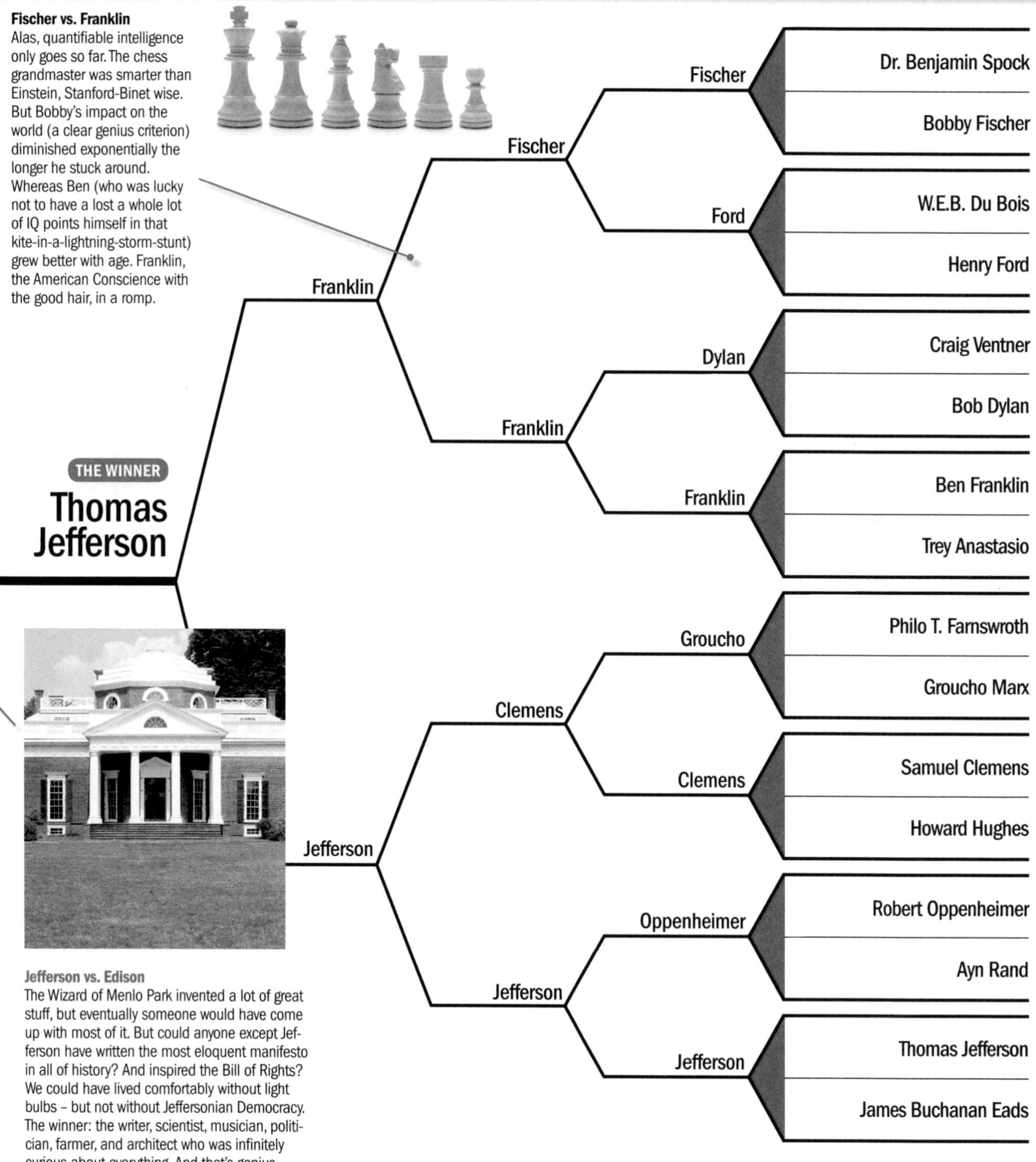
Dr. Benjamin Spock
Bobby Fischer
W.E.B. Du Bois
Henry Ford
Craig Ventner
Bob Dylan
Ben Franklin
Trey Anastasio
Philo T. Farnswroth
Groucho Marx
Samuel Clemens
Howard Hughes
Robert Oppenheimer
Ayn Rand
Thomas Jefferson
James Buchanan Eads
Fischer
Ford
Dylan
Franklin
Groucho
Clemens
Oppenheimer
Jefferson
Fischer
Franklin
Clemens
Jefferson
Franklin
Jefferson
THE WINNER
Thomas Jefferson

Fischer vs. Franklin
Alas, quantifiable intelligence only goes so far. The chess grandmaster was smarter than Einstein, Stanford-Binet wise. But Bobby's impact on the world (a clear genius criterion) diminished exponentially the longer he stuck around. Whereas Ben (who was lucky not to have a lost a whole lot of IQ points himself in that kite-in-a-lightning-storm-stunt) grew better with age. Franklin, the American Conscience with the good hair, in a romp.

Jefferson vs. Edison
The Wizard of Menlo Park invented a lot of great stuff, but eventually someone would have come up with most of it. But could anyone except Jefferson have written the most eloquent manifesto in all of history? And inspired the Bill of Rights? We could have lived comfortably without light bulbs – but not without Jeffersonian Democracy. The winner: the writer, scientist, musician, politician, farmer, and architect who was infinitely curious about everything. And that's genius.

Celebrity Baby Names

By Linda Rosenkrantz and Pamela Redmond Satran

Linda Rosenkrantz and Pamela Redmond Satran's shared obsession with names has led to a website, nameberry.com, and 10 bestselling books on the subject, including *Beyond Jennifer and Jason* and *The Baby Name Bible.*

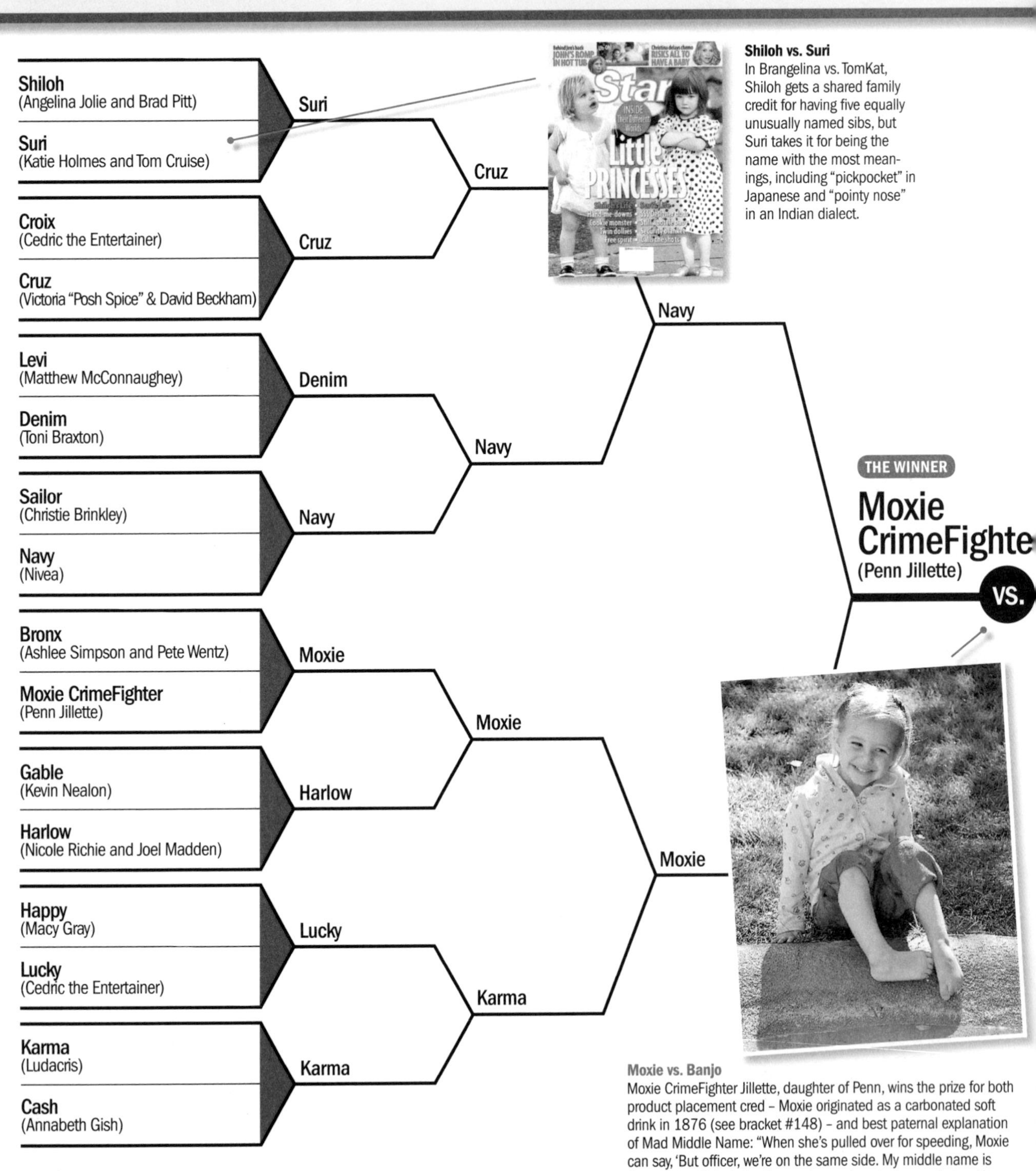
Shiloh
(Angelina Jolie and Brad Pitt)
Suri
(Katie Holmes and Tom Cruise)
Croix
(Cedric the Entertainer)
Cruz
(Victoria "Posh Spice" & David Beckham)
Levi
(Matthew McConnaughey)
Denim
(Toni Braxton)
Sailor
(Christie Brinkley)
Navy
(Nivea)
Bronx
(Ashlee Simpson and Pete Wentz)
Moxie CrimeFighter
(Penn Jillette)
Gable
(Kevin Nealon)
Harlow
(Nicole Richie and Joel Madden)
Happy
(Macy Gray)
Lucky
(Cedric the Entertainer)
Karma
(Ludacris)
Cash
(Annabeth Gish)
Suri
Cruz
Denim
Navy
Moxie
Harlow
Lucky
Karma
Cruz
Navy
Moxie
Karma
Navy
Moxie
Star
Little PRINCESSES
THE WINNER
Moxie CrimeFighte
(Penn Jillette)
VS.

Shiloh vs. Suri
In Brangelina vs. TomKat, Shiloh gets a shared family credit for having five equally unusually named sibs, but Suri takes it for being the name with the most meanings, including "pickpocket" in Japanese and "pointy nose" in an Indian dialect.

Moxie vs. Banjo
Moxie CrimeFighter Jillette, daughter of Penn, wins the prize for both product placement cred – Moxie originated as a carbonated soft drink in 1876 (see bracket #148) – and best paternal explanation of Mad Middle Name: "When she's pulled over for speeding, Moxie can say, 'But officer, we're on the same side. My middle name is CrimeFighter.'" And also for, you know, sheer baby-naming moxie.

THE COMPETITION AMONG CELEBS for most original (a.k.a. weirdest) baby name is as fierce as the Tour de France, with contenders constantly looking over their shoulders to make sure no other parent gets to their name first. Extra points for an equally outré middle name, equally iconoclastic sibling names, staying unique but creating a trend, and engendering a tsunami of outraged publicity

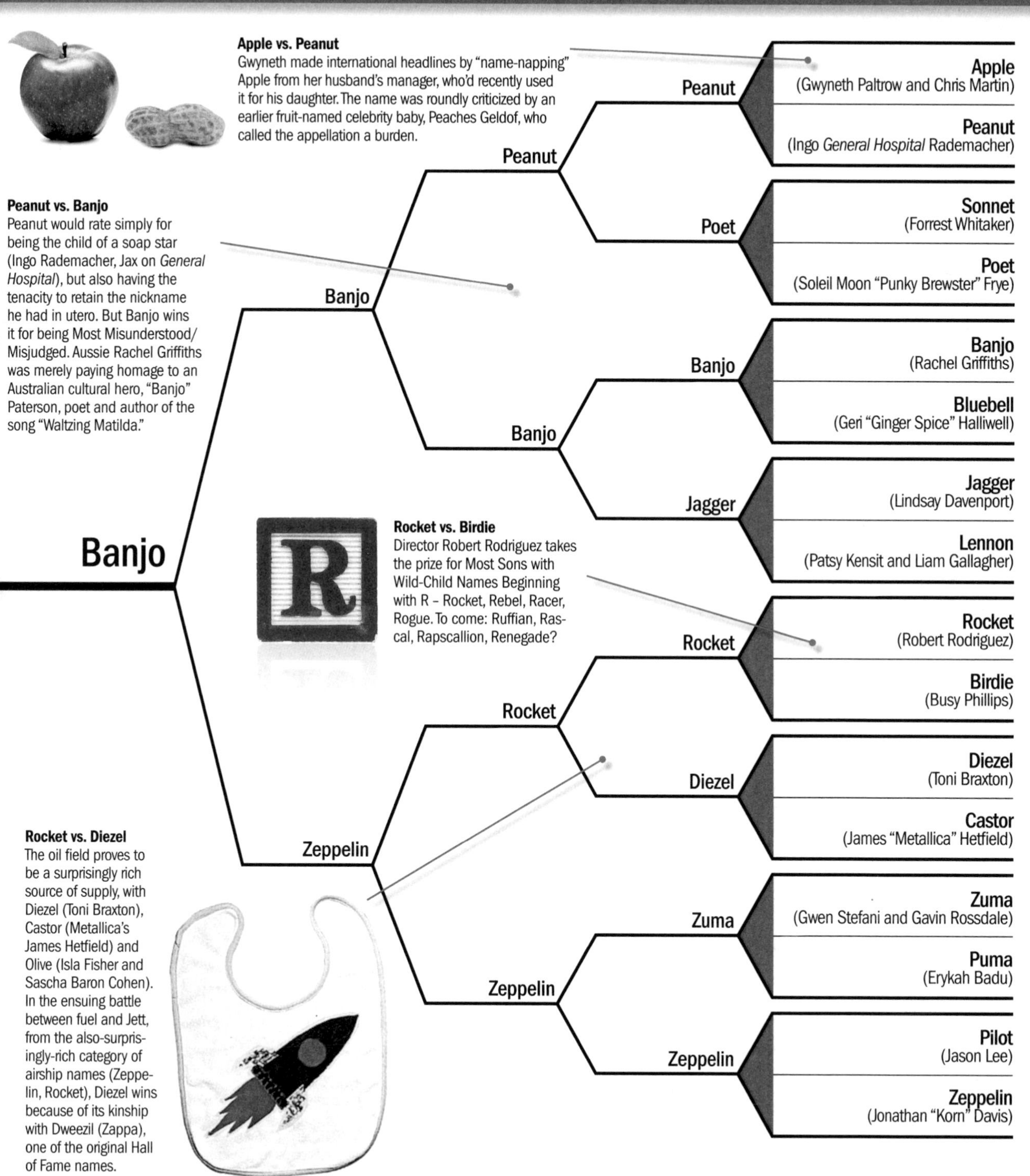

Apple
(Gwyneth Paltrow and Chris Martin)
Peanut
(Ingo *General Hospital* Rademacher)
Sonnet
(Forrest Whitaker)
Poet
(Soleil Moon "Punky Brewster" Frye)
Banjo
(Rachel Griffiths)
Bluebell
(Geri "Ginger Spice" Halliwell)
Jagger
(Lindsay Davenport)
Lennon
(Patsy Kensit and Liam Gallagher)
Rocket
(Robert Rodriguez)
Birdie
(Busy Phillips)
Diezel
(Toni Braxton)
Castor
(James "Metallica" Hetfield)
Zuma
(Gwen Stefani and Gavin Rossdale)
Puma
(Erykah Badu)
Pilot
(Jason Lee)
Zeppelin
(Jonathan "Korn" Davis)
Peanut
Poet
Banjo
Jagger
Rocket
Diezel
Zuma
Zeppelin
Peanut
Banjo
Rocket
Zeppelin
Banjo
Zeppelin
Banjo

Apple vs. Peanut
Gwyneth made international headlines by "name-napping" Apple from her husband's manager, who'd recently used it for his daughter. The name was roundly criticized by an earlier fruit-named celebrity baby, Peaches Geldof, who called the appellation a burden.

Peanut vs. Banjo
Peanut would rate simply for being the child of a soap star (Ingo Rademacher, Jax on *General Hospital*), but also having the tenacity to retain the nickname he had in utero. But Banjo wins it for being Most Misunderstood/Misjudged. Aussie Rachel Griffiths was merely paying homage to an Australian cultural hero, "Banjo" Paterson, poet and author of the song "Waltzing Matilda."

Rocket vs. Birdie
Director Robert Rodriguez takes the prize for Most Sons with Wild-Child Names Beginning with R – Rocket, Rebel, Racer, Rogue. To come: Ruffian, Rascal, Rapscallion, Renegade?

Rocket vs. Diezel
The oil field proves to be a surprisingly rich source of supply, with Diezel (Toni Braxton), Castor (Metallica's James Hetfield) and Olive (Isla Fisher and Sascha Baron Cohen). In the ensuing battle between fuel and Jett, from the also-surprisingly-rich category of airship names (Zeppelin, Rocket), Diezel wins because of its kinship with Dweezil (Zappa), one of the original Hall of Fame names.

Untimely Deaths

By Mark Reiter

Mark Reiter, co-editor of this book, is getting used to the fact that no one lives forever.

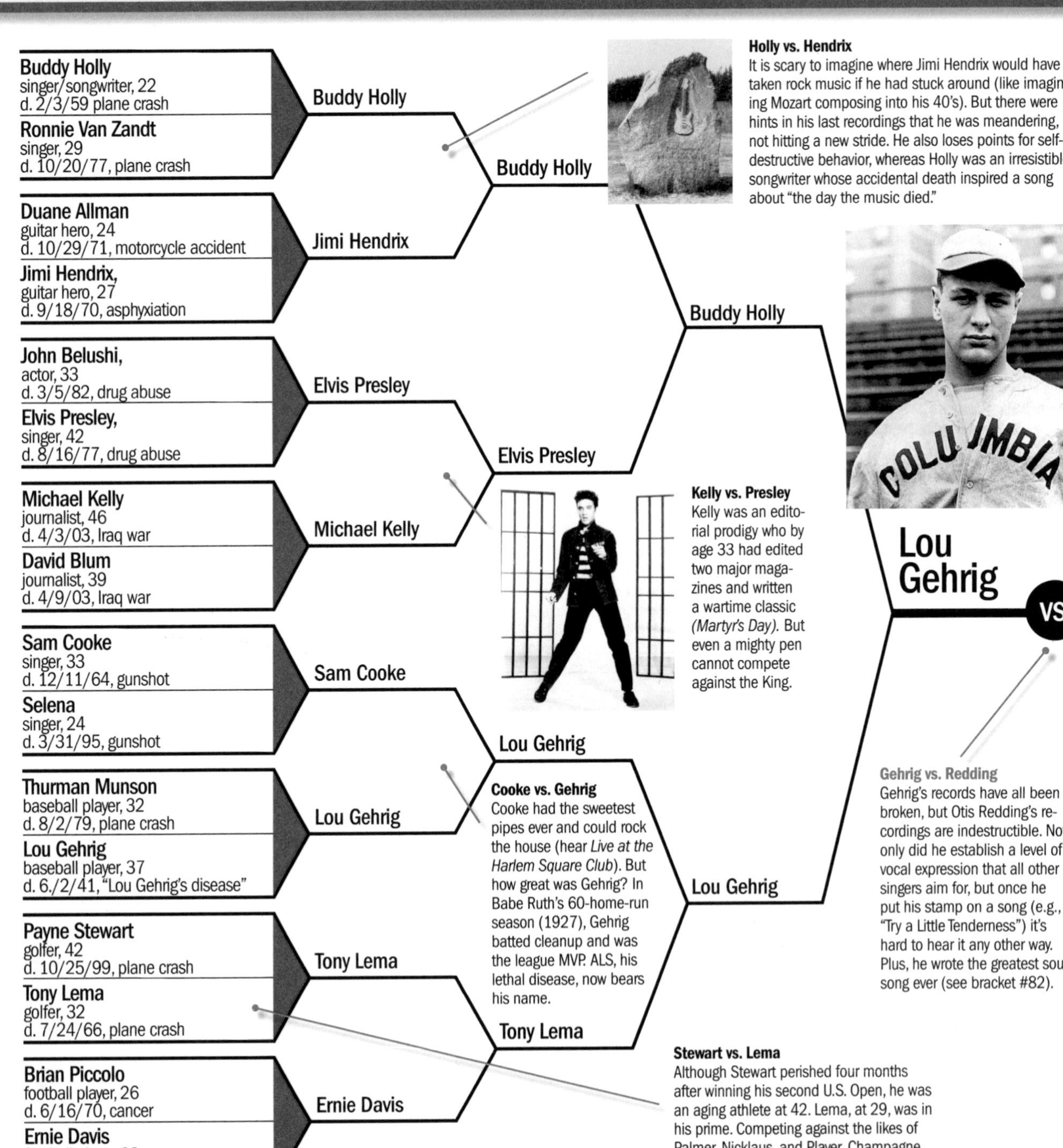

Buddy Holly
singer/songwriter, 22
d. 2/3/59 plane crash
Ronnie Van Zandt
singer, 29
d. 10/20/77, plane crash
Duane Allman
guitar hero, 24
d. 10/29/71, motorcycle accident
Jimi Hendrix,
guitar hero, 27
d. 9/18/70, asphyxiation
John Belushi,
actor, 33
d. 3/5/82, drug abuse
Elvis Presley,
singer, 42
d. 8/16/77, drug abuse
Michael Kelly
journalist, 46
d. 4/3/03, Iraq war
David Blum
journalist, 39
d. 4/9/03, Iraq war
Sam Cooke
singer, 33
d. 12/11/64, gunshot
Selena
singer, 24
d. 3/31/95, gunshot
Thurman Munson
baseball player, 32
d. 8/2/79, plane crash
Lou Gehrig
baseball player, 37
d. 6./2/41, "Lou Gehrig's disease"
Payne Stewart
golfer, 42
d. 10/25/99, plane crash
Tony Lema
golfer, 32
d. 7/24/66, plane crash
Brian Piccolo
football player, 26
d. 6/16/70, cancer
Ernie Davis
football player, 22
d. 5/18/63, leukemia
Buddy Holly
Jimi Hendrix
Elvis Presley
Michael Kelly
Sam Cooke
Lou Gehrig
Tony Lema
Ernie Davis
Buddy Holly
Elvis Presley
Lou Gehrig
Tony Lema
Buddy Holly
Lou Gehrig
Lou Gehrig
VS.
COLUMBIA

Holly vs. Hendrix
It is scary to imagine where Jimi Hendrix would have taken rock music if he had stuck around (like imagining Mozart composing into his 40's). But there were hints in his last recordings that he was meandering, not hitting a new stride. He also loses points for self-destructive behavior, whereas Holly was an irresistible songwriter whose accidental death inspired a song about "the day the music died."

Kelly vs. Presley
Kelly was an editorial prodigy who by age 33 had edited two major magazines and written a wartime classic *(Martyr's Day)*. But even a mighty pen cannot compete against the King.

Cooke vs. Gehrig
Cooke had the sweetest pipes ever and could rock the house (hear *Live at the Harlem Square Club*). But how great was Gehrig? In Babe Ruth's 60-home-run season (1927), Gehrig batted cleanup and was the league MVP. ALS, his lethal disease, now bears his name.

Gehrig vs. Redding
Gehrig's records have all been broken, but Otis Redding's recordings are indestructible. Not only did he establish a level of vocal expression that all other singers aim for, but once he put his stamp on a song (e.g., "Try a Little Tenderness") it's hard to hear it any other way. Plus, he wrote the greatest soul song ever (see bracket #82).

Stewart vs. Lema
Although Stewart perished four months after winning his second U.S. Open, he was an aging athlete at 42. Lema, at 29, was in his prime. Competing against the likes of Palmer, Nicklaus, and Player, Champagne Tony won 12 times in four seasons, including the '64 British Open. Macabre factor: Lema's plane crashed on a golf course.

WHILE NO DEATH IS TIMELY (unless you're 109 years old and pass in your sleep with a smile on your face), inevitably some passings are more tragic than others. You lose points for self-destructive behavior or taking your own life. You gain points for going in car accidents, plane crashes, or senseless shootings. No war heroes or assassination victims allowed either (so don't expect Abe Lincoln to be squaring off against MLK, JFK, RFK, or Harvey Milk in the final). This is a contest of interrupted potential and the magnitude of What If.

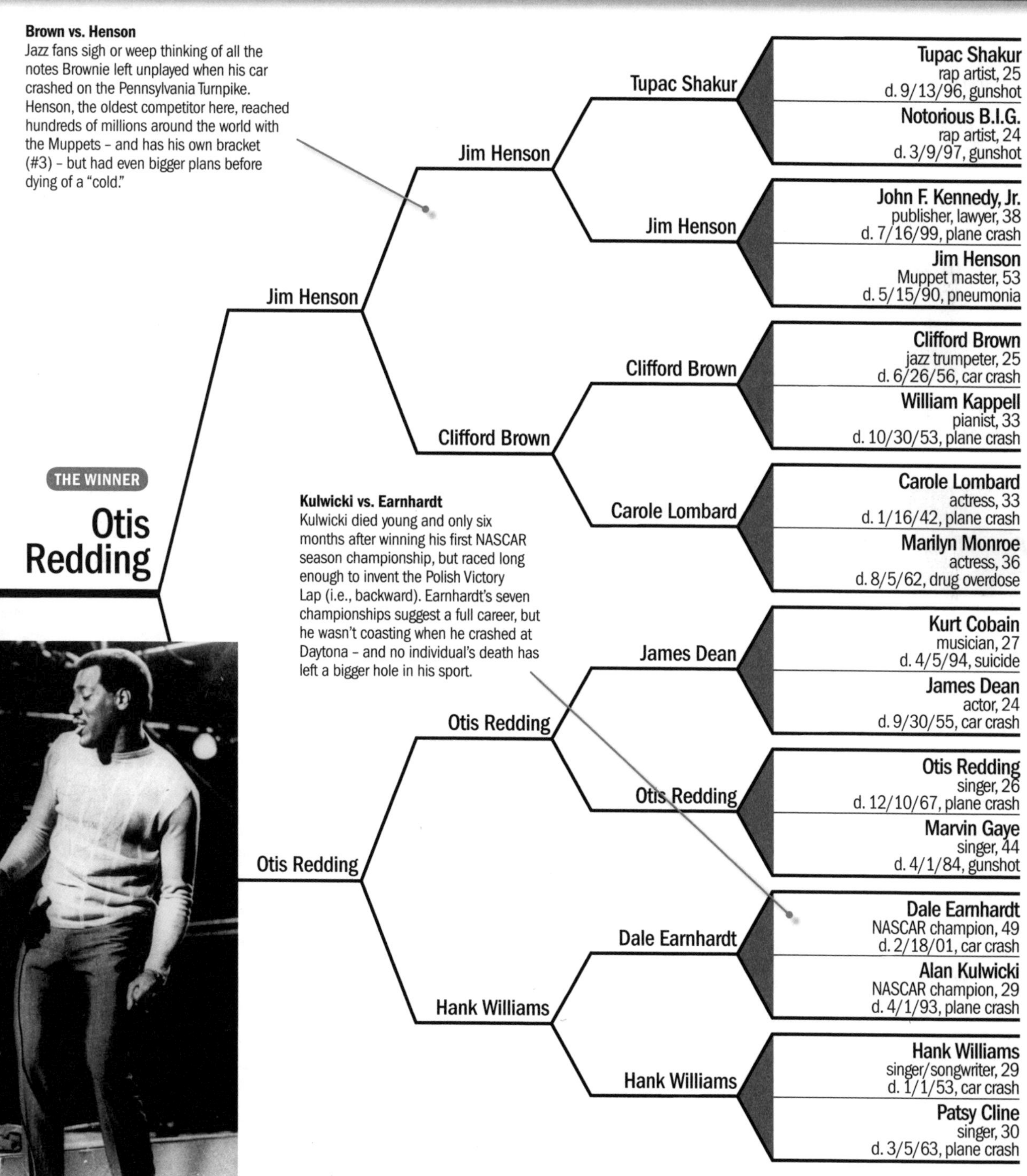

Tupac Shakur
rap artist, 25
d. 9/13/96, gunshot
Notorious B.I.G.
rap artist, 24
d. 3/9/97, gunshot
John F. Kennedy, Jr.
publisher, lawyer, 38
d. 7/16/99, plane crash
Jim Henson
Muppet master, 53
d. 5/15/90, pneumonia
Clifford Brown
jazz trumpeter, 25
d. 6/26/56, car crash
William Kappell
pianist, 33
d. 10/30/53, plane crash
Carole Lombard
actress, 33
d. 1/16/42, plane crash
Marilyn Monroe
actress, 36
d. 8/5/62, drug overdose
Kurt Cobain
musician, 27
d. 4/5/94, suicide
James Dean
actor, 24
d. 9/30/55, car crash
Otis Redding
singer, 26
d. 12/10/67, plane crash
Marvin Gaye
singer, 44
d. 4/1/84, gunshot
Dale Earnhardt
NASCAR champion, 49
d. 2/18/01, car crash
Alan Kulwicki
NASCAR champion, 29
d. 4/1/93, plane crash
Hank Williams
singer/songwriter, 29
d. 1/1/53, car crash
Patsy Cline
singer, 30
d. 3/5/63, plane crash
Tupac Shakur
Jim Henson
Clifford Brown
Carole Lombard
James Dean
Otis Redding
Dale Earnhardt
Hank Williams
Jim Henson
Clifford Brown
Otis Redding
Hank Williams
Jim Henson
Otis Redding
THE WINNER
Otis Redding

Brown vs. Henson
Jazz fans sigh or weep thinking of all the notes Brownie left unplayed when his car crashed on the Pennsylvania Turnpike. Henson, the oldest competitor here, reached hundreds of millions around the world with the Muppets – and has his own bracket (#3) – but had even bigger plans before dying of a "cold."

Kulwicki vs. Earnhardt
Kulwicki died young and only six months after winning his first NASCAR season championship, but raced long enough to invent the Polish Victory Lap (i.e., backward). Earnhardt's seven championships suggest a full career, but he wasn't coasting when he crashed at Daytona – and no individual's death has left a bigger hole in his sport.

David

By David Fisher

David Fisher has written or collaborated on 15 *New York Times* bestsellers. He lives happily in the Bronx, New York, with a beautiful wife, two sons, a dog, and a cat – none of whom is named David.

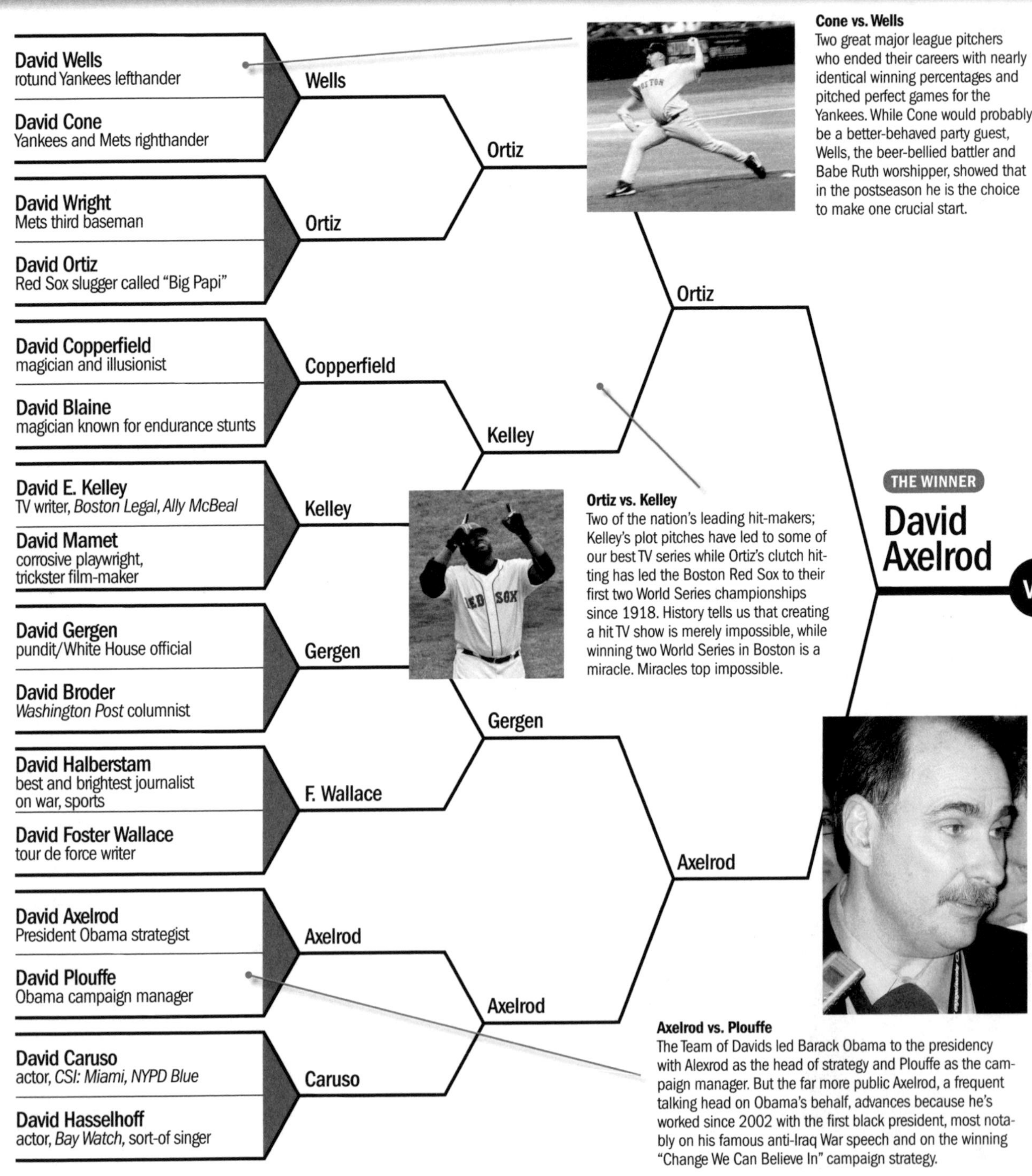

David Wells
rotund Yankees lefthander
David Cone
Yankees and Mets righthander
David Wright
Mets third baseman
David Ortiz
Red Sox slugger called "Big Papi"
David Copperfield
magician and illusionist
David Blaine
magician known for endurance stunts
David E. Kelley
TV writer, *Boston Legal*, *Ally McBeal*
David Mamet
corrosive playwright, trickster film-maker
David Gergen
pundit/White House official
David Broder
Washington Post columnist
David Halberstam
best and brightest journalist on war, sports
David Foster Wallace
tour de force writer
David Axelrod
President Obama strategist
David Plouffe
Obama campaign manager
David Caruso
actor, *CSI: Miami*, *NYPD Blue*
David Hasselhoff
actor, *Bay Watch*, sort-of singer
Wells
Ortiz
Copperfield
Kelley
Gergen
F. Wallace
Axelrod
Caruso
Ortiz
Kelley
Gergen
Axelrod
Ortiz
Axelrod
THE WINNER
David Axelrod
VS.

Cone vs. Wells
Two great major league pitchers who ended their careers with nearly identical winning percentages and pitched perfect games for the Yankees. While Cone would probably be a better-behaved party guest, Wells, the beer-bellied battler and Babe Ruth worshipper, showed that in the postseason he is the choice to make one crucial start.

Ortiz vs. Kelley
Two of the nation's leading hit-makers; Kelley's plot pitches have led to some of our best TV series while Ortiz's clutch hitting has led the Boston Red Sox to their first two World Series championships since 1918. History tells us that creating a hit TV show is merely impossible, while winning two World Series in Boston is a miracle. Miracles top impossible.

Axelrod vs. Plouffe
The Team of Davids led Barack Obama to the presidency with Alexrod as the head of strategy and Plouffe as the campaign manager. But the far more public Axelrod, a frequent talking head on Obama's behalf, advances because he's worked since 2002 with the first black president, most notably on his famous anti-Iraq War speech and on the winning "Change We Can Believe In" campaign strategy.

DAVID MEANS "BELOVED," an auspicious start for any name. Michelangelo's marble nude, *David,* beckons people from thousands of miles away. The statue's impressive namesake, the biblical King David, was a leading statesman, writer, musician, and soldier who vanquished the heavily-favored Goliath in history's greatest upset. In doing so he established the name as one with such potent simplicity that only the most loving parents bestowed it on their fortunate sons. Some of those sons turned into great guys. Some didn't.

Crockett vs. Axelrod
Crockett's mythical place in storybooks and American history is certain. But Axelrod turned a state senator from Illinois with a Muslim name into America's first African American president. He changed the way political campaigns will be conducted, and with Plouffe, kept internal battles quiet, created the most tech-savvy campaign ever, and raised $750 million to defeat Hillary Clinton and then John McCain. And he never needed a coonskin cap.

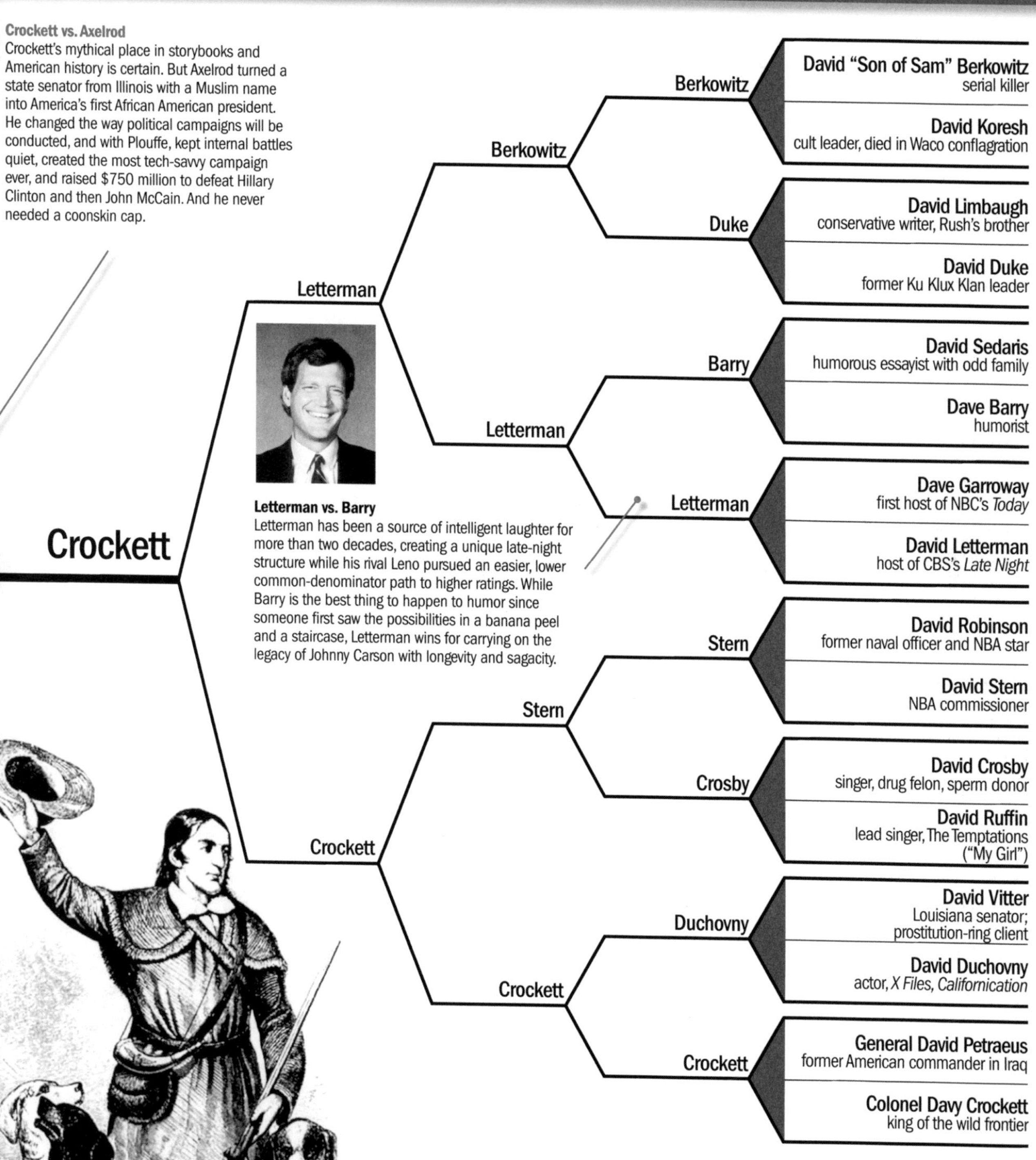

David "Son of Sam" Berkowitz
serial killer
David Koresh
cult leader, died in Waco conflagration
David Limbaugh
conservative writer, Rush's brother
David Duke
former Ku Klux Klan leader
David Sedaris
humorous essayist with odd family
Dave Barry
humorist
Dave Garroway
first host of NBC's *Today*
David Letterman
host of CBS's *Late Night*
David Robinson
former naval officer and NBA star
David Stern
NBA commissioner
David Crosby
singer, drug felon, sperm donor
David Ruffin
lead singer, The Temptations ("My Girl")
David Vitter
Louisiana senator; prostitution-ring client
David Duchovny
actor, *X Files, Californication*
General David Petraeus
former American commander in Iraq
Colonel Davy Crockett
king of the wild frontier
Berkowitz
Duke
Barry
Letterman
Stern
Crosby
Duchovny
Crockett
Berkowitz
Letterman
Stern
Crockett
Letterman
Crockett
Crockett

Letterman vs. Barry
Letterman has been a source of intelligent laughter for more than two decades, creating a unique late-night structure while his rival Leno pursued an easier, lower common-denominator path to higher ratings. While Barry is the best thing to happen to humor since someone first saw the possibilities in a banana peel and a staircase, Letterman wins for carrying on the legacy of Johnny Carson with longevity and sagacity.

Celebrity Memoirs

By Charles Leerhsen

Charles Leerhsen is a former assistant managing editor at *People* magazine and the survivor of five celebrity ghostwriting projects. He is also the author of *Crazy Good: The True Story of Dan Patch, the Most Famous Horse in America.*

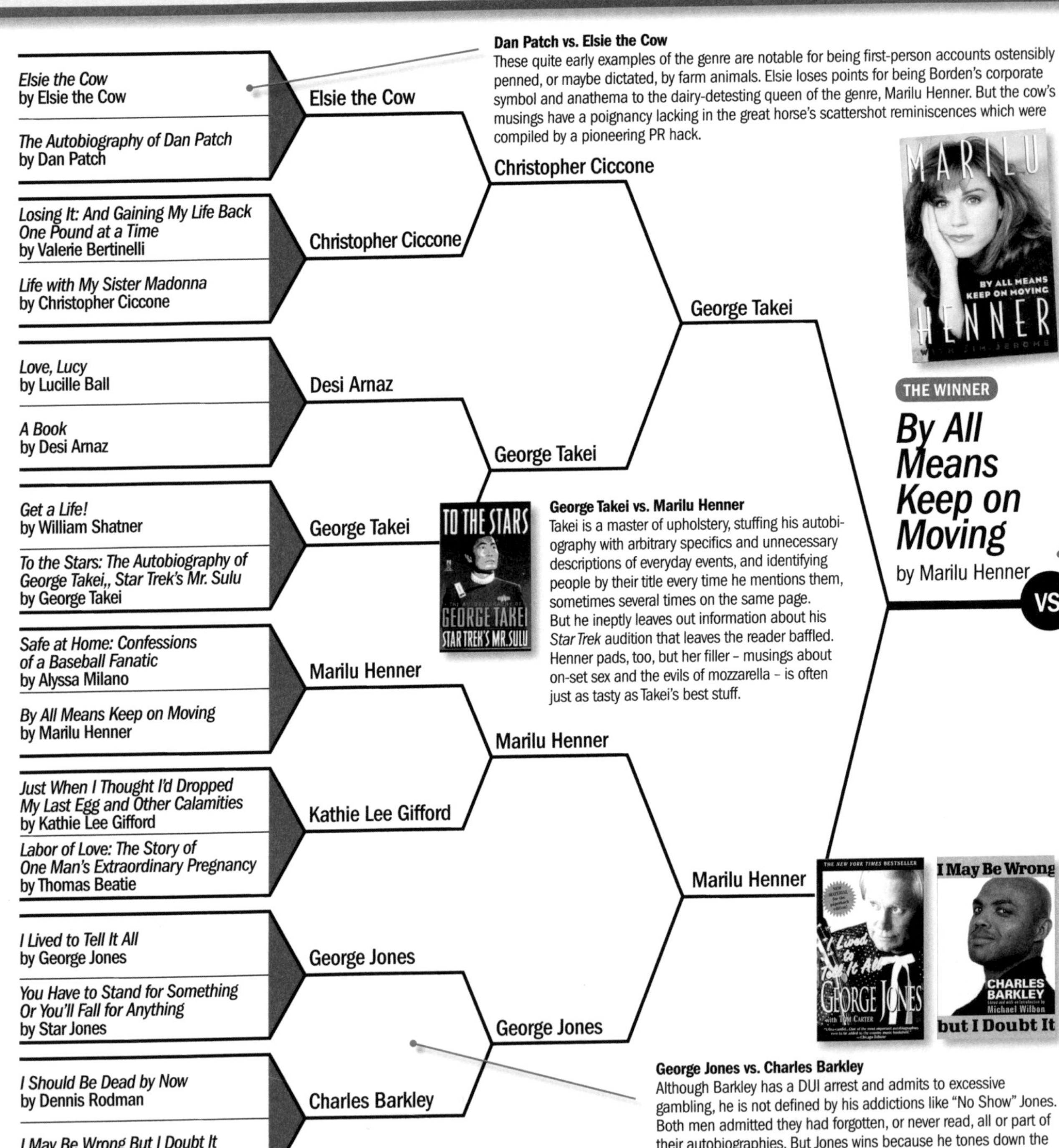
Elsie the Cow by Elsie the Cow
The Autobiography of Dan Patch by Dan Patch
Elsie the Cow
Losing It: And Gaining My Life Back One Pound at a Time by Valerie Bertinelli
Life with My Sister Madonna by Christopher Ciccone
Christopher Ciccone
Christopher Ciccone
Love, Lucy by Lucille Ball
A Book by Desi Arnaz
Desi Arnaz
Get a Life! by William Shatner
To the Stars: The Autobiography of George Takei,, Star Trek's Mr. Sulu by George Takei
George Takei
George Takei
George Takei
Safe at Home: Confessions of a Baseball Fanatic by Alyssa Milano
By All Means Keep on Moving by Marilu Henner
Marilu Henner
Just When I Thought I'd Dropped My Last Egg and Other Calamities by Kathie Lee Gifford
Labor of Love: The Story of One Man's Extraordinary Pregnancy by Thomas Beatie
Kathie Lee Gifford
Marilu Henner
I Lived to Tell It All by George Jones
You Have to Stand for Something Or You'll Fall for Anything by Star Jones
George Jones
I Should Be Dead by Now by Dennis Rodman
I May Be Wrong But I Doubt It by Charles Barkley
Charles Barkley
George Jones
Marilu Henner
MARILU HENNER
BY ALL MEANS KEEP ON MOVING
TO THE STARS
GEORGE TAKEI
STAR TREK'S MR. SULU
GEORGE JONES
I Lived to Tell It All
I May Be Wrong but I Doubt It
CHARLES BARKLEY
THE WINNER
By All Means Keep on Moving by Marilu Henner
VS.

Dan Patch vs. Elsie the Cow

These quite early examples of the genre are notable for being first-person accounts ostensibly penned, or maybe dictated, by farm animals. Elsie loses points for being Borden's corporate symbol and anathema to the dairy-detesting queen of the genre, Marilu Henner. But the cow's musings have a poignancy lacking in the great horse's scattershot reminiscences which were compiled by a pioneering PR hack.

George Takei vs. Marilu Henner

Takei is a master of upholstery, stuffing his autobiography with arbitrary specifics and unnecessary descriptions of everyday events, and identifying people by their title every time he mentions them, sometimes several times on the same page. But he ineptly leaves out information about his *Star Trek* audition that leaves the reader baffled. Henner pads, too, but her filler – musings about on-set sex and the evils of mozzarella – is often just as tasty as Takei's best stuff.

George Jones vs. Charles Barkley

Although Barkley has a DUI arrest and admits to excessive gambling, he is not defined by his addictions like "No Show" Jones. Both men admitted they had forgotten, or never read, all or part of their autobiographies. But Jones wins because he tones down the braggadocio and tells better stories, such as the time he sidled up to singer Porter Wagoner at a urinal and grabbed Wagoner's penis as a way of saying, "Listen, you, stay away from my gal."

REVIEWING *TRUMP: SURVIVING AT THE TOP*, which I cowrote with Donald Trump and considered my magnum opus until I learned a little Latin, smarty-pants author Michael Lewis called it a "sloppy job of façade-repair." Lewis thought he was insulting The Donald in the *New York Times* when in fact he was defining what a celebrity memoir should be: something not too fastidious and not too fair. I mean, who wants a celebrity with a flawless façade and impeccable judgment about what he puts down for posterity? Dish beats decorum every time.

Wilt Chamberlain vs. Marilu Henner

Chamberlain's claim that he shtupped 20,000 women is really all he's got. After two autobiographies (the better one came 18 years earlier) he seems sour and spent. Henner's banal blathering adds up to one gloriously unfiltered puff: she confesses to being "cross addicted to dairy and roast beef," reveals affairs with Tony Danza and Judd Hirsch, and admits to an (unconsummated) thing for Danny DeVito because he was charming, funny, and "already down there."

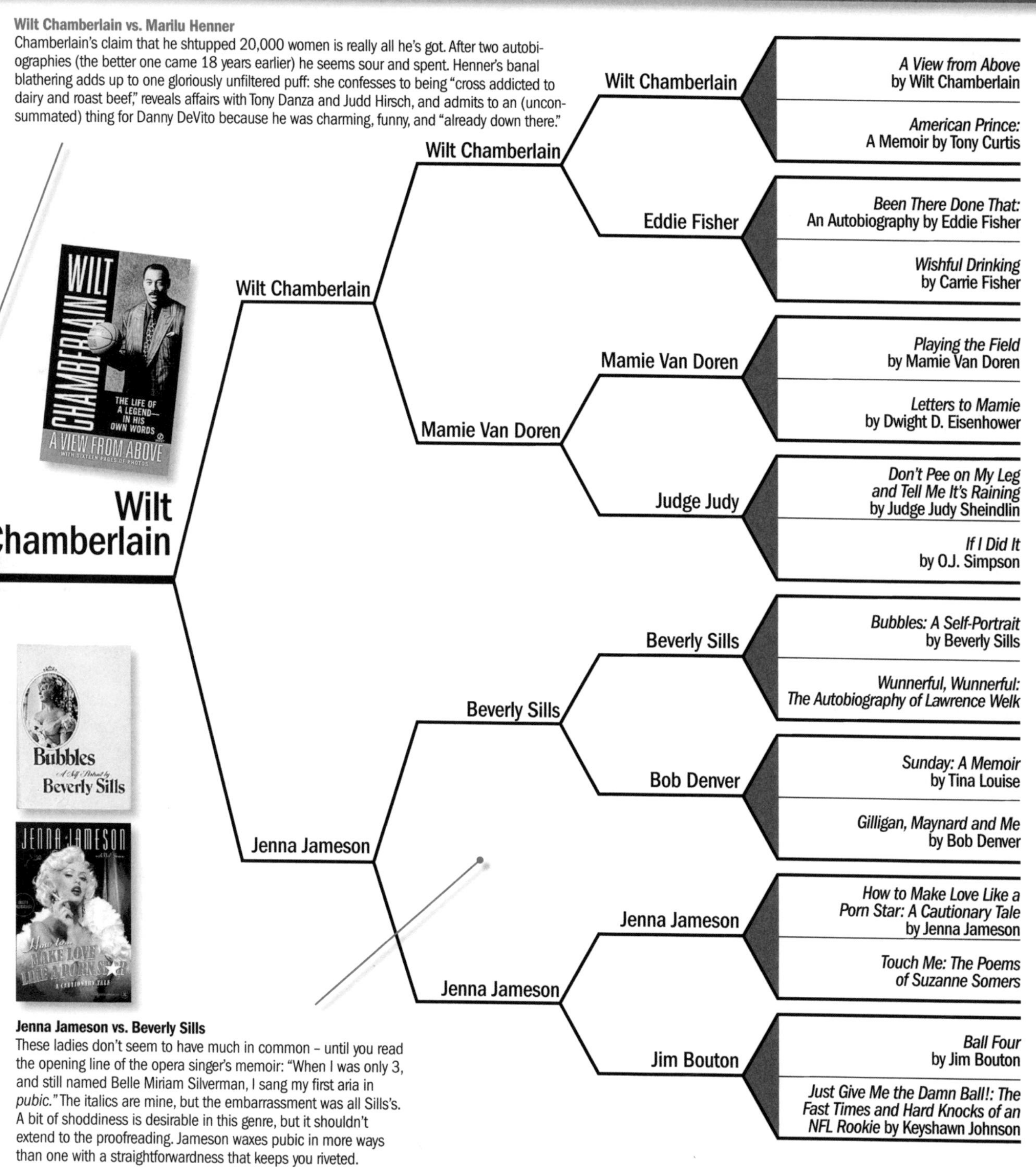

A View from Above by Wilt Chamberlain
American Prince: A Memoir by Tony Curtis
Been There Done That: An Autobiography by Eddie Fisher
Wishful Drinking by Carrie Fisher
Playing the Field by Mamie Van Doren
Letters to Mamie by Dwight D. Eisenhower
Don't Pee on My Leg and Tell Me It's Raining by Judge Judy Sheindlin
If I Did It by O.J. Simpson
Bubbles: A Self-Portrait by Beverly Sills
Wunnerful, Wunnerful: The Autobiography of Lawrence Welk
Sunday: A Memoir by Tina Louise
Gilligan, Maynard and Me by Bob Denver
How to Make Love Like a Porn Star: A Cautionary Tale by Jenna Jameson
Touch Me: The Poems of Suzanne Somers
Ball Four by Jim Bouton
Just Give Me the Damn Ball!: The Fast Times and Hard Knocks of an NFL Rookie by Keyshawn Johnson
Wilt Chamberlain
Eddie Fisher
Mamie Van Doren
Judge Judy
Beverly Sills
Bob Denver
Jenna Jameson
Jim Bouton
Wilt Chamberlain
Mamie Van Doren
Beverly Sills
Jenna Jameson
Wilt Chamberlain
Jenna Jameson
Wilt Chamberlain
WILT CHAMBERLAIN
THE LIFE OF A LEGEND—IN HIS OWN WORDS
A VIEW FROM ABOVE
WITH SIXTEEN PAGES OF PHOTOS
Bubbles
A Self-Portrait by
Beverly Sills
JENNA JAMESON
How to Make Love Like a Porn Star
A CAUTIONARY TALE

Jenna Jameson vs. Beverly Sills

These ladies don't seem to have much in common – until you read the opening line of the opera singer's memoir: "When I was only 3, and still named Belle Miriam Silverman, I sang my first aria in *pubic.*" The italics are mine, but the embarrassment was all Sills's. A bit of shoddiness is desirable in this genre, but it shouldn't extend to the proofreading. Jameson waxes pubic in more ways than one with a straightforwardness that keeps you riveted.

Lousy Husbands

By Kari Boyer

Kari Boyer, a veteran food reporter and editor, would never put her husband Peter on this list. Not yet.

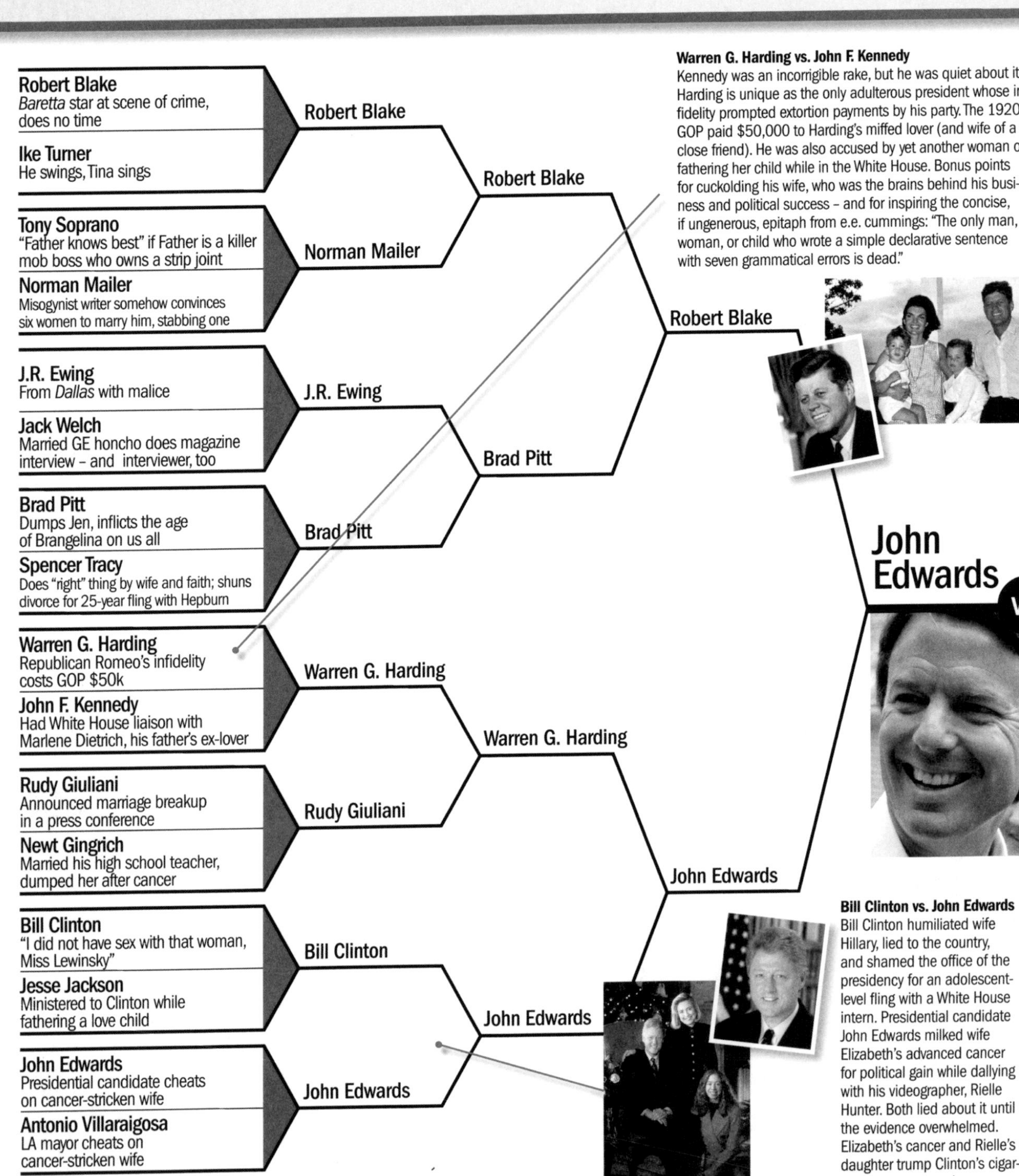

Robert Blake
Baretta star at scene of crime, does no time
Ike Turner
He swings, Tina sings
Tony Soprano
"Father knows best" if Father is a killer mob boss who owns a strip joint
Norman Mailer
Misogynist writer somehow convinces six women to marry him, stabbing one
J.R. Ewing
From *Dallas* with malice
Jack Welch
Married GE honcho does magazine interview – and interviewer, too
Brad Pitt
Dumps Jen, inflicts the age of Brangelina on us all
Spencer Tracy
Does "right" thing by wife and faith; shuns divorce for 25-year fling with Hepburn
Warren G. Harding
Republican Romeo's infidelity costs GOP $50k
John F. Kennedy
Had White House liaison with Marlene Dietrich, his father's ex-lover
Rudy Giuliani
Announced marriage breakup in a press conference
Newt Gingrich
Married his high school teacher, dumped her after cancer
Bill Clinton
"I did not have sex with that woman, Miss Lewinsky"
Jesse Jackson
Ministered to Clinton while fathering a love child
John Edwards
Presidential candidate cheats on cancer-stricken wife
Antonio Villaraigosa
LA mayor cheats on cancer-stricken wife
Robert Blake
Norman Mailer
J.R. Ewing
Brad Pitt
Warren G. Harding
Rudy Giuliani
Bill Clinton
John Edwards
Robert Blake
Brad Pitt
Warren G. Harding
John Edwards
Robert Blake
John Edwards
John Edwards
VS.

Warren G. Harding vs. John F. Kennedy

Kennedy was an incorrigible rake, but he was quiet about it. Harding is unique as the only adulterous president whose infidelity prompted extortion payments by his party. The 1920 GOP paid $50,000 to Harding's miffed lover (and wife of a close friend). He was also accused by yet another woman of fathering her child while in the White House. Bonus points for cuckolding his wife, who was the brains behind his business and political success – and for inspiring the concise, if ungenerous, epitaph from e.e. cummings: "The only man, woman, or child who wrote a simple declarative sentence with seven grammatical errors is dead."

Bill Clinton vs. John Edwards

Bill Clinton humiliated wife Hillary, lied to the country, and shamed the office of the presidency for an adolescent-level fling with a White House intern. Presidential candidate John Edwards milked wife Elizabeth's advanced cancer for political gain while dallying with his videographer, Rielle Hunter. Both lied about it until the evidence overwhelmed. Elizabeth's cancer and Rielle's daughter trump Clinton's cigar-and-intern escapade.

WHAT MAKES A BAD HUSBAND? Violence and emotional cruelty, certainly. Humiliation cuts deep, too. That's why so many politicians make world-class lousy husbands. Because American politics insists on the image of domestic perfection, a betrayed political wife is triply humiliated: first in the adoring spouse phase, then with the revelation of the betrayal, and finally during the stand-by-your-fallen-man press conference. Maybe some of them still have faith in their lout. But on the evidence here (including two fictional TV heels who are so vivid they serve as role models for others in the bracket), they shouldn't.

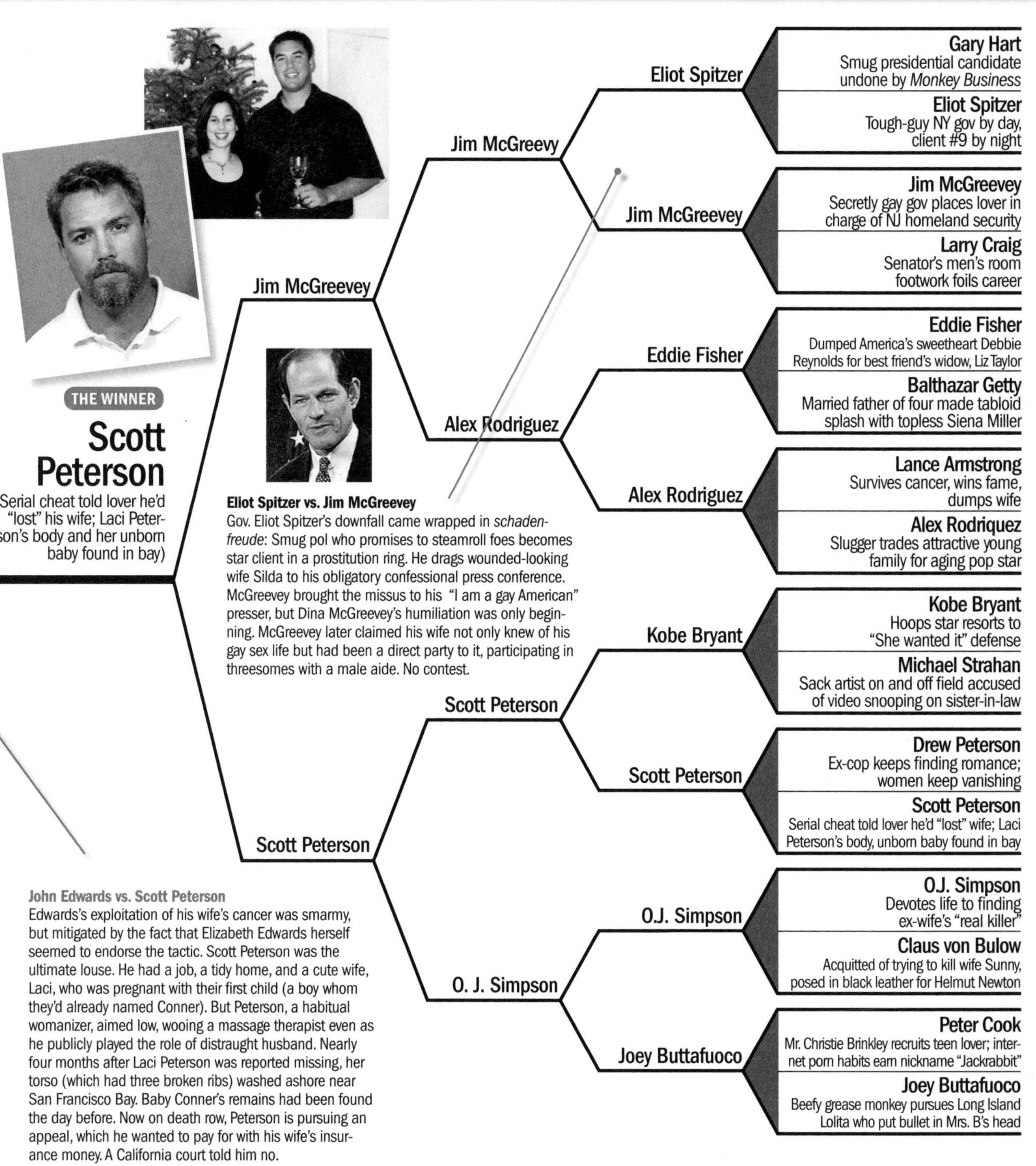
Gary Hart
Smug presidential candidate undone by *Monkey Business*
Eliot Spitzer
Tough-guy NY gov by day, client #9 by night
Jim McGreevey
Secretly gay gov places lover in charge of NJ homeland security
Larry Craig
Senator's men's room footwork foils career
Eddie Fisher
Dumped America's sweetheart Debbie Reynolds for best friend's widow, Liz Taylor
Balthazar Getty
Married father of four made tabloid splash with topless Siena Miller
Lance Armstrong
Survives cancer, wins fame, dumps wife
Alex Rodriquez
Slugger trades attractive young family for aging pop star
Kobe Bryant
Hoops star resorts to "She wanted it" defense
Michael Strahan
Sack artist on and off field accused of video snooping on sister-in-law
Drew Peterson
Ex-cop keeps finding romance; women keep vanishing
Scott Peterson
Serial cheat told lover he'd "lost" wife; Laci Peterson's body, unborn baby found in bay
O.J. Simpson
Devotes life to finding ex-wife's "real killer"
Claus von Bulow
Acquitted of trying to kill wife Sunny, posed in black leather for Helmut Newton
Peter Cook
Mr. Christie Brinkley recruits teen lover; internet porn habits earn nickname "Jackrabbit"
Joey Buttafuoco
Beefy grease monkey pursues Long Island Lolita who put bullet in Mrs. B's head
Eliot Spitzer
Jim McGreevey
Eddie Fisher
Alex Rodriguez
Kobe Bryant
Scott Peterson
O.J. Simpson
Joey Buttafuoco
Jim McGreevey
Alex Rodriguez
Scott Peterson
O. J. Simpson
Jim McGreevey
Scott Peterson
THE WINNER

Scott Peterson

(Serial cheat told lover he'd "lost" his wife; Laci Peterson's body and her unborn baby found in bay)

Eliot Spitzer vs. Jim McGreevey

Gov. Eliot Spitzer's downfall came wrapped in *schadenfreude*: Smug pol who promises to steamroll foes becomes star client in a prostitution ring. He drags wounded-looking wife Silda to his obligatory confessional press conference. McGreevey brought the missus to his "I am a gay American" presser, but Dina McGreevey's humiliation was only beginning. McGreevey later claimed his wife not only knew of his gay sex life but had been a direct party to it, participating in threesomes with a male aide. No contest.

John Edwards vs. Scott Peterson

Edwards's exploitation of his wife's cancer was smarmy, but mitigated by the fact that Elizabeth Edwards herself seemed to endorse the tactic. Scott Peterson was the ultimate louse. He had a job, a tidy home, and a cute wife, Laci, who was pregnant with their first child (a boy whom they'd already named Conner). But Peterson, a habitual womanizer, aimed low, wooing a massage therapist even as he publicly played the role of distraught husband. Nearly four months after Laci Peterson was reported missing, her torso (which had three broken ribs) washed ashore near San Francisco Bay. Baby Conner's remains had been found the day before. Now on death row, Peterson is pursuing an appeal, which he wanted to pay for with his wife's insurance money. A California court told him no.

William et. al.

By William/Bill Geist

Bill Geist is an Emmy Award-winning correspondent for CBS News and a *New York Times* bestselling author.

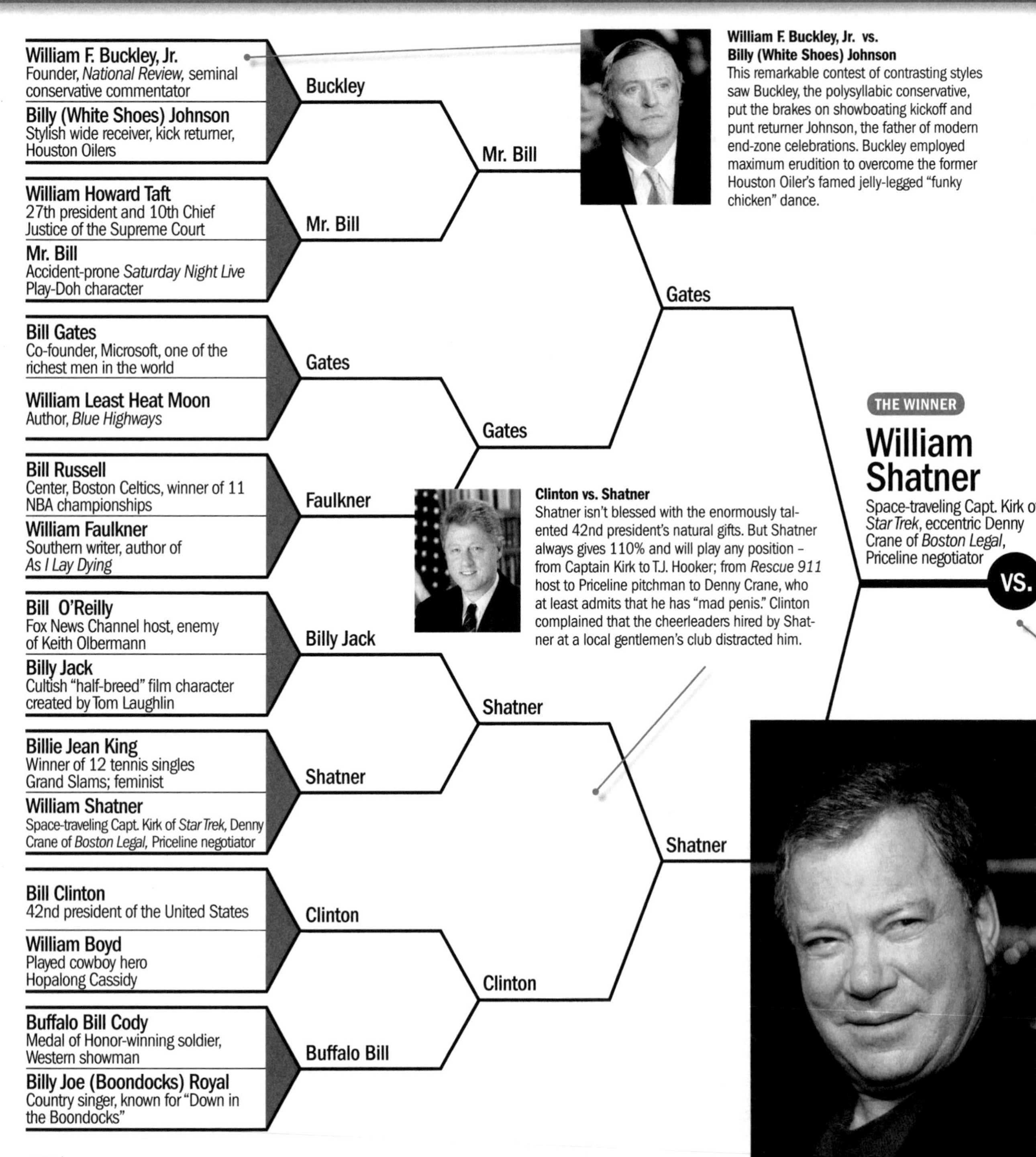

William F. Buckley, Jr.
Founder, *National Review,* seminal conservative commentator
Billy (White Shoes) Johnson
Stylish wide receiver, kick returner, Houston Oilers
William Howard Taft
27th president and 10th Chief Justice of the Supreme Court
Mr. Bill
Accident-prone *Saturday Night Live* Play-Doh character
Bill Gates
Co-founder, Microsoft, one of the richest men in the world
William Least Heat Moon
Author, *Blue Highways*
Bill Russell
Center, Boston Celtics, winner of 11 NBA championships
William Faulkner
Southern writer, author of *As I Lay Dying*
Bill O'Reilly
Fox News Channel host, enemy of Keith Olbermann
Billy Jack
Cultish "half-breed" film character created by Tom Laughlin
Billie Jean King
Winner of 12 tennis singles Grand Slams; feminist
William Shatner
Space-traveling Capt. Kirk of *Star Trek*, Denny Crane of *Boston Legal,* Priceline negotiator
Bill Clinton
42nd president of the United States
William Boyd
Played cowboy hero Hopalong Cassidy
Buffalo Bill Cody
Medal of Honor-winning soldier, Western showman
Billy Joe (Boondocks) Royal
Country singer, known for "Down in the Boondocks"
Buckley
Mr. Bill
Gates
Faulkner
Billy Jack
Shatner
Clinton
Buffalo Bill
Mr. Bill
Gates
Shatner
Clinton
Gates
Shatner
William F. Buckley, Jr. vs. Billy (White Shoes) Johnson
This remarkable contest of contrasting styles saw Buckley, the polysyllabic conservative, put the brakes on showboating kickoff and punt returner Johnson, the father of modern end-zone celebrations. Buckley employed maximum erudition to overcome the former Houston Oiler's famed jelly-legged "funky chicken" dance.
Clinton vs. Shatner
Shatner isn't blessed with the enormously talented 42nd president's natural gifts. But Shatner always gives 110% and will play any position – from Captain Kirk to T.J. Hooker; from *Rescue 911* host to Priceline pitchman to Denny Crane, who at least admits that he has "mad penis." Clinton complained that the cheerleaders hired by Shatner at a local gentlemen's club distracted him.
THE WINNER
William Shatner
Space-traveling Capt. Kirk of *Star Trek*, eccentric Denny Crane of *Boston Legal*, Priceline negotiator
VS.

I'VE BEEN A WILLIAM/BILL FOR AS LONG AS I CAN REMEMBER. I never liked Wilma or Wilhelmina, which is why I "stayed put" when the transgender thing hit. I was named for my uncle Bill and my son is Willie (a permutation of William that gets a dispensation here even if said Willies were not born as William). I wish more babies were named William/Bill instead of Baron or D'Brickashaw, but I'm elated by excesses such as the double Billing of William Carlos Williams and Billy Dee Williams. My favorite team: the Buffalo Bills.

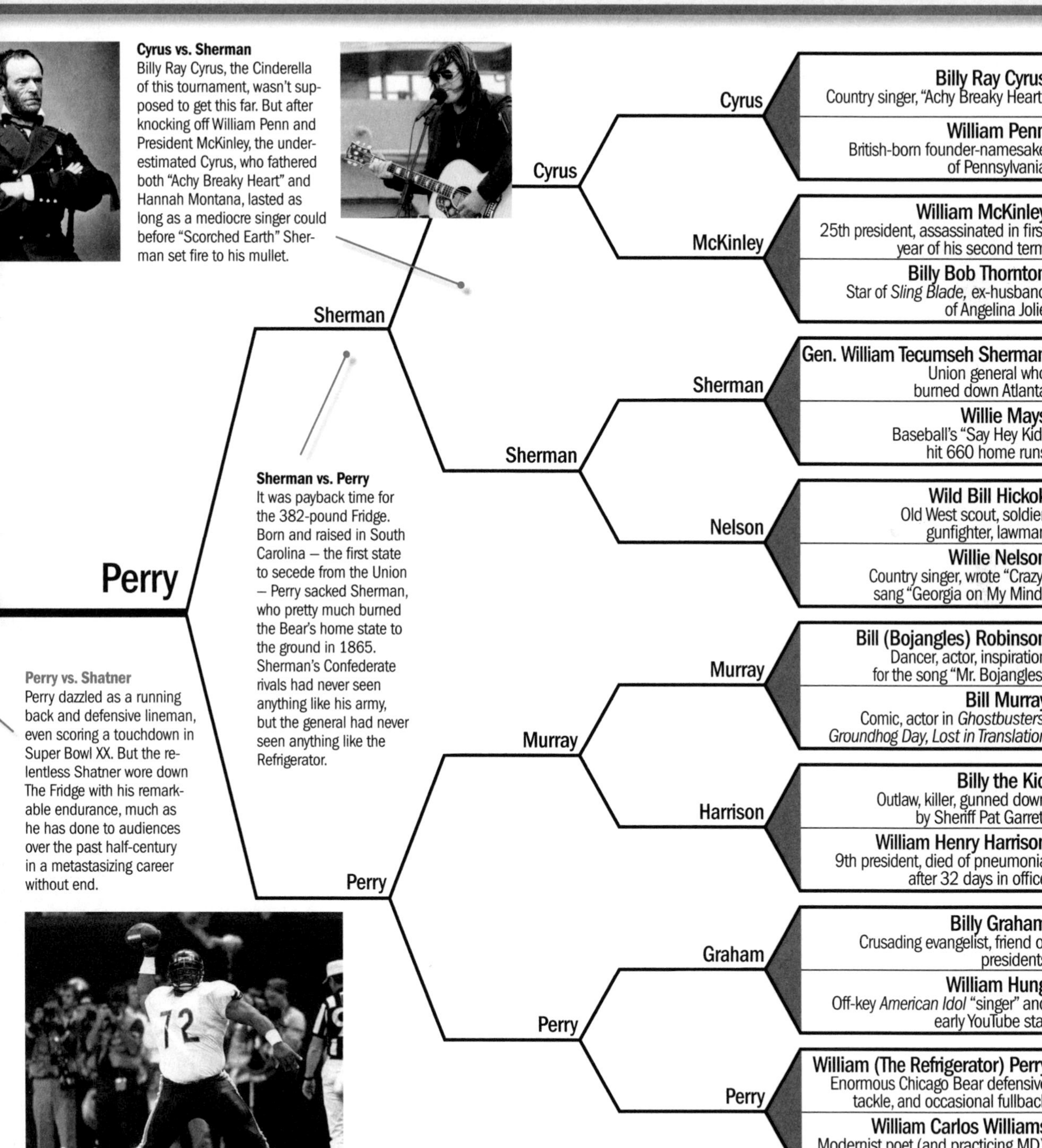

Billy Ray Cyrus
Country singer, "Achy Breaky Heart"
William Penn
British-born founder-namesake of Pennsylvania
William McKinley
25th president, assassinated in first year of his second term
Billy Bob Thornton
Star of *Sling Blade,* ex-husband of Angelina Jolie
Gen. William Tecumseh Sherman
Union general who burned down Atlanta
Willie Mays
Baseball's "Say Hey Kid" hit 660 home runs
Wild Bill Hickok
Old West scout, soldier, gunfighter, lawman
Willie Nelson
Country singer, wrote "Crazy," sang "Georgia on My Mind"
Bill (Bojangles) Robinson
Dancer, actor, inspiration for the song "Mr. Bojangles"
Bill Murray
Comic, actor in *Ghostbusters, Groundhog Day, Lost in Translation*
Billy the Kid
Outlaw, killer, gunned down by Sheriff Pat Garrett
William Henry Harrison
9th president, died of pneumonia after 32 days in office
Billy Graham
Crusading evangelist, friend of presidents
William Hung
Off-key *American Idol* "singer" and early YouTube star
William (The Refrigerator) Perry
Enormous Chicago Bear defensive tackle, and occasional fullback
William Carlos Williams
Modernist poet (and practicing MD), wrote "The Red Wheelbarrow"
Cyrus
McKinley
Sherman
Nelson
Murray
Harrison
Graham
Perry
Cyrus
Sherman
Murray
Perry
Sherman
Perry
Perry

Cyrus vs. Sherman
Billy Ray Cyrus, the Cinderella of this tournament, wasn't supposed to get this far. But after knocking off William Penn and President McKinley, the underestimated Cyrus, who fathered both "Achy Breaky Heart" and Hannah Montana, lasted as long as a mediocre singer could before "Scorched Earth" Sherman set fire to his mullet.

Sherman vs. Perry
It was payback time for the 382-pound Fridge. Born and raised in South Carolina – the first state to secede from the Union – Perry sacked Sherman, who pretty much burned the Bear's home state to the ground in 1865. Sherman's Confederate rivals had never seen anything like his army, but the general had never seen anything like the Refrigerator.

Perry vs. Shatner
Perry dazzled as a running back and defensive lineman, even scoring a touchdown in Super Bowl XX. But the relentless Shatner wore down The Fridge with his remarkable endurance, much as he has done to audiences over the past half-century in a metastasizing career without end.

Disappearing Acts

By Franz Lidz

Franz Lidz is the author of *Unstrung Heroes, Ghosty Men,* and *Fairway to Hell.* He lives quietly on Barmy Farm with 2 Great Pyrenees, 2 cats, 13 chickens, 8 guinea fowl, and 1 wife.

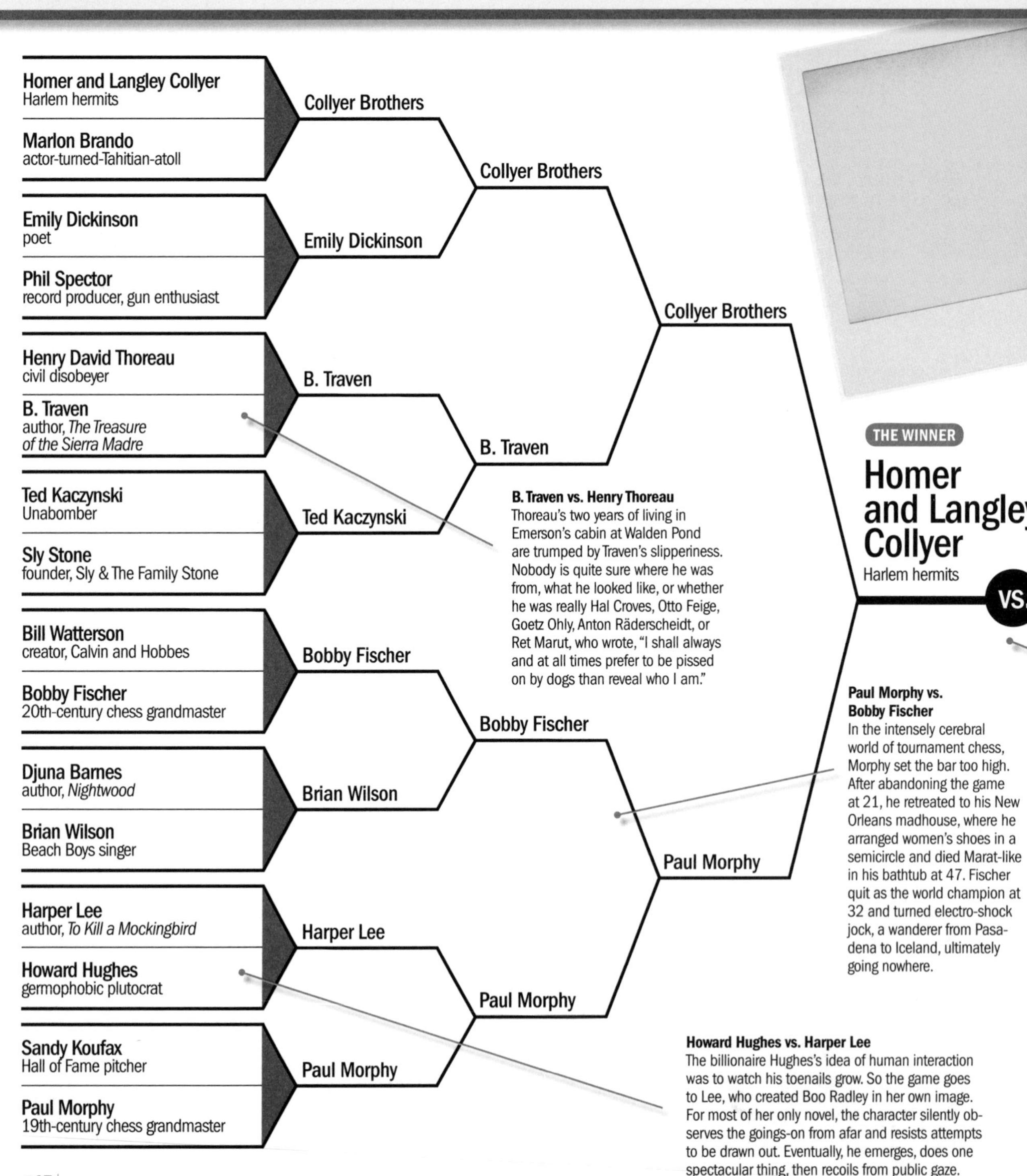
Homer and Langley Collyer
Harlem hermits
Marlon Brando
actor-turned-Tahitian-atoll
Emily Dickinson
poet
Phil Spector
record producer, gun enthusiast
Henry David Thoreau
civil disobeyer
B. Traven
author, The Treasure of the Sierra Madre
Ted Kaczynski
Unabomber
Sly Stone
founder, Sly & The Family Stone
Bill Watterson
creator, Calvin and Hobbes
Bobby Fischer
20th-century chess grandmaster
Djuna Barnes
author, Nightwood
Brian Wilson
Beach Boys singer
Harper Lee
author, To Kill a Mockingbird
Howard Hughes
germophobic plutocrat
Sandy Koufax
Hall of Fame pitcher
Paul Morphy
19th-century chess grandmaster
Collyer Brothers
Emily Dickinson
B. Traven
Ted Kaczynski
Bobby Fischer
Brian Wilson
Harper Lee
Paul Morphy
Collyer Brothers
B. Traven
Bobby Fischer
Paul Morphy
Collyer Brothers
Paul Morphy
THE WINNER
Homer and Langley Collyer
Harlem hermits
VS.

B. Traven vs. Henry Thoreau
Thoreau's two years of living in Emerson's cabin at Walden Pond are trumped by Traven's slipperiness. Nobody is quite sure where he was from, what he looked like, or whether he was really Hal Croves, Otto Feige, Goetz Ohly, Anton Räderscheidt, or Ret Marut, who wrote, "I shall always and at all times prefer to be pissed on by dogs than reveal who I am."

Paul Morphy vs. Bobby Fischer
In the intensely cerebral world of tournament chess, Morphy set the bar too high. After abandoning the game at 21, he retreated to his New Orleans madhouse, where he arranged women's shoes in a semicircle and died Marat-like in his bathtub at 47. Fischer quit as the world champion at 32 and turned electro-shock jock, a wanderer from Pasadena to Iceland, ultimately going nowhere.

Howard Hughes vs. Harper Lee
The billionaire Hughes's idea of human interaction was to watch his toenails grow. So the game goes to Lee, who created Boo Radley in her own image. For most of her only novel, the character silently observes the goings-on from afar and resists attempts to be drawn out. Eventually, he emerges, does one spectacular thing, then recoils from public gaze.

A LIFE OF SOLITUDE AND CONTEMPLATION WAS ONCE A VIRTUE. Nowadays, it's suspect. No longer just figures of mystery and fascination, recluses have devolved into a kind of sub-people to be pitied for their failure to appreciate the worth of TiVo, electric mascara, and Berry Chai Tazo Tea Infusions. The more famous the recluse or the longer the self-imposed exile, the more these disappearing acts' decisions to disappear and enjoy their privacy – basically to say no to human contact, no to everything – invites speculation about their psychological shortcomings. Sometimes fairly, often not.

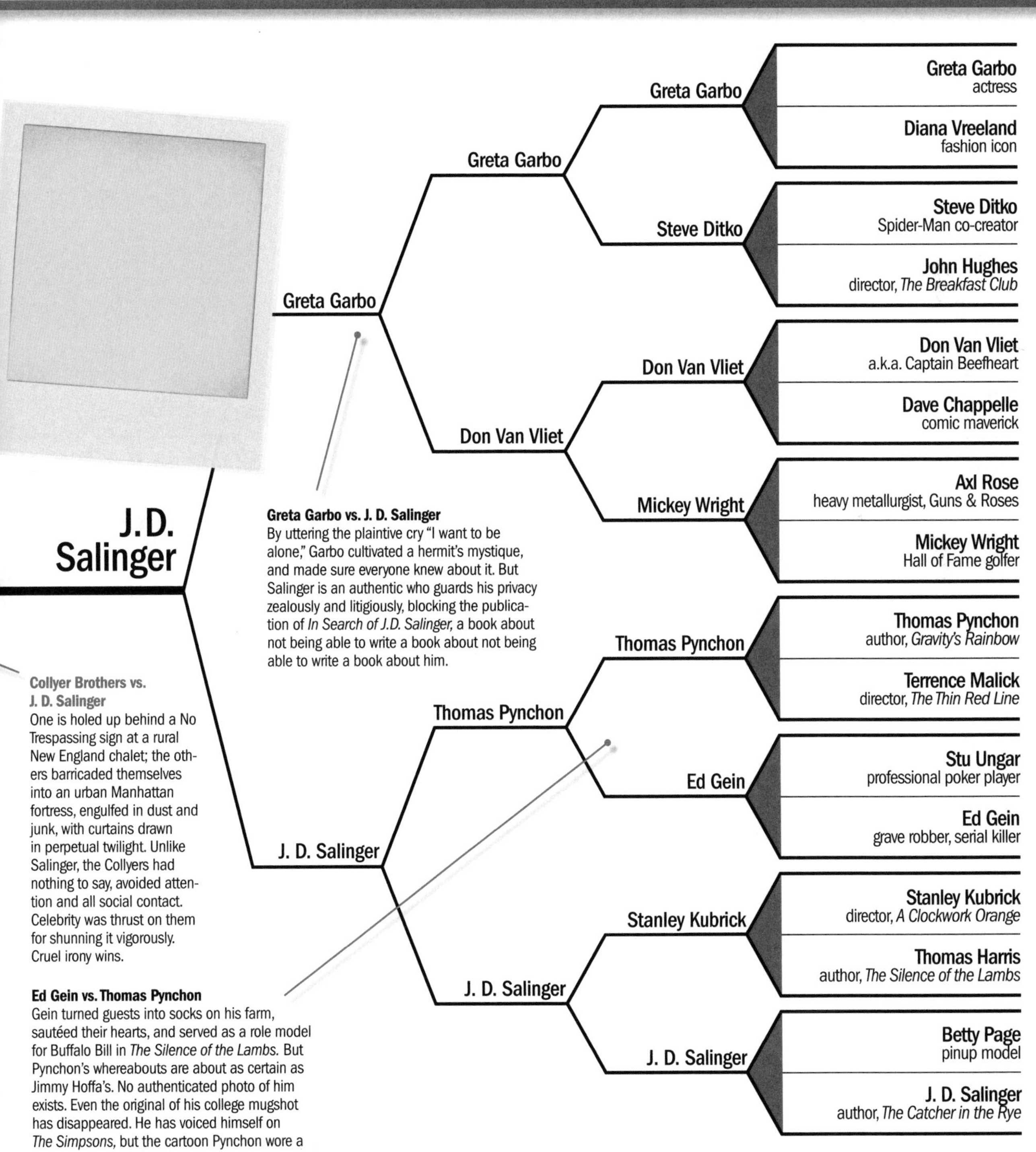
J.D. Salinger
Greta Garbo
J. D. Salinger
Greta Garbo
Don Van Vliet
Thomas Pynchon
J. D. Salinger
Greta Garbo
Steve Ditko
Don Van Vliet
Mickey Wright
Thomas Pynchon
Ed Gein
Stanley Kubrick
J. D. Salinger
Greta Garbo
actress
Diana Vreeland
fashion icon
Steve Ditko
Spider-Man co-creator
John Hughes
director, The Breakfast Club
Don Van Vliet
a.k.a. Captain Beefheart
Dave Chappelle
comic maverick
Axl Rose
heavy metallurgist, Guns & Roses
Mickey Wright
Hall of Fame golfer
Thomas Pynchon
author, Gravity's Rainbow
Terrence Malick
director, The Thin Red Line
Stu Ungar
professional poker player
Ed Gein
grave robber, serial killer
Stanley Kubrick
director, A Clockwork Orange
Thomas Harris
author, The Silence of the Lambs
Betty Page
pinup model
J. D. Salinger
author, The Catcher in the Rye

Greta Garbo vs. J. D. Salinger
By uttering the plaintive cry "I want to be alone," Garbo cultivated a hermit's mystique, and made sure everyone knew about it. But Salinger is an authentic who guards his privacy zealously and litigiously, blocking the publication of *In Search of J.D. Salinger,* a book about not being able to write a book about not being able to write a book about him.

Collyer Brothers vs. J. D. Salinger
One is holed up behind a No Trespassing sign at a rural New England chalet; the others barricaded themselves into an urban Manhattan fortress, engulfed in dust and junk, with curtains drawn in perpetual twilight. Unlike Salinger, the Collyers had nothing to say, avoided attention and all social contact. Celebrity was thrust on them for shunning it vigorously. Cruel irony wins.

Ed Gein vs. Thomas Pynchon
Gein turned guests into socks on his farm, sautéed their hearts, and served as a role model for Buffalo Bill in *The Silence of the Lambs.* But Pynchon's whereabouts are about as certain as Jimmy Hoffa's. No authenticated photo of him exists. Even the original of his college mugshot has disappeared. He has voiced himself on *The Simpsons,* but the cartoon Pynchon wore a paper bag over his head.

Richard vs. Dick

By Richard Sandomir

Richard Sandomir, the co-editor of this book, was born a Richard and rarely answers to anything but his full name, Rich or Richie. Only older men call him Dick, to which he will respond reluctantly.

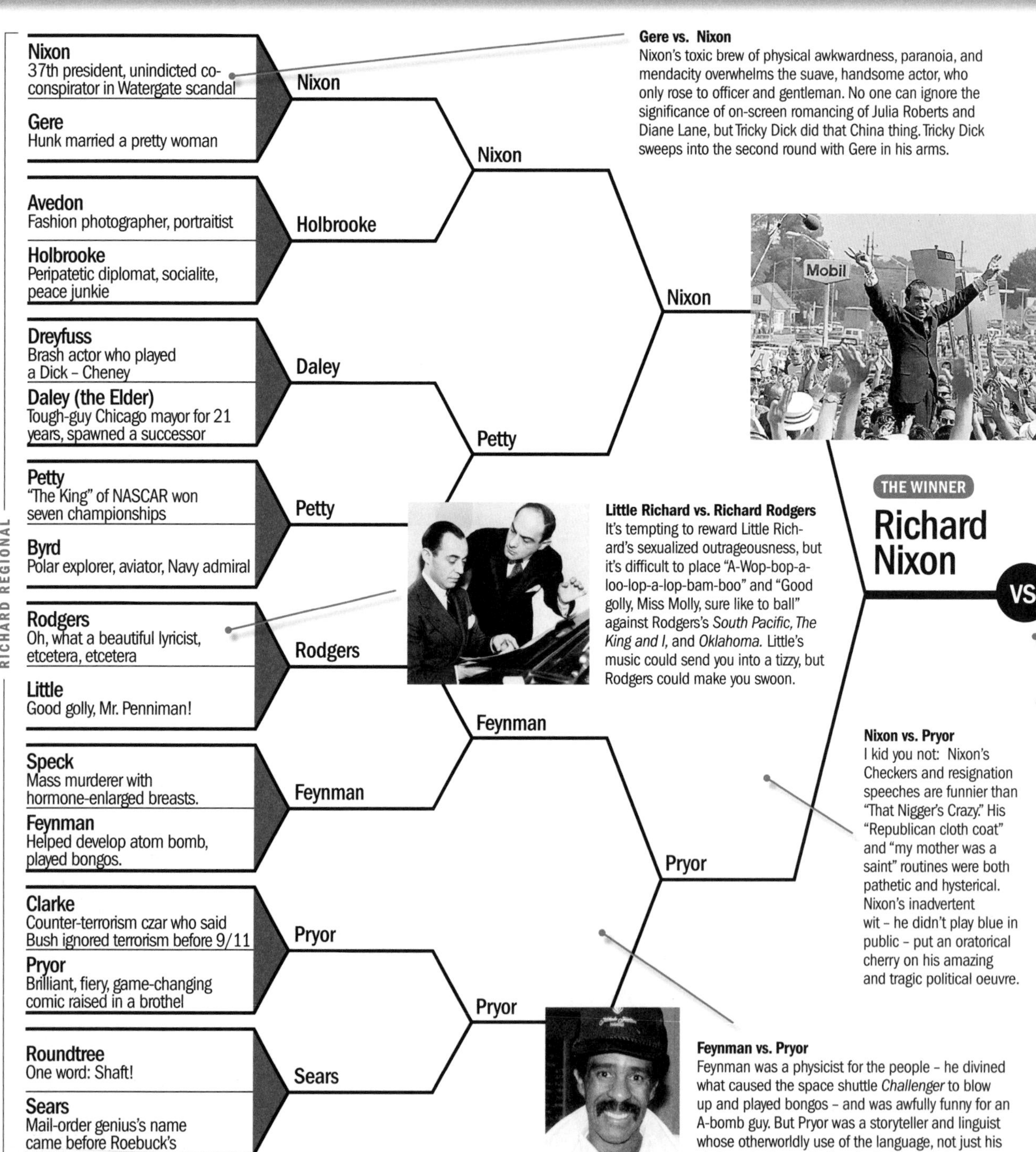

RICHARD REGIONAL
Nixon
37th president, unindicted co-conspirator in Watergate scandal
Gere
Hunk married a pretty woman
Avedon
Fashion photographer, portraitist
Holbrooke
Peripatetic diplomat, socialite, peace junkie
Dreyfuss
Brash actor who played a Dick – Cheney
Daley (the Elder)
Tough-guy Chicago mayor for 21 years, spawned a successor
Petty
"The King" of NASCAR won seven championships
Byrd
Polar explorer, aviator, Navy admiral
Rodgers
Oh, what a beautiful lyricist, etcetera, etcetera
Little
Good golly, Mr. Penniman!
Speck
Mass murderer with hormone-enlarged breasts.
Feynman
Helped develop atom bomb, played bongos.
Clarke
Counter-terrorism czar who said Bush ignored terrorism before 9/11
Pryor
Brilliant, fiery, game-changing comic raised in a brothel
Roundtree
One word: Shaft!
Sears
Mail-order genius's name came before Roebuck's
Nixon
Holbrooke
Daley
Petty
Rodgers
Feynman
Pryor
Sears
Nixon
Petty
Feynman
Pryor
Nixon
Pryor
Mobil
THE WINNER
Richard Nixon
VS.

Gere vs. Nixon
Nixon's toxic brew of physical awkwardness, paranoia, and mendacity overwhelms the suave, handsome actor, who only rose to officer and gentleman. No one can ignore the significance of on-screen romancing of Julia Roberts and Diane Lane, but Tricky Dick did that China thing. Tricky Dick sweeps into the second round with Gere in his arms.

Little Richard vs. Richard Rodgers
It's tempting to reward Little Richard's sexualized outrageousness, but it's difficult to place "A-Wop-bop-a-loo-lop-a-lop-bam-boo" and "Good golly, Miss Molly, sure like to ball" against Rodgers's *South Pacific, The King and I,* and *Oklahoma.* Little's music could send you into a tizzy, but Rodgers could make you swoon.

Nixon vs. Pryor
I kid you not: Nixon's Checkers and resignation speeches are funnier than "That Nigger's Crazy." His "Republican cloth coat" and "my mother was a saint" routines were both pathetic and hysterical. Nixon's inadvertent wit – he didn't play blue in public – put an oratorical cherry on his amazing and tragic political oeuvre.

Feynman vs. Pryor
Feynman was a physicist for the people – he divined what caused the space shuttle *Challenger* to blow up and played bongos – and was awfully funny for an A-bomb guy. But Pryor was a storyteller and linguist whose otherworldly use of the language, not just his glorious deployment of profanity, illustrated the possibilities of humor, not just black humor.

IN THIS BATTLE OF RICHARDS AND DICKS, we omit Ricks, Dickies, and Rickys as too much clutter, and foreign greats like Richard III, Dick Francis, or Richard the Lionheart, who aren't eligible. Despite Richard's enormous etymological edge (Old German for "powerful leader") over Dick (a genitalian. lunkheaded variant of Richard that flatters no one), both regions display an astonishing breadth of talent in politics, culture, sports, and science. And in any gathering of Dicks, a little Trickle must fall.

Cavett vs. Button
Cavett's version of the late-night talk show was about erudition and Groucho, but Button won Winter Olympic figure skating gold in 1948 and 1952, performed the first double axel and toe loop in competition, and then became TV's most influential and acerbic figure skating commentator.

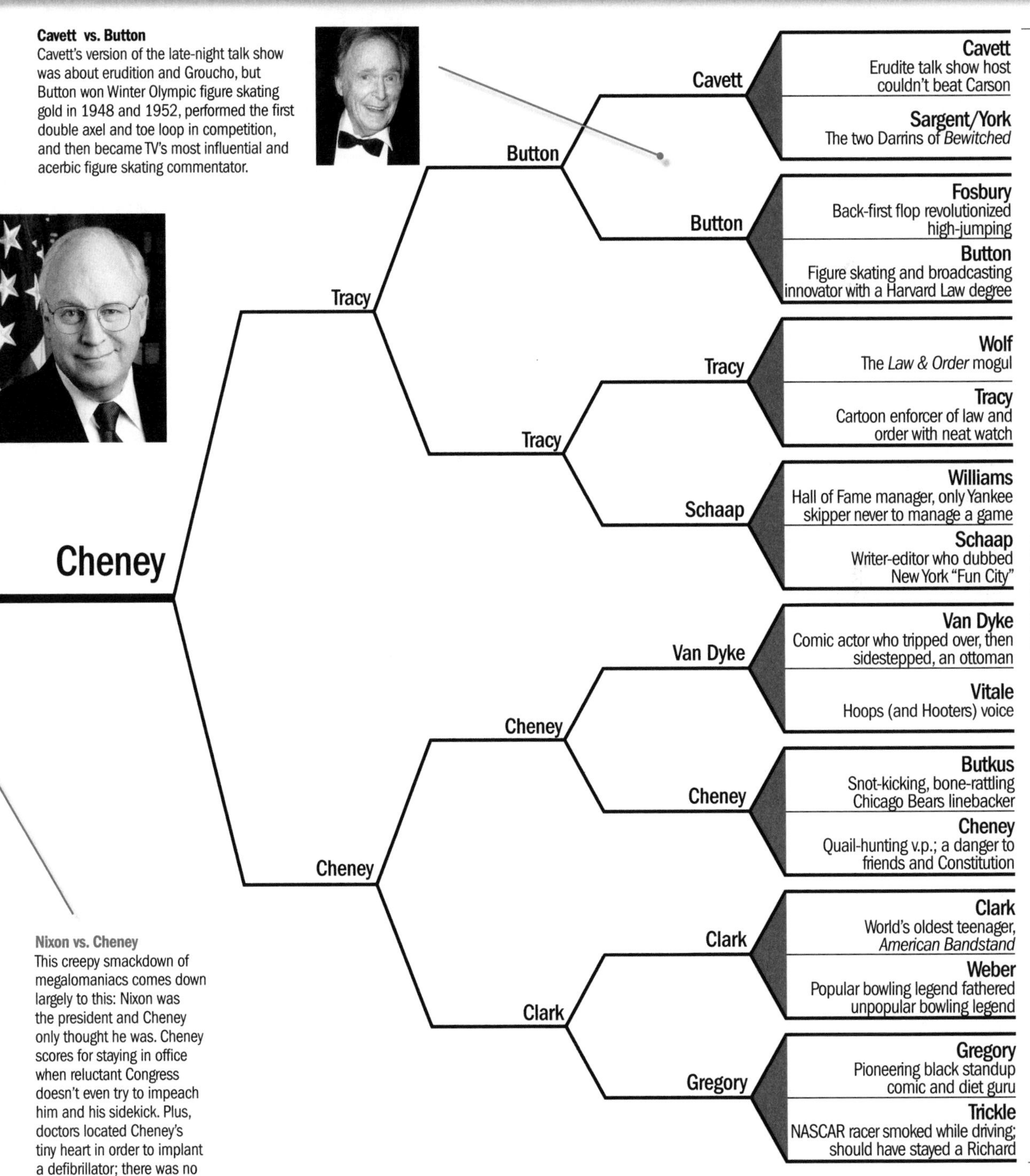
DICK REGIONAL
Cavett
Erudite talk show host couldn't beat Carson
Sargent/York
The two Darrins of *Bewitched*
Fosbury
Back-first flop revolutionized high-jumping
Button
Figure skating and broadcasting innovator with a Harvard Law degree
Wolf
The *Law & Order* mogul
Tracy
Cartoon enforcer of law and order with neat watch
Williams
Hall of Fame manager, only Yankee skipper never to manage a game
Schaap
Writer-editor who dubbed New York "Fun City"
Van Dyke
Comic actor who tripped over, then sidestepped, an ottoman
Vitale
Hoops (and Hooters) voice
Butkus
Snot-kicking, bone-rattling Chicago Bears linebacker
Cheney
Quail-hunting v.p.; a danger to friends and Constitution
Clark
World's oldest teenager, *American Bandstand*
Weber
Popular bowling legend fathered unpopular bowling legend
Gregory
Pioneering black standup comic and diet guru
Trickle
NASCAR racer smoked while driving; should have stayed a Richard
Cavett
Button
Tracy
Schaap
Van Dyke
Cheney
Clark
Gregory
Button
Tracy
Cheney
Clark
Tracy
Cheney
Cheney

Nixon vs. Cheney
This creepy smackdown of megalomaniacs comes down largely to this: Nixon was the president and Cheney only thought he was. Cheney scores for staying in office when reluctant Congress doesn't even try to impeach him and his sidekick. Plus, doctors located Cheney's tiny heart in order to implant a defibrillator; there was no evidence of Nixon's.

American Pinups

By Gregory Curtis

Gregory Curtis is the former editor of *Texas Monthly.* Until he wrote *Disarmed: The Story of the Venus de Milo,* he had never, ever, not even once, noticed a pinup.

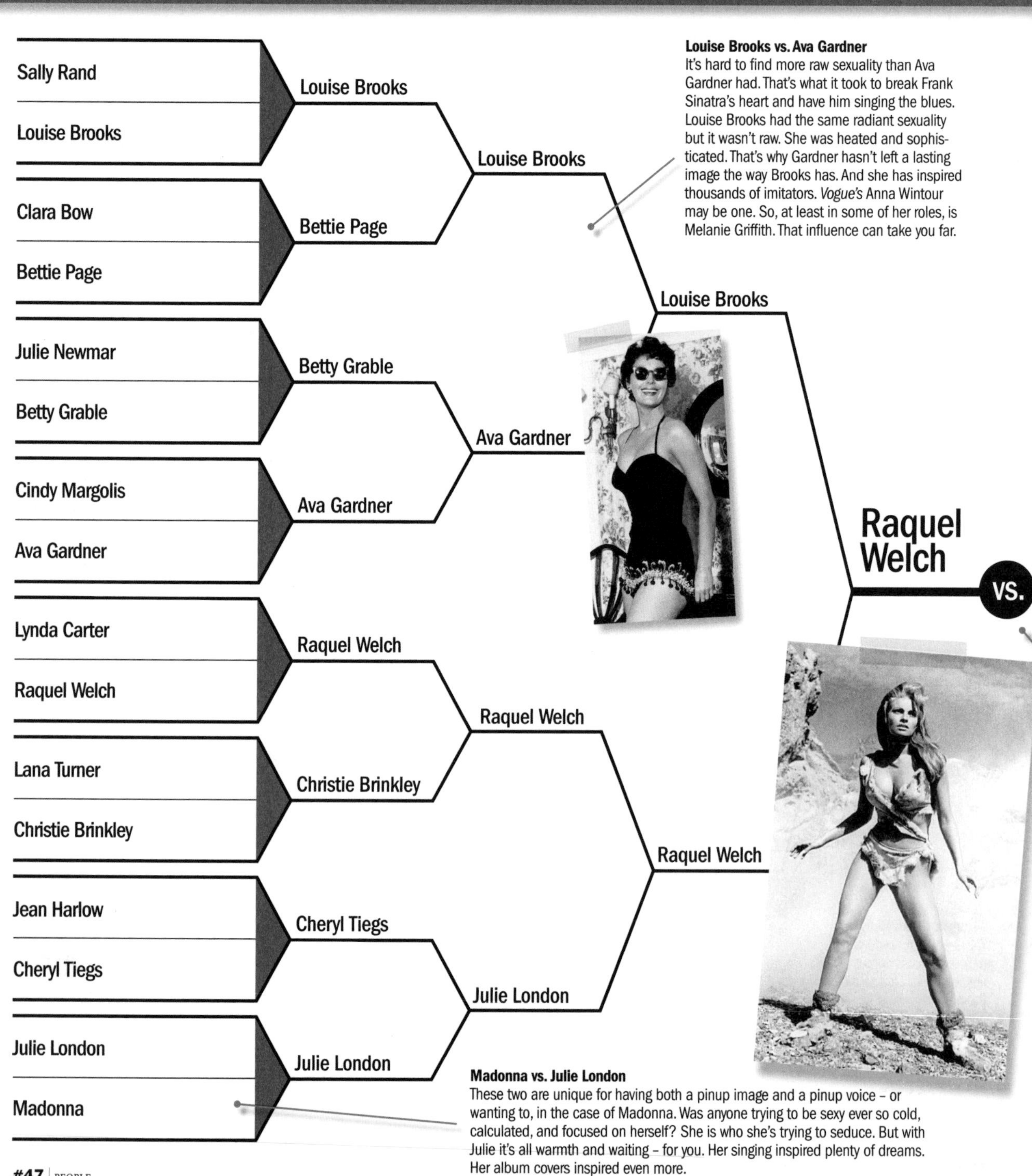

Sally Rand
Louise Brooks
Clara Bow
Bettie Page
Julie Newmar
Betty Grable
Cindy Margolis
Ava Gardner
Lynda Carter
Raquel Welch
Lana Turner
Christie Brinkley
Jean Harlow
Cheryl Tiegs
Julie London
Madonna
Louise Brooks
Bettie Page
Betty Grable
Ava Gardner
Raquel Welch
Christie Brinkley
Cheryl Tiegs
Julie London
Louise Brooks
Ava Gardner
Raquel Welch
Julie London
Louise Brooks
Raquel Welch
Raquel Welch
VS.

Louise Brooks vs. Ava Gardner
It's hard to find more raw sexuality than Ava Gardner had. That's what it took to break Frank Sinatra's heart and have him singing the blues. Louise Brooks had the same radiant sexuality but it wasn't raw. She was heated and sophisticated. That's why Gardner hasn't left a lasting image the way Brooks has. And she has inspired thousands of imitators. *Vogue's* Anna Wintour may be one. So, at least in some of her roles, is Melanie Griffith. That influence can take you far.

Madonna vs. Julie London
These two are unique for having both a pinup image and a pinup voice – or wanting to, in the case of Madonna. Was anyone trying to be sexy ever so cold, calculated, and focused on herself? She is who she's trying to seduce. But with Julie it's all warmth and waiting – for you. Her singing inspired plenty of dreams. Her album covers inspired even more.

PINUPS COME IN TWO VARIETIES. She can be the girl next door, turned into a goddess but still nice, e.g., Cheryl Tiegs, Christie Brinkley, Farrah Fawcett, even Bettie Page in bondage smiling sweetly. Or she can be Miss Va Va Voom, an extreme physical specimen that seems other-worldly, e.g., Jane Russell, Marilyn Monroe, Jayne Mansfield. A pinup of the first style is a nice girl. Miss Va Va Voom is beyond being a nice girl (or a bad girl) and so becomes soulless. A nice bust doesn't make up for that.

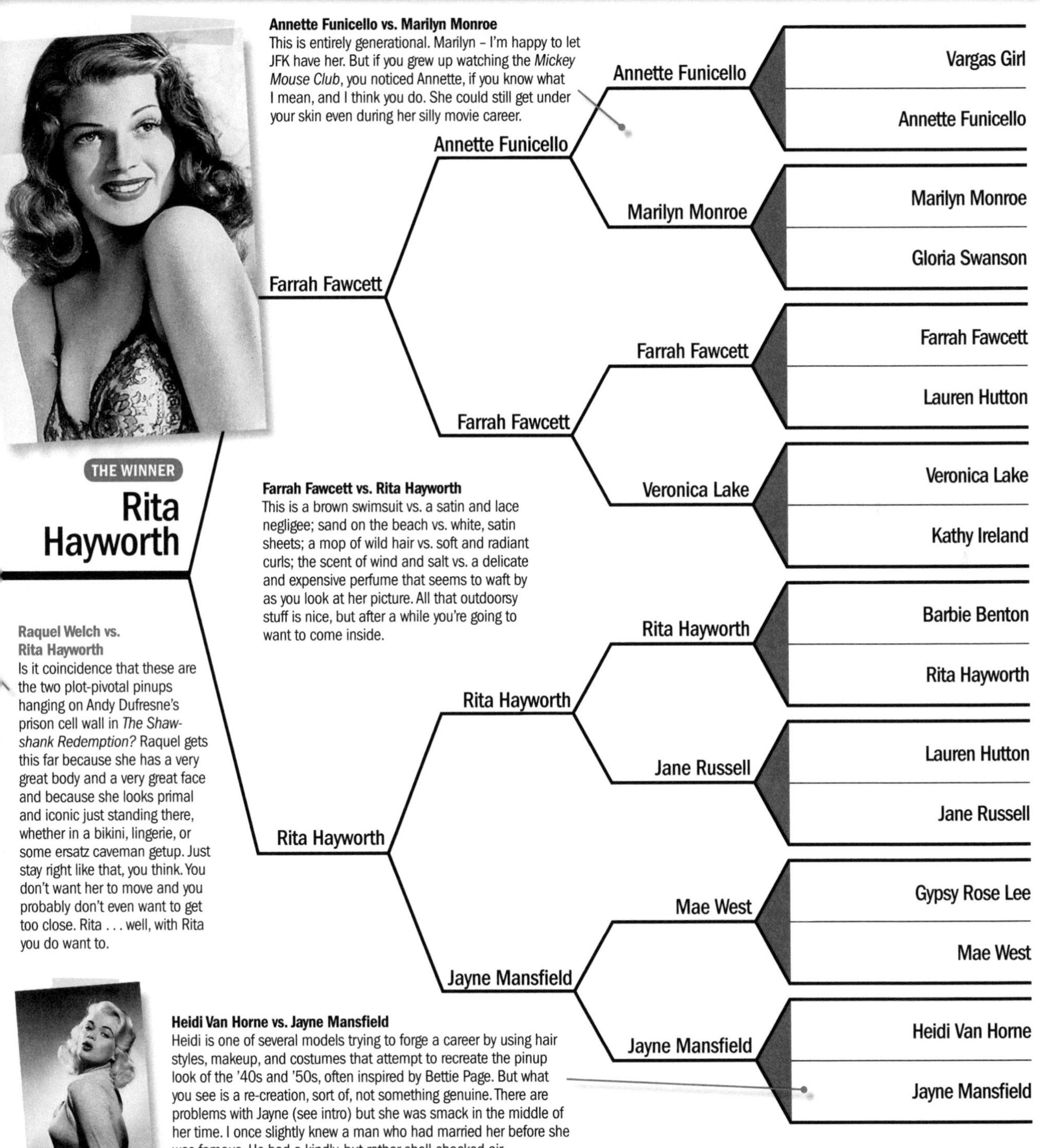

Vargas Girl
Annette Funicello
Marilyn Monroe
Gloria Swanson
Farrah Fawcett
Lauren Hutton
Veronica Lake
Kathy Ireland
Barbie Benton
Rita Hayworth
Lauren Hutton
Jane Russell
Gypsy Rose Lee
Mae West
Heidi Van Horne
Jayne Mansfield
Annette Funicello
Marilyn Monroe
Farrah Fawcett
Veronica Lake
Rita Hayworth
Jane Russell
Mae West
Jayne Mansfield
Annette Funicello
Farrah Fawcett
Rita Hayworth
Jayne Mansfield
Farrah Fawcett
Rita Hayworth
THE WINNER
Rita Hayworth

Annette Funicello vs. Marilyn Monroe
This is entirely generational. Marilyn – I'm happy to let JFK have her. But if you grew up watching the *Mickey Mouse Club*, you noticed Annette, if you know what I mean, and I think you do. She could still get under your skin even during her silly movie career.

Farrah Fawcett vs. Rita Hayworth
This is a brown swimsuit vs. a satin and lace negligee; sand on the beach vs. white, satin sheets; a mop of wild hair vs. soft and radiant curls; the scent of wind and salt vs. a delicate and expensive perfume that seems to waft by as you look at her picture. All that outdoorsy stuff is nice, but after a while you're going to want to come inside.

Raquel Welch vs. Rita Hayworth
Is it coincidence that these are the two plot-pivotal pinups hanging on Andy Dufresne's prison cell wall in *The Shawshank Redemption?* Raquel gets this far because she has a very great body and a very great face and because she looks primal and iconic just standing there, whether in a bikini, lingerie, or some ersatz caveman getup. Just stay right like that, you think. You don't want her to move and you probably don't even want to get too close. Rita . . . well, with Rita you do want to.

Heidi Van Horne vs. Jayne Mansfield
Heidi is one of several models trying to forge a career by using hair styles, makeup, and costumes that attempt to recreate the pinup look of the '40s and '50s, often inspired by Bettie Page. But what you see is a re-creation, sort of, not something genuine. There are problems with Jayne (see intro) but she was smack in the middle of her time. I once slightly knew a man who had married her before she was famous. He had a kindly, but rather shell-shocked air.

Pundits

By Franklin Foer

Franklin Foer is a pundit who lives among pundits in Washington, DC. He is editor of the *New Republic* and author of *How Soccer Explains the World: An Unlikely Theory of Globalization.*

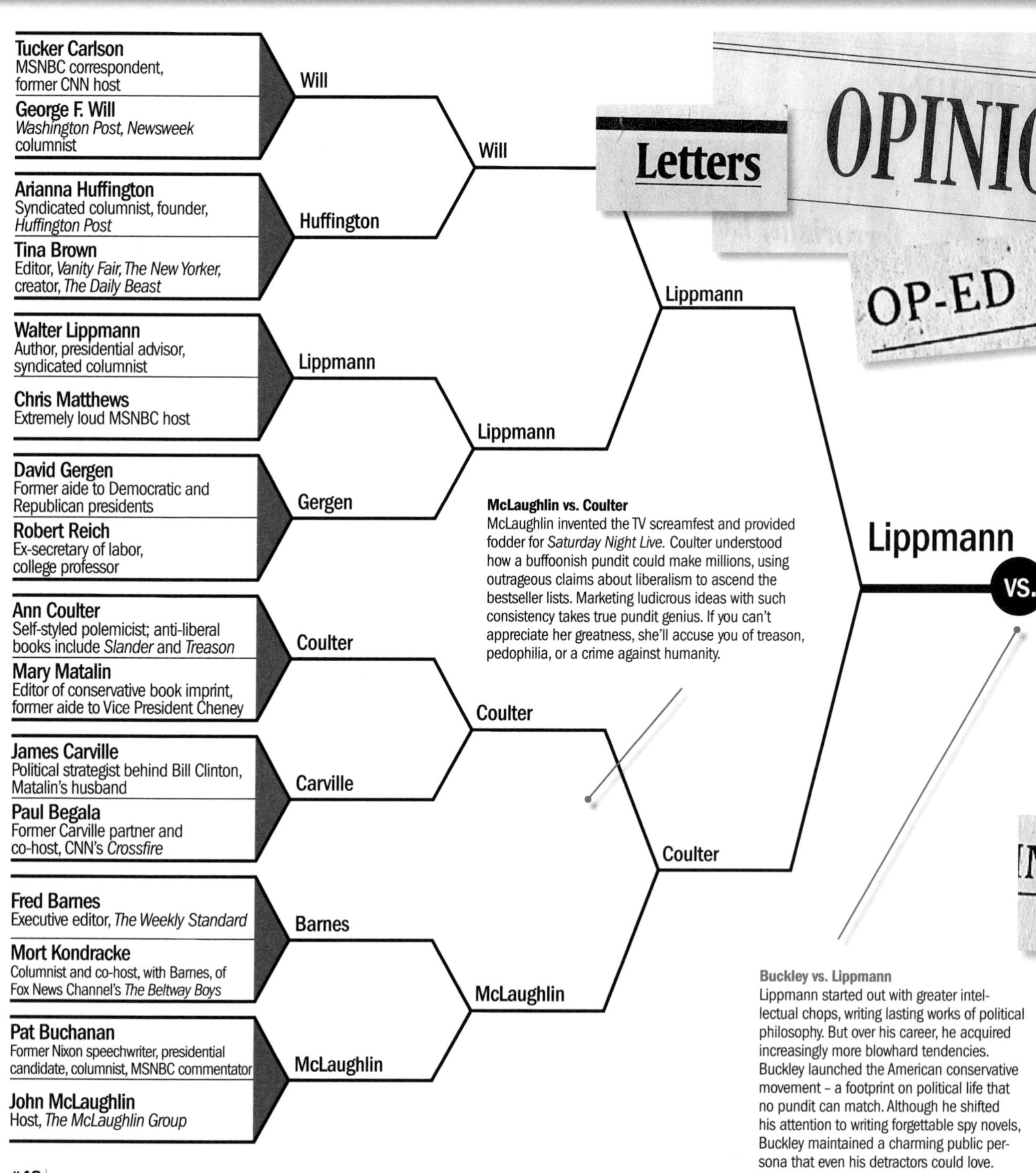

Tucker Carlson
MSNBC correspondent, former CNN host
George F. Will
Washington Post, Newsweek columnist
Arianna Huffington
Syndicated columnist, founder, Huffington Post
Tina Brown
Editor, Vanity Fair, The New Yorker, creator, The Daily Beast
Walter Lippmann
Author, presidential advisor, syndicated columnist
Chris Matthews
Extremely loud MSNBC host
David Gergen
Former aide to Democratic and Republican presidents
Robert Reich
Ex-secretary of labor, college professor
Ann Coulter
Self-styled polemicist; anti-liberal books include Slander and Treason
Mary Matalin
Editor of conservative book imprint, former aide to Vice President Cheney
James Carville
Political strategist behind Bill Clinton, Matalin's husband
Paul Begala
Former Carville partner and co-host, CNN's Crossfire
Fred Barnes
Executive editor, The Weekly Standard
Mort Kondracke
Columnist and co-host, with Barnes, of Fox News Channel's The Beltway Boys
Pat Buchanan
Former Nixon speechwriter, presidential candidate, columnist, MSNBC commentator
John McLaughlin
Host, The McLaughlin Group
Will
Huffington
Lippmann
Gergen
Coulter
Carville
Barnes
McLaughlin
Will
Lippmann
Coulter
McLaughlin
Lippmann
Coulter
Lippmann
VS.
Letters
OPINIO
OP-ED

McLaughlin vs. Coulter
McLaughlin invented the TV screamfest and provided fodder for *Saturday Night Live.* Coulter understood how a buffoonish pundit could make millions, using outrageous claims about liberalism to ascend the bestseller lists. Marketing ludicrous ideas with such consistency takes true pundit genius. If you can't appreciate her greatness, she'll accuse you of treason, pedophilia, or a crime against humanity.

Buckley vs. Lippmann
Lippmann started out with greater intellectual chops, writing lasting works of political philosophy. But over his career, he acquired increasingly more blowhard tendencies. Buckley launched the American conservative movement – a footprint on political life that no pundit can match. Although he shifted his attention to writing forgettable spy novels, Buckley maintained a charming public persona that even his detractors could love.

IN THE GOLDEN AGE OF PUNDITS – before bloggers, YouTube, and the slow demise of newspapers eroded their influence – creatures discoursed from television thrones and bejeweled columns with sage authority, even if their wisdom was only gleaned earlier that day over lunch at The Palm. Some were blowhards, some were more entrepreneur than commentator, but some were genuine intellectuals and great reporters. The best destroyed old strands of conventional wisdom in the course of creating new ones. The others, well, they shouted.

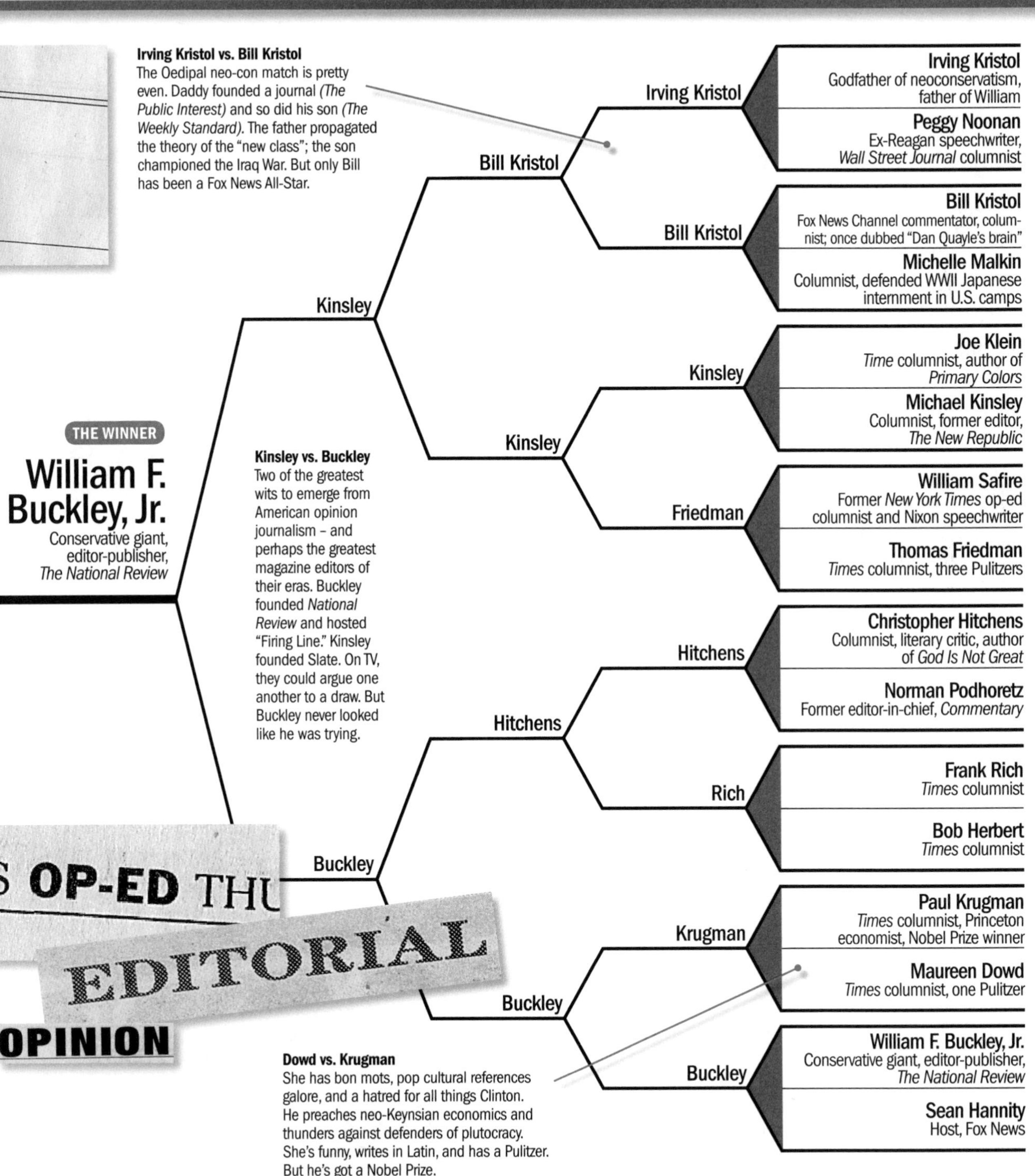

Irving Kristol
Godfather of neoconservatism, father of William
Peggy Noonan
Ex-Reagan speechwriter, Wall Street Journal columnist
Bill Kristol
Fox News Channel commentator, columnist; once dubbed "Dan Quayle's brain"
Michelle Malkin
Columnist, defended WWII Japanese internment in U.S. camps
Joe Klein
Time columnist, author of Primary Colors
Michael Kinsley
Columnist, former editor, The New Republic
William Safire
Former New York Times op-ed columnist and Nixon speechwriter
Thomas Friedman
Times columnist, three Pulitzers
Christopher Hitchens
Columnist, literary critic, author of God Is Not Great
Norman Podhoretz
Former editor-in-chief, Commentary
Frank Rich
Times columnist
Bob Herbert
Times columnist
Paul Krugman
Times columnist, Princeton economist, Nobel Prize winner
Maureen Dowd
Times columnist, one Pulitzer
William F. Buckley, Jr.
Conservative giant, editor-publisher, The National Review
Sean Hannity
Host, Fox News
Irving Kristol
Bill Kristol
Kinsley
Friedman
Hitchens
Rich
Krugman
Buckley
Bill Kristol
Kinsley
Hitchens
Buckley
Kinsley
Buckley
THE WINNER
William F. Buckley, Jr.
Conservative giant, editor-publisher, The National Review
S OP-ED THU
EDITORIAL
OPINION

Irving Kristol vs. Bill Kristol
The Oedipal neo-con match is pretty even. Daddy founded a journal *(The Public Interest)* and so did his son *(The Weekly Standard)*. The father propagated the theory of the "new class"; the son championed the Iraq War. But only Bill has been a Fox News All-Star.

Kinsley vs. Buckley
Two of the greatest wits to emerge from American opinion journalism – and perhaps the greatest magazine editors of their eras. Buckley founded *National Review* and hosted "Firing Line." Kinsley founded Slate. On TV, they could argue one another to a draw. But Buckley never looked like he was trying.

Dowd vs. Krugman
She has bon mots, pop cultural references galore, and a hatred for all things Clinton. He preaches neo-Keynsian economics and thunders against defenders of plutocracy. She's funny, writes in Latin, and has a Pulitzer. But he's got a Nobel Prize.

Great Brother Acts

By Mark Reiter

Mark Reiter, the co-editor of this book, has one brother but they live 6,000 miles apart, which makes it tough to get their act together.

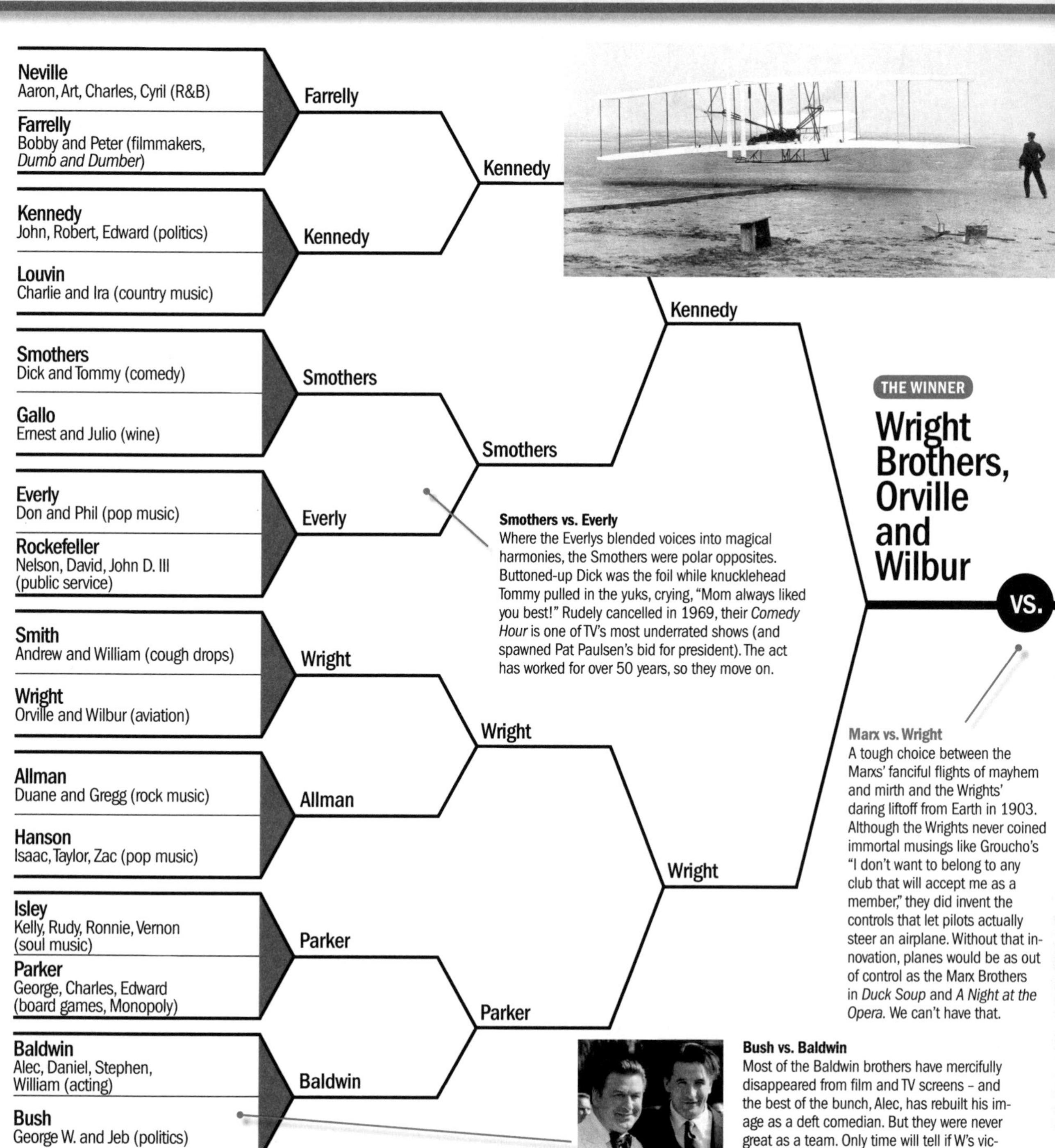

Neville
Aaron, Art, Charles, Cyril (R&B)
Farrelly
Bobby and Peter (filmmakers, *Dumb and Dumber*)
Kennedy
John, Robert, Edward (politics)
Louvin
Charlie and Ira (country music)
Smothers
Dick and Tommy (comedy)
Gallo
Ernest and Julio (wine)
Everly
Don and Phil (pop music)
Rockefeller
Nelson, David, John D. III (public service)
Smith
Andrew and William (cough drops)
Wright
Orville and Wilbur (aviation)
Allman
Duane and Gregg (rock music)
Hanson
Isaac, Taylor, Zac (pop music)
Isley
Kelly, Rudy, Ronnie, Vernon (soul music)
Parker
George, Charles, Edward (board games, Monopoly)
Baldwin
Alec, Daniel, Stephen, William (acting)
Bush
George W. and Jeb (politics)
Farrelly
Kennedy
Smothers
Everly
Wright
Allman
Parker
Baldwin
Kennedy
Smothers
Wright
Parker
Kennedy
Wright
THE WINNER
Wright Brothers, Orville and Wilbur
VS.

Smothers vs. Everly
Where the Everlys blended voices into magical harmonies, the Smothers were polar opposites. Buttoned-up Dick was the foil while knucklehead Tommy pulled in the yuks, crying, "Mom always liked you best!" Rudely cancelled in 1969, their *Comedy Hour* is one of TV's most underrated shows (and spawned Pat Paulsen's bid for president). The act has worked for over 50 years, so they move on.

Marx vs. Wright
A tough choice between the Marxs' fanciful flights of mayhem and mirth and the Wrights' daring liftoff from Earth in 1903. Although the Wrights never coined immortal musings like Groucho's "I don't want to belong to any club that will accept me as a member," they did invent the controls that let pilots actually steer an airplane. Without that innovation, planes would be as out of control as the Marx Brothers in *Duck Soup* and *A Night at the Opera*. We can't have that.

Bush vs. Baldwin
Most of the Baldwin brothers have mercifully disappeared from film and TV screens – and the best of the bunch, Alec, has rebuilt his image as a deft comedian. But they were never great as a team. Only time will tell if W's victory in the decisive 2000 Florida recount while brother Jeb was governor is passing strange or the greatest brother act in U.S. history.

TO BE A GREAT BROTHER ACT you have to operate as a team, creating a sum greater than the parts. It's not enough to be in the same line of work, like the brothers McEnroe in tennis or the DiMaggios in baseball. You have to complement and enhance each other, and one sib cannot overshadow the others so greatly that it sunders the act itself (which is why the Jacksons don't get past the second round). After that, the main criterion here is achievement and impact.

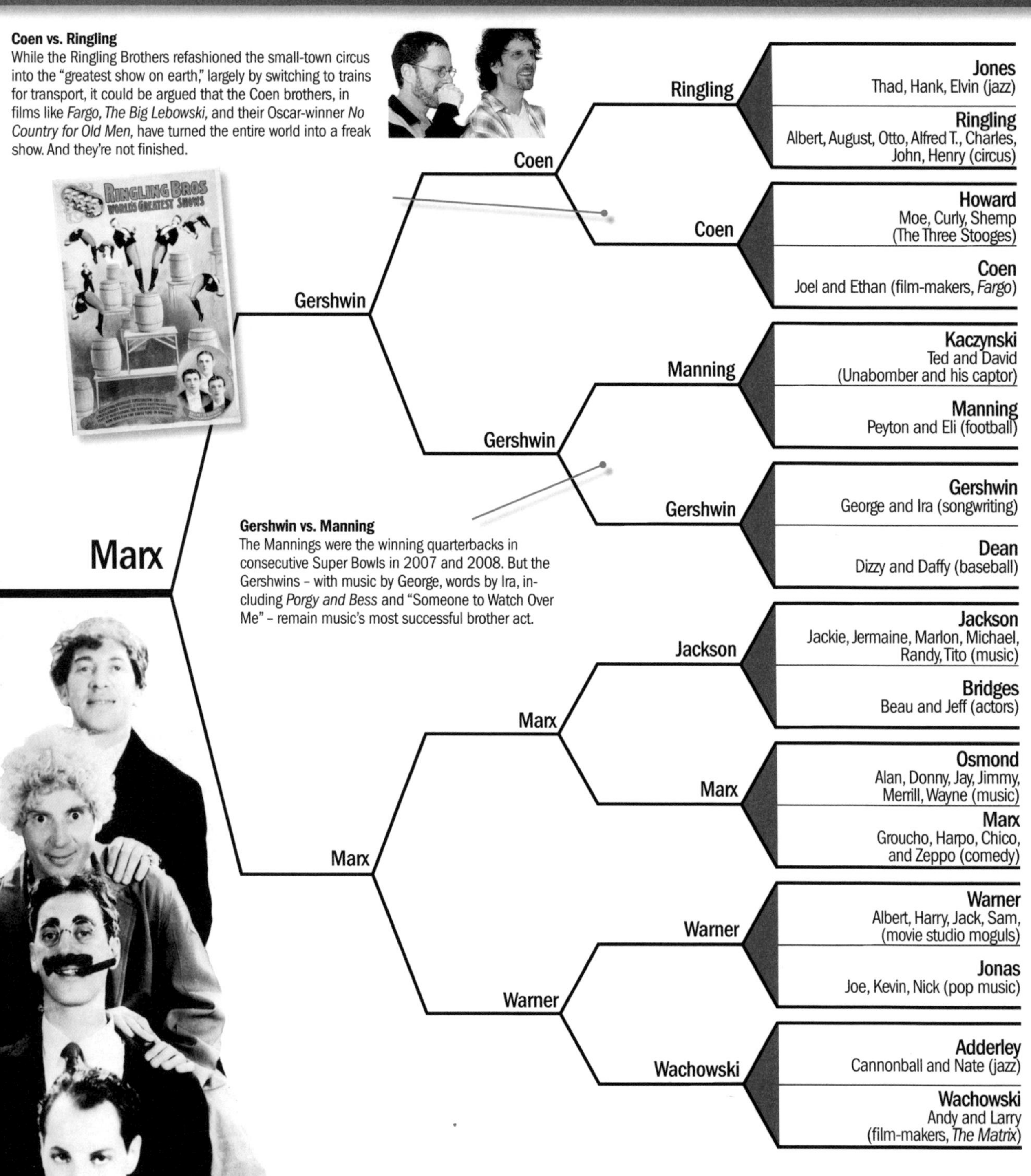

RINGLING BROS
WORLD'S GREATEST SHOWS
Jones
Thad, Hank, Elvin (jazz)
Ringling
Albert, August, Otto, Alfred T., Charles, John, Henry (circus)
Howard
Moe, Curly, Shemp (The Three Stooges)
Coen
Joel and Ethan (film-makers, *Fargo*)
Kaczynski
Ted and David (Unabomber and his captor)
Manning
Peyton and Eli (football)
Gershwin
George and Ira (songwriting)
Dean
Dizzy and Daffy (baseball)
Jackson
Jackie, Jermaine, Marlon, Michael, Randy, Tito (music)
Bridges
Beau and Jeff (actors)
Osmond
Alan, Donny, Jay, Jimmy, Merrill, Wayne (music)
Marx
Groucho, Harpo, Chico, and Zeppo (comedy)
Warner
Albert, Harry, Jack, Sam, (movie studio moguls)
Jonas
Joe, Kevin, Nick (pop music)
Adderley
Cannonball and Nate (jazz)
Wachowski
Andy and Larry (film-makers, *The Matrix*)
Ringling
Coen
Manning
Gershwin
Jackson
Marx
Warner
Wachowski
Coen
Gershwin
Marx
Warner
Gershwin
Marx
Marx

Coen vs. Ringling
While the Ringling Brothers refashioned the small-town circus into the "greatest show on earth," largely by switching to trains for transport, it could be argued that the Coen brothers, in films like *Fargo, The Big Lebowski,* and their Oscar-winner *No Country for Old Men*, have turned the entire world into a freak show. And they're not finished.

Gershwin vs. Manning
The Mannings were the winning quarterbacks in consecutive Super Bowls in 2007 and 2008. But the Gershwins – with music by George, words by Ira, including *Porgy and Bess* and "Someone to Watch Over Me" – remain music's most successful brother act.

Tom vs. Thomas

By Tom Chiarella

Tom Chiarella is fiction editor and writer-at-large for *Esquire* magazine. He is a visiting professor at DePauw University in Greencastle, Indiana. Author of three books, his next is *The Proposition*. No one calls him Thomas.

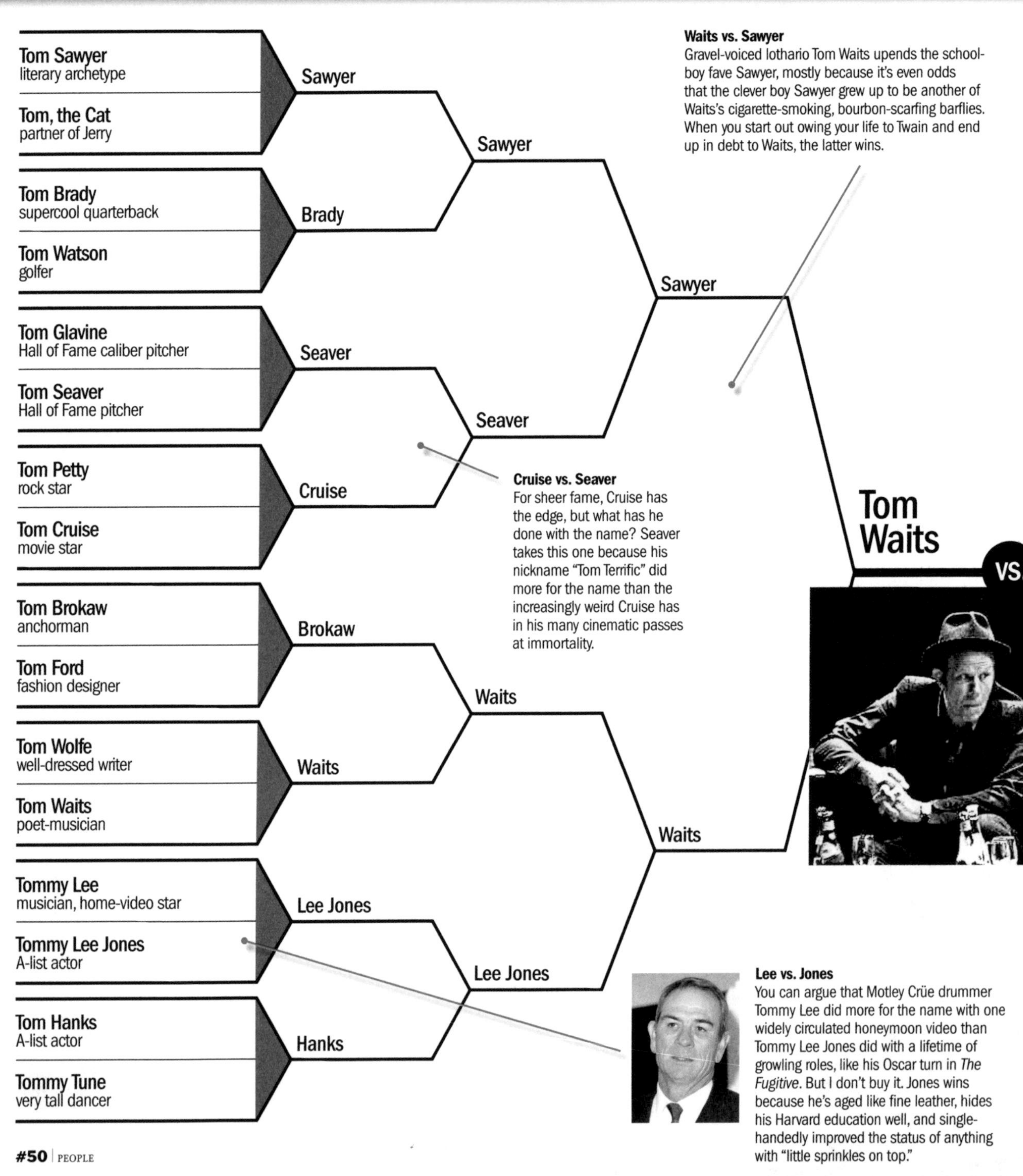

Tom Sawyer
literary archetype
Tom, the Cat
partner of Jerry
Tom Brady
supercool quarterback
Tom Watson
golfer
Tom Glavine
Hall of Fame caliber pitcher
Tom Seaver
Hall of Fame pitcher
Tom Petty
rock star
Tom Cruise
movie star
Tom Brokaw
anchorman
Tom Ford
fashion designer
Tom Wolfe
well-dressed writer
Tom Waits
poet-musician
Tommy Lee
musician, home-video star
Tommy Lee Jones
A-list actor
Tom Hanks
A-list actor
Tommy Tune
very tall dancer
Sawyer
Brady
Seaver
Cruise
Brokaw
Waits
Lee Jones
Hanks
Sawyer
Seaver
Waits
Lee Jones
Sawyer
Waits
Tom Waits
vs.

Waits vs. Sawyer
Gravel-voiced lothario Tom Waits upends the schoolboy fave Sawyer, mostly because it's even odds that the clever boy Sawyer grew up to be another of Waits's cigarette-smoking, bourbon-scarfing barflies. When you start out owing your life to Twain and end up in debt to Waits, the latter wins.

Cruise vs. Seaver
For sheer fame, Cruise has the edge, but what has he done with the name? Seaver takes this one because his nickname "Tom Terrific" did more for the name than the increasingly weird Cruise has in his many cinematic passes at immortality.

Lee vs. Jones
You can argue that Motley Crüe drummer Tommy Lee did more for the name with one widely circulated honeymoon video than Tommy Lee Jones did with a lifetime of growling roles, like his Oscar turn in *The Fugitive*. But I don't buy it. Jones wins because he's aged like fine leather, hides his Harvard education well, and single-handedly improved the status of anything with "little sprinkles on top."

GENERALLY SPEAKING, you'd want to have a beer with a Tom and have your taxes done by a guy named Thomas. As for Tommy, well, take my word for it: never lend money to a guy named Tommy. Tom is affable, Thomas self-serious, and Tommy flirts with edgy. Hence, two regionals here, one for Tom and the occasional Tommy, the other for Thomas. Only first names were invited, thus avoiding some tasty first-round match-ups (Clarence Thomas vs. Helen Thomas) and brand names like Tommy Gun and that nourishing semi-final lock, Thomas' English Muffins.

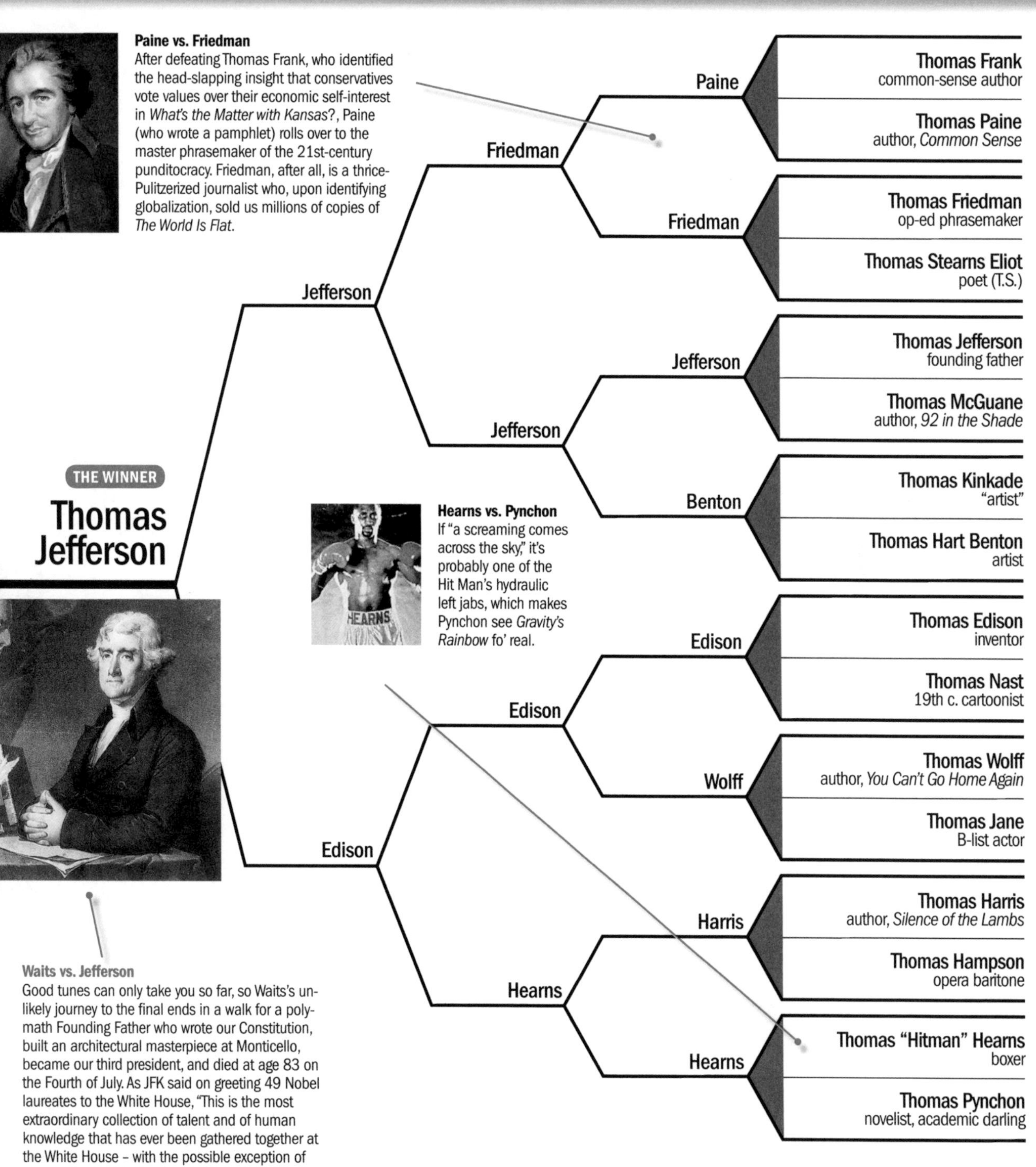

Thomas Frank
common-sense author
Thomas Paine
author, Common Sense
Thomas Friedman
op-ed phrasemaker
Thomas Stearns Eliot
poet (T.S.)
Thomas Jefferson
founding father
Thomas McGuane
author, 92 in the Shade
Thomas Kinkade
"artist"
Thomas Hart Benton
artist
Thomas Edison
inventor
Thomas Nast
19th c. cartoonist
Thomas Wolff
author, You Can't Go Home Again
Thomas Jane
B-list actor
Thomas Harris
author, Silence of the Lambs
Thomas Hampson
opera baritone
Thomas "Hitman" Hearns
boxer
Thomas Pynchon
novelist, academic darling
Paine
Friedman
Jefferson
Benton
Edison
Wolff
Harris
Hearns
Friedman
Jefferson
Edison
Hearns
Jefferson
Edison
HEARNS
THE WINNER
Thomas Jefferson

Paine vs. Friedman
After defeating Thomas Frank, who identified the head-slapping insight that conservatives vote values over their economic self-interest in *What's the Matter with Kansas?*, Paine (who wrote a pamphlet) rolls over to the master phrasemaker of the 21st-century punditocracy. Friedman, after all, is a thrice-Pulitzerized journalist who, upon identifying globalization, sold us millions of copies of *The World Is Flat*.

Hearns vs. Pynchon
If "a screaming comes across the sky," it's probably one of the Hit Man's hydraulic left jabs, which makes Pynchon see *Gravity's Rainbow* fo' real.

Waits vs. Jefferson
Good tunes can only take you so far, so Waits's unlikely journey to the final ends in a walk for a polymath Founding Father who wrote our Constitution, built an architectural masterpiece at Monticello, became our third president, and died at age 83 on the Fourth of July. As JFK said on greeting 49 Nobel laureates to the White House, "This is the most extraordinary collection of talent and of human knowledge that has ever been gathered together at the White House – with the possible exception of when Thomas Jefferson dined alone."

Immigrants

By Tony Quinn

Tony Quinn is the former editor of *Irish Connections* magazine and sports editor of *Home and Away* newspaper. He came to the U.S. from Newry in Ireland in 1993 and lives in Brooklyn.

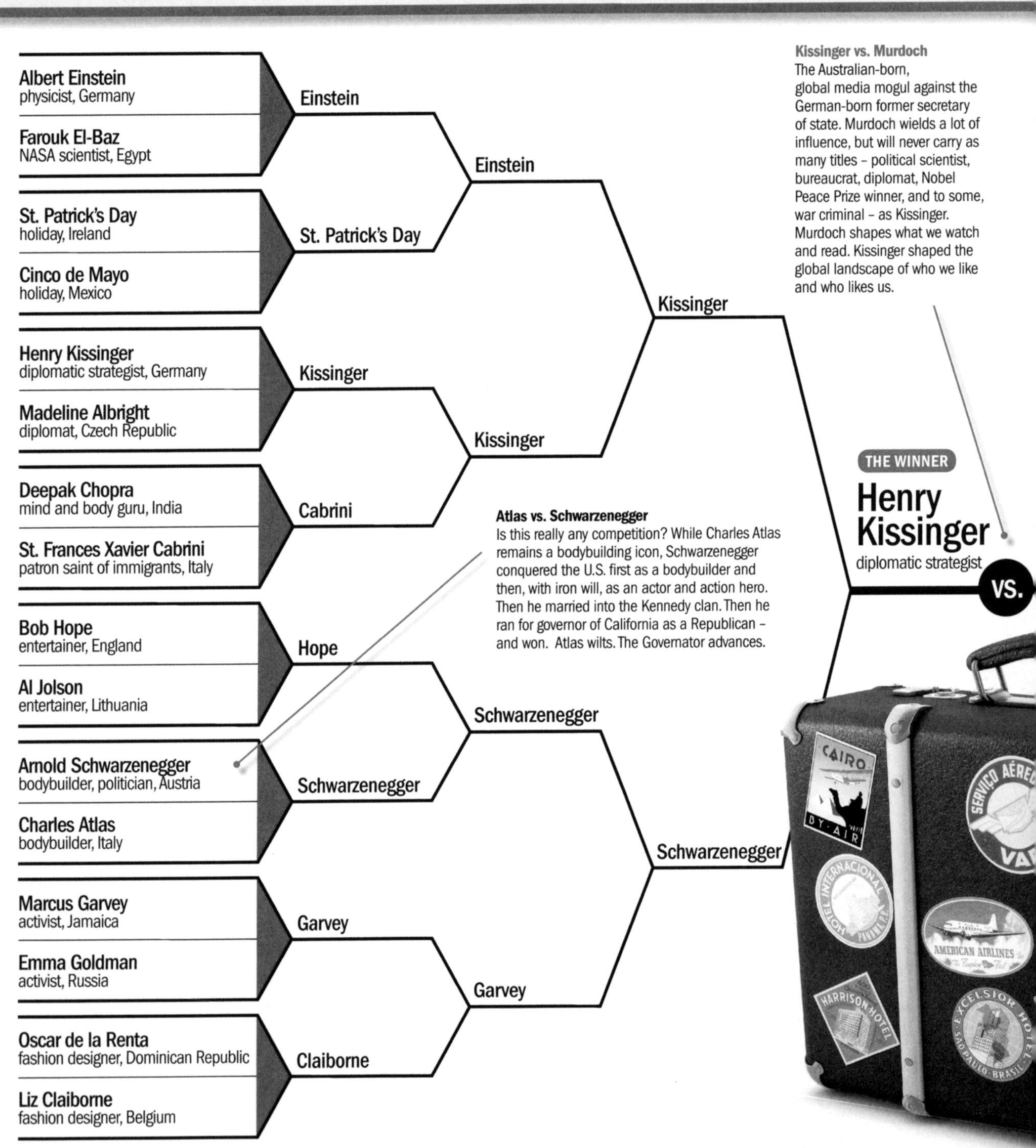

Albert Einstein
physicist, Germany
Farouk El-Baz
NASA scientist, Egypt
St. Patrick's Day
holiday, Ireland
Cinco de Mayo
holiday, Mexico
Henry Kissinger
diplomatic strategist, Germany
Madeline Albright
diplomat, Czech Republic
Deepak Chopra
mind and body guru, India
St. Frances Xavier Cabrini
patron saint of immigrants, Italy
Bob Hope
entertainer, England
Al Jolson
entertainer, Lithuania
Arnold Schwarzenegger
bodybuilder, politician, Austria
Charles Atlas
bodybuilder, Italy
Marcus Garvey
activist, Jamaica
Emma Goldman
activist, Russia
Oscar de la Renta
fashion designer, Dominican Republic
Liz Claiborne
fashion designer, Belgium
Einstein
St. Patrick's Day
Kissinger
Cabrini
Hope
Schwarzenegger
Garvey
Claiborne
Einstein
Kissinger
Schwarzenegger
Garvey
Kissinger
Schwarzenegger
THE WINNER
Henry Kissinger
diplomatic strategist
VS.
CAIRO
BY AIR
HOTEL INTERNACIONAL
PANAMA
AMERICAN AIRLINES
HARRISON HOTEL
EXCELSIOR HOTEL
SAO PAULO-BRASIL

Kissinger vs. Murdoch
The Australian-born, global media mogul against the German-born former secretary of state. Murdoch wields a lot of influence, but will never carry as many titles – political scientist, bureaucrat, diplomat, Nobel Peace Prize winner, and to some, war criminal – as Kissinger. Murdoch shapes what we watch and read. Kissinger shaped the global landscape of who we like and who likes us.

Atlas vs. Schwarzenegger
Is this really any competition? While Charles Atlas remains a bodybuilding icon, Schwarzenegger conquered the U.S. first as a bodybuilder and then, with iron will, as an actor and action hero. Then he married into the Kennedy clan. Then he ran for governor of California as a Republican – and won. Atlas wilts. The Governator advances.

A BRONZE PLAQUE OUTSIDE THE CHELSEA HOTEL in New York City reads: "To America, my new found land: The man that hates you hates the human race." Though the author of these words, the Irish writer Brendan Behan, never actually became a U.S. citizen, his words express the hope of every immigrant: to discover a love for a country that is not your own. America draws people from every corner of the world. Driven by ambition, curiosity, dreams of safety or freedom, we are a nation of immigrants. Here, some of the most influential.

Carnegie vs. Murdoch
The Scottish-born industrialist and businessman is often regarded as the second richest person in history. But he made his lasting mark as a philanthropist, giving most of his money away to fund schools and libraries. If there's a large, beautiful, imposing library in your home town, chances are Carnegie paid for it. Murdoch's News Corp is one of the world's largest media conglomerates and shows no signs of slowing down.

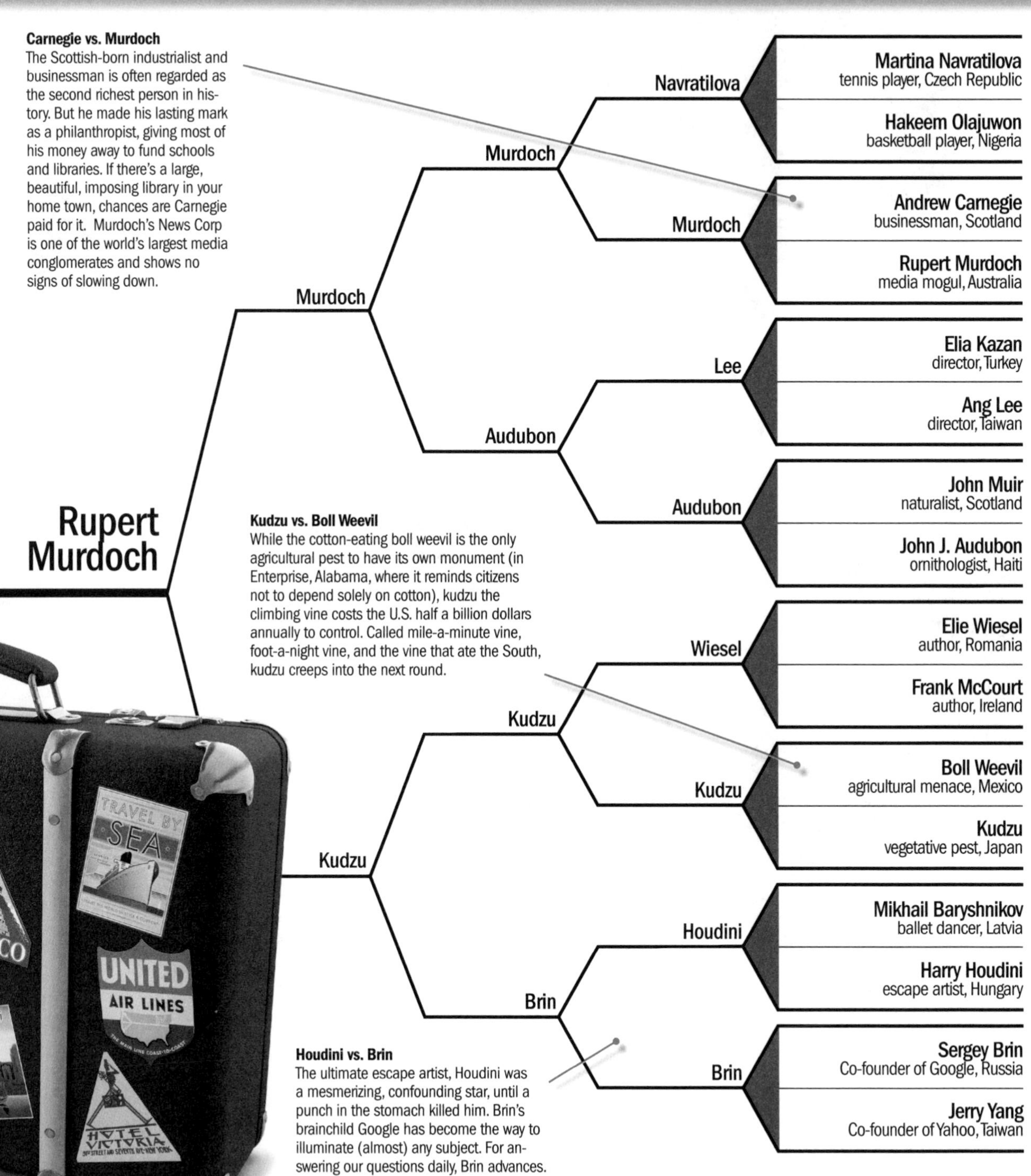

Martina Navratilova
tennis player, Czech Republic
Hakeem Olajuwon
basketball player, Nigeria
Andrew Carnegie
businessman, Scotland
Rupert Murdoch
media mogul, Australia
Elia Kazan
director, Turkey
Ang Lee
director, Taiwan
John Muir
naturalist, Scotland
John J. Audubon
ornithologist, Haiti
Elie Wiesel
author, Romania
Frank McCourt
author, Ireland
Boll Weevil
agricultural menace, Mexico
Kudzu
vegetative pest, Japan
Mikhail Baryshnikov
ballet dancer, Latvia
Harry Houdini
escape artist, Hungary
Sergey Brin
Co-founder of Google, Russia
Jerry Yang
Co-founder of Yahoo, Taiwan
Navratilova
Murdoch
Lee
Audubon
Wiesel
Kudzu
Houdini
Brin
Murdoch
Audubon
Kudzu
Brin
Murdoch
Kudzu
Rupert Murdoch
TRAVEL BY SEA
UNITED AIR LINES
HOTEL VICTORIA

Kudzu vs. Boll Weevil
While the cotton-eating boll weevil is the only agricultural pest to have its own monument (in Enterprise, Alabama, where it reminds citizens not to depend solely on cotton), kudzu the climbing vine costs the U.S. half a billion dollars annually to control. Called mile-a-minute vine, foot-a-night vine, and the vine that ate the South, kudzu creeps into the next round.

Houdini vs. Brin
The ultimate escape artist, Houdini was a mesmerizing, confounding star, until a punch in the stomach killed him. Brin's brainchild Google has become the way to illuminate (almost) any subject. For answering our questions daily, Brin advances.

SPORTS

Olympic Athletes *by David Maraniss* 52
NFL Team Logos *by D.W. Pine* 53
Dallas Cowboys *by Jeff Pearlman* 54
Jewish Baseball Players *by Daniel Okrent* 55
All-Time Fantasy Sports Performances *by Matt Pitzer* 56
21st-Century Sports Books *by Will Leitch* 57
Ringless Athletes *by Dick Friedman* 58
Donald Ross Courses *by Bob Carney* 59
American Hockey Players *by Nick Paumgarten* 60
Steroid-Era Moments *by Shaun Assael* 61
Sports Clichés *by Steve Rushin* 62
Instant Replays *by Alan Schwarz* 63
Sexually Inadequate Nicknames *by Hart Seely* 64
Baseball Moments *by John Thorn* 65
Absurd College Nicknames *by Richard Sandomir and Pete Thamel* 66
Toughest Golf Holes *by Chris Millard* 67
Dubious Sports Achievements *by Richard Hoffer* 68
From Athlete to Actor *by Mark Reiter* 69
Sportscasters *by Richard Deitsch* 70
SEC Athletes *by Steve Eubanks* 71
Pound-for-Pound Fighters *by Steve Farhood* 72
Field Goals and PATs *by Stefan Fatsis* 73
Golf Books *by John Garrity* 74
New York Athletes *by George Vecsey* 75
Boston Athletes *by Dan Shaughnessy* 76
Sportswriters *by Glenn Stout* 77
Advertising Icons *by Bryan Curtis* 78
Greatest Sports Year *by Mike Vaccaro* 79

Olympic Athletes

By David Maraniss

David Maraniss, an associate editor of the *Washington Post,* won a 1993 Pulitzer Prize for his articles on Bill Clinton. His books include *When Pride Still Mattered* and *Rome 1960.*

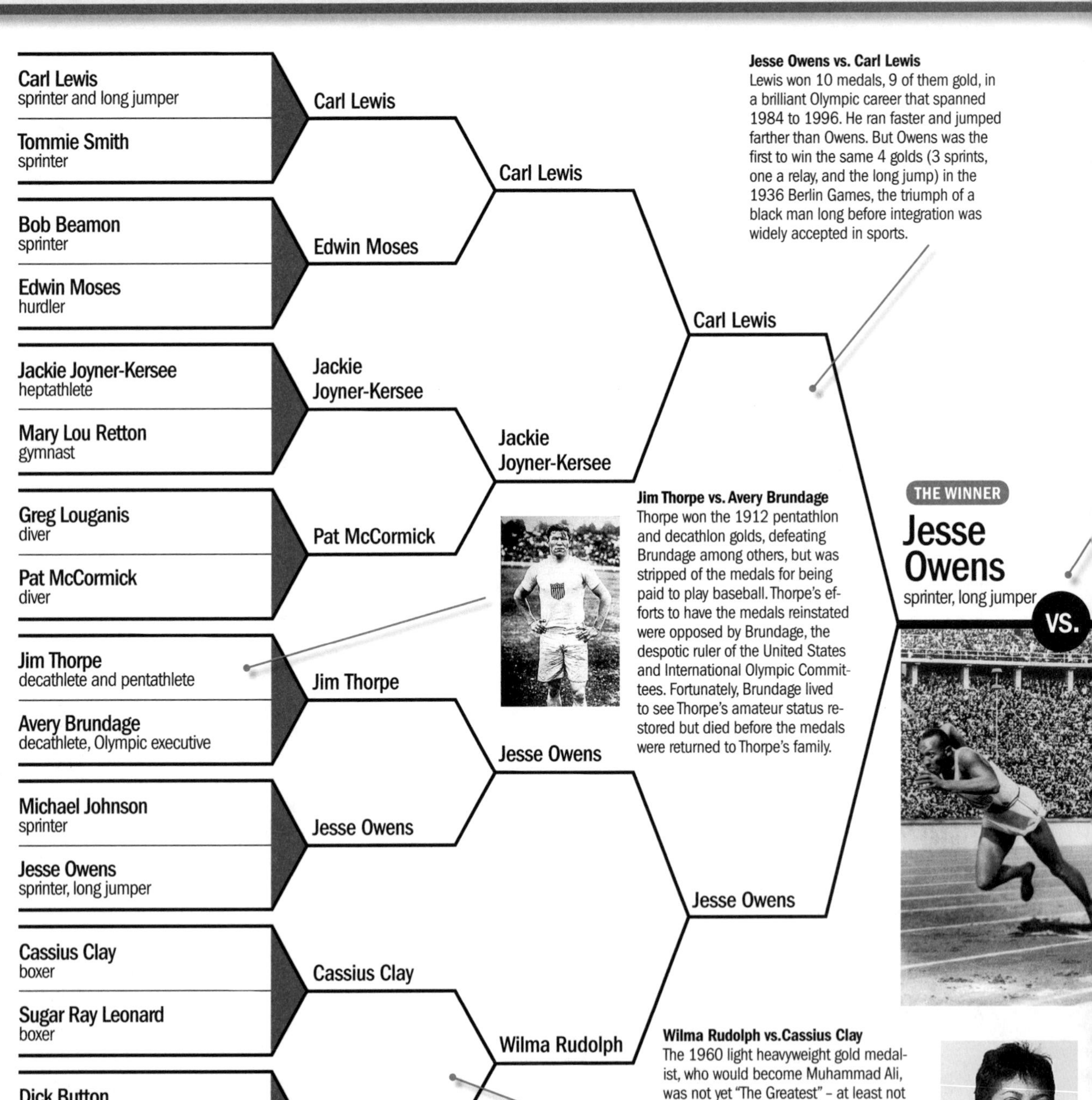

Carl Lewis
sprinter and long jumper
Tommie Smith
sprinter
Bob Beamon
sprinter
Edwin Moses
hurdler
Jackie Joyner-Kersee
heptathlete
Mary Lou Retton
gymnast
Greg Louganis
diver
Pat McCormick
diver
Jim Thorpe
decathlete and pentathlete
Avery Brundage
decathlete, Olympic executive
Michael Johnson
sprinter
Jesse Owens
sprinter, long jumper
Cassius Clay
boxer
Sugar Ray Leonard
boxer
Dick Button
figure skater
Wilma Rudolph
sprinter
Carl Lewis
Edwin Moses
Jackie Joyner-Kersee
Pat McCormick
Jim Thorpe
Jesse Owens
Cassius Clay
Wilma Rudolph
Carl Lewis
Jackie Joyner-Kersee
Jesse Owens
Wilma Rudolph
Carl Lewis
Jesse Owens
THE WINNER
Jesse Owens
sprinter, long jumper
VS.

Jesse Owens vs. Carl Lewis
Lewis won 10 medals, 9 of them gold, in a brilliant Olympic career that spanned 1984 to 1996. He ran faster and jumped farther than Owens. But Owens was the first to win the same 4 golds (3 sprints, one a relay, and the long jump) in the 1936 Berlin Games, the triumph of a black man long before integration was widely accepted in sports.

Jim Thorpe vs. Avery Brundage
Thorpe won the 1912 pentathlon and decathlon golds, defeating Brundage among others, but was stripped of the medals for being paid to play baseball. Thorpe's efforts to have the medals reinstated were opposed by Brundage, the despotic ruler of the United States and International Olympic Committees. Fortunately, Brundage lived to see Thorpe's amateur status restored but died before the medals were returned to Thorpe's family.

Wilma Rudolph vs. Cassius Clay
The 1960 light heavyweight gold medalist, who would become Muhammad Ali, was not yet "The Greatest" – at least not when it came to facing Wilma, the shining star of the U.S. track team who overcame childhood polio and won three golds that year in Rome. With Clay at age 18 more impressed by the 20-year-old Wilma than he would later be by Sonny Liston, Wilma races to the next heat.

THE BEAUTY OF THE OLYMPICS is that the world takes the same stage at the same time, performing a passion play of nations, races, ideologies, sports, talents, and aspirations unmatched in any other venue in the world. The greatest Olympians, including scores of Americans, cannot be fairly judged against each other over nearly 100 years because of the evolution in training techniques, field conditions, and equipment. Surely, Michael Phelps was better prepared in 2008 in Beijing than Johnny Weissmuller was 84 years earlier in Paris. So gut instinct and lasting social significance produced the gold medalists here.

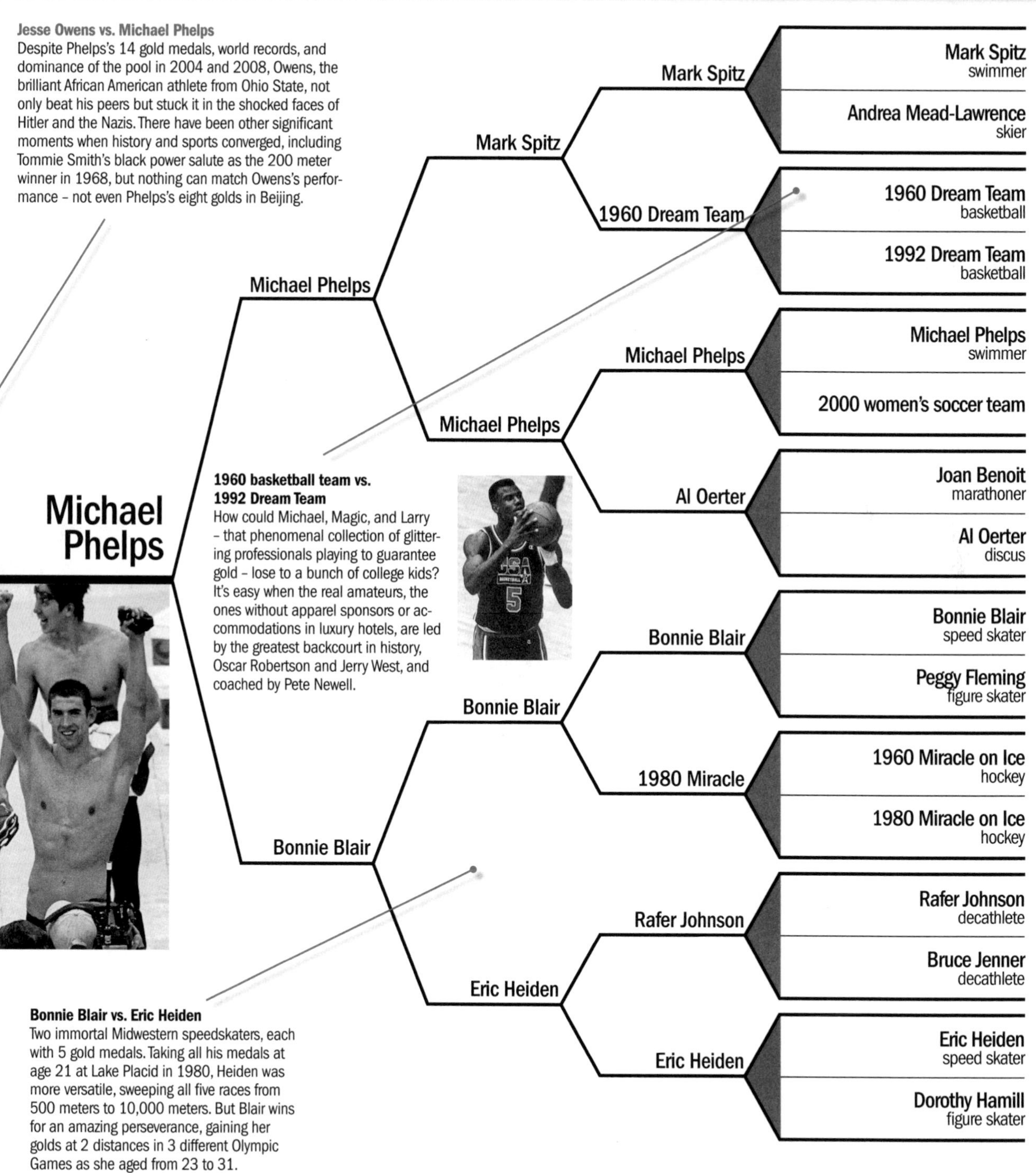

Michael Phelps
Michael Phelps
Bonnie Blair
Mark Spitz
Michael Phelps
Bonnie Blair
Eric Heiden
Mark Spitz
1960 Dream Team
Michael Phelps
Al Oerter
Bonnie Blair
1980 Miracle
Rafer Johnson
Eric Heiden
Mark Spitz
swimmer
Andrea Mead-Lawrence
skier
1960 Dream Team
basketball
1992 Dream Team
basketball
Michael Phelps
swimmer
2000 women's soccer team
Joan Benoit
marathoner
Al Oerter
discus
Bonnie Blair
speed skater
Peggy Fleming
figure skater
1960 Miracle on Ice
hockey
1980 Miracle on Ice
hockey
Rafer Johnson
decathlete
Bruce Jenner
decathlete
Eric Heiden
speed skater
Dorothy Hamill
figure skater

Jesse Owens vs. Michael Phelps
Despite Phelps's 14 gold medals, world records, and dominance of the pool in 2004 and 2008, Owens, the brilliant African American athlete from Ohio State, not only beat his peers but stuck it in the shocked faces of Hitler and the Nazis. There have been other significant moments when history and sports converged, including Tommie Smith's black power salute as the 200 meter winner in 1968, but nothing can match Owens's performance – not even Phelps's eight golds in Beijing.

1960 basketball team vs. 1992 Dream Team
How could Michael, Magic, and Larry – that phenomenal collection of glittering professionals playing to guarantee gold – lose to a bunch of college kids? It's easy when the real amateurs, the ones without apparel sponsors or accommodations in luxury hotels, are led by the greatest backcourt in history, Oscar Robertson and Jerry West, and coached by Pete Newell.

Bonnie Blair vs. Eric Heiden
Two immortal Midwestern speedskaters, each with 5 gold medals. Taking all his medals at age 21 at Lake Placid in 1980, Heiden was more versatile, sweeping all five races from 500 meters to 10,000 meters. But Blair wins for an amazing perseverance, gaining her golds at 2 distances in 3 different Olympic Games as she aged from 23 to 31.

NFL Team Logos

By D.W. Pine

D.W. Pine, the designer of this book, is the deputy art director of *Time* magazine, a former sportswriter for the *Atlanta Journal-Constitution* and a lifelong Steelers fan. He's currently crying into his Terrible Towel for picking the Browns.

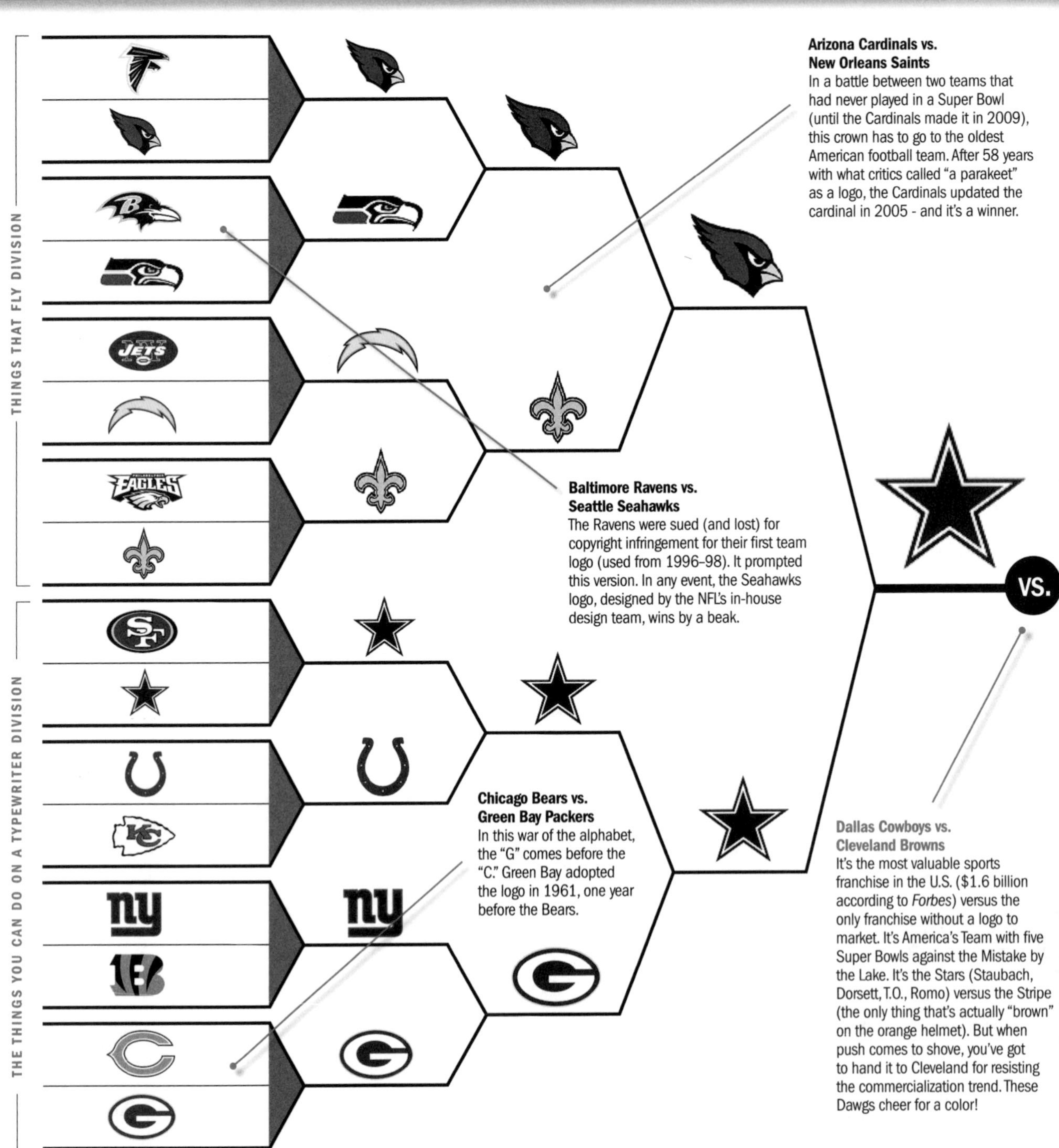

THINGS THAT FLY DIVISION
THE THINGS YOU CAN DO ON A TYPEWRITER DIVISION
VS.

Arizona Cardinals vs. New Orleans Saints
In a battle between two teams that had never played in a Super Bowl (until the Cardinals made it in 2009), this crown has to go to the oldest American football team. After 58 years with what critics called "a parakeet" as a logo, the Cardinals updated the cardinal in 2005 - and it's a winner.

Baltimore Ravens vs. Seattle Seahawks
The Ravens were sued (and lost) for copyright infringement for their first team logo (used from 1996–98). It prompted this version. In any event, the Seahawks logo, designed by the NFL's in-house design team, wins by a beak.

Chicago Bears vs. Green Bay Packers
In this war of the alphabet, the "G" comes before the "C." Green Bay adopted the logo in 1961, one year before the Bears.

Dallas Cowboys vs. Cleveland Browns
It's the most valuable sports franchise in the U.S. ($1.6 billion according to *Forbes*) versus the only franchise without a logo to market. It's America's Team with five Super Bowls against the Mistake by the Lake. It's the Stars (Staubach, Dorsett, T.O., Romo) versus the Stripe (the only thing that's actually "brown" on the orange helmet). But when push comes to shove, you've got to hand it to Cleveland for resisting the commercialization trend. These Dawgs cheer for a color!

WE SPEND NEARLY HALF A YEAR passionately pleading (praying) for our favorite NFL team to win a game — any game! But in the end, we're not cheering for the players (who are hidden behind helmets), we're rooting for the actual helmets. A color. A symbol. A design. Players come and go, but it's the logos that keep us coming back year after year.

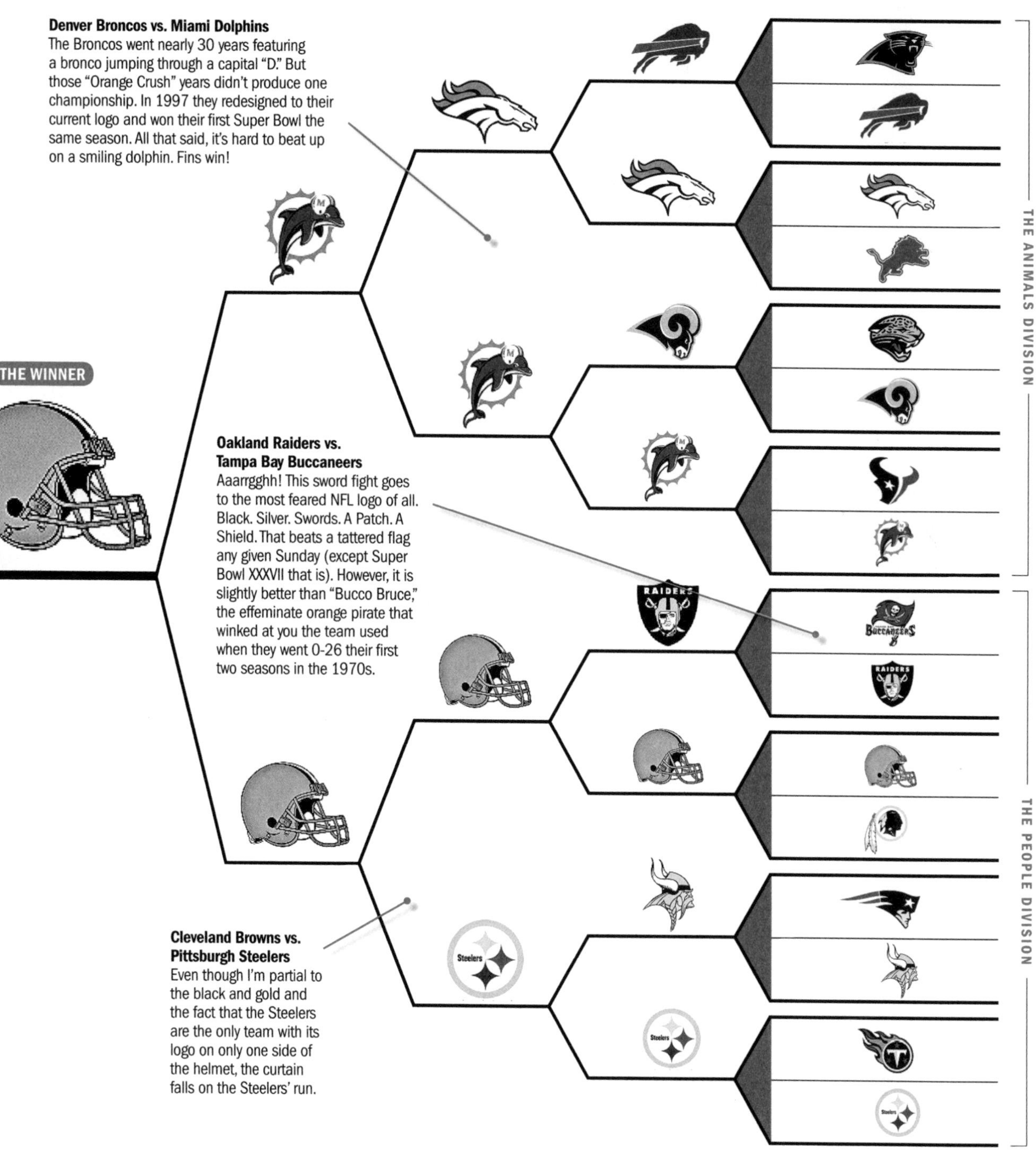

THE WINNER
THE ANIMALS DIVISION
THE PEOPLE DIVISION
RAIDERS
BUCCANEERS
Steelers

Denver Broncos vs. Miami Dolphins
The Broncos went nearly 30 years featuring a bronco jumping through a capital "D." But those "Orange Crush" years didn't produce one championship. In 1997 they redesigned to their current logo and won their first Super Bowl the same season. All that said, it's hard to beat up on a smiling dolphin. Fins win!

Oakland Raiders vs. Tampa Bay Buccaneers
Aaarrgghh! This sword fight goes to the most feared NFL logo of all. Black. Silver. Swords. A Patch. A Shield. That beats a tattered flag any given Sunday (except Super Bowl XXXVII that is). However, it is slightly better than "Bucco Bruce," the effeminate orange pirate that winked at you the team used when they went 0-26 their first two seasons in the 1970s.

Cleveland Browns vs. Pittsburgh Steelers
Even though I'm partial to the black and gold and the fact that the Steelers are the only team with its logo on only one side of the helmet, the curtain falls on the Steelers' run.

Dallas Cowboys

By Jeff Pearlman

Jeff Pearlman is the author of the *New York Times* bestseller *Boys Will Be Boys: The Glory Days and Party Nights of the Dallas Cowboys Dynasty.*

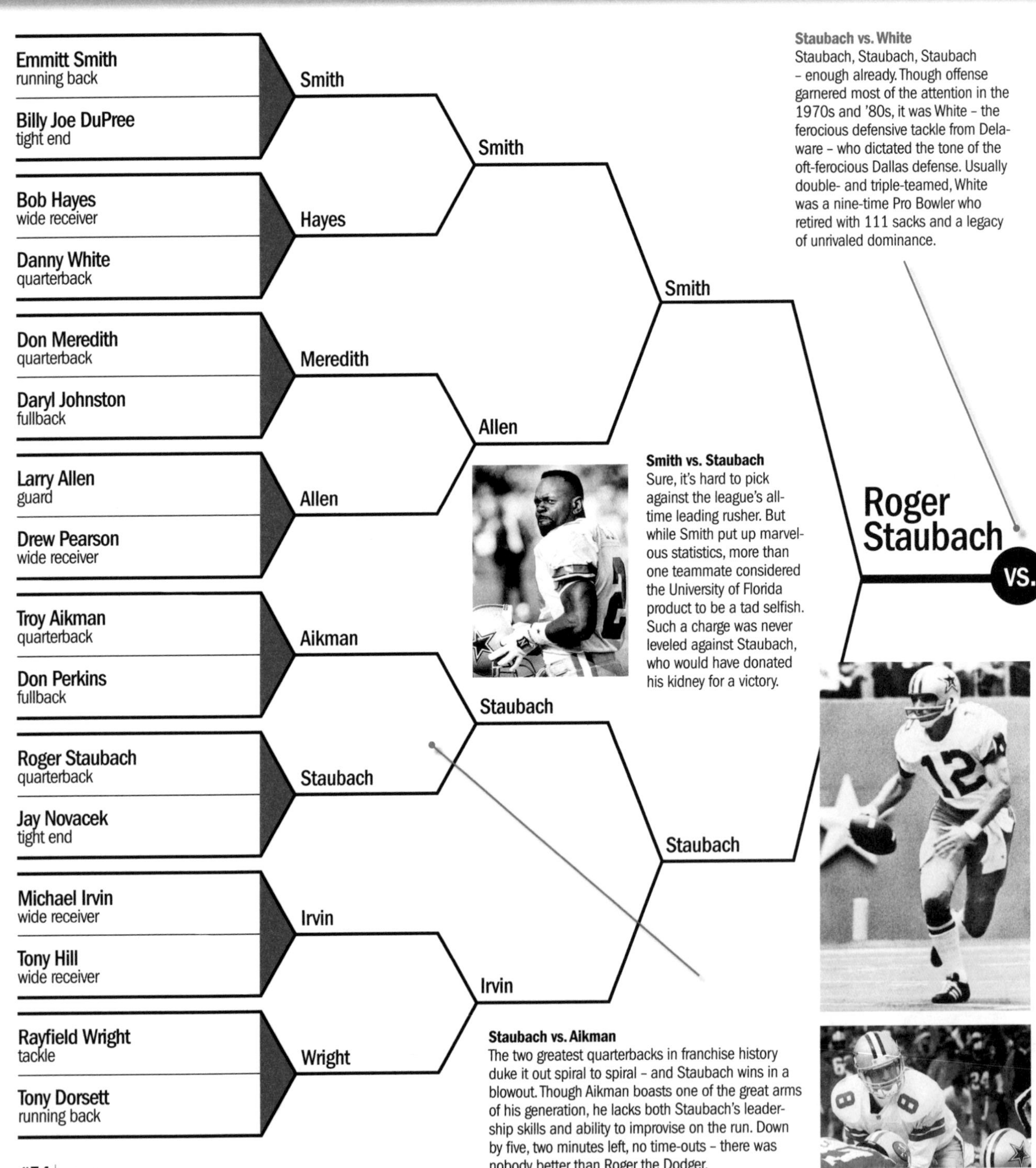
Emmitt Smith
running back
Billy Joe DuPree
tight end
Bob Hayes
wide receiver
Danny White
quarterback
Don Meredith
quarterback
Daryl Johnston
fullback
Larry Allen
guard
Drew Pearson
wide receiver
Troy Aikman
quarterback
Don Perkins
fullback
Roger Staubach
quarterback
Jay Novacek
tight end
Michael Irvin
wide receiver
Tony Hill
wide receiver
Rayfield Wright
tackle
Tony Dorsett
running back
Smith
Hayes
Meredith
Allen
Aikman
Staubach
Irvin
Wright
Smith
Allen
Staubach
Irvin
Smith
Staubach
Roger Staubach
VS.

Staubach vs. White
Staubach, Staubach, Staubach – enough already. Though offense garnered most of the attention in the 1970s and '80s, it was White – the ferocious defensive tackle from Delaware – who dictated the tone of the oft-ferocious Dallas defense. Usually double- and triple-teamed, White was a nine-time Pro Bowler who retired with 111 sacks and a legacy of unrivaled dominance.

Smith vs. Staubach
Sure, it's hard to pick against the league's all-time leading rusher. But while Smith put up marvelous statistics, more than one teammate considered the University of Florida product to be a tad selfish. Such a charge was never leveled against Staubach, who would have donated his kidney for a victory.

Staubach vs. Aikman
The two greatest quarterbacks in franchise history duke it out spiral to spiral – and Staubach wins in a blowout. Though Aikman boasts one of the great arms of his generation, he lacks both Staubach's leadership skills and ability to improvise on the run. Down by five, two minutes left, no time-outs – there was nobody better than Roger the Dodger.

IN THE LONG HISTORY OF THE NATIONAL FOOTBALL LEAGUE, no team has elicited both the love and hate of the average fan more than the Dallas Cowboys. They're amazing and arrogant, cocky and charismatic, boastful and blessed. The Cowboys are blonde, long-legged cheerleaders. They're Tom Landry's fedora, Jimmy Johnson's sideways grin, Jerry Jones's prideful strut, and the hole atop Texas Stadium. Yet most of all, they're the dazzling assortment of Pro Bowlers and Hall of Famers who, over 39 seasons, have not only dominated the league but often revolutionized it.

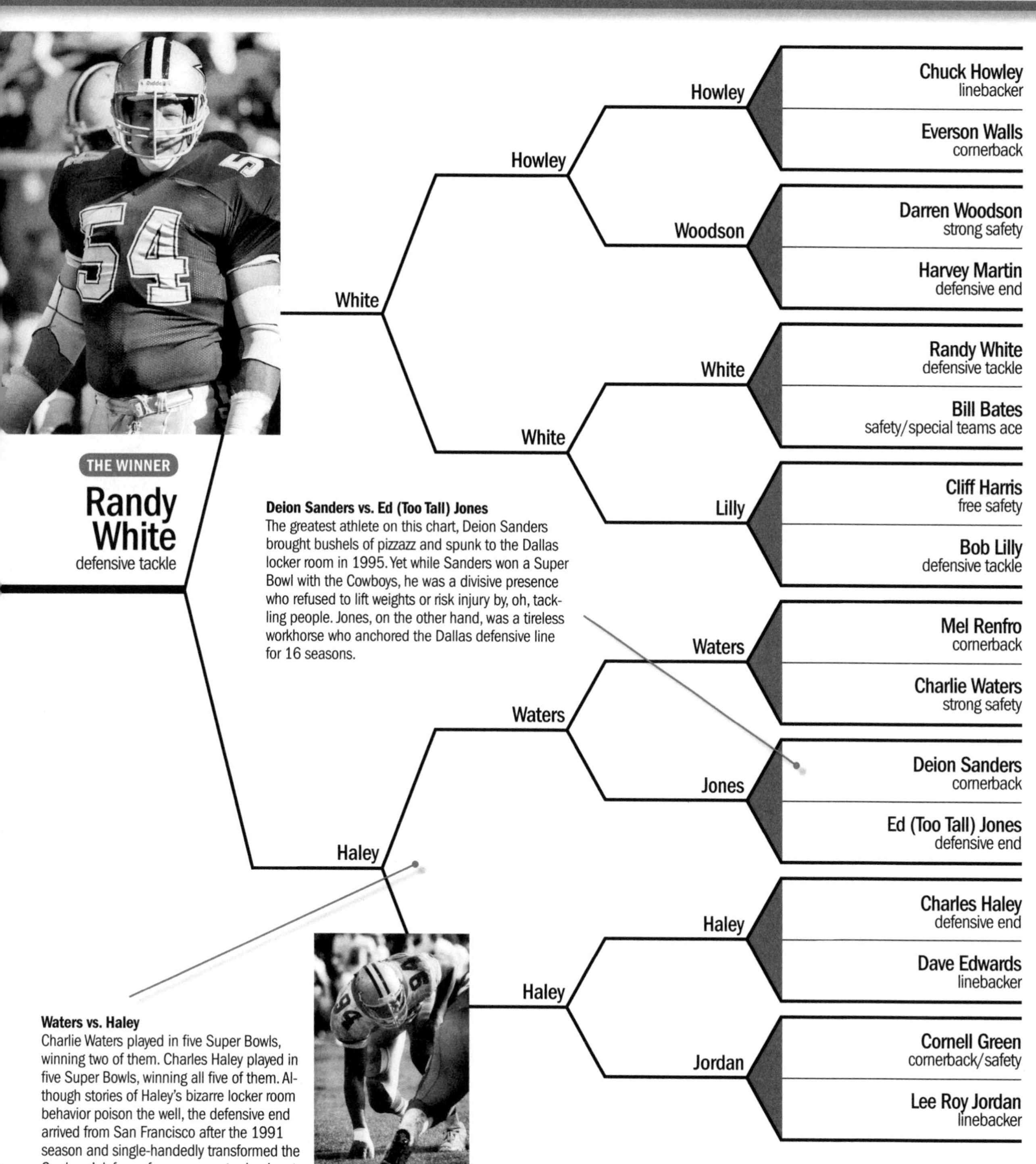

Chuck Howley
linebacker
Everson Walls
cornerback
Darren Woodson
strong safety
Harvey Martin
defensive end
Randy White
defensive tackle
Bill Bates
safety/special teams ace
Cliff Harris
free safety
Bob Lilly
defensive tackle
Mel Renfro
cornerback
Charlie Waters
strong safety
Deion Sanders
cornerback
Ed (Too Tall) Jones
defensive end
Charles Haley
defensive end
Dave Edwards
linebacker
Cornell Green
cornerback/safety
Lee Roy Jordan
linebacker
Howley
Woodson
White
Lilly
Waters
Jones
Haley
Jordan
Howley
White
Waters
Haley
White
Haley
THE WINNER
Randy White
defensive tackle

Deion Sanders vs. Ed (Too Tall) Jones
The greatest athlete on this chart, Deion Sanders brought bushels of pizzazz and spunk to the Dallas locker room in 1995. Yet while Sanders won a Super Bowl with the Cowboys, he was a divisive presence who refused to lift weights or risk injury by, oh, tackling people. Jones, on the other hand, was a tireless workhorse who anchored the Dallas defensive line for 16 seasons.

Waters vs. Haley
Charlie Waters played in five Super Bowls, winning two of them. Charles Haley played in five Super Bowls, winning all five of them. Although stories of Haley's bizarre locker room behavior poison the well, the defensive end arrived from San Francisco after the 1991 season and single-handedly transformed the Cowboys' defense from average to dominant.

Jewish Baseball Players

By Daniel Okrent

Daniel Okrent's books include the baseball classic *Nine Innings,* as well as *Great Fortune: The Epic of Rockefeller Center,* a finalist for the 2004 Pulitzer Prize in history. He was also the first public editor of the *New York Times.*

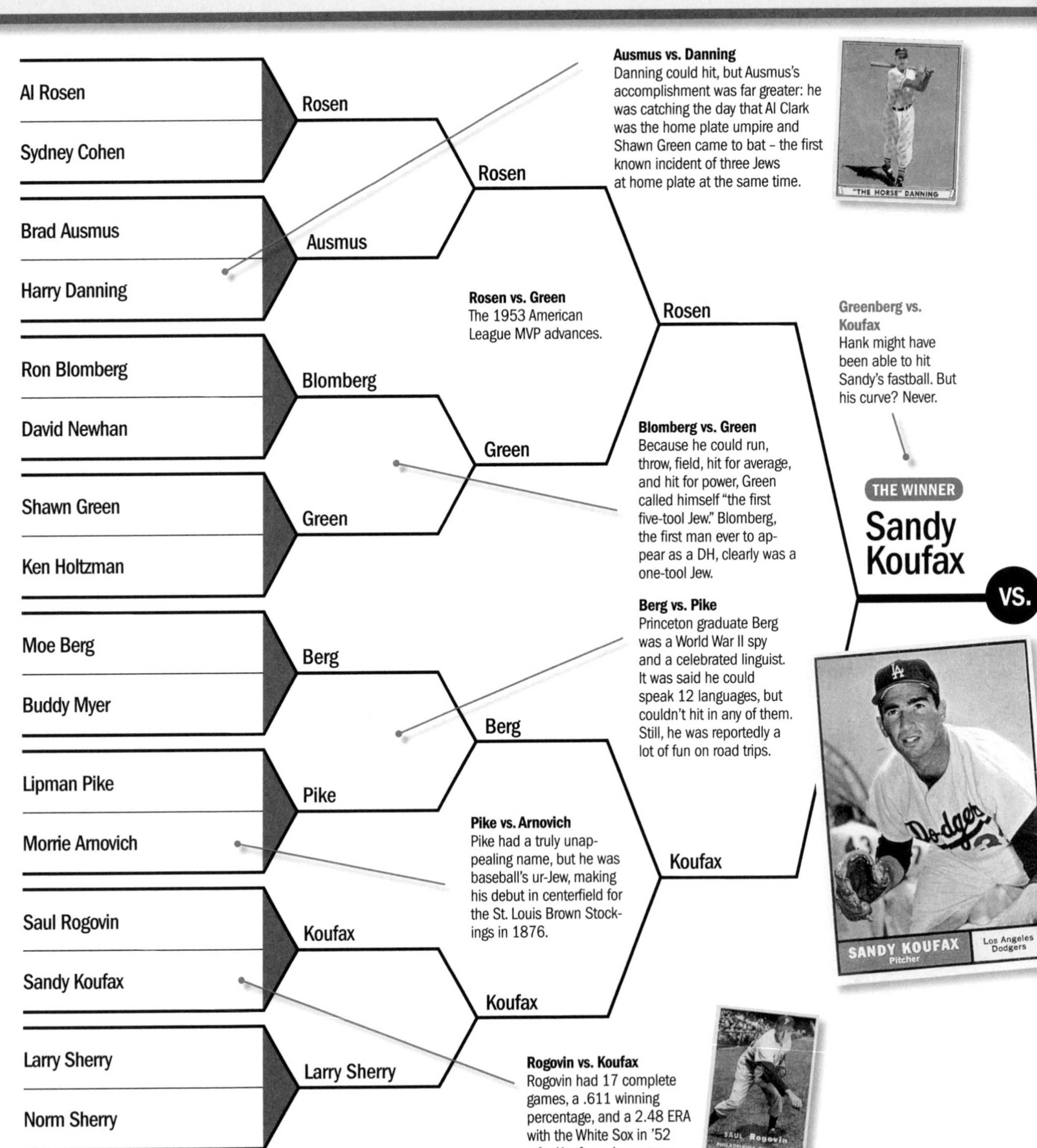
Al Rosen
Sydney Cohen
Brad Ausmus
Harry Danning
Ron Blomberg
David Newhan
Shawn Green
Ken Holtzman
Moe Berg
Buddy Myer
Lipman Pike
Morrie Arnovich
Saul Rogovin
Sandy Koufax
Larry Sherry
Norm Sherry
Rosen
Ausmus
Blomberg
Green
Berg
Pike
Koufax
Larry Sherry
Rosen
Green
Berg
Koufax
Rosen
Koufax
Ausmus vs. Danning
Danning could hit, but Ausmus's accomplishment was far greater: he was catching the day that Al Clark was the home plate umpire and Shawn Green came to bat – the first known incident of three Jews at home plate at the same time.
"THE HORSE" DANNING
Rosen vs. Green
The 1953 American League MVP advances.
Greenberg vs. Koufax
Hank might have been able to hit Sandy's fastball. But his curve? Never.
Blomberg vs. Green
Because he could run, throw, field, hit for average, and hit for power, Green called himself "the first five-tool Jew." Blomberg, the first man ever to appear as a DH, clearly was a one-tool Jew.
THE WINNER
Sandy Koufax
VS.
Berg vs. Pike
Princeton graduate Berg was a World War II spy and a celebrated linguist. It was said he could speak 12 languages, but couldn't hit in any of them. Still, he was reportedly a lot of fun on road trips.
Pike vs. Arnovich
Pike had a truly unappealing name, but he was baseball's ur-Jew, making his debut in centerfield for the St. Louis Brown Stockings in 1876.
SANDY KOUFAX
Pitcher
Los Angeles Dodgers
Rogovin vs. Koufax
Rogovin had 17 complete games, a .611 winning percentage, and a 2.48 ERA with the White Sox in '52 – for Koufax, a lousy year.
SAUL Rogovin
PHILADELPHIA PHILLIES

ONCE THERE WERE BALLPLAYERS WITH NAMES LIKE "Sydney Cohen" and "Moe Berg." Those days are gone, but the Jewish ballplayer remains. Only now, he's named "Ryan," or "Shawn," or "Kevin." In this tournament of 32 great, good, decent, or barely adequate Major League Jews (it's not as if there were thousands to choose from), face-offs are won by the better player – except when I don't like the outcome. That's when I turn to Diamond Semitology, allowing either "Hebraic pride" or "yiddishe irony" to trump on-field evidence. Take your base, Mose Solomon; doff your cap, Adam Greenberg.

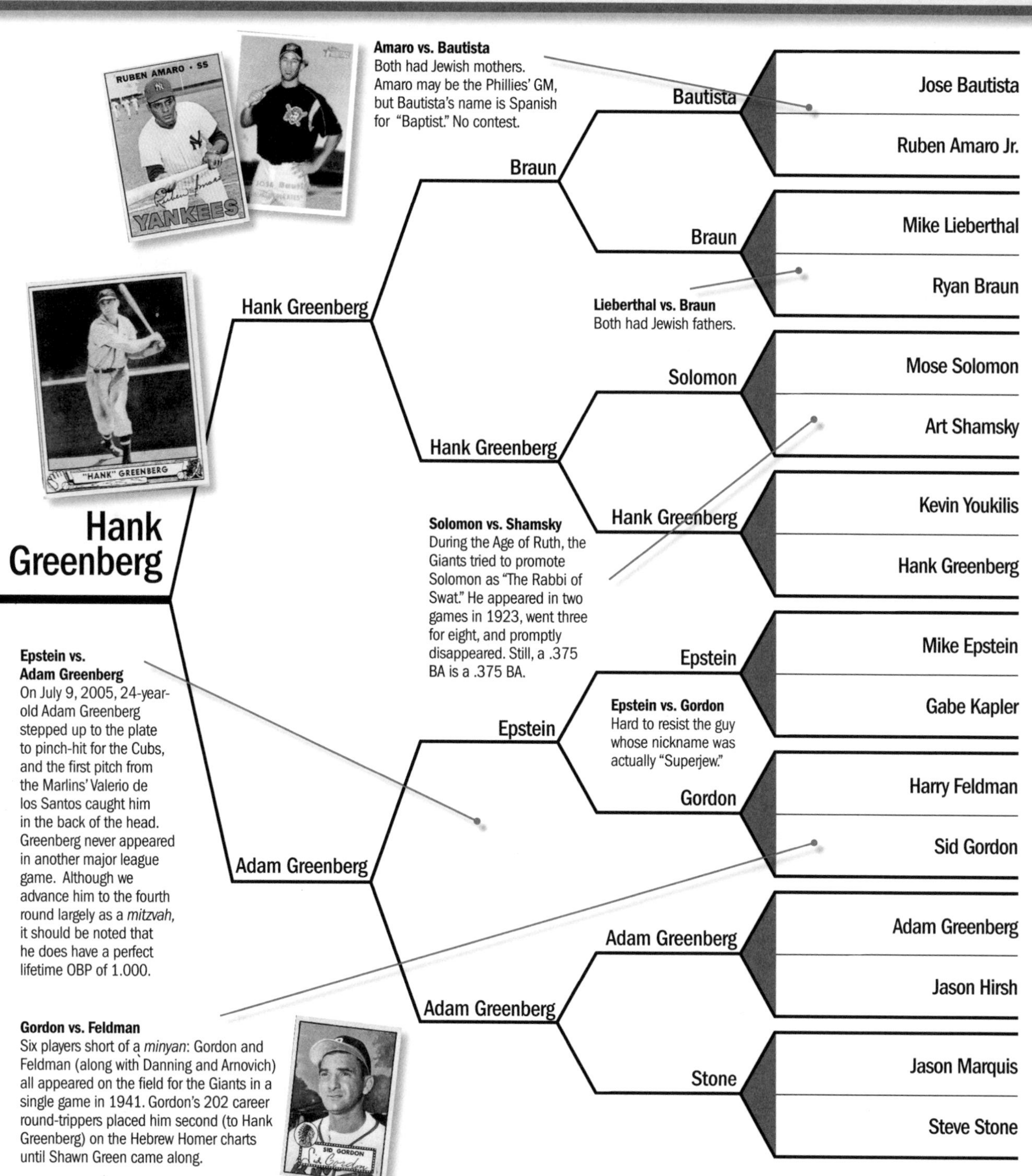

RUBEN AMARO · SS
YANKEES
"HANK" GREENBERG
SID GORDON
Jose Bautista
Ruben Amaro Jr.
Mike Lieberthal
Ryan Braun
Mose Solomon
Art Shamsky
Kevin Youkilis
Hank Greenberg
Mike Epstein
Gabe Kapler
Harry Feldman
Sid Gordon
Adam Greenberg
Jason Hirsh
Jason Marquis
Steve Stone
Bautista
Braun
Solomon
Hank Greenberg
Epstein
Gordon
Adam Greenberg
Stone
Braun
Hank Greenberg
Epstein
Adam Greenberg
Hank Greenberg
Adam Greenberg
Hank Greenberg

Amaro vs. Bautista
Both had Jewish mothers. Amaro may be the Phillies' GM, but Bautista's name is Spanish for "Baptist." No contest.

Lieberthal vs. Braun
Both had Jewish fathers.

Solomon vs. Shamsky
During the Age of Ruth, the Giants tried to promote Solomon as "The Rabbi of Swat." He appeared in two games in 1923, went three for eight, and promptly disappeared. Still, a .375 BA is a .375 BA.

Epstein vs. Gordon
Hard to resist the guy whose nickname was actually "Superjew."

Epstein vs. Adam Greenberg
On July 9, 2005, 24-year-old Adam Greenberg stepped up to the plate to pinch-hit for the Cubs, and the first pitch from the Marlins' Valerio de los Santos caught him in the back of the head. Greenberg never appeared in another major league game. Although we advance him to the fourth round largely as a *mitzvah*, it should be noted that he does have a perfect lifetime OBP of 1.000.

Gordon vs. Feldman
Six players short of a *minyan*: Gordon and Feldman (along with Danning and Arnovich) all appeared on the field for the Giants in a single game in 1941. Gordon's 202 career round-trippers placed him second (to Hank Greenberg) on the Hebrew Homer charts until Shawn Green came along.

All-Time Fantasy Sports Performances

By Matt Pitzer

Matt Pitzer writes about fantasy football for *USA Today*. Previously, he covered fantasy sports for the *Sporting News*. He occasionally leaves his basement.

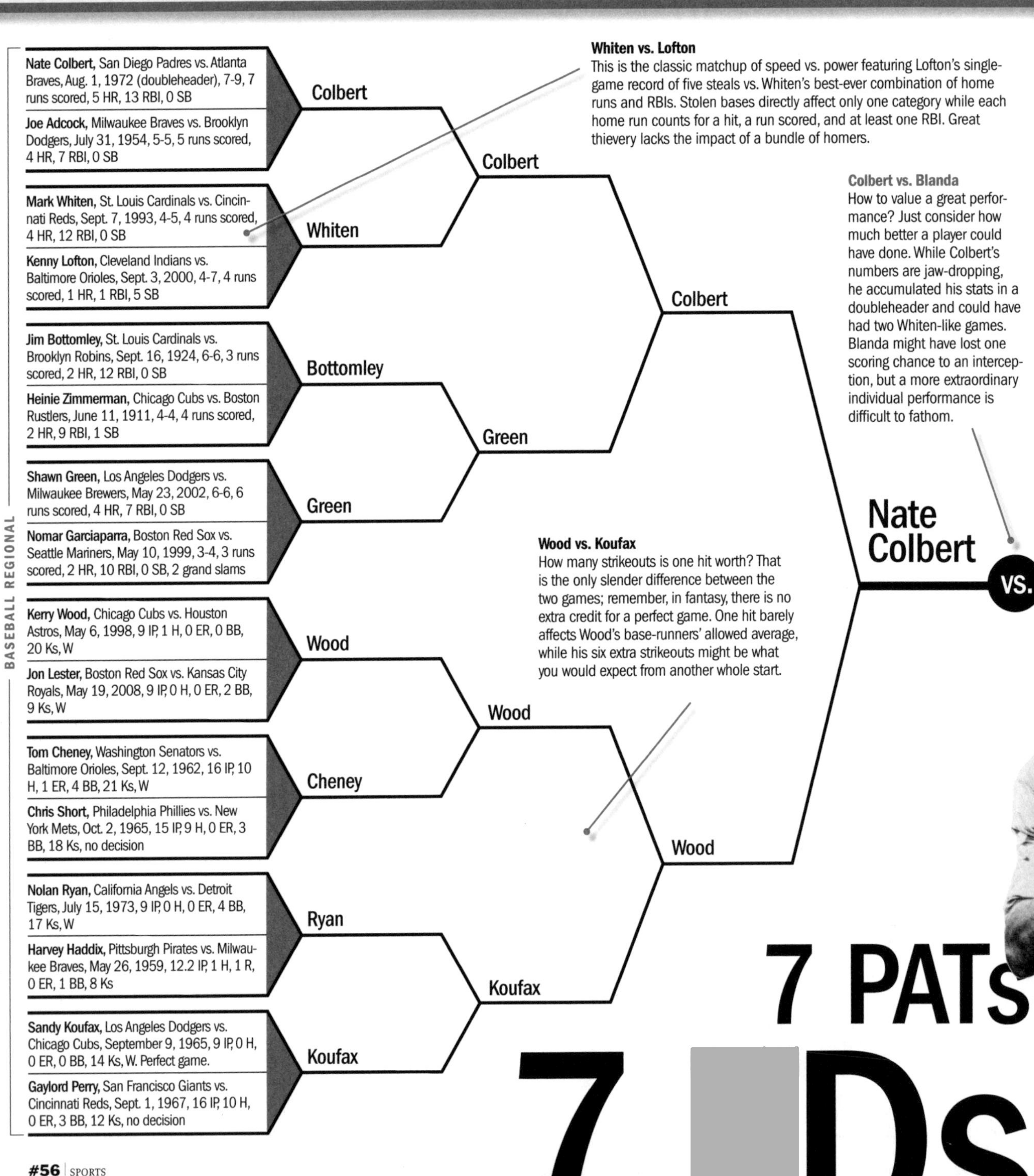
BASEBALL REGIONAL
Nate Colbert, San Diego Padres vs. Atlanta Braves, Aug. 1, 1972 (doubleheader), 7-9, 7 runs scored, 5 HR, 13 RBI, 0 SB
Joe Adcock, Milwaukee Braves vs. Brooklyn Dodgers, July 31, 1954, 5-5, 5 runs scored, 4 HR, 7 RBI, 0 SB
Mark Whiten, St. Louis Cardinals vs. Cincinnati Reds, Sept. 7, 1993, 4-5, 4 runs scored, 4 HR, 12 RBI, 0 SB
Kenny Lofton, Cleveland Indians vs. Baltimore Orioles, Sept. 3, 2000, 4-7, 4 runs scored, 1 HR, 1 RBI, 5 SB
Jim Bottomley, St. Louis Cardinals vs. Brooklyn Robins, Sept. 16, 1924, 6-6, 3 runs scored, 2 HR, 12 RBI, 0 SB
Heinie Zimmerman, Chicago Cubs vs. Boston Rustlers, June 11, 1911, 4-4, 4 runs scored, 2 HR, 9 RBI, 1 SB
Shawn Green, Los Angeles Dodgers vs. Milwaukee Brewers, May 23, 2002, 6-6, 6 runs scored, 4 HR, 7 RBI, 0 SB
Nomar Garciaparra, Boston Red Sox vs. Seattle Mariners, May 10, 1999, 3-4, 3 runs scored, 2 HR, 10 RBI, 0 SB, 2 grand slams
Kerry Wood, Chicago Cubs vs. Houston Astros, May 6, 1998, 9 IP, 1 H, 0 ER, 0 BB, 20 Ks, W
Jon Lester, Boston Red Sox vs. Kansas City Royals, May 19, 2008, 9 IP, 0 H, 0 ER, 2 BB, 9 Ks, W
Tom Cheney, Washington Senators vs. Baltimore Orioles, Sept. 12, 1962, 16 IP, 10 H, 1 ER, 4 BB, 21 Ks, W
Chris Short, Philadelphia Phillies vs. New York Mets, Oct. 2, 1965, 15 IP, 9 H, 0 ER, 3 BB, 18 Ks, no decision
Nolan Ryan, California Angels vs. Detroit Tigers, July 15, 1973, 9 IP, 0 H, 0 ER, 4 BB, 17 Ks, W
Harvey Haddix, Pittsburgh Pirates vs. Milwaukee Braves, May 26, 1959, 12.2 IP, 1 H, 1 R, 0 ER, 1 BB, 8 Ks
Sandy Koufax, Los Angeles Dodgers vs. Chicago Cubs, September 9, 1965, 9 IP, 0 H, 0 ER, 0 BB, 14 Ks, W. Perfect game.
Gaylord Perry, San Francisco Giants vs. Cincinnati Reds, Sept. 1, 1967, 16 IP, 10 H, 0 ER, 3 BB, 12 Ks, no decision
Colbert
Whiten
Bottomley
Green
Wood
Cheney
Ryan
Koufax
Colbert
Green
Wood
Koufax
Colbert
Wood
Nate Colbert
VS.
Whiten vs. Lofton
This is the classic matchup of speed vs. power featuring Lofton's single-game record of five steals vs. Whiten's best-ever combination of home runs and RBIs. Stolen bases directly affect only one category while each home run counts for a hit, a run scored, and at least one RBI. Great thievery lacks the impact of a bundle of homers.
Colbert vs. Blanda
How to value a great performance? Just consider how much better a player could have done. While Colbert's numbers are jaw-dropping, he accumulated his stats in a doubleheader and could have had two Whiten-like games. Blanda might have lost one scoring chance to an interception, but a more extraordinary individual performance is difficult to fathom.
Wood vs. Koufax
How many strikeouts is one hit worth? That is the only slender difference between the two games; remember, in fantasy, there is no extra credit for a perfect game. One hit barely affects Wood's base-runners' allowed average, while his six extra strikeouts might be what you would expect from another whole start.
7 PATs
7
Ds

IN DETERMINING THE BEST FANTASY PERFORMANCE, one must acknowledge that (a) fantasy is barely 20 years old and (b) football players have one-tenth fewer chances for single-game achievements than everyday baseball players (and half as many as most starting pitchers). So, as this bracket goes back and forth in time, we use modern fantasy's valuation tools to compare the feats of running backs, receivers, and quarterbacks against each other, and then, a slugger and quarterback's most astonishing days. If fantasy had existed in 1924, fans with Jim Bottomley would have drooled over his 12 RBIs in a single game.

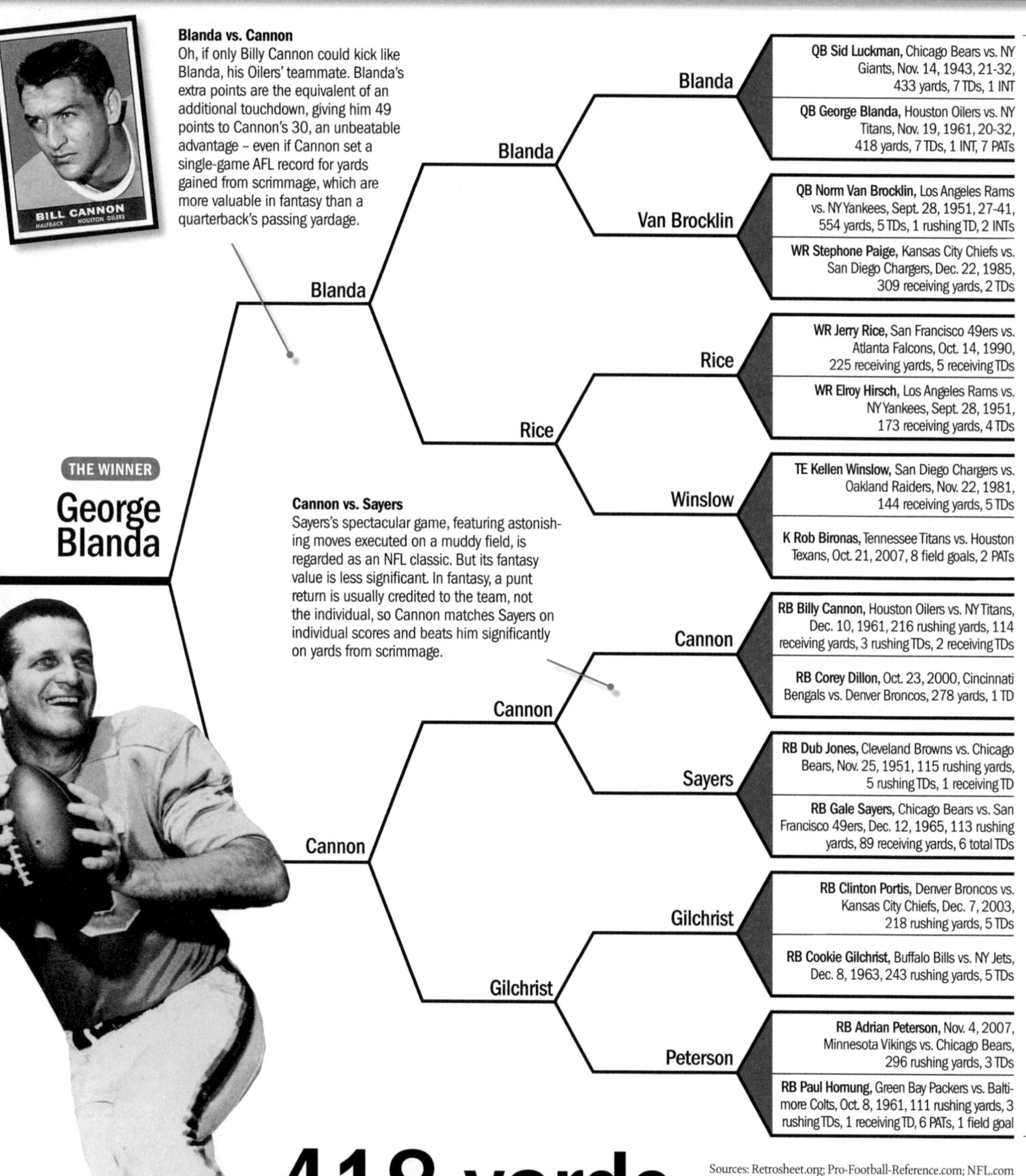
BILL CANNON
HALFBACK HOUSTON OILERS
FOOTBALL REGIONAL
THE WINNER
George Blanda
QB Sid Luckman, Chicago Bears vs. NY Giants, Nov. 14, 1943, 21-32, 433 yards, 7 TDs, 1 INT
QB George Blanda, Houston Oilers vs. NY Titans, Nov. 19, 1961, 20-32, 418 yards, 7 TDs, 1 INT, 7 PATs
Blanda
QB Norm Van Brocklin, Los Angeles Rams vs. NY Yankees, Sept. 28, 1951, 27-41, 554 yards, 5 TDs, 1 rushing TD, 2 INTs
WR Stephone Paige, Kansas City Chiefs vs. San Diego Chargers, Dec. 22, 1985, 309 receiving yards, 2 TDs
Van Brocklin
Blanda
WR Jerry Rice, San Francisco 49ers vs. Atlanta Falcons, Oct. 14, 1990, 225 receiving yards, 5 receiving TDs
WR Elroy Hirsch, Los Angeles Rams vs. NY Yankees, Sept. 28, 1951, 173 receiving yards, 4 TDs
Rice
TE Kellen Winslow, San Diego Chargers vs. Oakland Raiders, Nov. 22, 1981, 144 receiving yards, 5 TDs
K Rob Bironas, Tennessee Titans vs. Houston Texans, Oct. 21, 2007, 8 field goals, 2 PATs
Winslow
Rice
Blanda
RB Billy Cannon, Houston Oilers vs. NY Titans, Dec. 10, 1961, 216 rushing yards, 114 receiving yards, 3 rushing TDs, 2 receiving TDs
RB Corey Dillon, Oct. 23, 2000, Cincinnati Bengals vs. Denver Broncos, 278 yards, 1 TD
Cannon
RB Dub Jones, Cleveland Browns vs. Chicago Bears, Nov. 25, 1951, 115 rushing yards, 5 rushing TDs, 1 receiving TD
RB Gale Sayers, Chicago Bears vs. San Francisco 49ers, Dec. 12, 1965, 113 rushing yards, 89 receiving yards, 6 total TDs
Sayers
Cannon
RB Clinton Portis, Denver Broncos vs. Kansas City Chiefs, Dec. 7, 2003, 218 rushing yards, 5 TDs
RB Cookie Gilchrist, Buffalo Bills vs. NY Jets, Dec. 8, 1963, 243 rushing yards, 5 TDs
Gilchrist
RB Adrian Peterson, Nov. 4, 2007, Minnesota Vikings vs. Chicago Bears, 296 rushing yards, 3 TDs
RB Paul Hornung, Green Bay Packers vs. Baltimore Colts, Oct. 8, 1961, 111 rushing yards, 3 rushing TDs, 1 receiving TD, 6 PATs, 1 field goal
Peterson
Gilchrist
Cannon

Blanda vs. Cannon

Oh, if only Billy Cannon could kick like Blanda, his Oilers' teammate. Blanda's extra points are the equivalent of an additional touchdown, giving him 49 points to Cannon's 30, an unbeatable advantage – even if Cannon set a single-game AFL record for yards gained from scrimmage, which are more valuable in fantasy than a quarterback's passing yardage.

Cannon vs. Sayers

Sayers's spectacular game, featuring astonishing moves executed on a muddy field, is regarded as an NFL classic. But its fantasy value is less significant. In fantasy, a punt return is usually credited to the team, not the individual, so Cannon matches Sayers on individual scores and beats him significantly on yards from scrimmage.

418 yards

Sources: Retrosheet.org; Pro-Football-Reference.com; NFL.com

21st-Century Sports Books

By Will Leitch

Will Leitch is a contributing editor at *New York* magazine, a columnist for *Sporting News*, and the founder of Deadspin.com. He has written three books, *Life As A Loser* (2003), *Catch* (2005), and *God Save The Fan* (2008). He grew up in rural Mattoon, IL.

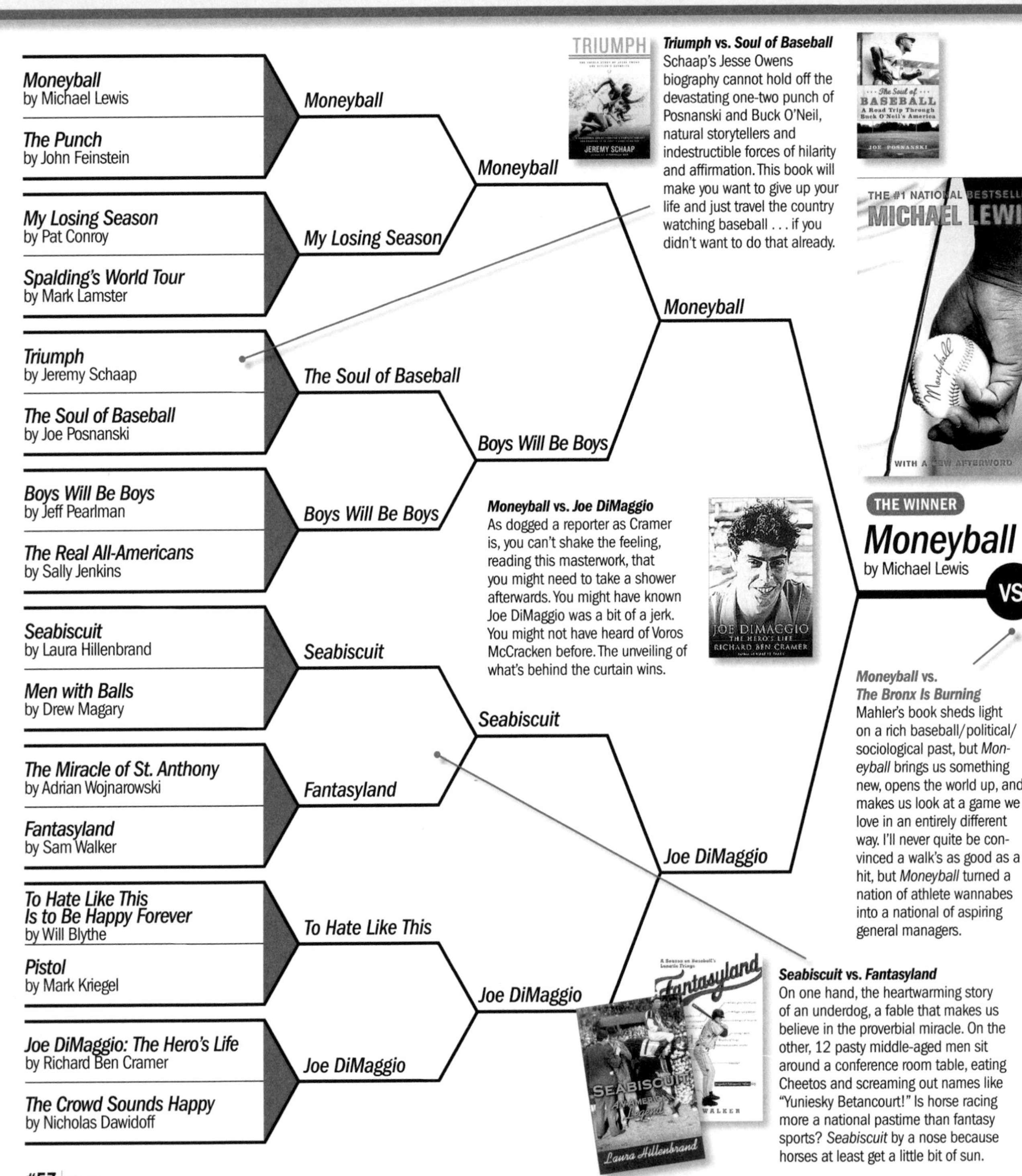

Moneyball by Michael Lewis
The Punch by John Feinstein
My Losing Season by Pat Conroy
Spalding's World Tour by Mark Lamster
Triumph by Jeremy Schaap
The Soul of Baseball by Joe Posnanski
Boys Will Be Boys by Jeff Pearlman
The Real All-Americans by Sally Jenkins
Seabiscuit by Laura Hillenbrand
Men with Balls by Drew Magary
The Miracle of St. Anthony by Adrian Wojnarowski
Fantasyland by Sam Walker
To Hate Like This Is to Be Happy Forever by Will Blythe
Pistol by Mark Kriegel
Joe DiMaggio: The Hero's Life by Richard Ben Cramer
The Crowd Sounds Happy by Nicholas Dawidoff
Moneyball
My Losing Season
The Soul of Baseball
Boys Will Be Boys
Seabiscuit
Fantasyland
To Hate Like This
Joe DiMaggio
Moneyball
Boys Will Be Boys
Seabiscuit
Joe DiMaggio
Moneyball
Joe DiMaggio
THE WINNER
Moneyball
by Michael Lewis
VS.

Triumph* vs. *Soul of Baseball
Schaap's Jesse Owens biography cannot hold off the devastating one-two punch of Posnanski and Buck O'Neil, natural storytellers and indestructible forces of hilarity and affirmation. This book will make you want to give up your life and just travel the country watching baseball . . . if you didn't want to do that already.

Moneyball* vs. *Joe DiMaggio
As dogged a reporter as Cramer is, you can't shake the feeling, reading this masterwork, that you might need to take a shower afterwards. You might have known Joe DiMaggio was a bit of a jerk. You might not have heard of Voros McCracken before. The unveiling of what's behind the curtain wins.

Moneyball* vs. *The Bronx Is Burning
Mahler's book sheds light on a rich baseball/political/sociological past, but *Moneyball* brings us something new, opens the world up, and makes us look at a game we love in an entirely different way. I'll never quite be convinced a walk's as good as a hit, but *Moneyball* turned a nation of athlete wannabes into a national of aspiring general managers.

Seabiscuit* vs. *Fantasyland
On one hand, the heartwarming story of an underdog, a fable that makes us believe in the proverbial miracle. On the other, 12 pasty middle-aged men sit around a conference room table, eating Cheetos and screaming out names like "Yuniesky Betancourt!" Is horse racing more a national pastime than fantasy sports? *Seabiscuit* by a nose because horses at least get a little bit of sun.

I PREFER BOOKS THAT EMPHASIZE the silliness and fun of sports rather than the mythos inherent in much sportswriting. Anytime you see a list of the top sports books, you're lucky to see so much as one or two books from the last 25 years. This is a shame, particularly when you consider how dramatically sportswriting has changed in the last decade. Not all of these can stand with Bernard Malamud, but they're closer than you think. Oh, and a third of the authors in this bracket also write blogs.

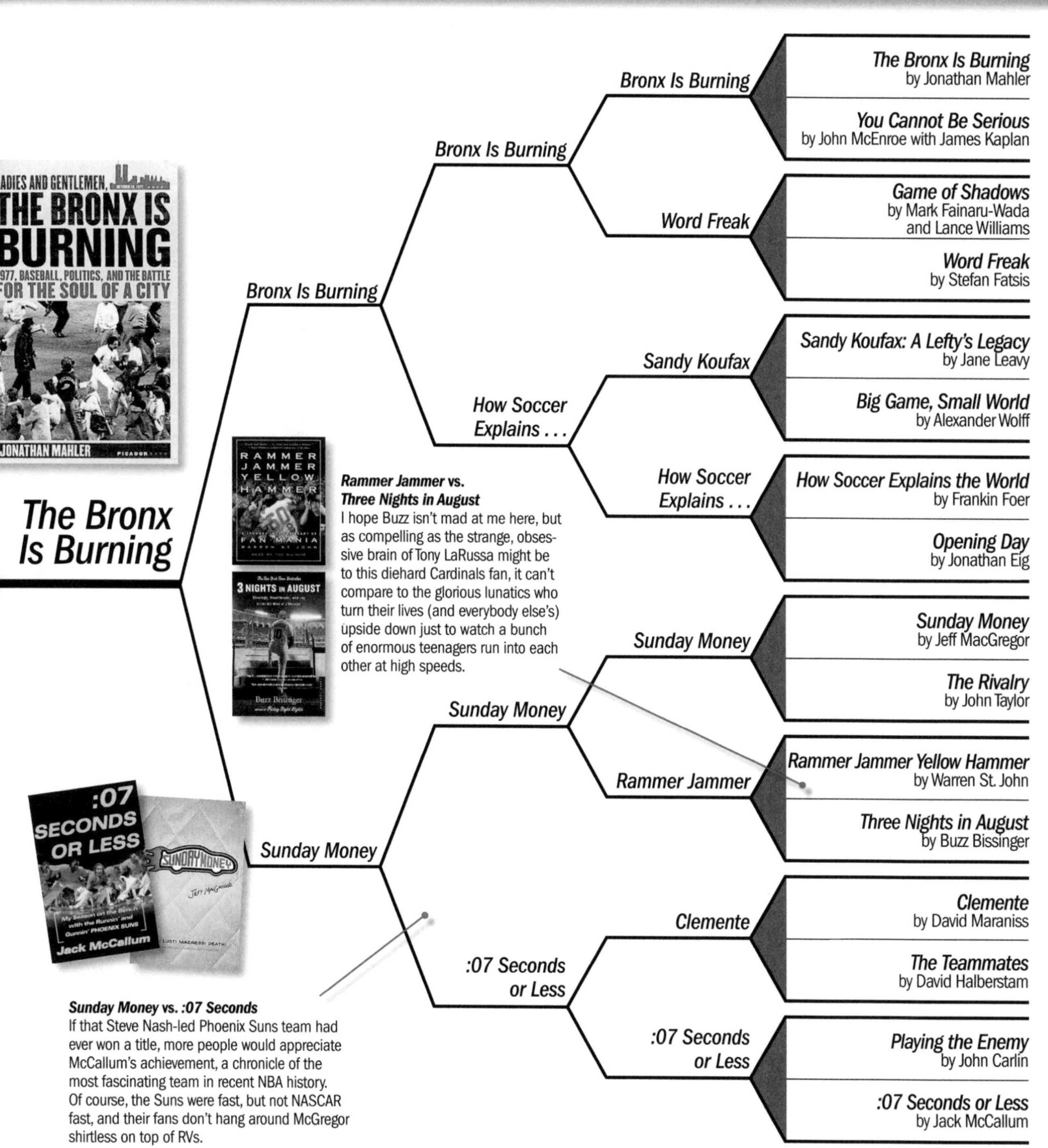

The Bronx Is Burning by Jonathan Mahler
You Cannot Be Serious by John McEnroe with James Kaplan
Game of Shadows by Mark Fainaru-Wada and Lance Williams
Word Freak by Stefan Fatsis
Sandy Koufax: A Lefty's Legacy by Jane Leavy
Big Game, Small World by Alexander Wolff
How Soccer Explains the World by Frankin Foer
Opening Day by Jonathan Eig
Sunday Money by Jeff MacGregor
The Rivalry by John Taylor
Rammer Jammer Yellow Hammer by Warren St. John
Three Nights in August by Buzz Bissinger
Clemente by David Maraniss
The Teammates by David Halberstam
Playing the Enemy by John Carlin
:07 Seconds or Less by Jack McCallum
Bronx Is Burning
Word Freak
Sandy Koufax
How Soccer Explains . . .
Sunday Money
Rammer Jammer
Clemente
:07 Seconds or Less
Bronx Is Burning
How Soccer Explains . . .
Sunday Money
:07 Seconds or Less
Bronx Is Burning
Sunday Money
The Bronx Is Burning
LADIES AND GENTLEMEN, THE BRONX IS BURNING
1977, BASEBALL, POLITICS, AND THE BATTLE FOR THE SOUL OF A CITY
JONATHAN MAHLER
RAMMER JAMMER YELLOW HAMMER
FAN MANIA
WARREN ST. JOHN
3 NIGHTS IN AUGUST
Buzz Bissinger
:07 SECONDS OR LESS
Jack McCallum
SUNDAY MONEY

Rammer Jammer* vs. *Three Nights in August
I hope Buzz isn't mad at me here, but as compelling as the strange, obsessive brain of Tony LaRussa might be to this diehard Cardinals fan, it can't compare to the glorious lunatics who turn their lives (and everybody else's) upside down just to watch a bunch of enormous teenagers run into each other at high speeds.

Sunday Money* vs. *:07 Seconds
If that Steve Nash-led Phoenix Suns team had ever won a title, more people would appreciate McCallum's achievement, a chronicle of the most fascinating team in recent NBA history. Of course, the Suns were fast, but not NASCAR fast, and their fans don't hang around McGregor shirtless on top of RVs.

Ringless Athletes

By Dick Friedman

A longtime editor at *Sports Illustrated,* Dick Friedman grew up in the Boston area and in his mind has won 27 rings: 17 with the Celtics, three with the Patriots, two each with the Bruins and Red Sox, and three with the Mad Dogs street hockey team.

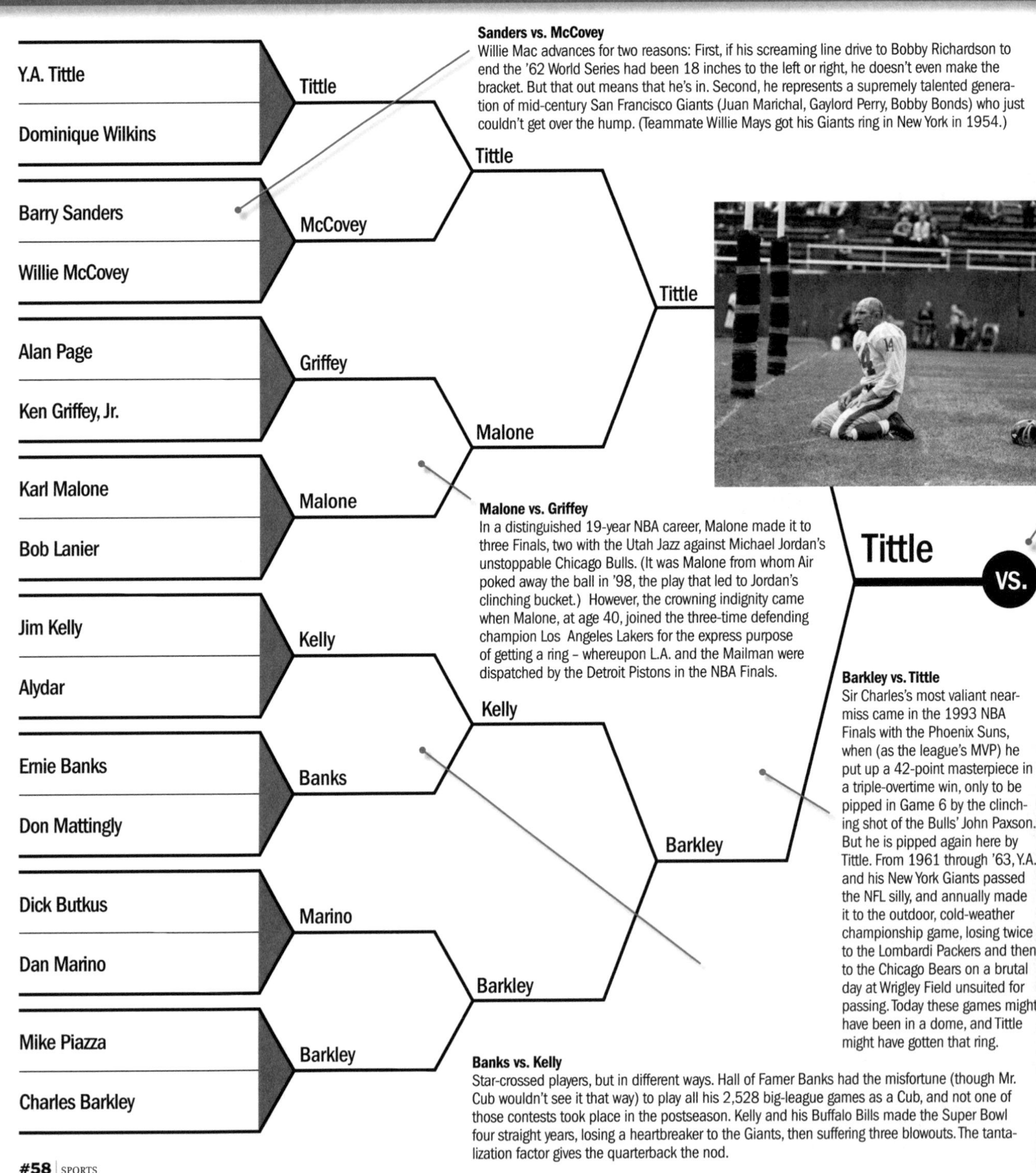
Y.A. Tittle
Dominique Wilkins
Barry Sanders
Willie McCovey
Alan Page
Ken Griffey, Jr.
Karl Malone
Bob Lanier
Jim Kelly
Alydar
Ernie Banks
Don Mattingly
Dick Butkus
Dan Marino
Mike Piazza
Charles Barkley
Tittle
McCovey
Griffey
Malone
Kelly
Banks
Marino
Barkley
Tittle
Malone
Kelly
Barkley
Tittle
Barkley
Tittle
VS.

Sanders vs. McCovey

Willie Mac advances for two reasons: First, if his screaming line drive to Bobby Richardson to end the '62 World Series had been 18 inches to the left or right, he doesn't even make the bracket. But that out means that he's in. Second, he represents a supremely talented generation of mid-century San Francisco Giants (Juan Marichal, Gaylord Perry, Bobby Bonds) who just couldn't get over the hump. (Teammate Willie Mays got his Giants ring in New York in 1954.)

Malone vs. Griffey

In a distinguished 19-year NBA career, Malone made it to three Finals, two with the Utah Jazz against Michael Jordan's unstoppable Chicago Bulls. (It was Malone from whom Air poked away the ball in '98, the play that led to Jordan's clinching bucket.) However, the crowning indignity came when Malone, at age 40, joined the three-time defending champion Los Angeles Lakers for the express purpose of getting a ring – whereupon L.A. and the Mailman were dispatched by the Detroit Pistons in the NBA Finals.

Barkley vs. Tittle

Sir Charles's most valiant near-miss came in the 1993 NBA Finals with the Phoenix Suns, when (as the league's MVP) he put up a 42-point masterpiece in a triple-overtime win, only to be pipped in Game 6 by the clinching shot of the Bulls' John Paxson. But he is pipped again here by Tittle. From 1961 through '63, Y.A. and his New York Giants passed the NFL silly, and annually made it to the outdoor, cold-weather championship game, losing twice to the Lombardi Packers and then to the Chicago Bears on a brutal day at Wrigley Field unsuited for passing. Today these games might have been in a dome, and Tittle might have gotten that ring.

Banks vs. Kelly

Star-crossed players, but in different ways. Hall of Famer Banks had the misfortune (though Mr. Cub wouldn't see it that way) to play all his 2,528 big-league games as a Cub, and not one of those contests took place in the postseason. Kelly and his Buffalo Bills made the Super Bowl four straight years, losing a heartbreaker to the Giants, then suffering three blowouts. The tantalization factor gives the quarterback the nod.

THE MONKEY ON THE BACK: That's usually the phrase employed to describe the plight of the great athlete who can't win a championship. Sometimes ringlessness arises from being stuck on the wrong franchise. Sometimes the superstar has the bad fortune to play in an era dominated by an opposing supernova (Bill Russell, Michael Jordan, Tiger Woods, Affirmed). And let's face it, sometimes he or she chokes. Our scale is subjective, but we give a lot of special consideration for multiple misses, with bonuses for multiple consecutive misses – and a wild card for gut-wrenching, rip-your-heart-out failure.

Tittle vs. Baylor

At least in this bracket, Elg is a champ! And what a swellagant, elegant heartbreak kid he is! Seven times his Lakers (Minneapolis and L.A.) lost to Bill Russell's Boston Celtics in the NBA Finals, three of the defeats in seven games, once after Elg had singed the Celts for 62 points. Add another seven-game Finals loss to the New York Knicks. To top it off: As a collegian, Baylor made the NCAA finals with Seattle, only to lose to Kentucky. Can't we at least give this man an honorary ring?

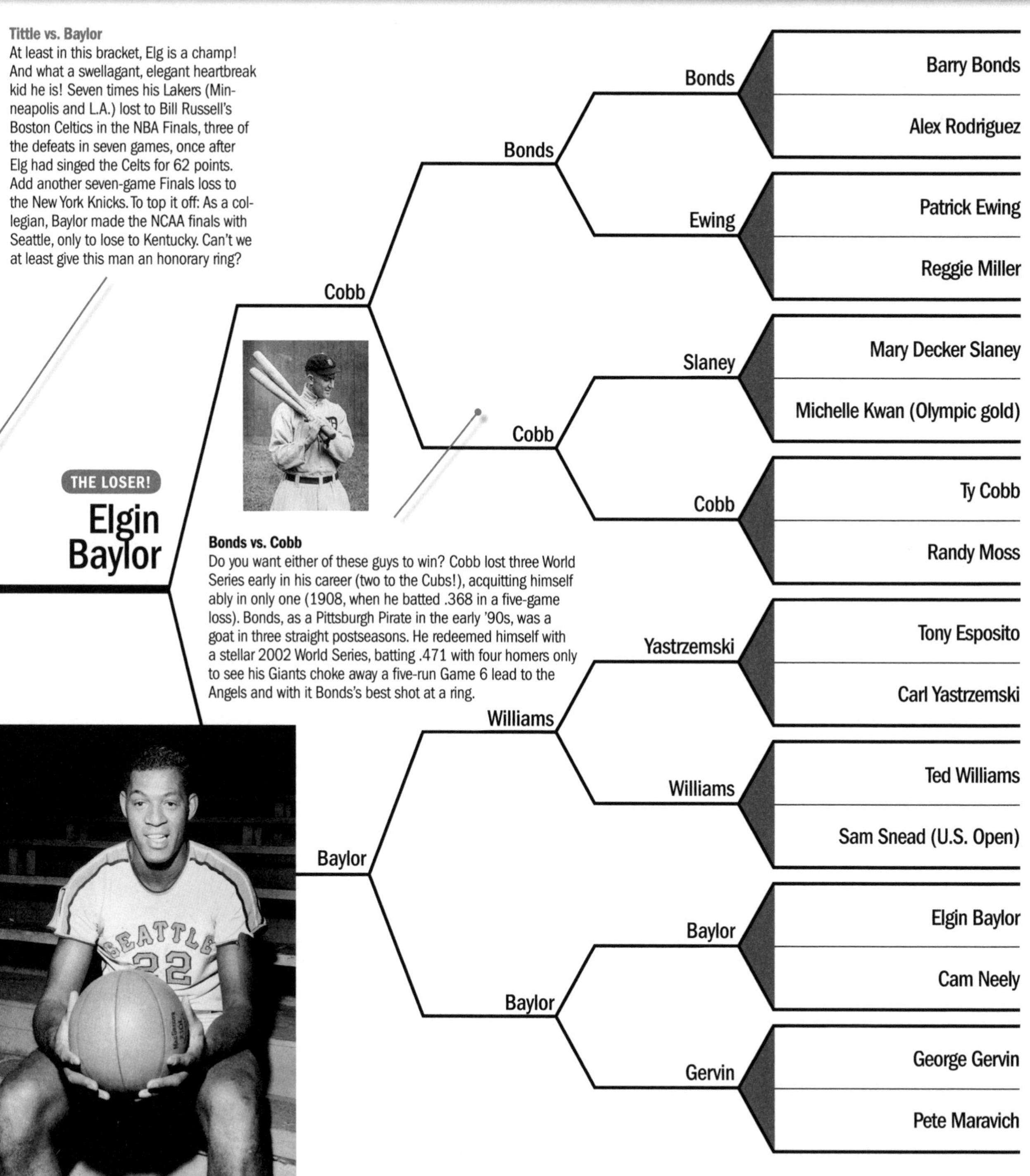
THE LOSER!
Elgin Baylor
Cobb
Bonds
Bonds
Ewing
Cobb
Slaney
Cobb
Baylor
Williams
Yastrzemski
Williams
Baylor
Baylor
Gervin
Barry Bonds
Alex Rodriguez
Patrick Ewing
Reggie Miller
Mary Decker Slaney
Michelle Kwan (Olympic gold)
Ty Cobb
Randy Moss
Tony Esposito
Carl Yastrzemski
Ted Williams
Sam Snead (U.S. Open)
Elgin Baylor
Cam Neely
George Gervin
Pete Maravich

Bonds vs. Cobb

Do you want either of these guys to win? Cobb lost three World Series early in his career (two to the Cubs!), acquitting himself ably in only one (1908, when he batted .368 in a five-game loss). Bonds, as a Pittsburgh Pirate in the early '90s, was a goat in three straight postseasons. He redeemed himself with a stellar 2002 World Series, batting .471 with four homers only to see his Giants choke away a five-run Game 6 lead to the Angels and with it Bonds's best shot at a ring.

Donald Ross Courses

By Bob Carney

Bob Carney, creative director at *Golf Digest,* oversees the magazine's course ranking. His home course, Brooklawn, is by Tillie, not Ross, but he's okay with that. Special thanks to caddy Ron Whitten.

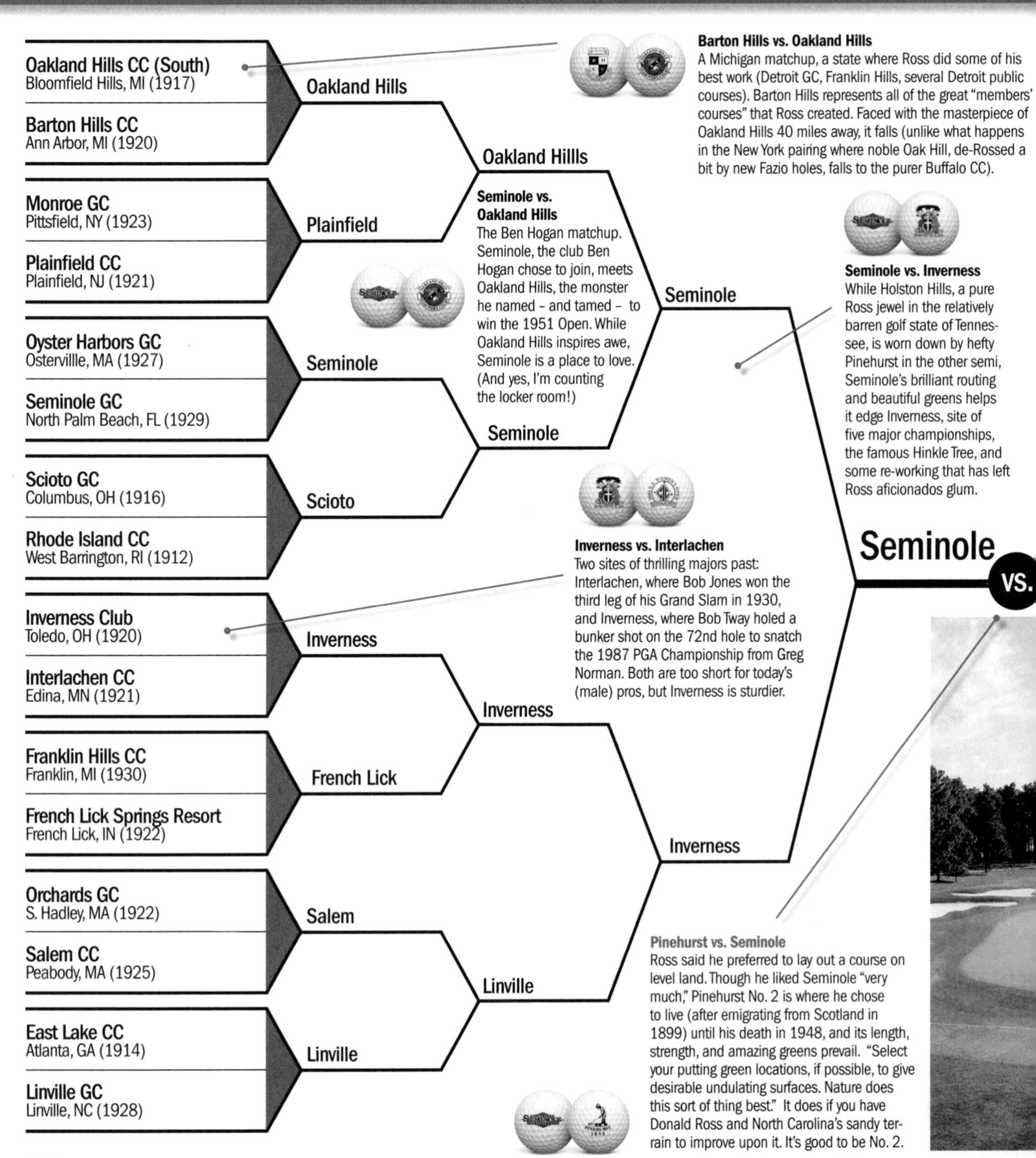

Oakland Hills CC (South)
Bloomfield Hills, MI (1917)
Barton Hills CC
Ann Arbor, MI (1920)
Monroe GC
Pittsfield, NY (1923)
Plainfield CC
Plainfield, NJ (1921)
Oyster Harbors GC
Osterville, MA (1927)
Seminole GC
North Palm Beach, FL (1929)
Scioto GC
Columbus, OH (1916)
Rhode Island CC
West Barrington, RI (1912)
Inverness Club
Toledo, OH (1920)
Interlachen CC
Edina, MN (1921)
Franklin Hills CC
Franklin, MI (1930)
French Lick Springs Resort
French Lick, IN (1922)
Orchards GC
S. Hadley, MA (1922)
Salem CC
Peabody, MA (1925)
East Lake CC
Atlanta, GA (1914)
Linville GC
Linville, NC (1928)
Oakland Hills
Plainfield
Seminole
Scioto
Inverness
French Lick
Salem
Linville
Oakland Hills
Seminole
Inverness
Linville
Seminole
Inverness
Seminole
VS.

Barton Hills vs. Oakland Hills
A Michigan matchup, a state where Ross did some of his best work (Detroit GC, Franklin Hills, several Detroit public courses). Barton Hills represents all of the great "members' courses" that Ross created. Faced with the masterpiece of Oakland Hills 40 miles away, it falls (unlike what happens in the New York pairing where noble Oak Hill, de-Rossed a bit by new Fazio holes, falls to the purer Buffalo CC).

Seminole vs. Oakland Hills
The Ben Hogan matchup. Seminole, the club Ben Hogan chose to join, meets Oakland Hills, the monster he named - and tamed - to win the 1951 Open. While Oakland Hills inspires awe, Seminole is a place to love. (And yes, I'm counting the locker room!)

Seminole vs. Inverness
While Holston Hills, a pure Ross jewel in the relatively barren golf state of Tennessee, is worn down by hefty Pinehurst in the other semi, Seminole's brilliant routing and beautiful greens helps it edge Inverness, site of five major championships, the famous Hinkle Tree, and some re-working that has left Ross aficionados glum.

Inverness vs. Interlachen
Two sites of thrilling majors past: Interlachen, where Bob Jones won the third leg of his Grand Slam in 1930, and Inverness, where Bob Tway holed a bunker shot on the 72nd hole to snatch the 1987 PGA Championship from Greg Norman. Both are too short for today's (male) pros, but Inverness is sturdier.

Pinehurst vs. Seminole
Ross said he preferred to lay out a course on level land. Though he liked Seminole "very much," Pinehurst No. 2 is where he chose to live (after emigrating from Scotland in 1899) until his death in 1948, and its length, strength, and amazing greens prevail. "Select your putting green locations, if possible, to give desirable undulating surfaces. Nature does this sort of thing best." It does if you have Donald Ross and North Carolina's sandy terrain to improve upon it. It's good to be No. 2.

OF GOLF'S "CULT" ARCHITECTS, from Tillinghast to Raynor to Dye, Donald Ross is the most prolific, credited in name or legitimate design with over 500 courses in the U.S. The first question about a Ross course is, "How Ross is it?" The second: "Who restored it?" These 32, though tweaked and toughened over the years, are "all Ross." Mostly. Which means they have skillful routing and greens that aren't all pushed-up, crowned surfaces resembling the top of a bowler hat (though many are). Choosing the greatest is like choosing the finest Frank Lloyd Wright home, if Wright had done subdivisions.

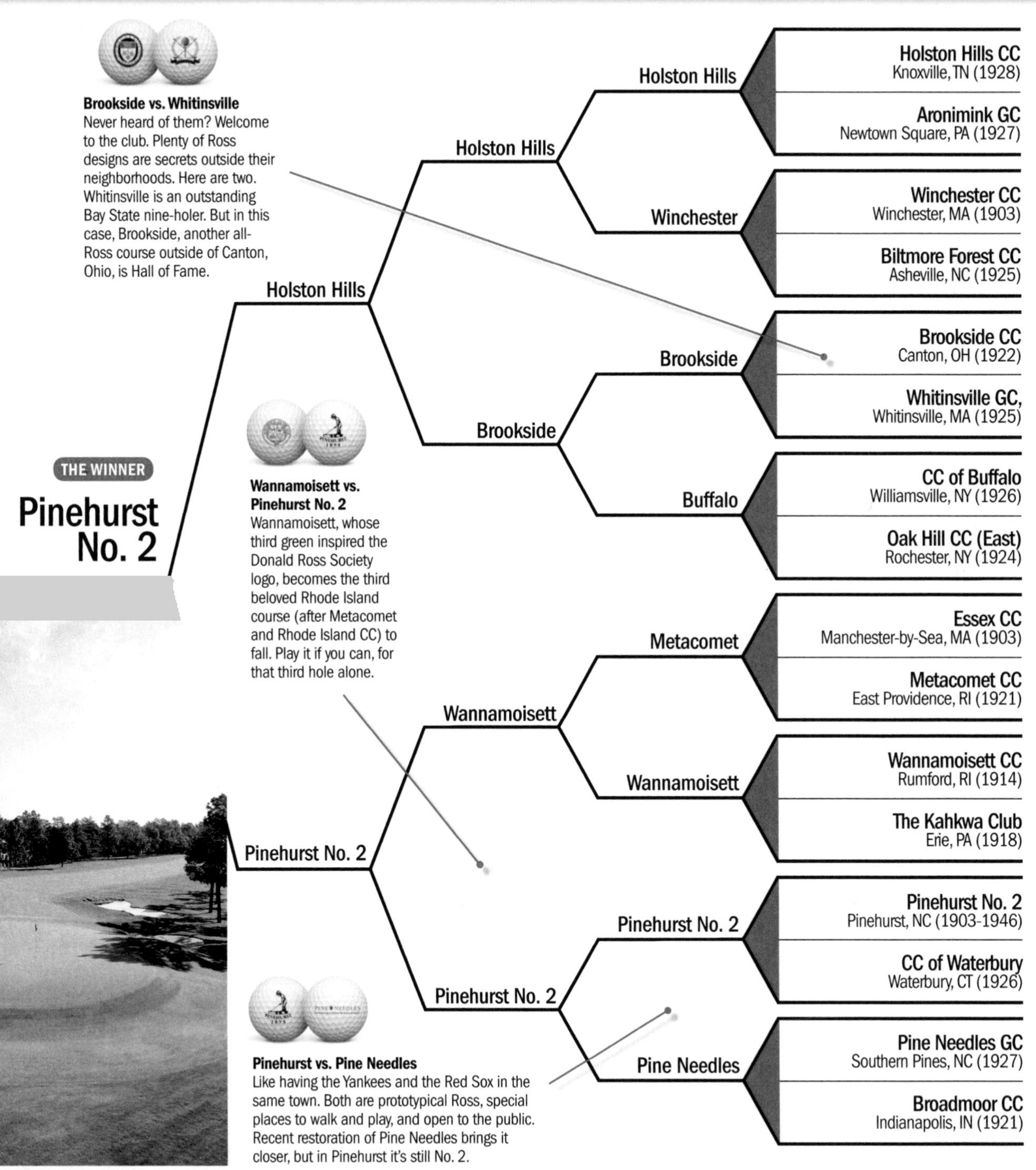

Holston Hills CC
Knoxville, TN (1928)
Aronimink GC
Newtown Square, PA (1927)
Winchester CC
Winchester, MA (1903)
Biltmore Forest CC
Asheville, NC (1925)
Brookside CC
Canton, OH (1922)
Whitinsville GC,
Whitinsville, MA (1925)
CC of Buffalo
Williamsville, NY (1926)
Oak Hill CC (East)
Rochester, NY (1924)
Essex CC
Manchester-by-Sea, MA (1903)
Metacomet CC
East Providence, RI (1921)
Wannamoisett CC
Rumford, RI (1914)
The Kahkwa Club
Erie, PA (1918)
Pinehurst No. 2
Pinehurst, NC (1903-1946)
CC of Waterbury
Waterbury, CT (1926)
Pine Needles GC
Southern Pines, NC (1927)
Broadmoor CC
Indianapolis, IN (1921)
Holston Hills
Winchester
Brookside
Buffalo
Metacomet
Wannamoisett
Pinehurst No. 2
Pine Needles
Holston Hills
Brookside
Wannamoisett
Pinehurst No. 2
Holston Hills
Pinehurst No. 2
THE WINNER
Pinehurst No. 2

Brookside vs. Whitinsville
Never heard of them? Welcome to the club. Plenty of Ross designs are secrets outside their neighborhoods. Here are two. Whitinsville is an outstanding Bay State nine-holer. But in this case, Brookside, another all-Ross course outside of Canton, Ohio, is Hall of Fame.

Wannamoisett vs. Pinehurst No. 2
Wannamoisett, whose third green inspired the Donald Ross Society logo, becomes the third beloved Rhode Island course (after Metacomet and Rhode Island CC) to fall. Play it if you can, for that third hole alone.

Pinehurst vs. Pine Needles
Like having the Yankees and the Red Sox in the same town. Both are prototypical Ross, special places to walk and play, and open to the public. Recent restoration of Pine Needles brings it closer, but in Pinehurst it's still No. 2.

American Hockey Players

By Nick Paumgarten

Nick Paumgarten is a staff writer at *The New Yorker,* and an American-born beer-league mucker.

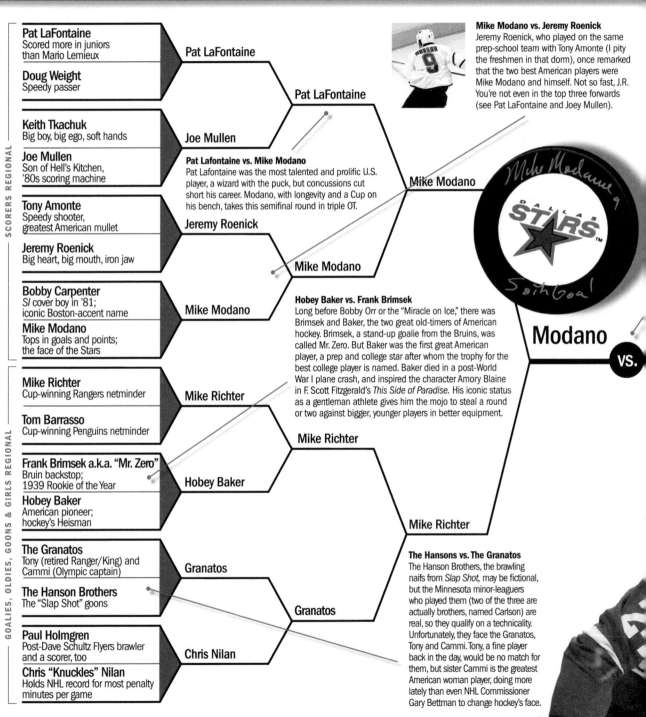

SCORERS REGIONAL

Pat LaFontaine
Scored more in juniors than Mario Lemieux

Doug Weight
Speedy passer

Keith Tkachuk
Big boy, big ego, soft hands

Joe Mullen
Son of Hell's Kitchen, '80s scoring machine

Tony Amonte
Speedy shooter, greatest American mullet

Jeremy Roenick
Big heart, big mouth, iron jaw

Bobby Carpenter
SI cover boy in '81; iconic Boston-accent name

Mike Modano
Tops in goals and points; the face of the Stars

GOALIES, OLDIES, GOONS & GIRLS REGIONAL

Mike Richter
Cup-winning Rangers netminder

Tom Barrasso
Cup-winning Penguins netminder

Frank Brimsek a.k.a. "Mr. Zero"
Bruin backstop; 1939 Rookie of the Year

Hobey Baker
American pioneer; hockey's Heisman

The Granatos
Tony (retired Ranger/King) and Cammi (Olympic captain)

The Hanson Brothers
The "Slap Shot" goons

Paul Holmgren
Post-Dave Schultz Flyers brawler and a scorer, too

Chris "Knuckles" Nilan
Holds NHL record for most penalty minutes per game

Second round: Pat LaFontaine, Joe Mullen, Jeremy Roenick, Mike Modano, Mike Richter, Hobey Baker, Granatos, Chris Nilan

Third round: Pat LaFontaine, Mike Modano, Mike Richter, Granatos

Regional finals: Mike Modano, Mike Richter

Modano vs.

Mike Modano vs. Jeremy Roenick
Jeremy Roenick, who played on the same prep-school team with Tony Amonte (I pity the freshmen in that dorm), once remarked that the two best American players were Mike Modano and himself. Not so fast, J.R. You're not even in the top three forwards (see Pat LaFontaine and Joey Mullen).

Pat Lafontaine vs. Mike Modano
Pat Lafontaine was the most talented and prolific U.S. player, a wizard with the puck, but concussions cut short his career. Modano, with longevity and a Cup on his bench, takes this semifinal round in triple OT.

Hobey Baker vs. Frank Brimsek
Long before Bobby Orr or the "Miracle on Ice," there was Brimsek and Baker, the two great old-timers of American hockey. Brimsek, a stand-up goalie from the Bruins, was called Mr. Zero. But Baker was the first great American player, a prep and college star after whom the trophy for the best college player is named. Baker died in a post-World War I plane crash, and inspired the character Amory Blaine in F. Scott Fitzgerald's *This Side of Paradise.* His iconic status as a gentleman athlete gives him the mojo to steal a round or two against bigger, younger players in better equipment.

The Hansons vs. The Granatos
The Hanson Brothers, the brawling naifs from *Slap Shot,* may be fictional, but the Minnesota minor-leaguers who played them (two of the three are actually brothers, named Carlson) are real, so they qualify on a technicality. Unfortunately, they face the Granatos, Tony and Cammi. Tony, a fine player back in the day, would be no match for them, but sister Cammi is the greatest American woman player, doing more lately than even NHL Commissioner Gary Bettman to change hockey's face.

ALTHOUGH AMERICAN HOCKEY TEAMS have won big international competitions (Olympics, World Cup, World Juniors) and various regions qualify as hockey hotbeds, puck has always been a marginal sport – one of the few areas where we let Canadians feel superior. We've bred many very good players, but few great ones, much less a Great One – which is why ranking American players, though a staple of rec-league locker rooms, has hardly been a high priority on sports talk radio. We correct that here.

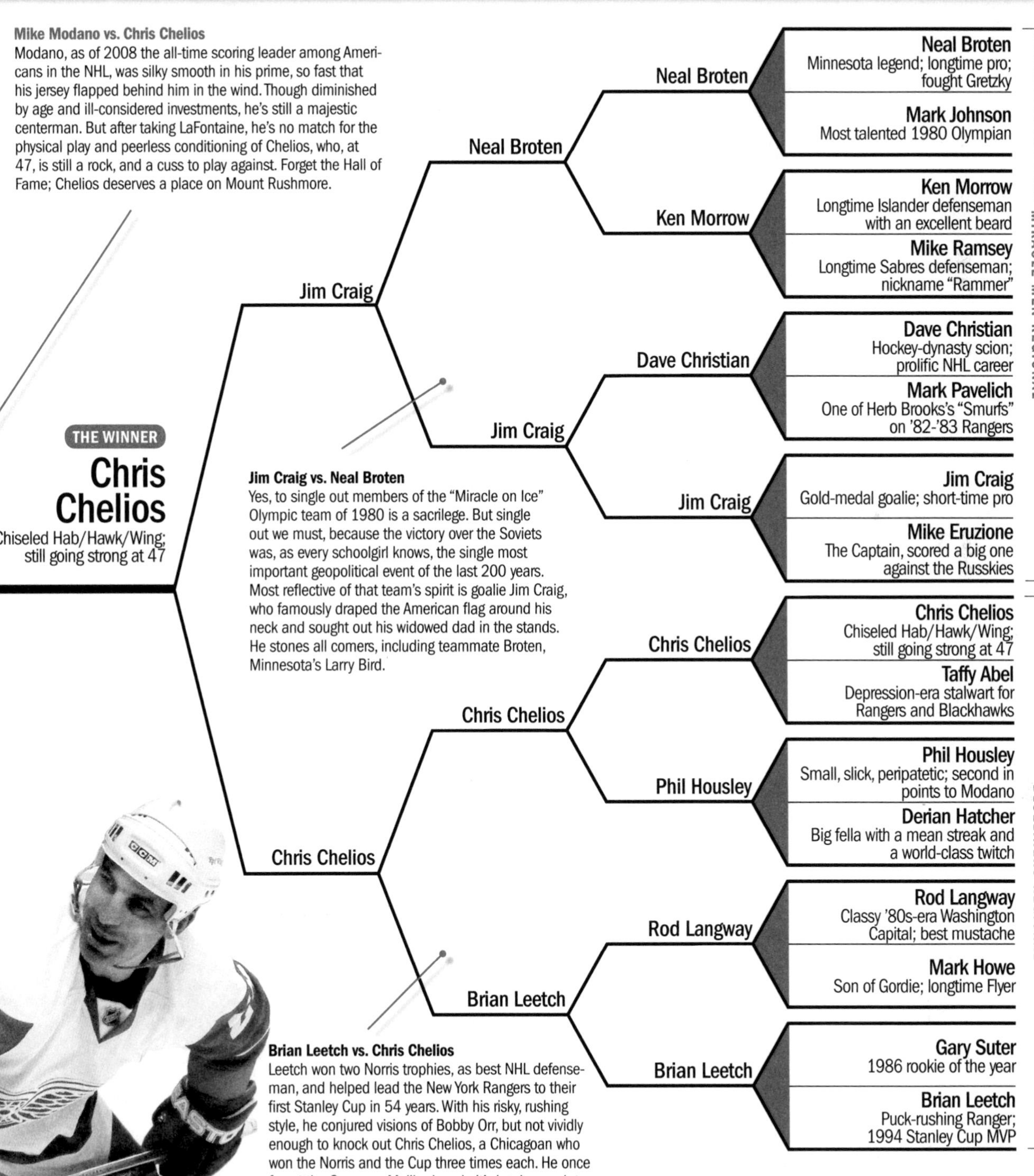

MIRACLE MEN REGIONAL
Neal Broten
Minnesota legend; longtime pro; fought Gretzky
Mark Johnson
Most talented 1980 Olympian
Ken Morrow
Longtime Islander defenseman with an excellent beard
Mike Ramsey
Longtime Sabres defenseman; nickname "Rammer"
Dave Christian
Hockey-dynasty scion; prolific NHL career
Mark Pavelich
One of Herb Brooks's "Smurfs" on '82-'83 Rangers
Jim Craig
Gold-medal goalie; short-time pro
Mike Eruzione
The Captain, scored a big one against the Russkies
Neal Broten
Ken Morrow
Dave Christian
Jim Craig
Neal Broten
Jim Craig
Jim Craig
BLUELINERS REGIONAL
Chris Chelios
Chiseled Hab/Hawk/Wing; still going strong at 47
Taffy Abel
Depression-era stalwart for Rangers and Blackhawks
Phil Housley
Small, slick, peripatetic; second in points to Modano
Derian Hatcher
Big fella with a mean streak and a world-class twitch
Rod Langway
Classy '80s-era Washington Capital; best mustache
Mark Howe
Son of Gordie; longtime Flyer
Gary Suter
1986 rookie of the year
Brian Leetch
Puck-rushing Ranger; 1994 Stanley Cup MVP
Chris Chelios
Phil Housley
Rod Langway
Brian Leetch
Chris Chelios
Brian Leetch
Chris Chelios
THE WINNER
Chris Chelios
Chiseled Hab/Hawk/Wing; still going strong at 47

Mike Modano vs. Chris Chelios

Modano, as of 2008 the all-time scoring leader among Americans in the NHL, was silky smooth in his prime, so fast that his jersey flapped behind him in the wind. Though diminished by age and ill-considered investments, he's still a majestic centerman. But after taking LaFontaine, he's no match for the physical play and peerless conditioning of Chelios, who, at 47, is still a rock, and a cuss to play against. Forget the Hall of Fame; Chelios deserves a place on Mount Rushmore.

Jim Craig vs. Neal Broten

Yes, to single out members of the "Miracle on Ice" Olympic team of 1980 is a sacrilege. But single out we must, because the victory over the Soviets was, as every schoolgirl knows, the single most important geopolitical event of the last 200 years. Most reflective of that team's spirit is goalie Jim Craig, who famously draped the American flag around his neck and sought out his widowed dad in the stands. He stones all comers, including teammate Broten, Minnesota's Larry Bird.

Brian Leetch vs. Chris Chelios

Leetch won two Norris trophies, as best NHL defenseman, and helped lead the New York Rangers to their first Stanley Cup in 54 years. With his risky, rushing style, he conjured visions of Bobby Orr, but not vividly enough to knock out Chris Chelios, a Chicagoan who won the Norris and the Cup three times each. He once forgot the Cup on a Malibu beach. It's hard enough to win the thing, but to leave it behind takes game.

Steroid-Era Moments

By Shaun Assael

Shaun Assael, a senior writer for *ESPN the Magazine*, is the author of three books, among them *Steroid Nation*, which had the ridiculously long subtitle: *Juiced Home Run Totals, Anti-aging Miracles, and a Hercules in Every High School: The Secret History of America's True Drug Addiction.*

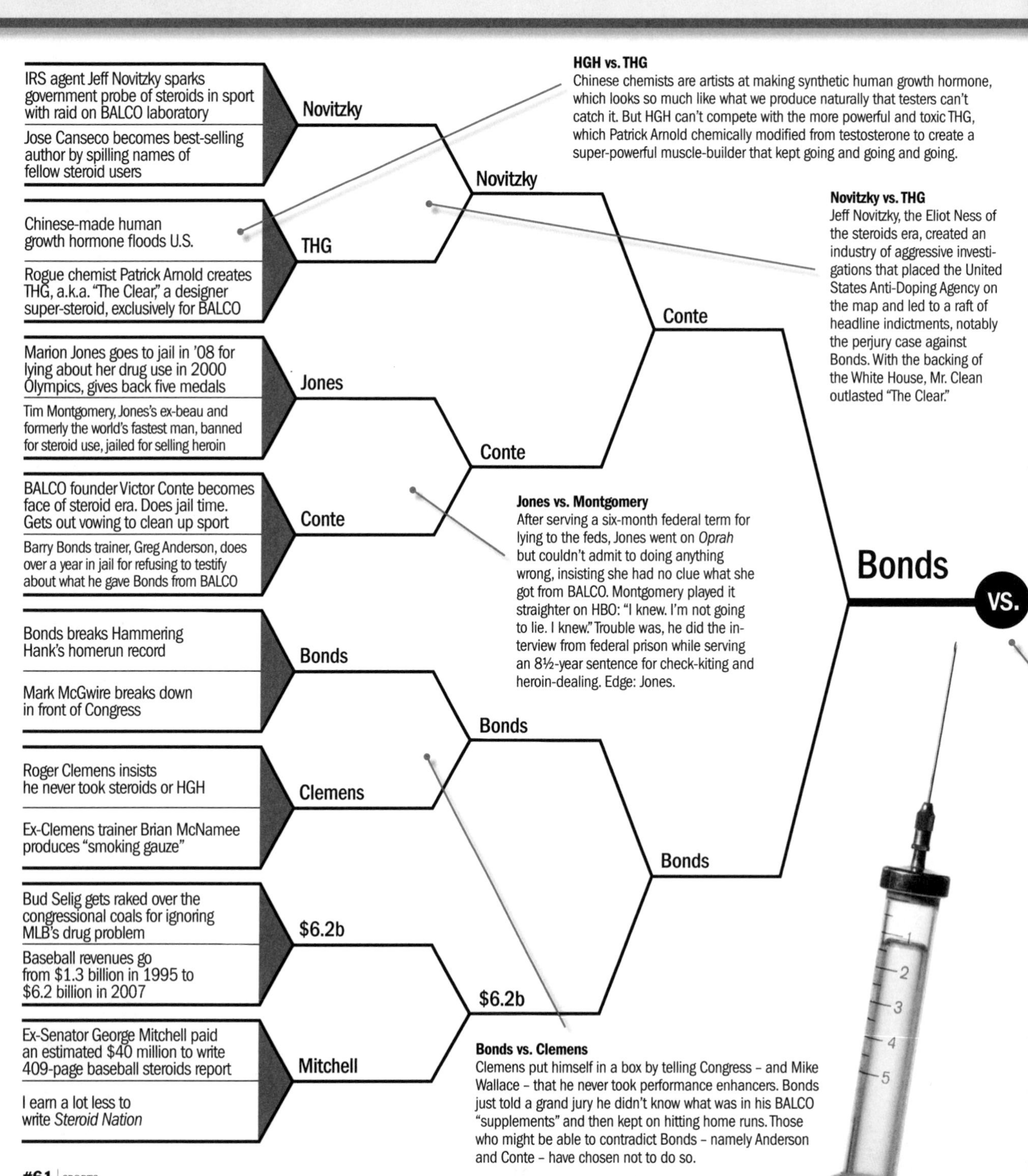

IRS agent Jeff Novitzky sparks government probe of steroids in sport with raid on BALCO laboratory
Jose Canseco becomes best-selling author by spilling names of fellow steroid users
Novitzky
Chinese-made human growth hormone floods U.S.
Rogue chemist Patrick Arnold creates THG, a.k.a. "The Clear," a designer super-steroid, exclusively for BALCO
THG
Novitzky
Marion Jones goes to jail in '08 for lying about her drug use in 2000 Olympics, gives back five medals
Tim Montgomery, Jones's ex-beau and formerly the world's fastest man, banned for steroid use, jailed for selling heroin
Jones
BALCO founder Victor Conte becomes face of steroid era. Does jail time. Gets out vowing to clean up sport
Barry Bonds trainer, Greg Anderson, does over a year in jail for refusing to testify about what he gave Bonds from BALCO
Conte
Conte
Conte
Bonds breaks Hammering Hank's homerun record
Mark McGwire breaks down in front of Congress
Bonds
Roger Clemens insists he never took steroids or HGH
Ex-Clemens trainer Brian McNamee produces "smoking gauze"
Clemens
Bonds
Bud Selig gets raked over the congressional coals for ignoring MLB's drug problem
Baseball revenues go from $1.3 billion in 1995 to $6.2 billion in 2007
$6.2b
Ex-Senator George Mitchell paid an estimated $40 million to write 409-page baseball steroids report
I earn a lot less to write *Steroid Nation*
Mitchell
$6.2b
Bonds
Bonds
VS.
1
2
3
4
5

HGH vs. THG
Chinese chemists are artists at making synthetic human growth hormone, which looks so much like what we produce naturally that testers can't catch it. But HGH can't compete with the more powerful and toxic THG, which Patrick Arnold chemically modified from testosterone to create a super-powerful muscle-builder that kept going and going and going.

Novitzky vs. THG
Jeff Novitzky, the Eliot Ness of the steroids era, created an industry of aggressive investigations that placed the United States Anti-Doping Agency on the map and led to a raft of headline indictments, notably the perjury case against Bonds. With the backing of the White House, Mr. Clean outlasted "The Clear."

Jones vs. Montgomery
After serving a six-month federal term for lying to the feds, Jones went on *Oprah* but couldn't admit to doing anything wrong, insisting she had no clue what she got from BALCO. Montgomery played it straighter on HBO: "I knew. I'm not going to lie. I knew." Trouble was, he did the interview from federal prison while serving an 8½-year sentence for check-kiting and heroin-dealing. Edge: Jones.

Bonds vs. Clemens
Clemens put himself in a box by telling Congress – and Mike Wallace – that he never took performance enhancers. Bonds just told a grand jury he didn't know what was in his BALCO "supplements" and then kept on hitting home runs. Those who might be able to contradict Bonds – namely Anderson and Conte – have chosen not to do so.

THE STEROID ERA WILL BE RECALLED AS A QUAINT TIME when the sports world cared little about the bizarre physical transformations unfolding before its eyes. Front-office execs saw nothing strange about cartoon-sized biceps, back acne, and strangely expanding heads. Fans ignored the reasons behind amazing home run and Olympic records. In this juiced-up game of cat and mouse between the alleged cheaters and those trying to catch them, players advance by winning the most, or losing the least.

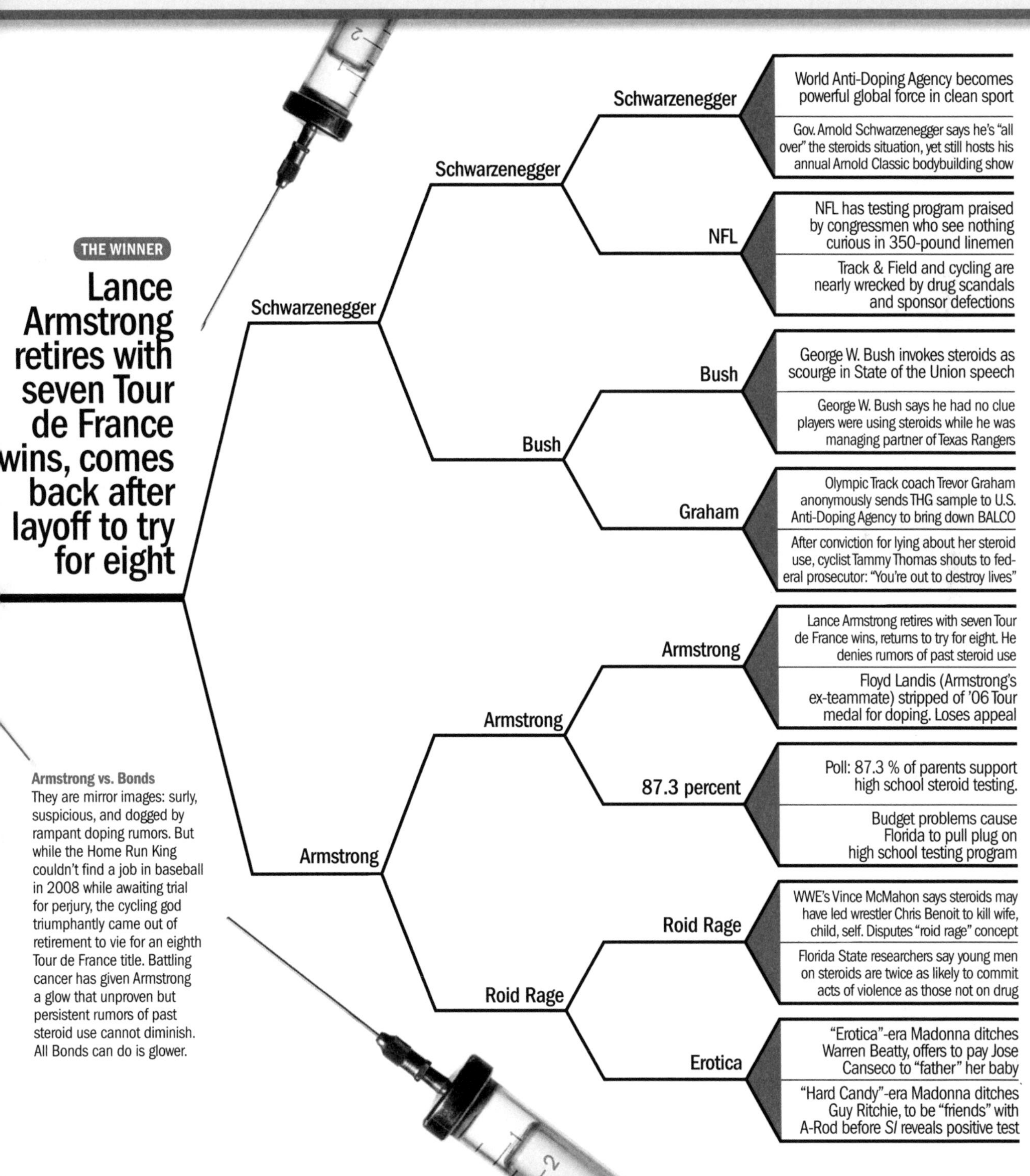

World Anti-Doping Agency becomes powerful global force in clean sport
Gov. Arnold Schwarzenegger says he's "all over" the steroids situation, yet still hosts his annual Arnold Classic bodybuilding show
NFL has testing program praised by congressmen who see nothing curious in 350-pound linemen
Track & Field and cycling are nearly wrecked by drug scandals and sponsor defections
George W. Bush invokes steroids as scourge in State of the Union speech
George W. Bush says he had no clue players were using steroids while he was managing partner of Texas Rangers
Olympic Track coach Trevor Graham anonymously sends THG sample to U.S. Anti-Doping Agency to bring down BALCO
After conviction for lying about her steroid use, cyclist Tammy Thomas shouts to federal prosecutor: "You're out to destroy lives"
Lance Armstrong retires with seven Tour de France wins, returns to try for eight. He denies rumors of past steroid use
Floyd Landis (Armstrong's ex-teammate) stripped of '06 Tour medal for doping. Loses appeal
Poll: 87.3 % of parents support high school steroid testing.
Budget problems cause Florida to pull plug on high school testing program
WWE's Vince McMahon says steroids may have led wrestler Chris Benoit to kill wife, child, self. Disputes "roid rage" concept
Florida State researchers say young men on steroids are twice as likely to commit acts of violence as those not on drug
"Erotica"-era Madonna ditches Warren Beatty, offers to pay Jose Canseco to "father" her baby
"Hard Candy"-era Madonna ditches Guy Ritchie, to be "friends" with A-Rod before SI reveals positive test
Schwarzenegger
NFL
Bush
Graham
Armstrong
87.3 percent
Roid Rage
Erotica
Schwarzenegger
Bush
Armstrong
Roid Rage
Schwarzenegger
Armstrong
THE WINNER
Lance Armstrong retires with seven Tour de France wins, comes back after layoff to try for eight

Armstrong vs. Bonds
They are mirror images: surly, suspicious, and dogged by rampant doping rumors. But while the Home Run King couldn't find a job in baseball in 2008 while awaiting trial for perjury, the cycling god triumphantly came out of retirement to vie for an eighth Tour de France title. Battling cancer has given Armstrong a glow that unproven but persistent rumors of past steroid use cannot diminish. All Bonds can do is glower.

Sports Clichés

By Steve Rushin

Steve Rushin is the author of the nonfiction books *Road Swing* and *The Caddie Was a Reindeer* and a forthcoming novel, *The Pint Man*. He has been a columnist for *Sports Illustrated* and an essayist for *Time*.

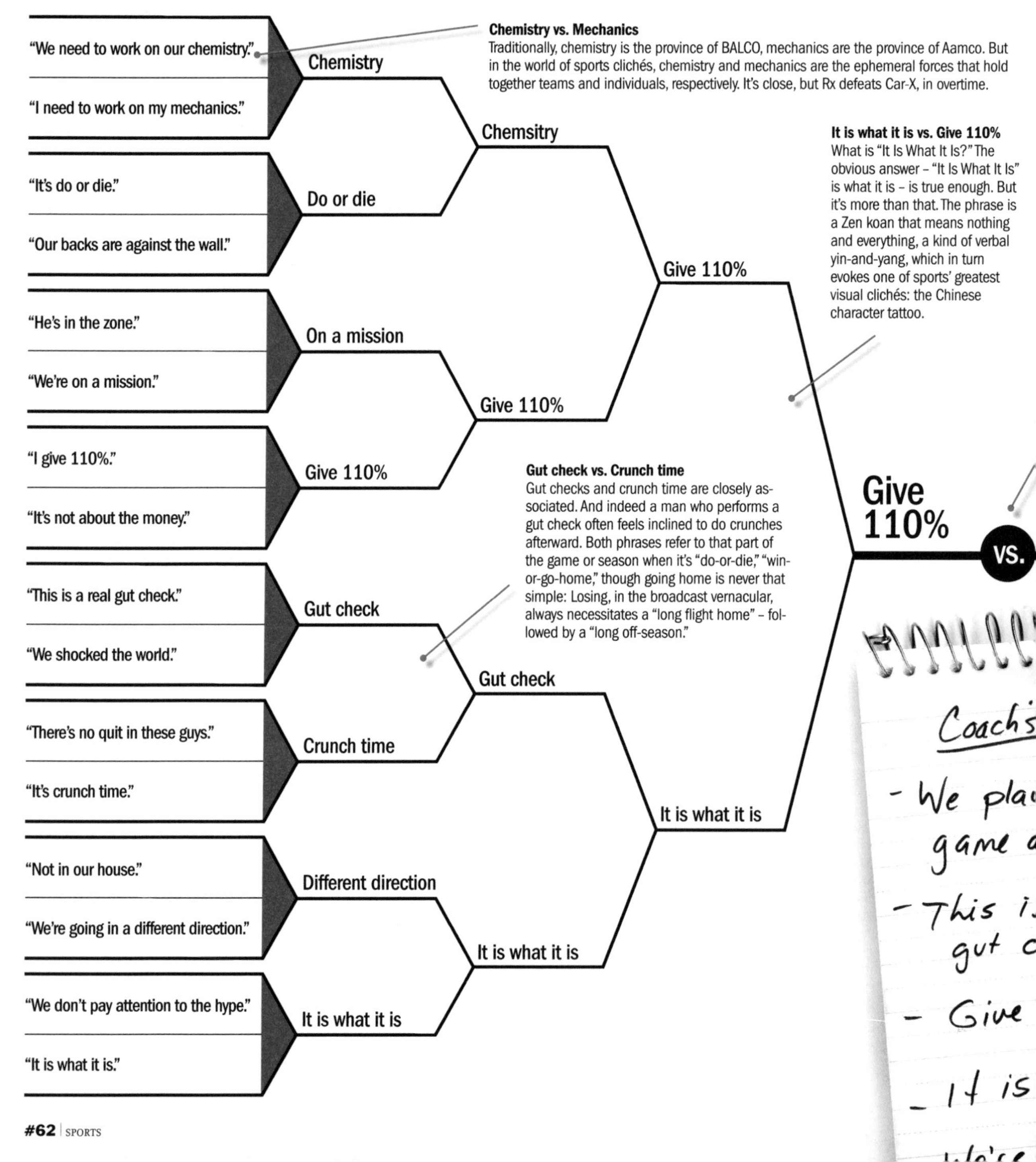
"We need to work on our chemistry."
"I need to work on my mechanics."
"It's do or die."
"Our backs are against the wall."
"He's in the zone."
"We're on a mission."
"I give 110%."
"It's not about the money."
"This is a real gut check."
"We shocked the world."
"There's no quit in these guys."
"It's crunch time."
"Not in our house."
"We're going in a different direction."
"We don't pay attention to the hype."
"It is what it is."
Chemistry
Do or die
On a mission
Give 110%
Gut check
Crunch time
Different direction
It is what it is
Chemsitry
Give 110%
Gut check
It is what it is
Give 110%
It is what it is
Give 110%
VS.
Chemistry vs. Mechanics
Traditionally, chemistry is the province of BALCO, mechanics are the province of Aamco. But in the world of sports clichés, chemistry and mechanics are the ephemeral forces that hold together teams and individuals, respectively. It's close, but Rx defeats Car-X, in overtime.
It is what it is vs. Give 110%
What is "It Is What It Is?" The obvious answer – "It Is What It Is" is what it is – is true enough. But it's more than that. The phrase is a Zen koan that means nothing and everything, a kind of verbal yin-and-yang, which in turn evokes one of sports' greatest visual clichés: the Chinese character tattoo.
Gut check vs. Crunch time
Gut checks and crunch time are closely associated. And indeed a man who performs a gut check often feels inclined to do crunches afterward. Both phrases refer to that part of the game or season when it's "do-or-die," "win-or-go-home," though going home is never that simple: Losing, in the broadcast vernacular, always necessitates a "long flight home" – followed by a "long off-season."
Coach's
Give

THE FRENCH HAVE MORE NAMES FOR BOREDOM THAN CHEESES, among them ennui and malaise and plat ("flat"), from which we get such touchstones of tedium as "platitude" and North Platte, Nebraska. But no word conveys existential weariness quite like cliché, and no cliché deadens the soul quite like a sports cliché, in which all fired coaches "step down" and all winning teams "step up." But you know that. The sports cliché, to use a cliché, needs no introduction.

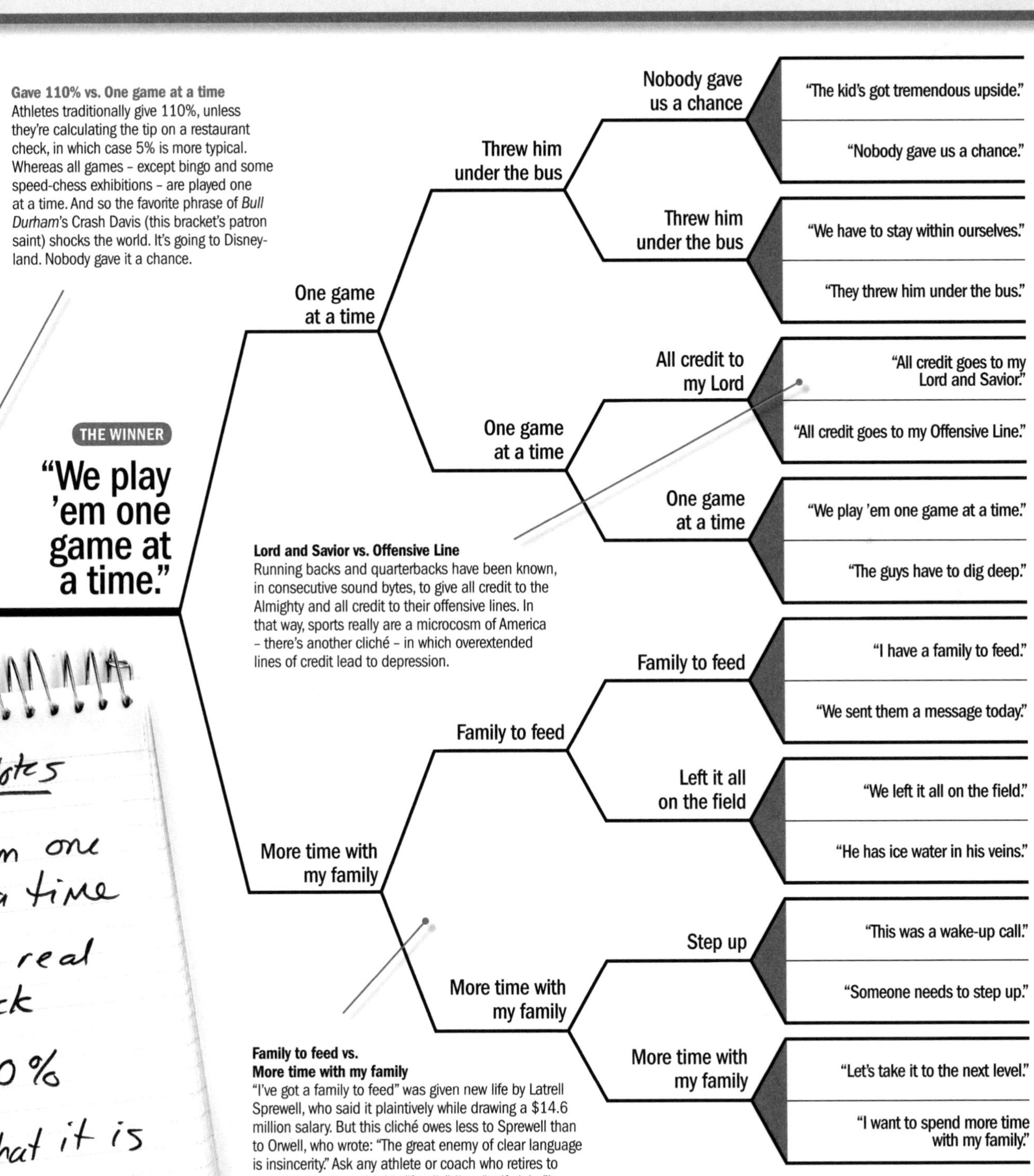

Nobody gave us a chance
"The kid's got tremendous upside."
"Nobody gave us a chance."
Threw him under the bus
Threw him under the bus
"We have to stay within ourselves."
"They threw him under the bus."
One game at a time
All credit to my Lord
"All credit goes to my Lord and Savior."
"All credit goes to my Offensive Line."
One game at a time
One game at a time
"We play 'em one game at a time."
"The guys have to dig deep."
THE WINNER
"We play 'em one game at a time."
Family to feed
"I have a family to feed."
"We sent them a message today."
Family to feed
Left it all on the field
"We left it all on the field."
"He has ice water in his veins."
More time with my family
Step up
"This was a wake-up call."
"Someone needs to step up."
More time with my family
More time with my family
"Let's take it to the next level."
"I want to spend more time with my family."

Gave 110% vs. One game at a time
Athletes traditionally give 110%, unless they're calculating the tip on a restaurant check, in which case 5% is more typical. Whereas all games – except bingo and some speed-chess exhibitions – are played one at a time. And so the favorite phrase of *Bull Durham*'s Crash Davis (this bracket's patron saint) shocks the world. It's going to Disneyland. Nobody gave it a chance.

Lord and Savior vs. Offensive Line
Running backs and quarterbacks have been known, in consecutive sound bytes, to give all credit to the Almighty and all credit to their offensive lines. In that way, sports really are a microcosm of America – there's another cliché – in which overextended lines of credit lead to depression.

Family to feed vs. More time with my family
"I've got a family to feed" was given new life by Latrell Sprewell, who said it plaintively while drawing a $14.6 million salary. But this cliché owes less to Sprewell than to Orwell, who wrote: "The great enemy of clear language is insincerity." Ask any athlete or coach who retires to spend more time with his "family" (i.e., "golf clubs").

Instant Replays

By Alan Schwarz

Alan Schwarz is a sports reporter for the *New York Times* and the author of *The Numbers Game: Baseball's Lifelong Fascination with Statistics.* Like most of the *Times* staff, he sits within earshot of this book's co-editor, Richard Sandomir.

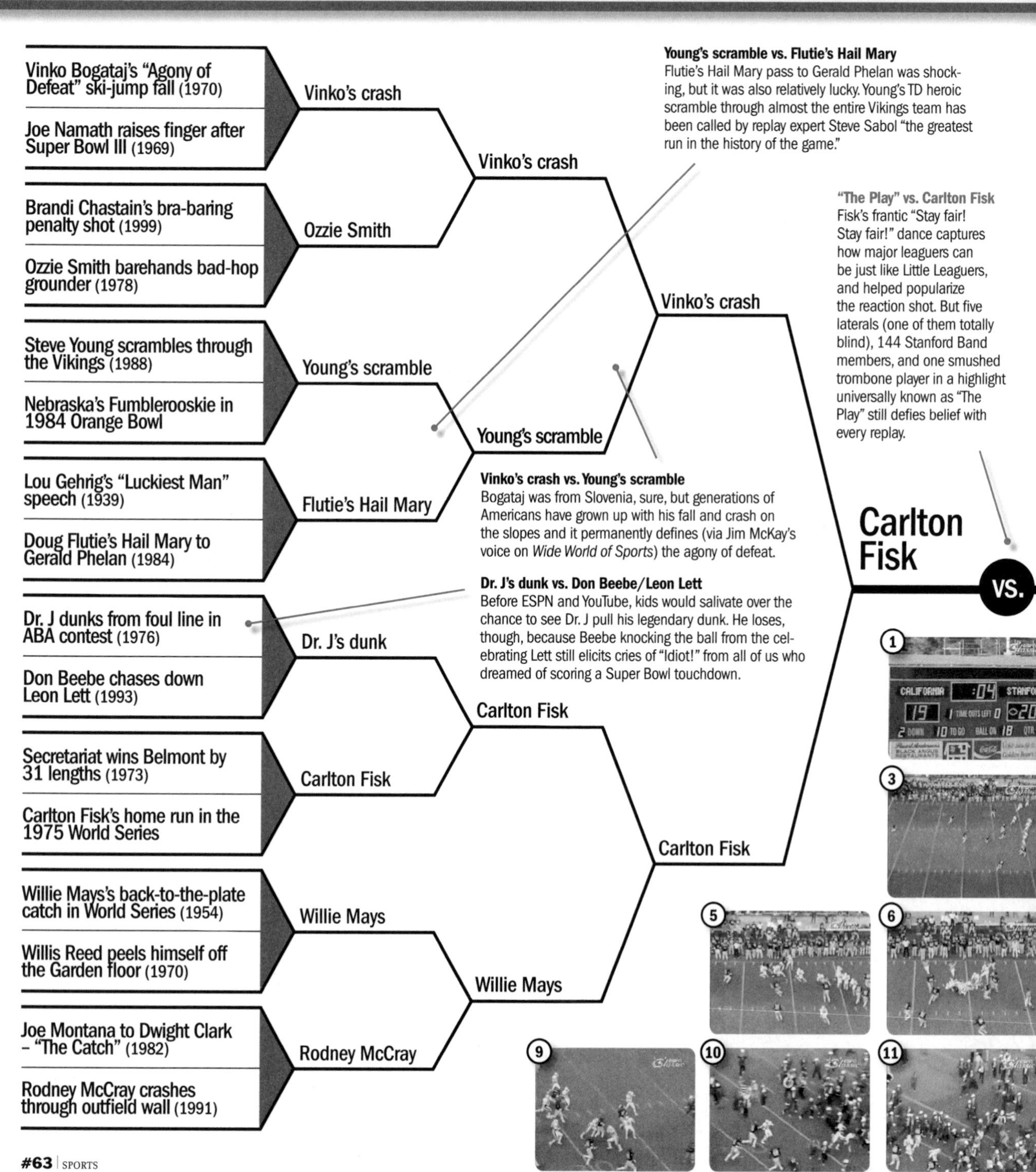
Vinko Bogataj's "Agony of Defeat" ski-jump fall (1970)
Joe Namath raises finger after Super Bowl III (1969)
Brandi Chastain's bra-baring penalty shot (1999)
Ozzie Smith barehands bad-hop grounder (1978)
Steve Young scrambles through the Vikings (1988)
Nebraska's Fumblerooskie in 1984 Orange Bowl
Lou Gehrig's "Luckiest Man" speech (1939)
Doug Flutie's Hail Mary to Gerald Phelan (1984)
Dr. J dunks from foul line in ABA contest (1976)
Don Beebe chases down Leon Lett (1993)
Secretariat wins Belmont by 31 lengths (1973)
Carlton Fisk's home run in the 1975 World Series
Willie Mays's back-to-the-plate catch in World Series (1954)
Willis Reed peels himself off the Garden floor (1970)
Joe Montana to Dwight Clark – "The Catch" (1982)
Rodney McCray crashes through outfield wall (1991)
Vinko's crash
Ozzie Smith
Young's scramble
Flutie's Hail Mary
Dr. J's dunk
Carlton Fisk
Willie Mays
Rodney McCray
Vinko's crash
Young's scramble
Carlton Fisk
Willie Mays
Vinko's crash
Carlton Fisk
Carlton Fisk
VS.
1
3
5
6
9
10
11

Young's scramble vs. Flutie's Hail Mary
Flutie's Hail Mary pass to Gerald Phelan was shocking, but it was also relatively lucky. Young's TD heroic scramble through almost the entire Vikings team has been called by replay expert Steve Sabol "the greatest run in the history of the game."

"The Play" vs. Carlton Fisk
Fisk's frantic "Stay fair! Stay fair!" dance captures how major leaguers can be just like Little Leaguers, and helped popularize the reaction shot. But five laterals (one of them totally blind), 144 Stanford Band members, and one smushed trombone player in a highlight universally known as "The Play" still defies belief with every replay.

Vinko's crash vs. Young's scramble
Bogataj was from Slovenia, sure, but generations of Americans have grown up with his fall and crash on the slopes and it permanently defines (via Jim McKay's voice on *Wide World of Sports*) the agony of defeat.

Dr. J's dunk vs. Don Beebe/Leon Lett
Before ESPN and YouTube, kids would salivate over the chance to see Dr. J pull his legendary dunk. He loses, though, because Beebe knocking the ball from the celebrating Lett still elicits cries of "Idiot!" from all of us who dreamed of scoring a Super Bowl touchdown.

SPORTS REPLAYS AREN'T JUST ABOUT GREAT MOMENTS – they have to be visually arresting, with rarely-seen moves or compelling audio that you want to experience over and over again. (Alan Ameche's TD in the 1958 Ice Bowl is a flashpoint in sports history, but the footage is actually quite dull.) If you were stranded on a desert island (with a DVD player), these catches, scrambles, and legendary maneuvers (some of them bloopers) would justify our fascination with sports, even if you only watched them with a volleyball named Wilson.

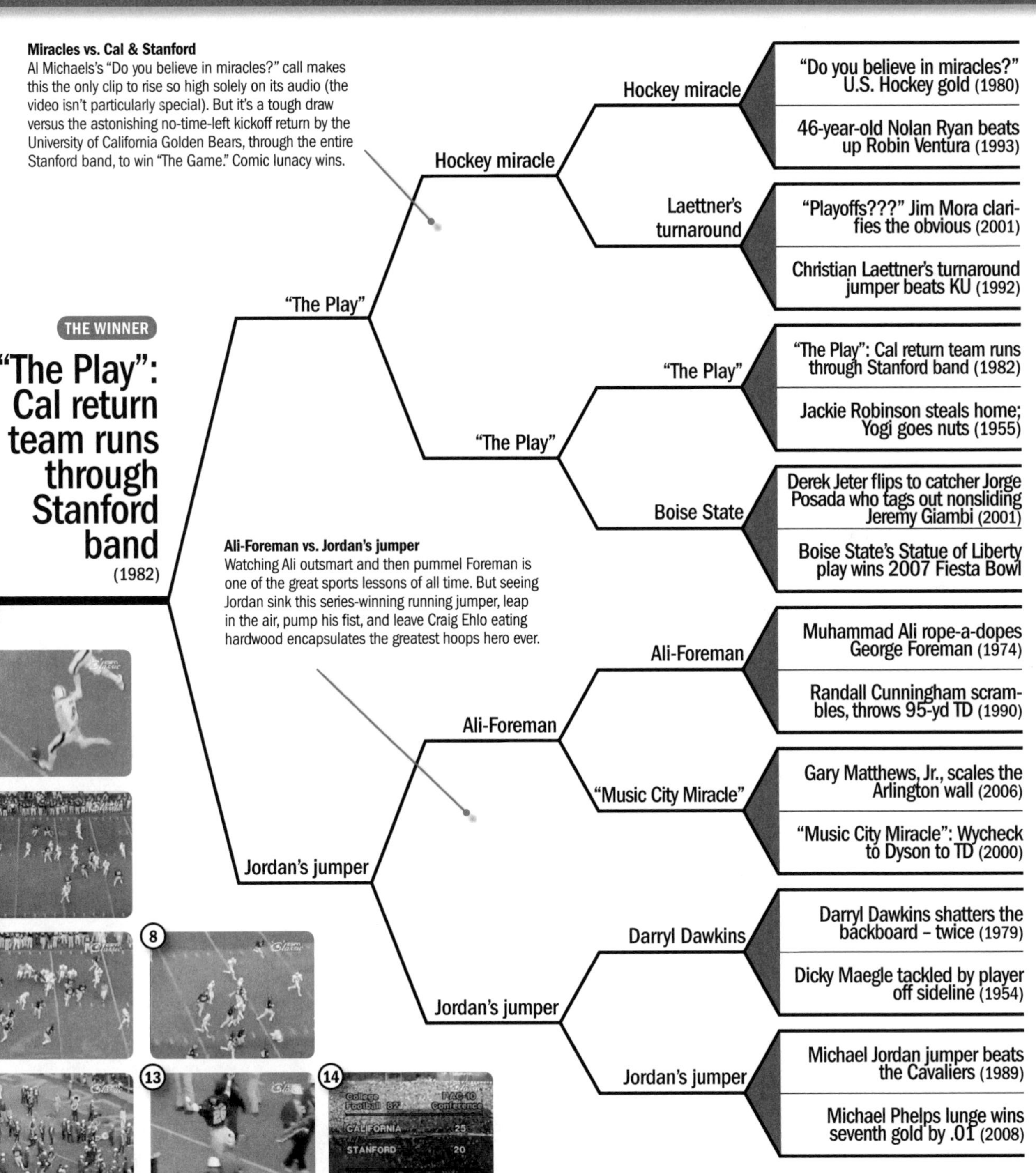

Miracles vs. Cal & Stanford
Al Michaels's "Do you believe in miracles?" call makes this the only clip to rise so high solely on its audio (the video isn't particularly special). But it's a tough draw versus the astonishing no-time-left kickoff return by the University of California Golden Bears, through the entire Stanford band, to win "The Game." Comic lunacy wins.
"Do you believe in miracles?" U.S. Hockey gold (1980)
46-year-old Nolan Ryan beats up Robin Ventura (1993)
Hockey miracle
"Playoffs???" Jim Mora clarifies the obvious (2001)
Christian Laettner's turnaround jumper beats KU (1992)
Laettner's turnaround
Hockey miracle
"The Play": Cal return team runs through Stanford band (1982)
Jackie Robinson steals home; Yogi goes nuts (1955)
"The Play"
Derek Jeter flips to catcher Jorge Posada who tags out nonsliding Jeremy Giambi (2001)
Boise State's Statue of Liberty play wins 2007 Fiesta Bowl
Boise State
"The Play"
"The Play"
THE WINNER
"The Play": Cal return team runs through Stanford band (1982)
Ali-Foreman vs. Jordan's jumper
Watching Ali outsmart and then pummel Foreman is one of the great sports lessons of all time. But seeing Jordan sink this series-winning running jumper, leap in the air, pump his fist, and leave Craig Ehlo eating hardwood encapsulates the greatest hoops hero ever.
Muhammad Ali rope-a-dopes George Foreman (1974)
Randall Cunningham scrambles, throws 95-yd TD (1990)
Ali-Foreman
Gary Matthews, Jr., scales the Arlington wall (2006)
"Music City Miracle": Wycheck to Dyson to TD (2000)
"Music City Miracle"
Ali-Foreman
Darryl Dawkins shatters the backboard – twice (1979)
Dicky Maegle tackled by player off sideline (1954)
Darryl Dawkins
Michael Jordan jumper beats the Cavaliers (1989)
Michael Phelps lunge wins seventh gold by .01 (2008)
Jordan's jumper
Jordan's jumper
Jordan's jumper
8
13
14
College Football 82
PAC-10 Conference
CALIFORNIA 25
STANFORD 20
FINAL

Sexually Inadequate Nicknames

By Hart Seely

Hart Seely, author of *Mrs. Goose Goes to Washington: Nursery Rhymes for the Political Barnyard,* ruminates daily about the New York Yankees on his website, *It Is High, It Is Far, It Is Caught.*

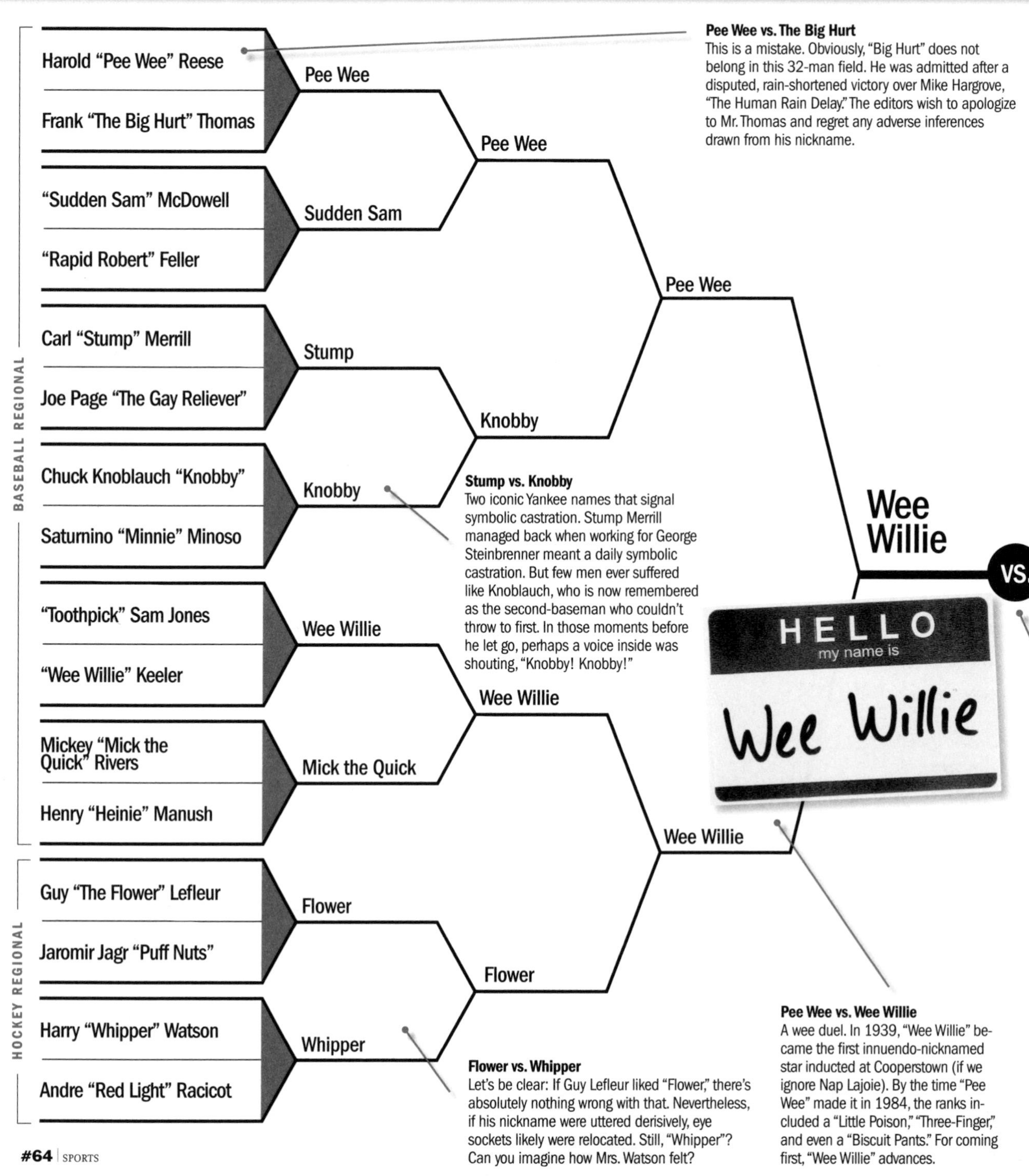

BASEBALL REGIONAL
Harold "Pee Wee" Reese
Frank "The Big Hurt" Thomas
"Sudden Sam" McDowell
"Rapid Robert" Feller
Carl "Stump" Merrill
Joe Page "The Gay Reliever"
Chuck Knoblauch "Knobby"
Saturnino "Minnie" Minoso
"Toothpick" Sam Jones
"Wee Willie" Keeler
Mickey "Mick the Quick" Rivers
Henry "Heinie" Manush
HOCKEY REGIONAL
Guy "The Flower" Lefleur
Jaromir Jagr "Puff Nuts"
Harry "Whipper" Watson
Andre "Red Light" Racicot
Pee Wee
Sudden Sam
Stump
Knobby
Wee Willie
Mick the Quick
Flower
Whipper
Pee Wee
Knobby
Wee Willie
Flower
Pee Wee
Wee Willie
Wee Willie
VS.
HELLO
my name is
Wee Willie

Pee Wee vs. The Big Hurt
This is a mistake. Obviously, "Big Hurt" does not belong in this 32-man field. He was admitted after a disputed, rain-shortened victory over Mike Hargrove, "The Human Rain Delay." The editors wish to apologize to Mr. Thomas and regret any adverse inferences drawn from his nickname.

Stump vs. Knobby
Two iconic Yankee names that signal symbolic castration. Stump Merrill managed back when working for George Steinbrenner meant a daily symbolic castration. But few men ever suffered like Knoblauch, who is now remembered as the second-baseman who couldn't throw to first. In those moments before he let go, perhaps a voice inside was shouting, "Knobby! Knobby!"

Flower vs. Whipper
Let's be clear: If Guy Lefleur liked "Flower," there's absolutely nothing wrong with that. Nevertheless, if his nickname were uttered derisively, eye sockets likely were relocated. Still, "Whipper"? Can you imagine how Mrs. Watson felt?

Pee Wee vs. Wee Willie
A wee duel. In 1939, "Wee Willie" became the first innuendo-nicknamed star inducted at Cooperstown (if we ignore Nap Lajoie). By the time "Pee Wee" made it in 1984, the ranks included a "Little Poison," "Three-Finger," and even a "Biscuit Pants." For coming first, "Wee Willie" advances.

FROM BASEBALL'S VLADIMIR GUERRERO ("Vlad the Impaler") to hockey's Georges Vezina ("The Chicoutimi Cucumber"), our great male athletes traditionally receive great phallic nicknames. Unfortunately, though, a few stars suffer nicknames on the field of play that imply mediocrity on the field of love. With each shout of his name, he hears a taunt of inadequacy, impotence, unhealthiness, or poor technique. Here, we honor those who overcame nicknames that would have sent lesser men to the bench.

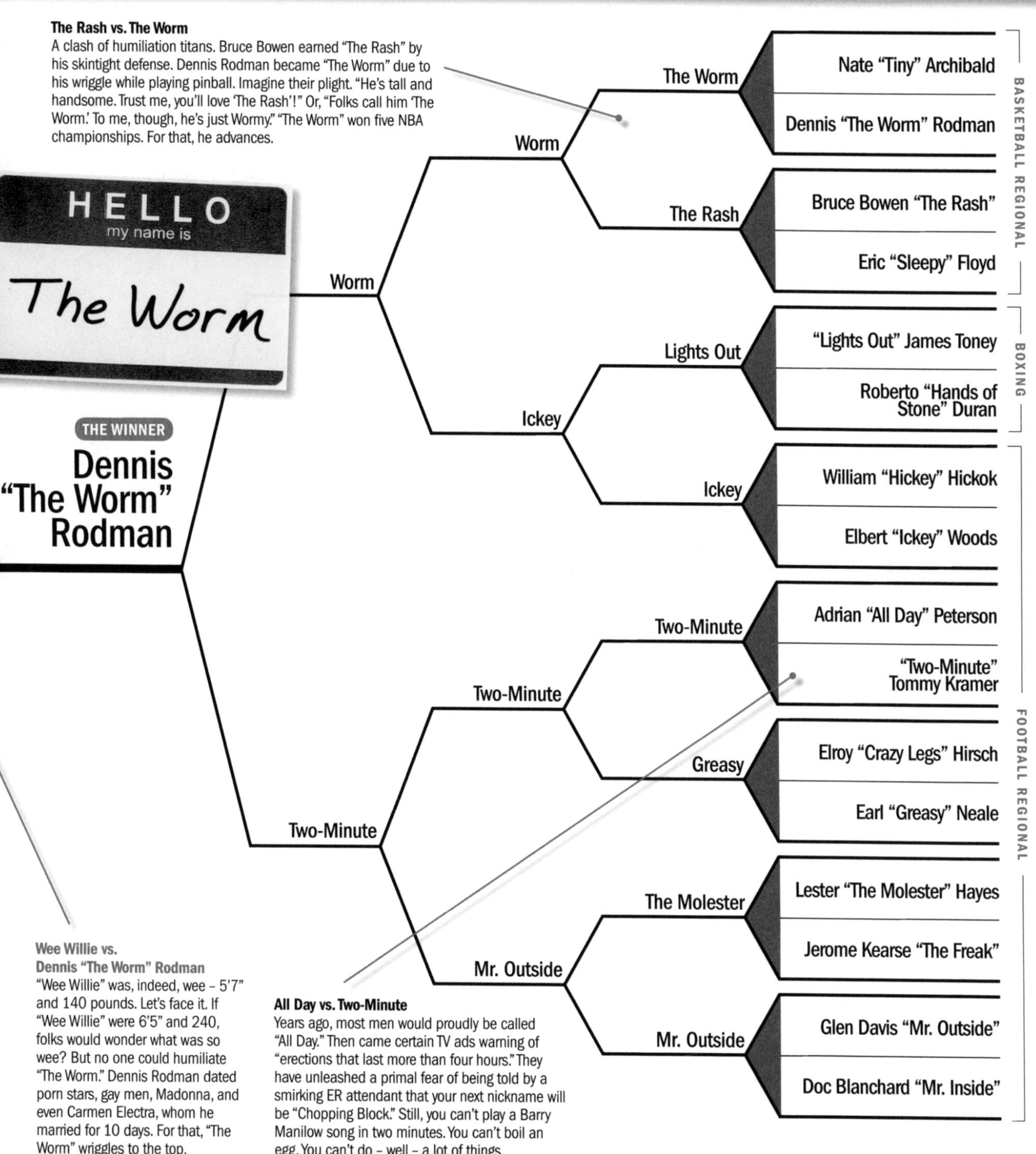

HELLO
my name is
The Worm
THE WINNER
Dennis "The Worm" Rodman
Worm
Worm
The Worm
The Rash
Ickey
Lights Out
Ickey
Two-Minute
Two-Minute
Two-Minute
Greasy
Mr. Outside
The Molester
Mr. Outside
Nate "Tiny" Archibald
Dennis "The Worm" Rodman
Bruce Bowen "The Rash"
Eric "Sleepy" Floyd
"Lights Out" James Toney
Roberto "Hands of Stone" Duran
William "Hickey" Hickok
Elbert "Ickey" Woods
Adrian "All Day" Peterson
"Two-Minute" Tommy Kramer
Elroy "Crazy Legs" Hirsch
Earl "Greasy" Neale
Lester "The Molester" Hayes
Jerome Kearse "The Freak"
Glen Davis "Mr. Outside"
Doc Blanchard "Mr. Inside"
BASKETBALL REGIONAL
BOXING
FOOTBALL REGIONAL

The Rash vs. The Worm
A clash of humiliation titans. Bruce Bowen earned "The Rash" by his skintight defense. Dennis Rodman became "The Worm" due to his wriggle while playing pinball. Imagine their plight. "He's tall and handsome. Trust me, you'll love 'The Rash'!" Or, "Folks call him 'The Worm.' To me, though, he's just Wormy." "The Worm" won five NBA championships. For that, he advances.

Wee Willie vs. Dennis "The Worm" Rodman
"Wee Willie" was, indeed, wee – 5'7" and 140 pounds. Let's face it. If "Wee Willie" were 6'5" and 240, folks would wonder what was so wee? But no one could humiliate "The Worm." Dennis Rodman dated porn stars, gay men, Madonna, and even Carmen Electra, whom he married for 10 days. For that, "The Worm" wriggles to the top.

All Day vs. Two-Minute
Years ago, most men would proudly be called "All Day." Then came certain TV ads warning of "erections that last more than four hours." They have unleashed a primal fear of being told by a smirking ER attendant that your next nickname will be "Chopping Block." Still, you can't play a Barry Manilow song in two minutes. You can't boil an egg. You can't do – well – a lot of things.

Baseball Moments

By John Thorn

John Thorn has written and edited many baseball books over the past 35 years, including *Total Baseball, Baseball's 10 Greatest Games,* and *Treasures of the Baseball Hall of Fame.*

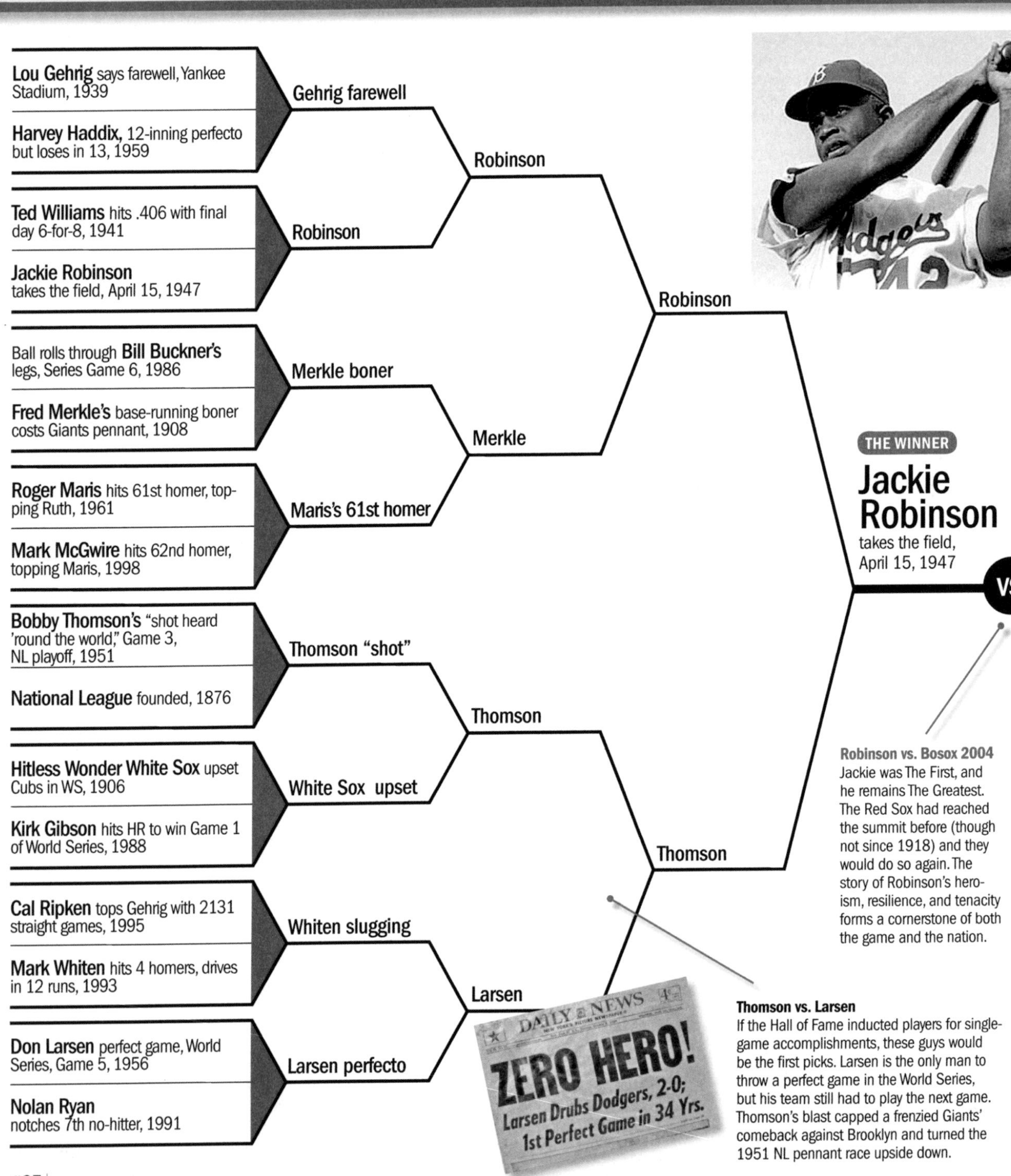
Lou Gehrig says farewell, Yankee Stadium, 1939
Harvey Haddix, 12-inning perfecto but loses in 13, 1959
Ted Williams hits .406 with final day 6-for-8, 1941
Jackie Robinson takes the field, April 15, 1947
Ball rolls through **Bill Buckner's** legs, Series Game 6, 1986
Fred Merkle's base-running boner costs Giants pennant, 1908
Roger Maris hits 61st homer, topping Ruth, 1961
Mark McGwire hits 62nd homer, topping Maris, 1998
Bobby Thomson's "shot heard 'round the world," Game 3, NL playoff, 1951
National League founded, 1876
Hitless Wonder White Sox upset Cubs in WS, 1906
Kirk Gibson hits HR to win Game 1 of World Series, 1988
Cal Ripken tops Gehrig with 2131 straight games, 1995
Mark Whiten hits 4 homers, drives in 12 runs, 1993
Don Larsen perfect game, World Series, Game 5, 1956
Nolan Ryan notches 7th no-hitter, 1991
Gehrig farewell
Robinson
Merkle boner
Maris's 61st homer
Thomson "shot"
White Sox upset
Whiten slugging
Larsen perfecto
Robinson
Merkle
Thomson
Larsen
Robinson
Thomson
THE WINNER
Jackie Robinson
takes the field, April 15, 1947
VS.
DAILY NEWS
ZERO HERO!
Larsen Drubs Dodgers, 2-0; 1st Perfect Game in 34 Yrs.

Robinson vs. Bosox 2004
Jackie was The First, and he remains The Greatest. The Red Sox had reached the summit before (though not since 1918) and they would do so again. The story of Robinson's heroism, resilience, and tenacity forms a cornerstone of both the game and the nation.

Thomson vs. Larsen
If the Hall of Fame inducted players for single-game accomplishments, these guys would be the first picks. Larsen is the only man to throw a perfect game in the World Series, but his team still had to play the next game. Thomson's blast capped a frenzied Giants' comeback against Brooklyn and turned the 1951 NL pennant race upside down.

SINCE, AS CASEY STENGEL MIGHT OBSERVE, most of our readers are above ground at the present time, most of these moments occurred after World War II. A moment is ideally a single play, or a game, or even an extended feat, that is epitomized in a single contest. Even a jaw-dropping accomplishment like Pedro Martinez's ERA of 1.74 in 2000, when the American League average was 5.07, does not reduce to a moment, any more than does Ichiro Suzuki's record of 262 hits in 2004. A great moment ought to be memorable or unique, preferably both.

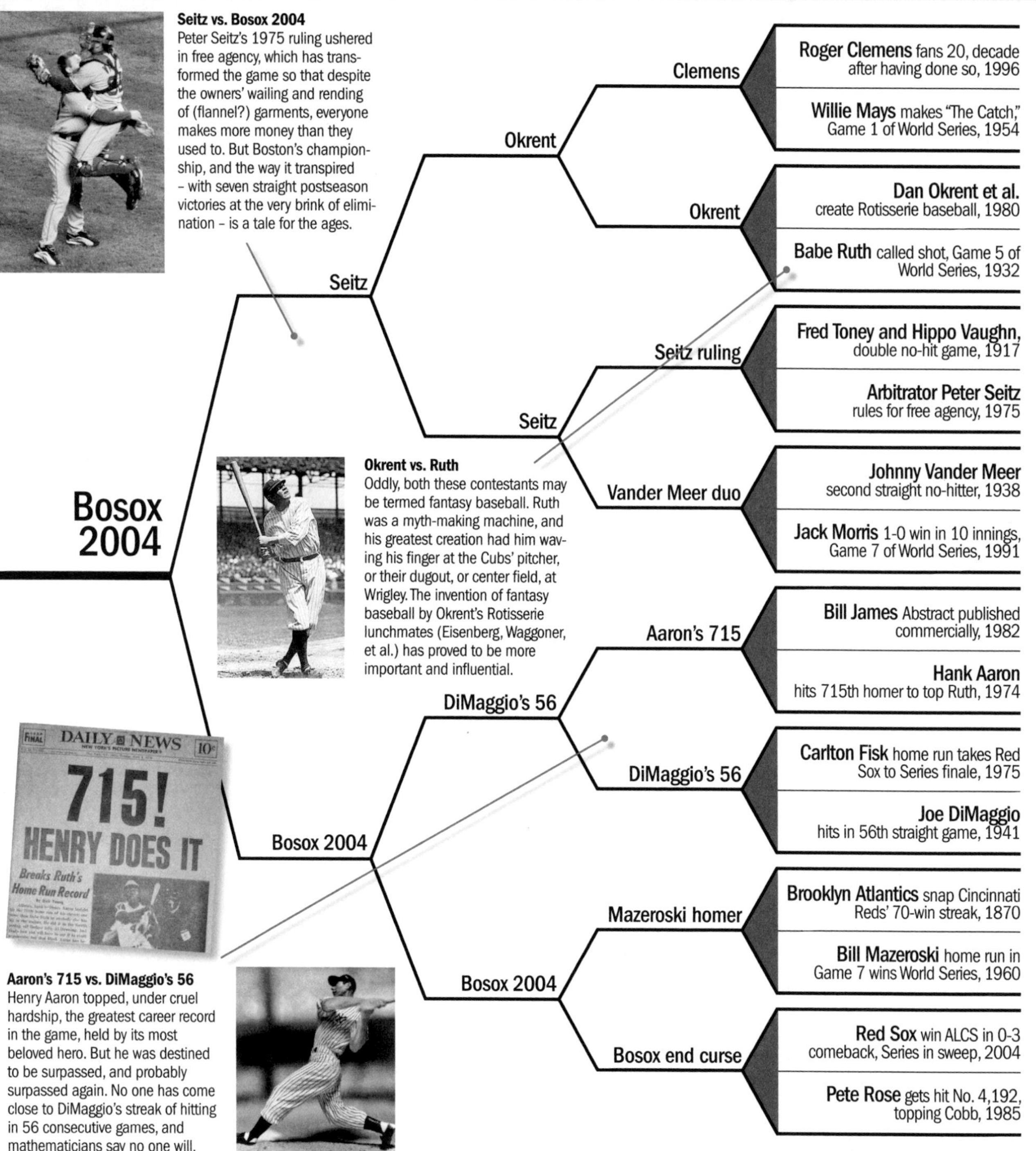
Roger Clemens fans 20, decade after having done so, 1996
Willie Mays makes "The Catch," Game 1 of World Series, 1954
Dan Okrent et al. create Rotisserie baseball, 1980
Babe Ruth called shot, Game 5 of World Series, 1932
Fred Toney and Hippo Vaughn, double no-hit game, 1917
Arbitrator Peter Seitz rules for free agency, 1975
Johnny Vander Meer second straight no-hitter, 1938
Jack Morris 1-0 win in 10 innings, Game 7 of World Series, 1991
Bill James Abstract published commercially, 1982
Hank Aaron hits 715th homer to top Ruth, 1974
Carlton Fisk home run takes Red Sox to Series finale, 1975
Joe DiMaggio hits in 56th straight game, 1941
Brooklyn Atlantics snap Cincinnati Reds' 70-win streak, 1870
Bill Mazeroski home run in Game 7 wins World Series, 1960
Red Sox win ALCS in 0-3 comeback, Series in sweep, 2004
Pete Rose gets hit No. 4,192, topping Cobb, 1985
Clemens
Okrent
Seitz ruling
Vander Meer duo
Aaron's 715
DiMaggio's 56
Mazeroski homer
Bosox end curse
Okrent
Seitz
DiMaggio's 56
Bosox 2004
Seitz
Bosox 2004
Bosox 2004
FINAL
DAILY NEWS
10¢
715!
HENRY DOES IT
Breaks Ruth's Home Run Record

Seitz vs. Bosox 2004
Peter Seitz's 1975 ruling ushered in free agency, which has transformed the game so that despite the owners' wailing and rending of (flannel?) garments, everyone makes more money than they used to. But Boston's championship, and the way it transpired – with seven straight postseason victories at the very brink of elimination – is a tale for the ages.

Okrent vs. Ruth
Oddly, both these contestants may be termed fantasy baseball. Ruth was a myth-making machine, and his greatest creation had him waving his finger at the Cubs' pitcher, or their dugout, or center field, at Wrigley. The invention of fantasy baseball by Okrent's Rotisserie lunchmates (Eisenberg, Waggoner, et al.) has proved to be more important and influential.

Aaron's 715 vs. DiMaggio's 56
Henry Aaron topped, under cruel hardship, the greatest career record in the game, held by its most beloved hero. But he was destined to be surpassed, and probably surpassed again. No one has come close to DiMaggio's streak of hitting in 56 consecutive games, and mathematicians say no one will.

Absurd College Nicknames

By Richard Sandomir and Pete Thamel

Richard Sandomir attended Queens College, where he watched, but did not play for, the Knights. He dropped gym class before he could fail it. Pete Thamel is the college sports reporter for the *New York Times* and a proud Syracuse graduate who eats only one fruit: orang

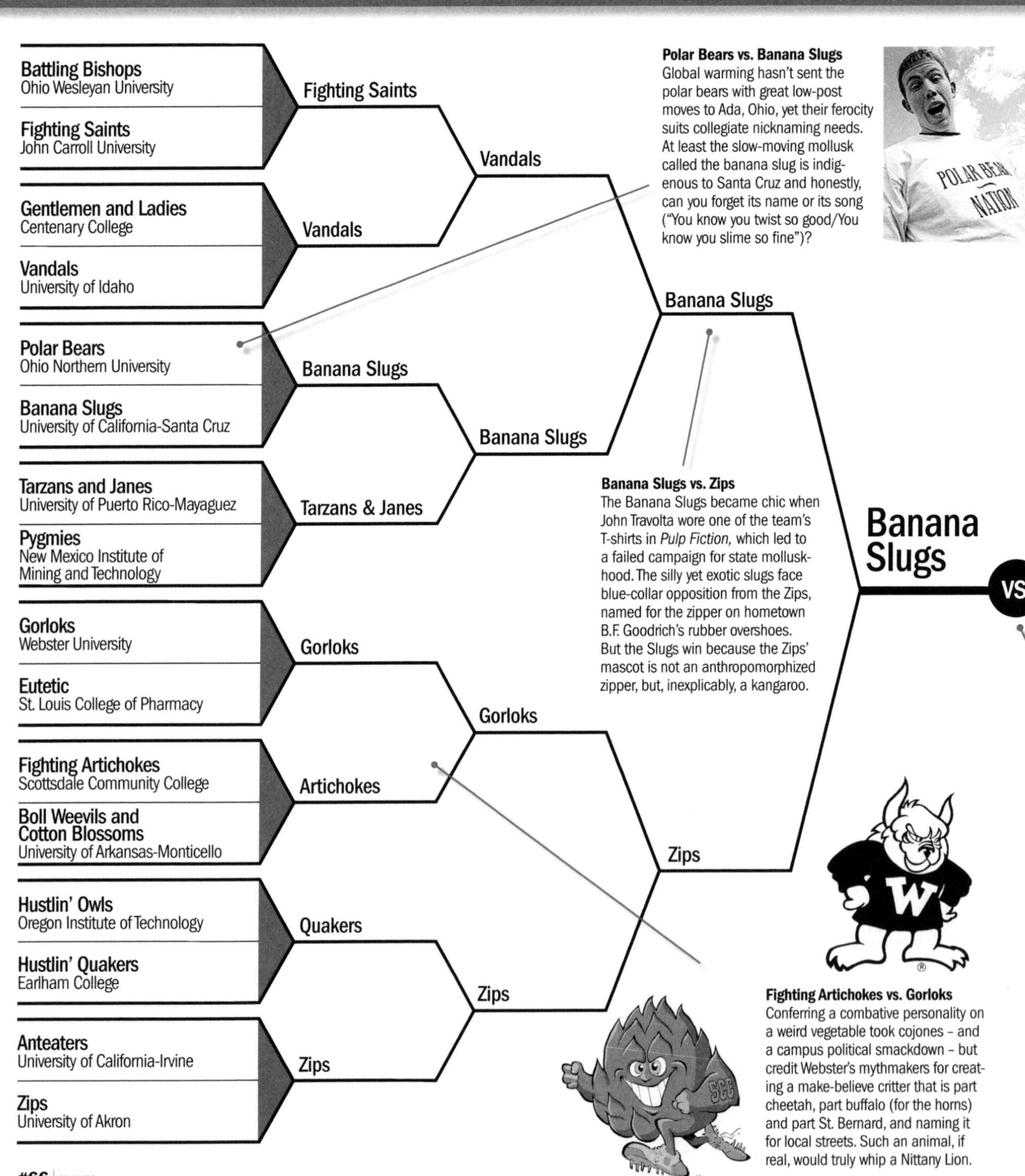

Battling Bishops
Ohio Wesleyan University
Fighting Saints
John Carroll University
Gentlemen and Ladies
Centenary College
Vandals
University of Idaho
Polar Bears
Ohio Northern University
Banana Slugs
University of California-Santa Cruz
Tarzans and Janes
University of Puerto Rico-Mayaguez
Pygmies
New Mexico Institute of Mining and Technology
Gorloks
Webster University
Eutetic
St. Louis College of Pharmacy
Fighting Artichokes
Scottsdale Community College
Boll Weevils and Cotton Blossoms
University of Arkansas-Monticello
Hustlin' Owls
Oregon Institute of Technology
Hustlin' Quakers
Earlham College
Anteaters
University of California-Irvine
Zips
University of Akron
Fighting Saints
Vandals
Banana Slugs
Tarzans & Janes
Gorloks
Artichokes
Quakers
Zips
Vandals
Banana Slugs
Gorloks
Zips
Banana Slugs
Zips
Banana Slugs
VS.
POLAR BEAR NATION
W
SCC

Polar Bears vs. Banana Slugs
Global warming hasn't sent the polar bears with great low-post moves to Ada, Ohio, yet their ferocity suits collegiate nicknaming needs. At least the slow-moving mollusk called the banana slug is indigenous to Santa Cruz and honestly, can you forget its name or its song ("You know you twist so good/You know you slime so fine")?

Banana Slugs vs. Zips
The Banana Slugs became chic when John Travolta wore one of the team's T-shirts in *Pulp Fiction,* which led to a failed campaign for state mollusk-hood. The silly yet exotic slugs face blue-collar opposition from the Zips, named for the zipper on hometown B.F. Goodrich's rubber overshoes. But the Slugs win because the Zips' mascot is not an anthropomorphized zipper, but, inexplicably, a kangaroo.

Fighting Artichokes vs. Gorloks
Conferring a combative personality on a weird vegetable took cojones – and a campus political smackdown – but credit Webster's mythmakers for creating a make-believe critter that is part cheetah, part buffalo (for the horns) and part St. Bernard, and naming it for local streets. Such an animal, if real, would truly whip a Nittany Lion.

(**OF ALL OF COLLEGE SPORTS' WONDERFUL RITUALS** – the bands, the chants, the tailgating – none is more absurd than team nicknames. Gators, Seminoles, Tigers, Trojans, Hoyas, Longhorns, Badgers, Wildcats, Eagles, and Fighting Irish (more believable in Hell's Kitchen than South Bend) dominate major college programs. But small, lesser-known schools that do not play in major conferences have inane monikers that are at least as inappropriate for sensate humans. So, go Eutetic, kill those Hustlin' Owls!)

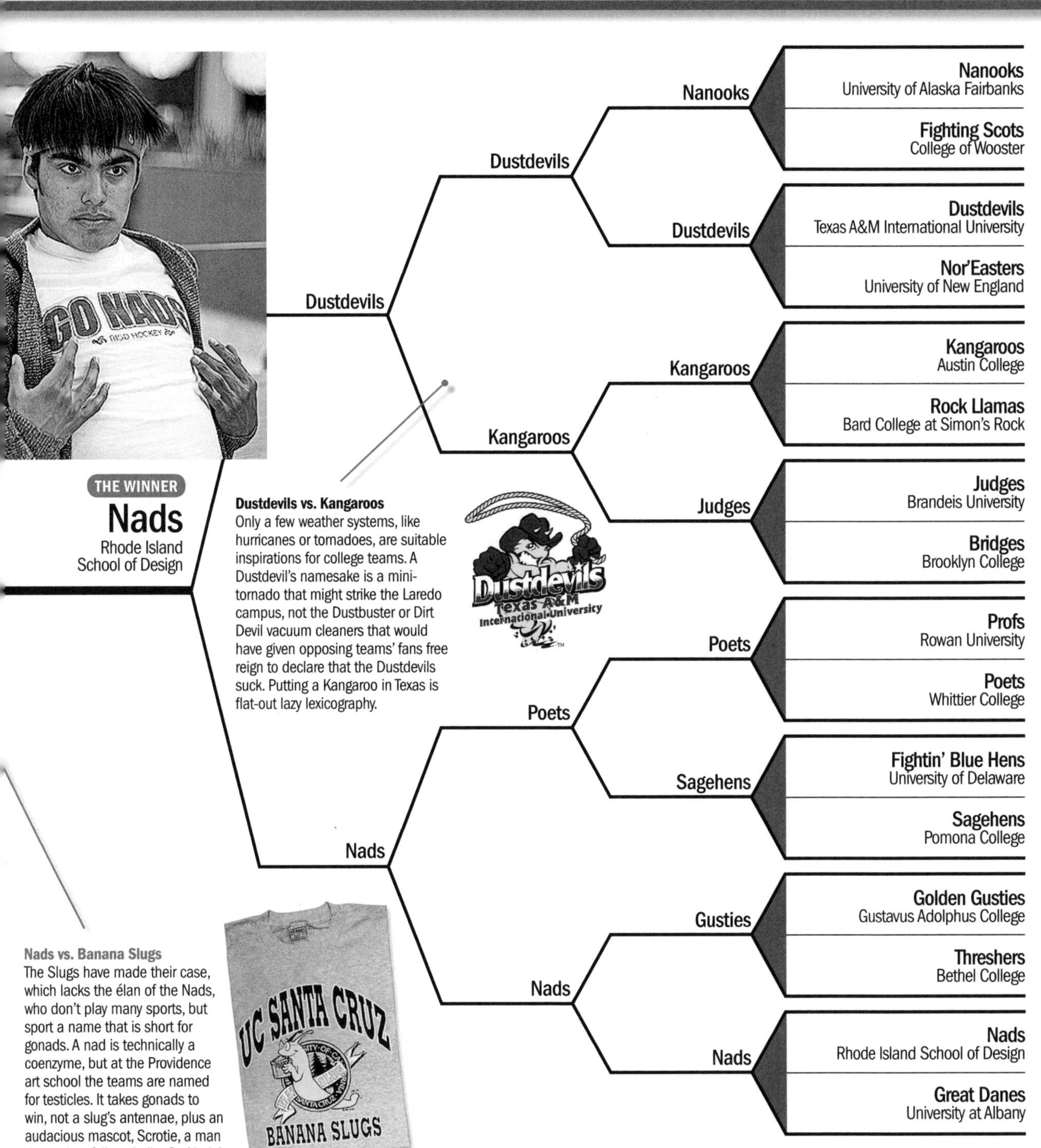
GO NADS
RISD HOCKEY
THE WINNER
Nads
Rhode Island School of Design
Dustdevils
Dustdevils
Nanooks
Nanooks
University of Alaska Fairbanks
Fighting Scots
College of Wooster
Dustdevils
Dustdevils
Texas A&M International University
Nor'Easters
University of New England
Kangaroos
Kangaroos
Kangaroos
Austin College
Rock Llamas
Bard College at Simon's Rock
Judges
Judges
Brandeis University
Bridges
Brooklyn College
Dustdevils
Texas A&M International University
Nads
Poets
Poets
Profs
Rowan University
Poets
Whittier College
Sagehens
Fightin' Blue Hens
University of Delaware
Sagehens
Pomona College
Nads
Gusties
Golden Gusties
Gustavus Adolphus College
Threshers
Bethel College
Nads
Nads
Rhode Island School of Design
Great Danes
University at Albany
UC SANTA CRUZ
BANANA SLUGS

Dustdevils vs. Kangaroos
Only a few weather systems, like hurricanes or tornadoes, are suitable inspirations for college teams. A Dustdevil's namesake is a mini-tornado that might strike the Laredo campus, not the Dustbuster or Dirt Devil vacuum cleaners that would have given opposing teams' fans free reign to declare that the Dustdevils suck. Putting a Kangaroo in Texas is flat-out lazy lexicography.

Nads vs. Banana Slugs
The Slugs have made their case, which lacks the élan of the Nads, who don't play many sports, but sport a name that is short for gonads. A nad is technically a coenzyme, but at the Providence art school the teams are named for testicles. It takes gonads to win, not a slug's antennae, plus an audacious mascot, Scrotie, a man dressed as full genitalia. Go Nads!

Toughest Golf Holes

By Chris Millard

Chris Millard is the author of *Golf's 100 Toughest Holes* and co-author with Jack Nicklaus of *Nicklaus By Design*. He thinks all holes are tough.

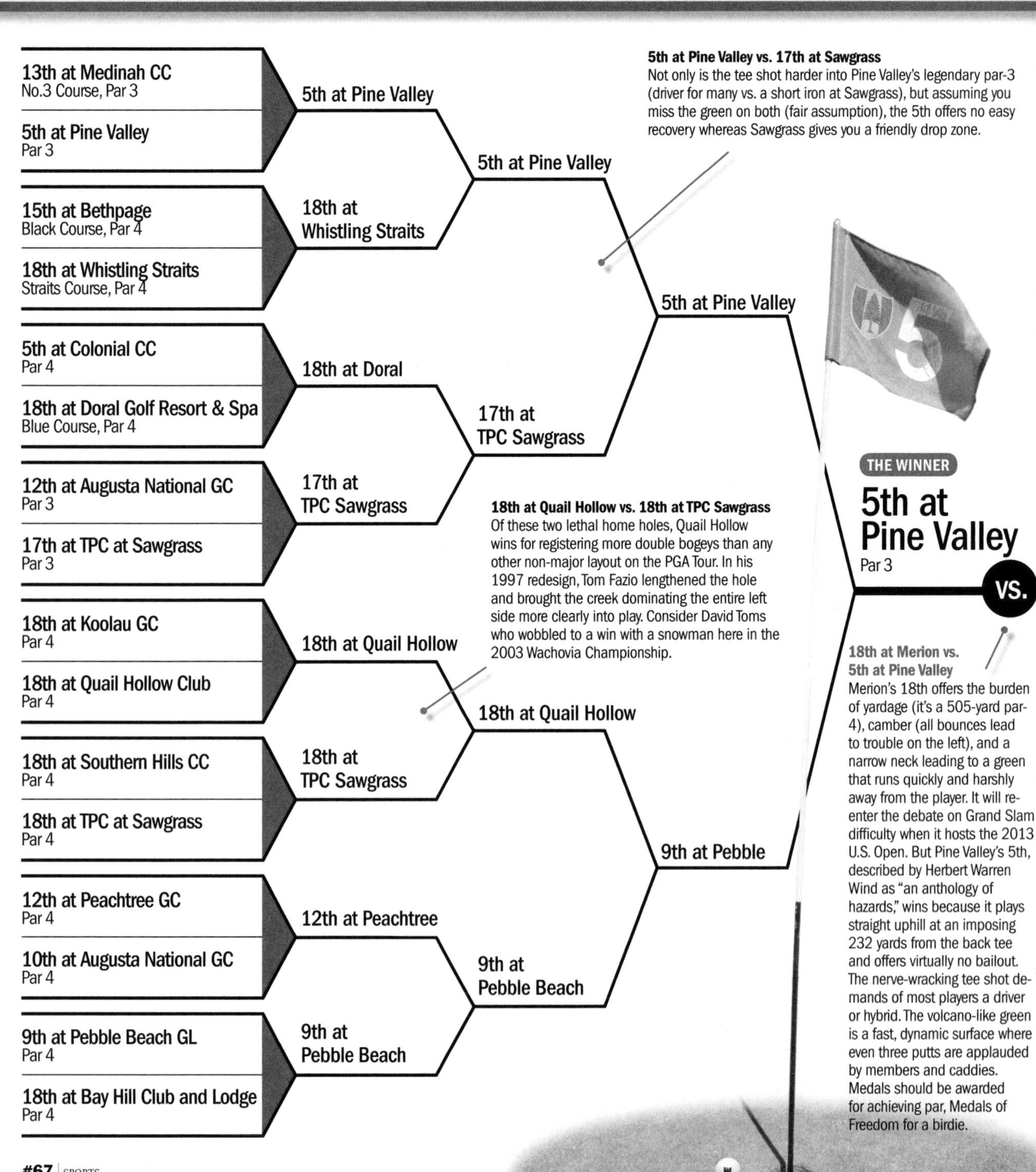
13th at Medinah CC
No.3 Course, Par 3
5th at Pine Valley
Par 3
15th at Bethpage
Black Course, Par 4
18th at Whistling Straits
Straits Course, Par 4
5th at Colonial CC
Par 4
18th at Doral Golf Resort & Spa
Blue Course, Par 4
12th at Augusta National GC
Par 3
17th at TPC at Sawgrass
Par 3
18th at Koolau GC
Par 4
18th at Quail Hollow Club
Par 4
18th at Southern Hills CC
Par 4
18th at TPC at Sawgrass
Par 4
12th at Peachtree GC
Par 4
10th at Augusta National GC
Par 4
9th at Pebble Beach GL
Par 4
18th at Bay Hill Club and Lodge
Par 4
5th at Pine Valley
18th at Whistling Straits
18th at Doral
17th at TPC Sawgrass
18th at Quail Hollow
18th at TPC Sawgrass
12th at Peachtree
9th at Pebble Beach
5th at Pine Valley
17th at TPC Sawgrass
18th at Quail Hollow
9th at Pebble Beach
5th at Pine Valley
9th at Pebble
THE WINNER
5th at Pine Valley
Par 3
VS.

5th at Pine Valley vs. 17th at Sawgrass
Not only is the tee shot harder into Pine Valley's legendary par-3 (driver for many vs. a short iron at Sawgrass), but assuming you miss the green on both (fair assumption), the 5th offers no easy recovery whereas Sawgrass gives you a friendly drop zone.

18th at Quail Hollow vs. 18th at TPC Sawgrass
Of these two lethal home holes, Quail Hollow wins for registering more double bogeys than any other non-major layout on the PGA Tour. In his 1997 redesign, Tom Fazio lengthened the hole and brought the creek dominating the entire left side more clearly into play. Consider David Toms who wobbled to a win with a snowman here in the 2003 Wachovia Championship.

18th at Merion vs. 5th at Pine Valley
Merion's 18th offers the burden of yardage (it's a 505-yard par-4), camber (all bounces lead to trouble on the left), and a narrow neck leading to a green that runs quickly and harshly away from the player. It will re-enter the debate on Grand Slam difficulty when it hosts the 2013 U.S. Open. But Pine Valley's 5th, described by Herbert Warren Wind as "an anthology of hazards," wins because it plays straight uphill at an imposing 232 yards from the back tee and offers virtually no bailout. The nerve-wracking tee shot demands of most players a driver or hybrid. The volcano-like green is a fast, dynamic surface where even three putts are applauded by members and caddies. Medals should be awarded for achieving par, Medals of Freedom for a birdie.

AMERICANS ARE ATTRACTED TO DIFFICULTY. How else to explain the audacity of moon launches, Microsoft Vista, or so many hackers playing the back tees? George Thomas, who designed the courses at Bel-Air, Riviera, and Los Angeles, said that difficulty contributes to the essence of the game. "Place the golf course on a level plane; have no traps of any kind; let the fairway be flat, the green unprotected and without rolls; let there be no rough . . . and the green itself absolutely level; and what would be the result? A thing . . . on which there is no thrill of accomplishment worthwhile."

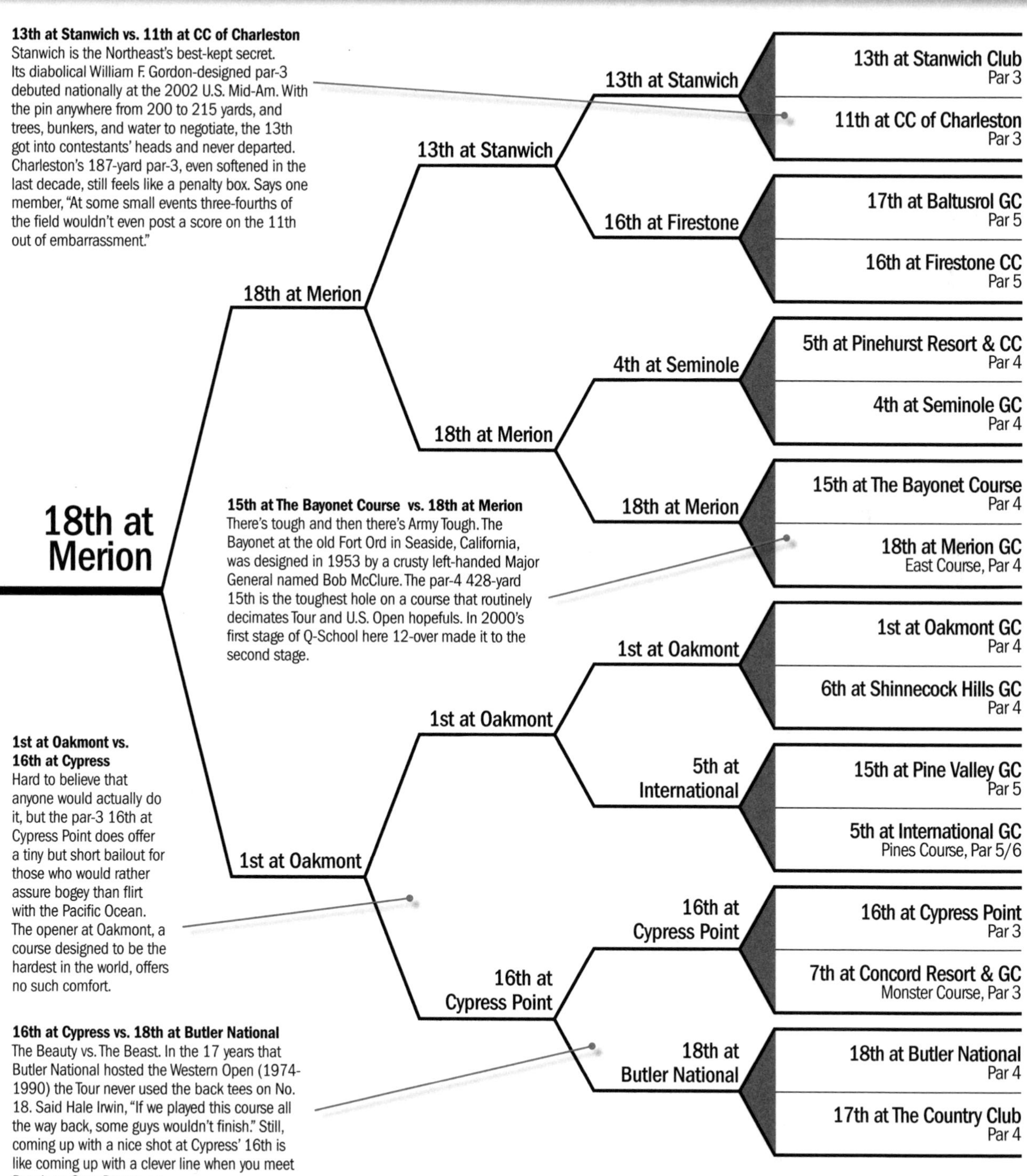

13th at Stanwich vs. 11th at CC of Charleston
Stanwich is the Northeast's best-kept secret. Its diabolical William F. Gordon-designed par-3 debuted nationally at the 2002 U.S. Mid-Am. With the pin anywhere from 200 to 215 yards, and trees, bunkers, and water to negotiate, the 13th got into contestants' heads and never departed. Charleston's 187-yard par-3, even softened in the last decade, still feels like a penalty box. Says one member, "At some small events three-fourths of the field wouldn't even post a score on the 11th out of embarrassment."
15th at The Bayonet Course vs. 18th at Merion
There's tough and then there's Army Tough. The Bayonet at the old Fort Ord in Seaside, California, was designed in 1953 by a crusty left-handed Major General named Bob McClure. The par-4 428-yard 15th is the toughest hole on a course that routinely decimates Tour and U.S. Open hopefuls. In 2000's first stage of Q-School here 12-over made it to the second stage.
1st at Oakmont vs. 16th at Cypress
Hard to believe that anyone would actually do it, but the par-3 16th at Cypress Point does offer a tiny but short bailout for those who would rather assure bogey than flirt with the Pacific Ocean. The opener at Oakmont, a course designed to be the hardest in the world, offers no such comfort.
16th at Cypress vs. 18th at Butler National
The Beauty vs. The Beast. In the 17 years that Butler National hosted the Western Open (1974-1990) the Tour never used the back tees on No. 18. Said Hale Irwin, "If we played this course all the way back, some guys wouldn't finish." Still, coming up with a nice shot at Cypress' 16th is like coming up with a clever line when you meet Penelope Cruz. Dream on.
18th at Merion
18th at Merion
13th at Stanwich
13th at Stanwich
13th at Stanwich Club
Par 3
11th at CC of Charleston
Par 3
16th at Firestone
17th at Baltusrol GC
Par 5
16th at Firestone CC
Par 5
18th at Merion
4th at Seminole
5th at Pinehurst Resort & CC
Par 4
4th at Seminole GC
Par 4
18th at Merion
15th at The Bayonet Course
Par 4
18th at Merion GC
East Course, Par 4
1st at Oakmont
1st at Oakmont
1st at Oakmont
1st at Oakmont GC
Par 4
6th at Shinnecock Hills GC
Par 4
5th at International
15th at Pine Valley GC
Par 5
5th at International GC
Pines Course, Par 5/6
16th at Cypress Point
16th at Cypress Point
16th at Cypress Point
Par 3
7th at Concord Resort & GC
Monster Course, Par 3
18th at Butler National
18th at Butler National
Par 4
17th at The Country Club
Par 4

Dubious Sports Achievements

By Richard Hoffer

Richard Hoffer, a long-time writer for *Sports Illustrated,* is the author of *A Savage Business,* which the magazine once included in its list of the 100 best sports books ever. As dubious as it gets.

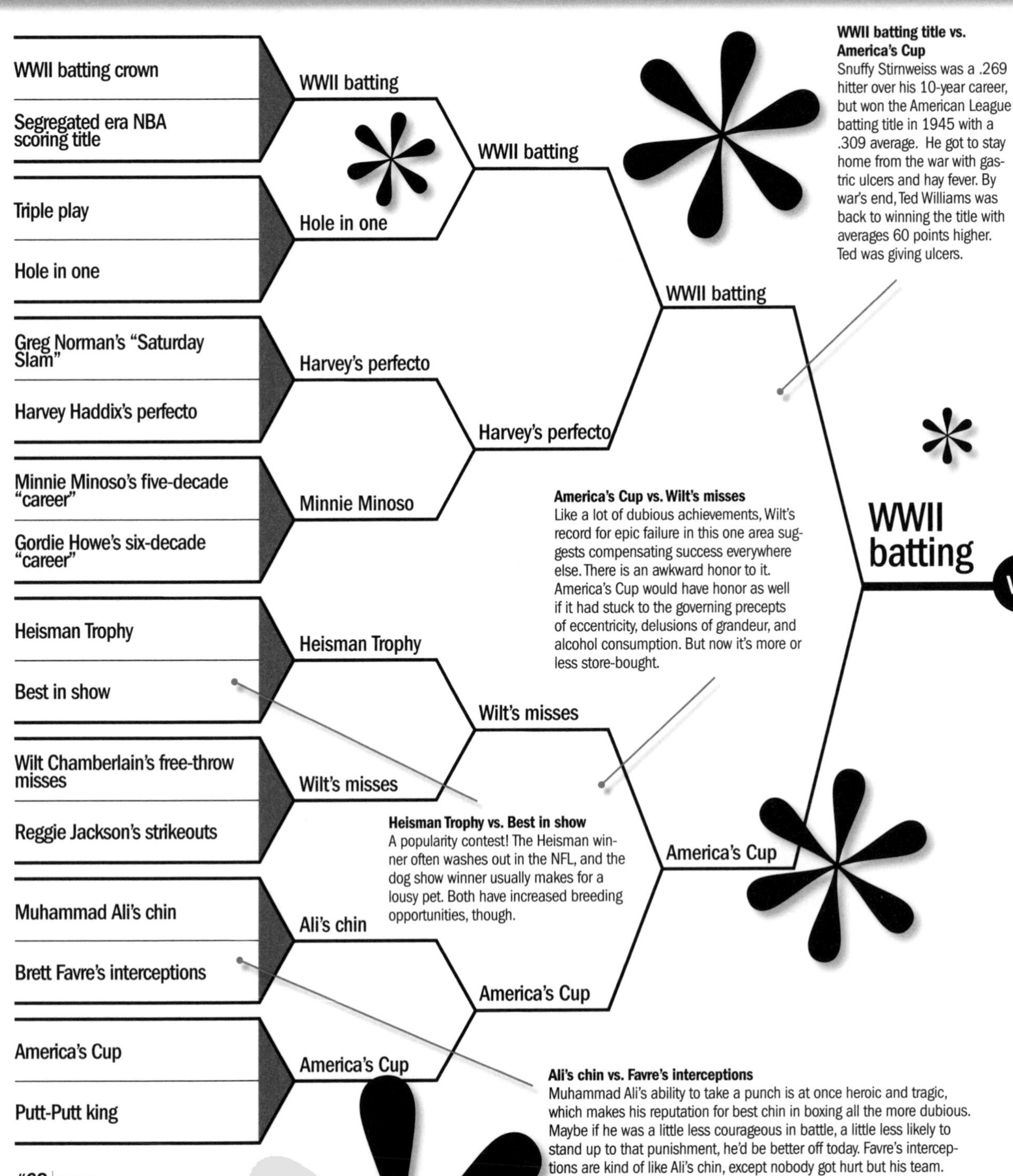
WWII batting crown
Segregated era NBA scoring title
Triple play
Hole in one
Greg Norman's "Saturday Slam"
Harvey Haddix's perfecto
Minnie Minoso's five-decade "career"
Gordie Howe's six-decade "career"
Heisman Trophy
Best in show
Wilt Chamberlain's free-throw misses
Reggie Jackson's strikeouts
Muhammad Ali's chin
Brett Favre's interceptions
America's Cup
Putt-Putt king
WWII batting
Hole in one
Harvey's perfecto
Minnie Minoso
Heisman Trophy
Wilt's misses
Ali's chin
America's Cup
WWII batting
Harvey's perfecto
Wilt's misses
America's Cup
WWII batting
America's Cup
WWII batting
VS.

WWII batting title vs. America's Cup
Snuffy Stirnweiss was a .269 hitter over his 10-year career, but won the American League batting title in 1945 with a .309 average. He got to stay home from the war with gastric ulcers and hay fever. By war's end, Ted Williams was back to winning the title with averages 60 points higher. Ted was giving ulcers.

America's Cup vs. Wilt's misses
Like a lot of dubious achievements, Wilt's record for epic failure in this one area suggests compensating success everywhere else. There is an awkward honor to it. America's Cup would have honor as well if it had stuck to the governing precepts of eccentricity, delusions of grandeur, and alcohol consumption. But now it's more or less store-bought.

Heisman Trophy vs. Best in show
A popularity contest! The Heisman winner often washes out in the NFL, and the dog show winner usually makes for a lousy pet. Both have increased breeding opportunities, though.

Ali's chin vs. Favre's interceptions
Muhammad Ali's ability to take a punch is at once heroic and tragic, which makes his reputation for best chin in boxing all the more dubious. Maybe if he was a little less courageous in battle, a little less likely to stand up to that punishment, he'd be better off today. Favre's interceptions are kind of like Ali's chin, except nobody got hurt but his team.

WE HAVE CAST A WIDE NET, mingling the merely embarrassing with the hopelessly irrelevant, the outright freakish with the downright felonious, the innocently unintended with the cynically pursued. Not every dubious achievement deserves shame. Mostly they're just a matter of somebody being in the wrong place at the wrong time, accepting a distinction neither sought nor earned. To qualify, a dubious sports achievement should demand explanations, asterisks, and at the very least, a sheepish shrug of the shoulders. In any case, nothing to be proud of here.

Steroid era vs. WWII batting
At least Snuffy competed honestly. But every slugger from the steroid era will be dogged by suspicion that he didn't. If they don't quite get an asterisk, they have a perpetual taint and premature hair loss. Do you have any idea how many home runs Joe Bauman could have hit at Roswell if he had had access to BALCO?

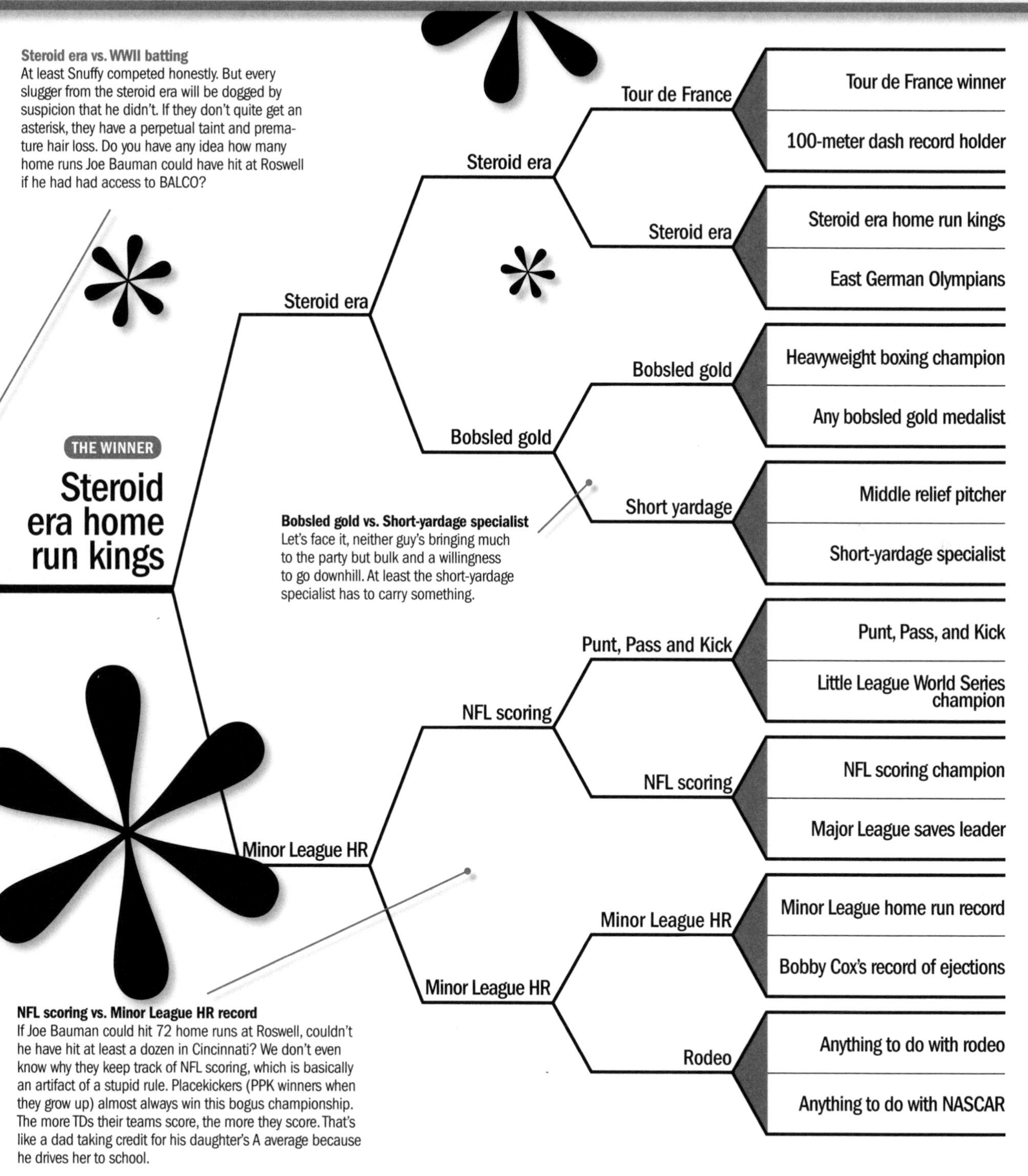

Tour de France winner
100-meter dash record holder
Steroid era home run kings
East German Olympians
Heavyweight boxing champion
Any bobsled gold medalist
Middle relief pitcher
Short-yardage specialist
Punt, Pass, and Kick
Little League World Series champion
NFL scoring champion
Major League saves leader
Minor League home run record
Bobby Cox's record of ejections
Anything to do with rodeo
Anything to do with NASCAR
Tour de France
Steroid era
Bobsled gold
Short yardage
Punt, Pass and Kick
NFL scoring
Minor League HR
Rodeo
Steroid era
Bobsled gold
NFL scoring
Minor League HR
Steroid era
Minor League HR
THE WINNER
Steroid era home run kings

Bobsled gold vs. Short-yardage specialist
Let's face it, neither guy's bringing much to the party but bulk and a willingness to go downhill. At least the short-yardage specialist has to carry something.

NFL scoring vs. Minor League HR record
If Joe Bauman could hit 72 home runs at Roswell, couldn't he have hit at least a dozen in Cincinnati? We don't even know why they keep track of NFL scoring, which is basically an artifact of a stupid rule. Placekickers (PPK winners when they grow up) almost always win this bogus championship. The more TDs their teams score, the more they score. That's like a dad taking credit for his daughter's A average because he drives her to school.

From Athlete to Actor

By Mark Reiter

Mark Reiter, co-editor of this book, has never acted and he's not much of an athlete either.

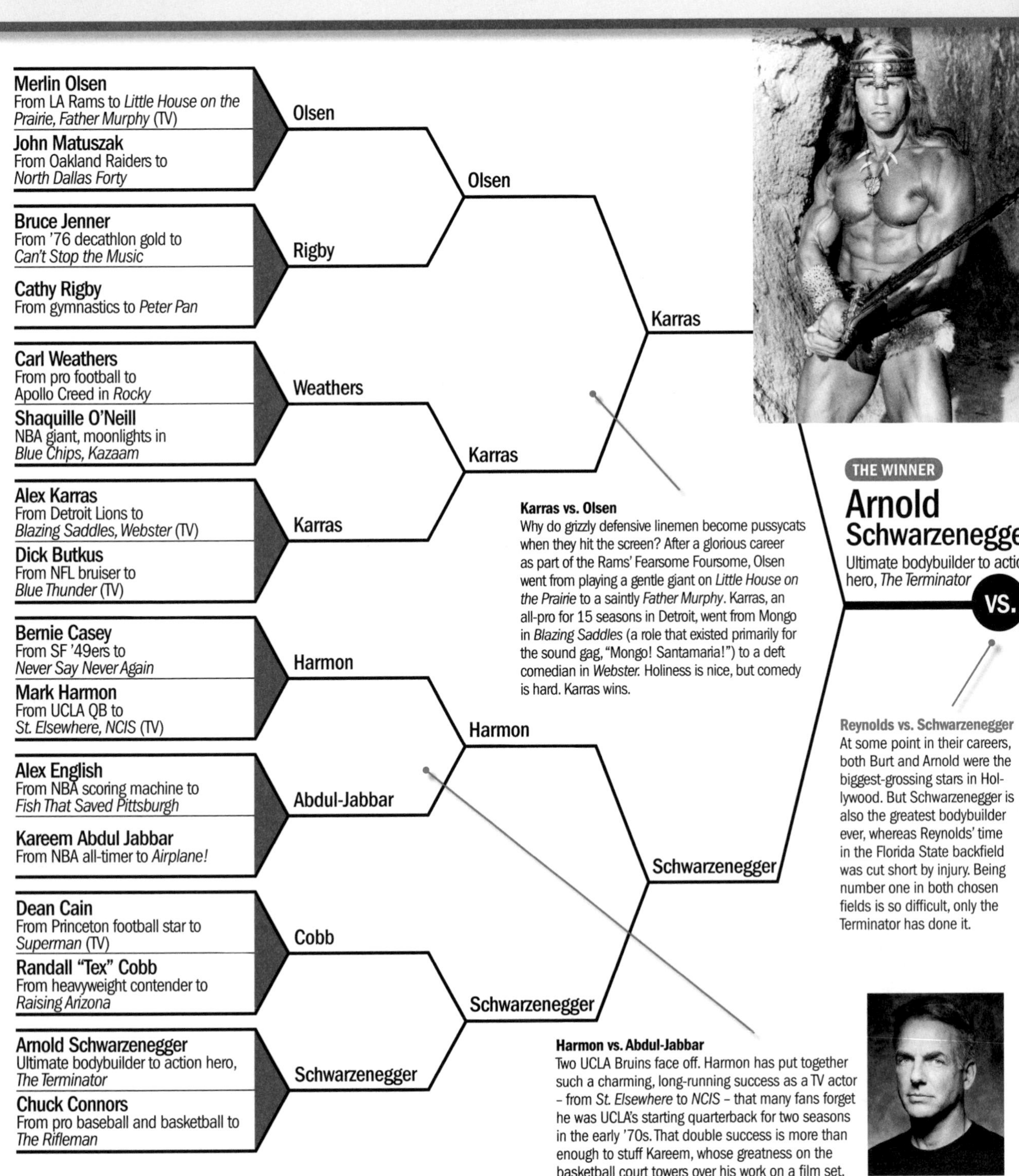

Merlin Olsen
From LA Rams to *Little House on the Prairie, Father Murphy* (TV)
John Matuszak
From Oakland Raiders to *North Dallas Forty*
Bruce Jenner
From '76 decathlon gold to *Can't Stop the Music*
Cathy Rigby
From gymnastics to *Peter Pan*
Carl Weathers
From pro football to Apollo Creed in *Rocky*
Shaquille O'Neill
NBA giant, moonlights in *Blue Chips, Kazaam*
Alex Karras
From Detroit Lions to *Blazing Saddles, Webster* (TV)
Dick Butkus
From NFL bruiser to *Blue Thunder* (TV)
Bernie Casey
From SF '49ers to *Never Say Never Again*
Mark Harmon
From UCLA QB to *St. Elsewhere, NCIS* (TV)
Alex English
From NBA scoring machine to *Fish That Saved Pittsburgh*
Kareem Abdul Jabbar
From NBA all-timer to *Airplane!*
Dean Cain
From Princeton football star to *Superman* (TV)
Randall "Tex" Cobb
From heavyweight contender to *Raising Arizona*
Arnold Schwarzenegger
Ultimate bodybuilder to action hero, *The Terminator*
Chuck Connors
From pro baseball and basketball to *The Rifleman*
Olsen
Rigby
Weathers
Karras
Harmon
Abdul-Jabbar
Cobb
Schwarzenegger
Olsen
Karras
Harmon
Schwarzenegger
Karras
Schwarzenegger
THE WINNER
Arnold Schwarzenegge
Ultimate bodybuilder to actio hero, *The Terminator*
VS.

Karras vs. Olsen
Why do grizzly defensive linemen become pussycats when they hit the screen? After a glorious career as part of the Rams' Fearsome Foursome, Olsen went from playing a gentle giant on *Little House on the Prairie* to a saintly *Father Murphy*. Karras, an all-pro for 15 seasons in Detroit, went from Mongo in *Blazing Saddles* (a role that existed primarily for the sound gag, "Mongo! Santamaria!") to a deft comedian in *Webster*. Holiness is nice, but comedy is hard. Karras wins.

Reynolds vs. Schwarzenegger
At some point in their careers, both Burt and Arnold were the biggest-grossing stars in Hollywood. But Schwarzenegger is also the greatest bodybuilder ever, whereas Reynolds' time in the Florida State backfield was cut short by injury. Being number one in both chosen fields is so difficult, only the Terminator has done it.

Harmon vs. Abdul-Jabbar
Two UCLA Bruins face off. Harmon has put together such a charming, long-running success as a TV actor – from *St. Elsewhere* to *NCIS* – that many fans forget he was UCLA's starting quarterback for two seasons in the early '70s. That double success is more than enough to stuff Kareem, whose greatness on the basketball court towers over his work on a film set.

IF YOU'RE AN ATHLETE WHO REALLY WANTS TO ACT, it helps to be a great athlete, but it's not essential. On the evidence, it's more important that you bulk up – which explains why so many large and tall people take on show biz. It also helps to be a man. In this tournament of athletes who made the switch from sports to acting, only one woman gets an invite. Advancement is a function of how well you performed as both athlete and actor, with bonus points for playing a role rather than yourself. Dominance in both, while rare, takes the prize.

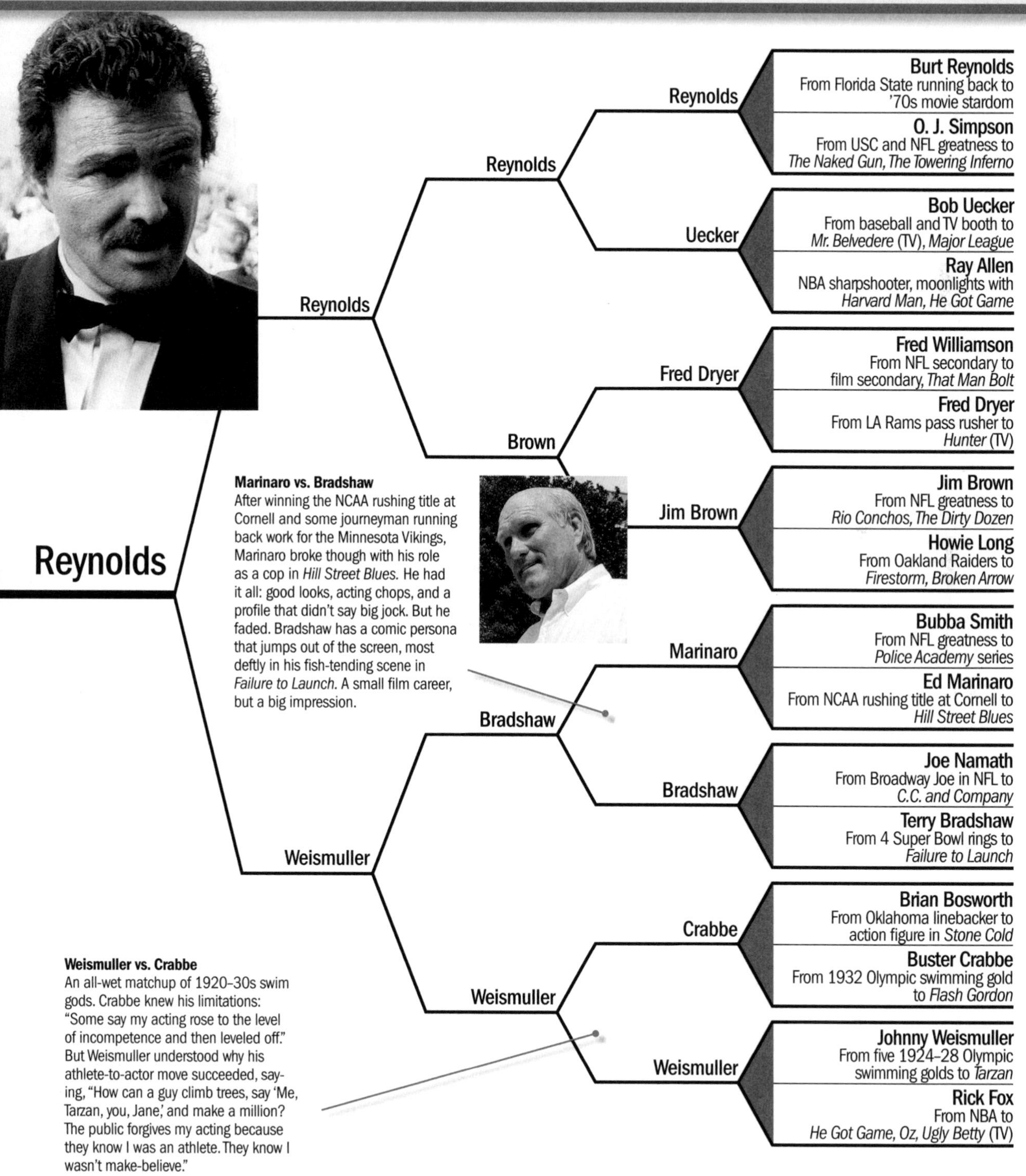

Burt Reynolds
From Florida State running back to '70s movie stardom
O. J. Simpson
From USC and NFL greatness to *The Naked Gun, The Towering Inferno*
Bob Uecker
From baseball and TV booth to *Mr. Belvedere* (TV), *Major League*
Ray Allen
NBA sharpshooter, moonlights with *Harvard Man, He Got Game*
Fred Williamson
From NFL secondary to film secondary, *That Man Bolt*
Fred Dryer
From LA Rams pass rusher to *Hunter* (TV)
Jim Brown
From NFL greatness to *Rio Conchos, The Dirty Dozen*
Howie Long
From Oakland Raiders to *Firestorm, Broken Arrow*
Bubba Smith
From NFL greatness to *Police Academy* series
Ed Marinaro
From NCAA rushing title at Cornell to *Hill Street Blues*
Joe Namath
From Broadway Joe in NFL to *C.C. and Company*
Terry Bradshaw
From 4 Super Bowl rings to *Failure to Launch*
Brian Bosworth
From Oklahoma linebacker to action figure in *Stone Cold*
Buster Crabbe
From 1932 Olympic swimming gold to *Flash Gordon*
Johnny Weismuller
From five 1924–28 Olympic swimming golds to *Tarzan*
Rick Fox
From NBA to *He Got Game, Oz, Ugly Betty* (TV)
Reynolds
Uecker
Fred Dryer
Jim Brown
Marinaro
Bradshaw
Crabbe
Weismuller
Reynolds
Brown
Bradshaw
Weismuller
Reynolds
Weismuller
Reynolds

Marinaro vs. Bradshaw
After winning the NCAA rushing title at Cornell and some journeyman running back work for the Minnesota Vikings, Marinaro broke though with his role as a cop in *Hill Street Blues.* He had it all: good looks, acting chops, and a profile that didn't say big jock. But he faded. Bradshaw has a comic persona that jumps out of the screen, most deftly in his fish-tending scene in *Failure to Launch.* A small film career, but a big impression.

Weismuller vs. Crabbe
An all-wet matchup of 1920–30s swim gods. Crabbe knew his limitations: "Some say my acting rose to the level of incompetence and then leveled off." But Weismuller understood why his athlete-to-actor move succeeded, saying, "How can a guy climb trees, say 'Me, Tarzan, you, Jane,' and make a million? The public forgives my acting because they know I was an athlete. They know I wasn't make-believe."

Sportscasters

By Richard Deitsch

Richard Deitsch is a sports media writer and special projects editor for *Sports Illustrated,* and writes the Media Circus column for SI.com.

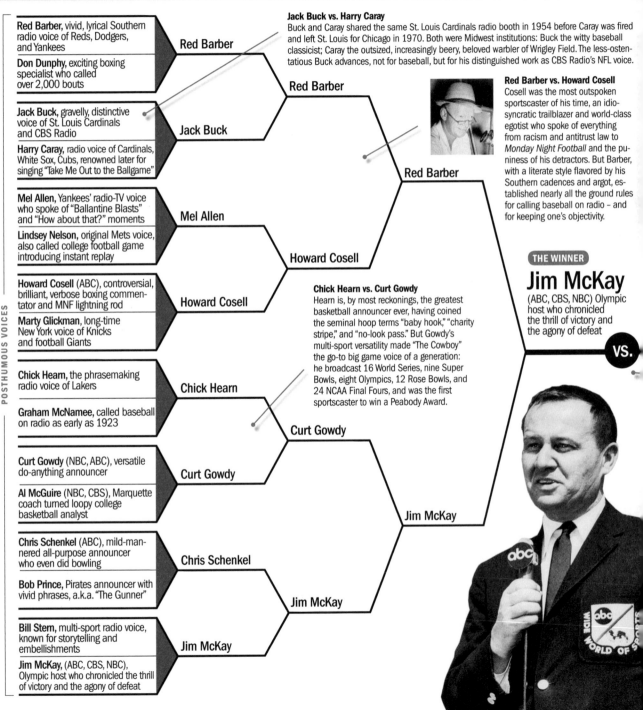

POSTHUMOUS VOICES

Red Barber, vivid, lyrical Southern radio voice of Reds, Dodgers, and Yankees

Don Dunphy, exciting boxing specialist who called over 2,000 bouts

Red Barber

Jack Buck, gravelly, distinctive voice of St. Louis Cardinals and CBS Radio

Harry Caray, radio voice of Cardinals, White Sox, Cubs, renowned later for singing "Take Me Out to the Ballgame"

Jack Buck

Mel Allen, Yankees' radio-TV voice who spoke of "Ballantine Blasts" and "How about that?" moments

Lindsey Nelson, original Mets voice, also called college football game introducing instant replay

Mel Allen

Howard Cosell (ABC), controversial, brilliant, verbose boxing commentator and MNF lightning rod

Marty Glickman, long-time New York voice of Knicks and football Giants

Howard Cosell

Chick Hearn, the phrasemaking radio voice of Lakers

Graham McNamee, called baseball on radio as early as 1923

Chick Hearn

Curt Gowdy (NBC, ABC), versatile do-anything announcer

Al McGuire (NBC, CBS), Marquette coach turned loopy college basketball analyst

Curt Gowdy

Chris Schenkel (ABC), mild-mannered all-purpose announcer who even did bowling

Bob Prince, Pirates announcer with vivid phrases, a.k.a. "The Gunner"

Chris Schenkel

Bill Stern, multi-sport radio voice, known for storytelling and embellishments

Jim McKay, (ABC, CBS, NBC), Olympic host who chronicled the thrill of victory and the agony of defeat

Jim McKay

Red Barber

Howard Cosell

Curt Gowdy

Jim McKay

Red Barber

Jim McKay

Jack Buck vs. Harry Caray

Buck and Caray shared the same St. Louis Cardinals radio booth in 1954 before Caray was fired and left St. Louis for Chicago in 1970. Both were Midwest institutions: Buck the witty baseball classicist; Caray the outsized, increasingly beery, beloved warbler of Wrigley Field. The less-ostentatious Buck advances, not for baseball, but for his distinguished work as CBS Radio's NFL voice.

Red Barber vs. Howard Cosell

Cosell was the most outspoken sportscaster of his time, an idiosyncratic trailblazer and world-class egotist who spoke of everything from racism and antitrust law to *Monday Night Football* and the puniness of his detractors. But Barber, with a literate style flavored by his Southern cadences and argot, established nearly all the ground rules for calling baseball on radio – and for keeping one's objectivity.

Chick Hearn vs. Curt Gowdy

Hearn is, by most reckonings, the greatest basketball announcer ever, having coined the seminal hoop terms "baby hook," "charity stripe," and "no-look pass." But Gowdy's multi-sport versatility made "The Cowboy" the go-to big game voice of a generation: he broadcast 16 World Series, nine Super Bowls, eight Olympics, 12 Rose Bowls, and 24 NCAA Final Fours, and was the first sportscaster to win a Peabody Award.

THE WINNER

Jim McKay

(ABC, CBS, NBC) Olympic host who chronicled the thrill of victory and the agony of defeat

VS.

COMPETENCE, EGO, HONESTY, intellect, showmanship, storytelling, and voice are commonplace traits with every great sportscaster. But most of all it is the underlying professionalism and an instinctive sense of what to say – and what not to say – that defines this small community.

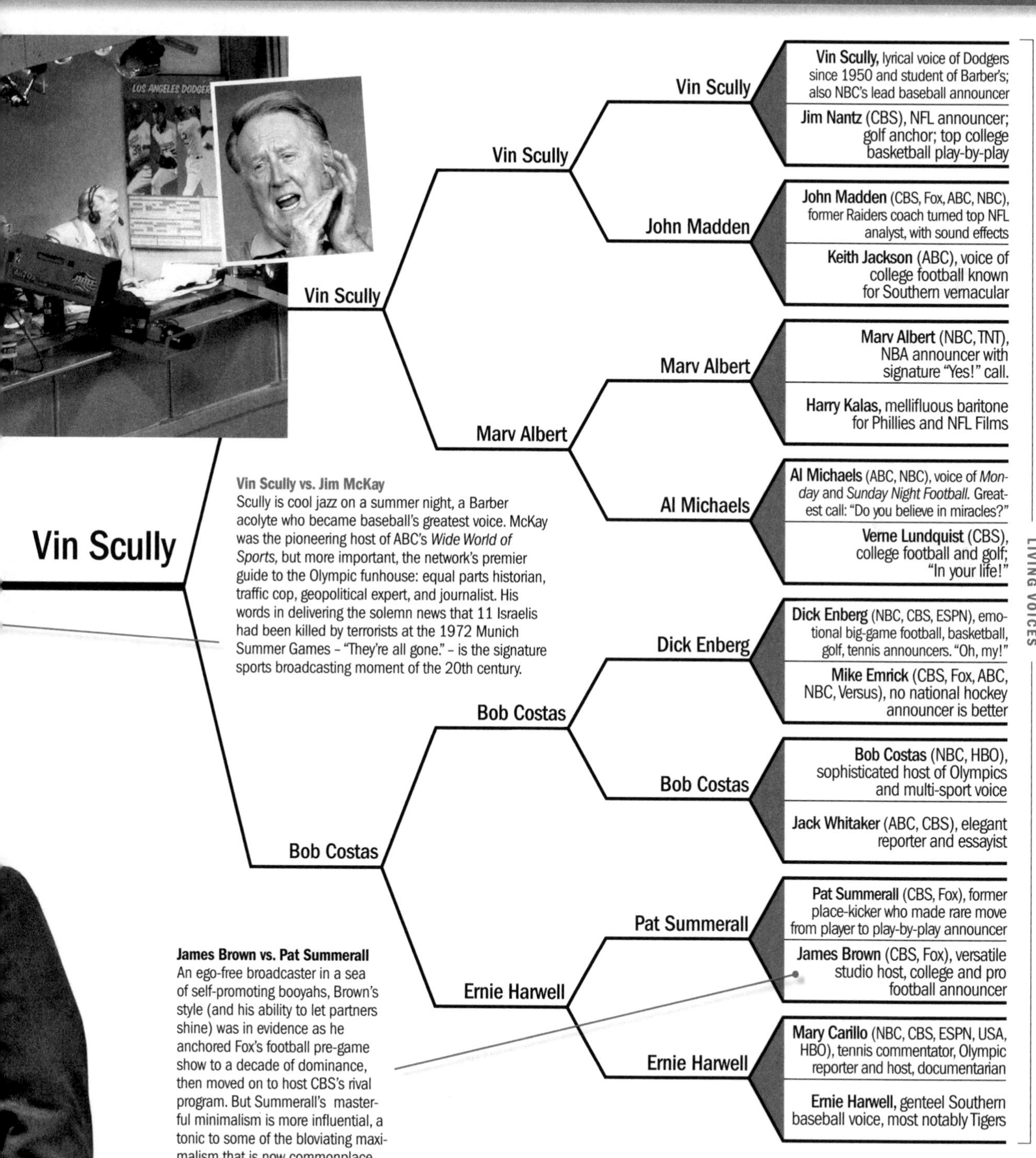
LIVING VOICES
Vin Scully, lyrical voice of Dodgers since 1950 and student of Barber's; also NBC's lead baseball announcer
Jim Nantz (CBS), NFL announcer; golf anchor; top college basketball play-by-play
John Madden (CBS, Fox, ABC, NBC), former Raiders coach turned top NFL analyst, with sound effects
Keith Jackson (ABC), voice of college football known for Southern vernacular
Marv Albert (NBC, TNT), NBA announcer with signature "Yes!" call.
Harry Kalas, mellifluous baritone for Phillies and NFL Films
Al Michaels (ABC, NBC), voice of *Monday* and *Sunday Night Football.* Greatest call: "Do you believe in miracles?"
Verne Lundquist (CBS), college football and golf; "In your life!"
Dick Enberg (NBC, CBS, ESPN), emotional big-game football, basketball, golf, tennis announcers. "Oh, my!"
Mike Emrick (CBS, Fox, ABC, NBC, Versus), no national hockey announcer is better
Bob Costas (NBC, HBO), sophisticated host of Olympics and multi-sport voice
Jack Whitaker (ABC, CBS), elegant reporter and essayist
Pat Summerall (CBS, Fox), former place-kicker who made rare move from player to play-by-play announcer
James Brown (CBS, Fox), versatile studio host, college and pro football announcer
Mary Carillo (NBC, CBS, ESPN, USA, HBO), tennis commentator, Olympic reporter and host, documentarian
Ernie Harwell, genteel Southern baseball voice, most notably Tigers
Vin Scully
John Madden
Marv Albert
Al Michaels
Dick Enberg
Bob Costas
Pat Summerall
Ernie Harwell
Vin Scully
Marv Albert
Bob Costas
Ernie Harwell
Vin Scully
Bob Costas
Vin Scully

Vin Scully vs. Jim McKay
Scully is cool jazz on a summer night, a Barber acolyte who became baseball's greatest voice. McKay was the pioneering host of ABC's *Wide World of Sports,* but more important, the network's premier guide to the Olympic funhouse: equal parts historian, traffic cop, geopolitical expert, and journalist. His words in delivering the solemn news that 11 Israelis had been killed by terrorists at the 1972 Munich Summer Games – "They're all gone." – is the signature sports broadcasting moment of the 20th century.

James Brown vs. Pat Summerall
An ego-free broadcaster in a sea of self-promoting booyahs, Brown's style (and his ability to let partners shine) was in evidence as he anchored Fox's football pre-game show to a decade of dominance, then moved on to host CBS's rival program. But Summerall's masterful minimalism is more influential, a tonic to some of the bloviating maximalism that is now commonplace.

SEC Athletes

By Steve Eubanks

Steve Eubanks is a contributing columnist for FoxSports.com and author of too many books. He lives in Peachtree City, Georgia, with his family and more animals than city ordinances allow.

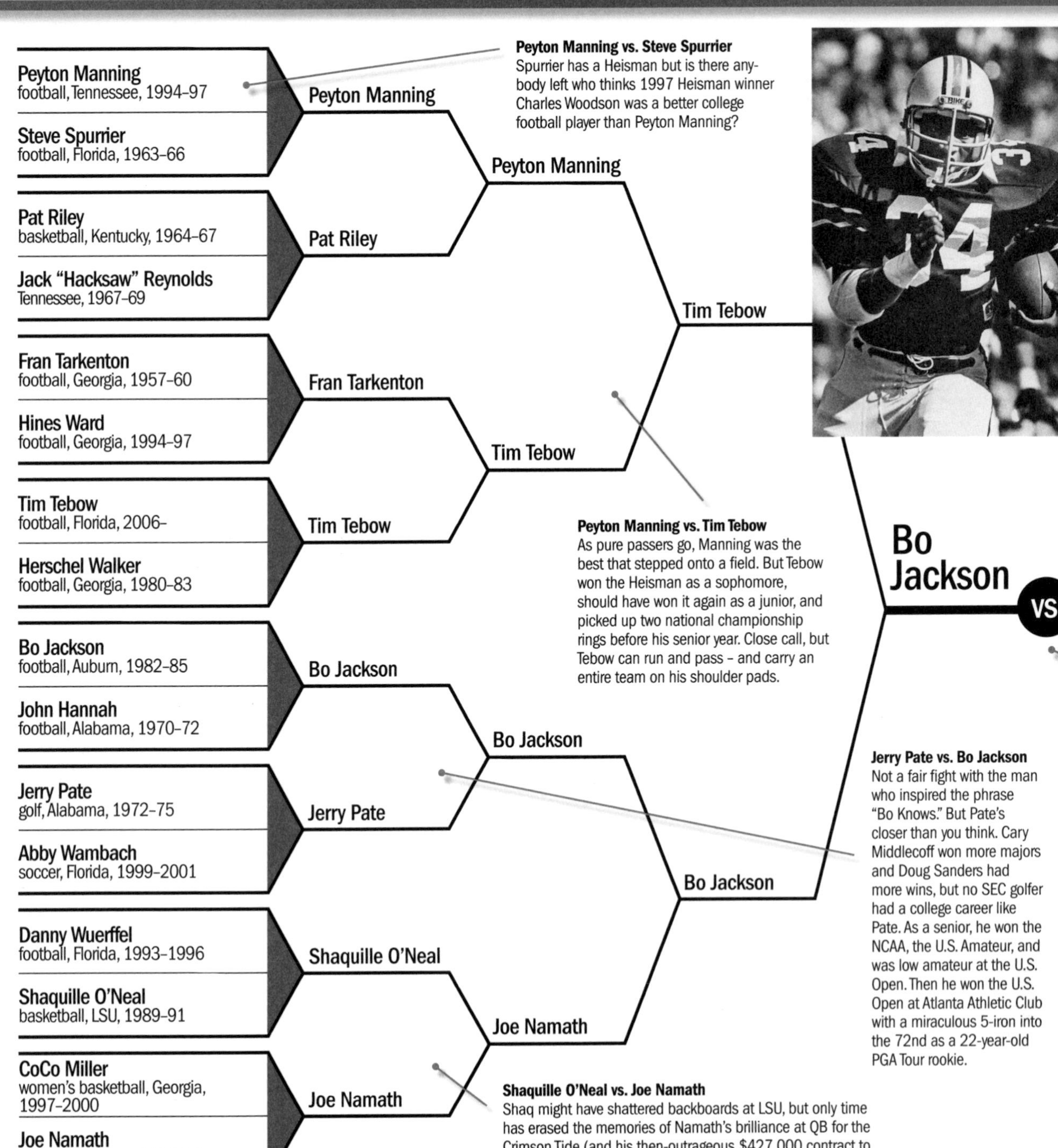

Peyton Manning
football, Tennessee, 1994–97
Steve Spurrier
football, Florida, 1963–66
Pat Riley
basketball, Kentucky, 1964–67
Jack "Hacksaw" Reynolds
Tennessee, 1967–69
Fran Tarkenton
football, Georgia, 1957–60
Hines Ward
football, Georgia, 1994–97
Tim Tebow
football, Florida, 2006–
Herschel Walker
football, Georgia, 1980–83
Bo Jackson
football, Auburn, 1982–85
John Hannah
football, Alabama, 1970–72
Jerry Pate
golf, Alabama, 1972–75
Abby Wambach
soccer, Florida, 1999–2001
Danny Wuerffel
football, Florida, 1993–1996
Shaquille O'Neal
basketball, LSU, 1989–91
CoCo Miller
women's basketball, Georgia, 1997–2000
Joe Namath
football, Alabama, 1962–64
Peyton Manning
Pat Riley
Fran Tarkenton
Tim Tebow
Bo Jackson
Jerry Pate
Shaquille O'Neal
Joe Namath
Peyton Manning
Tim Tebow
Bo Jackson
Joe Namath
Tim Tebow
Bo Jackson
Bo Jackson
VS.

Peyton Manning vs. Steve Spurrier
Spurrier has a Heisman but is there anybody left who thinks 1997 Heisman winner Charles Woodson was a better college football player than Peyton Manning?

Peyton Manning vs. Tim Tebow
As pure passers go, Manning was the best that stepped onto a field. But Tebow won the Heisman as a sophomore, should have won it again as a junior, and picked up two national championship rings before his senior year. Close call, but Tebow can run and pass – and carry an entire team on his shoulder pads.

Jerry Pate vs. Bo Jackson
Not a fair fight with the man who inspired the phrase "Bo Knows." But Pate's closer than you think. Cary Middlecoff won more majors and Doug Sanders had more wins, but no SEC golfer had a college career like Pate. As a senior, he won the NCAA, the U.S. Amateur, and was low amateur at the U.S. Open. Then he won the U.S. Open at Atlanta Athletic Club with a miraculous 5-iron into the 72nd as a 22-year-old PGA Tour rookie.

Shaquille O'Neal vs. Joe Namath
Shaq might have shattered backboards at LSU, but only time has erased the memories of Namath's brilliance at QB for the Crimson Tide (and his then-outrageous $427,000 contract to go to the fledgling AFL). Truly, he was the first college athlete since Red Grange with star power before he turned pro.

THE SOUTHEASTERN CONFERENCE is the best in college sports, with powerhouse teams in so many sports from Florida, Alabama, Tennessee, Kentucky, Auburn, LSU, Georgia, and more. If you want to argue the point, here's who didn't make the list: Cornelius Bennett, Garrison Hearst, Cris Collinsworth, Frank Thomas, Robert Horry, Shaun Alexander, Joaquim Noah, Cadillac Williams, DeLisa Milton-Jones, David Toms, and Champ Bailey, among others. Good doesn't cut it here; you have to be legendary. Bonus points for later success in the pros, but it's the college performance that counts here.

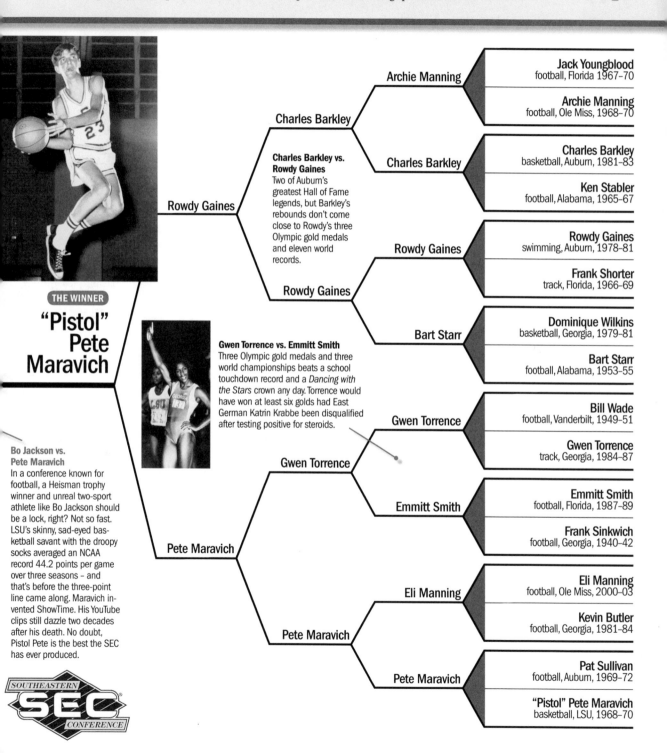

Jack Youngblood
football, Florida 1967–70

Archie Manning
football, Ole Miss, 1968–70

Charles Barkley
basketball, Auburn, 1981–83

Ken Stabler
football, Alabama, 1965–67

Rowdy Gaines
swimming, Auburn, 1978–81

Frank Shorter
track, Florida, 1966–69

Dominique Wilkins
basketball, Georgia, 1979–81

Bart Starr
football, Alabama, 1953–55

Bill Wade
football, Vanderbilt, 1949–51

Gwen Torrence
track, Georgia, 1984–87

Emmitt Smith
football, Florida, 1987–89

Frank Sinkwich
football, Georgia, 1940–42

Eli Manning
football, Ole Miss, 2000–03

Kevin Butler
football, Georgia, 1981–84

Pat Sullivan
football, Auburn, 1969–72

"Pistol" Pete Maravich
basketball, LSU, 1968–70

Archie Manning

Charles Barkley

Rowdy Gaines

Bart Starr

Gwen Torrence

Emmitt Smith

Eli Manning

Pete Maravich

Charles Barkley

Rowdy Gaines

Gwen Torrence

Pete Maravich

Rowdy Gaines

Pete Maravich

Charles Barkley vs. Rowdy Gaines
Two of Auburn's greatest Hall of Fame legends, but Barkley's rebounds don't come close to Rowdy's three Olympic gold medals and eleven world records.

Gwen Torrence vs. Emmitt Smith
Three Olympic gold medals and three world championships beats a school touchdown record and a *Dancing with the Stars* crown any day. Torrence would have won at least six golds had East German Katrin Krabbe been disqualified after testing positive for steroids.

THE WINNER

"Pistol" Pete Maravich

Bo Jackson vs. Pete Maravich
In a conference known for football, a Heisman trophy winner and unreal two-sport athlete like Bo Jackson should be a lock, right? Not so fast. LSU's skinny, sad-eyed basketball savant with the droopy socks averaged an NCAA record 44.2 points per game over three seasons – and that's before the three-point line came along. Maravich invented ShowTime. His YouTube clips still dazzle two decades after his death. No doubt, Pistol Pete is the best the SEC has ever produced.

SOUTHEASTERN
SEC
CONFERENCE

Pound-for-Pound Fighters

By Steve Farhood

Steve Farhood is a former editor-in-chief of *The Ring* and *KO* magazines, and is now an on-air analyst for Showtime.

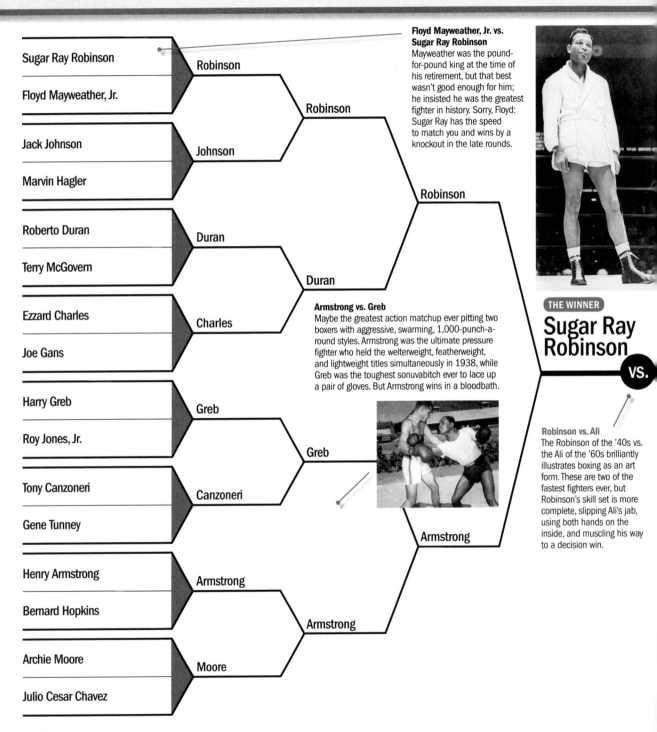

Sugar Ray Robinson
Floyd Mayweather, Jr.
Jack Johnson
Marvin Hagler
Roberto Duran
Terry McGovern
Ezzard Charles
Joe Gans
Harry Greb
Roy Jones, Jr.
Tony Canzoneri
Gene Tunney
Henry Armstrong
Bernard Hopkins
Archie Moore
Julio Cesar Chavez

Robinson
Johnson
Duran
Charles
Greb
Canzoneri
Armstrong
Moore

Robinson
Duran
Greb
Armstrong

Robinson
Armstrong

Floyd Mayweather, Jr. vs. Sugar Ray Robinson
Mayweather was the pound-for-pound king at the time of his retirement, but that best wasn't good enough for him; he insisted he was the greatest fighter in history. Sorry, Floyd: Sugar Ray has the speed to match you and wins by a knockout in the late rounds.

THE WINNER

Sugar Ray Robinson

VS.

Armstrong vs. Greb
Maybe the greatest action matchup ever pitting two boxers with aggressive, swarming, 1,000-punch-a-round styles. Armstrong was the ultimate pressure fighter who held the welterweight, featherweight, and lightweight titles simultaneously in 1938, while Greb was the toughest sonuvabitch ever to lace up a pair of gloves. But Armstrong wins in a bloodbath.

Robinson vs. Ali
The Robinson of the '40s vs. the Ali of the '60s brilliantly illustrates boxing as an art form. These are two of the fastest fighters ever, but Robinson's skill set is more complete, slipping Ali's jab, using both hands on the inside, and muscling his way to a decision win.

THE PROLIFERATION OF BOXING WORLD TITLES, with its alphabet soup's worth of sanctioning body confusion, has cluttered the sport, demeaned the value of championship belts, and elevated the importance of a best pound-for-pound fighter. The pound-for-pound standard lets us judge fighters from different eras through their accomplishments, skill, artistry, longevity, and quality of opposition. It breaks my heart to exclude greats who fought in America, like Emile Griffith, Bob Foster, Ruben Olivares, Ike Williams, and Sandy Saddler; and picking a winner was like going 12 rounds with my eventual champ.

Leonard vs. Ali

Leonard is the best fighter I've covered in my 30 years at ringside, but Ali is still "The Greatest." Leonard clearly can't outfinesse Ali. Leonard looks to brawl, but his aggressiveness works against him; he repeatedly walks into Ali's punching range and gets tagged by counter right hands. Ali wins by unanimous decision.

Ali vs. Louis

Ali and Louis are the two greatest heavyweights in history, and it's a long drop to number three. Louis's one edge, his punching power, is neutralized by Ali's fast feet and reliable chin. Ali jabs with persistence and precision, steals a couple of rounds with flurries, and recovers quickly from a knockdown to win by unanimous decision.

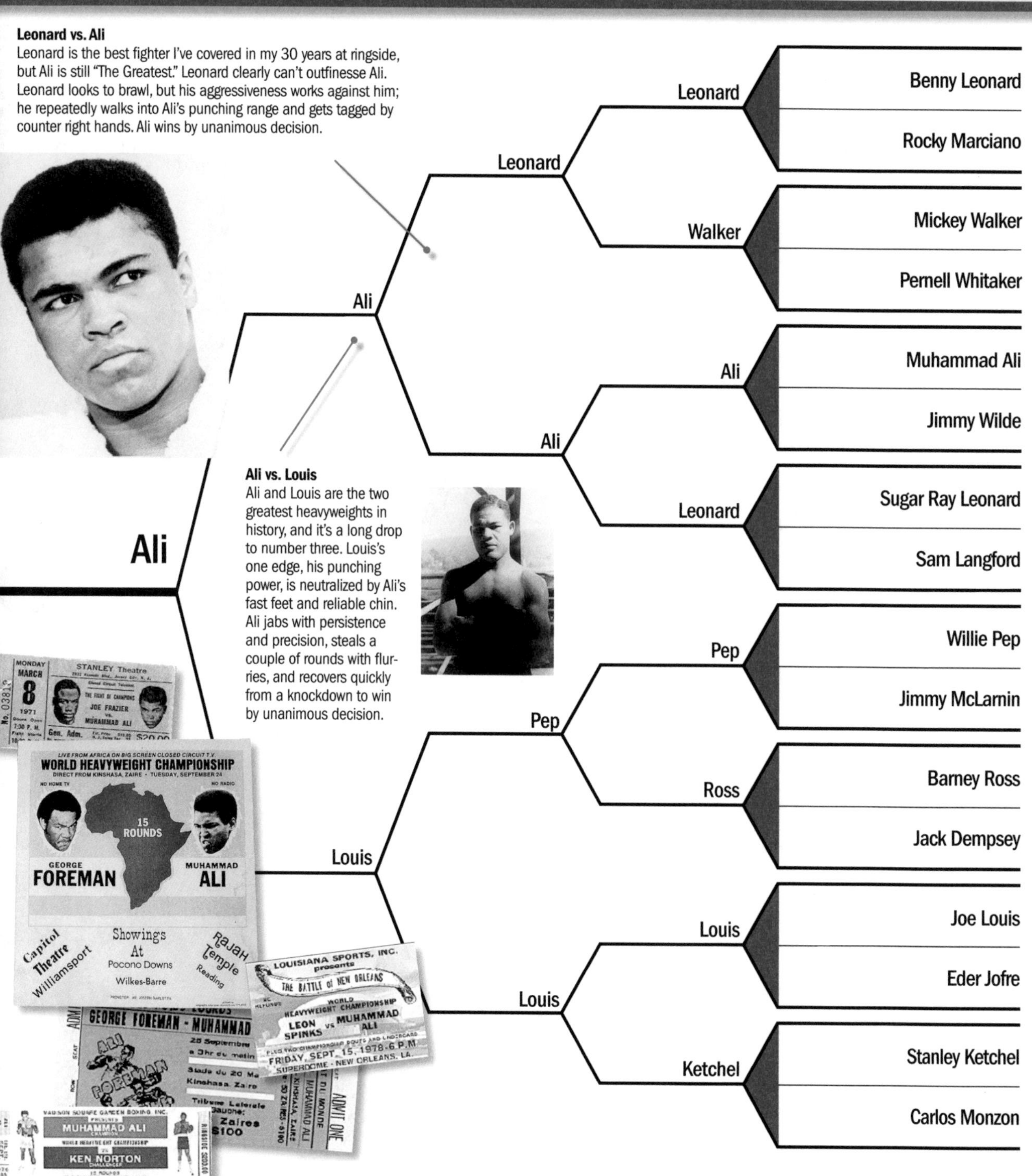

Benny Leonard
Rocky Marciano
Mickey Walker
Pernell Whitaker
Muhammad Ali
Jimmy Wilde
Sugar Ray Leonard
Sam Langford
Willie Pep
Jimmy McLarnin
Barney Ross
Jack Dempsey
Joe Louis
Eder Jofre
Stanley Ketchel
Carlos Monzon
Leonard
Walker
Ali
Leonard
Pep
Ross
Louis
Ketchel
Leonard
Ali
Pep
Louis
Ali
Louis
Ali
WORLD HEAVYWEIGHT CHAMPIONSHIP
15 ROUNDS
GEORGE FOREMAN
MUHAMMAD ALI
Showings At Pocono Downs Wilkes-Barre
Capitol Theatre Williamsport
Rajah Temple Reading
LOUISIANA SPORTS, INC. presents
THE BATTLE of NEW ORLEANS
LEON SPINKS vs MUHAMMAD ALI
FRIDAY, SEPT. 15, 1978-6 P.M.
SUPERDOME - NEW ORLEANS, LA.
GEORGE FOREMAN - MUHAMMAD
MUHAMMAD ALI
KEN NORTON
YANKEE STADIUM
STANLEY Theatre
JOE FRAZIER vs. MUHAMMAD ALI
MONDAY MARCH 8 1971

Field Goals and PATs

By Stefan Fatsis

Stefan Fatsis is the author of *A Few Seconds of Panic: A 5-foot-8, 170-pound, 43-year-old Sportswriter Plays in the NFL* and talks about sports on NPR's *All Things Considered.* He insists he can still make a 40-yard field goal. Or at least a 35.

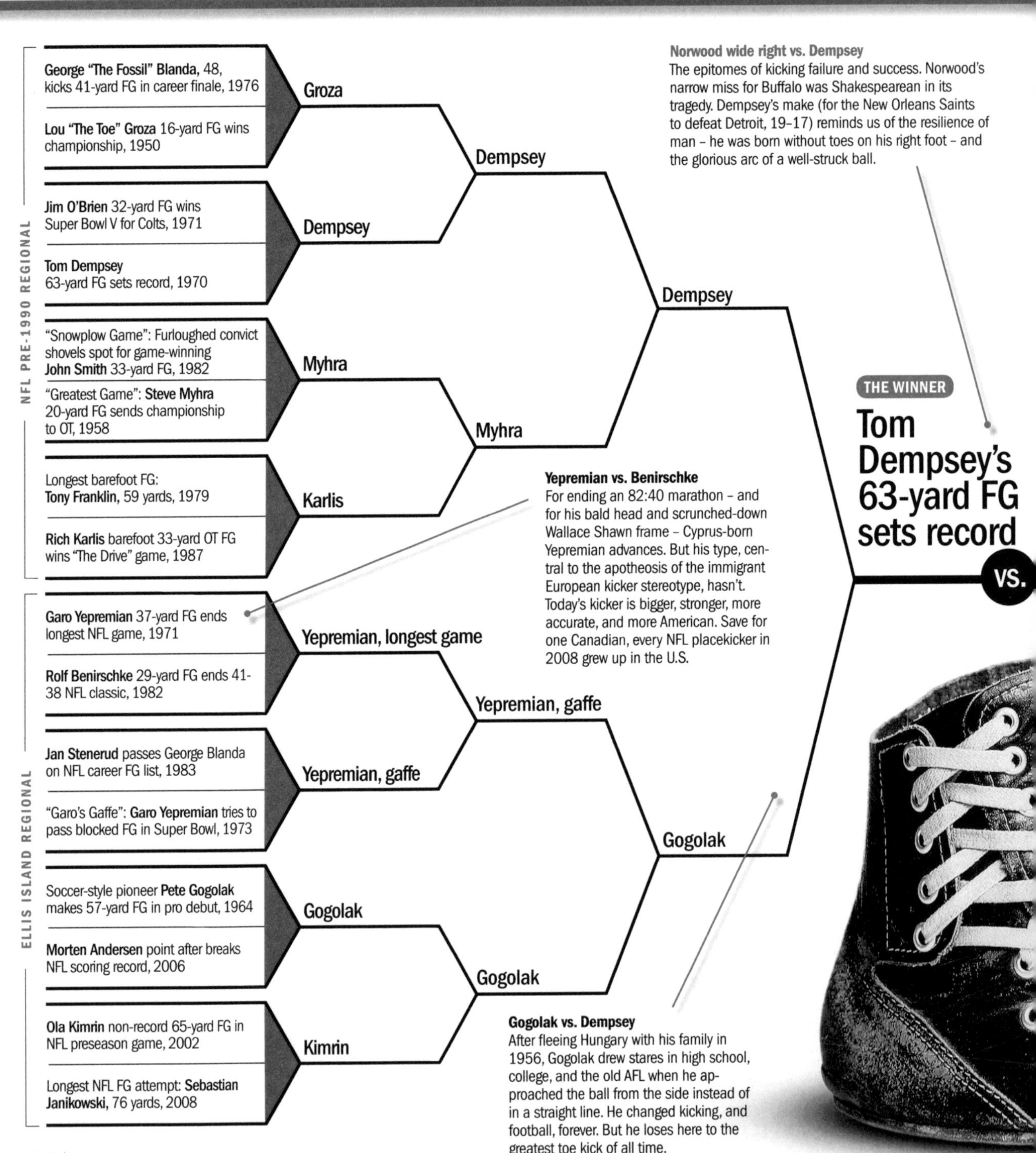
NFL PRE-1990 REGIONAL
George "The Fossil" Blanda, 48, kicks 41-yard FG in career finale, 1976
Lou "The Toe" Groza 16-yard FG wins championship, 1950
Jim O'Brien 32-yard FG wins Super Bowl V for Colts, 1971
Tom Dempsey 63-yard FG sets record, 1970
"Snowplow Game": Furloughed convict shovels spot for game-winning John Smith 33-yard FG, 1982
"Greatest Game": Steve Myhra 20-yard FG sends championship to OT, 1958
Longest barefoot FG: Tony Franklin, 59 yards, 1979
Rich Karlis barefoot 33-yard OT FG wins "The Drive" game, 1987
ELLIS ISLAND REGIONAL
Garo Yepremian 37-yard FG ends longest NFL game, 1971
Rolf Benirschke 29-yard FG ends 41-38 NFL classic, 1982
Jan Stenerud passes George Blanda on NFL career FG list, 1983
"Garo's Gaffe": Garo Yepremian tries to pass blocked FG in Super Bowl, 1973
Soccer-style pioneer Pete Gogolak makes 57-yard FG in pro debut, 1964
Morten Andersen point after breaks NFL scoring record, 2006
Ola Kimrin non-record 65-yard FG in NFL preseason game, 2002
Longest NFL FG attempt: Sebastian Janikowski, 76 yards, 2008
Groza
Dempsey
Myhra
Karlis
Yepremian, longest game
Yepremian, gaffe
Gogolak
Kimrin
Dempsey
Myhra
Yepremian, gaffe
Gogolak
Dempsey
Gogolak
Norwood wide right vs. Dempsey
The epitomes of kicking failure and success. Norwood's narrow miss for Buffalo was Shakespearean in its tragedy. Dempsey's make (for the New Orleans Saints to defeat Detroit, 19–17) reminds us of the resilience of man – he was born without toes on his right foot – and the glorious arc of a well-struck ball.
Yepremian vs. Benirschke
For ending an 82:40 marathon – and for his bald head and scrunched-down Wallace Shawn frame – Cyprus-born Yepremian advances. But his type, central to the apotheosis of the immigrant European kicker stereotype, hasn't. Today's kicker is bigger, stronger, more accurate, and more American. Save for one Canadian, every NFL placekicker in 2008 grew up in the U.S.
Gogolak vs. Dempsey
After fleeing Hungary with his family in 1956, Gogolak drew stares in high school, college, and the old AFL when he approached the ball from the side instead of in a straight line. He changed kicking, and football, forever. But he loses here to the greatest toe kick of all time.
THE WINNER
Tom Dempsey's 63-yard FG sets record
VS.

HATE THAT FOOTBALL GAMES are contested by brave and magnificent athletes but often decided by guys in clean uniforms and size-8 cleats? Get over it. From football's primordial 19th-century origins, no body part has been more important than the foot. Memorable kicks come from impossible distances, under unfathomable pressure, and, it seems, under the goofiest circumstances. Here's one kick that didn't make the cut: a 28-yarder that saved the Denver Broncos 30 minutes of meetings during training camp in 2006. The kicker? Me.

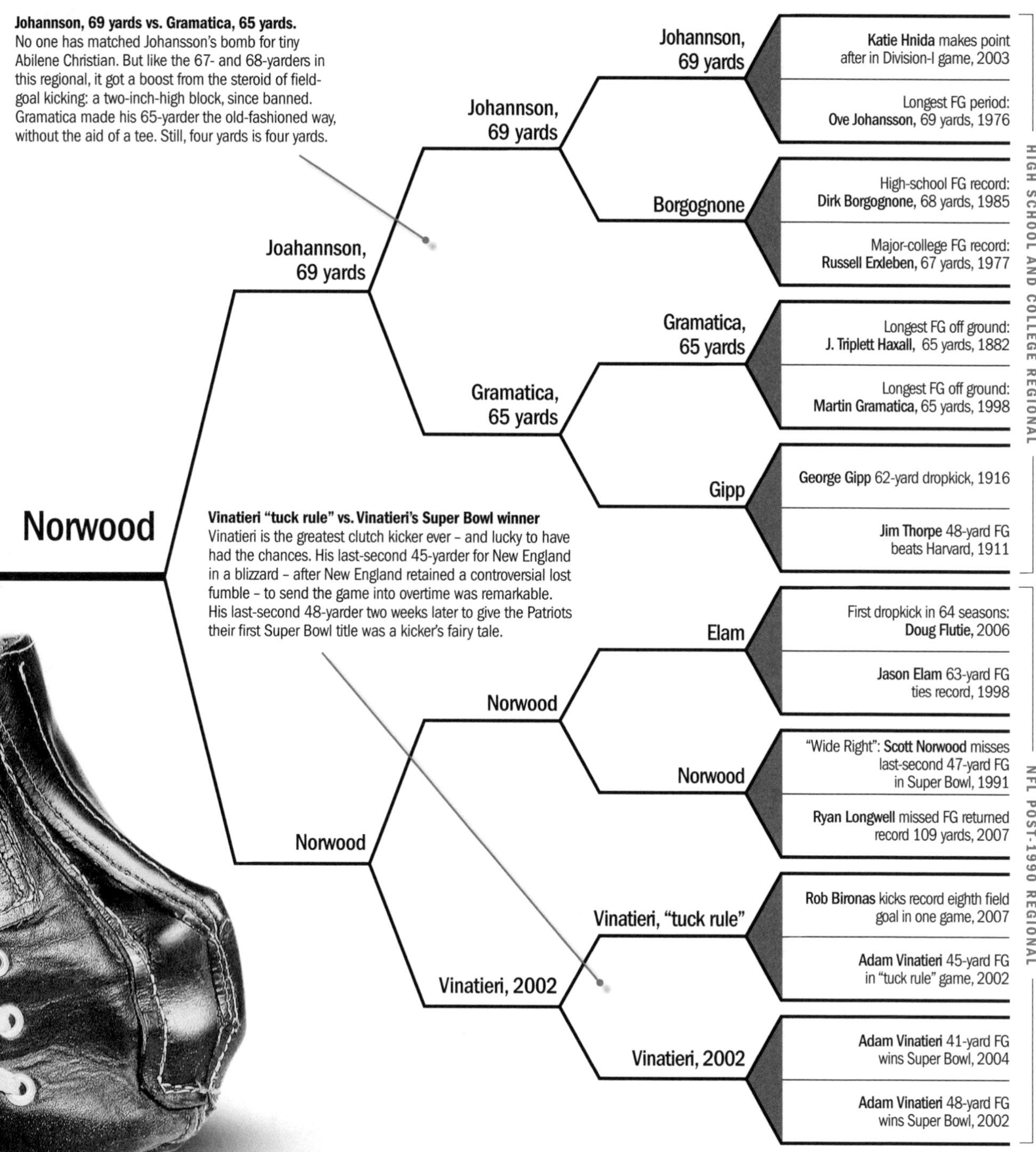

Johannson, 69 yards vs. Gramatica, 65 yards.
No one has matched Johansson's bomb for tiny Abilene Christian. But like the 67- and 68-yarders in this regional, it got a boost from the steroid of field-goal kicking: a two-inch-high block, since banned. Gramatica made his 65-yarder the old-fashioned way, without the aid of a tee. Still, four yards is four yards.
Katie Hnida makes point after in Division-I game, 2003
Longest FG period: Ove Johansson, 69 yards, 1976
High-school FG record: Dirk Borgognone, 68 yards, 1985
Major-college FG record: Russell Erxleben, 67 yards, 1977
Longest FG off ground: J. Triplett Haxall, 65 yards, 1882
Longest FG off ground: Martin Gramatica, 65 yards, 1998
George Gipp 62-yard dropkick, 1916
Jim Thorpe 48-yard FG beats Harvard, 1911
Johannson, 69 yards
Borgognone
Gramatica, 65 yards
Gipp
Johannson, 69 yards
Gramatica, 65 yards
Joahannson, 69 yards
HIGH SCHOOL AND COLLEGE REGIONAL
Norwood
Vinatieri "tuck rule" vs. Vinatieri's Super Bowl winner
Vinatieri is the greatest clutch kicker ever – and lucky to have had the chances. His last-second 45-yarder for New England in a blizzard – after New England retained a controversial lost fumble – to send the game into overtime was remarkable. His last-second 48-yarder two weeks later to give the Patriots their first Super Bowl title was a kicker's fairy tale.
First dropkick in 64 seasons: Doug Flutie, 2006
Jason Elam 63-yard FG ties record, 1998
"Wide Right": Scott Norwood misses last-second 47-yard FG in Super Bowl, 1991
Ryan Longwell missed FG returned record 109 yards, 2007
Rob Bironas kicks record eighth field goal in one game, 2007
Adam Vinatieri 45-yard FG in "tuck rule" game, 2002
Adam Vinatieri 41-yard FG wins Super Bowl, 2004
Adam Vinatieri 48-yard FG wins Super Bowl, 2002
Elam
Norwood
Vinatieri, "tuck rule"
Vinatieri, 2002
Norwood
Vinatieri, 2002
Norwood
NFL POST-1990 REGIONAL

Golf Books

By John Garrity

John Garrity, a longtime *Sports Illustrated* writer, has contributed numerous books to the golf underbracket, including *Tiger 2.0, Ancestral Links,* and *America's Worst Golf Courses* – and one that belongs here, *Tour Tempo,* co-authored with John Novosel.

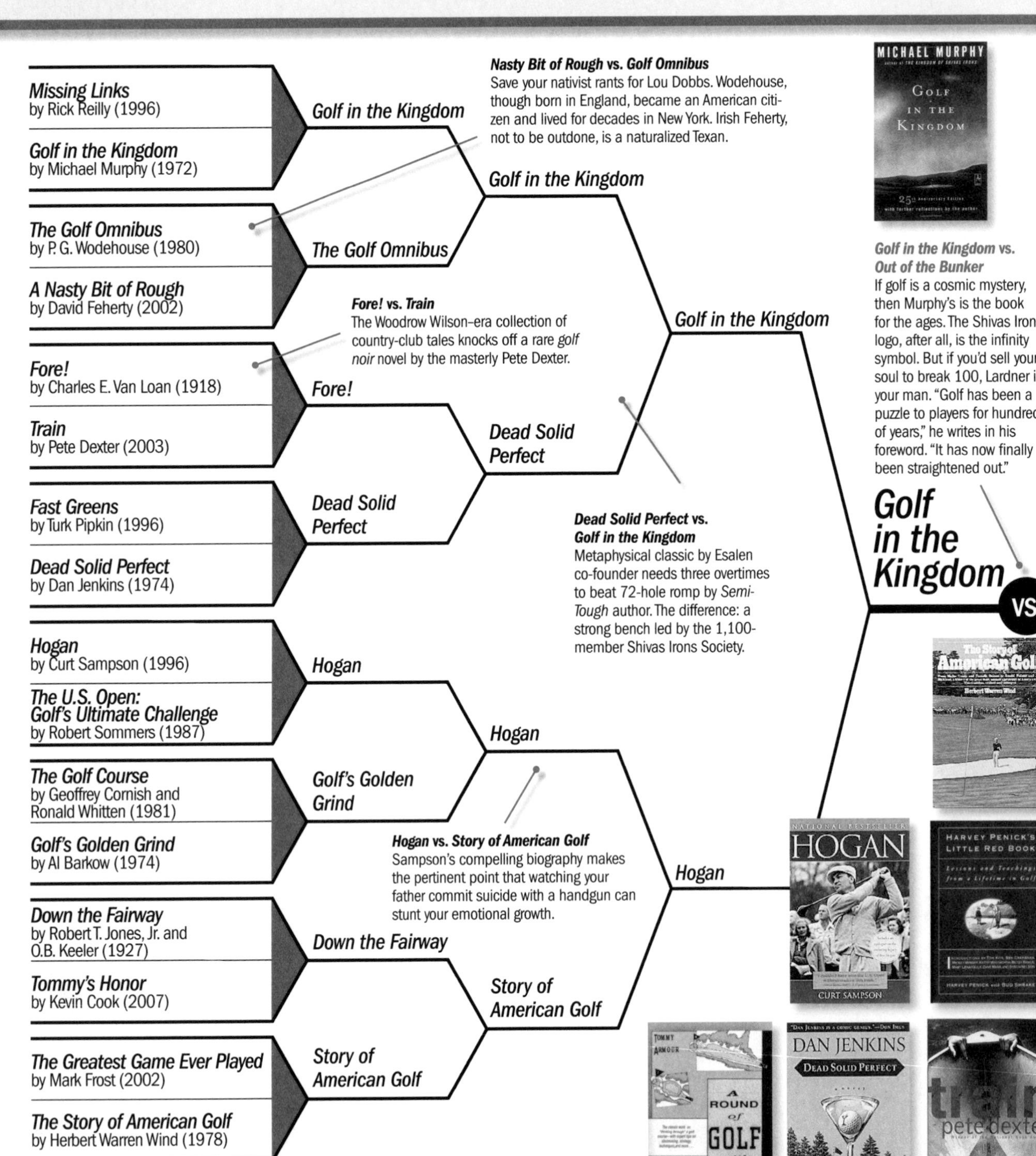

Missing Links
by Rick Reilly (1996)
Golf in the Kingdom
by Michael Murphy (1972)
The Golf Omnibus
by P. G. Wodehouse (1980)
A Nasty Bit of Rough
by David Feherty (2002)
Fore!
by Charles E. Van Loan (1918)
Train
by Pete Dexter (2003)
Fast Greens
by Turk Pipkin (1996)
Dead Solid Perfect
by Dan Jenkins (1974)
Hogan
by Curt Sampson (1996)
The U.S. Open: Golf's Ultimate Challenge
by Robert Sommers (1987)
The Golf Course
by Geoffrey Cornish and Ronald Whitten (1981)
Golf's Golden Grind
by Al Barkow (1974)
Down the Fairway
by Robert T. Jones, Jr. and O.B. Keeler (1927)
Tommy's Honor
by Kevin Cook (2007)
The Greatest Game Ever Played
by Mark Frost (2002)
The Story of American Golf
by Herbert Warren Wind (1978)
Golf in the Kingdom
The Golf Omnibus
Fore!
Dead Solid Perfect
Hogan
Golf's Golden Grind
Down the Fairway
Story of American Golf
Golf in the Kingdom
Dead Solid Perfect
Hogan
Story of American Golf
Golf in the Kingdom
Hogan
Nasty Bit of Rough vs. Golf Omnibus
Save your nativist rants for Lou Dobbs. Wodehouse, though born in England, became an American citizen and lived for decades in New York. Irish Feherty, not to be outdone, is a naturalized Texan.
Fore! vs. Train
The Woodrow Wilson–era collection of country-club tales knocks off a rare golf noir novel by the masterly Pete Dexter.
Dead Solid Perfect vs. Golf in the Kingdom
Metaphysical classic by Esalen co-founder needs three overtimes to beat 72-hole romp by Semi-Tough author. The difference: a strong bench led by the 1,100-member Shivas Irons Society.
Hogan vs. Story of American Golf
Sampson's compelling biography makes the pertinent point that watching your father commit suicide with a handgun can stunt your emotional growth.
Golf in the Kingdom vs. Out of the Bunker
If golf is a cosmic mystery, then Murphy's is the book for the ages. The Shivas Irons logo, after all, is the infinity symbol. But if you'd sell your soul to break 100, Lardner is your man. "Golf has been a puzzle to players for hundreds of years," he writes in his foreword. "It has now finally been straightened out."
Golf in the Kingdom
VS.
MICHAEL MURPHY
Golf in the Kingdom
The Story of American Golf
Herbert Warren Wind
HOGAN
CURT SAMPSON
HARVEY PENICK'S LITTLE RED BOOK
DAN JENKINS
DEAD SOLID PERFECT
A ROUND of GOLF with TOMMY ARMOUR
train
pete dexter

GOLF WRITERS TURN OUT DISTINGUISHED PROSE, George Plimpton said, because their attempts to play the game lead to "the state of contained melancholy that so often produces first-rate writing." In other words, golf writing flows from the same fountain of remorse, paranoia, and wounded self-esteem that makes comedians funny and tech tycoons rich. That said, the best golf writing shows no correlation between handicap and literary merit. Some golf writers actually play the game well, which is to be expected. If frustration were the magic ingredient, we'd have 26 million Hemingways.

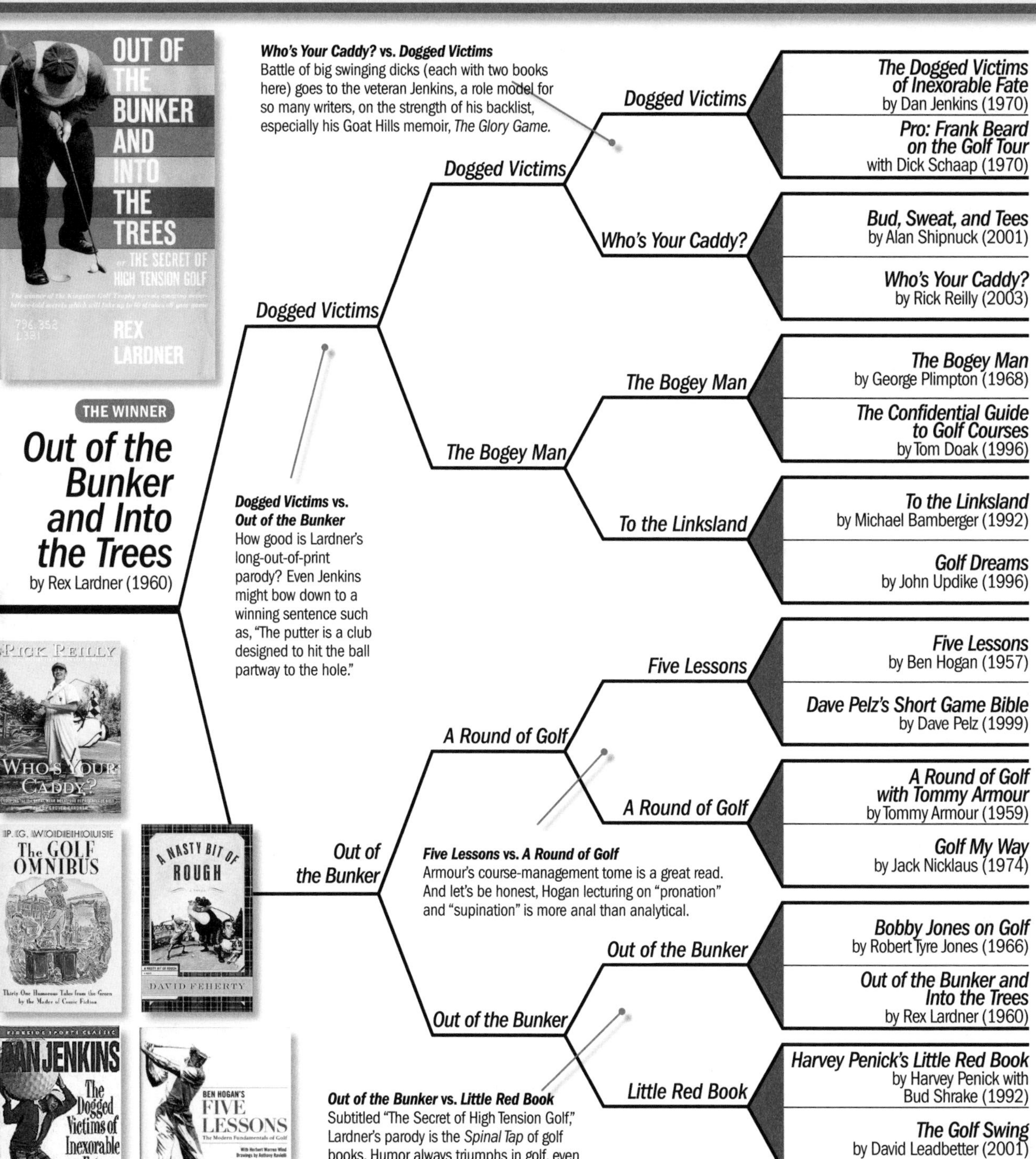

OUT OF THE BUNKER AND INTO THE TREES
or THE SECRET OF HIGH TENSION GOLF
REX LARDNER
THE WINNER
Out of the Bunker and Into the Trees
by Rex Lardner (1960)
Who's Your Caddy? vs. Dogged Victims
Battle of big swinging dicks (each with two books here) goes to the veteran Jenkins, a role model for so many writers, on the strength of his backlist, especially his Goat Hills memoir, The Glory Game.
Dogged Victims vs. Out of the Bunker
How good is Lardner's long-out-of-print parody? Even Jenkins might bow down to a winning sentence such as, "The putter is a club designed to hit the ball partway to the hole."
Five Lessons vs. A Round of Golf
Armour's course-management tome is a great read. And let's be honest, Hogan lecturing on "pronation" and "supination" is more anal than analytical.
Out of the Bunker vs. Little Red Book
Subtitled "The Secret of High Tension Golf," Lardner's parody is the Spinal Tap of golf books. Humor always triumphs in golf, even against one of the most earnest, sincere, well-written golf instructionals of all time.
Dogged Victims
Out of the Bunker
Dogged Victims
The Bogey Man
A Round of Golf
Out of the Bunker
Dogged Victims
Who's Your Caddy?
The Bogey Man
To the Linksland
Five Lessons
A Round of Golf
Out of the Bunker
Little Red Book
The Dogged Victims of Inexorable Fate
by Dan Jenkins (1970)
Pro: Frank Beard on the Golf Tour
with Dick Schaap (1970)
Bud, Sweat, and Tees
by Alan Shipnuck (2001)
Who's Your Caddy?
by Rick Reilly (2003)
The Bogey Man
by George Plimpton (1968)
The Confidential Guide to Golf Courses
by Tom Doak (1996)
To the Linksland
by Michael Bamberger (1992)
Golf Dreams
by John Updike (1996)
Five Lessons
by Ben Hogan (1957)
Dave Pelz's Short Game Bible
by Dave Pelz (1999)
A Round of Golf with Tommy Armour
by Tommy Armour (1959)
Golf My Way
by Jack Nicklaus (1974)
Bobby Jones on Golf
by Robert Tyre Jones (1966)
Out of the Bunker and Into the Trees
by Rex Lardner (1960)
Harvey Penick's Little Red Book
by Harvey Penick with Bud Shrake (1992)
The Golf Swing
by David Leadbetter (2001)
RICK REILLY
WHO'S YOUR CADDY?
P.G. WODEHOUSE
The GOLF OMNIBUS
Thirty One Humorous Tales from the Green by the Master of Comic Fiction
A NASTY BIT OF ROUGH
DAVID FEHERTY
DAN JENKINS
The Dogged Victims of Inexorable Fate
A LOVE-HATE CELEBRATION OF GOLFERS AND THEIR GAME
BEN HOGAN'S
FIVE LESSONS
The Modern Fundamentals of Golf

New York Athletes

By George Vecsey

George Vecsey has been in journalism since the late 1950s, covering high schools for *Newsday* and later the World Cup of soccer, his favorite event, for the *New York Times.* He moved away from New York for a few years and found himself critically homesick.

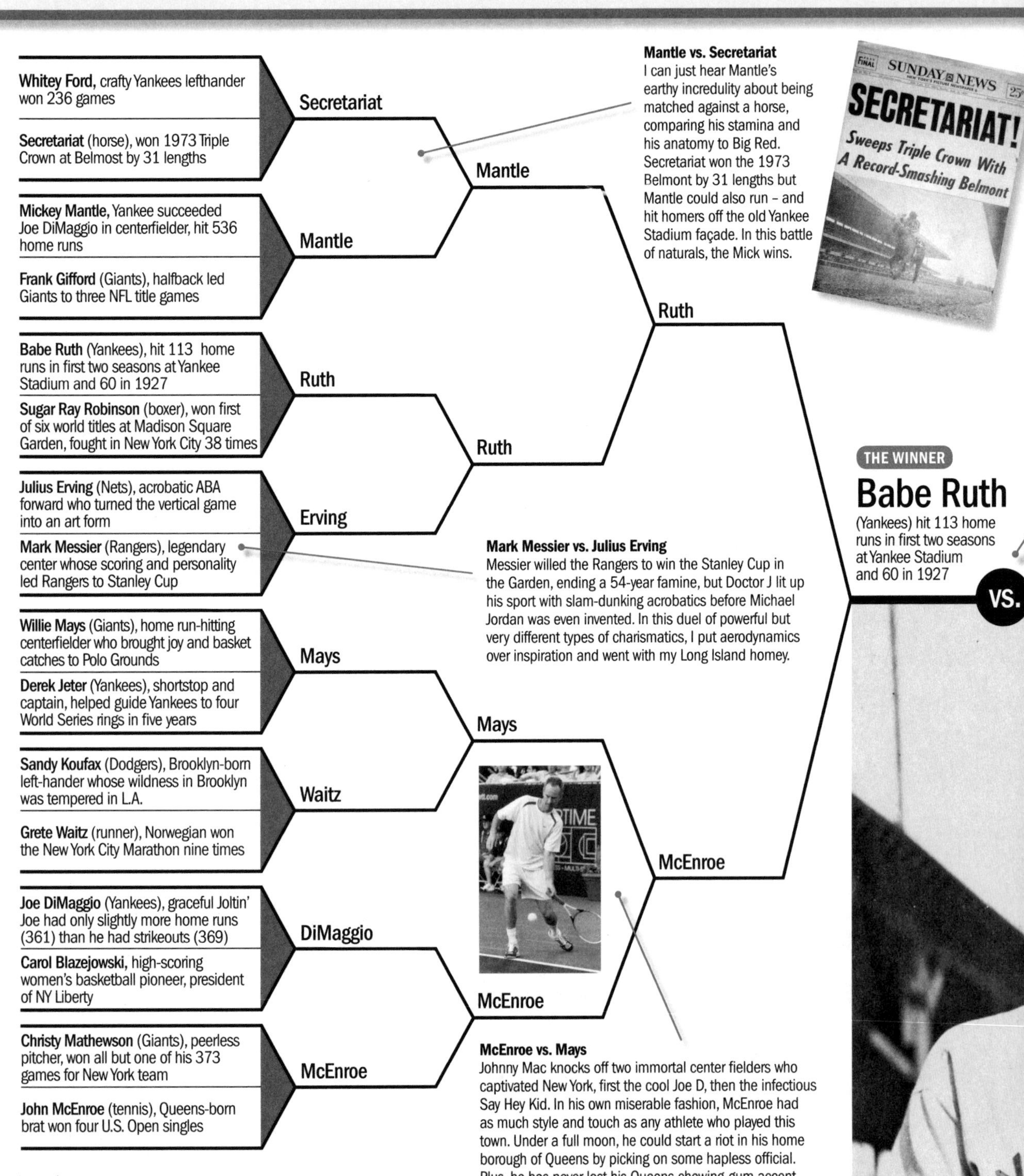

Whitey Ford, crafty Yankees lefthander won 236 games
Secretariat (horse), won 1973 Triple Crown at Belmost by 31 lengths
Mickey Mantle, Yankee succeeded Joe DiMaggio in centerfielder, hit 536 home runs
Frank Gifford (Giants), halfback led Giants to three NFL title games
Babe Ruth (Yankees), hit 113 home runs in first two seasons at Yankee Stadium and 60 in 1927
Sugar Ray Robinson (boxer), won first of six world titles at Madison Square Garden, fought in New York City 38 times
Julius Erving (Nets), acrobatic ABA forward who turned the vertical game into an art form
Mark Messier (Rangers), legendary center whose scoring and personality led Rangers to Stanley Cup
Willie Mays (Giants), home run-hitting centerfielder who brought joy and basket catches to Polo Grounds
Derek Jeter (Yankees), shortstop and captain, helped guide Yankees to four World Series rings in five years
Sandy Koufax (Dodgers), Brooklyn-born left-hander whose wildness in Brooklyn was tempered in L.A.
Grete Waitz (runner), Norwegian won the New York City Marathon nine times
Joe DiMaggio (Yankees), graceful Joltin' Joe had only slightly more home runs (361) than he had strikeouts (369)
Carol Blazejowski, high-scoring women's basketball pioneer, president of NY Liberty
Christy Mathewson (Giants), peerless pitcher, won all but one of his 373 games for New York team
John McEnroe (tennis), Queens-born brat won four U.S. Open singles
Secretariat
Mantle
Ruth
Erving
Mays
Waitz
DiMaggio
McEnroe
Mantle
Ruth
Mays
McEnroe
Ruth
McEnroe
SUNDAY NEWS
25¢
SECRETARIAT!
Sweeps Triple Crown With A Record-Smashing Belmont
THE WINNER
Babe Ruth
(Yankees) hit 113 home runs in first two seasons at Yankee Stadium and 60 in 1927
VS.

Mantle vs. Secretariat

I can just hear Mantle's earthy incredulity about being matched against a horse, comparing his stamina and his anatomy to Big Red. Secretariat won the 1973 Belmont by 31 lengths but Mantle could also run – and hit homers off the old Yankee Stadium façade. In this battle of naturals, the Mick wins.

Mark Messier vs. Julius Erving

Messier willed the Rangers to win the Stanley Cup in the Garden, ending a 54-year famine, but Doctor J lit up his sport with slam-dunking acrobatics before Michael Jordan was even invented. In this duel of powerful but very different types of charismatics, I put aerodynamics over inspiration and went with my Long Island homey.

McEnroe vs. Mays

Johnny Mac knocks off two immortal center fielders who captivated New York, first the cool Joe D, then the infectious Say Hey Kid. In his own miserable fashion, McEnroe had as much style and touch as any athlete who played this town. Under a full moon, he could start a riot in his home borough of Queens by picking on some hapless official. Plus, he has never lost his Queens chewing-gum accent.

WE NEW YORKERS BELIEVE WE ARE THE CENTER OF THE UNIVERSE and that everything comes to us, including superstar athletes. (We don't believe it; it's true.) I give style points to New York natives, New York residents, New York accents, New York noses, and New York attitude – athletes who could handle the fickle crowds, shrug off the media jokers, and in general, got it and thrived. I know, I know, I left off your favorite athlete. Stop hocking me! It's the Big City. It's got tough brackets, too.

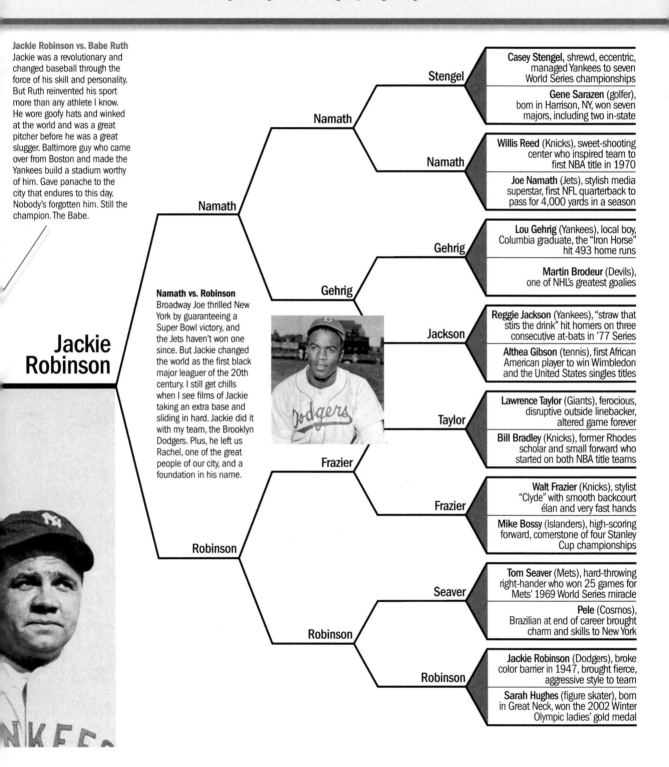

Jackie Robinson vs. Babe Ruth
Jackie was a revolutionary and changed baseball through the force of his skill and personality. But Ruth reinvented his sport more than any athlete I know. He wore goofy hats and winked at the world and was a great pitcher before he was a great slugger. Baltimore guy who came over from Boston and made the Yankees build a stadium worthy of him. Gave panache to the city that endures to this day. Nobody's forgotten him. Still the champion. The Babe.

Casey Stengel, shrewd, eccentric, managed Yankees to seven World Series championships

Gene Sarazen (golfer), born in Harrison, NY, won seven majors, including two in-state

Stengel

Willis Reed (Knicks), sweet-shooting center who inspired team to first NBA title in 1970

Joe Namath (Jets), stylish media superstar, first NFL quarterback to pass for 4,000 yards in a season

Namath

Namath

Lou Gehrig (Yankees), local boy, Columbia graduate, the "Iron Horse" hit 493 home runs

Martin Brodeur (Devils), one of NHL's greatest goalies

Gehrig

Reggie Jackson (Yankees), "straw that stirs the drink" hit homers on three consecutive at-bats in '77 Series

Althea Gibson (tennis), first African American player to win Wimbledon and the United States singles titles

Jackson

Gehrig

Namath

Lawrence Taylor (Giants), ferocious, disruptive outside linebacker, altered game forever

Bill Bradley (Knicks), former Rhodes scholar and small forward who started on both NBA title teams

Taylor

Walt Frazier (Knicks), stylist "Clyde" with smooth backcourt élan and very fast hands

Mike Bossy (Islanders), high-scoring forward, cornerstone of four Stanley Cup championships

Frazier

Frazier

Tom Seaver (Mets), hard-throwing right-hander who won 25 games for Mets' 1969 World Series miracle

Pele (Cosmos), Brazilian at end of career brought charm and skills to New York

Seaver

Jackie Robinson (Dodgers), broke color barrier in 1947, brought fierce, aggressive style to team

Sarah Hughes (figure skater), born in Great Neck, won the 2002 Winter Olympic ladies' gold medal

Robinson

Robinson

Robinson

Namath vs. Robinson
Broadway Joe thrilled New York by guaranteeing a Super Bowl victory, and the Jets haven't won one since. But Jackie changed the world as the first black major leaguer of the 20th century. I still get chills when I see films of Jackie taking an extra base and sliding in hard. Jackie did it with my team, the Brooklyn Dodgers. Plus, he left us Rachel, one of the great people of our city, and a foundation in his name.

Jackie Robinson

Boston Athletes

By Dan Shaughnessy

Dan Shaughnessy, a sports columnist for the *Boston Globe,* was born in Groton and lives in Newton, Massachusetts. He has written 11 books, including *The Curse of the Bambino* and *Senior Year: A Father, a Son, and High School Baseball.*

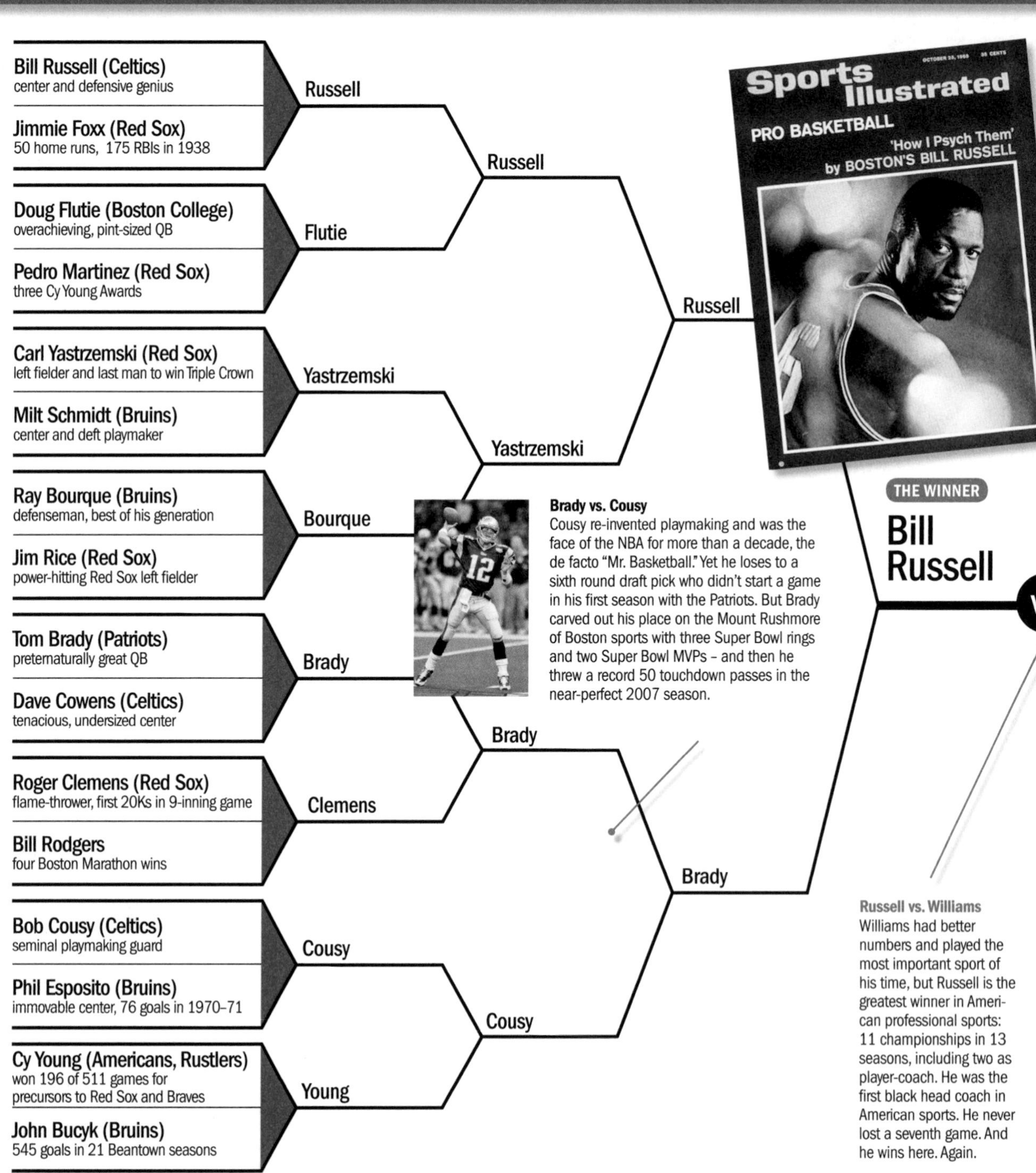

Bill Russell (Celtics)
center and defensive genius
Jimmie Foxx (Red Sox)
50 home runs, 175 RBIs in 1938
Doug Flutie (Boston College)
overachieving, pint-sized QB
Pedro Martinez (Red Sox)
three Cy Young Awards
Carl Yastrzemski (Red Sox)
left fielder and last man to win Triple Crown
Milt Schmidt (Bruins)
center and deft playmaker
Ray Bourque (Bruins)
defenseman, best of his generation
Jim Rice (Red Sox)
power-hitting Red Sox left fielder
Tom Brady (Patriots)
preternaturally great QB
Dave Cowens (Celtics)
tenacious, undersized center
Roger Clemens (Red Sox)
flame-thrower, first 20Ks in 9-inning game
Bill Rodgers
four Boston Marathon wins
Bob Cousy (Celtics)
seminal playmaking guard
Phil Esposito (Bruins)
immovable center, 76 goals in 1970–71
Cy Young (Americans, Rustlers)
won 196 of 511 games for precursors to Red Sox and Braves
John Bucyk (Bruins)
545 goals in 21 Beantown seasons
Russell
Flutie
Yastrzemski
Bourque
Brady
Clemens
Cousy
Young
Russell
Yastrzemski
Brady
Cousy
Russell
Brady
Sports Illustrated
PRO BASKETBALL
'How I Psych Them'
by BOSTON'S BILL RUSSELL
THE WINNER
Bill Russell
VS.

Brady vs. Cousy
Cousy re-invented playmaking and was the face of the NBA for more than a decade, the de facto "Mr. Basketball." Yet he loses to a sixth round draft pick who didn't start a game in his first season with the Patriots. But Brady carved out his place on the Mount Rushmore of Boston sports with three Super Bowl rings and two Super Bowl MVPs – and then he threw a record 50 touchdown passes in the near-perfect 2007 season.

Russell vs. Williams
Williams had better numbers and played the most important sport of his time, but Russell is the greatest winner in American professional sports: 11 championships in 13 seasons, including two as player-coach. He was the first black head coach in American sports. He never lost a seventh game. And he wins here. Again.

IN A CITY BLESSED WITH FOUR PROFESSIONAL TEAMS, multiple colleges and individual greats in road-running and boxing, the best in Boston are judged by heart, championships, and the love of the fans. It's not always about stats, which is why Tony Conigliaro and Harry Agganis, whose baseball careers (and lives) were far too short, make this roster over another Red Sox player, Dwight Evans, with better numbers and longer service. It didn't take the Red Sox' and Patriots' recent titles to pack this bracket – only one 21st century player, Patriots quarterback Tom Brady, is here, for his early, astonishing accomplishments.

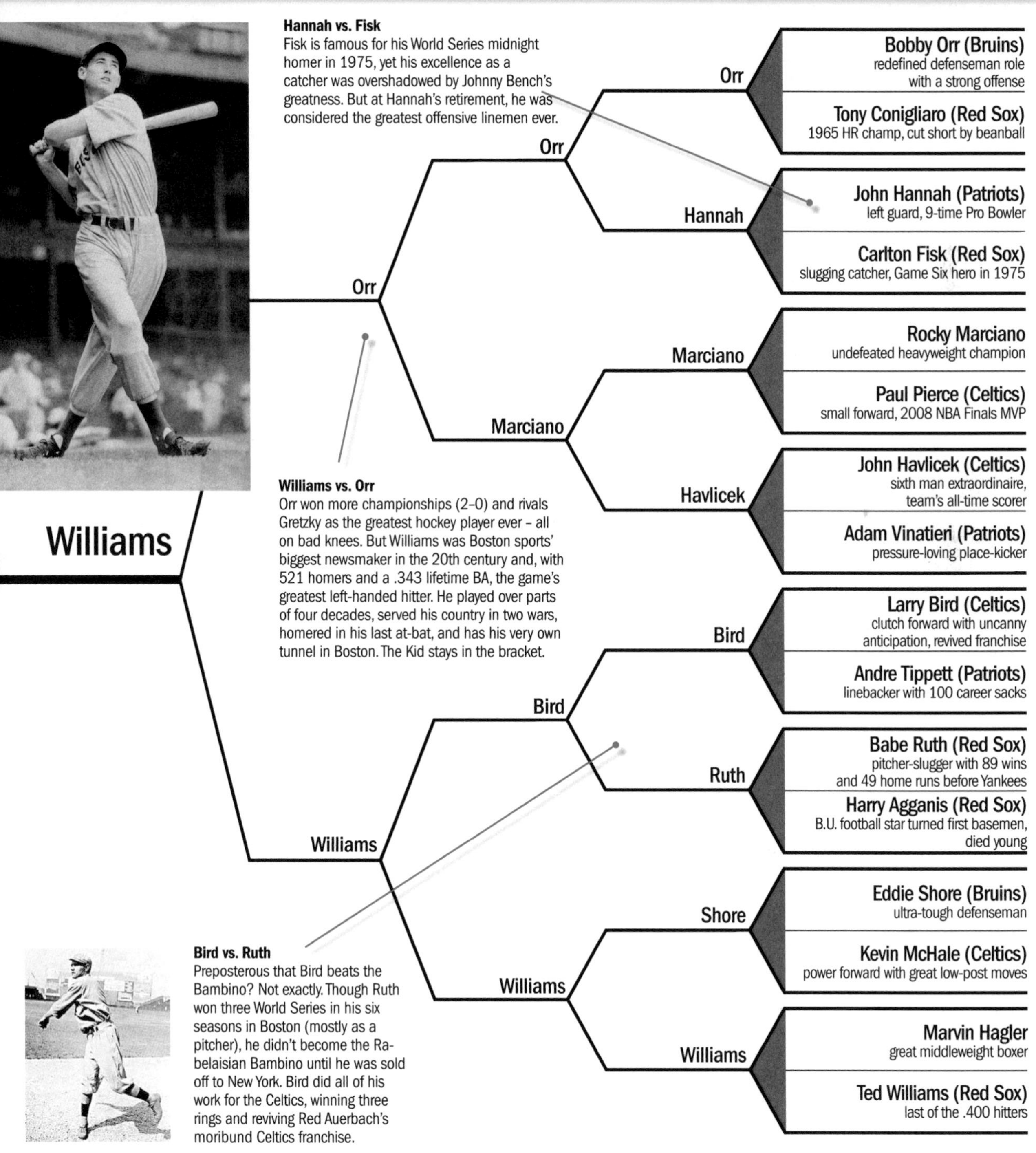
Bobby Orr (Bruins)
redefined defenseman role with a strong offense
Tony Conigliaro (Red Sox)
1965 HR champ, cut short by beanball
John Hannah (Patriots)
left guard, 9-time Pro Bowler
Carlton Fisk (Red Sox)
slugging catcher, Game Six hero in 1975
Rocky Marciano
undefeated heavyweight champion
Paul Pierce (Celtics)
small forward, 2008 NBA Finals MVP
John Havlicek (Celtics)
sixth man extraordinaire, team's all-time scorer
Adam Vinatieri (Patriots)
pressure-loving place-kicker
Larry Bird (Celtics)
clutch forward with uncanny anticipation, revived franchise
Andre Tippett (Patriots)
linebacker with 100 career sacks
Babe Ruth (Red Sox)
pitcher-slugger with 89 wins and 49 home runs before Yankees
Harry Agganis (Red Sox)
B.U. football star turned first basemen, died young
Eddie Shore (Bruins)
ultra-tough defenseman
Kevin McHale (Celtics)
power forward with great low-post moves
Marvin Hagler
great middleweight boxer
Ted Williams (Red Sox)
last of the .400 hitters
Orr
Hannah
Marciano
Havlicek
Bird
Ruth
Shore
Williams
Orr
Marciano
Bird
Williams
Orr
Williams
Williams

Hannah vs. Fisk

Fisk is famous for his World Series midnight homer in 1975, yet his excellence as a catcher was overshadowed by Johnny Bench's greatness. But at Hannah's retirement, he was considered the greatest offensive linemen ever.

Williams vs. Orr

Orr won more championships (2–0) and rivals Gretzky as the greatest hockey player ever – all on bad knees. But Williams was Boston sports' biggest newsmaker in the 20th century and, with 521 homers and a .343 lifetime BA, the game's greatest left-handed hitter. He played over parts of four decades, served his country in two wars, homered in his last at-bat, and has his very own tunnel in Boston. The Kid stays in the bracket.

Bird vs. Ruth

Preposterous that Bird beats the Bambino? Not exactly. Though Ruth won three World Series in his six seasons in Boston (mostly as a pitcher), he didn't become the Rabelaisian Bambino until he was sold off to New York. Bird did all of his work for the Celtics, winning three rings and reviving Red Auerbach's moribund Celtics franchise.

Sportswriters

By Glenn Stout

Glenn Stout has been series editor of *The Best American Sports Writing* series since its inception in 1991. Since he probably reads more sportswriting than anyone else on the planet, he is eternally grateful that so much of it is good, and occasionally great.

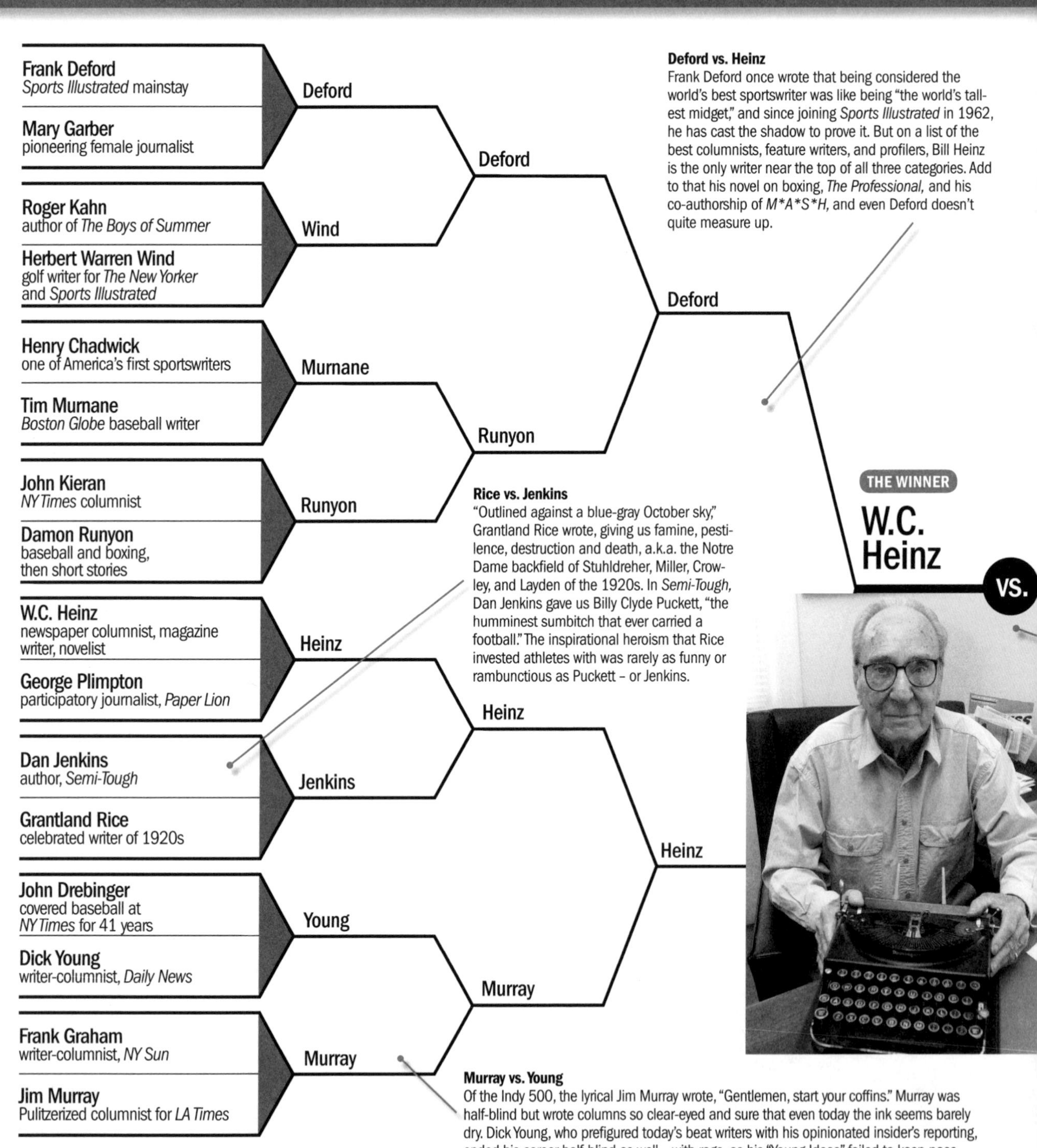
Frank Deford
Sports Illustrated mainstay
Mary Garber
pioneering female journalist
Roger Kahn
author of The Boys of Summer
Herbert Warren Wind
golf writer for The New Yorker and Sports Illustrated
Henry Chadwick
one of America's first sportswriters
Tim Murnane
Boston Globe baseball writer
John Kieran
NY Times columnist
Damon Runyon
baseball and boxing, then short stories
W.C. Heinz
newspaper columnist, magazine writer, novelist
George Plimpton
participatory journalist, Paper Lion
Dan Jenkins
author, Semi-Tough
Grantland Rice
celebrated writer of 1920s
John Drebinger
covered baseball at NY Times for 41 years
Dick Young
writer-columnist, Daily News
Frank Graham
writer-columnist, NY Sun
Jim Murray
Pulitzerized columnist for LA Times
Deford
Wind
Murnane
Runyon
Heinz
Jenkins
Young
Murray
Deford
Runyon
Heinz
Murray
Deford
Heinz
THE WINNER
W.C. Heinz
VS.

Deford vs. Heinz
Frank Deford once wrote that being considered the world's best sportswriter was like being "the world's tallest midget," and since joining *Sports Illustrated* in 1962, he has cast the shadow to prove it. But on a list of the best columnists, feature writers, and profilers, Bill Heinz is the only writer near the top of all three categories. Add to that his novel on boxing, *The Professional,* and his co-authorship of *M*A*S*H,* and even Deford doesn't quite measure up.

Rice vs. Jenkins
"Outlined against a blue-gray October sky," Grantland Rice wrote, giving us famine, pestilence, destruction and death, a.k.a. the Notre Dame backfield of Stuhldreher, Miller, Crowley, and Layden of the 1920s. In *Semi-Tough,* Dan Jenkins gave us Billy Clyde Puckett, "the humminest sumbitch that ever carried a football." The inspirational heroism that Rice invested athletes with was rarely as funny or rambunctious as Puckett – or Jenkins.

Murray vs. Young
Of the Indy 500, the lyrical Jim Murray wrote, "Gentlemen, start your coffins." Murray was half-blind but wrote columns so clear-eyed and sure that even today the ink seems barely dry. Dick Young, who prefigured today's beat writers with his opinionated insider's reporting, ended his career half-blind as well – with rage, as his "Young Ideas" failed to keep pace.

SPORTSWRITERS TODAY stand in the shadow of these 32 giants, nearly all of them writers of yesteryear. Some were pioneers, some were innovators, and some are and were first-rate stylists who never recognized the limitations of the genre. They all loved writing more than they loved sports, and combined curiosity, first-rate reporting, research, a good grasp of the fundamentals of the language, and, oh, a little music, an attentive ear, some empathy, and intelligence.

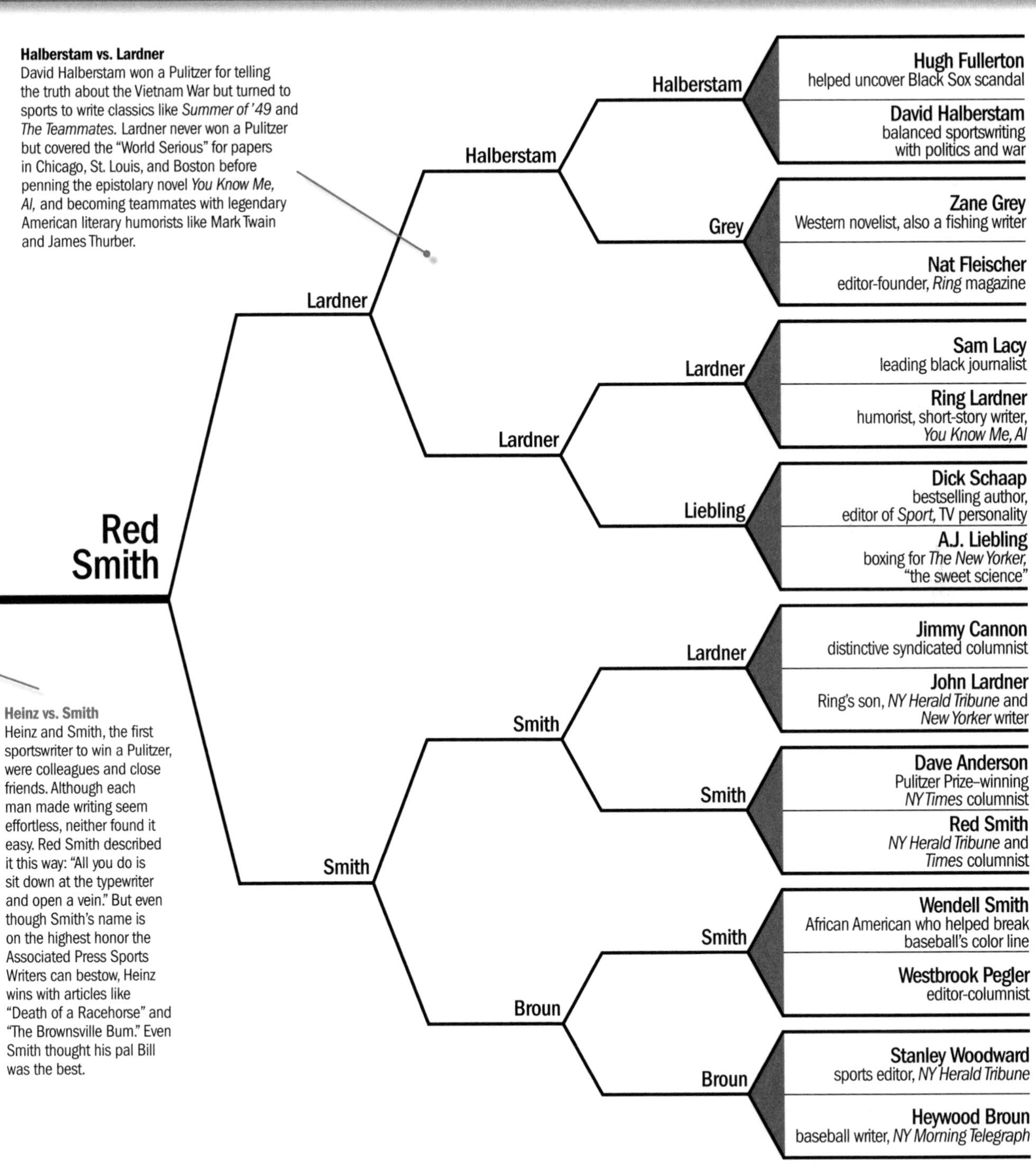

Hugh Fullerton
helped uncover Black Sox scandal
David Halberstam
balanced sportswriting with politics and war
Zane Grey
Western novelist, also a fishing writer
Nat Fleischer
editor-founder, Ring magazine
Sam Lacy
leading black journalist
Ring Lardner
humorist, short-story writer, You Know Me, Al
Dick Schaap
bestselling author, editor of Sport, TV personality
A.J. Liebling
boxing for The New Yorker, "the sweet science"
Jimmy Cannon
distinctive syndicated columnist
John Lardner
Ring's son, NY Herald Tribune and New Yorker writer
Dave Anderson
Pulitzer Prize–winning NY Times columnist
Red Smith
NY Herald Tribune and Times columnist
Wendell Smith
African American who helped break baseball's color line
Westbrook Pegler
editor-columnist
Stanley Woodward
sports editor, NY Herald Tribune
Heywood Broun
baseball writer, NY Morning Telegraph
Halberstam
Grey
Lardner
Liebling
Lardner
Smith
Smith
Broun
Halberstam
Lardner
Smith
Broun
Lardner
Smith
Red Smith

Halberstam vs. Lardner
David Halberstam won a Pulitzer for telling the truth about the Vietnam War but turned to sports to write classics like *Summer of '49* and *The Teammates.* Lardner never won a Pulitzer but covered the "World Serious" for papers in Chicago, St. Louis, and Boston before penning the epistolary novel *You Know Me, Al,* and becoming teammates with legendary American literary humorists like Mark Twain and James Thurber.

Heinz vs. Smith
Heinz and Smith, the first sportswriter to win a Pulitzer, were colleagues and close friends. Although each man made writing seem effortless, neither found it easy. Red Smith described it this way: "All you do is sit down at the typewriter and open a vein." But even though Smith's name is on the highest honor the Associated Press Sports Writers can bestow, Heinz wins with articles like "Death of a Racehorse" and "The Brownsville Bum." Even Smith thought his pal Bill was the best.

Advertising Icons

By Bryan Curtis

Bryan Curtis was a columnist at *Play: The New York Times Sports Magazine*, for its (too) short, (ludicrously) happy life. He is now a senior editor at *The Daily Beast*.

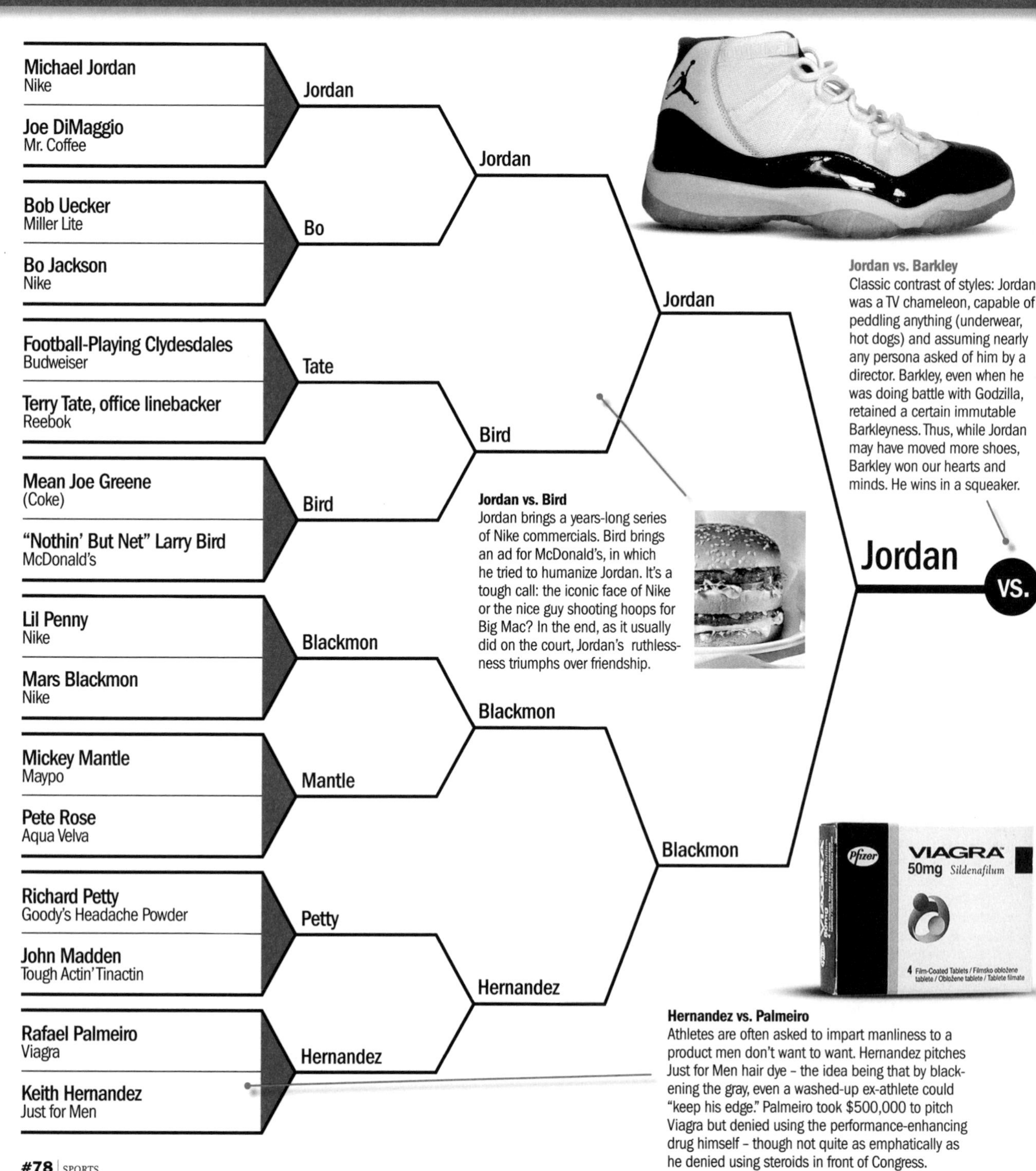
Michael Jordan
Nike
Joe DiMaggio
Mr. Coffee
Bob Uecker
Miller Lite
Bo Jackson
Nike
Football-Playing Clydesdales
Budweiser
Terry Tate, office linebacker
Reebok
Mean Joe Greene
(Coke)
"Nothin' But Net" Larry Bird
McDonald's
Lil Penny
Nike
Mars Blackmon
Nike
Mickey Mantle
Maypo
Pete Rose
Aqua Velva
Richard Petty
Goody's Headache Powder
John Madden
Tough Actin' Tinactin
Rafael Palmeiro
Viagra
Keith Hernandez
Just for Men
Jordan
Bo
Tate
Bird
Blackmon
Mantle
Petty
Hernandez
Jordan
Bird
Blackmon
Hernandez
Jordan
Blackmon
Jordan
VS.
Pfizer
VIAGRA
50mg Sildenafilum
4 Film-Coated Tablets / Filmsko obložene tablete / Obložene tablete / Tablete filmate

Jordan vs. Bird
Jordan brings a years-long series of Nike commercials. Bird brings an ad for McDonald's, in which he tried to humanize Jordan. It's a tough call: the iconic face of Nike or the nice guy shooting hoops for Big Mac? In the end, as it usually did on the court, Jordan's ruthlessness triumphs over friendship.

Jordan vs. Barkley
Classic contrast of styles: Jordan was a TV chameleon, capable of peddling anything (underwear, hot dogs) and assuming nearly any persona asked of him by a director. Barkley, even when he was doing battle with Godzilla, retained a certain immutable Barkleyness. Thus, while Jordan may have moved more shoes, Barkley won our hearts and minds. He wins in a squeaker.

Hernandez vs. Palmeiro
Athletes are often asked to impart manliness to a product men don't want to want. Hernandez pitches Just for Men hair dye – the idea being that by blackening the gray, even a washed-up ex-athlete could "keep his edge." Palmeiro took $500,000 to pitch Viagra but denied using the performance-enhancing drug himself – though not quite as emphatically as he denied using steroids in front of Congress.

AS FORMER BALTIMORE ORIOLE BOOG POWELL ONCE PUT IT, "You make one Miller Lite commercial, it's like then everyone forgets you played ball for 20 years." Indeed, sports advertising has taken jocks known for their jump shots and made them into catchphrase dispensers ("Tastes great!" "I'm going to Disney World!"). But not all athlete-pitchmen are created equally. Some slip into their product as comfortably as Hanes briefs, while others look positively mortified. Only a jock who truly embodies his product can make it to the top.

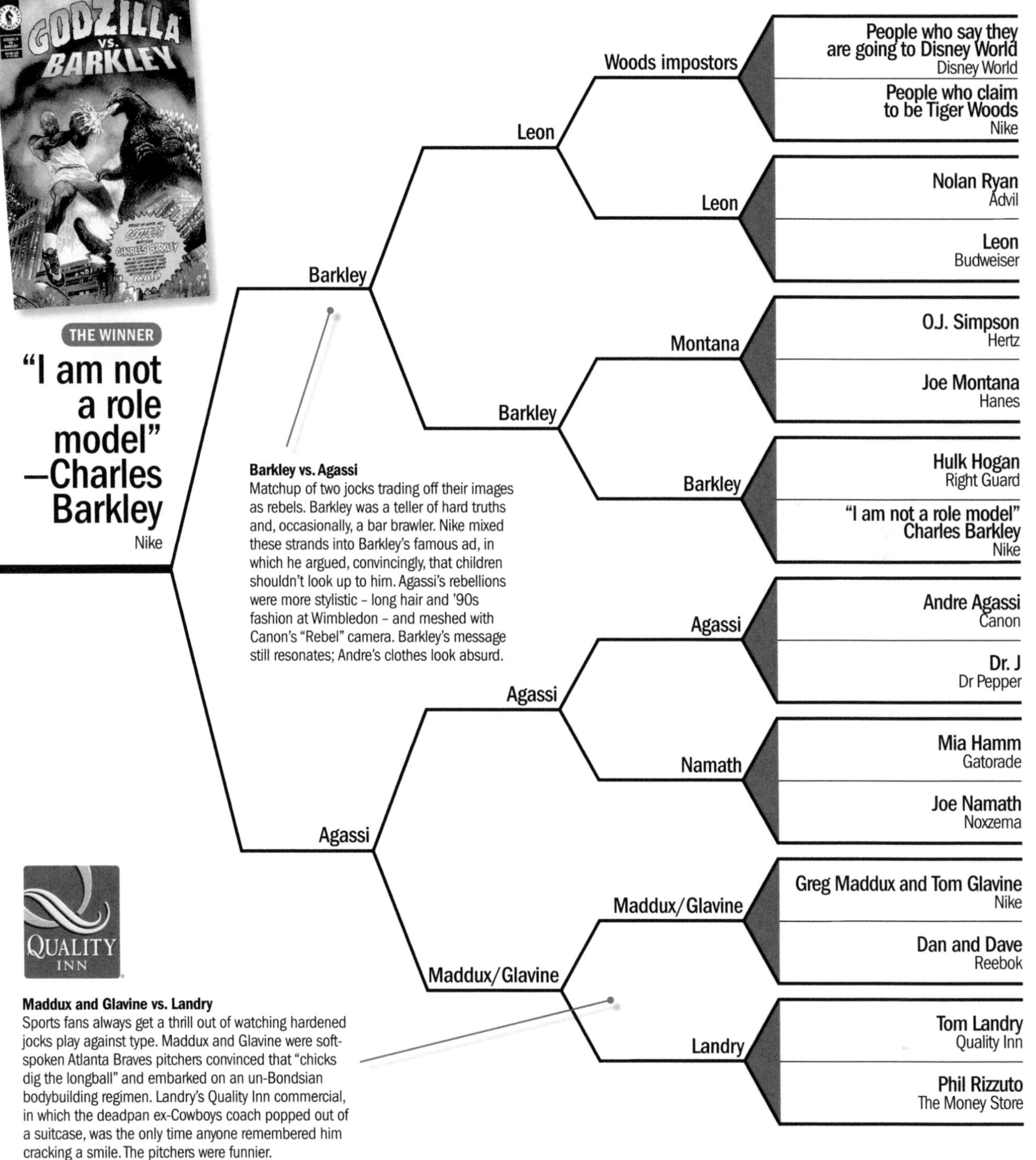

GODZILLA VS. BARKLEY
THE WINNER
"I am not a role model" —Charles Barkley
Nike
Barkley
Agassi
Leon
Barkley
Agassi
Maddux/Glavine
Woods impostors
Leon
Montana
Barkley
Agassi
Namath
Maddux/Glavine
Landry
People who say they are going to Disney World
Disney World
People who claim to be Tiger Woods
Nike
Nolan Ryan
Advil
Leon
Budweiser
O.J. Simpson
Hertz
Joe Montana
Hanes
Hulk Hogan
Right Guard
"I am not a role model" Charles Barkley
Nike
Andre Agassi
Canon
Dr. J
Dr Pepper
Mia Hamm
Gatorade
Joe Namath
Noxzema
Greg Maddux and Tom Glavine
Nike
Dan and Dave
Reebok
Tom Landry
Quality Inn
Phil Rizzuto
The Money Store
QUALITY INN

Barkley vs. Agassi
Matchup of two jocks trading off their images as rebels. Barkley was a teller of hard truths and, occasionally, a bar brawler. Nike mixed these strands into Barkley's famous ad, in which he argued, convincingly, that children shouldn't look up to him. Agassi's rebellions were more stylistic – long hair and '90s fashion at Wimbledon – and meshed with Canon's "Rebel" camera. Barkley's message still resonates; Andre's clothes look absurd.

Maddux and Glavine vs. Landry
Sports fans always get a thrill out of watching hardened jocks play against type. Maddux and Glavine were soft-spoken Atlanta Braves pitchers convinced that "chicks dig the longball" and embarked on an un-Bondsian bodybuilding regimen. Landry's Quality Inn commercial, in which the deadpan ex-Cowboys coach popped out of a suitcase, was the only time anyone remembered him cracking a smile. The pitchers were funnier.

Greatest Sports Year

By Mike Vaccaro

Mike Vaccaro, sports columnist for the *New York Post*, is author of *Emperors and Idiots*, a narrative history of the Yankees-Red Sox rivalry, plus another book whose title gives this bracket away.

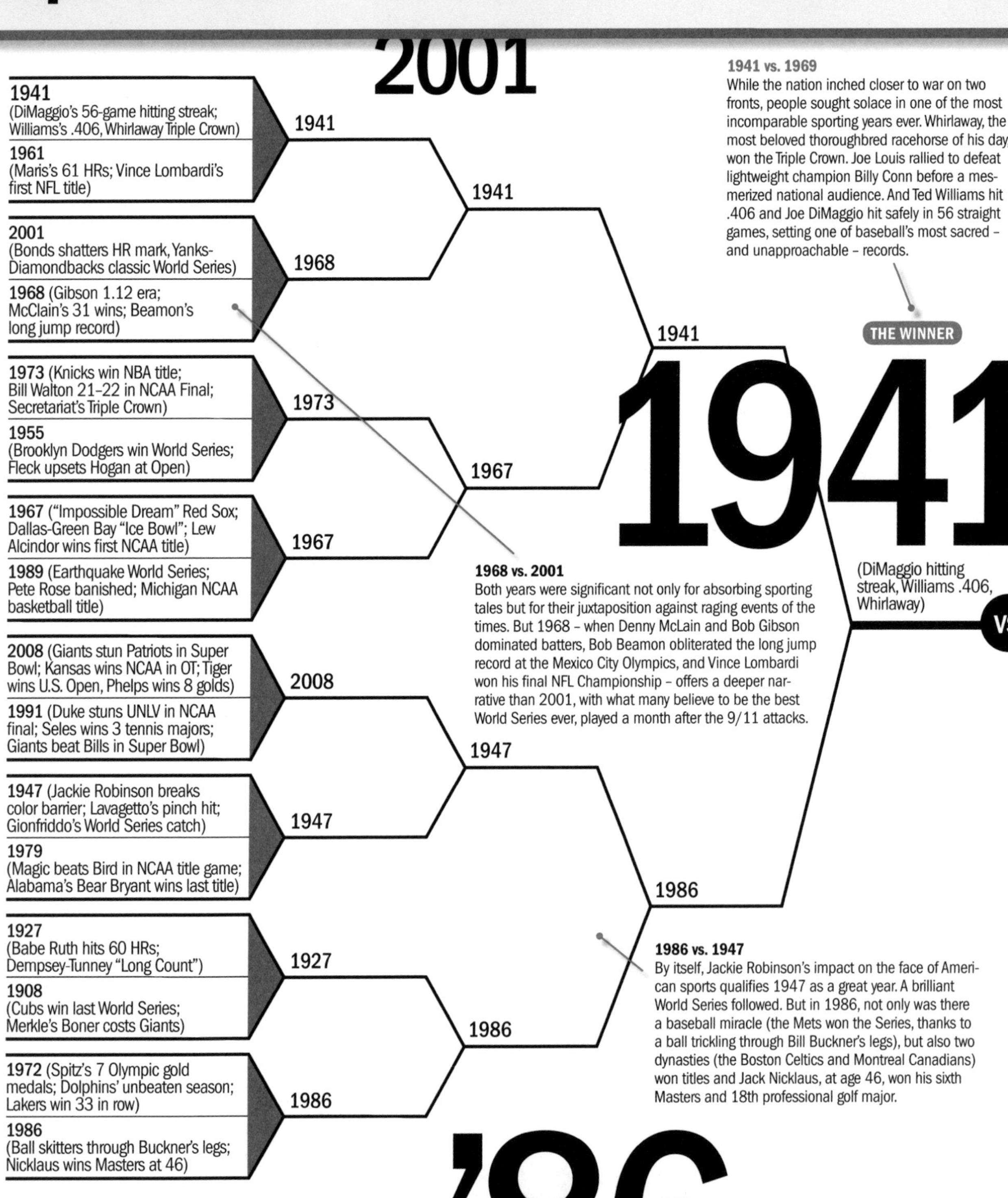

2001
1941
(DiMaggio's 56-game hitting streak; Williams's .406, Whirlaway Triple Crown)
1961
(Maris's 61 HRs; Vince Lombardi's first NFL title)
2001
(Bonds shatters HR mark, Yanks-Diamondbacks classic World Series)
1968 (Gibson 1.12 era; McClain's 31 wins; Beamon's long jump record)
1973 (Knicks win NBA title; Bill Walton 21-22 in NCAA Final; Secretariat's Triple Crown)
1955
(Brooklyn Dodgers win World Series; Fleck upsets Hogan at Open)
1967 ("Impossible Dream" Red Sox; Dallas-Green Bay "Ice Bowl"; Lew Alcindor wins first NCAA title)
1989 (Earthquake World Series; Pete Rose banished; Michigan NCAA basketball title)
2008 (Giants stun Patriots in Super Bowl; Kansas wins NCAA in OT; Tiger wins U.S. Open, Phelps wins 8 golds)
1991 (Duke stuns UNLV in NCAA final; Seles wins 3 tennis majors; Giants beat Bills in Super Bowl)
1947 (Jackie Robinson breaks color barrier; Lavagetto's pinch hit; Gionfriddo's World Series catch)
1979
(Magic beats Bird in NCAA title game; Alabama's Bear Bryant wins last title)
1927
(Babe Ruth hits 60 HRs; Dempsey-Tunney "Long Count")
1908
(Cubs win last World Series; Merkle's Boner costs Giants)
1972 (Spitz's 7 Olympic gold medals; Dolphins' unbeaten season; Lakers win 33 in row)
1986
(Ball skitters through Buckner's legs; Nicklaus wins Masters at 46)
1941
1968
1973
1967
2008
1947
1927
1986
1941
1967
1947
1986
1941
1986
THE WINNER
1941
(DiMaggio hitting streak, Williams .406, Whirlaway)
VS.
'86

1941 vs. 1969

While the nation inched closer to war on two fronts, people sought solace in one of the most incomparable sporting years ever. Whirlaway, the most beloved thoroughbred racehorse of his day, won the Triple Crown. Joe Louis rallied to defeat lightweight champion Billy Conn before a mesmerized national audience. And Ted Williams hit .406 and Joe DiMaggio hit safely in 56 straight games, setting one of baseball's most sacred – and unapproachable – records.

1968 vs. 2001

Both years were significant not only for absorbing sporting tales but for their juxtaposition against raging events of the times. But 1968 – when Denny McLain and Bob Gibson dominated batters, Bob Beamon obliterated the long jump record at the Mexico City Olympics, and Vince Lombardi won his final NFL Championship – offers a deeper narrative than 2001, with what many believe to be the best World Series ever, played a month after the 9/11 attacks.

1986 vs. 1947

By itself, Jackie Robinson's impact on the face of American sports qualifies 1947 as a great year. A brilliant World Series followed. But in 1986, not only was there a baseball miracle (the Mets won the Series, thanks to a ball trickling through Bill Buckner's legs), but also two dynasties (the Boston Celtics and Montreal Canadians) won titles and Jack Nicklaus, at age 46, won his sixth Masters and 18th professional golf major.

A GREAT SPORTS SEASON MUST ADVANCE with an almost unabated sense of drama, suspense, accomplishment, and excellence. It is helpful if great athletes perform great feats within those 12 months, but what is necessary is that the games that serve as yard markers for the 52-week grind are memorable, if not actually magical. Mostly, a great sports year makes you shake your head in wonder that so many different athletes from so many diverse sports could all leave their footprints so indelibly on that calendar year.

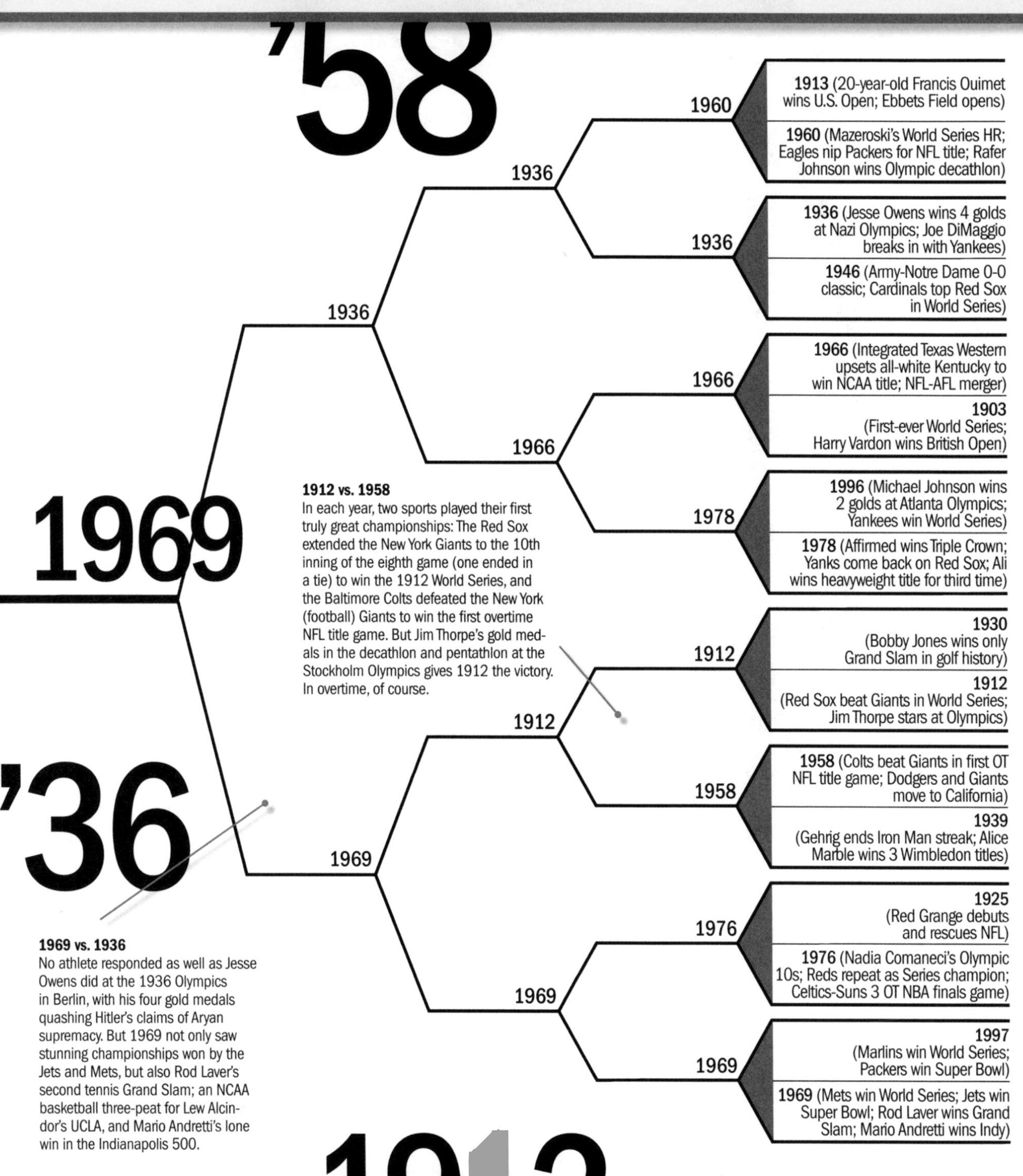

'58
1913 (20-year-old Francis Ouimet wins U.S. Open; Ebbets Field opens)
1960 (Mazeroski's World Series HR; Eagles nip Packers for NFL title; Rafer Johnson wins Olympic decathlon)
1936 (Jesse Owens wins 4 golds at Nazi Olympics; Joe DiMaggio breaks in with Yankees)
1946 (Army-Notre Dame 0-0 classic; Cardinals top Red Sox in World Series)
1966 (Integrated Texas Western upsets all-white Kentucky to win NCAA title; NFL-AFL merger)
1903 (First-ever World Series; Harry Vardon wins British Open)
1996 (Michael Johnson wins 2 golds at Atlanta Olympics; Yankees win World Series)
1978 (Affirmed wins Triple Crown; Yanks come back on Red Sox; Ali wins heavyweight title for third time)
1930 (Bobby Jones wins only Grand Slam in golf history)
1912 (Red Sox beat Giants in World Series; Jim Thorpe stars at Olympics)
1958 (Colts beat Giants in first OT NFL title game; Dodgers and Giants move to California)
1939 (Gehrig ends Iron Man streak; Alice Marble wins 3 Wimbledon titles)
1925 (Red Grange debuts and rescues NFL)
1976 (Nadia Comaneci's Olympic 10s; Reds repeat as Series champion; Celtics-Suns 3 OT NBA finals game)
1997 (Marlins win World Series; Packers win Super Bowl)
1969 (Mets win World Series; Jets win Super Bowl; Rod Laver wins Grand Slam; Mario Andretti wins Indy)
1960
1936
1936
1966
1966
1978
1936
1912
1912
1958
1969
1976
1969
1969
1969
'36
1912

1912 vs. 1958
In each year, two sports played their first truly great championships: The Red Sox extended the New York Giants to the 10th inning of the eighth game (one ended in a tie) to win the 1912 World Series, and the Baltimore Colts defeated the New York (football) Giants to win the first overtime NFL title game. But Jim Thorpe's gold medals in the decathlon and pentathlon at the Stockholm Olympics gives 1912 the victory. In overtime, of course.

1969 vs. 1936
No athlete responded as well as Jesse Owens did at the 1936 Olympics in Berlin, with his four gold medals quashing Hitler's claims of Aryan supremacy. But 1969 not only saw stunning championships won by the Jets and Mets, but also Rod Laver's second tennis Grand Slam; an NCAA basketball three-peat for Lew Alcindor's UCLA, and Mario Andretti's lone win in the Indianapolis 500.

POP CULTURE

Movie Gunfights *by Stephen Hunter* **80**
YouTube Videos *by Virginia Heffernan* **81**
Soul Songs *by John Leland* **82**
Paul Newman Roles *by Mark Reiter* **83**
Sitcom Dads *by Steven Reddicliffe* **84**
Sitcom Moms *by Richard Sandomir* **85**
Talk-Show Graveyard *by Bill Carter* **86**
Children's Books *by Jon Scieszka* **87**
Cinematic Interrogatories *by John Steinbreder* **88**
Comic Strips *by R.C. Harvey* **89**
High School Movies *by Rick Staehling* **90**
Stunt Scenes *by Kevin Conley* **91**
Impressionists *by Richard Sandomir* **92**
Literary Heroes *by B.R. Myers* **93**
Comedy Routines *by Bill Scheft* **94**
Worst Movies by Great Directors *by A.O. Scott* **95**
George Carlin Hunks *by Kelly Carlin-McCall* **96**
Cop Movies *by Lorenzo Carcaterra* **97**
Reality TV Stars *by Bob Boden* **98**
Fictional Lawyers *by Thane Rosenbaum* **99**
Good Imus vs. Evil Imus *by Richard Sandomir* **100**
Steve Earle Songs *by Mark Reiter* **101**
Most American Superhero *by Peter Coogan* **102**
Gangster Films *by Lorenzo Carcaterra* **103**
Disney Animated Films *by Richard Corliss* **104**
Honeymooners *by Peter Crescenti* **105**
You Call This Acting? *By Will Reiter* **106**
Talk Radio Hosts *by David Hinckley* **107**
Child Actors *by Griffin Miller* **108**
Detroit Celluloid *by Kevin Conley* **109**
Girl Singers *by Tom Moon* **110**
Cathartic Movie Deaths *by David Edelstein* **111**
Game-Show Hosts *by Mark Leblang* **112**
Grateful Dead Songs *by John Steinbreder* **113**
Romance Novels *by Isabel Swift* **114**
TV Catchphrases *by Robert J. Thompson* **115**
Jazz Solos *by Nick Trautwein* **116**
Romantic Comedies *by David Denby* **117**
Cats and Dogs *by Lon Tweeten* **118**
Clint Eastwood Films *by Manohla Dargis* **119**
Comedy Teams *by Robert Wuhl* **120**
Comic Book Superpowers *by Peter Coogan* **121**

Movie Gunfights

By Stephen Hunter

Stephen Hunter has written books called *American Gunfight, The Master Sniper,* and *Point of Impact* (which became the movie *Shooter*). He won a Pulitzer Prize for film criticism in 2003.

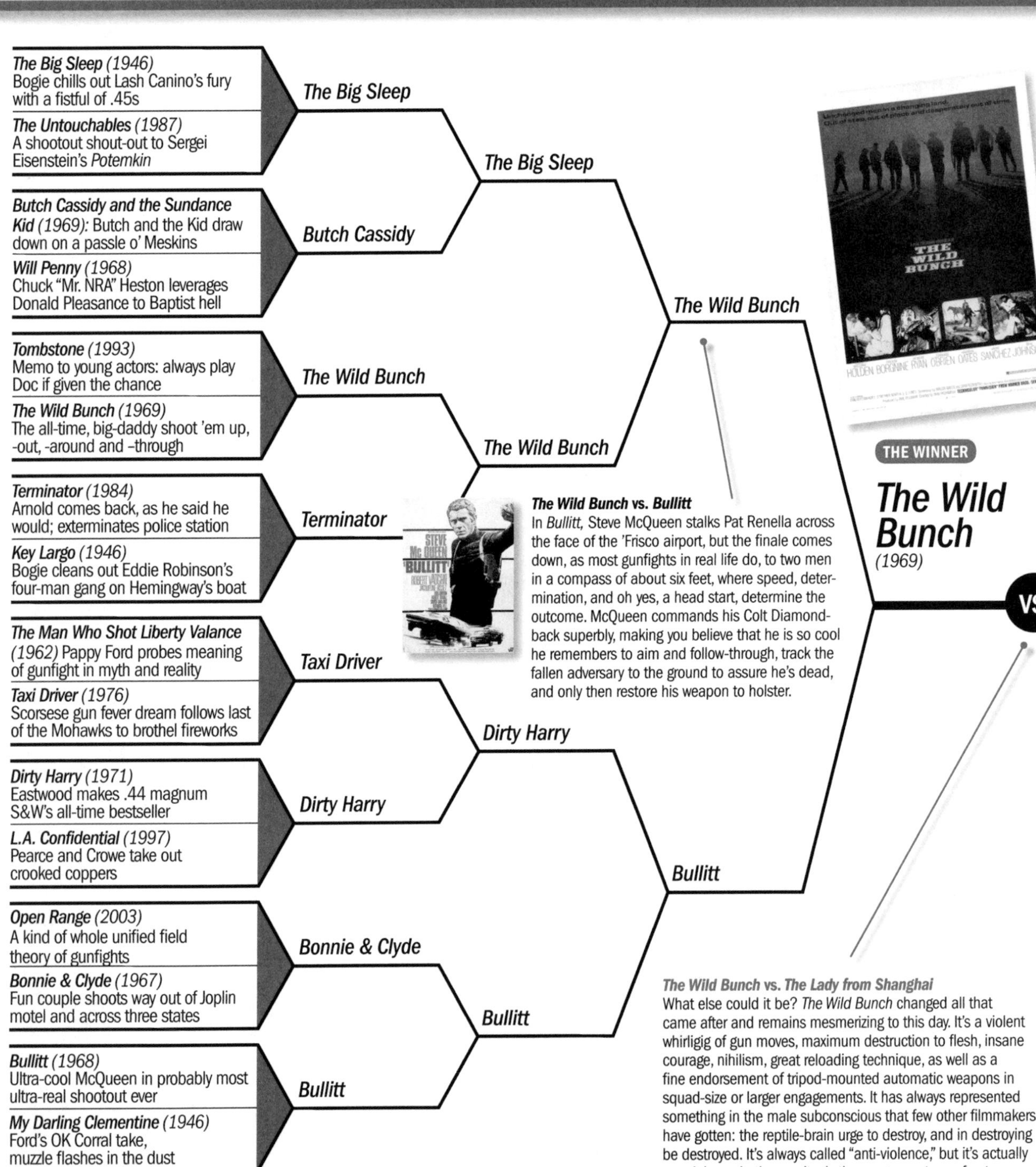

The Big Sleep (1946)
Bogie chills out Lash Canino's fury with a fistful of .45s
The Untouchables (1987)
A shootout shout-out to Sergei Eisenstein's *Potemkin*
Butch Cassidy and the Sundance Kid (1969): Butch and the Kid draw down on a passle o' Meskins
Will Penny (1968)
Chuck "Mr. NRA" Heston leverages Donald Pleasance to Baptist hell
Tombstone (1993)
Memo to young actors: always play Doc if given the chance
The Wild Bunch (1969)
The all-time, big-daddy shoot 'em up, -out, -around and -through
Terminator (1984)
Arnold comes back, as he said he would; exterminates police station
Key Largo (1946)
Bogie cleans out Eddie Robinson's four-man gang on Hemingway's boat
The Man Who Shot Liberty Valance (1962) Pappy Ford probes meaning of gunfight in myth and reality
Taxi Driver (1976)
Scorsese gun fever dream follows last of the Mohawks to brothel fireworks
Dirty Harry (1971)
Eastwood makes .44 magnum S&W's all-time bestseller
L.A. Confidential (1997)
Pearce and Crowe take out crooked coppers
Open Range (2003)
A kind of whole unified field theory of gunfights
Bonnie & Clyde (1967)
Fun couple shoots way out of Joplin motel and across three states
Bullitt (1968)
Ultra-cool McQueen in probably most ultra-real shootout ever
My Darling Clementine (1946)
Ford's OK Corral take, muzzle flashes in the dust
The Big Sleep
Butch Cassidy
The Wild Bunch
Terminator
Taxi Driver
Dirty Harry
Bonnie & Clyde
Bullitt
The Big Sleep
The Wild Bunch
Dirty Harry
Bullitt
The Wild Bunch
Bullitt
THE WILD BUNCH
HOLDEN BORGNINE RYAN O'BRIEN OATES SANCHEZ JOHNSON
STEVE McQUEEN
BULLITT
ROBERT VAUGHN
THE WINNER
The Wild Bunch (1969)
VS.

The Wild Bunch* vs. *Bullitt

In *Bullitt,* Steve McQueen stalks Pat Renella across the face of the 'Frisco airport, but the finale comes down, as most gunfights in real life do, to two men in a compass of about six feet, where speed, determination, and oh yes, a head start, determine the outcome. McQueen commands his Colt Diamondback superbly, making you believe that he is so cool he remembers to aim and follow-through, track the fallen adversary to the ground to assure he's dead, and only then restore his weapon to holster.

The Wild Bunch* vs. *The Lady from Shanghai

What else could it be? *The Wild Bunch* changed all that came after and remains mesmerizing to this day. It's a violent whirligig of gun moves, maximum destruction to flesh, insane courage, nihilism, great reloading technique, as well as a fine endorsement of tripod-mounted automatic weapons in squad-size or larger engagements. It has always represented something in the male subconscious that few other filmmakers have gotten: the reptile-brain urge to destroy, and in destroying be destroyed. It's always called "anti-violence," but it's actually pro-violence in the way its rhythms urge you to confront your own impulses. Maybe that's a good thing. Maybe not.

AMERICAN MOVIES INVENTED MEN WITH GUNS, but it sometimes seems movies are more about guns with men. Directors love lethal contests and the toys that make them lethal. The criterion here isn't realism (though some fights are realistic) or stylization (some are stylized unto abstraction), or even cool guns (though Thompsons are very cool). Originality of movement counts. No war movies, no executions, and no CGI. Just good old American gunwork, where speed and guts count as much as firepower and social authority.

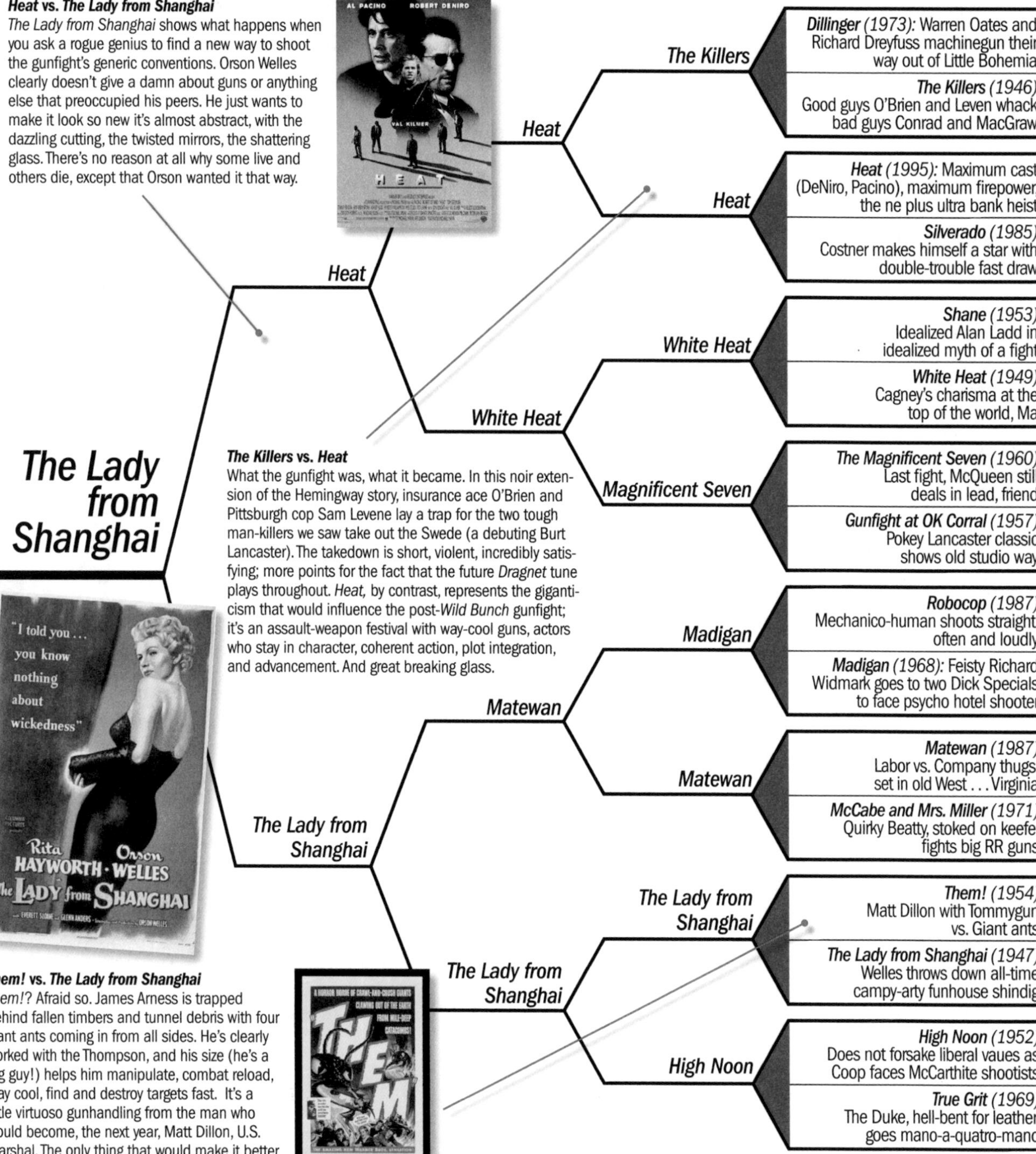

AL PACINO ROBERT DENIRO
VAL KILMER
HEAT
"I told you . . . you know nothing about wickedness"
Rita HAYWORTH · Orson WELLES
The LADY from SHANGHAI
THEM!
The Lady from Shanghai
Heat
The Lady from Shanghai
Heat
White Heat
The Killers
Heat
White Heat
Magnificent Seven
Madigan
Matewan
The Lady from Shanghai
High Noon
Matewan
The Lady from Shanghai
Dillinger (1973): Warren Oates and Richard Dreyfuss machinegun their way out of Little Bohemia
The Killers (1946) Good guys O'Brien and Leven whack bad guys Conrad and MacGraw
Heat (1995): Maximum cast (DeNiro, Pacino), maximum firepower, the ne plus ultra bank heist
Silverado (1985) Costner makes himself a star with double-trouble fast draw
Shane (1953) Idealized Alan Ladd in idealized myth of a fight
White Heat (1949) Cagney's charisma at the top of the world, Ma
The Magnificent Seven (1960) Last fight, McQueen still deals in lead, friend
Gunfight at OK Corral (1957) Pokey Lancaster classic shows old studio way
Robocop (1987) Mechanico-human shoots straight, often and loudly
Madigan (1968): Feisty Richard Widmark goes to two Dick Specials to face psycho hotel shooter
Matewan (1987) Labor vs. Company thugs, set in old West . . . Virginia
McCabe and Mrs. Miller (1971) Quirky Beatty, stoked on keefe, fights big RR guns
Them! (1954) Matt Dillon with Tommygun vs. Giant ants
The Lady from Shanghai (1947) Welles throws down all-time campy-arty funhouse shindig
High Noon (1952) Does not forsake liberal vaues as Coop faces McCarthite shootists
True Grit (1969) The Duke, hell-bent for leather, goes mano-a-quatro-mano

Heat* vs. *The Lady from Shanghai
The Lady from Shanghai shows what happens when you ask a rogue genius to find a new way to shoot the gunfight's generic conventions. Orson Welles clearly doesn't give a damn about guns or anything else that preoccupied his peers. He just wants to make it look so new it's almost abstract, with the dazzling cutting, the twisted mirrors, the shattering glass. There's no reason at all why some live and others die, except that Orson wanted it that way.

The Killers* vs. *Heat
What the gunfight was, what it became. In this noir extension of the Hemingway story, insurance ace O'Brien and Pittsburgh cop Sam Levene lay a trap for the two tough man-killers we saw take out the Swede (a debuting Burt Lancaster). The takedown is short, violent, incredibly satisfying; more points for the fact that the future *Dragnet* tune plays throughout. *Heat,* by contrast, represents the giganticism that would influence the post-*Wild Bunch* gunfight; it's an assault-weapon festival with way-cool guns, actors who stay in character, coherent action, plot integration, and advancement. And great breaking glass.

Them!* vs. *The Lady from Shanghai
Them!? Afraid so. James Arness is trapped behind fallen timbers and tunnel debris with four giant ants coming in from all sides. He's clearly worked with the Thompson, and his size (he's a big guy!) helps him manipulate, combat reload, stay cool, find and destroy targets fast. It's a little virtuoso gunhandling from the man who would become, the next year, Matt Dillon, U.S. Marshal. The only thing that would make it better would be if the ants were commies.

YouTube Videos

By Virginia Heffernan

Virginia Heffernan is "The Medium" columnist at the *New York Times Magazine* and is the co-author, with Mike Albo, of the comic novel *The Underminer.*

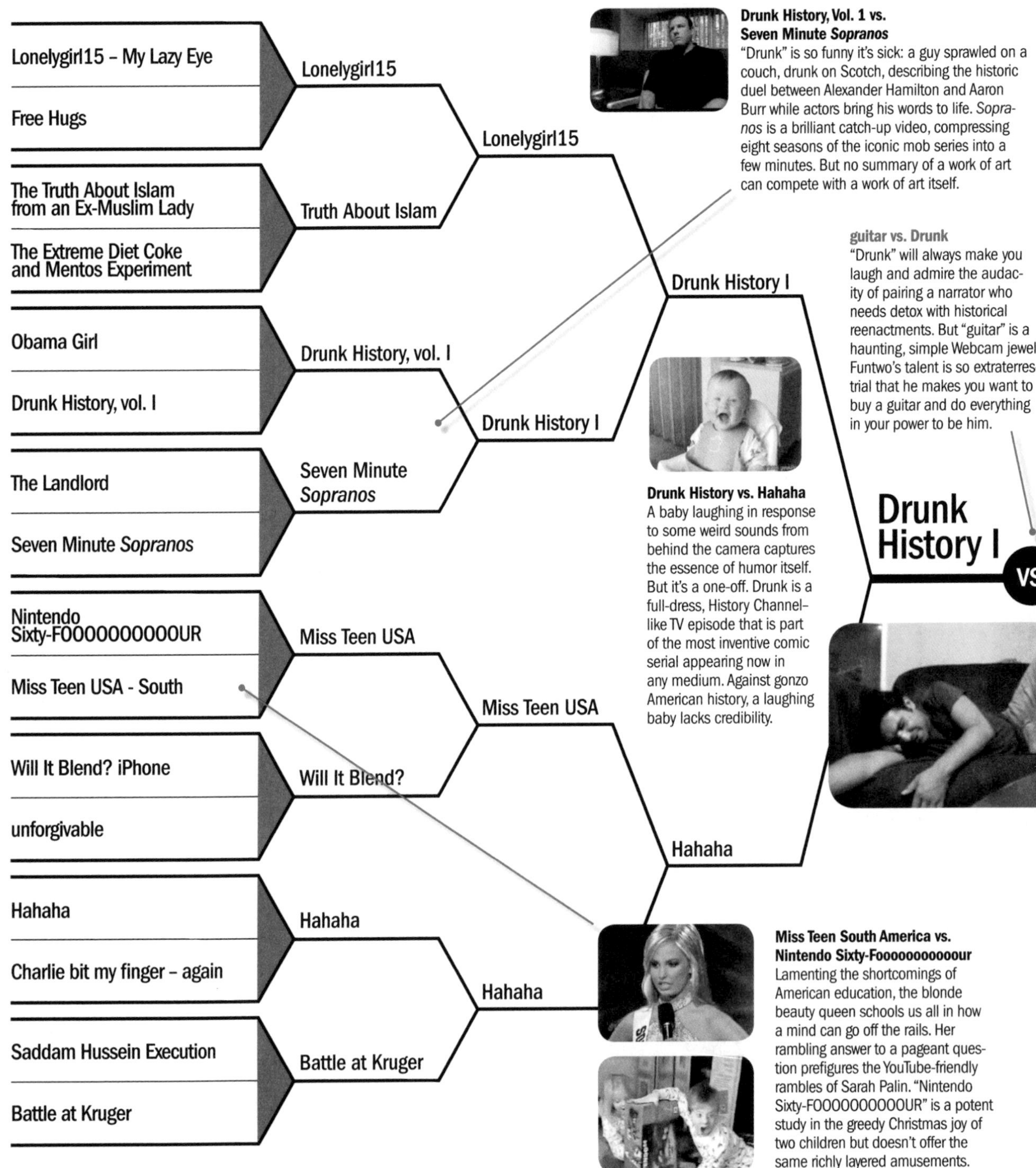
Lonelygirl15 – My Lazy Eye
Free Hugs
The Truth About Islam from an Ex-Muslim Lady
The Extreme Diet Coke and Mentos Experiment
Obama Girl
Drunk History, vol. I
The Landlord
Seven Minute *Sopranos*
Nintendo Sixty-FOOOOOOOOOOUR
Miss Teen USA - South
Will It Blend? iPhone
unforgivable
Hahaha
Charlie bit my finger – again
Saddam Hussein Execution
Battle at Kruger
Lonelygirl15
Truth About Islam
Drunk History, vol. I
Seven Minute *Sopranos*
Miss Teen USA
Will It Blend?
Hahaha
Battle at Kruger
Lonelygirl15
Drunk History I
Miss Teen USA
Hahaha
Drunk History I
Hahaha
Drunk History I
VS.

Drunk History, Vol. 1 vs. Seven Minute *Sopranos*
"Drunk" is so funny it's sick: a guy sprawled on a couch, drunk on Scotch, describing the historic duel between Alexander Hamilton and Aaron Burr while actors bring his words to life. *Sopranos* is a brilliant catch-up video, compressing eight seasons of the iconic mob series into a few minutes. But no summary of a work of art can compete with a work of art itself.

guitar vs. Drunk
"Drunk" will always make you laugh and admire the audacity of pairing a narrator who needs detox with historical reenactments. But "guitar" is a haunting, simple Webcam jewel: Funtwo's talent is so extraterrestrial that he makes you want to buy a guitar and do everything in your power to be him.

Drunk History vs. Hahaha
A baby laughing in response to some weird sounds from behind the camera captures the essence of humor itself. But it's a one-off. Drunk is a full-dress, History Channel–like TV episode that is part of the most inventive comic serial appearing now in any medium. Against gonzo American history, a laughing baby lacks credibility.

Miss Teen South America vs. Nintendo Sixty-Fooooooooooour
Lamenting the shortcomings of American education, the blonde beauty queen schools us all in how a mind can go off the rails. Her rambling answer to a pageant question prefigures the YouTube-friendly rambles of Sarah Palin. "Nintendo Sixty-FOOOOOOOOOOUR" is a potent study in the greedy Christmas joy of two children but doesn't offer the same richly layered amusements.

YOUTUBE IS FAMOUS FOR JUNK, but amid the garbage, what's gold glitters. That focus on eccentric or beautiful faces (Chris Crocker from "Leave Britney Alone") jostles against others using vérité and stagey mise-en-scène techniques that are entirely their own (the reverse-surveillance "Don't Tase Me, Bro"). Videos using visceral surprise ("George Bush Shoe Attack") bump into those built on juxtaposition ("Real Estate Downfall," which inserts subtitles on the economic crisis into a 2004 movie about Hitler). There's no sense comparing the genres, which is like equating bobby-pins with constitutional law.

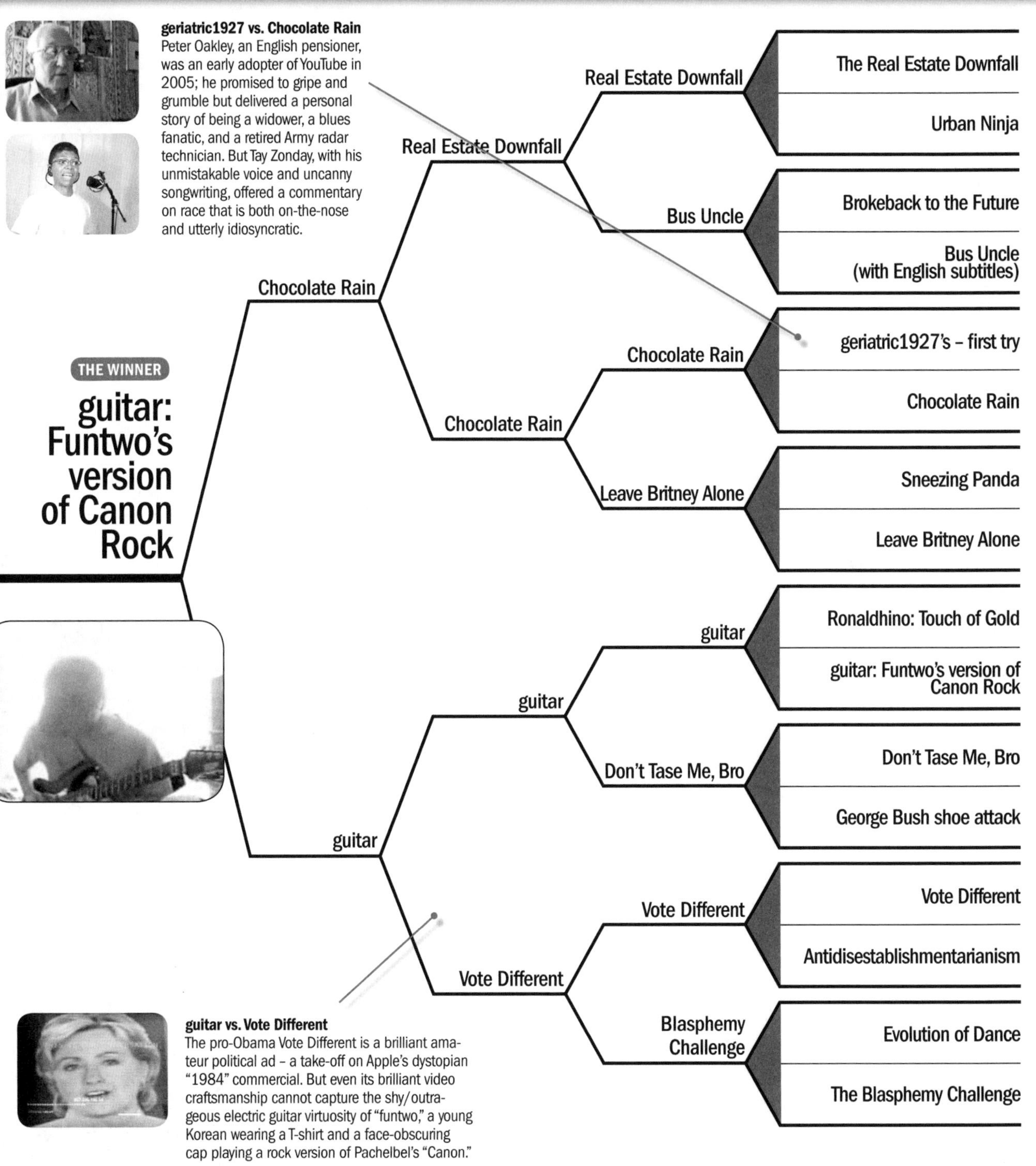

THE WINNER
guitar: Funtwo's version of Canon Rock
Chocolate Rain
Real Estate Downfall
Real Estate Downfall
The Real Estate Downfall
Urban Ninja
Bus Uncle
Brokeback to the Future
Bus Uncle (with English subtitles)
Chocolate Rain
Chocolate Rain
geriatric1927's – first try
Chocolate Rain
Leave Britney Alone
Sneezing Panda
Leave Britney Alone
guitar
guitar
guitar
Ronaldhino: Touch of Gold
guitar: Funtwo's version of Canon Rock
Don't Tase Me, Bro
Don't Tase Me, Bro
George Bush shoe attack
Vote Different
Vote Different
Vote Different
Antidisestablishmentarianism
Blasphemy Challenge
Evolution of Dance
The Blasphemy Challenge

geriatric1927 vs. Chocolate Rain
Peter Oakley, an English pensioner, was an early adopter of YouTube in 2005; he promised to gripe and grumble but delivered a personal story of being a widower, a blues fanatic, and a retired Army radar technician. But Tay Zonday, with his unmistakable voice and uncanny songwriting, offered a commentary on race that is both on-the-nose and utterly idiosyncratic.

guitar vs. Vote Different
The pro-Obama Vote Different is a brilliant amateur political ad – a take-off on Apple's dystopian "1984" commercial. But even its brilliant video craftsmanship cannot capture the shy/outrageous electric guitar virtuosity of "funtwo," a young Korean wearing a T-shirt and a face-obscuring cap playing a rock version of Pachelbel's "Canon."

Soul Songs

By John Leland

John Leland is a reporter at the *New York Times* and author of *Why Kerouac Matters: The Lessons of 'On the Road' (They're Not What You Think)* and *Hip: The History*. He can't carry a tune in a bucket.

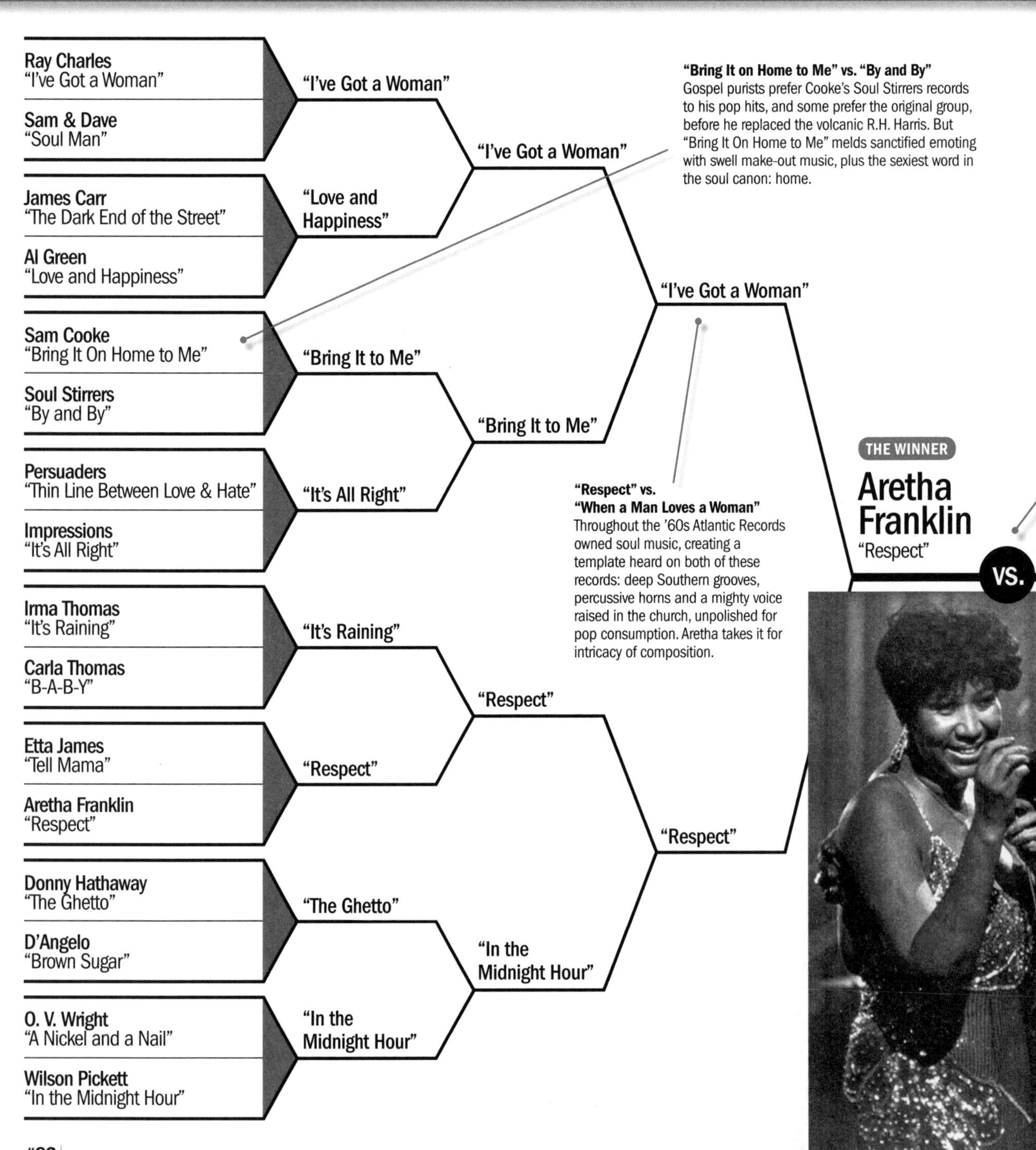

Ray Charles
"I've Got a Woman"
Sam & Dave
"Soul Man"
James Carr
"The Dark End of the Street"
Al Green
"Love and Happiness"
Sam Cooke
"Bring It On Home to Me"
Soul Stirrers
"By and By"
Persuaders
"Thin Line Between Love & Hate"
Impressions
"It's All Right"
Irma Thomas
"It's Raining"
Carla Thomas
"B-A-B-Y"
Etta James
"Tell Mama"
Aretha Franklin
"Respect"
Donny Hathaway
"The Ghetto"
D'Angelo
"Brown Sugar"
O. V. Wright
"A Nickel and a Nail"
Wilson Pickett
"In the Midnight Hour"
"I've Got a Woman"
"Love and Happiness"
"Bring It to Me"
"It's All Right"
"It's Raining"
"Respect"
"The Ghetto"
"In the Midnight Hour"
"I've Got a Woman"
"Bring It to Me"
"Respect"
"In the Midnight Hour"
"I've Got a Woman"
"Respect"
"Bring It on Home to Me" vs. "By and By"
Gospel purists prefer Cooke's Soul Stirrers records to his pop hits, and some prefer the original group, before he replaced the volcanic R.H. Harris. But "Bring It On Home to Me" melds sanctified emoting with swell make-out music, plus the sexiest word in the soul canon: home.
"Respect" vs. "When a Man Loves a Woman"
Throughout the '60s Atlantic Records owned soul music, creating a template heard on both of these records: deep Southern grooves, percussive horns and a mighty voice raised in the church, unpolished for pop consumption. Aretha takes it for intricacy of composition.
THE WINNER
Aretha Franklin
"Respect"
VS.

AMERICAN MUSIC IS ABOUT SYNTHESIS, and the soul music that emerged out of Holiness churches and hellified nightclubs in the early 1950s drew on two mighty mother-lodes: the unrelenting fury of gospel and the profane backbeat of rhythm and blues. It became a scandal to some church folks and the elevating soundtrack of the civil rights movement, a liturgy for a nation that knew both pain and the promised land.

Arthur Conley
"Sweet Soul Music"
William DeVaughn
"Be Thankful for What You Got"
Willie Nelson
"Night Life"
Isaac Hayes,
"Walk on By"
James Brown
"Cold Sweat"
Luther Ingram
"(If Loving You Is Wrong) I Don't Want to Be Right"
Aaron Neville
"Tell It Like It Is"
Simon and Garfunkel
"Bridge Over Troubled Water"
Otis Redding
"I've Been Loving You Too Long (To Stop Now)"
Bobby "Blue" Bland
"Ain't No Love in the Heart of the City"
King Curtis
"Memphis Soul Stew"
Young Holt Unlimited
"Soulful Strut"
Staple Singers
"I'll Take You There"
Ann Peebles
"I'm Gonna Tear Your Playhouse Down"
Percy Sledge
"When a Man Loves a Woman"
Solomon Burke
"Everybody Needs Somebody to Love"
"Sweet Soul Music"
"Walk on By"
"Cold Sweat"
"Bridge Over"
"Loving You"
"Soulful Strut"
"Take You There"
"When a Man Loves a Woman"
"Sweet Soul"
"Cold Sweat"
"Loving You"
"When a Man Loves a Woman"
"Cold Sweat"
"When a Man Loves a Woman"
"Cold Sweat"

"Respect" vs. "Cold Sweat"
Otis Redding wrote "Respect," but Aretha made it an anthem of an odd sort: She's giving her man all her money, and all she asks is a little of the sweet stuff. The slinky opening guitar is all the invitation she needs. What we want, baby she's got it. In heaps.

"Cold Sweat" vs. "When a Man Loves a Woman"
Brown ran the tightest and hardest working bands in show business, able to start and stop at the speed of grunt. Every instrument was a drum, including James's voice. "Cold Sweat" looks forward to his greasy funk. Alas, poor Percy, without him the world would be a less populous place.

"Bridge Over Troubled Water" vs. "Tell It Like It Is"
A second-round blowout, but don't sell Paul and Art short. Until Simon joins on the last verse, "Bridge Over Troubled Water" is pristine gospel soul, as healing as the funkier stuff. A hymn to holy friendship.

Paul Newman Roles

By Mark Reiter

Mark Reiter, co-editor of this book, deals with any dilemma by asking himself, "What would Paul Newman do?"

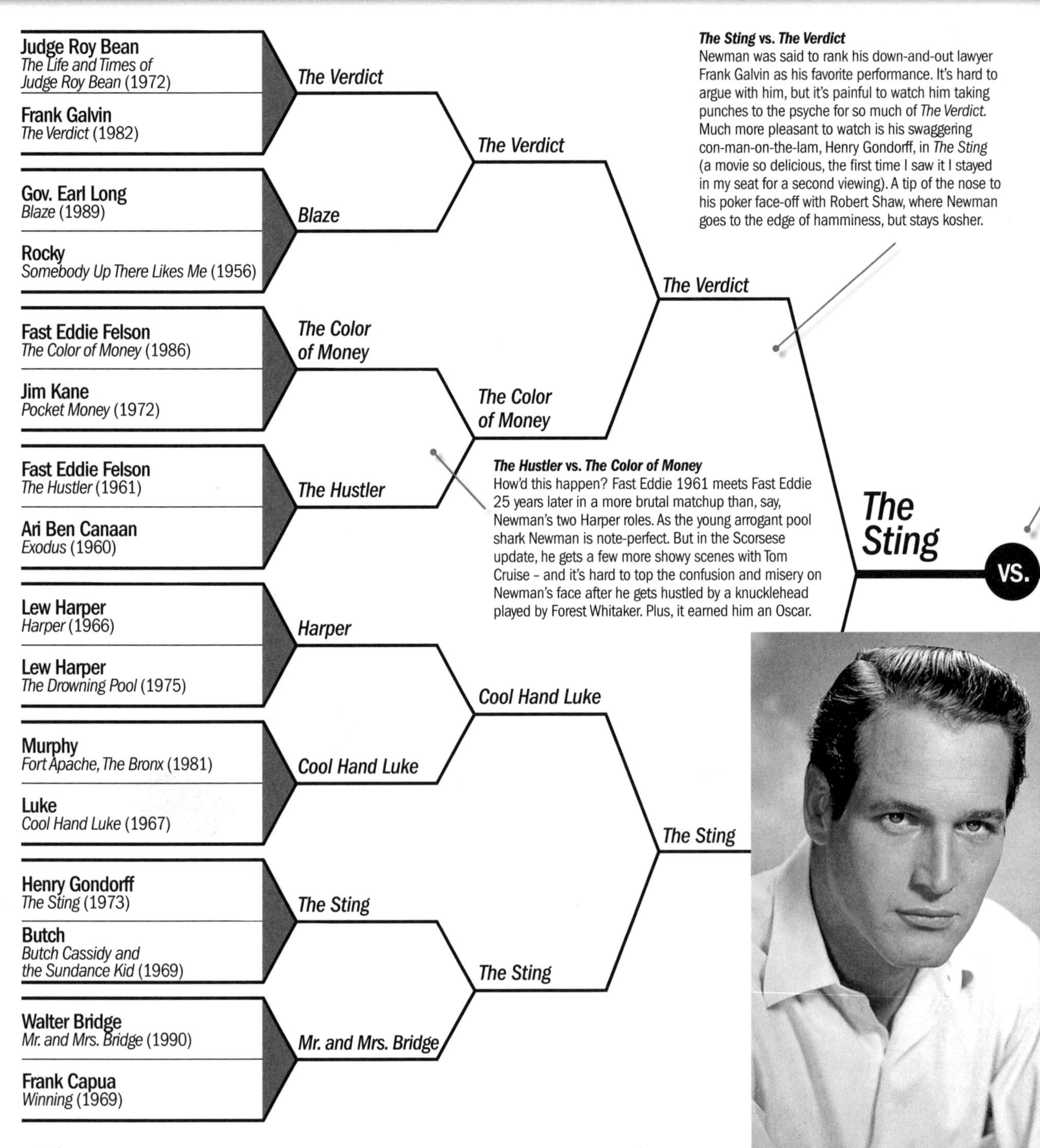
Judge Roy Bean
The Life and Times of Judge Roy Bean (1972)
Frank Galvin
The Verdict (1982)
Gov. Earl Long
Blaze (1989)
Rocky
Somebody Up There Likes Me (1956)
Fast Eddie Felson
The Color of Money (1986)
Jim Kane
Pocket Money (1972)
Fast Eddie Felson
The Hustler (1961)
Ari Ben Canaan
Exodus (1960)
Lew Harper
Harper (1966)
Lew Harper
The Drowning Pool (1975)
Murphy
Fort Apache, The Bronx (1981)
Luke
Cool Hand Luke (1967)
Henry Gondorff
The Sting (1973)
Butch
Butch Cassidy and the Sundance Kid (1969)
Walter Bridge
Mr. and Mrs. Bridge (1990)
Frank Capua
Winning (1969)
The Verdict
Blaze
The Color of Money
The Hustler
Harper
Cool Hand Luke
The Sting
Mr. and Mrs. Bridge
The Verdict
The Color of Money
Cool Hand Luke
The Sting
The Verdict
The Sting
The Sting
VS.

The Sting* vs. *The Verdict
Newman was said to rank his down-and-out lawyer Frank Galvin as his favorite performance. It's hard to argue with him, but it's painful to watch him taking punches to the psyche for so much of *The Verdict*. Much more pleasant to watch is his swaggering con-man-on-the-lam, Henry Gondorff, in *The Sting* (a movie so delicious, the first time I saw it I stayed in my seat for a second viewing). A tip of the nose to his poker face-off with Robert Shaw, where Newman goes to the edge of hamminess, but stays kosher.

The Hustler* vs. *The Color of Money
How'd this happen? Fast Eddie 1961 meets Fast Eddie 25 years later in a more brutal matchup than, say, Newman's two Harper roles. As the young arrogant pool shark Newman is note-perfect. But in the Scorsese update, he gets a few more showy scenes with Tom Cruise – and it's hard to top the confusion and misery on Newman's face after he gets hustled by a knucklehead played by Forest Whitaker. Plus, it earned him an Oscar.

PAUL NEWMAN WORKED LONG ENOUGH IN FILMS, from 1954 to 2006, that it's tempting to pigeonhole his career into convenient chronological phases, from newcomer through smoldering rogue to artisanal actor – and grade each on a curve. But the only criterion here is how good was the role and the performance? Could you forget the blue eyes and the legendary persona and only see the character he's playing? When Paul Newman disappears completely and yet invests the character with his charisma and wit, that's what wins here.

The Sting* vs. *Absence of Malice

A perverse choice for the actor who created Hud, Luke, Brick, and Butch? I don't think so. In *Absence of Malice,* Newman's Michael Gallagher is an average man forced, by perfidy and folly all around him, to do unto others as they have done unto him. No gunplay, no fighting, no dark suspense, just Newman's brainpower and guile at play. At every step, you never think this is the guy on the salad bottle. In the final scene, where everyone gets their comeuppance, Wilford Brimley's U.S. Attorney turns to Newman's Gallagher and asks, "Are you that smart?" He is, he was, and it doesn't get better than that.

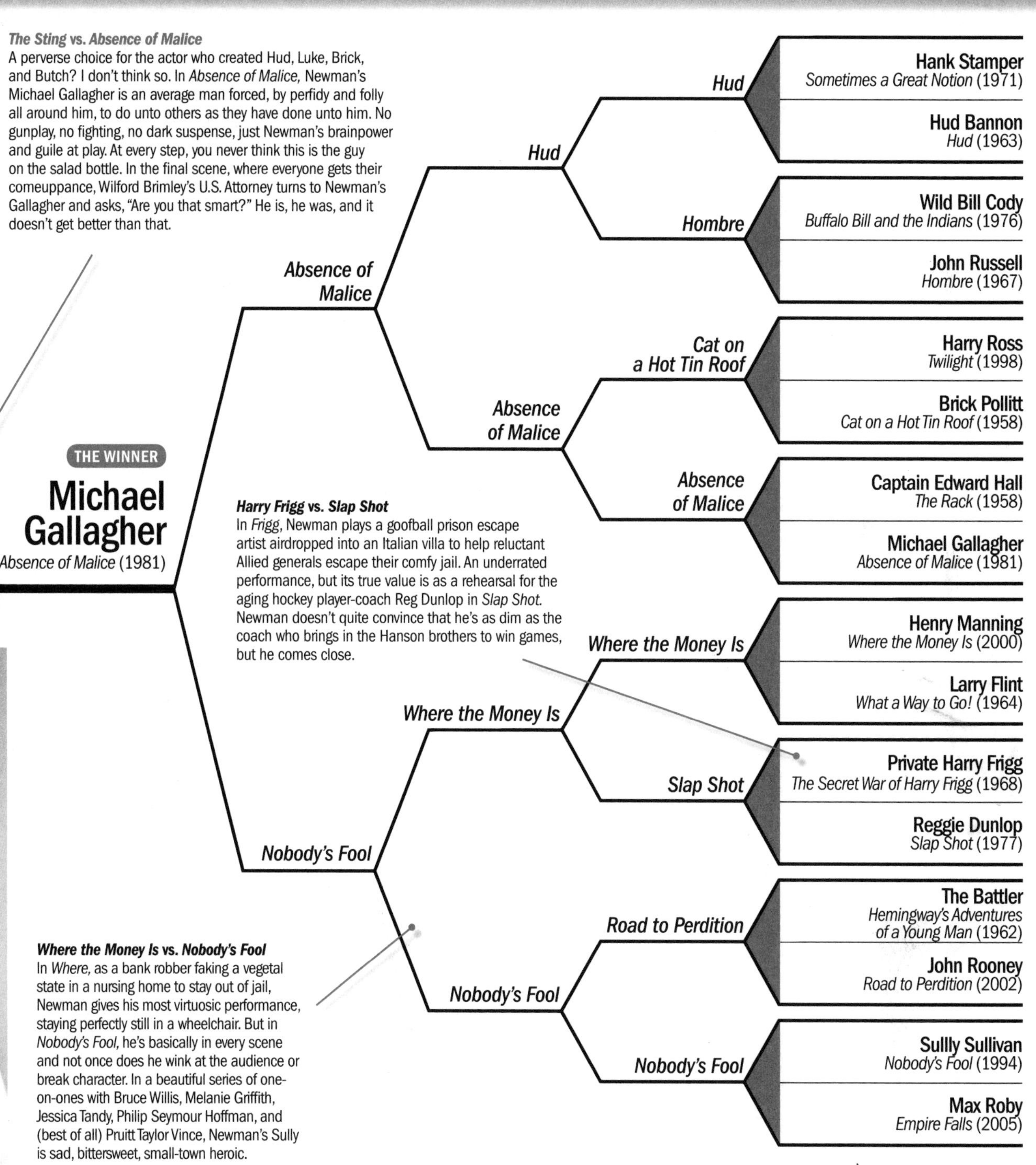

Hank Stamper
Sometimes a Great Notion (1971)
Hud Bannon
Hud (1963)
Wild Bill Cody
Buffalo Bill and the Indians (1976)
John Russell
Hombre (1967)
Harry Ross
Twilight (1998)
Brick Pollitt
Cat on a Hot Tin Roof (1958)
Captain Edward Hall
The Rack (1958)
Michael Gallagher
Absence of Malice (1981)
Henry Manning
Where the Money Is (2000)
Larry Flint
What a Way to Go! (1964)
Private Harry Frigg
The Secret War of Harry Frigg (1968)
Reggie Dunlop
Slap Shot (1977)
The Battler
Hemingway's Adventures of a Young Man (1962)
John Rooney
Road to Perdition (2002)
Sullly Sullivan
Nobody's Fool (1994)
Max Roby
Empire Falls (2005)
Hud
Hombre
Cat on a Hot Tin Roof
Absence of Malice
Where the Money Is
Slap Shot
Road to Perdition
Nobody's Fool
Hud
Absence of Malice
Where the Money Is
Nobody's Fool
Absence of Malice
Nobody's Fool
THE WINNER
Michael Gallagher
Absence of Malice (1981)

Harry Frigg* vs. *Slap Shot

In *Frigg,* Newman plays a goofball prison escape artist airdropped into an Italian villa to help reluctant Allied generals escape their comfy jail. An underrated performance, but its true value is as a rehearsal for the aging hockey player-coach Reg Dunlop in *Slap Shot.* Newman doesn't quite convince that he's as dim as the coach who brings in the Hanson brothers to win games, but he comes close.

Where the Money Is* vs. *Nobody's Fool

In *Where,* as a bank robber faking a vegetal state in a nursing home to stay out of jail, Newman gives his most virtuosic performance, staying perfectly still in a wheelchair. But in *Nobody's Fool,* he's basically in every scene and not once does he wink at the audience or break character. In a beautiful series of one-on-ones with Bruce Willis, Melanie Griffith, Jessica Tandy, Philip Seymour Hoffman, and (best of all) Pruitt Taylor Vince, Newman's Sully is sad, bittersweet, small-town heroic.

Sitcom Dads

By Steven Reddicliffe

Steven Reddicliffe, a media editor at the *New York Times,* has been a suburban dad for 18 years (his children contributed to the Danny Tanner entry here). He has always tried to be more Cleaver than Cheever.

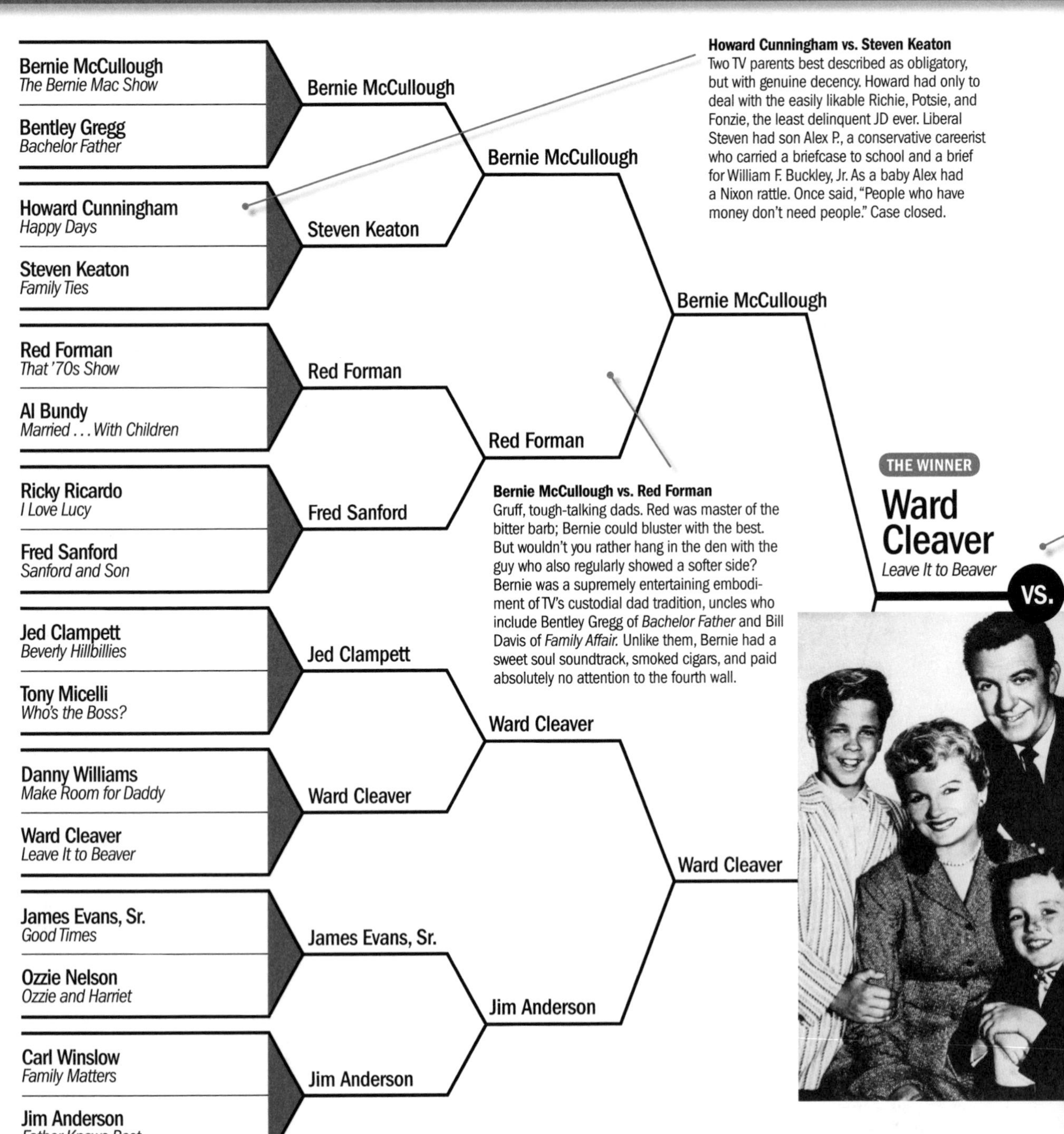

Bernie McCullough
The Bernie Mac Show
Bentley Gregg
Bachelor Father
Howard Cunningham
Happy Days
Steven Keaton
Family Ties
Red Forman
That '70s Show
Al Bundy
Married . . . With Children
Ricky Ricardo
I Love Lucy
Fred Sanford
Sanford and Son
Jed Clampett
Beverly Hillbillies
Tony Micelli
Who's the Boss?
Danny Williams
Make Room for Daddy
Ward Cleaver
Leave It to Beaver
James Evans, Sr.
Good Times
Ozzie Nelson
Ozzie and Harriet
Carl Winslow
Family Matters
Jim Anderson
Father Knows Best
Bernie McCullough
Steven Keaton
Red Forman
Fred Sanford
Jed Clampett
Ward Cleaver
James Evans, Sr.
Jim Anderson
Bernie McCullough
Red Forman
Ward Cleaver
Jim Anderson
Bernie McCullough
Ward Cleaver
THE WINNER
Ward Cleaver
Leave It to Beaver
VS.

Howard Cunningham vs. Steven Keaton
Two TV parents best described as obligatory, but with genuine decency. Howard had only to deal with the easily likable Richie, Potsie, and Fonzie, the least delinquent JD ever. Liberal Steven had son Alex P., a conservative careerist who carried a briefcase to school and a brief for William F. Buckley, Jr. As a baby Alex had a Nixon rattle. Once said, "People who have money don't need people." Case closed.

Bernie McCullough vs. Red Forman
Gruff, tough-talking dads. Red was master of the bitter barb; Bernie could bluster with the best. But wouldn't you rather hang in the den with the guy who also regularly showed a softer side? Bernie was a supremely entertaining embodiment of TV's custodial dad tradition, uncles who include Bentley Gregg of *Bachelor Father* and Bill Davis of *Family Affair.* Unlike them, Bernie had a sweet soul soundtrack, smoked cigars, and paid absolutely no attention to the fourth wall.

DAD'S A DOOFUS – that's the long-lived misconception when it comes to television. Although there may be the occasional dips and dorks, situation comedy dads are usually sane and sensitive fellows, wry guys who can impart useful life lessons between mowing the lawn and conducting goldfish funerals. There are exceptions, sure (Frank Costanza's discourse on the brassiere somehow leaps to mind), but mellow understanding prevails. As the '60s soul group The Winstons once put it, "I think I'll color this man love."

Cliff Huxtable vs. Ward Cleaver
No one ever should have been worried about the Beaver. Ward was the unshakable foundation for the admirable TV dad – affectionate, patient, good-humored, capable of making a mistake and of deftly repairing one. Also dried the dishes. Cliff played a genuinely funny, contemporary riff on Ward (he cooked, wife was a lawyer), but there can be no rancor or raised voices in this battle; wouldn't be fatherly. As both Cliff and Ward would tell their children, there is only one champion, and sometimes the good guy who gets there first wins the prize.

Herman Munster vs. Dan Conner
Physically imposing dads, one built in a laboratory, the other built with cholesterol. Herman, a genuine sweetheart, is challenged only by his vampire father-in-law; Dan's challenge comes from the most formidable wife in sitcom history. But winning the dad trophy often comes down to the better bowler, and based on bendability alone, that man would be Dan.

Danny Tanner vs. Steve Douglas
This one's strictly a numbers game. Tanner: kids D.J., Stephanie, and Michelle, a dog named Comet, Joey, Jesse, Jesse's wife Becky, and their twins Alex and Nicky. Douglas: three biological sons, one adopted son, triplet grandkids, a dog named Tramp, a wife late in the game, Bub, and Uncle Charley. That's a fuller house.

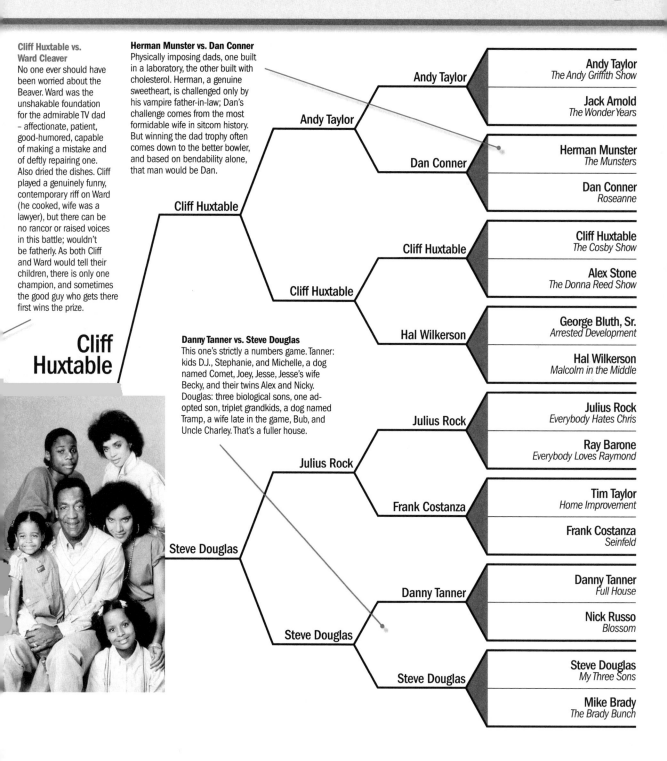

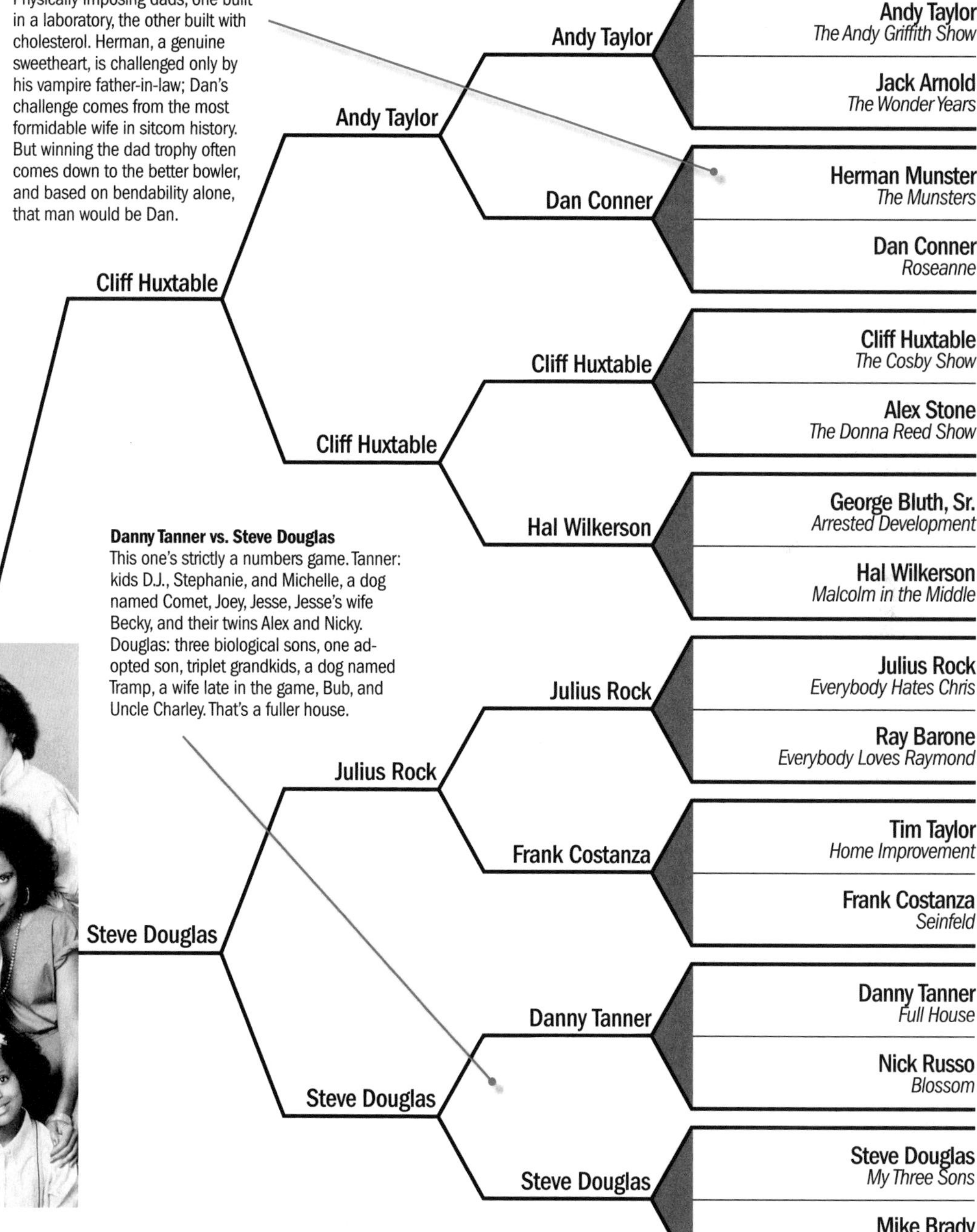
Cliff Huxtable
Cliff Huxtable
Andy Taylor
Andy Taylor
Dan Conner
Cliff Huxtable
Cliff Huxtable
Hal Wilkerson
Steve Douglas
Julius Rock
Julius Rock
Frank Costanza
Steve Douglas
Danny Tanner
Steve Douglas
Andy Taylor
The Andy Griffith Show
Jack Arnold
The Wonder Years
Herman Munster
The Munsters
Dan Conner
Roseanne
Cliff Huxtable
The Cosby Show
Alex Stone
The Donna Reed Show
George Bluth, Sr.
Arrested Development
Hal Wilkerson
Malcolm in the Middle
Julius Rock
Everybody Hates Chris
Ray Barone
Everybody Loves Raymond
Tim Taylor
Home Improvement
Frank Costanza
Seinfeld
Danny Tanner
Full House
Nick Russo
Blossom
Steve Douglas
My Three Sons
Mike Brady
The Brady Bunch

Sitcom Moms

By Richard Sandomir

Richard Sandomir's mother is most like Edith Bunker in her consummate decency, innocence, and depth of caring. But she loved watching *Maude.*

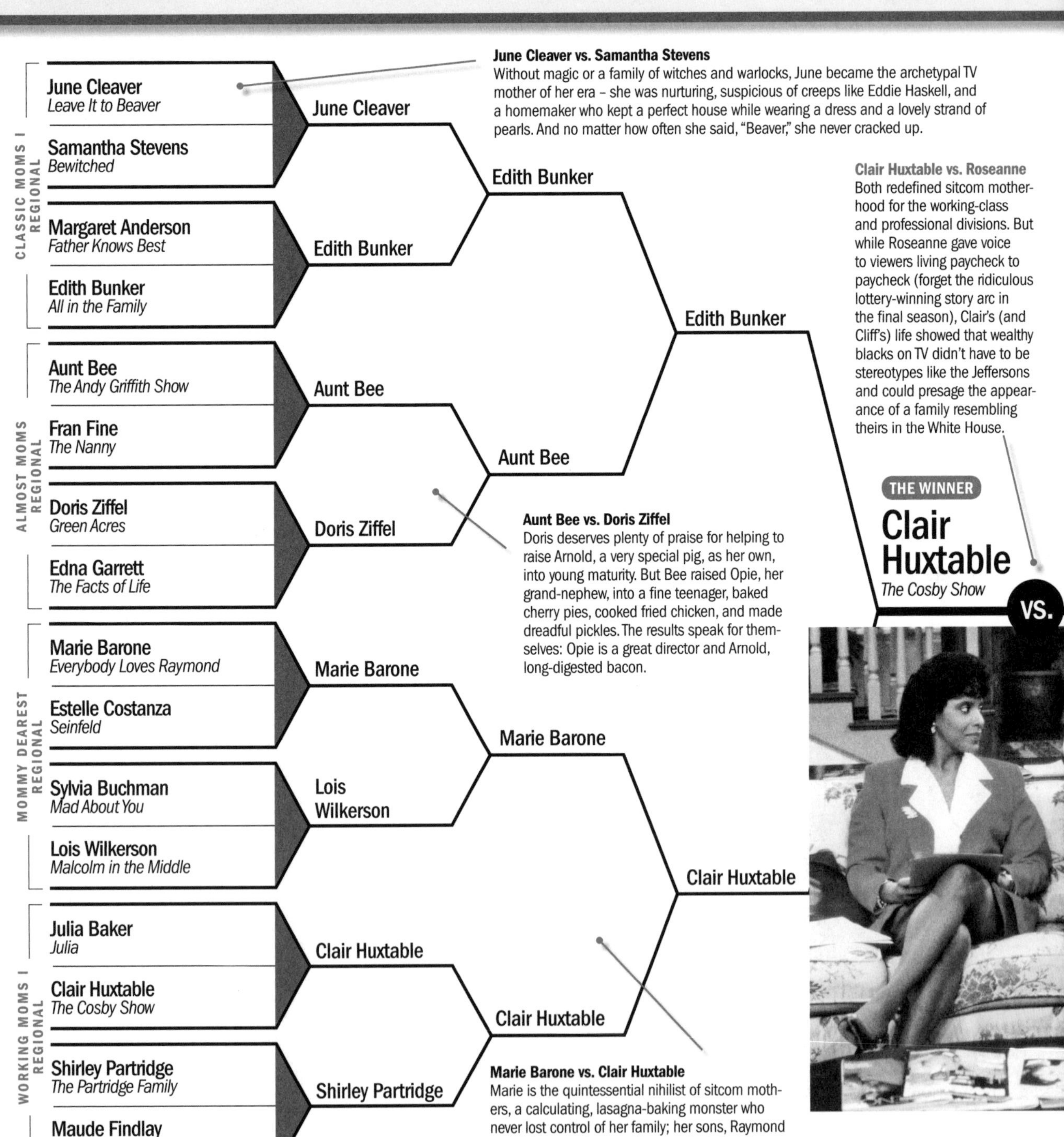

CLASSIC MOMS REGIONAL
June Cleaver
Leave It to Beaver
Samantha Stevens
Bewitched
Margaret Anderson
Father Knows Best
Edith Bunker
All in the Family
June Cleaver
Edith Bunker
Edith Bunker
ALMOST MOMS REGIONAL
Aunt Bee
The Andy Griffith Show
Fran Fine
The Nanny
Doris Ziffel
Green Acres
Edna Garrett
The Facts of Life
Aunt Bee
Doris Ziffel
Aunt Bee
Edith Bunker
MOMMY DEAREST REGIONAL
Marie Barone
Everybody Loves Raymond
Estelle Costanza
Seinfeld
Sylvia Buchman
Mad About You
Lois Wilkerson
Malcolm in the Middle
Marie Barone
Lois Wilkerson
Marie Barone
WORKING MOMS REGIONAL
Julia Baker
Julia
Clair Huxtable
The Cosby Show
Shirley Partridge
The Partridge Family
Maude Findlay
Maude
Clair Huxtable
Shirley Partridge
Clair Huxtable
Clair Huxtable
THE WINNER
Clair Huxtable
The Cosby Show
VS.

June Cleaver vs. Samantha Stevens
Without magic or a family of witches and warlocks, June became the archetypal TV mother of her era – she was nurturing, suspicious of creeps like Eddie Haskell, and a homemaker who kept a perfect house while wearing a dress and a lovely strand of pearls. And no matter how often she said, "Beaver," she never cracked up.

Clair Huxtable vs. Roseanne
Both redefined sitcom motherhood for the working-class and professional divisions. But while Roseanne gave voice to viewers living paycheck to paycheck (forget the ridiculous lottery-winning story arc in the final season), Clair's (and Cliff's) life showed that wealthy blacks on TV didn't have to be stereotypes like the Jeffersons and could presage the appearance of a family resembling theirs in the White House.

Aunt Bee vs. Doris Ziffel
Doris deserves plenty of praise for helping to raise Arnold, a very special pig, as her own, into young maturity. But Bee raised Opie, her grand-nephew, into a fine teenager, baked cherry pies, cooked fried chicken, and made dreadful pickles. The results speak for themselves: Opie is a great director and Arnold, long-digested bacon.

Marie Barone vs. Clair Huxtable
Marie is the quintessential nihilist of sitcom mothers, a calculating, lasagna-baking monster who never lost control of her family; her sons, Raymond and Robert, are her emotionally crippled victims. But Clair, a regal lawyer in a loving marriage where her husband is not a moronic boob, offered a new vision of the sitcom working mother.

THESE MOTHERS (sorry, Peg Bundy, Donna Stone, Sophia Petrillo) demonstrated wide and varied abilities to provide the glue to their families, with food (Marie Barone), magic (Samantha Stevens), wise-cracking tough-love (Roseanne Conner), husband-exasperating antics (Lucy Ricardo), perky sexuality (Laura Petrie), or in case of a doofus mate, steady practicality (Marge Simpson). Some, like June, Edith, and Laura, you'd really want for your mother; others, like Marie, Maude, or Estelle, you'd need lifelong therapy.

Marge Simpson vs. Roseanne
It's not easy being married to Homer (think of how often he's been naked in public), but Roseanne wasn't very nice, insulted her kids, didn't keep house very well, dressed without style, and argued loudly with Dan. Blue-collar life had been depicted on TV before (nobody was poorer than Alice Kramden), but never as a comedic primal scream.

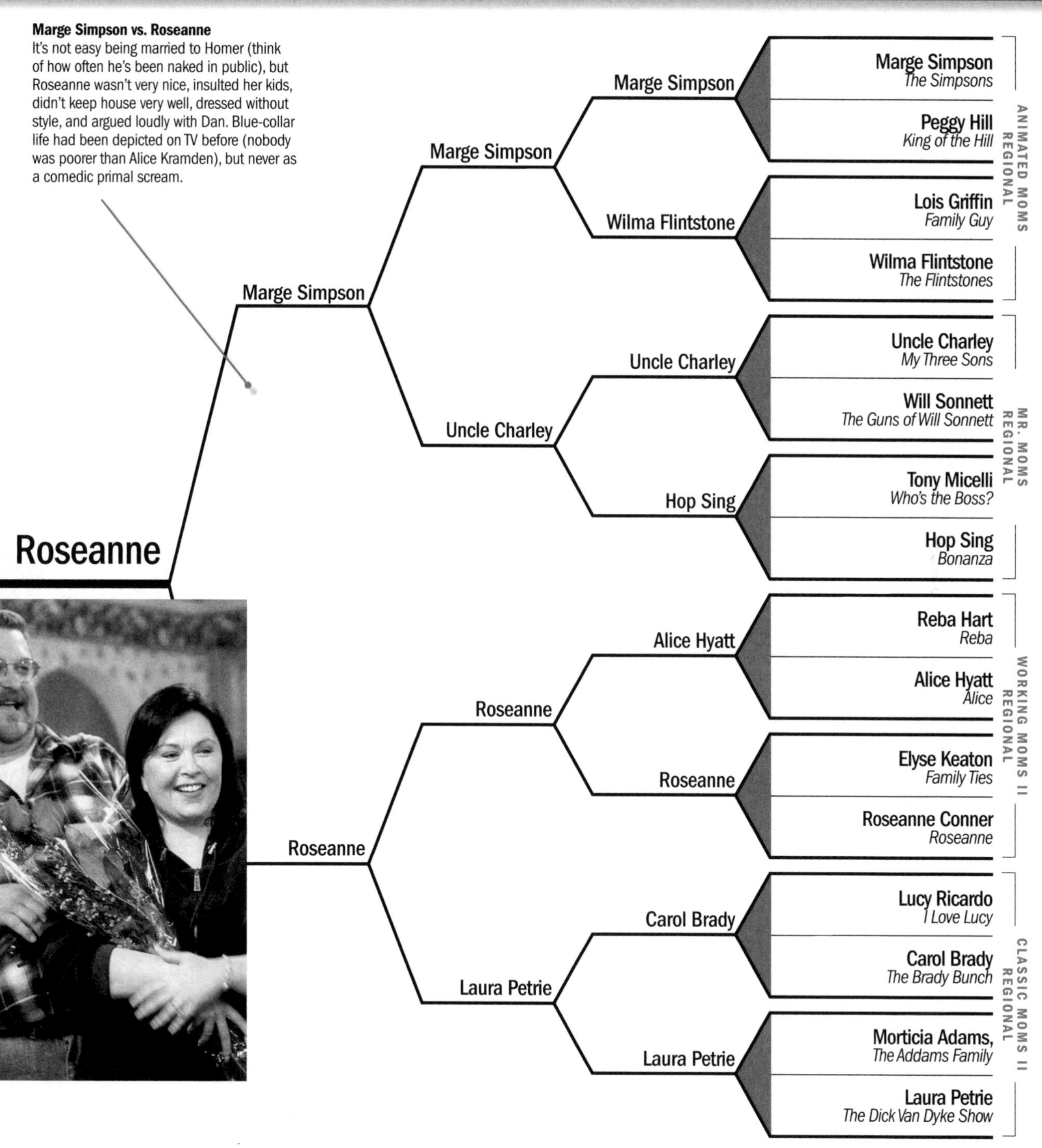

Roseanne
Marge Simpson
Roseanne
Marge Simpson
Uncle Charley
Roseanne
Laura Petrie
Marge Simpson
Wilma Flintstone
Uncle Charley
Hop Sing
Alice Hyatt
Roseanne
Carol Brady
Laura Petrie
ANIMATED MOMS REGIONAL
Marge Simpson
The Simpsons
Peggy Hill
King of the Hill
Lois Griffin
Family Guy
Wilma Flintstone
The Flintstones
MR. MOMS REGIONAL
Uncle Charley
My Three Sons
Will Sonnett
The Guns of Will Sonnett
Tony Micelli
Who's the Boss?
Hop Sing
Bonanza
WORKING MOMS II REGIONAL
Reba Hart
Reba
Alice Hyatt
Alice
Elyse Keaton
Family Ties
Roseanne Conner
Roseanne
CLASSIC MOMS II REGIONAL
Lucy Ricardo
I Love Lucy
Carol Brady
The Brady Bunch
Morticia Adams,
The Addams Family
Laura Petrie
The Dick Van Dyke Show

Talk-Show Graveyard

By Bill Carter

Bill Carter has covered the television industry for the *New York Times* for 20 years. He is the author of three books about the business: *Monday Night Mayhem* (with Marc Gunther), *The Late Shift*, and *Desperate Networks*.

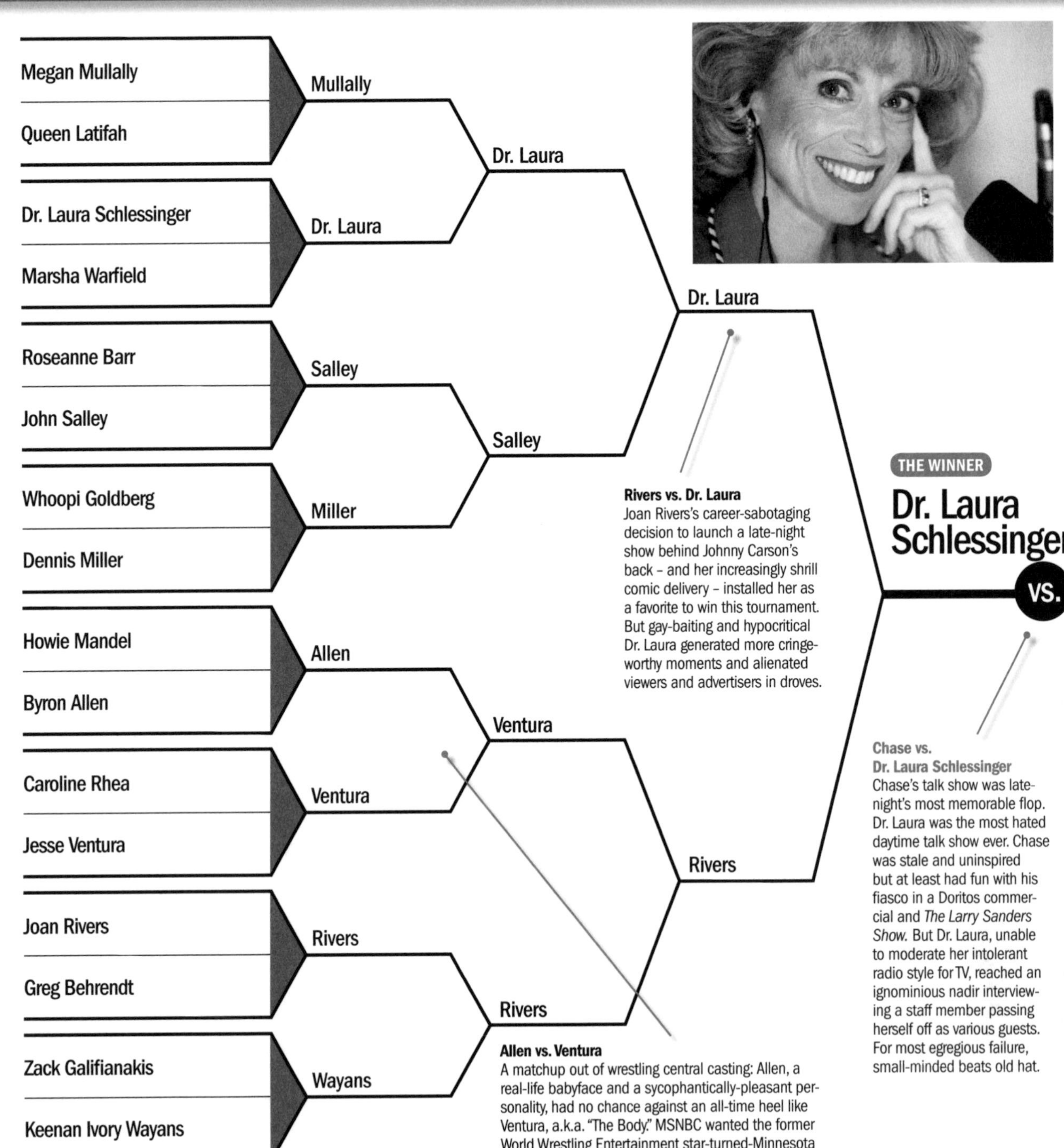
Megan Mullally
Queen Latifah
Dr. Laura Schlessinger
Marsha Warfield
Roseanne Barr
John Salley
Whoopi Goldberg
Dennis Miller
Howie Mandel
Byron Allen
Caroline Rhea
Jesse Ventura
Joan Rivers
Greg Behrendt
Zack Galifianakis
Keenan Ivory Wayans
Mullally
Dr. Laura
Salley
Miller
Allen
Ventura
Rivers
Wayans
Dr. Laura
Salley
Ventura
Rivers
Dr. Laura
Rivers
THE WINNER
Dr. Laura Schlessinger
VS.

Rivers vs. Dr. Laura
Joan Rivers's career-sabotaging decision to launch a late-night show behind Johnny Carson's back – and her increasingly shrill comic delivery – installed her as a favorite to win this tournament. But gay-baiting and hypocritical Dr. Laura generated more cringe-worthy moments and alienated viewers and advertisers in droves.

Allen vs. Ventura
A matchup out of wrestling central casting: Allen, a real-life babyface and a sycophantically-pleasant personality, had no chance against an all-time heel like Ventura, a.k.a. "The Body." MSNBC wanted the former World Wrestling Entertainment star-turned-Minnesota governor to host a nightly talk slugfest, but all he could manage was a low-rated Saturday night show that died meekly after less than three months.

Chase vs. Dr. Laura Schlessinger
Chase's talk show was late-night's most memorable flop. Dr. Laura was the most hated daytime talk show ever. Chase was stale and uninspired but at least had fun with his fiasco in a Doritos commercial and *The Larry Sanders Show.* But Dr. Laura, unable to moderate her intolerant radio style for TV, reached an ignominious nadir interviewing a staff member passing herself off as various guests. For most egregious failure, small-minded beats old hat.

MOST OF TELEVISION IS ABOUT FAILURE. Usually, it's not a disgrace: shows are mounted, viewers give them a look (or not) and reject them. But when talk shows flop, there is a special humiliation – a direct rejection of the "person behind the desk," as Johnny Carson called the host. Simple failures fade. But the colossal ones are memorable debacles that recall both the great expectations with which the shows started and questions about why you'd give a show to these people.

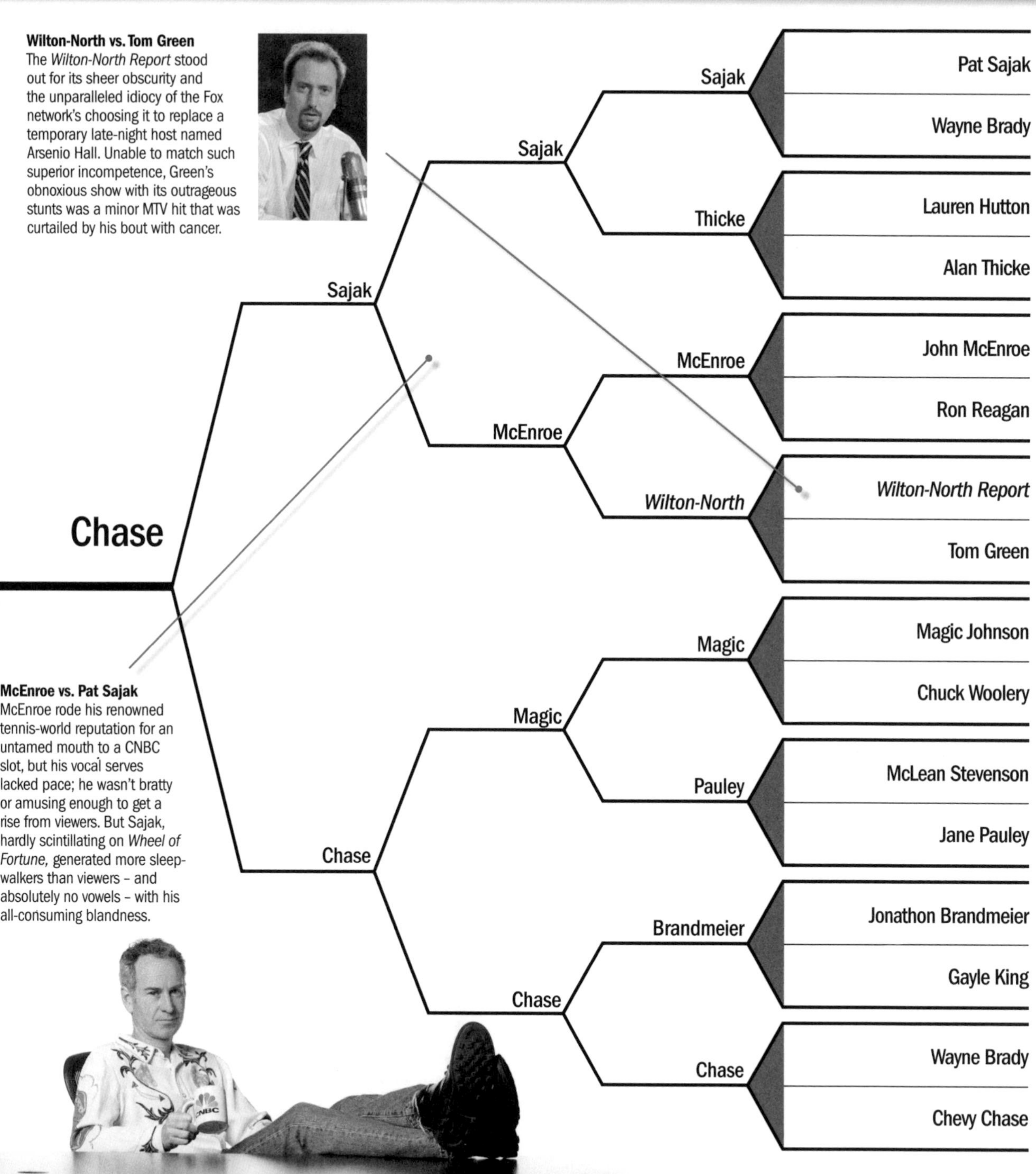

Pat Sajak
Wayne Brady
Lauren Hutton
Alan Thicke
John McEnroe
Ron Reagan
Wilton-North Report
Tom Green
Magic Johnson
Chuck Woolery
McLean Stevenson
Jane Pauley
Jonathon Brandmeier
Gayle King
Wayne Brady
Chevy Chase
Sajak
Thicke
McEnroe
Wilton-North
Magic
Pauley
Brandmeier
Chase
Sajak
McEnroe
Magic
Chase
Sajak
Chase
Chase

Wilton-North vs. Tom Green
The *Wilton-North Report* stood out for its sheer obscurity and the unparalleled idiocy of the Fox network's choosing it to replace a temporary late-night host named Arsenio Hall. Unable to match such superior incompetence, Green's obnoxious show with its outrageous stunts was a minor MTV hit that was curtailed by his bout with cancer.

McEnroe vs. Pat Sajak
McEnroe rode his renowned tennis-world reputation for an untamed mouth to a CNBC slot, but his vocal serves lacked pace; he wasn't bratty or amusing enough to get a rise from viewers. But Sajak, hardly scintillating on *Wheel of Fortune,* generated more sleepwalkers than viewers – and absolutely no vowels – with his all-consuming blandness.

Children's Books

By Jon Scieszka

Jon Scieszka, author of *The True Story of the 3 Little Pigs!* and *The Stinky Cheese Man,* was appointed the nation's first National Ambassador for Young People's Literature by the Librarian of Congress.

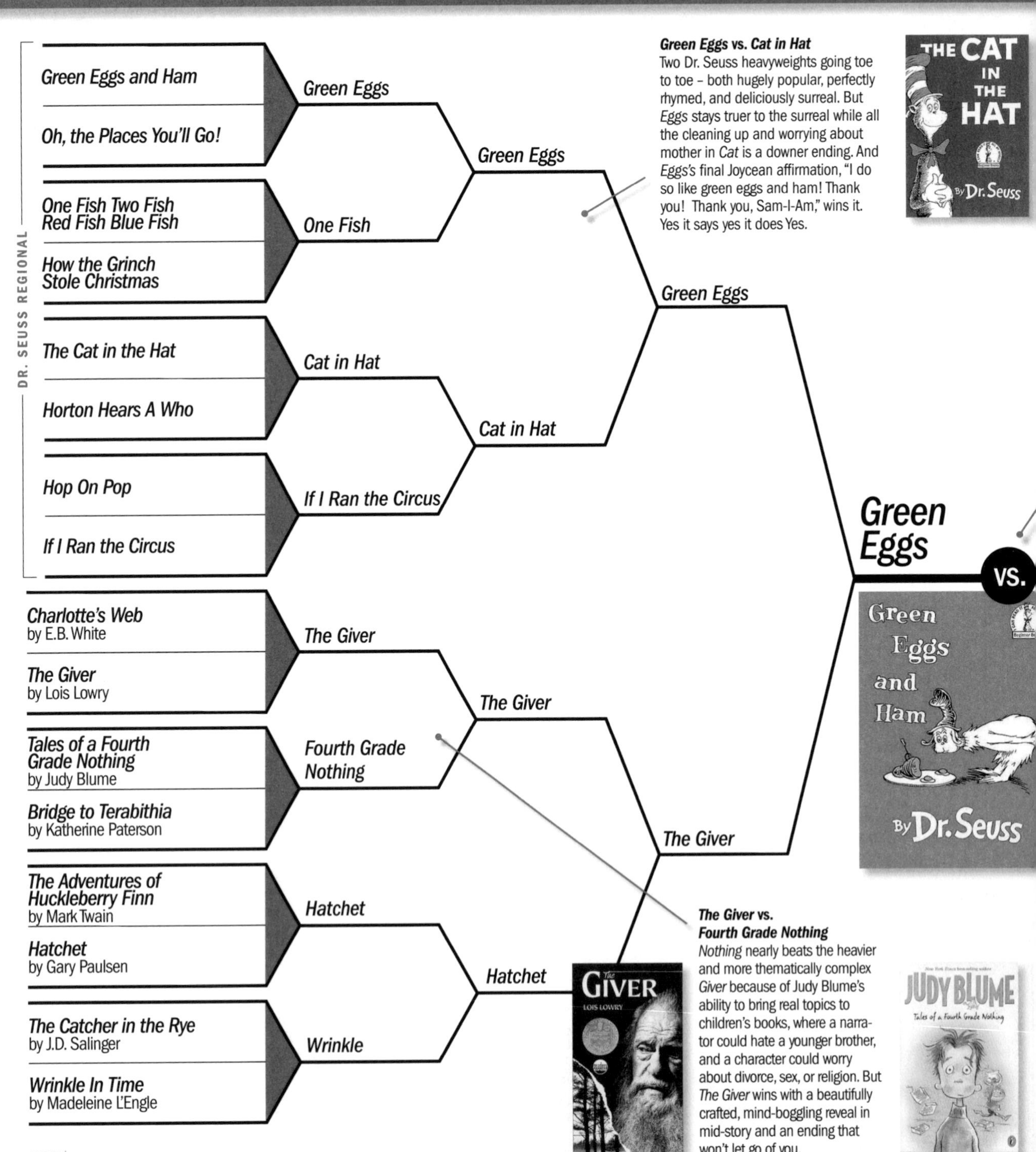

DR. SEUSS REGIONAL
Green Eggs and Ham
Oh, the Places You'll Go!
One Fish Two Fish Red Fish Blue Fish
How the Grinch Stole Christmas
The Cat in the Hat
Horton Hears A Who
Hop On Pop
If I Ran the Circus
Green Eggs
One Fish
Cat in Hat
If I Ran the Circus
Green Eggs
Cat in Hat
Green Eggs
Charlotte's Web by E.B. White
The Giver by Lois Lowry
Tales of a Fourth Grade Nothing by Judy Blume
Bridge to Terabithia by Katherine Paterson
The Adventures of Huckleberry Finn by Mark Twain
Hatchet by Gary Paulsen
The Catcher in the Rye by J.D. Salinger
Wrinkle In Time by Madeleine L'Engle
The Giver
Fourth Grade Nothing
Hatchet
Wrinkle
The Giver
Hatchet
The Giver
Green Eggs
VS.
Green Eggs vs. Cat in Hat
Two Dr. Seuss heavyweights going toe to toe – both hugely popular, perfectly rhymed, and deliciously surreal. But *Eggs* stays truer to the surreal while all the cleaning up and worrying about mother in *Cat* is a downer ending. And *Eggs's* final Joycean affirmation, "I do so like green eggs and ham! Thank you! Thank you, Sam-I-Am," wins it. Yes it says yes it does Yes.
THE CAT IN THE HAT By Dr. Seuss
Green Eggs and Ham By Dr. Seuss
The Giver vs. Fourth Grade Nothing
Nothing nearly beats the heavier and more thematically complex *Giver* because of Judy Blume's ability to bring real topics to children's books, where a narrator could hate a younger brother, and a character could worry about divorce, sex, or religion. But *The Giver* wins with a beautifully crafted, mind-boggling reveal in mid-story and an ending that won't let go of you.
The GIVER LOIS LOWRY
JUDY BLUME Tales of a Fourth Grade Nothing

JUDGING THE AWESOME RANGE OF CHILDREN'S LITERATURE – from beginning picture books and easy readers to young adult novels – is like comparing green eggs to talking dogs. It's a mind-bending mission, but bending kids' minds by giving them reasons to be a reader is what great children's literature is all about. The best books combine popularity, repeat-readability, kid-friendliness, longevity, and literary merit. Only Dr. Seuss got a regional of his own, because his books are a force and region all their own.

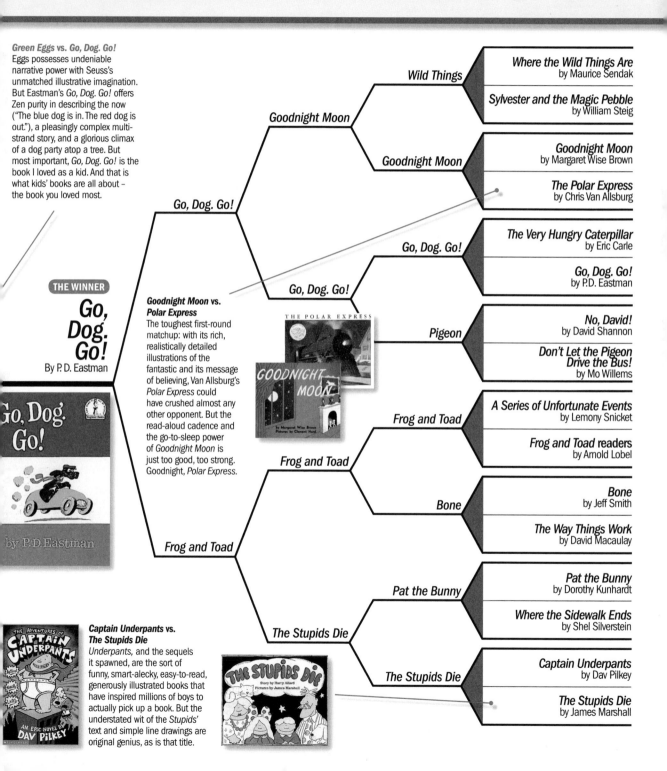

Green Eggs* vs. *Go, Dog. Go!
Eggs possesses undeniable narrative power with Seuss's unmatched illustrative imagination. But Eastman's *Go, Dog. Go!* offers Zen purity in describing the now ("The blue dog is in. The red dog is out."), a pleasingly complex multi-strand story, and a glorious climax of a dog party atop a tree. But most important, *Go, Dog. Go!* is the book I loved as a kid. And that is what kids' books are all about – the book you loved most.

THE WINNER

Go, Dog. Go!
By P. D. Eastman

Go, Dog. Go!
by P.D.Eastman

Goodnight Moon* vs. *Polar Express
The toughest first-round matchup: with its rich, realistically detailed illustrations of the fantastic and its message of believing, Van Allsburg's *Polar Express* could have crushed almost any other opponent. But the read-aloud cadence and the go-to-sleep power of *Goodnight Moon* is just too good, too strong. Goodnight, *Polar Express*.

THE POLAR EXPRESS

GOODNIGHT MOON
by Margaret Wise Brown
Pictures by Clement Hurd

Where the Wild Things Are by Maurice Sendak
Sylvester and the Magic Pebble by William Steig
— Wild Things

Goodnight Moon by Margaret Wise Brown
The Polar Express by Chris Van Allsburg
— Goodnight Moon

Wild Things vs. Goodnight Moon — Goodnight Moon

The Very Hungry Caterpillar by Eric Carle
Go, Dog. Go! by P.D. Eastman
— Go, Dog. Go!

No, David! by David Shannon
Don't Let the Pigeon Drive the Bus! by Mo Willems
— Pigeon

Go, Dog. Go! vs. Pigeon — Go, Dog. Go!

Goodnight Moon vs. Go, Dog. Go! — Go, Dog. Go!

A Series of Unfortunate Events by Lemony Snicket
Frog and Toad readers by Arnold Lobel
— Frog and Toad

Bone by Jeff Smith
The Way Things Work by David Macaulay
— Bone

Frog and Toad vs. Bone — Frog and Toad

Pat the Bunny by Dorothy Kunhardt
Where the Sidewalk Ends by Shel Silverstein
— Pat the Bunny

Captain Underpants by Dav Pilkey
The Stupids Die by James Marshall
— The Stupids Die

Pat the Bunny vs. The Stupids Die — The Stupids Die

Frog and Toad vs. The Stupids Die — Frog and Toad

Go, Dog. Go! vs. Frog and Toad — Go, Dog. Go!

THE ADVENTURES OF CAPTAIN UNDERPANTS
AN EPIC NOVEL BY DAV PILKEY

Captain Underpants* vs. *The Stupids Die
Underpants, and the sequels it spawned, are the sort of funny, smart-alecky, easy-to-read, generously illustrated books that have inspired millions of boys to actually pick up a book. But the understated wit of the *Stupids'* text and simple line drawings are original genius, as is that title.

THE STUPIDS DIE
Story by Harry Allard
Pictures by James Marshall

Cinematic Interrogatories

By John Steinbreder

John Steinbreder has written eight books, none about films. He's still asking himself why that is.

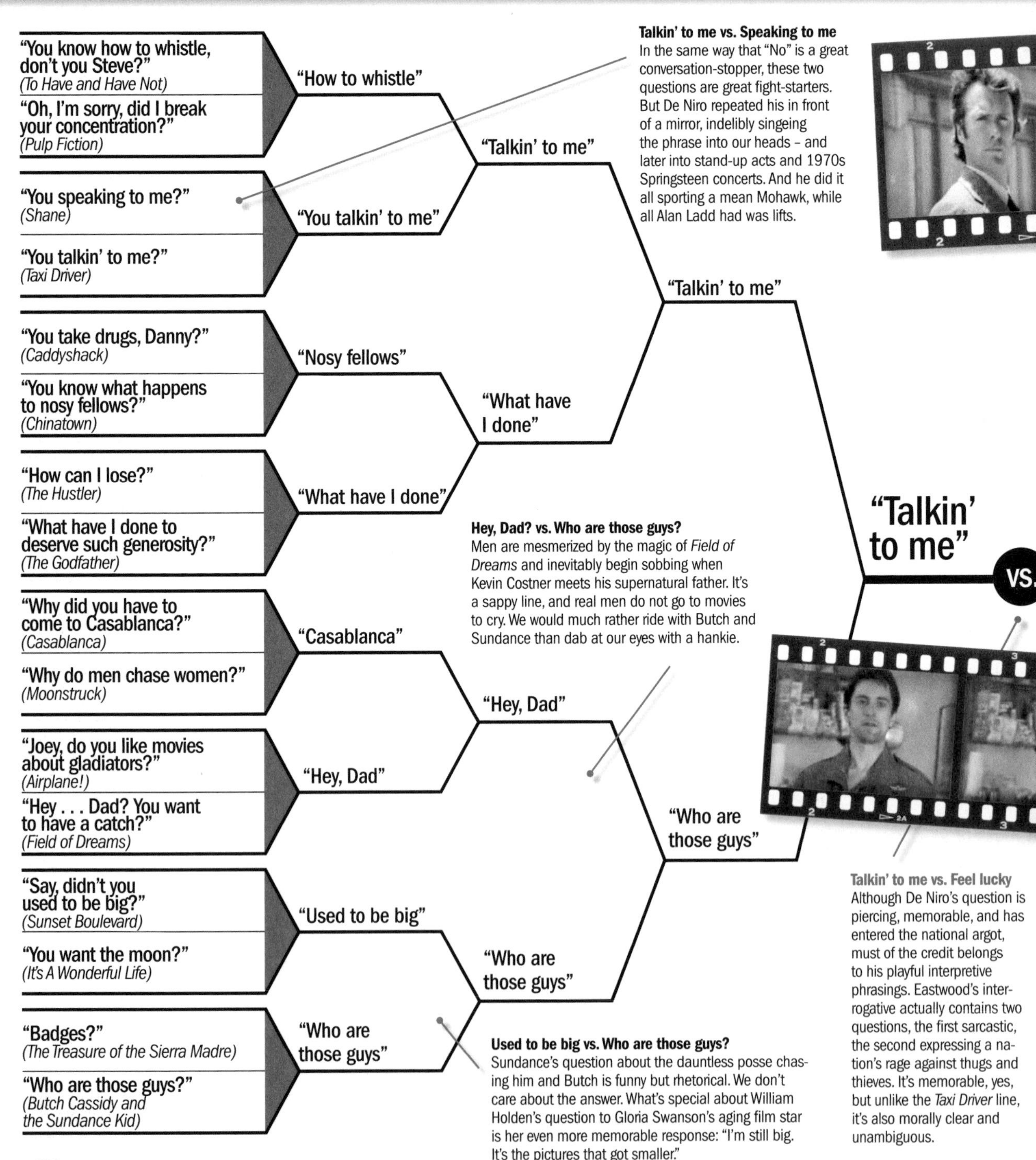
"You know how to whistle, don't you Steve?" (To Have and Have Not)
"Oh, I'm sorry, did I break your concentration?" (Pulp Fiction)
"How to whistle"
"You speaking to me?" (Shane)
"You talkin' to me?" (Taxi Driver)
"You talkin' to me"
"Talkin' to me"
"You take drugs, Danny?" (Caddyshack)
"You know what happens to nosy fellows?" (Chinatown)
"Nosy fellows"
"How can I lose?" (The Hustler)
"What have I done to deserve such generosity?" (The Godfather)
"What have I done"
"What have I done"
"Talkin' to me"
"Why did you have to come to Casablanca?" (Casablanca)
"Why do men chase women?" (Moonstruck)
"Casablanca"
"Joey, do you like movies about gladiators?" (Airplane!)
"Hey . . . Dad? You want to have a catch?" (Field of Dreams)
"Hey, Dad"
"Hey, Dad"
"Say, didn't you used to be big?" (Sunset Boulevard)
"You want the moon?" (It's A Wonderful Life)
"Used to be big"
"Badges?" (The Treasure of the Sierra Madre)
"Who are those guys?" (Butch Cassidy and the Sundance Kid)
"Who are those guys"
"Who are those guys"
"Who are those guys"
"Talkin' to me"
VS.

Talkin' to me vs. Speaking to me
In the same way that "No" is a great conversation-stopper, these two questions are great fight-starters. But De Niro repeated his in front of a mirror, indelibly singeing the phrase into our heads – and later into stand-up acts and 1970s Springsteen concerts. And he did it all sporting a mean Mohawk, while all Alan Ladd had was lifts.

Hey, Dad? vs. Who are those guys?
Men are mesmerized by the magic of *Field of Dreams* and inevitably begin sobbing when Kevin Costner meets his supernatural father. It's a sappy line, and real men do not go to movies to cry. We would much rather ride with Butch and Sundance than dab at our eyes with a hankie.

Used to be big vs. Who are those guys?
Sundance's question about the dauntless posse chasing him and Butch is funny but rhetorical. We don't care about the answer. What's special about William Holden's question to Gloria Swanson's aging film star is her even more memorable response: "I'm still big. It's the pictures that got smaller."

Talkin' to me vs. Feel lucky
Although De Niro's question is piercing, memorable, and has entered the national argot, must of the credit belongs to his playful interpretive phrasings. Eastwood's interrogative actually contains two questions, the first sarcastic, the second expressing a nation's rage against thugs and thieves. It's memorable, yes, but unlike the *Taxi Driver* line, it's also morally clear and unambiguous.

A GREAT MOVIE FEATURES AT LEAST ONE GREAT QUESTION. It could be the interrogative itself that shines. Or it's the answer that makes the query stand out. Still other questions stick in the mind because of constant repetition, as if recited by a Greek chorus (e.g., "Who are those guys?"). But the questions that go far here are the ones that define the individual asking them. For example, where would De Niro and Eastwood be as actor-icons if they never uttered a sharp interrogative early in their careers? Good question.

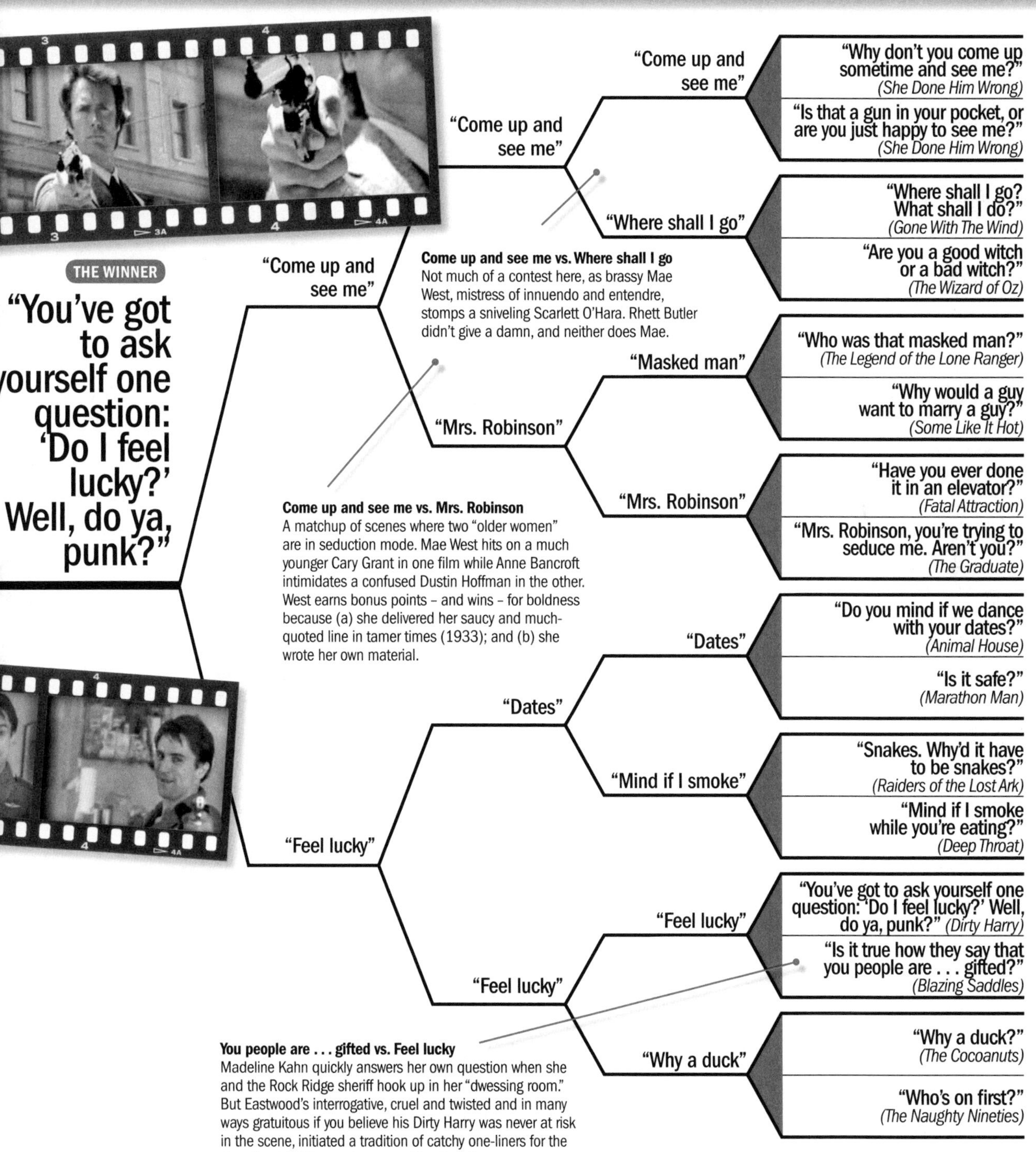
"Why don't you come up sometime and see me?" (She Done Him Wrong)
"Is that a gun in your pocket, or are you just happy to see me?" (She Done Him Wrong)
"Where shall I go? What shall I do?" (Gone With The Wind)
"Are you a good witch or a bad witch?" (The Wizard of Oz)
"Who was that masked man?" (The Legend of the Lone Ranger)
"Why would a guy want to marry a guy?" (Some Like It Hot)
"Have you ever done it in an elevator?" (Fatal Attraction)
"Mrs. Robinson, you're trying to seduce me. Aren't you?" (The Graduate)
"Do you mind if we dance with your dates?" (Animal House)
"Is it safe?" (Marathon Man)
"Snakes. Why'd it have to be snakes?" (Raiders of the Lost Ark)
"Mind if I smoke while you're eating?" (Deep Throat)
"You've got to ask yourself one question: 'Do I feel lucky?' Well, do ya, punk?" (Dirty Harry)
"Is it true how they say that you people are . . . gifted?" (Blazing Saddles)
"Why a duck?" (The Cocoanuts)
"Who's on first?" (The Naughty Nineties)
"Come up and see me"
"Where shall I go"
"Masked man"
"Mrs. Robinson"
"Dates"
"Mind if I smoke"
"Feel lucky"
"Why a duck"
"Come up and see me"
"Mrs. Robinson"
"Dates"
"Feel lucky"
"Come up and see me"
"Feel lucky"
THE WINNER
"You've got to ask yourself one question: 'Do I feel lucky?' Well, do ya, punk?"
Come up and see me vs. Where shall I go
Not much of a contest here, as brassy Mae West, mistress of innuendo and entendre, stomps a sniveling Scarlett O'Hara. Rhett Butler didn't give a damn, and neither does Mae.
Come up and see me vs. Mrs. Robinson
A matchup of scenes where two "older women" are in seduction mode. Mae West hits on a much younger Cary Grant in one film while Anne Bancroft intimidates a confused Dustin Hoffman in the other. West earns bonus points – and wins – for boldness because (a) she delivered her saucy and much-quoted line in tamer times (1933); and (b) she wrote her own material.
You people are . . . gifted vs. Feel lucky
Madeline Kahn quickly answers her own question when she and the Rock Ridge sheriff hook up in her "dwessing room." But Eastwood's interrogative, cruel and twisted and in many ways gratuitous if you believe his Dirty Harry was never at risk in the scene, initiated a tradition of catchy one-liners for the star. It made him number one, with a bullet.

Comic Strips

By R.C. Harvey

R.C. Harvey, one-time cartoonist and all-time comics chronicler, has authored nearly a dozen books about the arts and artisans of cartooning, all of which are described at his website, RCHarvey.com.

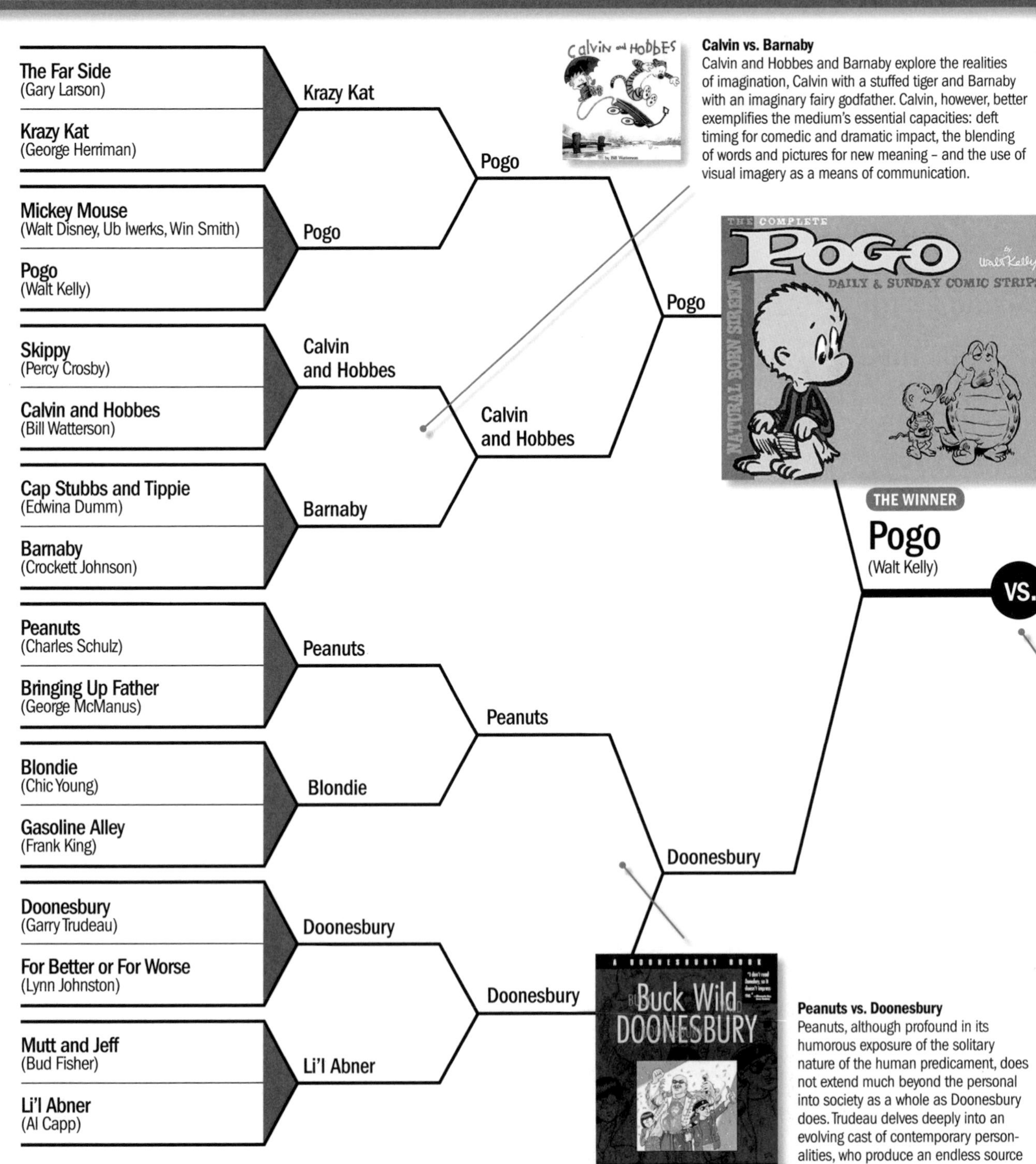

The Far Side (Gary Larson)
Krazy Kat (George Herriman)
Mickey Mouse (Walt Disney, Ub Iwerks, Win Smith)
Pogo (Walt Kelly)
Skippy (Percy Crosby)
Calvin and Hobbes (Bill Watterson)
Cap Stubbs and Tippie (Edwina Dumm)
Barnaby (Crockett Johnson)
Peanuts (Charles Schulz)
Bringing Up Father (George McManus)
Blondie (Chic Young)
Gasoline Alley (Frank King)
Doonesbury (Garry Trudeau)
For Better or For Worse (Lynn Johnston)
Mutt and Jeff (Bud Fisher)
Li'l Abner (Al Capp)
Krazy Kat
Pogo
Calvin and Hobbes
Barnaby
Peanuts
Blondie
Doonesbury
Li'l Abner
Pogo
Calvin and Hobbes
Peanuts
Doonesbury
Pogo
Doonesbury
THE WINNER
Pogo
(Walt Kelly)
VS.
Calvin and Hobbes
The Complete Pogo
by Walt Kelly
Daily & Sunday Comic Strips
A Doonesbury Book
Buck Wild Doonesbury
by G. B. Trudeau

Calvin vs. Barnaby
Calvin and Hobbes and Barnaby explore the realities of imagination, Calvin with a stuffed tiger and Barnaby with an imaginary fairy godfather. Calvin, however, better exemplifies the medium's essential capacities: deft timing for comedic and dramatic impact, the blending of words and pictures for new meaning – and the use of visual imagery as a means of communication.

Peanuts vs. Doonesbury
Peanuts, although profound in its humorous exposure of the solitary nature of the human predicament, does not extend much beyond the personal into society as a whole as Doonesbury does. Trudeau delves deeply into an evolving cast of contemporary personalities, who produce an endless source of satire and motivation.

THE BEST COMIC STRIPS over the past century blend the verbal and the visual to create a meaning that neither words nor pictures alone can achieve. Some of the of the masterworks are pace-setters (Mutt and Jeff, Wash Tubbs, The Far Side, Peanuts) or superb examples of the realistic illustration (Tarzan, Flash Gordon). Others are inimitable exploitations of the medium's capacities (Krazy Kat, Popeye, Calvin and Hobbes, Alley Oop) while still more are brilliantly satirical (Li'l Abner, Doonesbury, Pogo).

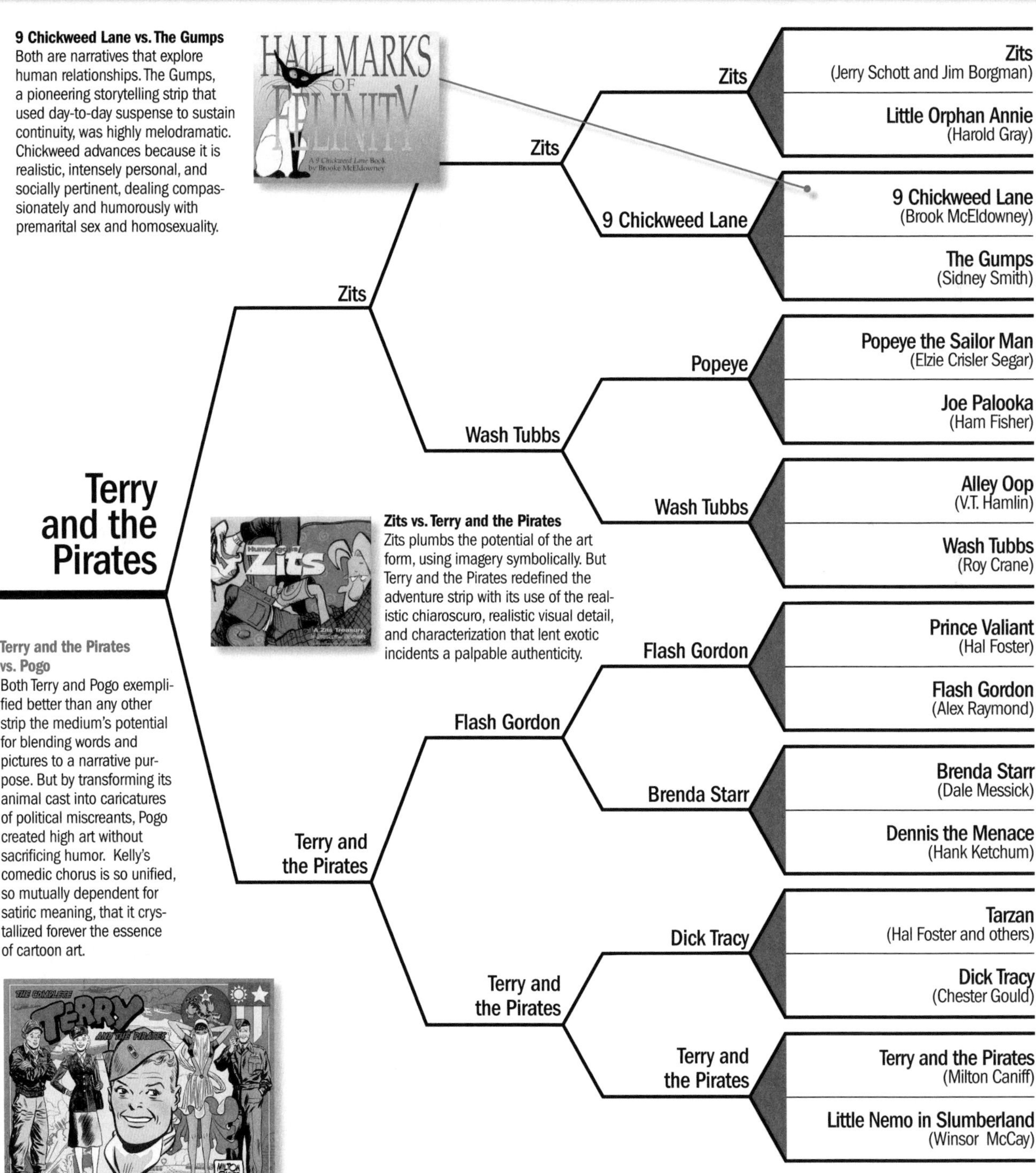
HALLMARKS OF FELINITY
A 9 Chickweed Lane Book by Brooke McEldowney
Zits
A Zits Treasury
THE COMPLETE TERRY AND THE PIRATES
MILTON CANIFF
Terry and the Pirates
Zits
Terry and the Pirates
Zits
Wash Tubbs
Flash Gordon
Terry and the Pirates
Zits
9 Chickweed Lane
Popeye
Wash Tubbs
Flash Gordon
Brenda Starr
Dick Tracy
Terry and the Pirates
Zits (Jerry Schott and Jim Borgman)
Little Orphan Annie (Harold Gray)
9 Chickweed Lane (Brook McEldowney)
The Gumps (Sidney Smith)
Popeye the Sailor Man (Elzie Crisler Segar)
Joe Palooka (Ham Fisher)
Alley Oop (V.T. Hamlin)
Wash Tubbs (Roy Crane)
Prince Valiant (Hal Foster)
Flash Gordon (Alex Raymond)
Brenda Starr (Dale Messick)
Dennis the Menace (Hank Ketchum)
Tarzan (Hal Foster and others)
Dick Tracy (Chester Gould)
Terry and the Pirates (Milton Caniff)
Little Nemo in Slumberland (Winsor McCay)

9 Chickweed Lane vs. The Gumps
Both are narratives that explore human relationships. The Gumps, a pioneering storytelling strip that used day-to-day suspense to sustain continuity, was highly melodramatic. Chickweed advances because it is realistic, intensely personal, and socially pertinent, dealing compassionately and humorously with premarital sex and homosexuality.

Zits vs. Terry and the Pirates
Zits plumbs the potential of the art form, using imagery symbolically. But Terry and the Pirates redefined the adventure strip with its use of the realistic chiaroscuro, realistic visual detail, and characterization that lent exotic incidents a palpable authenticity.

Terry and the Pirates vs. Pogo
Both Terry and Pogo exemplified better than any other strip the medium's potential for blending words and pictures to a narrative purpose. But by transforming its animal cast into caricatures of political miscreants, Pogo created high art without sacrificing humor. Kelly's comedic chorus is so unified, so mutually dependent for satiric meaning, that it crystallized forever the essence of cartoon art.

High School Movies

By Rick Staehling

Rick Staehling is the Canadian Broadcasting Corporation's film critic in British Columbia. His first published article, "The Truth About Teen Movies," appeared in *Rolling Stone* 40 years ago this year.

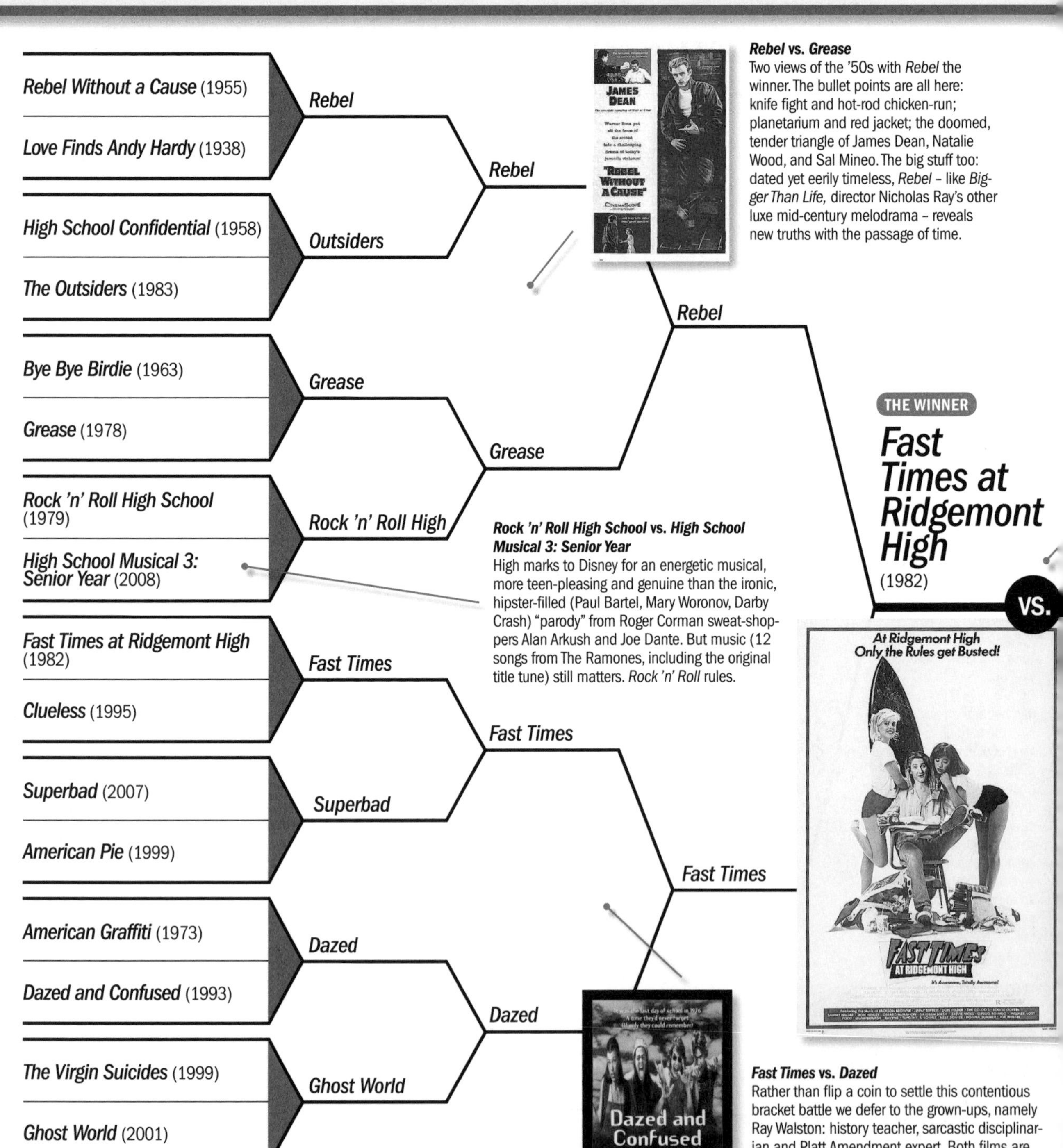
Rebel Without a Cause (1955)
Love Finds Andy Hardy (1938)
High School Confidential (1958)
The Outsiders (1983)
Bye Bye Birdie (1963)
Grease (1978)
Rock 'n' Roll High School (1979)
High School Musical 3: Senior Year (2008)
Fast Times at Ridgemont High (1982)
Clueless (1995)
Superbad (2007)
American Pie (1999)
American Graffiti (1973)
Dazed and Confused (1993)
The Virgin Suicides (1999)
Ghost World (2001)
Rebel
Outsiders
Grease
Rock 'n' Roll High
Fast Times
Superbad
Dazed
Ghost World
Rebel
Grease
Fast Times
Dazed
Rebel
Fast Times
JAMES DEAN
"REBEL WITHOUT A CAUSE"
THE WINNER
Fast Times at Ridgemont High (1982)
VS.
At Ridgemont High Only the Rules get Busted!
FAST TIMES AT RIDGEMONT HIGH
It's Awesome, Totally Awesome!
Dazed and Confused

Rebel* vs. *Grease
Two views of the '50s with *Rebel* the winner. The bullet points are all here: knife fight and hot-rod chicken-run; planetarium and red jacket; the doomed, tender triangle of James Dean, Natalie Wood, and Sal Mineo. The big stuff too: dated yet eerily timeless, *Rebel* – like *Bigger Than Life,* director Nicholas Ray's other luxe mid-century melodrama – reveals new truths with the passage of time.

Rock 'n' Roll High School* vs. *High School Musical 3: Senior Year
High marks to Disney for an energetic musical, more teen-pleasing and genuine than the ironic, hipster-filled (Paul Bartel, Mary Woronov, Darby Crash) "parody" from Roger Corman sweat-shoppers Alan Arkush and Joe Dante. But music (12 songs from The Ramones, including the original title tune) still matters. *Rock 'n' Roll* rules.

Fast Times* vs. *Dazed
Rather than flip a coin to settle this contentious bracket battle we defer to the grown-ups, namely Ray Walston: history teacher, sarcastic disciplinarian and Platt Amendment expert. Both films are loaded with stars-to-be and uncanny re-creations of period and place. But only *Fast Times* has Walston's Mr. Hand.

HIGH SCHOOL MOVIES, like first loves, summer songs, and out-of-business liquor stores, are potent reminders of our youth. They are also generational signifiers, as anyone who has witnessed unseemly arguments over the relative merits of *American Graffiti* and *Dazed and Confused* can attest. But unless you're like Matthew McConaughey's 22-year-old drivers' license bureau worker in *Dazed,* you eventually move on. Which is what we've done here: looking at 70 years of this enduring genre and making the calls based on merit, not personal memories.

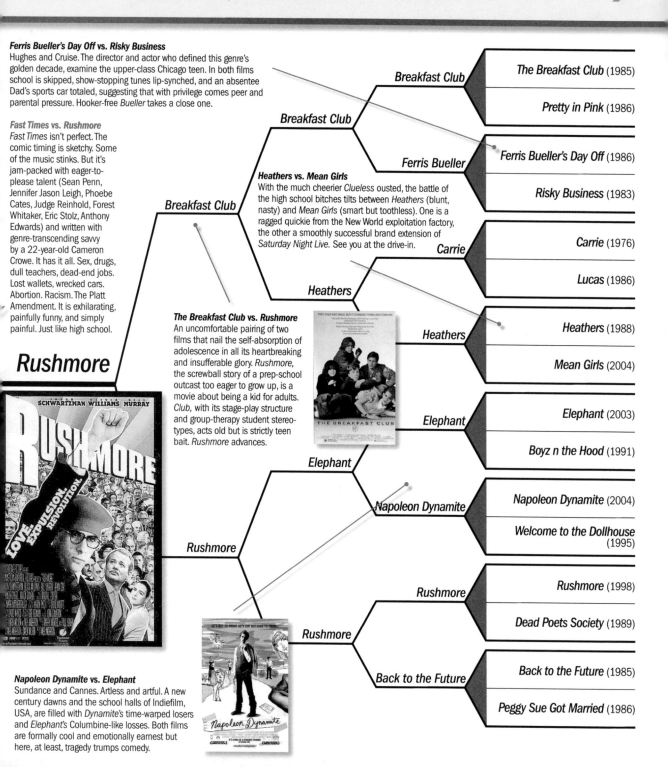

Ferris Bueller's Day Off* vs. *Risky Business
Hughes and Cruise. The director and actor who defined this genre's golden decade, examine the upper-class Chicago teen. In both films school is skipped, show-stopping tunes lip-synched, and an absentee Dad's sports car totaled, suggesting that with privilege comes peer and parental pressure. Hooker-free *Bueller* takes a close one.

Fast Times* vs. *Rushmore
Fast Times isn't perfect. The comic timing is sketchy. Some of the music stinks. But it's jam-packed with eager-to-please talent (Sean Penn, Jennifer Jason Leigh, Phoebe Cates, Judge Reinhold, Forest Whitaker, Eric Stolz, Anthony Edwards) and written with genre-transcending savvy by a 22-year-old Cameron Crowe. It has it all. Sex, drugs, dull teachers, dead-end jobs. Lost wallets, wrecked cars. Abortion. Racism. The Platt Amendment. It is exhilarating, painfully funny, and simply painful. Just like high school.

Heathers* vs. *Mean Girls
With the much cheerier *Clueless* ousted, the battle of the high school bitches tilts between *Heathers* (blunt, nasty) and *Mean Girls* (smart but toothless). One is a ragged quickie from the New World exploitation factory, the other a smoothly successful brand extension of *Saturday Night Live.* See you at the drive-in.

The Breakfast Club* vs. *Rushmore
An uncomfortable pairing of two films that nail the self-absorption of adolescence in all its heartbreaking and insufferable glory. *Rushmore,* the screwball story of a prep-school outcast too eager to grow up, is a movie about being a kid for adults. *Club,* with its stage-play structure and group-therapy student stereotypes, acts old but is strictly teen bait. *Rushmore* advances.

Napoleon Dynamite* vs. *Elephant
Sundance and Cannes. Artless and artful. A new century dawns and the school halls of Indiefilm, USA, are filled with *Dynamite's* time-warped losers and *Elephant's* Columbine-like losses. Both films are formally cool and emotionally earnest but here, at least, tragedy trumps comedy.

The Breakfast Club (1985)
Pretty in Pink (1986)
Ferris Bueller's Day Off (1986)
Risky Business (1983)
Carrie (1976)
Lucas (1986)
Heathers (1988)
Mean Girls (2004)
Elephant (2003)
Boyz n the Hood (1991)
Napoleon Dynamite (2004)
Welcome to the Dollhouse (1995)
Rushmore (1998)
Dead Poets Society (1989)
Back to the Future (1985)
Peggy Sue Got Married (1986)

Breakfast Club
Ferris Bueller
Carrie
Heathers
Elephant
Napoleon Dynamite
Rushmore
Back to the Future

Breakfast Club
Heathers
Elephant
Rushmore

Breakfast Club
Rushmore

Rushmore

Stunt Scenes
(or Greatest Gags)

By Kevin Conley

Kevin Conley has written two books, the latest being *The Full Burn: On the Set, At the Bar, Behind the Wheel, and Over the Edge with Hollywood Stuntmen,* during the course of which his interview subjects were kind enough to set him on fire.

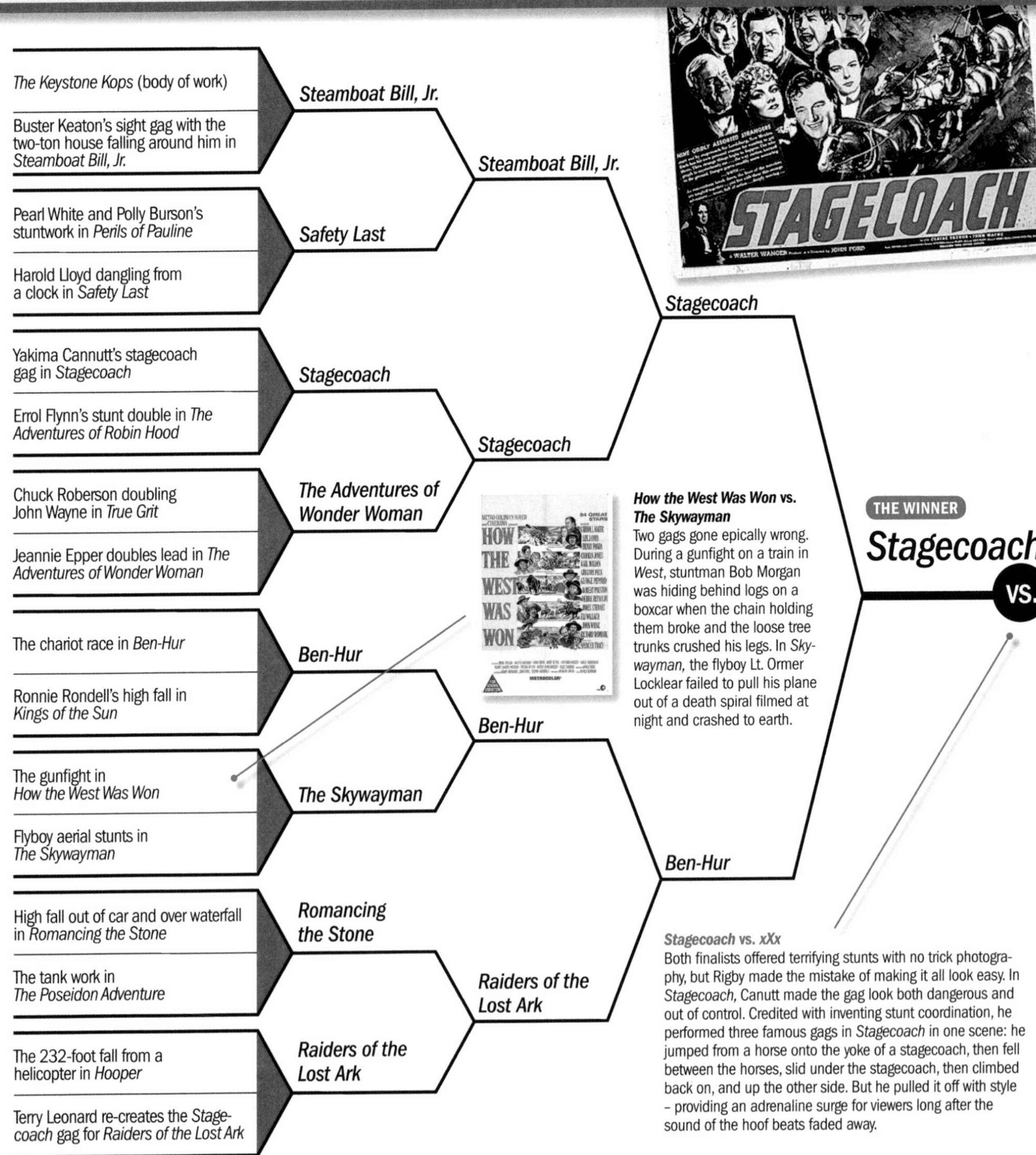

The Keystone Kops (body of work)
Buster Keaton's sight gag with the two-ton house falling around him in *Steamboat Bill, Jr.*
Pearl White and Polly Burson's stuntwork in *Perils of Pauline*
Harold Lloyd dangling from a clock in *Safety Last*
Yakima Cannutt's stagecoach gag in *Stagecoach*
Errol Flynn's stunt double in *The Adventures of Robin Hood*
Chuck Roberson doubling John Wayne in *True Grit*
Jeannie Epper doubles lead in *The Adventures of Wonder Woman*
The chariot race in *Ben-Hur*
Ronnie Rondell's high fall in *Kings of the Sun*
The gunfight in *How the West Was Won*
Flyboy aerial stunts in *The Skywayman*
High fall out of car and over waterfall in *Romancing the Stone*
The tank work in *The Poseidon Adventure*
The 232-foot fall from a helicopter in *Hooper*
Terry Leonard re-creates the *Stagecoach* gag for *Raiders of the Lost Ark*
Steamboat Bill, Jr.
Safety Last
Stagecoach
The Adventures of Wonder Woman
Ben-Hur
The Skywayman
Romancing the Stone
Raiders of the Lost Ark
Steamboat Bill, Jr.
Stagecoach
Ben-Hur
Raiders of the Lost Ark
Stagecoach
Ben-Hur
STAGECOACH
HOW THE WEST WAS WON
THE WINNER
Stagecoach
VS.

How the West Was Won* vs. *The Skywayman
Two gags gone epically wrong. During a gunfight on a train in *West*, stuntman Bob Morgan was hiding behind logs on a boxcar when the chain holding them broke and the loose tree trunks crushed his legs. In *Skywayman*, the flyboy Lt. Ormer Locklear failed to pull his plane out of a death spiral filmed at night and crashed to earth.

Stagecoach* vs. *xXx
Both finalists offered terrifying stunts with no trick photography, but Rigby made the mistake of making it all look easy. In *Stagecoach*, Canutt made the gag look both dangerous and out of control. Credited with inventing stunt coordination, he performed three famous gags in *Stagecoach* in one scene: he jumped from a horse onto the yoke of a stagecoach, then fell between the horses, slid under the stagecoach, then climbed back on, and up the other side. But he pulled it off with style – providing an adrenaline surge for viewers long after the sound of the hoof beats faded away.

HOLLYWOOD STUNTMEN refer to their feats as gags, a leftover from Keystone Kop days. A chase scene is a car gag; getting engulfed in flame is a fire gag; sliding beneath and between a stagecoach team moving at 35 miles an hour is a horse gag. Fame isn't a primary motivation for such derring-do. Stuntmen are contractually anonymous, and, what's worse, their greatest achievements often wind up in box-office losers. Determining the greatest stunts is left to stuntmen themselves, who know exactly what goes into their rough brand of movie magic. This tourney distills their shoptalk on the set.

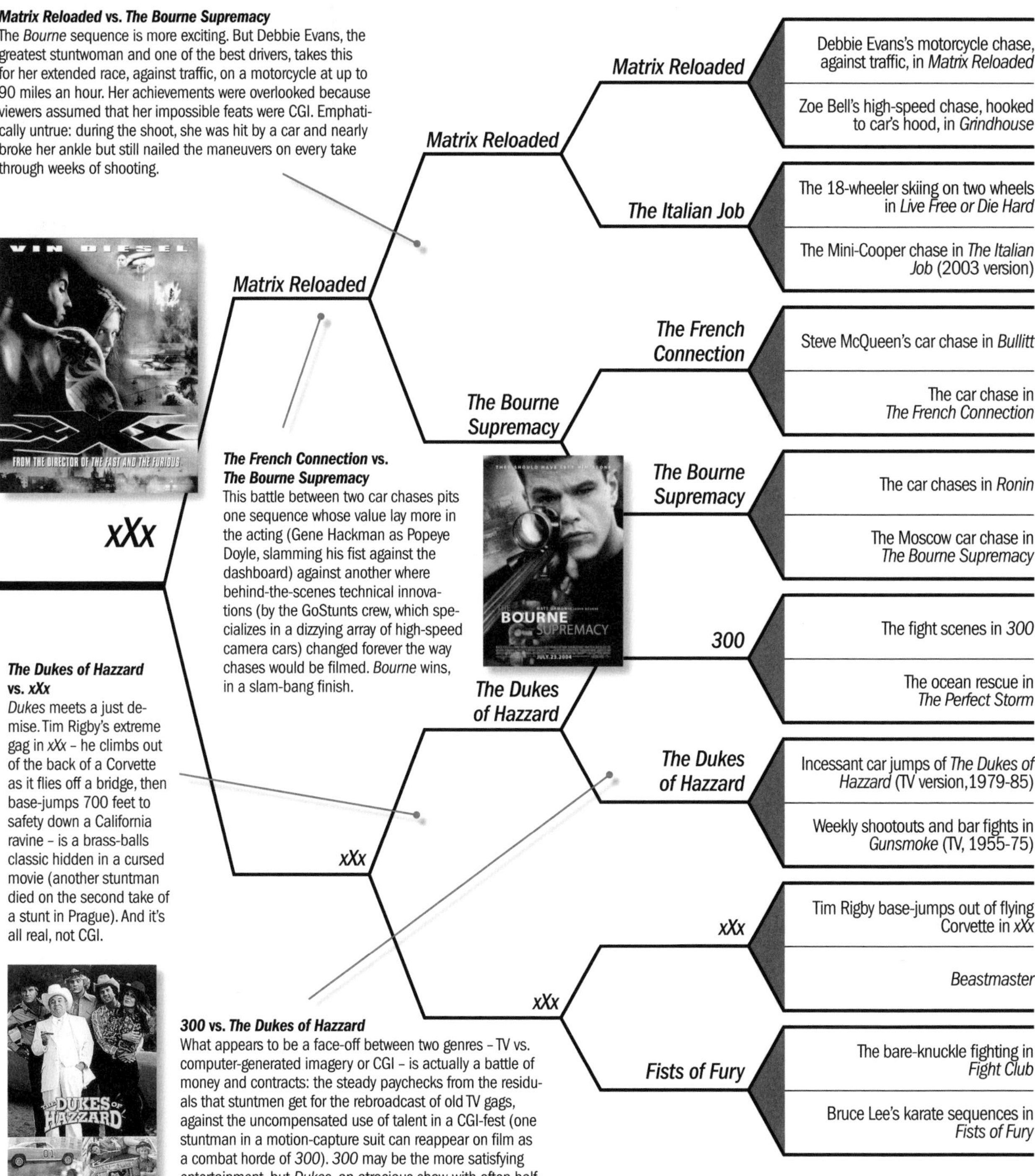

Debbie Evans's motorcycle chase, against traffic, in Matrix Reloaded
Zoe Bell's high-speed chase, hooked to car's hood, in Grindhouse
The 18-wheeler skiing on two wheels in Live Free or Die Hard
The Mini-Cooper chase in The Italian Job (2003 version)
Steve McQueen's car chase in Bullitt
The car chase in The French Connection
The car chases in Ronin
The Moscow car chase in The Bourne Supremacy
The fight scenes in 300
The ocean rescue in The Perfect Storm
Incessant car jumps of The Dukes of Hazzard (TV version,1979-85)
Weekly shootouts and bar fights in Gunsmoke (TV, 1955-75)
Tim Rigby base-jumps out of flying Corvette in xXx
Beastmaster
The bare-knuckle fighting in Fight Club
Bruce Lee's karate sequences in Fists of Fury
Matrix Reloaded
The Italian Job
The French Connection
The Bourne Supremacy
300
The Dukes of Hazzard
xXx
Fists of Fury
Matrix Reloaded
The Bourne Supremacy
The Dukes of Hazzard
xXx
Matrix Reloaded
xXx
xXx
VIN DIESEL
XXX
FROM THE DIRECTOR OF THE FAST AND THE FURIOUS
BOURNE SUPREMACY
DUKES OF HAZZARD

Matrix Reloaded* vs. *The Bourne Supremacy
The *Bourne* sequence is more exciting. But Debbie Evans, the greatest stuntwoman and one of the best drivers, takes this for her extended race, against traffic, on a motorcycle at up to 90 miles an hour. Her achievements were overlooked because viewers assumed that her impossible feats were CGI. Emphatically untrue: during the shoot, she was hit by a car and nearly broke her ankle but still nailed the maneuvers on every take through weeks of shooting.

The French Connection* vs. *The Bourne Supremacy
This battle between two car chases pits one sequence whose value lay more in the acting (Gene Hackman as Popeye Doyle, slamming his fist against the dashboard) against another where behind-the-scenes technical innovations (by the GoStunts crew, which specializes in a dizzying array of high-speed camera cars) changed forever the way chases would be filmed. *Bourne* wins, in a slam-bang finish.

The Dukes of Hazzard* vs. *xXx
Dukes meets a just demise. Tim Rigby's extreme gag in *xXx* – he climbs out of the back of a Corvette as it flies off a bridge, then base-jumps 700 feet to safety down a California ravine – is a brass-balls classic hidden in a cursed movie (another stuntman died on the second take of a stunt in Prague). And it's all real, not CGI.

300* vs. *The Dukes of Hazzard
What appears to be a face-off between two genres – TV vs. computer-generated imagery or CGI – is actually a battle of money and contracts: the steady paychecks from the residuals that stuntmen get for the rebroadcast of old TV gags, against the uncompensated use of talent in a CGI-fest (one stuntman in a motion-capture suit can reappear on film as a combat horde of *300*). *300* may be the more satisfying entertainment, but *Dukes*, an atrocious show with often half-ass stunts, paid full weight – and wins.

Impressionists

By Richard Sandomir

Richard Sandomir, the co-editor of this book, scares people with his Truman Capote impression.

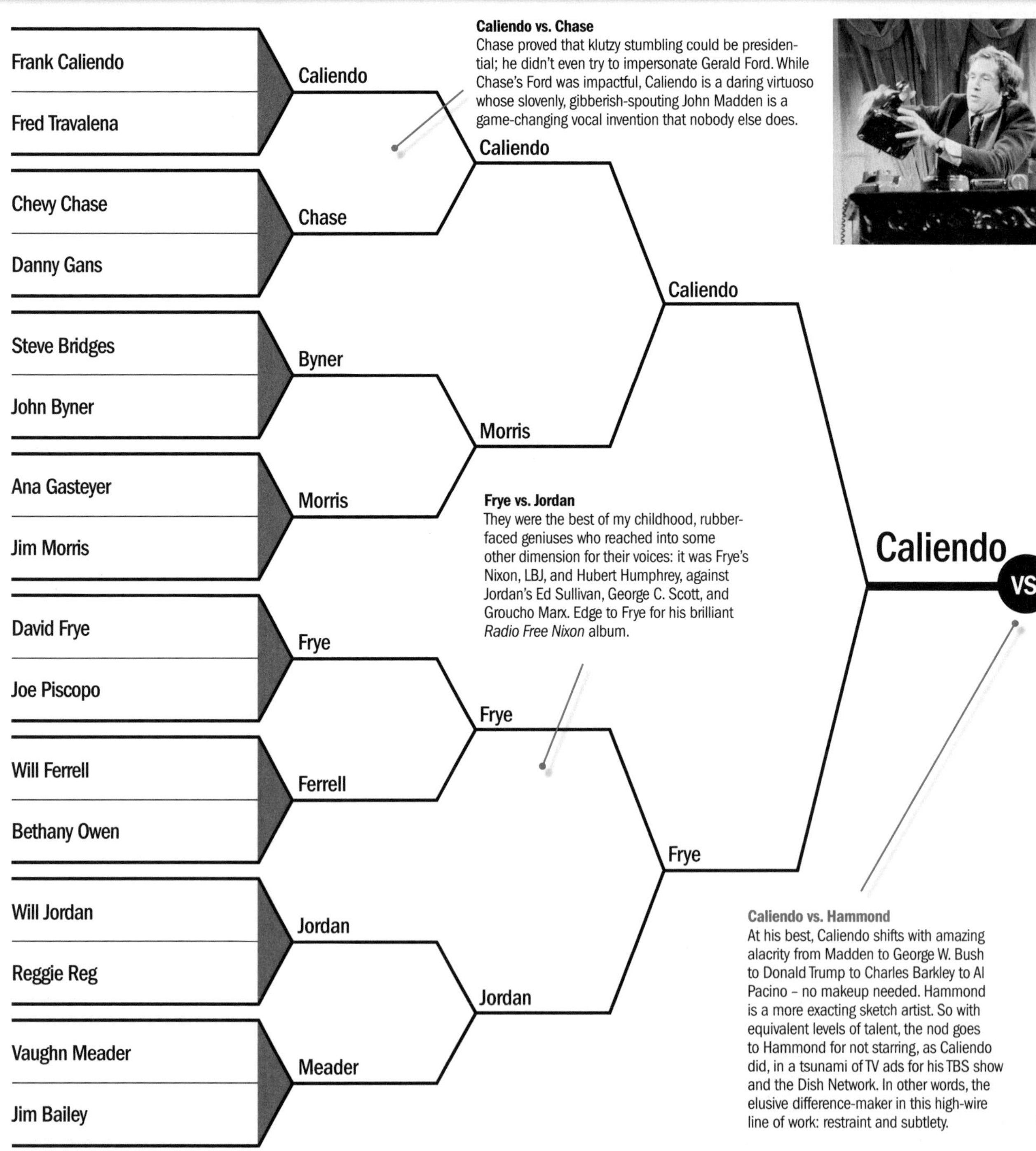

Frank Caliendo
Fred Travalena
Chevy Chase
Danny Gans
Steve Bridges
John Byner
Ana Gasteyer
Jim Morris
David Frye
Joe Piscopo
Will Ferrell
Bethany Owen
Will Jordan
Reggie Reg
Vaughn Meader
Jim Bailey
Caliendo
Chase
Byner
Morris
Frye
Ferrell
Jordan
Meader
Caliendo
Morris
Frye
Jordan
Caliendo
Frye
Caliendo
vs.

Caliendo vs. Chase
Chase proved that klutzy stumbling could be presidential; he didn't even try to impersonate Gerald Ford. While Chase's Ford was impactful, Caliendo is a daring virtuoso whose slovenly, gibberish-spouting John Madden is a game-changing vocal invention that nobody else does.

Frye vs. Jordan
They were the best of my childhood, rubber-faced geniuses who reached into some other dimension for their voices: it was Frye's Nixon, LBJ, and Hubert Humphrey, against Jordan's Ed Sullivan, George C. Scott, and Groucho Marx. Edge to Frye for his brilliant *Radio Free Nixon* album.

Caliendo vs. Hammond
At his best, Caliendo shifts with amazing alacrity from Madden to George W. Bush to Donald Trump to Charles Barkley to Al Pacino – no makeup needed. Hammond is a more exacting sketch artist. So with equivalent levels of talent, the nod goes to Hammond for not starring, as Caliendo did, in a tsunami of TV ads for his TBS show and the Dish Network. In other words, the elusive difference-maker in this high-wire line of work: restraint and subtlety.

I'VE BEEN DOING IMPRESSIONS SINCE I WAS A KID, starting with Frank Fontaine's Crazy Guggenheim from *The Jackie Gleason Show* and building to Ed Sullivan (my version of John Byner's) and Richard Nixon (a knockoff of David Frye's). I'm fascinated by the triggers that mimics find to capture a voice, such as Frank Caliendo developing his Charles Barkley around the Round Mound of Rebound's pronunciation of "terrible." Everyone here is talented but the edge goes to verbal skill coupled with great material, which a great mimic like Rich Little (a Canadian, thus not invited) has never had.

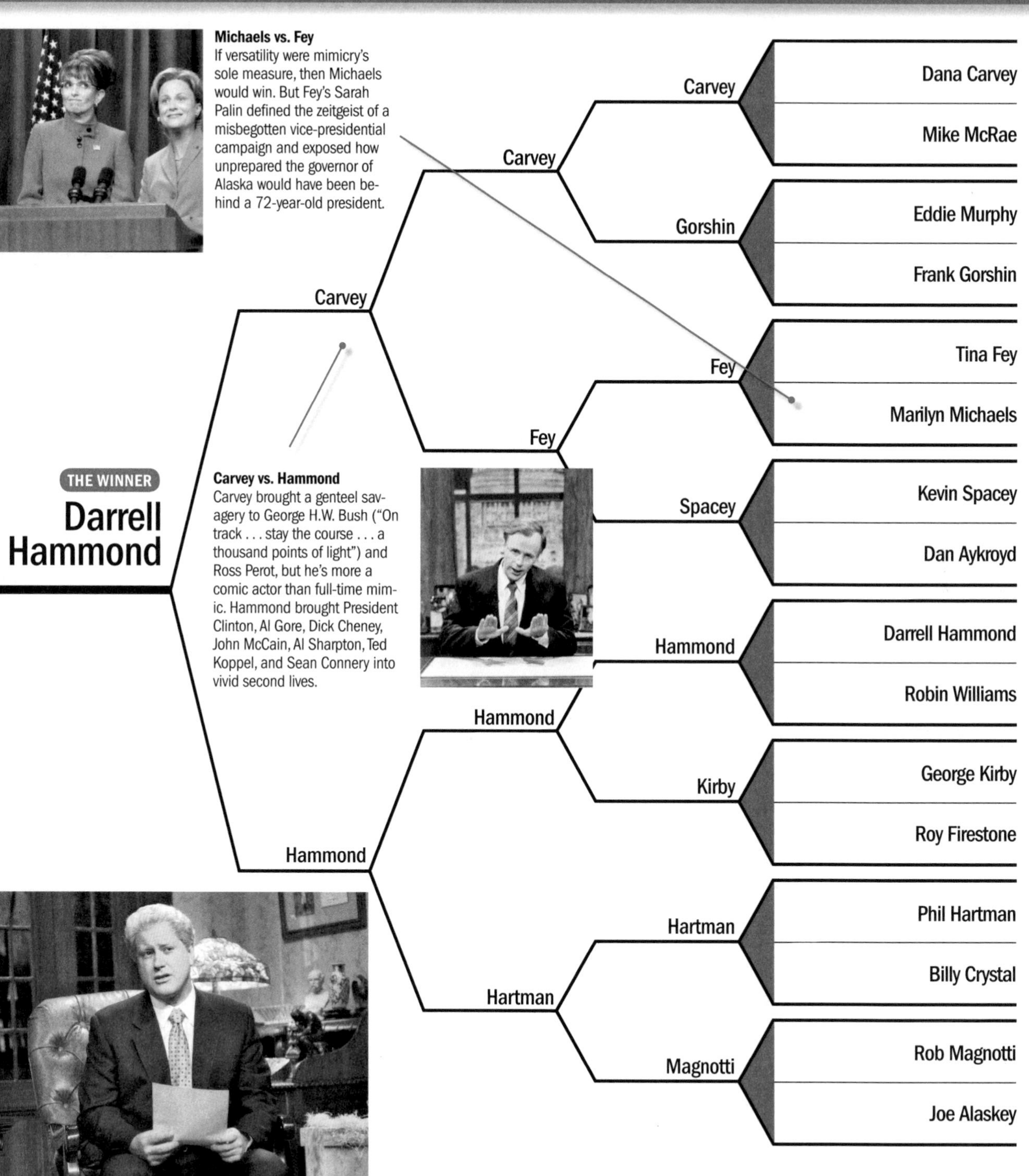

Dana Carvey
Mike McRae
Eddie Murphy
Frank Gorshin
Tina Fey
Marilyn Michaels
Kevin Spacey
Dan Aykroyd
Darrell Hammond
Robin Williams
George Kirby
Roy Firestone
Phil Hartman
Billy Crystal
Rob Magnotti
Joe Alaskey
Carvey
Gorshin
Fey
Spacey
Hammond
Kirby
Hartman
Magnotti
Carvey
Fey
Hammond
Hartman
Carvey
Hammond
THE WINNER
Darrell Hammond

Michaels vs. Fey
If versatility were mimicry's sole measure, then Michaels would win. But Fey's Sarah Palin defined the zeitgeist of a misbegotten vice-presidential campaign and exposed how unprepared the governor of Alaska would have been behind a 72-year-old president.

Carvey vs. Hammond
Carvey brought a genteel savagery to George H.W. Bush ("On track . . . stay the course . . . a thousand points of light") and Ross Perot, but he's more a comic actor than full-time mimic. Hammond brought President Clinton, Al Gore, Dick Cheney, John McCain, Al Sharpton, Ted Koppel, and Sean Connery into vivid second lives.

Literary Heroes

By B.R. Myers

B.R. Myers is a contributing editor of *The Atlantic* and the author of *A Reader's Manifesto.*

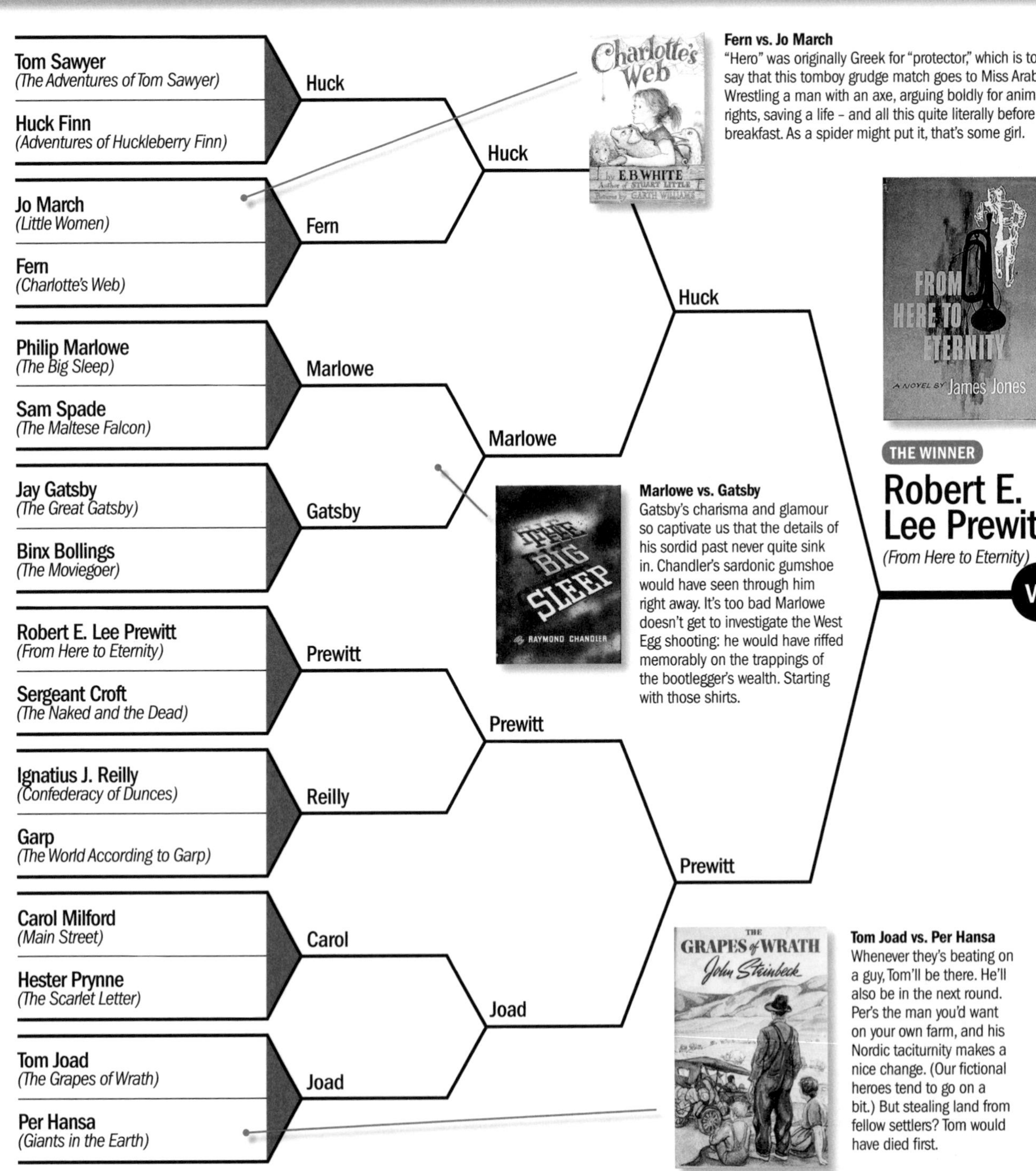
Tom Sawyer
(The Adventures of Tom Sawyer)
Huck Finn
(Adventures of Huckleberry Finn)
Jo March
(Little Women)
Fern
(Charlotte's Web)
Philip Marlowe
(The Big Sleep)
Sam Spade
(The Maltese Falcon)
Jay Gatsby
(The Great Gatsby)
Binx Bollings
(The Moviegoer)
Robert E. Lee Prewitt
(From Here to Eternity)
Sergeant Croft
(The Naked and the Dead)
Ignatius J. Reilly
(Confederacy of Dunces)
Garp
(The World According to Garp)
Carol Milford
(Main Street)
Hester Prynne
(The Scarlet Letter)
Tom Joad
(The Grapes of Wrath)
Per Hansa
(Giants in the Earth)
Huck
Fern
Marlowe
Gatsby
Prewitt
Reilly
Carol
Joad
Huck
Marlowe
Prewitt
Joad
Huck
Prewitt
Charlotte's Web
by E.B. WHITE
FROM HERE TO ETERNITY
A NOVEL BY James Jones
THE BIG SLEEP
By RAYMOND CHANDLER
THE GRAPES of WRATH
John Steinbeck
VS.

Fern vs. Jo March
"Hero" was originally Greek for "protector," which is to say that this tomboy grudge match goes to Miss Arable. Wrestling a man with an axe, arguing boldly for animal rights, saving a life – and all this quite literally before breakfast. As a spider might put it, that's some girl.

THE WINNER

Robert E. Lee Prewitt

(From Here to Eternity)

Marlowe vs. Gatsby
Gatsby's charisma and glamour so captivate us that the details of his sordid past never quite sink in. Chandler's sardonic gumshoe would have seen through him right away. It's too bad Marlowe doesn't get to investigate the West Egg shooting: he would have riffed memorably on the trappings of the bootlegger's wealth. Starting with those shirts.

Tom Joad vs. Per Hansa
Whenever they's beating on a guy, Tom'll be there. He'll also be in the next round. Per's the man you'd want on your own farm, and his Nordic taciturnity makes a nice change. (Our fictional heroes tend to go on a bit.) But stealing land from fellow settlers? Tom would have died first.

WOULD WE BE AS INTERESTED IN OUR LITERARY HEROES if they were real people? Take all those existential Everymen with their midlife crises and ridiculous names: we wouldn't cross the road to say hello, let alone emulate them. Literary purists may be outraged, but it's time to separate the protagonists from the heroes – using the latter word in its popular sense. Entrants hail from fiction of established literary standard or fame, but now they're on their own. To advance you need heroic qualities, with points subtracted for things like murder and rudeness.

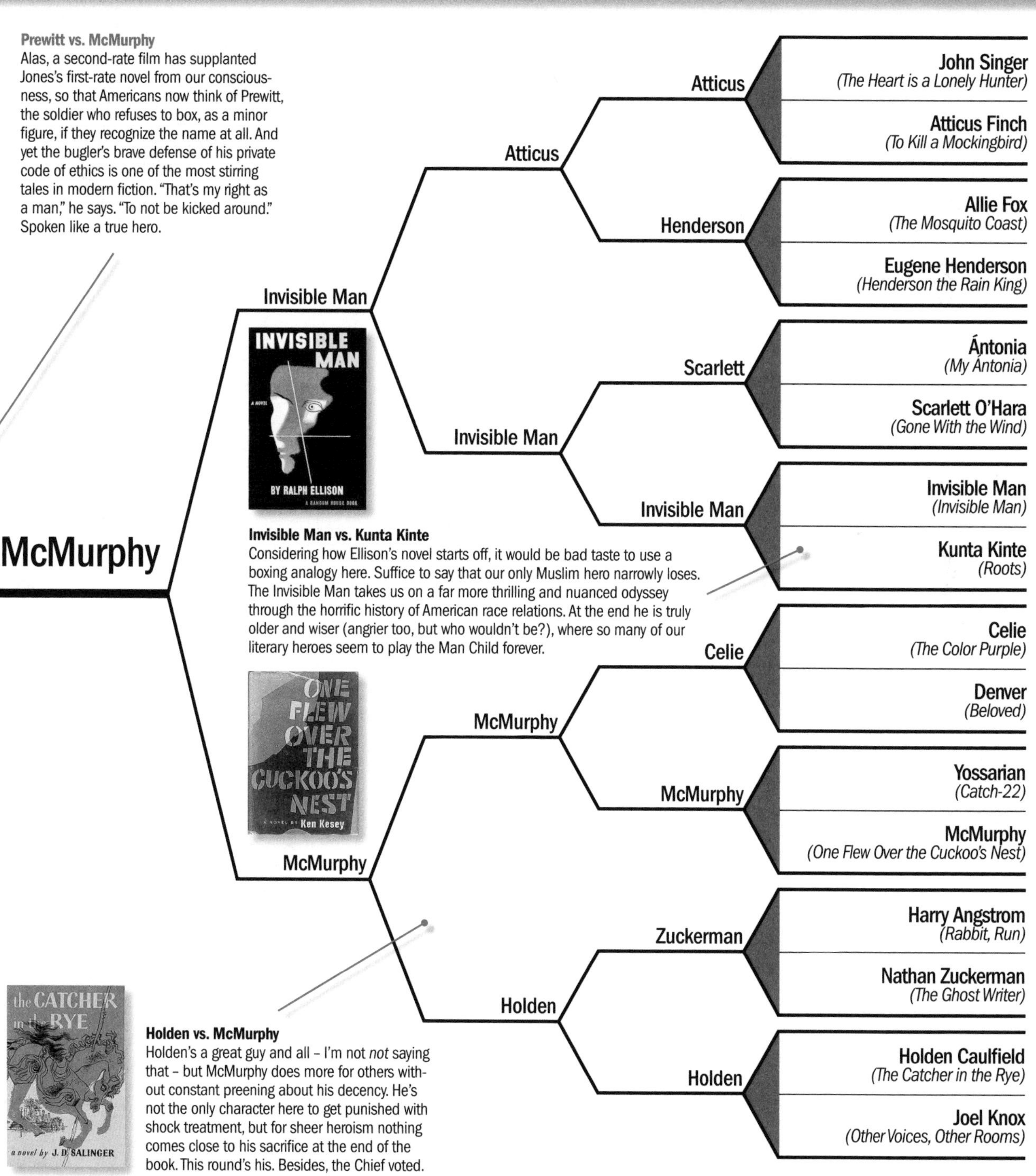

John Singer
(The Heart is a Lonely Hunter)
Atticus Finch
(To Kill a Mockingbird)
Allie Fox
(The Mosquito Coast)
Eugene Henderson
(Henderson the Rain King)
Ántonia
(My Ántonia)
Scarlett O'Hara
(Gone With the Wind)
Invisible Man
(Invisible Man)
Kunta Kinte
(Roots)
Celie
(The Color Purple)
Denver
(Beloved)
Yossarian
(Catch-22)
McMurphy
(One Flew Over the Cuckoo's Nest)
Harry Angstrom
(Rabbit, Run)
Nathan Zuckerman
(The Ghost Writer)
Holden Caulfield
(The Catcher in the Rye)
Joel Knox
(Other Voices, Other Rooms)
Atticus
Henderson
Scarlett
Invisible Man
Celie
McMurphy
Zuckerman
Holden
Atticus
Invisible Man
McMurphy
Holden
Invisible Man
McMurphy
McMurphy
INVISIBLE MAN
A NOVEL
BY RALPH ELLISON
ONE FLEW OVER THE CUCKOO'S NEST
A NOVEL BY Ken Kesey
the CATCHER in the RYE
a novel by J. D. SALINGER

Prewitt vs. McMurphy
Alas, a second-rate film has supplanted Jones's first-rate novel from our consciousness, so that Americans now think of Prewitt, the soldier who refuses to box, as a minor figure, if they recognize the name at all. And yet the bugler's brave defense of his private code of ethics is one of the most stirring tales in modern fiction. "That's my right as a man," he says. "To not be kicked around." Spoken like a true hero.

Invisible Man vs. Kunta Kinte
Considering how Ellison's novel starts off, it would be bad taste to use a boxing analogy here. Suffice to say that our only Muslim hero narrowly loses. The Invisible Man takes us on a far more thrilling and nuanced odyssey through the horrific history of American race relations. At the end he is truly older and wiser (angrier too, but who wouldn't be?), where so many of our literary heroes seem to play the Man Child forever.

Holden vs. McMurphy
Holden's a great guy and all – I'm not *not* saying that – but McMurphy does more for others without constant preening about his decency. He's not the only character here to get punished with shock treatment, but for sheer heroism nothing comes close to his sacrifice at the end of the book. This round's his. Besides, the Chief voted.

Comedy Routines

By Bill Scheft

Bill Scheft, a longtime writer for David Letterman, is the author of three novels, including *Everything Hurts*. Once a house MC at Catch a Rising Star in New York, he is not bitter about the less talented acts who wound up with bigger careers. Don't even go there.

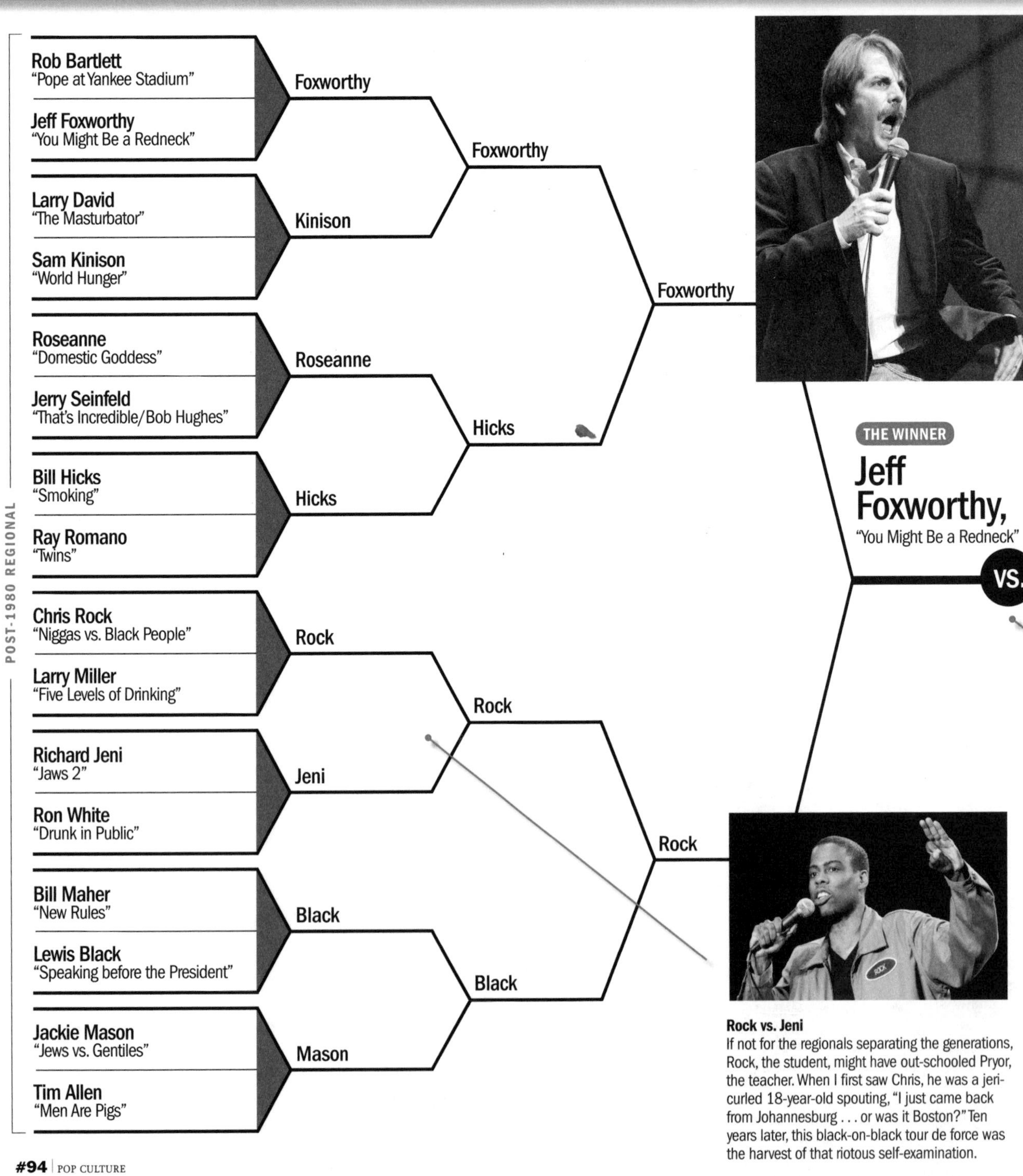

POST-1980 REGIONAL
Rob Bartlett
"Pope at Yankee Stadium"
Jeff Foxworthy
"You Might Be a Redneck"
Larry David
"The Masturbator"
Sam Kinison
"World Hunger"
Roseanne
"Domestic Goddess"
Jerry Seinfeld
"That's Incredible/Bob Hughes"
Bill Hicks
"Smoking"
Ray Romano
"Twins"
Chris Rock
"Niggas vs. Black People"
Larry Miller
"Five Levels of Drinking"
Richard Jeni
"Jaws 2"
Ron White
"Drunk in Public"
Bill Maher
"New Rules"
Lewis Black
"Speaking before the President"
Jackie Mason
"Jews vs. Gentiles"
Tim Allen
"Men Are Pigs"
Foxworthy
Kinison
Roseanne
Hicks
Rock
Jeni
Black
Mason
Foxworthy
Hicks
Rock
Black
Foxworthy
Rock
THE WINNER
Jeff Foxworthy,
"You Might Be a Redneck"
VS.

Rock vs. Jeni
If not for the regionals separating the generations, Rock, the student, might have out-schooled Pryor, the teacher. When I first saw Chris, he was a jeri-curled 18-year-old spouting, "I just came back from Johannesburg . . . or was it Boston?" Ten years later, this black-on-black tour de force was the harvest of that riotous self-examination.

THERE ARE TWO TYPES OF JOKES: The first makes you say, "Why didn't I think of that?" The second makes you say, "In a million years, I couldn't come up with that." Welcome to 32 people writing nothing but the second type. I know, I know. Many are missing but I limited the field to first-hand knowledge of self-contained bits by comics, which meant no line guys, non-sequitarians, or topical monologists. Regrets to, among others, Mitch Hedberg, Dave Atell, Steven Wright, Mort Sahl, Robin, Jon, Johnny, Joan. And um, Dave, I'll have my desk cleared out Monday.

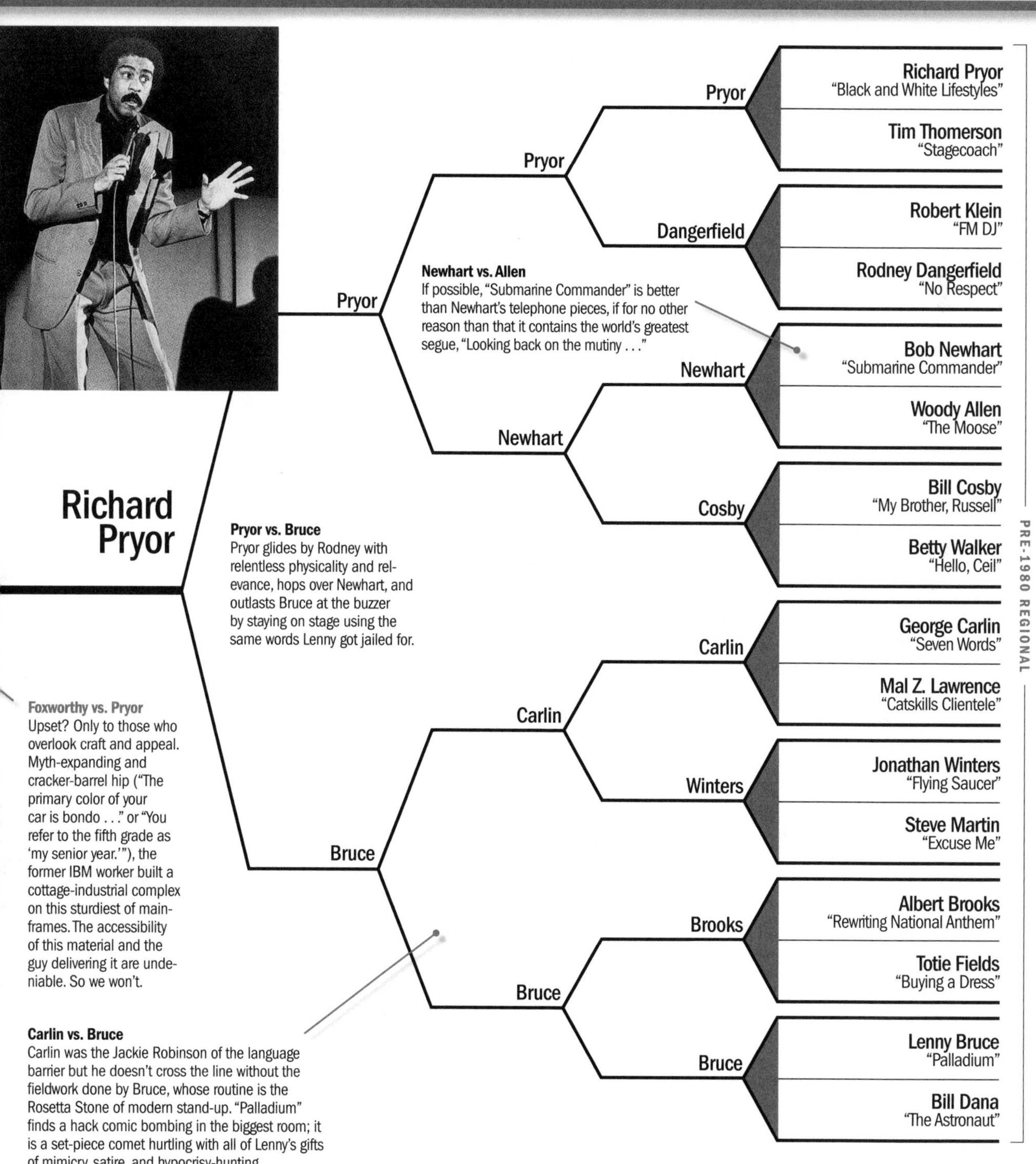

Richard Pryor
PRE-1980 REGIONAL
Richard Pryor
"Black and White Lifestyles"
Tim Thomerson
"Stagecoach"
Robert Klein
"FM DJ"
Rodney Dangerfield
"No Respect"
Bob Newhart
"Submarine Commander"
Woody Allen
"The Moose"
Bill Cosby
"My Brother, Russell"
Betty Walker
"Hello, Ceil"
George Carlin
"Seven Words"
Mal Z. Lawrence
"Catskills Clientele"
Jonathan Winters
"Flying Saucer"
Steve Martin
"Excuse Me"
Albert Brooks
"Rewriting National Anthem"
Totie Fields
"Buying a Dress"
Lenny Bruce
"Palladium"
Bill Dana
"The Astronaut"
Pryor
Dangerfield
Newhart
Cosby
Carlin
Winters
Brooks
Bruce
Pryor
Newhart
Carlin
Bruce
Pryor
Bruce

Newhart vs. Allen
If possible, "Submarine Commander" is better than Newhart's telephone pieces, if for no other reason than that it contains the world's greatest segue, "Looking back on the mutiny . . ."

Pryor vs. Bruce
Pryor glides by Rodney with relentless physicality and relevance, hops over Newhart, and outlasts Bruce at the buzzer by staying on stage using the same words Lenny got jailed for.

Foxworthy vs. Pryor
Upset? Only to those who overlook craft and appeal. Myth-expanding and cracker-barrel hip ("The primary color of your car is bondo . . ." or "You refer to the fifth grade as 'my senior year.'"), the former IBM worker built a cottage-industrial complex on this sturdiest of mainframes. The accessibility of this material and the guy delivering it are undeniable. So we won't.

Carlin vs. Bruce
Carlin was the Jackie Robinson of the language barrier but he doesn't cross the line without the fieldwork done by Bruce, whose routine is the Rosetta Stone of modern stand-up. "Palladium" finds a hack comic bombing in the biggest room; it is a set-piece comet hurtling with all of Lenny's gifts of mimicry, satire, and hypocrisy-hunting.

Worst Movies by Great Directors

By A.O. Scott

A.O. Scott is a film critic at the *New York Times.*

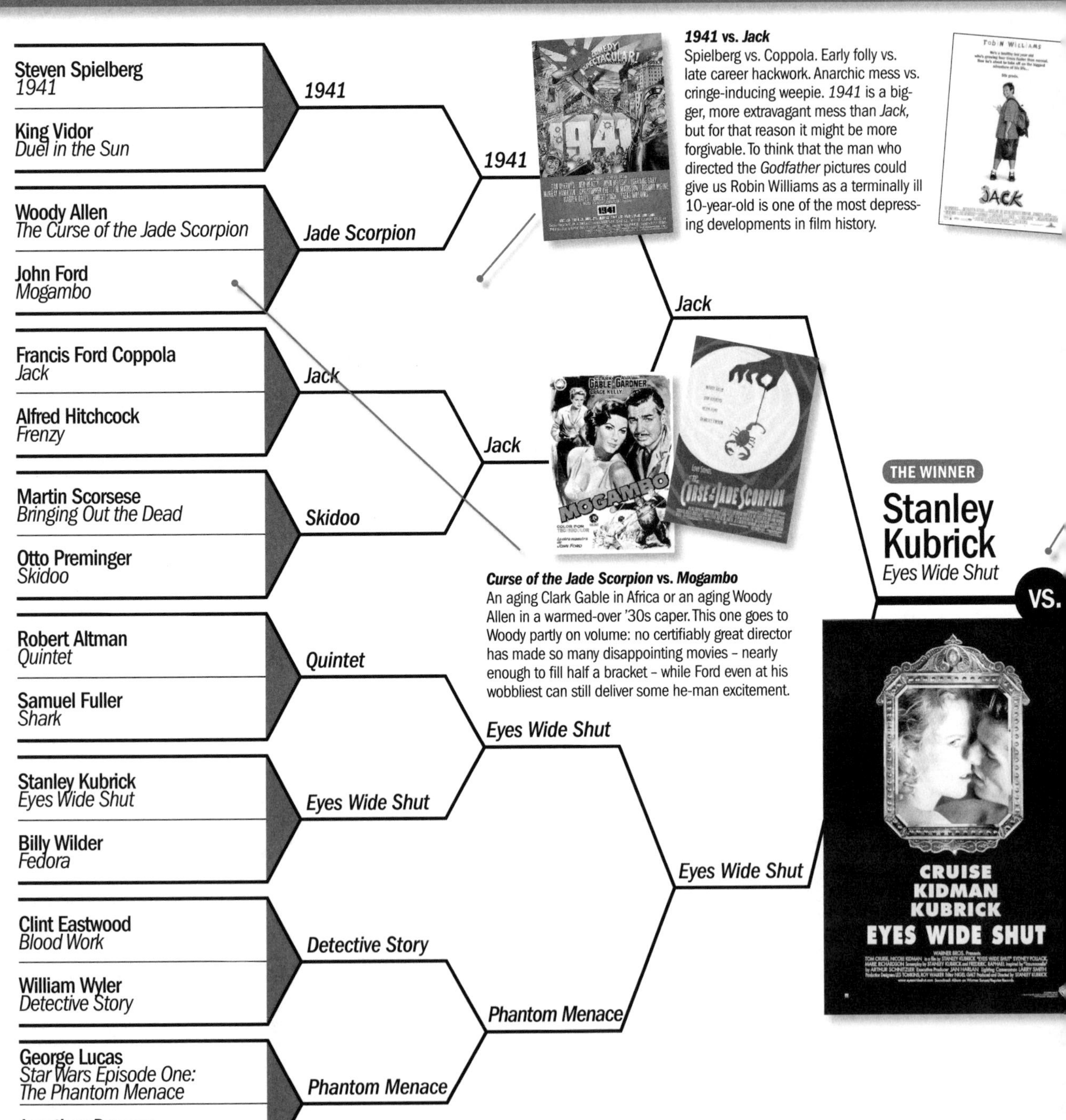

Steven Spielberg
1941
King Vidor
Duel in the Sun
Woody Allen
The Curse of the Jade Scorpion
John Ford
Mogambo
Francis Ford Coppola
Jack
Alfred Hitchcock
Frenzy
Martin Scorsese
Bringing Out the Dead
Otto Preminger
Skidoo
Robert Altman
Quintet
Samuel Fuller
Shark
Stanley Kubrick
Eyes Wide Shut
Billy Wilder
Fedora
Clint Eastwood
Blood Work
William Wyler
Detective Story
George Lucas
Star Wars Episode One: The Phantom Menace
Jonathan Demme
Beloved
1941
Jade Scorpion
Jack
Skidoo
Quintet
Eyes Wide Shut
Detective Story
Phantom Menace
1941
Jack
Eyes Wide Shut
Phantom Menace
Jack
Eyes Wide Shut
THE WINNER
Stanley Kubrick
Eyes Wide Shut
VS.
JACK
MOGAMBO
CRUISE
KIDMAN
KUBRICK
EYES WIDE SHUT

1941* vs. *Jack
Spielberg vs. Coppola. Early folly vs. late career hackwork. Anarchic mess vs. cringe-inducing weepie. *1941* is a bigger, more extravagant mess than *Jack,* but for that reason it might be more forgivable. To think that the man who directed the *Godfather* pictures could give us Robin Williams as a terminally ill 10-year-old is one of the most depressing developments in film history.

Curse of the Jade Scorpion* vs. *Mogambo
An aging Clark Gable in Africa or an aging Woody Allen in a warmed-over '30s caper. This one goes to Woody partly on volume: no certifiably great director has made so many disappointing movies – nearly enough to fill half a bracket – while Ford even at his wobbliest can still deliver some he-man excitement.

NOBODY SETS OUT TO MAKE A BAD MOVIE, and an old adage holds that a stinker is just as hard to produce as a masterpiece. But amid the heap of bombs, turkeys, and dogs that Hollywood has churned out, a special place is reserved for the failures of artists who should have known better. A Qualitative Inversion Formula™ is applied to the pictures below, whereby what is rewarded is not just the raw awfulness of a given movie, but also the gap between its putrescence and the awesomeness of its director's grandest accomplishments.

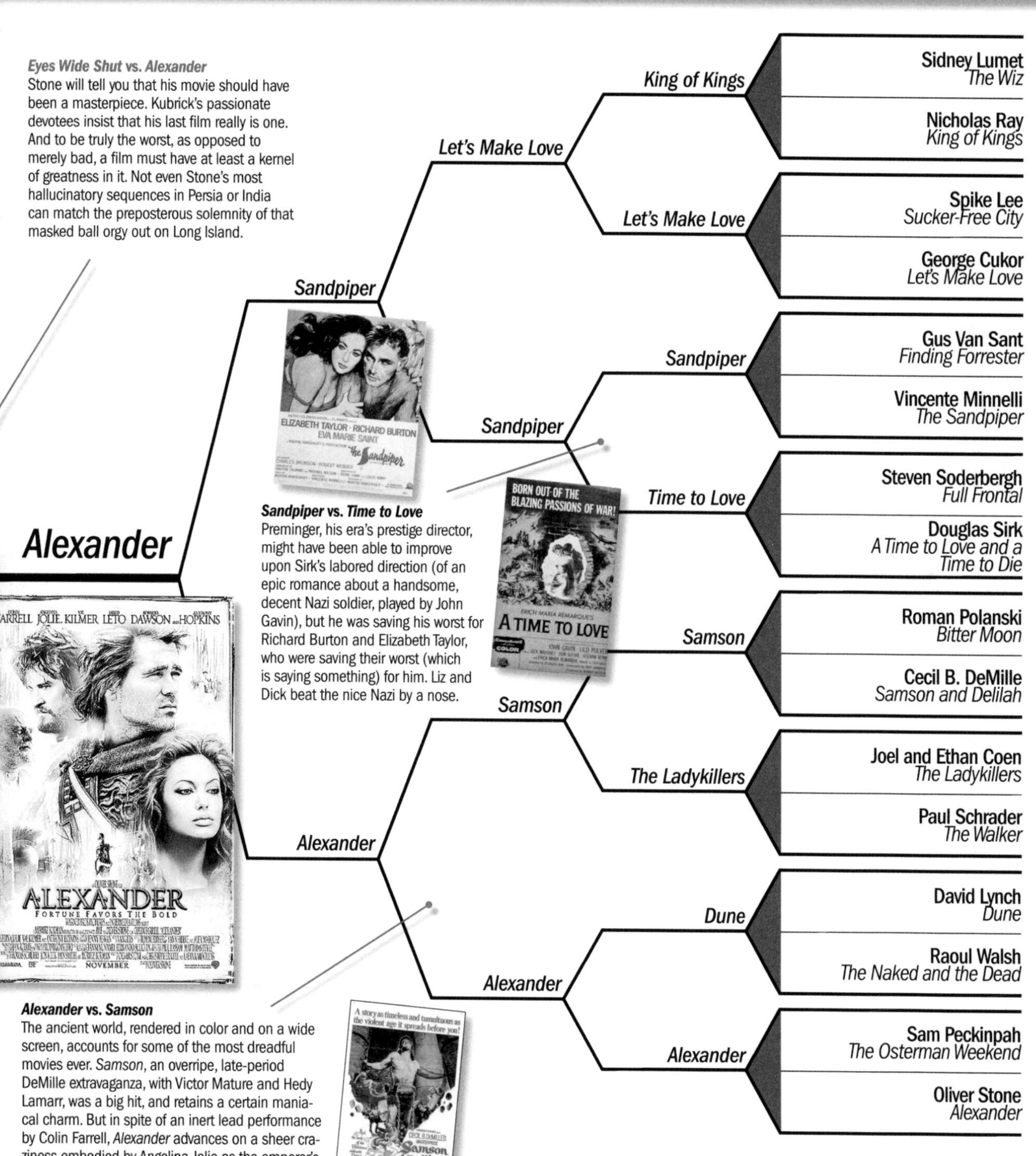

Sidney Lumet
The Wiz
Nicholas Ray
King of Kings
Spike Lee
Sucker-Free City
George Cukor
Let's Make Love
Gus Van Sant
Finding Forrester
Vincente Minnelli
The Sandpiper
Steven Soderbergh
Full Frontal
Douglas Sirk
A Time to Love and a Time to Die
Roman Polanski
Bitter Moon
Cecil B. DeMille
Samson and Delilah
Joel and Ethan Coen
The Ladykillers
Paul Schrader
The Walker
David Lynch
Dune
Raoul Walsh
The Naked and the Dead
Sam Peckinpah
The Osterman Weekend
Oliver Stone
Alexander
King of Kings
Let's Make Love
Sandpiper
Time to Love
Samson
The Ladykillers
Dune
Alexander
Let's Make Love
Sandpiper
Samson
Alexander
Sandpiper
Alexander
Alexander
ELIZABETH TAYLOR · RICHARD BURTON
EVA MARIE SAINT
The Sandpiper
BORN OUT OF THE BLAZING PASSIONS OF WAR!
A TIME TO LOVE
FARRELL JOLIE KILMER LETO DAWSON HOPKINS
ALEXANDER
FORTUNE FAVORS THE BOLD
NOVEMBER
A story as timeless and tumultuous as the violent age it spreads before you!
CECIL B. DeMILLE'S
Samson and Delilah

Eyes Wide Shut* vs. *Alexander

Stone will tell you that his movie should have been a masterpiece. Kubrick's passionate devotees insist that his last film really is one. And to be truly the worst, as opposed to merely bad, a film must have at least a kernel of greatness in it. Not even Stone's most hallucinatory sequences in Persia or India can match the preposterous solemnity of that masked ball orgy out on Long Island.

Sandpiper* vs. *Time to Love

Preminger, his era's prestige director, might have been able to improve upon Sirk's labored direction (of an epic romance about a handsome, decent Nazi soldier, played by John Gavin), but he was saving his worst for Richard Burton and Elizabeth Taylor, who were saving their worst (which is saying something) for him. Liz and Dick beat the nice Nazi by a nose.

Alexander* vs. *Samson

The ancient world, rendered in color and on a wide screen, accounts for some of the most dreadful movies ever. *Samson*, an overripe, late-period DeMille extravaganza, with Victor Mature and Hedy Lamarr, was a big hit, and retains a certain maniacal charm. But in spite of an inert lead performance by Colin Farrell, *Alexander* advances on a sheer craziness embodied by Angelina Jolie as the emperor's snake-fetishizing, Slavic-accented mama.

George Carlin Hunks

By Kelly Carlin-McCall

Kelly Carlin-McCall writes for *Fresh Yarn* and the *Huffington Post.* Oh, and she is George's daughter.

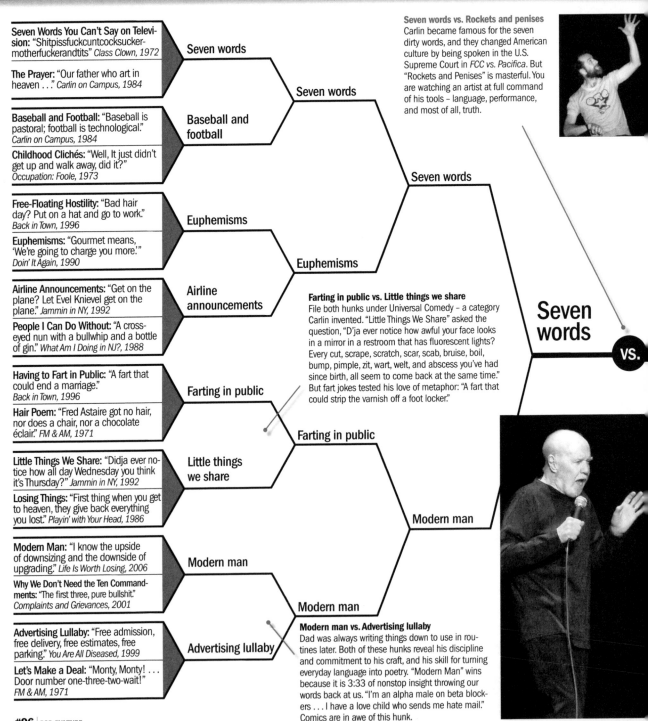

Seven Words You Can't Say on Television: "Shitpissfuckcuntcocksucker-motherfuckerandtits" *Class Clown, 1972*

The Prayer: "Our father who art in heaven . . ." *Carlin on Campus, 1984*

Baseball and Football: "Baseball is pastoral; football is technological." *Carlin on Campus, 1984*

Childhood Clichés: "Well, It just didn't get up and walk away, did it?" *Occupation: Foole, 1973*

Free-Floating Hostility: "Bad hair day? Put on a hat and go to work." *Back in Town, 1996*

Euphemisms: "Gourmet means, 'We're going to charge you more.'" *Doin' It Again, 1990*

Airline Announcements: "Get on the plane? Let Evel Knievel get on the plane." *Jammin in NY, 1992*

People I Can Do Without: "A cross-eyed nun with a bullwhip and a bottle of gin." *What Am I Doing in NJ?, 1988*

Having to Fart in Public: "A fart that could end a marriage." *Back in Town, 1996*

Hair Poem: "Fred Astaire got no hair, nor does a chair, nor a chocolate éclair." *FM & AM, 1971*

Little Things We Share: "Didja ever notice how all day Wednesday you think it's Thursday?" *Jammin in NY, 1992*

Losing Things: "First thing when you get to heaven, they give back everything you lost." *Playin' with Your Head, 1986*

Modern Man: "I know the upside of downsizing and the downside of upgrading." *Life Is Worth Losing, 2006*

Why We Don't Need the Ten Commandments: "The first three, pure bullshit." *Complaints and Grievances, 2001*

Advertising Lullaby: "Free admission, free delivery, free estimates, free parking." *You Are All Diseased, 1999*

Let's Make a Deal: "Monty, Monty! . . . Door number one-three-two-wait!" *FM & AM, 1971*

Seven words

Baseball and football

Euphemisms

Airline announcements

Farting in public

Little things we share

Modern man

Advertising lullaby

Seven words

Euphemisms

Farting in public

Modern man

Seven words

Modern man

Seven words vs.

Seven words vs. Rockets and penises
Carlin became famous for the seven dirty words, and they changed American culture by being spoken in the U.S. Supreme Court in *FCC vs. Pacifica*. But "Rockets and Penises" is masterful. You are watching an artist at full command of his tools – language, performance, and most of all, truth.

Farting in public vs. Little things we share
File both hunks under Universal Comedy – a category Carlin invented. "Little Things We Share" asked the question, "D'ja ever notice how awful your face looks in a mirror in a restroom that has fluorescent lights? Every cut, scrape, scratch, scar, scab, bruise, boil, bump, pimple, zit, wart, welt, and abscess you've had since birth, all seem to come back at the same time." But fart jokes tested his love of metaphor: "A fart that could strip the varnish off a foot locker."

Modern man vs. Advertising lullaby
Dad was always writing things down to use in routines later. Both of these hunks reveal his discipline and commitment to his craft, and his skill for turning everyday language into poetry. "Modern Man" wins because it is 3:33 of nonstop insight throwing our words back at us. "I'm an alpha male on beta blockers . . . I have a love child who sends me hate mail." Comics are in awe of this hunk.

UNTIL HIS DEATH AT 71 IN 2008, comedian George Carlin enjoyed a legendary performing career. But he also had a prolific "recording" career, from LPs to CDs to the DVDs of his 14 HBO specials. That's where his routines, which he called "hunks," are gathered for posterity as 10:51 or 6:54 of genius. The 32 hunks here cover five decades of biting social criticism, wordplay, and insight about small moments of human interaction. His body aged (whose doesn't?), but his body of work will not.

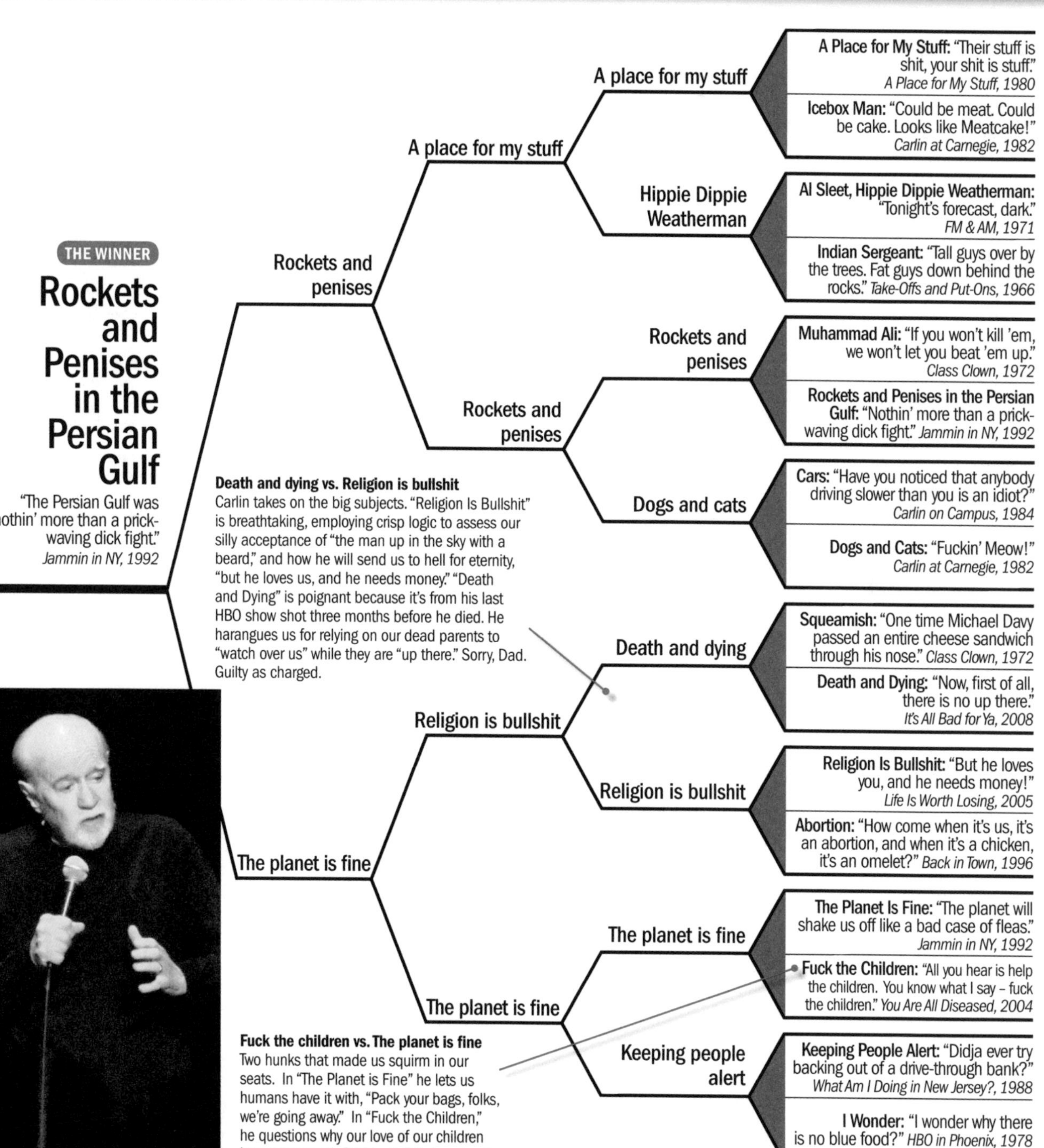

THE WINNER
Rockets and Penises in the Persian Gulf
"The Persian Gulf was nothin' more than a prick-waving dick fight." Jammin in NY, 1992
A Place for My Stuff: "Their stuff is shit, your shit is stuff." A Place for My Stuff, 1980
Icebox Man: "Could be meat. Could be cake. Looks like Meatcake!" Carlin at Carnegie, 1982
Al Sleet, Hippie Dippie Weatherman: "Tonight's forecast, dark." FM & AM, 1971
Indian Sergeant: "Tall guys over by the trees. Fat guys down behind the rocks." Take-Offs and Put-Ons, 1966
Muhammad Ali: "If you won't kill 'em, we won't let you beat 'em up." Class Clown, 1972
Rockets and Penises in the Persian Gulf: "Nothin' more than a prick-waving dick fight." Jammin in NY, 1992
Cars: "Have you noticed that anybody driving slower than you is an idiot?" Carlin on Campus, 1984
Dogs and Cats: "Fuckin' Meow!" Carlin at Carnegie, 1982
Squeamish: "One time Michael Davy passed an entire cheese sandwich through his nose." Class Clown, 1972
Death and Dying: "Now, first of all, there is no up there." It's All Bad for Ya, 2008
Religion Is Bullshit: "But he loves you, and he needs money!" Life Is Worth Losing, 2005
Abortion: "How come when it's us, it's an abortion, and when it's a chicken, it's an omelet?" Back in Town, 1996
The Planet Is Fine: "The planet will shake us off like a bad case of fleas." Jammin in NY, 1992
Fuck the Children: "All you hear is help the children. You know what I say – fuck the children." You Are All Diseased, 2004
Keeping People Alert: "Didja ever try backing out of a drive-through bank?" What Am I Doing in New Jersey?, 1988
I Wonder: "I wonder why there is no blue food?" HBO in Phoenix, 1978
A place for my stuff
Hippie Dippie Weatherman
Rockets and penises
Dogs and cats
Death and dying
Religion is bullshit
The planet is fine
Keeping people alert
A place for my stuff
Rockets and penises
Religion is bullshit
The planet is fine
Rockets and penises
The planet is fine
Death and dying vs. Religion is bullshit
Carlin takes on the big subjects. "Religion Is Bullshit" is breathtaking, employing crisp logic to assess our silly acceptance of "the man up in the sky with a beard," and how he will send us to hell for eternity, "but he loves us, and he needs money." "Death and Dying" is poignant because it's from his last HBO show shot three months before he died. He harangues us for relying on our dead parents to "watch over us" while they are "up there." Sorry, Dad. Guilty as charged.
Fuck the children vs. The planet is fine
Two hunks that made us squirm in our seats. In "The Planet is Fine" he lets us humans have it with, "Pack your bags, folks, we're going away." In "Fuck the Children," he questions why our love of our children is so sacrosanct. Prickly stuff, but we laugh. Planet wins here because he even manages to piss off environmentalists.

Cop Movies

By Lorenzo Carcaterra

Lorenzo Carcaterra is the author of *Sleepers* and *Apaches,* as well as a writer for *Law & Order.*

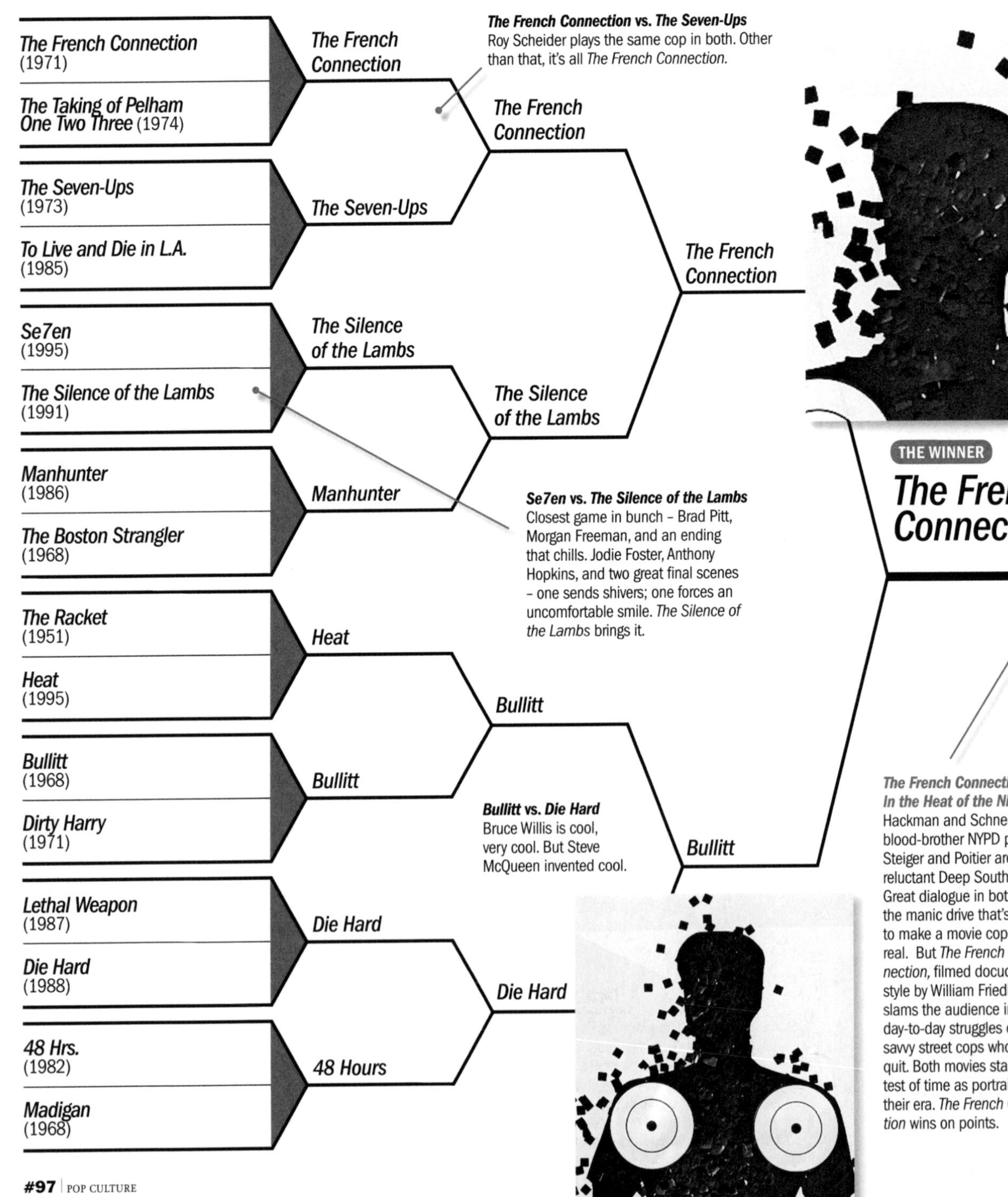

The French Connection (1971)
The Taking of Pelham One Two Three (1974)
The Seven-Ups (1973)
To Live and Die in L.A. (1985)
Se7en (1995)
The Silence of the Lambs (1991)
Manhunter (1986)
The Boston Strangler (1968)
The Racket (1951)
Heat (1995)
Bullitt (1968)
Dirty Harry (1971)
Lethal Weapon (1987)
Die Hard (1988)
48 Hrs. (1982)
Madigan (1968)
The French Connection
The Seven-Ups
The Silence of the Lambs
Manhunter
Heat
Bullitt
Die Hard
48 Hours
The French Connection
The Silence of the Lambs
Bullitt
Die Hard
The French Connection
Bullitt
THE WINNER
The French Connection
VS.

The French Connection* vs. *The Seven-Ups
Roy Scheider plays the same cop in both. Other than that, it's all *The French Connection.*

Se7en* vs. *The Silence of the Lambs
Closest game in bunch – Brad Pitt, Morgan Freeman, and an ending that chills. Jodie Foster, Anthony Hopkins, and two great final scenes – one sends shivers; one forces an uncomfortable smile. *The Silence of the Lambs* brings it.

Bullitt* vs. *Die Hard
Bruce Willis is cool, very cool. But Steve McQueen invented cool.

The French Connection* vs. *In the Heat of the Night
Hackman and Schneider are blood-brother NYPD partners. Steiger and Poitier are reluctant Deep South partners. Great dialogue in both with the manic drive that's needed to make a movie cop seem real. But *The French Connection,* filmed docudrama style by William Friedkin, body slams the audience into the day-to-day struggles of two savvy street cops who won't quit. Both movies stand the test of time as portraits of their era. *The French Connection* wins on points.

YOU MAY NOT WANT POPEYE DOYLE to date your daughter, but these are the movie cops you want knocking on your door in time of need. The rules were simple: The officer with the badge must propel the action, the more realistic the better. No joke movies, no private eyes. Our cops had to be members of a bureau or department, called to action by a crime, not by a hire. So, sit back, pour yourself a glass of Chianti, pick your feet if you're near Poughkeepsie, and make your day with our top cops.

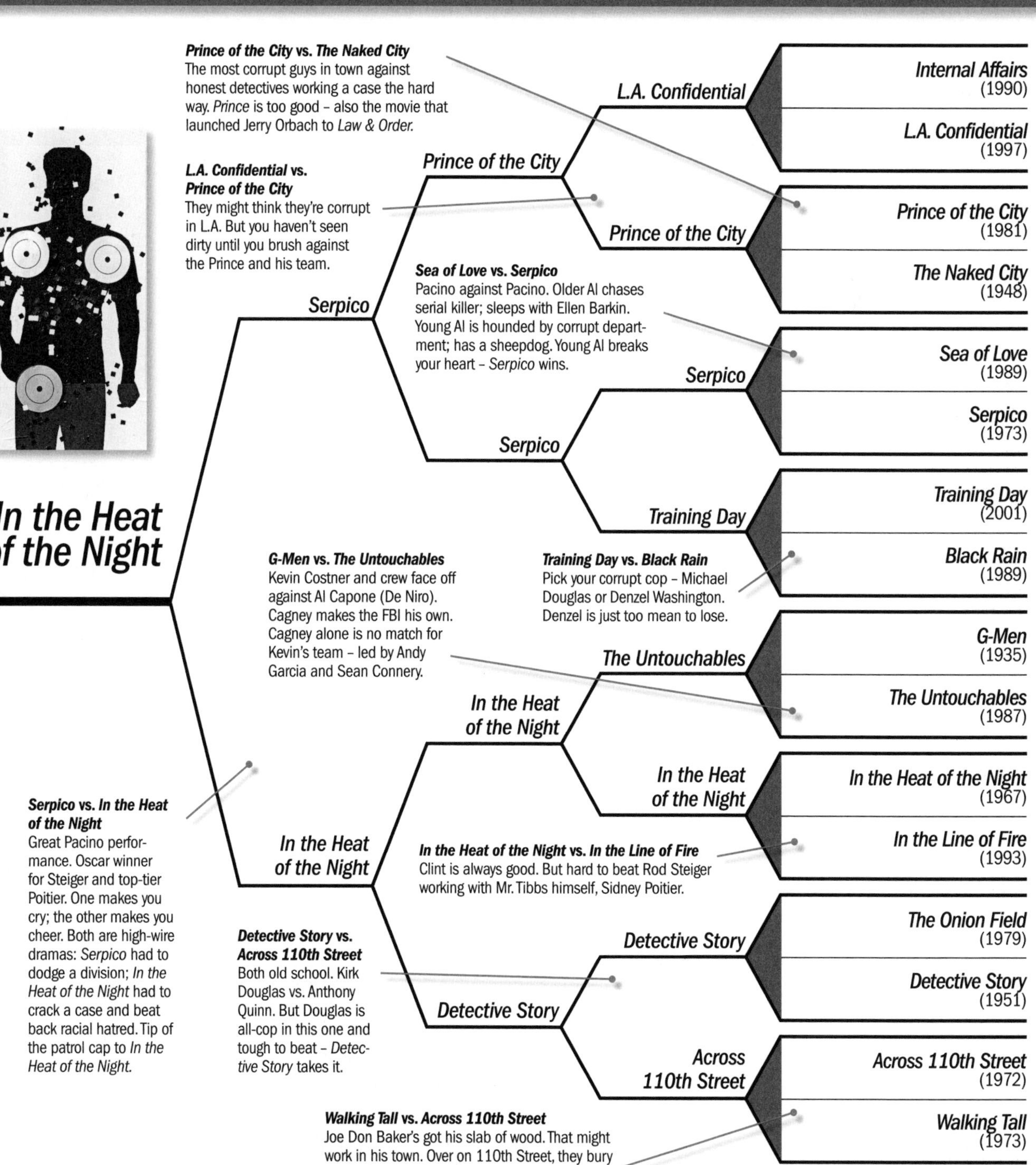

Internal Affairs (1990)
L.A. Confidential (1997)
Prince of the City (1981)
The Naked City (1948)
Sea of Love (1989)
Serpico (1973)
Training Day (2001)
Black Rain (1989)
G-Men (1935)
The Untouchables (1987)
In the Heat of the Night (1967)
In the Line of Fire (1993)
The Onion Field (1979)
Detective Story (1951)
Across 110th Street (1972)
Walking Tall (1973)
L.A. Confidential
Prince of the City
Serpico
Training Day
The Untouchables
In the Heat of the Night
Detective Story
Across 110th Street
Prince of the City
Serpico
In the Heat of the Night
Detective Story
Serpico
In the Heat of the Night
In the Heat of the Night

Prince of the City vs. The Naked City
The most corrupt guys in town against honest detectives working a case the hard way. *Prince* is too good – also the movie that launched Jerry Orbach to *Law & Order.*

L.A. Confidential vs. Prince of the City
They might think they're corrupt in L.A. But you haven't seen dirty until you brush against the Prince and his team.

Sea of Love vs. Serpico
Pacino against Pacino. Older Al chases serial killer; sleeps with Ellen Barkin. Young Al is hounded by corrupt department; has a sheepdog. Young Al breaks your heart – *Serpico* wins.

Training Day vs. Black Rain
Pick your corrupt cop – Michael Douglas or Denzel Washington. Denzel is just too mean to lose.

G-Men vs. The Untouchables
Kevin Costner and crew face off against Al Capone (De Niro). Cagney makes the FBI his own. Cagney alone is no match for Kevin's team – led by Andy Garcia and Sean Connery.

In the Heat of the Night vs. In the Line of Fire
Clint is always good. But hard to beat Rod Steiger working with Mr. Tibbs himself, Sidney Poitier.

Serpico vs. In the Heat of the Night
Great Pacino performance. Oscar winner for Steiger and top-tier Poitier. One makes you cry; the other makes you cheer. Both are high-wire dramas: *Serpico* had to dodge a division; *In the Heat of the Night* had to crack a case and beat back racial hatred. Tip of the patrol cap to *In the Heat of the Night.*

Detective Story vs. Across 110th Street
Both old school. Kirk Douglas vs. Anthony Quinn. But Douglas is all-cop in this one and tough to beat – *Detective Story* takes it.

Walking Tall vs. Across 110th Street
Joe Don Baker's got his slab of wood. That might work in his town. Over on 110th Street, they bury you in wood. Anthony Quinn packs a gun with lots of bullets. *Across 110th Street* wins.

Reality TV Stars

By Bob Boden

Bob Boden is senior vice president, Programming, Production and Development, for Fox Reality Channel, the only all-reality, all-the-time cable and satellite network and co-creator of the game show *GREED.*

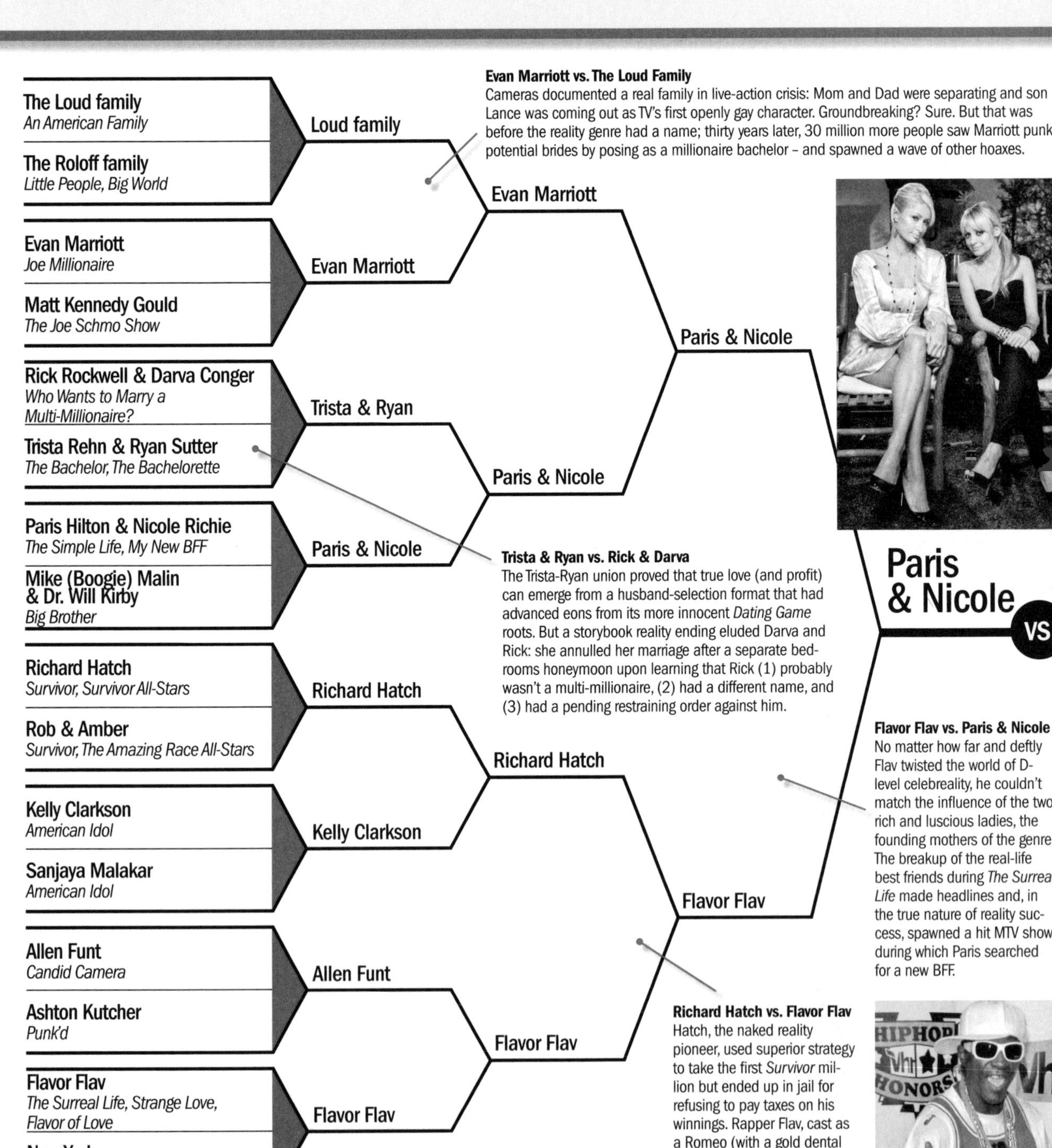

The Loud family
An American Family
The Roloff family
Little People, Big World
Evan Marriott
Joe Millionaire
Matt Kennedy Gould
The Joe Schmo Show
Rick Rockwell & Darva Conger
Who Wants to Marry a Multi-Millionaire?
Trista Rehn & Ryan Sutter
The Bachelor, The Bachelorette
Paris Hilton & Nicole Richie
The Simple Life, My New BFF
Mike (Boogie) Malin & Dr. Will Kirby
Big Brother
Richard Hatch
Survivor, Survivor All-Stars
Rob & Amber
Survivor, The Amazing Race All-Stars
Kelly Clarkson
American Idol
Sanjaya Malakar
American Idol
Allen Funt
Candid Camera
Ashton Kutcher
Punk'd
Flavor Flav
The Surreal Life, Strange Love, Flavor of Love
New York
Flavor of Love, I Love New York
Loud family
Evan Marriott
Trista & Ryan
Paris & Nicole
Richard Hatch
Kelly Clarkson
Allen Funt
Flavor Flav
Evan Marriott
Paris & Nicole
Richard Hatch
Flavor Flav
Paris & Nicole
Flavor Flav
Paris & Nicole
VS.
HIPHOP
VH1
HONORS

Evan Marriott vs. The Loud Family
Cameras documented a real family in live-action crisis: Mom and Dad were separating and son Lance was coming out as TV's first openly gay character. Groundbreaking? Sure. But that was before the reality genre had a name; thirty years later, 30 million more people saw Marriott punk potential brides by posing as a millionaire bachelor – and spawned a wave of other hoaxes.

Trista & Ryan vs. Rick & Darva
The Trista-Ryan union proved that true love (and profit) can emerge from a husband-selection format that had advanced eons from its more innocent *Dating Game* roots. But a storybook reality ending eluded Darva and Rick: she annulled her marriage after a separate bedrooms honeymoon upon learning that Rick (1) probably wasn't a multi-millionaire, (2) had a different name, and (3) had a pending restraining order against him.

Flavor Flav vs. Paris & Nicole
No matter how far and deftly Flav twisted the world of D-level celebreality, he couldn't match the influence of the two rich and luscious ladies, the founding mothers of the genre. The breakup of the real-life best friends during *The Surreal Life* made headlines and, in the true nature of reality success, spawned a hit MTV show during which Paris searched for a new BFF.

Richard Hatch vs. Flavor Flav
Hatch, the naked reality pioneer, used superior strategy to take the first *Survivor* million but ended up in jail for refusing to pay taxes on his winnings. Rapper Flav, cast as a Romeo (with a gold dental grille), delivered delicious, audacious, controversial parodies of *The Bachelor* when he filled a mansion with trashy ladies vying for his love.

WITH ITS OVERT APPEALS TO greed, self-image, sex, upward mobility, bitchiness, adventure, and competitiveness, reality television has created a generation of characters unimagined by scriptwriters: real people living in communal houses, vying for jobs, singing in talent shows, nabbing bail-jumpers. They are dysfunctional civilians and celebrities, survivors and bachelors, real and phony millionaires, and people with and without talent – the most successful ones impose (or inflict) their personalities on America.

Paris & Nicole vs. Omarosa
Omarosa, reality TV's first queen bitch, began as a liar and backstabber to get an edge on Donald Trump in *The Apprentice,* then challenged Janice Dickinson in the *Surreal Life* house and Piers Morgan on *Celebrity Apprentice.* Paris and Nicole are brilliant news manipulators, but Omarosa's bad girl archetype lives on in other shows and in references to other characters' evildoing as "pulling an Omarosa."

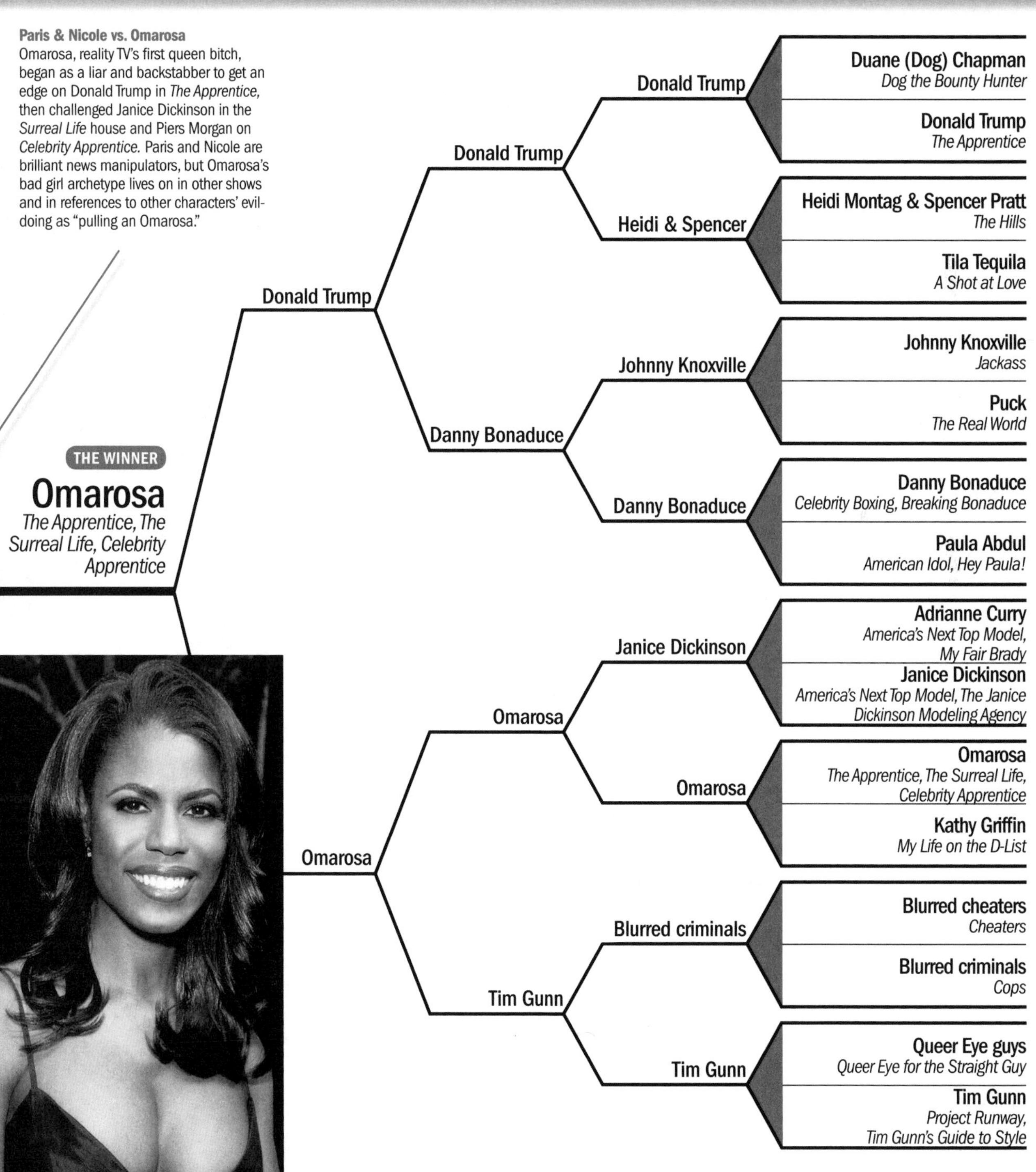
THE WINNER
Omarosa
The Apprentice, The Surreal Life, Celebrity Apprentice
Donald Trump
Omarosa
Donald Trump
Danny Bonaduce
Omarosa
Tim Gunn
Donald Trump
Heidi & Spencer
Johnny Knoxville
Danny Bonaduce
Janice Dickinson
Omarosa
Blurred criminals
Tim Gunn
Duane (Dog) Chapman
Dog the Bounty Hunter
Donald Trump
The Apprentice
Heidi Montag & Spencer Pratt
The Hills
Tila Tequila
A Shot at Love
Johnny Knoxville
Jackass
Puck
The Real World
Danny Bonaduce
Celebrity Boxing, Breaking Bonaduce
Paula Abdul
American Idol, Hey Paula!
Adrianne Curry
America's Next Top Model, My Fair Brady
Janice Dickinson
America's Next Top Model, The Janice Dickinson Modeling Agency
Omarosa
The Apprentice, The Surreal Life, Celebrity Apprentice
Kathy Griffin
My Life on the D-List
Blurred cheaters
Cheaters
Blurred criminals
Cops
Queer Eye guys
Queer Eye for the Straight Guy
Tim Gunn
Project Runway, Tim Gunn's Guide to Style

Fictional Lawyers

By Thane Rosenbaum

Thane Rosenbaum is the John Whelan Distinguished Lecturer in Law at Fordham Law School, where he teaches courses in law and literature and also directs the Forum on Law, Culture & Society

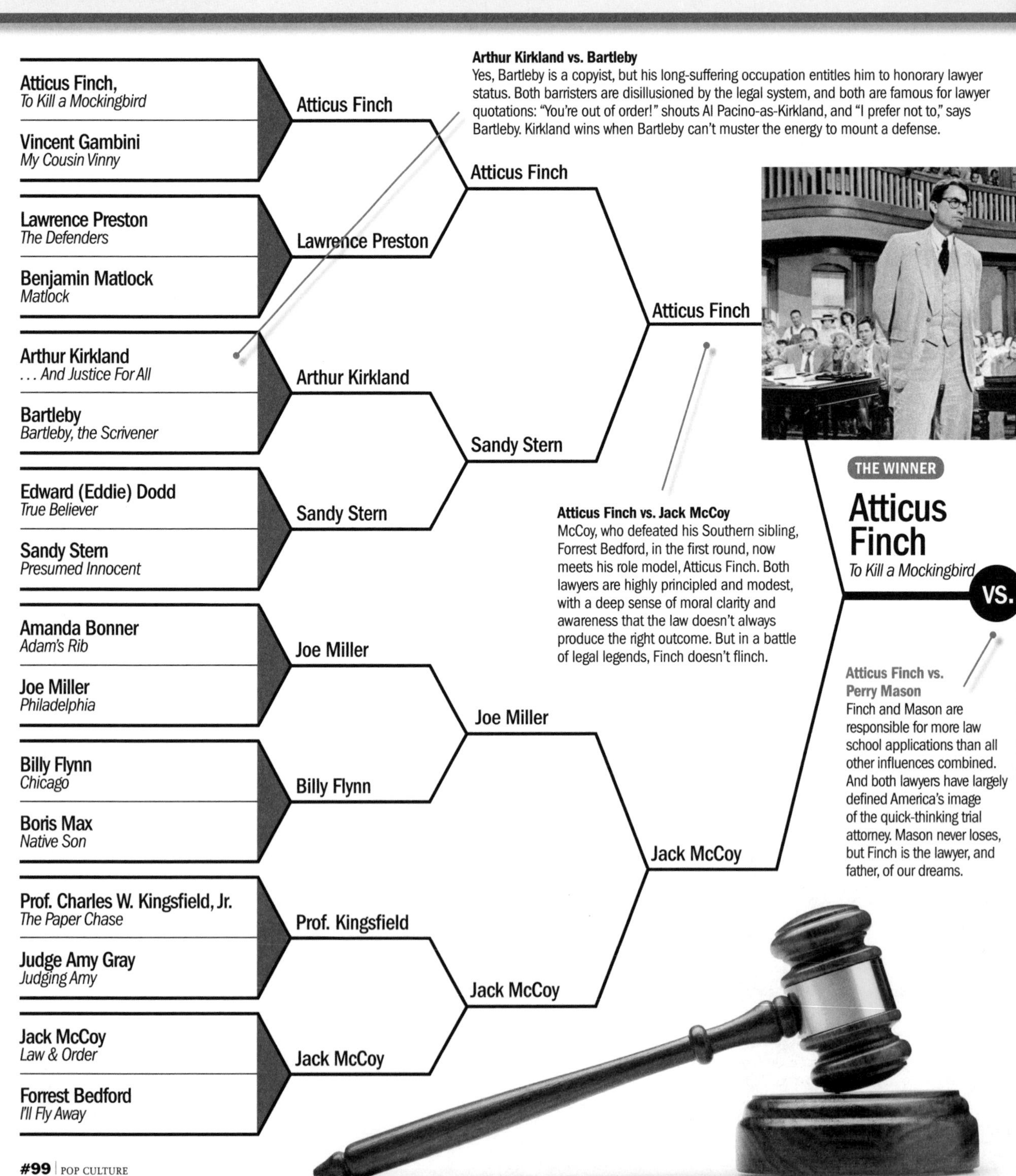
Atticus Finch, *To Kill a Mockingbird*
Vincent Gambini *My Cousin Vinny*
Lawrence Preston *The Defenders*
Benjamin Matlock *Matlock*
Arthur Kirkland *. . . And Justice For All*
Bartleby *Bartleby, the Scrivener*
Edward (Eddie) Dodd *True Believer*
Sandy Stern *Presumed Innocent*
Amanda Bonner *Adam's Rib*
Joe Miller *Philadelphia*
Billy Flynn *Chicago*
Boris Max *Native Son*
Prof. Charles W. Kingsfield, Jr. *The Paper Chase*
Judge Amy Gray *Judging Amy*
Jack McCoy *Law & Order*
Forrest Bedford *I'll Fly Away*
Atticus Finch
Lawrence Preston
Arthur Kirkland
Sandy Stern
Joe Miller
Billy Flynn
Prof. Kingsfield
Jack McCoy
Atticus Finch
Sandy Stern
Joe Miller
Jack McCoy
Atticus Finch
Jack McCoy
Arthur Kirkland vs. Bartleby
Yes, Bartleby is a copyist, but his long-suffering occupation entitles him to honorary lawyer status. Both barristers are disillusioned by the legal system, and both are famous for lawyer quotations: "You're out of order!" shouts Al Pacino-as-Kirkland, and "I prefer not to," says Bartleby. Kirkland wins when Bartleby can't muster the energy to mount a defense.
Atticus Finch vs. Jack McCoy
McCoy, who defeated his Southern sibling, Forrest Bedford, in the first round, now meets his role model, Atticus Finch. Both lawyers are highly principled and modest, with a deep sense of moral clarity and awareness that the law doesn't always produce the right outcome. But in a battle of legal legends, Finch doesn't flinch.
THE WINNER
Atticus Finch
To Kill a Mockingbird
VS.
Atticus Finch vs. Perry Mason
Finch and Mason are responsible for more law school applications than all other influences combined. And both lawyers have largely defined America's image of the quick-thinking trial attorney. Mason never loses, but Finch is the lawyer, and father, of our dreams.

AMERICANS LOVE LAWYER JOKES and seemingly hate lawyers, yet, paradoxically, the drama of fictional lawyers has become America's favorite pastime and guilty pleasure. The lawyers of our imagination, the ones who can't be retained but are still loved and loathed, have craftily argued, adjudicated, and plotted their way through novels, television dramas, and feature films, animating our culture with Lawyer Madness and a deep longing to see that justice is done – even if it exists only in art.

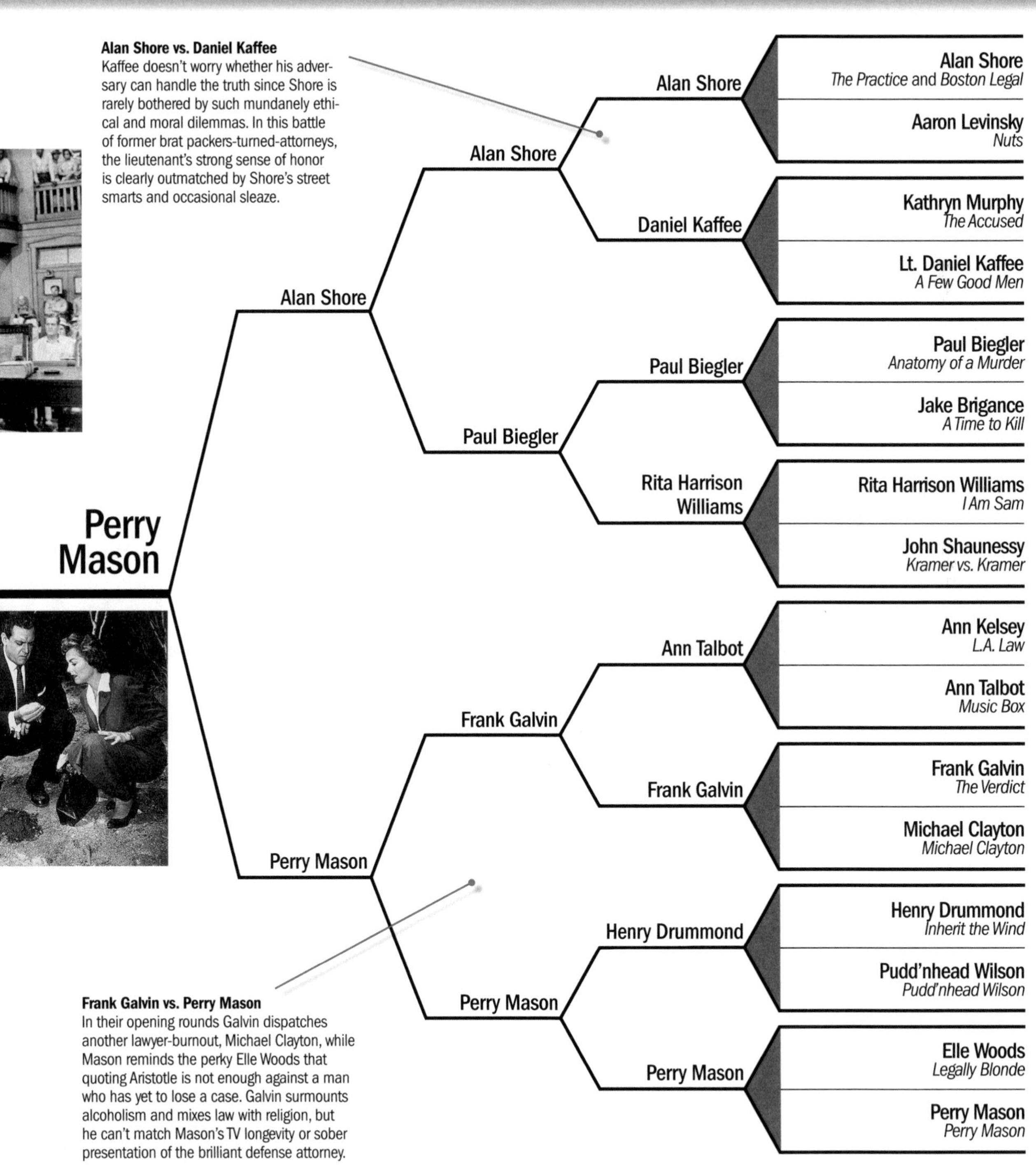

Alan Shore vs. Daniel Kaffee
Kaffee doesn't worry whether his adversary can handle the truth since Shore is rarely bothered by such mundanely ethical and moral dilemmas. In this battle of former brat packers-turned-attorneys, the lieutenant's strong sense of honor is clearly outmatched by Shore's street smarts and occasional sleaze.
Alan Shore
The Practice and Boston Legal
Aaron Levinsky
Nuts
Kathryn Murphy
The Accused
Lt. Daniel Kaffee
A Few Good Men
Paul Biegler
Anatomy of a Murder
Jake Brigance
A Time to Kill
Rita Harrison Williams
I Am Sam
John Shaunessy
Kramer vs. Kramer
Ann Kelsey
L.A. Law
Ann Talbot
Music Box
Frank Galvin
The Verdict
Michael Clayton
Michael Clayton
Henry Drummond
Inherit the Wind
Pudd'nhead Wilson
Pudd'nhead Wilson
Elle Woods
Legally Blonde
Perry Mason
Perry Mason
Alan Shore
Daniel Kaffee
Paul Biegler
Rita Harrison Williams
Ann Talbot
Frank Galvin
Henry Drummond
Perry Mason
Alan Shore
Paul Biegler
Frank Galvin
Perry Mason
Alan Shore
Perry Mason
Perry Mason
Frank Galvin vs. Perry Mason
In their opening rounds Galvin dispatches another lawyer-burnout, Michael Clayton, while Mason reminds the perky Elle Woods that quoting Aristotle is not enough against a man who has yet to lose a case. Galvin surmounts alcoholism and mixes law with religion, but he can't match Mason's TV longevity or sober presentation of the brilliant defense attorney.

Good Imus vs. Evil Imus

By Richard Sandomir

Richard Sandomir has interviewed Imus thrice. The first time, Imus confiscated his notebook. The second time, he took away his notebook and tape recorder. The third time, he showed off a recent surgical scar; a week later, he called Sandomir a "bald-headed pedophile" on the air.

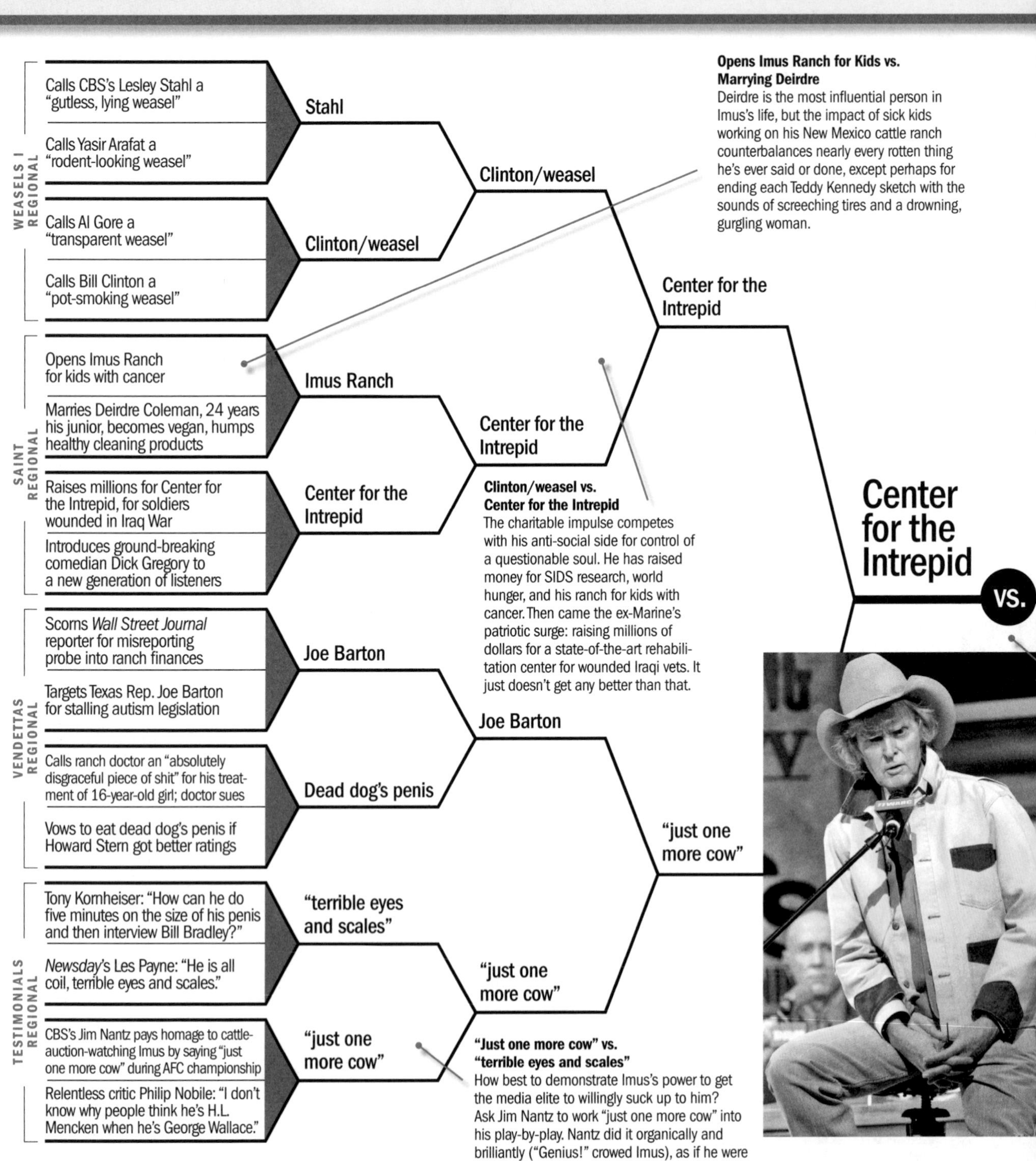

WEASELS I REGIONAL
Calls CBS's Lesley Stahl a "gutless, lying weasel"
Calls Yasir Arafat a "rodent-looking weasel"
Stahl
Calls Al Gore a "transparent weasel"
Calls Bill Clinton a "pot-smoking weasel"
Clinton/weasel
Clinton/weasel
SAINT REGIONAL
Opens Imus Ranch for kids with cancer
Marries Deirdre Coleman, 24 years his junior, becomes vegan, humps healthy cleaning products
Imus Ranch
Raises millions for Center for the Intrepid, for soldiers wounded in Iraq War
Introduces ground-breaking comedian Dick Gregory to a new generation of listeners
Center for the Intrepid
Center for the Intrepid
Center for the Intrepid
VENDETTAS REGIONAL
Scorns Wall Street Journal reporter for misreporting probe into ranch finances
Targets Texas Rep. Joe Barton for stalling autism legislation
Joe Barton
Calls ranch doctor an "absolutely disgraceful piece of shit" for his treatment of 16-year-old girl; doctor sues
Vows to eat dead dog's penis if Howard Stern got better ratings
Dead dog's penis
Joe Barton
TESTIMONIALS REGIONAL
Tony Kornheiser: "How can he do five minutes on the size of his penis and then interview Bill Bradley?"
Newsday's Les Payne: "He is all coil, terrible eyes and scales."
"terrible eyes and scales"
CBS's Jim Nantz pays homage to cattle-auction-watching Imus by saying "just one more cow" during AFC championship
Relentless critic Philip Nobile: "I don't know why people think he's H.L. Mencken when he's George Wallace."
"just one more cow"
"just one more cow"
"just one more cow"
Center for the Intrepid
VS.

Opens Imus Ranch for Kids vs. Marrying Deirdre
Deirdre is the most influential person in Imus's life, but the impact of sick kids working on his New Mexico cattle ranch counterbalances nearly every rotten thing he's ever said or done, except perhaps for ending each Teddy Kennedy sketch with the sounds of screeching tires and a drowning, gurgling woman.

Clinton/weasel vs. Center for the Intrepid
The charitable impulse competes with his anti-social side for control of a questionable soul. He has raised money for SIDS research, world hunger, and his ranch for kids with cancer. Then came the ex-Marine's patriotic surge: raising millions of dollars for a state-of-the-art rehabilitation center for wounded Iraqi vets. It just doesn't get any better than that.

"Just one more cow" vs. "terrible eyes and scales"
How best to demonstrate Imus's power to get the media elite to willingly suck up to him? Ask Jim Nantz to work "just one more cow" into his play-by-play. Nantz did it organically and brilliantly ("Genius!" crowed Imus), as if he were following an Imus-led game of "Simon Says." Calling Imus a snake? Exactly what he wants.

THERE ARE TWO ERAS IN DON IMUS'S RADIO HISTORY. In the first, he was a shock-jock, known for telephoning unsuspecting women to ask, "Are you naked?" In the second, the misanthropic Imus is no more mature (calling Venus Williams "Penis" is not a sign of wisdom) but he has turned his show into a salon for politicians, journalists, and singers seeking his approval, and a forum for his charitable causes. He still goads guests to say something that "ruins their life" – which he nearly did to himself.

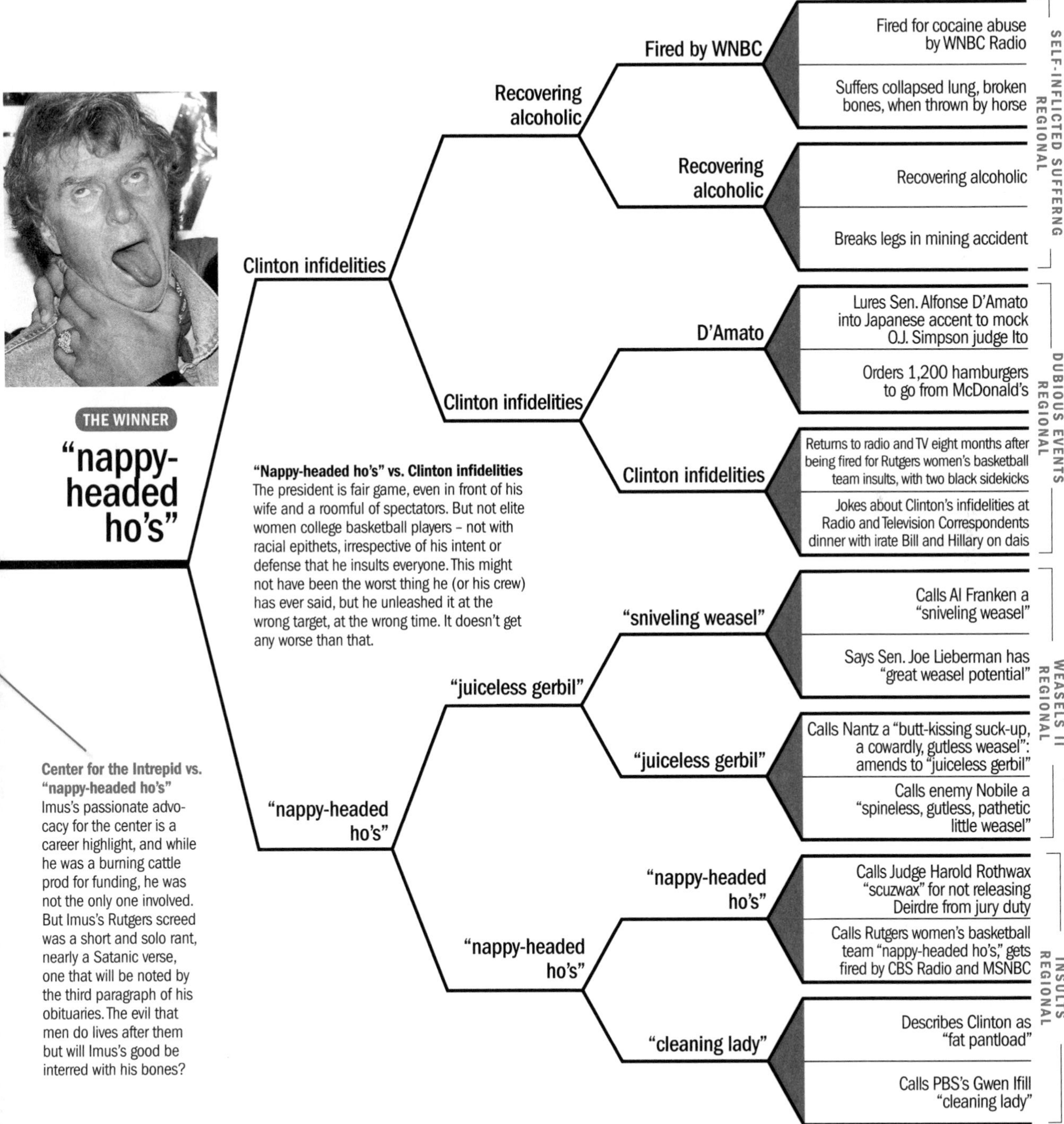

SELF-INFLICTED SUFFERNG REGIONAL
Fired for cocaine abuse by WNBC Radio
Suffers collapsed lung, broken bones, when thrown by horse
Fired by WNBC
Recovering alcoholic
Breaks legs in mining accident
Recovering alcoholic
Recovering alcoholic
DUBIOUS EVENTS REGIONAL
Lures Sen. Alfonse D'Amato into Japanese accent to mock O.J. Simpson judge Ito
Orders 1,200 hamburgers to go from McDonald's
D'Amato
Returns to radio and TV eight months after being fired for Rutgers women's basketball team insults, with two black sidekicks
Jokes about Clinton's infidelities at Radio and Television Correspondents dinner with irate Bill and Hillary on dais
Clinton infidelities
Clinton infidelities
Clinton infidelities
WEASELS II REGIONAL
Calls Al Franken a "sniveling weasel"
Says Sen. Joe Lieberman has "great weasel potential"
"sniveling weasel"
Calls Nantz a "butt-kissing suck-up, a cowardly, gutless weasel": amends to "juiceless gerbil"
Calls enemy Nobile a "spineless, gutless, pathetic little weasel"
"juiceless gerbil"
"juiceless gerbil"
INSULTS REGIONAL
Calls Judge Harold Rothwax "scuzwax" for not releasing Deirdre from jury duty
Calls Rutgers women's basketball team "nappy-headed ho's," gets fired by CBS Radio and MSNBC
"nappy-headed ho's"
Describes Clinton as "fat pantload"
Calls PBS's Gwen Ifill "cleaning lady"
"cleaning lady"
"nappy-headed ho's"
"nappy-headed ho's"
THE WINNER
"nappy-headed ho's"

"Nappy-headed ho's" vs. Clinton infidelities
The president is fair game, even in front of his wife and a roomful of spectators. But not elite women college basketball players – not with racial epithets, irrespective of his intent or defense that he insults everyone. This might not have been the worst thing he (or his crew) has ever said, but he unleashed it at the wrong target, at the wrong time. It doesn't get any worse than that.

Center for the Intrepid vs. "nappy-headed ho's"
Imus's passionate advocacy for the center is a career highlight, and while he was a burning cattle prod for funding, he was not the only one involved. But Imus's Rutgers screed was a short and solo rant, nearly a Satanic verse, one that will be noted by the third paragraph of his obituaries. The evil that men do lives after them but will Imus's good be interred with his bones?

Steve Earle Songs

By Mark Reiter

Mark Reiter, co-editor of this book, regrets all the other Earle songs he couldn't invite to this tournament.

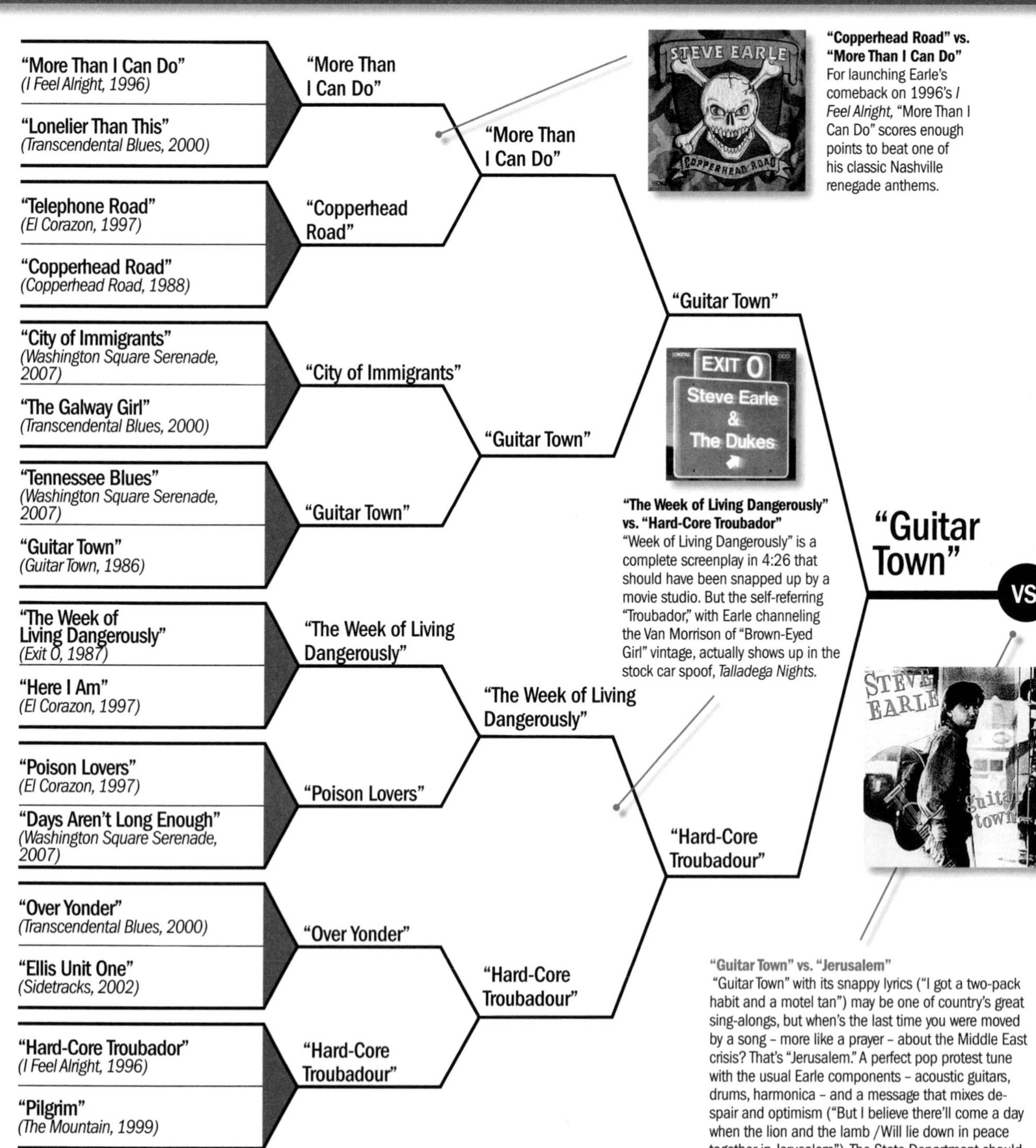

"More Than I Can Do" (I Feel Alright, 1996)
"Lonelier Than This" (Transcendental Blues, 2000)
"Telephone Road" (El Corazon, 1997)
"Copperhead Road" (Copperhead Road, 1988)
"City of Immigrants" (Washington Square Serenade, 2007)
"The Galway Girl" (Transcendental Blues, 2000)
"Tennessee Blues" (Washington Square Serenade, 2007)
"Guitar Town" (Guitar Town, 1986)
"The Week of Living Dangerously" (Exit 0, 1987)
"Here I Am" (El Corazon, 1997)
"Poison Lovers" (El Corazon, 1997)
"Days Aren't Long Enough" (Washington Square Serenade, 2007)
"Over Yonder" (Transcendental Blues, 2000)
"Ellis Unit One" (Sidetracks, 2002)
"Hard-Core Troubador" (I Feel Alright, 1996)
"Pilgrim" (The Mountain, 1999)
"More Than I Can Do"
"Copperhead Road"
"City of Immigrants"
"Guitar Town"
"The Week of Living Dangerously"
"Poison Lovers"
"Over Yonder"
"Hard-Core Troubadour"
"More Than I Can Do"
"Guitar Town"
"The Week of Living Dangerously"
"Hard-Core Troubadour"
"Guitar Town"
"Hard-Core Troubadour"
"Guitar Town"
VS.
STEVE EARLE
COPPERHEAD ROAD
EXIT 0
Steve Earle & The Dukes
STEVE EARLE
guitar town

"Copperhead Road" vs. "More Than I Can Do"
For launching Earle's comeback on 1996's *I Feel Alright,* "More Than I Can Do" scores enough points to beat one of his classic Nashville renegade anthems.

"The Week of Living Dangerously" vs. "Hard-Core Troubador"
"Week of Living Dangerously" is a complete screenplay in 4:26 that should have been snapped up by a movie studio. But the self-referring "Troubador," with Earle channeling the Van Morrison of "Brown-Eyed Girl" vintage, actually shows up in the stock car spoof, *Talladega Nights.*

"Guitar Town" vs. "Jerusalem"
"Guitar Town" with its snappy lyrics ("I got a two-pack habit and a motel tan") may be one of country's great sing-alongs, but when's the last time you were moved by a song – more like a prayer – about the Middle East crisis? That's "Jerusalem." A perfect pop protest tune with the usual Earle components – acoustic guitars, drums, harmonica – and a message that mixes despair and optimism ("But I believe there'll come a day when the lion and the lamb /Will lie down in peace together in Jerusalem"). The State Department should play this song once a week – for inspiration.

AS A SINGER-SONGWRITER, Steve Earle is Bruce Springsteen with a twang (but without the stadium-sized fan base). There's the guitar-driven hooks, the sharp lyric commentary, the high-pop taste. But Earle adds a willingness to expose every personal nerve ending. His backstory of addiction, jail time, and seven marriages is well known. But while artists like Billy Joel and Stevie Wonder are fading creatively, Earle, now past 50, keeps getting better. Had we a Final Four of Living American Songwriters, he'd be in there with Dylan, Simon, and Gill (as in Vince).

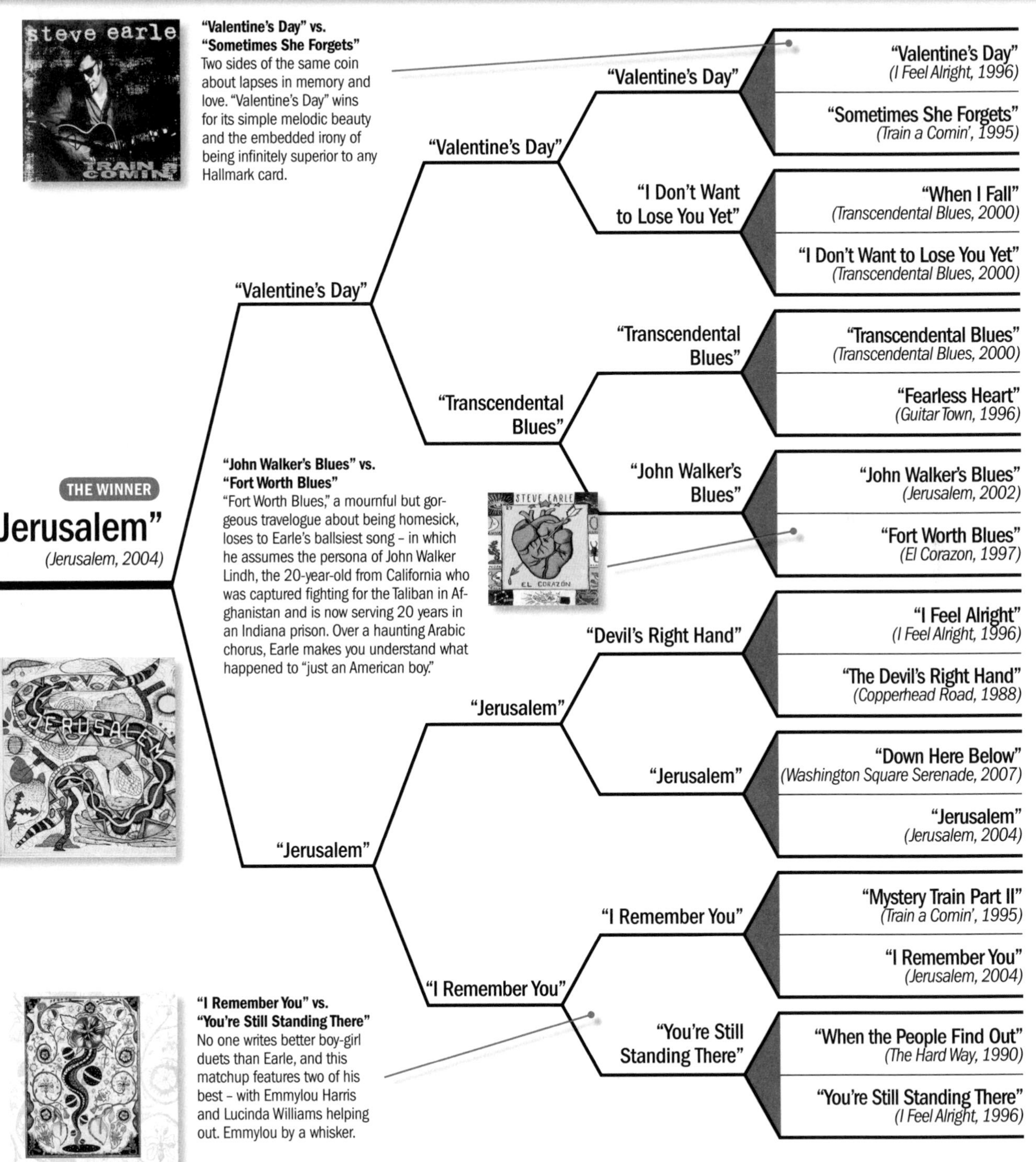

steve earle
"Valentine's Day" vs. "Sometimes She Forgets"
Two sides of the same coin about lapses in memory and love. "Valentine's Day" wins for its simple melodic beauty and the embedded irony of being infinitely superior to any Hallmark card.
"Valentine's Day" (I Feel Alright, 1996)
"Sometimes She Forgets" (Train a Comin', 1995)
"When I Fall" (Transcendental Blues, 2000)
"I Don't Want to Lose You Yet" (Transcendental Blues, 2000)
"Transcendental Blues" (Transcendental Blues, 2000)
"Fearless Heart" (Guitar Town, 1996)
"John Walker's Blues" (Jerusalem, 2002)
"Fort Worth Blues" (El Corazon, 1997)
"I Feel Alright" (I Feel Alright, 1996)
"The Devil's Right Hand" (Copperhead Road, 1988)
"Down Here Below" (Washington Square Serenade, 2007)
"Jerusalem" (Jerusalem, 2004)
"Mystery Train Part II" (Train a Comin', 1995)
"I Remember You" (Jerusalem, 2004)
"When the People Find Out" (The Hard Way, 1990)
"You're Still Standing There" (I Feel Alright, 1996)
"Valentine's Day"
"I Don't Want to Lose You Yet"
"Transcendental Blues"
"John Walker's Blues"
"Devil's Right Hand"
"Jerusalem"
"I Remember You"
"You're Still Standing There"
"Valentine's Day"
"Transcendental Blues"
"Jerusalem"
"I Remember You"
"Valentine's Day"
"Jerusalem"
THE WINNER
"Jerusalem" (Jerusalem, 2004)
"John Walker's Blues" vs. "Fort Worth Blues"
"Fort Worth Blues," a mournful but gorgeous travelogue about being homesick, loses to Earle's ballsiest song – in which he assumes the persona of John Walker Lindh, the 20-year-old from California who was captured fighting for the Taliban in Afghanistan and is now serving 20 years in an Indiana prison. Over a haunting Arabic chorus, Earle makes you understand what happened to "just an American boy."
STEVE EARLE
EL CORAZÓN
JERUSALEM
"I Remember You" vs. "You're Still Standing There"
No one writes better boy-girl duets than Earle, and this matchup features two of his best – with Emmylou Harris and Lucinda Williams helping out. Emmylou by a whisker.

Most American Superhero

By Peter Coogan

Dr. Peter Coogan, director of the Institute for Comics Studies and author of *Superhero: Th Secret Origin of a Genre,* has achieved his childhood dream of getting paid to read comics. His daughter fights for truth, justice, and her own way as the superheroine Flashgirl.

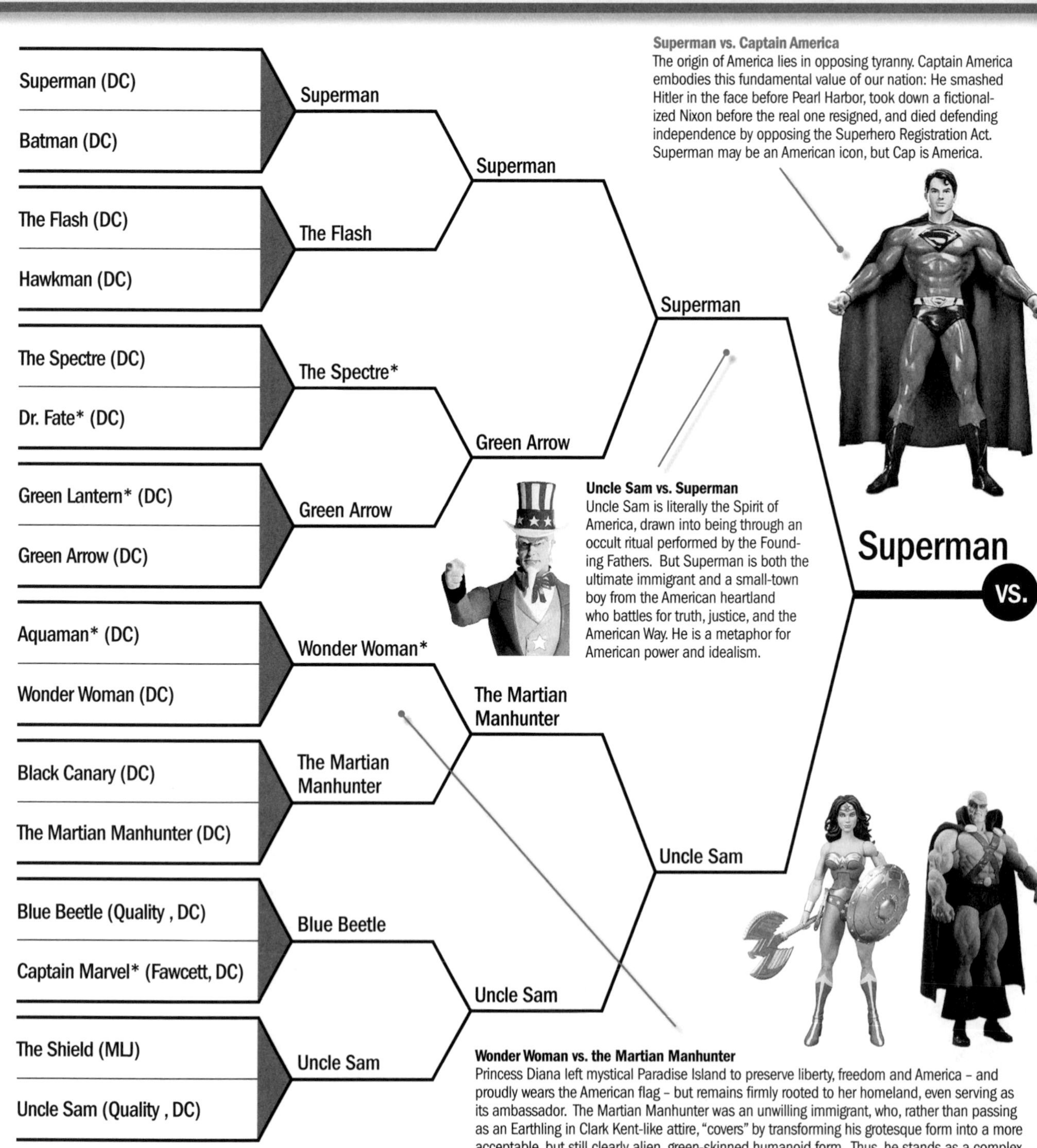
Superman (DC)
Batman (DC)
The Flash (DC)
Hawkman (DC)
The Spectre (DC)
Dr. Fate* (DC)
Green Lantern* (DC)
Green Arrow (DC)
Aquaman* (DC)
Wonder Woman (DC)
Black Canary (DC)
The Martian Manhunter (DC)
Blue Beetle (Quality , DC)
Captain Marvel* (Fawcett, DC)
The Shield (MLJ)
Uncle Sam (Quality , DC)
Superman
The Flash
The Spectre*
Green Arrow
Wonder Woman*
The Martian Manhunter
Blue Beetle
Uncle Sam
Superman
Green Arrow
The Martian Manhunter
Uncle Sam
Superman
Uncle Sam
Superman
vs.
Superman vs. Captain America
The origin of America lies in opposing tyranny. Captain America embodies this fundamental value of our nation: He smashed Hitler in the face before Pearl Harbor, took down a fictionalized Nixon before the real one resigned, and died defending independence by opposing the Superhero Registration Act. Superman may be an American icon, but Cap is America.
Uncle Sam vs. Superman
Uncle Sam is literally the Spirit of America, drawn into being through an occult ritual performed by the Founding Fathers. But Superman is both the ultimate immigrant and a small-town boy from the American heartland who battles for truth, justice, and the American Way. He is a metaphor for American power and idealism.
Wonder Woman vs. the Martian Manhunter
Princess Diana left mystical Paradise Island to preserve liberty, freedom and America – and proudly wears the American flag – but remains firmly rooted to her homeland, even serving as its ambassador. The Martian Manhunter was an unwilling immigrant, who, rather than passing as an Earthling in Clark Kent-like attire, "covers" by transforming his grotesque form into a more acceptable, but still clearly alien, green-skinned humanoid form. Thus, he stands as a complex symbol for minorities who reshape themselves to fit into American society.

WE TEND TO RANK SUPERHEROES BY THEIR POWER, but what makes them quintessentially American? Superheroes are vivid metaphors for the balance between power and responsibility, and the tension of the public and private self. But they also embody American mythology and the American creed. But most American? Is it Superman, the ultimate immigrant? Batman, the self-made man? Iron Man, the technological expression of the military-industrial complex? Green Arrow, the rebel-in-chief? The X-Men, the embodiment of every sort of diversity?

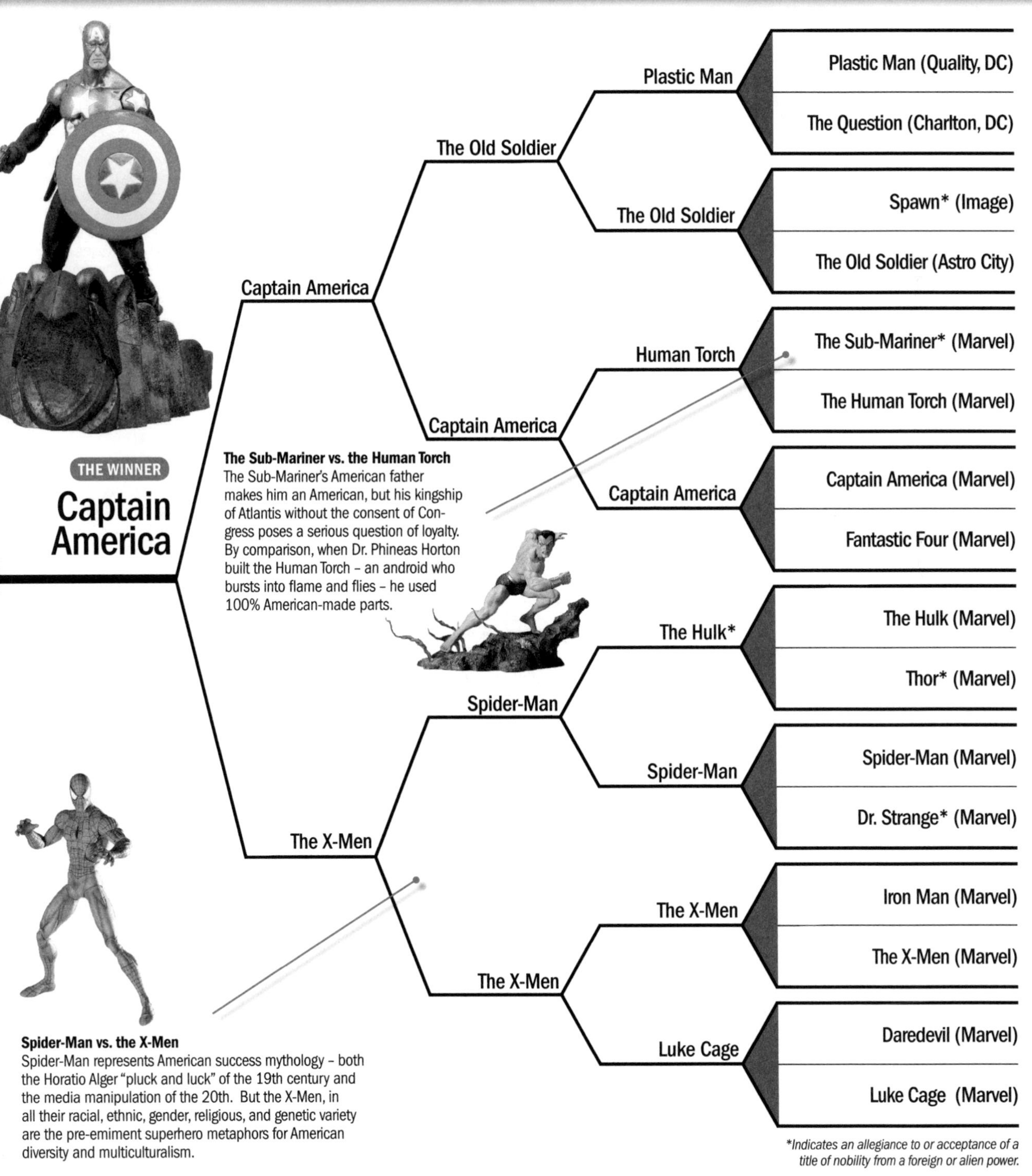

THE WINNER
Captain America
Captain America
The X-Men
The Old Soldier
Captain America
Spider-Man
The X-Men
Plastic Man
The Old Soldier
Human Torch
Captain America
The Hulk*
Spider-Man
The X-Men
Luke Cage
Plastic Man (Quality, DC)
The Question (Charlton, DC)
Spawn* (Image)
The Old Soldier (Astro City)
The Sub-Mariner* (Marvel)
The Human Torch (Marvel)
Captain America (Marvel)
Fantastic Four (Marvel)
The Hulk (Marvel)
Thor* (Marvel)
Spider-Man (Marvel)
Dr. Strange* (Marvel)
Iron Man (Marvel)
The X-Men (Marvel)
Daredevil (Marvel)
Luke Cage (Marvel)

The Sub-Mariner vs. the Human Torch
The Sub-Mariner's American father makes him an American, but his kingship of Atlantis without the consent of Congress poses a serious question of loyalty. By comparison, when Dr. Phineas Horton built the Human Torch – an android who bursts into flame and flies – he used 100% American-made parts.

Spider-Man vs. the X-Men
Spider-Man represents American success mythology – both the Horatio Alger "pluck and luck" of the 19th century and the media manipulation of the 20th. But the X-Men, in all their racial, ethnic, gender, religious, and genetic variety are the pre-emiment superhero metaphors for American diversity and multiculturalism.

**Indicates an allegiance to or acceptance of a title of nobility from a foreign or alien power.*

Gangster Films

By Lorenzo Carcaterra

Lorenzo Carcaterra, a novelist and screenwriter, is the author of *Sleepers* and *Gangster.*

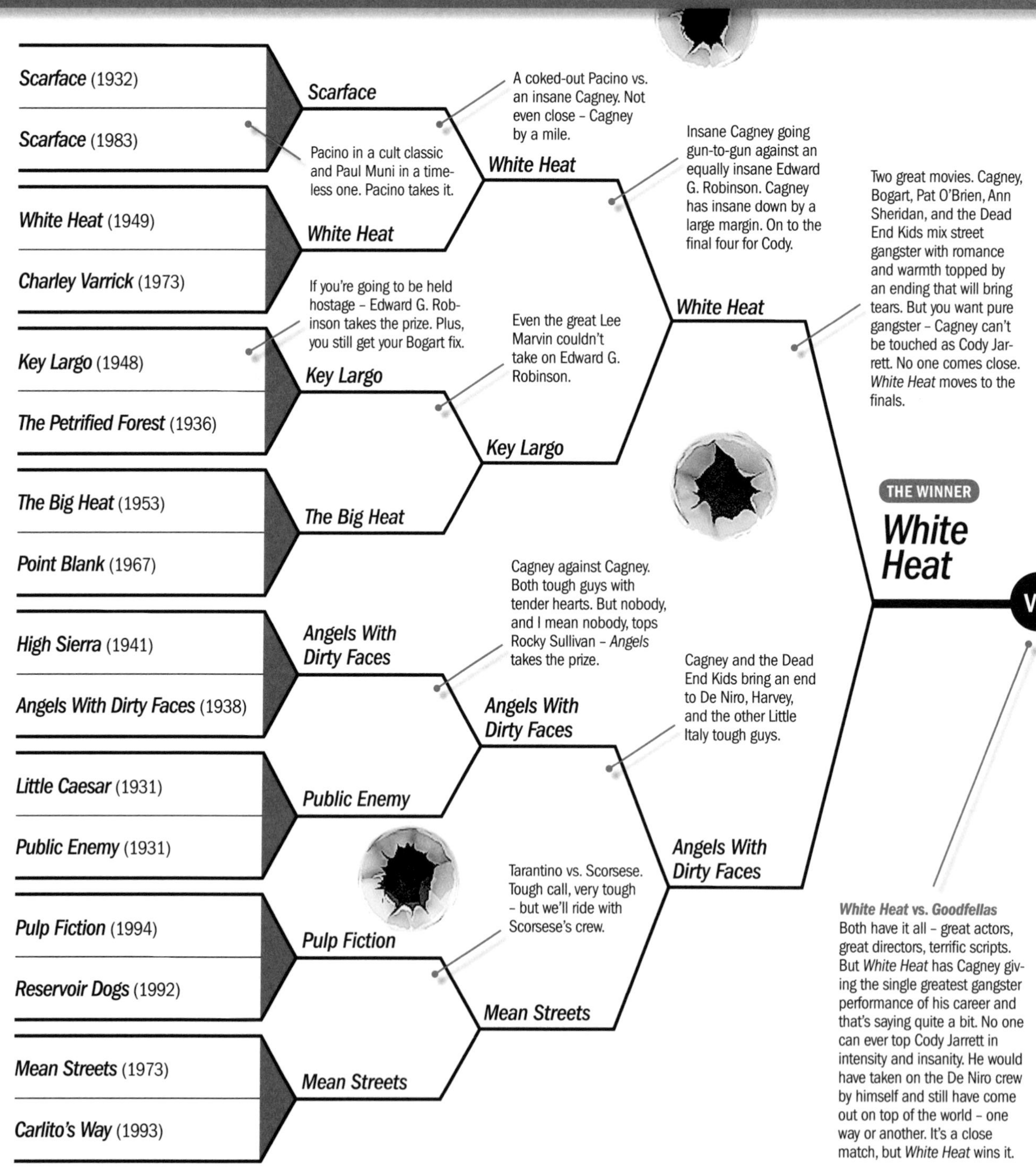
Scarface (1932)
Scarface (1983)
White Heat (1949)
Charley Varrick (1973)
Key Largo (1948)
The Petrified Forest (1936)
The Big Heat (1953)
Point Blank (1967)
High Sierra (1941)
Angels With Dirty Faces (1938)
Little Caesar (1931)
Public Enemy (1931)
Pulp Fiction (1994)
Reservoir Dogs (1992)
Mean Streets (1973)
Carlito's Way (1993)
Scarface
Pacino in a cult classic and Paul Muni in a timeless one. Pacino takes it.
White Heat
Key Largo
If you're going to be held hostage – Edward G. Robinson takes the prize. Plus, you still get your Bogart fix.
The Big Heat
Angels With Dirty Faces
Public Enemy
Pulp Fiction
Mean Streets
A coked-out Pacino vs. an insane Cagney. Not even close – Cagney by a mile.
White Heat
Even the great Lee Marvin couldn't take on Edward G. Robinson.
Key Largo
Cagney against Cagney. Both tough guys with tender hearts. But nobody, and I mean nobody, tops Rocky Sullivan – *Angels* takes the prize.
Angels With Dirty Faces
Tarantino vs. Scorsese. Tough call, very tough – but we'll ride with Scorsese's crew.
Mean Streets
Insane Cagney going gun-to-gun against an equally insane Edward G. Robinson. Cagney has insane down by a large margin. On to the final four for Cody.
White Heat
Cagney and the Dead End Kids bring an end to De Niro, Harvey, and the other Little Italy tough guys.
Angels With Dirty Faces
Two great movies. Cagney, Bogart, Pat O'Brien, Ann Sheridan, and the Dead End Kids mix street gangster with romance and warmth topped by an ending that will bring tears. But you want pure gangster – Cagney can't be touched as Cody Jarrett. No one comes close. *White Heat* moves to the finals.
THE WINNER
White Heat
VS.
White Heat vs. Goodfellas
Both have it all – great actors, great directors, terrific scripts. But *White Heat* has Cagney giving the single greatest gangster performance of his career and that's saying quite a bit. No one can ever top Cody Jarrett in intensity and insanity. He would have taken on the De Niro crew by himself and still have come out on top of the world – one way or another. It's a close match, but *White Heat* wins it.

IT'S NOT EASY CHOOSING THE BEST GANGSTER FILM – even when we slide *The Godfather* and *The Godfather II* into a category of their own. I chose only pure gangster movies, ruling out comedies (*Analyze This* would have been a contender) and any movie where the gangster does not propel the action (this eliminated *The Untouchables; Heat* with Pacino and DeNiro, not with Burt Reynolds; and *On The Waterfront*). To qualify, the films had to be all gangster all the time and the less we saw of men with badges the better.

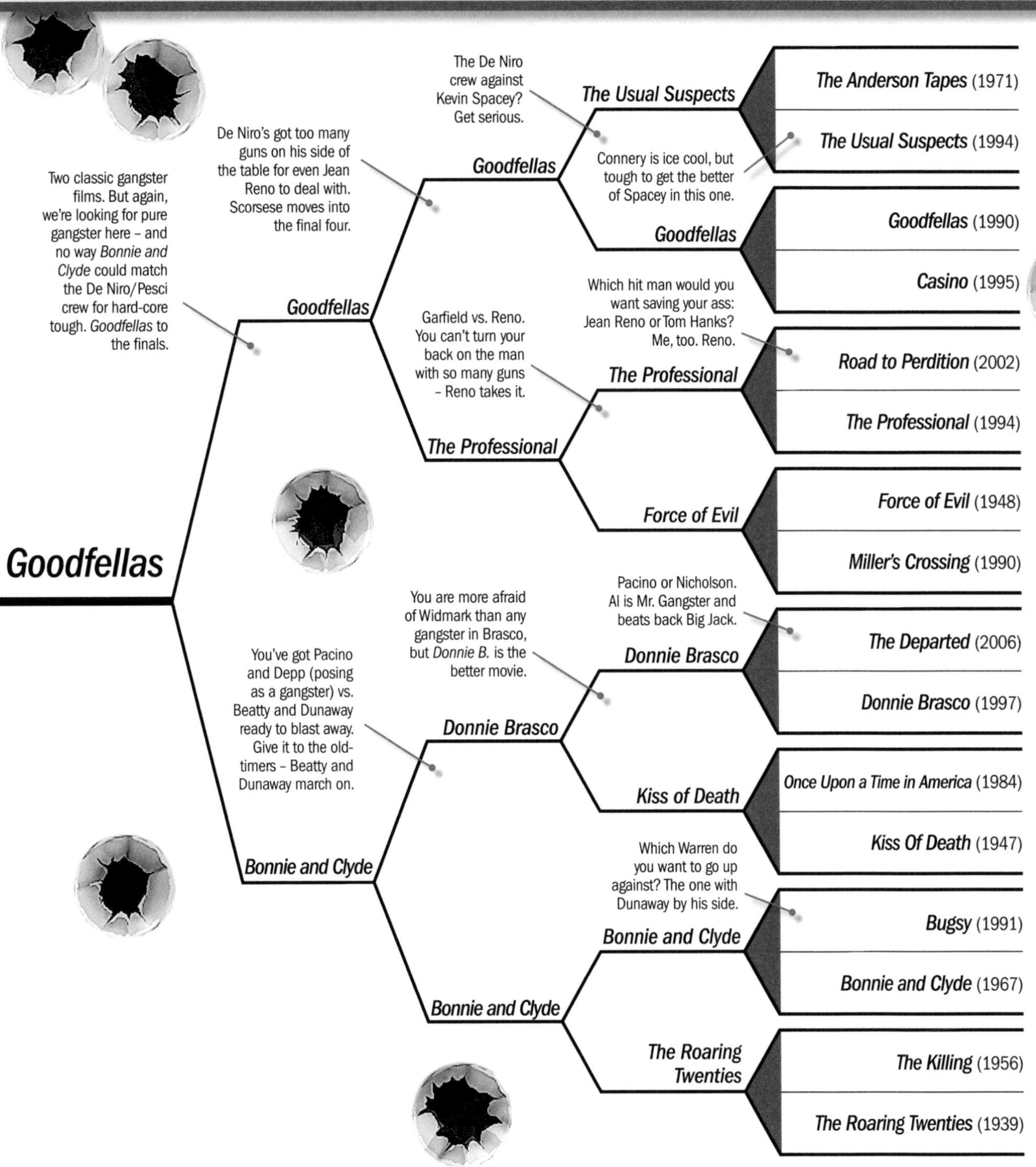

The De Niro crew against Kevin Spacey? Get serious.
The Usual Suspects
The Anderson Tapes (1971)
The Usual Suspects (1994)
De Niro's got too many guns on his side of the table for even Jean Reno to deal with. Scorsese moves into the final four.
Goodfellas
Connery is ice cool, but tough to get the better of Spacey in this one.
Two classic gangster films. But again, we're looking for pure gangster here – and no way Bonnie and Clyde could match the De Niro/Pesci crew for hard-core tough. Goodfellas to the finals.
Goodfellas
Goodfellas (1990)
Casino (1995)
Goodfellas
Which hit man would you want saving your ass: Jean Reno or Tom Hanks? Me, too. Reno.
Garfield vs. Reno. You can't turn your back on the man with so many guns – Reno takes it.
The Professional
Road to Perdition (2002)
The Professional (1994)
The Professional
Force of Evil
Force of Evil (1948)
Miller's Crossing (1990)
Goodfellas
Pacino or Nicholson. Al is Mr. Gangster and beats back Big Jack.
You are more afraid of Widmark than any gangster in Brasco, but Donnie B. is the better movie.
Donnie Brasco
The Departed (2006)
Donnie Brasco (1997)
You've got Pacino and Depp (posing as a gangster) vs. Beatty and Dunaway ready to blast away. Give it to the old-timers – Beatty and Dunaway march on.
Donnie Brasco
Kiss of Death
Once Upon a Time in America (1984)
Kiss Of Death (1947)
Bonnie and Clyde
Which Warren do you want to go up against? The one with Dunaway by his side.
Bonnie and Clyde
Bugsy (1991)
Bonnie and Clyde (1967)
Bonnie and Clyde
The Roaring Twenties
The Killing (1956)
The Roaring Twenties (1939)

Disney Animated Films

By Richard Corliss

Richard Corliss, a *Time* movie critic, has watched Disney films all his life, but he's really a Warner Bros. cartoon man.

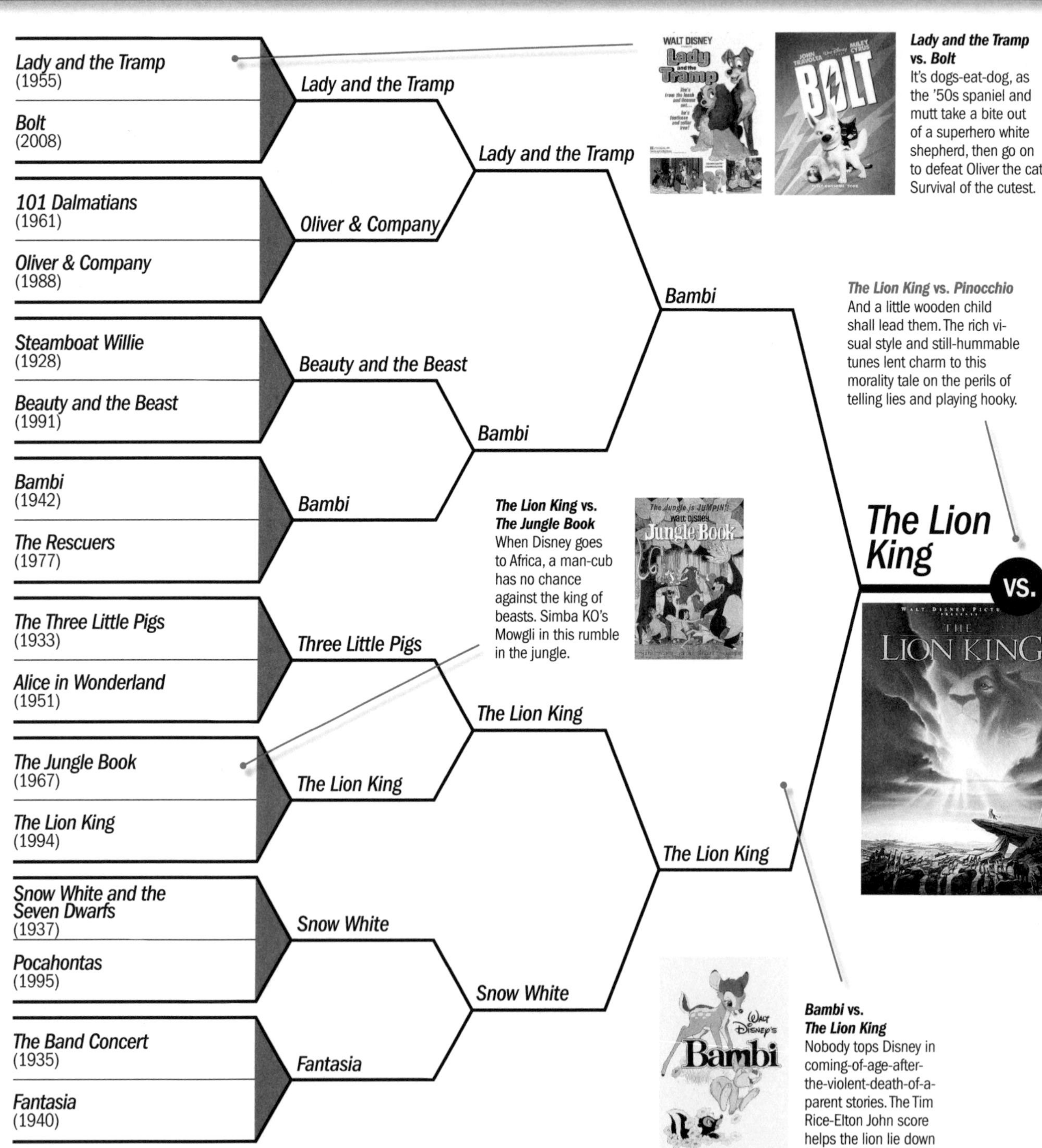

Lady and the Tramp (1955)
Bolt (2008)
101 Dalmatians (1961)
Oliver & Company (1988)
Steamboat Willie (1928)
Beauty and the Beast (1991)
Bambi (1942)
The Rescuers (1977)
The Three Little Pigs (1933)
Alice in Wonderland (1951)
The Jungle Book (1967)
The Lion King (1994)
Snow White and the Seven Dwarfs (1937)
Pocahontas (1995)
The Band Concert (1935)
Fantasia (1940)
Lady and the Tramp
Oliver & Company
Beauty and the Beast
Bambi
Three Little Pigs
The Lion King
Snow White
Fantasia
Lady and the Tramp
Bambi
The Lion King
Snow White
Bambi
The Lion King
The Lion King
VS.

Lady and the Tramp* vs. *Bolt
It's dogs-eat-dog, as the '50s spaniel and mutt take a bite out of a superhero white shepherd, then go on to defeat Oliver the cat. Survival of the cutest.

The Lion King* vs. *Pinocchio
And a little wooden child shall lead them. The rich visual style and still-hummable tunes lent charm to this morality tale on the perils of telling lies and playing hooky.

The Lion King* vs. *The Jungle Book
When Disney goes to Africa, a man-cub has no chance against the king of beasts. Simba KO's Mowgli in this rumble in the jungle.

Bambi* vs. *The Lion King
Nobody tops Disney in coming-of-age-after-the-violent-death-of-a-parent stories. The Tim Rice-Elton John score helps the lion lie down on the deer.

THE VERY FIRST MOVIES SEEN BY GENERATIONS OF KIDS, Disney animated features had pretty songs and cute animals. But in their plumbing of toddler fears – abandonment, humiliation, instant orphandom – these were also primal horror films that could literally scare the poo out of wee ones. A genre more or less created by one man, the Disney cartoon factory has enthralled and troubled audiences for 80-plus years. In this tournament, Walt's early shorts duke it out with some of the most widely seen feature films ever made. No Pixar movies, though; those wizards from the Bay Area would be ringers.

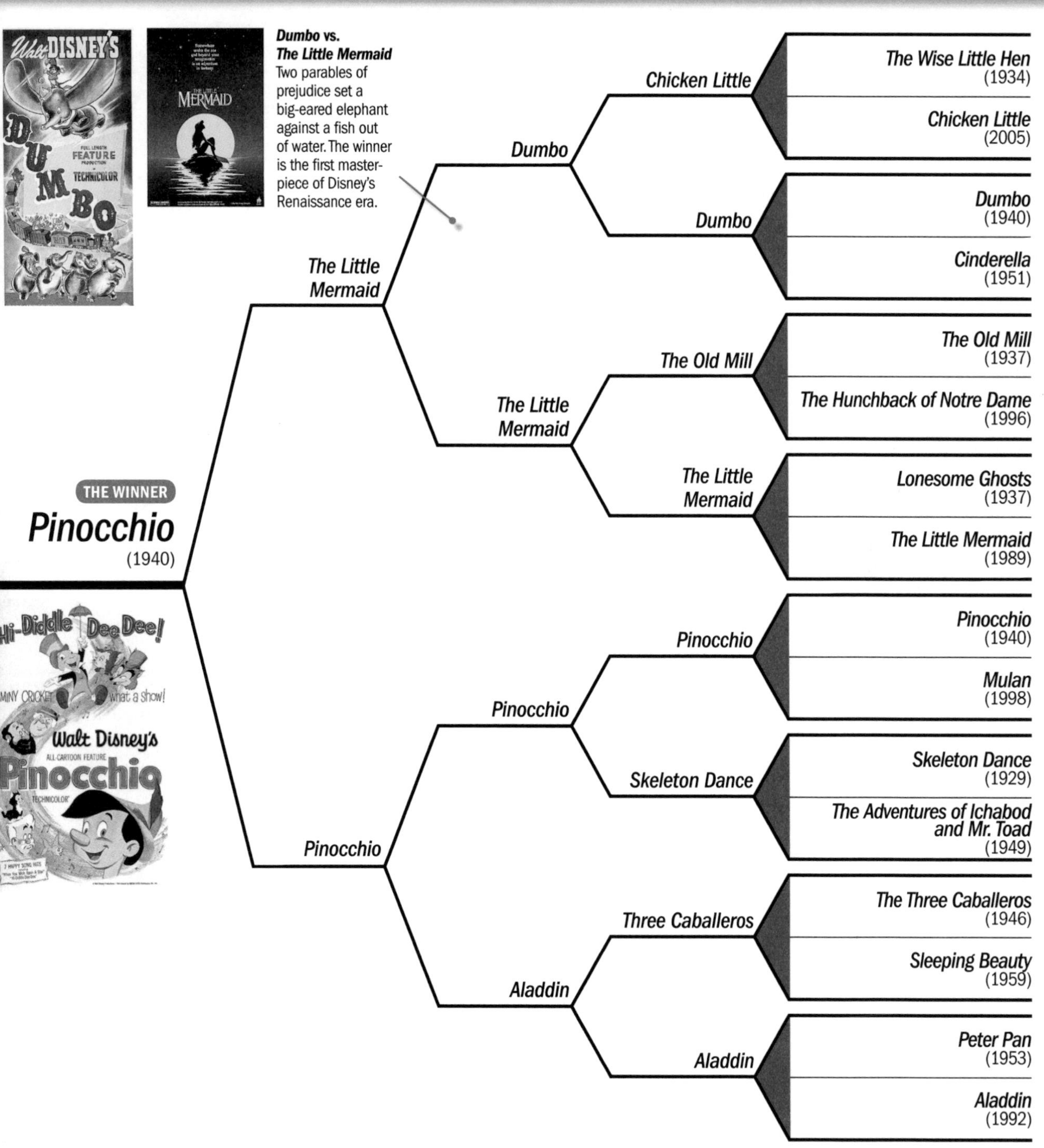

Walt DISNEY'S
DUMBO
FULL LENGTH FEATURE PRODUCTION
TECHNICOLOR
THE LITTLE MERMAID
Dumbo vs. The Little Mermaid
Two parables of prejudice set a big-eared elephant against a fish out of water. The winner is the first masterpiece of Disney's Renaissance era.
The Wise Little Hen (1934)
Chicken Little (2005)
Dumbo (1940)
Cinderella (1951)
The Old Mill (1937)
The Hunchback of Notre Dame (1996)
Lonesome Ghosts (1937)
The Little Mermaid (1989)
Pinocchio (1940)
Mulan (1998)
Skeleton Dance (1929)
The Adventures of Ichabod and Mr. Toad (1949)
The Three Caballeros (1946)
Sleeping Beauty (1959)
Peter Pan (1953)
Aladdin (1992)
Chicken Little
Dumbo
The Old Mill
The Little Mermaid
Pinocchio
Skeleton Dance
Three Caballeros
Aladdin
Dumbo
The Little Mermaid
Pinocchio
Aladdin
The Little Mermaid
Pinocchio
THE WINNER
Pinocchio (1940)
Hi-Diddle Dee Dee!
what a show!
Walt Disney's
ALL-CARTOON FEATURE
Pinocchio
TECHNICOLOR

The Honeymooners Lexicon

By Peter Crescenti

Peter Crescenti is co-founder of *The Honeymooners* fan club, RALPH (Royal Association for the Longevity and Preservation of the Honeymooners), and has authored/co-authored five books about the series.

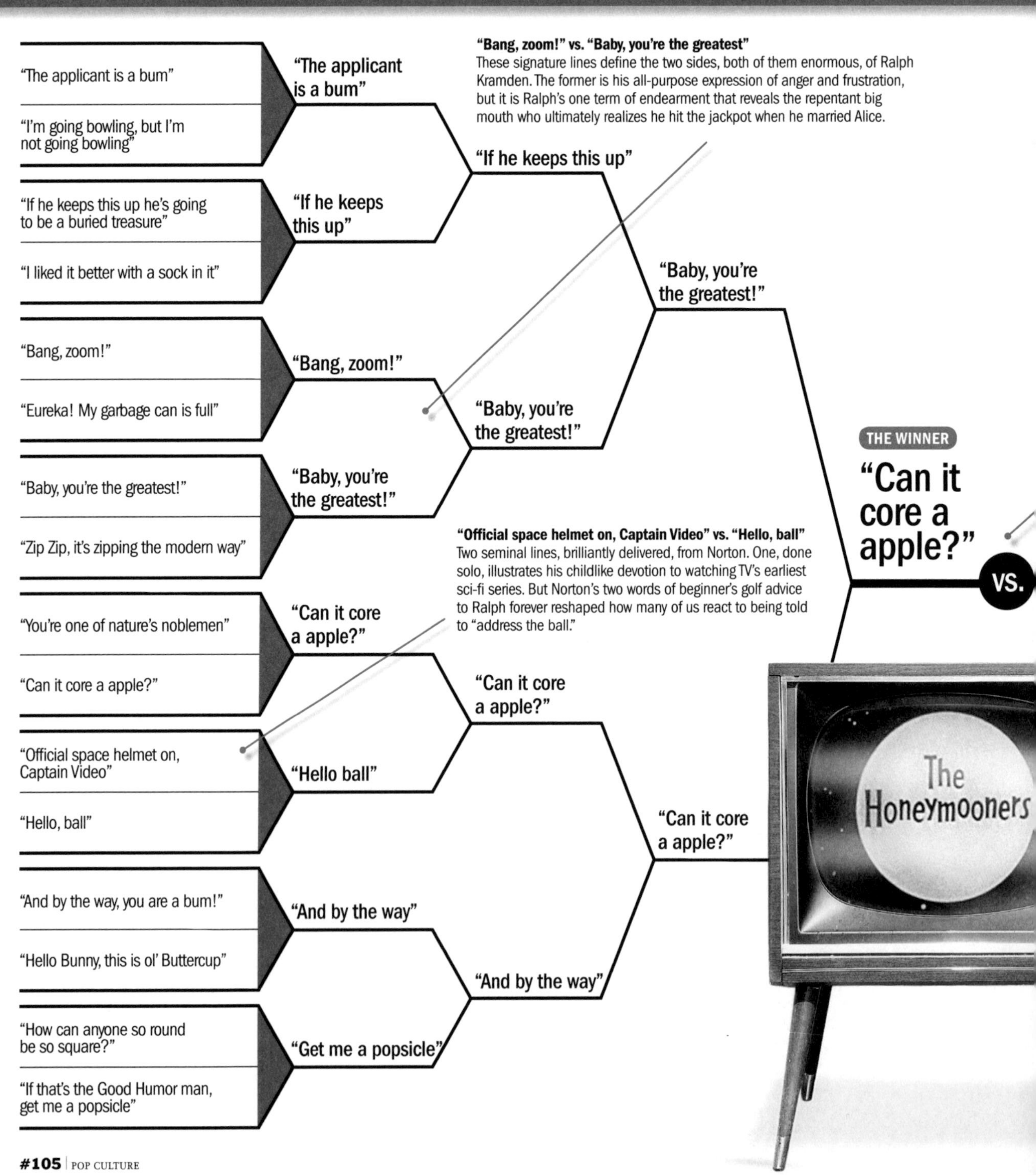

"The applicant is a bum"
"I'm going bowling, but I'm not going bowling"
"If he keeps this up he's going to be a buried treasure"
"I liked it better with a sock in it"
"Bang, zoom!"
"Eureka! My garbage can is full"
"Baby, you're the greatest!"
"Zip Zip, it's zipping the modern way"
"You're one of nature's noblemen"
"Can it core a apple?"
"Official space helmet on, Captain Video"
"Hello, ball"
"And by the way, you are a bum!"
"Hello Bunny, this is ol' Buttercup"
"How can anyone so round be so square?"
"If that's the Good Humor man, get me a popsicle"
"The applicant is a bum"
"If he keeps this up"
"Bang, zoom!"
"Baby, you're the greatest!"
"Can it core a apple?"
"Hello ball"
"And by the way"
"Get me a popsicle"
"If he keeps this up"
"Baby, you're the greatest!"
"Can it core a apple?"
"And by the way"
"Baby, you're the greatest!"
"Can it core a apple?"
THE WINNER
"Can it core a apple?"
VS.
The Honeymooners

"Bang, zoom!" vs. "Baby, you're the greatest"
These signature lines define the two sides, both of them enormous, of Ralph Kramden. The former is his all-purpose expression of anger and frustration, but it is Ralph's one term of endearment that reveals the repentant big mouth who ultimately realizes he hit the jackpot when he married Alice.

"Official space helmet on, Captain Video" vs. "Hello, ball"
Two seminal lines, brilliantly delivered, from Norton. One, done solo, illustrates his childlike devotion to watching TV's earliest sci-fi series. But Norton's two words of beginner's golf advice to Ralph forever reshaped how many of us react to being told to "address the ball."

MORE THAN 50 YEARS since the classic 39 episodes of *The Honeymooners* had their first TV run, they represent a perfect storm of once-in-a-lifetime cast chemistry, extraordinary comic talent, and first-class writing. In a dingy tenement in postwar Brooklyn, Ralph Kramden and Ed Norton strive, in hysterical and poignant ways, for the American Dream that they and their wives can never achieve. Kramden and Norton defined an exquisite black-and-white minimalism and set the standard for buddy sitcoms.

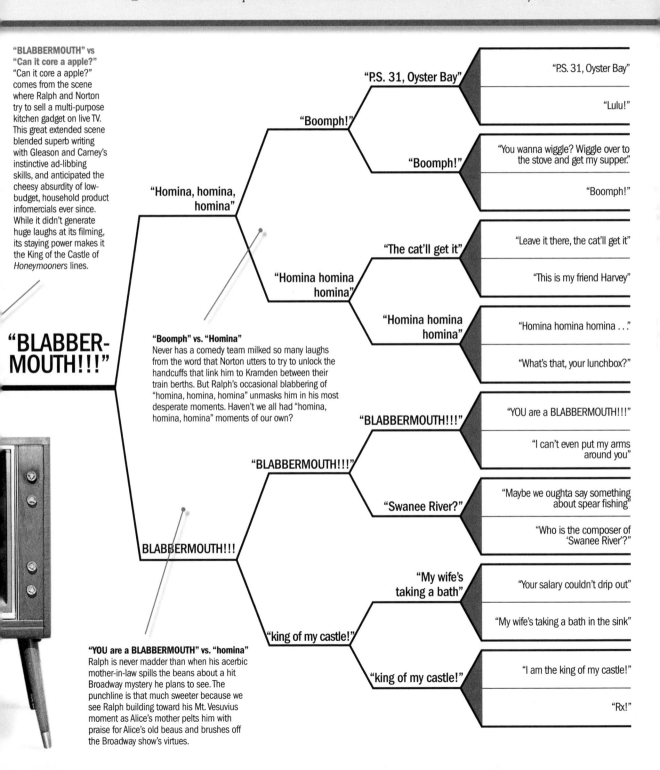

"BLABBERMOUTH" vs "Can it core a apple?"
"Can it core a apple?" comes from the scene where Ralph and Norton try to sell a multi-purpose kitchen gadget on live TV. This great extended scene blended superb writing with Gleason and Carney's instinctive ad-libbing skills, and anticipated the cheesy absurdity of low-budget, household product infomercials ever since. While it didn't generate huge laughs at its filming, its staying power makes it the King of the Castle of *Honeymooners* lines.

"P.S. 31, Oyster Bay"

"Lulu!"

"You wanna wiggle? Wiggle over to the stove and get my supper."

"Boomph!"

"Leave it there, the cat'll get it"

"This is my friend Harvey"

"Homina homina homina . . ."

"What's that, your lunchbox?"

"YOU are a BLABBERMOUTH!!!"

"I can't even put my arms around you"

"Maybe we oughta say something about spear fishing"

"Who is the composer of 'Swanee River'?"

"Your salary couldn't drip out"

"My wife's taking a bath in the sink"

"I am the king of my castle!"

"Rx!"

"P.S. 31, Oyster Bay"

"Boomph!"

"The cat'll get it"

"Homina homina homina"

"BLABBERMOUTH!!!"

"Swanee River?"

"My wife's taking a bath"

"king of my castle!"

"Boomph!"

"Homina homina homina"

"BLABBERMOUTH!!!"

"king of my castle!"

"Homina, homina, homina"

BLABBERMOUTH!!!

"BLABBER-MOUTH!!!"

"Boomph" vs. "Homina"
Never has a comedy team milked so many laughs from the word that Norton utters to try to unlock the handcuffs that link him to Kramden between their train berths. But Ralph's occasional blabbering of "homina, homina, homina" unmasks him in his most desperate moments. Haven't we all had "homina, homina, homina" moments of our own?

"YOU are a BLABBERMOUTH" vs. "homina"
Ralph is never madder than when his acerbic mother-in-law spills the beans about a hit Broadway mystery he plans to see. The punchline is that much sweeter because we see Ralph building toward his Mt. Vesuvius moment as Alice's mother pelts him with praise for Alice's old beaus and brushes off the Broadway show's virtues.

You Call This Acting?

By Will Reiter

Will Reiter, a former editorial staffer at *OK!* magazine, could easily play himself in the movie version.

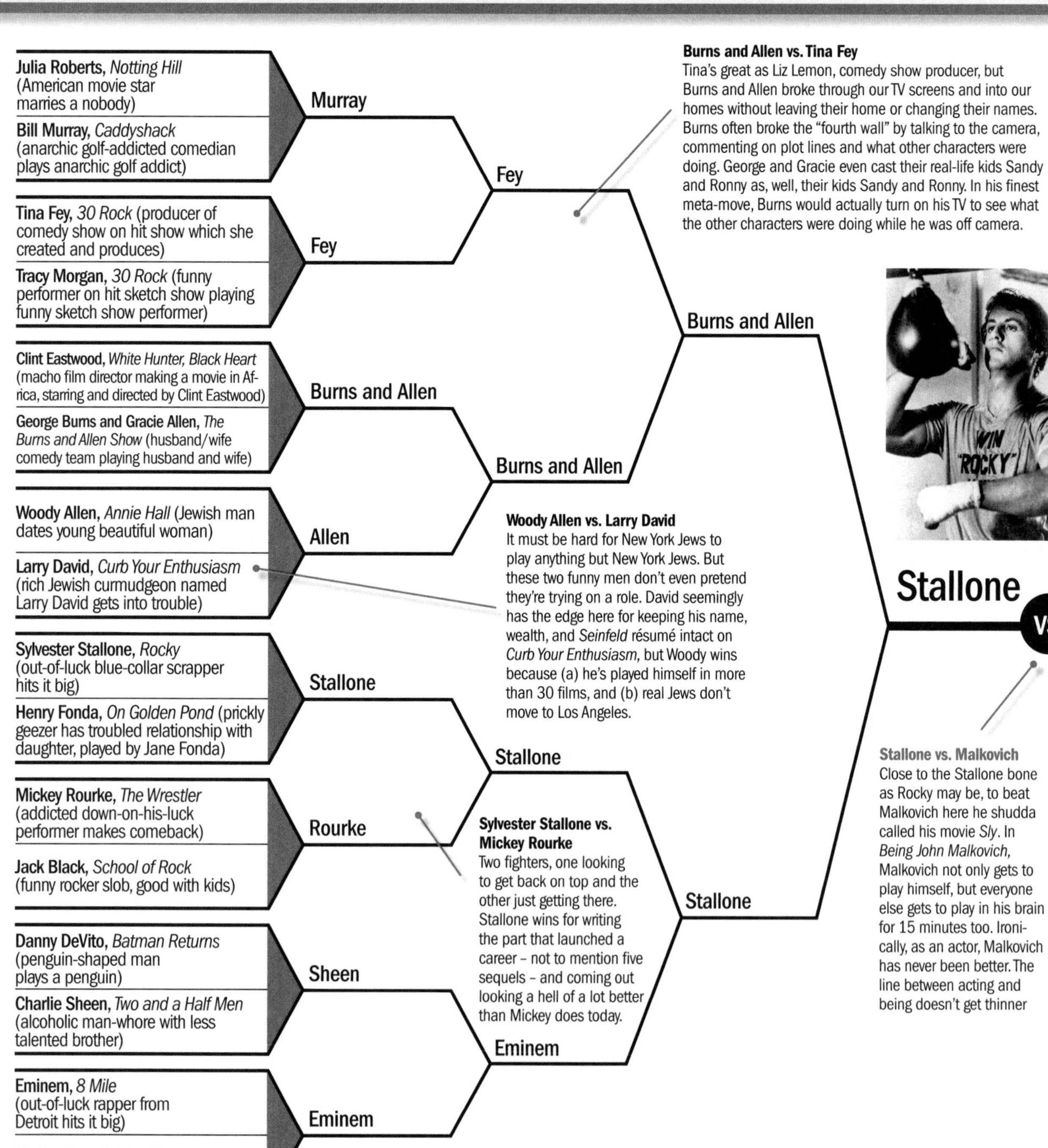

Julia Roberts, *Notting Hill* (American movie star marries a nobody)
Bill Murray, *Caddyshack* (anarchic golf-addicted comedian plays anarchic golf addict)
Tina Fey, *30 Rock* (producer of comedy show on hit show which she created and produces)
Tracy Morgan, *30 Rock* (funny performer on hit sketch show playing funny sketch show performer)
Clint Eastwood, *White Hunter, Black Heart* (macho film director making a movie in Africa, starring and directed by Clint Eastwood)
George Burns and Gracie Allen, *The Burns and Allen Show* (husband/wife comedy team playing husband and wife)
Woody Allen, *Annie Hall* (Jewish man dates young beautiful woman)
Larry David, *Curb Your Enthusiasm* (rich Jewish curmudgeon named Larry David gets into trouble)
Sylvester Stallone, *Rocky* (out-of-luck blue-collar scrapper hits it big)
Henry Fonda, *On Golden Pond* (prickly geezer has troubled relationship with daughter, played by Jane Fonda)
Mickey Rourke, *The Wrestler* (addicted down-on-his-luck performer makes comeback)
Jack Black, *School of Rock* (funny rocker slob, good with kids)
Danny DeVito, *Batman Returns* (penguin-shaped man plays a penguin)
Charlie Sheen, *Two and a Half Men* (alcoholic man-whore with less talented brother)
Eminem, *8 Mile* (out-of-luck rapper from Detroit hits it big)
Marlon Brando, *The Freshman* (the Godfather replays the Godfather)
Murray
Fey
Burns and Allen
Allen
Stallone
Rourke
Sheen
Eminem
Fey
Burns and Allen
Stallone
Eminem
Burns and Allen
Stallone
Stallone
VS.

Burns and Allen vs. Tina Fey

Tina's great as Liz Lemon, comedy show producer, but Burns and Allen broke through our TV screens and into our homes without leaving their home or changing their names. Burns often broke the "fourth wall" by talking to the camera, commenting on plot lines and what other characters were doing. George and Gracie even cast their real-life kids Sandy and Ronny as, well, their kids Sandy and Ronny. In his finest meta-move, Burns would actually turn on his TV to see what the other characters were doing while he was off camera.

Woody Allen vs. Larry David

It must be hard for New York Jews to play anything but New York Jews. But these two funny men don't even pretend they're trying on a role. David seemingly has the edge here for keeping his name, wealth, and *Seinfeld* résumé intact on *Curb Your Enthusiasm,* but Woody wins because (a) he's played himself in more than 30 films, and (b) real Jews don't move to Los Angeles.

Sylvester Stallone vs. Mickey Rourke

Two fighters, one looking to get back on top and the other just getting there. Stallone wins for writing the part that launched a career – not to mention five sequels – and coming out looking a hell of a lot better than Mickey does today.

Stallone vs. Malkovich

Close to the Stallone bone as Rocky may be, to beat Malkovich here he shudda called his movie *Sly*. In *Being John Malkovich,* Malkovich not only gets to play himself, but everyone else gets to play in his brain for 15 minutes too. Ironically, as an actor, Malkovich has never been better. The line between acting and being doesn't get thinner

ACTORS DREAM OF FINDING ROLES THAT THEY WERE "BORN TO PLAY." But how hard can it be to play a part where you're basically playing yourself? Was that Rocky we were rooting for in *Rocky,* or Sylvester Stallone? Were we watching a dancer in *Top Hat,* or Fred Astaire? In this bracket we aim to measure the thin line between what a star does on screen and who he or she really is. The thinner the line, the better – at least here.

Will Smith vs. Kid 'n Play
Both can rap and dance, '90s style. Both kept their name on screen. And both end up with the girl. But Smith shed the Fresh Prince persona and went on to bigger roles that expanded his acting chops, while Kid 'n Play never gave up on playing themselves. But Sydney, she's got a house! With a rec room!

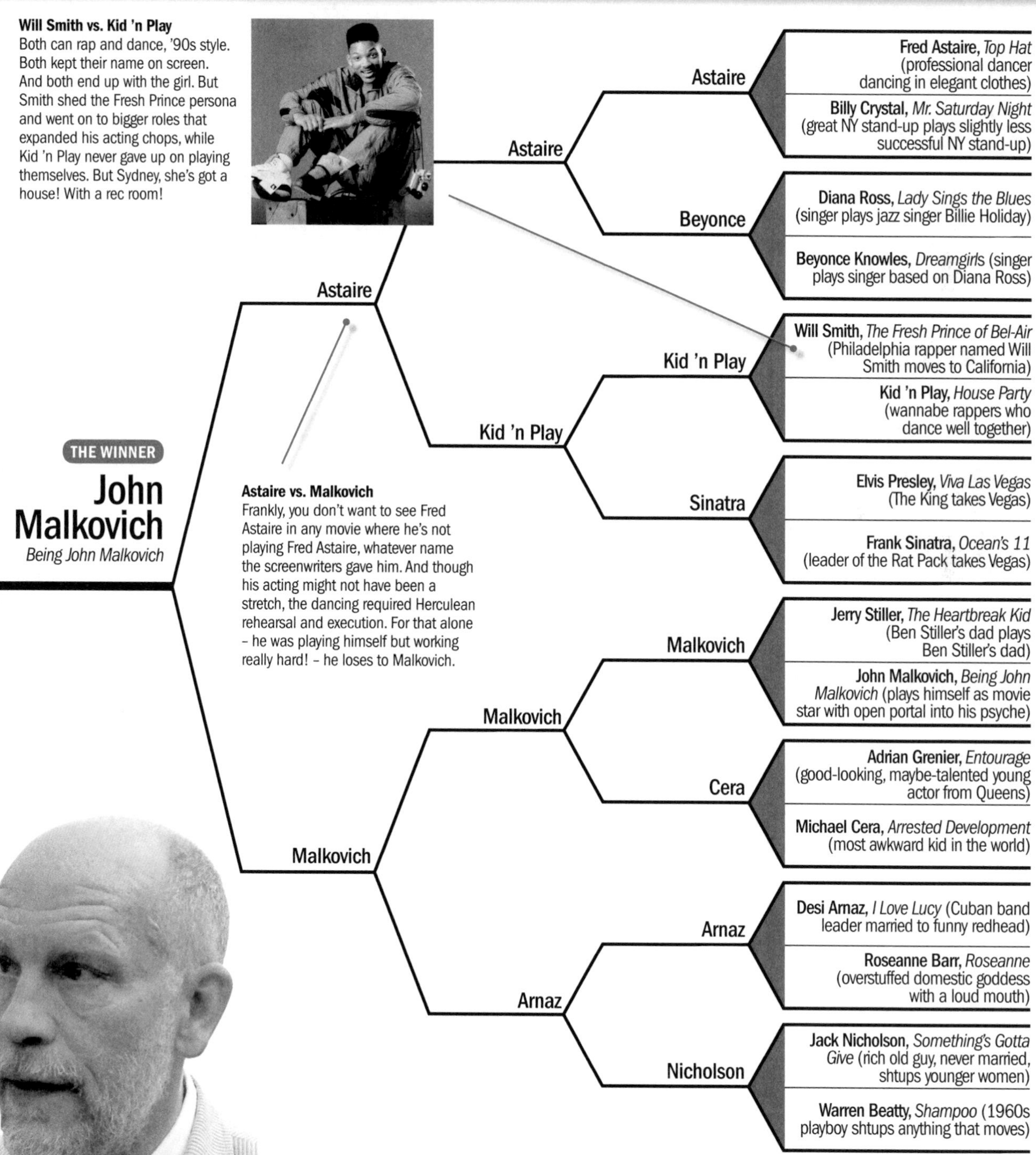

Fred Astaire, Top Hat (professional dancer dancing in elegant clothes)
Billy Crystal, Mr. Saturday Night (great NY stand-up plays slightly less successful NY stand-up)
Diana Ross, Lady Sings the Blues (singer plays jazz singer Billie Holiday)
Beyonce Knowles, Dreamgirls (singer plays singer based on Diana Ross)
Will Smith, The Fresh Prince of Bel-Air (Philadelphia rapper named Will Smith moves to California)
Kid 'n Play, House Party (wannabe rappers who dance well together)
Elvis Presley, Viva Las Vegas (The King takes Vegas)
Frank Sinatra, Ocean's 11 (leader of the Rat Pack takes Vegas)
Jerry Stiller, The Heartbreak Kid (Ben Stiller's dad plays Ben Stiller's dad)
John Malkovich, Being John Malkovich (plays himself as movie star with open portal into his psyche)
Adrian Grenier, Entourage (good-looking, maybe-talented young actor from Queens)
Michael Cera, Arrested Development (most awkward kid in the world)
Desi Arnaz, I Love Lucy (Cuban band leader married to funny redhead)
Roseanne Barr, Roseanne (overstuffed domestic goddess with a loud mouth)
Jack Nicholson, Something's Gotta Give (rich old guy, never married, shtups younger women)
Warren Beatty, Shampoo (1960s playboy shtups anything that moves)
Astaire
Beyonce
Kid 'n Play
Sinatra
Malkovich
Cera
Arnaz
Nicholson
Astaire
Kid 'n Play
Malkovich
Arnaz
Astaire
Malkovich
THE WINNER
John Malkovich
Being John Malkovich

Astaire vs. Malkovich
Frankly, you don't want to see Fred Astaire in any movie where he's not playing Fred Astaire, whatever name the screenwriters gave him. And though his acting might not have been a stretch, the dancing required Herculean rehearsal and execution. For that alone – he was playing himself but working really hard! – he loses to Malkovich.

Talk Radio Hosts

By David Hinckley

David Hinckley was first drawn to talk radio when he heard the late Joe Pyne tell a caller to "go gargle with razor blades." The image still intrigues him. He has spent the last 28 years as an editor and writer with the *New York Daily News*, covering, among other things, radio.

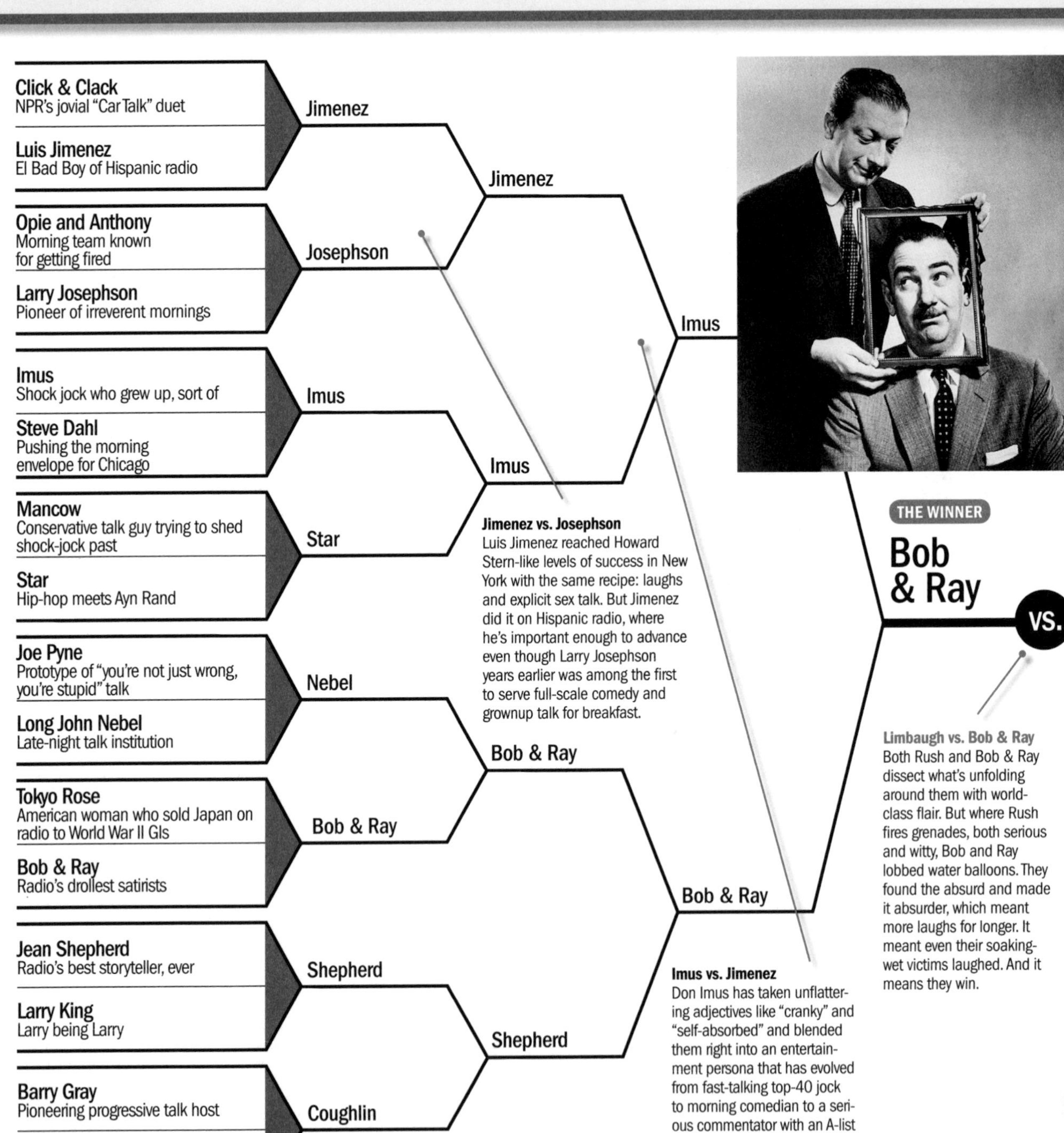
Click & Clack
NPR's jovial "Car Talk" duet
Luis Jimenez
El Bad Boy of Hispanic radio
Opie and Anthony
Morning team known for getting fired
Larry Josephson
Pioneer of irreverent mornings
Imus
Shock jock who grew up, sort of
Steve Dahl
Pushing the morning envelope for Chicago
Mancow
Conservative talk guy trying to shed shock-jock past
Star
Hip-hop meets Ayn Rand
Joe Pyne
Prototype of "you're not just wrong, you're stupid" talk
Long John Nebel
Late-night talk institution
Tokyo Rose
American woman who sold Japan on radio to World War II GIs
Bob & Ray
Radio's drollest satirists
Jean Shepherd
Radio's best storyteller, ever
Larry King
Larry being Larry
Barry Gray
Pioneering progressive talk host
Father Coughlin
Fiery priest of 1930s radio – populist, isolationist, anti-Semitic
Jimenez
Josephson
Imus
Star
Nebel
Bob & Ray
Shepherd
Coughlin
Jimenez
Imus
Bob & Ray
Shepherd
Imus
Bob & Ray
THE WINNER
Bob & Ray
VS.

Jimenez vs. Josephson
Luis Jimenez reached Howard Stern-like levels of success in New York with the same recipe: laughs and explicit sex talk. But Jimenez did it on Hispanic radio, where he's important enough to advance even though Larry Josephson years earlier was among the first to serve full-scale comedy and grownup talk for breakfast.

Imus vs. Jimenez
Don Imus has taken unflattering adjectives like "cranky" and "self-absorbed" and blended them right into an entertainment persona that has evolved from fast-talking top-40 jock to morning comedian to a serious commentator with an A-list roster of political and media guests. That chameleon-like adaptability puts him through this round.

Limbaugh vs. Bob & Ray
Both Rush and Bob & Ray dissect what's unfolding around them with world-class flair. But where Rush fires grenades, both serious and witty, Bob and Ray lobbed water balloons. They found the absurd and made it absurder, which meant more laughs for longer. It meant even their soaking-wet victims laughed. And it means they win.

TALK ON THE RADIO, like music, has always had a magnetic power, making the listener part of the American conversation. In recent years talk's dominant voice, or at least its loudest, has been conservative politics. But whatever ideological nudges it has given the country, talk radio remains primarily an entertainment medium, touching everything from sports to spanakopita. A host who can't make a show lively and fun doesn't get into the conversation at all.

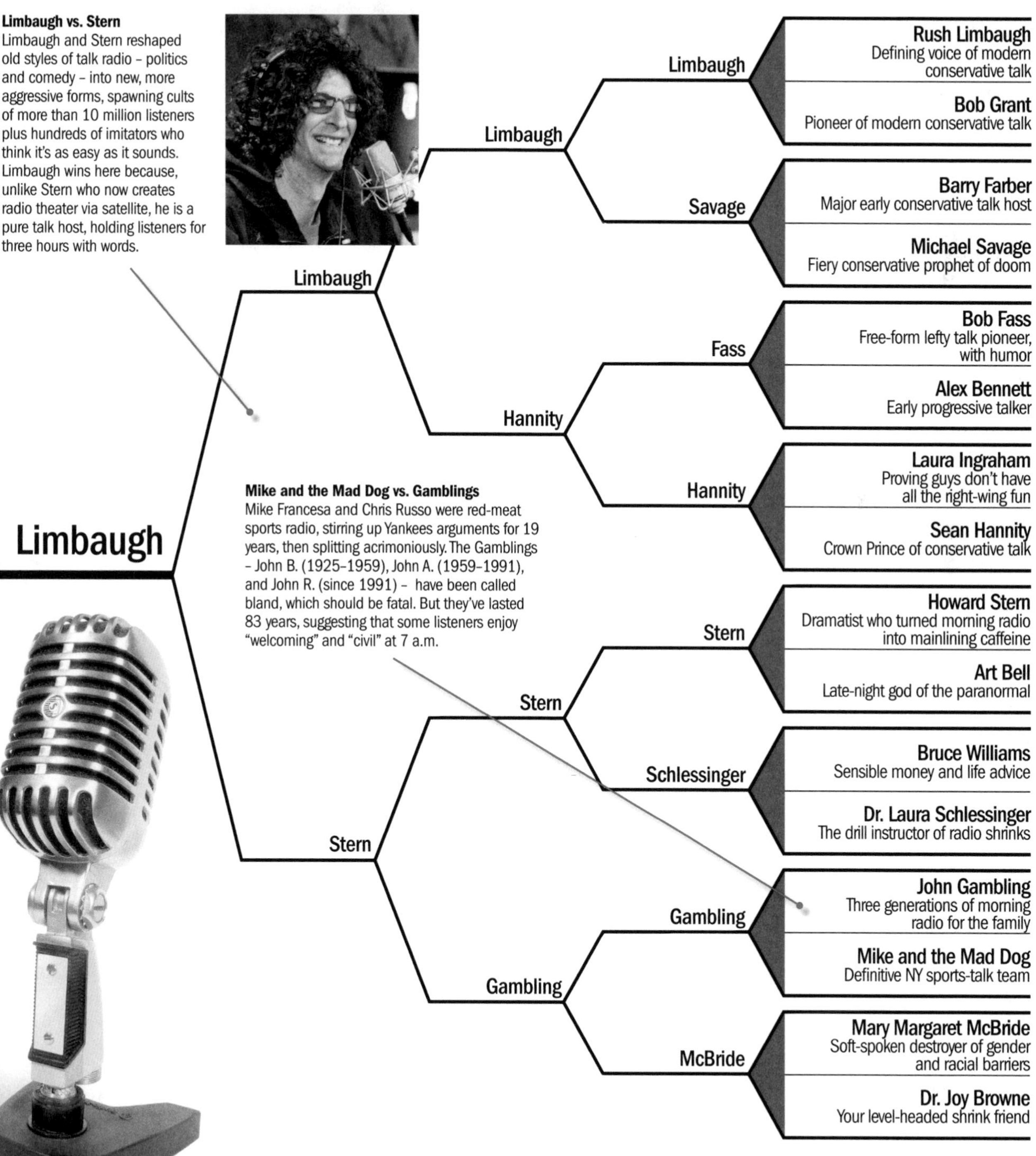

Limbaugh
Limbaugh
Limbaugh
Limbaugh
Savage
Hannity
Fass
Hannity
Stern
Stern
Schlessinger
Stern
Gambling
Gambling
McBride
Rush Limbaugh
Defining voice of modern conservative talk
Bob Grant
Pioneer of modern conservative talk
Barry Farber
Major early conservative talk host
Michael Savage
Fiery conservative prophet of doom
Bob Fass
Free-form lefty talk pioneer, with humor
Alex Bennett
Early progressive talker
Laura Ingraham
Proving guys don't have all the right-wing fun
Sean Hannity
Crown Prince of conservative talk
Howard Stern
Dramatist who turned morning radio into mainlining caffeine
Art Bell
Late-night god of the paranormal
Bruce Williams
Sensible money and life advice
Dr. Laura Schlessinger
The drill instructor of radio shrinks
John Gambling
Three generations of morning radio for the family
Mike and the Mad Dog
Definitive NY sports-talk team
Mary Margaret McBride
Soft-spoken destroyer of gender and racial barriers
Dr. Joy Browne
Your level-headed shrink friend

Limbaugh vs. Stern
Limbaugh and Stern reshaped old styles of talk radio – politics and comedy – into new, more aggressive forms, spawning cults of more than 10 million listeners plus hundreds of imitators who think it's as easy as it sounds. Limbaugh wins here because, unlike Stern who now creates radio theater via satellite, he is a pure talk host, holding listeners for three hours with words.

Mike and the Mad Dog vs. Gamblings
Mike Francesa and Chris Russo were red-meat sports radio, stirring up Yankees arguments for 19 years, then splitting acrimoniously. The Gamblings – John B. (1925–1959), John A. (1959–1991), and John R. (since 1991) – have been called bland, which should be fatal. But they've lasted 83 years, suggesting that some listeners enjoy "welcoming" and "civil" at 7 a.m.

Child Actors

By Griffin Miller

Griffin Miller is theater editor for the Davler Media publications "*City" Guide, Promenade,* and *NY Metro Parents.* Her inner child is the best (but unsung) kid actor ever.

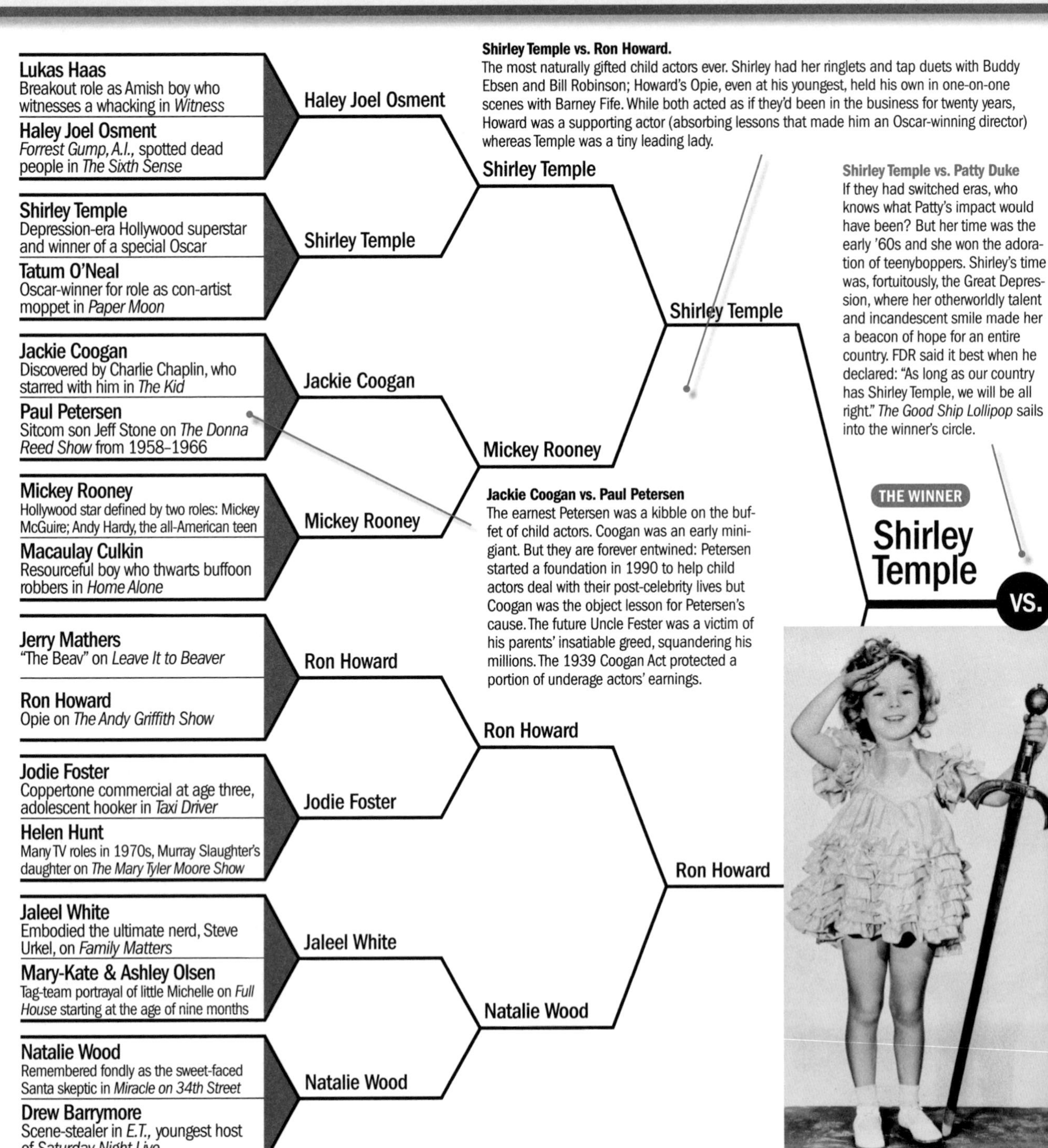

Lukas Haas
Breakout role as Amish boy who witnesses a whacking in *Witness*

Haley Joel Osment
Forrest Gump, A.I., spotted dead people in *The Sixth Sense*

Shirley Temple
Depression-era Hollywood superstar and winner of a special Oscar

Tatum O'Neal
Oscar-winner for role as con-artist moppet in *Paper Moon*

Jackie Coogan
Discovered by Charlie Chaplin, who starred with him in *The Kid*

Paul Petersen
Sitcom son Jeff Stone on *The Donna Reed Show* from 1958–1966

Mickey Rooney
Hollywood star defined by two roles: Mickey McGuire; Andy Hardy, the all-American teen

Macaulay Culkin
Resourceful boy who thwarts buffoon robbers in *Home Alone*

Jerry Mathers
"The Beav" on *Leave It to Beaver*

Ron Howard
Opie on *The Andy Griffith Show*

Jodie Foster
Coppertone commercial at age three, adolescent hooker in *Taxi Driver*

Helen Hunt
Many TV roles in 1970s, Murray Slaughter's daughter on *The Mary Tyler Moore Show*

Jaleel White
Embodied the ultimate nerd, Steve Urkel, on *Family Matters*

Mary-Kate & Ashley Olsen
Tag-team portrayal of little Michelle on *Full House* starting at the age of nine months

Natalie Wood
Remembered fondly as the sweet-faced Santa skeptic in *Miracle on 34th Street*

Drew Barrymore
Scene-stealer in *E.T.,* youngest host of *Saturday Night Live*

Haley Joel Osment
Shirley Temple
Jackie Coogan
Mickey Rooney
Ron Howard
Jodie Foster
Jaleel White
Natalie Wood

Shirley Temple
Mickey Rooney
Ron Howard
Natalie Wood

Shirley Temple
Ron Howard

Shirley Temple vs. Ron Howard.
The most naturally gifted child actors ever. Shirley had her ringlets and tap duets with Buddy Ebsen and Bill Robinson; Howard's Opie, even at his youngest, held his own in one-on-one scenes with Barney Fife. While both acted as if they'd been in the business for twenty years, Howard was a supporting actor (absorbing lessons that made him an Oscar-winning director) whereas Temple was a tiny leading lady.

Jackie Coogan vs. Paul Petersen
The earnest Petersen was a kibble on the buffet of child actors. Coogan was an early mini-giant. But they are forever entwined: Petersen started a foundation in 1990 to help child actors deal with their post-celebrity lives but Coogan was the object lesson for Petersen's cause. The future Uncle Fester was a victim of his parents' insatiable greed, squandering his millions. The 1939 Coogan Act protected a portion of underage actors' earnings.

Shirley Temple vs. Patty Duke
If they had switched eras, who knows what Patty's impact would have been? But her time was the early '60s and she won the adoration of teenyboppers. Shirley's time was, fortuitously, the Great Depression, where her otherworldly talent and incandescent smile made her a beacon of hope for an entire country. FDR said it best when he declared: "As long as our country has Shirley Temple, we will be all right." *The Good Ship Lollipop* sails into the winner's circle.

THE WINNER
Shirley Temple

VS.

FROM SILENT FILMS TO THE DISNEY CHANNEL, America's adorable, precocious, gifted, spunky, and bratty child actors have been known as much for their professional success as for their psychological meltdowns that often doomed their adult careers. But their happy/sad quotient cannot erase the charm they exuded when they were at their peak cuteness, demonstrating their preternatural talents. Since it would take another bracket to fit in the *Cosby* kids, the *Eight is Enoughers,* and the *Brady Bunches*, they were eliminated from consideration.

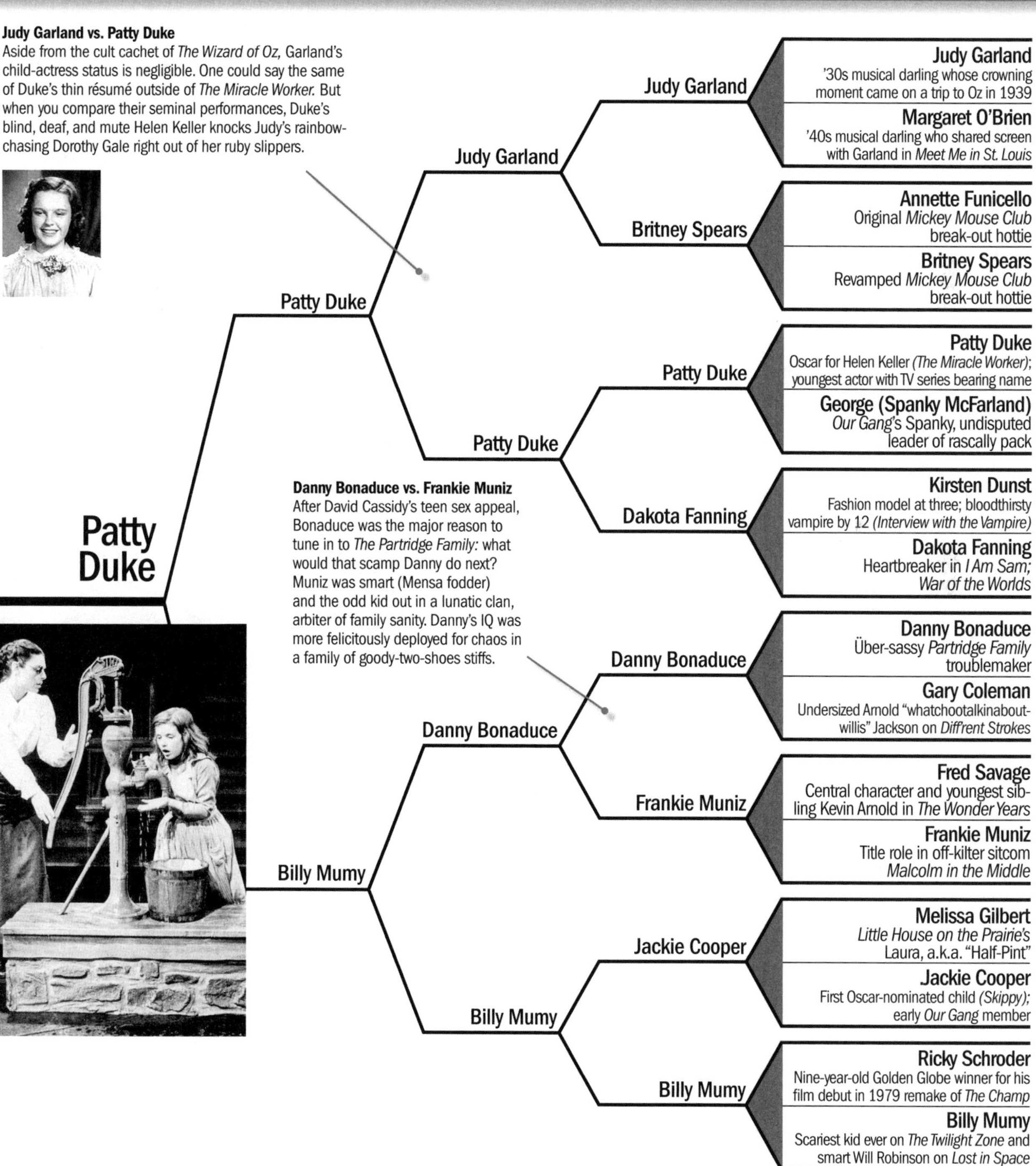

Judy Garland vs. Patty Duke
Aside from the cult cachet of The Wizard of Oz, Garland's child-actress status is negligible. One could say the same of Duke's thin résumé outside of The Miracle Worker. But when you compare their seminal performances, Duke's blind, deaf, and mute Helen Keller knocks Judy's rainbow-chasing Dorothy Gale right out of her ruby slippers.
Judy Garland
'30s musical darling whose crowning moment came on a trip to Oz in 1939
Margaret O'Brien
'40s musical darling who shared screen with Garland in Meet Me in St. Louis
Annette Funicello
Original Mickey Mouse Club break-out hottie
Britney Spears
Revamped Mickey Mouse Club break-out hottie
Patty Duke
Oscar for Helen Keller (The Miracle Worker); youngest actor with TV series bearing name
George (Spanky McFarland)
Our Gang's Spanky, undisputed leader of rascally pack
Kirsten Dunst
Fashion model at three; bloodthirsty vampire by 12 (Interview with the Vampire)
Dakota Fanning
Heartbreaker in I Am Sam; War of the Worlds
Danny Bonaduce
Über-sassy Partridge Family troublemaker
Gary Coleman
Undersized Arnold "whatchootalkinaboutwillis" Jackson on Diff'rent Strokes
Fred Savage
Central character and youngest sibling Kevin Arnold in The Wonder Years
Frankie Muniz
Title role in off-kilter sitcom Malcolm in the Middle
Melissa Gilbert
Little House on the Prairie's Laura, a.k.a. "Half-Pint"
Jackie Cooper
First Oscar-nominated child (Skippy); early Our Gang member
Ricky Schroder
Nine-year-old Golden Globe winner for his film debut in 1979 remake of The Champ
Billy Mumy
Scariest kid ever on The Twilight Zone and smart Will Robinson on Lost in Space
Judy Garland
Britney Spears
Patty Duke
Dakota Fanning
Danny Bonaduce
Frankie Muniz
Jackie Cooper
Billy Mumy
Judy Garland
Patty Duke
Danny Bonaduce
Billy Mumy
Patty Duke
Billy Mumy
Patty Duke
Danny Bonaduce vs. Frankie Muniz
After David Cassidy's teen sex appeal, Bonaduce was the major reason to tune in to The Partridge Family: what would that scamp Danny do next? Muniz was smart (Mensa fodder) and the odd kid out in a lunatic clan, arbiter of family sanity. Danny's IQ was more felicitously deployed for chaos in a family of goody-two-shoes stiffs.

Detroit Celluloid

By Kevin Conley

Kevin Conley grew up on Detroit's East Side and pretty much hasn't been scared since.

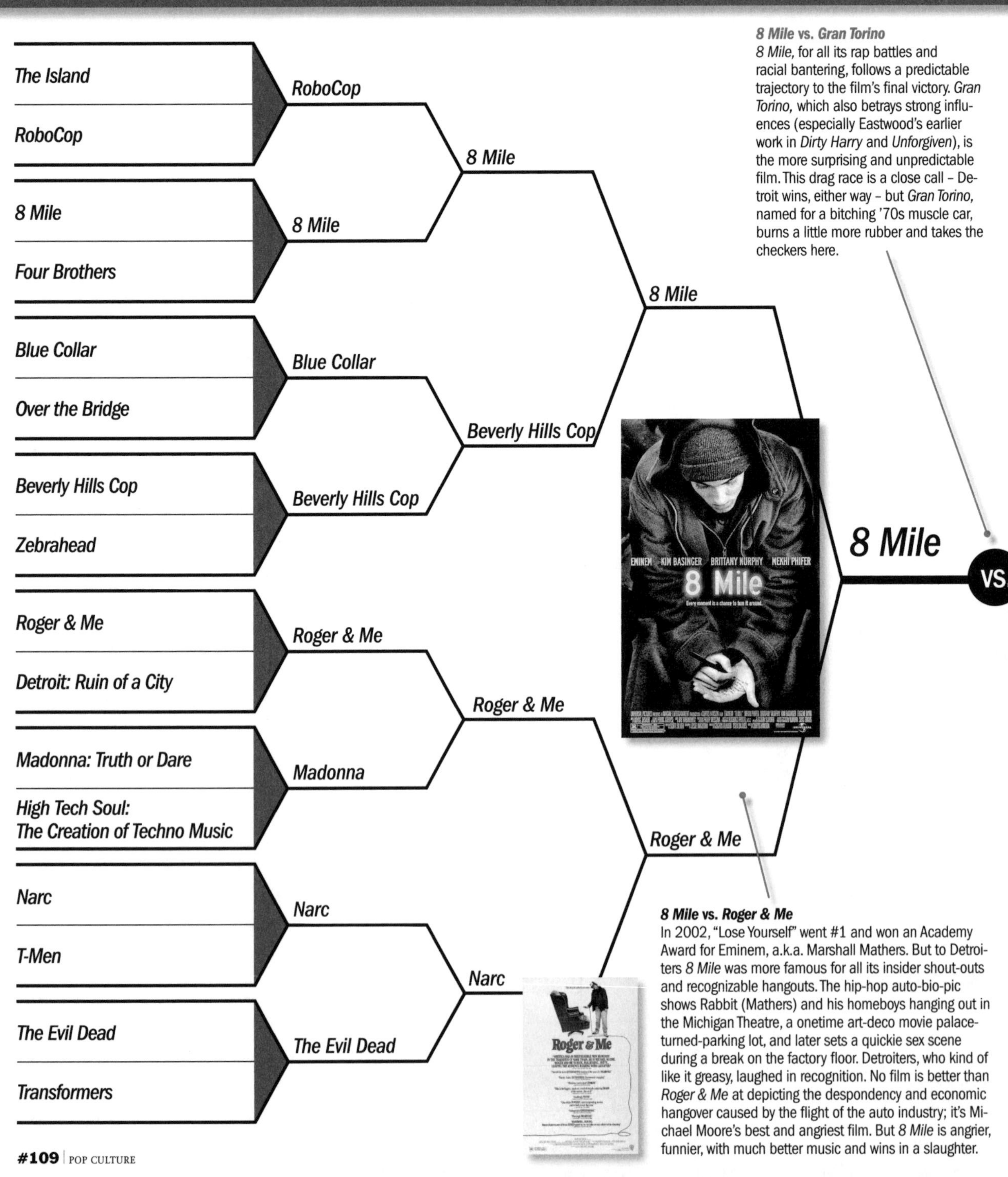

The Island
RoboCop
8 Mile
Four Brothers
Blue Collar
Over the Bridge
Beverly Hills Cop
Zebrahead
Roger & Me
Detroit: Ruin of a City
Madonna: Truth or Dare
High Tech Soul: The Creation of Techno Music
Narc
T-Men
The Evil Dead
Transformers
RoboCop
8 Mile
Blue Collar
Beverly Hills Cop
Roger & Me
Madonna
Narc
The Evil Dead
8 Mile
Beverly Hills Cop
Roger & Me
Narc
8 Mile
Roger & Me
EMINEM KIM BASINGER BRITTANY MURPHY MEKHI PHIFER
8 Mile
Roger & Me
8 Mile
VS.

8 Mile* vs. *Gran Torino
8 Mile, for all its rap battles and racial bantering, follows a predictable trajectory to the film's final victory. *Gran Torino,* which also betrays strong influences (especially Eastwood's earlier work in *Dirty Harry* and *Unforgiven*), is the more surprising and unpredictable film. This drag race is a close call – Detroit wins, either way – but *Gran Torino,* named for a bitching '70s muscle car, burns a little more rubber and takes the checkers here.

8 Mile* vs. *Roger & Me
In 2002, "Lose Yourself" went #1 and won an Academy Award for Eminem, a.k.a. Marshall Mathers. But to Detroiters *8 Mile* was more famous for all its insider shout-outs and recognizable hangouts. The hip-hop auto-bio-pic shows Rabbit (Mathers) and his homeboys hanging out in the Michigan Theatre, a onetime art-deco movie palace-turned-parking lot, and later sets a quickie sex scene during a break on the factory floor. Detroiters, who kind of like it greasy, laughed in recognition. No film is better than *Roger & Me* at depicting the despondency and economic hangover caused by the flight of the auto industry; it's Michael Moore's best and angriest film. But *8 Mile* is angrier, funnier, with much better music and wins in a slaughter.

HOLLYWOOD LOVES A GRITTY "Down and Out in Motor City" story, but it balks at actually filming there. Nearly half the films here were shot in safer locations. This is a shame, and to Detroiters, a betrayal. The D of today is the Mickey Rourke of locations: one look and you see all the decades of drugs, riot, late nights, bare knuckles. Though old photos of postwar Warsaw, with its bombed-out buildings and meadows of rubble, make native Detroiters feel homesick, the Motor City remains ready for its closeup.

Gran Torino vs. *Virgin Suicides*
Gran Torino ends with the title car driving beside the bright blue waters of Lake St. Clair, along Lakeshore, in Grosse Pointe Shores. It could be headed toward the private school attended by the Lisbon sisters, the suicides in Sofia Coppola's directorial debut. But Coppola copped out, transplanting the pitch-perfect suburban adolescents of the Eugenides novel to Toronto. The result is a dreamy, homogenous, hormonal tone poem that can't stand up to the challenge of Eastwood's foul-mouthed elegy for the working man. *Gran Torino* in a walkover.

True Romance* vs. *Detroit 9000
A Quentin Tarantino faceoff: the writer-director offered the first taste of his sado-weisenheimer style with his screenplay for *True Romance.* Five years later, after the success of *Pulp Fiction,* he arranged the re-release of *Detroit 9000,* a key 1973 Blaxploitation pic. In a squeaker, the ironic remake beats the cultural touchstone.

52 Pick-Up* vs. *Dreamgirls
Both of these movies should have been filmed in Detroit. *52 Pickup* takes a juicy Elmore Leonard story and transposes it to an antiseptic L.A. *Dreamgirls* takes a Motown origin myth – how Berry Gordy created the top soul group of the '60s, the Supremes, by demoting its most soulful voice to a backup singer – and profanes it by setting it in a generic midwestern city. *52 Pickup,* which at least retained Leonard's dialogue, wins this duel of disappointments.

Out of Sight* vs. *Shadows of Motown
Out of Sight is the best Elmore Leonard movie set in his adopted hometown. The city looks both rough and romantic, with a hotel love scene between George Clooney and Jennifer Lopez in Detroit's wishfully named Renaissance Center. The documentary *Standing in the Shadows* tells the story of Motown's studio musicians – largely anonymous during the label's heyday, then abruptly abandoned when Gordy moved production to LA. As in life, star power trounces the backup band.

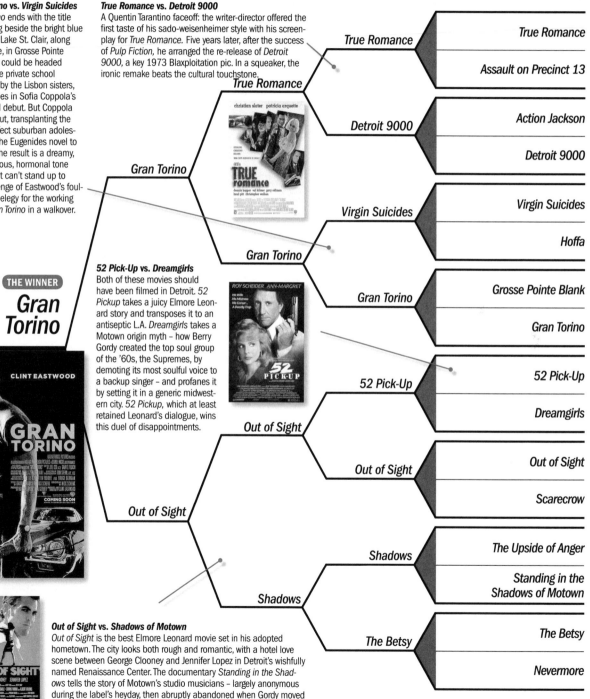

First round	Second round	Quarterfinal	Semifinal
True Romance / Assault on Precinct 13	True Romance	True Romance	Gran Torino
Action Jackson / Detroit 9000	Detroit 9000		
Virgin Suicides / Hoffa	Virgin Suicides	Gran Torino	
Grosse Pointe Blank / Gran Torino	Gran Torino		
52 Pick-Up / Dreamgirls	52 Pick-Up	Out of Sight	Out of Sight
Out of Sight / Scarecrow	Out of Sight		
The Upside of Anger / Standing in the Shadows of Motown	Shadows	Shadows	
The Betsy / Nevermore	The Betsy		

THE WINNER
Gran Torino

Girl Singers

By Tom Moon

Tom Moon, a former music critic at the *Philadelphia Inquirer,* is a regular contributor to NPR's *All Things Considered* and the author of the bestselling *1000 Recordings to Hear Before You Die.*

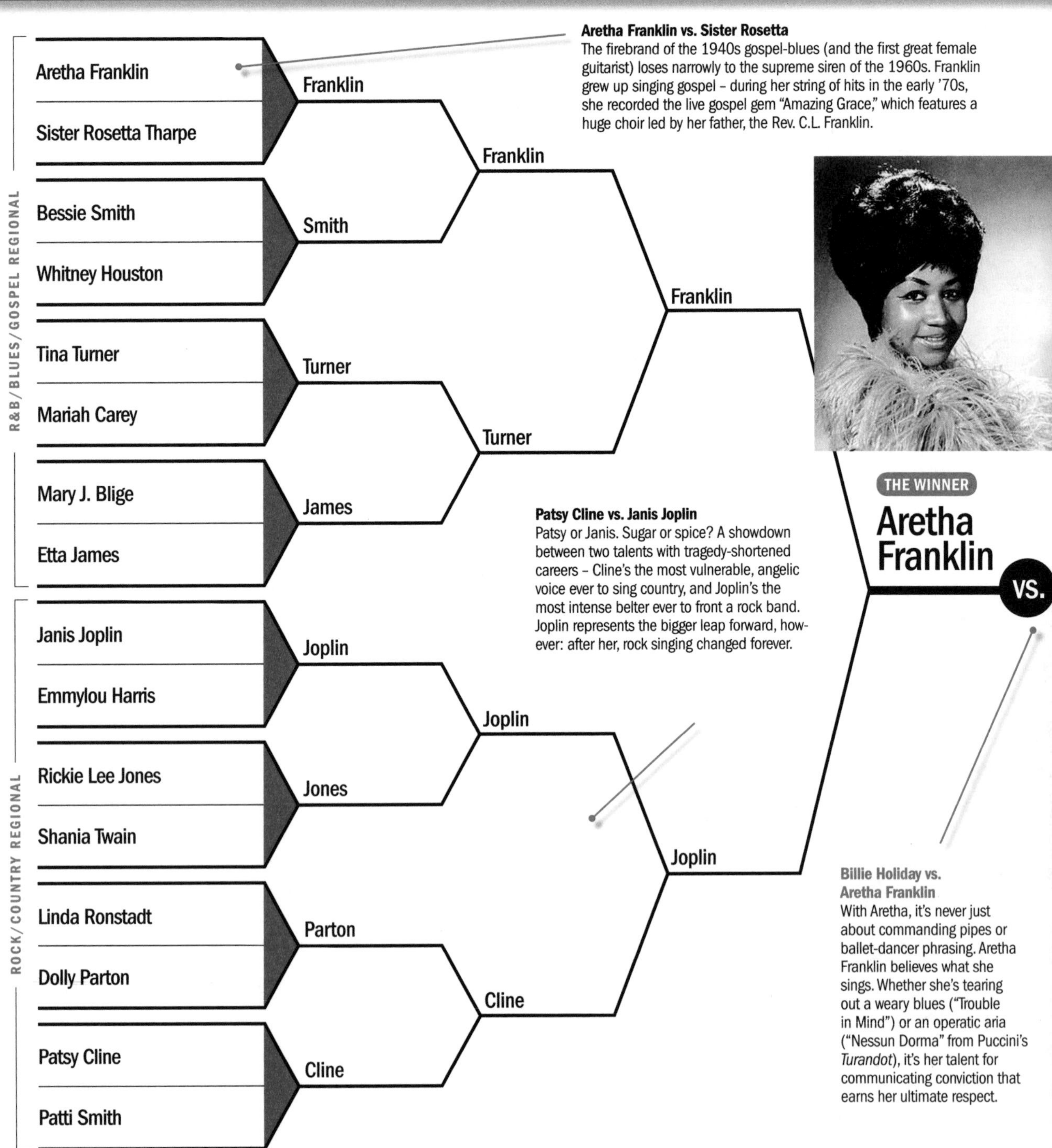
R&B/BLUES/GOSPEL REGIONAL
Aretha Franklin
Sister Rosetta Tharpe
Bessie Smith
Whitney Houston
Tina Turner
Mariah Carey
Mary J. Blige
Etta James
Franklin
Smith
Turner
James
Franklin
Turner
Franklin
ROCK/COUNTRY REGIONAL
Janis Joplin
Emmylou Harris
Rickie Lee Jones
Shania Twain
Linda Ronstadt
Dolly Parton
Patsy Cline
Patti Smith
Joplin
Jones
Parton
Cline
Joplin
Cline
Joplin
THE WINNER
Aretha Franklin
VS.

Aretha Franklin vs. Sister Rosetta

The firebrand of the 1940s gospel-blues (and the first great female guitarist) loses narrowly to the supreme siren of the 1960s. Franklin grew up singing gospel – during her string of hits in the early '70s, she recorded the live gospel gem "Amazing Grace," which features a huge choir led by her father, the Rev. C.L. Franklin.

Patsy Cline vs. Janis Joplin

Patsy or Janis. Sugar or spice? A showdown between two talents with tragedy-shortened careers – Cline's the most vulnerable, angelic voice ever to sing country, and Joplin's the most intense belter ever to front a rock band. Joplin represents the bigger leap forward, however: after her, rock singing changed forever.

Billie Holiday vs. Aretha Franklin

With Aretha, it's never just about commanding pipes or ballet-dancer phrasing. Aretha Franklin believes what she sings. Whether she's tearing out a weary blues ("Trouble in Mind") or an operatic aria ("Nessun Dorma" from Puccini's *Turandot*), it's her talent for communicating conviction that earns her ultimate respect.

SINCE THE DAWN OF RECORDED SOUND, the girl singer has exerted extraordinary pull on the American imagination – as a beacon of virtue/piety (Marian Anderson) or a corruptor of men (Bessie Smith), a take-no-bullshit realist (Aretha Franklin) or a weaver of dreams (Patsy Cline), a witness to love's anguish (Billie Holiday) or a witness to the cruelties of society (Nina Simone). To divine the fairest behind the microphone, we start with four basic styles – opera, jazz, rock/country, blues/R&B (including gospel). Advancement is determined by influence on the art of singing. Those who cast the longest shadow stay in the game.

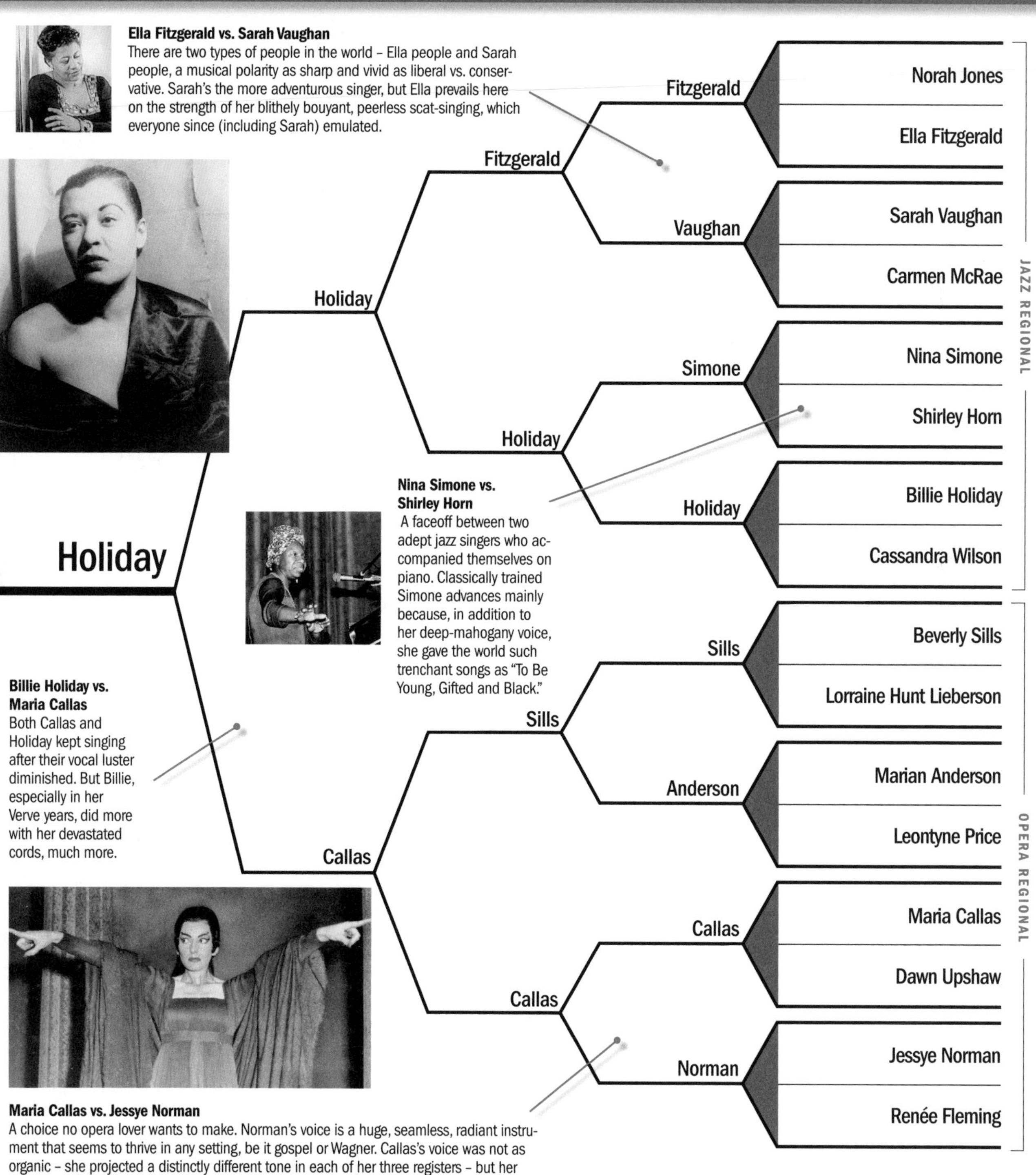
Norah Jones
Ella Fitzgerald
Sarah Vaughan
Carmen McRae
Nina Simone
Shirley Horn
Billie Holiday
Cassandra Wilson
Beverly Sills
Lorraine Hunt Lieberson
Marian Anderson
Leontyne Price
Maria Callas
Dawn Upshaw
Jessye Norman
Renée Fleming
Fitzgerald
Vaughan
Simone
Holiday
Sills
Anderson
Callas
Norman
Fitzgerald
Holiday
Sills
Callas
Holiday
Callas
Holiday
JAZZ REGIONAL
OPERA REGIONAL

Ella Fitzgerald vs. Sarah Vaughan
There are two types of people in the world – Ella people and Sarah people, a musical polarity as sharp and vivid as liberal vs. conservative. Sarah's the more adventurous singer, but Ella prevails here on the strength of her blithely bouyant, peerless scat-singing, which everyone since (including Sarah) emulated.

Nina Simone vs. Shirley Horn
A faceoff between two adept jazz singers who accompanied themselves on piano. Classically trained Simone advances mainly because, in addition to her deep-mahogany voice, she gave the world such trenchant songs as "To Be Young, Gifted and Black."

Billie Holiday vs. Maria Callas
Both Callas and Holiday kept singing after their vocal luster diminished. But Billie, especially in her Verve years, did more with her devastated cords, much more.

Maria Callas vs. Jessye Norman
A choice no opera lover wants to make. Norman's voice is a huge, seamless, radiant instrument that seems to thrive in any setting, be it gospel or Wagner. Callas's voice was not as organic – she projected a distinctly different tone in each of her three registers – but her dramatic interpretations redefined the meaning of "singing actress."

Cathartic Movie Deaths

By David Edelstein

David Edelstein is the film critic for *New York* magazine, NPR's *Fresh Air*, and CBS *Sunday Morning*.

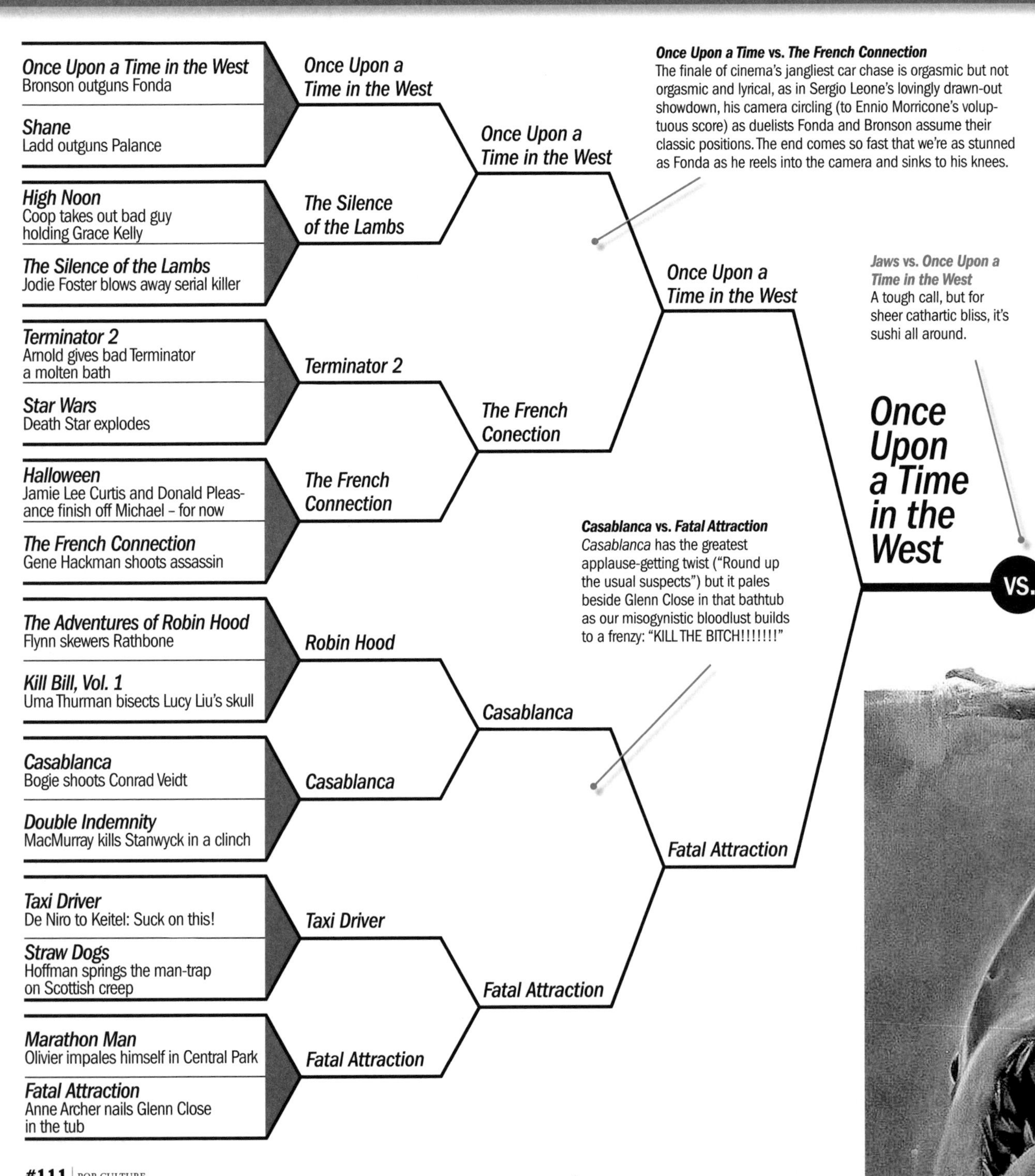
Once Upon a Time in the West
Bronson outguns Fonda
Shane
Ladd outguns Palance
High Noon
Coop takes out bad guy holding Grace Kelly
The Silence of the Lambs
Jodie Foster blows away serial killer
Terminator 2
Arnold gives bad Terminator a molten bath
Star Wars
Death Star explodes
Halloween
Jamie Lee Curtis and Donald Pleasance finish off Michael – for now
The French Connection
Gene Hackman shoots assassin
The Adventures of Robin Hood
Flynn skewers Rathbone
Kill Bill, Vol. 1
Uma Thurman bisects Lucy Liu's skull
Casablanca
Bogie shoots Conrad Veidt
Double Indemnity
MacMurray kills Stanwyck in a clinch
Taxi Driver
De Niro to Keitel: Suck on this!
Straw Dogs
Hoffman springs the man-trap on Scottish creep
Marathon Man
Olivier impales himself in Central Park
Fatal Attraction
Anne Archer nails Glenn Close in the tub
Once Upon a Time in the West
The Silence of the Lambs
Terminator 2
The French Connection
Robin Hood
Casablanca
Taxi Driver
Fatal Attraction
Once Upon a Time in the West
The French Conection
Casablanca
Fatal Attraction
Once Upon a Time in the West
Fatal Attraction
Once Upon a Time vs. The French Connection
The finale of cinema's jangliest car chase is orgasmic but not orgasmic and lyrical, as in Sergio Leone's lovingly drawn-out showdown, his camera circling (to Ennio Morricone's voluptuous score) as duelists Fonda and Bronson assume their classic positions. The end comes so fast that we're as stunned as Fonda as he reels into the camera and sinks to his knees.
Casablanca vs. Fatal Attraction
Casablanca has the greatest applause-getting twist ("Round up the usual suspects") but it pales beside Glenn Close in that bathtub as our misogynistic bloodlust builds to a frenzy: "KILL THE BITCH!!!!!!!"
Jaws vs. Once Upon a Time in the West
A tough call, but for sheer cathartic bliss, it's sushi all around.
Once Upon a Time in the West
VS.

FEW THINGS IN MOVIES give as much pleasure as the moment the villain gets it – gets it so it hurts, so the audience screams as one as in a giant cinematic orgasmatron. Alas, I've had to disqualify many fine old films because the bad guy gets arrested. Bummer. To make this list there must be no shades of gray, no twinge of sympathy for the devil. To paraphrase Shakespeare: "Nothing becomes these monsters' lives like the leaving of them."

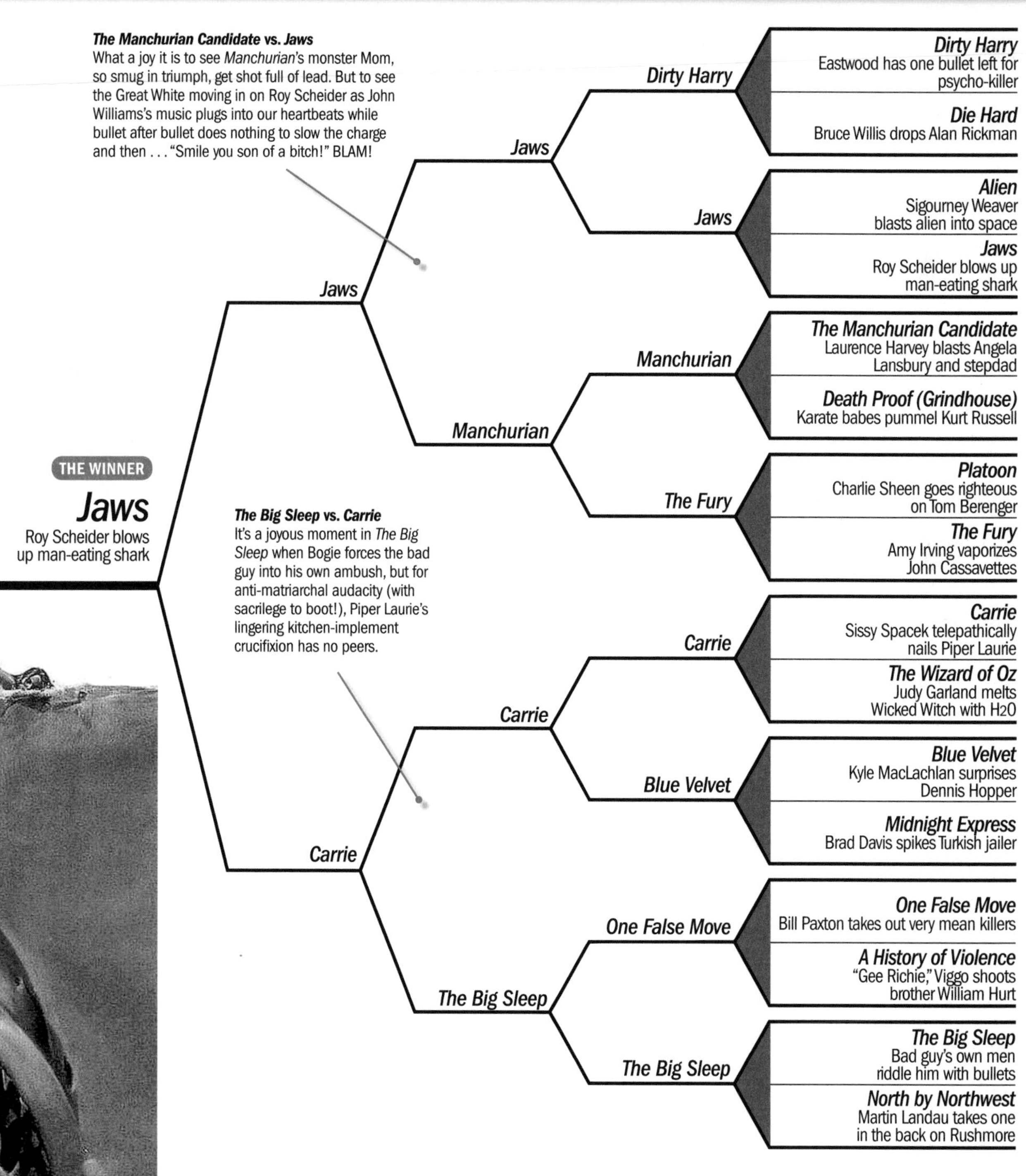

The Manchurian Candidate* vs. *Jaws
What a joy it is to see *Manchurian*'s monster Mom, so smug in triumph, get shot full of lead. But to see the Great White moving in on Roy Scheider as John Williams's music plugs into our heartbeats while bullet after bullet does nothing to slow the charge and then . . . "Smile you son of a bitch!" BLAM!

The Big Sleep* vs. *Carrie
It's a joyous moment in *The Big Sleep* when Bogie forces the bad guy into his own ambush, but for anti-matriarchal audacity (with sacrilege to boot!), Piper Laurie's lingering kitchen-implement crucifixion has no peers.

THE WINNER
Jaws
Roy Scheider blows up man-eating shark

Dirty Harry
Eastwood has one bullet left for psycho-killer
Die Hard
Bruce Willis drops Alan Rickman
Alien
Sigourney Weaver blasts alien into space
Jaws
Roy Scheider blows up man-eating shark
The Manchurian Candidate
Laurence Harvey blasts Angela Lansbury and stepdad
Death Proof (Grindhouse)
Karate babes pummel Kurt Russell
Platoon
Charlie Sheen goes righteous on Tom Berenger
The Fury
Amy Irving vaporizes John Cassavettes
Carrie
Sissy Spacek telepathically nails Piper Laurie
The Wizard of Oz
Judy Garland melts Wicked Witch with H2O
Blue Velvet
Kyle MacLachlan surprises Dennis Hopper
Midnight Express
Brad Davis spikes Turkish jailer
One False Move
Bill Paxton takes out very mean killers
A History of Violence
"Gee Richie," Viggo shoots brother William Hurt
The Big Sleep
Bad guy's own men riddle him with bullets
North by Northwest
Martin Landau takes one in the back on Rushmore

Dirty Harry
Jaws
Manchurian
The Fury
Carrie
Blue Velvet
One False Move
The Big Sleep
Jaws
Manchurian
Carrie
The Big Sleep
Jaws
Carrie

Game-Show Hosts

By Steve Leblang

Steve Leblang, a senior research executive for FOX's cable networks, frequently roamed NBC's Rockefeller Center (the 1970s home of *Jackpot* and *To Tell the Truth*) and the corner of West 58th Street and 7th Avenue in New York City (home to the *$20,000 Pyramid* and *The Big Showdown*).

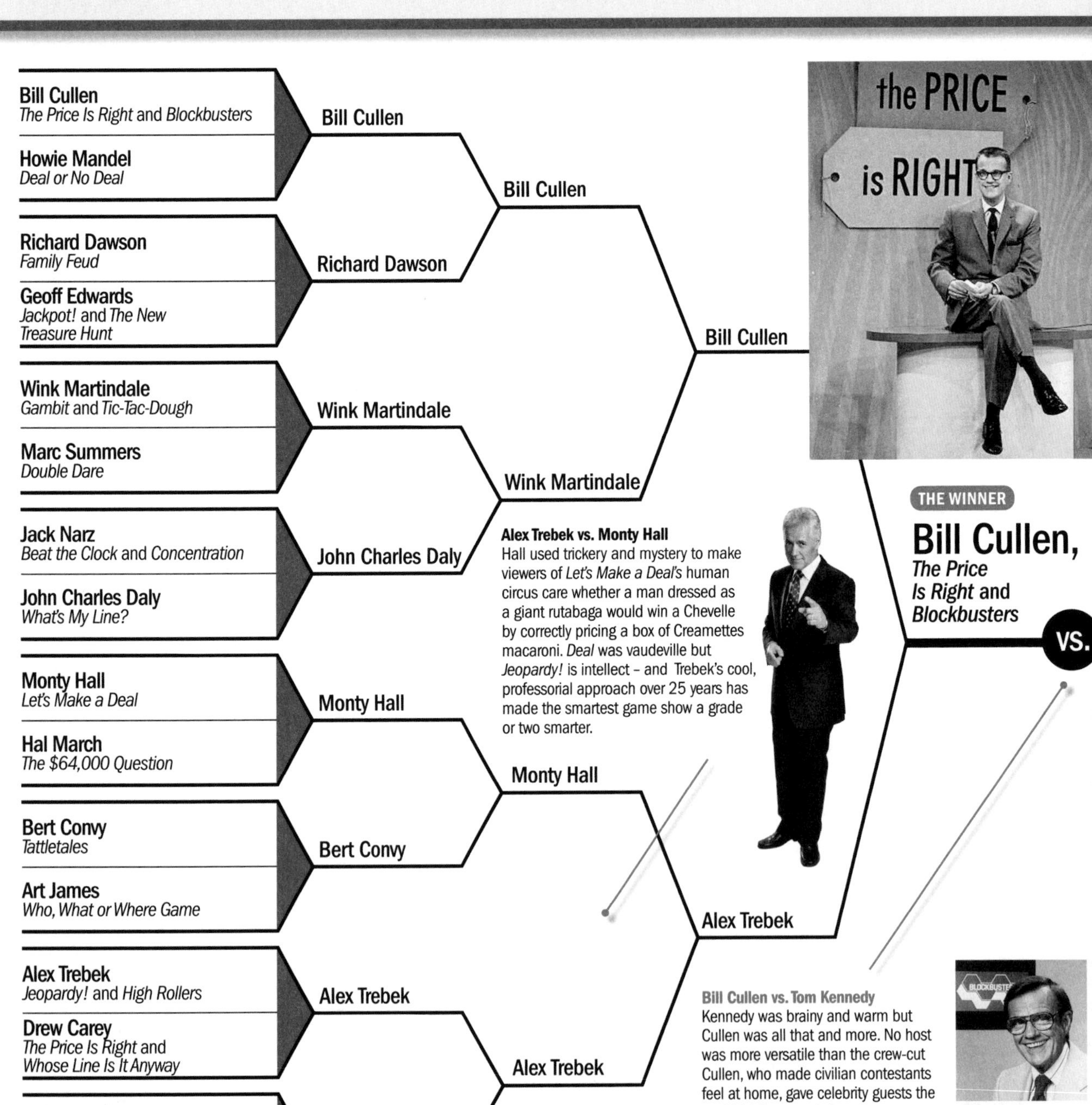

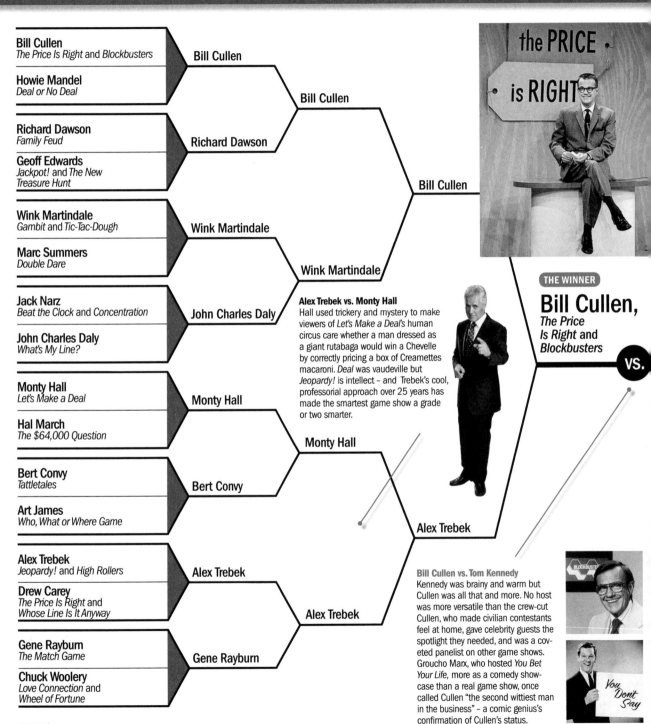

Bill Cullen
The Price Is Right and Blockbusters
Howie Mandel
Deal or No Deal
Richard Dawson
Family Feud
Geoff Edwards
Jackpot! and The New Treasure Hunt
Wink Martindale
Gambit and Tic-Tac-Dough
Marc Summers
Double Dare
Jack Narz
Beat the Clock and Concentration
John Charles Daly
What's My Line?
Monty Hall
Let's Make a Deal
Hal March
The $64,000 Question
Bert Convy
Tattletales
Art James
Who, What or Where Game
Alex Trebek
Jeopardy! and High Rollers
Drew Carey
The Price Is Right and Whose Line Is It Anyway
Gene Rayburn
The Match Game
Chuck Woolery
Love Connection and Wheel of Fortune
Bill Cullen
Richard Dawson
Wink Martindale
John Charles Daly
Monty Hall
Bert Convy
Alex Trebek
Gene Rayburn
Bill Cullen
Wink Martindale
Monty Hall
Alex Trebek
Bill Cullen
Alex Trebek
the PRICE is RIGHT
THE WINNER
Bill Cullen,
The Price Is Right and Blockbusters
VS.
BLOCKBUSTERS
You Don't Say

Alex Trebek vs. Monty Hall
Hall used trickery and mystery to make viewers of *Let's Make a Deal's* human circus care whether a man dressed as a giant rutabaga would win a Chevelle by correctly pricing a box of Creamettes macaroni. *Deal* was vaudeville but *Jeopardy!* is intellect – and Trebek's cool, professorial approach over 25 years has made the smartest game show a grade or two smarter.

Bill Cullen vs. Tom Kennedy
Kennedy was brainy and warm but Cullen was all that and more. No host was more versatile than the crew-cut Cullen, who made civilian contestants feel at home, gave celebrity guests the spotlight they needed, and was a coveted panelist on other game shows. Groucho Marx, who hosted *You Bet Your Life,* more as a comedy showcase than a real game show, once called Cullen "the second wittiest man in the business" – a comic genius's confirmation of Cullen's status.

FOR NEARLY SIXTY YEARS Americans have come on down, spun the wheel, beat the clock, named that tune, and become queen for a day, nearly always guided by suave, attractive purveyors of wealth, fantasy, and good luck. To contestants and viewers, the best game-show hosts are entertainers who inform and somehow make us feel they're our friend. They keep us returning to solve that rebus on *Concentration*, to guess what Monty Hall has in his jacket pocket, and to give the answer in the form of a question.

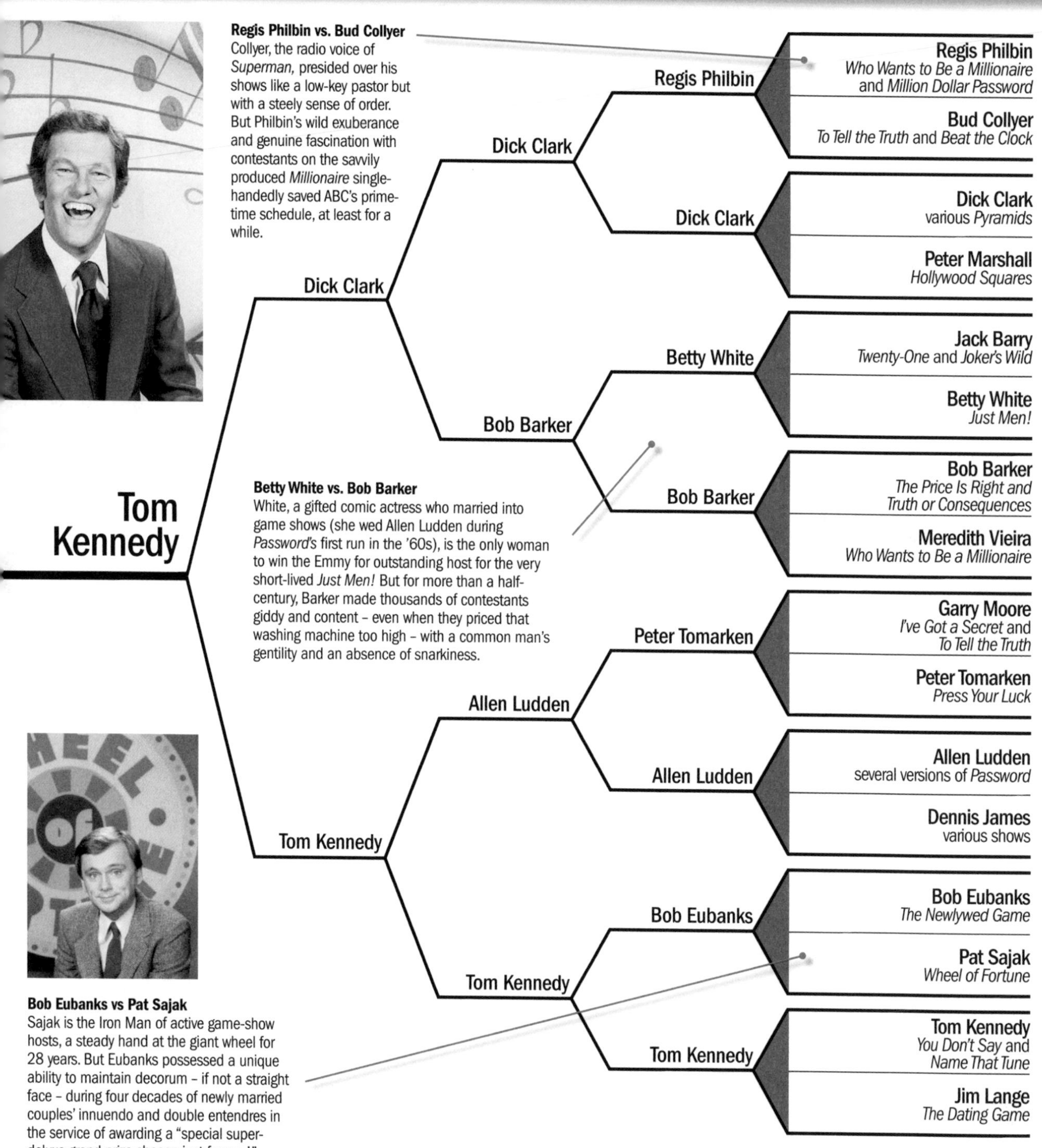

Regis Philbin
Who Wants to Be a Millionaire and Million Dollar Password
Bud Collyer
To Tell the Truth and Beat the Clock
Dick Clark
various Pyramids
Peter Marshall
Hollywood Squares
Jack Barry
Twenty-One and Joker's Wild
Betty White
Just Men!
Bob Barker
The Price Is Right and Truth or Consequences
Meredith Vieira
Who Wants to Be a Millionaire
Garry Moore
I've Got a Secret and To Tell the Truth
Peter Tomarken
Press Your Luck
Allen Ludden
several versions of Password
Dennis James
various shows
Bob Eubanks
The Newlywed Game
Pat Sajak
Wheel of Fortune
Tom Kennedy
You Don't Say and Name That Tune
Jim Lange
The Dating Game
Regis Philbin
Dick Clark
Betty White
Bob Barker
Peter Tomarken
Allen Ludden
Bob Eubanks
Tom Kennedy
Dick Clark
Bob Barker
Allen Ludden
Tom Kennedy
Dick Clark
Tom Kennedy
Tom Kennedy

Regis Philbin vs. Bud Collyer
Collyer, the radio voice of *Superman,* presided over his shows like a low-key pastor but with a steely sense of order. But Philbin's wild exuberance and genuine fascination with contestants on the savvily produced *Millionaire* single-handedly saved ABC's prime-time schedule, at least for a while.

Betty White vs. Bob Barker
White, a gifted comic actress who married into game shows (she wed Allen Ludden during *Password's* first run in the '60s), is the only woman to win the Emmy for outstanding host for the very short-lived *Just Men!* But for more than a half-century, Barker made thousands of contestants giddy and content – even when they priced that washing machine too high – with a common man's gentility and an absence of snarkiness.

Bob Eubanks vs Pat Sajak
Sajak is the Iron Man of active game-show hosts, a steady hand at the giant wheel for 28 years. But Eubanks possessed a unique ability to maintain decorum – if not a straight face – during four decades of newly married couples' innuendo and double entendres in the service of awarding a "special super-deluxe grand prize chosen just for you!"

Grateful Dead Songs

By John Steinbreder

John Steinbreder, who writes for *Golf Digest* and *Forbes Life*, has more than fifty Dead shows under his belt, the last in 1992. His daughter often borrows from his collection of *Dick's Picks*, and does not necessarily agree with his winner here.

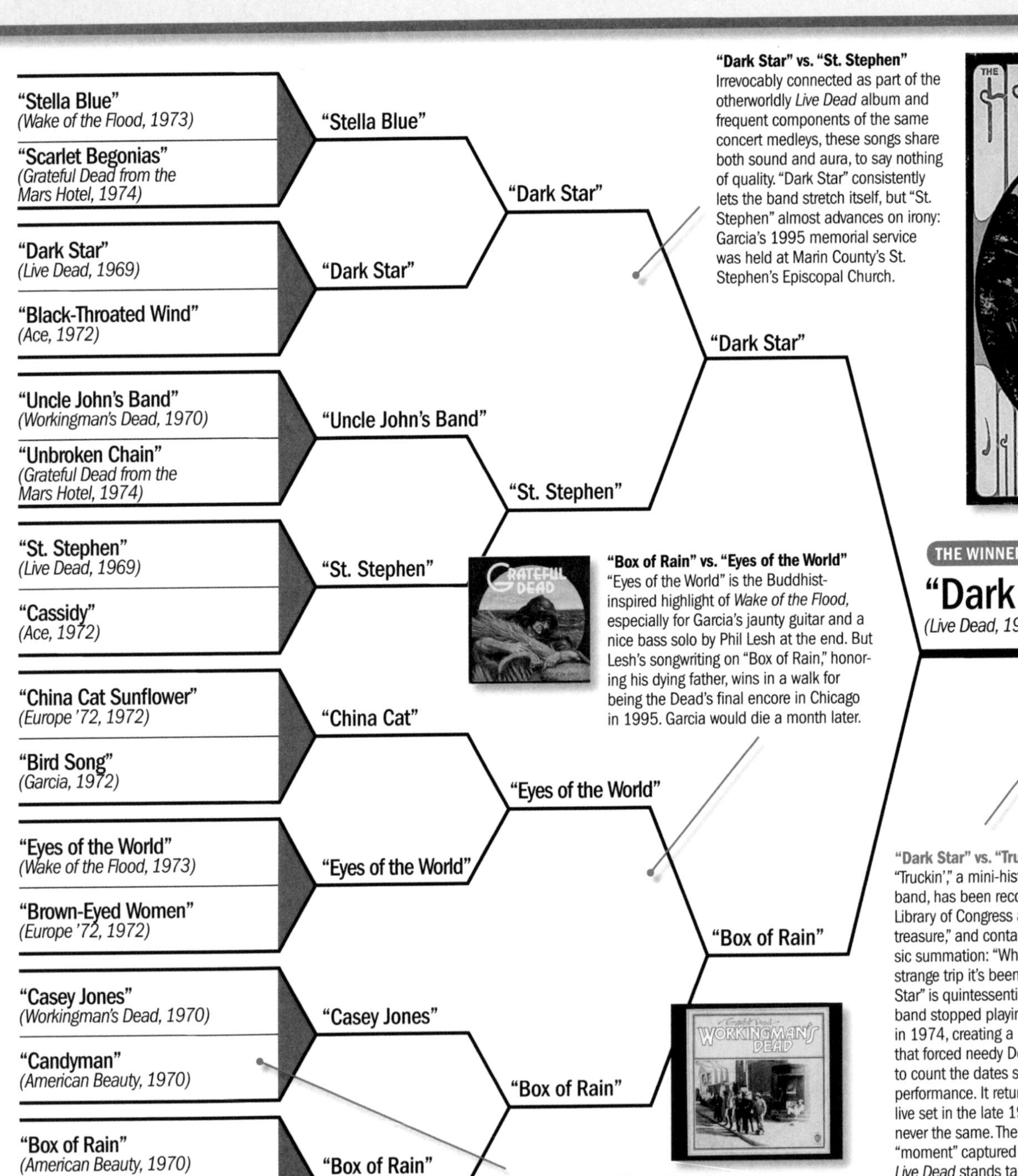

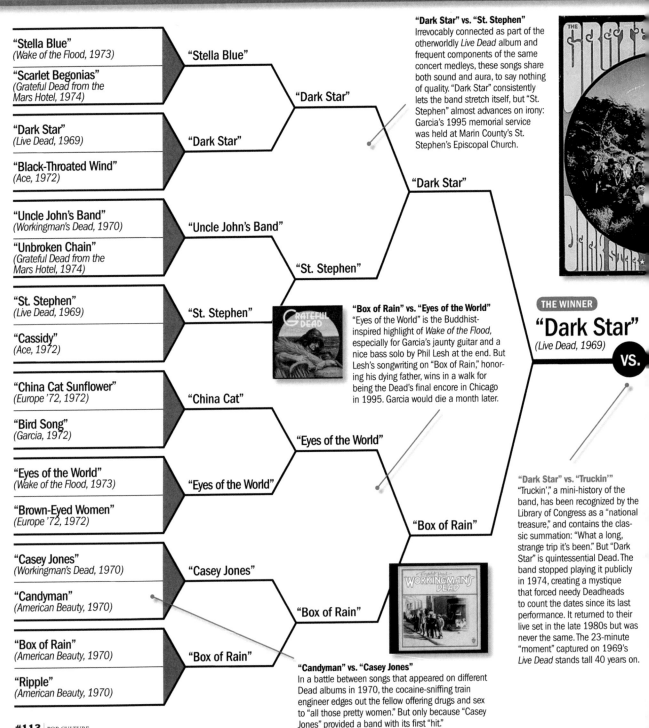

"Stella Blue" (Wake of the Flood, 1973)
"Scarlet Begonias" (Grateful Dead from the Mars Hotel, 1974)
"Dark Star" (Live Dead, 1969)
"Black-Throated Wind" (Ace, 1972)
"Uncle John's Band" (Workingman's Dead, 1970)
"Unbroken Chain" (Grateful Dead from the Mars Hotel, 1974)
"St. Stephen" (Live Dead, 1969)
"Cassidy" (Ace, 1972)
"China Cat Sunflower" (Europe '72, 1972)
"Bird Song" (Garcia, 1972)
"Eyes of the World" (Wake of the Flood, 1973)
"Brown-Eyed Women" (Europe '72, 1972)
"Casey Jones" (Workingman's Dead, 1970)
"Candyman" (American Beauty, 1970)
"Box of Rain" (American Beauty, 1970)
"Ripple" (American Beauty, 1970)
"Stella Blue"
"Dark Star"
"Uncle John's Band"
"St. Stephen"
"China Cat"
"Eyes of the World"
"Casey Jones"
"Box of Rain"
"Dark Star"
"St. Stephen"
"Eyes of the World"
"Box of Rain"
"Dark Star"
"Box of Rain"
THE WINNER
"Dark Star"
(Live Dead, 1969)
VS.

"Dark Star" vs. "St. Stephen"
Irrevocably connected as part of the otherworldly *Live Dead* album and frequent components of the same concert medleys, these songs share both sound and aura, to say nothing of quality. "Dark Star" consistently lets the band stretch itself, but "St. Stephen" almost advances on irony: Garcia's 1995 memorial service was held at Marin County's St. Stephen's Episcopal Church.

"Box of Rain" vs. "Eyes of the World"
"Eyes of the World" is the Buddhist-inspired highlight of *Wake of the Flood*, especially for Garcia's jaunty guitar and a nice bass solo by Phil Lesh at the end. But Lesh's songwriting on "Box of Rain," honoring his dying father, wins in a walk for being the Dead's final encore in Chicago in 1995. Garcia would die a month later.

"Dark Star" vs. "Truckin'"
"Truckin'," a mini-history of the band, has been recognized by the Library of Congress as a "national treasure," and contains the classic summation: "What a long, strange trip it's been." But "Dark Star" is quintessential Dead. The band stopped playing it publicly in 1974, creating a mystique that forced needy Deadheads to count the dates since its last performance. It returned to their live set in the late 1980s but was never the same. The 23-minute "moment" captured on 1969's *Live Dead* stands tall 40 years on.

"Candyman" vs. "Casey Jones"
In a battle between songs that appeared on different Dead albums in 1970, the cocaine-sniffing train engineer edges out the fellow offering drugs and sex to "all those pretty women." But only because "Casey Jones" provided a band with its first "hit."

THE GRATEFUL DEAD ARE CELEBRATED for their improvisatory live performances, often six hours long, and their staying power (returned by their devoted fan base of Deadheads), but not nearly enough for their songwriting. Jerry Garcia, Bob Weir, and Phil Lesh composed most of the music, while Robert Hunter and John Perry Barlow handled the words. The tunes vary in style, mood, and inspiration – and the winner, it can safely be said, could only have been written by the Dead.

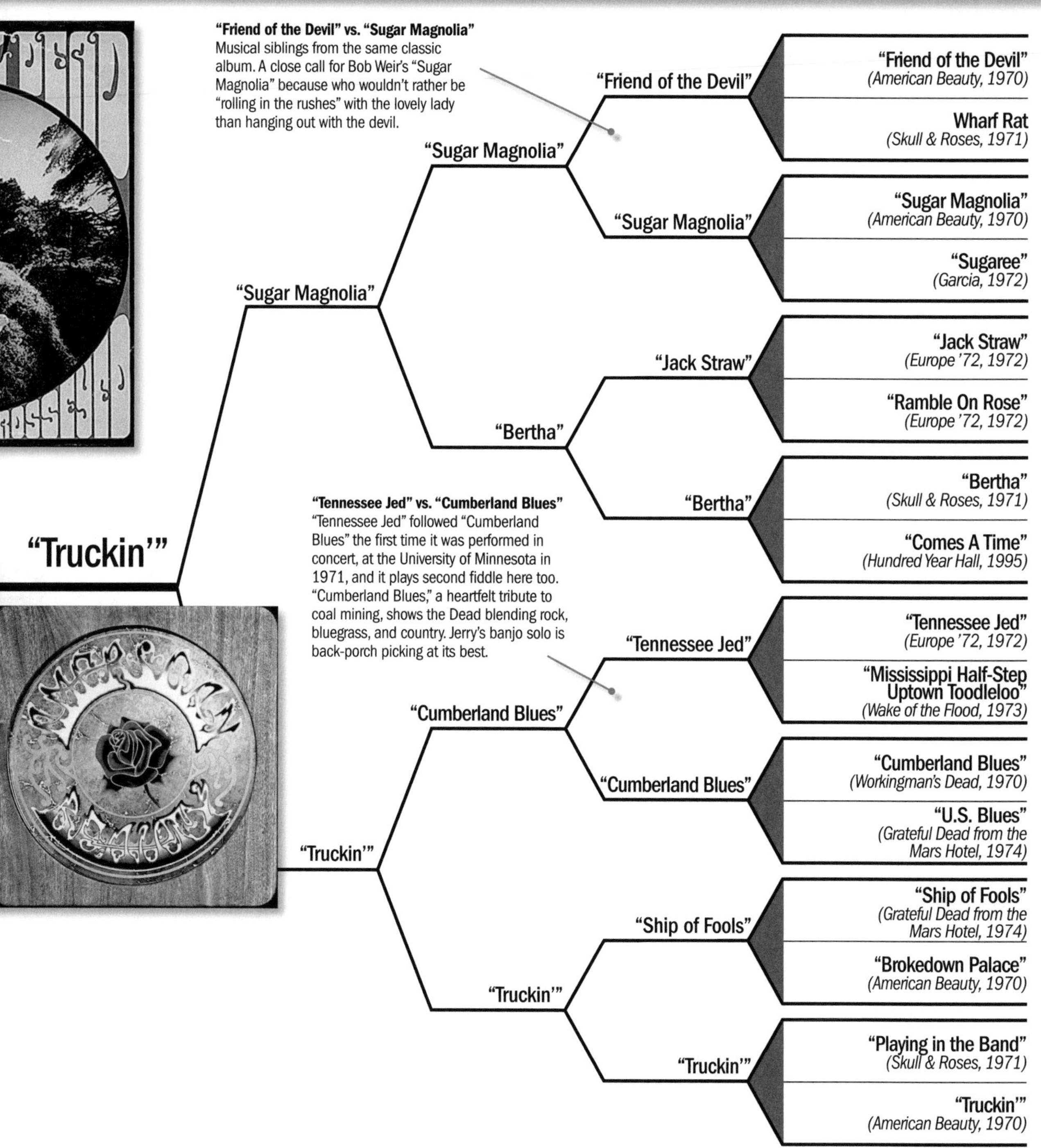

"Friend of the Devil" vs. "Sugar Magnolia"
Musical siblings from the same classic album. A close call for Bob Weir's "Sugar Magnolia" because who wouldn't rather be "rolling in the rushes" with the lovely lady than hanging out with the devil.
"Friend of the Devil" (American Beauty, 1970)
Wharf Rat (Skull & Roses, 1971)
"Sugar Magnolia" (American Beauty, 1970)
"Sugaree" (Garcia, 1972)
"Jack Straw" (Europe '72, 1972)
"Ramble On Rose" (Europe '72, 1972)
"Bertha" (Skull & Roses, 1971)
"Comes A Time" (Hundred Year Hall, 1995)
"Tennessee Jed" (Europe '72, 1972)
"Mississippi Half-Step Uptown Toodleloo" (Wake of the Flood, 1973)
"Cumberland Blues" (Workingman's Dead, 1970)
"U.S. Blues" (Grateful Dead from the Mars Hotel, 1974)
"Ship of Fools" (Grateful Dead from the Mars Hotel, 1974)
"Brokedown Palace" (American Beauty, 1970)
"Playing in the Band" (Skull & Roses, 1971)
"Truckin'" (American Beauty, 1970)
"Friend of the Devil"
"Sugar Magnolia"
"Jack Straw"
"Bertha"
"Tennessee Jed"
"Cumberland Blues"
"Ship of Fools"
"Truckin'"
"Sugar Magnolia"
"Bertha"
"Cumberland Blues"
"Truckin'"
"Sugar Magnolia"
"Truckin'"
"Truckin'"
"Tennessee Jed" vs. "Cumberland Blues"
"Tennessee Jed" followed "Cumberland Blues" the first time it was performed in concert, at the University of Minnesota in 1971, and it plays second fiddle here too. "Cumberland Blues," a heartfelt tribute to coal mining, shows the Dead blending rock, bluegrass, and country. Jerry's banjo solo is back-porch picking at its best.

Romance Novels

By Isabel Swift

Isabel Swift, a former editor at Harlequin, has been a spokesperson for the romance genre and has developed and launched romance lines for Pocket Books and Silhouette Books.

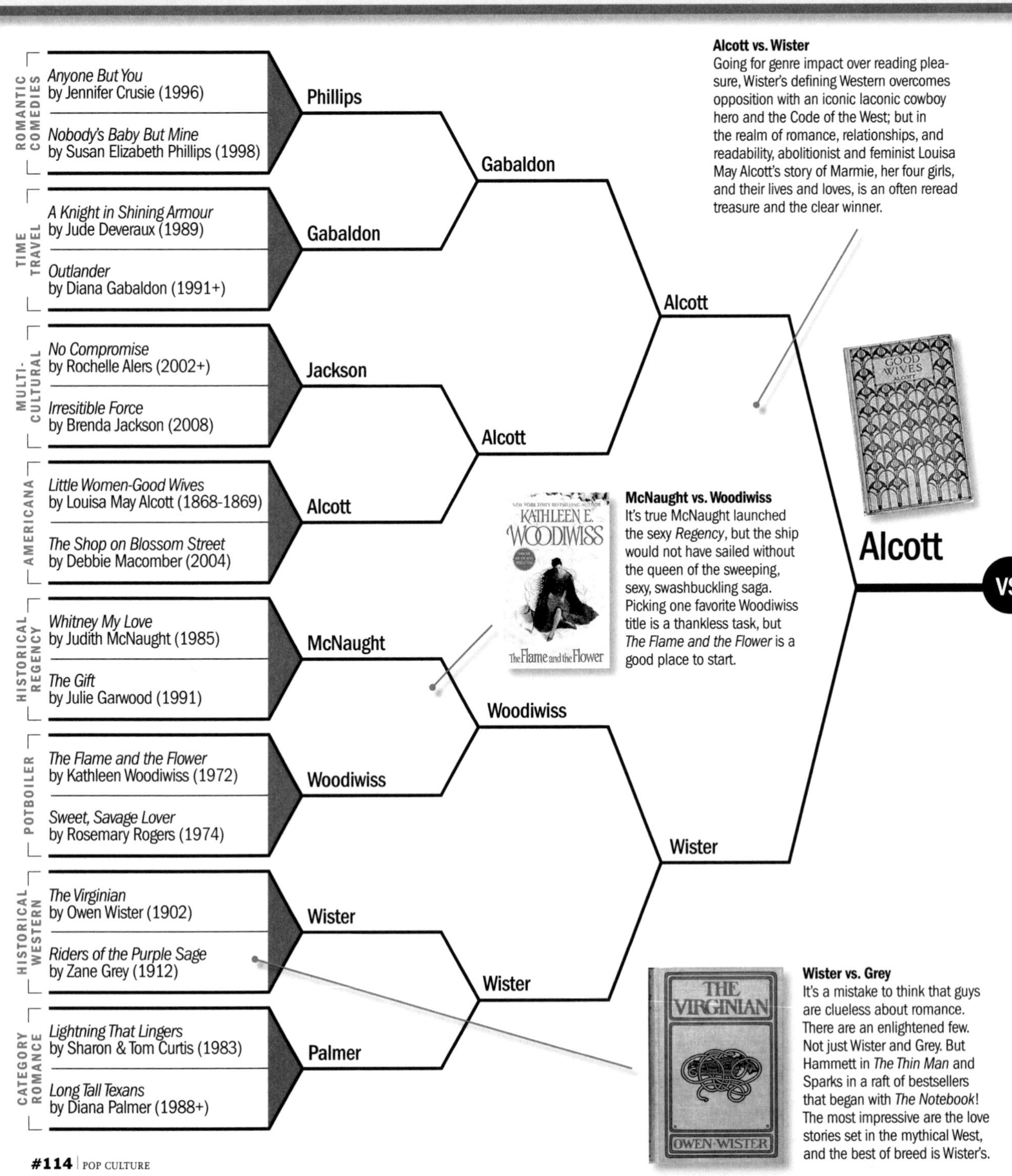

ROMANTIC COMEDIES
Anyone But You by Jennifer Crusie (1996)
Nobody's Baby But Mine by Susan Elizabeth Phillips (1998)
TIME TRAVEL
A Knight in Shining Armour by Jude Deveraux (1989)
Outlander by Diana Gabaldon (1991+)
MULTI-CULTURAL
No Compromise by Rochelle Alers (2002+)
Irresitible Force by Brenda Jackson (2008)
AMERICANA
Little Women-Good Wives by Louisa May Alcott (1868-1869)
The Shop on Blossom Street by Debbie Macomber (2004)
HISTORICAL REGENCY
Whitney My Love by Judith McNaught (1985)
The Gift by Julie Garwood (1991)
POTBOILER
The Flame and the Flower by Kathleen Woodiwiss (1972)
Sweet, Savage Lover by Rosemary Rogers (1974)
HISTORICAL WESTERN
The Virginian by Owen Wister (1902)
Riders of the Purple Sage by Zane Grey (1912)
CATEGORY ROMANCE
Lightning That Lingers by Sharon & Tom Curtis (1983)
Long Tall Texans by Diana Palmer (1988+)
Phillips
Gabaldon
Jackson
Alcott
McNaught
Woodiwiss
Wister
Palmer
Gabaldon
Alcott
Woodiwiss
Wister
Alcott
Wister
Alcott
VS.
GOOD WIVES
ALCOTT
KATHLEEN E. WOODIWISS
The Flame and the Flower
THE VIRGINIAN
OWEN WISTER

Alcott vs. Wister
Going for genre impact over reading pleasure, Wister's defining Western overcomes opposition with an iconic laconic cowboy hero and the Code of the West; but in the realm of romance, relationships, and readability, abolitionist and feminist Louisa May Alcott's story of Marmie, her four girls, and their lives and loves, is an often reread treasure and the clear winner.

McNaught vs. Woodiwiss
It's true McNaught launched the sexy *Regency*, but the ship would not have sailed without the queen of the sweeping, sexy, swashbuckling saga. Picking one favorite Woodiwiss title is a thankless task, but *The Flame and the Flower* is a good place to start.

Wister vs. Grey
It's a mistake to think that guys are clueless about romance. There are an enlightened few. Not just Wister and Grey. But Hammett in *The Thin Man* and Sparks in a raft of bestsellers that began with *The Notebook*! The most impressive are the love stories set in the mythical West, and the best of breed is Wister's.

THE BOOKS HERE MAY STRETCH the Romance Writers of America's definition of romance fiction: "A central love story and an emotionally satisfying and optimistic ending." Some have vampires in the mix, others are sweeping historicals, still others are set in the Wild West. But they all deliver satisfaction, touching readers' hearts, offering an uplifting reading experience, and reinforcing the belief in the transformative power of love.

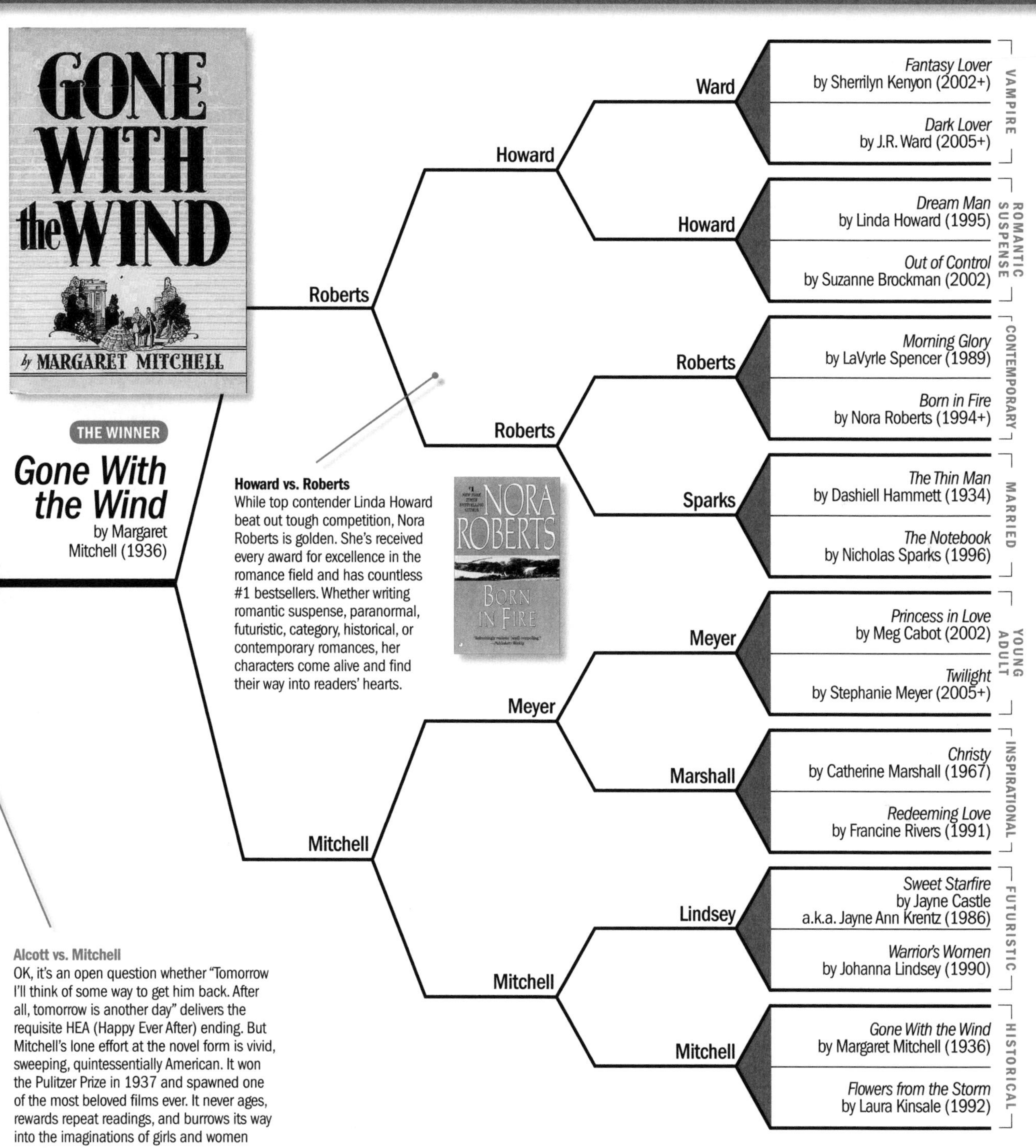
GONE WITH the WIND
by MARGARET MITCHELL
THE WINNER
Gone With the Wind
by Margaret Mitchell (1936)
Roberts
Howard
Ward
Howard
Roberts
Roberts
Sparks
Mitchell
Meyer
Meyer
Marshall
Mitchell
Lindsey
Mitchell
Fantasy Lover
by Sherrilyn Kenyon (2002+)
Dark Lover
by J.R. Ward (2005+)
VAMPIRE
Dream Man
by Linda Howard (1995)
Out of Control
by Suzanne Brockman (2002)
ROMANTIC SUSPENSE
Morning Glory
by LaVyrle Spencer (1989)
Born in Fire
by Nora Roberts (1994+)
CONTEMPORARY
The Thin Man
by Dashiell Hammett (1934)
The Notebook
by Nicholas Sparks (1996)
MARRIED
Princess in Love
by Meg Cabot (2002)
Twilight
by Stephanie Meyer (2005+)
YOUNG ADULT
Christy
by Catherine Marshall (1967)
Redeeming Love
by Francine Rivers (1991)
INSPIRATIONAL
Sweet Starfire
by Jayne Castle
a.k.a. Jayne Ann Krentz (1986)
Warrior's Women
by Johanna Lindsey (1990)
FUTURISTIC
Gone With the Wind
by Margaret Mitchell (1936)
Flowers from the Storm
by Laura Kinsale (1992)
HISTORICAL
NORA ROBERTS
BORN IN FIRE

Howard vs. Roberts
While top contender Linda Howard beat out tough competition, Nora Roberts is golden. She's received every award for excellence in the romance field and has countless #1 bestsellers. Whether writing romantic suspense, paranormal, futuristic, category, historical, or contemporary romances, her characters come alive and find their way into readers' hearts.

Alcott vs. Mitchell
OK, it's an open question whether "Tomorrow I'll think of some way to get him back. After all, tomorrow is another day" delivers the requisite HEA (Happy Ever After) ending. But Mitchell's lone effort at the novel form is vivid, sweeping, quintessentially American. It won the Pulitzer Prize in 1937 and spawned one of the most beloved films ever. It never ages, rewards repeat readings, and burrows its way into the imaginations of girls and women – and guys too.

TV Catchphrases

By Robert J. Thompson

Robert Thompson is director of the Bleier Center for Television and Popular Culture at Syracuse University, where he is also a Trustee professor. He has written or edited six books about American television.

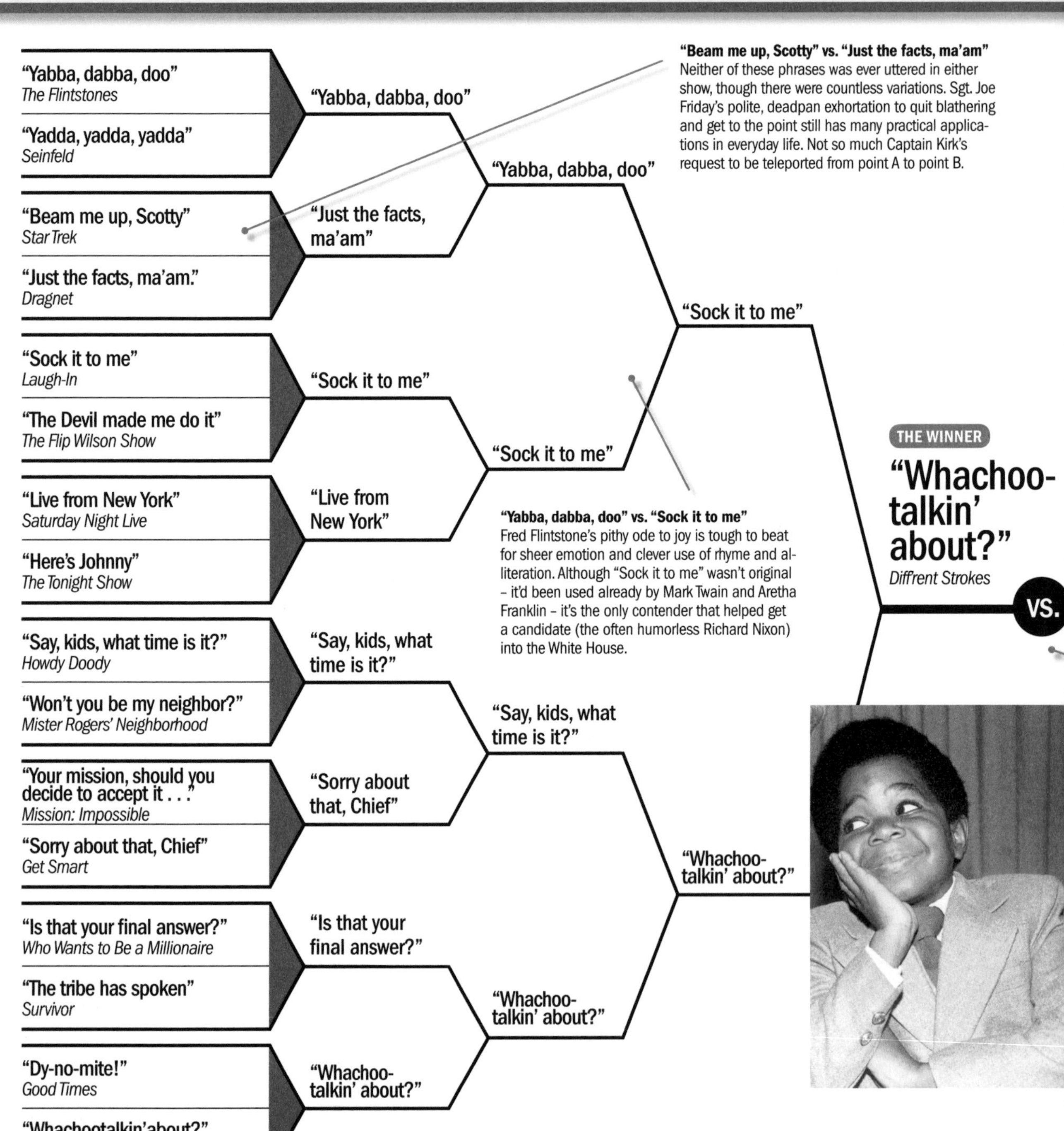
"Yabba, dabba, doo"
The Flintstones
"Yadda, yadda, yadda"
Seinfeld
"Beam me up, Scotty"
Star Trek
"Just the facts, ma'am."
Dragnet
"Sock it to me"
Laugh-In
"The Devil made me do it"
The Flip Wilson Show
"Live from New York"
Saturday Night Live
"Here's Johnny"
The Tonight Show
"Say, kids, what time is it?"
Howdy Doody
"Won't you be my neighbor?"
Mister Rogers' Neighborhood
"Your mission, should you decide to accept it . . ."
Mission: Impossible
"Sorry about that, Chief"
Get Smart
"Is that your final answer?"
Who Wants to Be a Millionaire
"The tribe has spoken"
Survivor
"Dy-no-mite!"
Good Times
"Whachootalkin'about?"
Diffrent Strokes
"Yabba, dabba, doo"
"Just the facts, ma'am"
"Sock it to me"
"Live from New York"
"Say, kids, what time is it?"
"Sorry about that, Chief"
"Is that your final answer?"
"Whachoo-talkin' about?"
"Yabba, dabba, doo"
"Sock it to me"
"Say, kids, what time is it?"
"Whachoo-talkin' about?"
"Sock it to me"
"Whachoo-talkin' about?"
THE WINNER
"Whachoo-talkin' about?"
Diffrent Strokes
VS.

"Beam me up, Scotty" vs. "Just the facts, ma'am"
Neither of these phrases was ever uttered in either show, though there were countless variations. Sgt. Joe Friday's polite, deadpan exhortation to quit blathering and get to the point still has many practical applications in everyday life. Not so much Captain Kirk's request to be teleported from point A to point B.

"Yabba, dabba, doo" vs. "Sock it to me"
Fred Flintstone's pithy ode to joy is tough to beat for sheer emotion and clever use of rhyme and alliteration. Although "Sock it to me" wasn't original – it'd been used already by Mark Twain and Aretha Franklin – it's the only contender that helped get a candidate (the often humorless Richard Nixon) into the White House.

THE HALCYON DAYS FOR TELEVISION CATCHPHRASES started in the mid-1950s and ended in the late 1970s. Weekly repetition on sitcoms, dramas, game shows, news programs, and cartoons seared these phrases into the American vernacular and they are still as easily accessed from our memory banks as the names of our closest relatives. But by the mid-1980s, the form came to be associated with high cheesiness – something to be mocked, albeit with affection. With a few notable exceptions (like *Seinfeld,* a mother lode of single-episode, zeitgeist-defining phrases), the catchphrase, like the jingle, was in bad decline.

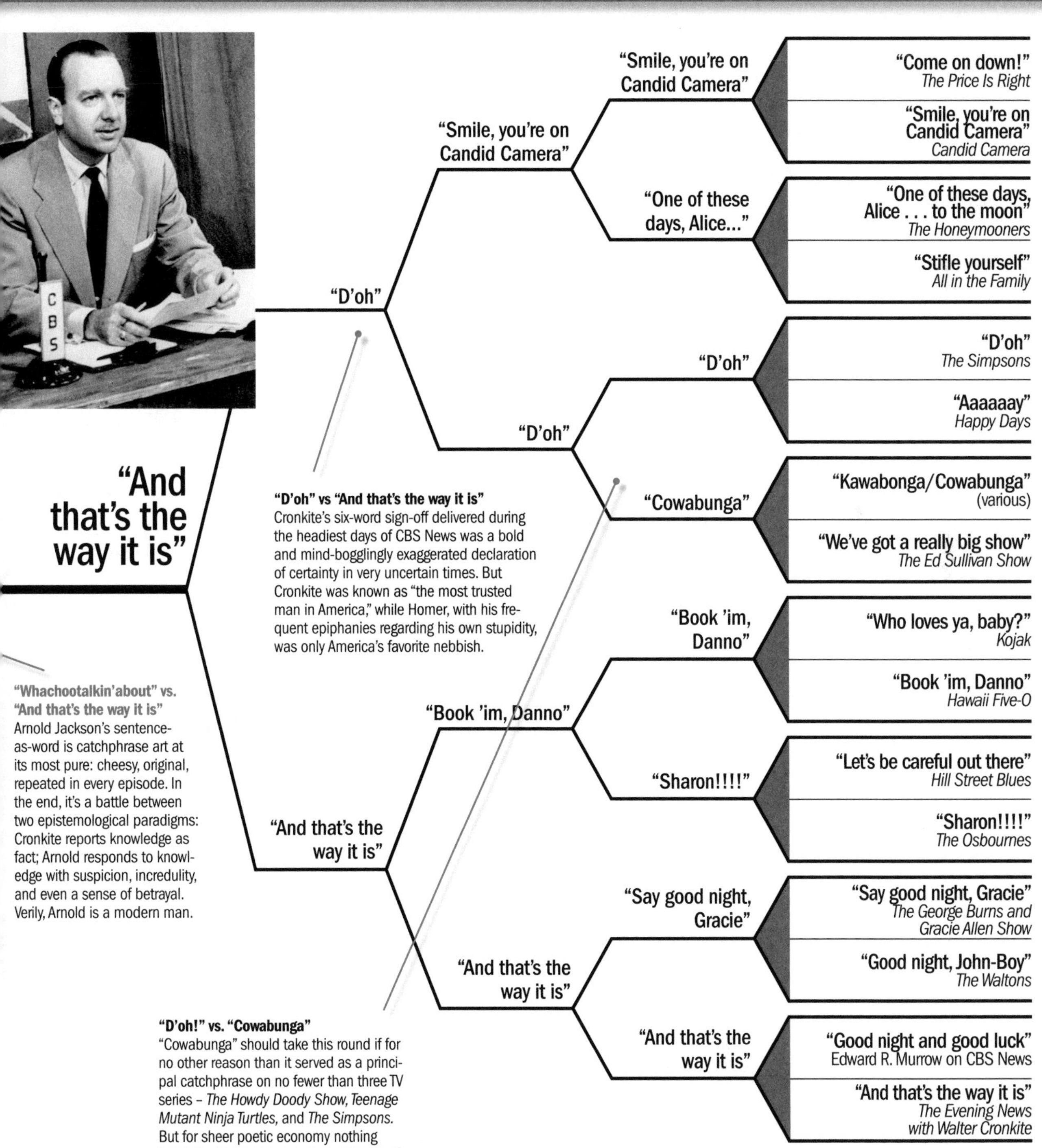

C B S
"And that's the way it is"
"D'oh"
"Smile, you're on Candid Camera"
"Smile, you're on Candid Camera"
"Come on down!" *The Price Is Right*
"Smile, you're on Candid Camera" *Candid Camera*
"One of these days, Alice..."
"One of these days, Alice . . . to the moon" *The Honeymooners*
"Stifle yourself" *All in the Family*
"D'oh"
"D'oh"
"D'oh" *The Simpsons*
"Aaaaaay" *Happy Days*
"Cowabunga"
"Kawabonga/Cowabunga" (various)
"We've got a really big show" *The Ed Sullivan Show*
"And that's the way it is"
"Book 'im, Danno"
"Book 'im, Danno"
"Who loves ya, baby?" *Kojak*
"Book 'im, Danno" *Hawaii Five-O*
"Sharon!!!!"
"Let's be careful out there" *Hill Street Blues*
"Sharon!!!!" *The Osbournes*
"And that's the way it is"
"Say good night, Gracie"
"Say good night, Gracie" *The George Burns and Gracie Allen Show*
"Good night, John-Boy" *The Waltons*
"And that's the way it is"
"Good night and good luck" Edward R. Murrow on CBS News
"And that's the way it is" *The Evening News with Walter Cronkite*

"D'oh" vs "And that's the way it is"
Cronkite's six-word sign-off delivered during the headiest days of CBS News was a bold and mind-bogglingly exaggerated declaration of certainty in very uncertain times. But Cronkite was known as "the most trusted man in America," while Homer, with his frequent epiphanies regarding his own stupidity, was only America's favorite nebbish.

"Whachootalkin'about" vs. "And that's the way it is"
Arnold Jackson's sentence-as-word is catchphrase art at its most pure: cheesy, original, repeated in every episode. In the end, it's a battle between two epistemological paradigms: Cronkite reports knowledge as fact; Arnold responds to knowledge with suspicion, incredulity, and even a sense of betrayal. Verily, Arnold is a modern man.

"D'oh!" vs. "Cowabunga"
"Cowabunga" should take this round if for no other reason than it served as a principal catchphrase on no fewer than three TV series – *The Howdy Doody Show, Teenage Mutant Ninja Turtles,* and *The Simpsons.* But for sheer poetic economy nothing beats the three-letters-and-apostrophe of Homer Simpson's emphatic "D'oh."

Jazz Solos

By Nick Trautwein

Nick Trautwein is an editor and saxophonist in New York City. His last gig was Friday night, at a dive on Avenue B. The piano player won.

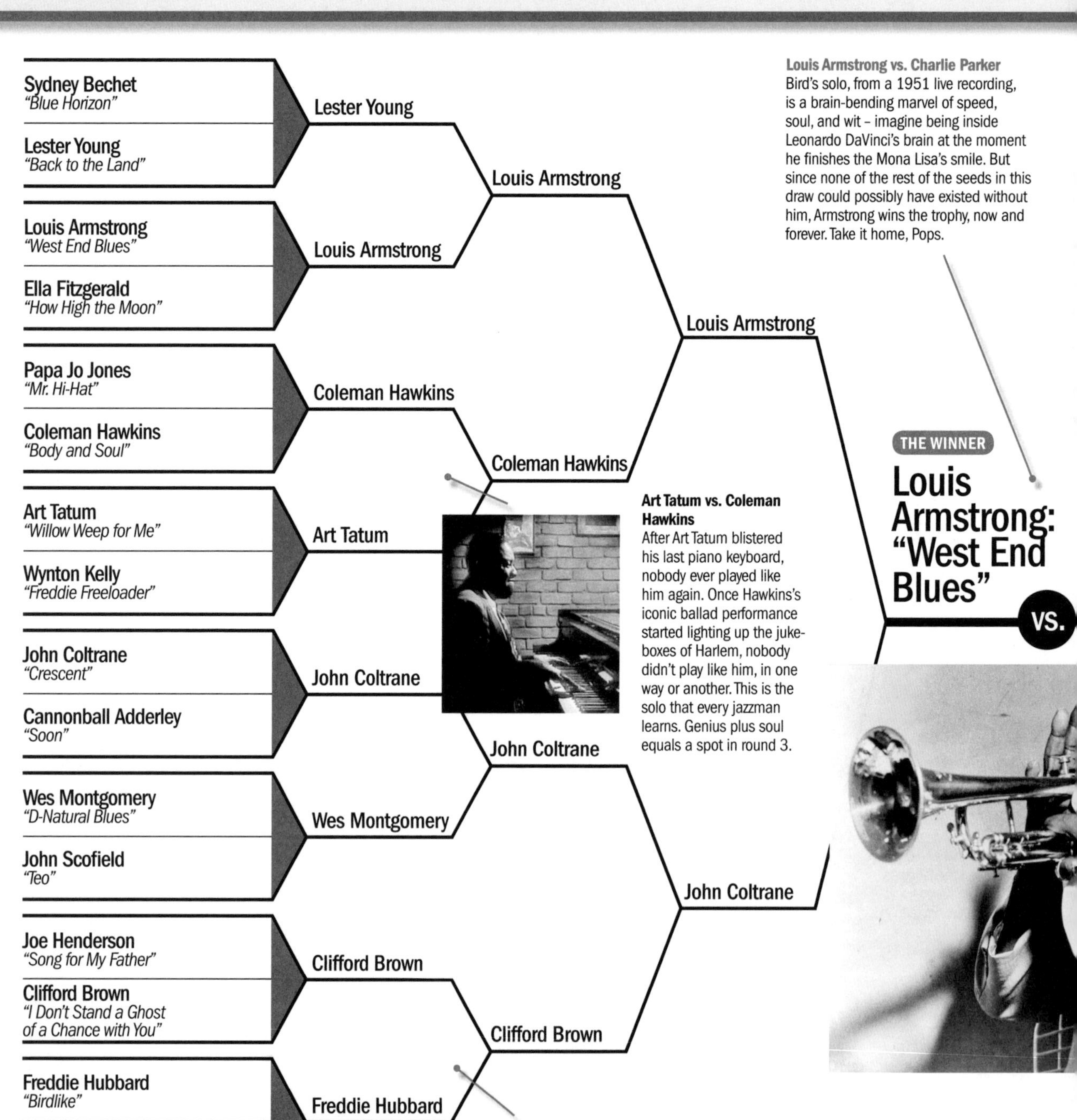
Sydney Bechet
"Blue Horizon"
Lester Young
"Back to the Land"
Louis Armstrong
"West End Blues"
Ella Fitzgerald
"How High the Moon"
Papa Jo Jones
"Mr. Hi-Hat"
Coleman Hawkins
"Body and Soul"
Art Tatum
"Willow Weep for Me"
Wynton Kelly
"Freddie Freeloader"
John Coltrane
"Crescent"
Cannonball Adderley
"Soon"
Wes Montgomery
"D-Natural Blues"
John Scofield
"Teo"
Joe Henderson
"Song for My Father"
Clifford Brown
"I Don't Stand a Ghost of a Chance with You"
Freddie Hubbard
"Birdlike"
Miles Davis
"So What"
Lester Young
Louis Armstrong
Coleman Hawkins
Art Tatum
John Coltrane
Wes Montgomery
Clifford Brown
Freddie Hubbard
Louis Armstrong
Coleman Hawkins
John Coltrane
Clifford Brown
Louis Armstrong
John Coltrane
THE WINNER
Louis Armstrong: "West End Blues"
VS.

Louis Armstrong vs. Charlie Parker
Bird's solo, from a 1951 live recording, is a brain-bending marvel of speed, soul, and wit – imagine being inside Leonardo DaVinci's brain at the moment he finishes the Mona Lisa's smile. But since none of the rest of the seeds in this draw could possibly have existed without him, Armstrong wins the trophy, now and forever. Take it home, Pops.

Art Tatum vs. Coleman Hawkins
After Art Tatum blistered his last piano keyboard, nobody ever played like him again. Once Hawkins's iconic ballad performance started lighting up the juke-boxes of Harlem, nobody didn't play like him, in one way or another. This is the solo that every jazzman learns. Genius plus soul equals a spot in round 3.

Clifford Brown vs. Freddie Hubbard
Two precociously fluent trumpeters go head to head, Freddie with 19 blues choruses that some trumpet player somewhere is guaranteed to be ripping off at this very moment, Clifford with a swoon-inducing ballad that goes from whispering in your ear to shouting from the rooftops. Sweet ain't easy on the trumpet; Clifford wins.

JAZZ, CHARLES MINGUS SAID, IS AMERICA'S ONLY INDIGENOUS ART FORM – that and the atomic bomb. While it's hard to imagine Robret Oppenheimer lighting up the crowd on a Saturday night, jazz musicians have always been happy to turn the bandstand into a zone of armed conflict. More than any other, jazz is an art form you can win. Points are given for spontaneous brilliance, individualism, virtuosity, and sex appeal. Winners stick around to play the late set.

Sonny Rollins vs. Sonny Stitt
This one's an actual recorded matchup, from the Dizzy Gillespie record Sonny Side Up, on which the two Sonnies take turns doing to the chords of "I've Got Rhythm" (and to each other) something like what Mike Tyson did to Peter McNeeley. Rough, inventive Rollins takes down silky-smooth Stitt.
McCoy Tyner
"Passion Dance"
Charlie Parker
"Lester Leaps In"
Sonny Stitt
"The Eternal Triangle"
Sonny Rollins
"The Eternal Triangle"
Illinois Jacquet
"Flying Home"
Paul Gonsalves
"Diminuendo and Crescendo in Blue"
Thelonious Monk
"Functional"
Oscar Peterson
"52nd Street Theme"
Kenny Garrett
"Human Nature"
Michael Brecker
"Syzygy"
Paul Chambers
"Straight, No Chaser"
Ornette Coleman
"Peace"
Keith Jarrett
"Too Young to Go Steady"
JJ Johnson
"Crazy Rhythm"
Bud Powell
"So Sorry Please"
Herbie Hancock
"All of You"
Charlie Parker
Sonny Rollins
Illinois Jacquet
Thelonious Monk
Kenny Garrett
Ornette Coleman
Keith Jarrett
Herbie Hancock
Charlie Parker
Illinois Jacquet
Ornette Coleman
Herbie Hancock
Charlie Parker
Herbie Hancock
Charlie Parker
Illinois Jacquet vs. Paul Gonsalves
According to legend, Gonsalves's side-splitting 27-chorus solo was thrust upon him by bandleader Duke Ellington as punishment for showing up to the gig at Newport too drunk to stand up right. Given the advantage of (relative) sobriety, the ferociously entertaining Jacquet moves on.
Ornette Coleman vs. Herbie Hancock
Ornette's free improvisation is a masterwork of melodic beauty (and also probably the best piece of evidence that he actually knows what the hell he's doing). But Herbie live at the Plugged Nickel is like Federer at the U.S. Open – cool, graceful, wickedly smart, and transportingly able to do anything he wants.

Romantic Comedies

By David Denby

David Denby, a film critic and staff writer at *The New Yorker* since 1998, is the author of *Great Books, American Sucker,* and *Snark.*

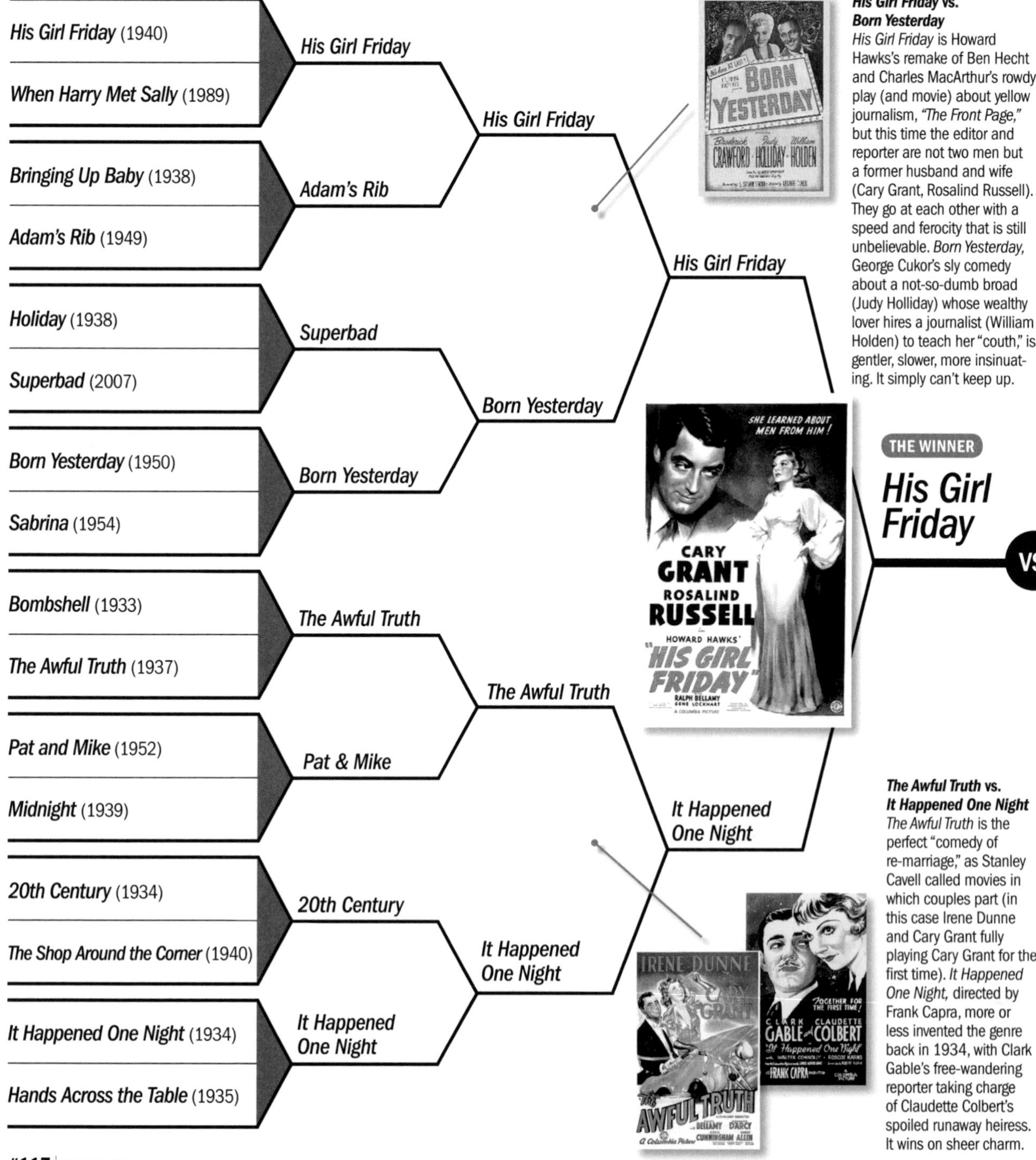

His Girl Friday (1940)
When Harry Met Sally (1989)
Bringing Up Baby (1938)
Adam's Rib (1949)
Holiday (1938)
Superbad (2007)
Born Yesterday (1950)
Sabrina (1954)
Bombshell (1933)
The Awful Truth (1937)
Pat and Mike (1952)
Midnight (1939)
20th Century (1934)
The Shop Around the Corner (1940)
It Happened One Night (1934)
Hands Across the Table (1935)
His Girl Friday
Adam's Rib
Superbad
Born Yesterday
The Awful Truth
Pat & Mike
20th Century
It Happened One Night
His Girl Friday
Born Yesterday
The Awful Truth
It Happened One Night
His Girl Friday
It Happened One Night
BORN YESTERDAY
CRAWFORD · HOLLIDAY · HOLDEN
SHE LEARNED ABOUT MEN FROM HIM!
CARY GRANT
ROSALIND RUSSELL
HOWARD HAWKS'
"HIS GIRL FRIDAY"
RALPH BELLAMY
GENE LOCKHART
A COLUMBIA PICTURE
IRENE DUNNE
CARY GRANT
THE AWFUL TRUTH
BELLAMY
D'ARCY
CUNNINGHAM
ALLEN
A Columbia Picture
TOGETHER FOR THE FIRST TIME!
CLARK GABLE and CLAUDETTE COLBERT
"It Happened One Night"
FRANK CAPRA
COLUMBIA PICTURE
THE WINNER
His Girl Friday
VS.

His Girl Friday* vs. *Born Yesterday

His Girl Friday is Howard Hawks's remake of Ben Hecht and Charles MacArthur's rowdy play (and movie) about yellow journalism, *"The Front Page,"* but this time the editor and reporter are not two men but a former husband and wife (Cary Grant, Rosalind Russell). They go at each other with a speed and ferocity that is still unbelievable. *Born Yesterday,* George Cukor's sly comedy about a not-so-dumb broad (Judy Holliday) whose wealthy lover hires a journalist (William Holden) to teach her "couth," is gentler, slower, more insinuating. It simply can't keep up.

The Awful Truth* vs. *It Happened One Night

The Awful Truth is the perfect "comedy of re-marriage," as Stanley Cavell called movies in which couples part (in this case Irene Dunne and Cary Grant fully playing Cary Grant for the first time). *It Happened One Night,* directed by Frank Capra, more or less invented the genre back in 1934, with Clark Gable's free-wandering reporter taking charge of Claudette Colbert's spoiled runaway heiress. It wins on sheer charm.

A GREAT ROMANTIC COMEDY IS ABOUT EQUALITY – of looks, temperament, or brains. The man and woman meet, quarrel, part, tentatively reunite, fight again, and finally become a couple in a courtship dance conducted with wit, invention, tooth, claw, romantic seduction. Despite all the anger, the conclusion is as fated as the two halves of a drawbridge falling into place. If there's been a drop-off in recent years, it's because loutish young men have been paired up with hard-driving women, and the genre's beautiful balance has been shattered. These movies all have that balance, some more than others.

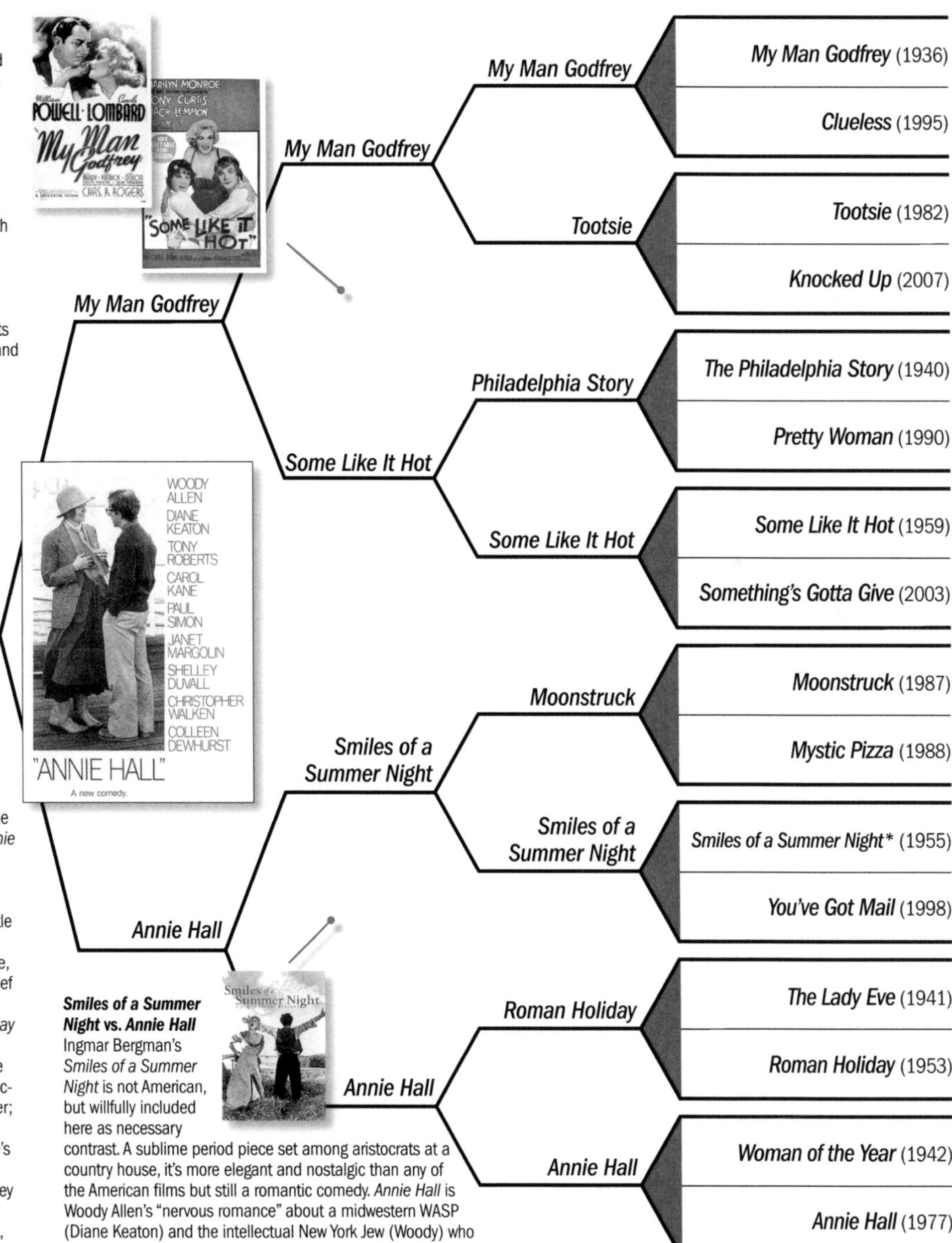

My Man Godfrey (1936)
Clueless (1995)
Tootsie (1982)
Knocked Up (2007)
The Philadelphia Story (1940)
Pretty Woman (1990)
Some Like It Hot (1959)
Something's Gotta Give (2003)
Moonstruck (1987)
Mystic Pizza (1988)
Smiles of a Summer Night* (1955)
You've Got Mail (1998)
The Lady Eve (1941)
Roman Holiday (1953)
Woman of the Year (1942)
Annie Hall (1977)
My Man Godfrey
Tootsie
Philadelphia Story
Some Like It Hot
Moonstruck
Smiles of a Summer Night
Roman Holiday
Annie Hall
My Man Godfrey
Some Like It Hot
Smiles of a Summer Night
Annie Hall
My Man Godfrey
Annie Hall
Annie Hall
William Powell · Carole Lombard
My Man Godfrey
Chas. R. Rogers
Marilyn Monroe
Tony Curtis
Jack Lemmon
"Some Like It Hot"
Woody Allen
Diane Keaton
Tony Roberts
Carol Kane
Paul Simon
Janet Margolin
Shelley Duvall
Christopher Walken
Colleen Dewhurst
"ANNIE HALL"
A new comedy.
Smiles of a Summer Night

My Man Godfrey vs. Some Like It Hot
Carol Lombard's giddy speed as another heiress who hires what she takes to be a bum (William Powell) as an East Side butler brings *My Man Godfrey* to life. *Some Like It Hot* is Billy Wilder's drag comedy in which Tony Curtis, imitating Grant, winds up with Marilyn and Jack Lemmon winds up with the elderly swain Joe E. Brown. It has the best last line ("Nobody's perfect"), but *Godfrey*, with its perfect balance of silliness and Depression-era blues, wins.

His Girl Friday vs. Annie Hall
His Girl Friday is about work – there's a roaring satire of corrupt journalistic technique in the middle of it – and *Annie Hall* is more about taste, which is the way Woody's urbanites send signals to each other. The working battle brings out the equality of editor and writer as a couple, and since equality is my chief criterion for successful romantic comedy, *His Girl Friday* wins. It goes at such a clip that you don't know how the microphones kept up. The actors don't blanket each other; all the gags come through. For sheer momentum, there's nothing like it. Even when Grant and Russell realize they need each other, the movie pauses only briefly. Combat, of course, is their form of romance. It's sexier than sex.

Smiles of a Summer Night vs. Annie Hall
Ingmar Bergman's *Smiles of a Summer Night* is not American, but willfully included here as necessary contrast. A sublime period piece set among aristocrats at a country house, it's more elegant and nostalgic than any of the American films but still a romantic comedy. *Annie Hall* is Woody Allen's "nervous romance" about a midwestern WASP (Diane Keaton) and the intellectual New York Jew (Woody) who tries to contol her and loses her. Nod to Woody for perfectly capturing a contemporary mood with bittersweet lyricism.

Cats and Dogs

By Lon Tweeten

Lon Tweeten, a wildly unsuccessful cartoonist working in NYC, has shared residence with over 20 cats and dogs over the years, though only once simultaneously . . . it ended badly.

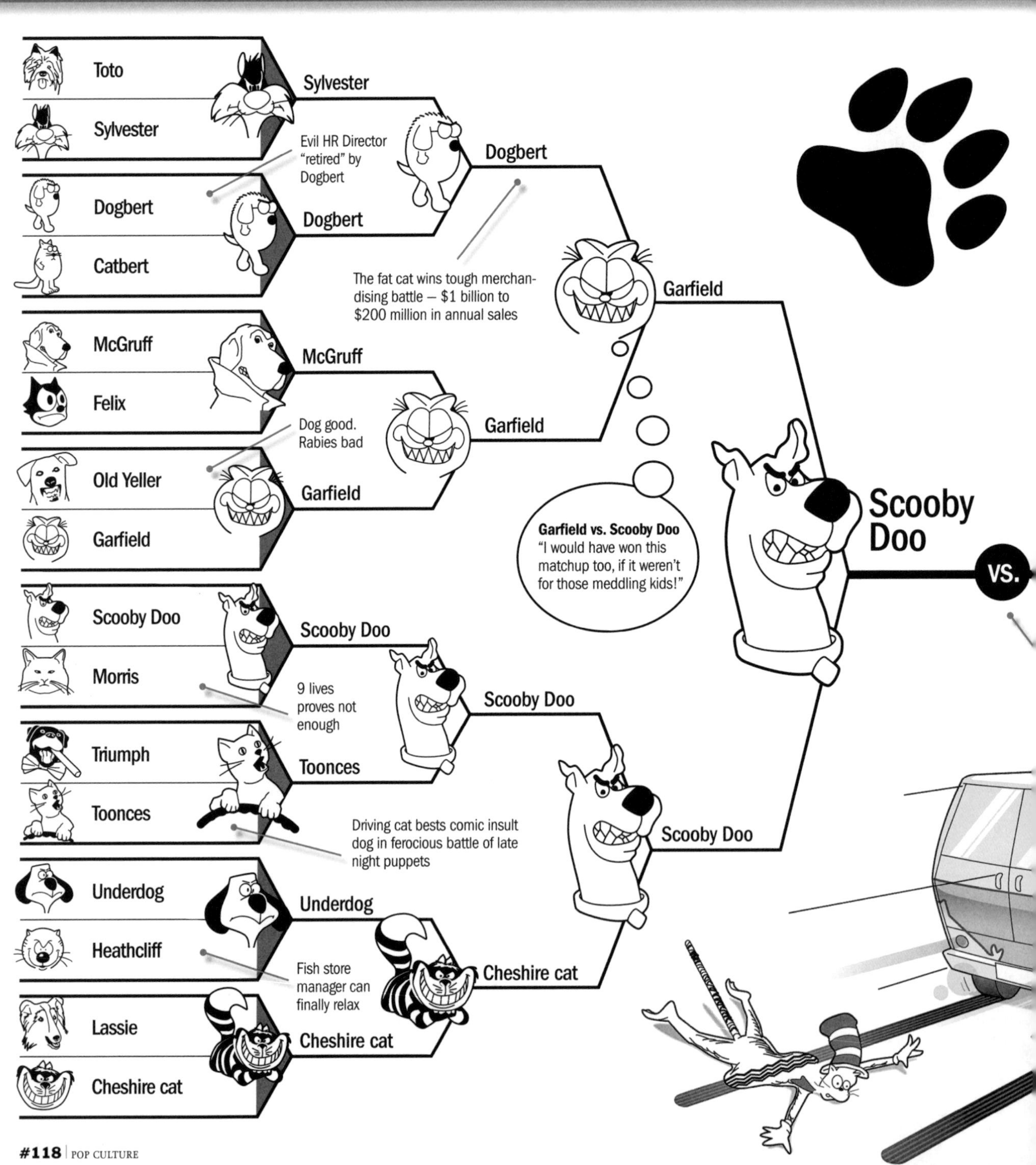
Toto
Sylvester
Dogbert
Catbert
McGruff
Felix
Old Yeller
Garfield
Scooby Doo
Morris
Triumph
Toonces
Underdog
Heathcliff
Lassie
Cheshire cat
Sylvester
Dogbert
McGruff
Garfield
Scooby Doo
Toonces
Underdog
Cheshire cat
Evil HR Director "retired" by Dogbert
Dog good. Rabies bad
9 lives proves not enough
Driving cat bests comic insult dog in ferocious battle of late night puppets
Fish store manager can finally relax
Dogbert
Garfield
Scooby Doo
Cheshire cat
The fat cat wins tough merchandising battle – $1 billion to $200 million in annual sales
Garfield
Scooby Doo
Garfield vs. Scooby Doo
"I would have won this matchup too, if it weren't for those meddling kids!"
Scooby Doo
VS.

MAN'S FAVORITE DOMESTICATED ANIMALS – *Felis Catus* and *Canis Lupus Familiaris* – share a deep genetic hatred for one another. With the world's cat and dog population estimated at over 500 million and growing, escalation of skirmishes is inevitable.

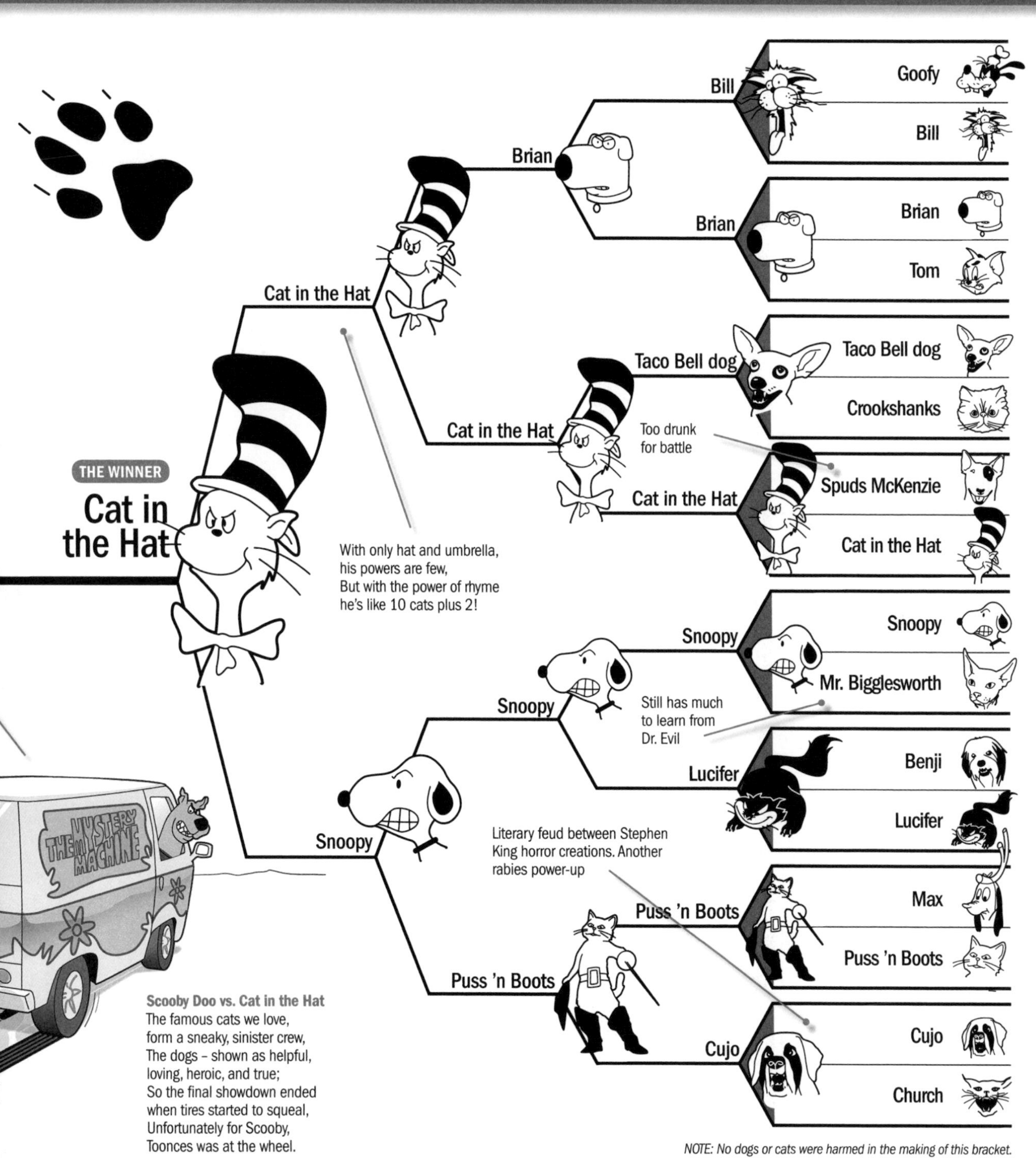

Goofy
Bill
Brian
Tom
Taco Bell dog
Crookshanks
Spuds McKenzie
Cat in the Hat
Snoopy
Mr. Bigglesworth
Benji
Lucifer
Max
Puss 'n Boots
Cujo
Church
Bill
Brian
Taco Bell dog
Cat in the Hat
Snoopy
Lucifer
Puss 'n Boots
Cujo
Brian
Cat in the Hat
Snoopy
Puss 'n Boots
Cat in the Hat
Snoopy
THE WINNER
Cat in the Hat
Too drunk for battle
With only hat and umbrella, his powers are few, But with the power of rhyme he's like 10 cats plus 2!
Still has much to learn from Dr. Evil
Literary feud between Stephen King horror creations. Another rabies power-up
THE MYSTERY MACHINE

Scooby Doo vs. Cat in the Hat
The famous cats we love,
form a sneaky, sinister crew,
The dogs – shown as helpful,
loving, heroic, and true;
So the final showdown ended
when tires started to squeal,
Unfortunately for Scooby,
Toonces was at the wheel.

NOTE: No dogs or cats were harmed in the making of this bracket.

Clint Eastwood Films

By Manohla Dargis

Manohla Dargis reviews films for the *New York Times*. She lives in Los Angeles and does not own a gun.

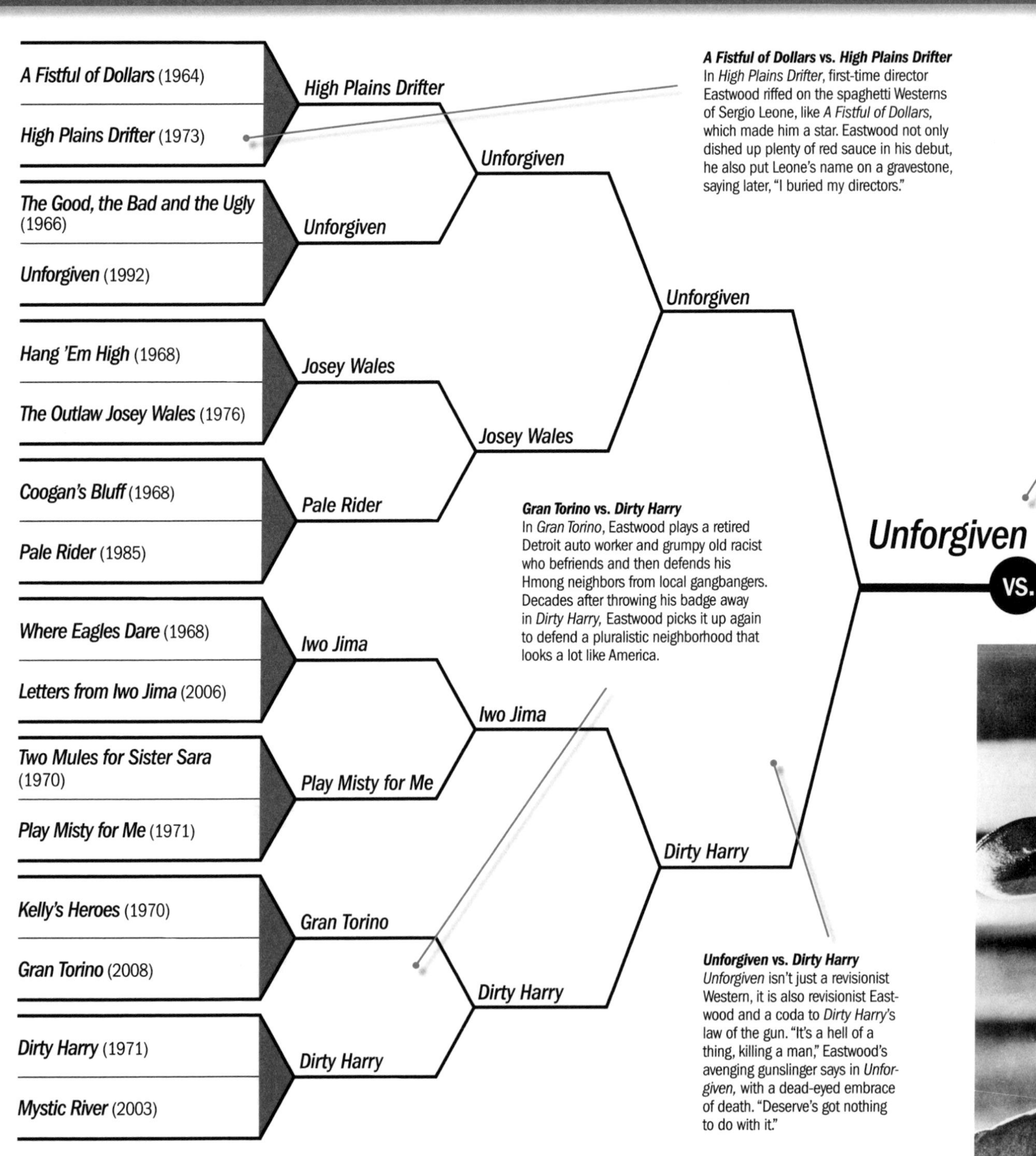

A Fistful of Dollars (1964)
High Plains Drifter (1973)
The Good, the Bad and the Ugly (1966)
Unforgiven (1992)
Hang 'Em High (1968)
The Outlaw Josey Wales (1976)
Coogan's Bluff (1968)
Pale Rider (1985)
Where Eagles Dare (1968)
Letters from Iwo Jima (2006)
Two Mules for Sister Sara (1970)
Play Misty for Me (1971)
Kelly's Heroes (1970)
Gran Torino (2008)
Dirty Harry (1971)
Mystic River (2003)
High Plains Drifter
Unforgiven
Josey Wales
Pale Rider
Iwo Jima
Play Misty for Me
Gran Torino
Dirty Harry
Unforgiven
Josey Wales
Iwo Jima
Dirty Harry
Unforgiven
Dirty Harry
Unforgiven
VS.

A Fistful of Dollars vs. High Plains Drifter
In *High Plains Drifter*, first-time director Eastwood riffed on the spaghetti Westerns of Sergio Leone, like *A Fistful of Dollars*, which made him a star. Eastwood not only dished up plenty of red sauce in his debut, he also put Leone's name on a gravestone, saying later, "I buried my directors."

Gran Torino vs. Dirty Harry
In *Gran Torino*, Eastwood plays a retired Detroit auto worker and grumpy old racist who befriends and then defends his Hmong neighbors from local gangbangers. Decades after throwing his badge away in *Dirty Harry*, Eastwood picks it up again to defend a pluralistic neighborhood that looks a lot like America.

Unforgiven vs. Dirty Harry
Unforgiven isn't just a revisionist Western, it is also revisionist Eastwood and a coda to *Dirty Harry*'s law of the gun. "It's a hell of a thing, killing a man," Eastwood's avenging gunslinger says in *Unforgiven*, with a dead-eyed embrace of death. "Deserve's got nothing to do with it."

CLINT EASTWOOD is to the last half of the 20th century what John Wayne was to the first: the embodiment of American radical individualism, plus guns. As the self-styled Hollywood outsider who has made some of its greatest films, Eastwood has spent much of his bifurcated career as an actor-turned-director reconsidering, reconceptualizing, and radically revising his own screen identity. His great subject is masculinity and its discontents, a gift that keeps on giving.

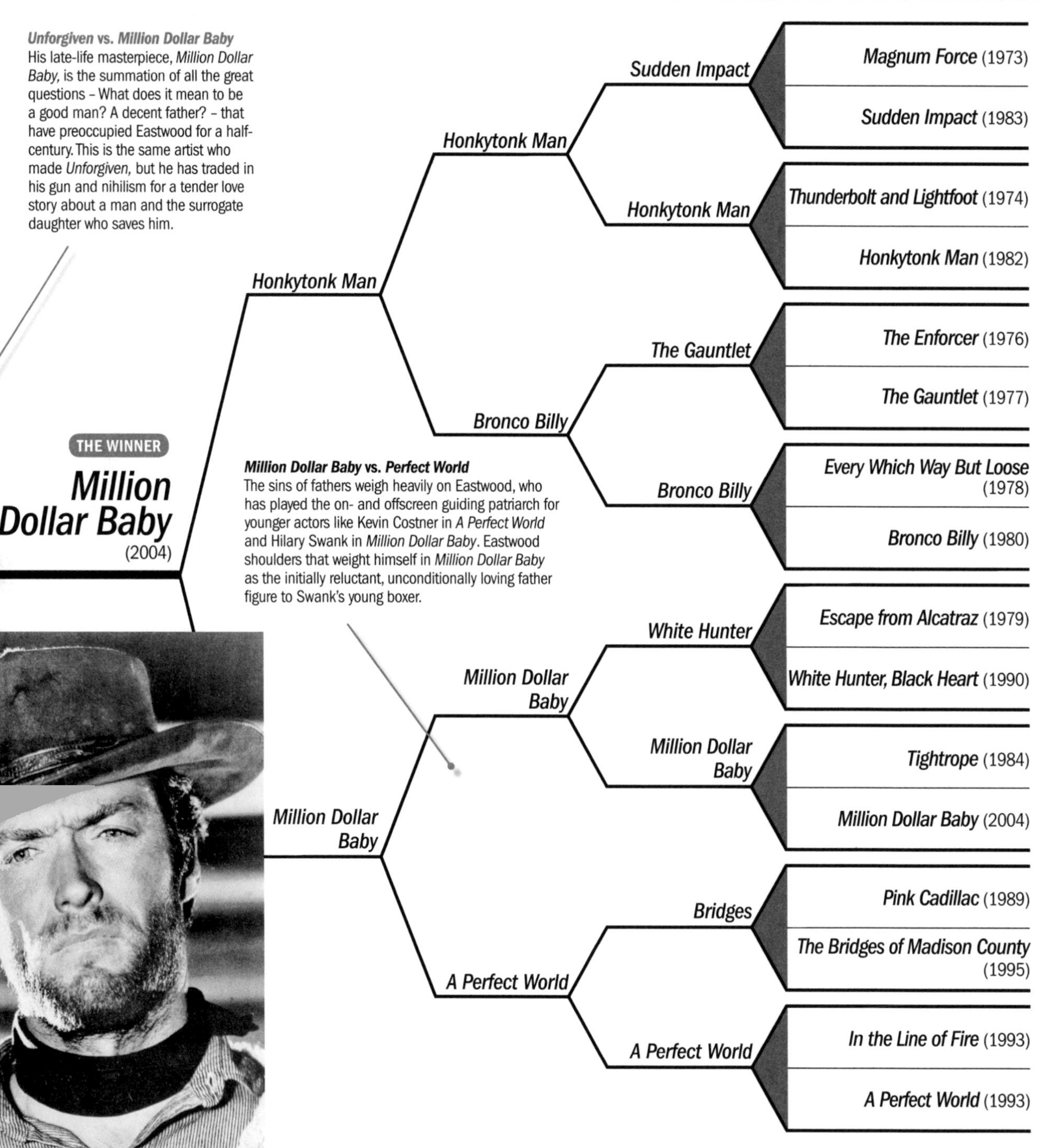

Magnum Force (1973)
Sudden Impact (1983)
Thunderbolt and Lightfoot (1974)
Honkytonk Man (1982)
The Enforcer (1976)
The Gauntlet (1977)
Every Which Way But Loose (1978)
Bronco Billy (1980)
Escape from Alcatraz (1979)
White Hunter, Black Heart (1990)
Tightrope (1984)
Million Dollar Baby (2004)
Pink Cadillac (1989)
The Bridges of Madison County (1995)
In the Line of Fire (1993)
A Perfect World (1993)
Sudden Impact
Honkytonk Man
The Gauntlet
Bronco Billy
White Hunter
Million Dollar Baby
Bridges
A Perfect World
Honkytonk Man
Bronco Billy
Million Dollar Baby
A Perfect World
Honkytonk Man
Million Dollar Baby
THE WINNER
Million Dollar Baby (2004)

Unforgiven vs. Million Dollar Baby
His late-life masterpiece, *Million Dollar Baby,* is the summation of all the great questions – What does it mean to be a good man? A decent father? – that have preoccupied Eastwood for a half-century. This is the same artist who made *Unforgiven,* but he has traded in his gun and nihilism for a tender love story about a man and the surrogate daughter who saves him.

Million Dollar Baby vs. Perfect World
The sins of fathers weigh heavily on Eastwood, who has played the on- and offscreen guiding patriarch for younger actors like Kevin Costner in *A Perfect World* and Hilary Swank in *Million Dollar Baby*. Eastwood shoulders that weight himself in *Million Dollar Baby* as the initially reluctant, unconditionally loving father figure to Swank's young boxer.

Comedy Teams

By Robert Wuhl

Robert Wuhl is a two-time Emmy Award–winning writer. Whether he's funny is, of course, based on one's point of view.

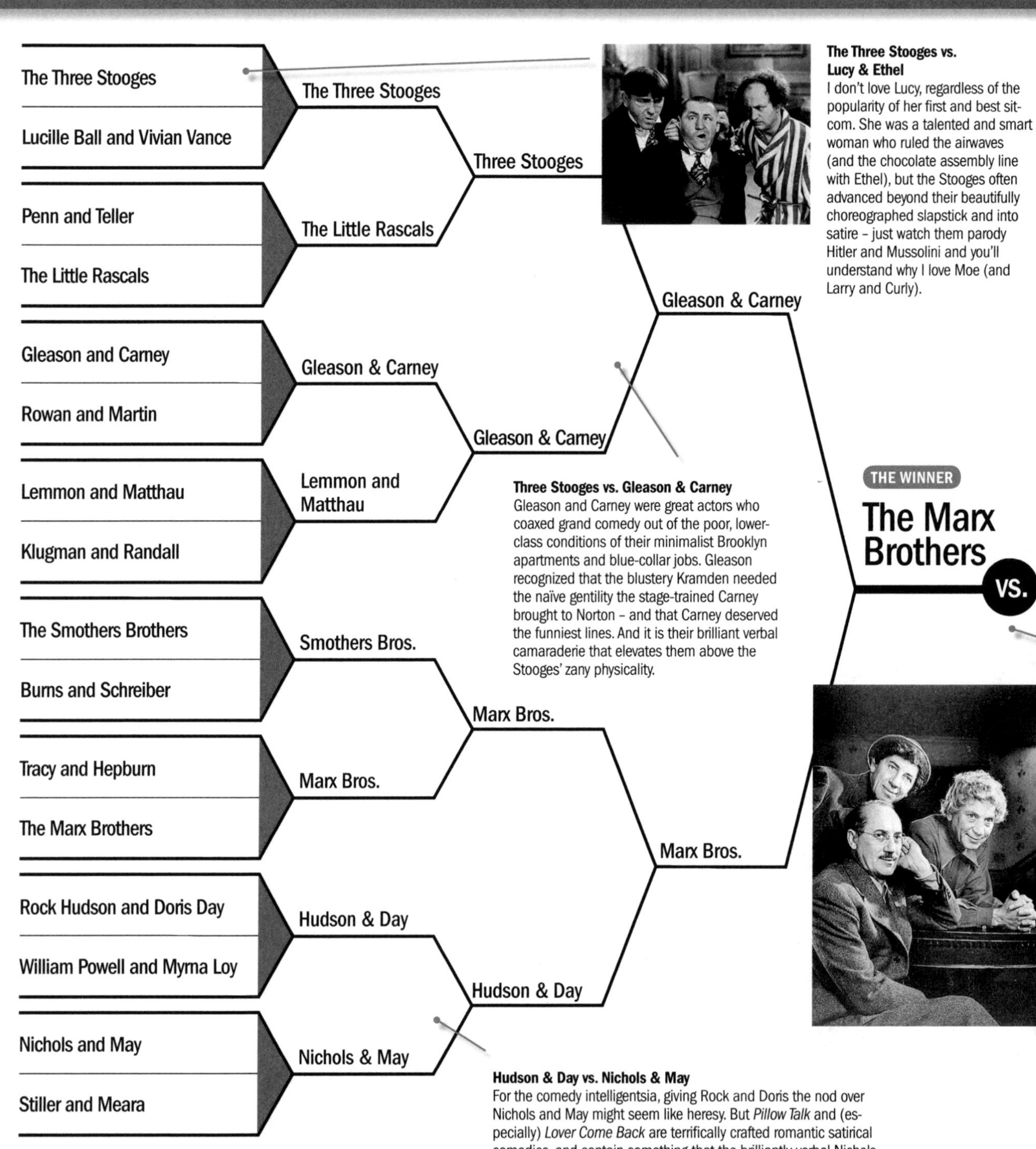

The Three Stooges
Lucille Ball and Vivian Vance
Penn and Teller
The Little Rascals
Gleason and Carney
Rowan and Martin
Lemmon and Matthau
Klugman and Randall
The Smothers Brothers
Burns and Schreiber
Tracy and Hepburn
The Marx Brothers
Rock Hudson and Doris Day
William Powell and Myrna Loy
Nichols and May
Stiller and Meara
The Three Stooges
The Little Rascals
Gleason & Carney
Lemmon and Matthau
Smothers Bros.
Marx Bros.
Hudson & Day
Nichols & May
Three Stooges
Gleason & Carney
Marx Bros.
Hudson & Day
Gleason & Carney
Marx Bros.
THE WINNER
The Marx Brothers
VS.

The Three Stooges vs. Lucy & Ethel
I don't love Lucy, regardless of the popularity of her first and best sitcom. She was a talented and smart woman who ruled the airwaves (and the chocolate assembly line with Ethel), but the Stooges often advanced beyond their beautifully choreographed slapstick and into satire – just watch them parody Hitler and Mussolini and you'll understand why I love Moe (and Larry and Curly).

Three Stooges vs. Gleason & Carney
Gleason and Carney were great actors who coaxed grand comedy out of the poor, lower-class conditions of their minimalist Brooklyn apartments and blue-collar jobs. Gleason recognized that the blustery Kramden needed the naïve gentility the stage-trained Carney brought to Norton – and that Carney deserved the funniest lines. And it is their brilliant verbal camaraderie that elevates them above the Stooges' zany physicality.

Hudson & Day vs. Nichols & May
For the comedy intelligentsia, giving Rock and Doris the nod over Nichols and May might seem like heresy. But *Pillow Talk* and (especially) *Lover Come Back* are terrifically crafted romantic satirical comedies, and contain something that the brilliantly verbal Nichols and May bits never contained – sexual tension.

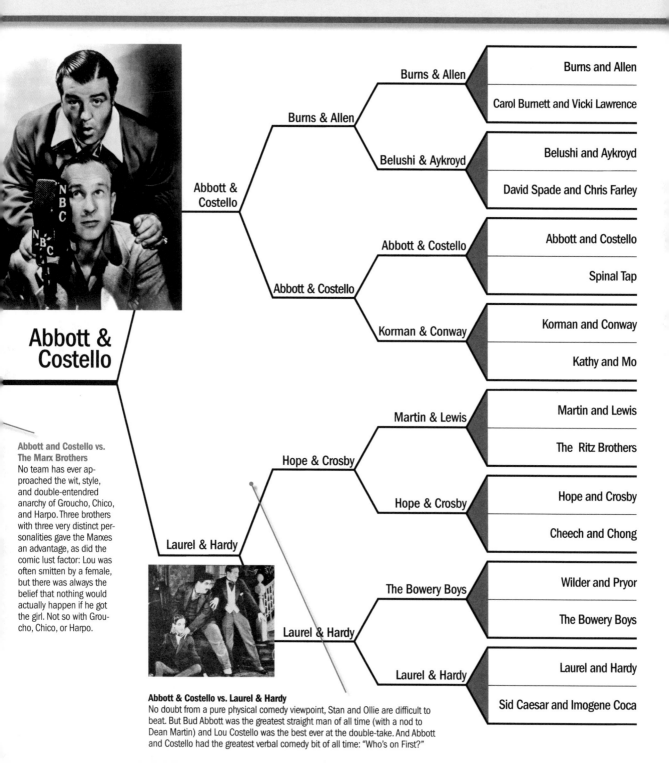

COMEDY IS DIFFICULT ENOUGH TO ACHIEVE, but try doing it night after night, film after film, or episode after episode. When it works — when it is delightfully artful, witty, silly, smart, or physical – it is a combination of music, rhythm, and choreography between two or more artists. What happens in the space between the players generates the chemistry we see, and for us, magic is made. It is very difficult to produce, and even more difficult to maintain. The greatest teams cross generations to create that most involuntary of human responses – making us laugh.

NBC
NBC

Abbott & Costello

- Abbott & Costello
  - Burns & Allen
    - Burns & Allen
      - Burns and Allen
      - Carol Burnett and Vicki Lawrence
    - Belushi & Aykroyd
      - Belushi and Aykroyd
      - David Spade and Chris Farley
  - Abbott & Costello
    - Abbott & Costello
      - Abbott and Costello
      - Spinal Tap
    - Korman & Conway
      - Korman and Conway
      - Kathy and Mo
- Laurel & Hardy
  - Hope & Crosby
    - Martin & Lewis
      - Martin and Lewis
      - The Ritz Brothers
    - Hope & Crosby
      - Hope and Crosby
      - Cheech and Chong
  - Laurel & Hardy
    - The Bowery Boys
      - Wilder and Pryor
      - The Bowery Boys
    - Laurel & Hardy
      - Laurel and Hardy
      - Sid Caesar and Imogene Coca

Abbott and Costello vs. The Marx Brothers
No team has ever approached the wit, style, and double-entendred anarchy of Groucho, Chico, and Harpo. Three brothers with three very distinct personalities gave the Marxes an advantage, as did the comic lust factor: Lou was often smitten by a female, but there was always the belief that nothing would actually happen if he got the girl. Not so with Groucho, Chico, or Harpo.

Abbott & Costello vs. Laurel & Hardy
No doubt from a pure physical comedy viewpoint, Stan and Ollie are difficult to beat. But Bud Abbott was the greatest straight man of all time (with a nod to Dean Martin) and Lou Costello was the best ever at the double-take. And Abbott and Costello had the greatest verbal comedy bit of all time: "Who's on First?"

Comic Book Superpowers

By Peter Coogan

Dr. Peter Coogan is co-chair of the Comics Arts Conference (held at the San Diego Comic-Con International).

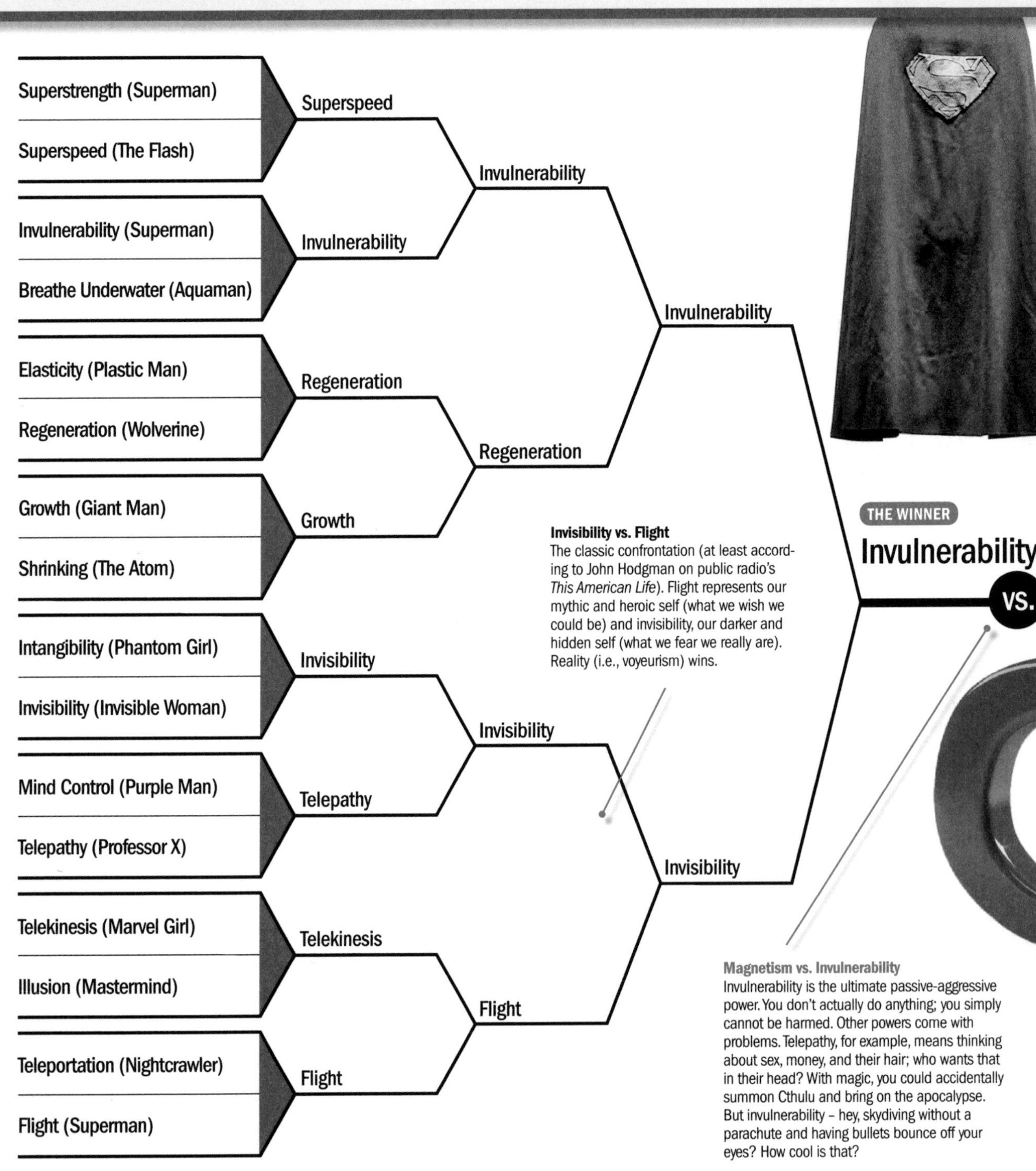
Superstrength (Superman)
Superspeed (The Flash)
Invulnerability (Superman)
Breathe Underwater (Aquaman)
Elasticity (Plastic Man)
Regeneration (Wolverine)
Growth (Giant Man)
Shrinking (The Atom)
Intangibility (Phantom Girl)
Invisibility (Invisible Woman)
Mind Control (Purple Man)
Telepathy (Professor X)
Telekinesis (Marvel Girl)
Illusion (Mastermind)
Teleportation (Nightcrawler)
Flight (Superman)
Superspeed
Invulnerability
Regeneration
Growth
Invisibility
Telepathy
Telekinesis
Flight
Invulnerability
Regeneration
Invisibility
Flight
Invulnerability
Invisibility
THE WINNER
Invulnerability
VS.

Invisibility vs. Flight
The classic confrontation (at least according to John Hodgman on public radio's *This American Life*). Flight represents our mythic and heroic self (what we wish we could be) and invisibility, our darker and hidden self (what we fear we really are). Reality (i.e., voyeurism) wins.

Magnetism vs. Invulnerability
Invulnerability is the ultimate passive-aggressive power. You don't actually do anything; you simply cannot be harmed. Other powers come with problems. Telepathy, for example, means thinking about sex, money, and their hair; who wants that in their head? With magic, you could accidentally summon Cthulu and bring on the apocalypse. But invulnerability – hey, skydiving without a parachute and having bullets bounce off your eyes? How cool is that?

THIS BRACKET STEMS FROM CHILDHOOD FANTASY, when we debated which is the best power to have, either in daily life or for fighting crime. I think we can admit now that none of us really wanted to dress up like a bat and spend our nights on patrol. It wasn't the costume; it's the actual superpower that's cool and fun. Ever since Gilgamesh went looking for immortality, people have dreamed of having superpowers to escape the monotony of mundane existence. But if you could only have one power – whether it's physical, mental, or meta – which would it be?

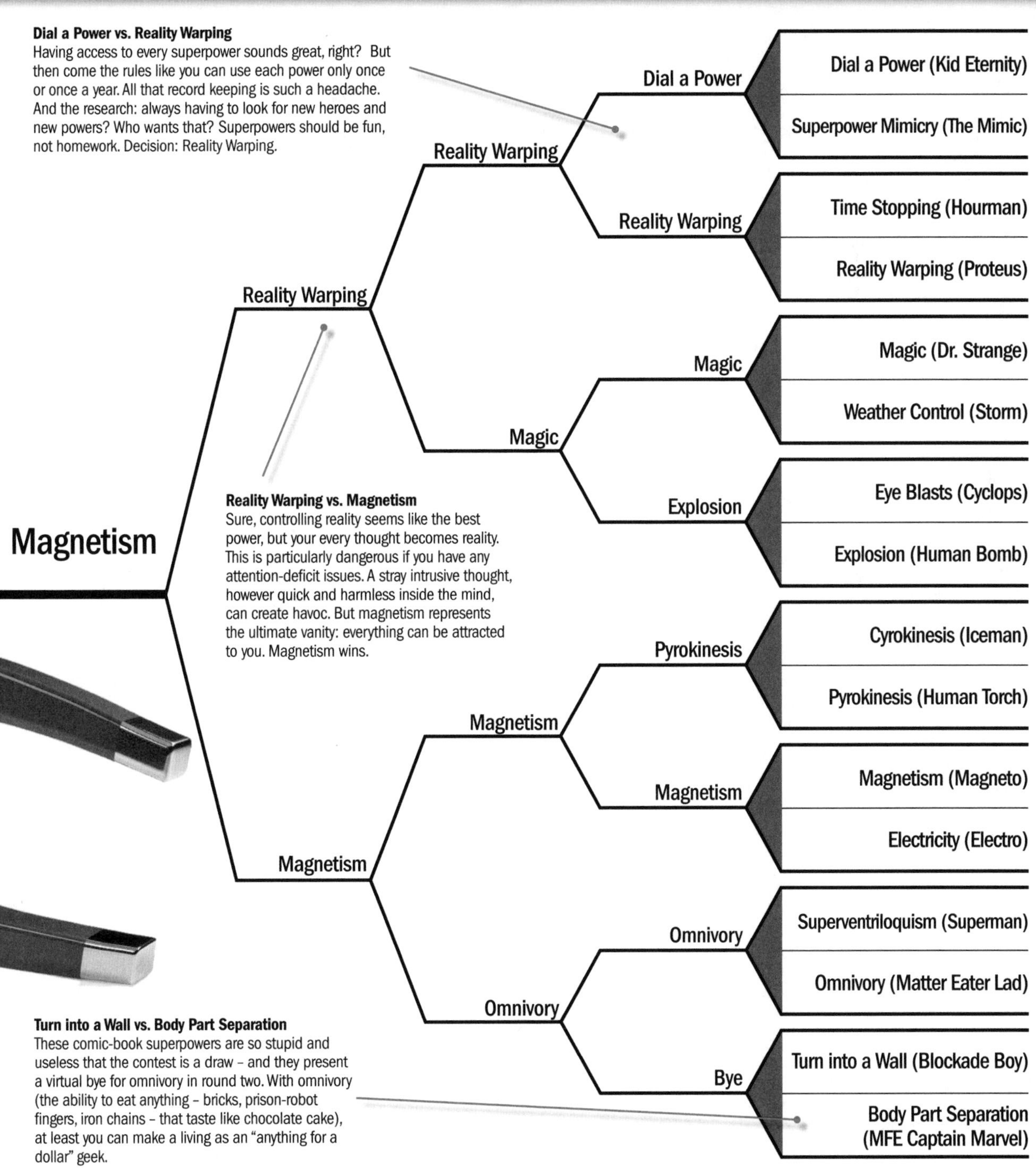

Dial a Power (Kid Eternity)
Superpower Mimicry (The Mimic)
Time Stopping (Hourman)
Reality Warping (Proteus)
Magic (Dr. Strange)
Weather Control (Storm)
Eye Blasts (Cyclops)
Explosion (Human Bomb)
Cyrokinesis (Iceman)
Pyrokinesis (Human Torch)
Magnetism (Magneto)
Electricity (Electro)
Superventriloquism (Superman)
Omnivory (Matter Eater Lad)
Turn into a Wall (Blockade Boy)
Body Part Separation (MFE Captain Marvel)
Dial a Power
Reality Warping
Magic
Explosion
Pyrokinesis
Magnetism
Omnivory
Bye
Reality Warping
Magic
Magnetism
Omnivory
Reality Warping
Magnetism
Magnetism

Dial a Power vs. Reality Warping
Having access to every superpower sounds great, right? But then come the rules like you can use each power only once or once a year. All that record keeping is such a headache. And the research: always having to look for new heroes and new powers? Who wants that? Superpowers should be fun, not homework. Decision: Reality Warping.

Reality Warping vs. Magnetism
Sure, controlling reality seems like the best power, but your every thought becomes reality. This is particularly dangerous if you have any attention-deficit issues. A stray intrusive thought, however quick and harmless inside the mind, can create havoc. But magnetism represents the ultimate vanity: everything can be attracted to you. Magnetism wins.

Turn into a Wall vs. Body Part Separation
These comic-book superpowers are so stupid and useless that the contest is a draw – and they present a virtual bye for omnivory in round two. With omnivory (the ability to eat anything – bricks, prison-robot fingers, iron chains – that taste like chocolate cake), at least you can make a living as an "anything for a dollar" geek.

NATURE

Fears and Phobias *by Roz Chast* 122

National Parks *by Scott Kirkwood* 123

Dangerous Animals *by Chris Jenkins* 124

Best Ski Runs *by Steve Cohen* 125

Nothing but the Tooth *by James Hudson, D.M.D.* 126

Fish Tales *by Peter Kaminsky* 127

Energy Alternatives *by Gwyneth Cravens* 128

My Prized Feathers *by Luke Dempsey* 129

Looking Younger *by David Leffell, M.D.* 130

Fears and Phobias

By Roz Chast
Roz Chast is a cartoonist for *The New Yorker* magazine.

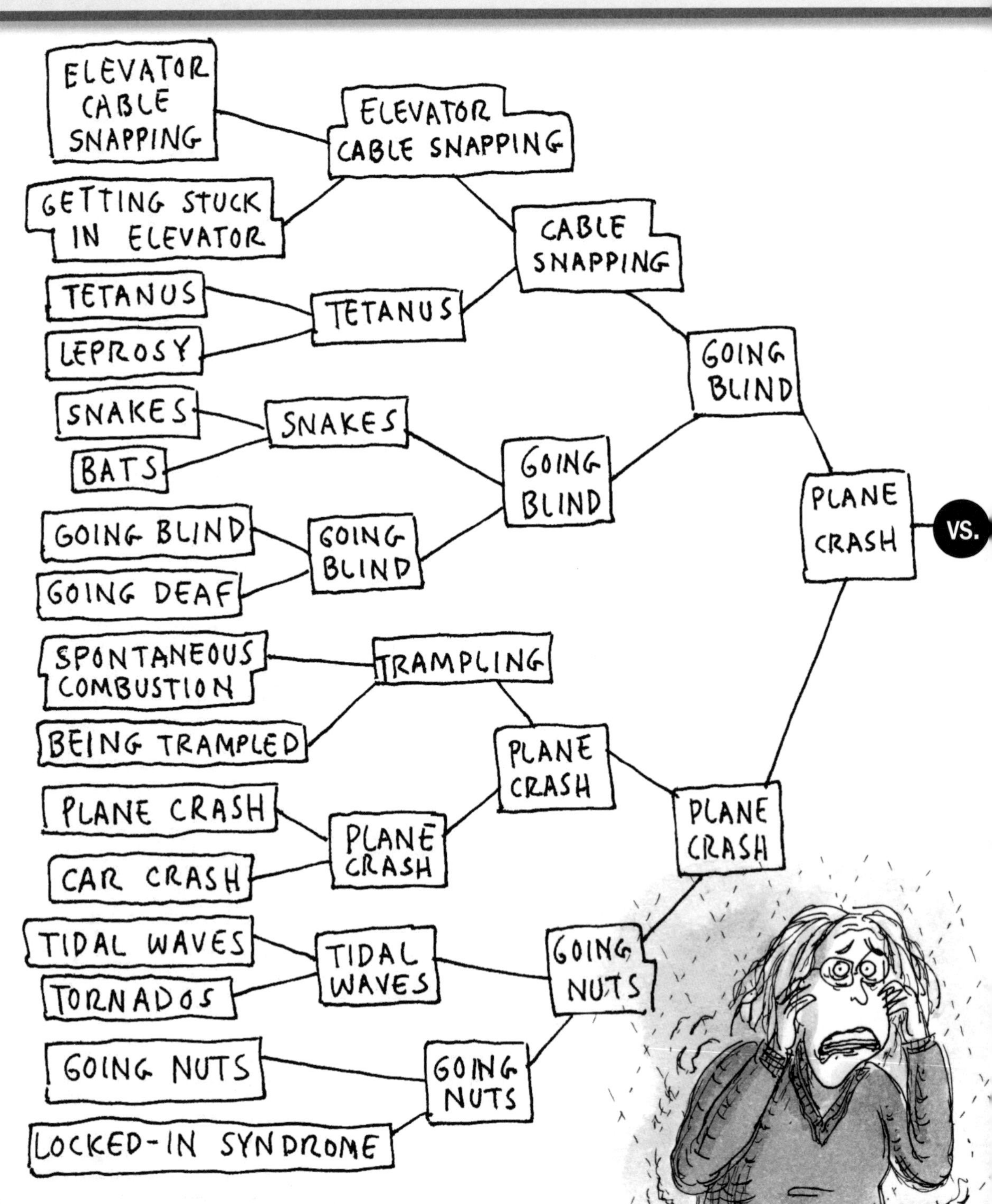
ELEVATOR CABLE SNAPPING
GETTING STUCK IN ELEVATOR
ELEVATOR CABLE SNAPPING
TETANUS
LEPROSY
TETANUS
CABLE SNAPPING
SNAKES
BATS
SNAKES
GOING BLIND
GOING DEAF
GOING BLIND
GOING BLIND
GOING BLIND
SPONTANEOUS COMBUSTION
BEING TRAMPLED
TRAMPLING
PLANE CRASH
CAR CRASH
PLANE CRASH
PLANE CRASH
TIDAL WAVES
TORNADOS
TIDAL WAVES
GOING NUTS
LOCKED-IN SYNDROME
GOING NUTS
GOING NUTS
PLANE CRASH
PLANE CRASH
VS.

EVER SINCE I WAS LITTLE, I have always had a lot of phobias. When I was a kid, the main ones were appendicitis (thank you, Ludwig Bemelmans); going blind; going cross-eyed; nightmares; losing my permanent teeth; kites; leprosy; spontaneous combustion; and balloons. I have outgrown most of these but not all. The bad news is that as I get older, I accumulate new ones.

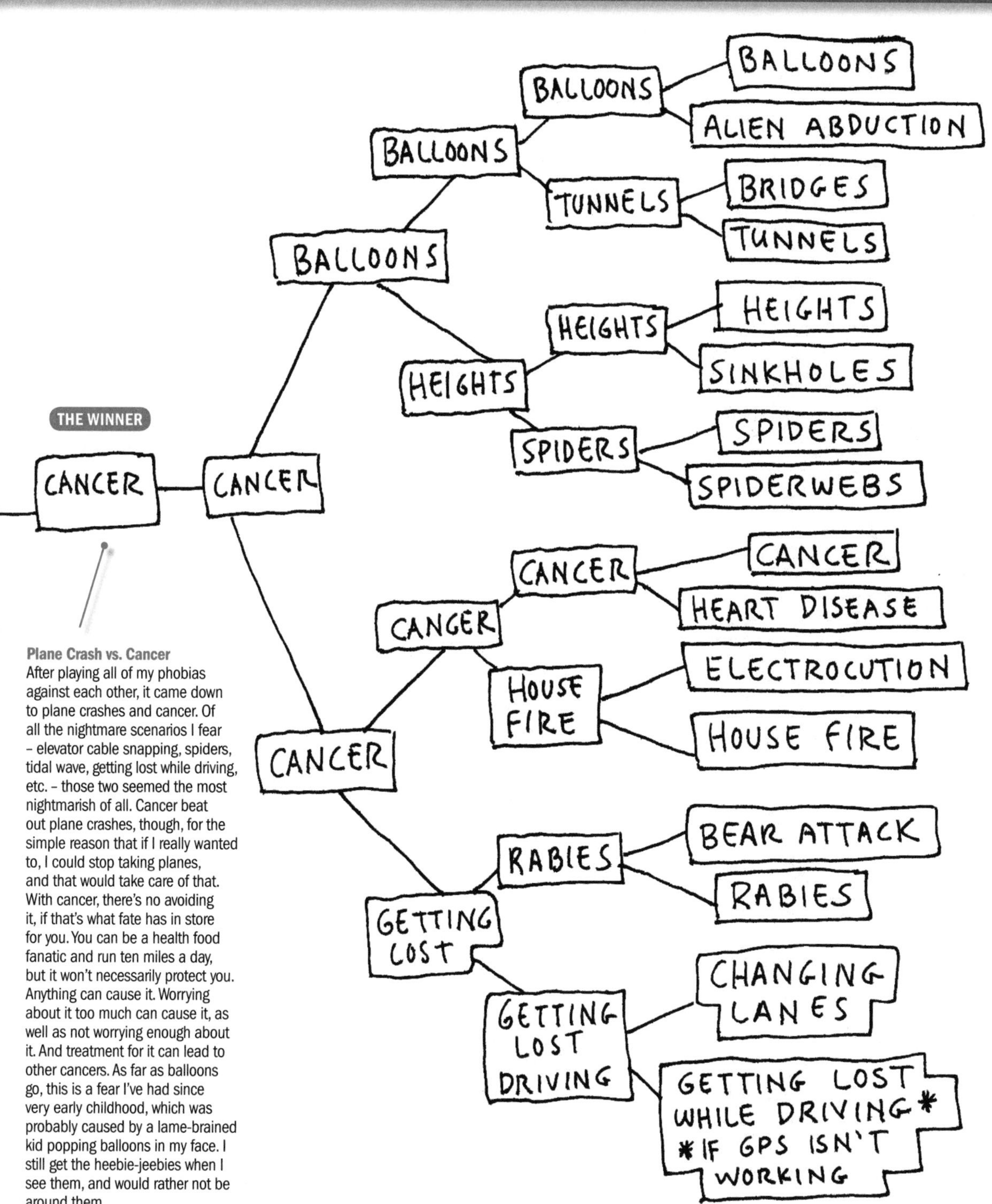

BALLOONS
ALIEN ABDUCTION
BALLOONS
BALLOONS
TUNNELS
BRIDGES
TUNNELS
BALLOONS
HEIGHTS
HEIGHTS
SINKHOLES
HEIGHTS
SPIDERS
SPIDERS
SPIDERWEBS
THE WINNER
CANCER
CANCER
CANCER
CANCER
HEART DISEASE
CANCER
HOUSE FIRE
ELECTROCUTION
HOUSE FIRE
CANCER
RABIES
BEAR ATTACK
RABIES
GETTING LOST
GETTING LOST DRIVING
CHANGING LANES
GETTING LOST WHILE DRIVING*
*IF GPS ISN'T WORKING

Plane Crash vs. Cancer
After playing all of my phobias against each other, it came down to plane crashes and cancer. Of all the nightmare scenarios I fear – elevator cable snapping, spiders, tidal wave, getting lost while driving, etc. – those two seemed the most nightmarish of all. Cancer beat out plane crashes, though, for the simple reason that if I really wanted to, I could stop taking planes, and that would take care of that. With cancer, there's no avoiding it, if that's what fate has in store for you. You can be a health food fanatic and run ten miles a day, but it won't necessarily protect you. Anything can cause it. Worrying about it too much can cause it, as well as not worrying enough about it. And treatment for it can lead to other cancers. As far as balloons go, this is a fear I've had since very early childhood, which was probably caused by a lame-brained kid popping balloons in my face. I still get the heebie-jeebies when I see them, and would rather not be around them.

National Parks

By Scott Kirkwood

Scott Kirkwood is the editor of *National Parks* magazine, published by the National Parks Conservation Association, a nonprofit group that fights to make sure all 391 park units are around for your kids and your kids' kids.

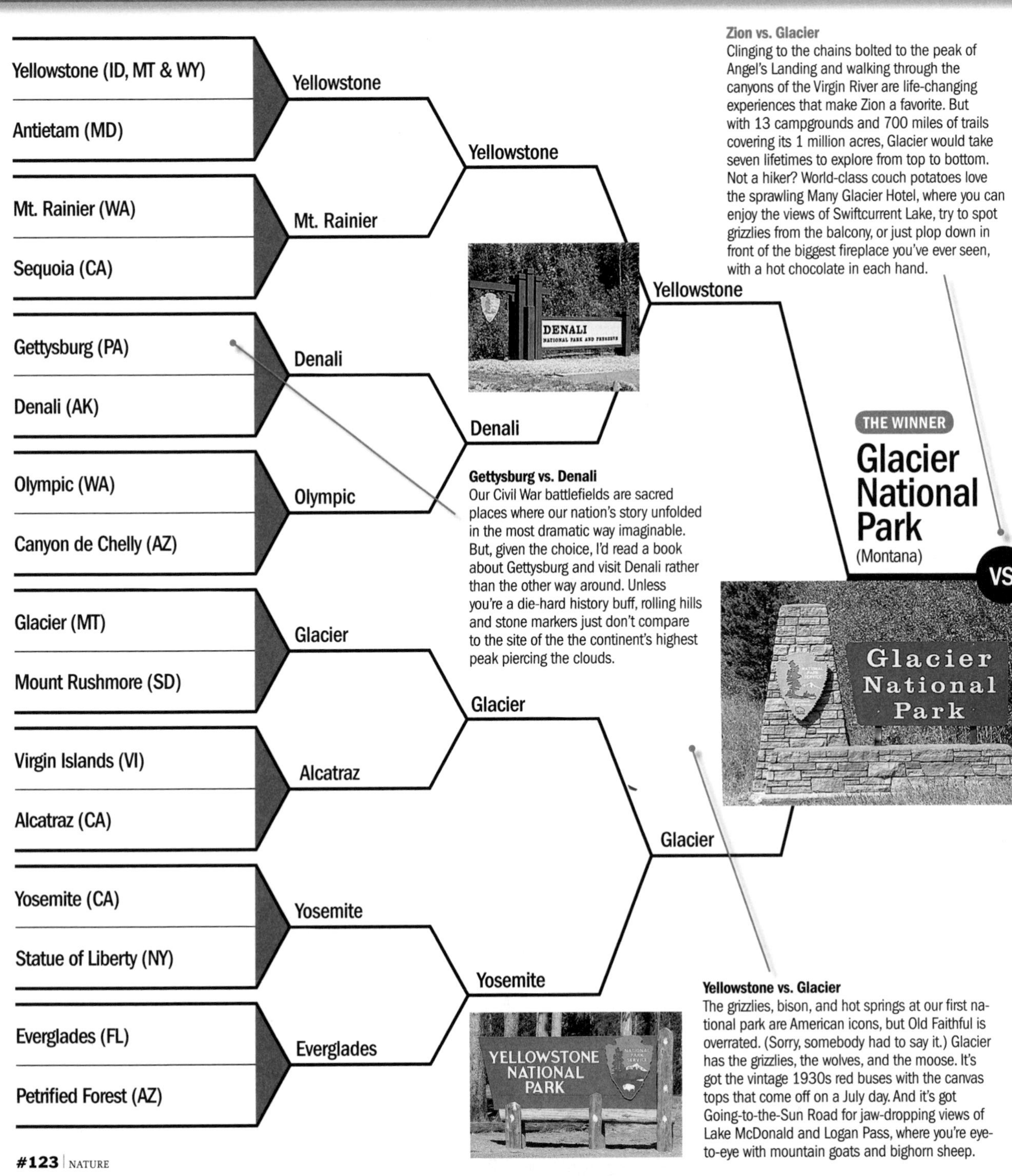

Yellowstone (ID, MT & WY)
Antietam (MD)
Mt. Rainier (WA)
Sequoia (CA)
Gettysburg (PA)
Denali (AK)
Olympic (WA)
Canyon de Chelly (AZ)
Glacier (MT)
Mount Rushmore (SD)
Virgin Islands (VI)
Alcatraz (CA)
Yosemite (CA)
Statue of Liberty (NY)
Everglades (FL)
Petrified Forest (AZ)
Yellowstone
Mt. Rainier
Denali
Olympic
Glacier
Alcatraz
Yosemite
Everglades
Yellowstone
Denali
Glacier
Yosemite
Yellowstone
Glacier
DENALI
NATIONAL PARK AND PRESERVE
THE WINNER
Glacier National Park
(Montana)
VS.
Glacier National Park
YELLOWSTONE NATIONAL PARK

Zion vs. Glacier
Clinging to the chains bolted to the peak of Angel's Landing and walking through the canyons of the Virgin River are life-changing experiences that make Zion a favorite. But with 13 campgrounds and 700 miles of trails covering its 1 million acres, Glacier would take seven lifetimes to explore from top to bottom. Not a hiker? World-class couch potatoes love the sprawling Many Glacier Hotel, where you can enjoy the views of Swiftcurrent Lake, try to spot grizzlies from the balcony, or just plop down in front of the biggest fireplace you've ever seen, with a hot chocolate in each hand.

Gettysburg vs. Denali
Our Civil War battlefields are sacred places where our nation's story unfolded in the most dramatic way imaginable. But, given the choice, I'd read a book about Gettysburg and visit Denali rather than the other way around. Unless you're a die-hard history buff, rolling hills and stone markers just don't compare to the site of the the continent's highest peak piercing the clouds.

Yellowstone vs. Glacier
The grizzlies, bison, and hot springs at our first national park are American icons, but Old Faithful is overrated. (Sorry, somebody had to say it.) Glacier has the grizzlies, the wolves, and the moose. It's got the vintage 1930s red buses with the canvas tops that come off on a July day. And it's got Going-to-the-Sun Road for jaw-dropping views of Lake McDonald and Logan Pass, where you're eye-to-eye with mountain goats and bighorn sheep.

ASK ANYONE WHO'S VISITED A HANDFUL of national parks to pick a favorite, and they'll tell you it's impossible. But as you can see, they're all wrong. Just like every parent secretly has a favorite child, we all find that one national park leaves us with a lasting impression. Whether it's the majestic wildlife, the stunning landscapes, or that tingling feeling that comes when you touch your own country's history, one of these spots will compel you to take dozens of mediocre photos and buy a horrible T-shirt. And go back again and again.

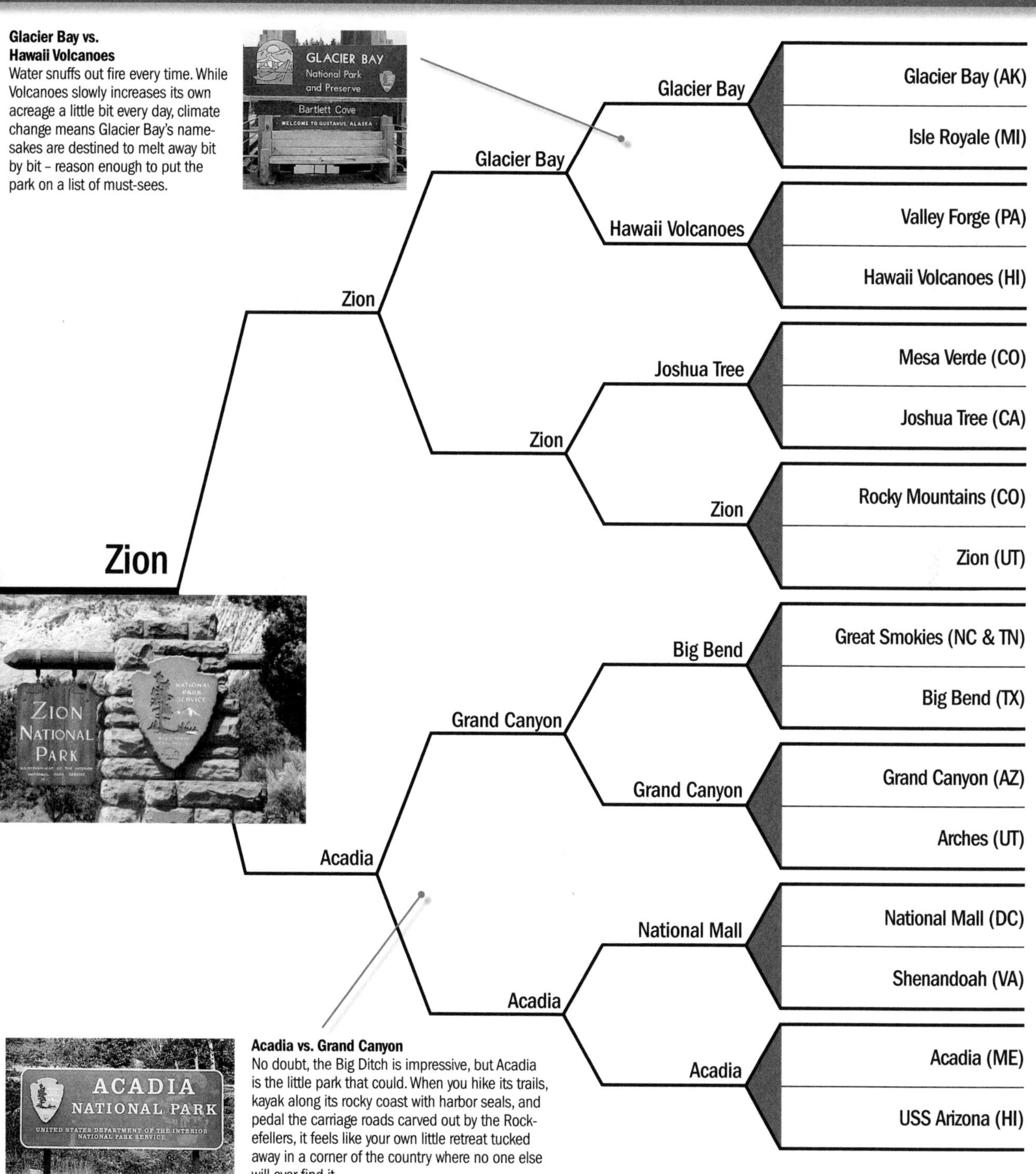
GLACIER BAY
National Park
and Preserve
Bartlett Cove
WELCOME TO GUSTAVUS, ALASKA
Glacier Bay (AK)
Isle Royale (MI)
Valley Forge (PA)
Hawaii Volcanoes (HI)
Mesa Verde (CO)
Joshua Tree (CA)
Rocky Mountains (CO)
Zion (UT)
Great Smokies (NC & TN)
Big Bend (TX)
Grand Canyon (AZ)
Arches (UT)
National Mall (DC)
Shenandoah (VA)
Acadia (ME)
USS Arizona (HI)
Glacier Bay
Hawaii Volcanoes
Joshua Tree
Zion
Big Bend
Grand Canyon
National Mall
Acadia
Glacier Bay
Zion
Grand Canyon
Acadia
Zion
Acadia
Zion
ZION
NATIONAL
PARK
NATIONAL PARK SERVICE
ACADIA
NATIONAL PARK
UNITED STATES DEPARTMENT OF THE INTERIOR
NATIONAL PARK SERVICE

Glacier Bay vs. Hawaii Volcanoes
Water snuffs out fire every time. While Volcanoes slowly increases its own acreage a little bit every day, climate change means Glacier Bay's namesakes are destined to melt away bit by bit – reason enough to put the park on a list of must-sees.

Acadia vs. Grand Canyon
No doubt, the Big Ditch is impressive, but Acadia is the little park that could. When you hike its trails, kayak along its rocky coast with harbor seals, and pedal the carriage roads carved out by the Rockefellers, it feels like your own little retreat tucked away in a corner of the country where no one else will ever find it.

Dangerous Animals

By Chris Jenkins

Chris Jenkins is a wildlife biologist working with "dangerous" animals, primarily venomous snakes, and helping people to let go of some of their greatest fears.

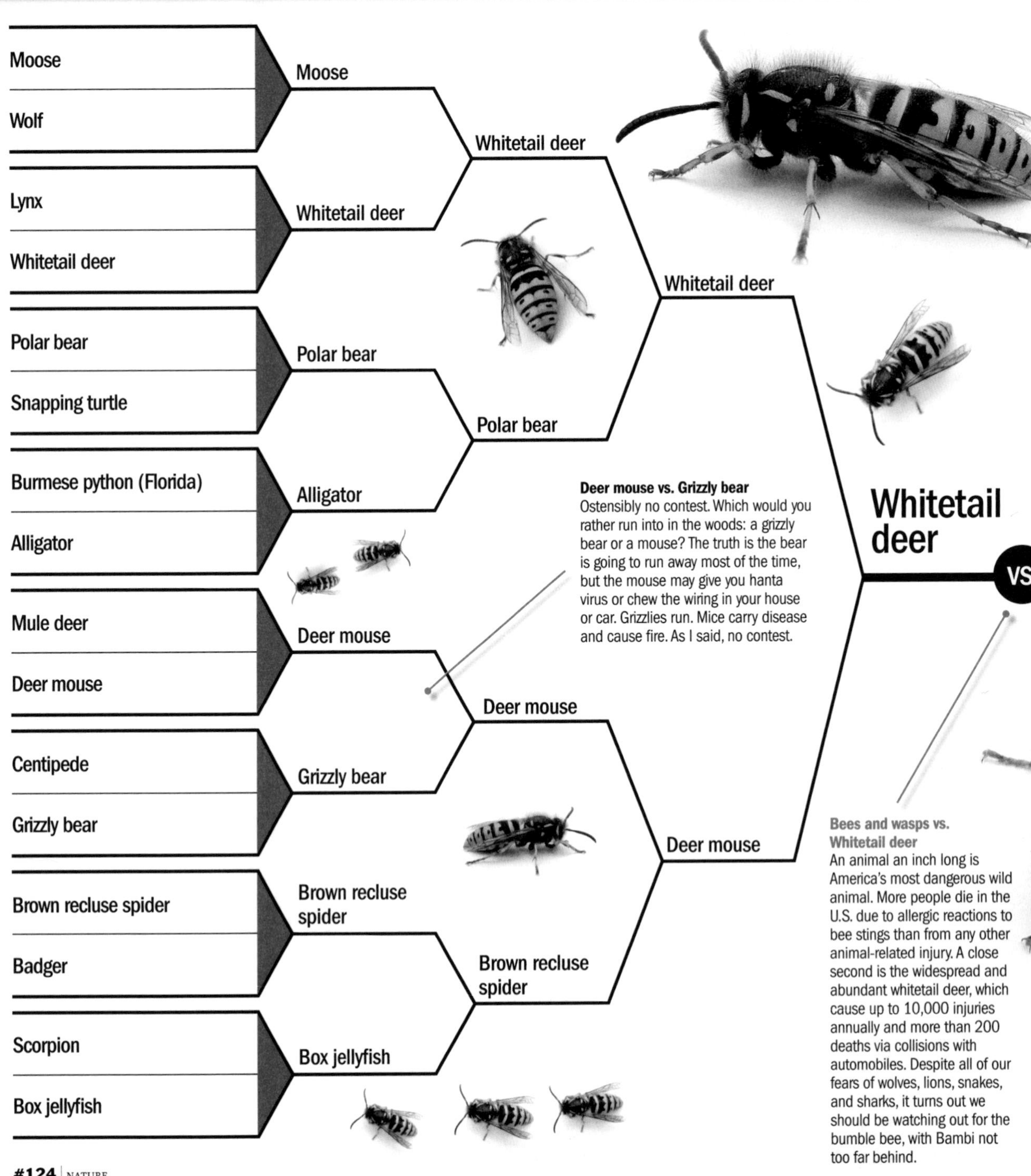
Moose
Wolf
Lynx
Whitetail deer
Polar bear
Snapping turtle
Burmese python (Florida)
Alligator
Mule deer
Deer mouse
Centipede
Grizzly bear
Brown recluse spider
Badger
Scorpion
Box jellyfish
Moose
Whitetail deer
Polar bear
Alligator
Deer mouse
Grizzly bear
Brown recluse spider
Box jellyfish
Whitetail deer
Polar bear
Deer mouse
Brown recluse spider
Whitetail deer
Deer mouse
Whitetail deer
VS.

Deer mouse vs. Grizzly bear
Ostensibly no contest. Which would you rather run into in the woods: a grizzly bear or a mouse? The truth is the bear is going to run away most of the time, but the mouse may give you hanta virus or chew the wiring in your house or car. Grizzlies run. Mice carry disease and cause fire. As I said, no contest.

Bees and wasps vs. Whitetail deer
An animal an inch long is America's most dangerous wild animal. More people die in the U.S. due to allergic reactions to bee stings than from any other animal-related injury. A close second is the widespread and abundant whitetail deer, which cause up to 10,000 injuries annually and more than 200 deaths via collisions with automobiles. Despite all of our fears of wolves, lions, snakes, and sharks, it turns out we should be watching out for the bumble bee, with Bambi not too far behind.

LET'S BEGIN WITH THE FACT that the most dangerous animals in the world are humans. Only then can we understand America's most dangerous wild animals. They range from those that can strike fear in our hearts, such as snakes and wolves, to animals that we don't typically think of as dangerous, such as mice. The criterion here is the animal's chance of causing human injury or death – and the element of surprise when we realize which animals are really scary and which are not.

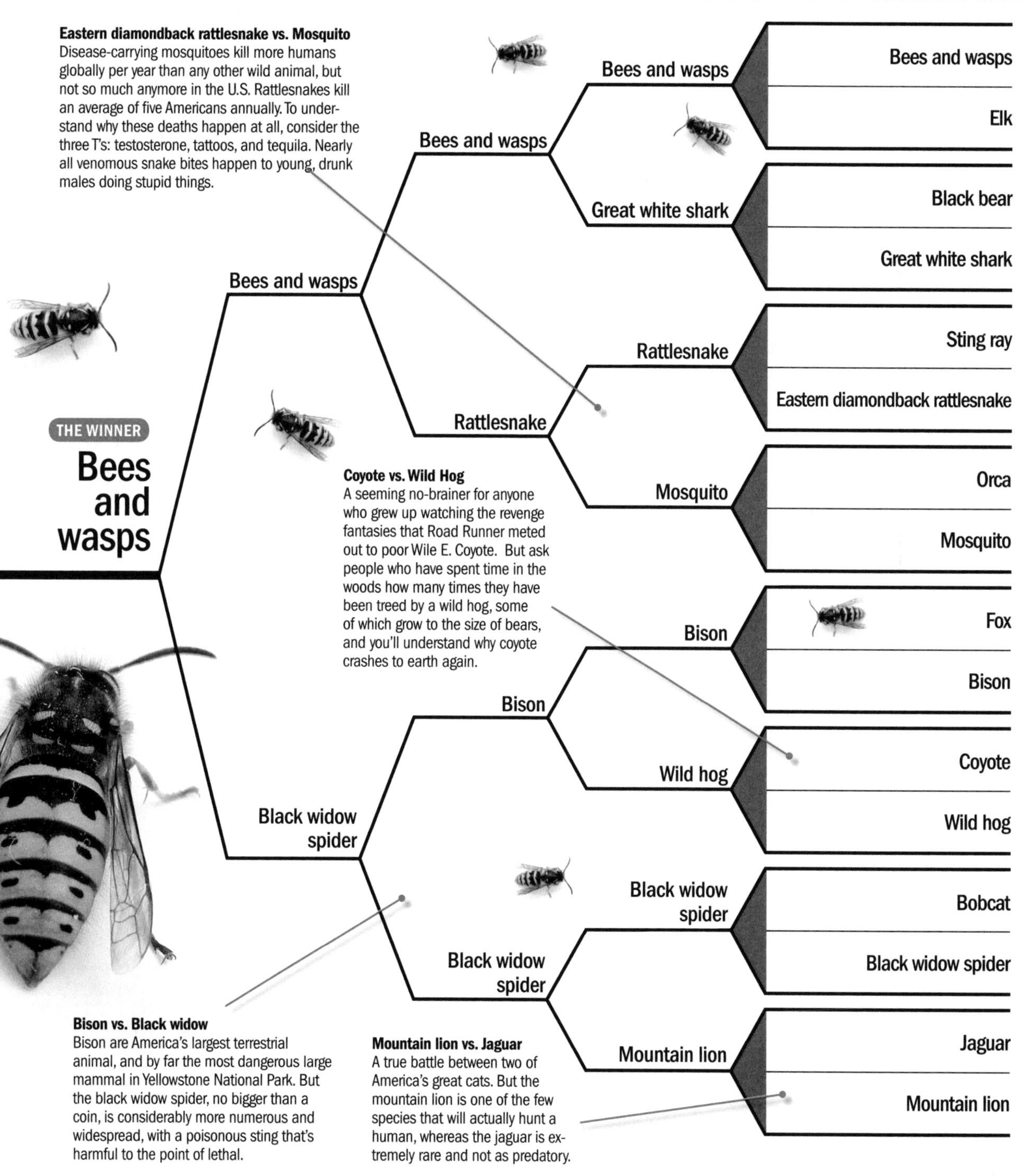

Bees and wasps
Elk
Black bear
Great white shark
Sting ray
Eastern diamondback rattlesnake
Orca
Mosquito
Fox
Bison
Coyote
Wild hog
Bobcat
Black widow spider
Jaguar
Mountain lion
Bees and wasps
Great white shark
Rattlesnake
Mosquito
Bison
Wild hog
Black widow spider
Mountain lion
Bees and wasps
Rattlesnake
Bison
Black widow spider
Bees and wasps
Black widow spider
THE WINNER
Bees and wasps

Eastern diamondback rattlesnake vs. Mosquito
Disease-carrying mosquitoes kill more humans globally per year than any other wild animal, but not so much anymore in the U.S. Rattlesnakes kill an average of five Americans annually. To understand why these deaths happen at all, consider the three T's: testosterone, tattoos, and tequila. Nearly all venomous snake bites happen to young, drunk males doing stupid things.

Coyote vs. Wild Hog
A seeming no-brainer for anyone who grew up watching the revenge fantasies that Road Runner meted out to poor Wile E. Coyote. But ask people who have spent time in the woods how many times they have been treed by a wild hog, some of which grow to the size of bears, and you'll understand why coyote crashes to earth again.

Bison vs. Black widow
Bison are America's largest terrestrial animal, and by far the most dangerous large mammal in Yellowstone National Park. But the black widow spider, no bigger than a coin, is considerably more numerous and widespread, with a poisonous sting that's harmful to the point of lethal.

Mountain lion vs. Jaguar
A true battle between two of America's great cats. But the mountain lion is one of the few species that will actually hunt a human, whereas the jaguar is extremely rare and not as predatory.

Best Ski Runs

By Steve Cohen

Steve Cohen is the former editor of *Ski* magazine. He has skied at more than 130 resorts on four continents and, unlike his Euro-sycophant peers, prefers North American skiing. Although his office desk's messiness doesn't show it, he adores the orderliness of American lift lines.

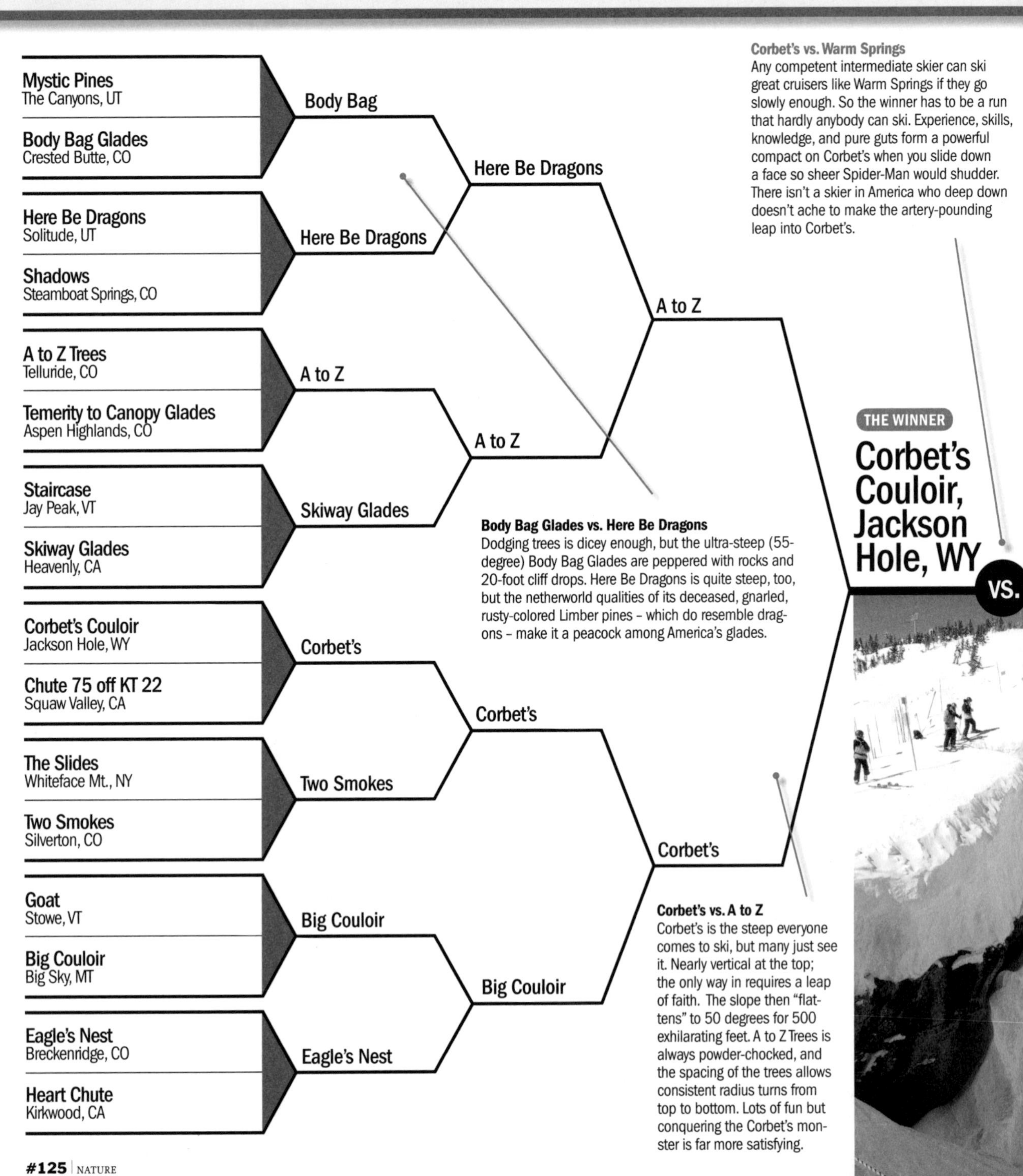

Mystic Pines
The Canyons, UT
Body Bag Glades
Crested Butte, CO
Here Be Dragons
Solitude, UT
Shadows
Steamboat Springs, CO
A to Z Trees
Telluride, CO
Temerity to Canopy Glades
Aspen Highlands, CO
Staircase
Jay Peak, VT
Skiway Glades
Heavenly, CA
Corbet's Couloir
Jackson Hole, WY
Chute 75 off KT 22
Squaw Valley, CA
The Slides
Whiteface Mt., NY
Two Smokes
Silverton, CO
Goat
Stowe, VT
Big Couloir
Big Sky, MT
Eagle's Nest
Breckenridge, CO
Heart Chute
Kirkwood, CA
Body Bag
Here Be Dragons
A to Z
Skiway Glades
Corbet's
Two Smokes
Big Couloir
Eagle's Nest
Here Be Dragons
A to Z
Corbet's
Big Couloir
A to Z
Corbet's
THE WINNER
Corbet's Couloir, Jackson Hole, WY
VS.

Corbet's vs. Warm Springs
Any competent intermediate skier can ski great cruisers like Warm Springs if they go slowly enough. So the winner has to be a run that hardly anybody can ski. Experience, skills, knowledge, and pure guts form a powerful compact on Corbet's when you slide down a face so sheer Spider-Man would shudder. There isn't a skier in America who deep down doesn't ache to make the artery-pounding leap into Corbet's.

Body Bag Glades vs. Here Be Dragons
Dodging trees is dicey enough, but the ultra-steep (55-degree) Body Bag Glades are peppered with rocks and 20-foot cliff drops. Here Be Dragons is quite steep, too, but the netherworld qualities of its deceased, gnarled, rusty-colored Limber pines – which do resemble dragons – make it a peacock among America's glades.

Corbet's vs. A to Z
Corbet's is the steep everyone comes to ski, but many just see it. Nearly vertical at the top; the only way in requires a leap of faith. The slope then "flattens" to 50 degrees for 500 exhilarating feet. A to Z Trees is always powder-chocked, and the spacing of the trees allows consistent radius turns from top to bottom. Lots of fun but conquering the Corbet's monster is far more satisfying.

SERIOUS SKIERS CARE MOST ABOUT THE TERRAIN that challenges them mentally and physically or lets them approach speeds that would get them pulled over on the Interstate. These desires are fulfilled on high-speed cruisers, moguls, glades, and steeps – ski runs that are defined by trees, rocks, or some other topographical feature. One rule is enforced here: no schlepping required. If you can't get off a lift and ski down without going up or sideways, it wasn't considered. Sure, that eliminates some great runs, but how do you rate oblivion?

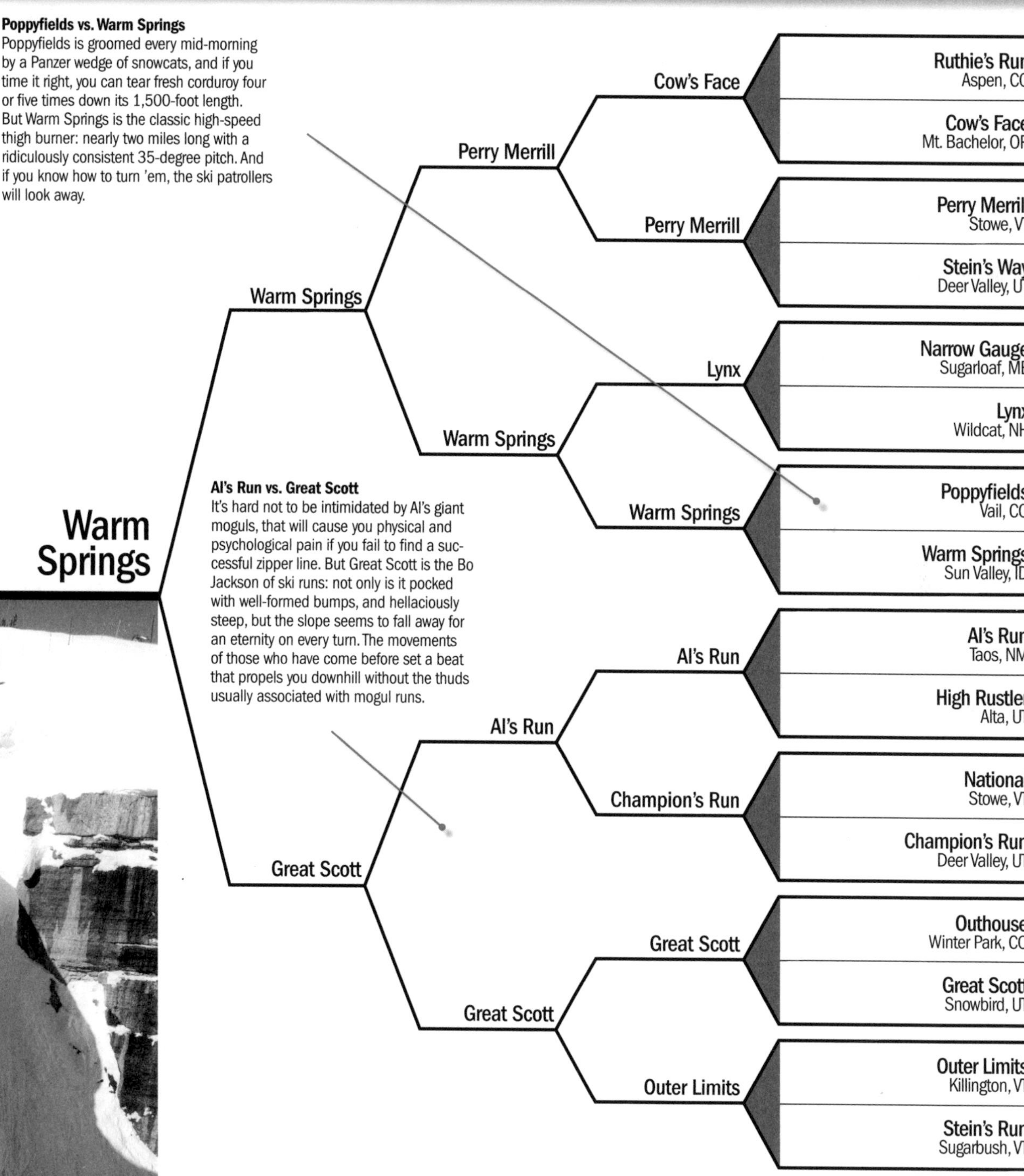
Ruthie's Run
Aspen, CO
Cow's Face
Mt. Bachelor, OR
Perry Merrill
Stowe, VT
Stein's Way
Deer Valley, UT
Narrow Gauge
Sugarloaf, ME
Lynx
Wildcat, NH
Poppyfields
Vail, CO
Warm Springs
Sun Valley, ID
Al's Run
Taos, NM
High Rustler
Alta, UT
National
Stowe, VT
Champion's Run
Deer Valley, UT
Outhouse
Winter Park, CO
Great Scott
Snowbird, UT
Outer Limits
Killington, VT
Stein's Run
Sugarbush, VT
Cow's Face
Perry Merrill
Lynx
Warm Springs
Al's Run
Champion's Run
Great Scott
Outer Limits
Perry Merrill
Warm Springs
Al's Run
Great Scott
Warm Springs
Great Scott
Warm Springs

Poppyfields vs. Warm Springs
Poppyfields is groomed every mid-morning by a Panzer wedge of snowcats, and if you time it right, you can tear fresh corduroy four or five times down its 1,500-foot length. But Warm Springs is the classic high-speed thigh burner: nearly two miles long with a ridiculously consistent 35-degree pitch. And if you know how to turn 'em, the ski patrollers will look away.

Al's Run vs. Great Scott
It's hard not to be intimidated by Al's giant moguls, that will cause you physical and psychological pain if you fail to find a successful zipper line. But Great Scott is the Bo Jackson of ski runs: not only is it pocked with well-formed bumps, and hellaciously steep, but the slope seems to fall away for an eternity on every turn. The movements of those who have come before set a beat that propels you downhill without the thuds usually associated with mogul runs.

Nothing but the Tooth

By James Hudson, D.M.D.

Dr. James Hudson has a private dental practice in New York City and serves as deputy chief forensic dentist for the city's office of Chief Medical Examiner. He, his wife, four children, and two dogs have a combined 244 teeth to care for daily.

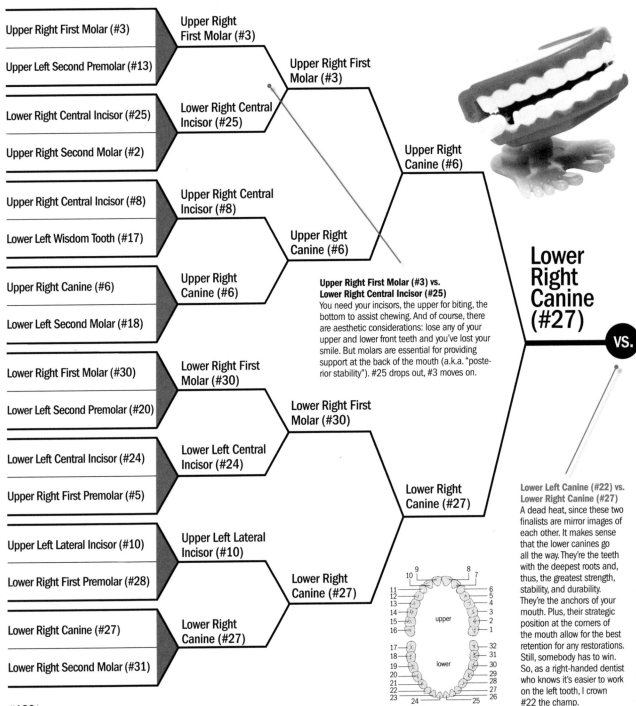

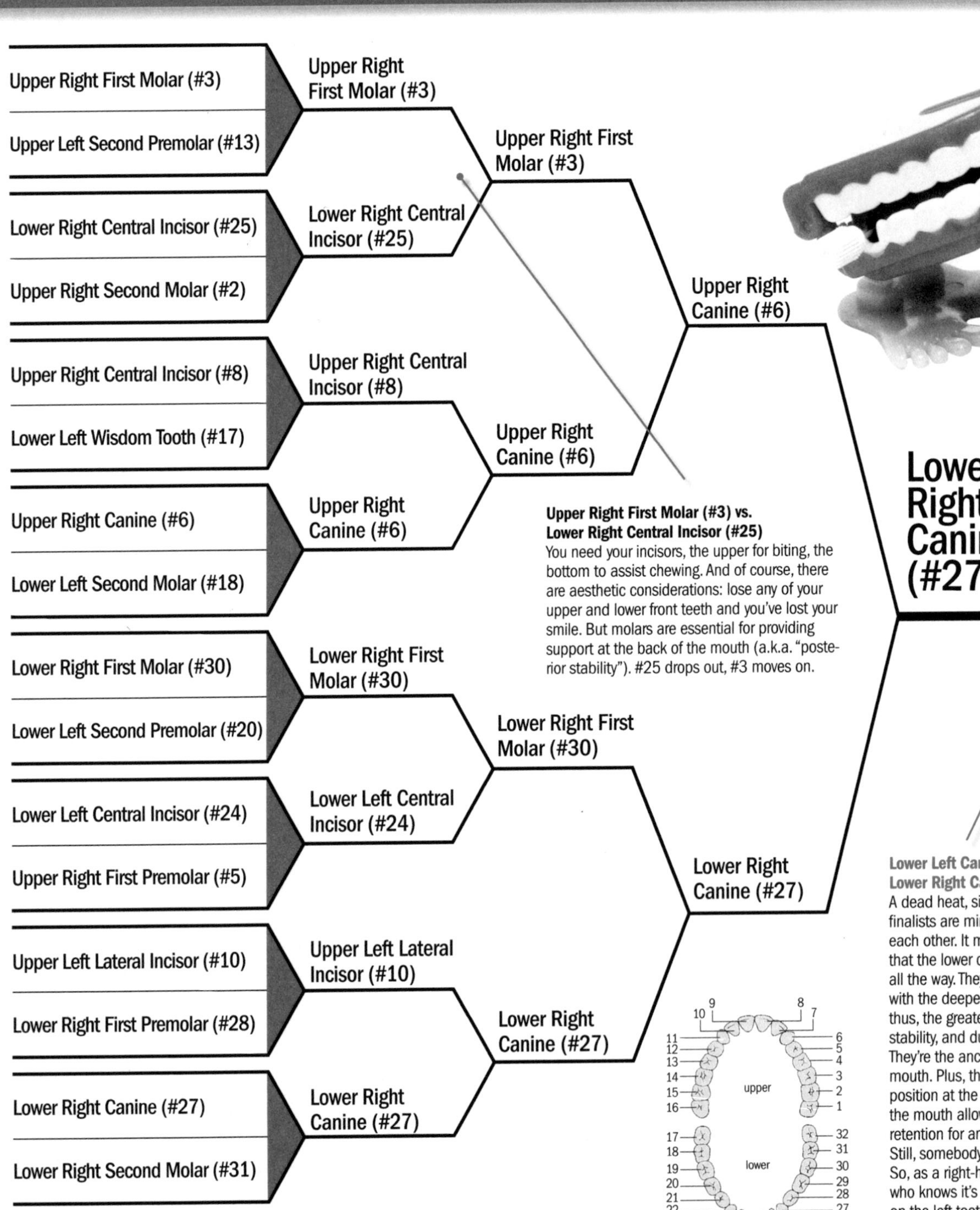
Upper Right First Molar (#3)
Upper Left Second Premolar (#13)
Lower Right Central Incisor (#25)
Upper Right Second Molar (#2)
Upper Right Central Incisor (#8)
Lower Left Wisdom Tooth (#17)
Upper Right Canine (#6)
Lower Left Second Molar (#18)
Lower Right First Molar (#30)
Lower Left Second Premolar (#20)
Lower Left Central Incisor (#24)
Upper Right First Premolar (#5)
Upper Left Lateral Incisor (#10)
Lower Right First Premolar (#28)
Lower Right Canine (#27)
Lower Right Second Molar (#31)
Upper Right First Molar (#3)
Lower Right Central Incisor (#25)
Upper Right Central Incisor (#8)
Upper Right Canine (#6)
Lower Right First Molar (#30)
Lower Left Central Incisor (#24)
Upper Left Lateral Incisor (#10)
Lower Right Canine (#27)
Upper Right First Molar (#3)
Upper Right Canine (#6)
Lower Right First Molar (#30)
Lower Right Canine (#27)
Upper Right Canine (#6)
Lower Right Canine (#27)
Lower Right Canine (#27)
VS.
upper
lower

Upper Right First Molar (#3) vs. Lower Right Central Incisor (#25)
You need your incisors, the upper for biting, the bottom to assist chewing. And of course, there are aesthetic considerations: lose any of your upper and lower front teeth and you've lost your smile. But molars are essential for providing support at the back of the mouth (a.k.a. "posterior stability"). #25 drops out, #3 moves on.

Lower Left Canine (#22) vs. Lower Right Canine (#27)
A dead heat, since these two finalists are mirror images of each other. It makes sense that the lower canines go all the way. They're the teeth with the deepest roots and, thus, the greatest strength, stability, and durability. They're the anchors of your mouth. Plus, their strategic position at the corners of the mouth allow for the best retention for any restorations. Still, somebody has to win. So, as a right-handed dentist who knows it's easier to work on the left tooth, I crown #22 the champ.

MOST OF US HAVE 32 TEETH, suggesting that the Intelligent Designer was the first bracketologist. But if you could keep only one tooth, which would it be? And what are your criteria? Aesthetics is important (as vanity is a prime motivator for seeking dental care). But there's no way that retaining only one tooth, or two or three for that matter, could ever look good. So functionality is important, too. Then there's the matter of whether that lone tooth can be a sound building block for future dental work that rebuilds a mouthful of teeth. Now, open your mouth please.

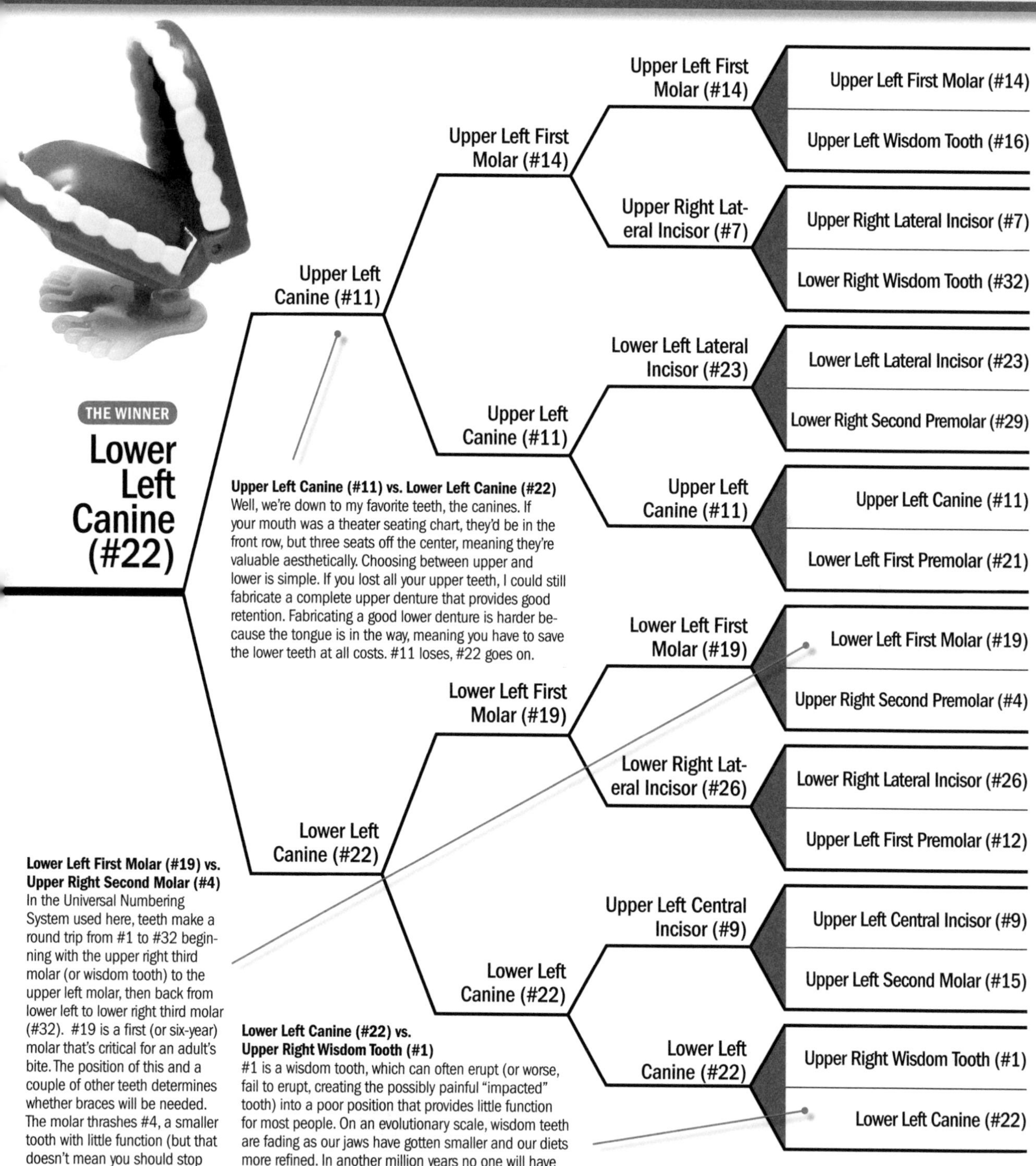

Upper Left First Molar (#14)
Upper Left Wisdom Tooth (#16)
Upper Right Lateral Incisor (#7)
Lower Right Wisdom Tooth (#32)
Lower Left Lateral Incisor (#23)
Lower Right Second Premolar (#29)
Upper Left Canine (#11)
Lower Left First Premolar (#21)
Lower Left First Molar (#19)
Upper Right Second Premolar (#4)
Lower Right Lateral Incisor (#26)
Upper Left First Premolar (#12)
Upper Left Central Incisor (#9)
Upper Left Second Molar (#15)
Upper Right Wisdom Tooth (#1)
Lower Left Canine (#22)
Upper Left First Molar (#14)
Upper Right Lateral Incisor (#7)
Lower Left Lateral Incisor (#23)
Upper Left Canine (#11)
Lower Left First Molar (#19)
Lower Right Lateral Incisor (#26)
Upper Left Central Incisor (#9)
Lower Left Canine (#22)
Upper Left First Molar (#14)
Upper Left Canine (#11)
Lower Left First Molar (#19)
Lower Left Canine (#22)
Upper Left Canine (#11)
Lower Left Canine (#22)
THE WINNER
Lower Left Canine (#22)

Upper Left Canine (#11) vs. Lower Left Canine (#22)
Well, we're down to my favorite teeth, the canines. If your mouth was a theater seating chart, they'd be in the front row, but three seats off the center, meaning they're valuable aesthetically. Choosing between upper and lower is simple. If you lost all your upper teeth, I could still fabricate a complete upper denture that provides good retention. Fabricating a good lower denture is harder because the tongue is in the way, meaning you have to save the lower teeth at all costs. #11 loses, #22 goes on.

Lower Left First Molar (#19) vs. Upper Right Second Molar (#4)
In the Universal Numbering System used here, teeth make a round trip from #1 to #32 beginning with the upper right third molar (or wisdom tooth) to the upper left molar, then back from lower left to lower right third molar (#32). #19 is a first (or six-year) molar that's critical for an adult's bite. The position of this and a couple of other teeth determines whether braces will be needed. The molar thrashes #4, a smaller tooth with little function (but that doesn't mean you should stop flossing or brushing around it).

Lower Left Canine (#22) vs. Upper Right Wisdom Tooth (#1)
#1 is a wisdom tooth, which can often erupt (or worse, fail to erupt, creating the possibly painful "impacted" tooth) into a poor position that provides little function for most people. On an evolutionary scale, wisdom teeth are fading as our jaws have gotten smaller and our diets more refined. In another million years no one will have them. The future champ advances.

Fish Tales

By Peter Kaminsky

Peter Kaminsky's many fishing books include *The Moon Pulled Up an Acre of Bass* and *The Flyfisherman's Guide to the Meaning of Life.*

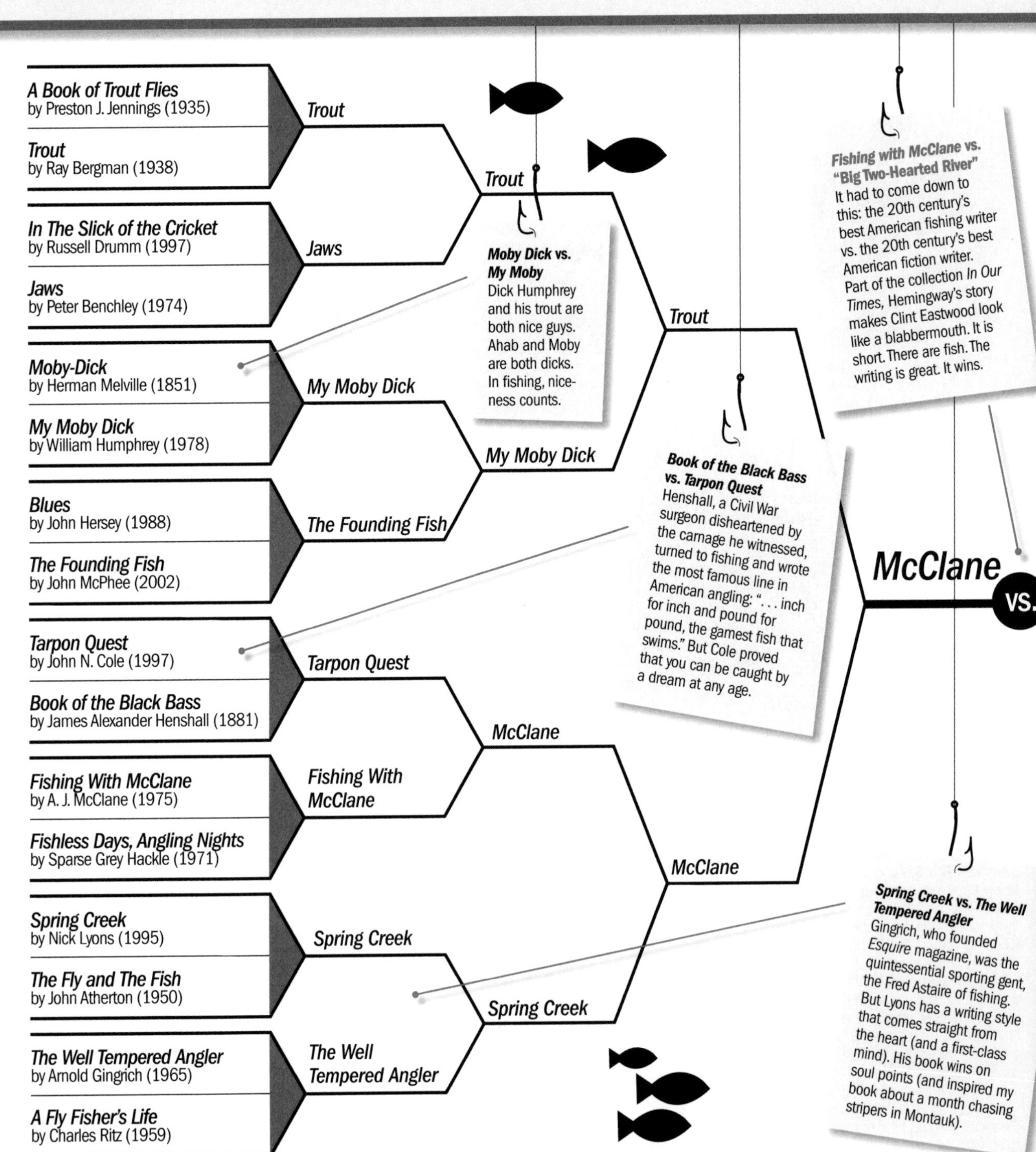

A Book of Trout Flies by Preston J. Jennings (1935)
Trout by Ray Bergman (1938)
In The Slick of the Cricket by Russell Drumm (1997)
Jaws by Peter Benchley (1974)
Moby-Dick by Herman Melville (1851)
My Moby Dick by William Humphrey (1978)
Blues by John Hersey (1988)
The Founding Fish by John McPhee (2002)
Tarpon Quest by John N. Cole (1997)
Book of the Black Bass by James Alexander Henshall (1881)
Fishing With McClane by A. J. McClane (1975)
Fishless Days, Angling Nights by Sparse Grey Hackle (1971)
Spring Creek by Nick Lyons (1995)
The Fly and The Fish by John Atherton (1950)
The Well Tempered Angler by Arnold Gingrich (1965)
A Fly Fisher's Life by Charles Ritz (1959)
Trout
Jaws
My Moby Dick
The Founding Fish
Tarpon Quest
Fishing With McClane
Spring Creek
The Well Tempered Angler
Trout
My Moby Dick
McClane
Spring Creek
Trout
McClane
McClane
vs.
Moby Dick vs. My Moby
Dick Humphrey and his trout are both nice guys. Ahab and Moby are both dicks. In fishing, niceness counts.
Fishing with McClane vs. "Big Two-Hearted River"
It had to come down to this: the 20th century's best American fishing writer vs. the 20th century's best American fiction writer. Part of the collection In Our Times, Hemingway's story makes Clint Eastwood look like a blabbermouth. It is short. There are fish. The writing is great. It wins.
Book of the Black Bass vs. Tarpon Quest
Henshall, a Civil War surgeon disheartened by the carnage he witnessed, turned to fishing and wrote the most famous line in American angling: ". . . inch for inch and pound for pound, the gamest fish that swims." But Cole proved that you can be caught by a dream at any age.
Spring Creek vs. The Well Tempered Angler
Gingrich, who founded Esquire magazine, was the quintessential sporting gent, the Fred Astaire of fishing. But Lyons has a writing style that comes straight from the heart (and a first-class mind). His book wins on soul points (and inspired my book about a month chasing stripers in Montauk).

WITH THE POSSIBLE EXCEPTION OF GOLF, FISHING IS THE WORDIEST SPORT. But not all words are created equal. Great fishing writing should enchant, seduce, excite, instruct, induce hunger, and most of all, make you want to grab a rod and get near water. Perhaps because it is a solitary sport (except on ESPN), the best fishing writing puts the reader in the soul and the world of the angler. In that sense, this bracket is about fishing as literature (and vice versa).

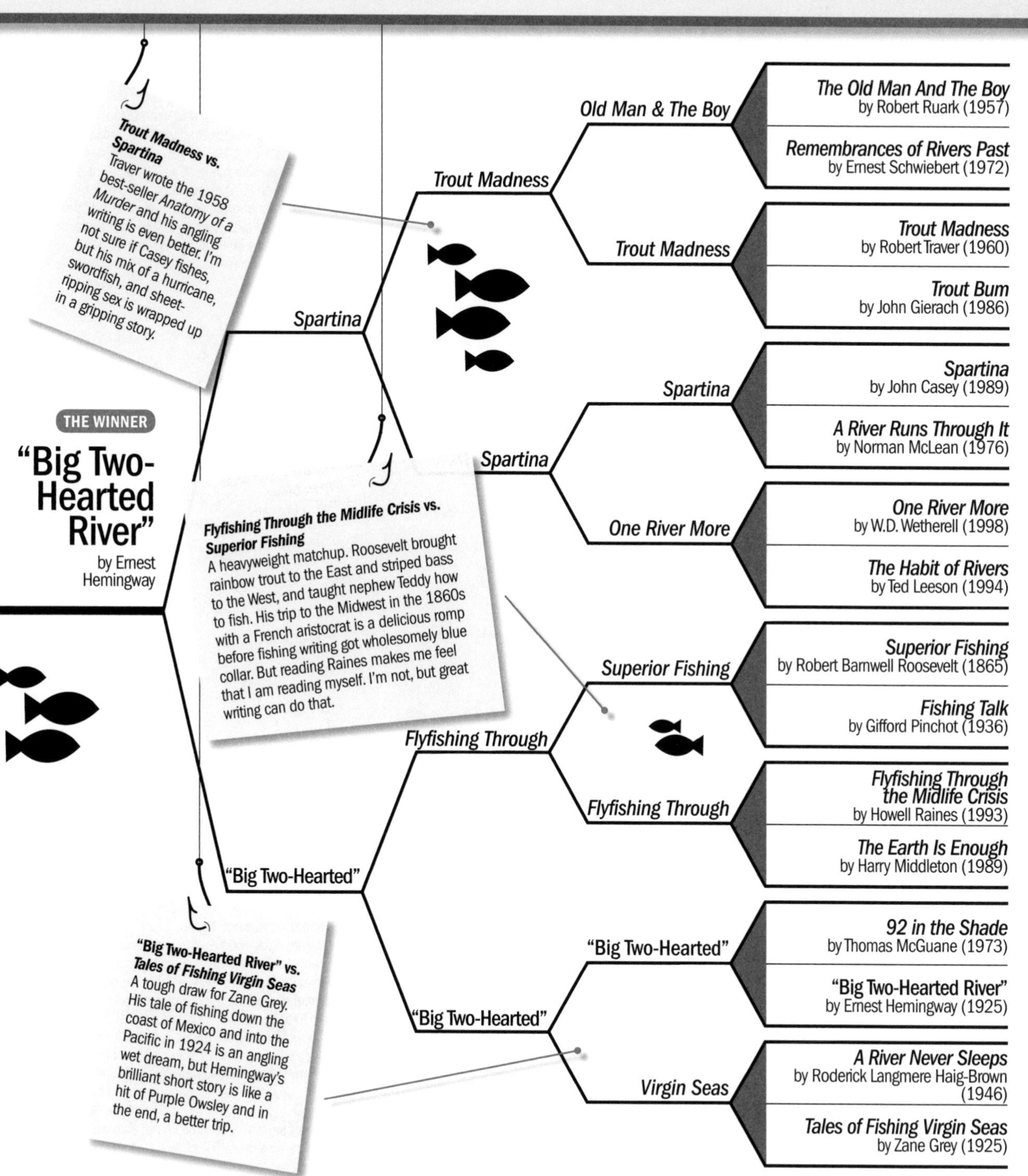

The Old Man And The Boy by Robert Ruark (1957)
Remembrances of Rivers Past by Ernest Schwiebert (1972)
Trout Madness by Robert Traver (1960)
Trout Bum by John Gierach (1986)
Spartina by John Casey (1989)
A River Runs Through It by Norman McLean (1976)
One River More by W.D. Wetherell (1998)
The Habit of Rivers by Ted Leeson (1994)
Superior Fishing by Robert Barnwell Roosevelt (1865)
Fishing Talk by Gifford Pinchot (1936)
Flyfishing Through the Midlife Crisis by Howell Raines (1993)
The Earth Is Enough by Harry Middleton (1989)
92 in the Shade by Thomas McGuane (1973)
"Big Two-Hearted River" by Ernest Hemingway (1925)
A River Never Sleeps by Roderick Langmere Haig-Brown (1946)
Tales of Fishing Virgin Seas by Zane Grey (1925)
Old Man & The Boy
Trout Madness
Spartina
One River More
Superior Fishing
Flyfishing Through
"Big Two-Hearted"
Virgin Seas
Trout Madness
Spartina
Flyfishing Through
"Big Two-Hearted"
Spartina
"Big Two-Hearted"
THE WINNER
"Big Two-Hearted River" by Ernest Hemingway
Trout Madness vs. Spartina
Traver wrote the 1958 best-seller Anatomy of a Murder and his angling writing is even better. I'm not sure if Casey fishes, but his mix of a hurricane, swordfish, and sheet-ripping sex is wrapped up in a gripping story.
Flyfishing Through the Midlife Crisis vs. Superior Fishing
A heavyweight matchup. Roosevelt brought rainbow trout to the East and striped bass to the West, and taught nephew Teddy how to fish. His trip to the Midwest in the 1860s with a French aristocrat is a delicious romp before fishing writing got wholesomely blue collar. But reading Raines makes me feel that I am reading myself. I'm not, but great writing can do that.
"Big Two-Hearted River" vs. Tales of Fishing Virgin Seas
A tough draw for Zane Grey. His tale of fishing down the coast of Mexico and into the Pacific in 1924 is an angling wet dream, but Hemingway's brilliant short story is like a hit of Purple Owsley and in the end, a better trip.

Energy Alternatives

By Gwyneth Cravens

Gwyneth Cravens is the author of *Power to Save the World: The Truth About Nuclear Energy.* She has published five novels. Her fiction and nonfiction have appeared in *Harper's* and *The New Yorker,* where she also worked as a fiction editor.

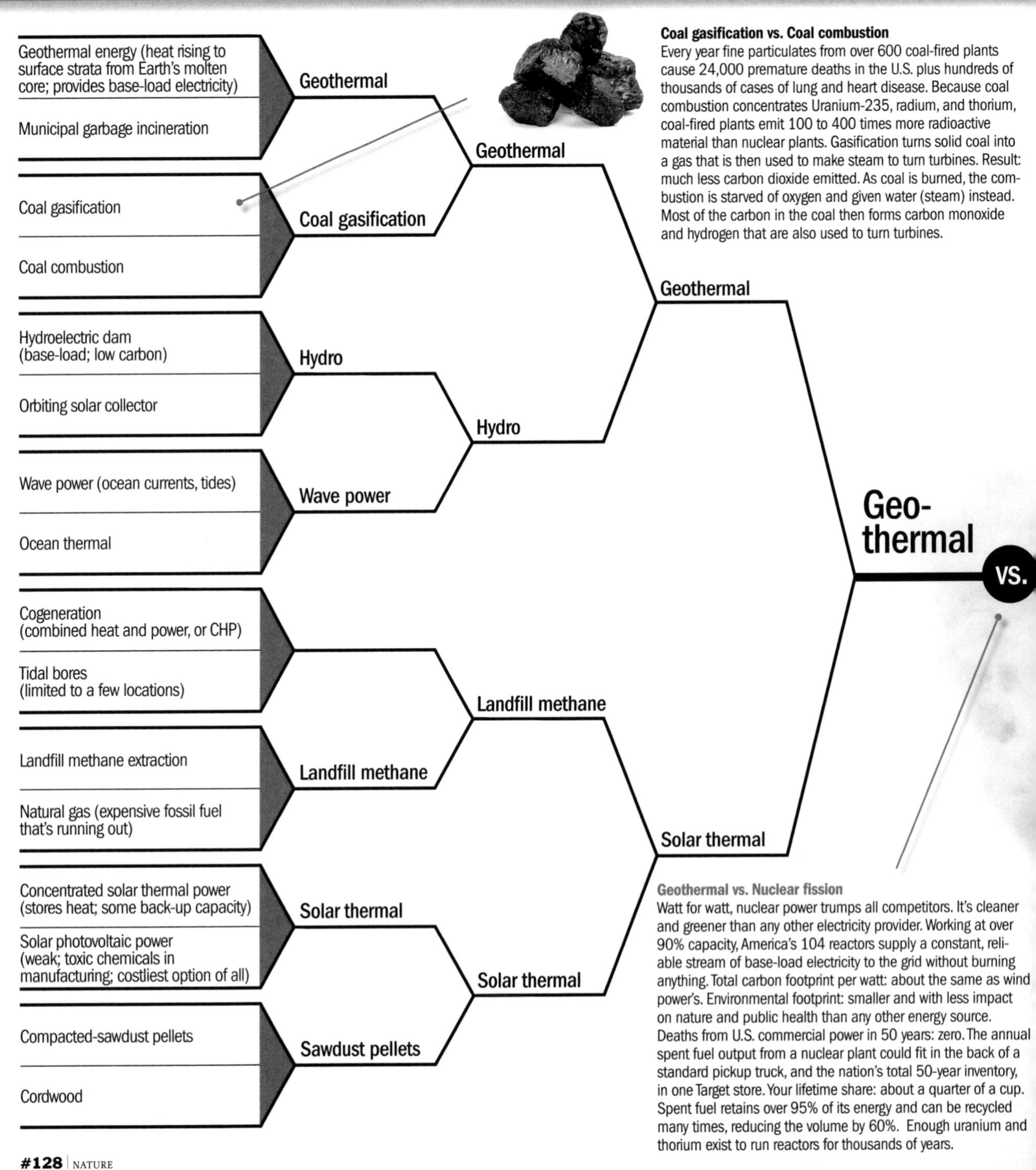
Geothermal energy (heat rising to surface strata from Earth's molten core; provides base-load electricity)
Municipal garbage incineration
Coal gasification
Coal combustion
Hydroelectric dam (base-load; low carbon)
Orbiting solar collector
Wave power (ocean currents, tides)
Ocean thermal
Cogeneration (combined heat and power, or CHP)
Tidal bores (limited to a few locations)
Landfill methane extraction
Natural gas (expensive fossil fuel that's running out)
Concentrated solar thermal power (stores heat; some back-up capacity)
Solar photovoltaic power (weak; toxic chemicals in manufacturing; costliest option of all)
Compacted-sawdust pellets
Cordwood
Geothermal
Coal gasification
Hydro
Wave power
Landfill methane
Solar thermal
Sawdust pellets
Geothermal
Hydro
Landfill methane
Solar thermal
Geothermal
Solar thermal
Geo-thermal
VS.

Coal gasification vs. Coal combustion

Every year fine particulates from over 600 coal-fired plants cause 24,000 premature deaths in the U.S. plus hundreds of thousands of cases of lung and heart disease. Because coal combustion concentrates Uranium-235, radium, and thorium, coal-fired plants emit 100 to 400 times more radioactive material than nuclear plants. Gasification turns solid coal into a gas that is then used to make steam to turn turbines. Result: much less carbon dioxide emitted. As coal is burned, the combustion is starved of oxygen and given water (steam) instead. Most of the carbon in the coal then forms carbon monoxide and hydrogen that are also used to turn turbines.

Geothermal vs. Nuclear fission

Watt for watt, nuclear power trumps all competitors. It's cleaner and greener than any other electricity provider. Working at over 90% capacity, America's 104 reactors supply a constant, reliable stream of base-load electricity to the grid without burning anything. Total carbon footprint per watt: about the same as wind power's. Environmental footprint: smaller and with less impact on nature and public health than any other energy source. Deaths from U.S. commercial power in 50 years: zero. The annual spent fuel output from a nuclear plant could fit in the back of a standard pickup truck, and the nation's total 50-year inventory, in one Target store. Your lifetime share: about a quarter of a cup. Spent fuel retains over 95% of its energy and can be recycled many times, reducing the volume by 60%. Enough uranium and thorium exist to run reactors for thousands of years.

FOR MILLENNIA, HUMANS HAVE FIGURED OUT HOW TO AVOID HARD WORK by exploiting the energy stored in other humans, animals, falling water, wind, wood, fossil fuels, and 70 years ago, the atomic nucleus. Fossil fuels – coal, oil, and gas – supply 73% of U.S. electricity, and their waste, which is stored in air, water, soil, and lungs, accounts for almost all human-caused greenhouse gases as well as toxic heavy metal and chemical pollution. But supplies are limited. What's the most efficient energy alternative that's also kind to our planet and health? Bracketology demands a single winner, but in reality there are many options.

Algae-produced fuels vs. Ethanol
To replace less than 1% of our gasoline consumption with ethanol requires about 5 million acres of land that might otherwise provide food for the hungry. In 2006 U.S. taxpayers spent $5.6 billion on ethanol production that reduced U.S. greenhouse gases by one-nineteenth of 1%. On the other hand, oil-producing micro-algae can be farmed in a nontoxic fashion – and cheaply provide about 20 to 80 times more biofuel per acre than corn or soybeans, which rely on petroleum-based fertilizers and pesticides. It would take an algae farm bigger than the state of Maryland to make all the gasoline the U.S. consumes. But can this much oil be extracted efficiently, and if so, by when?

Unobtainium vs. Hydrogen
Unobtainium is a term used by scientists to describe that mysterious energy source, substance, or device that's supposed to drive a space ship faster than light-speed, or provide power to a promising invention, or fill in the blanks of a newfangled energy scheme that looks great on paper but has yet to make it to the real world. In other words, it's fantasy – and loses.

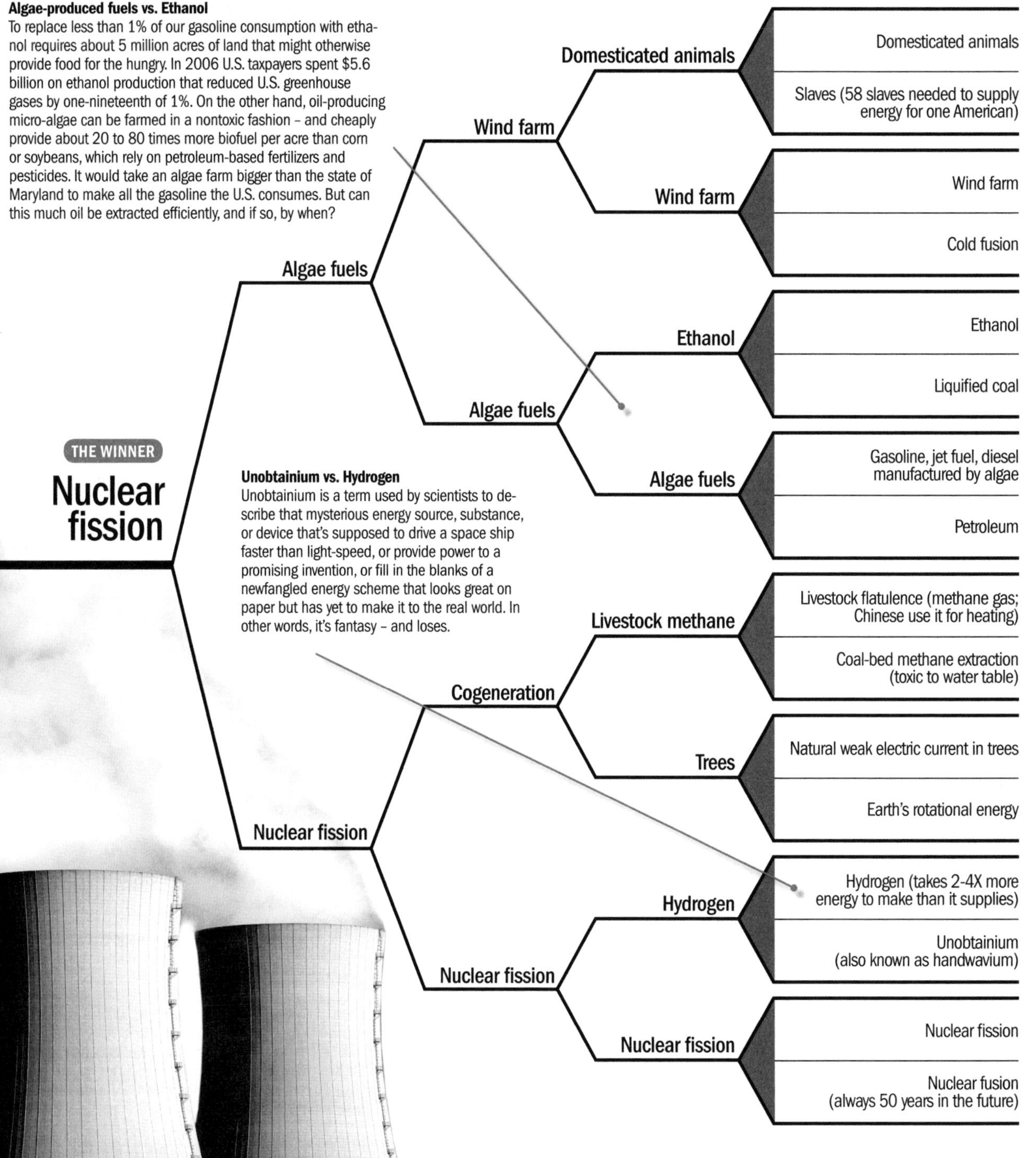

Domesticated animals
Slaves (58 slaves needed to supply energy for one American)
Wind farm
Cold fusion
Ethanol
Liquified coal
Gasoline, jet fuel, diesel manufactured by algae
Petroleum
Livestock flatulence (methane gas; Chinese use it for heating)
Coal-bed methane extraction (toxic to water table)
Natural weak electric current in trees
Earth's rotational energy
Hydrogen (takes 2-4X more energy to make than it supplies)
Unobtainium (also known as handwavium)
Nuclear fission
Nuclear fusion (always 50 years in the future)
Domesticated animals
Wind farm
Ethanol
Algae fuels
Livestock methane
Trees
Hydrogen
Nuclear fission
Wind farm
Algae fuels
Cogeneration
Nuclear fission
Algae fuels
Nuclear fission
THE WINNER
Nuclear fission

My Prized Feathers

By Luke Dempsey

Luke Dempsey is the author of *A Supremely Bad Idea: Three Mad Birders and Their Quest to See It All,* as well as "Paul Simon Songs" in *The Enlightened Bracketologist.*

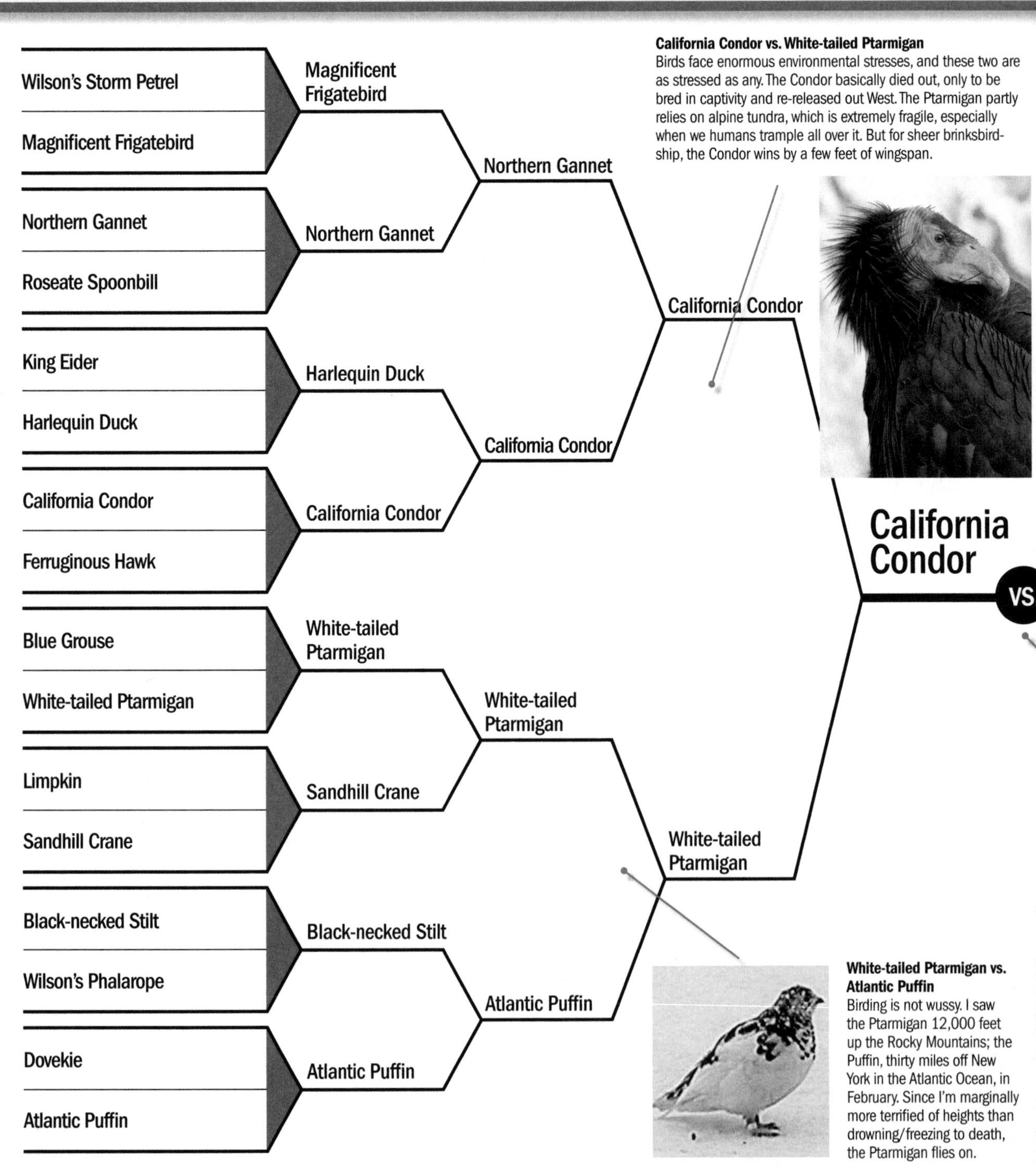

Wilson's Storm Petrel
Magnificent Frigatebird
Northern Gannet
Roseate Spoonbill
King Eider
Harlequin Duck
California Condor
Ferruginous Hawk
Blue Grouse
White-tailed Ptarmigan
Limpkin
Sandhill Crane
Black-necked Stilt
Wilson's Phalarope
Dovekie
Atlantic Puffin
Magnificent Frigatebird
Northern Gannet
Harlequin Duck
California Condor
White-tailed Ptarmigan
Sandhill Crane
Black-necked Stilt
Atlantic Puffin
Northern Gannet
California Condor
White-tailed Ptarmigan
Atlantic Puffin
California Condor
White-tailed Ptarmigan
California Condor
VS.

California Condor vs. White-tailed Ptarmigan
Birds face enormous environmental stresses, and these two are as stressed as any. The Condor basically died out, only to be bred in captivity and re-released out West. The Ptarmigan partly relies on alpine tundra, which is extremely fragile, especially when we humans trample all over it. But for sheer brinksbirdship, the Condor wins by a few feet of wingspan.

White-tailed Ptarmigan vs. Atlantic Puffin
Birding is not wussy. I saw the Ptarmigan 12,000 feet up the Rocky Mountains; the Puffin, thirty miles off New York in the Atlantic Ocean, in February. Since I'm marginally more terrified of heights than drowning/freezing to death, the Ptarmigan flies on.

LONG AGO I KNEW NOTHING ABOUT BIRDS. Then I started looking, and I haven't looked back. If I could turn back time, I would make a list of all the birds in North America that I must see. The list would include the beautiful, the hard to find, the endangered – and could only make sense if I knew something about birds, as I do now. This bracket is the list I would have made if I knew then what I know now. For the record, I've "gotten" all the birds here except the two finalists. One of them is barely alive; the other, so dazzling it makes your eyes hurt. (Or will, if I ever see it. That's why we bird.)

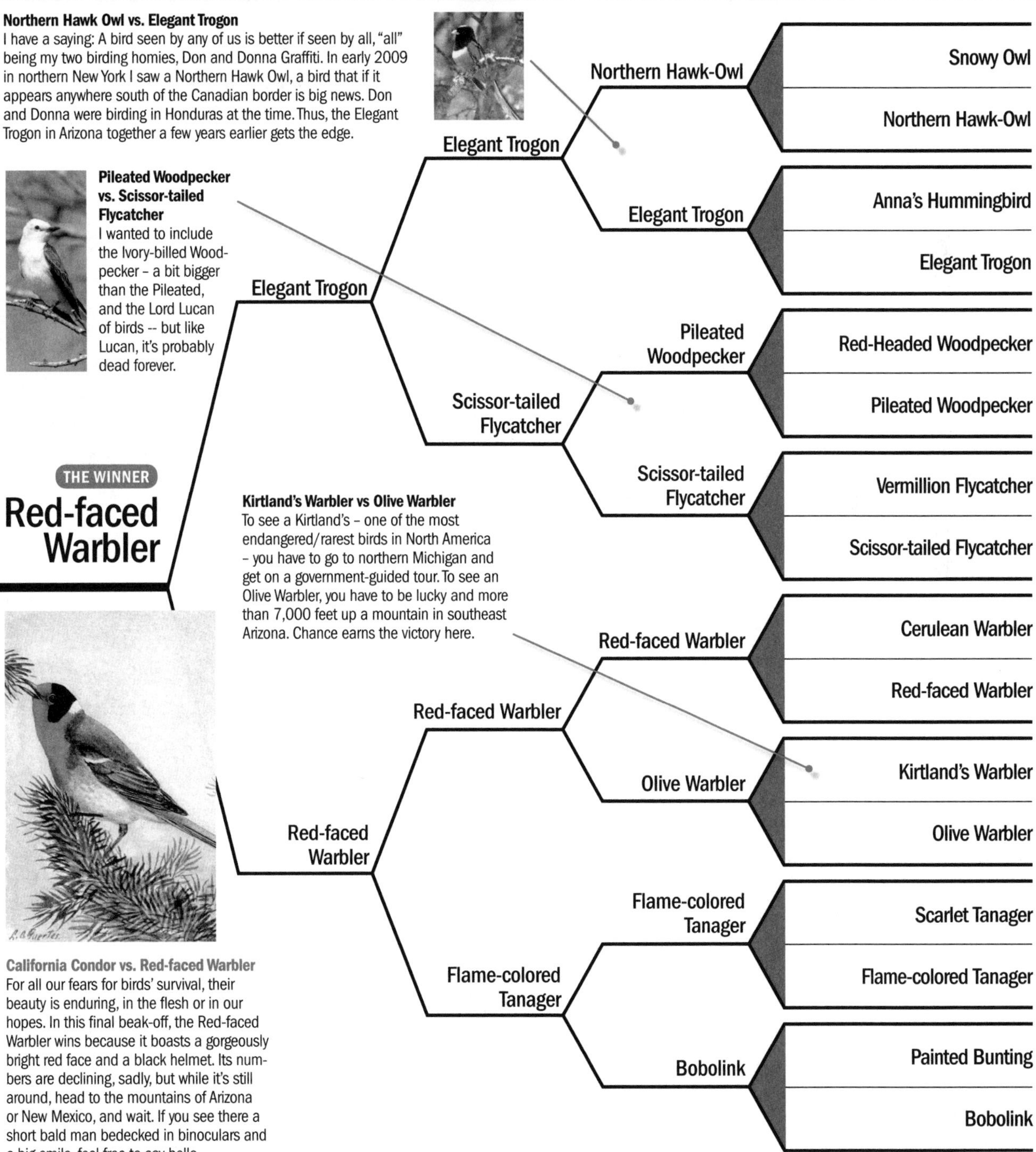

Snowy Owl
Northern Hawk-Owl
Anna's Hummingbird
Elegant Trogon
Red-Headed Woodpecker
Pileated Woodpecker
Vermillion Flycatcher
Scissor-tailed Flycatcher
Cerulean Warbler
Red-faced Warbler
Kirtland's Warbler
Olive Warbler
Scarlet Tanager
Flame-colored Tanager
Painted Bunting
Bobolink
Northern Hawk-Owl
Elegant Trogon
Pileated Woodpecker
Scissor-tailed Flycatcher
Red-faced Warbler
Olive Warbler
Flame-colored Tanager
Bobolink
Elegant Trogon
Scissor-tailed Flycatcher
Red-faced Warbler
Flame-colored Tanager
Elegant Trogon
Red-faced Warbler
THE WINNER
Red-faced Warbler

Northern Hawk Owl vs. Elegant Trogon
I have a saying: A bird seen by any of us is better if seen by all, "all" being my two birding homies, Don and Donna Graffiti. In early 2009 in northern New York I saw a Northern Hawk Owl, a bird that if it appears anywhere south of the Canadian border is big news. Don and Donna were birding in Honduras at the time. Thus, the Elegant Trogon in Arizona together a few years earlier gets the edge.

Pileated Woodpecker vs. Scissor-tailed Flycatcher
I wanted to include the Ivory-billed Woodpecker – a bit bigger than the Pileated, and the Lord Lucan of birds -- but like Lucan, it's probably dead forever.

Kirtland's Warbler vs Olive Warbler
To see a Kirtland's – one of the most endangered/rarest birds in North America – you have to go to northern Michigan and get on a government-guided tour. To see an Olive Warbler, you have to be lucky and more than 7,000 feet up a mountain in southeast Arizona. Chance earns the victory here.

California Condor vs. Red-faced Warbler
For all our fears for birds' survival, their beauty is enduring, in the flesh or in our hopes. In this final beak-off, the Red-faced Warbler wins because it boasts a gorgeously bright red face and a black helmet. Its numbers are declining, sadly, but while it's still around, head to the mountains of Arizona or New Mexico, and wait. If you see there a short bald man bedecked in binoculars and a big smile, feel free to say hello.

Looking Younger

By David J. Leffell, M.D.

Dr. David J. Leffell is the David Paige Smith Professor of Dermatology & Surgery at the Yale School of Medicine and author of *Total Skin.*

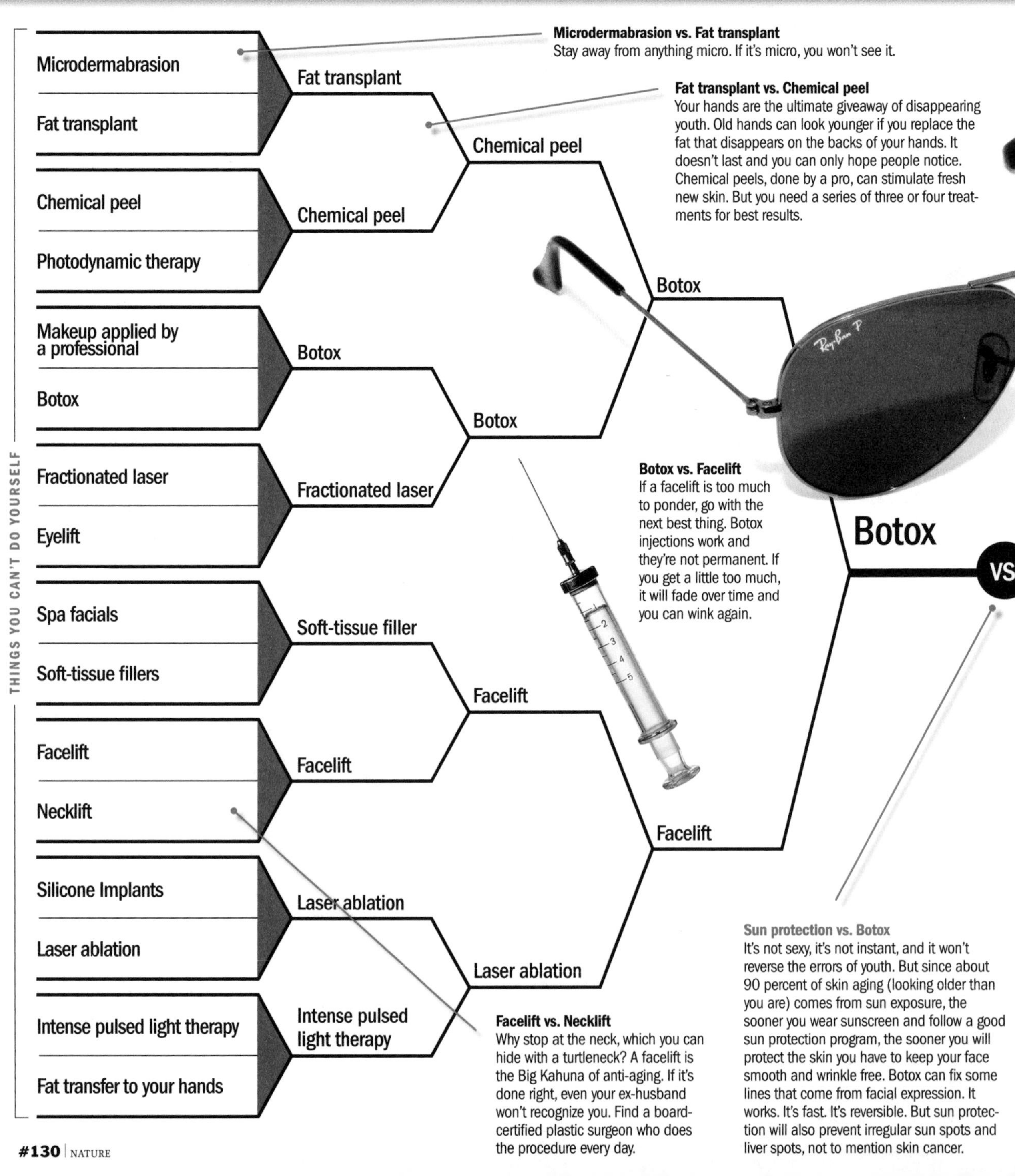
THINGS YOU CAN'T DO YOURSELF
Microdermabrasion
Fat transplant
Chemical peel
Photodynamic therapy
Makeup applied by a professional
Botox
Fractionated laser
Eyelift
Spa facials
Soft-tissue fillers
Facelift
Necklift
Silicone Implants
Laser ablation
Intense pulsed light therapy
Fat transfer to your hands
Fat transplant
Chemical peel
Botox
Fractionated laser
Soft-tissue filler
Facelift
Laser ablation
Intense pulsed light therapy
Chemical peel
Botox
Facelift
Laser ablation
Botox
Facelift
Botox
VS.

Microdermabrasion vs. Fat transplant
Stay away from anything micro. If it's micro, you won't see it.

Fat transplant vs. Chemical peel
Your hands are the ultimate giveaway of disappearing youth. Old hands can look younger if you replace the fat that disappears on the backs of your hands. It doesn't last and you can only hope people notice. Chemical peels, done by a pro, can stimulate fresh new skin. But you need a series of three or four treatments for best results.

Botox vs. Facelift
If a facelift is too much to ponder, go with the next best thing. Botox injections work and they're not permanent. If you get a little too much, it will fade over time and you can wink again.

Facelift vs. Necklift
Why stop at the neck, which you can hide with a turtleneck? A facelift is the Big Kahuna of anti-aging. If it's done right, even your ex-husband won't recognize you. Find a board-certified plastic surgeon who does the procedure every day.

Sun protection vs. Botox
It's not sexy, it's not instant, and it won't reverse the errors of youth. But since about 90 percent of skin aging (looking older than you are) comes from sun exposure, the sooner you wear sunscreen and follow a good sun protection program, the sooner you will protect the skin you have to keep your face smooth and wrinkle free. Botox can fix some lines that come from facial expression. It works. It's fast. It's reversible. But sun protection will also prevent irregular sun spots and liver spots, not to mention skin cancer.

THE DESIRE FOR IMMORTALITY is followed closely by the desire to appear immortal, to look young as the calendar pages peel off and fly away. More than $30 billion is spent in the United States annually on potions, creams, pills, and every manner of device and insertable creation – all intended to make you look younger than you are. Most of the products should be tossed into the closet where the "Emperor's New Clothes" hang, but some things can make a big difference, whether you do them to yourself or let others do them to you.

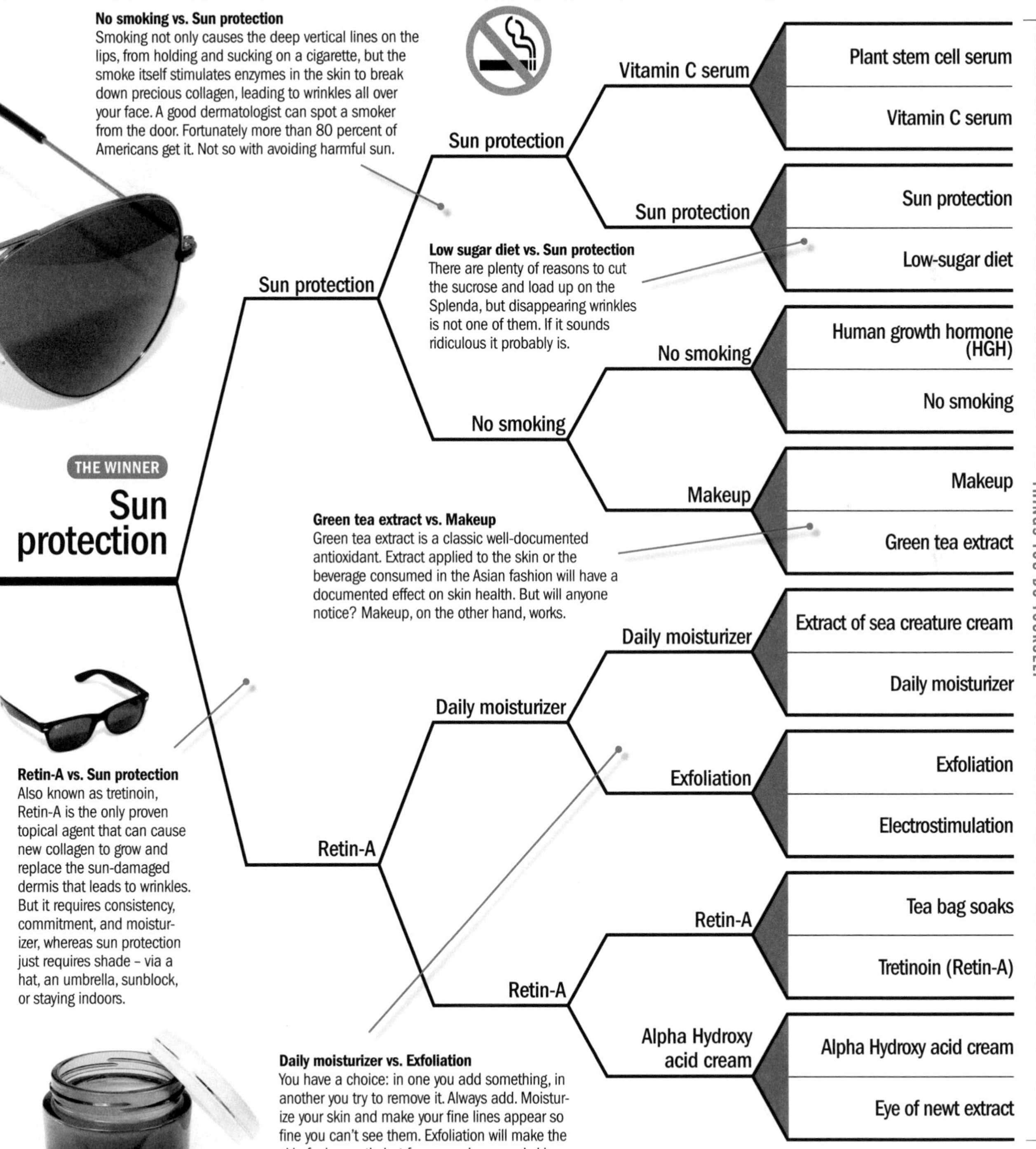

Plant stem cell serum
Vitamin C serum
Sun protection
Low-sugar diet
Human growth hormone (HGH)
No smoking
Makeup
Green tea extract
Extract of sea creature cream
Daily moisturizer
Exfoliation
Electrostimulation
Tea bag soaks
Tretinoin (Retin-A)
Alpha Hydroxy acid cream
Eye of newt extract
Vitamin C serum
Sun protection
No smoking
Makeup
Daily moisturizer
Exfoliation
Retin-A
Alpha Hydroxy acid cream
Sun protection
No smoking
Daily moisturizer
Retin-A
Sun protection
Retin-A
THE WINNER
Sun protection
THINGS YOU DO YOURSELF

No smoking vs. Sun protection
Smoking not only causes the deep vertical lines on the lips, from holding and sucking on a cigarette, but the smoke itself stimulates enzymes in the skin to break down precious collagen, leading to wrinkles all over your face. A good dermatologist can spot a smoker from the door. Fortunately more than 80 percent of Americans get it. Not so with avoiding harmful sun.

Low sugar diet vs. Sun protection
There are plenty of reasons to cut the sucrose and load up on the Splenda, but disappearing wrinkles is not one of them. If it sounds ridiculous it probably is.

Green tea extract vs. Makeup
Green tea extract is a classic well-documented antioxidant. Extract applied to the skin or the beverage consumed in the Asian fashion will have a documented effect on skin health. But will anyone notice? Makeup, on the other hand, works.

Retin-A vs. Sun protection
Also known as tretinoin, Retin-A is the only proven topical agent that can cause new collagen to grow and replace the sun-damaged dermis that leads to wrinkles. But it requires consistency, commitment, and moisturizer, whereas sun protection just requires shade – via a hat, an umbrella, sunblock, or staying indoors.

Daily moisturizer vs. Exfoliation
You have a choice: in one you add something, in another you try to remove it. Always add. Moisturize your skin and make your fine lines appear so fine you can't see them. Exfoliation will make the skin feel smooth, but for convenience and skin health, daily moisturizing is the way to go.

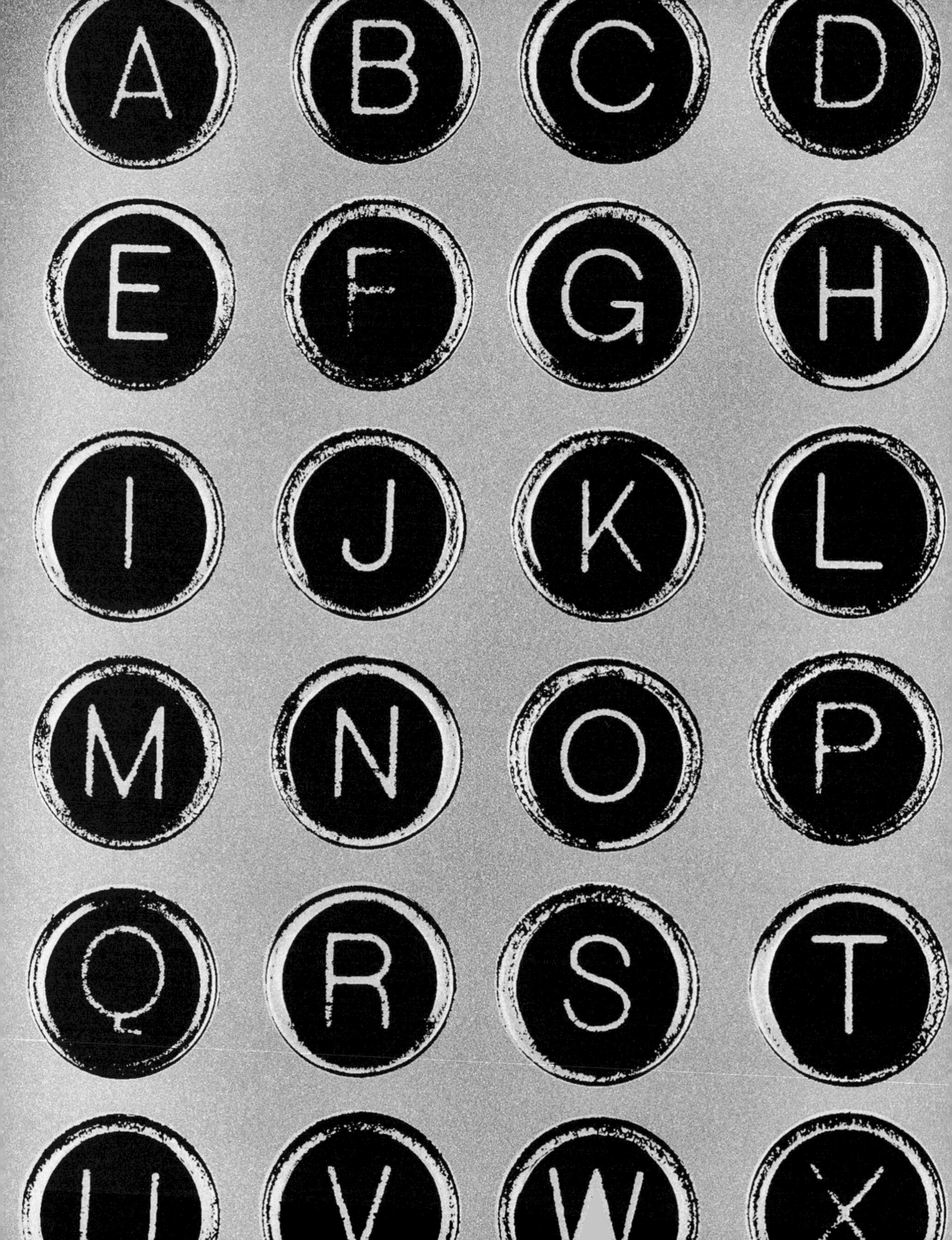
A
B
C
D
E
F
G
H
I
J
K
L
M
N
O
P
Q
R
S
T
U
V
W
X

WORDS

Fatherly Advice *by Jancee Dunn* 131
Motherly Advice *by Mark Reiter* 132
Acronyms *by Stefan Fatsis* 133
Lazy Wit *by Adi Ignatius* 134
Texas Sayings *by Anne Dingus* 135
Seductive Foreign Accents *by Asif Eydohno* 136
Yogi Berra Wisdom *by Dave Kaplan* 137
Fortune Cookies *by Jennifer 8. Lee* 138
All-Purpose Banalities *by Joe Queenan* 139
Deadly Sins of Emailing *by David Shipley and Will Schwalbe* 140
Politically Correct Terms *by Henry Beard and Christopher Cerf* 141
Woody Allen Wisdom *by Eric Lax* 142

Fatherly Advice

By Jancee Dunn

Jancee Dunn writes for the *New York Times*, *Vogue*, and *O, The Oprah Magazine*. Her third book is an essay collection, *Why Is My Mother Getting a Tattoo?*

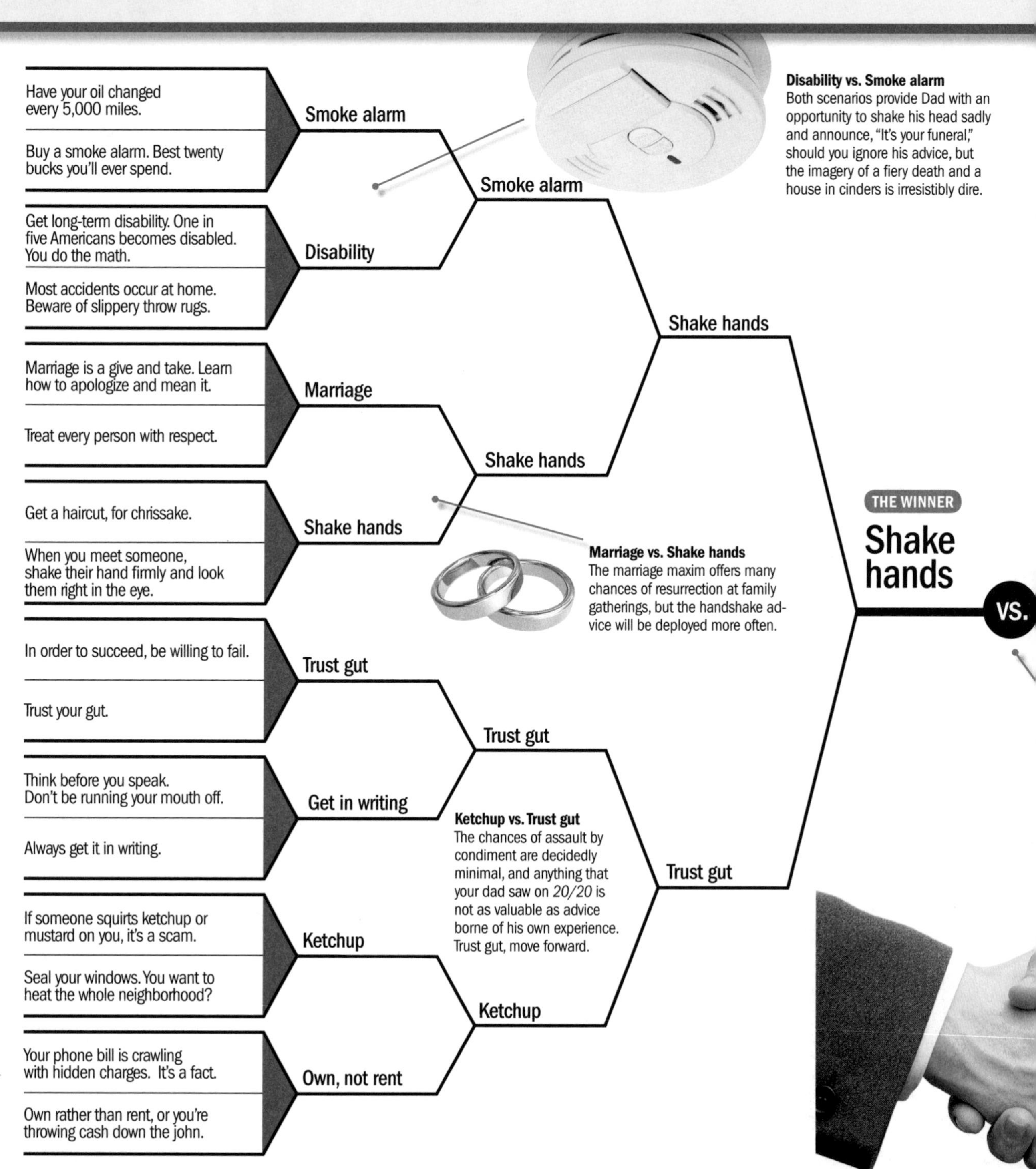
Have your oil changed every 5,000 miles.
Buy a smoke alarm. Best twenty bucks you'll ever spend.
Get long-term disability. One in five Americans becomes disabled. You do the math.
Most accidents occur at home. Beware of slippery throw rugs.
Marriage is a give and take. Learn how to apologize and mean it.
Treat every person with respect.
Get a haircut, for chrissake.
When you meet someone, shake their hand firmly and look them right in the eye.
In order to succeed, be willing to fail.
Trust your gut.
Think before you speak. Don't be running your mouth off.
Always get it in writing.
If someone squirts ketchup or mustard on you, it's a scam.
Seal your windows. You want to heat the whole neighborhood?
Your phone bill is crawling with hidden charges. It's a fact.
Own rather than rent, or you're throwing cash down the john.
Smoke alarm
Disability
Marriage
Shake hands
Trust gut
Get in writing
Ketchup
Own, not rent
Smoke alarm
Shake hands
Trust gut
Ketchup
Shake hands
Trust gut
THE WINNER
Shake hands
VS.

Disability vs. Smoke alarm
Both scenarios provide Dad with an opportunity to shake his head sadly and announce, "It's your funeral," should you ignore his advice, but the imagery of a fiery death and a house in cinders is irresistibly dire.

Marriage vs. Shake hands
The marriage maxim offers many chances of resurrection at family gatherings, but the handshake advice will be deployed more often.

Ketchup vs. Trust gut
The chances of assault by condiment are decidedly minimal, and anything that your dad saw on *20/20* is not as valuable as advice borne of his own experience. Trust gut, move forward.

I'VE NEVER HAD AN EXTENDED CONVERSATION WITH MY DAD that didn't end on some sort of teachable moment. Like many fathers, he just couldn't help himself: solicited or not, I was going to learn something. Over the years I've found that standard-issue Dad Wisdom contains one of three elements: preparedness (advice on financial planning, all forms of insurance, termite control), paranoia (potential health hazards, pyramid schemes, identity theft), and personal conduct (your word is your bond.)

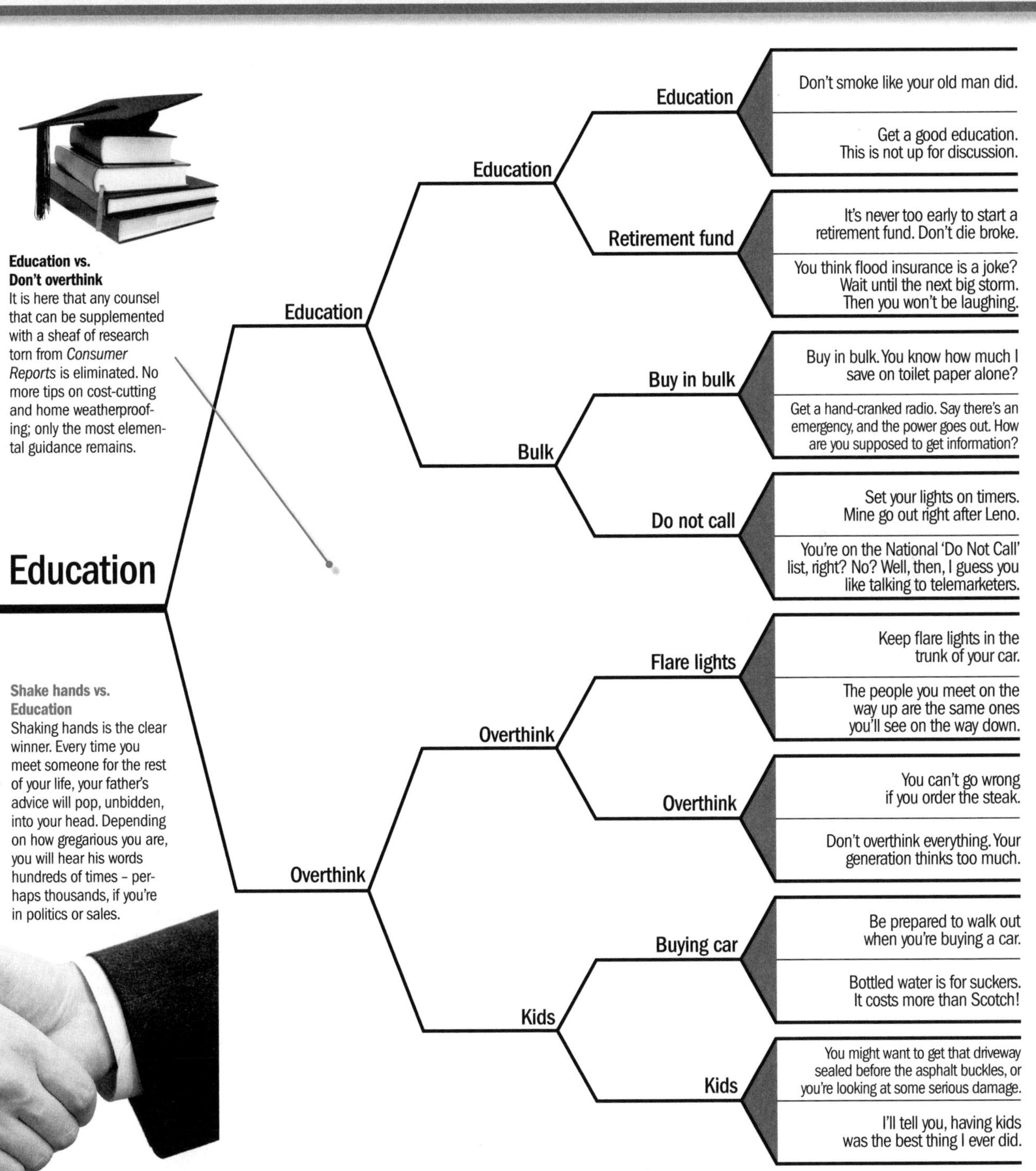
Don't smoke like your old man did.
Get a good education. This is not up for discussion.
It's never too early to start a retirement fund. Don't die broke.
You think flood insurance is a joke? Wait until the next big storm. Then you won't be laughing.
Buy in bulk. You know how much I save on toilet paper alone?
Get a hand-cranked radio. Say there's an emergency, and the power goes out. How are you supposed to get information?
Set your lights on timers. Mine go out right after Leno.
You're on the National 'Do Not Call' list, right? No? Well, then, I guess you like talking to telemarketers.
Keep flare lights in the trunk of your car.
The people you meet on the way up are the same ones you'll see on the way down.
You can't go wrong if you order the steak.
Don't overthink everything. Your generation thinks too much.
Be prepared to walk out when you're buying a car.
Bottled water is for suckers. It costs more than Scotch!
You might want to get that driveway sealed before the asphalt buckles, or you're looking at some serious damage.
I'll tell you, having kids was the best thing I ever did.
Education
Retirement fund
Buy in bulk
Do not call
Flare lights
Overthink
Buying car
Kids
Education
Bulk
Overthink
Kids
Education
Overthink
Education

Education vs. Don't overthink
It is here that any counsel that can be supplemented with a sheaf of research torn from *Consumer Reports* is eliminated. No more tips on cost-cutting and home weatherproofing; only the most elemental guidance remains.

Shake hands vs. Education
Shaking hands is the clear winner. Every time you meet someone for the rest of your life, your father's advice will pop, unbidden, into your head. Depending on how gregarious you are, you will hear his words hundreds of times – perhaps thousands, if you're in politics or sales.

Motherly Advice

By Mark Reiter

Mark Reiter, the co-editor of this book, has a mother who has very interesting theories about sleep, electric typewriters, QuickBooks, and automobiles painted red.

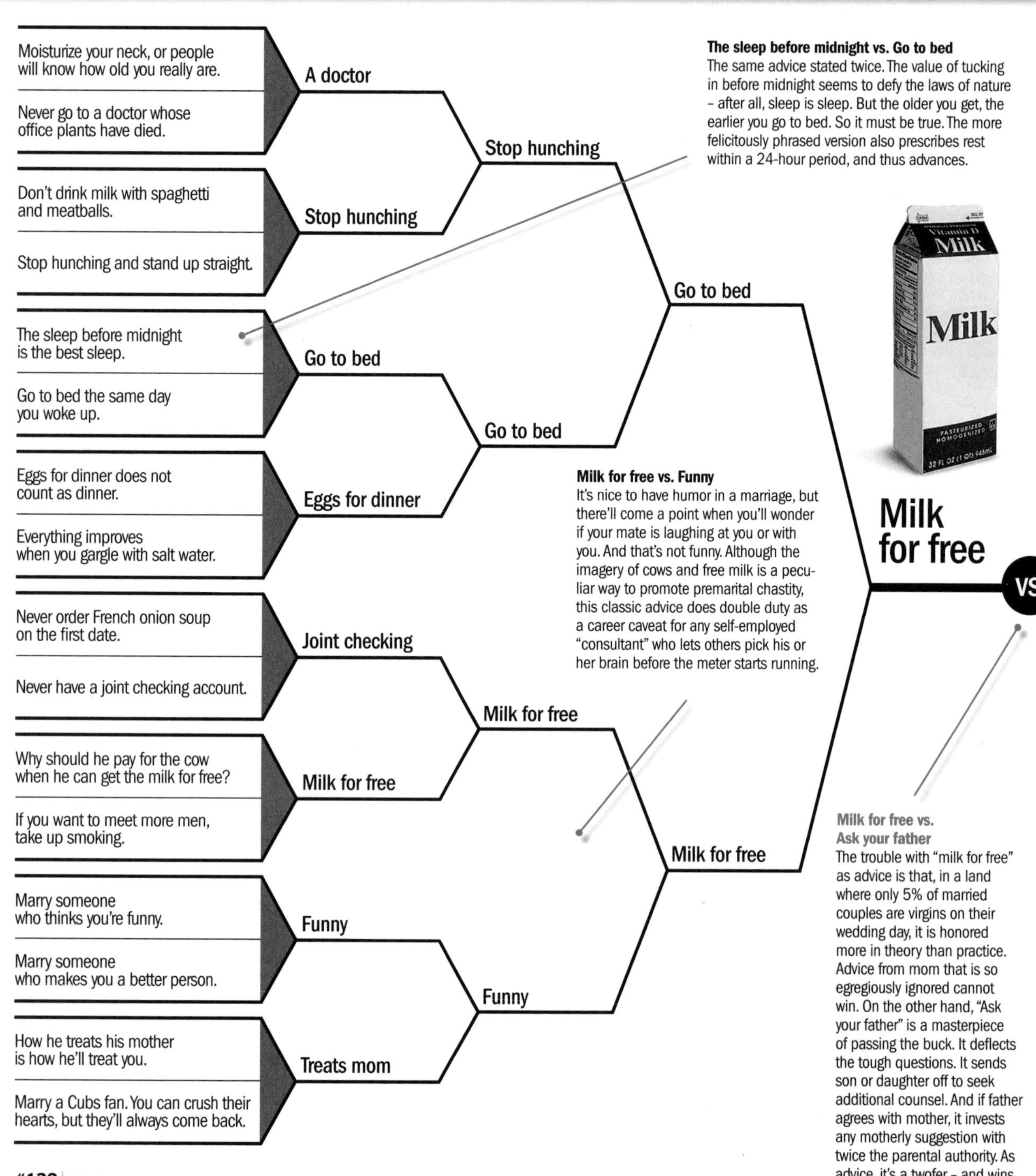

Moisturize your neck, or people will know how old you really are.
Never go to a doctor whose office plants have died.
Don't drink milk with spaghetti and meatballs.
Stop hunching and stand up straight.
The sleep before midnight is the best sleep.
Go to bed the same day you woke up.
Eggs for dinner does not count as dinner.
Everything improves when you gargle with salt water.
Never order French onion soup on the first date.
Never have a joint checking account.
Why should he pay for the cow when he can get the milk for free?
If you want to meet more men, take up smoking.
Marry someone who thinks you're funny.
Marry someone who makes you a better person.
How he treats his mother is how he'll treat you.
Marry a Cubs fan. You can crush their hearts, but they'll always come back.
A doctor
Stop hunching
Go to bed
Eggs for dinner
Joint checking
Milk for free
Funny
Treats mom
Stop hunching
Go to bed
Milk for free
Funny
Go to bed
Milk for free
Milk for free
VS.
Vitamin D
Milk
Milk
PASTEURIZED HOMOGENIZED
32 FL OZ (1 QT) 946mL

The sleep before midnight vs. Go to bed
The same advice stated twice. The value of tucking in before midnight seems to defy the laws of nature – after all, sleep is sleep. But the older you get, the earlier you go to bed. So it must be true. The more felicitously phrased version also prescribes rest within a 24-hour period, and thus advances.

Milk for free vs. Funny
It's nice to have humor in a marriage, but there'll come a point when you'll wonder if your mate is laughing at you or with you. And that's not funny. Although the imagery of cows and free milk is a peculiar way to promote premarital chastity, this classic advice does double duty as a career caveat for any self-employed "consultant" who lets others pick his or her brain before the meter starts running.

Milk for free vs. Ask your father
The trouble with "milk for free" as advice is that, in a land where only 5% of married couples are virgins on their wedding day, it is honored more in theory than practice. Advice from mom that is so egregiously ignored cannot win. On the other hand, "Ask your father" is a masterpiece of passing the buck. It deflects the tough questions. It sends son or daughter off to seek additional counsel. And if father agrees with mother, it invests any motherly suggestion with twice the parental authority. As advice, it's a twofer – and wins.

UNLIKE FATHERLY ADVICE, which tends toward the protective, motherly advice is all about creating a prettier, smarter, longer-living, more successful you. In other words, dads play defense, moms play offense. Moms want us to marry well and happily ever after. They think they know what we should put in our mouths. And they usually see our career paths more clearly than we do. Memorability and pithiness are the main criteria here, with bonus points for real-life effectiveness or absurdity. P.S. All variations on the Golden Rule ("Do unto others . . .") have been banned here, or else there would be no contest.

Thank You

"Thank you" vs. Ask your father
Of all the gems here, saying "Thank you" to a compliment is the easiest to do. You just put your lips together and say it. But it doesn't stand a chance against the mother of all delegating lines.

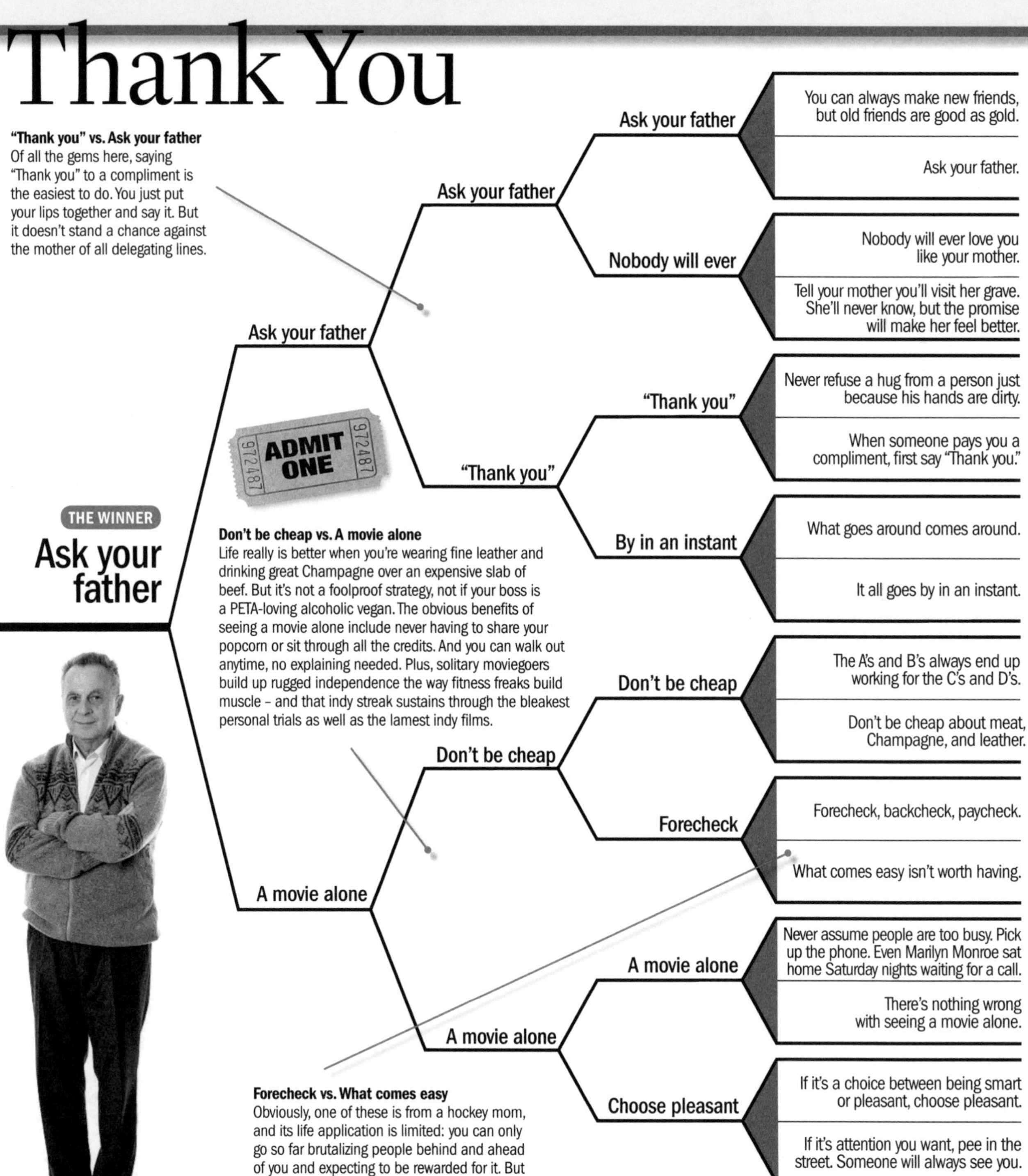

You can always make new friends, but old friends are good as gold.
Ask your father.
Nobody will ever love you like your mother.
Tell your mother you'll visit her grave. She'll never know, but the promise will make her feel better.
Never refuse a hug from a person just because his hands are dirty.
When someone pays you a compliment, first say "Thank you."
What goes around comes around.
It all goes by in an instant.
The A's and B's always end up working for the C's and D's.
Don't be cheap about meat, Champagne, and leather.
Forecheck, backcheck, paycheck.
What comes easy isn't worth having.
Never assume people are too busy. Pick up the phone. Even Marilyn Monroe sat home Saturday nights waiting for a call.
There's nothing wrong with seeing a movie alone.
If it's a choice between being smart or pleasant, choose pleasant.
If it's attention you want, pee in the street. Someone will always see you.
Ask your father
Nobody will ever
"Thank you"
By in an instant
Don't be cheap
Forecheck
A movie alone
Choose pleasant
Ask your father
"Thank you"
Don't be cheap
A movie alone
Ask your father
A movie alone
ADMIT ONE
972487
THE WINNER
Ask your father

Don't be cheap vs. A movie alone
Life really is better when you're wearing fine leather and drinking great Champagne over an expensive slab of beef. But it's not a foolproof strategy, not if your boss is a PETA-loving alcoholic vegan. The obvious benefits of seeing a movie alone include never having to share your popcorn or sit through all the credits. And you can walk out anytime, no explaining needed. Plus, solitary moviegoers build up rugged independence the way fitness freaks build muscle – and that indy streak sustains through the bleakest personal trials as well as the lamest indy films.

Forecheck vs. What comes easy
Obviously, one of these is from a hockey mom, and its life application is limited: you can only go so far brutalizing people behind and ahead of you and expecting to be rewarded for it. But it's short if not sweet, and moves on.

Acronyms

By Stefan Fatsis

Stefan Fatsis is the author of *Word Freak: Heartbreak, Triumph, Genius, and Obsession in the World of Competitive Scrabble Players* and *A Few Seconds of Panic: A 5-foot-8, 170-Pound, 43-Year-Old Sportswriter Plays in the NFL*. A former reporter for the *WSJ*, Fatsis talks on NPR and writes for the *NYT*, *SI*, et al.

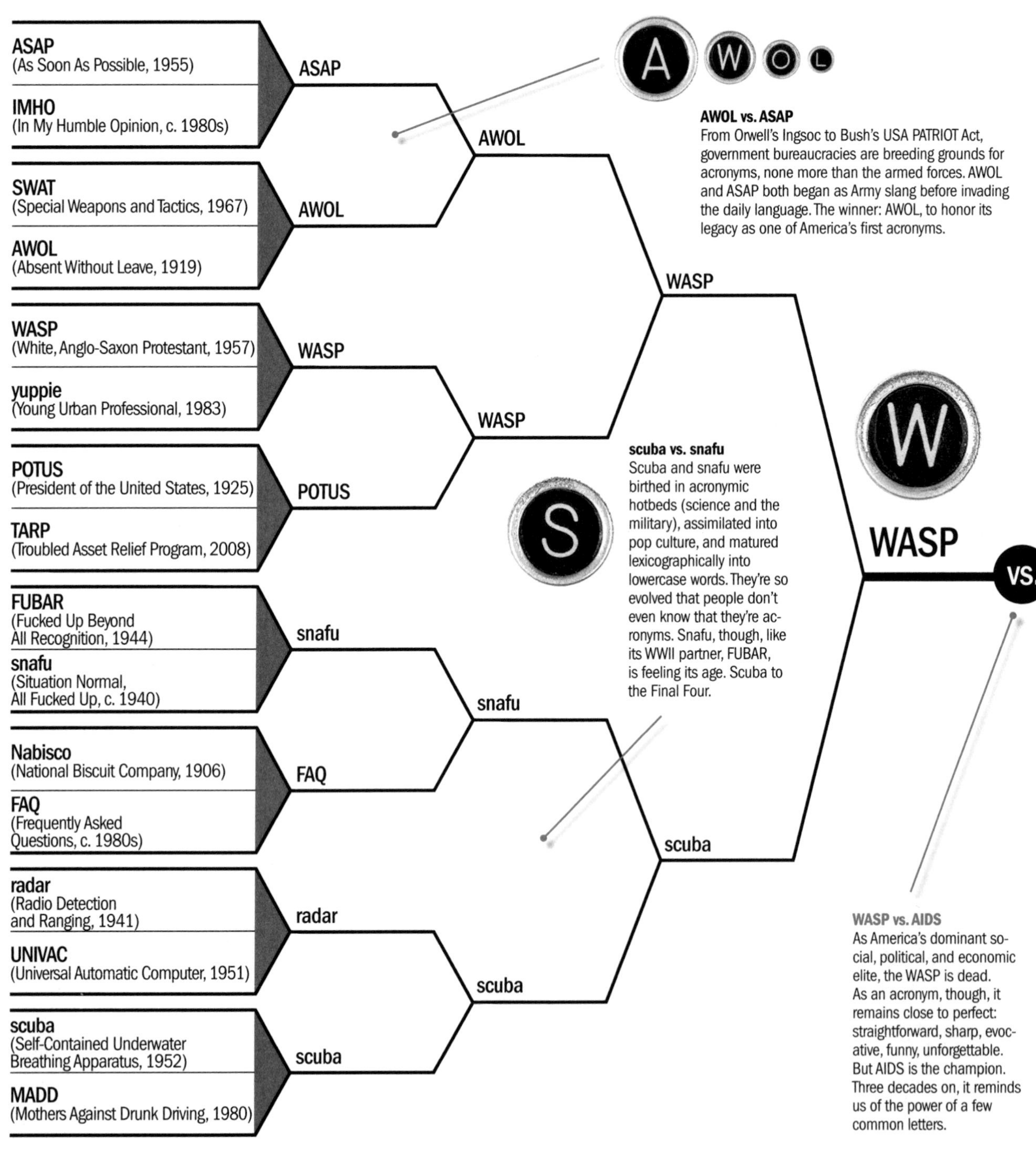

ASAP
(As Soon As Possible, 1955)
IMHO
(In My Humble Opinion, c. 1980s)
SWAT
(Special Weapons and Tactics, 1967)
AWOL
(Absent Without Leave, 1919)
WASP
(White, Anglo-Saxon Protestant, 1957)
yuppie
(Young Urban Professional, 1983)
POTUS
(President of the United States, 1925)
TARP
(Troubled Asset Relief Program, 2008)
FUBAR
(Fucked Up Beyond All Recognition, 1944)
snafu
(Situation Normal, All Fucked Up, c. 1940)
Nabisco
(National Biscuit Company, 1906)
FAQ
(Frequently Asked Questions, c. 1980s)
radar
(Radio Detection and Ranging, 1941)
UNIVAC
(Universal Automatic Computer, 1951)
scuba
(Self-Contained Underwater Breathing Apparatus, 1952)
MADD
(Mothers Against Drunk Driving, 1980)
ASAP
AWOL
WASP
POTUS
snafu
FAQ
radar
scuba
AWOL
WASP
snafu
scuba
WASP
scuba
WASP
VS.
A W O L
AWOL vs. ASAP
From Orwell's Ingsoc to Bush's USA PATRIOT Act, government bureaucracies are breeding grounds for acronyms, none more than the armed forces. AWOL and ASAP both began as Army slang before invading the daily language. The winner: AWOL, to honor its legacy as one of America's first acronyms.
W
S
scuba vs. snafu
Scuba and snafu were birthed in acronymic hotbeds (science and the military), assimilated into pop culture, and matured lexicographically into lowercase words. They're so evolved that people don't even know that they're acronyms. Snafu, though, like its WWII partner, FUBAR, is feeling its age. Scuba to the Final Four.
WASP vs. AIDS
As America's dominant social, political, and economic elite, the WASP is dead. As an acronym, though, it remains close to perfect: straightforward, sharp, evocative, funny, unforgettable. But AIDS is the champion. Three decades on, it reminds us of the power of a few common letters.

JOINING THE FIRST LETTER OR FIRST FEW LETTERS of multiple words into a single word is a 20th-century phenomenon, and a distinctly American one; the word "acronym" itself was coined at Bell Laboratories in 1943, from the Greek for "extreme" and "name." While some linguistic permissives consider initialisms – USA, BYOB, WWJD – to be acronyms, for our purposes an acronym has to be a pronounceable word. And real. Memo to KISS fans: your heroes are not Knights in Satan's Service.

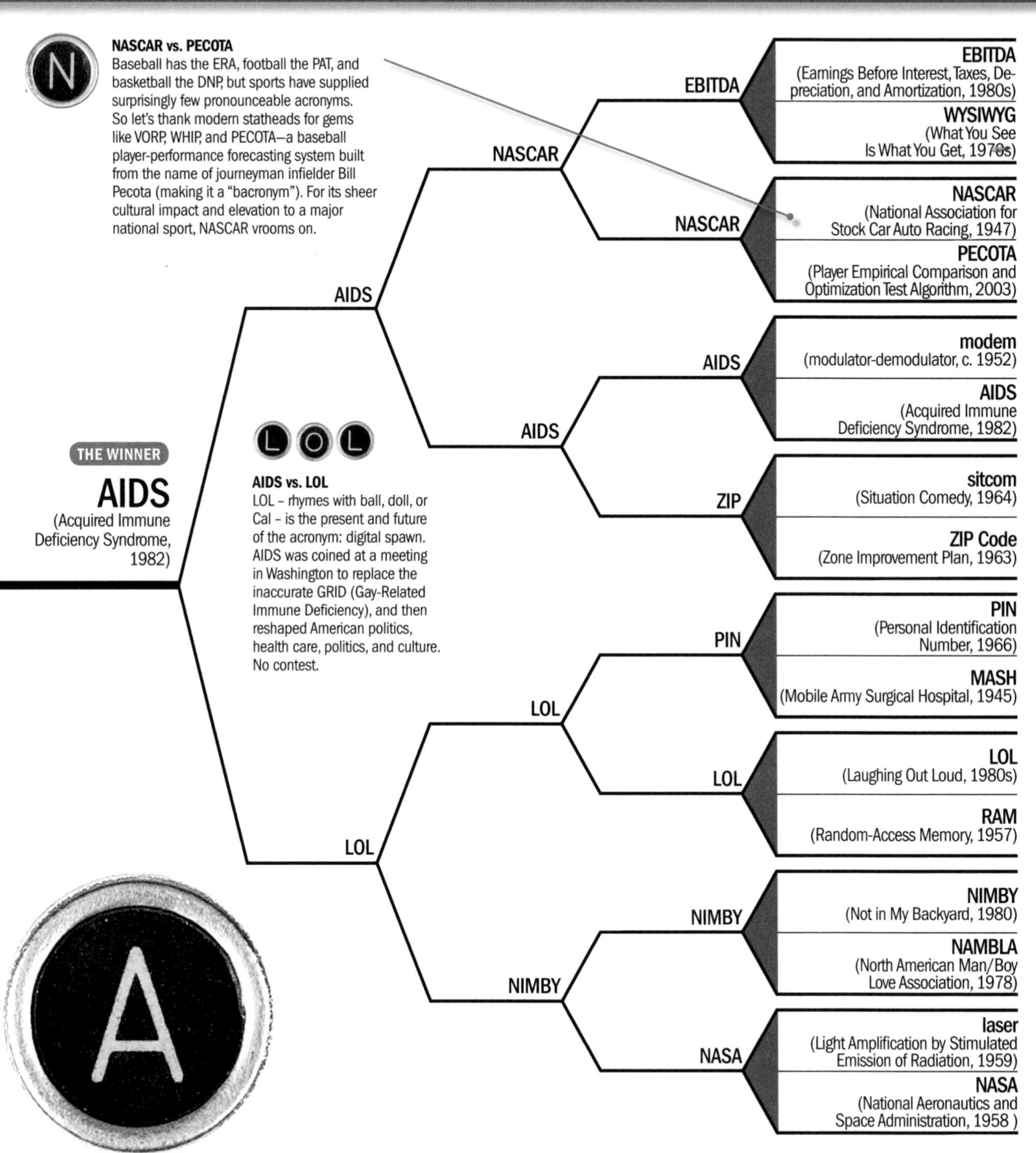

N
NASCAR vs. PECOTA
Baseball has the ERA, football the PAT, and basketball the DNP, but sports have supplied surprisingly few pronounceable acronyms. So let's thank modern statheads for gems like VORP, WHIP, and PECOTA—a baseball player-performance forecasting system built from the name of journeyman infielder Bill Pecota (making it a "bacronym"). For its sheer cultural impact and elevation to a major national sport, NASCAR vrooms on.
EBITDA
(Earnings Before Interest, Taxes, Depreciation, and Amortization, 1980s)
WYSIWYG
(What You See Is What You Get, 1970s)
NASCAR
(National Association for Stock Car Auto Racing, 1947)
PECOTA
(Player Empirical Comparison and Optimization Test Algorithm, 2003)
modem
(modulator-demodulator, c. 1952)
AIDS
(Acquired Immune Deficiency Syndrome, 1982)
sitcom
(Situation Comedy, 1964)
ZIP Code
(Zone Improvement Plan, 1963)
PIN
(Personal Identification Number, 1966)
MASH
(Mobile Army Surgical Hospital, 1945)
LOL
(Laughing Out Loud, 1980s)
RAM
(Random-Access Memory, 1957)
NIMBY
(Not in My Backyard, 1980)
NAMBLA
(North American Man/Boy Love Association, 1978)
laser
(Light Amplification by Stimulated Emission of Radiation, 1959)
NASA
(National Aeronautics and Space Administration, 1958)
EBITDA
NASCAR
PIN
LOL
NIMBY
NASA
AIDS
ZIP
NASCAR
AIDS
LOL
NIMBY
AIDS
LOL
THE WINNER
AIDS
(Acquired Immune Deficiency Syndrome, 1982)
LOL
AIDS vs. LOL
LOL – rhymes with ball, doll, or Cal – is the present and future of the acronym: digital spawn. AIDS was coined at a meeting in Washington to replace the inaccurate GRID (Gay-Related Immune Deficiency), and then reshaped American politics, health care, politics, and culture. No contest.
A

Lazy
Wit

By Adi Ignatius

Adi Ignatius, a journalist, relies on most of these lines to get through the day.

It's déjà vu all over again
Well, isn't that special
Fuggedaboutit!
Too much information
I'm just sayin'
That's what she said!
Oops. Did I say that out loud?
That's what I'm talkin' about!
I must have slept through the class on . . .
I must not have gotten the memo on . . .
. . . would be a great name for a rock band
I hate when that happens
LOL
OMG
Don't go there
Whatever

It's déjà vu all over again
Too much information
That's what she said!
That's what I'm talkin' about!
I must have slept through the class on . . .
I hate when that happens
LOL
Whatever

It's déjà vu all over again
That's what she said!
I hate when that happens
Whatever

That's what she said!
Whatever

Whatever

VS.

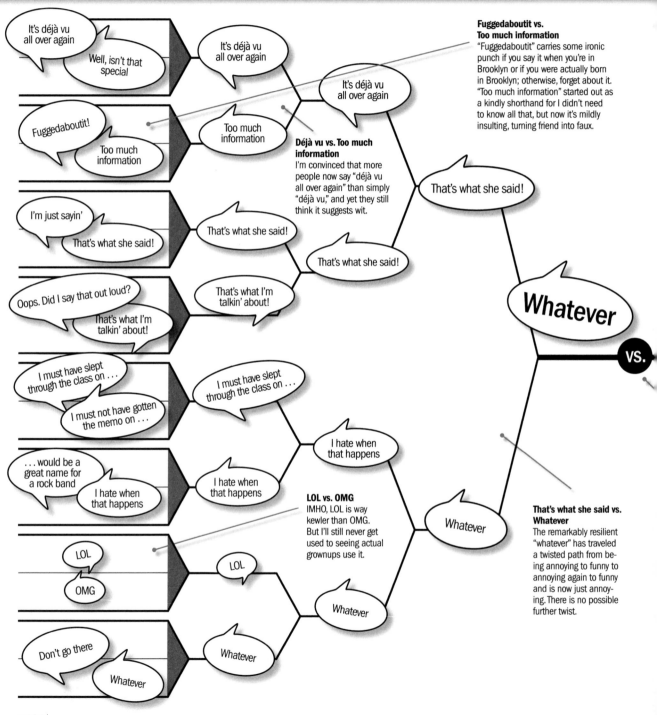

Fuggedaboutit vs. Too much information
"Fuggedaboutit" carries some ironic punch if you say it when you're in Brooklyn or if you were actually born in Brooklyn; otherwise, forget about it. "Too much information" started out as a kindly shorthand for I didn't need to know all that, but now it's mildly insulting, turning friend into faux.

Déjà vu vs. Too much information
I'm convinced that more people now say "déjà vu all over again" than simply "déjà vu," and yet they still think it suggests wit.

LOL vs. OMG
IMHO, LOL is way kewler than OMG. But I'll still never get used to seeing actual grownups use it.

That's what she said vs. Whatever
The remarkably resilient "whatever" has traveled a twisted path from being annoying to funny to annoying again to funny and is now just annoying. There is no possible further twist.

WE'VE ALL HEARD THEM. MOST OF US HAVE PROBABLY USED THEM: those handy catchphrases you store up and blurt out at opportune times with a twinkle in your eyes, as if you've just come up with a stunningly clever line. Only in truth, these phrases are used by everyone, of all ages, all the time. If they ever were witty, they certainly aren't by now. Which is the most expired? Follow the bracket.

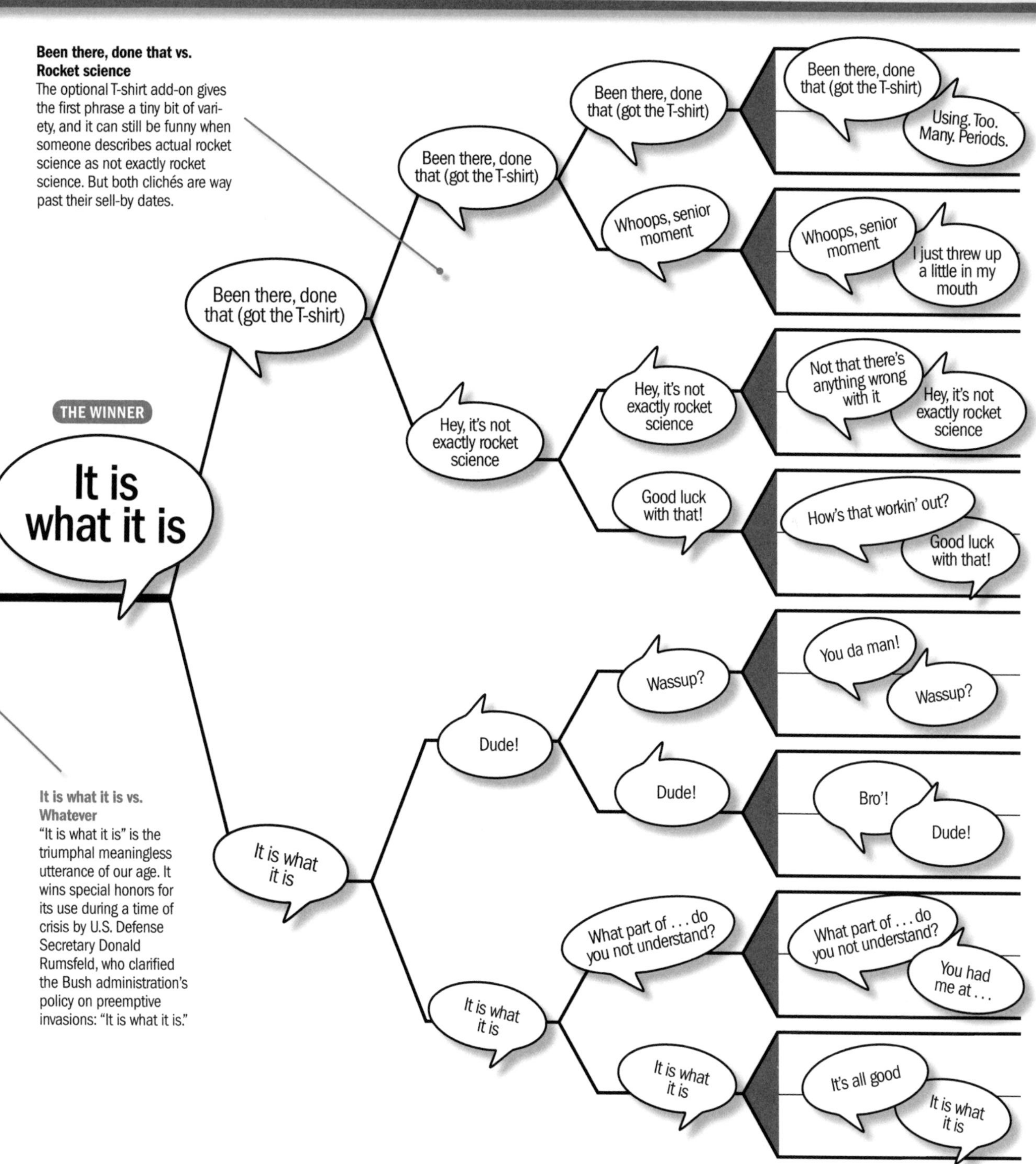

Been there, done that (got the T-shirt)
Using. Too. Many. Periods.
Whoops, senior moment
I just threw up a little in my mouth
Not that there's anything wrong with it
Hey, it's not exactly rocket science
How's that workin' out?
Good luck with that!
You da man!
Wassup?
Bro'!
Dude!
What part of . . . do you not understand?
You had me at . . .
It's all good
It is what it is
Been there, done that (got the T-shirt)
Whoops, senior moment
Hey, it's not exactly rocket science
Good luck with that!
Wassup?
Dude!
What part of . . . do you not understand?
It is what it is
Been there, done that (got the T-shirt)
Hey, it's not exactly rocket science
Dude!
It is what it is
Been there, done that (got the T-shirt)
It is what it is
THE WINNER
It is what it is

Been there, done that vs. Rocket science
The optional T-shirt add-on gives the first phrase a tiny bit of variety, and it can still be funny when someone describes actual rocket science as not exactly rocket science. But both clichés are way past their sell-by dates.

It is what it is vs. Whatever
"It is what it is" is the triumphal meaningless utterance of our age. It wins special honors for its use during a time of crisis by U.S. Defense Secretary Donald Rumsfeld, who clarified the Bush administration's policy on preemptive invasions: "It is what it is."

Texas Sayings

By Anne Dingus

Anne Dingus, a former columnist for *Texas Monthly*, is the author of *More Texas Sayings Than You Can Shake a Stick At*. She lives in Austin.

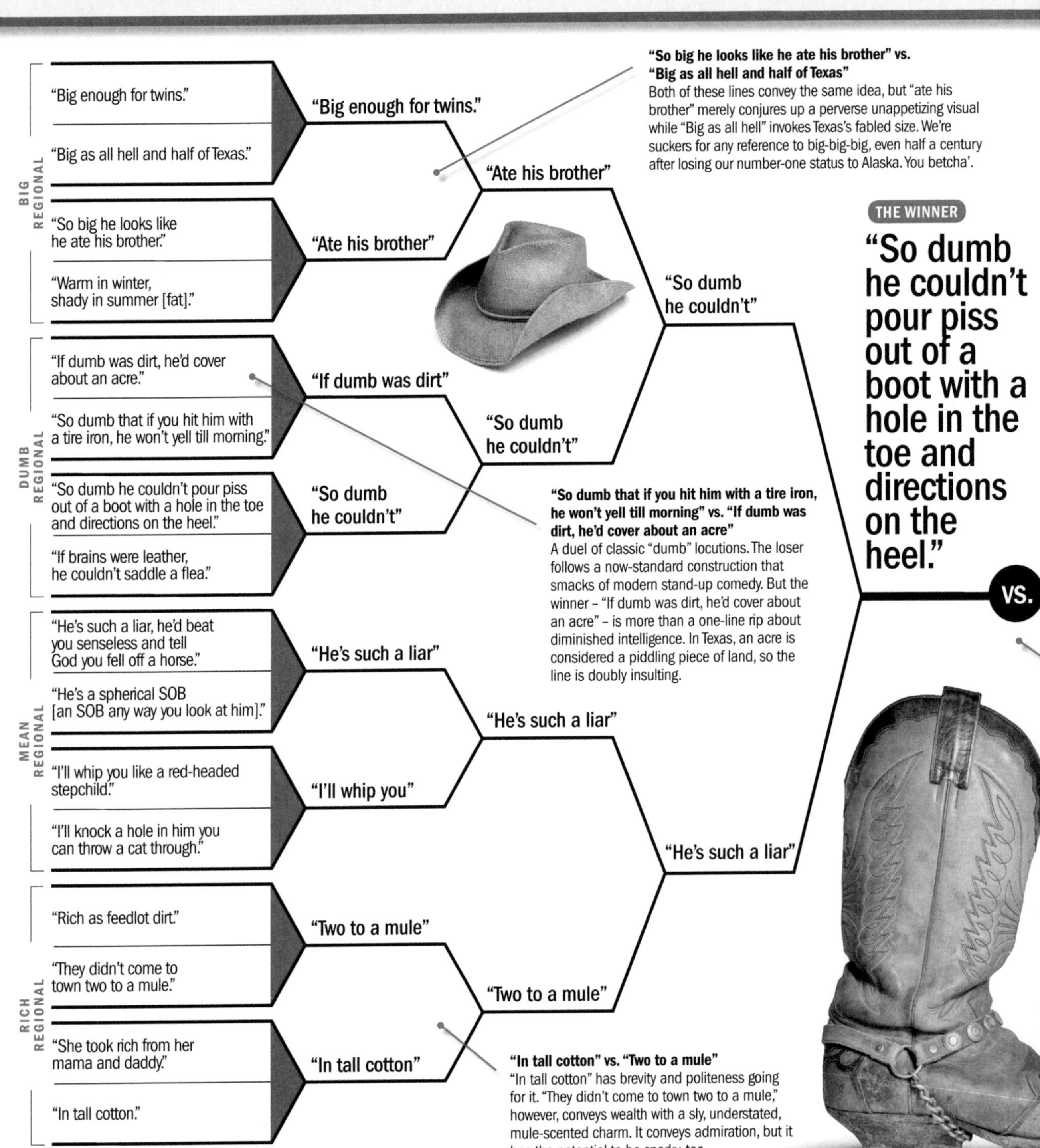
BIG REGIONAL
"Big enough for twins."
"Big as all hell and half of Texas."
"So big he looks like he ate his brother."
"Warm in winter, shady in summer [fat]."
DUMB REGIONAL
"If dumb was dirt, he'd cover about an acre."
"So dumb that if you hit him with a tire iron, he won't yell till morning."
"So dumb he couldn't pour piss out of a boot with a hole in the toe and directions on the heel."
"If brains were leather, he couldn't saddle a flea."
MEAN REGIONAL
"He's such a liar, he'd beat you senseless and tell God you fell off a horse."
"He's a spherical SOB [an SOB any way you look at him]."
"I'll whip you like a red-headed stepchild."
"I'll knock a hole in him you can throw a cat through."
RICH REGIONAL
"Rich as feedlot dirt."
"They didn't come to town two to a mule."
"She took rich from her mama and daddy."
"In tall cotton."
"Big enough for twins."
"Ate his brother"
"If dumb was dirt"
"So dumb he couldn't"
"He's such a liar"
"I'll whip you"
"Two to a mule"
"In tall cotton"
"Ate his brother"
"So dumb he couldn't"
"He's such a liar"
"Two to a mule"
"So dumb he couldn't"
"He's such a liar"
THE WINNER
"So dumb he couldn't pour piss out of a boot with a hole in the toe and directions on the heel."
VS.

"So big he looks like he ate his brother" vs. "Big as all hell and half of Texas"
Both of these lines convey the same idea, but "ate his brother" merely conjures up a perverse unappetizing visual while "Big as all hell" invokes Texas's fabled size. We're suckers for any reference to big-big-big, even half a century after losing our number-one status to Alaska. You betcha'.

"So dumb that if you hit him with a tire iron, he won't yell till morning" vs. "If dumb was dirt, he'd cover about an acre"
A duel of classic "dumb" locutions. The loser follows a now-standard construction that smacks of modern stand-up comedy. But the winner – "If dumb was dirt, he'd cover about an acre" – is more than a one-line rip about diminished intelligence. In Texas, an acre is considered a piddling piece of land, so the line is doubly insulting.

"In tall cotton" vs. "Two to a mule"
"In tall cotton" has brevity and politeness going for it. "They didn't come to town two to a mule," however, conveys wealth with a sly, understated, mule-scented charm. It conveys admiration, but it has the potential to be snarky, too.

WE TEXANS JUST LOVE TO HEAR OURSELVES TALK. No surprise, then, that we never settle for wimpy little adjectives or repressed ladylike exclamations. We prefer similes, metaphors, and colorful humor that channels Davy Crockett and Pecos Bill. We laugh at ourselves (and you, most likely), and we brag about everything from oil wells and pretty belles to at least one Texas president. Our sense of humor is big, rich, loud, hot, and occasionally dumb and mean, just like Texas. But always sprawling, out-size funny. Y'all talk back now, hear?

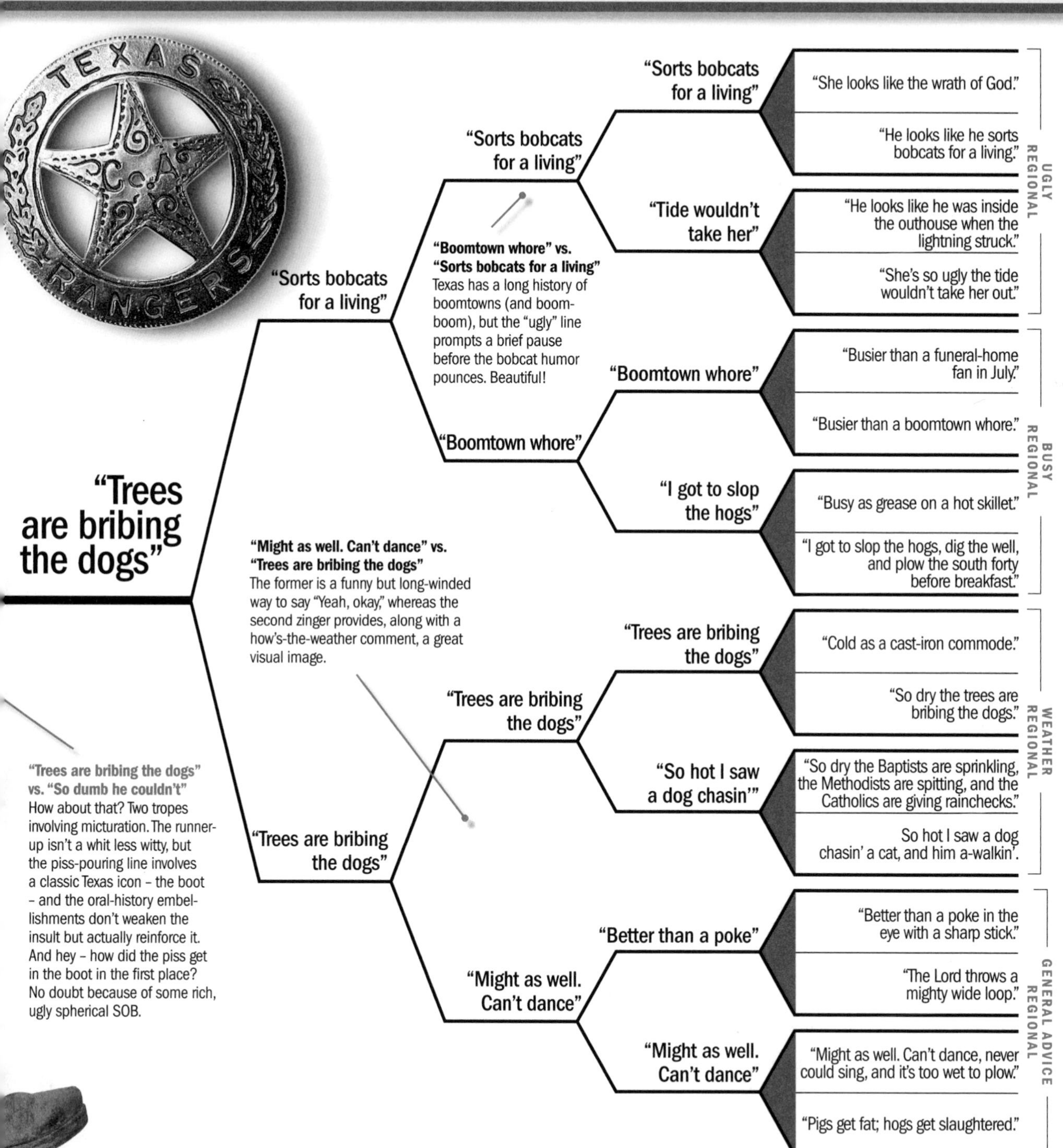

TEXAS RANGERS
"Trees are bribing the dogs"
"Sorts bobcats for a living"
"Trees are bribing the dogs"
"Sorts bobcats for a living"
"Boomtown whore"
"Trees are bribing the dogs"
"Might as well. Can't dance"
"Sorts bobcats for a living"
"Tide wouldn't take her"
"Boomtown whore"
"I got to slop the hogs"
"Trees are bribing the dogs"
"So hot I saw a dog chasin'"
"Better than a poke"
"Might as well. Can't dance"
"She looks like the wrath of God."
"He looks like he sorts bobcats for a living."
"He looks like he was inside the outhouse when the lightning struck."
"She's so ugly the tide wouldn't take her out."
UGLY REGIONAL
"Busier than a funeral-home fan in July."
"Busier than a boomtown whore."
"Busy as grease on a hot skillet."
"I got to slop the hogs, dig the well, and plow the south forty before breakfast."
BUSY REGIONAL
"Cold as a cast-iron commode."
"So dry the trees are bribing the dogs."
"So dry the Baptists are sprinkling, the Methodists are spitting, and the Catholics are giving rainchecks."
So hot I saw a dog chasin' a cat, and him a-walkin'.
WEATHER REGIONAL
"Better than a poke in the eye with a sharp stick."
"The Lord throws a mighty wide loop."
"Might as well. Can't dance, never could sing, and it's too wet to plow."
"Pigs get fat; hogs get slaughtered."
GENERAL ADVICE REGIONAL

"Boomtown whore" vs. "Sorts bobcats for a living" Texas has a long history of boomtowns (and boom-boom), but the "ugly" line prompts a brief pause before the bobcat humor pounces. Beautiful!

"Might as well. Can't dance" vs. "Trees are bribing the dogs" The former is a funny but long-winded way to say "Yeah, okay," whereas the second zinger provides, along with a how's-the-weather comment, a great visual image.

"Trees are bribing the dogs" vs. "So dumb he couldn't" How about that? Two tropes involving micturation. The runner-up isn't a whit less witty, but the piss-pouring line involves a classic Texas icon – the boot – and the oral-history embellishments don't weaken the insult but actually reinforce it. And hey – how did the piss get in the boot in the first place? No doubt because of some rich, ugly spherical SOB.

Seductive Foreign Accents

By Asif Eydohno

Asif Eydohno is a guest editor of this book. His native tongue is Hebrew, and he regards English as his most seductive foreign accent.

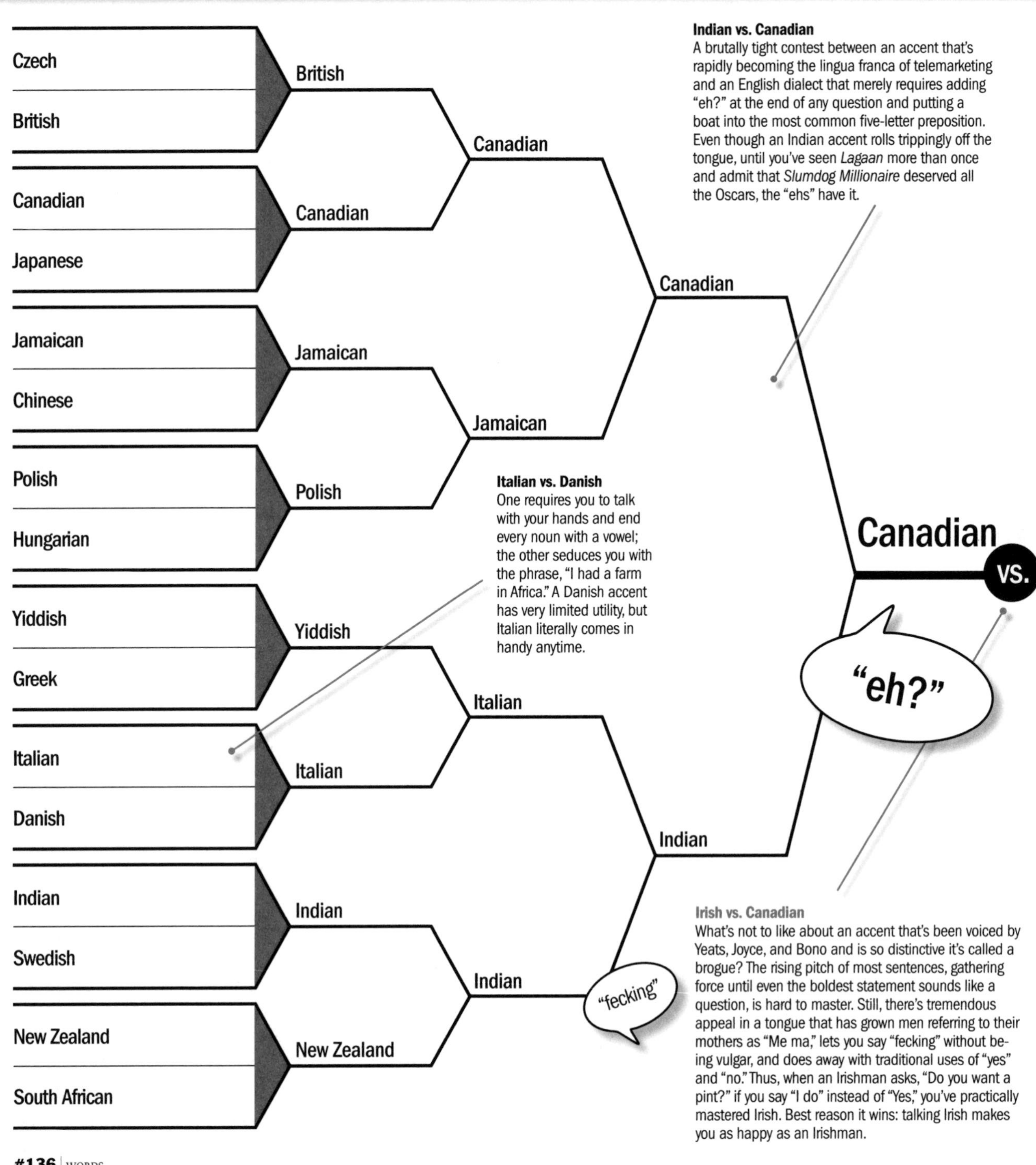

Czech
British
Canadian
Japanese
Jamaican
Chinese
Polish
Hungarian
Yiddish
Greek
Italian
Danish
Indian
Swedish
New Zealand
South African
British
Canadian
Jamaican
Polish
Yiddish
Italian
Indian
New Zealand
Canadian
Jamaican
Italian
Indian
Canadian
Indian
Canadian
VS.
"eh?"
"fecking"

Indian vs. Canadian
A brutally tight contest between an accent that's rapidly becoming the lingua franca of telemarketing and an English dialect that merely requires adding "eh?" at the end of any question and putting a boat into the most common five-letter preposition. Even though an Indian accent rolls trippingly off the tongue, until you've seen *Lagaan* more than once and admit that *Slumdog Millionaire* deserved all the Oscars, the "ehs" have it.

Italian vs. Danish
One requires you to talk with your hands and end every noun with a vowel; the other seduces you with the phrase, "I had a farm in Africa." A Danish accent has very limited utility, but Italian literally comes in handy anytime.

Irish vs. Canadian
What's not to like about an accent that's been voiced by Yeats, Joyce, and Bono and is so distinctive it's called a brogue? The rising pitch of most sentences, gathering force until even the boldest statement sounds like a question, is hard to master. Still, there's tremendous appeal in a tongue that has grown men referring to their mothers as "Me ma," lets you say "fecking" without being vulgar, and does away with traditional uses of "yes" and "no." Thus, when an Irishman asks, "Do you want a pint?" if you say "I do" instead of "Yes," you've practically mastered Irish. Best reason it wins: talking Irish makes you as happy as an Irishman.

EVER WATCH A CHARLES BOYER FILM and walk out of the theater talking like Pepe Le Pew? Or go to a Bengali restaurant and against every instinct of polite public behavior, order from the menu with a newfound Indian accent? Do you watch *Sophie's Choice* or *Out of Africa* and think "I could do what Meryl does." If so, this bracket's for you. A tournament to determine the most seductive (and maybe politically incorrect) foreign accent adopted by everyday Americans.

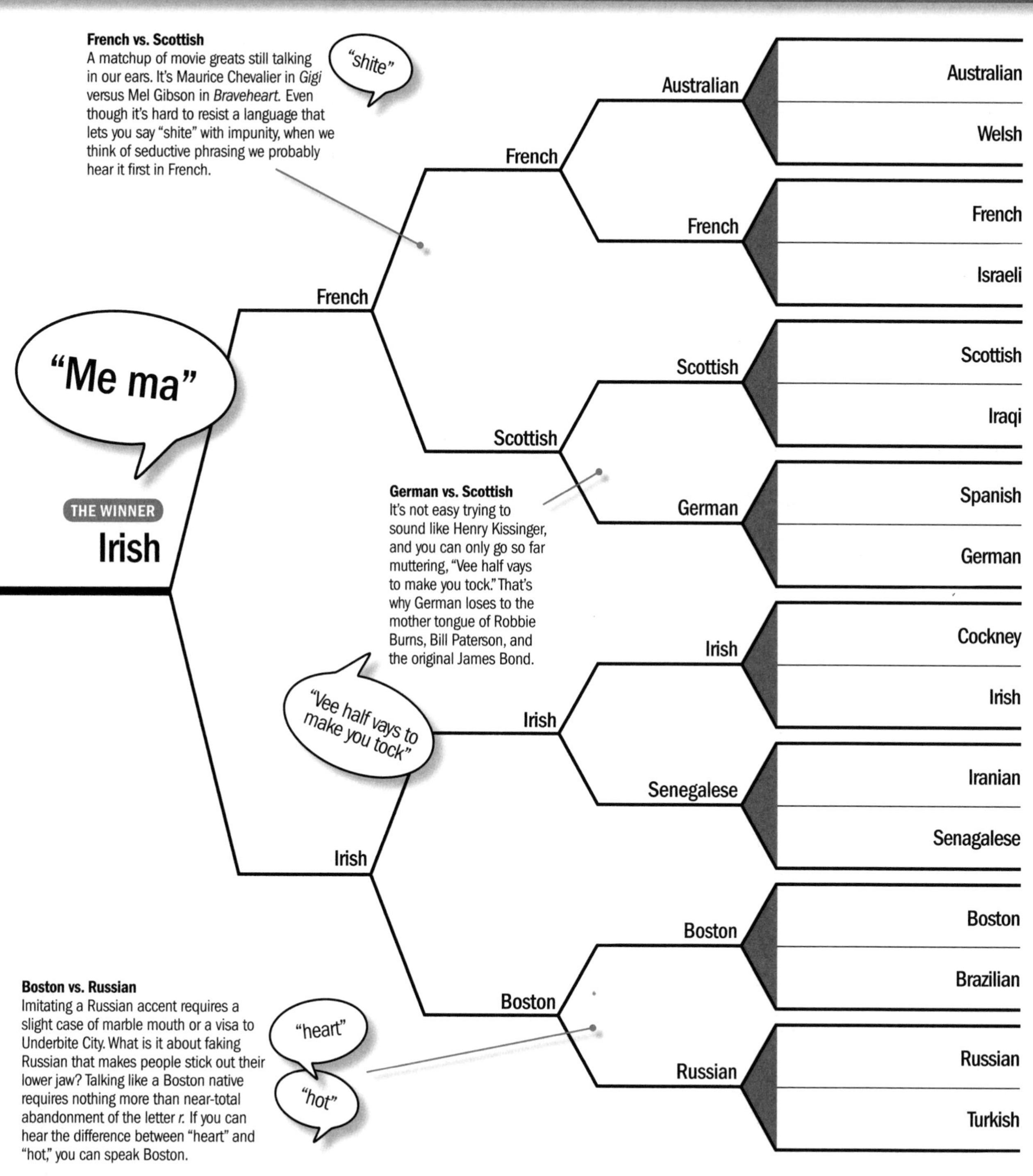

French vs. Scottish
A matchup of movie greats still talking in our ears. It's Maurice Chevalier in *Gigi* versus Mel Gibson in *Braveheart*. Even though it's hard to resist a language that lets you say "shite" with impunity, when we think of seductive phrasing we probably hear it first in French.
"shite"
"Me ma"
THE WINNER
Irish
German vs. Scottish
It's not easy trying to sound like Henry Kissinger, and you can only go so far muttering, "Vee half vays to make you tock." That's why German loses to the mother tongue of Robbie Burns, Bill Paterson, and the original James Bond.
"Vee half vays to make you tock"
Boston vs. Russian
Imitating a Russian accent requires a slight case of marble mouth or a visa to Underbite City. What is it about faking Russian that makes people stick out their lower jaw? Talking like a Boston native requires nothing more than near-total abandonment of the letter *r*. If you can hear the difference between "heart" and "hot," you can speak Boston.
"heart"
"hot"
French
Irish
French
Scottish
Irish
Boston
Australian
French
Scottish
German
Irish
Senegalese
Boston
Russian
Australian
Welsh
French
Israeli
Scottish
Iraqi
Spanish
German
Cockney
Irish
Iranian
Senagalese
Boston
Brazilian
Russian
Turkish

Yogi Berra Wisdom

By Dave Kaplan

Dave Kaplan is the founding director of the Yogi Berra Museum & Learning Center on the campus of Montclair State (NJ) University. He has collaborated with Yogi on four books, including the bestselling *When You Come to a Fork in the Road, Take It!*

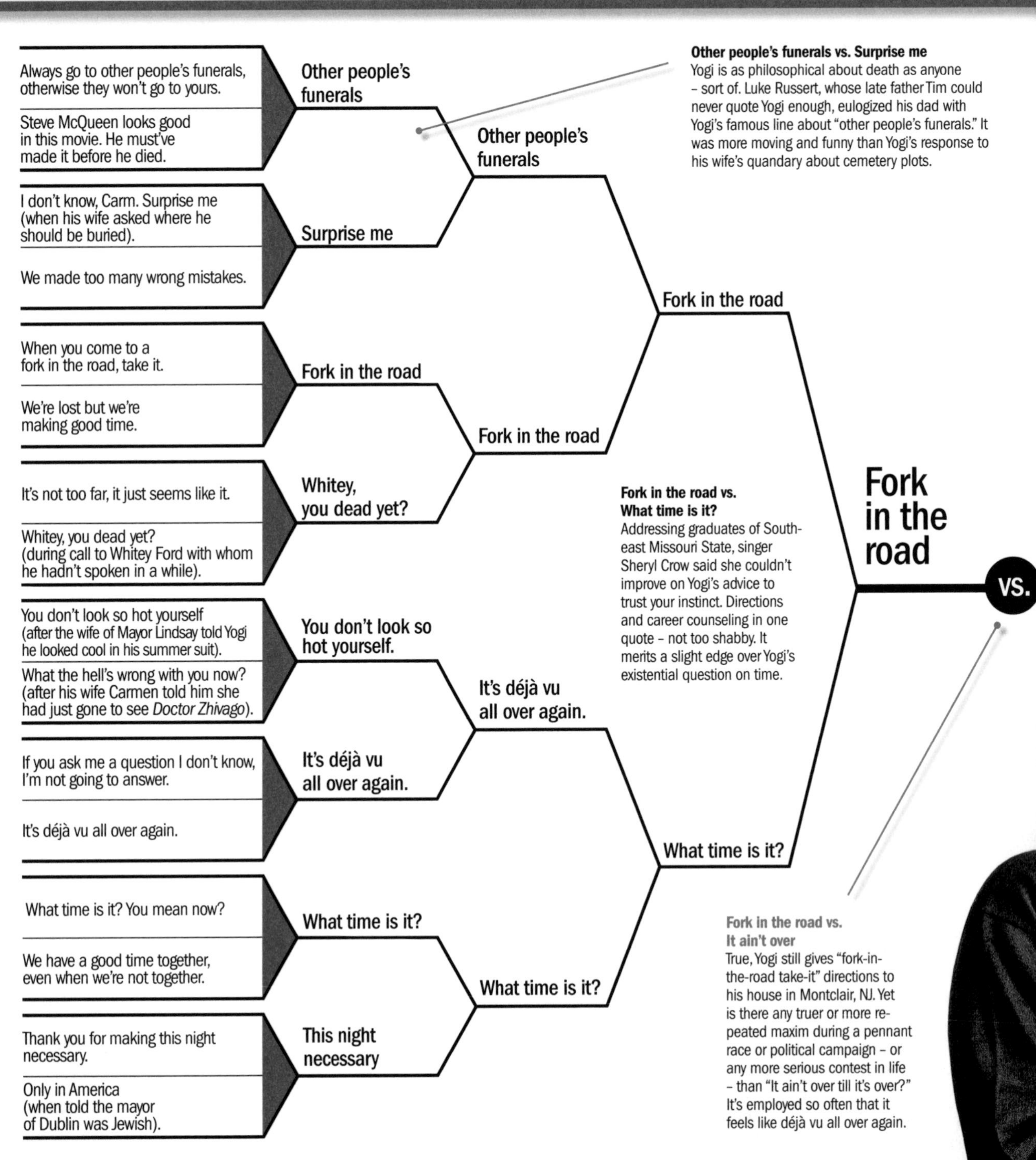
Always go to other people's funerals, otherwise they won't go to yours.
Steve McQueen looks good in this movie. He must've made it before he died.
I don't know, Carm. Surprise me (when his wife asked where he should be buried).
We made too many wrong mistakes.
When you come to a fork in the road, take it.
We're lost but we're making good time.
It's not too far, it just seems like it.
Whitey, you dead yet? (during call to Whitey Ford with whom he hadn't spoken in a while).
You don't look so hot yourself (after the wife of Mayor Lindsay told Yogi he looked cool in his summer suit).
What the hell's wrong with you now? (after his wife Carmen told him she had just gone to see *Doctor Zhivago*).
If you ask me a question I don't know, I'm not going to answer.
It's déjà vu all over again.
What time is it? You mean now?
We have a good time together, even when we're not together.
Thank you for making this night necessary.
Only in America (when told the mayor of Dublin was Jewish).
Other people's funerals
Surprise me
Fork in the road
Whitey, you dead yet?
You don't look so hot yourself.
It's déjà vu all over again.
What time is it?
This night necessary
Other people's funerals
Fork in the road
It's déjà vu all over again.
What time is it?
Fork in the road
What time is it?
Fork in the road
VS.

Other people's funerals vs. Surprise me
Yogi is as philosophical about death as anyone – sort of. Luke Russert, whose late father Tim could never quote Yogi enough, eulogized his dad with Yogi's famous line about "other people's funerals." It was more moving and funny than Yogi's response to his wife's quandary about cemetery plots.

Fork in the road vs. What time is it?
Addressing graduates of Southeast Missouri State, singer Sheryl Crow said she couldn't improve on Yogi's advice to trust your instinct. Directions and career counseling in one quote – not too shabby. It merits a slight edge over Yogi's existential question on time.

Fork in the road vs. It ain't over
True, Yogi still gives "fork-in-the-road take-it" directions to his house in Montclair, NJ. Yet is there any truer or more repeated maxim during a pennant race or political campaign – or any more serious contest in life – than "It ain't over till it's over?" It's employed so often that it feels like déjà vu all over again.

YOGI BERRA SEES THINGS DIFFERENTLY. Actually, he says things differently. Yet his inadvertent insights on baseball and life have a special logic. As the winner of 10 World Series rings with the Yankee dynasties of the late 1940s to early '60s and a three-time MVP on teams with DiMaggio and Mantle, he's not a Zen Master. He's simply Yogi. The winner here is the casual Berra brilliance that has most effectively wedged itself into America's conversation as all-purpose wisdom and truth.

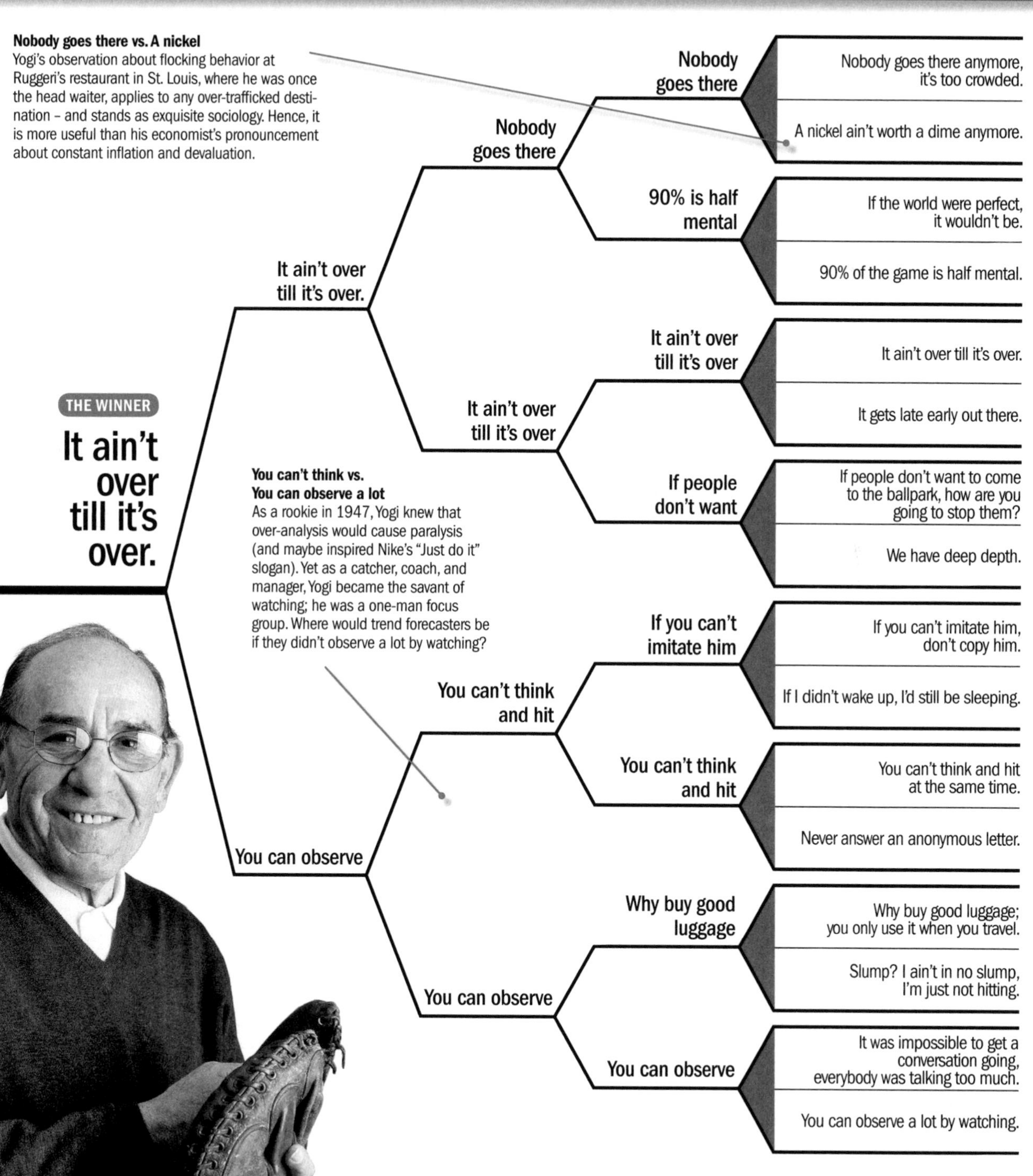

Nobody goes there
Nobody goes there anymore, it's too crowded.
A nickel ain't worth a dime anymore.
Nobody goes there
90% is half mental
If the world were perfect, it wouldn't be.
90% of the game is half mental.
It ain't over till it's over.
It ain't over till it's over
It ain't over till it's over.
It gets late early out there.
It ain't over till it's over
If people don't want
If people don't want to come to the ballpark, how are you going to stop them?
We have deep depth.
If you can't imitate him
If you can't imitate him, don't copy him.
If I didn't wake up, I'd still be sleeping.
You can't think and hit
You can't think and hit
You can't think and hit at the same time.
Never answer an anonymous letter.
You can observe
Why buy good luggage
Why buy good luggage; you only use it when you travel.
Slump? I ain't in no slump, I'm just not hitting.
You can observe
You can observe
It was impossible to get a conversation going, everybody was talking too much.
You can observe a lot by watching.
THE WINNER
It ain't over till it's over.

Nobody goes there vs. A nickel
Yogi's observation about flocking behavior at Ruggeri's restaurant in St. Louis, where he was once the head waiter, applies to any over-trafficked destination – and stands as exquisite sociology. Hence, it is more useful than his economist's pronouncement about constant inflation and devaluation.

You can't think vs. You can observe a lot
As a rookie in 1947, Yogi knew that over-analysis would cause paralysis (and maybe inspired Nike's "Just do it" slogan). Yet as a catcher, coach, and manager, Yogi became the savant of watching; he was a one-man focus group. Where would trend forecasters be if they didn't observe a lot by watching?

Fortune Cookies

By Jennifer 8. Lee

Jennifer 8. Lee, a *New York Times* reporter, traced the elusive history of the fortune cookie in her book, *The Fortune Cookie Chronicles: Adventures in the World of Chinese Food.*

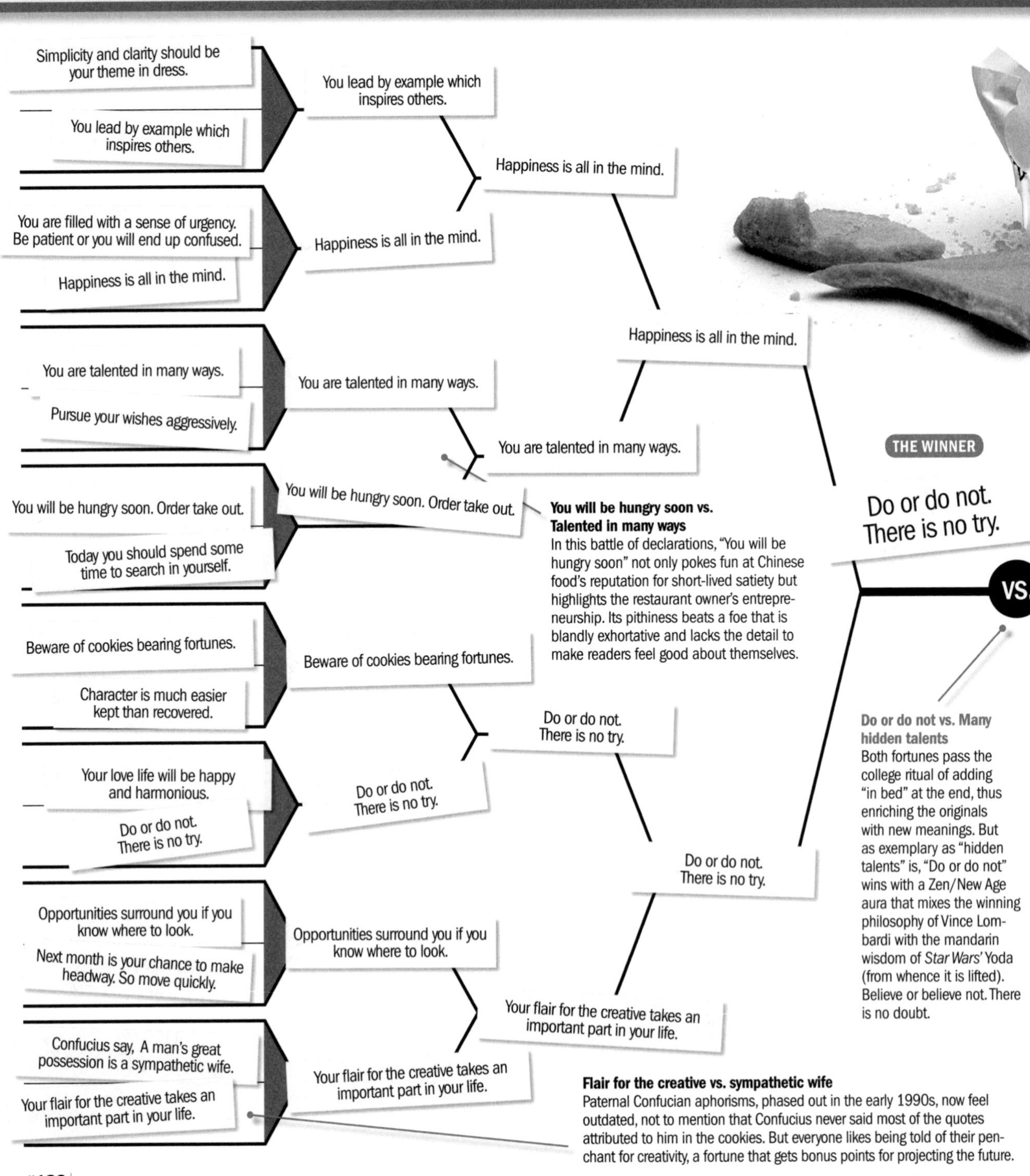

Simplicity and clarity should be your theme in dress.
You lead by example which inspires others.
You lead by example which inspires others.
You are filled with a sense of urgency. Be patient or you will end up confused.
Happiness is all in the mind.
Happiness is all in the mind.
Happiness is all in the mind.
Happiness is all in the mind.
You are talented in many ways.
Pursue your wishes aggressively.
You are talented in many ways.
You are talented in many ways.
You will be hungry soon. Order take out.
Today you should spend some time to search in yourself.
You will be hungry soon. Order take out.
Beware of cookies bearing fortunes.
Character is much easier kept than recovered.
Beware of cookies bearing fortunes.
Your love life will be happy and harmonious.
Do or do not. There is no try.
Do or do not. There is no try.
Do or do not. There is no try.
Do or do not. There is no try.
Opportunities surround you if you know where to look.
Next month is your chance to make headway. So move quickly.
Opportunities surround you if you know where to look.
Confucius say, A man's great possession is a sympathetic wife.
Your flair for the creative takes an important part in your life.
Your flair for the creative takes an important part in your life.
Your flair for the creative takes an important part in your life.
THE WINNER
Do or do not. There is no try.
VS.

You will be hungry soon vs. Talented in many ways
In this battle of declarations, "You will be hungry soon" not only pokes fun at Chinese food's reputation for short-lived satiety but highlights the restaurant owner's entrepreneurship. Its pithiness beats a foe that is blandly exhortative and lacks the detail to make readers feel good about themselves.

Do or do not vs. Many hidden talents
Both fortunes pass the college ritual of adding "in bed" at the end, thus enriching the originals with new meanings. But as exemplary as "hidden talents" is, "Do or do not" wins with a Zen/New Age aura that mixes the winning philosophy of Vince Lombardi with the mandarin wisdom of *Star Wars'* Yoda (from whence it is lifted). Believe or believe not. There is no doubt.

Flair for the creative vs. sympathetic wife
Paternal Confucian aphorisms, phased out in the early 1990s, now feel outdated, not to mention that Confucius never said most of the quotes attributed to him in the cookies. But everyone likes being told of their penchant for creativity, a fortune that gets bonus points for projecting the future.

THE "CONFUCIUS SAY" FORTUNE COOKIE PREAMBLE of decades past is deceptive. Fortune cookies were invented by the Japanese, popularized by the Chinese, but are ultimately consumed by Americans by the billions. As such, fortunes today are written by and for Americans seeking uplift with their General Tso's chicken. Writing fortunes is a demanding task: the best ones must be pithy enough to fit on a tiny slip of paper, generalized across a broad swath of the population, and possess a happy tone. Who wants to end dinner on a sour note?

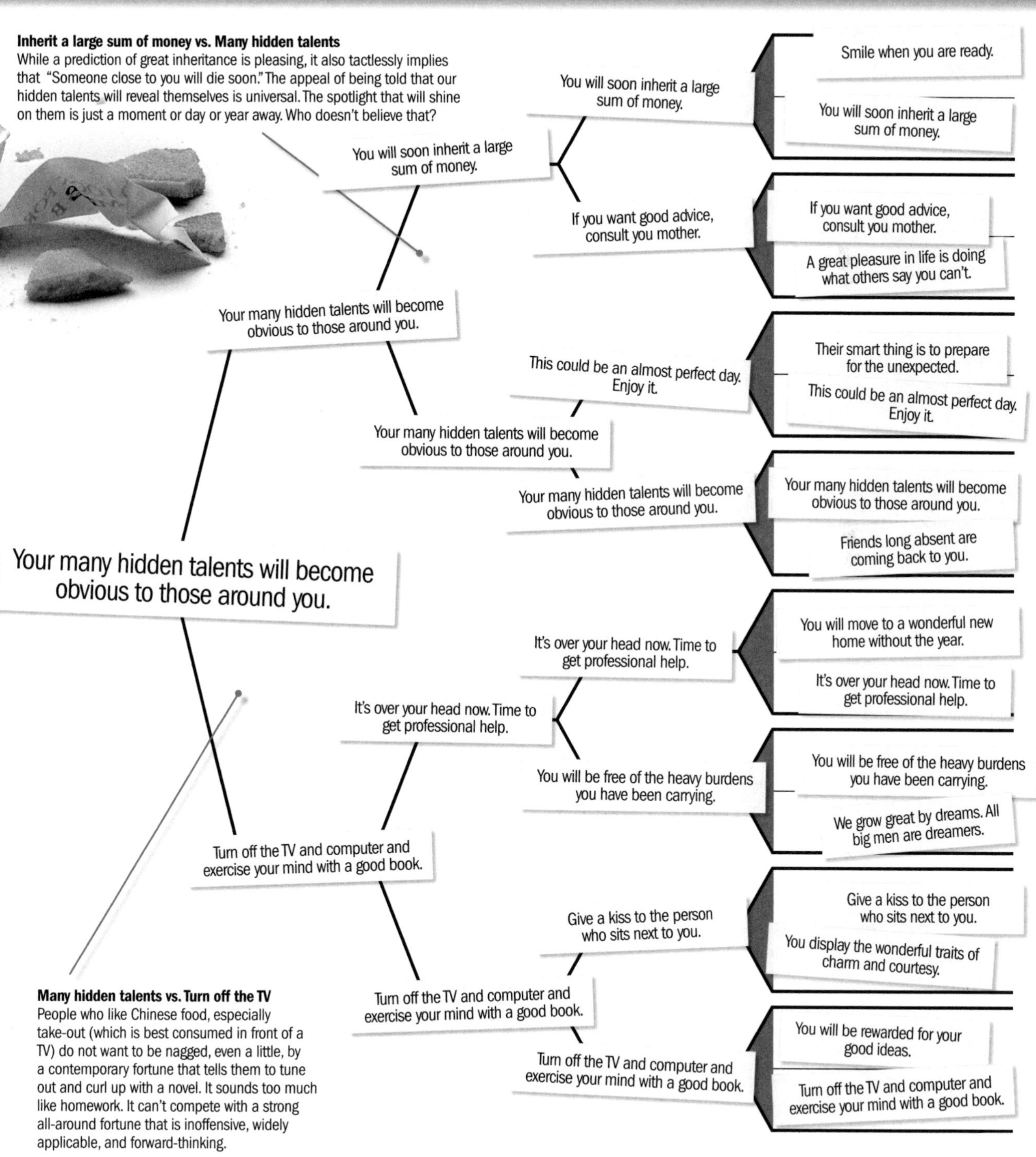

Inherit a large sum of money vs. Many hidden talents
While a prediction of great inheritance is pleasing, it also tactlessly implies that "Someone close to you will die soon." The appeal of being told that our hidden talents will reveal themselves is universal. The spotlight that will shine on them is just a moment or day or year away. Who doesn't believe that?
Smile when you are ready.
You will soon inherit a large sum of money.
You will soon inherit a large sum of money.
You will soon inherit a large sum of money.
If you want good advice, consult you mother.
If you want good advice, consult you mother.
A great pleasure in life is doing what others say you can't.
Your many hidden talents will become obvious to those around you.
Their smart thing is to prepare for the unexpected.
This could be an almost perfect day. Enjoy it.
This could be an almost perfect day. Enjoy it.
Your many hidden talents will become obvious to those around you.
Your many hidden talents will become obvious to those around you.
Your many hidden talents will become obvious to those around you.
Friends long absent are coming back to you.
Your many hidden talents will become obvious to those around you.
You will move to a wonderful new home without the year.
It's over your head now. Time to get professional help.
It's over your head now. Time to get professional help.
It's over your head now. Time to get professional help.
You will be free of the heavy burdens you have been carrying.
You will be free of the heavy burdens you have been carrying.
We grow great by dreams. All big men are dreamers.
Turn off the TV and computer and exercise your mind with a good book.
Give a kiss to the person who sits next to you.
Give a kiss to the person who sits next to you.
You display the wonderful traits of charm and courtesy.
Turn off the TV and computer and exercise your mind with a good book.
You will be rewarded for your good ideas.
Turn off the TV and computer and exercise your mind with a good book.
Turn off the TV and computer and exercise your mind with a good book.
Many hidden talents vs. Turn off the TV
People who like Chinese food, especially take-out (which is best consumed in front of a TV) do not want to be nagged, even a little, by a contemporary fortune that tells them to tune out and curl up with a novel. It sounds too much like homework. It can't compete with a strong all-around fortune that is inoffensive, widely applicable, and forward-thinking.

All-Purpose Banalities

By Joe Queenan

Joe Queenan is a freelance writer based in Tarrytown, NY. His latest book, *Closing Time,* contains none of the appalling clichés listed here.

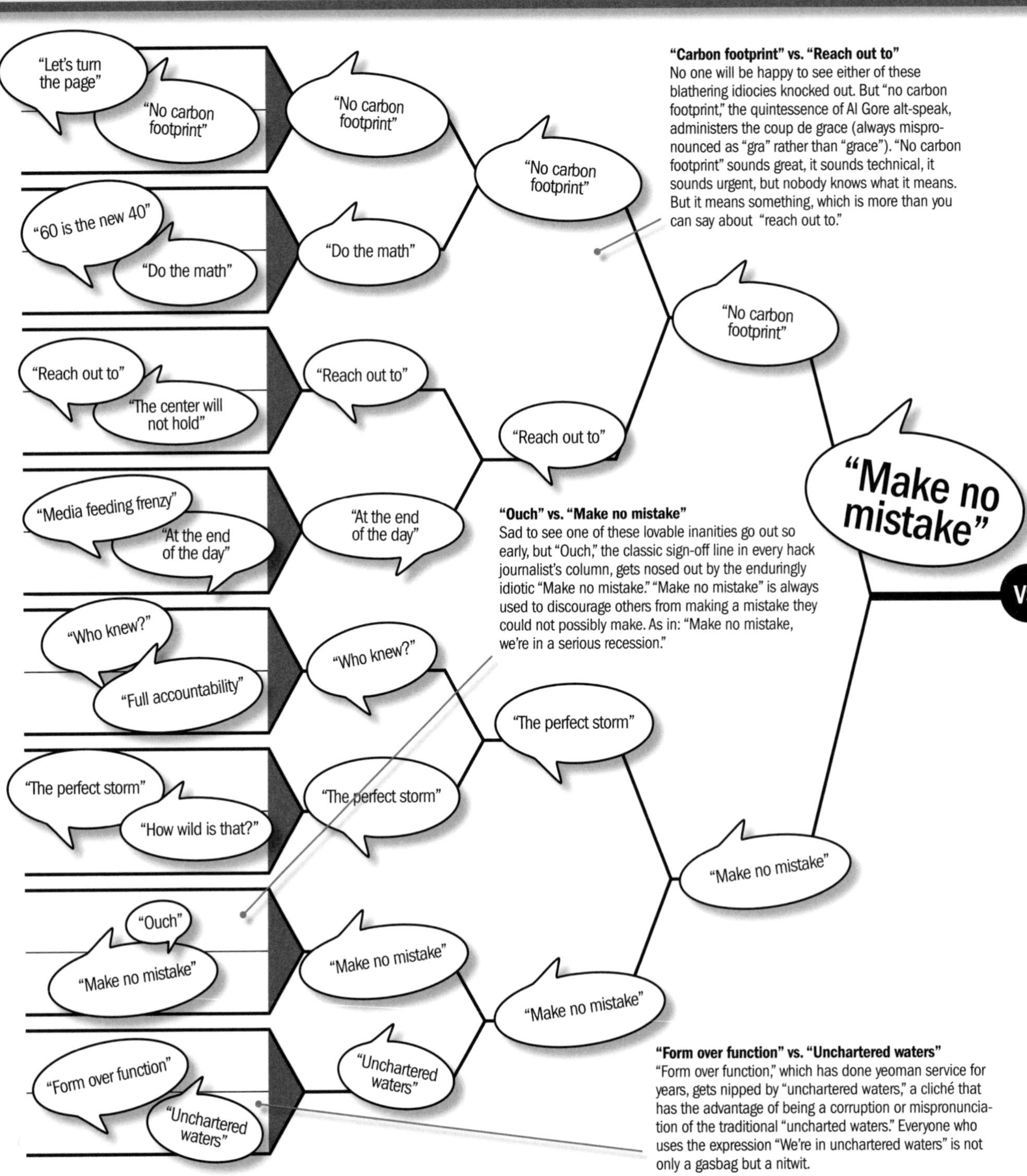

"Let's turn the page"
"No carbon footprint"
"60 is the new 40"
"Do the math"
"Reach out to"
"The center will not hold"
"Media feeding frenzy"
"At the end of the day"
"Who knew?"
"Full accountability"
"The perfect storm"
"How wild is that?"
"Ouch"
"Make no mistake"
"Form over function"
"Unchartered waters"
"No carbon footprint"
"Do the math"
"Reach out to"
"At the end of the day"
"Who knew?"
"The perfect storm"
"Make no mistake"
"Unchartered waters"
"No carbon footprint"
"Reach out to"
"The perfect storm"
"Make no mistake"
"No carbon footprint"
"Make no mistake"
"Make no mistake"
VS.
"Carbon footprint" vs. "Reach out to"
No one will be happy to see either of these blathering idiocies knocked out. But "no carbon footprint," the quintessence of Al Gore alt-speak, administers the coup de grace (always mispronounced as "gra" rather than "grace"). "No carbon footprint" sounds great, it sounds technical, it sounds urgent, but nobody knows what it means. But it means something, which is more than you can say about "reach out to."
"Ouch" vs. "Make no mistake"
Sad to see one of these lovable inanities go out so early, but "Ouch," the classic sign-off line in every hack journalist's column, gets nosed out by the enduringly idiotic "Make no mistake." "Make no mistake" is always used to discourage others from making a mistake they could not possibly make. As in: "Make no mistake, we're in a serious recession."
"Form over function" vs. "Unchartered waters"
"Form over function," which has done yeoman service for years, gets nipped by "unchartered waters," a cliché that has the advantage of being a corruption or mispronunciation of the traditional "uncharted waters." Everyone who uses the expression "We're in unchartered waters" is not only a gasbag but a nitwit.

ALL-PURPOSE BANALITIES CONFER A SENSE OF GRAVITAS on the person enunciating them or introduce a sinister, Rosie O'Donnell chumminess into the conversation, assuring the listener that the speaker holds the same salt-of-the-earth values as the common man. To qualify for this bracket, a banality must sound like something Nancy Pelosi would tell Jim Lehrer, something a major pundit might write, or something a White House press secretary would say to avoid talking about the Middle East situation, which is, it goes without saying, dire and fraught with peril.

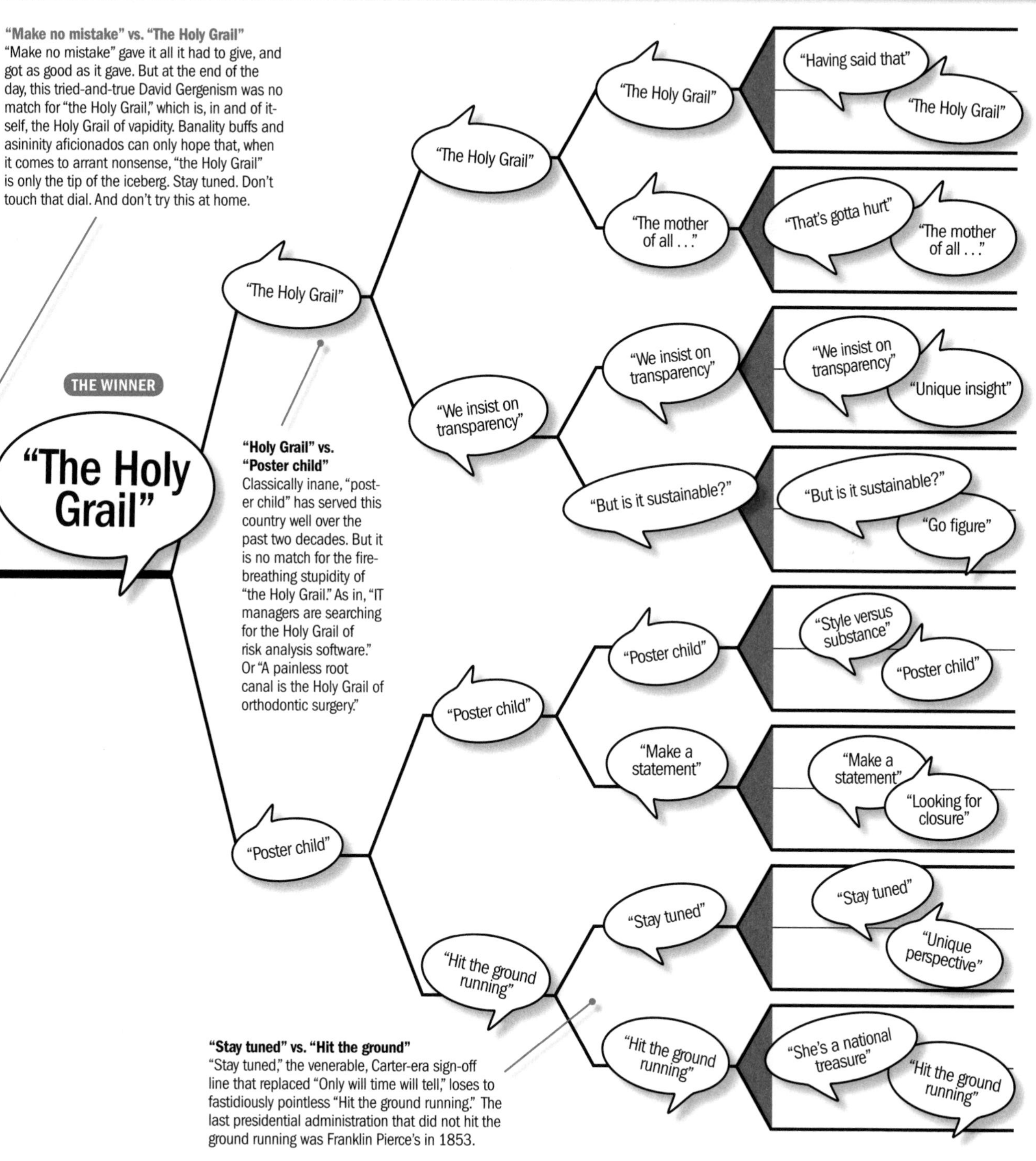
"Having said that"
"The Holy Grail"
"That's gotta hurt"
"The mother of all . . ."
"We insist on transparency"
"Unique insight"
"But is it sustainable?"
"Go figure"
"Style versus substance"
"Poster child"
"Make a statement"
"Looking for closure"
"Stay tuned"
"Unique perspective"
"She's a national treasure"
"Hit the ground running"
"The Holy Grail"
"The mother of all . . ."
"We insist on transparency"
"But is it sustainable?"
"Poster child"
"Make a statement"
"Stay tuned"
"Hit the ground running"
"The Holy Grail"
"We insist on transparency"
"Poster child"
"Hit the ground running"
"The Holy Grail"
"Poster child"
THE WINNER
"The Holy Grail"

"Make no mistake" vs. "The Holy Grail"
"Make no mistake" gave it all it had to give, and got as good as it gave. But at the end of the day, this tried-and-true David Gergenism was no match for "the Holy Grail," which is, in and of itself, the Holy Grail of vapidity. Banality buffs and asininity aficionados can only hope that, when it comes to arrant nonsense, "the Holy Grail" is only the tip of the iceberg. Stay tuned. Don't touch that dial. And don't try this at home.

"Holy Grail" vs. "Poster child"
Classically inane, "poster child" has served this country well over the past two decades. But it is no match for the fire-breathing stupidity of "the Holy Grail." As in, "IT managers are searching for the Holy Grail of risk analysis software." Or "A painless root canal is the Holy Grail of orthodontic surgery."

"Stay tuned" vs. "Hit the ground"
"Stay tuned," the venerable, Carter-era sign-off line that replaced "Only will time will tell," loses to fastidiously pointless "Hit the ground running." The last presidential administration that did not hit the ground running was Franklin Pierce's in 1853.

Deadly Sins of Emailing

By David Shipley and Will Schwalbe

David Shipley and Will Schwalbe are the authors of *SEND: Why People Email So Badly and How to Do It Better.* Shipley is the deputy editorial page editor and Op-Ed page editor of the *New York Times.* Schwalbe is the founder and CEO of Cookstr.com.

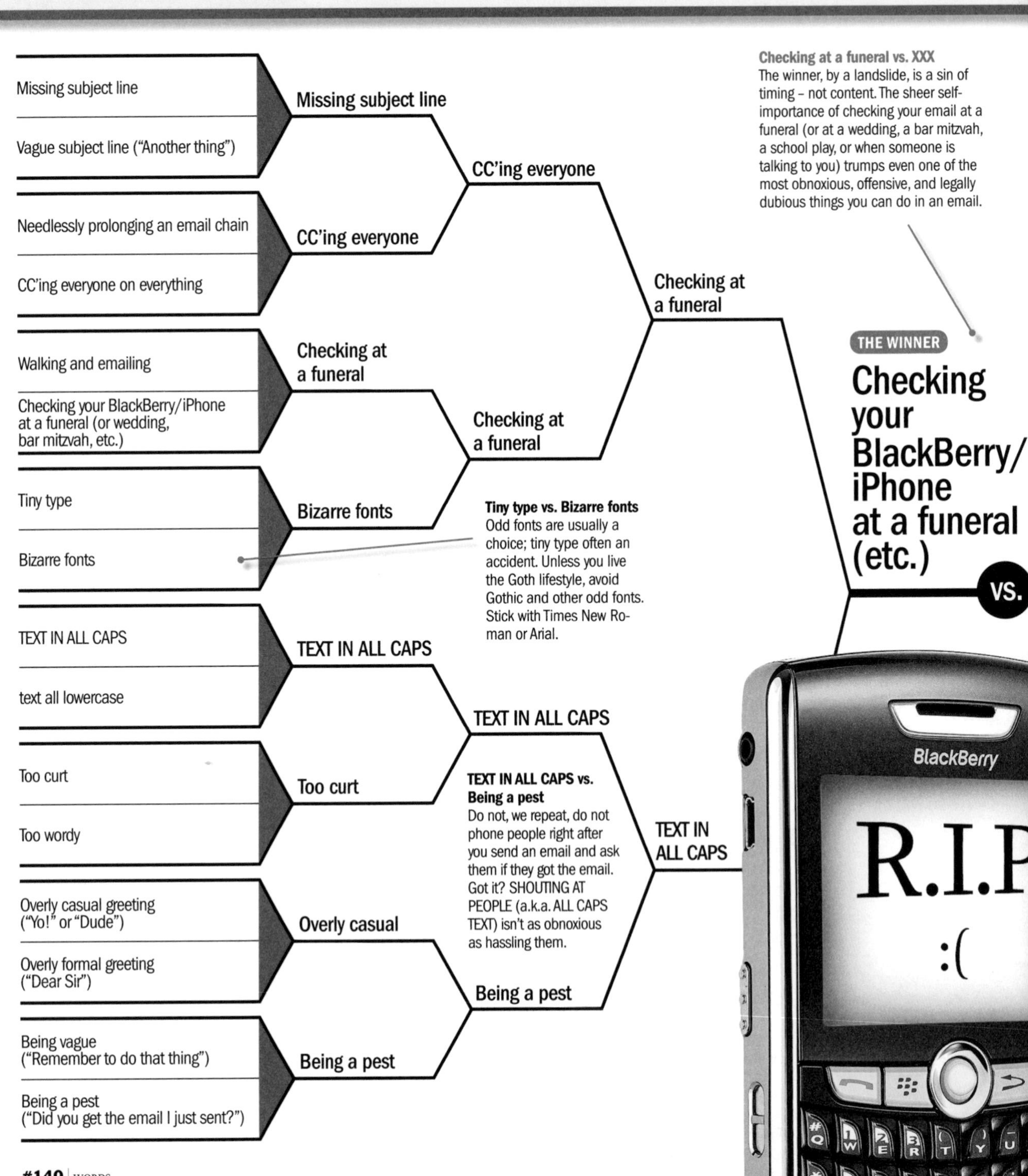
Missing subject line
Vague subject line ("Another thing")
Needlessly prolonging an email chain
CC'ing everyone on everything
Walking and emailing
Checking your BlackBerry/iPhone at a funeral (or wedding, bar mitzvah, etc.)
Tiny type
Bizarre fonts
TEXT IN ALL CAPS
text all lowercase
Too curt
Too wordy
Overly casual greeting ("Yo!" or "Dude")
Overly formal greeting ("Dear Sir")
Being vague ("Remember to do that thing")
Being a pest ("Did you get the email I just sent?")
Missing subject line
CC'ing everyone
Checking at a funeral
Bizarre fonts
TEXT IN ALL CAPS
Too curt
Overly casual
Being a pest
CC'ing everyone
Checking at a funeral
TEXT IN ALL CAPS
Being a pest
Checking at a funeral
TEXT IN ALL CAPS
THE WINNER
Checking your BlackBerry/iPhone at a funeral (etc.)
VS.
BlackBerry
R.I.P
:(

Checking at a funeral vs. XXX
The winner, by a landslide, is a sin of timing – not content. The sheer self-importance of checking your email at a funeral (or at a wedding, a bar mitzvah, a school play, or when someone is talking to you) trumps even one of the most obnoxious, offensive, and legally dubious things you can do in an email.

Tiny type vs. Bizarre fonts
Odd fonts are usually a choice; tiny type often an accident. Unless you live the Goth lifestyle, avoid Gothic and other odd fonts. Stick with Times New Roman or Arial.

TEXT IN ALL CAPS vs. Being a pest
Do not, we repeat, do not phone people right after you send an email and ask them if they got the email. Got it? SHOUTING AT PEOPLE (a.k.a. ALL CAPS TEXT) isn't as obnoxious as hassling them.

IN NO TIME AT ALL, email has taken over our lives. Don't get us wrong – we love email. But email comes with a host of boorish and terrible behaviors. Some behaviors make email hard to read (that's why missing subject lines, spelling errors, and bizarre fonts are so aggravating). Some are simply tough to take (is there anyone left who doesn't know that ALL CAPS is shouting?). Some are wildly dangerous to send in business ("this might not be legal") or affairs of the heart (emailing while drunk). Some, like our winner, are simply rude.

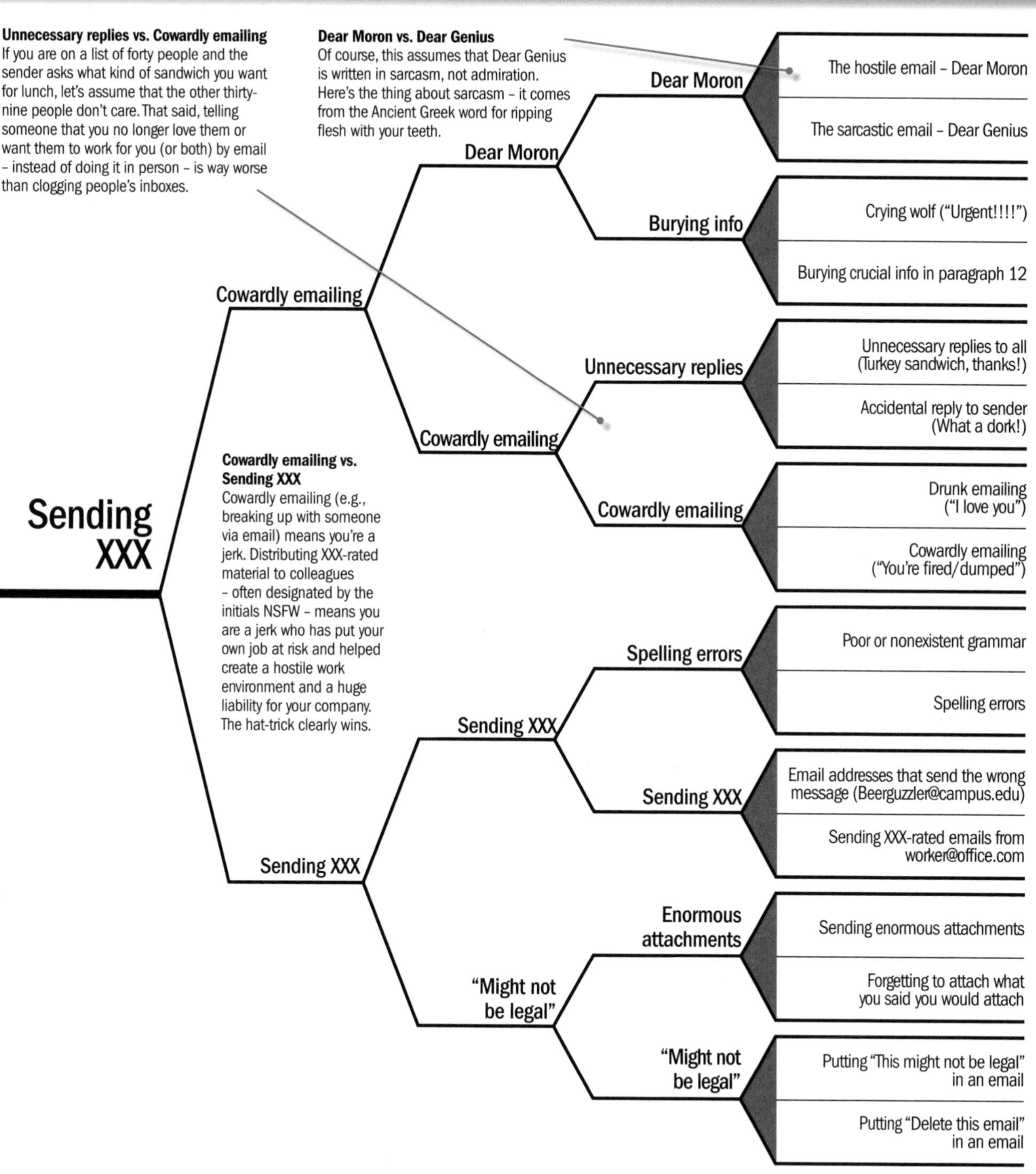

Unnecessary replies vs. Cowardly emailing
If you are on a list of forty people and the sender asks what kind of sandwich you want for lunch, let's assume that the other thirty-nine people don't care. That said, telling someone that you no longer love them or want them to work for you (or both) by email – instead of doing it in person – is way worse than clogging people's inboxes.
Dear Moron vs. Dear Genius
Of course, this assumes that Dear Genius is written in sarcasm, not admiration. Here's the thing about sarcasm – it comes from the Ancient Greek word for ripping flesh with your teeth.
Cowardly emailing vs. Sending XXX
Cowardly emailing (e.g., breaking up with someone via email) means you're a jerk. Distributing XXX-rated material to colleagues – often designated by the initials NSFW – means you are a jerk who has put your own job at risk and helped create a hostile work environment and a huge liability for your company. The hat-trick clearly wins.
Sending XXX
Cowardly emailing
Sending XXX
Dear Moron
Cowardly emailing
Sending XXX
"Might not be legal"
Dear Moron
Burying info
Unnecessary replies
Cowardly emailing
Spelling errors
Sending XXX
Enormous attachments
"Might not be legal"
The hostile email – Dear Moron
The sarcastic email – Dear Genius
Crying wolf ("Urgent!!!!")
Burying crucial info in paragraph 12
Unnecessary replies to all (Turkey sandwich, thanks!)
Accidental reply to sender (What a dork!)
Drunk emailing ("I love you")
Cowardly emailing ("You're fired/dumped")
Poor or nonexistent grammar
Spelling errors
Email addresses that send the wrong message (Beerguzzler@campus.edu)
Sending XXX-rated emails from worker@office.com
Sending enormous attachments
Forgetting to attach what you said you would attach
Putting "This might not be legal" in an email
Putting "Delete this email" in an email

Politically Correct Terms

By Henry Beard and Christopher Cerf

Henry Beard and Christopher Cerf are the co-authors of several processed tree carcasses, including *The Official Politically Correct Dictionary and Handbook* and its companion volume *The Official Sexually Correct Dictionary and Dating Guide.*

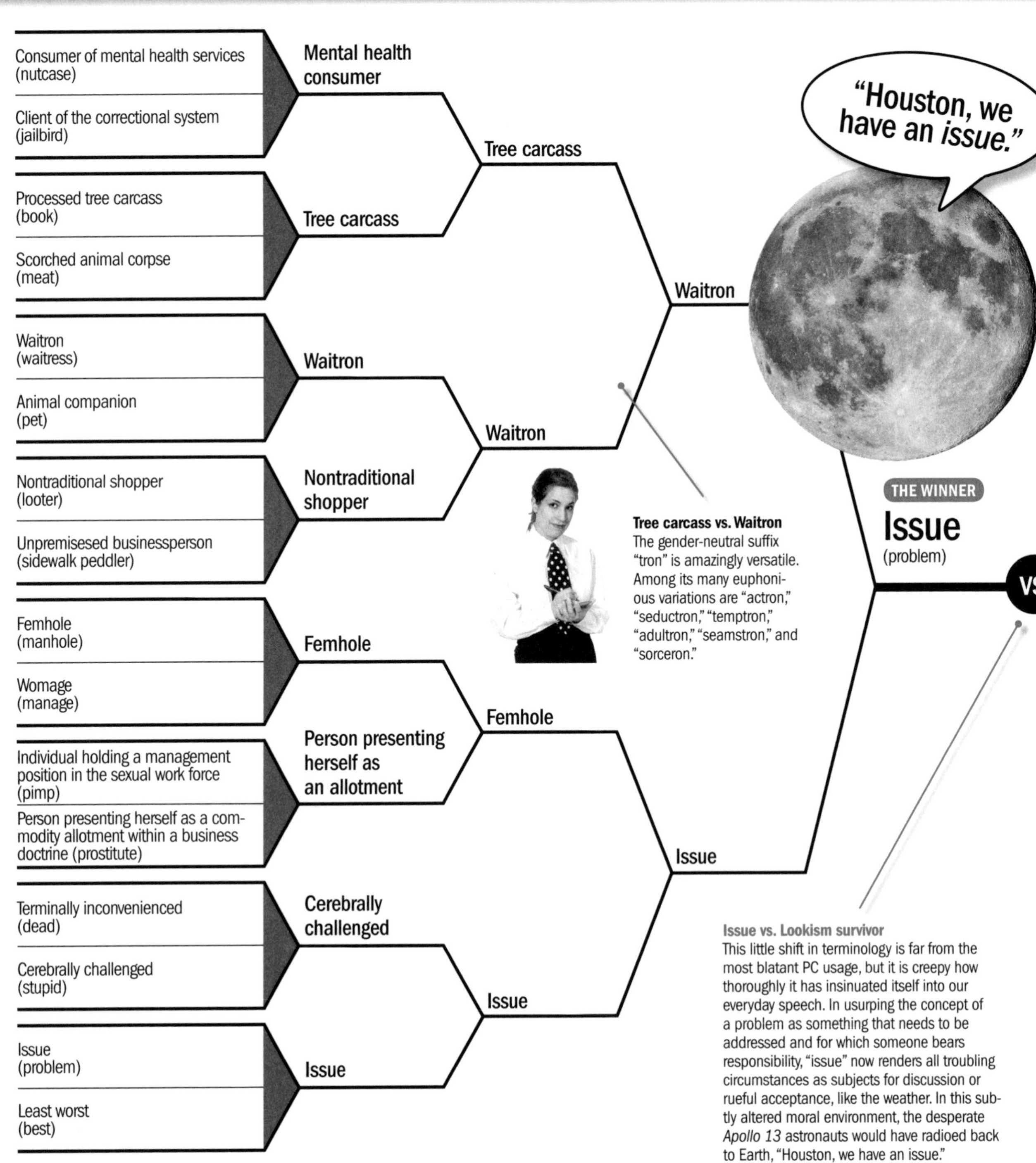
Consumer of mental health services (nutcase)
Client of the correctional system (jailbird)
Processed tree carcass (book)
Scorched animal corpse (meat)
Waitron (waitress)
Animal companion (pet)
Nontraditional shopper (looter)
Unpremisesed businessperson (sidewalk peddler)
Femhole (manhole)
Womage (manage)
Individual holding a management position in the sexual work force (pimp)
Person presenting herself as a commodity allotment within a business doctrine (prostitute)
Terminally inconvenienced (dead)
Cerebrally challenged (stupid)
Issue (problem)
Least worst (best)
Mental health consumer
Tree carcass
Waitron
Nontraditional shopper
Femhole
Person presenting herself as an allotment
Cerebrally challenged
Issue
Tree carcass
Waitron
Femhole
Issue
Waitron
Issue
"Houston, we have an *issue*."
THE WINNER
Issue
(problem)
VS.

Tree carcass vs. Waitron
The gender-neutral suffix "tron" is amazingly versatile. Among its many euphonious variations are "actron," "seductron," "temptron," "adultron," "seamstron," and "sorceron."

Issue vs. Lookism survivor
This little shift in terminology is far from the most blatant PC usage, but it is creepy how thoroughly it has insinuated itself into our everyday speech. In usurping the concept of a problem as something that needs to be addressed and for which someone bears responsibility, "issue" now renders all troubling circumstances as subjects for discussion or rueful acceptance, like the weather. In this subtly altered moral environment, the desperate *Apollo 13* astronauts would have radioed back to Earth, "Houston, we have an issue."

(POLITICALLY CORRECT SPEECH is not exclusively American, but we excel at it. The PC kerfuffle is a straw man – oops, "a person of straw" – for liberal-bashers desperate to portray any marginal movement as a vast conspiracy of behavior modification. That said, the idea of self-censorship has a disturbingly Orwellian Big Brother – er, Big Sibling – quality. Choosing a favorite implies winners and losers, which is a no-no because even the clunkiest turn of phrase is elegant in its own special way. Blame it on the bracketological tyranny of a male-dominant culture of sports hierarchicalism.)

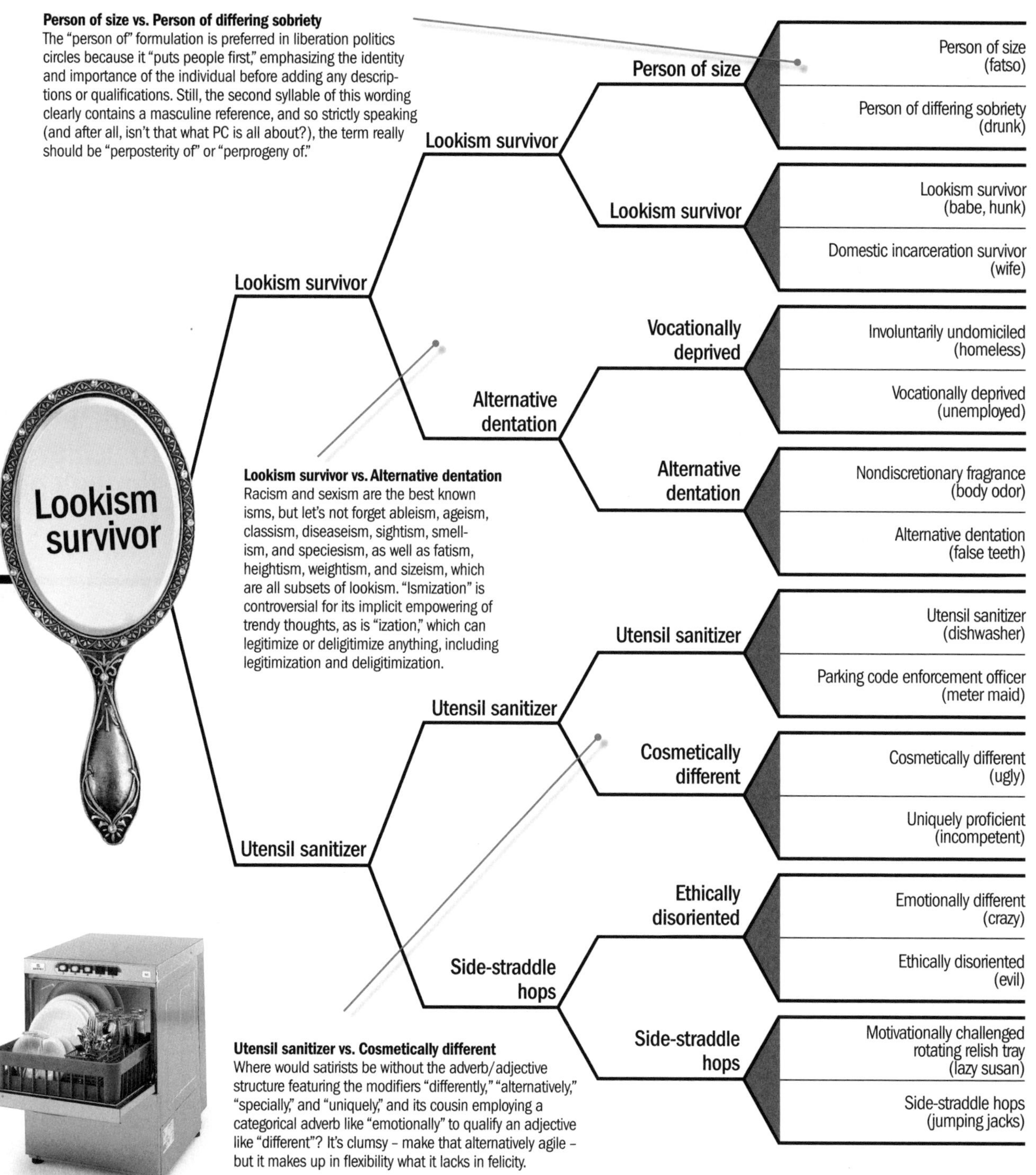

Person of size vs. Person of differing sobriety
The "person of" formulation is preferred in liberation politics circles because it "puts people first," emphasizing the identity and importance of the individual before adding any descriptions or qualifications. Still, the second syllable of this wording clearly contains a masculine reference, and so strictly speaking (and after all, isn't that what PC is all about?), the term really should be "perposterity of" or "perprogeny of."
Person of size
(fatso)
Person of differing sobriety
(drunk)
Lookism survivor
(babe, hunk)
Domestic incarceration survivor
(wife)
Involuntarily undomiciled
(homeless)
Vocationally deprived
(unemployed)
Nondiscretionary fragrance
(body odor)
Alternative dentation
(false teeth)
Utensil sanitizer
(dishwasher)
Parking code enforcement officer
(meter maid)
Cosmetically different
(ugly)
Uniquely proficient
(incompetent)
Emotionally different
(crazy)
Ethically disoriented
(evil)
Motivationally challenged rotating relish tray
(lazy susan)
Side-straddle hops
(jumping jacks)
Person of size
Lookism survivor
Vocationally deprived
Alternative dentation
Utensil sanitizer
Cosmetically different
Ethically disoriented
Side-straddle hops
Lookism survivor
Alternative dentation
Utensil sanitizer
Side-straddle hops
Lookism survivor
Utensil sanitizer
Lookism survivor
Lookism survivor vs. Alternative dentation
Racism and sexism are the best known isms, but let's not forget ableism, ageism, classism, diseaseism, sightism, smellism, and speciesism, as well as fatism, heightism, weightism, and sizeism, which are all subsets of lookism. "Ismization" is controversial for its implicit empowering of trendy thoughts, as is "ization," which can legitimize or deligitimize anything, including legitimization and deligitimization.
Utensil sanitizer vs. Cosmetically different
Where would satirists be without the adverb/adjective structure featuring the modifiers "differently," "alternatively," "specially," and "uniquely," and its cousin employing a categorical adverb like "emotionally" to qualify an adjective like "different"? It's clumsy – make that alternatively agile – but it makes up in flexibility what it lacks in felicity.

Woody Allen Wisdom

By Eric Lax

Besides *Woody Allen, a Biography,* and *Conversations with Woody Allen,* Eric Lax's books include *The Mold in Dr. Florey's Coat, Life and Death on 10 West,* and *On Being Funny.*

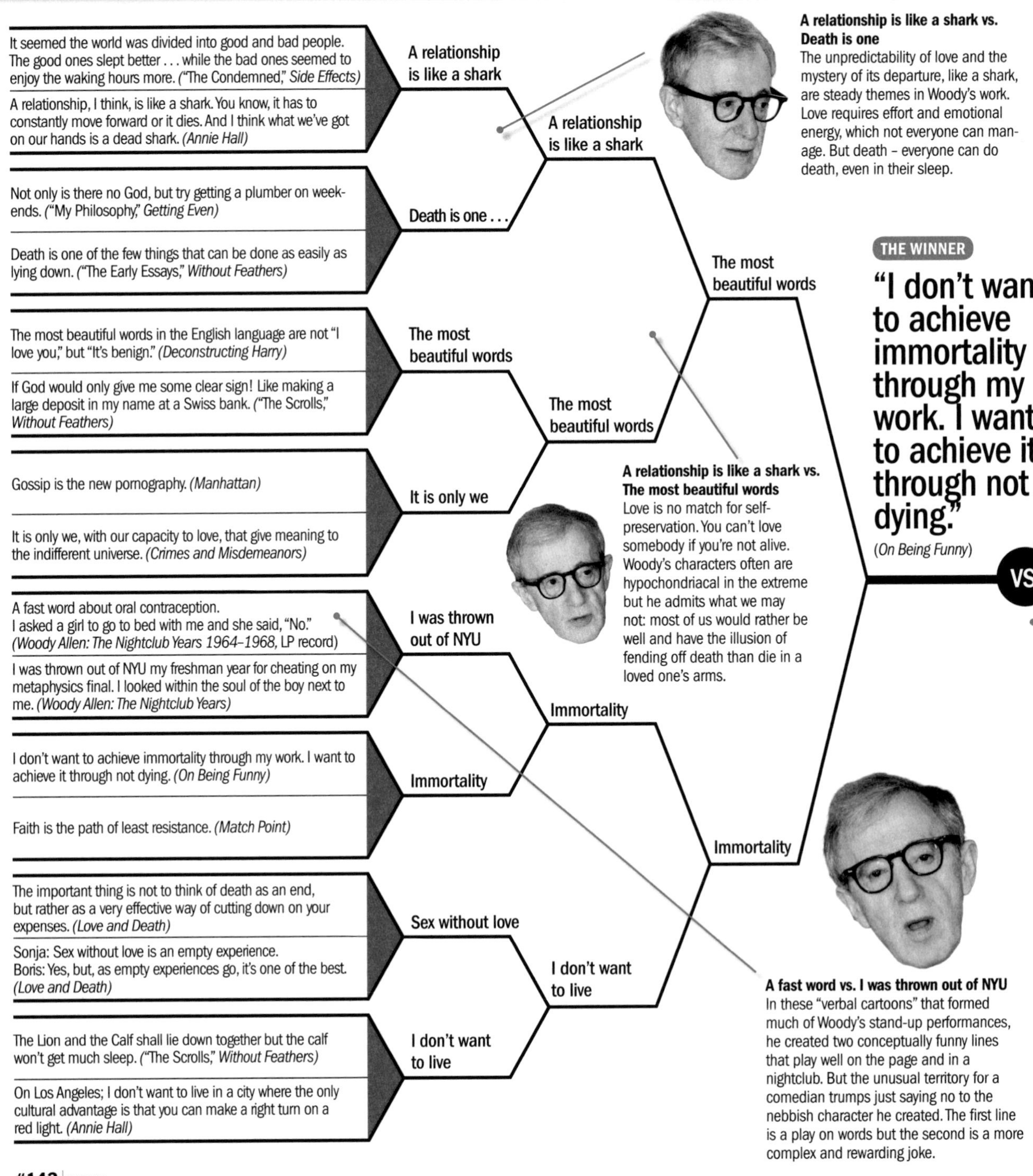

It seemed the world was divided into good and bad people. The good ones slept better . . . while the bad ones seemed to enjoy the waking hours more. ("The Condemned," *Side Effects*)
A relationship, I think, is like a shark. You know, it has to constantly move forward or it dies. And I think what we've got on our hands is a dead shark. (*Annie Hall*)
Not only is there no God, but try getting a plumber on weekends. ("My Philosophy," *Getting Even*)
Death is one of the few things that can be done as easily as lying down. ("The Early Essays," *Without Feathers*)
The most beautiful words in the English language are not "I love you," but "It's benign." (*Deconstructing Harry*)
If God would only give me some clear sign! Like making a large deposit in my name at a Swiss bank. ("The Scrolls," *Without Feathers*)
Gossip is the new pornography. (*Manhattan*)
It is only we, with our capacity to love, that give meaning to the indifferent universe. (*Crimes and Misdemeanors*)
A fast word about oral contraception. I asked a girl to go to bed with me and she said, "No." (*Woody Allen: The Nightclub Years 1964–1968,* LP record)
I was thrown out of NYU my freshman year for cheating on my metaphysics final. I looked within the soul of the boy next to me. (*Woody Allen: The Nightclub Years*)
I don't want to achieve immortality through my work. I want to achieve it through not dying. (*On Being Funny*)
Faith is the path of least resistance. (*Match Point*)
The important thing is not to think of death as an end, but rather as a very effective way of cutting down on your expenses. (*Love and Death*)
Sonja: Sex without love is an empty experience.
Boris: Yes, but, as empty experiences go, it's one of the best. (*Love and Death*)
The Lion and the Calf shall lie down together but the calf won't get much sleep. ("The Scrolls," *Without Feathers*)
On Los Angeles; I don't want to live in a city where the only cultural advantage is that you can make a right turn on a red light. (*Annie Hall*)
A relationship is like a shark
Death is one . . .
The most beautiful words
It is only we
I was thrown out of NYU
Immortality
Sex without love
I don't want to live
A relationship is like a shark
The most beautiful words
Immortality
I don't want to live
The most beautiful words
Immortality
A relationship is like a shark vs. Death is one
The unpredictability of love and the mystery of its departure, like a shark, are steady themes in Woody's work. Love requires effort and emotional energy, which not everyone can manage. But death – everyone can do death, even in their sleep.
A relationship is like a shark vs. The most beautiful words
Love is no match for self-preservation. You can't love somebody if you're not alive. Woody's characters often are hypochondriacal in the extreme but he admits what we may not: most of us would rather be well and have the illusion of fending off death than die in a loved one's arms.
A fast word vs. I was thrown out of NYU
In these "verbal cartoons" that formed much of Woody's stand-up performances, he created two conceptually funny lines that play well on the page and in a nightclub. But the unusual territory for a comedian trumps just saying no to the nebbish character he created. The first line is a play on words but the second is a more complex and rewarding joke.
THE WINNER
"I don't want to achieve immortality through my work. I want to achieve it through not dying."
(*On Being Funny*)
VS.

WOODY ALLEN'S QUIPS AND ONE-LINERS on love, death, sex, and the elusiveness of God combine a comic's insight with a poet's capacity to make the most of every word. His ease with ideas and his understanding of human frailty in films, stand-up comedy, essays, and interviews make for lines that are smart without being pedantic, biting without being rabid, and true in ways we had never considered, which is why they are funny, sage, and memorable.

If it turns out vs. Rather than live
God is speculative, death is absolute, as is Woody's desire to avoid it. One reason he is so prolific is that immersion in work distracts him from dwelling on eschatology. A God who lived up to His potential would let Woody live on in his beautiful home.

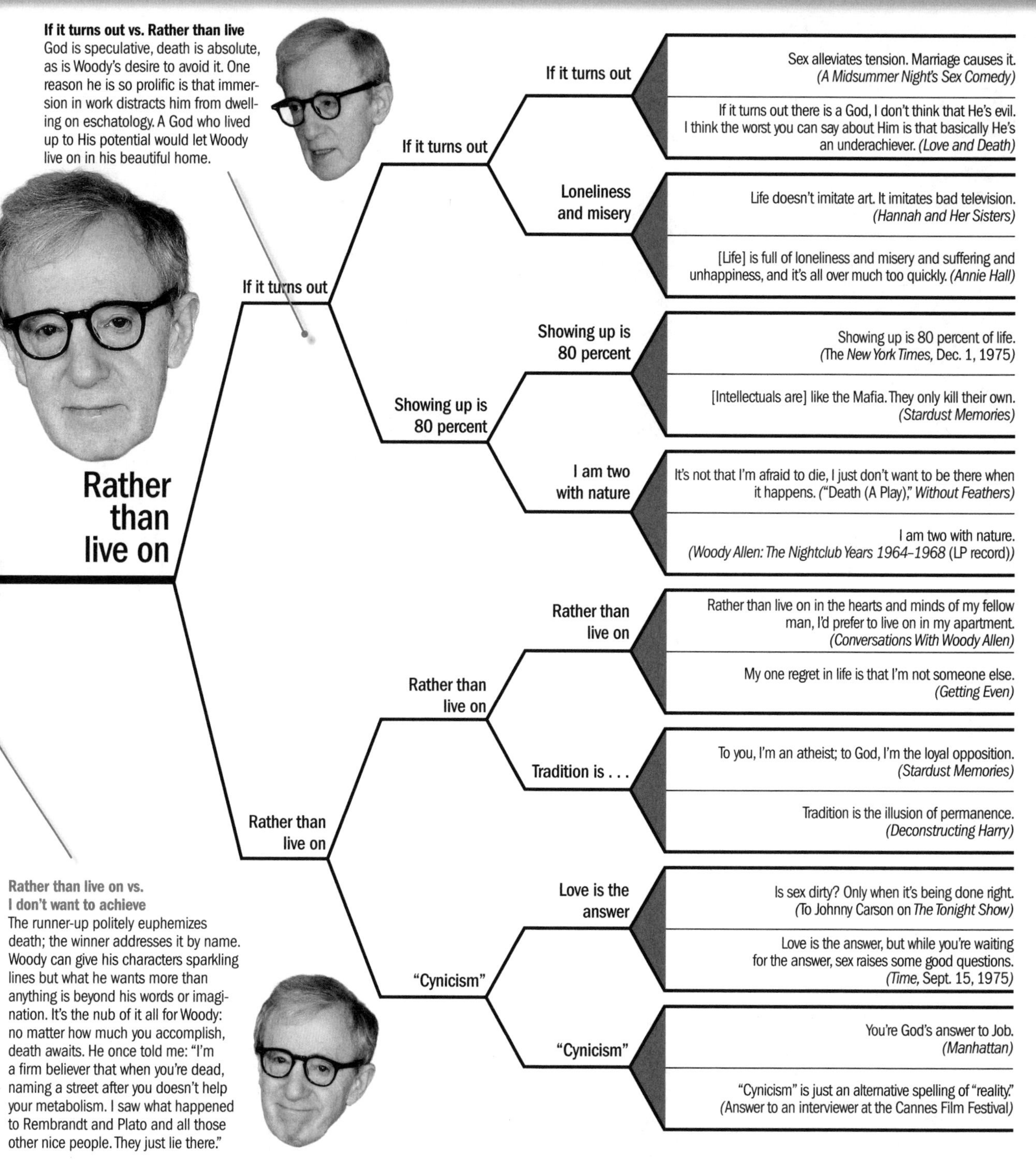

Rather than live on
If it turns out
If it turns out
If it turns out
Sex alleviates tension. Marriage causes it. (A Midsummer Night's Sex Comedy)
If it turns out there is a God, I don't think that He's evil. I think the worst you can say about Him is that basically He's an underachiever. (Love and Death)
Loneliness and misery
Life doesn't imitate art. It imitates bad television. (Hannah and Her Sisters)
[Life] is full of loneliness and misery and suffering and unhappiness, and it's all over much too quickly. (Annie Hall)
Showing up is 80 percent
Showing up is 80 percent
Showing up is 80 percent of life. (The New York Times, Dec. 1, 1975)
[Intellectuals are] like the Mafia. They only kill their own. (Stardust Memories)
I am two with nature
It's not that I'm afraid to die, I just don't want to be there when it happens. ("Death (A Play)," Without Feathers)
I am two with nature. (Woody Allen: The Nightclub Years 1964–1968 (LP record))
Rather than live on
Rather than live on
Rather than live on
Rather than live on in the hearts and minds of my fellow man, I'd prefer to live on in my apartment. (Conversations With Woody Allen)
My one regret in life is that I'm not someone else. (Getting Even)
Tradition is . . .
To you, I'm an atheist; to God, I'm the loyal opposition. (Stardust Memories)
Tradition is the illusion of permanence. (Deconstructing Harry)
"Cynicism"
Love is the answer
Is sex dirty? Only when it's being done right. (To Johnny Carson on The Tonight Show)
Love is the answer, but while you're waiting for the answer, sex raises some good questions. (Time, Sept. 15, 1975)
"Cynicism"
You're God's answer to Job. (Manhattan)
"Cynicism" is just an alternative spelling of "reality." (Answer to an interviewer at the Cannes Film Festival)

Rather than live on vs. I don't want to achieve
The runner-up politely euphemizes death; the winner addresses it by name. Woody can give his characters sparkling lines but what he wants more than anything is beyond his words or imagination. It's the nub of it all for Woody: no matter how much you accomplish, death awaits. He once told me: "I'm a firm believer that when you're dead, naming a street after you doesn't help your metabolism. I saw what happened to Rembrandt and Plato and all those other nice people. They just lie there."

FOOD & DRINK

It's Better with Bacon *by Peter Kaminksy* 143
Cocktails *by Jonathan Miles* 144
Breakfast Cereals *by Drew Magary* 145
Domestic Beers *by Maureen Ogle* 146
Artisan Cheeses *by Max McCalman and David Gibbons* 147
Regional Soda Pop *by Bob Roe* 148
American Wines *by Joseph S. Ward* 149
Classic Cookbooks *by Katie Workman* 150

It's Better with Bacon

By Peter Kaminsky

Peter Kaminsky is the author of *Pig Perfect: Encounters With Remarkable Swine,* and one of the world's leading hamthropologists.

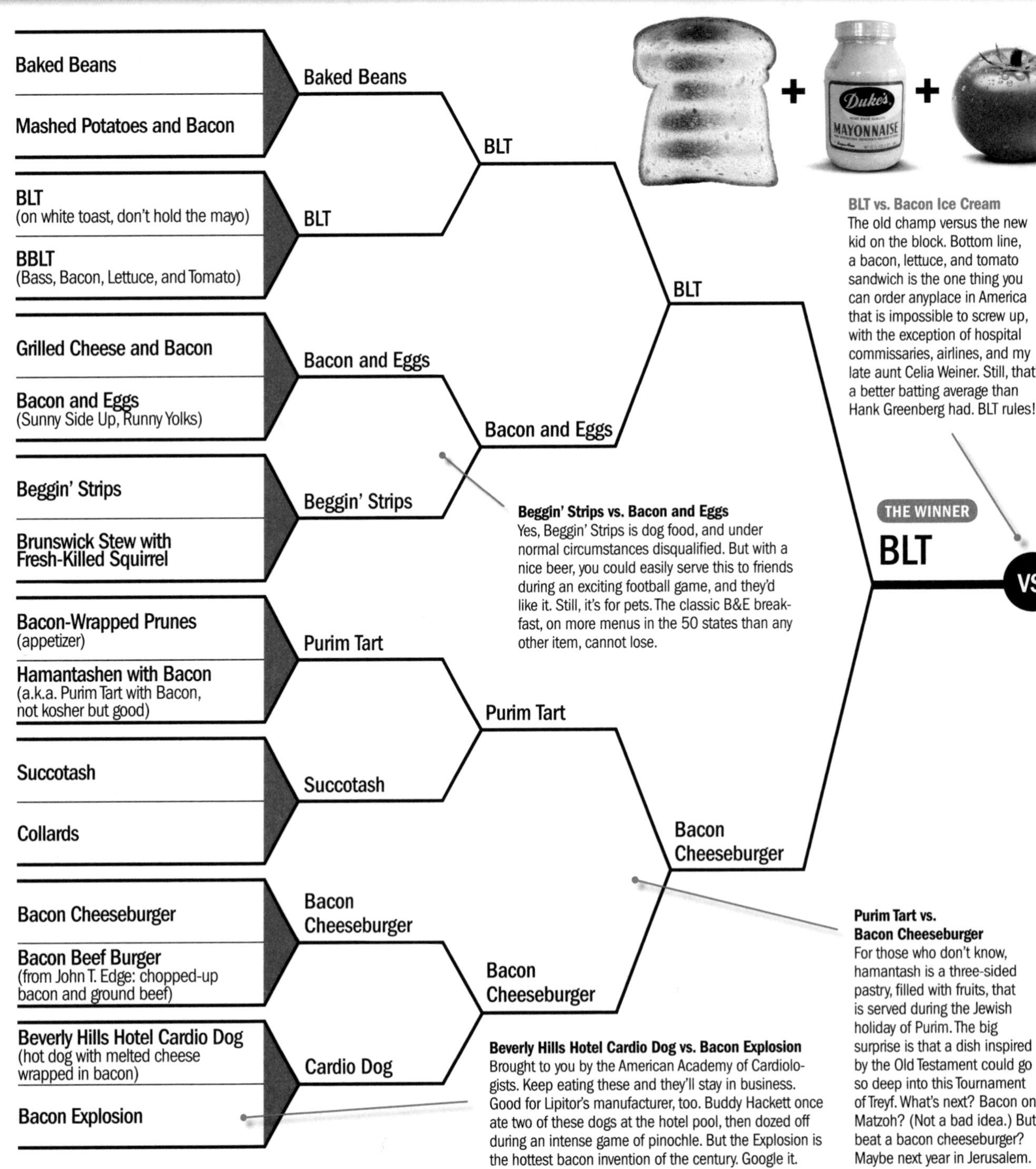
Baked Beans
Mashed Potatoes and Bacon
BLT
(on white toast, don't hold the mayo)
BBLT
(Bass, Bacon, Lettuce, and Tomato)
Grilled Cheese and Bacon
Bacon and Eggs
(Sunny Side Up, Runny Yolks)
Beggin' Strips
Brunswick Stew with Fresh-Killed Squirrel
Bacon-Wrapped Prunes
(appetizer)
Hamantashen with Bacon
(a.k.a. Purim Tart with Bacon, not kosher but good)
Succotash
Collards
Bacon Cheeseburger
Bacon Beef Burger
(from John T. Edge: chopped-up bacon and ground beef)
Beverly Hills Hotel Cardio Dog
(hot dog with melted cheese wrapped in bacon)
Bacon Explosion
Baked Beans
BLT
Bacon and Eggs
Beggin' Strips
Purim Tart
Succotash
Bacon Cheeseburger
Cardio Dog
BLT
Bacon and Eggs
Purim Tart
Bacon Cheeseburger
BLT
Bacon Cheeseburger
+
Duke's
MAYONNAISE
+
THE WINNER
BLT
VS.

BLT vs. Bacon Ice Cream
The old champ versus the new kid on the block. Bottom line, a bacon, lettuce, and tomato sandwich is the one thing you can order anyplace in America that is impossible to screw up, with the exception of hospital commissaries, airlines, and my late aunt Celia Weiner. Still, that's a better batting average than Hank Greenberg had. BLT rules!

Beggin' Strips vs. Bacon and Eggs
Yes, Beggin' Strips is dog food, and under normal circumstances disqualified. But with a nice beer, you could easily serve this to friends during an exciting football game, and they'd like it. Still, it's for pets. The classic B&E breakfast, on more menus in the 50 states than any other item, cannot lose.

Purim Tart vs. Bacon Cheeseburger
For those who don't know, hamantash is a three-sided pastry, filled with fruits, that is served during the Jewish holiday of Purim. The big surprise is that a dish inspired by the Old Testament could go so deep into this Tournament of Treyf. What's next? Bacon on Matzoh? (Not a bad idea.) But beat a bacon cheeseburger? Maybe next year in Jerusalem.

Beverly Hills Hotel Cardio Dog vs. Bacon Explosion
Brought to you by the American Academy of Cardiologists. Keep eating these and they'll stay in business. Good for Lipitor's manufacturer, too. Buddy Hackett once ate two of these dogs at the hotel pool, then dozed off during an intense game of pinochle. But the Explosion is the hottest bacon invention of the century. Google it.

THE HUMORIST SEAN KELLY CLAIMS that any literary work sounds funny when you insert the word "pork" into the title, as in "To Pork and Pork Not," "Gone with the Pork," or "The Porking Point." Likewise, there isn't a food on earth that isn't improved by the addition of bacon. Salty, crispy, fatty, meaty, funky – bacon is irresistible, which explains why I enjoy watching as one vegetarian after another steps on the steep slope that takes him from a first nibble of bacon in the morning to a bloody Porterhouse by dinner time. Bacon is the ultimate gateway drug.

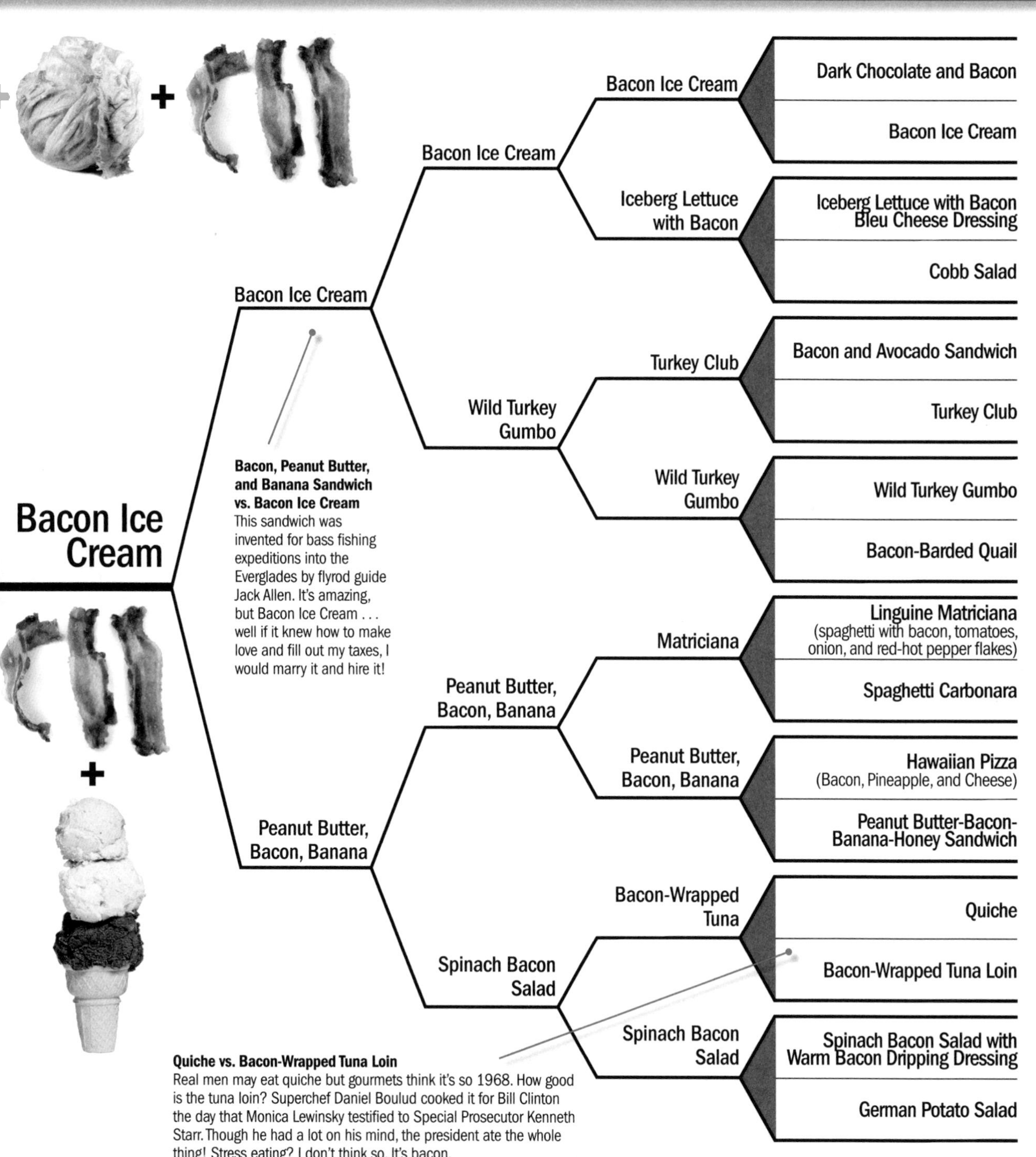

Dark Chocolate and Bacon
Bacon Ice Cream
Iceberg Lettuce with Bacon Bleu Cheese Dressing
Cobb Salad
Bacon and Avocado Sandwich
Turkey Club
Wild Turkey Gumbo
Bacon-Barded Quail
Linguine Matriciana (spaghetti with bacon, tomatoes, onion, and red-hot pepper flakes)
Spaghetti Carbonara
Hawaiian Pizza (Bacon, Pineapple, and Cheese)
Peanut Butter-Bacon-Banana-Honey Sandwich
Quiche
Bacon-Wrapped Tuna Loin
Spinach Bacon Salad with Warm Bacon Dripping Dressing
German Potato Salad
Bacon Ice Cream
Iceberg Lettuce with Bacon
Turkey Club
Wild Turkey Gumbo
Matriciana
Peanut Butter, Bacon, Banana
Bacon-Wrapped Tuna
Spinach Bacon Salad
Bacon Ice Cream
Wild Turkey Gumbo
Peanut Butter, Bacon, Banana
Spinach Bacon Salad
Bacon Ice Cream
Peanut Butter, Bacon, Banana
Bacon Ice Cream

Bacon, Peanut Butter, and Banana Sandwich vs. Bacon Ice Cream
This sandwich was invented for bass fishing expeditions into the Everglades by flyrod guide Jack Allen. It's amazing, but Bacon Ice Cream . . . well if it knew how to make love and fill out my taxes, I would marry it and hire it!

Quiche vs. Bacon-Wrapped Tuna Loin
Real men may eat quiche but gourmets think it's so 1968. How good is the tuna loin? Superchef Daniel Boulud cooked it for Bill Clinton the day that Monica Lewinsky testified to Special Prosecutor Kenneth Starr. Though he had a lot on his mind, the president ate the whole thing! Stress eating? I don't think so. It's bacon.

Cocktails

By Jonathan Miles

Jonathan Miles writes the "Shaken and Stirred" column for the Sunday Styles section of the *New York Times*, and is the author of a novel, *Dear American Airlines*.

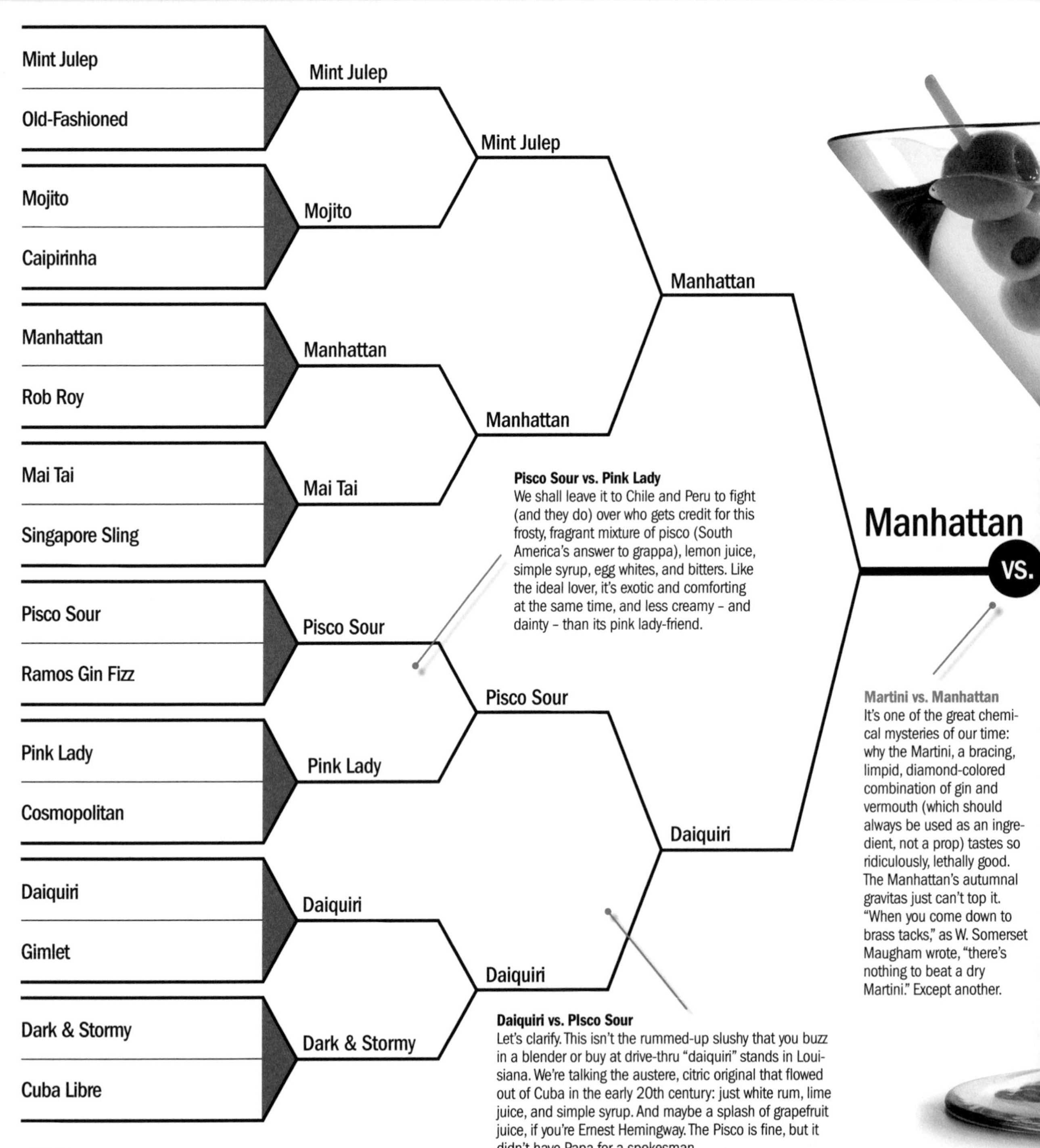

Mint Julep
Old-Fashioned
Mojito
Caipirinha
Manhattan
Rob Roy
Mai Tai
Singapore Sling
Pisco Sour
Ramos Gin Fizz
Pink Lady
Cosmopolitan
Daiquiri
Gimlet
Dark & Stormy
Cuba Libre
Mint Julep
Mojito
Manhattan
Mai Tai
Pisco Sour
Pink Lady
Daiquiri
Dark & Stormy
Mint Julep
Manhattan
Pisco Sour
Daiquiri
Manhattan
Daiquiri
Manhattan
VS.

Pisco Sour vs. Pink Lady
We shall leave it to Chile and Peru to fight (and they do) over who gets credit for this frosty, fragrant mixture of pisco (South America's answer to grappa), lemon juice, simple syrup, egg whites, and bitters. Like the ideal lover, it's exotic and comforting at the same time, and less creamy – and dainty – than its pink lady-friend.

Martini vs. Manhattan
It's one of the great chemical mysteries of our time: why the Martini, a bracing, limpid, diamond-colored combination of gin and vermouth (which should always be used as an ingredient, not a prop) tastes so ridiculously, lethally good. The Manhattan's autumnal gravitas just can't top it. "When you come down to brass tacks," as W. Somerset Maugham wrote, "there's nothing to beat a dry Martini." Except another.

Daiquiri vs. Pisco Sour
Let's clarify. This isn't the rummed-up slushy that you buzz in a blender or buy at drive-thru "daiquiri" stands in Louisiana. We're talking the austere, citric original that flowed out of Cuba in the early 20th century: just white rum, lime juice, and simple syrup. And maybe a splash of grapefruit juice, if you're Ernest Hemingway. The Pisco is fine, but it didn't have Papa for a spokesman.

THE COCKTAIL IS NOT ONLY AN AMERICAN INVENTION. It is, like jazz, an American symbol: the shaking and stirring of disparate components, many of them imports, to produce something greater than the sum of the parts. We herald our country as a "melting pot," but what the heck is a melting pot anyway and when might I have seen one? No, my country 'tis of thee is a cocktail shaker. The judging here was based on historical significance, lore and legend, and a prodigious series of semi-scientific tastings. Now if someone will just tell me on what page I can find the bracket for hangover remedies.

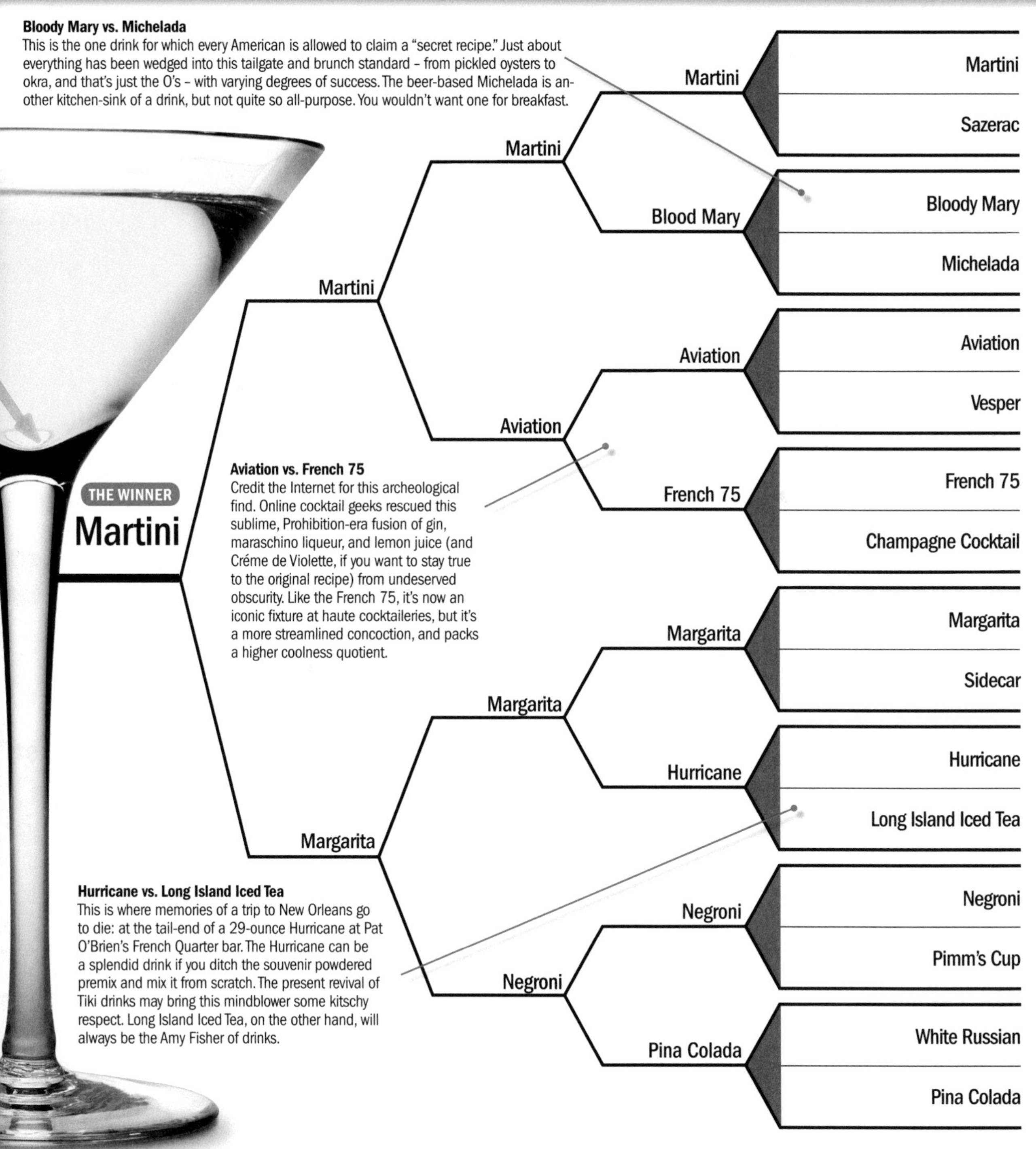

Martini
Sazerac
Bloody Mary
Michelada
Aviation
Vesper
French 75
Champagne Cocktail
Margarita
Sidecar
Hurricane
Long Island Iced Tea
Negroni
Pimm's Cup
White Russian
Pina Colada
Martini
Blood Mary
Aviation
French 75
Margarita
Hurricane
Negroni
Pina Colada
Martini
Aviation
Margarita
Negroni
Martini
Margarita
THE WINNER
Martini

Bloody Mary vs. Michelada
This is the one drink for which every American is allowed to claim a "secret recipe." Just about everything has been wedged into this tailgate and brunch standard – from pickled oysters to okra, and that's just the O's – with varying degrees of success. The beer-based Michelada is another kitchen-sink of a drink, but not quite so all-purpose. You wouldn't want one for breakfast.

Aviation vs. French 75
Credit the Internet for this archeological find. Online cocktail geeks rescued this sublime, Prohibition-era fusion of gin, maraschino liqueur, and lemon juice (and Créme de Violette, if you want to stay true to the original recipe) from undeserved obscurity. Like the French 75, it's now an iconic fixture at haute cocktaileries, but it's a more streamlined concoction, and packs a higher coolness quotient.

Hurricane vs. Long Island Iced Tea
This is where memories of a trip to New Orleans go to die: at the tail-end of a 29-ounce Hurricane at Pat O'Brien's French Quarter bar. The Hurricane can be a splendid drink if you ditch the souvenir powdered premix and mix it from scratch. The present revival of Tiki drinks may bring this mindblower some kitschy respect. Long Island Iced Tea, on the other hand, will always be the Amy Fisher of drinks.

Breakfast Cereals

By Drew Magary

Drew Magary is the author of *Men with Balls: The Professional Athlete's Handbook,* and the co-founder of Kissing Suzy Kolber. He has eaten cereal for dinner more often than he has eaten real food for dinner.

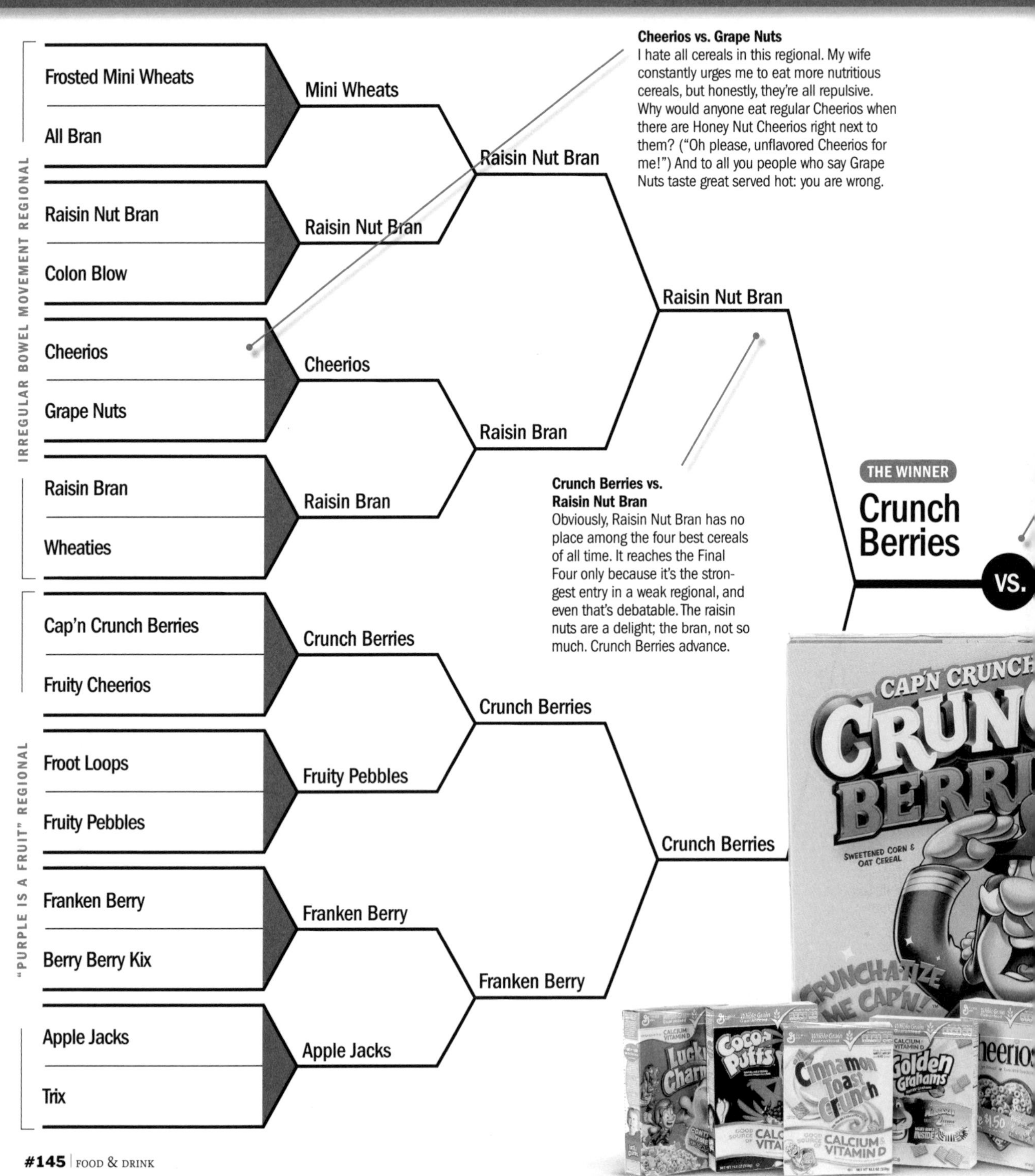
IRREGULAR BOWEL MOVEMENT REGIONAL
Frosted Mini Wheats
All Bran
Raisin Nut Bran
Colon Blow
Cheerios
Grape Nuts
Raisin Bran
Wheaties
Mini Wheats
Raisin Nut Bran
Cheerios
Raisin Bran
Raisin Nut Bran
Raisin Bran
Raisin Nut Bran
"PURPLE IS A FRUIT" REGIONAL
Cap'n Crunch Berries
Fruity Cheerios
Froot Loops
Fruity Pebbles
Franken Berry
Berry Berry Kix
Apple Jacks
Trix
Crunch Berries
Fruity Pebbles
Franken Berry
Apple Jacks
Crunch Berries
Franken Berry
Crunch Berries
THE WINNER
Crunch Berries
VS.
CAP'N CRUNCH
SWEETENED CORN & OAT CEREAL
CALCIUM & VITAMIN D

Cheerios vs. Grape Nuts
I hate all cereals in this regional. My wife constantly urges me to eat more nutritious cereals, but honestly, they're all repulsive. Why would anyone eat regular Cheerios when there are Honey Nut Cheerios right next to them? ("Oh please, unflavored Cheerios for me!") And to all you people who say Grape Nuts taste great served hot: you are wrong.

Crunch Berries vs. Raisin Nut Bran
Obviously, Raisin Nut Bran has no place among the four best cereals of all time. It reaches the Final Four only because it's the strongest entry in a weak regional, and even that's debatable. The raisin nuts are a delight; the bran, not so much. Crunch Berries advance.

I AM 32 YEARS OLD AND HAVE EATEN EVERY BREAKFAST CEREAL known to mankind. Ever have C3PO's? I have. Ever moan in ecstasy at the sight of a box of Oreo O's, which were discontinued in 2007 because they may or may not have caused instadiabetes in toddlers? I do. The best cereals stay crunchy in milk; leave tasty-flavored milk at the end; have enough sugar to destroy your pancreas; and have not-too-challenging mazes on the backs of their boxes.

Crunch Berries vs. Cinnamon Toast Crunch
In seventh grade, a friend of mine conducted a science experiment to determine which cereal stayed crunchy in milk the longest. All Cap'n Crunch varieties won by a mile. Unlike Cinnamon Toast Crunch, which de-crunches faster than I like, you could leave Crunch Berries in battery acid for a week and they'd still be intact – and they'd leave behind strawberry milk. If you don't think that's a great way to start a morning, I don't want to know you. You probably eat All Bran.

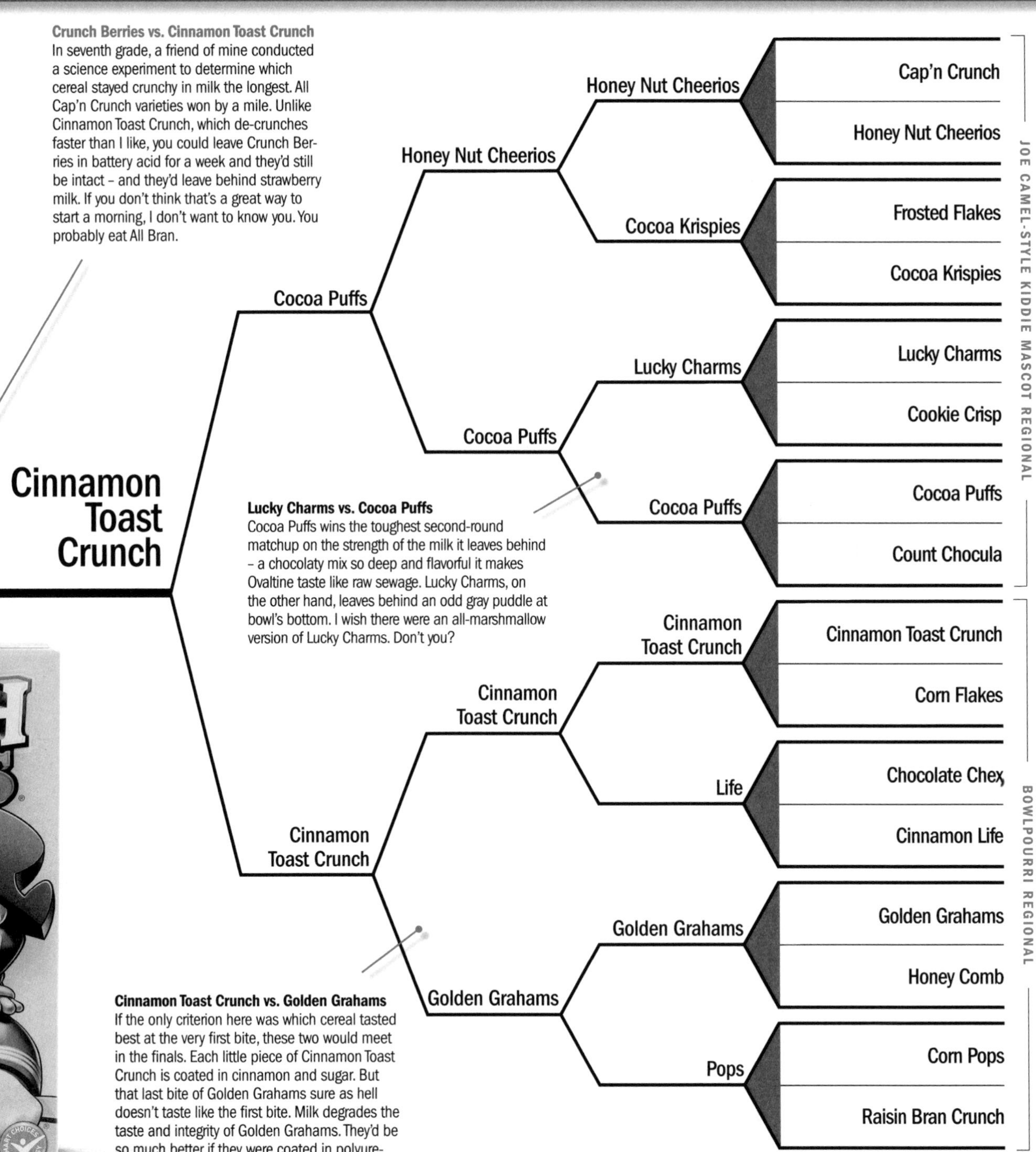

JOE CAMEL-STYLE KIDDIE MASCOT REGIONAL
Cap'n Crunch
Honey Nut Cheerios
Frosted Flakes
Cocoa Krispies
Lucky Charms
Cookie Crisp
Cocoa Puffs
Count Chocula
Honey Nut Cheerios
Cocoa Krispies
Lucky Charms
Cocoa Puffs
Honey Nut Cheerios
Cocoa Puffs
Cocoa Puffs
BOWLPOURRI REGIONAL
Cinnamon Toast Crunch
Corn Flakes
Chocolate Chex
Cinnamon Life
Golden Grahams
Honey Comb
Corn Pops
Raisin Bran Crunch
Cinnamon Toast Crunch
Life
Golden Grahams
Pops
Cinnamon Toast Crunch
Golden Grahams
Cinnamon Toast Crunch
Cinnamon Toast Crunch

Lucky Charms vs. Cocoa Puffs
Cocoa Puffs wins the toughest second-round matchup on the strength of the milk it leaves behind – a chocolaty mix so deep and flavorful it makes Ovaltine taste like raw sewage. Lucky Charms, on the other hand, leaves behind an odd gray puddle at bowl's bottom. I wish there were an all-marshmallow version of Lucky Charms. Don't you?

Cinnamon Toast Crunch vs. Golden Grahams
If the only criterion here was which cereal tasted best at the very first bite, these two would meet in the finals. Each little piece of Cinnamon Toast Crunch is coated in cinnamon and sugar. But that last bite of Golden Grahams sure as hell doesn't taste like the first bite. Milk degrades the taste and integrity of Golden Grahams. They'd be so much better if they were coated in polyurethane. I'm willing to accept the risks involved.

Domestic Beers

By Maureen Ogle

Maureen Ogle is the author of *Ambitious Brew: The Story of American Beer.* Beer, she has decided in middle age, is a portal to the meaning of life.

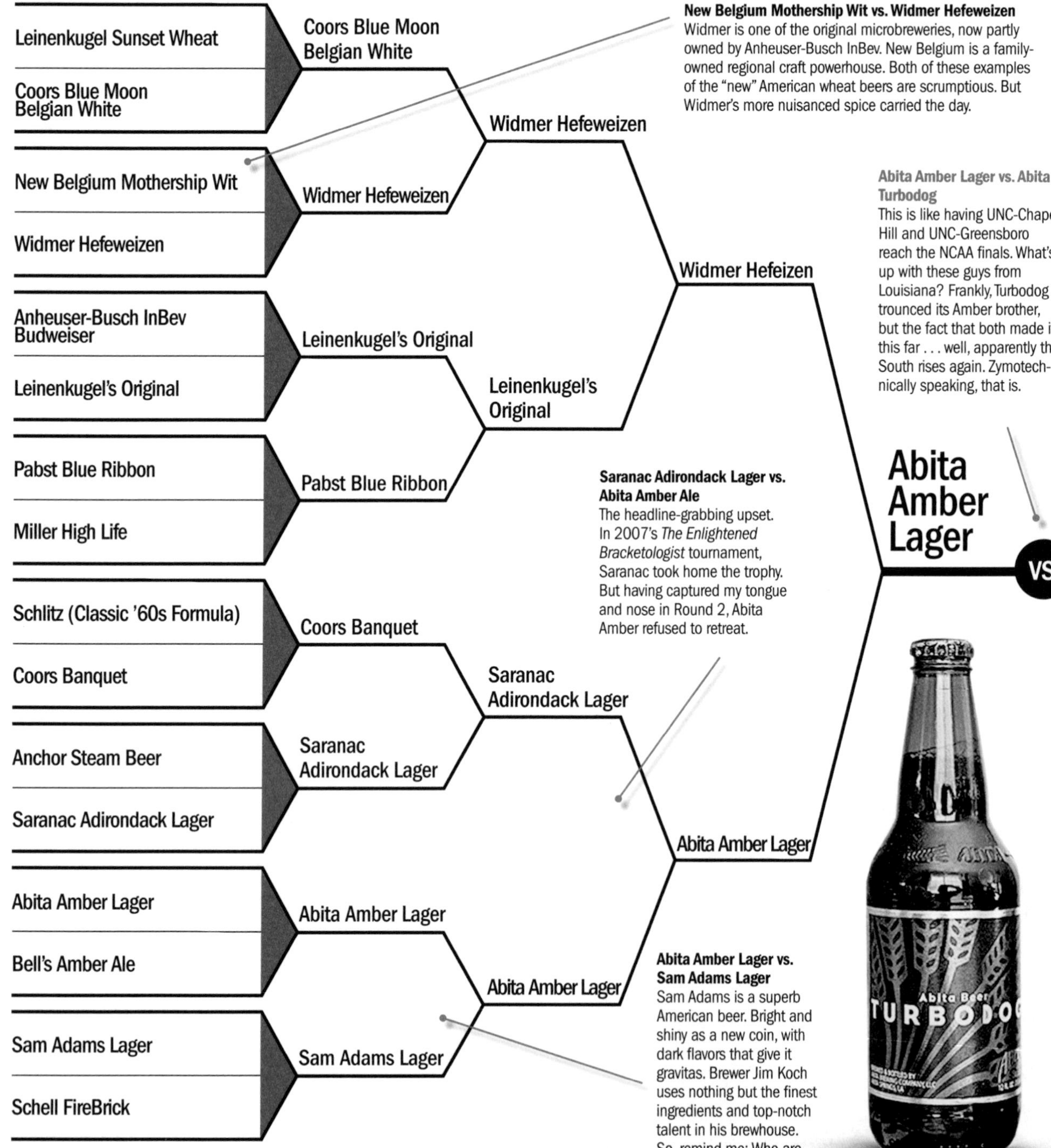
Leinenkugel Sunset Wheat
Coors Blue Moon Belgian White
New Belgium Mothership Wit
Widmer Hefeweizen
Anheuser-Busch InBev Budweiser
Leinenkugel's Original
Pabst Blue Ribbon
Miller High Life
Schlitz (Classic '60s Formula)
Coors Banquet
Anchor Steam Beer
Saranac Adirondack Lager
Abita Amber Lager
Bell's Amber Ale
Sam Adams Lager
Schell FireBrick
Coors Blue Moon Belgian White
Widmer Hefeweizen
Leinenkugel's Original
Pabst Blue Ribbon
Coors Banquet
Saranac Adirondack Lager
Abita Amber Lager
Sam Adams Lager
Widmer Hefeweizen
Leinenkugel's Original
Saranac Adirondack Lager
Abita Amber Lager
Widmer Hefeizen
Abita Amber Lager
Abita Amber Lager
VS.
Abita Beer
TURBODOG

New Belgium Mothership Wit vs. Widmer Hefeweizen
Widmer is one of the original microbreweries, now partly owned by Anheuser-Busch InBev. New Belgium is a family-owned regional craft powerhouse. Both of these examples of the "new" American wheat beers are scrumptious. But Widmer's more nuisanced spice carried the day.

Abita Amber Lager vs. Abita Turbodog
This is like having UNC-Chapel Hill and UNC-Greensboro reach the NCAA finals. What's up with these guys from Louisiana? Frankly, Turbodog trounced its Amber brother, but the fact that both made it this far . . . well, apparently the South rises again. Zymotechnically speaking, that is.

Saranac Adirondack Lager vs. Abita Amber Ale
The headline-grabbing upset. In 2007's *The Enlightened Bracketologist* tournament, Saranac took home the trophy. But having captured my tongue and nose in Round 2, Abita Amber refused to retreat.

Abita Amber Lager vs. Sam Adams Lager
Sam Adams is a superb American beer. Bright and shiny as a new coin, with dark flavors that give it gravitas. Brewer Jim Koch uses nothing but the finest ingredients and top-notch talent in his brewhouse. So, remind me: Who are these Abita people?

LAST TIME I TRIED THIS, Saranac Adirondack Lager won. Hey, life is about change, but the rules remain the same: American beers only (au revoir, Stella), available year-round (no pumpkin ales or other seasonals), and sold in Ames, Iowa, where I live. That narrowed the field because the vast majority of American beers are distributed locally; if I'd been sitting in Utah or Pennsylvania, I'd be bracketing different beers. Yes, the rule favors breweries with national distribution. But it's beer, right? It's all good!

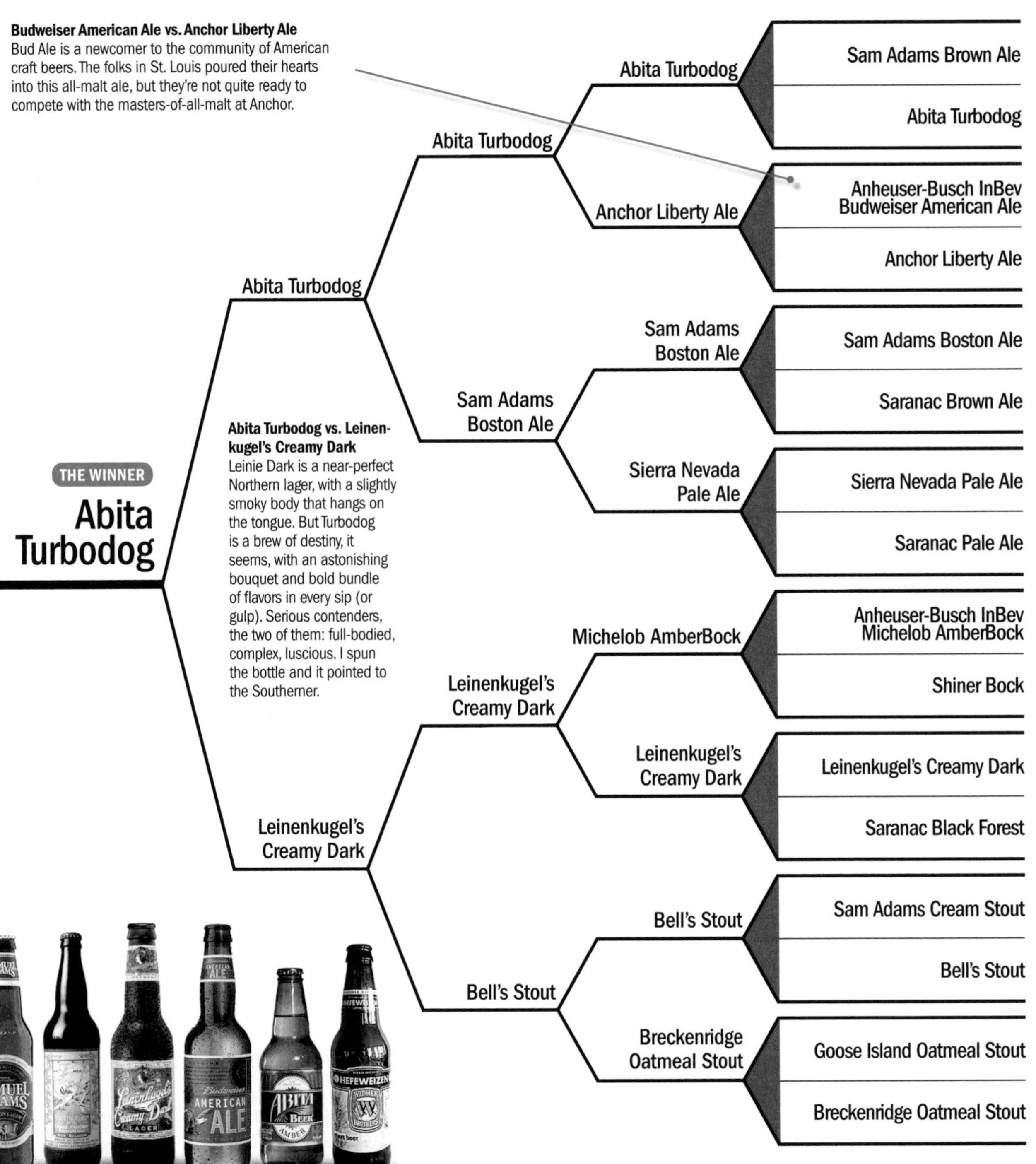
Budweiser American Ale vs. Anchor Liberty Ale
Bud Ale is a newcomer to the community of American craft beers. The folks in St. Louis poured their hearts into this all-malt ale, but they're not quite ready to compete with the masters-of-all-malt at Anchor.
Sam Adams Brown Ale
Abita Turbodog
Abita Turbodog
Abita Turbodog
Anheuser-Busch InBev Budweiser American Ale
Anchor Liberty Ale
Anchor Liberty Ale
Abita Turbodog
Sam Adams Boston Ale
Saranac Brown Ale
Sam Adams Boston Ale
Sierra Nevada Pale Ale
Saranac Pale Ale
Sierra Nevada Pale Ale
Sam Adams Boston Ale
Abita Turbodog vs. Leinenkugel's Creamy Dark
Leinie Dark is a near-perfect Northern lager, with a slightly smoky body that hangs on the tongue. But Turbodog is a brew of destiny, it seems, with an astonishing bouquet and bold bundle of flavors in every sip (or gulp). Serious contenders, the two of them: full-bodied, complex, luscious. I spun the bottle and it pointed to the Southerner.
THE WINNER
Abita Turbodog
Anheuser-Busch InBev Michelob AmberBock
Shiner Bock
Michelob AmberBock
Leinenkugel's Creamy Dark
Saranac Black Forest
Leinenkugel's Creamy Dark
Leinenkugel's Creamy Dark
Leinenkugel's Creamy Dark
Sam Adams Cream Stout
Bell's Stout
Bell's Stout
Goose Island Oatmeal Stout
Breckenridge Oatmeal Stout
Breckenridge Oatmeal Stout
Bell's Stout

Artisan Cheeses

By Max McCalman and David Gibbons

Max McCalman and David Gibbons are authors of *The Cheese Plate and Cheese: A Connoisseur's Guide to the World's Best,* which won a James Beard Award. Their third book, *Mastering Cheese,* is a compilation of nearly two decades of cheese tastings and research.

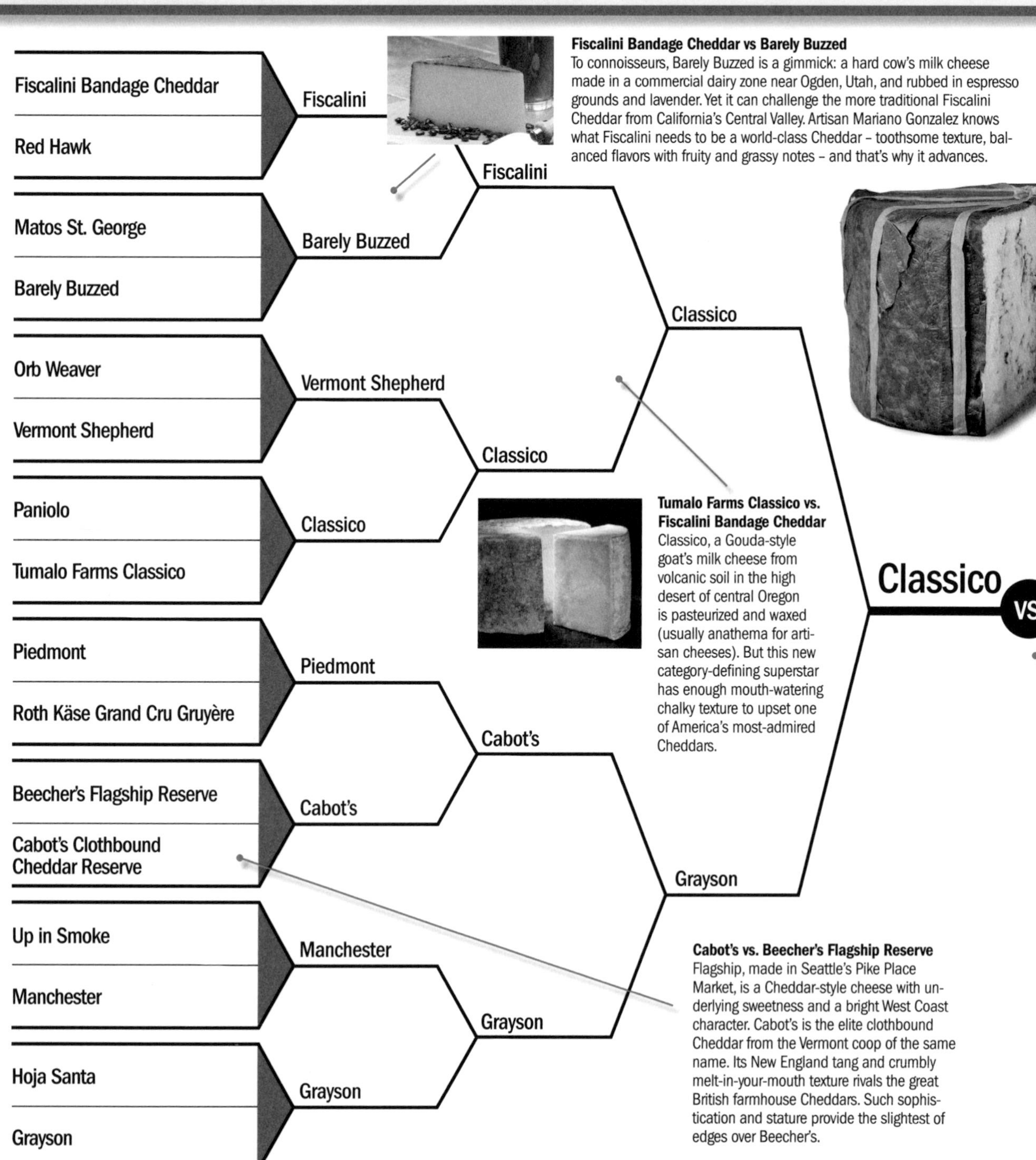

Fiscalini Bandage Cheddar
Red Hawk
Matos St. George
Barely Buzzed
Orb Weaver
Vermont Shepherd
Paniolo
Tumalo Farms Classico
Piedmont
Roth Käse Grand Cru Gruyère
Beecher's Flagship Reserve
Cabot's Clothbound Cheddar Reserve
Up in Smoke
Manchester
Hoja Santa
Grayson
Fiscalini
Barely Buzzed
Vermont Shepherd
Classico
Piedmont
Cabot's
Manchester
Grayson
Fiscalini
Classico
Cabot's
Grayson
Classico
Grayson
Classico
VS.

Fiscalini Bandage Cheddar vs Barely Buzzed
To connoisseurs, Barely Buzzed is a gimmick: a hard cow's milk cheese made in a commercial dairy zone near Ogden, Utah, and rubbed in espresso grounds and lavender. Yet it can challenge the more traditional Fiscalini Cheddar from California's Central Valley. Artisan Mariano Gonzalez knows what Fiscalini needs to be a world-class Cheddar – toothsome texture, balanced flavors with fruity and grassy notes – and that's why it advances.

Tumalo Farms Classico vs. Fiscalini Bandage Cheddar
Classico, a Gouda-style goat's milk cheese from volcanic soil in the high desert of central Oregon is pasteurized and waxed (usually anathema for artisan cheeses). But this new category-defining superstar has enough mouth-watering chalky texture to upset one of America's most-admired Cheddars.

Cabot's vs. Beecher's Flagship Reserve
Flagship, made in Seattle's Pike Place Market, is a Cheddar-style cheese with underlying sweetness and a bright West Coast character. Cabot's is the elite clothbound Cheddar from the Vermont coop of the same name. Its New England tang and crumbly melt-in-your-mouth texture rivals the great British farmhouse Cheddars. Such sophistication and stature provide the slightest of edges over Beecher's.

AMERICAN CHEESE HAS COME A LONG WAY since the year 2000, when barely 20 U.S. farmstead cheesemakers qualified for world-class status. Now more than five dozen artisans rank with the best. The cradles of artisan cheese used to be Vermont and California (and nine of the 32 entrants are from those two states). But eleven other states are represented, most impressively Oregon, which is eco-friendly and supportive of its small sustainable dairy farming and creamery operators – and performs well and deep into our tournament.

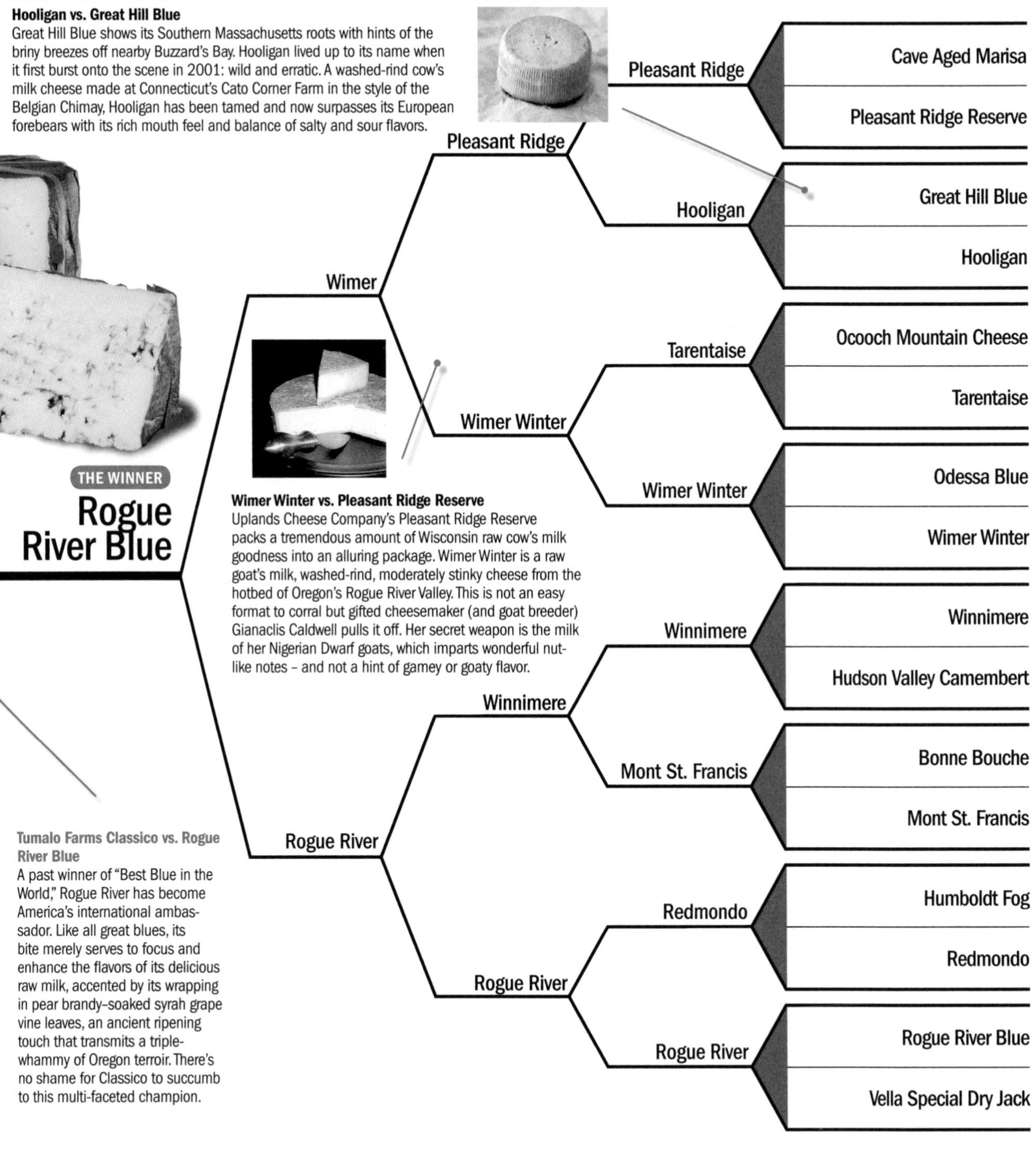

Cave Aged Marisa
Pleasant Ridge Reserve
Great Hill Blue
Hooligan
Ocooch Mountain Cheese
Tarentaise
Odessa Blue
Wimer Winter
Winnimere
Hudson Valley Camembert
Bonne Bouche
Mont St. Francis
Humboldt Fog
Redmondo
Rogue River Blue
Vella Special Dry Jack
Pleasant Ridge
Hooligan
Tarentaise
Wimer Winter
Winnimere
Mont St. Francis
Redmondo
Rogue River
Pleasant Ridge
Wimer Winter
Winnimere
Rogue River
Wimer
Rogue River
THE WINNER
Rogue River Blue

Hooligan vs. Great Hill Blue
Great Hill Blue shows its Southern Massachusetts roots with hints of the briny breezes off nearby Buzzard's Bay. Hooligan lived up to its name when it first burst onto the scene in 2001: wild and erratic. A washed-rind cow's milk cheese made at Connecticut's Cato Corner Farm in the style of the Belgian Chimay, Hooligan has been tamed and now surpasses its European forebears with its rich mouth feel and balance of salty and sour flavors.

Wimer Winter vs. Pleasant Ridge Reserve
Uplands Cheese Company's Pleasant Ridge Reserve packs a tremendous amount of Wisconsin raw cow's milk goodness into an alluring package. Wimer Winter is a raw goat's milk, washed-rind, moderately stinky cheese from the hotbed of Oregon's Rogue River Valley. This is not an easy format to corral but gifted cheesemaker (and goat breeder) Gianaclis Caldwell pulls it off. Her secret weapon is the milk of her Nigerian Dwarf goats, which imparts wonderful nut-like notes – and not a hint of gamey or goaty flavor.

Tumalo Farms Classico vs. Rogue River Blue
A past winner of "Best Blue in the World," Rogue River has become America's international ambassador. Like all great blues, its bite merely serves to focus and enhance the flavors of its delicious raw milk, accented by its wrapping in pear brandy–soaked syrah grape vine leaves, an ancient ripening touch that transmits a triple-whammy of Oregon terroir. There's no shame for Classico to succumb to this multi-faceted champion.

Regional Soda Pop

By Bob Roe

Bob Roe grew up in Southern California, fueled mainly by Wampums (imagine a bag of Fritos with some hair on its chest) washed down with Bubble-Up. His beverage of choice these days is a Chinotto, an Italian soda that his wife says tastes like cough medicine.

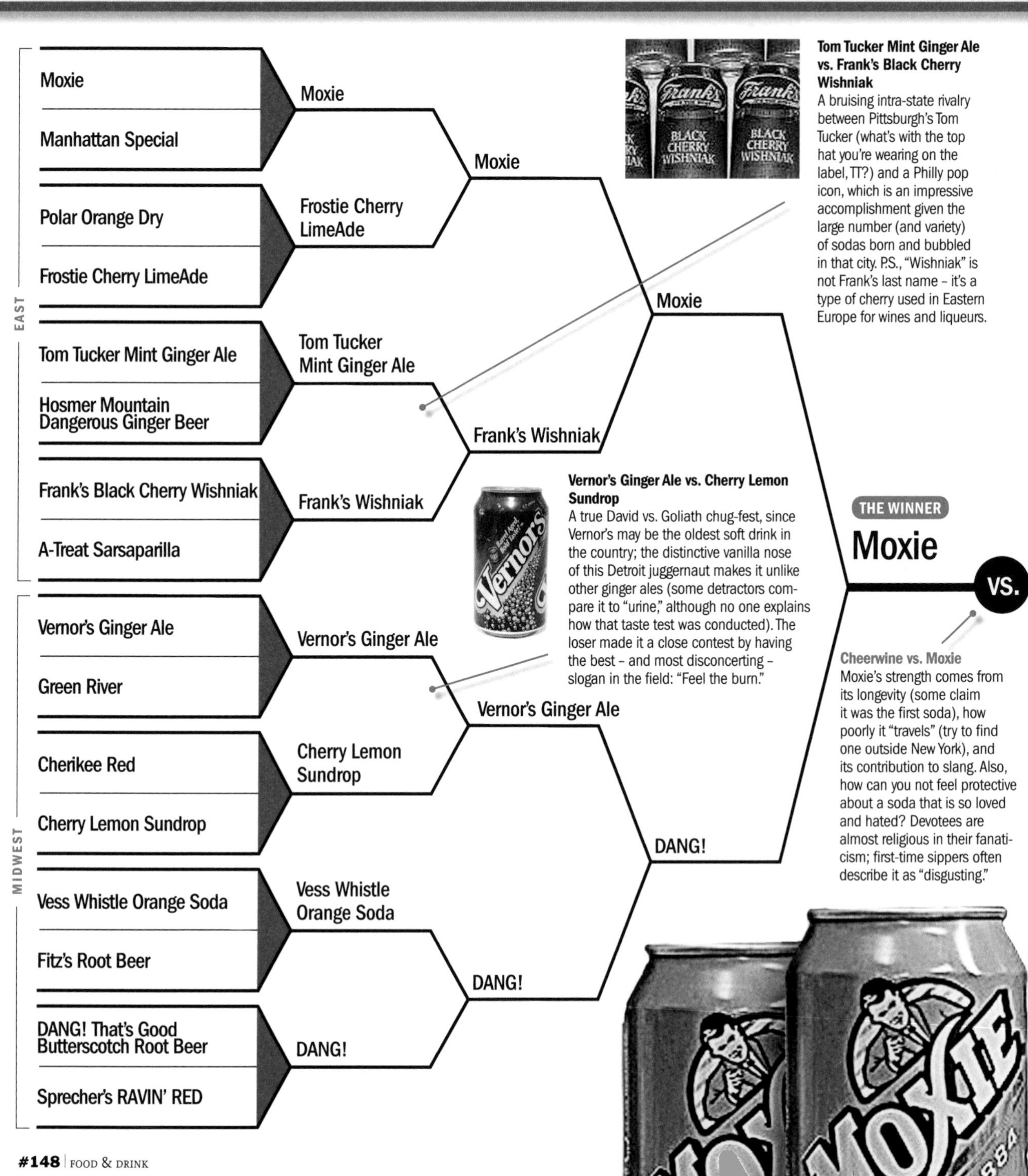
EAST
Moxie
Manhattan Special
Polar Orange Dry
Frostie Cherry LimeAde
Tom Tucker Mint Ginger Ale
Hosmer Mountain Dangerous Ginger Beer
Frank's Black Cherry Wishniak
A-Treat Sarsaparilla
Moxie
Frostie Cherry LimeAde
Tom Tucker Mint Ginger Ale
Frank's Wishniak
Moxie
Frank's Wishniak
Moxie
MIDWEST
Vernor's Ginger Ale
Green River
Cherikee Red
Cherry Lemon Sundrop
Vess Whistle Orange Soda
Fitz's Root Beer
DANG! That's Good Butterscotch Root Beer
Sprecher's RAVIN' RED
Vernor's Ginger Ale
Cherry Lemon Sundrop
Vess Whistle Orange Soda
DANG!
Vernor's Ginger Ale
DANG!
DANG!
THE WINNER
Moxie
VS.
Frank's
BLACK CHERRY WISHNIAK
Vernors
MOXIE
1884

Tom Tucker Mint Ginger Ale vs. Frank's Black Cherry Wishniak
A bruising intra-state rivalry between Pittsburgh's Tom Tucker (what's with the top hat you're wearing on the label, TT?) and a Philly pop icon, which is an impressive accomplishment given the large number (and variety) of sodas born and bubbled in that city. P.S., "Wishniak" is not Frank's last name – it's a type of cherry used in Eastern Europe for wines and liqueurs.

Vernor's Ginger Ale vs. Cherry Lemon Sundrop
A true David vs. Goliath chug-fest, since Vernor's may be the oldest soft drink in the country; the distinctive vanilla nose of this Detroit juggernaut makes it unlike other ginger ales (some detractors compare it to "urine," although no one explains how that taste test was conducted). The loser made it a close contest by having the best – and most disconcerting – slogan in the field: "Feel the burn."

Cheerwine vs. Moxie
Moxie's strength comes from its longevity (some claim it was the first soda), how poorly it "travels" (try to find one outside New York), and its contribution to slang. Also, how can you not feel protective about a soda that is so loved and hated? Devotees are almost religious in their fanaticism; first-time sippers often describe it as "disgusting."

IF YOU ONLY DRINK COKE OR PEPSI, you need more fizz in our life. America has a long, often goofy legacy of regional sodas that stretches back to the 1890s. In judging the best regional pops today, points were awarded for longevity, quality, uniqueness, and a defiantly regional appeal – in other words, a "brew" that might taste odd to someone who hadn't been weaned on it. As has happened in March Madness, the West was so weak that powerhouses from other areas had to be imported to fill out the regional.

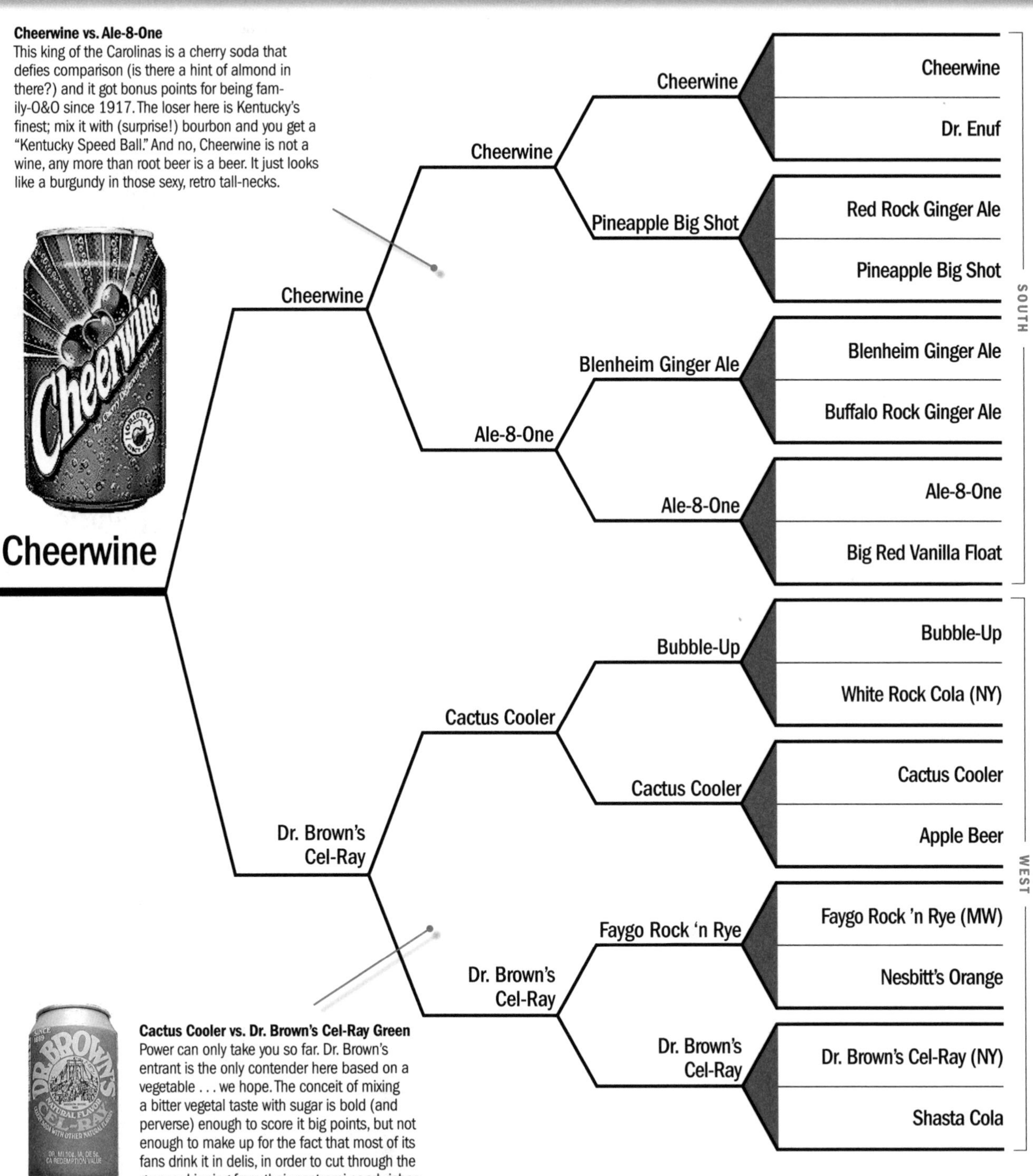
Cheerwine
Dr. Enuf
Red Rock Ginger Ale
Pineapple Big Shot
Blenheim Ginger Ale
Buffalo Rock Ginger Ale
Ale-8-One
Big Red Vanilla Float
SOUTH
Bubble-Up
White Rock Cola (NY)
Cactus Cooler
Apple Beer
Faygo Rock 'n Rye (MW)
Nesbitt's Orange
Dr. Brown's Cel-Ray (NY)
Shasta Cola
WEST
Cheerwine
Pineapple Big Shot
Blenheim Ginger Ale
Ale-8-One
Bubble-Up
Cactus Cooler
Faygo Rock 'n Rye
Dr. Brown's Cel-Ray
Cheerwine
Ale-8-One
Cactus Cooler
Dr. Brown's Cel-Ray
Cheerwine
Dr. Brown's Cel-Ray
Cheerwine

Cheerwine vs. Ale-8-One
This king of the Carolinas is a cherry soda that defies comparison (is there a hint of almond in there?) and it got bonus points for being family-O&O since 1917. The loser here is Kentucky's finest; mix it with (surprise!) bourbon and you get a "Kentucky Speed Ball." And no, Cheerwine is not a wine, any more than root beer is a beer. It just looks like a burgundy in those sexy, retro tall-necks.

Cactus Cooler vs. Dr. Brown's Cel-Ray Green
Power can only take you so far. Dr. Brown's entrant is the only contender here based on a vegetable . . . we hope. The conceit of mixing a bitter vegetal taste with sugar is bold (and perverse) enough to score it big points, but not enough to make up for the fact that most of its fans drink it in delis, in order to cut through the grease dripping from their pastrami sandwiches.

American Wines

By Joseph S. Ward

Joseph S. Ward is the wine editor for *Condé Nast Traveler* and the co-author, with Steven Spurrier, of *How to Buy Fine Wines: Practical Advice for the Investor and Connoisseur.*

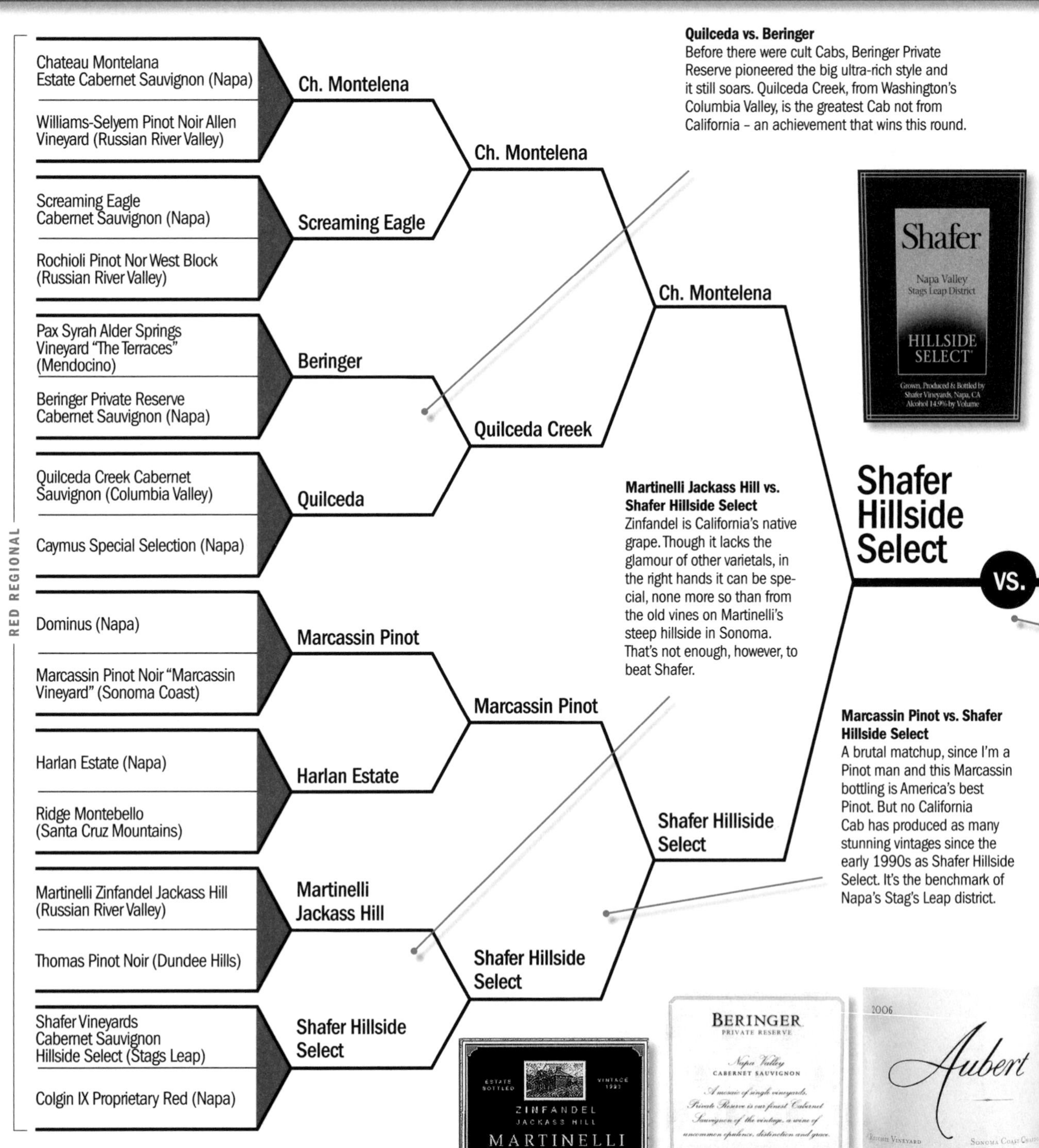

RED REGIONAL
Chateau Montelana Estate Cabernet Sauvignon (Napa)
Williams-Selyem Pinot Noir Allen Vineyard (Russian River Valley)
Screaming Eagle Cabernet Sauvignon (Napa)
Rochioli Pinot Nor West Block (Russian River Valley)
Pax Syrah Alder Springs Vineyard "The Terraces" (Mendocino)
Beringer Private Reserve Cabernet Sauvignon (Napa)
Quilceda Creek Cabernet Sauvignon (Columbia Valley)
Caymus Special Selection (Napa)
Dominus (Napa)
Marcassin Pinot Noir "Marcassin Vineyard" (Sonoma Coast)
Harlan Estate (Napa)
Ridge Montebello (Santa Cruz Mountains)
Martinelli Zinfandel Jackass Hill (Russian River Valley)
Thomas Pinot Noir (Dundee Hills)
Shafer Vineyards Cabernet Sauvignon Hillside Select (Stags Leap)
Colgin IX Proprietary Red (Napa)
Ch. Montelena
Screaming Eagle
Beringer
Quilceda
Marcassin Pinot
Harlan Estate
Martinelli Jackass Hill
Shafer Hillside Select
Ch. Montelena
Quilceda Creek
Marcassin Pinot
Shafer Hillside Select
Ch. Montelena
Shafer Hillside Select
Shafer Hillside Select
VS.
Shafer
Napa Valley
Stags Leap District
HILLSIDE SELECT
Grown, Produced & Bottled by Shafer Vineyards, Napa, CA
Alcohol 14.9% by Volume
ESTATE BOTTLED
VINTAGE
ZINFANDEL
JACKASS HILL
MARTINELLI
BERINGER
PRIVATE RESERVE
Napa Valley
CABERNET SAUVIGNON
A mosaic of single vineyards, Private Reserve is our finest Cabernet Sauvignon of the vintage, a wine of uncommon opulence, distinction and grace.
2006
Aubert

Quilceda vs. Beringer
Before there were cult Cabs, Beringer Private Reserve pioneered the big ultra-rich style and it still soars. Quilceda Creek, from Washington's Columbia Valley, is the greatest Cab not from California – an achievement that wins this round.

Martinelli Jackass Hill vs. Shafer Hillside Select
Zinfandel is California's native grape. Though it lacks the glamour of other varietals, in the right hands it can be special, none more so than from the old vines on Martinelli's steep hillside in Sonoma. That's not enough, however, to beat Shafer.

Marcassin Pinot vs. Shafer Hillside Select
A brutal matchup, since I'm a Pinot man and this Marcassin bottling is America's best Pinot. But no California Cab has produced as many stunning vintages since the early 1990s as Shafer Hillside Select. It's the benchmark of Napa's Stag's Leap district.

AMERICAN WINEMAKERS haven't had an inferiority complex for decades now. The 16 reds and 16 whites here certainly don't. The main criterion in this tournament, high quality and consistency being givens, is a wine that not only matches the Old World classics but creates a new archetype that stands on its own. From vintage to vintage, it is the benchmark other Americans aim for. If you see any of these on a wine list (and can handle the price), order a bottle.

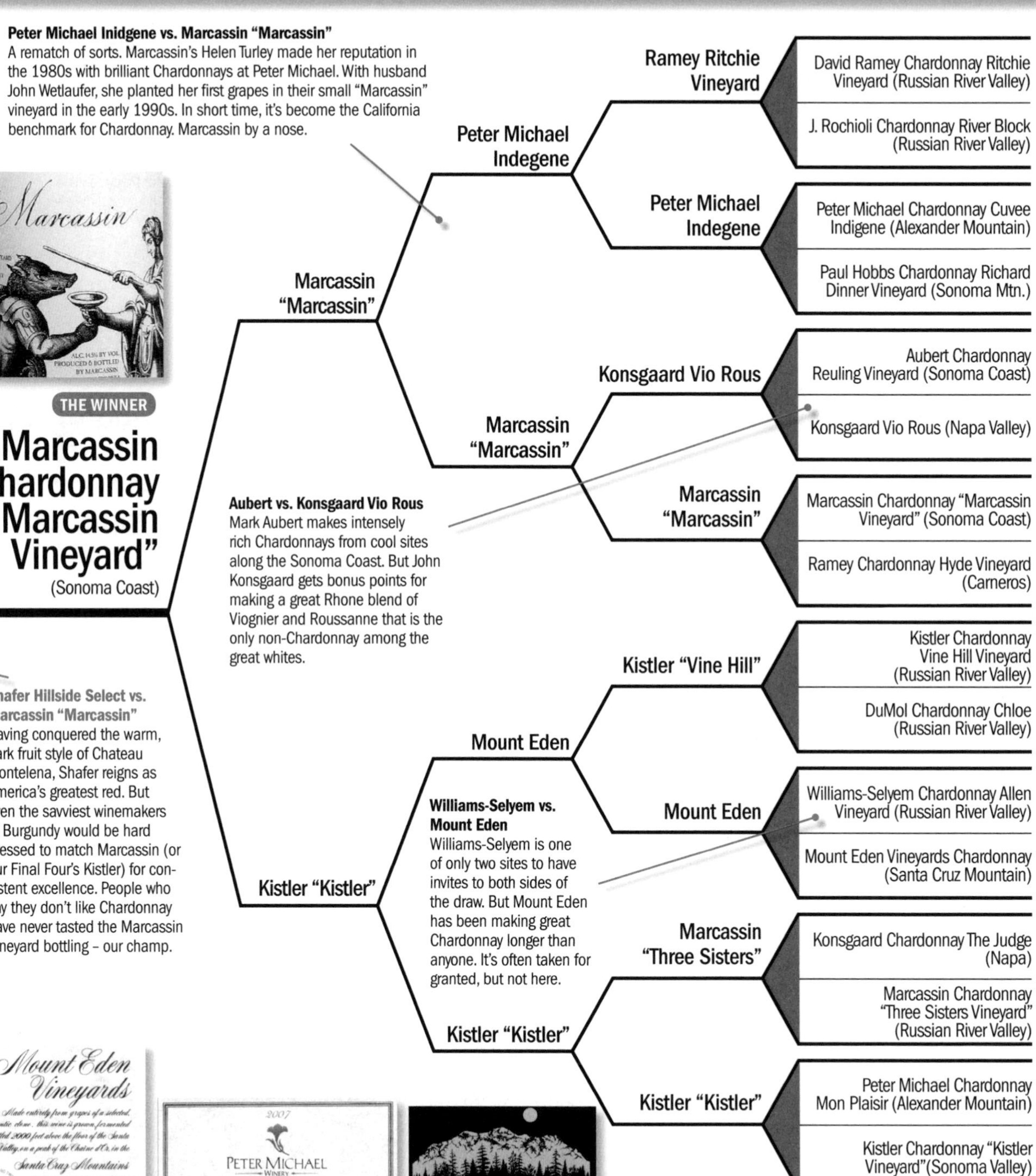

Peter Michael Inidgene vs. Marcassin "Marcassin"
A rematch of sorts. Marcassin's Helen Turley made her reputation in the 1980s with brilliant Chardonnays at Peter Michael. With husband John Wetlaufer, she planted her first grapes in their small "Marcassin" vineyard in the early 1990s. In short time, it's become the California benchmark for Chardonnay. Marcassin by a nose.
Marcassin
THE WINNER
Marcassin Chardonnay "Marcassin Vineyard" (Sonoma Coast)
Shafer Hillside Select vs. Marcassin "Marcassin"
Having conquered the warm, dark fruit style of Chateau Montelena, Shafer reigns as America's greatest red. But even the savviest winemakers of Burgundy would be hard pressed to match Marcassin (or our Final Four's Kistler) for consistent excellence. People who say they don't like Chardonnay have never tasted the Marcassin Vineyard bottling – our champ.
Aubert vs. Konsgaard Vio Rous
Mark Aubert makes intensely rich Chardonnays from cool sites along the Sonoma Coast. But John Konsgaard gets bonus points for making a great Rhone blend of Viognier and Roussanne that is the only non-Chardonnay among the great whites.
Williams-Selyem vs. Mount Eden
Williams-Selyem is one of only two sites to have invites to both sides of the draw. But Mount Eden has been making great Chardonnay longer than anyone. It's often taken for granted, but not here.
Marcassin "Marcassin"
Kistler "Kistler"
Peter Michael Indegene
Marcassin "Marcassin"
Mount Eden
Kistler "Kistler"
Ramey Ritchie Vineyard
Peter Michael Indegene
Konsgaard Vio Rous
Marcassin "Marcassin"
Kistler "Vine Hill"
Mount Eden
Marcassin "Three Sisters"
Kistler "Kistler"
David Ramey Chardonnay Ritchie Vineyard (Russian River Valley)
J. Rochioli Chardonnay River Block (Russian River Valley)
Peter Michael Chardonnay Cuvee Indigene (Alexander Mountain)
Paul Hobbs Chardonnay Richard Dinner Vineyard (Sonoma Mtn.)
Aubert Chardonnay Reuling Vineyard (Sonoma Coast)
Konsgaard Vio Rous (Napa Valley)
Marcassin Chardonnay "Marcassin Vineyard" (Sonoma Coast)
Ramey Chardonnay Hyde Vineyard (Carneros)
Kistler Chardonnay Vine Hill Vineyard (Russian River Valley)
DuMol Chardonnay Chloe (Russian River Valley)
Williams-Selyem Chardonnay Allen Vineyard (Russian River Valley)
Mount Eden Vineyards Chardonnay (Santa Cruz Mountain)
Konsgaard Chardonnay The Judge (Napa)
Marcassin Chardonnay "Three Sisters Vineyard" (Russian River Valley)
Peter Michael Chardonnay Mon Plaisir (Alexander Mountain)
Kistler Chardonnay "Kistler Vineyard"(Sonoma Valley)
Mount Eden Vineyards
Santa Cruz Mountains
CHARDONNAY
2005
2007
PETER MICHAEL
WINERY
'CUVÉE INDIGÈNE'
QUILCEDA CREEK
CABERNET SAUVIGNON

WHITE REGIONAL

Classic Cookbooks*

By Katie Workman

Katie Workman is the editor in chief and chief marketing officer of Cookstr.com, a recipe site dedicated to great recipes from respected cookbook authors and chefs.

***by authors who are no longer with us**

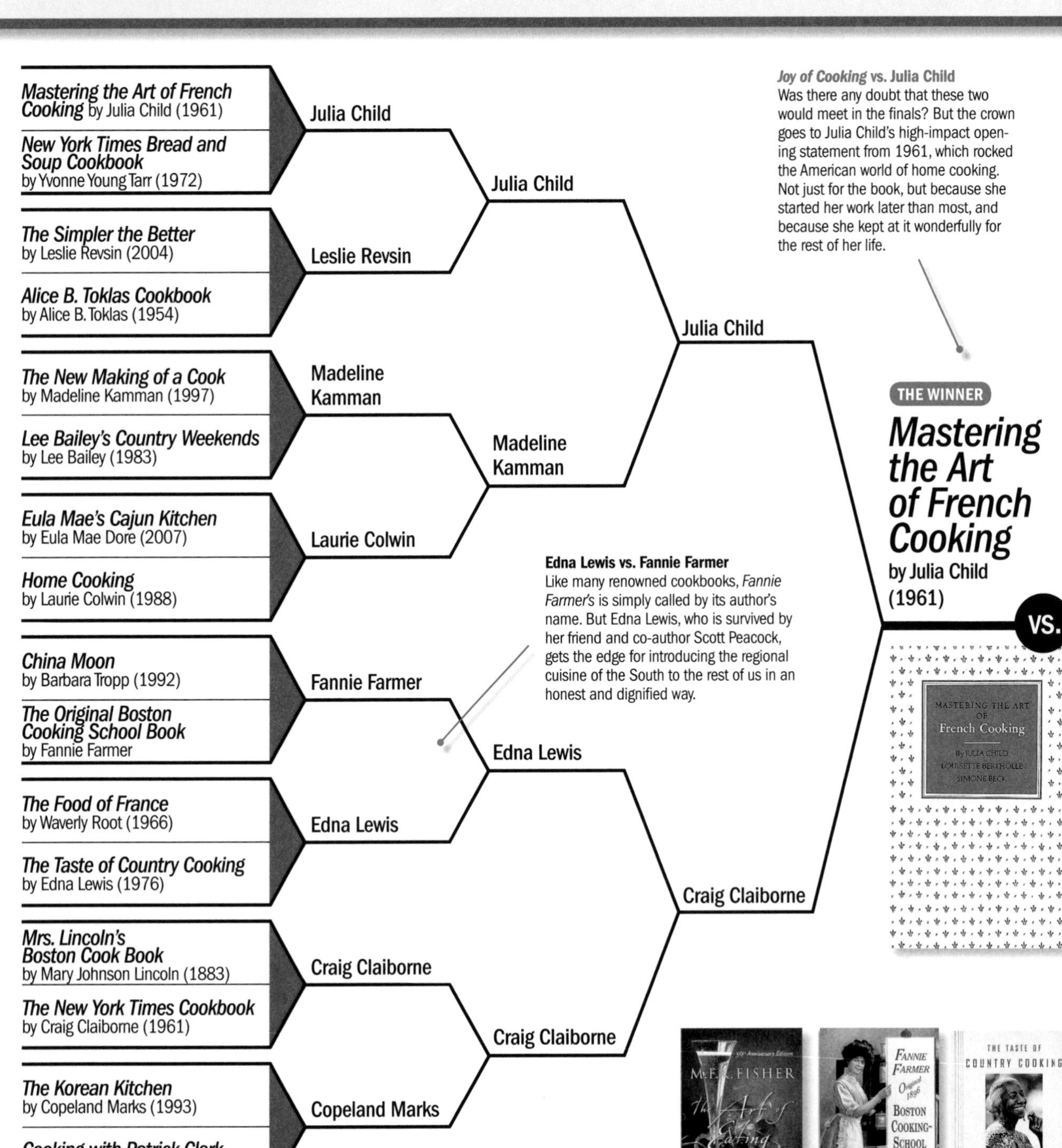

Mastering the Art of French Cooking by Julia Child (1961)
New York Times Bread and Soup Cookbook by Yvonne Young Tarr (1972)
Julia Child
The Simpler the Better by Leslie Revsin (2004)
Alice B. Toklas Cookbook by Alice B. Toklas (1954)
Leslie Revsin
Julia Child
The New Making of a Cook by Madeline Kamman (1997)
Lee Bailey's Country Weekends by Lee Bailey (1983)
Madeline Kamman
Eula Mae's Cajun Kitchen by Eula Mae Dore (2007)
Home Cooking by Laurie Colwin (1988)
Laurie Colwin
Madeline Kamman
Julia Child
China Moon by Barbara Tropp (1992)
The Original Boston Cooking School Book by Fannie Farmer
Fannie Farmer
The Food of France by Waverly Root (1966)
The Taste of Country Cooking by Edna Lewis (1976)
Edna Lewis
Edna Lewis
Mrs. Lincoln's Boston Cook Book by Mary Johnson Lincoln (1883)
The New York Times Cookbook by Craig Claiborne (1961)
Craig Claiborne
The Korean Kitchen by Copeland Marks (1993)
Cooking with Patrick Clark by Patrick Clark et al (1999)
Copeland Marks
Craig Claiborne
Craig Claiborne
***Joy of Cooking* vs. Julia Child**
Was there any doubt that these two would meet in the finals? But the crown goes to Julia Child's high-impact opening statement from 1961, which rocked the American world of home cooking. Not just for the book, but because she started her work later than most, and because she kept at it wonderfully for the rest of her life.
Edna Lewis vs. Fannie Farmer
Like many renowned cookbooks, *Fannie Farmer's* is simply called by its author's name. But Edna Lewis, who is survived by her friend and co-author Scott Peacock, gets the edge for introducing the regional cuisine of the South to the rest of us in an honest and dignified way.
THE WINNER
Mastering the Art of French Cooking
by Julia Child (1961)
VS.
MASTERING THE ART OF French Cooking
By JULIA CHILD
LOUISETTE BERTHOLLE
SIMONE BECK
M.F.K. FISHER
The Art of Eating
FANNIE FARMER
Original 1896
BOSTON COOKING-SCHOOL COOK BOOK
THE TASTE OF COUNTRY COOKING
EDNA LEWIS

COOKBOOKS CAN BE CLASSICS while their authors are still living. But they take on mythic stature after their authors pass on. Comparing the ur-texts written by the late and great of American cookery collected here is not an apples-to-apples thing; it's more like apples to rambutans. Some are broad in scope, others very specific, but they all aim to stir excitement in your kitchen. The greater the impact, the further they go.

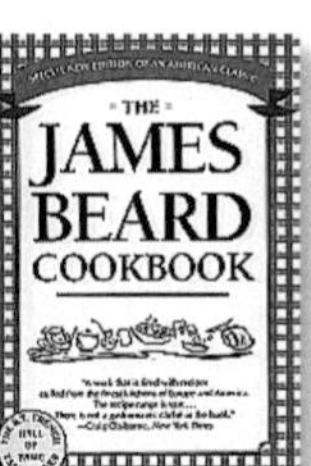
THE
JAMES
BEARD
COOKBOOK

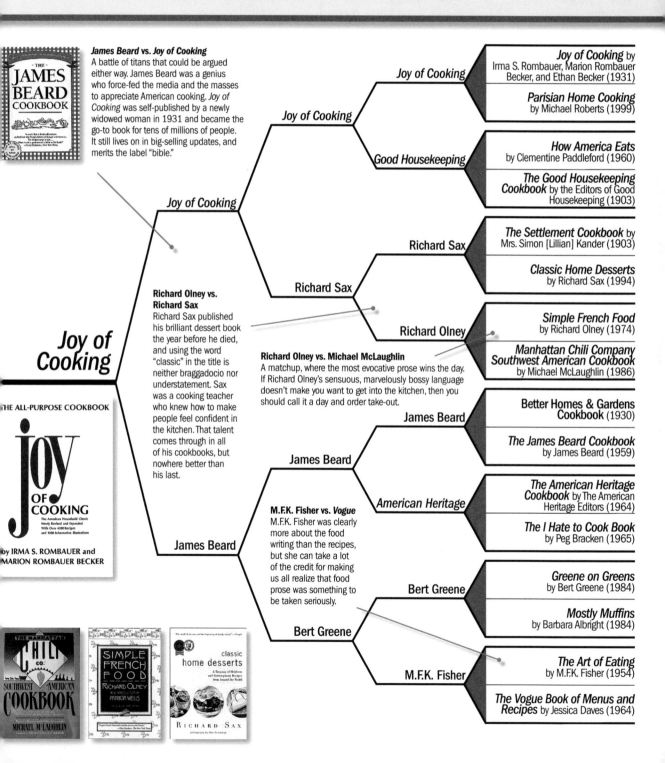

James Beard* vs. *Joy of Cooking
A battle of titans that could be argued either way. James Beard was a genius who force-fed the media and the masses to appreciate American cooking. *Joy of Cooking* was self-published by a newly widowed woman in 1931 and became the go-to book for tens of millions of people. It still lives on in big-selling updates, and merits the label "bible."

Richard Olney vs. Richard Sax
Richard Sax published his brilliant dessert book the year before he died, and using the word "classic" in the title is neither braggadocio nor understatement. Sax was a cooking teacher who knew how to make people feel confident in the kitchen. That talent comes through in all of his cookbooks, but nowhere better than his last.

Richard Olney vs. Michael McLaughlin
A matchup, where the most evocative prose wins the day. If Richard Olney's sensuous, marvelously bossy language doesn't make you want to get into the kitchen, then you should call it a day and order take-out.

M.F.K. Fisher vs. *Vogue*
M.F.K. Fisher was clearly more about the food writing than the recipes, but she can take a lot of the credit for making us all realize that food prose was something to be taken seriously.

Round 1:
- *Joy of Cooking* by Irma S. Rombauer, Marion Rombauer Becker, and Ethan Becker (1931) vs. *Parisian Home Cooking* by Michael Roberts (1999)
- *How America Eats* by Clementine Paddleford (1960) vs. *The Good Housekeeping Cookbook* by the Editors of Good Housekeeping (1903)
- *The Settlement Cookbook* by Mrs. Simon [Lillian] Kander (1903) vs. *Classic Home Desserts* by Richard Sax (1994)
- *Simple French Food* by Richard Olney (1974) vs. *Manhattan Chili Company Southwest American Cookbook* by Michael McLaughlin (1986)
- **Better Homes & Gardens Cookbook** (1930) vs. *The James Beard Cookbook* by James Beard (1959)
- *The American Heritage Cookbook* by The American Heritage Editors (1964) vs. *The I Hate to Cook Book* by Peg Bracken (1965)
- *Greene on Greens* by Bert Greene (1984) vs. *Mostly Muffins* by Barbara Albright (1984)
- *The Art of Eating* by M.F.K. Fisher (1954) vs. *The Vogue Book of Menus and Recipes* by Jessica Daves (1964)

Round 2: *Joy of Cooking*; *Good Housekeeping*; Richard Sax; Richard Olney; James Beard; *American Heritage*; Bert Greene; M.F.K. Fisher

Round 3: *Joy of Cooking*; Richard Sax; James Beard; Bert Greene

Round 4: *Joy of Cooking*; James Beard

Winner: *Joy of Cooking*

THE ALL-PURPOSE COOKBOOK
JOY
OF
COOKING
by IRMA S. ROMBAUER and
MARION ROMBAUER BECKER

THE MANHATTAN
CHILI
CO.
SOUTHWEST AMERICAN
COOKBOOK
MICHAEL McLAUGHLIN

SIMPLE
FRENCH
FOOD
RICHARD OLNEY
PATRICIA WELLS

classic
home desserts
RICHARD SAX

Name of Bracket

Your Name

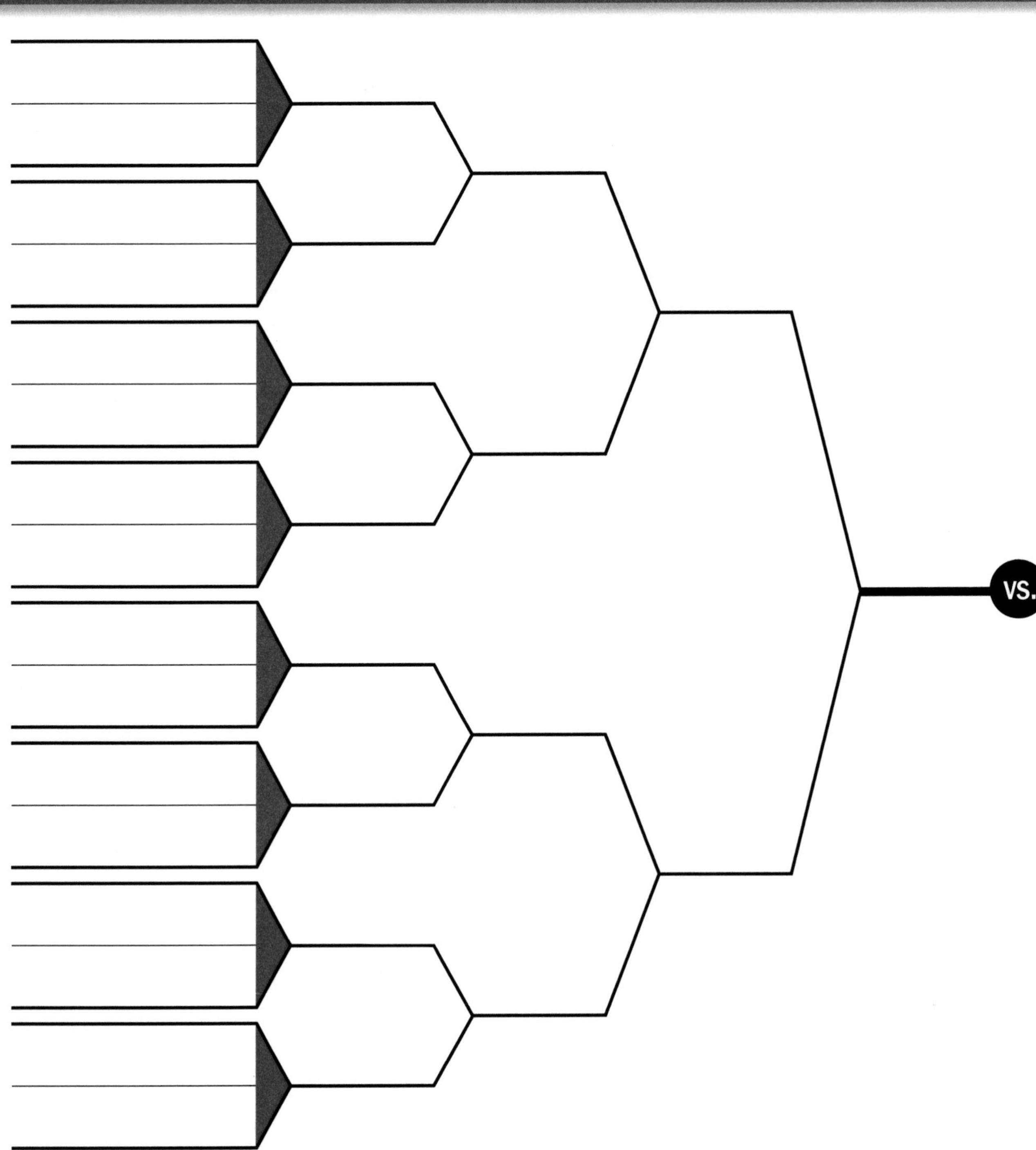
VS.

Introduction

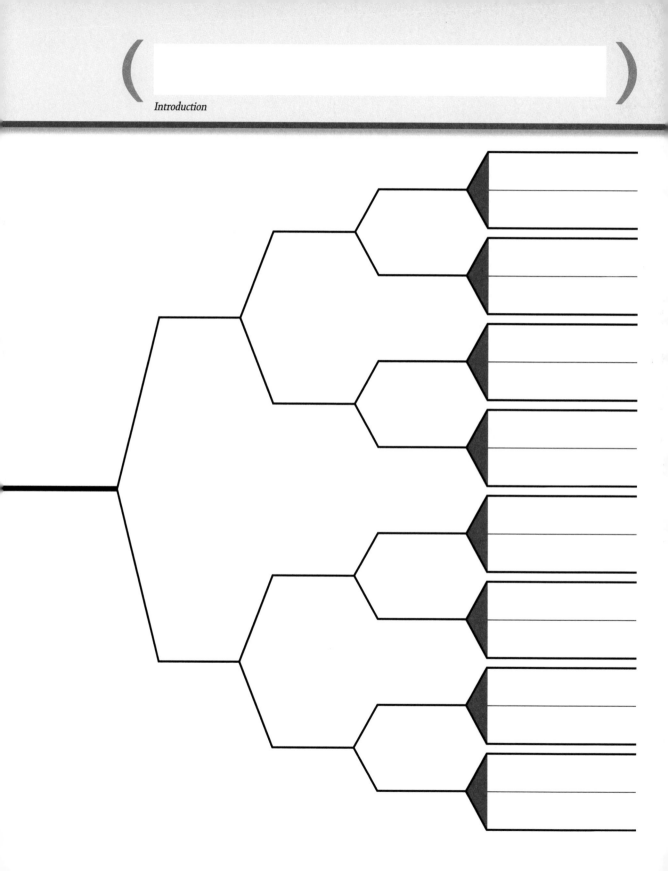

Acknowledgments

The Final Four of Everything

Our heartfelt thanks go to:

Our contributors, for getting the idea, dropping what they were doing, and jumping in with unbridled enthusiasm. When their brackets started coming in, every day seemed like Christmas.

Our publisher David Rosenthal, for getting the ball rolling with a simple but shrewd tweak.

Our editor Priscilla Painton, for her brilliant suggestions and steady hand on a project that resembles herding cats – and for bringing our attention to . . .

Our designer D.W. Pine, who got the concept immediately and then took it further than we imagined.

Our picture editor Skye Gurney, whose cleverness and work ethic are humbling.

Our fact-man Will Reiter, for checking the results.

Our web gurus Nina Schwartz and Michael Szczerban, for their proactive belief in the e-potential of brackets.

Our Simon & Schuster production team, for their infinite patience.

And for their ideas, connective tissue, and support: David McCormick, Annik Lafarge, David Hirshey, Ted Shaker, Sheryl Shaker, Zoe Pagnamenta, Theresa Park, Candy Lee, Susan Bolotin, Susan Mercandetti, Rachel Klayman, Susan Reed, Michael Solomon, Emily Sklar, Lisa Queen, Ben Adams, Dan Cabrera, Nick Reiter, Vince Wladika, Stefan Fatsis, Chris LaPlaca, Mark Mandel, Tom Jolly, Sandy Keenan, Will Leitch, Alan Schwarz, and our dear friend, Wikipedia.

To our spouses, Marie Rama and Griffin Miller, who moved easily into the finals of the Great Wives bracket.

Photo Credits

The Final Four of Everything

Introduction: Mugshot: www.thesmokinggun.com; Michael Jordan © Joshua Massel; Mary Tyler Moore: AP; George Carlin: Bonnie Murphy; William Shatner: David Gabber/PR Photos

Americana: #3: AP; #6 iStockPhoto; #7 www.15q.net; #8 Bluebird: Elaine R. Wilson; pelican: Calibus; oriole: Mdf; #10 "Moonrise, Hernandez, 1941": Photograph by Ansel Adams. © 2009 The Ansel Adams Publishing Rights Trust; #11 Jar of hair: © 2009 MastroAuctions.com; Buddy Holly: AP ;#14 All photographs courtesy of Scott Rutherford; #15 Water bottle: Answer sheet; alarm clock: iStockPhoto; #16 John Wayne: courtesy of www.doctormacro1.info

History & Politics: #18 Foam finger: iStockPhoto; #23 Cathode ray tube: iStockPhoto; #31 Jerry Falwell: Liberty University

People: Opener: Rita Hayworth: AP; #33 All photographs: NASA; #34 Cindy Crawford: Terry Thompson/PR photos; Dell'Orefice: The Heart Truth; Lauren Hutton: Lauren Hutton; Dovima: David Clarkson McJonathan-Swarm; #35. All photographs courtesy of www.thesmokinggun.com; #36 Mary Tyler Moore: AP; Mary Wilson: Jay D. Schwartz; #37 Michael Jordan © Joshua Massel; #38 Cat in the Hat © Dr. Seuss Enterprises, L.P.; lightbulb, chess pieces, and Monticello: iStockPhoto; #39 Moxie CrimeFighter Jillette courtesy of her parents; apple, peanut, and block: iStockPhoto; #40 Otis Redding: AP; #41 David Letterman: AP; David Axelrod: Newshour; David Ortiz: Aaron Donovan; David Wells: imagesbyferg/Ferguson; #43 John Edwards: David Victor Feldman; #44 William Shatner: David Gabber/PR Photos; William Perry: AP; #46 Richard Pryor: Alan Light; Dick Cavett: Christopher Peterson; #47 Rita Hayworth: AP; #49 Baldwins: AP; Wrights: AP; Coens: Rita Molnar; #50 Tommy Lee Jones: Jay Kravetz/PR Photos

Sports: #52 Michael Phelps: Bryan Allison; #54 Roger Staubach: AP; all other photographs courtesy of George Kitrinos; #55 Personal collection; #56 George Blanda: AP; #58 Y.A.Tittle: AP; Elgin Baylor: AP ; #59 Pinehurst No. 2 © Pinehurst, LLC 2007; #60 Chris Chelios: Dan4th Nicholas; Mike Modano: Elliot Lowe; puck: Tait Lifto; #61 iStockPhoto; #63 © YouTube; #65 Bosox: Leif Hedstrom; Joe DiMaggio by Gallerygal, available from geringlopez.com; #66 Polar bear: Ken Colwell; Nads: Jeffrey Daniel; #67 iStockPhoto; #69 Arnold Schwarzenegger: AP; Burt Reynolds: Alan Light; Mark Harmon: Jerry Avenaim; #70 Jim McKay: AP; Vin Scully: Dennis Ralutin; inset of Vin Scully: Craig Y. Fujii; #71 Tim Tebow: AP; Pete Maravich: AP; Gwen Torrence: courtesy of UGA Sports; #72 Joe Louis: Carl Van Vechten; ticket images courtesy of www.championsofthering.com; #73 Courtesy of Micah Larsen; #74 Personal collection; #75 Babe Ruth: AP; Jackie Robinson: AP; John McEnroe: Brett Weinstein; #76 Ted Williams: AP; Tom Brady: AP ; #77 AP

Pop Culture: Opener: Paul Newman: AP; #81 All photographs © YouTube; #82-#86 All photographs: AP; #88 film strip: iStockPhoto; #92 All photographs: AP; #94 Jeff Foxworthy: AP; Chris Rock: AP; Richard Pryor: Alan Light; #96 Top: Kevin Armstrong; bottom two photographs: Bonnie Murphy; #97 All images: iStockPhoto; #98 Omarosa: Glenn Francis; Paris Hilton and Nicole Richie: AP; Flavor Flav: PR Photos; #99 Atticus Finch: AP; gavel: iStockphoto; #100 All photographs: AP; #105 TV: iStockPhoto; #106 Will Smith: AP; Sylvester Stallone: AP; John Malkovich: Victor Felder; #107 Howard Stern: AP; #108 Shirley Temple: AP; Patty Duke: AP; #110 Maria Callas: AP; Nina Simone: Roland Godefroy; #112 Bill Cullen and Tom Kennedy: Adam Nedeff, GameShowUtopia.net; Pat Sajak: AP; #115 All photographs: AP; #116 Charlie Parker: AP; #118 Lon Tweeten; #119 AP; #120 Abbott and Costello: AP; #121 Magnet: iStockPhoto

Nature: Opener: iStockPhoto; #122 Roz Chast; #124 Trounce–Wikimedia; #125 Courtesy of Alan Ng; #126 Teeth: iStockPhoto; #128 All photographs: iStockPhoto; #129 Condor: Cszmurlo; trogon: Dominic Sherony; #130 syringe and lotion: iStockPhoto

Words: Opener: iStockPhoto; #131 All photographs: iStockPhoto; #133 iStockPhoto; #135 All photographs: iStockPhoto; #137 Courtesy of the Yogi Berra Museum & Learning Center; #138 iStockPhotos; #141 Mirror and waitress: iStockPhoto; #142 All photographs: PR Photos

Food & Drink: Opener: Courtesy of Rogue Creamery; #143 All photographs: iStockPhoto; #144: iStockPhoto